LITTLE, BROWN AND COMPANY

Law School Casebook Series

Constitutional Law: Cases and Other Problems. Second Edition. PAUL A. FREUND, Carl M. Loeb University Professor, Harvard University, ARTHUR E. SUTHERLAND, Bussey Professor of Law, Harvard University, MARK DE WOLFE HOWE, Professor of Law, Harvard University, and ERNEST J. BROWN, Professor of Law, Harvard University

Cases and Materials on Torts. CHARLES O. GREGORY, John B. Minor Professor of Law, University of Virginia, and HARRY KALVEN, JR., Professor of Law, University of Chicago

Land-use Planning: A Casebook on the Use, Misuse, and Re-use of Urban Land. CHARLES M. HAAR, Professor of Law, Harvard University

Administrative Law: Cases and Materials. Second Edition. LOUIS L. JAFFE, Byrne Professor of Administrative Law, Harvard University, and NATHANIEL L. NATHANSON, Professor of Law, Northwestern University

Trials and Appeals: Cases, Text, Statutes, Rules, and Forms. CHARLES W. JOINER, Professor of Law and Associate Dean, University of Michigan

Constitutional Law: Cases and Materials. Third Edition. PAUL G. KAUPER, Professor of Law, University of Michigan

Contracts: Cases and Materials. FRIEDRICH KESSLER, Hotchkiss Professor of Law, Yale University, and MALCOLM PITMAN SHARP, Professor of Law, Emeritus, University of Chicago

Basic Business Associations: Cases, Text and Problems. ELVIN R. LATTY, Professor of Law, Duke University School of Law, and GEORGE T. FRAMPTON, Professor of Law, University of Illinois

Cases and Text on the Law of Wills. Second Edition, 1960 Revision. W. BARTON LEACH, Story Professor of Law, Harvard University

Legislation: Cases and Materials. FRANK C. NEWMAN, Dean and Professor of Law, University of California at Berkeley, and STANLEY S. SURREY, formerly Jeremiah Smith, Jr., Professor of Law, Harvard University

Criminal Law and Its Processes: Cases and Materials. MONRAD G. PAULSEN, Professor of Law, Columbia University, and SANFORD H. KADISH, Professor of Law, University of California at Berkeley

Family Law: Cases and Materials. MORRIS PLOSCOWE, Adjunct Associate Professor of Law, New York University, and DORIS JONAS FREED, of the New York and Maryland Bars

Problems and Materials on Decedents' Estates and Trusts. EUGENE F. SCOLES, Professor of Law, University of Illinois, and EDWARD C. HALBACH, JR., Dean and Professor of Law, University of California at Berkeley

Cases and Other Materials on Civil Procedure. AUSTIN W. SCOTT, Dane Professor of Law, Emeritus, Harvard University, and ROBERT B. KENT, Professor of Law, Boston University

Select Cases and Other Authorities on the Law of Trusts. AUSTIN W. SCOTT, Dane Professor of Law, Emeritus, Harvard University, and AUSTIN W. SCOTT, JR., late Professor of Law, University of Colorado

An Introduction to Criminal Justice. Text and Cases. ORVILL C. SNYDER, Professor of Law, Brooklyn Law School

The Civil Law System: Cases and Materials for the Comparative Study of Law. ARTHUR TAYLOR VON MEHREN, Professor of Law, Harvard University

The Law of Multistate Problems: Cases and Materials on Conflict of Laws. ARTHUR TAYLOR VON MEHREN, Professor of Law, Harvard University, and DONALD THEODORE TRAUTMAN, Professor of Law, Harvard University

Cases on Contracts. SAMUEL WILLISTON, late Dane Professor of Law, Harvard University, Revised Sixth Edition by WILLIAM T. LAUBE, Professor of Law, University of California at Berkeley

Labor Relations and the Law. Third Edition. Edited by JERRE WILLIAMS, Co-Chairman, Labor Law Group Trust, and BENJAMIN AARON, Professor of Law and Director, Institute of Industrial Relations, University of California at Los Angeles

Law School Textbook Series

American Civil Procedure. WILLIAM WIRT BLUME, Professor of Law, University of California, Hastings College of Law

Readings in Jurisprudence and Legal Philosophy. Edited by MORRIS R. COHEN, late Professor of Law, City College of New York, and FELIX S. COHEN, late Visiting Professor of Law, City College of New York, and Visiting Lecturer, Yale University

The Elements of Law. THOMAS E. DAVITT, S.J., Professor of Jurisprudence, Marquette University

Handbook of Modern Equity. Second Edition. WILLIAM Q. DE FUNIAK, Professor of Law, University of San Francisco

Judicial Control of Administrative Action. Abridged Student Edition. LOUIS L. JAFFE, Byrne Professor of Administrative Law, Harvard University

Civil Procedure. FLEMING JAMES, JR., Lafayette S. Foster Professor of Law, Yale University

Trial Tactics and Methods. ROBERT E. KEETON, Professor of Law, Harvard University

Securities Regulation. Student's Edition. LOUIS LOSS, Professor of Law, Harvard University

Effective Legal Research: Student Edition Revised. MILES O. PRICE, Law Librarian and Professor of Law, Emeritus, Columbia University, and HARRY BITNER, Professor of Law and Law Librarian, Cornell University

Scott's Abridgment of the Law of Trusts. AUSTIN W. SCOTT, Dane Professor of Law, Emeritus, Harvard University

Handbook of Law Study. FERDINAND FAIRFAX STONE, Professor of Law and Director of Institute of Comparative Law, Tulane University

Materials on the Lawyer's Professional Responsibility. WILLIAM M. TRUMBULL, Professor of Law, Northwestern University

Political and Civil Rights
in the United States

Student Edition

A collection of legal and related
materials in two volumes

Thomas I. Emerson   *Lines Professor of Law,*
Yale University

David Haber   *Professor of Law,*
Rutgers University

Norman Dorsen   *Professor of Law and Director of the*
Arthur Garfield Hays Civil Liberties
Program, New York University

Vol. I

Little, Brown and Company
Boston   1967   Toronto

*Published simultaneously in Canada
by Little, Brown & Company (Canada) Limited*

PRINTED IN THE UNITED STATES OF AMERICA

PREFACE

Our effort in this third edition, as in the two previous editions, has been to present, primarily from the legal point of view, some of the basic materials which must be considered in seeking an answer to questions concerning the fundamental rights of the individual in modern society. In the rather elaborate notes and references we have undertaken to call attention to some of the ramifications of the problems, to trace background and development, to furnish a compilation of the major legal sources of information, and to give some introduction to the non-legal materials which are relevant to issues framed in legal terms.

The book grew originally out of a law school course in political and civil rights. It was undertaken in the first instance as a collection of materials for law students. As the project developed the authors were motivated by another consideration, that of making the book useful to the growing number of lawyers who deal in matters involving political and civil rights, or who have an interest in that field. Our purpose was to compensate, in part at least, for the lack of a comprehensive legal treatise on this branch of the law.

It has also been our hope that the book would have a wider appeal. As we said in our introduction to the first edition, the law of political and civil rights is too important a matter to be left to the lawyers. Solution of the problems involved requires the combined assistance of all intellectual disciplines. Above all it requires the fullest attention and understanding of all citizens. We therefore dare to encourage students of all kinds, and also the general reader, to make use of these materials. We have not stinted on the legal technicalities or attempted to simplify the legal issues. Some of the extracts may prove difficult going for the non-lawyer. But actually the law, at least in the field of political and civil rights, is not as mysterious as many laymen may suppose. And even legal writing can have literary merit. In any event the particular problems with which the materials deal are human, vital, and all-important.

In contrast with the first edition, when Supreme Court cases on political and civil rights were comparatively scarce, the mounting volume of court decisions, commentaries, studies, reports, and other materials has caused us many agonizing decisions in the selection process. And, even as was the case when materials were less abundant, we have been forced to omit or slight important segments. Our most painful omission, as in the second edition, has been the material on the rights of individuals in criminal proceedings. Our justification for the deletion of this traditional aspect of political and civil rights is that the material is treated in courses and texts on criminal law and is more readily available than most other aspects of the field. We have also been compelled to omit, as in both earlier editions, an adequate treatment of the rights of aliens, and virtually all consideration of political and civil rights in periods of emergency, problems of military law, and human rights in the world community. We have, however, kept up with the times by adding chapters on the rights of individuals in private associations and the right of privacy, as well as a fuller treatment of discrimination.

As in the earlier editions, the materials have been organized in terms of problems rather than of legal doctrine. Thus, issues of freedom of speech under the First Amendment, or "state action" under the Fourteenth, run through a number of chapters. We have used this organization in order to emphasize the concrete issues at stake and to bring to bear on those issues all relevant considerations, whether from legal or other sources. In order to facilitate use of the book along doctrinal lines, however, we have striven to make the index as complete as possible.

Although many of the footnotes attached to extracts reprinted have been retained, many others have been omitted. Except where we have wished to call the omitted footnote to the reader's attention, we have not indicated the omission. Nor have we attempted to renumber the footnotes.

As to a cut-off date — always a troublesome problem — we have attempted to include a complete reference to the major material through the first four months of 1966. Thereafter we have tried to include important developments up to the middle of the year. The Supreme Court decisions through the end of the term closing June 20, 1966, are incorporated. But there has not always been sufficient space or time for an adequate treatment of later developments.

This Student Edition is largely a response to the increased interest in the subject matter at law schools over the past decade, and it is designed to make the book more readily available for use in courses and seminars. The abridgement process has been difficult, but we are satisfied that all material essential for teaching purposes remains. The Standard Edition is of course available for the student who wishes to delve further into some of the problems.

We are, as usual, indebted to many persons for assistance in the preparation of these volumes. We are particularly grateful to Ronald Berger and Seymour Wishman for research assistance; to Mrs. Helen Minor and to Miss Florence Witherspoon and her staff for secretarial work; and to the staffs of the Yale, Rutgers, and New York University law libraries for effective help at all times. We acknowledge a special debt to Diana C. Haber for assistance in some of the typing, and to Ruth Calvin Emerson who performed unusual feats of research in the long, hot summer of 1966.

The two original editors warmly welcome Professor Norman Dorsen to the undertaking.

THOMAS I. EMERSON
DAVID HABER
NORMAN DORSEN

September, 1966

ADDENDUM

For two reasons I feel obliged to supplement the above Preface. First of all, not having participated in the preparation of the first two editions of Political and Civil Rights in the United States, I wish to record the enthusiasm with which I joined Professors Emerson and Haber and the pleasure and stimulation that I have derived from them throughout the enterprise.

Second, I owe a special debt to the Arthur Garfield Hays Civil Liberties Program of the New York University School of Law, which I have served for six years. Without its support, and particularly the massive assistance of several generations of graduate and undergraduate Arthur Garfield Hays and Robert Marshall Civil Liberties Fellows, it is doubtful whether I could have managed. The contribution of the Civil Liberties Fellows appears in every chapter of Part Three, for which I had special responsibility. The heaviest load was carried by Hillel J. Hoffman, Albert W. Overby, Robert J. Rabin, Paul S. Schreiber, and Bonnie P. Winawer. Also making valuable contributions were Norman J. Chachkin, William E. Crain, John C. Murphy, David Rudovsky, Robert F. Van Lierop, and Benjamin J. Zinkin.

Professor Bernard E. Harvith (himself a former Hays Graduate Fellow) and Michael B. Rosen, of the Project on Social Welfare Law of the Hays Program, provided the material on which the Note on Discrimination in Welfare Services in Chapter XXIV is based.

I also acknowledge the research assistance of Peter A. Winograd, an Instructor at the Law School, and Joel A. Brenner and John A. Ruskey. Susan M. Halpern and Edward A. Meilman bore the brunt of checking citations.

The immense load of stenographic responsibility fell primarily on as efficient a secretary as one could imagine, Dede N. Fuchs. She was assisted by Alethea Overby, Pat Stephens, and William Randolph.

A special word of thanks is due Michael Meltsner, Staff Attorney of the NAACP Legal Defense and Educational Fund, for his numerous helpful suggestions in a field in which he has professional competence.

Finally, the historical record should contain the fact that only after Harriette and I tied the knot did the work really sing along.

NORMAN DORSEN

SUMMARY OF CONTENTS

VOLUME I

CONTENTS

VOLUME I

(Listing of untitled Notes and
References has been omitted.)

Volume II

Part Three. DISCRIMINATION

TABLE OF CASES

Italic type has been used to indicate principal and excerpted cases and the pages on which they have been set out at length.

Q

R

Political and Civil Rights
in the United States

PART ONE

Freedom of Expression

CHAPTER I

Theoretical Framework

A. THE BASIC THEORY

MILTON, AREOPAGITICA
A Speech for the Liberty of Unlicensed Printing,
To the Parliament of England (1644)
Everyman's Library, pp. 23-38 (1927)

[Milton's speech was directed against an order of Parliament of June 14, 1643, which among other things provided that no book "shall from henceforth be printed or put to sale, unless the same be first approved of and licensed by such person or persons as both or either of the said Houses (of Parliament) shall appoint for the licensing of the same." After discussing the history of licensing, the values of reading, the ineffectiveness of the order to suppress scandalous, seditious, or libellous books, and the inhibitions it places upon scholars and writers, Milton goes on to consider the effect of the licensing system upon the growth and development of the country as a whole.]

And as it is a particular disesteem of every knowing person alive, and most injurious to the written labours and monuments of the dead, so to me it seems an undervaluing and vilifying of the whole Nation. I cannot set so light by all the invention, the art, the wit, the grave and solid judgment which is in England, as that it can be comprehended in any twenty capacities how good soever, much less that it should not pass except their superintendence be over it, except it be sifted and strained with their strainers, that it should be uncurrent without their manual stamp. Truth and understanding are not such wares as to be monopolised and traded in by tickets and statutes and standards. We must not think to make a staple commodity of all the knowledge in the land, to mark and licence it like our broadcloth and our woolpacks. What is it but a servitude like that imposed by the Philistines, not

1

to be allowed the sharpening of our own axes and coulters, but we must repair from all quarters to twenty licensing forges? Had anyone written and divulged erroneous things and scandalous to honest life, misusing and forfeiting the esteem had of his reason among men, if after conviction this only censure were adjudged him that he should never henceforth write but what were first examined by an appointed officer, whose hand should be annexed to pass his credit for him that now he might be safely read; it could not be apprehended less than a disgraceful punishment. Whence to include the whole Nation, and those that never yet thus offended, under such a diffident and suspectful prohibition, may plainly be understood what a disparagement it is. So much the more, whenas debtors and delinquents may walk abroad without a keeper, but unoffensive books must not stir forth without a visible jailer in their title.

Nor is it to the common people less than a reproach; for if we be so jealous over them, as that we dare not trust them with an English pamphlet, what do we but censure them for a giddy, vicious, and ungrounded people; in such a sick and weak state of faith and discretion, as to be able to take nothing down but through the pipe of a licenser? That this is care or love of them, we cannot pretend, whenas, in those popish places where the laity are most hated and despised, the same strictness is used over them. Wisdom we cannot call it, because it stops but one breach of licence, nor that neither: whenas those corruptions, which it seeks to prevent, break in faster at other doors which cannot be shut. . . .

Well knows he who uses to consider, that our faith and knowledge thrives by exercise, as well as our limbs and complexion. Truth is compared in Scripture to a streaming fountain; if her waters flow not in a perpetual progression, they sicken into a muddy pool of conformity and tradition. A man may be a heretic in the truth; and if he believe things only because his Pastor says so, or the Assembly so determines, without knowing other reason, though his belief be true, yet the very truth he holds becomes his heresy. . . .

There be who perpetually complain of schisms and sects, and make it such a calamity that any man dissents from their maxims. 'Tis their own pride and ignorance which causes the disturbing, who neither will hear with meekness, nor can convince; yet all must be suppressed which is not found in their Syntagma. They are the troublers, they are the dividers of unity, who neglect and permit not others to unite those dissevered pieces which are yet wanting to the body of Truth. To be still searching what we know not by what we know, still closing up truth to truth as we find it (for all her body is homogeneal and proportional), this is the golden rule in theology as well as in arithmetic, and makes up the best harmony in a Church; not the forced and outward union of cold and neutral, and inwardly divided minds.

Lords and Commons of England, consider what Nation it is whereof ye are, and whereof ye are the governors: a Nation not slow and dull, but of a quick, ingenious and piercing spirit, acute to invent, subtle and sinewy to discourse, not beneath the reach of any point, the highest that human capacity can soar to. . . .

Behold now this vast City: a city of refuge, the mansion house of liberty, encompassed and surrounded with His protection; the shop of war hath not there more anvils and hammers waking, to fashion out the plates and instruments of armed Justice in defence of beleaguered Truth, than there be pens and heads there, sitting by their studious lamps, musing, searching, revolving new notions and ideas wherewith to present, as with their homage and their fealty, the approaching Reformation: others as fast reading, trying all things, assenting to the force of reason and convincement. What could a man require more from a Nation so pliant and so prone to seek after knowledge? What wants there to such a towardly and pregnant soil, but wise and faithful labourers, to make a knowing people, a Nation of Prophets, of Sages, and of Worthies? We reckon more than five months yet to harvest; there need not be five weeks; had we but eyes to lift up, the fields are white already.

Where there is much desire to learn, there of necessity will be much arguing, much writing, many opinions; for opinion in good men is but knowledge in the making. Under these fantastic terrors of sect and schism, we wrong the earnest and zealous thirst after knowledge and understanding which God hath stirred up in this city. What some lament of, we rather should rejoice at, should rather praise this pious forwardness among men, to reassume the ill-reputed care of their Religion into their own hands again. A little generous prudence, a little forbearance of one another, and some grain of charity might win all these diligences to join, and unite in one general and brotherly search after Truth. . . .

Yet these are the men cried out against for schismatics and sectaries; as if, while the temple of the Lord was building, some cutting, some squaring the marble, others hewing the cedars, there should be a sort of irrational men who could not consider there must be many schisms and many dissections made in the quarry and in the timber, ere the house of God can be built. And when every stone is laid artfully together, it cannot be united into a continuity, it can but be contiguous in this world; neither can every piece of the building be of one form; nay rather the perfection consists in this, that, out of many moderate varieties and brotherly dissimilitudes that are not vastly disproportional, arises the goodly and the graceful symmetry that commends the whole pile and structure. . . .

The adversary again applauds, and waits the hour: When they have branched themselves out, saith he, small enough into parties and partitions, then will be our time. Fool! he sees not the firm root, out of which we all grow, though into branches: nor will be ware until he see our small divided maniples cutting through at every angle of his ill-united and unwieldy brigade. And that we are to hope better of all these supposed sects and schisms, and that we shall not need that solicitude, honest perhaps though overtimorous of them that vex in his behalf, but shall laugh in the end at those malicious applauders of our differences, I have these reasons to persuade me.

First, when a City shall be as it were besieged and blocked about, her navigable river infested, inroads and incursions round, defiance and battle oft rumoured to be marching up even to her walls and suburb trenches, that then the people, or the greater part, more than at other times, wholly taken up with the study of highest and most important matters to be reformed, should be disputing, reasoning, reading, inventing, discoursing, even to a rarity and admiration, things not before discoursed or written of, argues first a singular goodwill, contentedness and confidence in your prudent foresight and safe government, Lords and Commons; and from thence derives itself to a gallant bravery and well-grounded contempt of their enemies, as if there were no small number of as great spirits among us, as his was, who when Rome was nigh besieged by Hannibal, being in the city, bought that piece of ground at no cheap rate, whereon Hannibal himself encamped his own regiment.

Next, it is a lively and cheerful presage of our happy success and victory. For as in a body, when the blood is fresh, the spirits pure and vigorous, not only to vital but to rational faculties, and those in the acutest and the pertest operations of wit and subtlety, it argues in what good plight and constitution the body is so when the cheerfulness of the people is so sprightly up, as that it has not only wherewith to guard well its own freedom and safety, but to spare, and to bestow upon the solidest and sublimest points of controversy and new invention, it betokens us not degenerated, nor drooping to a fatal decay, but casting off the old and wrinkled skin of corruption to outlive these pangs and wax young again, entering the glorious ways of truth and prosperous virtue, destined to become great and honourable in these latter ages. Methinks I see in my mind a noble and puissant nation rousing herself like a strong man after sleep, and shaking her invincible locks. Methinks I see her as an eagle mewing her mighty youth, and kindling her undazzled eyes at the full midday beam; purging and unscaling her long-abused sight at the fountain itself of heavenly radiance; while the whole noise of timorous and flocking birds, with those also that love the twilight, flutter about, amazed at what she means, and in their envious gabble would prognosticate a year of sects and schisms.

What would ye do then? should ye suppress all this flowery crop of knowledge and new light sprung up and yet springing daily in this city? should ye set an oligarchy of twenty engrossers over it, to bring a famine upon our minds again, when we shall know nothing but what is measured to us by their bushel? . . .

And now the time in special is, by privilege to write and speak what may help to the further discussing of matters in agitation. The temple of Janus with his two controversial faces might now not unsignificantly be set open. And though all the winds of doctrine were let loose to play upon the earth, so

Truth be in the field, we do injuriously, by licensing and prohibiting, to misdoubt her strength. Let her and Falsehood grapple; who ever knew Truth put to the worse, in a free and open encounter? Her confuting is the best and surest suppressing. . . .

I fear yet this iron yoke of outward conformity hath left a slavish print upon our necks; the ghost of a linen decency yet haunts us. We stumble and are impatient at the least dividing of one visible congregation from another, though it be not in fundamentals; and through our forwardness to suppress, and our backwardness to recover any enthralled piece of truth out of the gripe of custom, we care not to keep truth separated from truth, which is the fiercest rent and disunion of all. We do not see that, while we still affect by all means a rigid external formality, we may as soon fall again into a gross conforming stupidity, a stark and dead congealment of wood and hay and stubble, forced and frozen together, which is more to the sudden degenerating of a Church than many subdichotomies of petty schisms.

Not that I can think well of every light separation, or that all in a Church is to be expected gold and silver and precious stones: it is not possible for man to sever the wheat from the tares, the good fish from the other fry; that must be the Angels' Ministry at the end of mortal things. Yet if all cannot be of one mind — as who looks they should be? — this doubtless is more wholesome, more prudent, and more Christian that many be tolerated, rather than all compelled. I mean not tolerated popery, and open superstition, which, as it extirpates all religions and civil supremacies, so itself should be extirpate, provided first that all charitable and compassionate means be used to win and regain the weak and the misled: that also which is impious or evil absolutely either against faith or manners no law can possibly permit, that intends not to unlaw itself: but those neighbouring differences, or rather indifferences, are what I speak of, whether in some point of doctrine or of discipline, which, though they may be many, yet need not interrupt the unity of Spirit, if we could but find among us the bond of peace.

In the meantime if any one would write, and bring his helpful hand to the slow-moving Reformation which we labour under, if Truth have spoken to him before others, or but seemed at least to speak, who hath so bejesuited us that we should trouble that man with asking licence to do so worthy a deed? and not consider this, that if it come to prohibiting, there is not aught more likely to be prohibited than truth itself; whose first appearance to our eyes, bleared and dimmed with prejudice and custom, is more unsightly and un-plausible than many errors, even as the person is of many a great man slight and contemptible to see to. And what do they tell us vainly of new opinions, when this very opinion of theirs, that none must be heard, but whom they like, is the worst and newest opinion of all others; and is the chief cause why sects and schisms do so much abound, and true knowledge is kept at distance from us. . . .

DECLARATION OF INDEPENDENCE
July 4, 1776

When in the Course of human events, it becomes necessary for one people to dissolve the political bands, which have connected them with another, and to assume, among the powers of the earth, the separate and equal station, to which the Laws of Nature and of Nature's God entitle them, a decent respect to the Opinions of mankind requires that they should declare the causes which impel them to the separation. — We hold these truths to be self-evident, that all men are created equal, that they are endowed by their Creator with certain unalienable Rights, that among these are Life, Liberty and the pursuit of Happiness. — That to secure these rights, Governments are instituted among Men, deriving their just powers from the consent of the governed, — That whenever any Form of Government becomes destructive of these ends, it is the Right of the People to alter or to abolish it, and to institute new Government, laying its foundation on such principles and organizing its powers in such form, as to them shall seem most likely to effect their Safety and Happiness. Prudence, indeed, will dictate that Governments long established should not be changed for light and transient causes; and accordingly all experience hath shewn, that mankind are more disposed to suffer, while evils are sufferable, than to right themselves by abolishing the forms to which they are accustomed. But when a long train of abuses and usurpations, pursuing invariably the same Object evinces a design to reduce them under absolute Despotism, it is their right, it is their duty to throw off such Government, and to provide new Guards for their future security. — Such has been the patient sufferance of these Colonies; and such is now the necessity which constrains them to alter their former Systems of Government.

JEFFERSON, FIRST INAUGURAL ADDRESS
March 4, 1801
The Complete Jefferson 384-385 (Padover ed. 1943)

During the contest of opinion through which we have passed, the animation of discussion and of exertions has sometimes worn an aspect which might impose on strangers unused to think freely and to speak and to write what they think; but this being now decided by the voice of the nation, announced according to the rules of the constitution, all will, of course, arrange themselves under the will of the law, and unite in common efforts for the common good. All, too, will bear in mind this sacred principle, that though the will of the majority is in all cases to prevail, that will, to be rightful, must be reasonable; that the minority possess their equal rights, which equal laws must protect, and to violate which would be oppression. Let us, then, fellow-citizens, unite with one heart and one mind. Let us restore to social intercourse that harmony and affection without which liberty and even life itself are but dreary things. And let us reflect that having banished from our land that religious intolerance under which mankind so long bled and suffered, we have yet gained little if we countenance a political intolerance as despotic, as wicked, and capable of as bitter and bloody persecutions. During the throes and convulsions of the ancient world, during the agonizing spasms of infuriated man, seeking through blood and slaughter his long lost liberty, it was not wonderful that the agitation of the billows should reach even this distant and peaceful shore; that this should be more felt and feared by some and less by others; that this should divide opinions as to measures of safety. But every difference of opinion is not a difference of principle. We have called by different names brethren of the same principle. We are all republicans — we are federalists. If there be any among us who would wish to dissolve this Union or to change its republican form, let them stand undisturbed as monuments of the safety with which error of opinion may be tolerated where reason is left free to combat it. I know, indeed, that some honest men fear that a republican government cannot be strong; that this govenment is not strong enough. But would the honest patriot, in the full tide of successful experiment, abandon a government which has so far kept us free and firm, on the theoretic and visionary fear that this government, the world's best hope, may by possibility want energy to preserve itself? I trust not. I believe this, on the contrary, the strongest government on earth. I believe it is the only one where every man, at the call of the laws, would fly to the standard of the law, and would meet invasions of the public order as his own personal concern. Sometimes it is said that man cannot be trusted with the government of himself. Can he, then, be trusted with the government of others? Or have we found angels in the forms of kings to govern him? Let history answer this question.

JOHN STUART MILL, ON LIBERTY
1859
15, 24-25, 30-31, 40-41, 47-48 (McCallum ed. 1946)

First: The opinion which it is attempted to suppress by authority may possibly be true. Those who desire to suppress it, of course deny its truth; but they are not infallible. They have no authority to decide the question for all mankind, and exclude every other person from the means of judging. To refuse a hearing to an opinion, because they are sure that it is false, is to assume that *their* certainty is the same thing as *absolute* certainty. All silencing of discussion is an assumption of infallibility. Its condemnation may be allowed to rest on this common argument, not the worse for being common. . . .

But, indeed, the dictum that truth always triumphs over persecution is one of those pleasant falsehoods which men repeat after one another till they pass into commonplaces, but which all experience refutes. History teems with instances of truth put down by persecution. If not suppressed for ever, it may be thrown back for centuries. To speak only of religious opinions: the Reformation broke out at least twenty times before Luther, and was put down. Arnold of Brescia was put down. Fra Dolcino was put down. Savonarola was put down. The Albigeois were put down. The Vaudois were put down. The Lollards were put down. The Hussites were put down. Even after the era of Luther, wherever persecution was persisted in, it was successful. In Spain, Italy, Flanders, the Austrian Empire, Protestantism was rooted out; and, most likely, would have been so in England, had Queen Mary lived, or Queen Elizabeth died. Persecution has always succeeded, save where the heretics were too strong a party to be effectually persecuted. No reasonable person can doubt that Christianity might have been extirpated in the Roman Empire. It spread, and became predominant, because the persecutions were only occasional, lasting but a short time, and separated by long intervals of almost undisturbed propagandism. It is a piece of idle sentimentality that truth, merely as truth, has any inherent power denied to error of prevailing against the dungeon and the stake. Men are not more zealous for truth than they often are for error, and a sufficient application of legal or even of social penalties will generally succeed in stopping the propagation of either. The real advantage which truth has consists in this, that when an opinion is true, it may be extinguished once, twice, or many times, but in the course of ages there will generally be found persons to rediscover it, until some one of its reappearances falls on a time when from favourable circumstances it escapes persecution until it has made such head as to withstand all subsequent attempts to suppress it. . . .

Let us now pass to the second division of the argument, and dismissing the supposition that any of the received opinions may be false, let us assume them to be true, and examine into the worth of the manner in which they are likely to be held, when their truth is not freely and openly canvassed. However unwillingly a person who has a strong opinion may admit the possibility that his opinion may be false he ought to be moved by the consideration that, however true it may be, if it is not fully, frequently, and fearlessly discussed, it will be held as a dead dogma, not a living truth.

There is a class of persons (happily not quite so numerous as formerly) who think it enough if a person assents undoubtingly to what they think true, though he has not knowledge whatever of the grounds of the opinion, and could not make a tenable defence of it against the most superficial objections. Such persons, if they can once get their creed taught from authority, naturally think that no good, and some harm, comes of its being allowed to be questioned. Where their influence prevails, they make it nearly impossible for the received opinion to be rejected wisely and considerately, though it may still be rejected rashly and ignorantly; for to shut out discussion entirely is seldom possible, and when it once gets in, beliefs not grounded on conviction are apt to give way before the slightest semblance of an argument. Waiving, however, this possibility — assuming that the true opinion abides in the mind, but abides as a prejudice, a belief independent of, and proof against, argument — this is not the way in which truth ought to be held by a rational being. This is not knowing the truth. Truth, thus held, is but one superstition the more, accidentally clinging to the words which enunciate a truth. . . .

It still remains to speak of one of the principal causes which make diversity of opinion advantageous, and will continue to do so until mankind shall have entered a stage of intellectual advancement which at present seems at an incalculable distance. We have hitherto considered only two possibilities: that the received opinion may be false, and some other opinion, consequently, true; or that, the received opinion being true, a conflict with the opposite error is essential to a clear apprehension and deep feeling of its truth. But there is a commoner case than either of these; when the conflicting doctrines, instead of being one true and the other false, share the truth between them; and the nonconforming opinion is needed to supply the remainder of the truth, of which the received doctrine embodies only a part. Popular opinions, on subjects not palpable to sense, are often true, but seldom or never the whole truth. They are a part of the truth; sometimes a greater, sometimes a smaller part, but exaggerated, distorted, and disjointed from the truths by which they ought to be accompanied and limited. Heretical opinions, on the other hand, are generally some of these suppressed and neglected truths, bursting the bonds which kept them down, and either seeking reconciliation with the truth contained in the common opinion, or fronting it as enemies, and setting themselves up, with similar exclusiveness, as the whole truth. The latter case is hitherto the most frequent, as, in the human mind, one-sidedness has always been the rule, and many-sidedness the exception. Hence, even in revolutions of opinion, one part of the truth usually sets while another rises. Even progress, which ought to superadd, for the most part only substitutes, one partial and incomplete truth for another; improvement consisting chiefly in this, that the new fragment of truth is more wanted, more adapted to the needs of the time, than that which it displaces. Such being the partial character of prevailing opinions, even when resting on a true foundation, every opinion which embodies somewhat of the portion of truth which the common opinion omits, ought to be considered precious, with whatever amount of error and confusion that truth may be blended. No sober judge of human affairs will feel bound to be indignant because those who force on our notice truths which we should otherwise have overlooked, overlook some of those which we see. Rather, he will think that so long as popular truth is one-sided, it is more desirable than otherwise that unpopular truth should have one-sided assertors too; such being usually the most energetic, and the most likely to compel reluctant attention to the fragment of wisdom which they proclaim as if it were the whole. . . .

Before quitting the subject of freedom of opinion, it is fit to take some notice of those who say, that the free expression of all opinions should be permitted, on condition that the manner be temperate, and do not pass the bounds of fair discussion. Much might be said on the impossibility of fixing where these supposed bounds are to be placed; for if the test be offence to those whose opinions are attacked, I think experience testifies that this offence is given whenever the attack is telling and powerful, and that every opponent who pushes them hard, and whom they find it difficult to answer, appears to them, if he shows any strong feeling on the subject, an intemperate opponent. But this, though an important consideration in a practical point of view, merges in a more fundamental objection. Undoubtedly the manner of asserting an opinion, even though it be a true one, may be very objectionable, and may justly incur severe censure. But the principal offences of the kind are such as it is mostly impossible, unless by accidental self-betrayal, to bring home to conviction. The gravest of them is, to argue sophistically, to suppress facts or arguments, to misstate the elements of the case, or misrepresent the opposite opinion. But all this, even to the most aggravated degree, is so continually done in perfect good faith, by persons who are not considered, and in many other respects may not deserve to be considered, ignorant or incompetent, that it is rarely possible, on adequate grounds, conscientiously to stamp the misrepresentation as morally culpable; and still less could law presume to interfere with this kind of controversial misconduct. With regard to what is commonly meant by intemperate discussion, namely invective, sarcasm, personality, and the like, the denunciation of these weapons would deserve more sympathy if it were ever proposed to interdict them equally to both sides; but it is only desired to restrain the employment of them against the prevailing opinion: against the unprevailing they may not only be used without general disapproval, but will be likely to obtain for him who uses them the praise of honest zeal and righteous indignation. Yet whatever mischief arises from their use, is greatest when they are employed against the comparatively defenceless; and whatever unfair advantage can be derived by any opinion from this mode of asserting it, accrues almost exclusively to received opinions. The worst offence of this kind which can be committed by a polemic, is to stigmatise those who hold the contrary opinion as bad and immoral men. To calumny of this sort, those who hold any unpopular opinion are peculiarly exposed, because they are in general few and uninfluential, and nobody but themselves feels much interested in seeing justice done them; but this weapon is, from the nature of the case, denied to those who attack a prevailing opinion: they can neither use it with safety to themselves, nor, if they could, would it do anything but recoil on their own cause. In general, opinions contrary to those commonly received can only obtain a hearing by studied moderation of language, and the most cautious avoidance of unnecessary offence, from which they hardly ever deviate even in a slight degree without losing ground: while unmeasured vituperation employed on the side of the prevailing opinion really does deter people from professing contrary opinions, and from listening to those who profess them. For the interest, therefore, of truth and justice, it is far more important to restrain this employment of vituperative language than the other; and, for example, if it were necessary to choose, there would be much more need to discourage offensive attacks on infidelity than on religion. It is, however, obvious that law and authority have no business with restraining either, while opinion ought, in every instance, to determine its verdict by the circumstances of the individual case; condemning every one, on whichever side of the argument he places himself, in whose mode of advocacy either want of candour, or malignity, bigotry, or intolerance of feeling manifest themselves; but not inferring these vices from the side which a person takes, though it be the contrary side of the question to our own: and giving merited honour to every one, whatever opinion he may hold, who has calmness to see and honesty to state what his opponents and their opinions really are, exaggerating nothing to their discredit, keeping nothing back which tells, or can be supposed to tell, in their favour. This is the real morality of public discussion: and if often violated, I am happy to think that there are many controversialists who to a great extent observe it, and a still greater number who conscientiously strive towards it.

ABRAMS v. UNITED STATES
250 U.S. 616, 630-631, 40 S. Ct. 17, 22, 63 L. Ed. 1173, 1180 (1919)

HOLMES, J. . . .

Persecution for the expression of opinions seems to me perfectly logical. If you have no doubt of your premises or your power and want a certain result with all your heart you naturally express your wishes in law and sweep away all opposition. To allow opposition by speech seems to indicate that you think the speech impotent, as when a man says that he has squared the circle, or that you do not care wholeheartedly for the result, or that you doubt either your power or your premises. But when men have realized that time has upset many fighting faiths, they may come to believe even more than they believe the very foundations of their own conduct that the ultimate good desired is better reached by free trade in ideas — that the best test of truth is the power of the thought to get itself accepted in the competition of the market, and that truth is the only ground upon which their wishes safely can be carried out. That at any rate is the theory of our Constitution. It is an experiment, as all life is an experiment. Every year if not every day we have to wager our salvation upon some prophecy based upon imperfect knowledge. While that experiment is part of our system I think that we should be eternally vigilant against attempts to check the expression of opinions that we loathe and believe to be fraught with death, unless they so imminently threaten immediate interference with the lawful and pressing purposes of the law that an immediate check is required to save the country. . . . Only the emergency that makes it immediately dangerous to leave the correction of evil counsels to time warrants making any exception to the sweeping command, "Congress shall make no law . . . abridging the freedom of speech."

WHITNEY v. CALIFORNIA
274 U.S. 357, 375-376, 47 S. Ct. 641, 648, 71 L. Ed. 1095, 1105-1106 (1927)

BRANDEIS, J. . . .

Those who won our independence believed that the final end of the State was to make men free to develop their faculties; and that in its government the deliberative forces should prevail over the arbitrary. They valued liberty both as an end and as a means. They believed liberty to be the secret of happiness and courage to be the secret of liberty. They believed that freedom to think as you will and to speak as you think are means indispensable to the discovery and spread of political truth; that without free speech and assembly discussion would be futile; that with them, discussion affords ordinarily adequate protection against the dissemination of noxious doctrine; that the greatest menace to freedom is an inert people; that public discussion is a political duty; and that this should be a fundamental principle of the American government. They recognized the risks to which all human institutions are subject. But they knew that order cannot be secured merely through fear of punishment for its infraction; that it is hazardous to discourage thought, hope and imagination; that fear breeds repression; that repression breeds hate; that hate menaces stable government; that the path of safety lies in the opportunity to discuss freely supposed grievances and proposed remedies; and that the fitting remedy for evil counsels is good ones. Believing in the power of reason as applied through public discussion, they eschewed silence coerced by law — the argument of force in its worst form. Recognizing the occasional tyrannies of governing majorities, they amended the Constitution so that free speech and assembly should be guaranteed.

MEIKLEJOHN, POLITICAL FREEDOM *
18-19, 26-28

Our preliminary remarks about the Constitution of the United States may, then, be briefly summarized. That Constitution is based upon a twofold political agreement. It is ordained that all authority to exercise control, to determine common action, belongs to "We, the People." We, and we alone, are the rulers. But it is ordained also that We, the People, are, all alike, subject to control. Every one of us may be told what he is allowed to do, what he is not allowed to do, what he is required to do. But this agreed-upon requirement of obedience does not transform a ruler into a slave. Citizens do not become puppets of the state when, having created it by common consent, they pledge allegiance to it and keep their pledge. Control by a self-governing nation is

* Copyright 1948, 1960, by Harper & Row.

utterly different in kind from control by an irresponsible despotism. And to confuse these two is to lose all understanding of what political freedom is. Under actual conditions, there is no freedom for men except by the authority of government. Free men are not non-governed. They are governed — by themselves. . . .

The First Amendment, then, is not the guardian of unregulated talkativeness. It does not require that, on every occasion, every citizen shall take part in public debate. Nor can it even give assurance that everyone shall have opportunity to do so. . . . What is essential is not that everyone shall speak, but that everything worth saying shall be said. To this end, for example, it may be arranged that each of the known conflicting points of view shall have, and shall be limited to, an assigned share of the time available. But however it be arranged, the vital point, as stated negatively, is that no suggestion of policy shall be denied a hearing because it is on one side of the issue rather than another. And this means that though citizens may, on other grounds, be barred from speaking, they may not be barred because their views are thought to be false or dangerous. No plan of action shall be outlawed because someone in control thinks it unwise, unfair, un-American. No speaker may be declared "out of order" because we disagree with what he intends to say. And the reason for this equality of status in the field of ideas lies deep in the very foundations of the self-governing process. When men govern themselves, it is they — and no one else — who must pass judgment upon unwisdom and unfairness and danger. And that means that unwise ideas must have a hearing as well as wise ones, unfair as well as fair, dangerous as well as safe, un-American as well as American. Just so far as, at any point, the citizens who are to decide an issue are denied acquaintance with information or opinion or doubt or disbelief or criticism which is relevant to that issue, just so far the result must be ill-considered, ill-balanced planning for the general good. *It is that mutilation of the thinking process of the community against which the First Amendment to the Constitution is directed.* The principle of the freedom of speech springs from the necessities of the program of self-government. It is not a Law of Nature or of Reason in the abstract. It is a deduction from the basic American agreement that public issues shall be decided by universal suffrage.

If, then, on any occasion in the United States it is allowable to say that the Constitution is a good document it is equally allowable, in that situation, to say that the Constitution is a bad document. If a public building may be used in which to say, in time of war, that the war is justified, then the same building may be used in which to say that it is not justified. If it be publicly argued that conscription for armed service is moral and necessary, it may likewise be publicly argued that it is immoral and unnecessary. If it may be said that American political institutions are superior to those of England or Russia or Germany, it may, with equal freedom, be said that those of England or Russia or Germany are superior to ours. These conflicting views may be expressed, must be expressed, not because they are valid, but because they are relevant. If they are responsibly entertained by anyone, we, the voters, need to hear them. When a question of policy is "before the house," free men choose to meet it not with their eyes shut, but with their eyes open. To be afraid of ideas, any idea, is to be unfit for self-government. Any such suppression of ideas about the common good, the First Amendment condemns with its absolute disapproval. The freedom of ideas shall not be abridged.

REFERENCES

1. Sources of the theory and tradition of freedom of expression, in addition to those quoted above, include Locke, The Second Treatise of Civil Government (1690) and Letters on Toleration (1689-1704); Hume, Essays Moral, Political, and Literary (1741-1777), in David Hume's Political Essays (Hendel ed. 1953); Paine, The Rights of Man (1791); Condorcet, Outlines of an Historical View of the Progress of the Human Mind (1796); Jefferson, The Kentucky Resolutions (1798), in The Complete Jefferson 128-134 (Padover ed. 1943); de Tocqueville, Democracy in America (1835); Bagehot, Physics and Politics (1873) and The Metaphysical Basis of Toleration (1874); Acton's lectures and essays (1861-1895) in Essays on Freedom and Power (Himmelfarb ed. 1948). Reference to the contributions of numerous English and American writers of the seventeenth and eighteenth centuries may be found in Levy, Legacy of Suppression (1960). For an account of the views and actions of Thomas Jefferson contrary to the liberal tradition, see Levy, Jefferson and Civil Liberties: The Darker Side (1963). On Voltaire, see Rowe, Voltaire and the State (1955). See also Lieber, On Civil Liberty and Self-Government (3d ed. rev. 1874).

2. Modern exponents of the traditional theory of freedom of expression include Laski, Authority in the Modern State (1919) and Liberty in the Modern State (1930); Chafee, Free Speech in the United States (1941) and The Blessings of Liberty (1956); Riesman, Civil Liberties in a Period of Transition, in 3 Public Policy (Friedrich and Mason eds. 1942); Becker, The Declaration of Independence (1942), and Freedom and Responsibility in the American Way of Life (1945); A. Meiklejohn, Political Freedom (1960) (originally published in part under the title, Free Speech and Its Relation to Self-Government (1948)); Hand, The Spirit of Liberty (Dillard ed. 1953); Commager, Freedom, Loyalty, Dissent (1954); Bay, The Structure of Freedom (1958); Douglas, The Right of the People (1958); Gellhorn, American Rights (1960); Tussman, Obligation and the Body Politic (1960); Emerson, Toward a General Theory of the First Amendment, 72 Yale L.J. 877 (1963). For the Catholic view see Ryan and Boland, Catholic Principles of Politics (1940); O'Meara, Freedom of Inquiry Versus Authority: Some Legal Aspects, 31 Notre Dame Law. 3 (1955); Gardiner, Catholic Viewpoint on Censorship (1958); Murray, We Hold These Truths (1960). See also Hocking, Freedom of the Press (1947); Hook, Heresy, Yes — Conspiracy, No! (1953) and The Paradoxes of Freedom (1962); Lippmann, The Public Philosophy (1955); Harding (ed.), Free Man Versus His Government (1958); and various decisions of the Supreme Court and discussions thereof, infra.

3. Materials dealing generally with issues of freedom or liberty are voluminous. Among those more relevant to the theory of freedom of expression are Kallen (ed.), Freedom in the Modern World (1928) and A Study of Liberty (1959); Maritain, Freedom in the Modern World (1936) and Man and the State (1951); Dewey, Freedom and Culture (1939); Anshen (ed.), Freedom, Its Meaning (1940); Barker, Reflections on Government (1942); Mumford, The Conduct of Life (1951); Gordon Walker, Restatement of Liberty (1951); MacIver (ed.), Conflict of Loyalties (1952); Popper, The Open

Society and Its Enemies (2d ed. 1952); Bryson et al. (eds.), Freedom and Authority in Our Time (1953); Fuller, Freedom — A Suggested Analysis, 68 Harv. L. Rev. 1305 (1955); Neumann, The Democratic and the Authoritarian State (1957); Adler, The Idea of Freedom (1958, 1961) (a survey of the various concepts of freedom, containing an extensive bibliography); Berlin, Two Concepts of Liberty (1958); Hook, Political Power and Personal Freedom (1959); Sabine, A History of Political Theory (rev. ed. 1959); Muller, Issues of Freedom (1960); Spiller (ed.), Social Control in a Free Society (1960); Bronowski and Mazlish, The Western Intellectual Tradition (1960); Cahn, The Predicament of Democratic Man (1961); Oppenheim, Dimensions of Freedom (1961); Frankel, The Democratic Prospect (1962); Friedrich (ed.), Liberty (1962); D. Meiklejohn, Freedom and the Public (1965).

4. Historical accounts of the development and practice of freedom, including freedom of expression, may be found in Bury, A History of Freedom of Thought (2d ed. 1952); Robertson, A Short History of Freethought (1957); Muller, Freedom in the Ancient World (1961), Freedom in the Western World: From the Dark Ages to the Rise of Democracy (1963), and Freedom in the Modern World (1966); Shotwell, The Long Way to Freedom (1960); Lecky, A History of the Rise and Influence of the Spirit of Rationalism in Europe (rev. ed. 1895); Levy, Legacy of Suppression (1960); Siebert, Freedom of the Press in England 1476-1776 (1952); Patterson, Free Speech and a Free Press (1939); Laski, The Rise of European Liberalism (1936); Bryce, Modern Democracies (1921); Castberg, Freedom of Speech in the West (1960); Kirchheimer, Political Justice (1961); Brant, The Bill of Rights (1965). For the historical development in America, see Chapter II.

5. Collections of basic documents, writings, and similar materials include Smith, The Democratic Spirit (1941); Coker, Democracy, Liberty and Property (1942); Jones, Primer of Intellectual Freedom (1949); MacIver, Great Expressions of Human Rights (1950); Chafee, Documents on Fundamental Human Rights (prelim. ed. 1951, 1952, rev. ed. 1963); Mayer, The Tradition of Freedom (1957); Bachrack, Problems in Freedom (1954); Smith and Murphy, Liberty and Justice (1958); Perry, Sources of Our Liberties (1959); Downs, The First Freedom: Liberty and Justice in the World of Reading (1960); McCormick and MacInnis, Versions of Censorship (1962); Newman, The Freedom Reader (rev. 2d ed. 1963). See also Hacker, The Shaping of the American Tradition (1947); Commager, Documents of American History (5th ed. 1949) and Living Ideas in America (1951). Collections of American court decisions and legal comment are cited in Chapter II, Section H.

6. Discussions of political and economic factors bearing on the maintenance of a system of freedom of political expression include Hayek, The Road to Serfdom (1944) and The Constitution of Liberty (1960); Wootton, Freedom Under Planning (1945); Knight, Freedom and Reform (1947); Russell, Authority and the Individual (1949); Mannheim, Freedom, Power, and Democratic Planning (1950); M. Polyani, The Logic of Liberty (1951); Schumpeter, Capitalism, Socialism and Democracy (4th ed. 1952); Mason, Security Through Freedom (1955); Mills, The Power Elite (1956); Loewenstein, Political Power and the Governmental Process (1957); Berle, Economic Power and the Free Society (1957); Friedrich (ed.), Authority (1958); Miller, The Constitutional Law of the "Security State," 10 Stan. L. Rev. 620 (1958), and Technology, Social Change, and the Constitution, 33 Geo. Wash. L. Rev. 17 (1964); Spitz, Democracy and the Challenge of Power (1958); C. B. Hoover, The Economy, Liberty and the State (1959); Mendelson, Capitalism, Democracy and the Supreme Court (1960); D'Antonio and Ehrlich (eds.), Power and Democracy in America (1961) (bibliography at 154-181); Woodard, Reality and Social Reform: The Transition From Laissez-Faire to the Welfare State, 72 Yale L.J. 286 (1962); Reich, The New Property, 73 Yale L.J. 733 (1964). Studies of organization, political and other, include Michels, Political Parties (E. and C. Paul trs. 1915); Simon, Administrative Behavior (1947, 2d ed. 1957); Merton et al.

(eds.), Reader in Bureaucracy (1952); Blau, Bureaucracy in Modern Society (1956); Selznick, The Organizational Weapon (1960).

Studies of psychological attitudes toward freedom include Fromm, Escape from Freedom (1941), Man for Himself (1947), and The Sane Society (1955); Riesman, The Lonely Crowd (1950), and Individualism Reconsidered (1953); Mills, White Collar (1953); May, Man's Search for Himself (1953); Whyte, The Organization Man (1956); M. Stein et al. (eds.), Identity and Anxiety (1960); Schaar, Escape from Authority (1961). See also Hoffer, The True Believer (1951). Materials dealing particularly with antidemocratic thought processes may be found in Alexander, The Emotional Structure of Totalitarianism, in Our Age of Unreason (rev. ed. 1951); Spitz, Patterns of Anti-Democratic Thought (1949); Adorno et al., The Authoritarian Personality (1950); Arendt, The Origins of Totalitarianism (1951, 2d ed. 1958); Allport, The Nature of Prejudice (1955); Bettelheim and Janowitz, Social Change and Prejudice (1964). For discussion of the social function of conflict see Simmel, Conflict (Wolff tr. 1955); Coser, The Functions of Social Conflict (1956); Rapoport, Fights, Games, and Debates (1960); for a recent survey of the literature see Angell, The Sociology of Human Conflict, in McNeil (ed.), The Nature of Human Conflict (1965).

Other material from the social sciences relevant to issues of freedom includes Malinowski, Freedom and Civilization (1944); West, Conscience and Society (1942); Flugel, Man, Morals and Society (1945); deGrazia, The Political Community: A Study of Anomie (1948); Kluckholn, Mirror for Man (1949); Hacker, Liberal Democracy and Social Control, 51 Am. Pol. Sci. Rev. 1009 (1957), and critique by Cook, id. at 1027; Berger et al. (eds.), Freedom and Control in Modern Society (1954); Bell (ed.), The New American Right (1955); Stouffer, Communism, Conformity, and Civil Liberties (1955); Dobzhansky, The Biological Basis of Human Freedom (1956); Festinger, A Theory of Cognitive Dissonance (1957); Bay, The Structure of Freedom (1958); Hyman, Political Socialization (1959); Kornhauser, The Politics of Mass Society (1959); Lipset, Political Man (1960); White and Lippitt, Autocracy and Democracy (1960); Rokeach, The Open and Closed Mind (1960); Gusfield, Mass Society and Extremist Politics, 27 Am. Soc. Rev. 19 (1962); Blau, Exchange and Power in Social Life (1964). For a compilation of propositions considered to be established by the behavioral sciences, see Berelson and Steiner, Human Behavior: An Inventory of Scientific Findings (1964).

7. For philosophic critiques of democratic thought, see Hobbes, Leviathan (1651); Nietzsche, Beyond Good and Evil, and the Will to Power (Complete Works of Friedrich Nietzsche, 1925); Pareto, The Mind and Society (1935); Plato, The Republic. See also Vishinsky, The Law of the State (1948, Russian original published in 1938). For an account of individual rights in various authoritarian societies, see Metz and Thomson, Authoritarianism and the Individual (1950). A vigorous criticism of the liberal tradition of freedom of expression appears in Berns, Freedom, Virtue and the First Amendment (1957).

For material challenging the theory that freedom of expression should be granted to antidemocratic groups, see Durbin, The Politics of Democratic Socialism (1940); Popper, The Open Society and Its Enemies (2d ed. 1952); Lippmann, Essays in the Public Philosophy 131-134 (1955); Lippincott, Democracy's Dilemma: The Totalitarian Party in a Free Society (1965) (bibliography at 239-268).

8. An extensive general bibliography is Brooks, A Bibliography of Civil Rights and Civil Liberties (1962).

B.   The Dynamics of Limitation

EMERSON, TOWARD A GENERAL THEORY
OF THE FIRST AMENDMENT
72 Yale L.J. 877, 887-891 (1963)

In constructing and maintaining a system of freedom of expression, the principal problems and major controversies have arisen when the attempt is made to fit the affirmative theory — that is, the affirmative functions served by the system — into a more comprehensive scheme of social values and social goals. The crucial issues have revolved around the question of what limitations, if any, ought to be imposed upon freedom of expression in order to reconcile that interest with other individual and social interests sought by the good society. Most of our efforts in the past to formulate rules for limiting freedom of expression have been seriously defective through failure to take into consideration the realistic context in which such limitations are administered. The crux of the problem is that the limitations, whatever they may be, must be applied by one group of human beings to other human beings. In order to take adequate account of this factor it is necessary to have some understanding of the forces in conflict, the practical difficulties in formulating limitations, the state apparatus necessary to enforce them, the possibility of distorting them to attain ulterior purposes, and the impact of the whole process upon achieving an effective system of free expression.

The starting point is a recognition of the powerful forces that impel men toward the elimination of unorthodox expression. Most men have a strong inclination to suppress opposition even where differences in viewpoint are comparatively slight. But a system of free expression must be framed to withstand far greater stress. The test of any such system is not whether it tolerates minor deviations but whether it permits criticism of the fundamental beliefs and practices of the society. And in this area the drives to repress, both irrational and rational, tend to become overwhelming.

. . . The strong innate drive to suppress deviant opinion has also been stressed in modern studies of the authoritarian personality. An attack upon cherished premises tends to create anxiety, especially in those who have a strong inner need for certainty. The deviant opinion is felt as a threat to personal security. And the response tends to be fear, hatred or a similar emotion, from which springs a compulsion to eliminate the source of the danger. In such circumstances it is natural to turn to the state for protection against the supposed evil. Such factors play a prominent part in the formulation of restrictions upon expression and, equally important, in their administration.[10]

It is necessary to take into account not only the psychology of the orthodox

---

[10] See, e.g., Adorno, Frenkel-Brunswik, Levinson and Sanford, The Authoritarian Personality 654-726 (1950).

but also the psychology of the dissenter. Persons who stand up against society and challenge the traditional view often have strong feelings for the issues they raise. Others may be influenced by inner tensions which make it difficult for them to "adjust" to the prevailing order. In any event, the dissent is often not pitched in conventional terms; nor does it follow customary standards of polite expression. This tends to increase the anxiety and hostility of the orthodox and thus compounds the problem.[11]

Apart from these inner compulsions at work in a system which undertakes to limit freedom of expression, difficulties arise at the more rational level. To many people their immediate and personal affairs are the most vivid and most compelling. Those who currently dominate a society naturally cling to their economic, political and social position of advantage. Vested interests in the status quo, or in the continuing ignorance of other people, tend to take precedence over the broader interests of society as a whole. Forces of this nature vigorously resist the expression of new ideas or the pressures of the underprivileged who would change existing conditions in the society.

Nor is the longer-run logic of the traditional theory immediately apparent to untutored participants in political conflict. . . .

Suppression of opinion thus may seem an entirely plausible course of action. Toleration may appear inconsistent with maintaining order or achieving other ends desired by the majority or the group in power. The dialectics of freedom and order are not always perceived; the apparent paradox is not always readily resolved.

That full understanding and readiness to accept the theory of freedom of expression tends to be an acquired attitude is apparent from the entire history of free expression. It has been common for individuals and groups who demanded freedom of expression for themselves to insist that it be denied to others. Until the nineteenth century most of the theoretical supporters of freedom of expression took this position. And even those who urged a broader view have sought to impose restrictions upon their opponents when they achieved power. Thomas Jefferson himself, after being elected President, wrote to Governor McKean of Pennsylvania objecting to the "licentiousness" and "lying" of the Federalist press and saying, "I have therefore long thought that a few prosecutions of the most prominent offenders would have a wholesome effect in restoring the integrity of the presses." [13] It is not surprising then that few nations in the past have succeeded in maintaining any substantial degree of freedom of expression, and that even those have suffered serious relapses in times of pressure.

Similar attitudes prevail in our own times. Studies of public support for freedom of expression reveal an alarmingly high proportion of the population who are unwilling to apply the basic principles of the theory in practice. . . .

[11] See, e.g., Mill, On Liberty and Other Essays 63-65 (Neff ed. 1926).
[13] Letter to Governor McKean, Feb. 19, 1803, in 8 The Writings of Thomas Jefferson 216, 218 (Ford ed. 1897).

Taking all these factors into account it is clear that the problem of maintaining a system of freedom of expression in a society is one of the most complex any society has to face. Self-restraint, self-discipline and maturity are required. The theory is essentially a highly sophisticated one. The members of the society must be willing to sacrifice individual and short-term advantage for social and long-range goals. And the process must operate in a context that is charged with emotion and subject to powerful conflicting forces of self-interest.

These considerations must be weighed in attempting to construct a theory of limitations. A system of free expression can be successful only when it rests upon the strongest possible commitment to the positive right and the narrowest possible basis for exceptions. And any such exceptions must be clear-cut, precise and readily controlled. Otherwise the forces that press toward restriction will break through the openings, and freedom of expression will become the exception and suppression the rule.

A second major element in the problem is the inherent difficulty of framing limitations on expression. Expression in itself is not normally harmful, and the objective of the limitation is not normally to suppress the communication as such. Those who seek to impose limitation on expression do so ordinarily in order to forestall some anticipated effect of expression in causing or influencing other conduct. It is difficult enough to trace the effect of the expression after the event. But it is even more difficult to calculate in advance what its effect will be. The inevitable result is that the limitation is framed and administered to restrict a much broader area of expression than is necessary to protect against the harmful conduct feared. In other words, limitations of expression are by nature attempts to prevent the possibility of certain events occurring rather than a punishment of the undesired conduct after it has taken place. To accomplish this end, especially because the effect of the expression is so uncertain, the prohibition is bound to cut deeply into the right of expression.

Moreover, the infinite varieties and subtleties of language and other forms of communication make it impossible to construct a limitation upon expression in definite or precise terms. It is not easy to frame a prohibition against certain forms of conduct; but to formulate a prohibition which will embrace the multiplicity of words and meanings which might influence conduct can only be done through language exceedingly broad in scope. Men for generations have found ingenious ways to evade mechanical formulae of censorship. The allegory and the historical allusion are only two of the devices that have been used for such purposes. In order to accomplish what the framers of the limitation seek, the limitation must be couched in a sweeping generalization. This means, of course, that a wide area of expression is brought within the reach of the limitation and enormous discretionary power placed in the hands of those who administer it.

This brings us to a third factor in the dynamics of limitation — the apparatus required for administration and enforcement. Those who are assigned this task already have or soon develop a tendency to pursue it with zeal. At the very least they have a job to do, the continued existence of which depends upon their activeness in performing it. Often their efficiency and possibility of advancement are measured in terms of their success, which means success in restricting expression. Prosecution of unpopular opinion is frequently an important avenue of political advancement, and hence has a special appeal for the politically ambitious. While there has been little study of the psychology of the censor, security officer and investigator, experience demonstrates that many of those attracted to these positions are likely to be more than ordinarily influenced by the fears, prejudices or emotions which furnish the driving force for suppression. Much of the day-to-day work of administration is controlled by persons in the lower echelons of a bureaucracy, where narrow adherence to rigid rules, fear of superiors, and sensitivity to pressures carry the application of restrictions to their extreme limits. And the accompanying techniques of enforcement in the area of expression — the investigations, surveillance, searches and seizures, secret informers, voluminous files on the suspect — all tend to exercise a repressive influence on freedom of expression.

Other features of the administration of a limitation on expression press in the same direction. Thus the very bringing of a prosecution or other governmental proceeding, even where it is not successful, or the simple fact of investigating, can have the most serious impact. The essential point is that the forces inherent in any system of administration tend to drive to excess, and the mere existence of an enforcement apparatus is in itself restrictive.

A fourth element in the practical administration of limitations on freedom of expression is that the objectives of the limitation are readily subject to distortion and to use for ulterior purposes. Many persons do not easily separate the conduct or threatened conduct of those who express unwanted ideas from their expression of hated and feared opinions. Thus opposition to the conduct, or to the potential conduct, readily merges into suppression of opinion. The irresistible drive is not only to oppose the action sought by the minority group but to suppress their advocacy of it. Frequently prosecution of unpopular opinion is used as a screen for opposing necessary social change. And often the limitation becomes a weapon in a political struggle, employed primarily for partisan advantage.

Finally, in analyzing limitations on freedom of expression, there must be taken into account the whole impact of restriction on the healthy functioning of a free society. Limitations are seldom applied except in an atmosphere of public fear and hysteria. This may be deliberately aroused or may simply be the inevitable accompaniment of repression. Under such circumstances the doctrines and institutions for enforcing the limitations are subjected to intense pressures. Moreover, while some of the more hardy may be willing to defy the opposition and suffer the consequences, the more numerous are likely to be unwilling to run the risks. Similarly persons whose cooperation is needed to permit the full flow of open discussion — those who own the means of publication or the facilities for communication — are likely to be frightened into withholding their patronage and assistance.

REFERENCES

There is very little material specifically addressed to the dynamics of limitation. The problems were, however, recognized by the framers of the First Amendment. See Madison, The Virginia Report of 1799, 4 Elliot's Debates 546-558 (2d ed. 1836). Among the most realistic writers of the modern era is Zechariah Chafee. See his Free Speech in the United States (1941). See also Kirchheimer, Political Justice (1961), especially chs. V-VII. Other data may be gleaned from the various historical accounts of repression, particularly during crisis periods such as the era of the Alien and Sedition laws, the abolitionist controversy, the "red scare" following World War I, and "McCarthyism" after World War II. See Chapter II.

C. THE ROLE OF LAW AND LEGAL INSTITUTIONS IN MAINTAINING A SYSTEM OF FREE EXPRESSION

LEARNED HAND, THE BILL OF RIGHTS *
66-74

. . . The authority of courts to annul statutes (and a fortiori, acts of the Executive) may, and indeed must, be inferred, although it is nowhere expressed, for without it we should have to refer all disputes between the "Departments" and states to popular decision, patently an impractical means of relief, whatever Thomas Jefferson may have thought. However, this power should be confined to occasions when the statute or order was outside the grant of power to the grantee, and should not include a review of how the power has been exercised. This distinction in the case of legislation demands an analysis of its component factors. These are an estimate of the relevant existing facts and a forecast of the changes that the proposed measure will bring about. In addition it involves an appraisal of the values that the change will produce, as to which there are no postulates specific enough to serve as guides on concrete occasions. In the end all that can be asked on review by a court is that the appraisals and the choice shall be impartial. The statute may be far from the best solution of the conflicts with which it deals; but if it is the result of an honest effort to embody that compromise or adjustment that will secure the widest acceptance and most avoid resentment, it is "Due Process of Law" and conforms to the First Amendment. In theory any statute is always open to challenge upon the ground that it was not in truth the result of an impartial effort, but from the outset it was seen that any such inquiry was almost always practically impossible, and moreover it would be to the last degree "political."

I am well aware that the decisions do not so narrowly circumscribe the power of courts to intervene under the authority of the First Amendment and the "Due Process Clause." I have not tried to say how far those decisions have in fact extended the scope of these clauses. Frankly, I should despair of succeeding. On the contrary I have been only trying to say what is the measure of judicial intervention that can be thought to be implicit, though unexpressed, in the Constitution. You may well ask, however, what difference it makes at long last if the courts do exceed those implicit limits. Even though until about a century ago it was the accepted role of courts to confine themselves to occasions when Congress or the states had stepped over their borders, why should we now retreat, if it has become the custom to go further and correct patent deviations from a court's notions of justice? It is a "constitution," you may go on to remind me, that we are "expounding," and constitutions have the habit of organic growth. Ours is no different from other constitutions, and it has by now been modified to protect the basic privileges of any free society by means of an agency made irresponsive to the pressure of public hysteria, public panic and public greed.

There may be much to be said for the existence of some such organ in a democratic state, especially if its power be confined to a suspensive veto, like that for example of the present British House of Lords. The recuperative powers of a government that has no such curb are indeed great, but in the interval between the damage and the restoration great permanent injury may be done, and in any event the suffering of individuals will never be repaired. Those who advocate such relief at times concede too scanty importance to the provisions very carefully devised at least in the federal Constitution to check hasty and ill-considered legislation. The veto and independent tenure of the President, unlike that of the ministry in most democracies, are obvious curbs upon sudden swings of popular obsession; so too is the Senate, whose control is in the hands of a small minority of the population, representing a facet of public opinion quite different from that of the urban sections. However, I am not going to discuss whether it might not be desirable to have a third chamber, but on the contrary I shall assume for argument that it would be. The question still remains whether the courts should be that chamber. Let me try to sum up the case on both sides: and first that of those who wish to give the courts power to review the merits.

I agree that they have the better argument so far as concerns Free Speech. The most important issues here arise when a majority of the voters are hostile, often bitterly hostile, to the dissidents against whom the statute is directed; and legislatures are more likely than courts to repress what ought to be free. It is true that the periods of passion or panic are ordinarily not very long, and that they are usually succeeded by a serener and more tolerant temper; but, as I have just said, serious damage may have been done that cannot be undone, and no restitution is ordinarily possible for the individuals who have suffered. This is a substantial and important advantage of wide judicial review.

When one comes to the other interests covered by the "Bill of Rights" it seems to me impossible to be sure on which side the advantage lies. Judges are perhaps more apt than legislators to take a long view, but that varies so much with the individual that generalization is hazardous. We are faced with the ever present problem in all popular government: how far the will of immediate majorities should prevail. Even assuming, as I am, that a suspensive veto would be desirable, the power to annul a statute is much more than that. It does not send back the challenged measure for renewed deliberation; it forbids it by making a different appraisal of the values, which, as I have just said, is the essence of legislation. Moreover, judges are seldom content merely to annul the particular solution before them; they do not, indeed they may not, say that taking all things into consideration, the legislators' solution is too strong for the judicial stomach. On the contrary they wrap up their veto in a protective veil of adjectives such as "arbitrary," "artificial," "normal," "reasonable," "inherent," "fundamental," or "essential," whose office usually, though quite innocently, is to disguise what they are doing and impute to it a derivation far more impressive than their personal preferences, which are all that in fact lie behind the decision. If we do need a third chamber it should appear for what it is, and not as the interpreter of inscrutable principles.

Another supposed advantage of the wider power of review seems to be that by "the moral radiation of its decision" a court may point the way to a resolution of the social conflicts involved better than any likely to emerge from a legislature. In other words, courts may light the way to a saner world and ought to be encouraged to do so. I should indeed be glad to believe it, and it may be that my failure hitherto to observe it is owing to some personal defect of vision; but at any rate judges have large areas left unoccupied by legislation within which to exercise this benign function. Besides, for a judge to serve as communal mentor appears to me a very dubious addition to his duties and one apt to interfere with their proper discharge.

So much for the advantages that may result from a judicial review. In what respect is it inexpedient? In the first place it is apparent, I submit, that in so far as it is made part of the duties of judges to take sides in political controversies, their known or expected convictions or predilections will, and indeed should, be at least one determinant in their appointment and an important one. There has been plenty of past experience that confirms this; indeed, we have become so used to it that we accept it as a matter of course. No doubt it is inevitable, however circumscribed his duty may be, that the personal proclivities of an interpreter will to some extent interject themselves into the meaning he imputes to a text, but in very much the greater part of a judge's duties he is charged with freeing himself as far as he can from all personal preferences, and that becomes difficult in proportion as these are strong. The degree to which he will secure compliance with his commands depends in large measure upon how far the community believes him to be the mouthpiece of a public will, conceived as the resultant of many conflicting strains that have come, at least provisionally, to a consensus. This sanction disappears in so far as it is supposed permissible for him covertly to smuggle into his decisions his personal notions of what is desirable, however disinterested personally those may be. Compliance will then much more depend upon a resort to force, not a desirable expedient when it can be avoided.

This consideration becomes especially important in appellate courts. It is often hard to secure unanimity about the borders of legislative power, but that is much easier than to decide how far a particular adjustment diverges from what the judges deem tolerable. On such issues experience has over and over again shown the difficulty of securing unanimity. This is disastrous because disunity cancels the impact of monolithic solidarity on which the authority of a bench of judges so largely depends. People become aware that the answer to the controversy is uncertain, even to those best qualified, and they feel free, unless especially docile, to ignore it if they are reasonably sure that they will not be caught. The reasoning of both sides is usually beyond their comprehension, and is apt to appear as verbiage designed to sustain one side of a dispute that in the end might be decided either way, which is generally the truth. Moreover, it certainly does not accord with the underlying presuppositions of popular government to vest in a chamber, unaccountable to anyone but itself, the power to suppress social experiments which it does not approve. Nothing, I submit, could warrant such a censorship except a code of paramount law that not only measured the scope of legislative authority but regulated how it should be exercised.

Each one of us must in the end choose for himself how far he would like to leave our collective fate to the wayward vagaries of popular assemblies. No one can fail to recognize the perils to which the last forty years have exposed such governments. We are not indeed forced to choose between absolutism and the kind of democracy that so often prevailed in Greek cities during the sixth to fourth centuries before our era. The Founding Fathers were acutely, perhaps overacutely, aware of the dangers that had followed that sort of rule, though, as you all know, they differed widely as to what curbs to impose. For myself it would be most irksome to be ruled by a bevy of Platonic Guardians, even if I knew how to choose them, which I assuredly do not. If they were in charge, I should miss the stimulus of living in a society where I have, at least theoretically, some part in the direction of public affairs. Of course I know how illusory would be the belief that my vote determined anything; but nevertheless when I go to the polls I have a satisfaction in the sense that we are all engaged in a common venture. If you retort that a sheep in the flock may feel something like it; I reply, following Saint Francis, "My brother, the Sheep."

EMERSON, TOWARD A GENERAL THEORY OF THE FIRST AMENDMENT

72 Yale L.J. 877, 893-895 (1963)

The American people have frequently been warned that they must not count too heavily upon the legal system for the preservation of democratic liberties. Judge Learned Hand, one of the most eloquest exponents of this view, has made the point in the strongest language:

"I often wonder whether we do not rest our hopes too much upon constitutions, upon laws and upon courts. These are false hopes; believe me, these are false hopes. Liberty lies in the hearts of men and women; when it dies there, no constitution, no law, no court can save it; no constitution, no law, no court can even do much to help it. While it lies there it needs no constitution, no law, no court to save it." [19]

Certainly this admonition must be taken to heart. Obviously a perfect set of legal rules and an ideal array of judicial institutions could not by themselves assure an effective system of free expression. Many other factors are critical. There must be a substantial consensus on the values and goals of the society — some minimum area of agreement or acquiescence. The economic structure must provide a certain standard of material welfare, shared broadly by all elements of the population. Political institutions must have some basis in the traditions of the people, must receive some degree of acceptance, must prove reasonably effective in meeting the problems of the society, and must remain capable of adjustment and change. Other institutions, such as private corporations and labor organizations, must permit communication on a diverse scale in important areas of decision-making. There must be some feeling of security in relation to other nations or societies. The educational system, the media of communication, and similar institutions moulding public opinion must have some capacity to produce mature and independent members of the local and national community. The general philosophy, attitudes and mental health of the citizenry must be favorable. In short, basic conditions for a viable democratic society must be present.

Yet surely Judge Hand has overstated the case. The legal system is not so peripheral to the maintenance of free expression as his words imply. The experience of mankind demonstrates the contrary. Wherever the principles of free expression have prevailed in a society they have been closely supported by law and legal institutions. This is particularly true, of course, in the United States. The main elements of that role, especially as it has changed in recent years, must be kept in mind in formulating a satisfactory theory of the first amendment. . . .

The legal system is, of course, one of the most effective instruments availa-

[19] The Spirit of Liberty, Papers and Addresses of Learned Hand 144 (Dilliard ed, 1959).

ble to a society for controlling the behavior of its members so as to realize the values and goals sought by that society. Because of certain characteristics of a system of free expression, the role of law is of peculiar significance in any social effort to maintain such a system.

First, a system of free expression is designed to encourage a necessary degree of conflict within a society. To be sure, it attempts to avoid resort to force or violence by channelling this conflict into the area of expression and persuasion. And it contemplates that a longer-range consensus will ultimately be achieved. Yet, because it recognizes the right of the citizen to disagree with, arouse, antagonize and shock his fellow citizens and the government, such an arrangement of human affairs is hardly likely to be self-operating. In its short-term effects it may indeed be highly volatile. Hence the system needs the legitimizing and harmonizing influence of the legal process to keep it in successful balance.

Other features of a system of free expression likewise demonstrate the need for buttressing it through law and legal institutions. The full benefits of the system can be realized only when the individual knows the extent of his rights and has some assurance of protection in exercising them. Thus the governing principles of such a system need to be articulated with some precision and clarity. Doubt or uncertainty negates the process. Furthermore, the theory rests upon subordination of immediate interests in favor of long-term benefits. This can be achieved only through the application of principle, not by ad hoc resolution of individual cases. And it requires procedures adequate to relieve immediate pressures and facilitate objective consideration. All these elements a legal system is equipped to supply.

Further, as already observed, the theory of freedom of expression is a sophisticated and even complex one. It does not come naturally to the ordinary citizen, but needs to be learned. It must be restated and reiterated not only for each generation but for each new situation. It leans heavily upon understanding and education, both for the individual and the community as a whole. The legal process is one of the most effective methods for providing the kind of social comprehension essential for the attainment of society's higher and more remote ideals.

Finally, the principles of the system must be constantly reshaped and expanded to meet new conditions and new threats to its existence. This requires the deliberate attention of an institution entrusted with that specific obligation and possessing the expertise to perform such a function.

The function of the legal process is not only to provide a means whereby a society shapes and controls the behavior of its individual members in the interests of the whole. It also supplies one of the principal methods by which a society controls itself, limiting its own powers in the interests of the individual. The role of law here is to mark and guard the line between the sphere of social power, organized in the form of the state, and the area of private right. The legal problems involved in maintaining a system of free expression fall largely into this realm. In essence, legal support for such a system involves the protection of individual rights against interference or unwarranted control by the government. More specifically the legal structure must provide:

(1) Protection of the individual's right to freedom of expression against interference by the government in its efforts to achieve other social objectives or to advance its own interests. This has been in the past the main area of legal concern, and it remains so, although other phases of the problem are assuming increasing importance.

(2) The use, and simultaneous restriction, of government in regulating conflicts between individuals or groups within the system of free expression itself; in protecting individuals or groups from non-governmental interference in the exercise of their rights; and in eliminating obstacles to the effective functioning of the system.

(3) Restriction of the government in so far as the government itself participates in the system of expression.

All these requirements involve control over the state. The use of law to achieve this kind of control has been one of the central concerns of freedom-seeking societies over the ages. Legal recognition of individual rights, enforced through the legal process, has become the core of free society.

REFERENCES

1. On the function of written constitutions and institutions such as judicial review in protecting individual liberties, see McIlwain, Constitutionalism: Ancient and Modern (rev. ed. 1947); Patterson, The Evolution of Constitutionalism, 32 Minn. L. Rev. 427 (1948); Wormuth, The Origins of Modern Constitutionalism (1949); Dowling, Cases on Constitutional Law, ch. I (5th ed. 1954) (bibliography at 83-84); Pound, The Development of Constitutional Guarantees of Liberty (1957); Roche, Courts and Rights: The American Judiciary in Action (1961); Sutherland, Constitutionalism in America: Origins and Evolution of Its Fundamental Ideas (1965). More generally see Read (ed.), The Constitution Reconsidered (1938); Beard, The Republic (1943); Pekelis, Law and Social Action (1950); Dahl, A Preface to Democratic Theory (1956), and Decision-Making in a Democracy: The Supreme Court as a National Policy-Maker, 6 J. Pub. Law 279 (1957); Jones, The Rule of Law and the Welfare State, 58 Colum. L. Rev. 143 (1958); Swisher, The Growth of Constitutional Power in the United States (2d ed. 1963). See also McWhinney, Judicial Review in the English-Speaking World (rev. ed. 1960).

Broader treatments of the role of law in social control include Pound, Social Control Through Law (1942); Stone, The Province and Function of Law (1946); Hale, Freedom Through Law (1952); Hurst, Law and the Conditions of Freedom in the Nineteenth-Century United States (1956); Newman and Newman (eds.), The Role of Law in Society (1958); Auerbach, Law and Social Change in the United States, 6 U.C.L.A.L. Rev. 516 (1959); Friedmann, Law in a Changing Society (1959); Shklar, Legalism (1964).

2. A voluminous literature exists on the role of the United States Supreme Court. Most of this deals generally with the whole problem of the Court's function in a democratic society, rather than specifically with its role in maintaining a system of freedom of

expression. The so-called "passivist" approach derives mainly from Thayer, The Origin and Scope of the American Doctrine of Constitutional Law, 7 Harv. L. Rev. 129 (1893), and is represented by Richardson, Freedom of Expression and the Function of Courts, 65 Harv. L. Rev. 1 (1951); Jackson, The Supreme Court in the American System of Government (1955); Hand, The Bill of Rights (1958); Wechsler, Toward Neutral Principles of Constitutional Law, 73 Harv. L. Rev. 1 (1959), reprinted in Principles, Politics and Fundamental Law (1961); McCloskey, The American Supreme Court (1960); Freund, The Supreme Court of the United States (1961); Mendelson, Justices Black and Frankfurter (1961); Hook, The Paradoxes of Freedom (1962). See also Bickel, The Least Dangerous Branch (1962). The so-called "activist" position is represented by Rostow, The Democratic Character of Judicial Review, 66 Harv. L. Rev. 193 (1952), reprinted in The Sovereign Prerogative (1962); Beth, The Case for Judicial Protection of Civil Liberties, 17 J. of Pol. 100 (1955); Cahn, The Firstness of the First Amendment, 65 Yale L.J. 464 (1956); Douglas, The Right of the People (1958); McKay, The Preference for Freedom, 34 N.Y.U.L. Rev. 1182 (1959); Rodell, Judicial Activists, Judicial Self-Deniers, Judicial Review and the First Amendment, 47 Geo. L.J. 483 (1959); C. L. Black, The People and the Court (1960); Miller and Howell, The Myth of Neutrality in Constitutional Adjudication, 27 U. Chi. L. Rev. 661 (1960); Shapiro, Judicial Modesty, Political Reality, and Preferred Position, 47 Cornell L.Q. 175 (1962), and Freedom of Speech: The Supreme Court and Judicial Review (1966). See also Cahn (ed.), Supreme Court and Supreme Law (1954); Swisher, The Supreme Court in Modern Role (1958); Schubert, Constitutional Politics (1960); Schmidhauser, Constitutional Law in the Political Process (1963); Dorsen (ed.), The Proper Role of the United States Supreme Court in Civil Liberties Cases, 10 Wayne L. Rev. 457 (1964); Shapiro, Law and Politics in the Supreme Court (1964) (contains references to additional writings on the subject).

3. For legislative and other reaction to the Supreme Court's performance of its functions, see Jackson, The Struggle for Judicial Supremacy (1941); Pritchett, Congress Versus the Supreme Court (1961); Murphy, Congress and the Court (1962); Hyneman, The Supreme Court on Trial (1963) (bibliography at 281-302). Recent literature appraising the Supreme Court's operations from a more technical viewpoint are cited in Miller, A Note on the Criticism of Supreme Court Decisions, 10 J. Pub. Law 139 (1961).

4. On the role of an independent bar in maintaining a system of freedom of expression, see Stone, The Public Influence of the Bar, 48 Harv. L. Rev. 1 (1934); Jackson, The Advocate: Guardian of Our Traditional Liberties, 36 A.B.A.J. 607 (1950); Jaworski, The Unpopular Cause, 47 A.B.A.J. 714 (1961); Kirchheimer, Political Justice 242-256, ch. VII (1961); Rostow, The Lawyer and his Client, 48 A.B.A.J. 25, 146 (1926); Pollitt, Counsel for the Unpopular Cause: The "Hazard of Being Undone," 43 N.C.L. Rev. 9 (1964). See generally Hurst, The Growth of American Law: The Law Makers, chs. 12, 13 (1950); Pound, The Lawyer from Antiquity to Modern Times (1953). See also Note, Private Attorneys-General: Group Action in the Fight for Civil Liberties, 58 Yale L.J. 574 (1949).

CHAPTER II

Development of Freedom of Expression in the United States

A. BACKGROUND OF THE FIRST AMENDMENT

The main source of constitutional protection for freedom of expression in the United States is the First Amendment. Other constitutional guarantees — such as the requirement of due process, the privilege against self-incrimination, and the prohibition against unreasonable searches and seizures — are significant elements in maintaining a system of freedom of expression. See, e.g., Cahn, The Firstness of the First Amendment, 65 Yale L.J. 464 (1956). But the principal emphasis, and the main focus of attention in Part One of this book, concern the provisions of the First Amendment.

The United States Constitution, as originally adopted in 1789, contained no provision dealing expressly with the right to freedom of expression. The delegates to the Constitutional Convention seemed to have assumed that the Federal Government, possessing only the enumerated powers, would not be authorized to legislate in the field of expression and that no explicit limitation upon its power in that area was necessary. But popular pressure forced the adoption of the Bill of Rights in 1791, the first provision of which contained an express guarantee of freedom of expression.

THE FIRST AMENDMENT
U.S. Constitution, adopted 1791

Congress shall make no law respecting an establishment of religion, or prohibiting the free exercise thereof; or abridging the freedom of speech, or of the press, or the right of the people peaceably to assemble, and to petition the Government for a redress of grievances.

The meaning and significance of the First Amendment to the people of the new nation is to be found in the existing law of England and the colonies dealing with restrictions upon freedom of speech, press and assembly. Apart from the law of civil libel and slander, the law dealing with blasphemy, and the law concerning obscenity, there were two significant legal doctrines with which the First Amendment was concerned. One was the law of censorship; the other was the law of seditious libel.

The history of English censorship has been summarized by Story:

"The art of printing soon after its introduction, we are told, was looked upon, as well in England as in other countries, as merely a matter of state, and subject to the coercion of the crown. It was therefore, regulated in England by the king's proclamations, prohibitions, charters of privilege, and licenses, and finally by the decrees of the Court of Star-Chamber, which limited the number of printers and of presses which each should employ, and prohibited new publications, unless previously approved by proper licensers. On the demolition of this odious jurisdiction, in 1641, the Long Parliament of Charles the First, after their rupture with that prince, assumed the same powers which the Star-Chamber exercised with respect to licensing books; and during the Commonwealth (such is human frailty and the love of power even in republics!) they issued their ordinances for that purpose, founded principally upon a Star-Chamber decree in 1637. After the restoration of Charles the Second, a statute on the same subject was passed, copied, with some few alterations, from the parliamentary ordinances. The act expired in 1679, and was revived and continued for a few years after the revolution of 1688. Many attempts were made by the government to keep it in force; but it was so strongly resisted by Parliament that it expired in 1694, and has never since been revived." [1]

The law of seditious libel, however, was effectively and vigorously enforced in the pre-Revolutionary period. In England some 70 prosecutions for seditious libel took place in the three decades before adoption of the First Amendment, resulting in 50 convictions. These included such well known cases as the prosecution of John Wilkes and the publishers of Junius' Letter to the King. Prosecutions for seditious libel had also occurred in the colonies, of which the most famous was that of Peter Zenger, New York printer, in 1734.

Professor Chafee, in the following extract, discusses the significance of the First Amendment in the light of this background.

CHAFEE, FREE SPEECH IN THE UNITED STATES *
18-21

If we apply Coke's test of statutory construction, and consider what mischief in the existing law the framers of the First Amendment wished to remedy by a new safeguard, we can be sure that it was not the censorship. This had expired in England in 1695, and in the colonies by 1725.[34] They knew from books that it destroyed liberty of the press; and if they ever thought of

[1] 2 Story, Commentaries on the Constitution of the United States §1882 (5th ed. 1891).

* Copyright 1941, by Harvard University Press.

[34] Macaulay, History of England, chap. xxi; C. A. Duniway, Freedom of Speech in Massachusetts, p. 89 n. . . . .

its revival as within the range of practical possibilities, they must have regarded it as clearly prohibited by the First Amendment. But there was no need to go to all the trouble of pushing through a constitutional amendment just to settle an issue that had been dead for decades. What the framers did have plenty of reason to fear was an entirely different danger to political writers and speakers.

For years the government here and in England had substituted for the censorship rigorous and repeated prosecutions for seditious libel, which were directed against political discussion, and for years these prosecutions were opposed by liberal opinion and popular agitation. Primarily the controversy raged around two legal contentions of the great advocates for the defense, such as Erskine and Andrew Hamilton. They argued, first, that the jury and not the judge ought to decide whether the writing was seditious, and secondly, that the truth of the charge ought to prevent conviction. The real issue, however, lay much deeper. Two different views of the relation of rulers and people were in conflict. According to one view, the rulers were the superiors of the people, and therefore must not be subjected to any censure that would tend to diminish their authority. The people could not make adverse criticism in newspapers or pamphlets, but only through their lawful representatives in the legislature, who might be petitioned in an orderly manner. According to the other view, the rulers were agents and servants of the people, who might therefore find fault with their servants and discuss questions of their punishment or dismissal, and of governmental policy.

Under the first view, which was officially accepted until the close of the eighteenth century, developed the law of seditious libel. This was defined as "the intentional publication, without lawful excuse or justification, of written blame of any public man, or of the law, or of any institution established by law." There was no need to prove any intention on the part of the defendant to produce disaffection or excite an insurrection. It was enough if he intended to publish the blame, because it was unlawful in him merely to find fault with his masters and betters. Such, in the opinion of the best authorities, was the common law of sedition.[36]

It is obvious that under this law liberty of the press was nothing more than absence of the censorship, as Blackstone said. All through the eighteenth century, however, there existed beside this definite legal meaning of liberty of the press, a definite popular meaning: the right of unrestricted discussion of public affairs. There can be no doubt that this was in a general way what freedom of speech meant to the framers of the Constitution. Thus Madison, who drafted the First Amendment, bases his explanation of it in 1799 on "the essential difference between the British Government and the American constitutions." In the United States the people and not the government possess

---

[36] Madison, Report on the Virginia Resolutions, 1799, Elliot's Debates (2d ed.), IV, 596 ff.; Stephen, History of the Criminal Law, II, 299, 353, and chap. xxiv, passim; Schofield [Freedom of Speech in the United States, in II Essays on Constitutional Law of Equity (1914)], 511 ff., gives an excellent summary with especial reference to American conditions. . . .

the absolute sovereignty, and the legislature as well as the executive is under limitations of power. Hence, Congress is not free to punish anything which was criminal at English common law. A government which is "elective, limited and responsible" in all its branches may well be supposed to require "a greater freedom of animadversion" [37] than might be tolerated by one that is composed of an irresponsible hereditary king and upper house, and an omnipotent legislature. . . .

There are a few early judicial decisions to the contrary, but they ought not to weigh against the statements of Madison and the general temper of the time. . . . I must therefore strongly dissent, with Justice Holmes,[40] from the position sometimes taken in arguments on the Espionage Act, that the founders of our government left the common law as to seditious libel in force and merely intended by the First Amendment "to limit the new government's statutory powers to penalize utterances as seditious, to those which were seditious under the then accepted common-law rule." [41] The founders had seen seventy English prosecutions for libel since 1760, and fifty convictions under that common-law rule, which made conviction easy.[42] That rule had been detested in this country ever since it was repudiated by jury and populace in the famous trial of Peter Zenger, the New York printer, the account of which went through fourteen editions before 1791.[43] The close relation between the Zenger trial and the prosecutions under George III in England and America is shown by the quotations on reprints of the trial and the dedication of the 1784 London edition to Erskine, as well as by reference to Zenger in the disscussions preceding the First Amendment. Nor was this the only colonial sedition prosecution under the common law, and many more were threatened. All the American cases before 1791 prove that our common law of sedition was exactly like that of England, and it would be extraordinary if the First Amendment enacted the English sedition law of that time, which was repudiated by every American and every liberal Englishman,[44] and altered through Fox's Libel Act by Parliament itself in the very next year, 1792. . . . The First Amendment was written by men to whom Wilkes and Junius were household words, who intended to wipe out

[37] Madison's Report on the Virginia Resolutions, Elliot's Debates (2d ed.), IV, 596-598. As draftsman of the Amendment, Madison's views about its interpretation carry great weight, although they were written down eight years after its adoption and may have been somewhat modified during the interval by his opposition to the Sedition Act of 1798. The same distinction was made by Erastus Root, Report of the New York Constitutional Convention of 1821, p. 489. See also Speeches of Charles Pinckney (1800), pp. 116 ff.

[40] Abrams v. U.S., 250 U.S. 616 (1919).

[41] W. R. Vance, in "Freedom of Speech and the Press," 2 Minnesota Law Review, 239, 259.

[42] May, Constitutional History of England (2d ed.), II, 9 n.

[43] 17 How. St. Tr. 675 (1735); Rutherford, John Peter Zenger (New York, 1904). See also the life of Zenger's counsel, Andrew Hamilton, by William Henry Loyd, in Great American Lawyers, I, 1.

[44] May, Constitutional History of England, vol. II, chap. ix; Stephen, History of the Criminal Law, vol. II, chap. xxiv.

the common law of sedition, and make further prosecutions for criticism of the government, without any incitement to law-breaking, forever impossible in the United States of America.

NOTE

Leonard W. Levy, in his Legacy of Suppression, amasses evidence to challenge the Chafee view that the framers of the First Amendment "intended to wipe out the common law of sedition." Levy's thesis is set forth in the Preface to his book in the following terms:

"This book presents a revisionist interpretation of the origins and original understanding of the First Amendment's clause on freedom of speech and press. I have been reluctantly forced to conclude that the generation which adopted the Constitution and the Bill of Rights did not believe in a broad scope for freedom of expression, particularly in the realm of politics.

"I find that libertarian theory from the time of Milton to the ratification of the First Amendment substantially accepted the right of the state to suppress seditious libel. I find also that the American experience with freedom of political expression was as slight as the theoretical inheritance was narrow. Indeed, the American legislatures, especially during the colonial period, were far more oppressive than the supposedly tyrannous common-law courts. The evidence drawn particularly from the period 1776 to 1791 indicates that the generation that framed the first state declarations of rights and the First Amendment was hardly as libertarian as we have traditionally assumed. They did not intend to give free rein to criticism of the government that might be deemed seditious libel, although the concept of seditious libel was — and still is — the principal basis of muzzling political dissent. There is even reason to believe that the Bill of Rights was more the chance product of political expediency on all sides than of principled commitment to personal liberties. A broad libertarian theory of freedom of speech and press did not emerge in the United States until Jeffersonians, when a minority party, were forced to defend themselves against the Federalist Sedition Act of 1798. In power, however, the Jeffersonians were not much more tolerant of their political critics than the Federalists had been." Levy, Legacy of Suppression: Freedom of Speech and Press in Early American History vii-viii (1960).

More specifically, Levy summarizes his conclusions as to what the framers meant by freedom of speech and freedom of the press in a subsequent passage:

"No one can say for certain what the Framers had in mind, for although the evidence all points in one direction there is not enough of it to justify cocksure conclusions. It is not even certain that the Framers themselves knew what they had in mind; that is, at the time of the drafting and ratification of the First Amendment, few among them if any at all clearly understood what they meant by the free speech-and-press clause, and it is perhaps doubtful that those few agreed except in a generalized way and equally doubtful that they represented a consensus. Considerable disagreement existed, for example, on the question whether freedom of expression meant the right to print the truth about government measures and officials if the truth was defamatory or revealed for unworthy motives. There was also disagreement about the function of juries in trials for criminal libel.

"What is clear is that there exists no evidence to suggest an understanding that a constitutional guarantee of free speech or press meant the impossibility of future prosecutions of seditious utterances. The traditional libertarian interpretation of the original meaning of the First Amendment is surely subject to the Scottish verdict: not proven. Freedom of speech and press, as all the scattered evidence suggests, was not understood to include a right to broadcast sedition by words. The security of the state against libelous advocacy or attack was always regarded as outweighing any social interest in open expression, at least through the period of the adoption of the First Amendment. The thought and experience of a lifetime, indeed the taught traditions of law and politics extending back many generations, supplied an a priori belief that freedom of political discourse, however broadly conceived, stopped short of seditious libel. . . ." Id. at 236-237.

That the First Amendment, as now construed, has abolished the law of seditious libel, see New York Times v. Sullivan, 376 U.S. 254, 84 S. Ct. 710, 11 L. Ed. 2d 686 (1964).

REFERENCES

1. For criticism of the Levy thesis see, Anastaplo, Book Review of Legacy of Suppression, 39 N.Y.U.L. Rev. 735 (1964). See also book reviews by D. Meiklejohn, 35 So. Calif. L. Rev. 111 (1961), and Leavitt, 49 Calif. L. Rev. 589 (1961).

2. In addition to the material cited above see, on the background of the English law, Donogh, The History and the Law of Sedition and Cognate Offences (3d ed. 1917); Holdsworth, Press Control and Copyright in the 16th and 17th Centuries, 29 Yale L.J. 841 (1920); Patterson, Free Speech and a Free Press (1939); Shientag, From Seditious Libel to Freedom of the Press, 11 Brook. L. Rev. 125 (1942); Chafee, How Human Rights Got Into the Constitution (1952); Siebert, Freedom of the Press in England 1476-1776 (1952); Kelly, Criminal Libel and Free Speech, 6 Kan. L. Rev. 295 (1958); Brant, The Bill of Rights (1965). On freedom of debate in Parliament, a right related to freedom of speech outside the legislature, see Chafee, Three Human Rights in the Constitution of 1787 4-89 (1956); Levy, Legacy of Suppression 5-6, 15-16, 108-109, 295-296 (1960).

3. On the American law background see, in addition to Patterson, Shientag, Chafee, Kelly and Brant, cited in reference note 2 supra, Schuyler, The Liberty of the Press in the American Colonies (1905); Duniway, The Development of Freedom of the Press in Massachusetts (1906); Rutland, The Birth of the Bill of Rights, 1776-1791 (1955); Kelly (ed.), Foundations of Freedom in the American Constitution (1958); Nelson, Seditious Libel in Colonial America, 3 Am. J. Leg. Hist. 160 (1959); Levy, Liberty and the First Amendment: 1790-1800, 68 Am. Hist. Rev. 22 (1962); Anastaplo, Notes on the First Amendment to the Constitution of the United States (U. Chi. thesis, 1964). See also Corwin, Freedom of Speech and Press Under the First Amendment: A Resumé, 30 Yale L.J. 48 (1920); Walsh, Is the New Judicial and Legislative Interpretation of Freedom of Speech, and of the Freedom of the Press, Sound Constitutional Development? 21 Geo. L.J. 35, 161 (1932-1933); Brandwen, The Battle of the First Amendment: A Study in Judicial Interpretation, 40 N.C.L. Rev. 273 (1962).

On the broader background of the First Amendment in America, see Rossiter, Seedtime of the Republic: The Origin of the American Tradition of Political Liberty (1953); Pound, The Development of Constitutional Guarantees of Liberty (1957); Roche, American Liberty: An Examination of the "Tradition" of Freedom, in Konvitz and Rossiter (eds.), Aspects of Liberty (1958); Hyman, To Try Men's Souls: Loyalty Tests in American History (1959); Haskins, Law and Authority in Early Massachusetts (1960); Ostrander, The Rights of Man in America 1606-1861 (1960); Wright, Fabric of Freedom 1763-1800 (1961). Material on the two principal architects of the Bill of Rights includes

Brant, James Madison: Father of the Constitution (1950); Malone, Jefferson and the Ordeal of Liberty (1962); Levy, Jefferson and Civil Liberties: The Darker Side (1963).

4. Accounts of the actual adoption of the First Amendment are given in Warren, Congress, The Constitution and the Supreme Court, ch. 3 (rev. ed. 1935); U.S. Constitution Sesquicentennial Commission, History of the Formation of the Union Under the Constitution 62-63, 280-328 (1941); Rutland, cited in reference note 3 supra; Dumbauld, The Bill of Rights and What It Means Today (1957) (bibliography at 223-235). A summary of the debate in Congress may be found in Konvitz, Fundamental Liberties of a Free People 345-361 (1957).

5. On the Peter Zenger case, one of the formative episodes of the period, see, in addition to the material cited by Chafee in How Human Rights Got Into the Constitution (1952), Buranelli (ed.), The Trial of Peter Zenger (1957) (with extensive bibliography); Alexander, A Brief Narrative of the Case and Trial of John Peter Zenger, Printer of the New York Weekly Journal (S.N. Katz ed. 1963). See also Crosman, The Legal and Journalistic Significance of the Trial of John Peter Zenger, 10 Rocky Mt. L. Rev. 258 (1938); H. H. Miller, The Case for Liberty, ch. II (1965) (bibliography at 233-235).

6. No comprehensive history of freedom of expression in the United States, bringing the story down to the present date, exists. Numerous accounts of particular periods or events are listed subsequently in this chapter and in later chapters. Legal developments are also treated infra. At this point the following general references to the history of civil liberties, primarily dealing with the 18th and 19th centuries, may be cited: McMaster, The Acquisition of Political, Social and Industrial Rights of Man in America (1903, reprinted 1961); Schofield, Freedom of the Press in the United States, in his Essays on Constitutional Law and Equity 510-571 (1921); Whipple, The Story of Civil Liberty in the United States (1927); Patterson, Free Speech and a Free Press (1939); Hallgren, Landscape of Freedom: The Story of American Liberty and Bigotry (1941); Myers, History of Bigotry in the United States (1943); Brant, James Madison: Father of the Constitution (1950) and The Bill of Rights (1965); Biddle, The Fear of Freedom (1951); Roche, American Liberty: An Examination of the "Tradition" of Freedom, in Konvitz and Rossiter (eds.), Aspects of Liberty (1958); Ostrander, The Rights of Man in America 1601-1861 (1960); and Handlin, The Dimensions of Liberty (1961). See also Douglas, An Almanac of Liberty (1954); H. H. Miller, cited in reference note 5 supra. On a more general level see Parrington, Main Currents in American Thought (1927-1930); Gabriel, The Course of American Democratic Thought (1940); Hartz, The Liberal Tradition in America (1955). See also U.S. Library of Congress, The Bill of Rights: A List of References (1940).

B. THE ALIEN AND SEDITION ACTS

The first serious challenge to freedom of political expression came with the Alien and Sedition Acts, passed in 1798. The United States at the time was on the verge of war with France. The impact of ideas generated by the French Revolution aroused fear and hostility in some segments of the American population. Rumors of French plots and charges of French espionage were sweeping the country. Antagonism to French and Irish immigrants ran high in some quarters. A bitter controversy raged between the Federalists, then in power, and the Republicans. Spearheading the Republican attack was an aggressive press, many of the editors of which were non-citizens. The polemics hurled by both sides were violent in tone, frequently scurrilous.

Under these circumstances the more extreme among the Federalists proposed a series of measures to curb the power of aliens and of the Republican party and press. Although not supported by some Federalists such as Marshall, the laws were passed by Congress. The Naturalization Act extended the period of residence required for naturalization from five to fourteen years. 1 Stat. 566. The Enemy Alien Act provided that in the event of war, "or any invasion or predatory incursion . . . perpetuated, attempted, or threatened," all subjects of the hostile nation within the United States who were not naturalized "shall be liable to be apprehended, restrained, secured and removed, as alien enemies." 1 Stat. 577. The important parts of the Alien Act and the Sedition Act are set forth below.

AN ACT CONCERNING ALIENS
1 Stat. 570, June 25, 1798

Section 1. *Be it enacted by the Senate and House of Representatives of the United States of America in Congress assembled,* That it shall be lawful for the President of the United States at any time during the continuance of this act, to *order* all such *aliens* as he shall judge dangerous to the peace and safety of the United States, or shall have reasonable grounds to suspect are concerned in any treasonable or secret machinations against the government thereof, to depart out of the territory of the United States, within such time as shall be expressed in such order. . . . And in case any alien, so ordered to depart, shall be found at large within the United States after the time limited in such order for his departure, and not having obtained a *license* from the President to reside therein, or having obtained such *license* shall not have conformed thereto, every such alien shall, on conviction thereof, be imprisoned for a term not exceeding three years, and shall never after be admitted to become a citizen of the United States. . . .

AN ACT IN ADDITION TO THE ACT, ENTITLED
"AN ACT FOR THE PUNISHMENT OF CERTAIN
CRIMES AGAINST THE UNITED STATES"
1 Stat. 596, July 14, 1798

Sec. 2. *And be it further enacted,* That if any person shall write, print, utter or publish, or shall cause to procure to be written, printed, uttered or published, or shall knowingly and willingly assist or aid in writing, printing, uttering or publishing any false, scandalous and malicious writing or writings against the government of the United States, or either house of the Congress of the United States, or the President of the United States, with intent to defame the said government, or either house of the said Congress, or the said President, or to bring them, or either of them, into contempt or disrepute; or to excite against them, or either or any of them, the hatred of the good people of the United States, or to stir up sedition within the United States, or to excite any unlawful combinations therein, for opposing or resisting any law of the United States, or any act of the President of the United States, done in pursuance of any such law, or of the powers in him vested by the constitution of the United States, or to resist, oppose, or defeat any such law or act, or to aid, encourage or abet any hostile designs of any foreign nation against the United States, their people or government, then such person, being thereof convicted before any court of the United States having jurisdiction thereof, shall be punished by a fine not exceeding two thousand dollars, and by imprisonment not exceeding two years.

Sec. 3. *And be it further enacted and declared,* That if any person shall be prosecuted under this act, for the writing or publishing any libel aforesaid, it shall be lawful for the defendant, upon the trial of the cause, to give in evidence in his defence, the truth of the matter contained in the publication charged as a libel. And the jury who shall try the cause, shall have a right to determine the law and the fact, under the direction of the court, as in other cases.

The Alien Act was never formally invoked but its very existence forced a number of aliens to leave the country or go into hiding. By its terms this act expired in two years.

The Sedition Act was vigorously enforced, the victims in all cases being members of the Republican Party. Republican newspapers were scanned for seditious material and prosecutions were brought against the four leading Republican papers as well as against some of those less influential. Cases were also instituted against at least three of the more outspoken Republican office holders. The number of arrests made is not entirely certain but there were at least 25, with at least 15 indictments. Prosecutions were brought in every state except New Hampshire and Rhode Island, where Republican strength was low, and the states of the far South and West. The cases, often tried before openly hostile Federalist judges, resulted in 10 convictions.

The nature of these prosecutions is revealed by the first one brought, against Congressman Matthew Lyon, Republican of Vermont. Lyon, who was one of the Republican politicians most hated by the Federalists, was indicted for (1) publishing an article in which he vigorously attacked the Adams administration, asserting that under President Adams "every consideration of the public welfare was swallowed up in a continual grasp for power, in an unbounded thirst for ridiculous pomp, foolish adulation, and selfish avarice"; (2) publishing a letter from Joel Barlow, then in France, in which Barlow stated that Congress should commit President Adams to the mad house, but, instead, treated him "with more servility than ever George III experienced from either House of Parliament." Lyon was convicted and sentenced to a fine of $1000 and four months in prison. He was immediately hurried off to jail and thrown into a filthy cell. While in jail Lyon was re-elected to Congress.

Another prosecution, of less significant figures, arose out of an incident in Dedham, Massachusetts. Here some of the inhabitants erected a liberty pole on which they placed the inscription: "No Stamp Act, no Sedition, no Alien bills, no Land Tax; downfall to the Tyrants of America, peace and retirement to the President." Federalist officials obtained the indictment of two of those responsible. One of these recanted and received a fine of $5 and 6 hours in prison — the only lenient sentence imposed under the Sedition Act. The other participant remained obdurate, refused to disclose the names of his associates, and was sentenced to a fine of $400 and 18 months in jail. Unable to pay his fine at the end of his term, he remained in prison altogether for two years.

The constitutional issues raised by the Alien and Sedition Acts never reached the Supreme Court. The validity of the Sedition Act, however, was sustained by the lower federal courts and by three Supreme Court Justices sitting on circuit. It was argued in support that the Act merely restated, with some liberalizing modifications, the common law of seditious libel, that the First Amendment prohibited only prior censorship, and that the exercise of federal power was derived from the necessary and proper clause. The Act was attacked on the ground that it lay outside the sphere of federal power and violated the First Amendment. Jefferson and Madison led the campaign against the Alien and Sedition Acts, the most famous expressions of their views being embodied in the Kentucky and Virginia Resolutions.

It is generally agreed that the Alien and Sedition laws profoundly shocked the country and were a major factor in the defeat of the Federalists in the election of 1800. The Sedition Act expired on March 3, 1801. Jefferson pardoned all those who had been convicted under it and eventually Congress repaid most of the fines.

REFERENCES

1. The most comprehensive account of the Alien and Sedition Acts is Smith, Freedom's Fetters (1956), reviewed by Roche in 70 Harv. L. Rev. 946 (1957); see also Miller, Crisis in Freedom (1951). Both books contain bibliographies. For a vivid description of Matthew Lyon's case and the general background, see Bowers, Jefferson and Hamilton 374-380 (1928). Also on the background see Miller, The Federalist Era (1960); Malone, Jefferson and the Ordeal of Liberty (1962).

2. The Federalist argument for constitutionality was incorporated in Report of a Select Committee to Consider Petitions for Repeal of the Alien and Sedition Laws, 5 Annals (5th Cong.) 2985. The opposition argument was set forth in the Kentucky and Virginia Resolutions, reprinted in Commager, Documents of American History 178-183 (1948); and in a report prepared by Madison known as The Virginia Report of 1799, 4 Elliot's Debates 546 (2d ed. 1836), reprinted as Sen. Doc. No. 873, 62d Cong., 2d Sess. (1921).

3. The four trials that are fully reported are United States v. Lyon, Wharton's St. Tr. 333 (1798); United States v. Haswell, Wharton's St. Tr. 684 (1800); United States v.

Cooper, Wharton's St. Tr. 659 (1800); United States v. Callender, Wharton's St. Tr. 688 (1800). None of the cases reached the Supreme Court.

4. For further discussion of the enforcement and legal issues, see Anderson, The Enforcement of the Alien and Sedition Laws, Annual Report of the American Historical Association 115 (1912); Carroll, Freedom of Speech and of the Press in the Federalist Period: The Sedition Act, 18 Mich. L. Rev. 615 (1920); Corwin, Freedom of Speech and Press Under the First Amendment: A Resumé, 30 Yale L.J. 48 (1920); Hudon, Freedom of Speech and Press in America, ch. V (1963).

5. For the impact of the French Revolution on prosecutions for seditious libel in England and on the Alien and Sedition Laws, see Brown, The French Revolution in English History (1918); 2 McMaster, A History of the People of the United States, ch. X (1928); Warren, Jacobin and Junto, chs. III, IV (1931); Sutherland, British Trials for Disloyal Association During the French Revolution, 34 Cornell L.Q. 303 (1949); Smelser, The Jacobin Phrenzy, 13 Rev. of Pol. 457 (1951).

6. After the Jeffersonians came to power in 1800 the Federal Government brought prosecutions in Connecticut against several Federalists, charging them with the common law crime of seditious libel. Upon appeal from the lower court's ruling on a demurrer, the Supreme Court held that the federal courts had no jurisdiction over common law crimes. The Court found it unnecessary to pass upon the question of whether Congress had power under the First Amendment to legislate on the subject. United States v. Hudson and Goodwin, 7 Cranch 32, 3 L. Ed. 259 (1812). For a discussion of the Connecticut cases, as well as state prosecutions in New York and Pennsylvania against Federalists for seditious libel, see Levy, Legacy of Suppression 297-307 (1960). For an account of other state prosecutions for seditious libel in the early decades of the new republic, see Duniway, Freedom of the Press in Massachusetts, ch. IX (1906); Kelly, Criminal Libel and Free Speech, 6 Kan. L. Rev. 295 (1958); Levy, id. at 205-214.

C. The First Half of the Nineteenth Century

Following the period of the Alien and Sedition Acts the question of whether the Federal Government should impose restrictions upon expression did not arise as a prominent issue until the crisis presented by the Civil War. Hence there was no occasion to invoke the legal protections of the First Amendment with respect to federal action. And in Barron v. Baltimore, 7 Peters 243, 8 L. Ed. 672, decided in 1833, the Supreme Court ruled that the guarantees of the Bill of Rights did not apply to state or local authorities, or to private individuals.

During this period, however, freedom of expression was subject to significant limitations, frequently from non-governmental sources, at various times and in various areas. The two most significant problems arose out of the nativist movements beginning in the 1830's and the controversy over abolition which mounted in intensity up to the Civil War. Abridgement of speech, press and assembly, as well as other civil liberties, growing out of the opposition to Catholics, aliens and dissenters are described in the following extract.

WHIPPLE, THE STORY OF CIVIL LIBERTY IN
THE UNITED STATES
51 (1927)

From 1828 to 1855, and especially from 1833 to 1843, came a veritable mob era. The masses, charmed by this idea of the rule of the people, were convinced that it made small difference whether you downed the minority by ballots or by brick-bats, which they understood better. This form of tyranny by majority had not been anticipated by the statesmen who expected the colder process of voting down the minority to prevail over the warmer sport of killing them.

Social conditions helped establish these notions. Urban centralization had begun. Immigration, encouraged to bring in cheap labor, first the Irish and later the Chinese, aroused economic, racial and religious prejudices. There was an ardent "nativism," by citizens who had themselves but yesterday come from foreign shores. There was an almost inexplicable dread of secret political or religious organizations, expressed in crusades against the Masons, Catholics, and Mormons. Beneath all, the growing machine industry was producing a proletariat. Wage-labor was slowly reaching economic self-consciousness, later to align itself against the wageless institution of Negro slavery. In a few places, direct action by the people approximated a rough sort of government, as in the Vigilantes and other extemporized "law and order" bodies of the frontier. They did some necessary natural policing before courts or State arrived.

NOTE

John P. Roche also concludes that, in practice, restrictions on freedom of expression in nineteenth century America were prevalent:

"When the historian looks back at the intellectual and social history of the early United States, he notes an enormous diversity of opinion. From this it is an easy step to conclude that there was toleration of divergent views among the population at large. From a different vantage point, however, tolerance as the precondition for diversity seems to be a non sequitur: what has been overlooked is the fact that until at least the beginning of the twentieth century, and in extensive areas of the nation later, the United States was an extremely heterogeneous country, dotted with subcultures. It is my contention that the diversity of opinion was a consequence not of tolerance and mutual respect — an over-all ideology of freedom — but of the existence of many communities within the society each with its own canons of orthodoxy. In other words, if one looked hard enough, it was probable that he could find somewhere in the United States a community that shared his own peculiar views — whether religious, vegetarian, polygamous, socialist, or whatever — and, joining it, he could help impose group beliefs on all within reach. . . .

"Again it must be emphasized that to say this is not to claim that persecution was rife: the average white Protestant American went through life with complete freedom and reciprocated by bestowing on other white Protestant Americans the blessings of liberty. Moreover, if things got too rough for a minority, it could probably emulate the Latter-Day Saints by finding an isolated spot beyond the long arm of the vicinage and the direct democracy of irate neighbors. And before one weeps too vigorously for the poor, persecuted victims, it should also be recalled that persecution was a two-way proposition: the Presbyterian who attempted to explain the evils of Romish domination to an Irish Catholic community, or the Baptist who tried to explain to the Mormons of Nauvoo or Salt Lake City that Joseph Smith was a blasphemer and forger, was seldom greeted in the spirit of Christian love." American Liberty: An Examination of the "Tradition" of Freedom, in Konvitz and Rossiter (eds.), Aspects of Liberty 134, 146 (1958).

REFERENCES

1. Other accounts of the state of civil liberties in the period prior to the Civil War may be found in Williams, The Shadow of the Pope 51-94 (1932); Billington, The Protestant Crusade 1800-1860 (1938) (bibliography at 498-504); Myers, History of Bigotry in the United States, chs. XIII-XIX (1943); Curti, The Roots of American Loyalty, ch. III (1946); Valentine, Vigilante Justice (1956); Beals, Brass-Knuckle Crusade: The Know-Nothing Conspiracy: 1820-1860 (1960).

2. Other than Barron v. Baltimore, there were no significant decisions of the federal courts dealing with freedom of expression during this pre-Civil War period. For the indirect impact of the Supreme Court in establishing conditions favorable to civil liberties during the first three decades of the century, see Morgan, The Marshall Court and Civil Liberties, in Konvitz and Rossiter (eds.), Aspects of Liberty 163 (1958).

The abolitionist movement created the most acute strain on freedom of expression in the pre-Civil War era, perhaps in any era of our history, and in the South the most complete suppression of discussion over the slavery issue resulted. The situation in the South is summarized in the following extract.

NYE, FETTERED FREEDOM: CIVIL LIBERTIES AND THE SLAVERY CONTROVERSY 1830-1860 *
174-177 (rev. ed. 1963)

Before 1830, though sensitive to antislavery talk, the South nevertheless allowed a limited amount of free discussion. Yet at the same time signs of displeasure indicated a growing public uneasiness about the slavery question. One "Hieronymous" in 1825 complained of newspaper comments on slavery; a meeting in Smithfield, Virginia, was broken up by local magistrates in 1827; and the Manumission Society of North Carolina in 1826 deplored the increasing tendency in the South to stifle criticism of its domestic institutions. The most rigid control of antislavery discussion before 1830 existed in South Caro-

* Copyright 1963, by The Michigan State University Press.

lina, but after that date fears of Garrisonian abolition and slave revolt spread suspicion of antislavery opinion throughout the South in general.

It was imperative, after the beginnings of the aggressive phase of abolition, for the dominant slaveholding group to prevent the dissemination of antislavery doctrines. The South could be self-critical; a decade of reports from Southern commercial conventions reprinted in DeBow's Review shows that slaveholders themselves recognized that slavery had its faults, yet it is significant that none of the resolutions passed by these conventions ever had really practical results. To retain political and economic control of the South, the slaveholders believed that no deep-seated criticism of slavery could safely be tolerated. This group, with its chief institution at stake, could not allow frank discussion of it, and, for obvious reasons, hoped to identify its private interests with the public welfare of the South at large.

In the deep South the suppression of antislavery criticism after 1830 was relatively simple, for there, as one historian phrased it, "existed the most perfect agreement known in Anglo-Saxon history." In the upper South, where cotton and Negroes were less of an issue, repression was more difficult, and though independent thinkers were discouraged, recalcitrants continued to appear in the border states until the Civil War. But throughout the South it was possible by the passage of state and local legislation to control and minimize, and, if need be, to prohibit entirely antislavery opinion and discussion among Southerners, and to prevent the spread of such doctrines in the region by Northerners.

With the exception of Kentucky, every Southern state eventually passed laws controlling and limiting speech, press, and discussion. The decision of an Alabama court in 1837, for example, made any person "who shall proclaim to our slaves the doctrine of universal emancipation . . . a subject for criminal justice." The Virginia Code of 1849 punished by imprisonment up to a year, and a fine up to $500, any person who "by speaking or writing maintains that owners have no right of property in slaves," while Louisiana's penalty for conversation "having a tendency to promote discontent among free colored people, or insubordination among slaves" ranged from twenty-one years at hard labor to death.[4] The passage of such laws was justified as a means of preventing slave revolts, presumably stirred up by abolitionists.[5] Not all Southerners agreed that these measures were necessary. The Richmond Whig thought the Virginia law of 1836 "far worse than lynching or lynch law," while the Louisville Gazette, applauding Kentucky's refusal to pass restrictive legislation, thought the preservation of free speech more important than the suppression of antislavery opinion.[6] Such objections were unusual, how-

[4] Helen T. Catterall, Judicial Cases Concerning Slavery, II:141; and William Goodell, The American Slave Code, 384.
[5] Catherine E. Beecher, Essay on Slavery and Abolition, 89; and R. W. Bailey, The Issue, Presented in a Series of Letters on Slavery, 54-55.
[6] Clement Eaton, Freedom of Thought in the Old South, 127; and the Cincinnati Philanthropist, December 18, 1838.

ever, and the laws remained on the statute books, reaffirmed and strengthened in subsequent years.

Though these statutes served to hamper free expression of antislavery opinion in the South, they did not fully suppress it. Most of the laws dealt out punishment for "incendiary" talk, or "opinions tending to incite insurrection," — terms vaguely defined and charges difficult to establish — a fact recognized by Southern courts, whose verdicts were usually lenient. Legal processes were often slow, loopholes could be found, and there were strong feelings in the South that better ways of controlling antislavery opinions ought to be found. To remedy these defects and to provide swifter and more effective punishment, the South turned to the citizen-mob, long known on the frontier as "lynch law." [8] Though isolated cases of mob action occurred before 1833, the development of the mob as a means of suppressing abolitionism reached its climax during the period 1833-1840, receding in the North after 1845 and continuing with undiminished force in the South until the Civil War.[9]

NOTE

In addition to enforcing legislation of the kind noted above the southern states, with assistance at times from the Federal Government, also undertook to ban abolitionist literature from the mails. See, e.g., Va. Acts, 1836, p. 44. Academic freedom was seriously curtailed, and various other forms of suppression were employed.

As stated by Nye, throughout this period suppression of abolitionist views also resulted from extra-legal sanctions enforced by private individuals and groups. Mob action in both North and South became common. Thus in Boston William Lloyd Garrison was mobbed and dragged through the streets. And a series of violent outbreaks occurred in St. Louis and Alton, Illinois, where the offices and printing presses of Rev. E. P. Lovejoy, publisher of a religious journal, were destroyed and Lovejoy himself killed. During these years lynch law, hitherto known only in frontier areas, spread through many parts of the country. As the Civil War neared, the abolitionists gradually received a better reception in the North, but in the South expressions of opinion favoring abolition were in effect totally suppressed.

Again, the legal issues involved in repression of the abolitionist movement did not reach the Supreme Court. This was largely precluded by the decision in Barron

---

[8] James E. Cutter, Lynch Law, 91 ff. The Savannah Republican, reprinted in The National Anti Slavery Standard, June 28, 1849, believed that while Southern laws were satisfactory, they were often too unwieldy and their punishments too light for abolitionist incendiaries. Excellent discussions of why the South was especially prone to the use of extra-legal methods are Clement Eaton, "Mob Violence in the South," Mississippi Valley Historical Review XXIX (Dec., 1942), 351-71, and C. S. Sydnor, "The Southerner and the Laws," Journal of Southern History VI (Feb., 1940), 3-24.

[9] Hezekia Niles, from his reading and clipping of hundreds of newspapers, thought 1835 the worst mob year. In one week he clipped five hundred items of mob violence, many of them over the slave question; Niles' Register, 49:1, 49. Notable too were the Irish riots in New York and New Orleans, anti-Catholic and labor riots in Massachusetts, and election riots in New York.

v. Baltimore. In the North the ultimate effect of the campaign of suppression, in which freedom of speech, press and assembly were linked with the anti-slavery movement, was probably to strengthen the theory and practice of free expression. In the South two results of the suppression, as noted by Nye, are worthy of attention:

"In the end, the refusal of the South to allow freedom of discussion in its institutions of higher learning proved disastrous. It led ultimately to a complete misunderstanding of the plantation system, and fostered intolerance of frank discussion of other problems connected with slavery. The intelligent Southerner who might have been a constructive critic of his region's economic and political structure was forced, by 1850, to maintain a sterile silence. As a consequence, during the decade when the South most needed discussion of its problems, the universities and colleges, which should have been fruitful sources of progressive thought, found themselves unable to speak. The trend toward sectionalism and insularity in the South found no corrective. The 'positive good' argument for slavery developed absurdities which no Southerner of intellectual prestige dared deny; the faults of slavery, of which an earlier South had been well aware, were glossed over by indiscriminate, enthusiastic praise of its virtues. By 1855 the South had lost all sense of proportion in regard to slavery, making claims for the system that few intelligent slaveholders thirty years earlier would have accepted as reasonable. Because Southern teachers and scholars had been denied their function for thirty years, the South could neither understand nor tolerate self-criticism." Id. at 100-101.

"An important factor in turning Northern sentiment against the South (which could then be translated into sentiment against slavery) was the South's tendency to identify all anti-slavery opinion with the extremists. The South, as time passed, refused to allow consideration of its own problems even by Southerners, and its growing distrust and suspicion made discussion of vital issues as impossible with "fire-eaters" as with Garrisonians. The institution whose supporters could not permit discussion or criticism, and who showed themselves willing to sacrifice the most cherished traditional liberties in its defense, wrote its own doom." Id. at 283.

REFERENCES

1. The two most detailed treatments of the subject are Nye, Fettered Freedom, supra, and from a more southern point of view, Eaton, The Freedom-of-Thought Struggle in the Old South (rev. ed. 1964). Both books contain numerous references to the original sources. In addition, see 2 Wilson, History of the Rise and Fall of the Slave Power in America (1872 and 1874); Johnson, William Lloyd Garrison and His Times (1879); 6 von Holst, The Constitutional and Political History of the United States, ch. VI (1889); Cutler, Lynch-Law, ch. IV (1905); Whipple, The Story of Civil Liberty in the United States, ch. III (1927); Savage, Abolitionist Literature in the Mails, 1835-1836, 13 J. Negro Hist. 150 (1928); Ruchames (ed.), The Abolitionists: A Collection of Their Writings (1963). A recent biography of Lovejoy is Dillon, Elijah P. Lovejoy, Abolitionist Editor (1961).

2. With reference to the impact on academic freedom, see Beale, A History of Freedom of Teaching in American Schools 111-167 (1941); Hofstadter, Academic Freedom in the Age of the College 253-261 (1961 ed.).

3. On enforcement of the fugitive slave laws, which involved a conflict of federal law and state "personal liberty laws," see 2 Warren, The Supreme Court in United States History, ch. XXV (rev. ed. 1935).

D.   The Civil War

The Civil War raised critical problems of freedom of expression in a military emergency, the more troublesome because much of the opposition to the war or its conduct involved expression intertwined with overt acts of rebellion. With the outbreak of the war President Lincoln, acting under the executive power, took a series of measures to meet the crisis. Those which directly affected freedom of expression were a direction that the Post Office be closed to "treasonable correspondence," subjection of "passengers to and from foreign countries" to passport controls, and suspension of the writ of habeas corpus. Under the latter action he "caused persons who were represented to him as being or about to engage in disloyal and treasonable practices to be arrested by special civil as well as military agencies and detained in military custody when necessary to prevent them or deter others from such practices." Richardson, Messages and Papers of the Presidents 3304 (1897). All of these actions were taken in the eleven weeks between the firing on Fort Sumter, April 12, 1861, and the convening of a special session of Congress on July 4, 1861. Suspension of the privilege of the writ of habeas corpus was later ratified by Congress. Act of March 3, 1863, 12 Stat. 755 (1863). The story of the period is suggested in the following extracts.

HALL, FREE SPEECH IN WARTIME
21 Colum. L. Rev. 526, 527 (1921)

During the Civil War it was deemed politically inexpedient to legislate against disloyal utterances in general. In the earlier stages of the contest Lincoln earnestly sought to hold the border slave states in the Union. He was represented as praying: "Oh, Lord, we earnestly hope that Thou will favor our cause, but we must have Kentucky." Men not irreconcilably of Southern sympathies were to be won over, if possible, by the methods of persuasion. Many utterances that in Massachusetts would have been treated as clearly indicative of disloyalty, in Kentucky were the natural expressions of men sorely perplexed and reluctant to make a decision that either way was fraught with sorrow. Legislation applying to all alike would have been unjust and alienating to the border state doubters, and would have been widely criticized as an illustration of the despotism so often charged against Lincoln by his opponents. But, without the sanction of the legislation, the federal government arrested by the thousand men whom it knew or suspected to be dangerous or disaffected, and confined them without charges and without trial in military prisons as long as it saw fit — and public opinion generally acquiesced in this as a fairly necessary measure of war-time precaution. The number of such executive arrests has been variously estimated up to as high as 38,000. The War Department records, confessedly very incomplete, show over 13,000.

LINCOLN'S DEFENSE OF HIS SUSPENSION OF HABEAS CORPUS

Message to Congress in Special Session, July 4, 1861
2 Nicolay and Hay, Lincoln, Complete Works 55 (1894)

Of course some consideration was given to the questions of power and propriety before this matter was acted upon. The whole of the laws which were required to be faithfully executed were being resisted and failing of execution in nearly one third of the States. Must they be allowed to finally fail of execution, even had it been perfectly clear that by the use of the means necessary to their execution some single law, made in such extreme tenderness of the citizen's liberty that, practically, it relieves more of the guilty than of the innocent should to a very limited extent be violated? To state the question more directly, are all the laws but one to go unexecuted, and the government itself go to pieces lest that one be violated? Even in such a case, would not the official oath be broken if the government should be overthrown, when it was believed that disregarding the single law would tend to preserve it? But it was not believed that this question was presented. It was not believed that any law was violated. The provision of the Constitution that "the privilege of the writ of habeas corpus shall not be suspended, unless when, in cases of rebellion or invasion, the public safety may require it," is equivalent to a provision — is a provision — that such privilege may be suspended when, in case of rebellion or invasion, the public safety does require it. It was decided that we have a case of rebellion, and that the public safety does require the qualified suspension of the privilege of the writ which was authorized to be made. Now it is insisted that Congress and not the executive, is vested with this power. But the Constitution itself is silent as to which or who is to exercise the power; and as the provision was plainly made for a dangerous emergency, it cannot be believed the framers of the instrument intended that in every case the danger should run its course until Congress could be called together, the very assembling of which might be prevented, as was intended in this case, by the rebellion.

NOTES

1. The constitutional problems raised by Lincoln's actions restricting freedom of expression were never passed upon by the Supreme Court during the war. In 1861 Chief Justice Taney, sitting in the circuit court in Baltimore, held that the President did not have authority to suspend the writ of habeas corpus, but the military

authorities and Lincoln ignored the Court's order. Ex parte Merryman, Fed. Cas. No. 9,487 (C.C. Md. 1861). And a similar issue was avoided by the full Court on procedural grounds in Ex parte Vallandigham, 68 U.S. 243, 17 L. Ed. 589 (1864). Other issues never reached the Court. Attorney General Bates' opinion upholding Lincoln's right to suspend habeas corpus is reported in 10 A.G. Opin. 74 (1861).

2. For a full discussion of Lincoln's measures and the role of the courts during the Civil War, see Randall, Constitutional Problems Under Lincoln (rev. ed. 1951), and Silver, Lincoln's Supreme Court (Illinois Studies in the Social Sciences 1956). Both books contain extensive bibliographies. See also Rossiter, Constitutional Dictatorship, ch. XV (1948); Halbert, The Suspension of the Writ of Habeas Corpus by President Lincoln, 2 Am. J. Leg. Hist. 95 (1958); Sprague, Freedom Under Lincoln (1965).

3. The issue of the authority of a military commission to arrest and try a citizen on criminal or other charges came before the Supreme Court after the war was over in Ex parte Milligan, 71 U.S. 2, 18 L. Ed. 281 (1866). A majority held that a military commission could have no such jurisdiction, and the writ of habeas corpus could not be suspended, so long as the courts were open and functioning. "Martial law cannot arise from a *threatened* invasion. The necessity must be actual and present; the invasion real, such as effectually closes the courts and deposes the civil administration." 71 U.S. at 127. Four justices concurred in the result, holding that a military commission had not been authorized by Congress but that Congress had power to set up such a commission if it chose to do so.

The Milligan case has long been famous as an outstanding statement of the right to constitutional protections in a period of emergency. For material on the case see Klaus, The Milligan Case (1929) (a complete text of the record and arguments, with bibliography); 2 Warren, The Supreme Court in United States History, 1836-1918, ch. XXIX (1932); Fairman, Mr. Justice Miller and the Supreme Court 90-97 (1939); Frank, Ex parte Milligan v. The Five Companies: Martial Law in Hawaii, 44 Colum. L. Rev. 639 (1944).

4. Another problem with major ramifications in the field of political expression grew out of the Civil War — the imposition of loyalty oaths as a condition of voting, of holding public office or public employment, or of engaging in certain occupations. After the war the Supreme Court dealt with this issue in two famous cases. In Cummings v. Missouri, 4 Wall. 277, 18 L. Ed. 356 (1867), a Roman Catholic priest had been convicted of teaching and preaching without having subscribed to one of these oaths imposed by the state of Missouri. The oath in question was described by the Court as follows:

"The oath prescribed by the constitution, divided into its separable parts, embraces more than thirty distinct affirmations or tests. Some of the acts, against which it is directed, constitute offences of the highest grade, to which, upon conviction, heavy penalties are attached. Some of the acts have never been classed as offences in the laws of any State, and some of the acts, under many circumstances, would not even be blameworthy. It requires the affiant to deny not only that he has ever 'been in armed hostility to the United States, or to the lawful authorities thereof,' but, among other things, that he has ever, 'by act or word,' manifested his adherence to the cause of the enemies of the United States, foreign or domestic, or his desire for their triumph over the arms of the United States, or his sympathy with those engaged in rebellion, or has ever harbored or aided any person engaged in guerrilla warfare against the loyal inhabitants of the United States, or has ever entered or left the State for the purpose of avoiding enrolment or draft in the military service of the United States; or, to escape the performance of duty in the militia of the United States, has ever indicated, in any terms, his disaffection to the government of the United States in its contest with the Rebellion." 4 Wall. at 316-317.

The Court reversed the conviction, holding the oath unconstitutional as a bill of attainder and an ex post facto law. In Ex Parte Garland, 4 Wall. 333, 18 L. Ed. 366 (1867), the Court struck down a similar oath, required as a condition of practicing law, on the same grounds.

The Civil War loyalty oaths are discussed in Russ, The Lawyer's Test Oath During Reconstruction, 10 Miss. L.J. 154 (1938); Hyman, Era of the Oath: Northern Loyalty Tests During the Civil War and Reconstruction (1954). On the "war crimes" problem arising out of the Civil War, see Arens, Vicarious Punishment and War Crimes Prosecution: The Civil War or Alice Through the Looking Glass, 1951 Wash. U.L.Q. 62.

REFERENCES

For additional material concerning the impact of the Civil War on civil liberties, including restrictions on the press, see Whipple, The Story of Civil Liberty in the United States, ch. IV (1927); Dunning, Essays on the Civil War and Reconstruction, ch. 1 (1898); Schlesinger, Political and Social History of the United States, 1829-1925, 215-216 (1932); 3 Rhodes, History of the United States 554-558 (1902); Stephenson, Abraham Lincoln and the Union 160-167 (1918); 2 Beard, The Rise of American Civilization 78-81 (1928); Cummings and McFarland, Federal Justice, ch. X (1937); Coulter, The Confederate States of America, 1861-1865 (1950); Ekirch, The Decline of American Liberalism, ch. 9 (1955).

E. From the Civil War to World War I

During the period from the end of the Civil War to the outbreak of World War I legal controls over freedom or restriction of expression continued primarily in the hands of state and local authorities. The Fourteenth Amendment, and to a lesser extent the Thirteenth and Fifteenth Amendments, adopted immediately after the Civil War, contained the seeds of a vast expansion of federal power in this area; but this potential remained undeveloped. In the Slaughter-House Cases, 16 Wall. 36, 21 L. Ed. 394 (1873), the Supreme Court declined to employ the privileges and immunities clause of the Fourteenth Amendment as a basis for federal power in the protection of individual rights against state action. The Supreme Court did assert, by way of dictum in United States v. Cruikshank, that the "right of the people peaceably to assemble for the purpose of petitioning Congress for a redress of grievances, or for anything else connected with the powers or the duties of the national government, is an attribute of national citizenship, and, as such, under the protection of, and guaranteed by, the United States." 92 U.S. 542, 552, 23 L.

Ed. 588, 591 (1875). But the doctrine thus anounced was never further crystalized or utilized during this period. By 1877, the Federal Government had largely withdrawn from the whole problem of reconstruction. See Chapter XIII.

At the state and local level, the extent of freedom of expression varied with the time, place and issue. After 1877 in the South the Negro's right of expression, along with many other of his political and civil rights, was virtually non-existent. See Chapter XIII. Throughout the country efforts to maintain freedom of expression encountered the forces that troubled the rapid and haphazard growth of an industrialized and urbanized society. The pressures against free expression centered around three somewhat overlapping groups — aliens, workers seeking to organize and political radicals. By 1910, out of a population of 92 million, roughly a third were foreign-born immigrants or the first American-born generation, and the gradually increasing demands from this source alarmed many members of the established population. The struggles of a rising labor movement, often accompanied with violence, created bitterness and aroused fears. And the militant activities of small groups of political extremists, such as the anarchists and later the Industrial Workers of the World, received widespread attention and added to the tensions of a turbulent period.

NOTES

Three series of events during the period exemplify the nature of the issues and the character of the restrictive responses.

1. In 1886 the country was in a state of agitation over the growth of the Knights of Labor, the demand for an eight-hour day, the activities of the anarchists, and similar matters. A meeting of labor sympathizers was being held in Haymarket Square, Chicago, when a detachment of police approached to disperse the crowd. At this moment someone threw a bomb at the police, the explosion killing eight policemen and wounding a number of other persons. It was never discovered who had thrown the bomb. But eight anarchists were tried for murder and convicted on the ground that their speeches and publications had been responsible for the killing. One of the convicted men committed suicide and four were hanged. The others, who were in prison, were pardoned three years later by Governor Altgeld.[1]

2. In 1902, shortly after the assassination of President McKinley, New York passed the first state anti-sedition law. This statute made it a criminal offense to advocate "criminal anarchy," defined as "the doctrine that organized government

---

[1] The convictions were affirmed by the Illinois Supreme Court in Spies v. People, 122 Ill. 1 (1887). A petition for writ of error to the United States Supreme Court was dismissed. Spies v. Illinois, 123 U.S. 131, 8 S. Ct. 21, 31 L. Ed. 80 (1887). Although petitioners claimed that the Illinois aiding and abetting statute, in making "mere advice, not to do the particular crime charged, but advice to a general revolutionary movement" a criminal offense, violated their privileges and immunities and due process rights under the Fourteenth Amendment, the Supreme Court did not refer to this claim in its opinion.

should be overthrown by force or violence," or to join any organization which taught or advocated the doctrine.[2]

3. The free speech struggles of the I.W.W are described in Brissenden, The I.W.W.: A Study of American Syndicalism (1919):

"It was in this same year that the I.W.W. made its bow to the American public as the militant jail and soap-box belligerent in the free-speech fight. As early as April, 1906, there was a minor clash between the police and the 'Wobblies,' but it was not until nearly three years later that the I.W.W. free-speech epidemic assumed national proportions. Since 1909 the I.W.W.s have attracted quite as much attention by their dramatic free-speech controversies with municipal authorities here and there as they have by the time-honored resort to the strike. During the next few years after the schism of 1908 these free-speech struggles became rather frequent. The Pacific slope is the most fruitful soil for these conflicts. Labor is more mobile there, and when the organizers in any particular town are arrested for preaching revolution a more effective call to 'foot-loose Wobblies' for an 'invasion' is possible. On the Pacific slope the 'Wobblies' almost literally broke into the jails by hundreds. They came to speak, but with the nearly certain foreknowledge that they would be collared by the police before they said many words. They simply crowded the jails, and in this way, as they intended, clogged the machinery of municipal administration by making themselves the guests of the city in such numbers as to be no inconsiderable burden to their real hosts, the taxpayers. . . . The same tactics are pursued in nearly every instance — a policy of sullen non-resistance on the part of the I.W.W. and of wholesale jailing by the authorities. The trouble always seems to begin because local authorities are revolted by — or at least nervously apprehensive about — either the substance of the I.W.W. speeches or the language in which their ideas are conveyed, or both. The remarks are alleged to be seditious, incendiary, unpatriotic, immoral, etc., or, whether they are any or all these or none of them, they are alleged to be profane or vulgar beyond the limits of forbearance. In the judgment of the writer the latter charge can be laid at the door of the I.W.W. with far greater justification than can the former. Refinement is not the Wobblies' long suit. . . ." (260-261.)

"In the fall of 1909 there were no less than three important free-speech campaigns conducted by the I.W.W. These were staged at Missoula, Montana; Spokane, Washington; and New Castle, Pennsylvania. In 1910 small 'fights' were conducted in the spring and summer in Wenatchee and Walla Walla, Washington, and during the fall a much more important one at Fresno, California. This latter struggle continued until March, 1911. From this time until the end of the year 1913 hardly a month elapsed that did not witness a more or less important free-speech controversy between the Wobblies and the municipal authorities in some part of the United States. In the five-year period, 1909-1913, there were at least twenty free-speech campaigns of importance, continuing under definite I.W.W. direction for periods ranging from a few days to more than six months. The most important of these disturbances was that at San Diego, which broke out about February 1, 1912, and continued until late the following summer. Since 1913 free speech has been a less important issue with the I.W.W., and there have been comparatively few such disturbances. Paterson, New Jersey, Aberdeen, South Da-

---

[2] N.Y. Laws of 1902, ch. 371. This was the statute involved in Gitlow v. New York, set forth in Chapter III, Section C.

kota, Old Forge, Pennsylvania, and Everett, Washington, are almost the only cases of any great importance. The most serious of these was the Everett free-speech controversy which culminated in the fatal tragedy of November 6, 1916." (263-264.)

Preston concludes as to the I.W.W. "free-speech fights": "While the Wobblies won the right to free speech, in the long run they lost, for 'the net effect on the public mind was that the violence was chiefly on the part of the I.W.W. or directly incited by them.' " Preston, Aliens and Dissenters: Federal Suppression of Radicals 1903-1933 (1963), at p. 44.

REFERENCES

1. For accounts of the struggles over freedom of expression during this period see, in addition to Preston and Brissenden, supra, Whipple, The Story of Civil Liberty in the United States, chs. VI, VII (1927); Higham, Strangers in the Land: Patterns of American Nativism 1860-1925 (2d ed. 1963); Roche, The Quest for the Dream, ch. I (1963), and Civil Liberties in the Age of Enterprise, 31 U. Chi. L. Rev. 103 (1963). On the general background, see Filler, Crusaders for American Liberalism (1939, new ed. 1961); Hofstadter, The Age of Reform (1955).

2. For accounts of the Haymarket prosecutions see Altgeld, Reasons for Pardoning Fielden, Neebe and Schwab (1893); The Chicago Martyrs: The Famous Speeches of the Eight Anarchists in Judge Gary's Court and Atlgeld's Reasons for Pardoning Fielden, Neebe and Schwab, No. 1, Free Society Library (1889); Browne, Altgeld of Illinois 74-115 (1924); Barnard, Eagle Forgotten 165-267 (1938); Zeisler, The Haymarket Riot (1956); David, The History of the Haymarket Affair (2d ed. 1958). See also Ginger, Altgeld's America, chs. 3, 4 (1958).

3. With respect to immigration and the problems of aliens see, in addition to Higham, Strangers in the Land: Patterns of American Nativism 1860-1925 (2d ed. 1963), and Preston, supra, Handlin, The Uprooted (1951) and The American People in the Twentieth Century (1954).

4. On the I.W.W., in addition to Brissenden and Preston, supra, see Gambs, The Decline of the I.W.W. (1943); O'Connor, Revolution in Seattle (1964); Kornbluh (ed.), Rebel Voices: An I.W.W. Anthology (1964); Foner, The Industrial Workers of the World 1905-1917 (1966). On the socialist and other radical movements of the period, see Fine, Labor and Farmer Parties in the United States, 1828-1928 (1928); Greer, American Social Reform Movements (1949); Egbert and Persons (eds.), Socialism and American Life (1952); Shannon, The Socialist Party in America (1955). See also Saposs, Left-Wing Unionism: A Study of Radical Policies and Tactics (1926); Ginger, The Bending Cross: A Biography of Eugene Victor Debs (1949).

5. For accounts of the celebrated Mooney-Billings case — involving prosecution for alleged participation in the exploding of a bomb which killed nine and wounded 40 people during a Preparedness Parade in San Francisco on July 22, 1916 — see Hunt, The Case of Thomas J. Mooney and Warren K. Billings (1929) (abstract and analysis of record); Draft of Mooney–Billings Report, submitted to the National Commission on Law Observance and Enforcement by the Section on Lawless Enforcement of the Law (1931), reprinted in The Mooney–Billings Report (1932); Hopkins, What Happened in the Mooney Case (1932). Mooney was sentenced to death but the sentence was later commuted to life imprisonment; he was released from prison and pardoned in 1939. Billings was released in 1939 and pardoned in 1961. N.Y. Times, Dec. 22, 1961.

F. World War I and Aftermath

In World War I and the years immediately following, the right of expression in the United States was subjected to restrictions more widespread than at any previous time in our history, and more intensive than at any other period except during the controversy over slavery in the pre-Civil War South. To the accumulating pressures of the preceding decades were now added, first the problems of conducting a war amid deliberately encouraged public excitement and hysteria, and later the fears, insecurities, and conflicts engendered by the changes in post-war America, stimulated and intensified by the Bolshevik Revolution. The period is notable as marking the beginning of an extensive use of federal power in controlling expression. It is significant also as the starting point in the development of First Amendment doctrine and application, as limiting both federal and state powers.

During the war itself the administration of the federal Espionage Act and similar state legislation constituted one of the principal restrictions upon the right of expression. Professor Chafee's account of these matters both reveals the temper of the times and outlines the events out of which First Amendment doctrine began to emerge.

CHAFEE, FREE SPEECH IN THE UNITED STATES *
37-41, 51-52, 100-101

[T]he government had at its disposal several criminal statutes enacted during the Civil War. These it could and did use to punish conspiracies by Emma Goldman and others aiming to resist recruiting and conscription by riots and other forcible means, or seeking by speeches and publications to induce men to evade the draft.[3] In some respects, however, these statutes were felt by the Department of Justice to be incomplete. (1) It was not a crime to persuade a man not to enlist voluntarily. (2) Inasmuch as one man cannot make a conspiracy all by himself, a deliberate attempt by an isolated individual to obstruct the draft, if unsuccessful, was beyond the reach of the law, except when his conduct was sufficiently serious to amount to treason. The treason statute, the only law on the books affecting the conduct of the individual, was of little service,[4] since there was considerable doubt whether it

---

* Copyright 1941, by Harvard University Press.

[3] These statutes are now 18 U.S.C.A. (1926), §§4, 6, 88, 550. . . . World War conspiracy cases thereunder include Emma Goldman v. United States, 245 U.S. 474 (1918); Wells v. U.S., 257 Fed. 605 (C.C.A., 1919); U.S. v. Phillips, Bull. Dept. Just., No. 14 (1917); Bryant v. U.S., 257 Fed. 378 (C.C.A., 1919); Orear v. U.S., 261 Fed. 267 (C.C.A., 1919); U.S. v. Reeder, Bull. Dept. Just., No. 161 (1918).

[4] O'Brian, [Civil Liberty in War Time, 42 Rep. N.Y. Bar Assn. 275, 277 (1919)]. The treason statute is now 18 U.S.C.A. (1926) §§1, 2; see Warren, "What is Giving Aid and Comfort to the Enemy?" 27 Yale Law Journal 331 (1918). . . . World War treason cases include U.S. v. Werner, 247 Fed. 708 (1918); U.S. v. Robinson, 259 Fed. 685 (1919); U.S. v. Fricke, 259 Fed. 673 (1919).

applied to utterances. Therefore, although it is probable that under the circumstances the existing conspiracy statutes would have taken care of any serious danger to the prosecution of the war, new legislation was demanded.

If the government had been content to limit itself to meeting the tangible needs just mentioned, the effect on discussion of the war would probably have been very slight, for treason, conspiracies, and actual attempts constitute a direct and dangerous interference with the war, outside the protection of freedom of speech as defined in the preceding chapter. Two additional factors, however, influenced the terms of the new statutes, and even more the spirit in which they were enforced. First came the recollection of the opposition during the Civil War, which was handled under martial law in so far as it was suppressed at all. Some persons, full of old tales of Copperheads, were eager to treat all opponents of this war as spies and traitors. A bill was actually introduced into the Senate which made the whole United States "a part of the zone of operations conducted by the enemy," and declared that any person who published anything endangering the successful operation of our forces could be tried as a spy by a military tribunal and put to death. President Wilson wished to head off such legislation as unwise and unconstitutional.[5] A turmoil would arise if army officers could thus dispose of the liberties and lives of civilians. Any control of the government over civilians outside actual war areas ought to be exercised through judges and juries. And yet the legal advisers of the administration felt that the conspiracy statutes were not enough to enable the ordinary courts to handle on a large scale dangerous activities short of treason. So it would be easier to resist pressure to take matters away from judges and juries, if a new criminal statute gave judges and juries wider and stiffer powers. The second factor was the fear of German propaganda, and the knowledge of legislation and administrative regulations guarding against it in Great Britain and Canada.[6] Although we did not adopt the British administrative control, which combined flexibility with possibilities of despotism, it was easy to forget our own policy of non-interference with minorities and put the United States also in a position to deal severely with written and spoken opposition to the war. . . .

The result of these various influences was the third section of Title I of the Espionage Act. As originally enacted on June 15, 1917 (and still in force in 1940), this section established three new offenses:

"(1) Whoever, when the United States is at war, shall willfully make or convey false reports or false statements with intent to interfere with the operation or success of the military or naval forces of the United States or to promote the success of its enemies (2) and whoever, when the United States is at war, shall willfully cause or attempt to cause insubordination, disloyalty,

[5] On this Chamberlain bill and similar proposals, see Thomas F. Carroll, "Freedom of Speech and of the Press in War Time: The Espionage Act," 17 Michigan Law Review 621, 663 note (1919); cited hereafter as Carroll. The bill seems clearly unconstitutional under Ex parte Milligan, 4 Wallace 2 (1866). . . .

[6] As to England, see 31 Harvard Law Review 296 (by Laski); Laski, Authority in the Modern State, p. 101. As to Canada, see Carroll, at 621 note.

mutiny, or refusal of duty, in the military or naval forces of the United States, (3) or shall willfully obstruct the recruiting or enlistment service of the United States, to the injury of the service or of the United States, shall be punished by a fine of not more than $10,000 or imprisonment for not more than twenty years, or both." [7]

Although most of the Espionage Act deals with entirely different subjects, like actual espionage, the protection of military secrets and the enforcement of neutrality in future conflicts between other nations, the section just quoted is buttressed by several provisions. Section 4 of the same Title (50 U.S.C.A. §34) punishes persons conspiring to violate section 3, if any one of them does any act to effect the object of the conspiracy. Title XI (18 U.S.C.A. §§611-633) authorizes the issue of search warrants for the seizure of property used as the means of committing a felony, which would include violations of the section just quoted. It was under this provision that the moving-picture film was confiscated in the Spirit of '76 case, and raids were made on the offices of anti-war organizations. Finally, Title XII (18 U.S.C.A. §§343, 344) makes non-mailable any matter violating the Act, or advocating treason, insurrection, or forcible resistance to any law of the United States, directs that it shall not be conveyed or delivered, and imposes heavy penalties for attempting to use the mails for its transmission.

Eleven months later the Espionage Act was greatly expanded by a second statute. Attorney General Gregory thought the original 1917 Act did not go far enough in some respects. He stated that although it had proved an effective instrumentality against deliberate or organized disloyal propaganda, it did not reach the individual casual or impulsive disloyal utterances. Also some District Courts gave what he considered a narrow construction of the word "obstruct" in clause 3, so that, as he described it, "most of the teeth which we tried to put in were taken out." [9] . . .

The history of subsequent events shows what is likely to happen in times of panic, when sedate lawyers ask for "just a wee drappie mair of suppression, and where's the harm in that." The Attorney General requested only a brief amendment of the Espionage Act by the addition of attempts to obstruct the recruiting service, and the punishment of efforts intentionally made to discredit and interfere with the flotation of war loans. The Senate Committee on the Judiciary, being thus stirred up, took the bit in its teeth, and decided to stamp on all utterances of a disloyal character. It went for a model of legislation affecting freedom of discussion to a recent sweeping sedition statute of the state of Montana, and inserted most of its clauses into the new federal law.

This amendment of May 16, 1918 (repealed in 1921),[11] which is sometimes

---

[7] Act of June 15, 1917, c. 30, Title I, §3, now 50 U.S.C.A. (1926), §33. The numerals are inserted by me. As to the provisions of this statute against real spying, see Gorin v. United States, 61 S. Ct. 429 (1941).

[9] 4 American Bar Association Journal 306.

[11] 40 Stat. 553 (1918). As to the repeal in 1921, see 41 Stat. 1359-1360; 60 Congressional Record 293-4, 4207-8.

called the Sedition Act, inserted "attempts to obstruct" in the third of the original offenses, and added nine more offenses, as follows: (4) saying or doing anything with intent to obstruct the sale of United States bonds, except by way of bona fide and not disloyal advice; (5) uttering, printing, writing, or publishing any disloyal, profane, scurrilous, or abusive language, or language intended to cause contempt, scorn, contumely or disrepute as regards the form of government of the United States; (6) or the Constitution; (7) or the flag; (8) or the uniform of the Army or Navy; (9) or any language intended to incite resistance to the United States or promote the cause of its enemies; (10) urging any curtailment of production of any things necessary to the prosecution of the war with intent to hinder its prosecution; (11) advocating, teaching, defending, or suggesting the doing of any of these acts; and (12) words or acts supporting or favoring the cause of any country at war with us, or opposing the cause of the United States therein. Whoever committed any one of these offenses during the war was liable to the maximum penalty of the original Act, $10,000 fine or twenty years' imprisonment, or both. . . .

It is unnecessary to review the two thousand Espionage Act prosecutions in detail, but a few general results may be presented here. The courts treated opinions as statements of fact and then condemned them as false because they differed from the President's speech or the resolution of Congress declaring war. . . . Under the second and third clauses against causing insubordination or obstructing recruiting, only a few persons were convicted for actually urging men to evade the draft or not to enlist. Almost all the convictions were for expressions of opinion about the merits and conduct of the war.

It became criminal to advocate heavier taxation instead of bond issues, to state that conscription was unconstitutional though the Supreme Court had not yet held it valid, to say that the sinking of merchant vessels was legal, to urge that a referendum should have preceded our declaration of war, to say that war was contrary to the teachings of Christ. Men have been punished for criticising the Red Cross and the Y.M.C.A., while under the Minnesota Espionage Act it has been held a crime to discourage women from knitting by the remark, "No soldier ever sees these socks." [30] It was in no way necessary that

---

[30] State v. Freerks, 140 Minn. 349 (1918). Among the many cases illustrating the statements of this paragraph, I cite the following convictions: Sandberg (revd. in 257 Fed. 643); Miller (Bull. 104); Nagler (Bull. 127, 252 Fed. 217); Goldsmith (Bull. 133); Kaufman (Bull. 134); Weist (Bull. 169); Kirchner (Bulls. 69, 174, 255 Fed. 301); Shaffer (Bulls. 125, 190, 255 Fed. 886); Albers (Bull. 191, 263 Fed. 27); Krafft (Bulls. 6, 84, 249 Fed. 919, 247 U.S. 520); Boutin (251 Fed. 313); Granzow (revd. in 261 Fed. 172); Hitchcock (Bull. 122); Weinsberg (Bull. 123); Denson (Bull. 142); Von Bank (Bull. 164, revd. in 258 Fed. 641); White (263 Fed. 17). A few of these convictions have been reversed as noted above and most of the other sentences were considerably reduced by the President after the armistice, but that does not excuse the conduct of the trial courts. . . .

A great many of the Espionage Act cases have never been reported in detail in print. The total number of persons convicted was stated by the Attorney General in his annual Reports as 877, out of 1,956 cases commenced. His Reports also show pardons and commutations of sentences.

these expressions of opinion should be addressed to soldiers or men on the point of enlisting or being drafted. Most judges held it enough if the words might conceivably reach such men. They have made it impossible for an opponent of the war to write an article or even a letter in a newspaper of general circulation because it will be read in some training camp where it might cause insubordination or interfere with military success. He cannot address a large audience because it is liable to include a few men in uniform; and some judges have held him punishable if it contains men between eighteen and forty-five, since they may be called into the army eventually; some have emphasized the possible presence of shipbuilders and munition-makers. All genuine discussion among civilians of the justice and wisdom of continuing a war thus becomes perilous. . . .

One would have supposed that the federal Espionage Act was a sufficient safeguard against opposition to the war, but many states were not satisfied with either its terms or its enforcement, and enacted similar but more drastic laws of their own.[107] These were particularly common in western states, where feeling ran high against the Non-Partisan League or the I.W.W. The most important of these statutes, that of Minnesota, made it unlawful to say "that men should not enlist in the military or naval forces of the United States or the State of Minnesota," or that residents of that state should not aid the United States in carrying on war with the public enemies.[108] There were a very large number of prosecutions and many convictions under this statute, chiefly of members of the Non-Partisan League, culminating in the condemnation of its president, A. C. Townley. . . .

REFERENCES

1. For a full discussion of the federal and state statutes and their administration in the War and post-War period, see Chafee, Free Speech in the United States (1941) at Parts I and II; Peterson and Fite, Opponents of War, 1917-1918 (1957). Supreme Court decisions dealing with these laws are considered in Chapter III, Section B.

2. The most complete accounts of the period, including the war and its aftermath, are Murray, Red Scare: A Study of National Hysteria, 1919-1920 (1955); and Preston, Aliens

---

A main source for these prosecutions is Bulletins of the Department of Justice on the Interpretation of War Statutes, cited herein as Bull. For other sources, see 32 Harvard Law Review 417.

[107] These statutes are listed in Appendix III. On the constitutionality of the Minnesota war statute and similar laws, see Chapter VII, section I. . . .

Other state cases arising out of war utterances involved breaches of the peace; municipal ordinances regulating newspapers (see Pound, Cases on Equitable Relief against Defamation, 2d ed., p. 44n.); conspiracy to compel newsdealer to handle distasteful newspaper; libel in war controversy; expulsion of college student for pacifism (id. 108); ordinance prohibiting German opera (infra, Chapter IV, note 29); ordinance making opponent of war a vagrant (Ex parte Taft v. Shaw, 284 Mo. 531; 27 Illinois Law Review 67).

[108] Minn. Laws, 1917, c. 463. This was superseded in 1919 by a still more drastic act, to take care of future wars — Laws, 1919, c. 93; Mason's Minn. Stat. (1927), §9972.

and Dissenters: Federal Suppression of Radicals 1903-1933 (1963). Both books contain bibliographies. See also Beale, Are American Teachers Free? ch. III (1936); Cummings and McFarland, Federal Justice, ch. XX (1937); Mock, Censorship — 1917 (1941); Hyman, To Try Men's Souls, chs. XI-XIII (1959); Scheiber, The Wilson Administration and Civil Liberties (Cornell Studies in American History, Literature and Folklore, 1960); Higham, Strangers in the Land: Patterns of American Nativism 1860-1925 (1963) (bibliography at 408-411); Johnson, The Challenge to American Freedoms: World War I and the Rise of the American Civil Liberties Union (1963) (bibliography at 205-227); Roche, The Quest for the Dream: The Development of Civil Rights and Human Relations in Modern America, chs. III, IV (1963).

3. For the more general background of the times, see Slosson, The Great Crusade and After, 1914-1928, chs. I-III (1930); Allen, Only Yesterday 45-77 (1931); V and VI Sullivan, Our Times: The United States, 1900-1925 (1933 and 1935); Paxson, American Democracy and the World War (3 vols. 1936-1948); Leuchtenburg, The Perils of Prosperity, 1914-1932 (1957) (bibliography at 277-297). See also Dos Passos, 1919 (1932).

4. On the use of federal powers to exclude material from the mails, see Chaffee, Free Speech in the United States 42-51, 97-100, 298-305 (1941); Mock, Censorship — 1917 110-130 (1941); Johnson, The Challenge to American Freedoms: World War I and the Rise of the American Civil Liberties Union 56-63, 73-84 (1963); and Preston, Aliens and Dissenters: Federal Suppression of Radicals 1903-1933 144-149 (1963). Federal laws excluding and expelling aliens because of political views and activities were strengthened by the Act of February 5, 1917, ch. 29, 39 Stat. 874, but the principal campaign to bar or deport aliens came after the war under the Act of October 16, 1918, ch. 186, 40 Stat. 1012, and later amendments. See infra. Federal power was also exercised to suppress radical groups, especially the I.W.W. in the early months of the war before the 1918 amendments to the Espionage Act, by the use of military forces. See Johnson, id, at ch. 4; Preston, id. at ch. IV. On the treatment of conscientious objectors see Johnson, id. at ch. 2 (bibliography at 212-217). With regard to government measures to arouse public opinion, see Creel, How We Advertised America (1920); Mock and Larson, Words That Won the War: The Story of the Committee on Public Information, 1917-1919 (1939).

5. Harassment and suppression of radicals and dissenters by private groups, such as the American Protective League with its 350,000 members, was widespread. See Hyman, To Try Men's Souls, chs. XI, XII (1959); Higham, Strangers in the Land: Patterns of American Nativism 1860-1925 (1963) at ch. 8; Johnson, supra at 63-69; Roche, The Quest for the Dream: The Development of Civil Rights and Human Relations in Modern America 43-46 (1963); Mock, supra, passim. See also Hough, The Web (1919). Roche summarizes the situation as follows: "The suppression of dissent affected every sector of American life: books, films, newspapers were censored and banned; teachers and ministers were disciplined or dismissed; lawful opposition to conscription was extirpated by methods both legal and illegal. (The difficulties of labor and radical groups were legion . . .). Everywhere one went, he found the gospel of 'Positive Americanism' preached as the highest truth and enforced by indiscriminate and savage sanctions of the patriotic mob. Freedom of speech, press, petition, or assembly had no standing in competition with this truth; the 'disloyal' had no rights." (id. at 45.)

NOTES

Although the federal Espionage Act was no longer in force upon the termination of the war, federal power was exerted through the immigration laws, congressional investigations, and in other ways. The activities of state and local authorities and private groups continued at an equal or increased tempo. The highlights of the period, often referred to as the era of the Red Scare, include:

1. *Passage of additional state criminal anarchy, criminal syndicalism, and similar anti-sedition laws.* These laws were similar to the New York law of 1902 and the California statute discussed in Whitney v. California, but some were more restrictive. Two thirds of the states passed such laws from 1917 to 1921. See Chafee, Free Speech in the United States (1941), chs. 4, 7, 8, 10, and App. III; Dowell, A History of Criminal Syndicalism Legislation in the United States (1939); Smith, Subversive Propaganda. The Past and the Present, 39 Geo. L.J. 809 (1941); Johnson, The Challenge to American Freedoms: World War I and the Rise of the American Civil Liberties Union 165-171 (1963). In addition 33 states passed red flag laws. See Chafee, id. at 159-163. It has been estimated that some 1400 persons were arrested and about 300 convicted under state sedition and red flag laws during the years 1919-1920. Murray, Red Scare: A Study of National Hysteria, 1919-1920 233-235 (1955). The California criminal syndicalism law was also used as a basis for a restraining order and temporary injunction against the I.W.W. and various of its officers and members, seriously crippling the operation of that organization in California. See Chafee, id. at ch. 10.

2. *Deportations.* As noted above, the immigration laws were amended in 1918 to permit the exclusion and deportation of additional types of aliens found to hold radical political views. These laws were vigorously enforced, most notably in the Palmer raids. Thus in January 1920 Attorney General Palmer conducted a nation-wide raid on aliens who were members of the Communist Party or the Communist Labor Party. Some 4000 aliens were rounded up; many were arrested and held without warrants; papers, documents, and other evidence were seized, also frequently without warrant; many of the raids were conducted at night and the persons arrested immediately hustled off to jail. Subsequent hearings before immigration officials violated some of the basic elements of due process and in many instances were reversed by the courts. In the end only a relatively few of the aliens were deported, but the effect upon political expression was obviously substantial. See Report Upon the Illegal Practices of the United States Department of Justice, prepared under the auspices of the National Popular Government League by 12 eminent lawyers (including Professor Chafee, Felix Frankfurter, Ernst Freund, Dean Roscoe Pound, and Frank P. Walsh) (1920); Post, The Deportations Delirium of Nineteen-Twenty (1923); Brown, The Disloyalty of Socialism, 53 Am. L. Rev. 681 (1919); Chafee, supra, at ch. 5; Dunn (ed.), The Palmer Raids (1948); Johnson, supra, at chs. 5, 6 (bibliography at 224-225); Murray, supra, at ch. 13 (bibliography at 293); Preston, Aliens and Dissenters: Federal Suppression of Radicals 1903-1933, chs. VII-IX (1963). See also Johnson, The Political Career of A. Mitchell Palmer, XXV Pa. History 345 (1958); Coben, A. Mitchell Palmer: Politician, chs. I, XII (1963). On the role of the F.B.I. see Lowenthal, The Federal Bureau of Investigation, ch. 14 (1950); cf. Whitehead, The F.B.I. Story, ch. 6 (1956). See also Cummings and McFarland, Federal Justice 429-430 (1937). For the judicial reaction see Colyer v. Skeffington, 265 Fed. 17 (D. Mass. 1920); cf. U.S. ex rel. Abern v. Wallis, 268 Fed. 413 (S.D. N.Y. 1920).

3. *Expulsion of Socialists from legislature.* Victor L. Berger, a leader of the Socialist Party, was indicted for conspiracy under the Espionage Act. In November 1918, before the trial, he was elected to Congress as a Representative from Wisconsin. At the opening of Congress in the spring of 1919 the House of Representatives refused to seat him. A special election was held in November 1919 and Berger was

again the victor. He was again refused his seat in Congress. Berger was convicted at his trial in December 1918 and sentenced to 20 years' imprisonment. On appeal the Supreme Court reversed on the ground that the judge should have disqualified himself for prejudice. Berger v. United States, 255 U.S. 22, 41 S. Ct. 230, 65 L. Ed. 481 (1921). Berger lost a third election in November 1920, but won again in 1922. This time he was allowed to take his seat. See Chafee, Free Speech in the United States 247-269 (1941). In January 1920 five members of the Socialist Party, who had been sworn in as members of the New York Assembly, were ousted from their seats pending investigation of their eligibility. In spite of strong protest, led by Charles Evans Hughes, the Judiciary Committee recommended expulsion and the Assembly voted overwhelmingly to expel. See State of New York, Legis. Doc. No. 30, Jan. 26, 1920; Chafee, id. at 269-282; Chamberlain, Loyalty and Legislative Action 48-51 (1951).

4. *Legislative investigating committees.* In 1919 two legislative committees — the first in modern times — undertook to investigate the loyalty of private citizens. The Overman Committee, a subcommittee of the Senate Judiciary Committee, made an investigation of the general strike in Seattle. It held hearings and published a lengthy report exposing the evils of Bolshevism and recommending new sedition legislation. Bolshevik Propaganda, Hearings before a Subcommittee of the Judiciary Committee of the U.S. Senate, pursuant to S. Res. 439 and 469, 65th Cong., 3d Sess. (1919). See also Murray, Red Scare: A Study of National Hysteria, 1919-1920 94-98 (1955).

The other committee, the Lusk Committee in New York, became more famous. Professor Chafee describes its operations: "On March 26, 1919, the [New York] legislature set up a joint committee of six under the chairmanship of Senator Lusk to investigate seditious activities and report to the legislature. Although in no sense a body for the prosecution of crime, it proceeded to conduct a series of spectacular illegal raids on the offices of the Rand School and other radical organizations, instigate prosecutions of radical leaders like Gitlow, and fill the press with a flow of terrorizing descriptions of the Red menace. And now it was the moving spirit in ousting the Socialist Assemblymen." Chafee, supra, at 271. For an account of the operation of the Lusk Committee see Chamberlain, supra, at 9-52; Murray, id. at 98-103. Governor Alfred E. Smith's well-known statements on vetoing the Lusk Bill in 1920 and signing the bill repealing the Lusk Laws in 1923 may be found in Public Papers of Governor Smith, 227 et seq. (1920), and Public Papers of Alfred E. Smith, Governor, 1923, 292 et seq. (1924).

5. *Teacher's loyalty oaths.* Many states passed legislation requiring loyalty oaths of teachers and restraining teachers in their political views and activities. See Chapter III, Section E.

6. *Sacco–Vanzetti case.* Sacco and Vanzetti were tried, convicted, and executed for a murder committed in connection with a hold-up. The controversy, which raged for years, involved the question of whether they had had a fair trial or had been prejudiced by their radical views. For the case in the courts, see Commonwealth v. Sacco, 255 Mass. 369, 151 N.E. 839 (1926) (overruling exceptions); 259 Mass. 128, 156 N.E. 57 (1927) (overruling exceptions to order denying new trial on the basis of new evidence); 261 Mass. 12, 158 N.E. 167 (1927), cert. dis., 275 U.S. 574 (1927) (overruling exceptions to order denying new trial and refusing to set aside sentences). There is now a voluminous literature on the Sacco–Vanzetti

case. Among the more significant materials are F. Frankfurter, The Case of Sacco and Vanzetti (1927); Fraenkel, The Sacco-Vanzetti Case (1931); Joughin and Morgan, The Legacy of Sacco and Vanzetti (1948) (extensive bibliography at 557-580); Ehrmann, The Untried Case (2d ed. 1960) (argument for thesis that the Morelli gang committed the crime), first edition reviewed by Morgan in 47 Harv. L. Rev. 538 (1934); Montgomery, Sacco–Vanzetti: The Murder and the Myth (1960) (concludes the trial was fair; critically reviewed by O'Connor in 14 Vand. L. Rev. 987 (1961) and Musmanno in 22 U. Pitt. L. Rev. 651 (1961)); Russell, Tragedy in Dedham (1962) (suggests Sacco guilty, Vanzetti innocent), disputed by Ehrmann in 79 Harv. L. Rev. 571 (1966); Cook, Sacco–Vanzetti: The Missing Fingerprints, The Nation, Dec. 22, 1962, p. 442; Felix, Protest: Sacco-Vanzetti and the Intellectuals (1965) (takes position that trial was fair and defendants guilty). See also M.D. Frankfurter and Jackson (eds.), The Letters of Sacco and Vanzetti (1928).

7. Harassment by private individuals and organizations, particularly of radicals but also of ethnic and religious groups, continued in the aftermath of the war. See Higham, Strangers in the Land: Patterns of American Nativism 1860-1925, chs. 9, 10 (1963); Murray, Red Scare: A Study of National Hysteria, 1919-1920, ch. 11 (1955); Roche, The Quest for the Dream, ch. IV (1963). For two extreme examples of the literature of the Red Scare, see Whitney, Reds in America (1924); Coán, The Red Web (1925); see also Dilling, The Red Network (1934). Other literature relating to the period is cited in Murray, Red Scare in America: A Study of National Hysteria, 1919-1920 294-295 (1955). This period also witnessed a revival of the Ku Klux Klan. See Frost, The Challenge of the Klan (1924); Rice, The Ku Klux Klan in American Politics (1962); Higham, id. at 286-299 (bibliography at 410); Alexander, The Ku Klux Klan in the Southwest (1965); Chalmers, Hooded Americanism: The First Century of the Ku Klux Klan, 1865-1965 (1965) (bibliography at 388-408). On the problems of labor see Murray, id. at chs. 7-10, citing also the standard histories of the labor movement.

8. The first organization devoted exclusively to protection of civil liberties grew out of the conflicts of this period. Organized in 1917 as the National Civil Liberties Bureau, it became the American Civil Liberties Union in January 1920. See Johnson, The Challenge to American Freedoms: World War I and the Rise of the American Civil Liberties Union (1963); L. Milner, The Education of an American Liberal (1954); Markmann, The Noblest Cry: A History of the American Civil Liberties Union (1965). The American Jewish Committee had already been organized in 1906, and the National Association for the Advancement of Colored People in 1909, but these organizations dealt primarily with specialized aspects of the civil liberties problem. See Schachner, The Price of Liberty: A History of the American Jewish Committee (1948); Jack, History of the National Association for the Advancement of Colored People (1943); Hughes, Fight for Freedom: The Story of the NAACP (1962) (bibliography at 207-208). On the role of civil liberties organizations in maintaining a system of individual rights in the United States, see Note, Private Attorneys-General: Group Action in the Fight for Civil Liberties, 58 Yale L.J. 574 (1949); Robison, Organizations Promoting Civil Rights and Liberties, 275 Annals of the Am. Acad. of Pol. and Soc. Sci. 18 (1951); Roche, We've Never Had More Freedom, The New Republic, Jan. 23 and 30, Feb. 6, 1956.

G. From World War I Through World War II

Beginning with the cases arising out of the federal Espionage Act, the major issues involving freedom of expression in the United States came more and more to be translated into legal terms and to become the subject of decisions by the Supreme Court. The course of events need not be detailed here since matters of chief interest are referred to in subsequent chapters dealing with the development of the law in the various specific areas of concern.

In general the years from the Red Scare to the beginning of the New Deal in 1933 marked a distinct relaxation in federal measures directed against radicals and other dissenters. Existing federal legislation — such as the statutes on insurrection and conspiracy to engage in acts of violence — were not invoked. The main impact of federal action was felt by the alien, to whom the laws on exclusion, deportation, naturalization, and denaturalization continued to be applied with substantial strictness. The New Deal, and the forces that made it up, brought a new and liberal outlook, in which freedom of expression came to be realized on a broader and deeper scale than at any previous time in our history. As the country moved toward war, however, new tensions began to mount. These were reflected in the Alien Registration Act of 1940, which included the Smith Act, the first federal peacetime sedition law since the Alien and Sedition Acts. Likewise the Dies Committee, predecessor of the House Committee on Un-American Activities, commenced operations in 1938. Loyalty tests for government employees began to take form at the same time.

At the state and local levels, prosecutions under state sedition laws dwindled off during the 1920's. They were revived to some extent in the depression years of the 1930's. Other state and local measures, such as the teacher loyalty oaths, continued in force. But on the whole state and local restrictions, as well as repression emanating from non-governmental sources, posed a diminishing problem for freedom of expression. The new role of the federal courts began to be manifest as state and local controls over press, assembly, association, and the distribution of literature commenced to reach the Supreme Court for adjudication. Again, the advent of the war brought some increase in restrictions. An outstanding example was the Rapp-Coudert Committee of the New York State legislature, which in 1940 and 1941 undertook a vigorous investigation of "subversives" in government, particularly among New York City teachers.

During World War II, however, there was no repetition of the excesses of the World War I period. The nation remained relatively calm, and expression in opposition to the war was not suppressed. The major exception to this was the exclusion of persons of Japanese ancestry from the West Coast and their detention in relocation centers. Two other events which raised issues of freedom of expression, though not assuming major proportions, were the prosecutions under the Smith Act of members of the Socialist Workers Party in Minneapolis and of a group of pro-Nazis in Washington, D.C. See Chapter III, Section B.

REFERENCES

1. Developments in civil liberties during the period between the two wars are recounted in Chafee, Free Speech in the United States, Pt. III (1941), and The Blessings of Liberty, ch. III (1956); Chamberlain, Loyalty and Legislative Action: A Survey of Activity by the New York State Legislature, 1919-1949, chs. II-IV (1951) (Chapter III deals with the Rapp-Coudert Committee); Hyman, To Try Men's Souls: Loyalty Tests in American History, ch. XIII (1959); Preston, Aliens and Dissenters, ch. IX (1963); Roche, The Quest for the Dream, chs. V-VII (1963). The annual reports of the American Civil Liberties Union contain contemporary accounts of major events year by year. For the story of some of the well-known trials of the period see Hays, Let Freedom Ring (1928) and Trial By Prejudice (1933).

2. On the state of civil liberties during World War II, see Chafee, The Blessings of Liberty 79 (1956); Hyman, supra, at 327-333; Roche, supra, at ch. VIII; Biddle, In Brief Authority (1962). See also A Symposium on Constitutional Rights in Wartime, 29 Iowa L. Rev. 379 (1944); cf. In re Yamashita, 327 U.S. 1, 66 S. Ct. 340, 90 L. Ed. 499 (1946), especially the Murphy and Rutledge dissents. With respect to censorship during the war see Summers, Wartime Censorship of Press and Radio (1942). Material on the Japanese relocation and the Smith Act prosecutions is cited in Chapter III, Section C. Likewise the legal aspects of the civil liberties issues from World War I through World War II are treated in detail in subsequent chapters dealing with particular problems.

3. For the general background of the period between the two wars, see Schlesinger, The Age of Roosevelt, vols. I-III (1957-1960); Leuchtenburg, The Perils of Prosperity, 1914-1932 (1957) (bibliography at 277-297); Bernstein, The Lean Years: A History of the American Worker 1920-1933 (1960). On the war period, see Burns, Roosevelt: The Lion and the Fox (1956), and other biographies of Roosevelt; Perkins, The New Age of Franklin Roosevelt, 1932-1945 (1957).

H. Since World War II

The years following World War II were dominated by the rise and then decline of the phenomenon known as "McCarthyism." As cold war tensions mounted, restrictions on freedom of expression designed to promote national security steadily increased. In March 1947 President Truman promulgated an Executive Order establishing a comprehensive loyalty program for federal government employees. Similar state and local programs were instituted or intensified. In 1948 the Federal Government commenced a series of prosecutions against Communist Party leaders under the Smith Act. The Internal Security Act, providing for registration of "Communist-action" and "Communist-front" organizations and for emergency detention, was enacted in 1950, and enforcement of this legislation began. The Communist Control Act, apparently "outlawing" the Communist Party, followed in 1954. In addition, an unprecedented series of measures — federal, state and local — undertook to deny government benefits or positions of influence to "subversives." Meantime an intensive series of legislative investigations of "subversive activities," by federal and state committees, was being pressed. After 1955, "McCarthyism" began to ebb, but most of the measures taken in those years remained in effect.

The rise of the civil rights movement, after the Supreme Court decision in the school segregation cases in 1954, brought another group of problems. Many of these related to the right of assembly, marches, various forms of demonstrations, and other issues in the area of internal order. But they also included additional significant matters, such as libel of public officials, miscellaneous restrictions on the right of association, and federal protection of First Amendment rights against state and local infringement. Apart from these issues growing out of the civil rights movement, various other questions pertaining to freedom of expression came to the fore. Among these were problems in the fields of obscenity and censorship, election and lobbying practices, fair trial and free press, government action to facilitate operation of the system of free expression, including control over radio and television, and government participation in the process of expression itself.

As the courts began to deal with all these questions, First Amendment doctrine became more elaborate and refined.

The various problems of the period are treated separately in subsequent chapters. Materials relating to the specific issues are collected in those sections. Materials dealing generally with the course of events in the post-World War II period, and the literature which embodies the more general surveys of Supreme Court decisions and doctrine on freedom of expression, are cited below.

REFERENCES

For general accounts of the post-World War I period, see McWilliams, Witch Hunt (1950); Biddle, The Fear of Freedom (1951); Davies, The Urge to Persecute (1953); Davis, But We Were Born Free (1954); Thomas, The Test of Freedom (1954); Chafee, The Blessings of Liberty (1956); Cushman, Civil Liberties in the United States (1956); Lamont, Freedom Is As Freedom Does (1956); Caughey, In Clear and Present Danger (1958); Hook, Political Power and Personal Freedom (1959); Williams, One Man's Freedom (1962); Roche, The Quest for the Dream, chs. IX, X (1963); Kunstler, . . . And Justice For All (1963) (account of some of the famous cases of the period); Congressional Quarterly, Congress and the Nation, ch. 16 (1965). See also the annual reports of the American Civil Liberties Union for the period. Material of a similar nature, but dealing more narrowly with issues of national security, is cited in Chapter III, Section C. The major literature specifically on Senator McCarthy is also cited in the same section.

BIBLIOGRAPHY OF GENERAL LEGAL LITERATURE
ON FREEDOM OF EXPRESSION

1. The most comprehensive surveys of the Supreme Court decisions on freedom of expression are Fraenkel, Our Civil Liberties (1944) and The Supreme Court and Civil Liberties (2d ed. 1963); Konvitz, Fundamental Liberties of a Free People: Religion, Speech, Press, Assembly (1957); Rogge, The First and the Fifth (1960); Hudon, Freedom of Speech and Press in America (1963); Pfeffer, The Liberties of an American (2d ed. 1963); Konvitz, Expanding Liberties: Freedom's Gains in Postwar America (1966). See also Ernst, The First Freedom (1946); Reppy, Civil Rights in the United States (1951); Pritchett, Civil Liberties and the Vinson Court (1954) and The Political Offender and the Warren Court (1958); Gellhorn, Individual Freedom and Governmental Restraints (1956) and American Rights (1960); Newman, Civil Liberty and Civil Rights (rev. ed. 1957); Douglas, The Right of the People (1958); Fellman, The Limits of Freedom (1959); Roche, Courts and Rights (1961); Kauper, Civil Liberties and the Constitution (1962). See also the material cited in Chapter I.

2. Discussions of First Amendment doctrine include: Chafee, Free Speech in the United States (1941); Lusky, Minority Rights and the Public Interest, 52 Yale L.J. 1 (1942); Meiklejohn, Free Speech and Its Relation to Self-Government (1948), reprinted in Political Freedom (1960), reviewed by Chafee in 62 Harv. L. Rev. 891 (1949); Cushman, "Clear and Present Danger" in Free Speech Cases: A Study in Judicial Semantics, in Konvitz and Murphy (eds.), Essays in Political Theory Presented to George H. Sabine 311 (1948); Hyman, Judicial Standards for the Protection of Basic Freedoms, 1 Buffalo L. Rev. 221 (1952); Note, Legislative Inquiry into Political Activity: First Amendment Immunity from Committee Interrogation, 65 Yale L.J. 1159 (1956); Freeman, Civil Liberties — Acid Test of Democracy, 43 Minn. L. Rev. 511 (1959); Murphy, Mr. Justice Jackson, Free Speech, and the Judicial Function, 12 Vand. L. Rev. 1019 (1959); Mr. Justice Black, The Bill of Rights, 35 N.Y.U.L. Rev. 865 (1960); Carr, The Seesaw Between Freedom and Power, 57 U. Ill. Bull. 3 (1960); Thomas, Felix Frankfurter: Scholar on the Bench (1960); Freund, The Supreme Court of the United States, ch. III (1961); Jacobs, Justice Frankfurter and Civil Liberties (1961); Meiklejohn, The Balancing of Self-Preservation Against Political Freedom, 49 Calif. L. Rev. 4 (1961), and The First Amendment Is an Absolute, 1961 Sup. Ct. Rev. 245; Mendelson, Justices Black and Frankfurter: Conflict in the Court (1961); Nutting, Is the First Amendment Obsolete? 30 Geo. Wash. L. Rev. 167 (1961); Note, The Constitutional Right to Anonymity: Free Speech, Disclosure and the Devil, 70 Yale L.J. 1084 (1961); Cahn, Mr. Justice Black and First Amendment "Absolutes" — A Public Interview, 37 N.Y.U.L. Rev. 549 (1962); Frantz, The First Amendment in the Balance, 71 Yale L.J. 1424 (1962); Mendelson, On the Meaning of the First Amendment: Absolutes in the Balance, 50 Calif. L. Rev. 821 (1962); further Frantz-Mendelson exchange in 51 Calif. L. Rev. 729 (1963) and 17 Vand. L. Rev. 479 (1964); Emerson, Toward a General Theory of the First Amendment, 72 Yale L.J. 877 (1963); Fried, Two Concepts of Interests: Some Reflections on the Supreme Court's Balancing Test, 76 Harv. L. Rev. 755 (1963); Anastaplo, Freedom of Speech and the First Amendment, 42 U. Det. L. Rev. 55 (1964); Alfange, The Balancing of Interests in Free Speech Cases: In Defense of an Abused Doctrine, 2 Law in Trans. Q. 35 (1965); Brennan, The Supreme Court and the Meiklejohn Interpretation of the First Amendment, 79 Harv. L. Rev. 1 (1965); Kalven, The Negro and the First Amendment (1965); Shapiro, Freedom of Speech: The Supreme Court and Judicial Review (1966).

Material discussing the legal implications of the theory that freedom of expression should not be granted to antidemocratic groups, includes: Wiener, "Freedom for the Thought That We Hate": Is It a Principle of the Constitution? 37 A.B.A.J. 177 (1951), answered by Katz in 37 A.B.A.J. 901 (1951); Auerbach, The Communist Control Act of 1954: A Proposed Legal-Political Theory of Free Speech, 23 U. Chi. L. Rev. 173 (1956). See also Westin, A Critique of Civil Libertarian Reactions to the "Communist Problem," 50 Nw. U.L. Rev. 58 (1955); Chase, The Libertarian Case for Making It a Crime to Be a Communist, 29 Temple L.Q. 121 (1956).

3. Collections of cases and legal materials include Konvitz, Bill of Rights Reader (3d ed. 1965); Dowling and Gunther, Cases and Materials on Constitutional Law (7th ed. 1965); Lockhart, Kamisar, and Choper, Cases and Materials on Constitutional Rights and Liberties (1964); Freund, Sutherland, Howe, and Brown, Constitutional Law: Cases and Other Problems (2d ed. 1961). Annual supplements are published to all the above except the Konvitz book. See also Starr, Human Rights in the United States (rev. ed. 1964); Barker and Barker, Freedoms, Courts, Politics: Studies in Civil Liberties (1965); Haiman, Freedom of Speech: Issues and Cases (1965).

Annual surveys of the Supreme Court decisions are published in the Harvard Law Review, New York University Law Review, and the American Political Science Review. The Supreme Court Review, published annually, contains detailed discussions of significant cases decided during the term.

A summary of current cases pending in the civil liberties field may be found in the Civil Liberties Docket, published four times a year by the National Lawyers Guild. The weekly press releases and annual reports of the American Civil Liberties Union also contain material on current cases.

4. On the law of freedom of expression in England, see Street, Freedom, the Individual, and the Law (1963); in Canada, see Schmeiser, Civil Liberties in Canada (1964); in France and Germany, see Castberg, Freedom of Speech in the West (1960).

5. Generally on international protection of human rights, see Holcombe, Human Rights in the Modern World (1948); Symposium, International Human Rights, 14 Law & Contemp. Prob. 411, 545 (1949); Lauterpacht, International Law and Human Rights (1950); Green, United Nations and Human Rights (1957); Christol, Remedies For Individuals Under World Law, 56 Nw. U.L. Rev. 65 (1961); McDougal and Bebr, Human Rights in the United Nations, 58 Am. J. Int. L. 603 (1964); Schwelb, Human Rights and the International Community (1964) (bibliography at 75-76); Symposium on the International Law of Human Rights, 11 How. L.J. 257 (1965).

With respect to the European Convention on Human Rights, see Weil, The Evolution of the European Convention on Human Rights, 57 Am. J. Int. L. 804 (1963); Greenberg and Shalit, New Horizons for Human Rights: The European Convention, Court, and Commission of Human Rights, 63 Colum. L. Rev. 1384 (1963); del Russo, The European Bill of Rights, 4 Santa Clara L. Rev. 8 (1963); Schwelb, On the Operation of the European Convention on Human Rights, 18 Int. Org. 558 (1964); Mosler, The Protection of Human Rights By International Legal Procedure, 52 Geo. L.J. 800 (1964).

Problems with regard to United States participation in an international system of human rights are discussed in Holman, An "International Bill of Rights"; Proposals Have Dangerous Implications for U.S., 34 A.B.A.J. 984 (1948); Rix, Human Rights and International Law: Effect of the Covenant Under Our Constitution, 35 A.B.A.J. 551 (1949); McDougal and Leighton, The Rights of Man in The World Community: Constitutional Illusions Versus Rational Action, 14 Law and Contemp. Prob. 490 (1949), 59 Yale L.J. 60 (1949); Chafee, Federal and State Powers Under the UN Covenant on Human Rights, 1951 Wis. L. Rev. 389, 623; Sorensen, Federal States and the International Protection of Human Rights, 46 Am. J. Int. L. 195 (1952); Nathanson, Constitutional Problems Involved in Adherence by the United States to a Convention for the Protection of Human Rights and Fundamental Freedoms, 50 Cornell L.Q. 235 (1965).

CHAPTER III

National Security

The right to freedom of expression has usually met its severest test when it has been thought to impair the social interest in national security. Used in this context, the term national security embraces both protection against external or foreign dangers and the need for maintaining the general system of law and order within the society. In its first aspect, issues in reconciling national security with freedom of expression have largely centered around restrictions on expression which it is feared may interfere with a war effort or with defense against outside potential enemies. In its second aspect, the questions have turned upon the control of expression which is thought to imperil the basic structure of government or the fundamental institutions of society. This area may be distinguished, at least for purposes of presenting these materials, from controls over expression which is deemed to pose local and relatively isolated threats to law and order, as in the conduct of local meetings, parades and demonstrations. These latter issues are treated separately in Chapter IV. The materials in this chapter are concerned rather with those situations where, generally speaking, the anticipated danger affects the country on a broader scale, arises out of a context of organizational activity of major scope, and tends to involve the relation of the state to a whole social or political movement.

This chapter first sets out the background of laws relating to treason, rebellion, insurrection, espionage, sabotage, and similar conduct which clearly falls outside the field of expression (Section A). It then takes up restrictions designed to eliminate interference with a war or defense effort (Section B). The ensuing section deals with peacetime sedition or "seditious libel" laws, both federal and state, and other direct restrictions of expression, primarily the Internal Security Act, the Communist Control Act, and counterpart state legislation (Section C). Indirect restrictions aimed at denying certain persons government privileges or positions of influence are considered thereafter (Section D), with the special problem of employee loyalty programs treated in a separate section (Section E). Finally, the chapter concludes with materials dealing with problems of legislative investigating committees (Section F).

A. Background of Laws on Treason, Rebellion, Insurrection, Espionage, Sabotage, and Similar Conduct

Reconciliation of the right to freedom of expression with the interest in national security must be considered against the background of existing legislation which protects society against conduct that traditionally falls outside any area of protected expression. The constitutional provisions relating to treason, and the basic statutes against rebellion, insurrection, and seditious conspiracy are set forth below.

U.S. CONSTITUTION, ARTICLE III, SECTION 3

Treason against the United States, shall consist only in levying War against them, or in adhering to their Enemies, giving them Aid and Comfort. No Person shall be convicted of Treason unless on the Testimony of two Witnesses to the same overt Act, or on Confession in open Court.

REBELLION OR INSURRECTION
18 U.S.C. §2383

Whoever incites, sets on foot, assists, or engages in any rebellion or insurrection against the authority of the United States or the laws thereof, or gives aid or comfort thereto, shall be fined not more than $10,000 or imprisoned not more than ten years, or both; and shall be incapable of holding any office under the United States.

SEDITIOUS CONSPIRACY
18 U.S.C. §2384

If two or more persons in any State or Territory, or in any place subject to the jurisdiction of the United States, conspire to overthrow, put down, or to destroy by force the Government of the United States, or to levy war against them, or to oppose by force the authority thereof, or by force to prevent, hinder, or delay the execution of any law of the United States, or by force to seize, take, or possess any property of the United States contrary to the authority thereof, they shall each be fined not more than $20,000 or imprisoned not more than twenty years, or both.

The constitutional provision on treason has been implemented by specific legislation, which also makes it a crime to conceal knowledge of treason. 18 U.S.C. §§2381-2382. The laws against espionage and sabotage were strengthened and expanded by the Espionage and Sabotage Act of 1954. 68 Stat. 1216

(1954), 18 U.S.C. §§792-798, 2151-2157. Other provisions dealing with specific aspects of these offenses are also on the statute books.

In addition other federal laws, which touch more closely the area of expression, exist. The Logan Act provides that "correspondence or intercourse with any foreign government or any officer or agent thereof, with intent to influence the measures or conduct of any foreign government or of any officer or agent thereof, in relation to any disputes or controversies with the United States, or to defeat the measures of the United States," constitutes a criminal offense. 62 Stat. 744 (originally enacted Jan. 30, 1799), 18 U.S.C. §953. Under the Foreign Agents Registration Act, also known as the McCormack Act, any individual acting as agent for a foreign principal must register with the Attorney General. 52 Stat. 631 (1938), 22 U.S.C. §§611-621. The Voorhis Act requires every organization, including an organization subject to foreign control, the purpose of which in whole or in part is to establish, control, conduct, seize or overthrow a government by force or threats of force, to register with the Attorney General. 54 Stat. 1201 (1940), 18 U.S.C. §2386.

A conspiracy to commit any of these offenses is punishable under the general conspiracy statute (18 U.S.C. §371) and, in some cases, under specific conspiracy provisions.

Prosecutions under the foregoing laws, especially in espionage cases, have had a significant effect upon the attitude of legislators and the general public toward legislative and administrative restrictions going beyond the area of concededly illegal action.

REFERENCES

1. For a complete compilation of statutes, Executive Orders, and regulations relating to national security see Internal Security Manual (rev.), Sen. Doc. No. 126, 86th Cong., 2d Sess. (G.P.O., 1961). A collection of the more important cases arising under these statutes may be found in Federal Case Law Concerning the Security of the United States, prepared by the Library of Congress for the Special Subcommittee on Security Affairs of the Senate Committee on Foreign Relations, 83rd Cong., 2d Sess. (G.P.O., 1954); Digest of the Public Record of Communism in the United States 1-38 (published by the Fund for the Republic, 1955).

2. On the history and application of the law of treason, see Cramer v. United States, 325 U.S. 1, 65 S. Ct. 918, 89 L. Ed. 1441 (1945); Hurst, Treason in the United States, 58 Harv. L. Rev. 226, 395, 806 (1945), and English Sources of the American Law of Treason, 1945 Wis. L. Rev. 315. See also Chapin, The American Law of Treason: Revolutionary and Early National Origins (1964); Simon, The Evolution of Treason, 35 Tulane L. Rev. 669 (1961); Westbrook, The Mental Element as a Limitation on the Law of Treason, 68 Dick. L. Rev. 1 (1963). Prosecutions growing out of World War II, in addition to the Cramer case, include Haupt v. United States, 330 U.S. 631, 67 S. Ct. 874, 91 L. Ed. 1145 (1947); Chandler v. United States, 171 F.2d 921 (1st Cir. 1948), cert. den., 336 U.S. 918 (1949); Best v. United States, 184 F.2d 131 (1st Cir. 1950), cert. den., 340 U.S. 939 (1951); D'Aquino v. United States, 192 F.2d 338 (9th Cir. 1951), cert. den., 343 U.S. 935 (1952) (Tokyo Rose); Kawakita v. United States, 343 U.S. 717, 72 S. Ct. 950, 96 L. Ed. 1249 (1952); United States v. Provoo, 215 F.2d 531 (2d Cir. 1954) (re-

versing conviction), 17 F.R.D. 183 (D. Md. 1955) (dismissing for delay in prosecution), aff'd 350 U.S. 857 (1955). For discussion of these cases see Steinhaus, Treason: A Brief History With Some Modern Applications, 22 Brooklyn L. Rev. 254 (1956); Olshausen, D'Aquino v. United States, The So-Called "Tokyo Rose" Case, 15 Law. Guild Rev. 6 (1955); Notes, 31 Marq. L. Rev. 249 (1947); 6 Cath. U.L. Rev. 56 (1956). See generally, Weyl, Treason: The Story of Disloyalty and Betrayal in American History (1950); West, The Meaning of Treason (1947), and the revised and expanded edition entitled The New Meaning of Treason (1964); Boveri, Treason in the Twentieth Century (1956, transl. by Steinberg 1961).

In 1945 Ezra Pound, the poet, was indicted on charges of treason based on his pro-Fascist broadcasts from Italy during the war. The case was never tried because Pound was declared insane and confined in St. Elizabeth's Hospital in Washington. In 1958 the indictment was dismissed with the consent of the Government. N.Y. Times, April 15 and 19, 1958. Thereafter Pound left the United States to reside in Italy. N.Y. Times, July 2 and 10, 1958. See on the Pound case, O'Connor and Stone, Casebook on Ezra Pound (1959); Cornell, The Trial of Ezra Pound (1966).

On other aspects of the law of treason, see Powers, Treason by Domiciled Aliens, Military Law Rev., July 1962, p. 123 (Dept. of Army Pamphlet 27-100-17); Garcia-Mora, Treason, Sedition and Espionage as Political Offenses Under the Law of Extradition, 26 U. Pitt. L. Rev. 65 (1964), and International Responsibility for Subversive Activities and Hostile Propaganda by Private Persons Against Foreign States, 35 Ind. L.J. 306 (1960).

3. A recent prosecution for seditious conspiracy under 18 U.S.C. §2384 involved a group of members of the Nationalist Party of Puerto Rico who were responsible for the attempted assassination of President Truman in October 1950 and the firing from the gallery of the House of Representatives in March 1954 which resulted in the wounding of five Congressmen. See United States v. Lebron, 22 F.2d 531 (2d Cir. 1955), cert. den., 350 U.S. 876 (1955). See, for a prior case involving members of the same Party, Albizu v. United States, 88 F.2d 138 (1st Cir. 1937), cert. den., 301 U.S. 707 (1937).

4. For discussion of the espionage and sabotage laws as revised by the 1954 Act, see Note, Federal Anti-Subversive Legislation of 1954, 55 Colum. L. Rev. 631, 659-663 (1955). The espionage laws were further amended in 1956 to reinstate a provision of the Internal Security Act (§20), dropped in the 1954 amendments, which requires (with some exceptions) every person to register with the Attorney General "who had knowledge of, or has received instruction or assignment in, the espionage, counterespionage, or sabotage service or tactics of a government of a foreign country or of a foreign political party." 70 Stat. 899, 50 U.S.C. §§851-857. The laws were further amended in 1961 to eliminate any geographical limitation. 75 Stat. 795, repealing 18 U.S.C. §791. For a brief survey of espionage and sabotage legislation see Brown, Loyalty and Security, chs. 8 and 9 (1958).

The major espionage case of the post-war period was the prosecution of Julius and Ethel Rosenberg and Morton Sobell for atomic espionage. The Rosenbergs were given the death penalty and executed on July 19, 1953. Sobell received a 30-year sentence. The principal court decisions are United States v. Rosenberg, 195 F.2d 583 (2d Cir. 1952) (affirming the conviction, Judge Frank dissenting as to Sobell on the ground that he was entitled to a separate trial), cert. den., 344 U.S. 838, 850, 889 (1952); 108 F. Supp. 798 (S.D. N.Y. 1952) (denying petition to set aside conviction and sentence), aff'd, 200 F.2d 666 (2d Cir. 1952), cert. den., 345 U.S. 965 (1953); 109 F. Supp. 108 (S.D. N.Y. 1953) (denying motion to reduce death sentences); Rosenberg v. United States, 346 U.S. 273, 73 S. Ct. 1152, 97 L. Ed. 1607 (1953) (vacating stay of execution issued by Justice Douglas). For a full account of the various proceedings in the case and a discussion of the legal issues, see Note, The Rosenberg Case: Some Reflections on Federal Criminal Law, 54 Colum. L. Rev. 219 (1954) (citation of court decisions is in footnote 208, p. 260); see also Note, 48 Nw. U.L. Rev. 751 (1954). For general discussion of the case see Pilat, The

Atom Spies (1952); Fineberg, The Rosenberg Case (1953); Reuben, The Atom Spy Hoax (1954); Beier and Sand, The Rosenberg Case: History and Hysteria, 40 A.B.A.J. 1046 (1954); Wexley, The Judgment of Julius and Ethel Rosenberg (1955); Sharp, Was Justice Done?: The Rosenberg-Sobell Case (1956) (chronology of case on pp. vii-xi), reviewed by Mann in 67 Yale L.J. 528 (1958); W. and M. Schneir, Invitation to An Inquest (1965).

In 1956 Sobell sought to reopen his case, chiefly on the grounds that the court had lacked jurisdiction because he had been kidnaped from Mexico with the connivance of the F.B.I. and that the prosecution had knowingly suppressed evidence and introduced perjured testimony. His efforts were unsuccessful. United States v. Sobell, 142 F. Supp. 515 (S.D. N.Y. 1956), aff'd, 244 F.2d 520 (2d Cir. 1957), cert. den., 355 U.S. 873 (1957). Two other attempts were also unsuccessful. Sobell v. United States, unreported in the Southern District of New York and the Court of Appeals for the Second Circuit, cert. den., 347 U.S. 904 (1954); 355 U.S. 860 (1957) (motion to vacate 1952 order denying certiorari denied). In 1962 Sobell again filed motions to set aside the conviction or, in the alternative, to correct the sentence, claiming that the trial judge had permitted improper cross-examination of co-defendant Ethel Rosenberg concerning her claim of the privilege against self-incrimination before the grand jury, and that the trial judge's conduct of the trial had displayed bias. The motions were denied. Sobell v. United States, 204 F. Supp. 225 (S.D. N.Y. 1962), aff'd, 314 F.2d 314 (2d Cir. 1963), cert. den., 374 U.S. 857 (1963). The Sobell case continued to be a center of controversy. See, e.g., Schneir, id. at 323-343; Love, The Sobell Case, The Nation, June 23, 1956, p. 526. A further petition under 28 U.S.C. §2255, based primarily upon data presented in the Schneir book, was filed in May 1966. S.D. N.Y. No. C 134-245.

Other prosecutions for espionage which have reached the appellate courts include United States v. Coplon, 185 F.2d 629 (2d Cir. 1950), cert. den., 342 U.S. 920 (1952), and Coplon v. United States, 191 F.2d 749 (D.C. Cir. 1951), cert. den., 342 U.S. 926 (1952), both cases reversing convictions; Abel v. United States, 362 U.S. 217, 80 S. Ct. 683, 4 L. Ed. 2d 668 (1960); United States v. Soblen, 199 F. Supp. 11 and 203 F. Supp. 542 (S.D. N.Y. 1961), aff'd, 301 F.2d 236 (2d Cir. 1962), cert. den., 370 U.S. 944 (1962). Soblen fled to Israel, was deported, and wounded himself with a steak knife just before his plane from Israel landed in London. He was hospitalized in London, was ordered deported from London, and died from an overdose of barbiturates on his way to the London airport. N.Y. Times, Sept. 12, 1962. For a discussion of the legal proceedings in England, see Thornberry, Dr. Soblen and the Alien Law of the United Kingdom, 12 Intl. and Comp. L.Q. 414 (1963). See also Gorin v. United States, 312 U.S. 19, 61 S. Ct. 429, 85 L. Ed. 488 (1941); Note, Espionage Prosecutions in the United States, 4 Catholic U.L. Rev. 44 (1954).

Generally on the subject of espionage directed against the United States see, Brown, Loyalty and Security, chs. 8 and 9 (1958); House Committee on Un-American Activities, The Shameful Years — 30 Years of Soviet Espionage in the United States, H. R. Rep. 1229, 82d Cong., 2d Sess. (1952); Burnham, The Web of Subversion (1954); Dallin, Soviet Espionage (1955); Whitehead, The FBI Story (1956); other reports by the House Committee on Un-American Activities, the Internal Security Sub-Committee of the Senate Judiciary Committee, and other Congressional Committees, listed in Internal Security Manual (rev.), Sen. Doc. No 126, 86th Cong., 2d Sess. (G.P.O., 1961), at Parts IV and V; and the materials cited below in connection with the Alger Hiss case. On counterespionage, particularly the operations of the Central Intelligence Agency, see Ransom, Central Intelligence and National Security (1958); Tully, CIA: The Inside Story (1962); Wise and Ross, The Invisible Government (1964); Blackstock, The Strategy of Subversion (1965); N.Y. Times, April 25-29, 1966.

5. Prosecutions for perjury growing out of investigations into alleged subversive activity include United States v. Hiss, 185 F.2d 822 (2d Cir. 1950), cert. den., 340 U.S. 948

(1951); 107 F. Supp. 128 (S.D. N.Y. 1952) (motion for new trial on newly discovered evidence denied), aff'd, 201 F.2d 372 (2d Cir. 1953), cert. den., 345 U.S. 942 (1953); United States v. Remington, 191 F.2d 246 (2d Cir. 1951) (reversing first conviction), cert. den., 343 U.S. 907 (1952); 208 F.2d 567 (2d Cir. 1953) (affirming second conviction), cert. den., 347 U.S. 913 (1954). The Hiss case, which had a significant influence on public attitudes toward security problems in the post-war period, is discussed in De Toledano and Lasky, Seeds of Treason (1950); Bentley, Out of Bondage (1951); Chambers, Witness (1952); Cooke, A Generation on Trial (2d ed. 1952); Morris, Fair Trial, ch. XIV (1952); Jowitt, The Strange Case of Alger Hiss (1953); Weyl, I Was in a Communist Unit With Hiss, U.S. News & World Report, Jan. 9, 1953, p. 22; Hiss, In the Court of Public Opinion (1957); Cook, The Unfinished Story of Alger Hiss (1958); Packer, A Tale of Two Typewriters, 10 Stan. L. Rev. 409 (1958); Altman, The Added Witness, The Nation, Oct. 1, 1960; B. and P. Andrews, A Tragedy of History (1962); Nixon, Six Crises (1962); Cook, Nixon Kicks a Hole in the Hiss Case, The Nation, Apr. 7, 1962, and The Ghost of a Typewriter, May 12, 1962. On the Remington case, see Cook, The Remington Tragedy, A Study of Injustice, The Nation, Dec. 28, 1957.

6. For the legislative history of the Logan Act, see Waldron v. British Petroleum Co., 231 F. Supp. 72, 89 (S.D. N.Y. 1964). There is no record that any prosecutions have been instituted under the Logan Act. Suggestions that the Act should be invoked, however, have been made on occasion. See, e.g., Preston, Aliens and Dissenters 241-242 (1963) (prosecution of American Communists in 1924 considered); McDougal, Gideon's Army 136-137 (1965) (prosecution of Henry A. Wallace for conduct on European tour in 1947 urged).

7. For further consideration of the Foreign Agents Registration Act and the Voorhis Act, see Section C, subsection 3, infra.

8. Of course all states, and many municipalities, have general legislation directed against the use of force or violence, or other forms of coercion, which is also applicable to such conduct occurring in connection with political activity. In addition, all states have laws against treason, and most states have laws against insurrection, rebellion, sabotage, and the like. For a collection of state laws and cases on internal security, see Internal Security and Subversion: Principal State Laws and Cases, A Study Prepared for the Subcommittee to Investigate the Administration of the Internal Security Act and Other Internal Security Laws of the Senate Committee on the Judiciary, by Legislative Reference Service, Library of Congress, 89th Cong., 1st Sess. (1965). See also Digest of the Public Record of Communism in the United States 241-265 (Fund for the Republic 1955); Gellhorn, The States and Subversion, Apps. A and B (1952); Groner, State Control of Subversive Activities in the United States, 9 Fed. B.J. 61 (1947). But see also the material dealing with federal pre-emption, Section C, subsection 5, infra.

B. Interference with War or Defense Effort

The first major decisions of the United States Supreme Court dealing with the constitutional principles underlying freedom of expression came in a series of cases involving prosecutions under the Federal Espionage Acts of 1917 and 1918 for interference with war effort (see Chapter II, Section F, supra, for the texts of these acts). Actually none of these cases reached the Supreme Court until the war was over. The initial decision, in which the Court first stated the famous "clear and present danger" test, was Schenck v. United States.

SCHENCK v. UNITED STATES
249 U.S. 47, 39 S. Ct. 247, 63 L. Ed. 470 (1919)

Mr. Justice Holmes delivered the opinion of the Court.

This is an indictment in three counts. The first charges a conspiracy to violate the Espionage Act of June 15, 1917, c. 30, §3, 40 Stat. 217, 219, by causing and attempting to cause insubordination, &c., in the military and naval forces of the United States, and to obstruct the recruiting and enlistment service of the United States, when the United States was at war with the German Empire, to-wit, that the defendants wilfully conspired to have printed and circulated to men who had been called and accepted for military service under the Act of May 18, 1917, a document set forth and alleged to be calculated to cause such insubordination and obstruction. The count alleges overt acts in pursuance of the conspiracy, ending in the distribution of the document set forth. The second count alleges a conspiracy to commit an offence against the United States, to-wit, to use the mails for the transmission of matter declared to be non-mailable by Title XII, §2 of the Act of June 15, 1917, to-wit, the above mentioned document, with an averment of the same overt acts. The third count charges an unlawful use of the mails for the transmission of the same matter and otherwise as above. The defendants were found guilty on all the counts. They set up the First Amendment to the Constitution forbidding Congress to make any law abridging the freedom of speech, or of the press, and bringing the case here on that ground have argued some other points also of which we must dispose.

It is argued that the evidence, if admissible, was not sufficient to prove that the defendant Schenck was concerned in sending the documents. According to the testimony Schenck said he was general secretary of the Socialist party and had charge of the Socialist headquarters from which the documents were sent. He identified a book found there as the minutes of the Executive Committee of the party. The book showed a resolution of August 13, 1917, that 15,000 leaflets should be printed on the other side of one of them in use, to be mailed to men who had passed exemption boards, and for distribution. Schenck personally attended to the printing. On August 20 the general secretary's report said "Obtained new leaflets from printer and started work addressing envelopes" &c.; and there was a resolve that Comrade Schenck be allowed $125 for sending leaflets through the mail. He said that he had about fifteen or sixteen thousand printed. There were files of the circular in question in the inner office which he said were printed on the other side of the one sided circular and were there for distribution. Other copies were proved to have been sent through the mails to drafted men. Without going into confirmatory details that were proved, no reasonable man could doubt that the defendant Schenck was largely instrumental in sending the circulars about. As to the defendant Baer there was evidence that she was a member of the

Executive Board and that the minutes of its transactions were hers. The argument as to the sufficiency of the evidence that the defendants conspired to send the documents only impairs the seriousness of the real defence. . . .

The document in question upon its first printed side recited the first section of the Thirteenth Amendment, said that the idea embodied in it was violated by the Conscription Act and that a conscript is little better than a convict. In impassioned language it intimated that conscription was despotism in its worst form and a monstrous wrong against humanity in the interest of Wall Street's chosen few. It said "Do not submit to intimidation," but in form at least confined itself to peaceful measures such as a petition for the repeal of the act. The other and later printed side of the sheet was headed "Assert Your Rights." It stated reasons for alleging that any one violated the Constitution when he refused to recognize "your right to assert your opposition to the draft," and went out "If you do not assert and support your rights, you are helping to deny or disparage rights which it is the solemn duty of all citizens and residents of the United States to retain." It described the arguments on the other side as coming from cunning politicians and a mercenary capitalist press, and even silent consent to the conscription law as helping to support an infamous conspiracy. It denied the power to send our citizens away to foreign shores to shoot up the people of other lands, and added that words could not express the condemnation such cold-blooded ruthlessness deserves, &c., &c., winding up "You must do your share to maintain, support and uphold the rights of the people of this country." Of course the document would not have been sent unless it had been intended to have some effect, and we do not see what effect it could be expected to have upon persons subject to the draft except to influence them to obstruct the carrying of it out. The defendants do not deny that the jury might find against them on this point.

But it is said, suppose that that was the tendency of this circular, it is protected by the First Amendment to the Constitution. Two of the strongest expressions are said to be quoted respectively from well-known public men. It well may be that the prohibition of laws abridging the freedom of speech is not confined to previous restraints, although to prevent them may have been the main purpose, as intimated in Patterson v. Colorado, 205 U.S. 454, 462. We admit that in many places and in ordinary times the defendants in saying all that was said in the circular would have been within their constitutional rights. But the character of every act depends upon the circumstances in which it is done. Aikens v. Wisconsin, 195 U.S. 194, 205, 206. The most stringent protection of free speech would not protect a man in falsely shouting fire in a theatre and causing a panic. It does not even protect a man from an injunction against uttering words that may have all the effect of force. Gompers v. Buck's Stove & Range Co., 221 U.S. 418, 439. The question in every case is whether the words used are used in such circumstances and are of such a nature as to create a clear and present danger that they will bring about the substantive evils that Congress has a right to prevent. It is a question of proximity and degree. When a nation is at war many things that might be said in time of peace are such a hindrance to its effort that their utterance will not be endured so long as men fight and that no Court could regard them as protected by any constitutional right. It seems to be admitted that if an actual obstruction of the recruiting service were proved, liability for words that produced that effect might be enforced. The Statute of 1917, in §4, punishes conspiracies to obstruct as well as actual obstruction. If the act (speaking, or circulating a paper,) its tendency and the intent with which it is done, are the same, we perceive no ground for saying that success alone warrants making the act a crime. Goldman v. United States, 245 U.S. 474, 477. Indeed that case might be said to dispose of the present contention if the precedent covers all media concludendi. But as the right to free speech was not referred to specially, we have thought fit to add a few words. . . .

NOTES

Similar results were reached in three other cases decided at the same time or shortly afterwards, all involving prosecutions for creating insubordination in the armed forces. The best known of these was the prosecution of Eugene V. Debs. Debs had made a speech on the general theme of socialism and opposition to the war, in the course of which he had praised certain individuals who had been convicted for resisting the draft or causing insubordination in the armed forces. His most extreme statement was "you need to know that you are fit for something better than slavery and cannon fodder." The jury had held Debs guilty, thus finding that the intent of the speech was to encourage his hearers to obstruct the recruiting service. Holding the First Amendment issue decided by the Schenck case the Court unanimously affirmed the conviction. The sentence was 10 years' imprisonment. Debs v. United States, 249 U.S. 211, 39 S. Ct. 252, 63 L. Ed. 566 (1919).[1]

The only case to come before the Court that involved the 1918 amendments to the Espionage Act was Abrams v. United States, 250 U.S. 616, 40 S. Ct. 17, 63 L. Ed. 1173 (1919). Here the defendants were indicted for publishing abusive language about the form of government, for publishing language intended to bring the form of government into contempt, for encouraging resistance to the United States in the war, and for inciting curtailment of production of war materials. The charges were based upon two leaflets which the defendants had printed and distributed by throwing them out the window of a building. The first leaflet denounced President Wilson as a coward and hypocrite for sending troops to Russia, and ended:

"The Russian Revolution cries: Workers of the World! Awake! Rise! Put down your enemy and mine!

---

[1] Debs began his sentence on April 13, 1919 at the age of 63. In 1920, while in prison, he was the Socialist candidate for President, receiving 919,799 votes. President Harding released him on Christmas Day, 1921, without restoration of citizenship. 5 Dictionary of American Biography 183. On the Debs speech, trial and imprisonment, see Ginger. The Bending Cross, chs. XVII-XX (1949).

The other two cases mentioned in the text are Sugarman v. United States, 249 U.S. 182, 39 S. Ct. 191, 63 L. Ed. 550 (1919), and Frohwerk v. United States, 249 U.S. 204, 39 S. Ct. 249, 63 L. Ed. 561 (1919).

"Yes! friends, there is only one enemy of the workers of the world and that is CAPITALISM.

"Awake! Awake, you Workers of the World."

"Revolutionists."

The second leaflet, addressed primarily to workers in the factories, declared, ". . . you are producing bullets, bayonets, cannon, to murder not only the Germans, but also your dearest, best, who are in Russia and are fighting for freedom"; "our reply to the barbaric intervention has to be a general strike!"; "workers, up to fight"; "woe unto those who will be in the way of progress. Let solidarity live!" It was signed, "The Rebels."

The majority of the Court held that "the plain purpose of their propaganda was to excite, at the supreme crisis of the war, disaffection, sedition, riots, and, as they hoped, revolution, in this country for the purpose of embarrassing and if possible defeating the military plans of the Government in Europe." 250 U.S. at 623. It thus found evidence to sustain the conviction on the third and fourth charges.

For the first time Justices Holmes and Brandeis dissented. The opinion of Mr. Justice Holmes goes on the ground that the intent required by the statute, to hinder the prosecution of the war, was not shown. Mr. Justice Holmes elaborated his remarks in the Schenck case in the following language:

"I never have seen any reason to doubt that the questions of law that alone were before this Court in the cases of Schenck, Frohwerk and Debs, 249 U.S. 47, 204, 211, were rightly decided. I do not doubt for a moment that by the same reasoning that would justify punishing persuasion to murder, the United States constitutionally may punish speech that produces or is intended to produce a clear and imminent danger that it will bring about forthwith certain substantive evils that the United States constitutionally may seek to prevent. The power undoubtedly is greater in time of war than in time of peace because war opens dangers that do not exist at other times.

"But as against dangers peculiar to war, as against others, the principle of the right to free speech is always the same. It is only the present danger of immediate evil or an intent to bring it about that warrants Congress in setting a limit to the expression of opinion where private rights are not concerned. Congress certainly cannot forbid all effort to change the mind of the country. Now nobody can suppose that the surreptitious publishing of a silly leaflet by an unknown man, without more, would present any immediate danger that its opinions would hinder the success of the government arms or have any appreciable tendency to do so. Publishing those opinions for the very purpose of obstructing however, might indicate a greater danger and at any rate would have the quality of an attempt. So I assume that the second leaflet if published for the purposes alleged in the fourth count might be punishable. But it seems pretty clear to me that nothing less than that would bring these papers within the scope of this law." 250 U.S. at 627-628.

REFERENCES

1. Other important cases arising under the Espionage Act were:

Schaefer v. United States, 251 U.S. 466, 40 S. Ct. 259, 64 L. Ed. 360 (1920), in which convictions were upheld of the officers of a German-language newspaper charged with printing false and distorted accounts of the war. Justices Holmes and Brandeis dissented on free speech grounds; Mr. Justice Clark dissented on grounds of error in the conduct of the trial.

Pierce v. United States, 252 U.S. 239, 40 S. Ct. 205, 64 L. Ed. 542 (1920), in which convictions were upheld of three Socialists who had distributed a pamphlet denouncing the war. Justices Holmes and Brandeis again dissented.

United States ex rel. Milwaukee Social Democrat Publishing Co. v. Burleson, 255 U.S. 407, 41 S. Ct. 352, 65 L. Ed. 704 (1921), in which the Court upheld the Postmaster General's revocation of the second-class mailing privileges of Victor Berger's Milwaukee Leader. The action was taken under Title XII of the Espionage Act which made nonmailable any matter violating the Act. The Court sanctioned not only denial of the second-class mailing privilege to issues of the newspaper found to violate the law but denial of the privilege to all future issues. Justices Holmes and Brandeis once more dissented.

The remaining cases, of less significance, were Stilson v. United States, 250 U.S. 583, 40 S. Ct. 28, 63 L. Ed. 1154 (1919); O'Connell v. United States, 253 U.S. 142, 40 S. Ct. 444, 64 L. Ed. 827 (1920).

2. One of the earliest, and most interesting, cases under the Espionage Act was Masses Publishing Co. v. Patten, 244 Fed. 535 (S.D. N.Y. 1917), in which Judge Learned Hand enjoined the New York Postmaster from excluding from the mails the August 1917 issue of The Masses, a left wing publication. Holding that the Espionage Act, in its original form, could not be construed to prohibit the statements involved, Judge Hand attempted to draw the line between protected and unprotected speech:

"One may not counsel or advise others to violate the law as it stands. Words are not only the keys of persuasion, but the triggers of action, and those which have no purport but to counsel the violation of law cannot by any latitude of interpretation be a part of that public opinion which is the final source of government in a democratic state. . . . Political agitation, by the passions it arouses or the convictions it engenders, may in fact stimulate men to the violation of law. Detestation of existing policies is easily transformed into forcible resistance of the authority which puts them in execution, and it would be folly to disregard the causal relation between the two. Yet to assimilate agitation, legitimate as such, with direct incitement to violent resistance, is to disregard the tolerance of all methods of political agitation which in normal times is a safeguard of free government. The distinction is not a scholastic subterfuge, but a hard-bought acquisition in the fight for freedom, and the purpose to disregard it must be evident when the power exists. If one stops short of urging upon others that it is their duty or their interest to resist the law, it seems to me one should not be held to have attempted to cause its violation. If that be not the test, I can see no escape from the conclusion that under this section every political agitation which can be shown to be apt to create a seditious temper is illegal. I am confident that by such language Congress had no such revolutionary purpose in view." 244 Fed. at 540.

On appeal Judge Hand's decision was reversed. 246 Fed. 24 (2d Cir. 1917).

3. In Gilbert v. Minnesota, 254 U.S. 325, 41 S. Ct. 125, 65 L. Ed. 287 (1920), the Supreme Court upheld the Minnesota statute, comparable to the Federal Espionage Act, which prohibited teaching or advocating that men should not enlist or aid in prosecution of the war. The Court ruled that (1) the subject matter of the statute was within the power of the states and not exclusively within federal power; and (2) assuming the right of free speech to be guaranteed against state action, the legislation did not violate any such right. Mr. Justice Brandeis dissented, arguing that "the right to speak freely concerning functions of the Federal Government is a privilege or immunity of every citizen of the United States which, even before the adoption of the Fourteenth Amendment, a State was powerless to curtail." 254 U.S. at 337.

4. For a full discussion of the federal and state statutes and cases see Chafee, Free Speech in the United States, chs. 2, 3, and 7 (1941). The cases up to July 1918, including

many not elsewhere reported, are collected in Nelles, Espionage Cases, published by the National Civil Liberties Bureau (1918). See also Wigmore, Abrams v. U.S.: Freedom of Speech and Freedom of Thuggery in War-Time and Peace-Time, 14 Ill. L. Rev. 539 (1920); Black, Debs v. The United States — A Judicial Milepost on the Road to Absolutism, 81 U. Pa. L. Rev. 160 (1932); Million, Political Crimes: I, 5 Mo. L. Rev. 164 (1940); Note, Legal Techniques for Protecting Free Discussion in Wartime, 51 Yale L.J. 798 (1942); Hudon, Freedom of Speech and Press in America, ch. VI (bibliography at 194-195) (1963).

For other materials on the clear and present danger test, as employed in World War I cases, see Section C, infra.

NOTES

1. The Espionage Act of 1918 was repealed in 1920 (41 Stat. 1359), leaving the original 1917 Act in effect (now 18 U.S.C.A. §2388). The statute is applicable only "when the United States is at war." Following World War II, however, Congress enacted legislation providing that §2388 should remain in force "until six months after the termination of the national emergency proclaimed by the President on December 16, 1950 . . . or such earlier date as may be prescribed by concurrent resolution of the Congress." 67 Stat. 134, 18 U.S.C.A. §2391. The 1950 proclamation of national emergency has continued in effect. Proclamation No. 2914, 15 Fed. Reg. 9029, 50 U.S.C.A. App. p. 6.

During World War II there were relatively few prosecutions under the statute. See Chafee, The Blessings of Liberty 79 (1956); Hyman, To Try Men's Souls 329 (1959). In the only case considered by the Supreme Court on the merits the defendant was convicted for disseminating three pamphlets calling for an abandonment of our allies and a conversion of the war into a racial conflict, some of which were mailed to persons in the armed forces or registered under the draft. The Court, without reaching First Amendment questions, reversed on the ground there was not "sufficient evidence from which a jury could infer beyond a reasonable doubt that he intended to bring about the specific consequences prohibited by the Act." Hartzel v. United States, 322 U.S. 680, 689, 64 S. Ct. 1233, 1237-1238, 88 L. Ed. 1534, 1540 (1944). Cf. United States v. Pelley, 132 F.2d 170 (7th Cir. 1942), cert. den., 318 U.S. 764 (1943).

There has been only one post-war prosecution under the statute. In 1956 three editors of the China Monthly Review, published in Shanghai, were charged with publishing false reports and creating insubordination in the armed forces by statements derogatory to the United States during 1950 to 1953. United States v. Powell, 156 F. Supp. 526 (N.D. Cal. 1957). After long delays the case went to trial, but a mistrial was declared because of prejudicial newspaper publicity. 171 F. Supp. 202 (N.D. Cal. 1959). Treason charges were then filed by the government but the grand jury failed to indict. N.Y. Times, July 14, 1959. The sedition charges were later dropped. N.Y. Times, May 3, 1961. For an account of the case see Marine, Sedition or Press Freedom? The Nation, Feb. 16, 1957, p. 136.

2. In addition to the Espionage Act of 1917, two other statutes prohibit interference with the armed forces. A provision of the Smith Act of 1940 punishes by 10 years in prison or $10,000 fine, or both, anyone who "with intent to interfere with, impair, or influence the loyalty, morale, or discipline of the military or naval forces of the United States (1) advises, counsels, urges, or in any manner causes or

attempts to cause insubordination, disloyalty, mutiny, or refusal of duty by any member of the military or naval forces of the United States; or (2) distributes or attempts to distribute any written or printed matter which advises, counsels, or urges insubordination, disloyalty, mutiny or refusal of duty by any member of the military or naval forces of the United States." 18 U.S.C.A. §2387. In 1941, 18 members of the Socialist Workers Party were convicted under this provision as well as other provisions of the Smith Act. Dunne v. United States, 138 F.2d 137 (8th Cir. 1943), cert. den., 320 U.S. 790 (1943), discussed in Section C, infra. In 1944, 28 alleged pro-Nazis were indicted for conspiracy to violate this portion of the Smith Act. United States v. McWilliams, 54 F. Supp. 791 (D. D.C. 1944). The trial went on for seven and a half months in 1944 before Judge Eicher in the District of Columbia. Judge Eicher died before completion of the trial and no re-trial was had. The indictment was later dismissed for failure to prosecute. 163 F.2d 695 (D.C. Cir. 1947). See Rogge, The First and the Fifth 92-93 (1960); St. George and Dennis, A Trial On Trial: The Great Sedition Trial of 1944 (1946).

3. The Universal Military Training and Service Act of 1948 provides that any-one "who knowingly counsels, aids, or abets another to refuse or evade registration or service in the armed forces or any of the requirements of this title" is guilty of an offense punishable by 5 years or $10,000 or both. 50 U.S.C.A. App. §462 (a). There are few reported cases under this provision. In one the defendant, dean of men at a college where one of the students was being arrested for refusal to register, told the student, "Do not let them coerce you into registering." The de-fendant was convicted and the Court of Appeals affirmed. Gara v. United States, 178 F.2d 38 (6th Cir. 1949). The Supreme Court affirmed by an equally divided vote. 340 U.S. 857 (1950). In another case the defendant, stepfather of the regis-trant, counseled his stepson not to register. The stepson rejected the advice and registered. The conviction was affirmed. Warren v. United States, 177 F.2d 596 (10th Cir. 1949), cert. den., 338 U.S. 947 (1950). See also United States v. Miller, 233 F.2d 171 (2d Cir. 1956); Keegan v. United States, 325 U.S. 478, 65 S. Ct. 1203, 89 L. Ed. 1745 (1945).

4. In 1965 and 1966 opposition to the war in Vietnam and to the draft again raised questions under the statutes prohibiting interference with the war effort. The protest took many forms, including marches and demonstrations, distribution of leaflets opposing the war and the draft, giving information about draft exemp-tions available to conscientious objectors, urging refusal of registration, giving advice on methods of feigning insanity, drug addiction or homosexuality to avoid the draft, and lying down in front of troop trains. Attorney General Katzenbach in a public statement said, "We may very well have some prosecutions." N.Y. Times, Oct. 18, 1965. See generally Finman and Macaulay, Freedom to Dissent: The Vietnam Protests and the Words of Public Officials, 1966 Wis. L. Rev. 632.

In August 1965 Congress amended the Universal Military Training and Service Act to bring within the penal provisions of that statute anyone who "knowingly destroys" or "knowingly mutilates" a draft card. 79 Stat. 586, 50 U.S.C.A. App. §462 (b). A number of prosecutions for burning draft cards were brought. The first indictment was upheld against a motion to dismiss in United States v. Miller, 249 F. Supp. 59 (S.D. N.Y. 1965). Miller was subsequently convicted, and received a three-year suspended sentence. N.Y. Times, Mar. 16, 1966. The statute was also upheld in United States v. Smith, 249 F. Supp. 515 (S.D. Iowa 1966).

5. The only state prosecution to reach the Supreme Court during World War II was Taylor v. Mississippi, 319 U.S. 583, 63 S. Ct. 1200, 87 L. Ed. 1600 (1943). That case involved the conviction of three Jehovah's Witnesses for violation of a Mississippi statute which, among other things, prohibited teaching or disseminating literature "designed and calculated to encourage violence, sabotage, or disloyalty to the government of the United States, or the state of Mississippi," or which "reasonably tends to create an attitude of stubborn refusal to salute, honor or respect the flag or government." The conviction of all three defendants for advocating and teaching refusal to salute the flag was set aside on the basis of West Virginia State Board of Education v. Barnette, 319 U.S. 624, 63 S. Ct. 1178, 87 L. Ed. 1628 (1943), decided the same day. Two of the defendants were also convicted for stating that "it was wrong for the President to send our boys across in uniform to fight our enemies," that "these boys were being shot down for no purpose at all," and other remarks to the same effect. Their convictions for encouragingly disloyalty by these statements were also set aside:

"The statute as construed in these cases makes it a criminal offense to communicate to others views and opinions respecting government policies, and prophecies concerning the future of our own and other nations. As applied to the appellants, it punishes them although what they communicated is not claimed or shown to have been done with an evil or sinister purpose, to have advocated or incited subversive action against the nation or state, or to have threatened any clear and present danger to our institutions or our Government. What these appellants communicated were their beliefs and opinions concerning domestic measures and trends in national and world affairs.

"Under our decisions criminal sanctions cannot be imposed for such communication." 319 U.S. at 589-590.

6. Prosecutions for failure to take cover during an air raid drill were upheld in People v. Parilli, 1 Misc. 2d 201, 499, 147 N.Y.S.2d 618 (Mag. Ct. 1955), aff'd sub nom. People v. Peck, 7 N.Y.2d 76, 195 N.Y.S.2d 637, 163 N.E.2d 866 (1959), app. dis. and cert. den., 364 U.S. 662 (1961); State v. Congdon, 76 N.J. Super. 493, 185 A.2d 21 (1962).

C. ANTI-SEDITION LAWS AND SIMILAR DIRECT RESTRICTIONS ON POLITICAL EXPRESSION

1. Developments Prior to the Smith Act Prosecutions

State anti-sedition laws first reached the Supreme Court in Gitlow v. New York. For the background of these laws see Chapter II, Section F.

GITLOW v. NEW YORK
268 U.S. 652, 45 S. Ct. 625, 69 L. Ed. 1138 (1925)

[Benjamin Gitlow and three others were convicted of violating a New York statute (N.Y. Penal Laws §§160, 161), originally enacted in 1902, which provided:

"§160. *Criminal anarchy defined.* Criminal anarchy is the doctrine that organized government should be overthrown by force or violence, or by assassination of the executive head or of any of the executive officials of government, or by any unlawful means. The advocacy of such doctrine either by word of mouth or writing is a felony.

"§161. *Advocacy of criminal anarchy.* Any person who:

"1. By word of mouth or writing advocates, advises or teaches the duty, necessity or propriety of overthrowing or overturning organized government by force or violence, or by assassination of the executive head or of any of the executive officials of government, or by any unlawful means; or,

"2. Prints, publishes, edits, issues or knowingly circulates, sells, distributes or publicly displays any book, paper, document, or written or printed matter in any form, containing or advocating, advising or teaching the doctrine that organized government should be overthrown by force, violence or any unlawful means . . . ,

"Is guilty of a felony and punishable" by imprisonment or fine, or both.

Gitlow was a member of the National Council of the Left Wing Section of the Socialist Party. In June 1919 the Council adopted a "Left Wing Manifesto" which it published in its paper, The Revolutionary Age. Defendants supervised the publication and distribution, by mail and by sales from the Council's office, of 16,000 copies. There was "no evidence of any effect resulting from the publication and circulation of the Manifesto."]

MR. JUSTICE SANFORD delivered the opinion of the Court.

. . . Coupled with a review of the rise of Socialism, [the Manifesto] condemned the dominant "moderate Socialism" for its recognition of the necesity of the democratic parliamentary state; repudiated its policy of introducing Socialism by legislative measures; and advocated, in plain and unequivocal language, the necessity of accomplishing the "Communist Revolution" by a militant and "revolutionary Socialism," based on "the class struggle" and mobilizing the "power of the proletariat in action," through mass industrial revolts developing into mass political strikes and "revolutionary mass action," for the purpose of conquering and destroying the parliamentary state and establishing in its place, through a "revolutionary dictatorship of the proletariat," the system of Communist Socialism. The then recent strikes in Seattle and Winnipeg were cited as instances of a development already verging on revolutionary action and suggestive of proletarian dictatorship, in which the strike-workers were "trying to usurp the functions of municipal government"; and revolutionary Socialism, it was urged, must use these mass industrial revolts to broaden the strike, make it general and militant, and develop it into mass political strikes and revolutionary mass action for the annihilation of the parliamentary state. . . .

The sole contention here is, essentially, that as there was no evidence of any concrete result flowing from the publication of the Manifesto or of circumstances showing the likelihood of such result, the statute as construed and applied by the trial court penalizes the mere utterance, as such, of "doctrine" having no quality of incitement, without regard either to the circumstances of its utterance or to the likelihood of unlawful sequences; and that, as the exercise of the right of free expression with relation to government is only punishable "in circumstances involving the likelihood of substantive evil," the statute contravenes the due process clause of the Fourteenth Amendment. The argument in support of this contention rests primarily upon the following propositions: 1st, That the "liberty" protected by the Fourteenth Amendment includes the liberty of speech and of the press; and 2nd, That while liberty of expression "is not absolute," it may be restrained "only in circumstances where its exercise bears a causal relation with some substantive evil, consummated, attempted or likely," and as the statute "takes no account of circumstances," it unduly restrains this liberty and is therefore unconstitutional.

The precise question presented, and the only question which we can consider under this writ of error, then is, whether the statute, as construed and applied in this case by the state courts, deprived the defendant of his liberty of expression in violation of the due process clause of the Fourteenth Amendment.

The statute does not penalize the utterance or publication of abstract "doctrine" or academic discussion having no quality of incitement to any concrete action. It is not aimed against mere historical or philosophical essays. It does not restrain the advocacy of changes in the form of government by constitutional and lawful means. What it prohibits is language advocating, advising or teaching the overthrow of organized government by unlawful means. These words imply urging to action. Advocacy is defined in the Century Dictionary as: "1. The act of pleading for, supporting, or recommending; active espousal." It is not the abstract "doctrine" of overthrowing organized government by unlawful means which is denounced by the statute, but the advocacy of action for the accomplishment of that purpose. . . .

The Manifesto, plainly, is neither the statement of abstract doctrine nor, as suggested by counsel, mere prediction that industrial disturbances and revolutionary mass strikes will result spontaneously in an inevitable process of evolution in the economic system. It advocates and urges in fervent language mass action which shall progressively foment industrial disturbances and through political mass strikes and revolutionary mass action overthrow and destroy organized parliamentary government. It concludes with a call to action in these words: "The proletariat revolution and the Communist reconstruction of society — *the struggle for these* — is now indispensable. . . . The Communist International calls the proletariat of the world to the final struggle!" This is not the expression of philosophical abstraction, the mere prediction of future events; it is the language of direct incitement.

The means advocated for bringing about the destruction of organized parliamentary government, namely, mass industrial revolts usurping the functions of municipal government, political mass strikes directed against the parliamentary state, and revolutionary mass action for its final destruction, necessarily imply the use of force and violence, and in their essential nature are inherently unlawful in a constitutional government of law and order. That the jury were warranted in finding that the Manifesto advocated not merely the abstract doctrine of overthrowing organized government by force, violence and unlawful means, but action to that end, is clear.

For present purposes we may and do assume that freedom of speech and of the press — which are protected by the First Amendment from abridgment by Congress — are among the fundamental personal rights and "liberties" protected by the due process clause of the Fourteenth Amendment from impairment by the States. We do not regard the incidental statement in Prudential Ins. Co. v. Cheek, 259 U.S. 530, 543, that the Fourteenth Amendment imposes no restrictions on the States concerning freedom of speech, as determinative of this question.

It is a fundamental principle, long established, that the freedom of speech and of the press which is secured by the Constitution, does not confer an absolute right to speak or publish, without responsibility, whatever one may choose, or an unrestricted and unbridled license that gives immunity for every possible use of language and prevents the punishment of those who abuse this freedom. 2 Story on the Constitution, 5th ed., §1580, p. 634; Robertson v. Baldwin, 165 U.S. 275, 281; Patterson v. Colorado, 205 U.S. 454, 462; Fox v. Washington, 236 U.S. 273, 276; Schenck v. United States, 249 U.S. 47, 52 . . .

That a State in the exercise of its police power may punish those who abuse this freedom by utterances inimical to the public welfare, tending to corrupt public morals, incite to crime, or disturb the public peace, is not open to question. Robertson v. Baldwin, supra, p. 281; Patterson v. Colorado, supra, p. 462; Fox v. Washington, supra, p. 277; Gilbert v. Minnesota [254 U.S. 325, 339]; People v. Most, 171 N.Y. 423, 431; State v. Holm, 139 Minn. 267, 275; State v. Hennessy, 114 Wash. 351, 359; State v. Boyd, 86 N.J.L. 75, 79; State v. Mc Kee, 73 Conn. 18, 27. Thus it was held by this Court in the Fox Case, that a State may punish publications advocating and encouraging a breach of its criminal laws; and, in the Gilbert Case, that a State may punish utterances teaching or advocating that its citizens should not assist the United States in prosecuting or carrying on war with its public enemies.

And, for yet more imperative reasons, a State may punish utterances endangering the foundations of organized government and threatening its overthrow by unlawful means. These imperil its own existence as a constitutional State. Freedom of speech and press, said Story (supra), does not protect disturbances to the public peace or the attempt to subvert the government. It does not protect publications or teachings which tend to subvert or imperil the government or to impede or hinder it in the performance of its governmental duties. State v. Holm, supra, p. 275. It does not protect publications prompting the overthrow of government by force; the punishment of those who publish articles which tend to destroy organized society being essential to the security of freedom and the stability of the State. People v. Most, supra, pp. 431, 432. And a State may penalize utterances which openly advocate the overthrow of the representative and constitutional form of government of the United States and the several States, by violence or other unlawful means. People v. Lloyd, 304 Ill. 23, 34. See also, State v. Tachin, 92 N.J.L. 269, 274; and People v. Steelik, 187 Cal. 361, 375. In short this freedom does not deprive a State of the primary and essential right of self preservation; which, so long as human governments endure, they cannot be denied. Turner v. Williams, 194 U.S. 279, 294. . . .

By enacting the present statute the State has determined, through its legislative body, that utterances advocating the overthrow of organized government by force, violence and unlawful means, are so inimical to the general welfare and involve such danger of substantive evil that they may be penalized in the exercise of its police power. That determination must be given great weight. Every presumption is to be indulged in favor of the validity of the statute. Mugler v. Kansas, 123 U.S. 623, 661. And the case is to be considered "in the light of the principle that the State is primarily the judge of regulations required in the interest of public safety and welfare;" and that its police "statutes may only be declared unconstitutional where they are arbitrary or unreasonable attempts to exercise authority vested in the State in the public interest." Great Northern Ry. v. Clara City, 246 U.S. 434, 439. That utterances inciting to the overthrow of organized government by unlawful means, present a sufficient danger of substantive evil to bring their punishment within the range of legislative discretion, is clear. Such utterances, by their very nature, involve danger to the public peace and to the security of the State. They threaten breaches of the peace and ultimate revolution. And the immediate danger is none the less real and substantial, because the effect of a given utterance cannot be accurately foreseen. The State cannot reasonably be required to measure the danger from every such utterance in the nice balance of a jeweler's scale. A single revolutionary spark may kindle a fire that, smouldering for a time, may burst into a sweeping and destructive conflagration. It cannot be said that the State is acting arbitrarily or unreasonably when in the exercise of its judgment as to the measures necessary to protect the public peace and safety, it seeks to extinguish the spark without waiting until it has enkindled the flame or blazed into the conflagration. It cannot reasonably be required to defer the adoption of measures for its own peace and safety until the revolutionary utterances lead to actual disturbances of the public peace or imminent and immediate danger of its own destruction; but it may, in the exercise of its judgment, suppress the threatened danger in its incipiency. . . .

We cannot hold that the present statute is an arbitrary or unreasonable exercise of the police power of the State unwarrantably infringing the freedom of speech or press; and we must and do sustain its constitutionality.

This being so it may be applied to every utterance — not too trivial to be beneath the notice of the law — which is of such a character and used with such intent and purpose as to bring it within the prohibition of the statute. . . . In other words, when the legislative body has determined generally, in the constitutional exercise of its discretion, that utterances of a certain kind involve such danger of substantive evil that they may be punished, the question whether any specific utterance coming within the prohibited class is likely, in and of itself, to bring about the substantive evil, is not open to consideration. It is sufficient that the statute itself be constitutional and that the use of the language comes within its prohibition.

It is clear that the question in such cases is entirely different from that involved in those cases where the statute merely prohibits certain acts involving the danger of substantive evil, without any reference to language itself, and it is sought to apply its provisions to language used by the defendant for the purpose of bringing about the prohibited results. There, if it be contended that the statute cannot be applied to the language used by the defendant because of its protection by the freedom of speech or press, it must necessarily be found, as an original question, without any previous determination by the legislative body, whether the specific language used involved such likelihood of bringing about the substantive evil as to deprive it of the constitutional protection. In such cases it has been held that the general provisions of the statute may be constitutionally applied to the specific utterance of the defendant if its natural tendency and probable effect was to bring about the substantive evil which the legislative body might prevent. Schenck v. United States, supra, p. 51; Debs v. United States [249 U.S. at 215, 216]. And the general statement in the Schenck Case (p. 52) that the "question in every case is whether the words are used in such circumstances and are of such a nature as to create a clear and present danger that they will bring about the substantive evils," — upon which great reliance is placed in the defendant's argument — was manifestly intended, as shown by the context, to apply only in cases of this class, and has no application to those like the present, where the legislative body itself has previously determined the danger of substantive evil arising from utterances of a specified character. . . .

It was not necessary, within the meaning of the statute, that the defendant should have advocated "some definite or immediate act or acts" of force, violence or unlawfulness. It was sufficient if such acts were advocated in general terms; and it was not essential that their immediate execution should have been advocated. Nor was it necessary that the language should have been "reasonably and ordinarily calculated to incite certain persons" to acts of force, violence or unlawfulness. The advocacy need not be addressed to specific persons. Thus, the publication and circulation of a newspaper article may be an encouragement or endeavor to persuade to murder, although not addressed to any person in particular. Queen v. Most, L.R., 7 Q.B.D. 244.

We need not enter upon a consideration of the English common law rule of seditious libel or the Federal Sedition Act of 1798, to which reference is made in the defendant's brief. These are so unlike the present statute, that we think the decisions under them cast no helpful light upon the questions here.

And finding, for the reasons stated, that the statute is not in itself unconstitutional, and that it has not been applied in the present case in derogation of any constitutional right, the judgment of the Court of Appeals is

Affirmed.

MR. JUSTICE HOLMES, dissenting.

Mr. Justice Brandeis and I are of opinion that this judgment should be reversed. The general principle of free speech, it seems to me, must be taken to be included in the Fourteenth Amendment, in view of the scope that has been given to the word "liberty" as there used, although perhaps it may be accepted with a somewhat larger latitude of interpretation than is allowed to Congress by the sweeping language that governs, or ought to govern, the laws of the United States. If I am right, then I think that the criterion sanctioned by the full Court in Schenck v. United States, 249 U.S. 47, 52, applies. "The question in every case is whether the words used are used in such circumstances and are of such a nature as to create a clear and present danger that they will bring about the substantive evils that [the State] has a right to prevent." It is true that in my opinion this criterion was departed from in Abrams v. United States, 250 U.S. 616, but the convictions that I expressed in that case are too deep for it to be possible for me as yet to believe that it and Schaefer v. United States, 251 U.S. 466, have settled the law. If what I think the correct test is applied, it is manifest that there was no present danger of an attempt to overthrow the government by force on the part of the admittedly small minority who shared the defendant's views. It is said that this manifesto was more than a theory, that it was an incitement. Every idea is an incitement. It offers itself for belief and if believed it is acted on unless some other belief outweighs it or some failure of energy stifles the movement at its birth. The only difference between the expression of an opinion and an incitement in the narrower sense is the speaker's enthusiasm for the result. Eloquence may set fire to reason. But whatever may be thought of the redundant discourse before us it had no chance of starting a present conflagration. If in the long run the beliefs expressed in proletarian dictatorship are destined to be accepted by the dominant forces of the community, the only meaning of free speech is that they should be given their chance and have their way.

If the publication of this document had been laid as an attempt to induce an uprising against government at once and not at some indefinite time in the future it would have presented a different question. The object would have been one with which the law might deal, subject to the doubt whether there was any danger that the publication could produce any result, or in other words, whether it was not futile and too remote from possible consequences. But the indictment alleges the publication and nothing more.

NOTES

1. In a second major case dealing with the same issues — Whitney v. California, 274 U.S. 357, 47 S. Ct. 641, 71 L. Ed. 1095 (1927) — the Supreme Court upheld the conviction of Miss Anita Whitney (a niece of Justice Stephen J. Field) for violation of the California Criminal Syndicalism Act. Calif. Stats. 1919, c. 188, p. 281. That statute provided:

"Section 1. The term 'criminal syndicalism' as used in this act is hereby defined as any doctrine or precept advocating, teaching or aiding and abetting the commission of crime, sabotage (which word is hereby defined as meaning wilful and malicious physical damage or injury to physical property), or unlawful acts of force and violence or unlawful methods of terrorism as a means of accomplishing a change in industrial ownership or control, or effecting any political change.

"Sec. 2. Any person who: . . . 4. Organizes or assists in organizing, or is or knowingly becomes a member of, any organization, society, group or assemblage of persons organized or assembled to advocate, teach or aid and abet criminal syndicalism . . .

"Is guilty of a felony and punishable by imprisonment."

Miss Whitney, a member of the Oakland branch of the Socialist Party, attended a convention in Chicago in 1919 which resulted in a split in the Socialist Party, the more militant group seceding to form the Communist Labor Party. The new party adopted a platform which, inter alia, rejected parliamentary methods and urged "a revolutionary class struggle." Miss Whitney joined the new party and participated in meetings, but actively opposed adoption of that portion of the platform which urged revolutionary methods. At her trial she testified that "it was not her intention that the Communist Labor Party of California should be an instrument of terrorism or violence, and that it was not her purpose or that of the Convention to violate any known law."

With respect to the free speech argument Justice Sanford, writing for the majority, said:

"Nor is the Syndicalism Act as applied in this case repugnant to the due process clause as a restraint of the rights of free speech, assembly, and association.

"That the freedom of speech which is secured by the Constitution does not confer an absolute right to speak, without responsibility, whatever one may choose, or an unrestricted and unbridled license giving immunity for every possible use of language and preventing the punishment of those who abuse this freedom; and that a State in the exercise of its police power may punish those who abuse this freedom by utterances inimical to the public welfare, tending to incite to crime, disturb the public peace, or endanger the foundations of organized government and threaten its overthrow by unlawful means, is not open to question. Gitlow v. New York, 268 U.S. 652, 666-668, and cases cited. . . .

"The essence of the offense denounced by the Act is the combining with others in an association for the accomplishment of the desired ends through the advocacy and use of criminal and unlawful methods. It partakes of the nature of a criminal conspiracy. . . . That such united and joint action involves even greater danger to the public peace and security than the isolated utterances and acts of individuals, is clear. We cannot hold that, as here applied, the Act is an unreasonable or arbitrary exercise of the police power of the State, unwarrantably infringing any right of free speech, assembly or association, or that those persons are protected from punishment by the due process clause who abuse such rights by joining and furthering an organization thus menacing the peace and welfare of the State. . . ." 274 U.S. at 371-372.

In a notable opinion, in which Justice Holmes joined, Justice Brandeis concurred, but only on the ground that the free speech issue had not been properly raised below:

"The felony which the statute created is a crime very unlike the old felony of conspiracy or the old misdemeanor of unlawful assembly. The mere act of assisting in forming a society for teaching syndicalism, of becoming a member of it, or of assembling with others for that purpose is given the dynamic quality of crime. There is guilt although the society may not contemplate immediate promulgation of the doctrine. Thus the accused is to be punished, not for contempt, incitement or conspiracy, but for a step in preparation, which, if it threatens the public order at all, does so only remotely. The novelty in the prohibition introduced is that the statute aims, not at the practice of criminal syndicalism, nor even directly at the preaching of it, but at association with those who propose to preach it.

"The right of free speech, the right to teach and the right of assembly are, of course, fundamental rights. . . . These may not be denied or abridged. But, although the rights of free speech and assembly are fundamental, they are not in their nature absolute. Their exercise is subject to restriction, if the particular restriction proposed is required in order to protect the State from destruction or from serious injury, political, economic or moral. That the necessity which is essential to a valid restriction does not exist unless speech would produce, or is intended to produce, a clear and imminent danger of some substantive evil which the State constitutionally may seek to prevent has been settled. See Schenck v. United States, 249 U.S. 47, 52. . . .

"This Court has not yet fixed the standard by which to determine when a danger shall be deemed clear; how remote the danger may be and yet be deemed present; and what degree of evil shall be deemed sufficiently substantial to justify resort to abridgement of free speech and assembly as the means of protection. To reach sound conclusions on these matters, we must bear in mind why a State is, ordinarily, denied the power to prohibit dissemination of social, economic and political doctrine which a vast majority of its citizens believes to be false and fraught with evil consequence.

[Here follows the passage quoted in Chapter I, supra.]

"Fear of serious injury cannot alone justify suppression of free speech and assembly. Men feared witches and burnt women. It is the function of speech to free men from the bondage of irrational fears. To justify suppression of free speech there must be reasonable ground to fear that serious evil will result if free speech is practiced. There must be reasonable ground to believe that the danger apprehended is imminent. There must be reasonable ground to believe that the evil to be prevented is a serious one. Every denunciation of existing law tends in some measure to increase the probability that there will be violation of it. Condonation of a breach enhances the probability. Expressions of approval add to the probability. Propagation of the criminal state of mind by teaching syndicalism increases it. Advocacy of law-breaking heightens it still further. But even advocacy of violation, however reprehensible morally, is not a justification for denying free speech where the advocacy falls short of incitement and there is nothing to indicate that the advocacy would be immediately acted on. The wide difference between advocacy and incitement, between preparation and attempt, between assembling and conspiracy, must be borne in mind. In order to support a finding of clear and present danger it must be shown either that immediate serious violence was to be expected or was advocated, or that the past conduct furnished reason to believe that such advocacy was then contemplated.

"Those who won our independence by revolution were not cowards. They did not fear political change. They did not exalt order at the cost of liberty. To courageous, self-reliant men, with confidence in the power of free and fearless reasoning applied through the processes of popular government, no danger flowing from speech can be deemed clear and present, unless the incidence of the evil apprehended is so imminent that it may befall before there is opportunity for full discussion. If there be time to expose through discussion the falsehoods and fallacies, to avert the evil by the processes of education, the remedy to be applied is more speech, not enforced silence. Only an emergency can justify repression. Such must be the rule if authority is to be reconciled with freedom. Such, in my opinion, is the command of the Constitution. It is therefore always open to Americans to challenge a law abridging free speech and assembly by showing that there was no emergency justifying it.

"Moreover, even imminent danger cannot justify resort to prohibition of these functions essential to effective democracy, unless the evil apprehended is relatively serious. Prohibition of free speech and assembly is a measure so stringent that it would be inappropriate as the means for averting a relatively trivial harm to society. A police measure may be unconstitutional merely because the remedy, although effective as means of protection, is unduly harsh or oppressive. Thus, a State might, in the exercise of its police power, make any trespass upon the land of another a crime, regardless of the results or of the intent or purpose of the trespasser. It might, also, punish an attempt, a conspiracy, or an incitement to commit the trespass. But it is hardly conceivable that this Court would hold constitutional a statute which punished as a felony the mere voluntary assembly with a society formed to teach that pedestrians had the moral right to cross unenclosed, unposted. waste lands and to advocate their doing so, even if there was imminent danger that advocacy would lead to a trespass. The fact that speech is likely to result in some violence or in destruction of property is not enough to justify its suppression. There must be the probability of serious injury to the State. Among free men, the deterrents ordinarily to be applied to prevent crime are education and punishment for violations of the law, not abridgment of the rights of free speech and assembly." 274 U.S. at 372-378.

In accord with the Whitney case is Burns v. United States, 274 U.S. 328, 47 S. Ct. 650, 71 L. Ed. 1077 (1927).

2. On the same day the Supreme Court also decided Fiske v. Kansas, 274 U.S. 380, 47 S. Ct. 665, 71 L. Ed. 1108 (1927), involving the Kansas Criminal Syndicalism Act. In that case an organizer for the I.W.W. had been convicted under the

Kansas statute on charges of advocating criminal syndicalism and procuring members for a local union of the I.W.W. The only evidence introduced against him consisted of the preamble to the I.W.W. Constitution, which included such statements as, "Between these two classes a struggle must go on until the workers of the World organize as a class, take possession of the earth, and the machinery of production and abolish the wage system." A unanimous Court held that the proof did not constitute evidence of advocacy of the use of unlawful methods and that the Kansas statute, as thus applied, violated the due process clause of the Fourteenth Amendment. Fiske was the first defendant to be successful in the Supreme Court.

REFERENCES

1. Benjamin Gitlow and his associates, after three years in prison, were pardoned by Governor Alfred E. Smith of New York. See Roche, The Quest for the Dream 128 (1963). Miss Whitney was pardoned by Governor Young of California and did not go to prison. See obituary in N.Y. Times, Feb. 5, 1955.

2. In the Prudential case, mentioned in the Gitlow opinion, the Supreme Court had stated only three years before unequivocally — though largely by way of dictum — that "neither the Fourteenth Amendment nor any other provision of the Constitution of the United States imposes upon the States any restrictions about 'freedom of speech' or the 'liberty of silence.'" Prudential Ins. Co. v. Cheek, 259 U.S. 530, 543, 42 S. Ct. 516, 522, 66 L. Ed. 1044, 1053 (1922). The Gitlow and Fiske decisions, however, established the doctrine that the First Amendment was in effect incorporated into the Fourteenth and hence applicable to the states. For comment on this aspect of the cases, see Chafee, Free Speech in the United States 320-325 (1941); Warren, The New "Liberty" Under the Fourteenth Amendment, 39 Harv. L. Rev. 431; Green, Liberty Under the Fourteenth Amendment, 27 Wash. U.L.Q. 497, 497-516 (1942); Note, 14 Va. L. Rev. 49 (1927). The Supreme Court has consistently adhered to this position, although it has been questioned by Mr. Justice Jackson in Beauharnais v. Illinois, 343 U.S. 250, 287-295, 72 S. Ct. 725, 96 L. Ed. 919 (1952); and more recently by Mr. Justice Harlan in Roth v. United States, 354 U.S. 476, 501-508, 77 S. Ct. 1304, 1 L. Ed. 2d 1498 (1957). In support of the Jackson-Harlan position see Rogge, The First and the Fifth, especially ch. III (1960). For other comment see Gordon, The First Amendment Incorporated, 12 Law. Guild Rev. 78 (1952); Antieau, The Federalism of Freedom, 42 Ky. L.J. 404 (1954); Note, Limiting State Action by the Fourteenth Amendment: Consequences of Abandoning the Theory of First Amendment Incorporation, 67 Harv. L. Rev. 1016 (1954).

3. The state anti-sedition laws of the period and state decisions are collected in Chafee, id. at chs. 4, 9, and 10, App. II; Lipsig, Sedition, Criminal Syndicalism, Criminal Anarchy Laws (mimeographed publication of American Civil Liberties Union 1937); Dowell, A History of Criminal Syndicalism Legislation in the United States (1939); Groner, State Control of Subversive Activities in the United States, 9 Fed. B.J. 61 (1947). See also Million, Political Crimes: II, 5 Mo. L. Rev. 293 (1940); Note, 36 Ill. L. Rev. 357 (1941). These laws were uniformly upheld by the state courts, and in applying the laws the state courts did not normally follow the clear and present danger test. See Antieau, The Rule of Clear and Present Danger: Scope of Its Applicability, 48 Mich. L. Rev. 811, 813, 817 (1950). For other discussion of the Gitlow, Whitney, Fiske, and the state cases, see Walsh, Is the New Judicial and Legislative Interpretation of Freedom of Speech, and of the Freedom of the Press, Sound Constitutional Development? 21 Geo. L.J. 161, 168-191 (1933); Notes, 33 Harv. L. Rev. 442 (1920); 35 Colum. L. Rev. 917 (1935); 84 U. Pa. L. Rev. 390 (1936); 61 Harv. L. Rev. 1215 (1948).

4. As noted in Chapter II, Section G, supra, prosecutions under state anti-sedition laws dwindled off during the 1920's. They were revived to some extent in the depression years of the 1930's. See Note, 35 Colum. L. Rev. 917 (1935). The most significant decision of the Supreme Court during this period was De Jonge v. Oregon, set forth below.

DE JONGE v. OREGON
299 U.S. 353, 57 S. Ct. 255, 81 L. Ed. 278 (1937)

MR. CHIEF JUSTICE HUGHES delivered the opinion of the Court.

Appellant, Dirk De Jonge, was indicted in Multonomah County, Oregon, for violation of the Criminal Syndicalism Law of that State. The act . . . defines "criminal syndicalism" as "the doctrine which advocates crime, physical violence, sabotage or any unlawful acts or methods as a means of accomplishing or effecting industrial or political change or revolution." With this preliminary definition the Act proceeds to describe a number of offenses, embracing the teaching of criminal syndicalism, the printing or distribution of books, pamphlets, etc., advocating that doctrine, the organization of a society or assemblage which advocates it, and presiding at or assisting in conducting a meeting of such an organization, society or group. The prohibited acts are made felonies, punishable by imprisonment for not less than one year nor more than ten years, or by a fine of not more than $1,000, or by both.

We are concerned with but one of the described offenses and with the validity of the statute in this particular application. The charge is that appellant assisted in the conduct of a meeting which was called under the auspices of the Communist Party, an organization advocating criminal syndicalism. The defense was that the meeting was public and orderly and was held for a lawful purpose; that while it was held under the auspices of the Communist Party, neither criminal syndicalism nor any unlawful conduct was taught or advocated at the meeting either by appellant or by others. Appellant moved for a direction of acquittal, contending that the statute as applied to him, for merely assisting at a meeting called by the Communist Party at which nothing unlawful was done or advocated, violated the due process clause of the Fourteenth Amendment of the Constitution of the United States.

This contention was overruled. Appellant was found guilty as charged and was sentenced to imprisonment for seven years. . . .

[A stipulation of the facts adduced at the trial stated that the meeting was called "as a protest against illegal raids on workers' halls and homes and against the shooting of striking longshoremen by Portland police." De Jonge, a speaker at the meeting, discussed the raids and police activities in the strike, "asked those present to do more work in obtaining members for the Communist Party," and "urged the purchase of certain communist literature which was sold at the meeting." There was no showing the literature "contained any advocacy of criminal syndicalism or of any unlawful conduct."]

The broad reach of the statute as thus applied is plain. While defendant was a member of the Communist Party, that membership was not necessary to conviction on such a charge. A like fate might have attended any speaker, although not a member, who "assisted in the conduct" of the meeting. However innocuous the object of the meeting, however lawful the subjects and tenor of the addresses, however reasonable and timely the discussion, all those assisting in the conduct of the meeting would be subject to imprisonment as felons if the meeting were held by the Communist Party. This manifest result was brought out sharply at this bar by the concessions which the Attorney General made, and could not avoid, in the light of the decision of the state court. Thus if the Communist Party had called a public meeting in Portland to discuss the tariff, or the foreign policy of the Government, or taxation, or relief, or candidacies for the offices of President, members of Congress, Governor, or state legislators, every speaker who assisted in the conduct of the meeting would be equally guilty with the defendant in this case, upon the charge as here defined and sustained. The list of illustrations might be indefinitely extended to every variety of meetings under the auspices of the Communist Party although held for the discussion of political issues or to adopt protests and pass resolutions of an entirely innocent and proper character.

While the States are entitled to protect themselves from the abuse of the privileges of our institutions through an attempted substitution of force and violence in the place of peaceful political action in order to effect revolutionary changes in government, none of our decisions go to the length of sustaining such a curtailment of the right of free speech and assembly as the Oregon statute demands in its present application. In Gitlow v. New York, 268 U.S. 652, under the New York statute defining criminal anarchy, the defendant was found to be responsible for a "manifesto" advocating the overthrow of the government by violence and unlawful means. Id., pp. 656, 662, 663. In Whitney v. California, 274 U.S. 357, under the California statute relating to criminal syndicalism, the defendant was found guilty of wilfully and deliberately assisting in the forming of an organization for the purpose of carrying on a revolutionary class struggle by criminal methods. The defendant was convicted of participation in what amounted to a conspiracy to commit serious crimes. Id., pp. 363, 364, 367, 379. The case of Burns v. United States, 274 U.S. 328, involved a similar ruling under the California statute as extended to the Yosemite National Park. Id., pp. 330, 331. On the other hand, in Fiske v. Kansas, 274 U.S. 380, the criminal syndicalism act of that State was held to have been applied unconstitutionally and the judgment of conviction was reversed, where it was not shown that unlawful methods had been advocated. Id., p. 387. See, also, Stromberg v. California, 283 U.S. 359.

Freedom of speech and of the press are fundamental rights which are safeguarded by the due process clause of the Fourteenth Amendment of the Federal Constitution. Gitlow v. New York, supra, p. 666; Stromberg v. California, supra, p. 368; Near v. Minnesota, 283 U.S. 697, 707; Grosjean v. American Press Co., 297 U.S. 233, 243, 244. The right of peaceable assembly is a right cognate to those of free speech and free press and is equally fundamental. As this Court said in United States v. Cruikshank, 92 U.S. 542, 552: "The very idea of a government, republican in form, implies a right on the part of its citizens to meet peaceably for consultation in respect to public affairs and to petition for a redress of grievances." The First Amendment of the Federal Constitution expressly guarantees that right against abridgment by Congress. But explicit mention there does not argue exclusion elsewhere. For the right is one that cannot be denied without violating those fundamental principles of liberty and justice which lie at the base of all civil and political institutions, — principles which the Fourteenth Amendment embodies in the general terms of its due process clause. Hebert v. Louisiana, 272 U.S. 312, 316; Powell v. Alabama, 287 U.S. 45, 67; Grosjean v. American Press Co., supra.

These rights may be abused by using speech or press or assembly in order to incite to violence and crime. The people through their legislatures may protect themselves against that abuse. But the legislative intervention can find constitutional justification only by dealing with the abuse. The rights themselves must not be curtailed. The greater the importance of safeguarding the community from incitements to the overthrow of our institutions by force and violence, the more imperative is the need to preserve inviolate the constitutional rights of free speech, free press and free assembly in order to maintain the opportunity for free political discussion, to the end that government may be responsive to the will of the people and that changes, if desired, may be obtained by peaceful means. Therein lies the security of the Republic, the very foundation of constitutional government.

It follows from these considerations that, consistently with the Federal Constitution, peaceable assembly for lawful discussion cannot be made a crime. The holding of meetings for peaceable political action cannot be proscribed. Those who assist in the conduct of such meetings cannot be branded as criminals on that score. The question, if the rights of free speech and peaceable assembly are to be preserved, is not as to the auspices under which the meeting is held but as to its purpose; not as to the relations of the speakers, but whether their utterances transcend the bounds of the freedom of speech which the Constitution protects. If the persons assembling have committed crimes elsewhere, if they have formed or are engaged in a conspiracy against the public peace and order, they may be prosecuted for their conspiracy or other violation of valid laws. But it is a different matter when the State, instead of prosecuting them for such offenses, seizes upon mere participation in a peaceable assembly and a lawful public discussion as the basis for a criminal charge.

We are not called upon to review the findings of the state court as to the objectives of the Communist Party. Notwithstanding those objectives, the defendant still enjoyed his personal right of free speech and to take part in a peaceable assembly having a lawful purpose, although called by that Party. The defendant was none the less entitled to discuss the public issues of the day and thus in a lawful manner, without incitement to violence or crime to seek redress of alleged grievances. That was of the essence of his guaranteed personal liberty.

We hold that the Oregon statute as applied to the particular charge as defined by the state court is repugnant to the due process clause of the Fourteenth Amendment. The judgment of conviction is reversed and the cause is remanded for further proceedings not inconsistent with this opinion.

Reversed.

Mr. Justice Stone took no part in the consideration or decision of this case.

NOTES

1. The only case to reach the Supreme Court involving the red flag laws was Stromberg v. California, 283 U.S. 359, 51 S. Ct. 532, 75 L. Ed. 1117 (1931). There the defendant was convicted under a California law which provided that "any person who displays a red flag, banner or badge . . . as a sign, symbol or emblem of opposition to organized government or as an invitation or stimulus to anarchistic action or as an aid to propaganda that is of a seditious character is guilty of a felony." The defendant, who conducted a children's camp, had daily raised "a camp-made reproduction of the flag of Soviet Russia, which was also the flag of the Communist Party in the United States." The California court defined the statutory terms "anarchistic action" and "seditious character" to mean unlawful and violent action. But it interpreted the term "opposition to organized government" broadly to include "peaceful and orderly opposition to government by legal means." Under the judge's charge the defendant could have been found guilty if she had displayed the flag for any of the three purposes set forth in the statute.

The Supreme Court, speaking through Chief Justice Hughes, said, "We have no reason to doubt the validity of the second and third clauses of the statute as construed by the state court to relate to such incitements to violence." But it held the first clause invalid and, since the defendant might have been found guilty under that clause, reversed the conviction:

"The maintenance of the opportunity for free political discussion to the end that government may be responsive to the will of the people and that changes may be obtained by lawful means, an opportunity essential to the security of the Republic, is a fundamental principle of our constitutional system. A statute which upon its face, and as authoritatively construed, is so vague and indefinite as to permit the punishment of the fair use of this opportunity is repugnant to the guaranty of liberty contained in the Fourteenth Amendment." 283 U.S. at 369.

2. The other significant decision of the period was Herndon v. Lowry, 301 U.S. 242, 57 S. Ct. 732, 81 L. Ed. 1066 (1937). Here the defendant was convicted under a Georgia insurrection statute which prohibited "any attempt, by persuasion or otherwise, to induce others to join in any combined resistance to the lawful authority of the State." The evidence showed that the defendant, a Communist Party organizer, had procured members for the Communist Party in Atlanta and that he had in his possession Communist literature which stated the Communist Party was based "upon the revolutionary theory of Marxism," referred to the need for

"overthrow of . . . class rule in the Black Belt" as necessary for the "self-determi-nation" of the Negroes, and contained similar references to the "revolutionary struggle for power." The Georgia Supreme Court interpreted the statute to re-quire an intent to resort to force but that it did not require "that the alleged offender should have intended that an insurrection should follow instantly or at any given time, but as to this element it would be sufficient if he intended that it should happen at any time within which he might reasonably expect his influence to continue to be directly operative in causing such action by those whom he sought to induce . . ." 301 U.S. at 254-255.

The Supreme Court reversed, saying that the Gitlow case did not hold that under a general law "the standard of guilt may be made the 'dangerous tendency' of his words," and that the statute, "as construed and applied in the appellant's trial does not furnish a sufficiently ascertainable standard of guilt." 301 U.S. at 258, 261. For an earlier stage of the case see Herndon v. Georgia, 295 U.S. 441, 55 S. Ct. 794, 79 L. Ed. 1530 (1935).

REFERENCES

1. The De Jonge case is discussed in Notes, 46 Yale L.J. 862 (1937); 4 U. Chi. L. Rev. 489 (1937); 37 Colum. L. Rev. 857 (1937); 25 Calif. L. Rev. 496 (1937). For further material on the right of assembly see Chapter IV.

2. The red flag laws and decisions are reviewed in Chafee, Free Speech in the United States 159-162, 362-366 (1941); Groner, State Control of Subversive Activities in the United States, 9 Fed. B.J. 61, 85-88 (1947); Hotes and Hotes, Freedom of Association, 10 Clev.-Mar. L. Rev. 104, 109-111 (1961). Massachusetts once had a statute prohibiting a red or black flag. It was repealed because it would have made the Harvard Crimson illegal. Said Professor Chafee, he hoped "other portions of the land of the brave will also be willing to face valiantly a piece of cloth." Chafee, id. at 162.

3. Related cases decided during the World War II period are Taylor v. Mississippi, 319 U.S. 583, 63 S. Ct. 1200, 87 L. Ed. 1600 (1943), discussed in Section B supra; and Schneiderman v. United States, 320 U.S. 118, 63 S. Ct. 1333, 87 L. Ed. 1796 (1943), and Bridges v. Wixon, 326 U.S. 135, 65 S. Ct. 1443, 89 L. Ed. 2103 (1945).

4. For general discussion of the 1931-1945 decisions and the legal doctrines enunciated therein, see Chafee, id. at ch. 11; Fraenkel, One Hundred and Fifty Years of the Bill of Rights, 23 Minn. L. Rev. 719 (1939); Wechsler in Symposium on Civil Liberties, 9 Am. L.S. Rev. 881 (1941); The Constitutional Right to Advocate Political, Social and Eco-nomic Change, 7 Law. Guild Rev. 57 (1947); Pritchett, The Roosevelt Court (1948); Green, The Supreme Court, The Bill of Rights and the States, 97 U. Pa. L. Rev. 608 (1949); Antieau, Judicial Delimitation of the First Amendment Freedoms, 34 Marq. L. Rev. 57 (1950); Konvitz, Fundamental Liberties of a Free People (1957); Drinker, Some Observations on the Four Freedoms of the First Amendment (1957); Hudon, Freedom of Speech and Press in America, chs. VIII and IX (1963); Pfeffer, The Liberties of an American (2d ed. 1963).

5. For discussion of the various specific doctrines developed during the period see, in addition to the material in the bibliography at the end of Chapter II:

Presumption in favor of rights guaranteed by the First Amendment: United States v. Carolene Products Co., 304 U.S. 144, 152-3 n. 4, 58 S. Ct. 778, 82 L. Ed. 1234 (1938); Schneider v. State, 308 U.S. 147, 161, 60 S. Ct. 146, 84 L. Ed. 155 (1939); Thomas v. Collins, 328 U.S. 516, 65 S. Ct. 315, 89 L. Ed. 430 (1945); see also compilation of cases in concurrence of Mr. Justice Frankfurter in Kovacs v. Cooper, 336 U.S. 77, 90-94 (and comment of Mr. Justice Rutledge at 106), 69 S. Ct. 448, 93 L. Ed. 513 (1949); Note,

Presumption of Constitutionality not Applicable to Statutes Dealing with Civil Liberties, 40 Colum. L. Rev. 531 (1940); Richardson, Freedom of Expression and the Function of Courts, 65 Harv. L. Rev. 1, 2 n. 3, 47-51 (1951); Kauper, The First Ten Amendments, 37 A.B.A.J. 717 (1951); Mason, The Core of Free Government, 1938-40: Mr. Justice Stone and the "Preferred Freedoms," 65 Yale L.J. 597 (1956); Cahn, Fact-Skepticism and Fundamental Law, 33 N.Y.U.L. Rev. 1, 13-16 (1958); Frantz, Two Kinds of Judicial Review, 19 Law. Guild Rev. 75 (1959); McKay, The Preference for Freedom, 34 N.Y.U.L. Rev. 1182 (1959).

Clear and present danger test: Thornhill v. Alabama, 310 U.S. 88, 60 S. Ct. 736, 84 L. Ed. 1093 (1940); Thomas v. Collins, id. at 527 n. 12, 530; Green, Liberty Under the Fourteenth Amendment, 27 Wash. U.L.Q. 497, 539-560 (1942); Antieau, The Rule of Clear and Present Danger — Its Origin and Application, 13 U. Detroit L.J. 198 (1950); The Rule of Clear and Present Danger: Scope of its Applicability, 48 Mich. L. Rev. 811 (1950); "Clear and Present Danger" — Its Meaning and Significance, 25 Notre Dame Law. 603 (1950); Mendelson, Clear and Present Danger — From Schenck to Dennis, 52 Colum. L. Rev. 313 (1952); Boudin, "Seditious Doctrines" and the "Clear and Present Danger" Rule, 38 Va. L. Rev. 143, 154-177 (1952).

Rule against vagueness: Lanzetta v. N.J., 306 U.S. 451, 59 S. Ct. 618, 83 L. Ed. 888 (1939); Musser v. Utah, 333 U.S. 95, 97, 68 S. Ct. 397, 92 L. Ed. 562 (1948); see also concurrence of Mr. Justice Rutledge, United States v. C.I.O., 335 U.S. 106, 150-155, 68 S. Ct. 1349, 92 L. Ed. 1849 (1948); Winters v. N.Y., 333 U.S. 507, 68 S. Ct. 665, 92 L. Ed. 840 (1948); Aigler, Legislation in Vague or General Terms, 21 Mich. L. Rev. 831 (1923); Note, Due Process Requirements of Definiteness in Statutes, 62 Harv. L. Rev. 77 (1948); Collings, Unconstitutional Uncertainty — An Appraisal, 40 Cornell L.Q. 195 (1955); Notes, 23 Ind. L.J. 272 (1948); 53 Mich. L. Rev. 264 (1954); Amsterdam, The Void for Vagueness Doctrine in the Supreme Court, 109 U. Pa. L. Rev. 67 (1960).

Statute must be narrowly drawn: Lovell v. Griffin, 303 U.S. 444, 451, 58 S. Ct. 666, 82 L. Ed. 949 (1938); Schneider v. State, id. at 162-164; Hague v. C.I.O., 307 U.S. 496, 516, 59 S. Ct. 954, 83 L. Ed. 1423 (1939); Thornhill v. Alabama, id. at 97-98; Carlson v. California, 310 U.S. 106, 112, 60 S. Ct. 746, 84 L. Ed. 1104 (1940); Cantwell v. Connecticut, 310 U.S. 296, 307-308, 60 S. Ct. 900, 84 L. Ed. 1213, 128 A.L.R. 1352 (1940); see also United States v. C.I.O., id. at 153; and Saia v. N.Y., 334 U.S. 558, 68 S. Ct. 1148, 92 L. Ed. 1574 (1948); Notes, 47 Colum. L. Rev. 595, 606-607 (1947); 61 Harv. L. Rev., 1208 (1948).

Guilt by association: Bridges v. Wixon, supra, concurrence of Mr. Justice Murphy at 163; but see Kessler v. Strecker, 307 U.S. 22, 29-31, 59 S. Ct. 694, 83 L. Ed. 1082 (1939); O'Brian, Loyalty Tests and Guilt by Association, 61 Harv. L. Rev. 592 (1948); Emerson and Helfeld, Loyalty Among Government Employees, 58 Yale L.J. 1, 91-94 (1948); Notes, 32 Geo. L.J. 405 (1944); 17 U. Chi. L. Rev. 148 (1949). Cf. Arens, Nuremberg and Group Prosecution, 1951 Wash. U.L.Q. 329.

For materials discussing the doctrine of prior restraint, see Chapter VII, infra.

BIBLIOGRAPHY ON THE COMMUNIST MOVEMENT AND AMERICAN REACTION TO IT IN THE POST-WORLD WAR II PERIOD

In the period following World War II issues of national security in the United States grew primarily out of concern over the Communist movement at home and abroad. See Chapter II, Section H, supra. As background to the Smith Act prosecution, as well as other matters considered later in this chapter, there are collected below some of the more significant materials dealing with the Communist movement and American reaction to it.

1. Materials emphasizing the threat of the Communist movement at home and abroad, the dangers of subversive activity, and the need for severe restrictive measures include: (1) the annual and other reports of the House Committee on Un-American Activities, especially The Communist Party of the United States as an Agent of a Foreign Power, H.R. Rep. No. 209, 80th Cong., 1st Sess. (1947); Report on the Communist Party of the United States as an Advocate of Overthrow of Government by Force and Violence, H.R. Rep. No. 1920, 80th Cong., 2d Sess. (1948); Organized Communism in the United States, H.R. Rep. No. 1694, 83rd Cong., 2d Sess. (1953, rev. 1958); The Communist Conspiracy — Strategy and Tactics of World Communism, H.R. Rep. No. 2240-4, 84th Cong., 2d Sess. (1956); Guide to Subversive Organizations and Publications (1961). (2) The annual and other reports of the Subcommittee on Internal Security of the Senate Judiciary Committee, especially Interlocking Subversion in Government Departments, 83rd Cong., 1st Sess. (1953); The Communist Party of the United States of America: What It Is — How It Works: A Handbook for Americans, Sen. Doc. 117, 84th Cong., 1st Sess. (1955). (3) Other Congressional Committee reports, such as House Committee on Foreign Affairs, The Strategy and Tactics of World Communism, H.R. Doc. No. 619, 80th Cong., 2d Sess. (1948); reports of the committees recommending passage of the Internal Security Act of 1950 and the Communist Control Act of 1954 (see subsection 3, infra); and materials collected in Internal Security Manual (rev.), Sen. Doc. No. 126, 86th Cong., 2d Sess., Parts IV and V, and Part VIII, Sec. C (G.P.O. 1961). See also Senate Committee on Government Operations, Congressional Investigations of Communism and Subversive Activities, Summary-Index 1918-1956, Sen. Doc. Nos. 1 and 8, 84th Cong., 2d Sess. (1956). (4) Individual authors, especially Ober, Communism vs. the Constitution, 34 A.B.A.J. 645 (1948); American Bar Association, Brief on Communism: Marxism-Leninism (1951); Weyl, The Battle Against Disloyalty (1951); Hook, Heresy, Yes — Conspiracy, No! (1953), and Political Power and Personal Freedom (1959); Cook, Democratic Rights Versus Communist Activity (1954); Burnham, The Web of Subversion (1954); Hoover, Masters of Deceit (1958), and A Study of Communism (1962); H. and B. Overstreet, What We Must Know About Communism (1958). See also the opinion of Justice Jackson in American Communications Assn. v. Douds, 339 U.S. 382, 424-433, 70 S. Ct. 674, 94 L. Ed. 925 (1950); Report of the Subversive Activities Control Board in Brownell v. Communist Party, reprinted as Sen. Doc. No. 41, 83rd Cong., 1st Sess. (1953).

2. Materials expressing concern over the restrictions upon political freedom and suggesting a more positive approach include McWilliams, Biddle, Davies, Davis, Thomas, Chafee, Cushman, Lamont and Caughey, cited in Chapter II, Section H; Fosdick, We Must Not Be Afraid of Change, N.Y. Times Magazine, April 3, 1949, p. 7; Rogge, Our Vanishing Civil Liberties (1949); Gellhorn, Security, Loyalty, and Science (1950); MacIver, The Ramparts We Guard (1950); Lasswell, National Security and Individual Freedom (1950); Barth, The Loyalty of Free Men (1951); Wilcox (ed.), Civil Liberties Under Attack (1951); Douglas, The Black Silence of Fear, N.Y. Times Magazine, Jan. 13, 1952, p. 7; Commager, Freedom, Loyalty, Dissent (1954); O'Brian, National Security and Individual Freedom (1955), and articles in 9 Wash. & Lee L. Rev. 157 (1952) and 66 Harv. L. Rev. 1 (1952); Harris, The Impact of the Cold War Upon Civil Liberties, 18 J. of Politics 3 (1956); Millis, Individual Freedom and the Common Defense (Fund for the Republic 1957); Brown, Loyalty and Security (1958); Ginzburg, Rededication to Freedom (1959); Aptheker, Dare We Be Free? (1961). For a statement of the argument that political restrictions ostensibly directed against extreme radicals may in reality be aimed at any social change, see Lerner, Freedom: Image and Reality in Safeguarding Civil Liberty Today (Cornell U. Press, 1945).

See also the hearings conducted in 1955 and 1956 by Senator Henning's Subcommittee on Constitutional Rights of the Senate Committee on the Judiciary, Security and Constitutional Rights, pursuant to S. Res. 94, 84th Cong., 2d Sess. (1955 and 1956); Community Security vs. Man's Right to Knowledge, May 1954 issue of Columbia Law Review, 54 Colum. L. Rev. 667; Internal Security and Civil Rights, 300 Annals of the Am. Acad. of Pol. and Soc. Sci. (July 1955); Security in a Free Society, October 1955 issue of Current History; Peltason, Constitutional Liberty and Seditious Activity (Freedom Agenda Pamphlet, published by Carrie Chapman Catt Memorial Fund, 1954); Morison, Freedom in Contemporary Society (1956); Chase, Security and Liberty: The Problem of Native Communists 1947-1955 (1955). For studies of the security problem from the viewpoint of sociology and political science, see Almond, The Appeals of Communism (1954); Stouffer, Communism, Conformity and Civil Liberties (1955) (a study of attitudes toward Communism and civil liberties based on public opinion polls); Grodzins, The Loyal and the Disloyal (1956); Shils, The Torment of Secrecy (1956); Schaar, Loyalty in America (1957); Selznick, The Organizational Weapon (new ed. 1960); Glazer, The Social Basis of American Communism (1961).

3. On the history and operations of the Communist Party in the United States the most recent and extensive account is the series Communism and American Life, of which Professor Clinton Rossiter is General Editor; see particularly Draper, The Roots of American Communism (1957) and American Communism and Soviet Russia (1960); Shannon, The Decline of American Communism (1959); and Latham, The Communist Controversy in Washington: From the New Deal to McCarthy (1966). See also, in addition to materials cited earlier in this note, Oneal and Werner, American Communism (1947); Egbert and Persons, Socialism and American Life (1952) (the most comprehensive study of radical movements in the U.S.); Howe and Coser, The American Communist Party: A Critical History (1919-1957) (1957). For the Communist view, see Foster, History of the Communist Party of the United States (1952); Aptheker, History and Reality (1955); see also Gates, The Story of an American Communist (1958). On Communism and the labor movement, see Kampelman, The Communist Party vs. The CIO (1957). With respect to the Communist Party and the Negro, see Nolan, Communism versus the Negro (1951); Record, The Negro and the Communist Party (1951) and Race and Radicalism (1964); Wynn, The NAACP Versus Revolutionary Protest (1955). See also Roy, Communism and the Churches (1960). Bibliographies include Bibliography on the Communist Problem in the United States (Fund for the Republic 1955); and Delaney, The Literature of Communism in America (1962).

4. On Senator McCarthy and "McCarthyism" see, for some of the critical literature: Anderson and May, McCarthy: The Man, The Senator, The "Ism" (1952); Rorty and Decter, McCarthy and the Communists (1954); Sweezy and Huberman, The Roots and Prospects of McCarthyism, Monthly Review, Jan. 1954; McCarthy: A Documented Record, The Progressive, April 1954; Millis, The Rise and Fall of the Radical Right, 44 Va. L. Rev. 1291 (1958); Rovere, Senator Joe McCarthy (1959); Polsby, Towards an Explanation of McCarthyism, 8 Political Studies (England 1960); Potter, Days of Shame (1965). For some of the favorable literature, see McCarthy, McCarthyism: The Fight For America (1952); Buckley and Bozell, McCarthy and His Enemies (1954).

For literature on the radical right, see Bell (ed.), The New American Right (1955), and the later edition entitled The Radical Right (1963); Burlingame, The Sixth Column (1962); Cook, The Ultras, The Nation, June 30, 1962; Ellsworth and Harris, The American Right Wing (1962); Janson and Eisman, The Far Right (1963); Broyles, The John Birch Society: Anatomy of a Protest (1964 rev. ed. 1966); Forster and Epstein, Danger on the Right (1964), and Report on the John Birch Society (1966).

5. Popular accounts of the liberal and left-wing movements of the 30's and 40's include Schlesinger, The Vital Center (1949); Wechsler, Age of Suspicion (1953); Hicks, Where We Came Out (1954); Kempton, Part of Our Time (1955); Warren, Liberals and Communism (1966). Exposés by former Communist Party members include Gitlow, I

Confess (1940); Budenz, This Is My Story (1947) and Men Without Faces (1950); Bentley, Out of Bondage (1951); Chambers, Witness (1952); Philbrick, I Led Three Lives (1952).

6. Discussions of the legal problems, in addition to the materials cited in Chapter II and previously in this chapter, include Cohen and Fuchs, Communisms's Challenge and the Constitution, 34 Cornell L.Q. 182, 352 (1948 and 1949); Note, Restraints on American Communist Activities, 96 U. Pa. L. Rev. 381 (1948); Note, Impact of the First Amendment on Federal Legislation Affecting "Subversive" Movements, 49 Colum. L. Rev. 363 (1949); Note, Control of Communist Activities, 1 Stan. L. Rev. 85 (1948); Sutherland, Freedom and Internal Security, 64 Harv. L. Rev. 383 (1951); Wyzanski, The Communist Party and the Law, The Atlantic Monthly, May 1951, p. 27; Barber, The Legal Status of the American Communist Party, 15 J. Pub. L. 94 (1966).

Microfilm records of 22 major trials involving issues of subversive activities have been prepared by the Fund for the Republic and are available in the Library of Congress, the New York Public Library, and the libraries at the Universities of California, Chicago, Harvard, Cornell, Texas, Washington, and Florida State. For the list see Digest of the Public Record of Communism in the United States 707-710 (Fund for the Republic 1955).

For materials dealing with more specific aspects of the problem see the following sections of this chapter.

2. The Smith Act Prosecutions

The Smith Act, named after its sponsor, Congressman Howard W. Smith of Virginia, was passed by Congress in 1940 as Title I of the Alien Registration Act. 54 Stat. 670. Section 1, now incorporated in 18 U.S.C. §2387, deals with impairing the morale of the armed forces and has been set forth above. Section B, supra. Sections 2 and 3, the remaining substantive provisions, are now incorporated in 18 U.S.C. §2385, set forth below.

THE SMITH ACT
18 U.S.C. §2385

Whoever knowingly or willfully advocates, abets, advises, or teaches the duty, necessity, desirability, or propriety of overthrowing or destroying the government of the United States or the government of any State, Territory, District or Possession thereof, or the government of any political subdivision therein, by force or violence, or by the assassination of any officer of any such government; or

Whoever, with intent to cause the overthrow or destruction of any such government, prints, publishes, edits, issues, circulates, sells, distributes, or publicly displays any written or printed matter advocating, advising, or teaching the duty, necessity, desirability, or propriety of overthrowing or destroying any government in the United States by force or violence, or attempts to do so; or

Whoever organizes or helps or attempts to organize any society, group, or assembly of persons who teach, advocate, or encourage the overthrow or destruction of any such government by force or violence; or becomes or is a member of, or affiliates with, any such society, group, or assembly of persons, knowing the purposes thereof —

Shall be fined not more than $20,000 or imprisoned not more than twenty years, or both, and shall be ineligible for employment by the United States or any department or agency thereof, for the five years next following his conviction.

If two or more persons conspire to commit any offense named in this section, each shall be fined not more than $20,000 or imprisoned not more than twenty years, or both, and shall be ineligible for employment by the United States or any department or agency thereof, for the five years next following his conviction.

As used in this section, the terms "organizes" and "organize," with respect to any society, group, or assembly of persons, include the recruiting of new members, the forming of new units, and the regrouping or expansion of existing clubs, classes, and other units of such society, group, or assembly of persons.

REFERENCES

1. The Smith Act was modeled on the New York Criminal Anarchy Act of 1902, involved in the Gitlow case. See subsection 1, supra. The legislative history is as follows:

The original bill, H.R. 5138, was introduced by Representative Howard W. Smith of Virginia on March 20, 1939. 84 Cong. Rec. 3013 (1939). It is set out at 84 Cong. Rec. 10355. Title I, Section 1 of the bill provided: "It shall be unlawful for any person by word of mouth or in writing, or by transmission by radio, to advocate, abet, advise, or teach the duty, necessity, desirability, or propriety of overthrowing or destroying the Government of the United States, or the government of any State of the United States, or the government of any subdivision thereof, by force or violence, or by the assassination of any officer . . . or by any other unlawful means." The House Judiciary Committee reported the bill without this provision. See 84 Cong. Rec. 9533. The provision was put back during the debate in the House, 84 Cong. Rec. 9532-9541, 10445-10456, and the bill passed on June 29, 1939. 84 Cong. Rec. 10456. Congress adjourned before the Senate could consider it. The following year, when the bill reached the Senate floor, a substitute bill was passed on June 15, 1940, without roll call vote, containing essentially the present version of Sections 2 and 3. 86 Cong. Rec. 8340-8347 (1940). The Conference Committee adopted the Senate version with slight modifications. 86 Cong. Rec. 9029. The conference version was debated in the House and passed on June 22, 1940. 86 Cong. Rec. 9031-9036. It passed the Senate, again without a roll call vote, on the same day. 86 Cong. Rec. 8950-8952. The President signed the measure on June 29, 1940. 86 Cong. Rec. 9127. For reference to previous bills and hearings, see Chafee, Free Speech in the United States 440-441 (1941).

With the adoption of the new Title 18, Crimes and Criminal Procedure, in 1948 the conspiracy provisions of Section 3 were incorporated into the general conspiracy statute, 18 U.S.C. §371, with the effect of reducing the penalty for conspiracy from ten to five years. In 1956 an amendment increased the penalties for violation of Section 2 to a fine of $20,000 or imprisonment for not more than 20 years, or both; the amendment also restored the special conspiracy provision for violation of Section 2, establishing the same penalty. 70 Stat. 623. The definition of the terms "organizes" and "organize" was added in 1962 for the purpose of changing the Supreme Court's interpretation of those words in the Yates case, set forth below. 76 Stat. 103; for the legislative history, see 1 U.S. Cong. and Admin. News 1709-1712 (87th Cong., 2d Sess., 1962).

2. For discussion of the background of the Smith Act see Chafee, id. at 439-490; Note, Recent Federal Legislation Against Subversive Influences, 41 Colum. L. Rev. 159 (1941); Note, Recent Legislative Attempts to Curb Subversive Activities in the United States, 10 Geo. Wash. L. Rev. 104 (1941). See also Note, Federal Sedition Bills, 35 Colum. L. Rev. 917 (1935).

NOTES

Prior to the Dennis case, infra, the Smith Act had been invoked only twice. In 1941, 18 members of the Socialist Workers Party were convicted of conspiracy to violate Sections 1 and 2 of the Act. The convictions were sustained by the Court of Appeals, relying upon the Gitlow case, and the Supreme Court denied certiorari. Dunne v. United States, 138 F.2d 137 (8th Cir. 1943), cert. den., 320 U.S. 790 (1943). The second case was the indictment in 1942 of 28 alleged pro-Nazis in the District of Columbia for conspiracy to violate Section 1. See Section B, supra.

In July 1948 the government indicted twelve members of the Central Committee of the Communist Party of the United States, the controlling group in the Party, for conspiracy under Section 3 of the Smith Act. The case as to William Z. Foster, Chairman of the Committee, was severed on grounds of ill health and the remaining defendants went to trial. The defendants challenged the jury list as not representative of a cross section of the community, and the trial on that issue extended from January 26 to March 1, 1949. The trial on the merits began the following week and went on continuously until September 23, 1949. The defendants were convicted and their convictions were sustained by the Court of Appeals for the Second Circuit. United States v. Dennis, 183 F.2d 201 (2d Cir. 1950). The case came before the Supreme Court in Dennis v. United States, set forth below.

DENNIS et al. v. UNITED STATES
341 U.S. 494, 71 S. Ct. 857, 95 L. Ed. 1137 (1951)

Mr. Chief Justice Vinson announced the judgment of the Court and an opinion in which Mr. Justice Reed, Mr. Justice Burton and Mr. Justice Minton join.

Petitioners were indicted in July, 1948, for violation of the conspiracy provisions of the Smith Act, 54 Stat. 671, 18 U.S.C. (1946 ed.) §11, during the period of April, 1945, to July, 1948. The pretrial motion to quash the indictment on the grounds, inter alia, that the statute was unconstitutional was denied, United States v. Foster, 80 F. Supp. 479, and the case was set for trial on January 17, 1949. A verdict of guilty as to all the petitioners was returned by the jury on October 14, 1949. The Court of Appeals affirmed the convictions. 183 F.2d 201. We granted certiorari, 340 U.S. 863, limited to the following two questions: (1) Whether either §2 or §3 of the Smith Act, inherently or as construed and applied in the instant case, violates the First Amendment and other provisions of the Bill of Rights; (2) whether either §2 or §3 of the

Act, inherently or as construed and applied in the instant case, violates the First and Fifth Amendments because of indefiniteness. . . .

The indictment charged the petitioners with wilfully and knowingly conspiring (1) to organize as the Communist Party of the United States of America a society, group and assembly of persons who teach and advocate the overthrow and destruction of the Government of the United States by force and violence, and (2) knowingly and wilfully to advocate and teach the duty and necessity of overthrowing and destroying the Government of the United States by force and violence. The indictment further alleged that §2 of the Smith Act proscribes these acts and that any conspiracy to take such action is a violation of §3 of the Act.

The trial of the case extended over nine months, six of which were devoted to the taking of evidence, resulting in a record of 16,000 pages. Our limited grant of the writ of certiorari has removed from our consideration any question as to the sufficiency of the evidence to support the jury's determination that petitioners are guilty of the offense charged. Whether on this record petitioners did in fact advocate the overthrow of the Government by force and violence is not before us, and we must base any discussion of this point upon the conclusions stated in the opinion of the Court of Appeals, which treated the issue in great detail. That court held that the record in this case amply supports the necessary finding of the jury that petitioners, the leaders of the Communist Party in this country, were unwilling to work within our framework of democracy, but intended to initiate a violent revolution whenever the propitious occasion appeared. Petitioners dispute the meaning to be drawn from the evidence, contending that the Marxist-Leninist doctrine they advocated taught that force and violence to achieve a Communist form of government in an existing democratic state would be necessary only because the ruling classes of that state would never permit the transformation to be accomplished peacefully, but would use force and violence to defeat any peaceful political and economic gain the Communists could achieve. But the Court of Appeals held that the record supports the following broad conclusions: By virtue of their control over the political apparatus of the Communist Political Association,[1] petitioners were able to transform that organization into the Communist Party; that the policies of the Association were changed from peaceful cooperation with the United States and its economic and political structure to a policy which had existed before the United States and the Soviet Union were fighting a common enemy, namely, a policy which worked for the overthrow of the Government by force and violence; that the Communist Party is a highly disciplined organization, adept at infiltration into strategic positions, use of aliases, and double-meaning language;

[1] Following the dissolution of the Communist International in 1943, the Communist Party of the United States dissolved and was reconstituted as the Communist Political Association. The program of this Association was one of cooperation between labor and management, and, in general, one designed to achieve national unity and peace and prosperity in the post-war period.

that the Party is rigidly controlled; that Communists, unlike other political parties, tolerate no dissension from the policy laid down by the guiding forces, but that the approved program is slavishly followed by the members of the Party; that the literature of the Party and the statements and activities of its leaders, petitioners here, advocate, and the general goal of the Party was, during the period in question, to achieve a successful overthrow of the existing order by force and violence.

I

It will be helpful in clarifying the issues to treat next the contention that the trial judge improperly interpreted the statute by charging that the statute required an unlawful intent before the jury could convict. More specifically, he charged that the jury could not find the petitioners guilty under the indictment unless they found that petitioners had the intent "to overthrow . . . the Government of the United States by force and violence as speedily as circumstances would permit." . . .

[The Chief Justice held that "the structure and purpose of the statute demand the inclusion of intent as an element of the crime."]

II

The obvious purpose of the statute is to protect existing Government, not from change by peaceable, lawful and constitutional means, but from change by violence, revolution and terrorism. That it is within the *power* of the Congress to protect the Government of the United States from armed rebellion is a proposition which requires little discussion. Whatever theoretical merit there may be to the argument that there is a "right" to rebellion against dictatorial governments is without force where the existing structure of the government provides for peaceful and orderly change. We reject any principle of governmental helplessness in the face of preparation for revolution, which principle, carried to its logical conclusion, must lead to anarchy. No one could conceive that it is not within the power of Congress to prohibit acts intended to overthrow the Government by force and violence. The question with which we are concerned here is not whether Congress has such *power,* but whether the *means* which it has employed conflict with the First and Fifth Amendments to the Constitution.

One of the bases for the contention that the means which Congress has employed are invalid takes the form of an attack on the face of the statute on the grounds that by its terms it prohibits academic discussion of the merits of Marxism-Leninism, that it stifles ideas and is contrary to all concepts of a free speech and a free press. Although we do not agree that the language itself has that significance, we must bear in mind that it is the duty of the federal courts to interpret federal legislation in a manner not inconsistent with the demands of the Constitution. American Communications Assn. v. Douds, 339 U.S. 382, 407 (1950). . . .

The very language of the Smith Act negates the interpretation which petitioners would have us impose on that Act. It is directed at advocacy, not discussion. Thus, the trial judge properly charged the jury that they could not convict if they found that petitioners did "no more than pursue peaceful studies and discussions or teachings and advocacy in the realm of ideas." He further charged that it was not unlawful "to conduct in an American college and university a course explaining the philosophical theories set forth in the books which have been placed in evidence." Such a charge is in strict accord with the statutory language, and illustrates the meaning to be placed on those words. Congress did not intend to eradicate the free discussion of political theories, to destroy the traditional rights of Americans to discuss and evaluate ideas without fear of governmental sanction. Rather Congress was concerned with the very kind of activity in which the evidence showed these petitioners engaged.

III

But although the statute is not directed at the hypothetical cases which petitioners have conjured, its application in this case has resulted in convictions for the teaching and advocacy of the overthrow of the Government by force and violence, which, even though coupled with the intent to accomplish that overthrow, contains an element of speech. For this reason, we must pay special heed to the demands of the First Amendment marking out the boundaries of speech.

We pointed out in Douds, supra, that the basis of the First Amendment is the hypothesis that speech can rebut speech, propaganda will answer propaganda, free debate of ideas will result in the wisest governmental policies. It is for this reason that this Court has recognized the inherent value of free discourse. An analysis of the leading cases in this Court which have involved direct limitations on speech, however, will demonstrate that both the majority of the Court and the dissenters in particular cases have recognized that this is not an unlimited, unqualified right, but that the societal value of speech must, on occasion, be subordinated to other values and considerations. . . .

[The Chief Justice here discusses the Supreme Court decisions in the Espionage Act cases of World War I, noted in Section B, supra.]

The rule we deduce from these cases is that where an offense is specified by a statute in nonspeech or nonpress terms, a conviction relying upon speech or press as evidence of violation may be sustained only when the speech or publication created a "clear and present danger" of attempting or accomplishing the prohibited crime, e.g., interference with enlistment. The dissents, we repeat, in emphasizing the value of speech, were addressed to the argument of the sufficiency of the evidence.

[The Chief Justice then discusses the Gitlow and Whitney cases, noted in subsection 1, supra.]

Although no case subsequent to Whitney and Gitlow has expressly overruled the majority opinions in those cases, there is little doubt that subsequent opinions have inclined toward the Holmes-Brandeis rationale. . . . But . . . neither Justice Holmes nor Justice Brandeis ever envisioned that a shorthand phrase should be crystallized into a rigid rule to be applied inflexibly without regard to the circumstances of each case. Speech is not an absolute, above and beyond control by the legislature when its judgment, subject to review here, is that certain kinds of speech are so undesirable as to warrant criminal sanction. Nothing is more certain in modern society than the principle that there are no absolutes, that a name, a phrase, a standard has meaning only when associated with the considerations which gave birth to the nomenclature. See American Communications Assn. v. Douds, 339 U.S. at 397. To those who would paralyze our Government in the face of impending threat by encasing it in a semantic strait-jacket we must reply that all concepts are relative.

In this case we are squarely presented with the application of the "clear and present danger" test, and must decide what that phrase imports. We first note that many of the cases in which this Court has reversed convictions by use of this or similar tests have been based on the fact that the interest which the State was attempting to protect was itself too insubstantial to warrant restriction of speech. In this category we may put such cases as Schneider v. State, 308 U.S. 147 (1939); Cantwell v. Connecticut, 310 U.S. 296 (1940); Martin v. Struthers, 319 U.S. 141 (1943); West Virginia State Board of Education v. Barnette, 319 U.S. 624 (1943); Thomas v. Collins, 323 U.S. 516 (1945); Marsh v. Alabama, 326 U.S. 501 (1946); but cf. Prince v. Massachusetts, 321 U.S. 158 (1944); Cox v. New Hampshire, 312 U.S. 569 (1941). Overthrow of the Government by force and violence is certainly a substantial enough interest for the Government to limit speech. Indeed, this is the ultimate value of any society, for if a society cannot protect its very structure, from armed internal attack, it must follow that no subordinate value can be protected. If, then, this interest may be protected, the literal problem which is presented is what has been meant by the use of the phrase "clear and present danger" of the utterances bringing about the evil within the power of Congress to punish.

Obviously, the words cannot mean that before the Government may act, it must wait until the putsch is about to be executed, the plans have been laid and the signal is awaited. If Government is aware that a group aiming at its overthrow is attempting to indoctrinate its members and to commit them to a course whereby they will strike when the leaders feel the circumstances permit, action by the Government is required. The argument that there is no need for Government to concern itself, for Government is strong, it possesses ample powers to put down a rebellion, it may defeat the revolution with ease needs no answer. For that is not the question. Certainly an attempt to overthrow the Government by force, even though doomed from the outset because of inadequate numbers or power of the revolutionists, is a sufficient evil for Congress to prevent. The damage which such attempts create both physically and politically to a nation makes it impossible to measure the validity in terms of the probability of success, or the immediacy of a successful attempt. In the instant case the trial judge charged the jury that they could not convict unless they found the petitioners intended to overthrow the Government "as speedily as circumstances would permit." This does not mean, and could not properly mean, that they would not strike until there was certainty of success. What was meant was that the revolutionists would strike when they thought the time was ripe. We must therefore reject the contention that success or probability of success is the criterion.

The situation with which Justices Holmes and Brandeis were concerned in Gitlow was a comparatively isolated event, bearing little relation in their minds to any substantial threat to the safety of the community. Such also is true of cases like Fiske v. Kansas, 274 U.S. 380 (1927), and DeJonge v. Oregon, 299 U.S. 353 (1937); but cf. Lazar v. Pennsylvania, 286 U.S. 532 (1932). They were not confronted with any situation comparable to the instant one — the development of an apparatus designed and dedicated to the overthrow of the Government, in the context of world crisis after crisis.

Chief Judge Learned Hand, writing for the majority below, interpreted the phrase as follows: "In each case [courts] must ask whether the gravity of the 'evil,' discounted by its improbability, justifies such invasion of free speech as is necessary to avoid the danger." 183 F.2d at 212. We adopt this statement of the rule. As articulated by Chief Judge Hand, it is as succinct and inclusive as any other we might devise at this time. It takes into consideration those factors which we deem relevant, and relates their significances. More we cannot expect from words.

Likewise, we are in accord with the court below, which affirmed the trial court's finding that the requisite danger existed. The mere fact that from the period 1945 to 1948 petitioners' activities did not result in an attempt to overthrow the Government by force and violence is of course no answer to the fact that there was a group that was ready to make the attempt. The formation by petitioners of such a highly organized conspiracy, with rigidly disciplined members subject to call when the leaders, these petitioners, felt that the time had come for action, coupled with the inflammable nature of world conditions, similar uprisings in other countries, and the touch-and-go nature of our relations with countries with whom petitioners were in the very least ideologically attuned, convince us that their convictions were justified on this score. And this analysis disposes of the contention that a conspiracy to advocate, as distinguished from the advocacy itself, cannot be constitutionally restrained, because it comprises only the preparation. It is the existence of the conspiracy which creates the danger. Cf. Pinkerton v. United States, 328 U.S. 640 (1946); Goldman v. United States, 245 U.S. 474 (1918); United States v. Rabinowich, 238 U.S. 78 (1915). If the ingredients of the reaction are present, we cannot bind the Government to wait until the catalyst is added.

I V

Although we have concluded that the finding that there was a sufficient danger to warrant the application of the statute was justified on the merits, there remains the problem of whether the trial judge's treatment of the issue was correct. He charged the jury, in relevant part, as follows:

"In further construction and interpretation of the statute I charge you that it is not the abstract doctrine of overthrowing or destroying organized government by unlawful means which is denounced by this law, but the teaching and advocacy of action for the accomplishment of that purpose, by language reasonably and ordinarily calculated to incite persons to such action. Accordingly, you cannot find the defendants or any of them guilty of the crime charged unless you are satisfied beyond a reasonable doubt that they conspired to organize a society, group and assembly of persons who teach and advocate the overthrow or destruction of the Government of the United States by force and violence and to advocate and teach the duty and necessity of overthrowing or destroying the Government of the United States by force and violence, with the intent that such teaching and advocacy be of a rule or principle of action and by language reasonably and ordinarily calculated to incite persons to such action, all with the intent to cause the overthrow or destruction of the Government of the United States by force and violence as speedily as circumstances would permit. . . .

"If you are satisfied that the evidence establishes beyond a reasonable doubt that the defendants, or any of them, are guilty of a violation of the statute, as I have interpreted it to you, I find as a matter of law that there is sufficient danger of a substantive evil that the Congress has a right to prevent to justify the application of the statute under the First Amendment of the Constitution.

"This is matter of law about which you have no concern. It is a finding on a matter of law which I deem essential to support my ruling that the case should be submitted to you to pass upon the guilt or innocence of the defendants. . . ."

It is thus clear that he reserved the question of the existence of the danger for his own determination, and the question becomes whether the issue is of such a nature that it should have been submitted to the jury.

The first paragraph of the quoted instructions calls for the jury to find the facts essential to establish the substantive crime, violation of §§2(a)(1) and

2(a)(3) of the Smith Act, involved in the conspiracy charge. There can be no doubt that if the jury found those facts against the petitioners violation of the Act would be established. The argument that the action of the trial court is erroneous, in declaring as a matter of law that such violation shows sufficient danger to justify the punishment despite the First Amendment, rests on the theory that a jury must decide a question of the application of the First Amendment. We do not agree.

When facts are found that establish the violation of a statute the protection against conviction afforded by the First Amendment is a matter of law. The doctrine that there must be a clear and present danger of a substantive evil that Congress has a right to prevent is a judicial rule to be applied as a matter of law by the courts. The guilt is established by proof of facts. Whether the First Amendment protects the activity which constitutes the violation of the statute must depend upon a judicial determination of the scope of the First Amendment applied to the circumstances of the case. . . .

V

There remains to be discussed the question of vagueness — whether the statute as we have interpreted it is too vague, not sufficiently advising those who would speak of the limitations upon their activity. It is urged that such vagueness contravenes the First and Fifth Amendments. [The Court rejected this argument.]

. . . Where there is doubt as to the intent of the defendants, the nature of their activities, or their power to bring about the evil, this Court will review the convictions with the scrupulous care demanded by our Constitution. But we are not convinced that because there may be borderline cases at some time in the future, these convictions should be reversed because of the argument that these petitioners could not know that their activities were constitutionally proscribed by the statute.

We have not discussed many of the questions which could be extracted from the record, although they were treated in detail by the court below. Our limited grant of the writ of certiorari has withdrawn from our consideration at this date those questions, which include, inter alia, sufficiency of the evidence, composition of jury, and conduct of the trial.

We hold that §§2(a)(1), 2(a)(3) and 3 of the Smith Act do not inherently, or as construed or applied in the instant case, violate the First Amendment and other provisions of the Bill of Rights, or the First and Fifth Amendments because of indefiniteness. Petitioners intended to overthrow the Government of the United States as speedily as the circumstances would permit. Their conspiracy to organize the Communist Party and to teach and advocate the overthrow of the Government of the United States by force and violence created a "clear and present danger" of an attempt to overthrow the

Government by force and violence. They were properly and constitutionally convicted for violation of the Smith Act. The judgments of conviction are
Affirmed.

Mr. Justice Clark took no part in the consideration or decision of this case.

MR. JUSTICE FRANKFURTER, concurring in affirmance of the judgment. . . .
Few questions of comparable import have come before this Court in recent years. The appellants maintain that they have a right to advocate a political theory, so long, at least, as their advocacy does not create an immediate danger of obvious magnitude to the very existence of our present scheme of society. On the other hand, the Government asserts the right to safeguard the security of the Nation by such a measure as the Smith Act. Our judgment is thus solicited on a conflict of interests of the utmost concern to the well-being of the country. This conflict of interests cannot be resolved by a dogmatic preference for one or the other, nor by a sonorous formula which is in fact only a euphemistic disguise for an unresolved conflict. If adjudication is to be a rational process we cannot escape a candid examination of the conflicting claims with full recognition that both are supported by weighty title-deeds. . . .

In all fairness, the argument cannot be met by reinterpreting the Court's frequent use of "clear" and "present" to mean an entertainable "probability." In giving this meaning to the phrase "clear and present danger," the Court of Appeals was fastidiously confining the rhetoric of opinions to the exact scope of what was decided by them. We have greater responsibility for having given constitutional support, over repeated protests, to uncritical libertarian generalities. . . .

[Mr. Justice Frankfurter then reviewed six types of cases in which the Court has "recognized and resolved conflicts between speech and competing interests."]

I must leave to others the ungrateful task of trying to reconcile all these decisions. . . . Viewed as a whole, however, the decisions express an attitude toward the judicial function and a standard of values which for me are decisive of the case before us.

First. — Free-speech cases are not an exception to the principle that we are not legislators, that direct policy-making is not our province. How best to reconcile competing interests is the business of legislatures, and the balance they strike is a judgment not to be displaced by ours, but to be respected unless outside the pale of fair judgment. . . .

Second. — A survey of the relevant decisions indicates that the results which we have reached are on the whole those that would ensue from careful weighing of conflicting interests. The complex issues presented by regulation of speech in public places, by picketing, and by legislation prohibiting advocacy of crime have been resolved by scrutiny of many factors besides the imminence and gravity of the evil threatened. The matter has been well summarized by a reflective student of the Court's work. "The truth is that the clear-and-present danger test is an over-simplified judgment unless it takes account also of a number of other factors: the relative seriousness of the danger in comparison with the value of the occasion for speech or political activity; the availability of more moderate controls than those which the state has imposed; and perhaps the specific intent with which the speech or activity is launched. No matter how rapidly we utter the phrase 'clear and present danger,' or how closely we hyphenate the words, they are not a substitute for the weighing of values. They tend to convey a delusion of certitude when what is most certain is the complexity of the strands in the web of freedoms which the judge must disentangle." Freund, On Understanding the Supreme Court, 27-28. . . .

Third. — Not every type of speech occupies the same position on the scale of values. There is no substantial public interest in permitting certain kinds of utterances: "the lewd and obscene, the profane, the libelous, and the insulting or 'fighting' words — those which by their very utterance inflict injury or tend to incite an immediate breach of the peace." Chaplinsky v. New Hampshire, 315 U.S. 568, 572. We have frequently indicated that interest in protecting speech depends on the circumstances of the occasion. See Niemotko v. Maryland, 340 U.S. at 275-283. It is pertinent to the decision before us to consider where on the scale of values we have in the past placed the type of speech now claiming constitutional immunity.

The defendants have been convicted of conspiring to organize a party of persons who advocate the overthrow of the Government by force and violence. The jury has found that the object of the conspiracy is advocacy as "a rule or principle of action," "by language reasonably and ordinarily calculated to incite persons to such action," and with the intent to cause the overthrow "as speedily as circumstances would permit."

On any scale of values which we have hitherto recognized, speech of this sort ranks low. . . .

These general considerations underlie decision of the case before us.

On the one hand is the interest in security. The Communist Party was not designed by these defendants as an ordinary political party. For the circumstances of its organization, its aims and methods, and the relation of the defendants to its organization and aims we are concluded by the jury's verdict. The jury found that the Party rejects the basic premise of our political system — that change is to be brought about by nonviolent constitutional process. The jury found that the Party advocates the theory that there is a duty and necessity to overthrow the Government by force and violence. It found that the Party entertains and promotes this view, not as a prophetic insight or as a bit of unworldly speculation, but as a program for winning adherents and as a policy to be translated into action.

In finding that the defendants violated the statute, we may not treat as established fact that the Communist Party in this country is of significant size, well-organized, well-disciplined, conditioned to embark on unlawful activity when given the command. But in determining whether application of the statute to the defendants is within the constitutional powers of Congress, we are not limited to the facts found by the jury. We must view such a question in the light of whatever is relevant to a legislative judgment. We may take judicial notice that the Communist doctrines which these defendants have conspired to advocate are in the ascendency in powerful nations who cannot be acquitted of unfriendliness to the institutions of this country. We may take account of evidence brought forward at this trial and elsewhere, much of which has long been common knowledge. In sum, it would amply justify a legislature in concluding that recruitment of additional members for the Party would create a substantial danger to national security.

In 1947, it has been reliably reported, at least 60,000 members were enrolled in the Party.[11] Evidence was introduced in this case that the membership was organized in small units, linked by an intricate chain of command, and protected by elaborate precautions designed to prevent disclosure of individual identity. There are no reliable data tracing acts of sabotage or espionage directly to these defendants. But a Canadian Royal Commission appointed in 1946 to investigate espionage reported that it was "overwhelmingly established" that "the Communist movement was the principal base within which the espionage network was recruited." [12] The most notorious spy in recent history was led into the service of the Soviet Union through Communist indoctrination.[13] Evidence supports the conclusion that members of the Party seek and occupy positions of importance in political and labor organizations.[14] Congress was not barred by the Constitution from believing that indifference to such experience would be an exercise not of freedom but of irresponsibility.

On the other hand is the interest in free speech. The right to exert all

[11] See the testimony of the Director of the Federal Bureau of Investigation. Hearings before the House Committee on Un-American Activities, on H.R. 1884 and H.R. 2122, 80th Cong., 1st Sess., Part 2, p. 37.

[12] Report of the Royal Commission to Investigate Communication of Secret and Confidential Information to Agents of a Foreign Power, June 27, 1946, p. 44. There appears to be little reliable evidence demonstrating directly that the Communist Party in this country has recruited persons willing to engage in espionage or other unlawful activity on behalf of the Soviet Union. The defection of a Soviet diplomatic employee, however, led to a careful investigation of an espionage network in Canada, and has disclosed the effectiveness of the Canadian Commuist Party in conditioning its members to disclose to Soviet agents vital information of a secret character. According to the Report of the Royal Commission investigating the network, conspiratorial characteristics of the Party similar to those shown in the evidence now before us were instrumental in developing the necessary motivation to cooperate in the espionage. See pp. 43-83 of the Report.

[13] The Communist background of Dr. Klaus Fuchs was brought out in the proceedings against him. See The [London] Times, Mar. 2, 1950, p. 2, col. 6.

[14] See American Communications Assn. v. Douds, 339 U.S. 382. Former Senator Robert M. La Follette, Jr., has reported his experience with infiltration of Communist sympathizers into congressional committee staffs. Collier's, Feb. 8, 1947, p. 22.

governmental powers in aid of maintaining our institutions and resisting their physical overthrow does not include intolerance of opinions and speech that cannot do harm although opposed and perhaps alien to dominant, traditional opinion. The treatment of its minorities, especially their legal position, is among the most searching tests of the level of civilization attained by a society. It is better for those who have almost unlimited power of government in their hands to err on the side of freedom. We have enjoyed so much freedom for so long that we are perhaps in danger of forgetting how much blood it cost to establish the Bill of Rights.

Of course no government can recognize a "right" of revolution, or a "right" to incite revolution if the incitement has no other purpose or effect. But speech is seldom restricted to a single purpose, and its effects may be manifold. A public interest is not wanting in granting freedom to speak their minds even to those who advocate the overthrow of the Government by force. For, as the evidence in this case abundantly illustrates, coupled with such advocacy is criticism of defects in our society. Criticism is the spur to reform; and Burke's admonition that a healthy society must reform in order to conserve has not lost its force. Astute observers have remarked that one of the characteristics of the American Republic is indifference to fundamental criticism. Bryce, The American Commonwealth, c. 84. It is a commonplace that there may be a grain of truth in the most uncouth doctrine, however false and repellent the balance may be. Suppressing advocates of overthrow inevitably will also silence critics who do not advocate overthrow but fear that their criticism may be so construed. No matter how clear we may be that the defendants now before us are preparing to overthrow the Government at the propitious moment, it is self-delusion to think that we can punish them for their advocacy without adding to the risks run by loyal citizens who honestly believe in some of the reforms these defendants advance. It is a sobering fact that in sustaining the conviction before us we can hardly escape restriction on the interchange of ideas.

We must not overlook the value of that interchange. Freedom of expression is the well-spring of our civilization — the civilization we seek to maintain and further by recognizing the right of Congress to put some limitation upon expression. Such are the paradoxes of life. For social development of trial and error, the fullest possible opportunity for the free play of the human mind is an indispensable prerequisite. The history of civilization is in considerable measure the displacement of error which once held sway as official truth by beliefs which in turn have yielded to other truths. Therefore the liberty of man to search for truth ought not to be fettered, no matter what orthodoxies he may challenge. Liberty of thought soon shrivels without freedom of expression. Nor can truth be pursued in an atmosphere hostile to the endeavor or under dangers which are hazarded only by heroes. . . .

It is not for us to decide how we would adjust the clash of interests which this case presents were the primary responsibility for reconciling it ours. Congress has determined that the danger created by advocacy of overthrow justifies the ensuing restriction on freedom of speech. The determination was made after due deliberation, and the seriousness of the congressional purpose is attested by the volume of legislation passed to effectuate the same ends.

Can we then say that the judgment Congress exercised was denied it by the Constitution? Can we establish a constitutional doctrine which forbids the elected representatives of the people to make this choice? Can we hold that the First Amendment deprives Congress of what it deemed necessary for the Government's protection?

To make validity of legislation depend on judicial reading of events still in the womb of time — a forecast, that is, of the outcome of forces at best appreciated only with knowledge of the topmost secrets of nations — is to charge the judiciary with duties beyond its equipment. We do not expect courts to pronounce historic verdicts on bygone events. Even historians have conflicting views to this day on the origin and conduct of the French Revolution. . . . It is as absurd to be confident that we can measure the present clash of forces and their outcome as to ask us to read history still enveloped in clouds of controversy. . . .

The wisdom of the assumptions underlying the legislation and prosecution is another matter. In finding that Congress has acted within its power, a judge does not remotely imply that he favors the implications that lie beneath the legal issues. Considerations there enter which go beyond the criteria that are binding upon judges within the narrow confines of their legitimate authority. . . .

Civil liberties draw at best only limited strength from legal guaranties. Preoccupation by our people with the constitutionality, instead of with the wisdom of legislation or of executive action, is preoccupation with a false value. Even those who would most freely use the judicial brake on the democratic process by invalidating legislation that goes deeply against their grain, acknowledge, at least by paying lip service, that constitutionality does not exact a sense of proportion or the sanity of humor or an absence of fear. Focusing attention on constitutionality tends to make constitutionality synonymous with wisdom. When legislation touches freedom of thought and freedom of speech, such a tendency is a formidable enemy of the free spirit. Much that should be rejected as illiberal, because repressive and envenoming, may well be not unconstitutional. The ultimate reliance for the deepest needs of civilization must be found outside their vindication in court of law; apart from all else, judges, howsoever they may seek to discipline themselves against it, unconsciously are too apt to be moved by the deep undercurrents of public feeling. A persistent, positive translation of the liberating faith into the feelings and thoughts and actions of men and women is the real protection against attempts to strait-jacket the human mind. Such temptations will have their way, if fear and hatred are not exorcised. The mark of a truly civilized man is confidence in the strength and security derived from the inquiring mind. We may be grateful for such honest comforts as it supports, but we must be unafraid of its uncertitudes. Without open minds there can be no open society. And if society be not open the spirit of man is mutilated and becomes enslaved.

[The Appendix to Mr. Justice Frankfurter's opinion, analyzing the cases requiring an imminent danger, is omitted.]

MR. JUSTICE JACKSON, concurring. . . .

The "clear and present danger" test was an innovation by Mr. Justice Holmes in the Schenck case, reiterated and refined by him and Mr. Justice Brandeis in later cases, all arising before the era of World War II revealed the subtlety and efficacy of modernized revolutionary techniques used by totalitarian parties. In these cases, they were faced with convictions under so-called criminal syndicalism statutes aimed at anarchists but which, loosely construed, had been applied to punish socialism, pacifism, and left-wing ideologies, the charges often resting on far-fetched inferences which, if true, would establish only technical or trivial violations. They proposed "clear and present danger" as a test for the sufficiency of evidence in particular cases.

I would save it, unmodified, for application as a "rule of reason" in the kind of case for which it was devised. When the issue is criminality of a hot-headed speech on a street corner, or circulation of a few incendiary pamphlets, or parading by some zealots behind a red flag, or refusal by a handful of school children to salute our flag, it is not beyond the capacity of judicial process to gather, comprehend, and weigh the necessary materials for decision whether it is a clear and present danger of substantive evil or a harmless letting off of steam. It is not a prophecy, for the danger in such cases has matured by the time of trial or it was never present. . . .

I think reason is lacking for applying that test to this case.

If we must decide that this Act and its application are constitutional only if we are convinced that petitioner's conduct creates a "clear and present danger" of violent overthrow, we must appraise imponderables, including international and national phenomena which baffle the best informed foreign offices and our most experienced politicians. We would have to foresee and predict the effectiveness of Communist propaganda, opportunities for infiltration, whether, and when, a time will come that they consider propitious for action, and whether and how fast our existing government will deteriorate. And we would have to speculate as to whether an approaching Communist coup would not be anticipated by a nationalistic fascist movement. No doctrine can be sound whose application requires us to make a prophecy of that sort in the guise of a legal decision. The judicial process simply is not adequate to a trial of such far-flung issues. The answers given would reflect our own political predilections and nothing more. . . .

What really is under review here is a conviction of conspiracy, after a trial for conspiracy, on an indictment charging conspiracy, brought under a statute outlawing conspiracy. . . .

The Constitution does not make conspiracy a civil right. The Court has never before done so, and I think it should not do so now. Conspiracies of labor unions, trade associations, and news agencies have been condemned, although accomplished, evidenced and carried out, like the conspiracy here, chiefly by letter-writing, meetings, speeches and organization. Indeed, this Court seems, particularly in cases where the conspiracy has economic ends, to be applying its doctrines with increasing severity. While I consider criminal conspiracy a dragnet device capable of perversion into an instrument of injustice in the hands of a partisan or complacent judiciary, it has an established place in our system of law, and no reason appears for applying it only to concerted action claimed to disturb interstate commerce and withholding it from those claimed to undermine our whole Government.[13] . . .

I do not suggest that Congress could punish conspiracy to advocate something, the doing of which it may not punish. Advocacy or exposition of the doctrine of communal property ownership, or any political philosophy unassociated with advocacy of its imposition by force or seizure of government by unlawful means could not be reached through conspiracy prosecution. But it is not forbidden to put down force or violence, it is not forbidden to punish its teaching or advocacy, and the end being punishable, there is no doubt of the power to punish conspiracy for the purpose. . . .

When our constitutional provisions were written, the chief forces recognized as antagonists in the struggle between authority and liberty were the Government on the one hand and the individual citizen on the other. It was thought that if the state could be kept in its place the individual could take care of himself.

In more recent times these problems have been complicated by the intervention between the state and the citizen of permanently organized, well-financed, semisecret and highly disciplined political organizations. Totalitarian groups here and abroad perfected the technique of creating private paramilitary organizations to coerce both the public government and its citizens. These organizations assert as against our Government all of the constitutional rights and immunities of individuals and at the same time exercise over their followers much of the authority which they deny to the Government. The Communist Party realistically is a state within a state, an authoritarian dictatorship within a republic. It demands these freedoms, not for its members, but for the organized party. It denies to its own members at the same time the freedom to dissent, to debate, to deviate from the party line, and enforces its authoritarian rule by crude purges, if nothing more violent.

The law of conspiracy has been the chief means at the Government's dis-

[13] These dangers were more fully set out in Krulewitch v. United States, 336 U.S. 440, 445.

posal to deal with the growing problems created by such organizations. I happen to think it is an awkward and inept remedy, but I find no constitutional authority for taking this weapon from the Government. There is no constitutional right to "gang up" on the Government.

While I think there was power in Congress to enact this statute and that, as applied in this case, it cannot be held unconstitutional, I add that I have little faith in the long-range effectiveness of this conviction to stop the rise of the Communist movement. Communism will not go to jail with these Communists. No decision by this Court can forestall revolution whenever the existing government fails to command the respect and loyalty of the people and sufficient distress and discontent is allowed to grow up among the masses. Many failures by fallen governments attest that no government can long prevent revolution by outlawry. Corruption, ineptitude, inflation, oppressive taxation, militarization, injustice, and loss of leadership capable of intellectual initiative in domestic or foreign affairs are allies on which the Communists count to bring opportunity knocking to their door. Sometimes I think they may be mistaken. But the Communists are not building just for today — the rest of us might profit by their example.

MR. JUSTICE BLACK, dissenting.

Here again, as in Breard v. Alexandria [341 U.S. 622], decided this day, my basic disagreement with the Court is not as to how we should explain or reconcile what was said in prior decisions but springs from a fundamental difference in constitutional approach. Consequently, it would serve no useful purpose to state my position at length.

At the outset I want to emphasize what the crime involved in this case is, and what it is not. These petitioners were not charged with an attempt to overthrow the Government. They were not charged with overt acts of any kind designed to overthrow the Government. They were not even charged with saying anything or with writing anything designed to overthrow the Government. The charge was that they agreed to assemble and to talk and to publish certain ideas at a later date: The indictment is that they conspired to organize the Communist Party and to use speech or newspapers and other publications in the future to teach and advocate the forcible overthrow of the Government. No matter how it is worded, this is a virulent form of prior censorship of speech and press, which I believe the First Amendment forbids. I would hold §3 of the Smith Act authorizing this prior restraint unconstitutional on its face and as applied.

But let us assume, contrary to all constitutional ideas of fair criminal procedure, that petitioners although not indicted for the crime of actual advocacy, may be punished for it. Even on this radical assumption, the other opinions in this case show that the only way to affirm these convictions is to repudiate directly or indirectly the established "clear and present danger" rule. This the Court does in a way which greatly restricts the protections afforded by the

First Amendment. The opinions for affirmance indicate that the chief reason for jettisoning the rule is the expressed fear that advocacy of Communist doctrine endangers the safety of the Republic. Undoubtedly, a governmental policy of unfettered communication of ideas does entail dangers. To the Founders of this Nation, however, the benefits derived from free expression were worth the risk. They embodied this philosophy in the First Amendment's command that "Congress shall make no law abridging . . . the freedom of speech, or of the press. . . ." I have always believed that the First Amendment is the keystone of our Government, that the freedoms it guarantees provide the best insurance against destruction of all freedom. At least as to speech in the realm of public matters, I believe that the "clear and present danger" test does not "mark the furthermost constitutional boundaries of protected expression" but does "no more than recognize a minimum compulsion of the Bill of Rights." Bridges v. California, 314 U.S. 252, 263.

So long as this Court exercises the power of judicial review of legislation, I cannot agree that the First Amendment permits us to sustain laws suppressing freedom of speech and press on the basis of Congress' or our own notions of mere "reasonableness." Such a doctrine waters down the First Amendment so that it amounts to little more than an admonition to Congress. The Amendment as so construed is not likely to protect any but those "safe" or orthodox views which rarely need its protection. I must also express my objection to the holding because, as MR. JUSTICE DOUGLAS' dissent shows, it sanctions the determination of a crucial issue of fact by the judge rather than by the jury. . . .

Public opinion being what it now is, few will protest the conviction of these Communist petitioners. There is hope, however, that in calmer times, when present pressures, passions and fears subside, this or some later Court will restore the First Amendment liberties to the high preferred place where they belong in a free society.

MR. JUSTICE DOUGLAS, dissenting.

If this were a case where those who claimed protection under the First Amendment were teaching the techniques of sabotage, the assassination of the President, the filching of documents from public files, the planting of bombs, the art of street warfare, and the like, I would have no doubts. The freedom to speak is not absolute; the teaching of methods of terror and other seditious conduct should be beyond the pale along with obscenity and immorality. This case was argued as if those were the facts. The argument imported much seditious conduct into the record. That is easy and it has popular appeal, for the activities of Communists in plotting and scheming against the free world are common knowledge. But the fact is that no such evidence was introduced at the trial. There is a statute which makes a seditious conspiracy unlawful. Petitioners, however, were not charged with a "conspiracy to overthrow" the Government. They were charged with a conspiracy to form a party and groups and assemblies of people who teach and advocate the overthrow of our Government by force or violence and with a conspiracy to advocate and teach its overthrow by force and violence. It may well be that indoctrination in the techniques of terror to destroy the Government would be indictable under either statute. But the teaching which is condemned here is of a different character.

So far as the present record is concerned, what petitioners did was to organize people to teach and themselves teach the Marxist-Leninist doctrine contained chiefly in four books: Stalin, Foundations of Leninism (1924); Marx and Engels, Manifesto of the Communist Party (1848); Lenin, The State and Revolution (1917); History of the Communist Party of the Soviet Union (B.) (1939).

Those books are to Soviet Communism what Mein Kampf was to Nazism. If they are understood, the ugliness of Communism is revealed, its deceit and cunning are exposed, the nature of its activities becomes apparent, and the chances of its success less likely. That is not, of course, the reason why petitioners chose these books for their classrooms. They are fervent Communists to whom these volumes are gospel. They preached the creed with the hope that some day it would be acted upon.

The opinion of the Court does not outlaw these texts nor condemn them to the fire, as the Communists do literature offensive to their creed. But if the books themselves are not outlawed, if they can lawfully remain on library shelves, by what reasoning does their use in a classroom become a crime? It would not be a crime under the Act to introduce these books to a class, though that would be teaching what the creed of violent overthrow of the government is. The Act, as construed, requires the element of intent — that those who teach the creed believe in it. The crime then depends not on what is taught but on who the teacher is. That is to make freedom of speech turn not on *what is said,* but on the *intent* with which it is said. Once we start down that road we enter territory dangerous to the liberties of every citizen.

There was a time in England when the concept of constructive treason flourished. Men were punished not for raising a hand against the king but for thinking murderous thoughts about him. The Framers of the Constitution were alive to that abuse and took steps to see that the practice would not flourish here. Treason was defined to require overt acts — the evolution of a plot against the country into an actual project. The present case is not one of treason. But the analogy is close when the illegality is made to turn on intent, not on the nature of the act. We then start probing men's minds for motive and purpose; they become entangled in the law not for what they did but *for what they thought;* they get convicted not for what they said but for the purpose with which they said it.

Intent, of course, often makes the difference in law. An act otherwise excusable or carrying minor penalties may grow to an abhorrent thing if the evil intent is present. We deal here, however, not with ordinary acts but with speech, to which the Constitution has given a special sanction. . . .

Free speech has occupied an exalted position because of the high service it has given our society. Its protection is essential to the very existence of a democracy. The airing of ideas releases pressures which otherwise might become destructive. When ideas compete in the market for acceptance, full and free discussion exposes the false and they gain few adherents. Full and free discussion even of ideas we hate encourages the testing of our own prejudices and preconceptions. Full and free discussion keeps a society from becoming stagnant and unprepared for the stresses and strains that work to tear all civilizations apart.

Full and free discussion has indeed been the first article of our faith. We have founded our political system on it. It has been the safeguard of every religious, political, philosophical, economic, and racial group amongst us. We have counted on it to keep us from embracing what is cheap and false; we have trusted the common sense of our people to choose the doctrine true to our genius and to reject the rest. This has been the one single outstanding tenet that has made our institutions the symbol of freedom and equality. We have deemed it more costly to liberty to suppress a despised minority than to let them vent their spleen. We have above all else feared the political censor. We have wanted a land where our people can be exposed to all the diverse creeds and cultures of the world.

There comes a time when even speech loses its constitutional immunity. Speech innocuous one year may at another time fan such destructive flames that it must be halted in the interests of the safety of the Republic. That is the meaning of the clear and present danger test. When conditions are so critical that there will be no time to avoid the evil that the speech threatens, it is time to call a halt. Otherwise, free speech which is the strength of the Nation will be the cause of its destruction.

Yet free speech is the rule, not the exception. The restraint to be constitutional must be based on more than fear, on more than passionate opposition against the speech, on more than a revolted dislike for its contents. There must be some immediate injury to society that is likely if speech is allowed. The classic statement of these conditions was made by Mr. Justice Brandeis in his concurring opinion in Whitney v. California, 274 U.S. 357, 376-377. . . .

I had assumed that the question of the clear and present danger, being so critical an issue in the case, would be a matter for submission to the jury. It was squarely held in Pierce v. United States, 252 U.S. 239, 244, to be a jury question. Mr. Justice Pitney, speaking for the Court, said, "Whether the statement contained in the pamphlet had a natural tendency to produce the forbidden consequences, as alleged, was a question to be determined not upon demurrer but by the jury at the trial." That is the only time the Court has passed on the issue. None of our other decisions is contrary. Nothing said in any of the nonjury cases has detracted from that ruling. The statement in Pierce v. United States, supra, states the law as it has been and as it should be. The Court, I think, errs when it treats the question as one of law.

Yet whether the question is one for the Court or the jury, there should be evidence of record on the issue. This record, however, contains no evidence whatsoever showing that the acts charged, viz., the teaching of the Soviet theory of revolution with the hope that it will be realized, have created any clear and present danger to the Nation. The Court, however, rules to the contrary. It says, "The formation by petitioners of such a highly organized conspiracy, with rigidly disciplined members subject to call when the leaders, these petitioners, felt that the time had come for action, coupled with the inflammable nature of world conditions, similar uprisings in other countries, and the touch-and-go nature of our relations with countries with whom petitioners were in the very least ideologically attuned, convince us that their convictions were justified on this score."

That ruling in my view is not responsive to the issue in the case. We might as well say that the speech of petitioners is outlawed because Soviet Russia and her Red Army are a threat to world peace.

The nature of Communism as a force on the world scene would, of course, be relevant to the issue of clear and present danger of petitioners' advocacy within the United States. But the primary consideration is the strength and tactical position of petitioners and their converts in this country. On that there is no evidence in the record. If we are to take judicial notice of the threat of Communists within the nation, it should not be difficult to conclude that *as a political party* they are of little consequence. Communists in this country have never made a respectable or serious showing in any election. I would doubt that there is a village, let alone a city or county or state which the Communists could carry. Communism in the world scene is no bogeyman; but Communism as a political faction or party in this country plainly is. Communism has been so thoroughly exposed in this country that it has been crippled as a political force. Free speech has destroyed it as an effective political party. It is inconceivable that those who went up and down this country preaching the doctrine of revolution which petitioners espouse would have any success. In days of trouble and confusion when bread lines were long, when the unemployed walked the streets, when people were starving, the advocates of a short-cut by revolution might have a chance to gain adherents. But today there are no such conditions. The country is not in despair; the people know Soviet Communism; the doctrine of Soviet revolution is exposed in all of its ugliness and the American people want none of it.

How it can be said that there is a clear and present danger that this advocacy will succeed is, therefore, a mystery. Some nations less resilient than the United States, where illiteracy is high and where democratic traditions are only budding, might have to take drastic steps and jail these men for merely speaking their creed. But in America they are miserable merchants of unwanted ideas; their wares remain unsold. The fact that their ideas are abhorrent does not make them powerful.

The political impotence of the Communists in this country does not, of course, dispose of the problem. Their numbers; their positions in industry and government; the extent to which they have in fact infiltrated the police, the armed services, transportation, stevedoring, power plants, munitions works, and other critical places — these facts all bear on the likelihood that their advocacy of the Soviet theory of revolution will endanger the Republic. But the record is silent on these facts. If we are to proceed on the basis of judicial notice, it is impossible for me to say that the Communists in this country are so potent or so strategically deployed that they must be suppressed for their speech. I could not so hold unless I were willing to conclude that the activities in recent years of committees of Congress, of the Attorney General, of labor unions, of state legislatures, and of Loyalty Boards were so futile as to leave the country on the edge of grave peril. To believe that petitioners and their following are placed in such critical positions as to endanger the Nation is to believe the incredible. It is safe to say that the followers of the creed of Soviet Communism are known to the F.B.I.; that in case of war with Russia they will be picked up overnight as were all prospective saboteurs at the commencement of World War II; that the invisible army of petitioners is the best known, the most beset, and the least thriving of any fifth column in history. Only those held by fear and panic could think otherwise.

This is my view if we are to act on the basis of judicial notice. But the mere statement of the opposing views indicates how important it is that we know the facts before we act. Neither prejudices nor hate nor senseless fear should be the basis of this solemn act. Free speech — the glory of our system of government — should not be sacrificed on anything less than plain and objective proof of danger that the evil advocated is imminent. On this record no one can say that petitioners and their converts are in such a strategic position as to have even the slightest chance of achieving their aims. . . .

[The Appendix to Mr. Justice Douglas' opinion, analyzing the cases on whether the existence of clear and present danger is a question for the court or jury, is omitted.]

REFERENCES

1. The Dennis case has been the subject of extensive comment. See Nathanson, The Communist Trial and the Clear-and-Present Danger Test, 63 Harv. L. Rev. 1167 (1950); Gorfinkel and Mack, Dennis v. United States and the Clear and Present Danger Rule, 39 Calif. L. Rev. 475 (1951); Boudin, "Seditious Doctrines" and the "Clear and Present Danger" Rule, 38 Va. L. Rev. 143, 315 (1952); Corwin, Bowing Out "Clear and Present Danger," 27 Notre Dame Law. 325 (1952); Hook, Heresy, Yes — Conspiracy, No! ch. 5 (1952); Meiklejohn, What Does the First Amendment Mean? 20 U. Chi. L. Rev. 461

(1953); Wormuth, Learned Legerdemain: A Grave but Implausible Hand, Western Pol. Q., Sept. 1953, p. 543; Konvitz, Fundamental Liberties of a Free People, chs. 27 and 28 (1957). See also Note, Clear and Present Danger Re-Examined, 51 Colum. L. Rev. 98 (1951); McClosky, Free Speech, Sedition and the Constitution, 45 Am. Pol. Sci. Rev. 662 (1951); Richardson, Freedom of Expression and the Function of Courts, 65 Harv. L. Rev. 1 (1951); Rostow, The Democratic Character of Judicial Review, 66 Harv. L. Rev. 193 (1952); American Civil Liberties Union, The Smith Act and the Supreme Court (1952); Antieau, Dennis v. United States — Precedent, Principle or Perversion? 5 Vand. L. Rev. 141 (1952); Mendelson, The Clear and Present Danger Test — A Reply to Mr. Meiklejohn, 5 Vand. L. Rev. 792 (1952), and Clandestine Speech and the First Amendment, 51 Mich. L. Rev. 553 (1953).

2. For other comments on the case, see Biddle, In Brief Authority 151-152 (1962) (the Attorney General who instituted the prosecution); Medina, The Anatomy of Freedom, ch. 1 (1959) (the trial judge); Marion, The Communist Trial (2d ed. 1950) (from the defendants' viewpoint).

3. With respect to the question of whether the issue of clear and present danger should be decided by the judge or the jury, see Hudon, Freedom of Speech and Press in America 116-121 (1963).

NOTES

Following the Supreme Court's decision in the Dennis case the Department of Justice commenced a series of further prosecutions under the Smith Act in various parts of the United States. Most of these prosecutions involved the secondary leadership of the Communist Party — state leaders and secondary national officials. A total of 15 prosecutions, involving approximately 121 defendants, were brought under the conspiracy provisions, and 8 prosecutions against individual defendants under the membership provision. The trials of these cases normally lasted three to six months. By the time of the Supreme Court's decision in the Yates case, on June 17, 1957, infra, the Government had secured convictions, in addition to the 11 Dennis defendants, of 96 defendants. Of these, four were convicted in membership cases and the remainder in conspiracy cases. In four of the conspiracy cases individual defendants were acquitted, a total of nine, four by the court and five by the jury. As to one additional defendant the jury disagreed. The remaining defendants had not been brought to trial.[1]

In the first two post-Dennis prosecutions to reach the Courts of Appeals, conspiracy convictions were affirmed and the Supreme Court denied certiorari. United States v. Frankfeld, 198 F.2d 679 (4th Cir. 1952) (six defendants tried in Baltimore convicted), cert. den., 344 U.S. 922 (1953); for preliminary rulings see 100 F. Supp. 934, 101 F. Supp. 449, 103 F. Supp. 48, noted in 12 Law. Guild Rev. 177 (1952). United States v. Flynn, 216 F.2d 354 (2d Cir. 1954) (13 defendants tried in New York convicted, 2 acquitted by the trial court), cert. den., 348 U.S. 909

---

[1] The above figures are based upon the reports of the proceedings in the Civil Liberties Docket (published by the National Lawyers Guild). See also Annual Report of the Attorney General of the United States, 1956, p. 65, which states that the total number of convictions, including the 11 Dennis defendants, was 108. Since the Attorney General's report does not list the individual cases, it is not possible to reconcile the discrepancy and the figures in this and the Note following the Yates case are based upon a total of 107 convictions.

(1955); verdict set aside as to two defendants and new trial ordered on ground of false testimony by prosecution witness, 130 F. Supp. 412 (S.D. N.Y. 1955); for preliminary rulings see 103 F. Supp. 925, 106 F. Supp. 966, 190 F.2d 672.

Thereafter, prior to the Yates decision in the Supreme Court, the Courts of Appeals affirmed convictions in three other conspiracy cases: Yates v. United States, 225 F.2d 146 (9th Cir. 1955) (14 defendants tried in Los Angeles convicted); for other aspects of the case see 106 F. Supp. 892, 906, 941; 107 F. Supp. 408, 412. United States v. Mesarosh (Nelson), 223 F.2d 449 (3d Cir. 1955) (Judges Hastie and Maris dissenting) (five defendants tried in Pittsburgh convicted); for trial court rulings see 13 F.R.D. 180, 115 F. Supp. 332, 116 F. Supp. 345. Wellman v. United States, 227 F.2d 757 (6th Cir. 1955) (six defendants tried in Detroit convicted). Convictions in two membership cases were likewise affirmed by the Courts of Appeals. Scales v. United States, 227 F.2d 581 (4th Cir. 1955) (M.D. N.C.), noted in 44 Geo. L.J. 515 (1956); United States v. Lightfoot, 228 F.2d 861 (7th Cir. 1956) (N.D. Ill.).

In the spring of 1956 the Supreme Court granted certiorari in the Yates, Mesarosh, Scales and Lightfoot cases. 350 U.S. 860, 922, 992 (1956). In September 1956, prior to the argument in the Mesarosh case, the Government filed a motion to remand the case to the District Court for a hearing on the credibility of one of the Government's witnesses, the informer Mazzei. The motion was based upon the fact that Mazzei had given testimony in other proceedings which the Government, on information in its possession, believed to be untrue. The Supreme Court, rejecting the Government's motion for a remand, ordered a new trial:

"Either this Court or the District Court should accept the statements of the Solicitor General as indicating the unreliability of this Government witness. The question of whether his untruthfulness in these other proceedings constituted perjury or was caused by a psychiatric condition can make no material difference here. Whichever explanation might be found to be correct in this regard, Mazzei's credibility has been wholly discredited by the disclosures of the Solicitor General. No other conclusion is possible. The dignity of the United States Government will not permit the conviction of any person on tainted testimony. This conviction is tainted, and there can be no other just result than to accord petitioners a new trial." Mesarosh v. United States, 352 U.S. 1, 9, 77 S. Ct. 1, 1 L. Ed. 2d 1 (1956).

For comment on the Mesarosh decision, see Notes, 45 Geo. L.J. 508 (1957); 1957 Wash. U.L.Q. 170.

The Scales and Lightfoot cases were argued and, in June, restored to the docket for further argument. 353 U.S. 979. On June 17, 1957 the Court decided the Yates case, set forth below.

REFERENCES

For discussion of the issues raised in the administration of the Smith Act prior to the Yates case, see Note, Post-Dennis Prosecutions Under the Smith Act, 31 Ind. L.J. 104 (1955); Fraenkel, The Smith Act Reconsidered, 16 Law. Guild Rev. 149 (1956). See also Somerville, The Communist Trials and the American Tradition (1956) (a discussion of the force and violence issues by a witness who testified as an expert for the defense in three Smith Act trials). A study of one of the Government's chief witnesses, John Lautner, may be found in Packer, Ex-Communist Witnesses, ch. 5 (1962). A summary of the prosecutions up to March 23, 1954 appears in Digest of the Public Record of Communism in the United States 194-205 (Fund for the Republic 1955).

YATES v. UNITED STATES
354 U.S. 298, 77 S. Ct. 1064, 1 L. Ed. 2d 1356 (1957)

MR. JUSTICE HARLAN delivered the opinion of the Court.

We brought these cases here to consider certain questions arising under the Smith Act which have not heretofore been passed upon by this Court, and otherwise to review the convictions of these petitioners for conspiracy to violate that Act. Among other things, the convictions are claimed to rest upon an application of the Smith Act which is hostile to the principles upon which its constitutionality was upheld in Dennis v. United States, 341 U.S. 494.

These 14 petitioners stand convicted, after a jury trial in the United States District Court for the Southern District of California, upon a single count indictment charging them with conspiring (1) to advocate and teach the duty and necessity of overthrowing the Government of the United States by force and violence, and (2) to organize, as the Communist Party of the United States, a society of persons who so advocate and teach, all with the intent of causing the overthrow of the Government by force and violence as speedily as circumstances would permit. Act of June 28, 1940, §2(a)(1) and (3), 54 Stat. 670, 671, 18 U.S.C. §§371, 2385. The conspiracy is alleged to have originated in 1940 and continued down to the date of the indictment in 1951. The indictment charged that in carrying out the conspiracy the defendants and their co-conspirators would (a) become members and officers of the Communist Party, with knowledge of its unlawful purposes, and assume leadership in carrying out its policies and activities; (b) cause to be organized units of the Party in California and elsewhere; (c) write and publish, in the "Daily Worker" and other Party organs, articles on the proscribed advocacy and teaching; (d) conduct schools for the indoctrination of Party members in such advocacy and teaching, and (e) recruit new Party members, particularly from among persons employed in the key industries of the nation. Twenty-three overt acts in furtherance of the conspiracy were alleged.

Upon conviction each of the petitioners was sentenced to five years' imprisonment and a fine of $10,000. The Court of Appeals affirmed. 225 F.2d 146. We granted certiorari for the reasons already indicated. 350 U.S. 860.

In the view we take of this case, it is necessary for us to consider only the following of petitioners' contentions: (1) that the term "organize" as used in the Smith Act was erroneously construed by the two lower courts; (2) that the trial court's instructions to the jury erroneously excluded from the case the issue of "incitement to action"; (3) that the evidence was so insufficient as to require this Court to direct the acquittal of these petitioners; and (4) that petitioner Schneiderman's conviction was precluded by this Court's judgment in Schneiderman v. United States, 320 U.S. 118, under the doctrine of collateral estoppel. For reasons given hereafter, we conclude that these convictions must be reversed and the case remanded to the District Court with instructions to enter judgments of acquittal as to certain of the petitioners, and to grant a new trial as to the rest.

[The Court first held that the term "organize" as used in the statute "refers only to acts entering into the creation of a new organization, and not to acts thereafter performed in carrying on its activities, even though such acts may loosely be termed 'organizational.' " The Communist Party was originally founded in 1919 but in 1944 it became the Communist Political Association. In July 1945 the Association was disbanded and reconstituted as the Communist Party. Hence the organizing count of the indictment was barred by the three-year statute of limitations. Since the jury might have based its verdict on the organizing count, or found overt acts relating only to that count, the verdict must be set aside on this ground.]

I I. *Instructions to the Jury*

Petitioners contend that the instructions to the jury were fatally defective in that the trial court refused to charge that, in order to convict, the jury must find that the advocacy which the defendants conspired to promote was of a kind calculated to "incite" persons to action for the forcible overthrow of the Government. It is argued that advocacy of forcible overthrow as mere *abstract doctrine* is within the free speech protection of the First Amendment; that the Smith Act, consistently with that constitutional provision, must be taken as proscribing only the sort of advocacy which incites to illegal *action;* and that the trial court's charge, by permitting conviction for mere advocacy, unrelated to its tendency to produce forcible action, resulted in an unconstitutional application of the Smith Act. The Government, which at the trial also requested the court to charge in terms of "incitement," now takes the position, however, that the true constitutional dividing line is not between inciting and abstract advocacy of forcible overthrow, but rather between advocacy as such, irrespective of its inciting qualities, and the mere discussion or exposition of violent overthrow as an abstract theory.

We print in the margin the pertinent parts of the trial court's instructions.[18] After telling the jury that it could not convict the defendants for holding or expressing mere opinions, beliefs, or predictions relating to violent overthrow, the trial court defined the content of the proscribed advocacy or teaching in the following terms, which are crucial here:

"Any advocacy or teaching which does not include the urging of force and

[18] [Footnote omitted. In addition to the paragraphs quoted in the text the trial court charged:

"The word 'wilfully', as used in the indictment, means a statement or declaration made or other act done with the specific intent to cause or bring about the overthrow and destruction of the Government of the United States by force and violence as speedily as circumstances will permit."]

violence as the means of overthrowing and destroying the Government of the United States is not within the issue of the indictment here and can constitute no basis for any finding against the defendants.

"The kind of advocacy and teaching which is charged and upon which your verdict must be reached is not merely a desirability but a necessity that the Government of the United States be overthrown and destroyed by force and violence and not merely a propriety but a duty to overthrow and destroy the Government of the United States by force and violence."

There can be no doubt from the record that in so instructing the jury the court regarded as immaterial, and intended to withdraw from the jury's consideration, any issue as to the character of the advocacy in terms of its capacity to stir listeners to forcible action. Both the petitioners and the Government submitted proposed instructions which would have required the jury to find that the proscribed advocacy was not of a mere abstract doctrine of forcible overthrow, but of action to that end, by the use of language reasonably and ordinarily calculated to incite persons to such action. The trial court rejected these proposed instructions on the ground that any necessity for giving them which may have existed at the time the Dennis case was tried was removed by this Court's subsequent decision in that case. The court made it clear in colloquy with counsel that in its view the illegal advocacy was made out simply by showing that what was said dealt with forcible overthrow and that it was uttered with a specific intent to accomplish that purpose, insisting that all such advocacy was punishable "whether it is language of incitement or not." . . .

We are thus faced with the question whether the Smith Act prohibits advocacy and teaching of forcible overthrow as an abstract principle, divorced from any effort to instigate action to that end, so long as such advocacy or teaching is engaged in with evil intent. We hold that it does not.

The distinction between advocacy of abstract doctrine and advocacy directed at promoting unlawful action is one that has been consistently recognized in the opinions of this Court, beginning with Fox v. Washington, 236 U.S. 273, and Schenck v. United States, 249 U.S. 47. This distinction was heavily underscored in Gitlow v. New York, 268 U.S. 652, in which the statute involved was nearly identical with the one now before us . . .

We need not, however, decide the issue before us in terms of constitutional compulsion, for our first duty is to construe this statute. In doing so we should not assume that Congress chose to disregard a constitutional danger zone so clearly marked, or that it used the words "advocate" and "teach" in their ordinary dictionary meanings when they had already been construed as terms of art carrying a special and limited connotation. . . . The Gitlow case and the New York Criminal Anarchy Act there involved, which furnished the prototype for the Smith Act, were both known and adverted to by Congress in the course of the legislative proceedings. . . . The legislative history of the Smith Act and related bills shows beyond all question that Congress was aware of the distinction between the advocacy or teaching of abstract doctrine and the advocacy or teaching of action, and that it did not intend to disregard it. The statute was aimed at the advocacy and teaching of concrete action for the forcible overthrow of the Government, and not of principles divorced from action.

The Government's reliance on this Court's decision in Dennis is misplaced. The jury instructions which were refused here were given there, and were referred to by this Court as requiring "the jury to find the facts *essential* to establish the substantive crime." 341 U.S., at 512 (emphasis added). It is true that at one point in the late Chief Justice's opinion it is stated that the Smith Act "is directed at advocacy, not discussion," id., at 502, but it is clear that the reference was to advocacy of action, not ideas, for in the very next sentence the opinion emphasizes that the jury was properly instructed that there could be no conviction for "advocacy in the realm of ideas." The two concurring opinions in that case likewise emphasize the distinction with which we are concerned. Id., at 518, 534, 536, 545, 546, 547, 571, 572.

In failing to distinguish between advocacy of forcible overthrow as an abstract doctrine and advocacy of action to that end, the District Court appears to have been led astray by the holding in Dennis that advocacy of violent action to be taken at some future time was enough. It seems to have considered that, since "inciting" speech is usually thought of as something calculated to induce immediate action, and since Dennis held advocacy of action for future overthrow sufficient, this meant that advocacy, irrespective of its tendency to generate action, is punishable, provided only that it is uttered with a specific intent to accomplish overthrow. In other words, the District Court apparently thought that Dennis obliterated the traditional dividing line between advocacy of abstract doctrine and advocacy of action.

This misconceives the situation confronting the Court in Dennis and what was held there. Although the jury's verdict, interpreted in light of the trial court's instructions, did not justify the conclusion that the defendants' advocacy was directed at, or created any danger of, immediate overthrow, it did establish that the advocacy was aimed at building up a seditious group and maintaining it in readiness for action at a propitious time. In such circumstances, said Chief Justice Vinson, the Government need not hold its hand "until the putsch is about to be executed, the plans have been laid and the signal is awaited. If Government is aware that a group aiming at its overthrow is attempting to indoctrinate its members and to commit them to a course whereby they will strike when the leaders feel the circumstances permit, action by the Government is required." 341 U.S., at 509. The essence of the Dennis holding was that indoctrination of a group in preparation for future violent action, as well as exhortation to immediate action, by advocacy found to be directed to "action for the accomplishment" of forcible overthrow, to violence as "a rule or principle of action," and employing "language of incitement," id., at 511-512, is not constitutionally protected when the group is of sufficient size and cohesiveness, is sufficiently oriented towards action, and other circumstances are such as reasonably to justify apprehension that action will occur. This is quite a different thing from the view of the District Court here that mere doctrinal justification of forcible overthrow, if engaged in with the intent to accomplish overthrow, is punishable per se under the Smith Act. That sort of advocacy, even though uttered with the hope that it may ultimately lead to violent revolution, is too remote from concrete action to be regarded as the kind of indoctrination preparatory to action which was condemned in Dennis. As one of the concurring opinions in Dennis put it: "Throughout our decisions there has recurred a distinction between the statement of an idea which may prompt its hearers to take unlawful action, and advocacy that such action be taken." Id., at 545. There is nothing in Dennis which makes that historic distinction obsolete. . . .

In light of the foregoing we are unable to regard the District Court's charge upon this aspect of the case as adequate. The jury was never told that the Smith Act does not denounce advocacy in the sense of preaching abstractly the forcible overthrow of the Government. We think that the trial court's statement that the proscribed advocacy must include the "urging," "necessity," and "duty" of forcible overthrow, and not merely its "desirability" and "propriety," may not be regarded as a sufficient substitute for charging that the Smith Act reaches only advocacy of action for the overthrow of government by force and violence. The essential distinction is that those to whom the advocacy is addressed must be urged to *do* something, now or in the future, rather than merely to *believe* in something. At best the expressions used by the trial court were equivocal, since in the absence of any instructions differentiating advocacy of abstract doctrine from advocacy of action, they were as consistent with the former as they were with the latter. . . .

Nor can we accept the Government's argument that the District Court was justified in not charging more than it did because the refused instructions proposed by both sides specified that the advocacy must be of a character reasonably calculated to "incite" to forcible overthrow, a term which, it is now argued, might have conveyed to the jury an implication that the advocacy must be of immediate action. Granting that some qualification of the proposed instructions would have been permissible to dispel such an implication, and that it was not necessary even that the trial court should have employed the particular term "incite," it was nevertheless incumbent on the court to make clear in some fashion that the advocacy must be of action and not merely abstract doctrine. The instructions given not only do not employ the word "incite," but also avoid the use of such terms and phrases as "action," "call for action," "as a rule or principle of action," and so on, all of which were offered in one form or another by both the petitioners and the Government. . . .

We recognize that distinctions between advocacy or teaching of abstract doctrines, with evil intent, and that which is directed to stirring people to action, are often subtle and difficult to grasp, for in a broad sense, as Mr. Justice Holmes said in his dissenting opinion in Gitlow, supra, 268 U.S., at 673: "Every idea is an incitement." But the very subtlety of these distinctions required the most clear and explicit instructions with reference to them, for they concerned an issue which went to the very heart of the charges against these petitioners. The need for precise and understandable instructions on this issue is further emphasized by the equivocal character of the evidence in this record, with which we deal in Part III of this opinion. Instances of speech that could be considered to amount to "advocacy of action" are so few and far between as to be almost completely overshadowed by the hundreds of instances in the record in which overthrow, if mentioned at all, occurs in the course of doctrinal disputation so remote from action as to be almost wholly lacking in probative value. Vague references to "revolutionary" or "militant" action of an unspecified character, which are found in the evidence, might in addition be given too great weight by the jury in the absence of more precise instructions. Particularly in light of this record, we must regard the trial court's charge in this respect as furnishing wholly inadequate guidance to the jury on this central point in the case. We cannot allow a conviction to stand on such "an equivocal direction to the jury on a basic issue." Bollenbach v. United States, 326 U.S. 607, 613.

I I I. *The Evidence*

The determinations already made require a reversal of these convictions. Nevertheless, in the exercise of our power under 28 U.S.C. §2106 to "direct the entry of such appropriate judgment . . . as may be just under the circumstances," we have conceived it to be our duty to scrutinize this lengthy record with care, in order to determine whether the way should be left open for a new trial of all or some of these petitioners. Such a judgment, we think, should, on the one hand, foreclose further proceedings against those of the petitioners as to whom the evidence in this record would be palpably insufficient upon a new trial, and should, on the other hand, leave the Government free to retry the other petitioners under proper legal standards, especially since it is by no means clear that certain aspects of the evidence against them could not have been clarified to the advantage of the Government had it not been under a misapprehension as to the burden cast upon it by the Smith Act. In judging the record by these criteria we do not apply to these cases the rigorous standards of review which, for example, the Court of Appeals would be required to apply in reviewing the evidence if any of these petitioners are convicted upon a retrial. Compare Dennis v. United States, supra, at 516. Rather, we have scrutinized the record to see whether there are individuals as to whom acquittal is unequivocally demanded. We do this because it is in general too hypothetical and abstract an inquiry to try to judge whether the evidence would have been inadequate had the cases been submitted under a proper charge, and had the Government realized that all its evidence must be channeled into the "advocacy" rather than the "organizing" charge. We think we may do this by drawing on our power under 28 U.S.C. §2106, because under that statute we would no doubt be justified in refusing to order acquittal even where the evidence might be deemed palpably insufficient, particularly since petitioners have asked in the alternative for a new trial as well as for acquittal. See Bryan v. United States, 338 U.S. 552.

On this basis we have concluded that the evidence against petitioners Connelly, Kusnitz, Richmond, Spector, and Steinberg is so clearly insufficient that their acquittal should be ordered, but that as to petitioners Carlson, Dobbs, Fox, Healey (Mrs. Connelly), Lambert, Lima, Schneiderman, Stack, and Yates, we would not be justified in closing the way to their retrial. We proceed to the reasons for these conclusions.

At the outset, in view of the conclusions reached in Part I of this opinion, we must put aside as against all petitioners the evidence relating to the "organizing" aspect of the alleged conspiracy, except insofar as it bears upon the "advocacy" charge. That, indeed, dilutes in a substantial way a large part of the evidence, for the record unmistakably indicates that the Government relied heavily on its "organizing" charge. Two further general observations should also be made about the evidence as to the "advocacy" charge. The first is that both the Government and the trial court evidently proceeded on the theory that advocacy of abstract doctrine was enough to offend the Smith Act, whereas, as we have held, it is only advocacy of forcible action that is proscribed. The second observation is that both the record and the Government's brief in this Court make it clear that the Government's thesis was that the Communist Party, or at least the Communist Party of California, constituted the conspiratorial group, and that membership in the conspiracy could therefore be proved by showing that the individual petitioners were actively identified with the Party's affairs and thus inferentially parties to its tenets. This might have been well enough towards making out the Government's case if advocacy of the abstract doctrine of forcible overthrow satisfied the Smith Act, for we would at least have little difficulty in saying on this record that a jury could justifiably conclude that such was one of the tenets of the Communist Party; and there was no dispute as to petitioners' active identification with Party affairs. But when it comes to Party advocacy or teaching in the sense of a call to forcible action at some future time we cannot but regard this record as strikingly deficient. At best this voluminous record shows but a half dozen or so scattered incidents which, even under the loosest standards, could be deemed to show such advocacy. Most of these were not connected with any of the petitioners, or occurred many years before the period covered by the indictment. We are unable to regard this sporadic showing as sufficient to justify viewing the Communist Party as the nexus between these petitioners and the conspiracy charged. We need scarcely say that however much one may abhor even the abstract preaching of forcible overthrow of government, or believe that forcible overthrow is the ultimate purpose to which the Communist Party is dedicated, it is upon the evidence in the record that the petitioners must be judged in this case.

We must, then, look elsewhere than to the evidence concerning the Communist Party as such for the existence of the conspiracy to advocate charged in the indictment. As to the petitioners Connelly, Kusnitz, Richmond, Spector, and Steinberg we find no adequate evidence in the record which would permit a jury to find that they were members of such a conspiracy. For all purposes relevant here, the sole evidence as to them was that they had long been members, officers or functionaries of the Communist Party of California; and that standing alone, as Congress has enacted in §4(f) of the Internal Security Act of 1950, makes out no case against them. So far as this record shows, none of them has engaged in or been associated with any but what appear to have been wholly lawful activities, or has ever made a single remark or been present when someone else made a remark, which would tend to prove the charges against them. Connelly and Richmond were, to be sure, the Los Angeles and Executive Editors, respectively, of the Daily People's World, the West Coast Party organ, but we can find nothing in the material introduced into evidence from that newspaper which advances the Government's case.

Moreover, apart from the inadequacy of the evidence to show, at best, more than the abstract advocacy and teaching of forcible overthrow by the Party, it is difficult to perceive how the requisite specific intent to accomplish such overthrow could be deemed proved by a showing of mere membership or the holding of office in the Communist Party. We therefore think that as to these petitioners the evidence was entirely too meagre to justify putting them to a new trial, and that their acquittal should be ordered.

As to the nine remaining petitioners, we consider that a different conclusion should be reached. There was testimony from the witness Foard, and other evidence, tying Fox, Healey, Lambert, Lima, Schneiderman, Stack, and Yates to Party classes conducted in the San Francisco area during the year 1946, where there occurred what might be considered to be the systematic teaching and advocacy of illegal action which is condemned by the statute. It might be found that one of the purposes of such classes was to develop in the members of the group a readiness to engage at the crucial time, perhaps during war or during attack upon the United States from without, in such activities as sabotage and street fighting, in order to divert and diffuse the resistance of the authorities and if possible to seize local vantage points. There was also testimony as to activities in the Los Angeles area, during the period covered by the indictment, which might be considered to amount to "advocacy of action," and with which petitioners Carlson and Dobbs were linked. From the testimony of the witness Scarletto, it might be found that individuals considered to be particularly trustworthy were taken into an "underground" apparatus and there instructed in tasks which would be useful when the time for violent action arrived. Scarletto was surreptitiously indoctrinated in methods, as he said, of moving "masses of people in time of crisis." It might be found, under all the circumstances, that the purpose of this teaching was to prepare the members of the underground apparatus to engage in, to facilitate, and to cooperate with violent action directed against government when the time was ripe. In short, while the record contains evidence of little more than a general program of educational activity by the Communist Party which included advocacy of violence as a theoretical matter, we are not prepared to say, at this stage of the case, that it would be impossible for a jury, resolving all conflicts in favor of the Government and giving the evidence as to these San Francisco and Los Angeles episodes its utmost sweep, to find that advocacy of action was also engaged in when the group involved was thought particularly trustworthy, dedicated, and suited for violent tasks.

Nor can we say that the evidence linking these nine petitioners to that sort of advocacy, with the requisite specific intent, is so tenuous as not to justify their retrial under proper legal standards. Fox, Healey, Lambert, Lima, Schneiderman, Stack, and Yates, as members of the State and San Francisco County Boards, were shown to have been closely associated with Ida Rothstein, the principal teacher of the San Francisco classes, who also during this same period arranged in a devious and conspiratorial manner for the holding of Board meetings at the home of the witness Honig, which were attended by these petitioners. It was also shown that from time to time instructions emanated from the Boards or their members to instructors of groups at lower levels. And while none of the written instructions produced at the trial were invidious in themselves, it might be inferred that additional instructions were given which were not reduced to writing. Similarly, there was evidence of close association between petitioners Carlson and Dobbs and associates or superiors of the witness Scarletto, which might be taken as indicating that these two petitioners had knowledge of the apparatus in which Scarletto was active. And finally, all of these nine petitioners were shown either to have made statements themselves, or apparently approved statements made in their presence, which a jury might take as some evidence of their participation with the requisite intent in a conspiracy to advocate illegal action.

As to these nine petitioners, then, we shall not order an acquittal. . . .

[The Court then rejected Schneiderman's defense of collateral estoppel.]

Since there must be a new trial, we have not found it necessary to deal with the contentions of the petitioners as to the fairness of the trial already held. The judgment of the Court of Appeals is reversed and the case remanded to the District Court for further proceedings consistent with this opinion.

It is so ordered.

MR. JUSTICE BURTON, concurring in the result.

I agree with the result reached by the Court, and with the opinion of the Court except as to its interpretation of the term "organize" as used in the

Smith Act. As to that I agree with the interpretation given it by the Court of Appeals. 225 F.2d 146.

Mr. Justice Brennan and Mr. Justice Whittaker took no part in the consideration or decision of this case.

MR. JUSTICE BLACK, with whom MR. JUSTICE DOUGLAS joins, concurring in part and dissenting in part.

I would reverse every one of these convictions and direct that all the defendants be acquitted. In my judgment the statutory provisions on which these prosecutions are based abridge freedom of speech, press and assembly in violation of the First Amendment to the United States Constitution. See my dissent and that of Mr. Justice Douglas in Dennis v. United States, 341 U.S. 494, 579, 581. Also see my opinion in American Communications Assn. v. Douds, 339 U.S. 382, 445.

The kind of trials conducted here are wholly dissimilar to normal criminal trials. Ordinarily these "Smith Act" trials are prolonged affairs lasting for months. In part this is attributable to the routine introduction in evidence of massive collections of books, tracts, pamphlets, newspapers, and manifestoes discussing Communism, Socialism, Capitalism, Feudalism and governmental institutions in general, which, it is not too much to say, are turgid, diffuse, abtruse, and just plain dull. Of course, no juror can or is expected to plow his way through this jungle of verbiage. The testimony of witnesses is comparatively insignificant. Guilt or innocence may turn on what Marx or Engels or someone else wrote or advocated as much as a hundred or more years ago. Elaborate, refined distinctions are drawn between "Communism," "Marxism," "Leninism," "Trotskyism," and "Stalinism." When the propriety of obnoxious or unorthodox views about government is in reality made the crucial issue, as it must be in cases of this kind, prejudice makes conviction inevitable except in the rarest circumstances. . . .

In essence, petitioners were tried upon the charge that they believe in and want to foist upon this country a different and to us a despicable form of authoritarian government in which voices criticizing the existing order are summarily silenced. I fear that the present type of prosecutions are more in line with the philosophy of authoritarian government than with that expressed by our First Amendment.

Doubtlessly, dictators have to stamp out causes and beliefs which they deem subversive to their evil regimes. But governmental suppression of causes and beliefs seems to me to be the very antithesis of what our Constitution stands for. The choice expressed in the First Amendment in favor of free expression was made against a turbulent background by men such as Jefferson, Madison, and Mason — men who believed that loyalty to the provisions of this Amendment was the best way to assure a long life for this new nation and its Government. Unless there is complete freedom for expression of all ideas, whether we like them or not, concerning the way government should be run and who shall run it, I doubt if any views in the long run can be secured against the censor. The First Amendment provides the only kind of security system that can preserve a free government — one that leaves the way wide open for people to favor, discuss, advocate, or incite causes and doctrines however obnoxious and antagonistic such views may be to the rest of us.

MR. JUSTICE CLARK, dissenting. . . .

The conspiracy includes the same group of defendants as in the Dennis case though petitioners here occupied a lower echelon in the party hierarchy. They, nevertheless, served in the same army and were engaged in the same mission. The convictions here were based upon evidence closely paralleling that adduced in Dennis and in United States v. Flynn, 216 F.2d 354 (2d Cir. 1954), both of which resulted in convictions. This Court laid down in Dennis the principles governing such prosecutions and they were closely adhered to here, although the nature of the two cases did not permit identical handling.

I would affirm the convictions. However, the Court has freed five of the convicted petitioners and ordered new trials for the remaining nine. As to the five, it says that the evidence is "clearly insufficient." I agree with the Court of Appeals, the District Court, and the jury that the evidence showed guilt beyond a reasonable doubt.[1] It paralleled that in Dennis and Flynn and was

---

[1] Petitioners Richmond, Connelly, Kusnitz, Steinberg, and Spector are set free.

Richmond at the time of his indictment had for many years been the editor-in-chief of the Daily People's World, the official organ of the Party on the West Coast. He had joined the Party in 1931 and received his indoctrination in Communist technique at the offices of the Daily Worker, the official Party paper on the East Coast. In 1937 he was chosen by the Party's Central Committee to be managing editor of the Daily People's World and was transferred to California. From 1946 through 1948 he regularly attended secret meetings of the state and county boards of the Party, admission to which was by identification from a special list of Party members prepared by the Party chairman or its security chief. Party strategy was mapped out at "very secret meetings" attended by Richmond and the core of the Party machinery, including at least seven of the petitioners here. Richmond served on a special committee to help develop "preconvention discussion" with petitioner Yates; he represented the state committee at the 1950 convention; he addressed many Party meetings preaching the "vanguard role" of the Party and the importance of the People's World in the Communist movement; and his articles in the paper urged the "Leninist and Marxist approach."

Connelly, a Party member since at least 1938, was the Los Angeles editor of the People's World. During the mobilization effort early in World War II he devoted his efforts to "building up sentiment against . . . the war effort" among steel, aircraft, and shipyard workers. He attended the same secret meetings attended by Richmond.

There can be no question that the proof sustained the charges against Richmond and Connelly in the conspiracy. Their newspaper was the conduit through which the Party announced its aims, policies, and decisions, sought its funds, and recruited its members. It is the height of naiveté to claim that the People's World does not publish appeals to its readers to follow Party doctrine in seeking the overthrow of the Government by force, but it is stark reality to conclude that such a publication provides an incomparable means of promoting the Party's aim of forcible seizure when the time is ripe.

Petitioner Spector has been active in the California Party since the early 1930's. He taught "Marxism-Leninism" in Party schools and was "division organizer" in Los Angeles County. He attended "underground meetings" with petitioners Lambert,

equally as strong. In any event, this Court should not acquit anyone here. In its long history I find no case in which an acquittal has been ordered by this Court solely on the *facts*. It is somewhat late to start in now usurping the function of the jury, especially where new trials are to be held covering the same charges. It may be — although after today's opinion it is somewhat doubtful — that under the new theories announced by the Court for Smith Act prosecutions sufficient evidence might be available on remand. To say the least, the Government should have an opportunity to present its evidence under these changed conditions. . . .

NOTES

1. Two weeks prior to the Yates decision the Supreme Court had held in the Jencks case that criminal defendants had a right to inspect and use on cross-examination reports and statements made by prosecution witnesses to the F.B.I. pertaining to matters about which such witnesses had testified at the trial. Jencks v. United States, 353 U.S. 657, 77 S. Ct. 1007, 1 L. Ed. 2d 1103 (1957). The Yates case and the Jencks case had a decisive influence upon the administration of the Smith Act. No further prosecutions were brought. In the Yates case the indictment against the remaining nine defendants was dismissed by the trial court upon the Government's statement that "we cannot satisfy the evidentiary requirements laid down by the Supreme Court in its opinion reversing the conviction in this matter." N.Y. Times, Dec. 3, 1957. In all other pending cases, except for one membership case (Scales), the indictments were ultimately dismissed by the courts or dropped by the Government.

William Z. Foster, head of the Communist Party, was indicted in 1948 with the original Dennis defendants, but his case was severed because of ill-health. In 1959

Dobbs, Healey, Carlson, and Schneiderman. The witness Rosser testified that these meetings were "so hid that you couldn't get to them unless you were invited and taken there." In 1946 he "conducted classes" for Party members in Hollywood, and in 1947 as a member of a committee of three Party officials examined the witness Russell, a student in one of his classes, on charges of being a Party "police spy."

Petitioner Kusnitz, following an organizational indoctrination period in New York City, became a Party leader in California in 1946, served as "section organizer," and later as "organizational secretary" in Los Angeles. Her position was directly below that of the local chairman in Party hierarchy. She attended many secret meetings and was present at a Party meeting with petitioner Yates when Yates advocated the necessity of "Soviet support" and "Marxist-Leninist training" as a means of bringing about the Soviet "type of government . . . all over the world." She contributed articles to Communist publications and was very active in the "regrouping of . . . clubs into smaller units;" conducting a "six session leadership training seminar;" carrying on campaigns for subscriptions to the People's World; and leading the "Party Building drive" for the recruitment of members.

Petitioner Henry Steinberg, active in the Young Communist League, and associated with the Party since 1936, was the "educational director." He took part in the creation of the program for the Party's training schools in Los Angeles County. His "education department" sponsored several meetings, one honoring the 25th anniversary of the death of Lenin. He worked with petitioner Schneiderman, the Party Chairman in California, attended meetings regularly, was active in circulation drives for the People's World, and was the principal speaker at many meetings.

he moved to dismiss the indictments on the ground that his health would never permit a trial. The motion was denied. United States v. Foster, 278 F.2d 567 (2d Cir. 1960), cert. den., 364 U.S. 834 (1960). Foster was never tried. He died in 1961. N.Y. Times, Sept. 2, 1961.

With respect to the eight membership cases, the Scales and Lightfoot cases, which had reached the Supreme Court at the same time as Yates (see supra), were reversed per curiam on the basis of the Jencks case, the Government confessing error. Scales v. United States, 355 U.S. 1, 78 S. Ct. 9, 2 L. Ed. 2d 19 (1957); Lightfoot v. United States, 355 U.S. 2, 78 S. Ct. 10, 2 L. Ed. 2d 19 (1957). Scales was retried and convicted again, and the Supreme Court sustained the conviction in Scales v. United States, set forth below. The other seven membership cases were reversed on appeal or dropped by the Government.

In summary, of the 141 persons indicted for violation of the Smith Act only 29 served prison terms. These were the defendants in the Dennis, Frankfeld and Flynn cases (supra), plus Scales. With the exception of Scales, no defendant went to prison after the Yates decision.

2. Two of the original Dennis defendants, Green and Winston, were still serving their sentences at the time of the Yates decision and petitioned the Supreme Court for a rehearing upon the basis of the Yates case. The petition was denied. Dennis v. United States, 355 U.S. 936 (1958).

3. In the Connecticut prosecution, Judge Anderson received in evidence the testimony of four expert witnesses presented by the defense on the issue of whether in fact the statements charged to the defendants constituted a clear and present danger. The witnesses were Professor Broadus Mitchell of Rutgers University, testifying as an expert on economic conditions; Professor H. H. Wilson of Princeton University, testifying as an expert on political and social conditions; Professor Ralph S. Brown, Jr., of Yale Law School, testifying as an expert upon security problems; and Professor Stringfellow Barr, then visiting professor at Rutgers University, testifying as an expert upon international law. The Government having waived the right to cross-examine or rebut, the evidence was received in writing. Judge Anderson found a clear and present danger to exist: "The prospect of the activities of a communist group within the United States in aid of and in conjunction with a communist nation at war with the United States cannot be dismissed as of so little consequence that it cannot be considered a clear and present danger." United States v. Silverman, D. Conn., Mar. 24, 1956 (unreported); rev'd on other grounds, 248 F.2d 671 (2d Cir. 1957), cert. den., 355 U.S. 942 (1958).

In the Bary case, supra, the trial court refused to receive evidence on the clear and present danger issue, and this ruling was sustained by the Court of Appeals. Bary v. United States, 248 F.2d 201, 208 (10th Cir. 1957).

REFERENCES

1. For comment on the Yates case see The Supreme Court 1956 Term, 71 Harv. L. Rev. 85, 123-126 (1957); Pritchett, The Political Offender and the Warren Court 21-25 (1958); Notes, 4 How. L.J. 60, 60-72 (1958); 60 W. Va. L. Rev. 91 (1957); 42 Minn. L. Rev. 301 (1957) (on the organizing issue); Somerville, Law, Logic and Revolution: The Smith Act Decisions, 14 Western Pol. Q. 839 (1961); Mollan, Smith Act Prosecutions: The Effect of the Dennis and Yates Decisions, 26 U. Pitt. L. Rev. 705 (1965); Note, 1965

Duke L.J. 369. The Mollan article contains a full account of the various prosecutions and their disposition following the Yates case. Current accounts of the prosecutions may be found in Civil Liberties Docket (published by the National Lawyers Guild).

2. On the issues arising out of the use of the conspiracy provisions in Smith Act prosecutions, see Note, The Conspiracy Dilemma: Prosecution of Group Crime or Protection of Individual Defendants, 62 Harv. L. Rev. 276 (1948); Arens, Conspiracy Revisited, 3 Buffalo L. Rev. 242 (1954), and Nuremberg and Group Prosecutions, 1951 Wash. U.L.Q. 329; Goldstein, Conspiracy to Defraud the United States, 68 Yale L.J. 405 (1959); Note, Developments in the Law — Criminal Conspiracy, 72 Harv. L. Rev. 920 (1959); Wechsler, Jones and Korn, The Treatment of Inchoate Crimes in the Model Penal Code of the American Law Institute: Attempt, Solicitation, and Conspiracy, 61 Colum. L. Rev. 957 (1961); Goldstein, The Krulewitch Warning: Guilt by Association, 54 Geo. L.J. 133 (1965).

SCALES v. UNITED STATES
367 U.S. 203, 81 S. Ct. 1469, 6 L. Ed. 2d 782 (1961)

Mr. Justice Harlan delivered the opinion of the Court.

Our writ issued in this case (358 U.S. 917) to review a judgment of the Court of Appeals (260 F.2d 21) affirming petitioner's conviction under the so-called membership clause of the Smith Act. 18 U.S.C. §2385. The Act, among other things, makes a felony the acquisition or holding of knowing membership in any organization which advocates the overthrow of the Government of the United States by force or violence. The indictment charged that from January 1946 to the date of its filing (November 18, 1954) the Communist Party of the United States was such an organization, and that petitioner throughout that period was a member thereof, with knowledge of the Party's illegal purpose and a specific intent to accomplish overthrow "as speedily as circumstances would permit."

The validity of this conviction is challenged on statutory, constitutional, and evidentiary grounds, and further on the basis of certain alleged trial and procedural errors. . . . For reasons given in this opinion we affirm the Court of Appeals.

[The Court rejected the contention that §4(f) of the Internal Security Act of 1950 constituted a pro tanto repeal of the membership clause of the Smith Act. See Subsection 3, infra.]

Constitutional Challenge to the Membership Clause on its Face

Petitioner's constitutional attack goes both to the statute on its face and as applied. At this point we deal with the first aspect of the challenge and with one part of its second aspect. The balance of the latter, which essentially concerns the sufficiency of the evidence, is discussed in the next section of this opinion.

It will bring the constitutional issues into clearer focus to notice first the premises on which the case was submitted to the jury. The jury was instructed that in order to convict it must find that within the three-year limitations period (1) the Communist Party advocated the violent overthrow of the Government, in the sense of present "advocacy of action" to accomplish that end as soon as circumstances were propitious; and (2) petitioner was an "active" member of the Party, and not merely "a nominal, passive, inactive or purely technical" member, with knowledge of the Party's illegal advocacy and a specific intent to bring about violent overthrow "as speedily as circumstances would permit."

The constitutional attack upon the membership clause, as thus construed, is that the statute offends (1) the Fifth Amendment, in that it impermissibly imputes guilt to an individual merely on the basis of his associations and sympathies, rather than because of some concrete personal involvement in criminal conduct; and (2) the First Amendment, in that it infringes on free political expression and association. . . .

[The Court concluded that "the membership clause permissibly bears the construction put upon it below." The discussion is omitted.]

Fifth Amendment

In our jurisprudence guilt is personal, and when the imposition of punishment on a status or on conduct can only be justified by reference to the relationship of that status or conduct to other concededly criminal activity (here advocacy of violent overthrow), that relationship must be sufficiently substantial to satisfy the concept of personal guilt in order to withstand attack under the Due Process Clause of the Fifth Amendment. Membership, without more, in an organization engaged in illegal advocacy, it is now said, has not heretofore been recognized by this Court to be such a relationship.[16] This claim stands, and we shall examine it, independently of the claim made under the First Amendment.

Any thought that due process puts beyond the reach of the criminal law all individual associational relationships, unless accompanied by the commission of specific acts of criminality, is dispelled by familiar concepts of the law of conspiracy and complicity. While both are commonplace in the landscape of the criminal law, they are not natural features. Rather they are particular legal concepts manifesting the more general principle that society, having the power to punish dangerous behavior, cannot be powerless against those who work to bring about that behavior. The fact that Congress has not resorted to either of these familiar concepts means only that the enquiry here must direct itself to an analysis of the relationship between the fact of membership and the underlying substantive illegal conduct, in order to determine whether that

---

[16] But compare Whitney v. California, 274 U.S. 357; Burns v. United States, 274 U.S. 328, sustaining state convictions under the organizing and membership provisions of the California Criminal Syndicalism Act.

relationship is indeed too tenuous to permit its use as the basis of criminal liability. In this instance it is an organization which engages in criminal activity,[18] and we can perceive no reason why one who actively and knowingly works in the ranks of that organization, intending to contribute to the success of those specifically illegal activities, should be any more immune from prosecution than he to whom the organization has assigned the task of carrying out the substantive criminal act. Nor should the fact that Congress has focussed here on "membership," the characteristic relationship between an individual and the type of conspiratorial quasi-political associations with the criminal aspect of whose activities Congress was concerned, of itself require the conclusion that the legislature has traveled outside the familiar and permissible bounds of criminal imputability. In truth, the specificity of the proscribed relationship is not necessarily a vice; it provides instruction and warning.

What must be met, then, is the argument that membership, even when accompanied by the elements of knowledge and specific intent, affords an insufficient quantum of participation in the organization's alleged criminal activity, that is, an insufficiently significant form of aid and encouragement to permit the imposition of criminal sanctions on that basis. It must indeed be recognized that a person who merely becomes a member of an illegal organization, by that "act" alone need be doing nothing more than signifying his assent to its purposes and activities on one hand, and providing, on the other, only the sort of moral encouragement which comes from the knowledge that others believe in what the organization is doing. It may indeed be argued that such assent and encouragement do fall short of the concrete, practical impetus given to a criminal enterprise which is lent for instance by a commitment on the part of a conspirator to act in furtherance of that enterprise. A member, as distinguished from a conspirator, may indicate his approval of a criminal enterprise by the very fact of his membership without thereby necessarily committing himself to further it by any act or course of conduct whatever.

In an area of the criminal law which this Court has indicated more than once demands its watchful scrutiny [citing Dennis, Yates and Noto], these factors have weight and must be found to be overborne in a total constitu-

---

[18] The problems in attributing criminal behavior to an abstract entity rather than to specified individuals, though perhaps difficult theoretically, as a practical matter resolve themselves into problems of proof. Whether it has been successfully shown that a particular group engages in forbidden advocacy must depend on the nature of the organization, the occasions on which such advocacy took place, the frequency of such occasions, and the position within the group of the persons engaging in the advocacy. . . . Understood in this way, there is no great difference between a charge of being a member in a group which engages in criminal conduct and being a member of a large conspiracy, many of whose participants are unknown or not before the court. Whatever difficulties might be thought to inhere in ascribing a course of criminal conduct to an abstract entity are certainly cured, so far as any particular defendant is concerned, by the requirement of proof that he knew that the *organization* engages in criminal advocacy, and that it was his purpose to further that criminal advocacy.

tional assessment of the statute. We think, however, they are duly met when the statute is found to reach only "active" members having also a guilty knowledge and intent, and which therefore prevents a conviction on what otherwise might be regarded as merely an expression of sympathy with the alleged criminal enterprise, unaccompanied by any significant action in its support or any commitment to undertake such action.

Thus, given the construction of the membership clause already discussed, we think the factors called for in rendering members criminally responsible for the illegal advocacy of the organization fall within established, and therefore presumably constitutional, standards of criminal imputability.

First Amendment

Little remains to be said concerning the claim that the statute infringes First Amendment freedoms. It was settled in Dennis that the advocacy with which we are here concerned is not constitutionally protected speech, and it was further established that a combination to promote such advocacy, albeit under the aegis of what purports to be a political party, is not such association as is protected by the First Amendment. We can discern no reason why membership, when it constitutes a purposeful form of complicity in a group engaging in this same forbidden advocacy, should receive any greater degree of protection from the guarantees of that Amendment.

If it is said that the mere existence of such an enactment tends to inhibit the exercise of constitutionally protected rights, in that it engenders an unhealthy fear that one may find himself unwittingly embroiled in criminal liability, the answer surely is that the statute provides that a defendant must be proven to have knowledge of the proscribed advocacy before he may be convicted. It is, of course, true that quasi-political parties or other groups that may embrace both legal and illegal aims differ from a technical conspiracy, which is defined by its criminal purpose, so that *all* knowing association with the conspiracy is a proper subject for criminal proscription as far as First Amendment liberties are concerned. If there were a similar blanket prohibition of association with a group having both legal and illegal aims, there would indeed be a real danger that legitimate political expression or association would be impaired, but the membership clause, as here construed, does not cut deeper into the freedom of association than is necessary to deal with "the substantive evils that Congress has a right to prevent." Schenck v. United States, 249 U.S. 47, 52. The clause does not make criminal all association with an organization which has been shown to engage in illegal advocacy. There must be clear proof that a defendant "specifically intend[s] to accomplish [the aims of the organization] by resort to violence." Noto v. United States, [367 U.S. at 299]. Thus the member for whom the organization is a vehicle for the advancement of legitimate aims and policies does not fall within the ban of the statute: he lacks the requisite specific intent "to bring about the overthrow of the government as speedily as circumstances would permit." Such a person may be foolish, deluded, or perhaps merely optimistic, but he is not by this statute made a criminal.

We conclude that petitioner's constitutional challenge must be overruled.[21]

Evidentiary Challenge

Only in rare instances will this Court review the general sufficiency of the evidence to support a criminal conviction, for ordinarily that is a function which properly belongs to and ends with the Court of Appeals. We do so in this case and in No. 9, Noto v. United States, [367 U.S. 290] — our first review of convictions under the membership clause of the Smith Act — not only to make sure that substantive constitutional standards have not been thwarted, but also to provide guidance for the future to the lower courts in an area which borders so closely upon constitutionally protected rights. . . .

First, Yates makes clear what type of evidence is not in itself sufficient to show illegal advocacy. This category includes evidence of the following: the teaching of Marxism-Leninism and the connected use of Marxist "classics" as textbooks; the official general resolutions and pronouncements of the Party at past conventions; dissemination of the Party's general literature, including the standard outlines on Marxism; the Party's history and organizational structure; the secrecy of meetings and the clandestine nature of the Party generally; statements by officials evidencing sympathy for and alliance with the U.S.S.R. It was the predominance of evidence of this type which led the Court to order the acquittal of several Yates defendants, with the comment that they had not themselves "made a single remark or been present when someone else made a remark which would tend to prove the charges against them." However, this kind of evidence, while insufficient in itself to sustain a conviction, is not irrelevant. Such evidence, in the context of other evidence, may be of value in showing illegal advocacy.

Second, the Yates opinion also indicates what kind of evidence is sufficient. There the Court pointed to two series of events which justified the denial of directed acquittals as to nine of the Yates defendants. The Court noted that with respect to seven of the defendants, meetings in San Francisco which were described by the witness Foard might be considered to be "the systematic teaching and advocacy of illegal action which is condemned by the statute." 354 U.S., at 331. In those meetings, a small group of members were not only taught that violent revolution was inevitable, but they were also taught techniques for achieving that end. For example, the Yates record reveals that members were directed to be prepared to convert a general strike into a revo-

---

[21] As both sides appear to agree that the "clear and present danger" doctrine, as viewed and applied in Dennis, supra, at 508-511, also reaches the membership clause of the Smith Act, and since the petition for certiorari tenders no issue as to the method of applying it here, we do not consider either question.

lution and to deal with Negroes so as to prepare them specifically for revolution. In addition to the San Francisco meetings, the Court referred to certain activities in the Los Angeles area "which might be considered to amount to 'advocacy of action'" and with which two Yates defendants were linked. Id.. 331-332. Here again, the participants did not stop with teaching of the inevitability of eventual revolution, but went on to explain techniques, both legal and illegal, to be employed in preparation for or in connection with the revolution. Thus, one member was "surreptitiously indoctrinated in methods . . . of moving 'masses of people in time of crisis'"; others were told to adopt such Russian prerevolutionary techniques as the development of a special communication system through a newspaper similar to Pravda. Id., 332. Viewed together, these events described in Yates indicate at least two patterns of evidence sufficient to show illegal advocacy: (a) the teaching of forceful overthrow, accompanied by directions as to the type of illegal action which must be taken when the time for the revolution is reached; and (b) the teaching of forceful overthrow, accompanied by a contemporary, though legal, course of conduct clearly undertaken for the specific purpose of rendering effective the later illegal activity which is advocated. Compare Noto v. United States, [367 U.S. at 297-299].

Finally, Yates is also relevant here in indicating, at least by implication, the type and quantum of evidence necessary to attach liability for illegal advocacy to the Party. In discussing the Government's "conspiratorial-nexus theory" the Court found that the evidence there was insufficient because the incidents of illegal advocacy were infrequent, sporadic, and not fairly related to the period covered by the indictment. In addition, the Court indicated that the illegal advocacy was not sufficiently tied to officials who spoke for the Party as such.

Thus, in short, Yates imposes a strict standard of proof, and indicates the kind of evidence that is insufficient to show illegal advocacy under that standard, the kind of evidence that is sufficient, and what pattern of evidence is necessary to hold the Party responsible for such advocacy. With these criteria in mind, we now proceed to an examination of the evidence in this case. . . . [The Court's detailed discussion of the evidence is omitted.]

We conclude that this evidence sufficed to make a case for the jury on the issue of illegal Party advocacy. Dennis and Yates have definitely laid at rest any doubt that present advocacy of *future* action for violent overthrow satisfies statutory and constitutional requirements equally with advocacy of *immediate* action to that end. 341 U.S., at 509; 354 U.S., at 321. Hence this record cannot be considered deficient because it contains no evidence of advocacy for immediate overthrow.

Since the evidence amply showed that Party leaders were continuously preaching during the indictment period the inevitability of eventual forcible overthrow, the first and basic question is a narrow one: whether the jury could permissibly infer that such preaching, in whole or in part, "was aimed at building up a seditious group and maintaining it in readiness for action at a propitious time . . . the kind of indoctrination preparatory to action which was condemned in Dennis." Yates, supra, at 321-322. On this score, we think that the jury, under instructions which fully satisfied the requirements of Yates, was entitled to infer from this systematic preaching that where the explicitness and concreteness, of the sort described previously, seemed necessary and prudent, the doctrine of violent revolution — elsewhere more a theory of historical predictability than a rule of conduct — was put forward as a guide to future action, in whatever tone, be it emotional or calculating, that the audience and occasion required; in short, that "advocacy of action" was engaged in.

The only other question on this phase of the case is whether such advocacy was sufficiently broadly based to permit its attribution to the Party. We think it was. The advocacy of action was not "sporadic," . . . the instances of it being neither infrequent, remote in time nor casual.[28] It cannot be said that the jury could not have found that the criminal advocacy was fully authorized and condoned by the Party. We regard the testimony of the witnesses, whose credibility, of course, is not for us, as indicating a sufficiently systematic and substantial course of utterances and conduct on the part of those high in the councils of the Party, including the petitioner himself, to entitle the jury to infer that such activities reflected tenets of the Party. The testimony described activities in various States, including the teaching at some seven schools, among them the national Party school. The witnesses told of advocacy by high Party officials, including that of leaders of the Party in nine States. Further, there was testimony that the Party followed the principle of "democratic-centralism" whereby a position once adopted by the Party must be unquestionably adhered to by the whole membership. The conformity of the views expressed and the terms employed in advocating violent overthrow in such States as Washington, North Carolina, Missouri, Colorado and Virginia could reasonably be taken by the jury as a practical manifestation of "democratic-centralism." Another concrete illustration of this principle could have been found in the circumstance that in almost every instance where a speaker engaged in advocacy of violent overthrow, he not only advocated violence to his audience but urged others to go out and do likewise. All of these factors combine to justify the inference that the illegal individual advocacy as to which testimony was adduced was in truth the expression of Party policy and purpose.

The requirement of Party imputability is adequately met in the record. (See note 18, supra.) . . .

The judgment of the Court of Appeals must be

[28] Although most of the particularized evidence related to events not within the limitations period, it was of course open to the jury, under proper instructions which were given, to infer that such events reflected the character of Party advocacy during the limitations period. Petitioner does not contend to the contrary.

Affirmed.

[The dissenting opinion of Mr. Justice Black is omitted.]

MR. JUSTICE DOUGLAS, dissenting.

When we allow petitioner to be sentenced to prison for six years for being a "member" of the Communist Party, we make a sharp break with traditional concepts of First Amendment rights and make serious Mark Twain's light-hearted comment that "It is by the goodness of God that in our country we have those three unspeakably precious things: freedom of speech, freedom of conscience, and the prudence never to practice either of them." [1]

Even the Alien and Sedition Laws — shameful reminders of an early chapter in intolerance — never went so far as we go today. They were aimed at conspiracy and advocacy of insurrection and at the publication of "false, scandalous and malicious" writing against the Government, 1 Stat. 596. The Government then sought control over the press "in order to strike at one of the chief sources of disaffection and sedition." Miller, Crisis in Freedom (1951), p. 56. There is here no charge of conspiracy, no charge of any overt act to overthrow the Government by force and violence, no charge of any other criminal act. The charge is being a "member" of the Communist Party, "well-knowing" that it advocated the overthrow of the Government by force and violence, "said defendant intending to bring about such overthrow by force and violence as speedily as circumstances would permit." That falls far short of a charge of conspiracy. Conspiracy rests not in intention alone but in an agreement with one or more others to promote an unlawful project. United States v. Falcone, 311 U.S. 205, 210; Direct Sales Co. v. United States, 319 U.S. 703, 713. No charge of any kind or sort of agreement hitherto embraced in the concept of a conspiracy is made here.

We legalize today guilt by association, sending a man to prison when he committed no unlawful act. Today's break with tradition is a serious one. It borrows from the totalitarian philosophy. . . .

The case is not saved by showing that petitioner was an active member. None of the activity constitutes a crime. The record contains evidence that Scales was the Chairman of the North and South Carolina Districts of the Communist Party. He recruited new members into the Party, and promoted the advanced education of selected young Party members in the theory of communism to be undertaken at secret schools. He was a director of one such school. He explained the principles of the Party to an FBI agent who posed as someone interested in joining the Party, and furnished him literature, including articles which criticized in vivid language the American "aggression" in Korea and described American "atrocities" committed on Korean citizens. He once remarked that the Party was setting up underground means of communication, and in 1951 he himself "went underground." At the school of which Scales was director, students were told (by someone else) that one of

[1] Following the Equator (1903), Vol. I, p. 198.

the Party's weaknesses was in failing to place people in key industrial positions. One witness told of a meeting arranged by Scales at which the staff of the school urged him to remain in his position in an industrial plant rather than return to college. In Scales' presence, students at the school were once shown how to kill a person with a pencil, a device which, it was said, might come in handy on a picket line. Other evidence showed Scales to have made several statements or distributed literature containing implicating passages. Among them were comments to the effect that the Party line was that the Negroes in the South and the working classes should be used to foment a violent revolution; that a Communist government could not be voted into power in this country because the Government controlled communication media, newspapers, the military, and the educational systems, and that force was the only way to achieve the revolution; that if a depression were to come the Communist America would be closer at hand than predicted by William Z. Foster; that the revolution would come within a generation; that it would be easier in the United States than in Russia to effectuate the revolution because of assistance and advice from Russian Communists. Petitioner at different times said or distributed literature which said that the goals of communism could only be achieved by violent revolution that would have to start internally with the working classes.

Not one single illegal act is charged to petitioner. That is why the essence of the crime covered by the indictment is merely belief — belief in the proletarian revolution, belief in Communist creed. . . .

Nothing but beliefs is on trial in this case. They are unpopular and to most of us revolting. But they are nonetheless ideas or dogmas or faiths within the broad framework of the First Amendment. . . .

Belief in the principle of revolution is deep in our traditions. The Declaration of Independence proclaims it:

"whenever any Form of Government becomes destructive of these Ends, it is the Right of the People to alter or to abolish it, and to institute new Government, laying its Foundation on such Principles, and organizing its Powers in such Form, as to them shall seem most likely to effect their Safety and Happiness."

This right of revolution has been and is a part of the fabric of our institutions.[5] . . .

Of course, Government can move against those who take up arms against it. Of course, the constituted authority has the right of self-preservation. But we deal in this prosecution of Scales only with the legality of ideas and beliefs, not with overt acts. The Court speaks of the prevention of "dangerous behavior" by punishing those "who work to bring about that behavior." That formula returns man to the dark days when government determined what behavior was "dangerous" and then policed the dissidents for tell-tale signs of advocacy. . . .

[5] See the Appendix to this opinion [omitted].

In recent years we have been departing, I think, from the theory of government expressed in the First Amendment. We have too often been "balancing" the right of speech and association against other values in society to see if we, the judges, feel that a particular need is more important than those guaranteed by the Bill of Rights. . . . This approach, which treats the commands of the First Amendment as "no more than admonitions of moderation" (see Hand, The Spirit of Liberty (1960 ed.), p. 278), runs counter to our prior decisions. See Lovell v. Griffin, 303 U.S. 444, 450; Murdock v. Pennsylvania, 319 U.S. 105, 108; Board of Education v. Barnette, 319 U.S. 624, 639. . . .

What we lose by majority vote today may be reclaimed at a future time when the fear of advocacy, dissent, and nonconformity no longer cast a shadow over us.

[Mr. Justice Brennan, in an opinion joined by Mr. Chief Justice Warren, Mr. Justice Black, and Mr. Justice Douglas, dissented on the ground that "in §4(f) of the Internal Security Act Congress legislated immunity from prosecution under the membership clause of the Smith Act."]

NOTES

1. Scales was sentenced to six years in prison. In December 1962 President Kennedy granted a petition for clemency and Scales was released. See N.Y. Times, Dec. 28, 1962 (Western ed.); 8 Civil Liberties Docket 75 (1963).

2. In Noto v. United States, 367 U.S. 290, 81 S. Ct. 1517, 6 L. Ed. 2d 836 (1961), decided the same day as Scales, the Supreme Court reversed a conviction under the membership clause of the Smith Act on the ground that "the evidence of illegal Party advocacy was insufficient to support this conviction." Mr. Justice Harlan, again writing for the majority, concluded as follows:

"We held in Yates, and we reiterate now, that the mere abstract teaching of Communist theory, including the teaching of the moral propriety or even moral necessity for a resort to force and violence, is not the same as preparing a group for violent action and steeling it to such action. There must be some substantial direct or circumstantial evidence of a call to violence now or in the future which is both sufficiently strong and sufficiently pervasive to lend color to the otherwise ambiguous theoretical material regarding Communist Party teaching, and to justify the inference that such a call to violence may fairly be imputed to the Party as a whole, and not merely to some narrow segment of it.

"Surely the offhand remarks that certain individuals hostile to the Party would one day be shot cannot demonstrate more than the venomous or spiteful attitude of the Party towards its enemies, and might indicate what could be expected from the Party if it should ever succeed to power. The 'industrial concentration' program, as to which the witness Regan testified in some detail, does indeed come closer to the kind of concrete and particular program on which a criminal conviction in this sort of case must be based. But in examining that evidence it appears to us that, in the context of this record, this too fails to establish that the Communist Party was an organization which presently advocated violent overthrow of the Government now or in the future, for that is what must be proven. The most that can be said is that the evidence as to that program might justify an inference that the leadership of the Party was preparing the way for a situation in which future acts of sabotage might be facilitated, but there is no evidence that such acts of sabotage were presently advocated; and it is *present* advocacy, and not an intent to advocate in the future or a conspiracy to advocate in the future once a groundwork has been laid, which is an element of the crime under the membership clause. To permit an inference of present advocacy from evidence showing at best only a purpose or conspiracy to advocate in the future would be to allow the jury to blur the lines of distinction between the various offenses punishable under the Smith Act." 367 U.S. at 297-299.

The four Justices who dissented in Scales concurred. Mr. Justice Black added:

"The conviction of the petitioner here is being reversed because the Government has failed to produce evidence the Court believes sufficient to prove that the Communist Party presently advocates the overthrow of the Government by force. The Government is being told, in effect, that if it wishes to get convictions under the Smith Act, it must maintain a permanent staff of informers who are prepared to give up-to-date information with respect to the present policies of the Communist Party. Given the fact that such prosecutions are to be permitted at all, I do not disagree with the wisdom of the Court's decision to compel the Government to come forward with evidence to prove its charges in each particular case. But I think that it is also important to realize the overriding pre-eminence that such a system of laws gives to the perpetuation and encouragement of the practice of informing — a practice which, I think it is fair to say, has not always been considered the sort of system to which a wise government would entrust the security of a Nation. I have always thought, as I still do think, that this Government was built upon a foundation strong enough to assure its endurance without resort to practices which most of us think of as being associated only with totalitarian governments.

"I cannot join an opinion which implies that the existence of liberty is dependent upon the efficiency of the Government's informers. I prefer to rest my concurrence in the judgment reversing petitioner's conviction on what I regard as the more solid ground that the First Amendment forbids the Government to abridge the rights of freedom of speech, press and assembly." 367 U.S. at 301-302.

3. As noted above, the six other membership cases were dismissed by the courts or dropped by the Government.

4. The original defendants in the Dennis case were indicted not only under the conspiracy provisions of the Smith Act, but also under the membership provisions. Upon leaving prison after serving their sentences for the conspiracy conviction they were re-arrested under the membership indictment and released on bail. Two of the defendants were permitted to take up residence in other countries, Foster and Dennis died, and the indictments against the remaining defendants were dismissed in 1963 at the Government's request. N.Y. Times, May 31, 1963; National Guardian, June 6, 1963.

REFERENCES

1. Legal comment on the membership cases appears in Note, Communism and the First Amendment: The Membership Clause of the Smith Act, 52 Nw. U.L. Rev. 527 (1957); Notes, 75 Harv. L. Rev. 40, 111-117 (1961); 37 Notre Dame Law. 239 (1961); 15

Vand. L. Rev. 279 (1961); 17 Miami L. Rev. 223 (1962); 23 Ohio St. L.J. 761 (1962); 31 U. Cinc. L. Rev. 152 (1962); Emerson, Freedom of Association and Freedom of Expression, 74 Yale L.J. 1, 9-10, 32-35 (1964); Mollan, Smith Act Prosecutions: The Effect of the Dennis and Yates Decisions, 26 U. Pitt. L. Rev. 705 (1965). The Mollan article gives a detailed account of the membership cases. For a popular account of the Scales case, see Wechsler, The Case of Junius Scales, The Progressive, Jan. 1962.

Issues concerning the disabilities which may be attached to membership in the Communist Party or other organizations have also arisen in cases involving the non-Communist affidavit of the Taft-Hartley Act, government loyalty programs, legislative investigations, naturalization and deportation, and many other areas. See infra. For continuation of the Scales discussion in a Taft-Hartley case case, see Killian v. United States, 368 U.S. 231, 82 S. Ct. 302, 7 L. Ed. 2d 256 (1961). Materials dealing generally with freedom of association and guilt by association are collected in Section E of this chapter and in Chapter V.

2. For a case holding that, in a deportation proceeding, the Government had failed to prove that the Socialist Workers Party advocated overthrow of the government by force and violence, see Scythes v. Webb, 307 F.2d 905 (7th Cir. 1962).

3. On the problem of bail see, e.g., Stack v. Boyle, 342 U.S. 1, 72 S. Ct. 1, 96 L. Ed. 3 (1951); Noto v. United States, 76 S. Ct. 255, 100 L. Ed. 1518 (1955); United States v. Flynn, 190 F.2d 672 (2d Cir. 1951); United States v. Mesarosh, 115 F. Supp. 332 (W.D. Pa. 1953).

4. For conviction by a military court of a soldier for violation of the Smith Act in fleeing to East Germany and there "affiliating" with the Communist secret police, see N.Y. Times, Nov. 1, 1953. See also Note, Military Personnel and the First Amendment: "Discreditable Conduct" as a Standard for Restricting Political Activity, 65 Yale L.J. 1207 (1956); Vagts, Free Speech in the Armed Forces, 57 Colum. L. Rev. 187 (1957).

5. The New York Times of September 30, 1949, reports a speech of John Foster Dulles, then candidate for U.S. Senator from New York, as including the following remarks:

" 'If we don't do that here' [preserve our liberty], he continued, 'we will go down with the tide and we will have our children and our grandchildren fighting their way back — a bloody way — against the all-powerful state.'

"Mr. Dulles quoted Thomas Jefferson as having said that the danger of an all-powerful state was so great that there ought to be a revolution every few years to preserve liberty and freedom.

" 'I don't believe that we need to have a violent revolution, certainly not today,' said the candidate. 'The people still have it in their power peacefully to check this thing, but if we don't do it and do it soon, we will have to fight our way back, as Thomas Jefferson said, through revolution.' " N.Y. Times, Sept. 30, 1949.

3. The Internal Security Act and the Communist Control Act

Deeming the Smith Act insufficient protection to national security against the Communist movement, Congress enacted the Internal Security Act in 1950 and the Communist Control Act in 1954. The Internal Security Act was passed, shortly after the outbreak of hostilities in Korea, over President Truman's veto. Apart from certain provisions amending the alien laws, which were superseded by the Immigration and Nationality Act of 1952, its principal features were (1) the legislative findings as to the nature of the Communist movement; (2) the provisions of Section 4(a) extending anti-sedition legislation; (3) the registration provisions, and (4) the detention provisions.

The Communist Control Act amended the Internal Security Act in certain particulars, provided that the Communist Party was not entitled to any of the "rights, privileges, and immunities attendant upon legal bodies," and listed various factors to be considered in determining membership or participation in the Party.

INTERNAL SECURITY ACT OF 1950
64 Stat. 987 (1950); 50 U.S.C. §§781-794, 811-826

Title I—Subversive Activities Control

Section 1. (a) This title may be cited as the "Subversive Activities Control Act of 1950."

(b) Nothing in this Act shall be construed to authorize, require, or establish military or civilian censorship or in any way to limit or infringe upon freedom of the press or of speech as guaranteed by the Constitution of the United States and no regulation shall be promulgated hereunder having that effect.

Necessity for Legislation

Sec. 2. As a result of evidence adduced before various committees of the Senate and House of Representatives, the Congress hereby finds that —

(1) There exists a world Communist movement which, in its origins, its development, and its present practice, is a worldwide revolutionary movement whose purpose it is, by treachery, deceit, infiltration into other groups (governmental and otherwise), espionage, sabotage, terrorism, and any other means deemed necessary, to establish a Communist totalitarian dictatorship in the countries throughout the world through the medium of a world-wide Communist organization.

(2) The establishment of a totalitarian dictatorship in any country results in the suppression of all opposition to the party in power, the subordination of the rights of individuals to the state, the denial of fundamental rights and liberties which are characteristic of a representative form of government, such as freedom of speech, of the press, of assembly, and of religious worship, and results in the maintenance of control over the people through fear, terrorism, and brutality.

(3) The system of government known as a totalitarian dictatorship is characterized by the existence of a single political party, organized on a dictatorial basis, and by substantial identity between such party and its policies and the government and governmental policies of the country in which it exists.

(4) The direction and control of the world Communist movement is vested in and exercised by the Communist dictatorship of a foreign country.

(5) The Communist dictatorship of such foreign country, in exercising such direction and control and in furthering the purposes of the world Communist movement, establishes or causes the establishment of, and utilizes, in various countries, action organizations which are not free and independent organizations, but are sections of a world-wide Communist organization and are controlled, directed, and subject to the discipline of the Communist dictatorship of such foreign country.

(6) The Communist action organizations so established and utilized in various countries, acting under such control, direction, and discipline, endeavor to carry out the objectives of the world Communist movement by bringing about the overthrow of existing governments by any available means, including force if necessary, and setting up Communist totalitarian dictatorships which will be subservient to the most powerful existing Communist totalitarian dictatorship. Although such organizations usually designate themselves as political parties, they are in fact constituent elements of the world-wide Communist movement and promote the objectives of such movement by conspiratorial and coercive tactics, instead of through the democratic processes of a free elective system or through the freedom-preserving means employed by a political party which operates as an agency by which people govern themselves.

(7) In carrying on the activities referred to in paragraph (6), such Communist organizations in various countries are organized on a secret, conspiratorial basis and operate to a substantial extent through organizations, commonly known as "Communist fronts," which in most instances are created and maintained, or used, in such manner as to conceal the facts as to their true character and purposes and their membership. One result of this method of operation is that such affiliated organizations are able to obtain financial and other support from persons who would not extend such support if they knew the true purposes of, and the actual nature of the control and influence exerted upon, such "Communist fronts."

(8) Due to the nature and scope of the world Communist movement, with the existence of affiliated constituent elements working toward common objectives in various countries of the world, travel of Communist members, representatives, and agents from country to country facilitates communication and is a prerequisite for the carrying on of activities to further the purposes of the Communist movement.

(9) In the United States those individuals who knowingly and willfully participate in the world Communist movement, when they so participate, in effect repudiate their allegiance to the United States, and in effect transfer their allegiance to the foreign country in which is vested the direction and control of the world Communist movement.

(10) In pursuance of communism's stated objectives, the most powerful existing Communist dictatorship has, by the methods referred to

above, already caused the establishment in numerous foreign countries of Communist totalitarian dictatorships, and threatens to establish similar dictatorships in still other countries.

(11) The agents of communism have devised clever and ruthless espionage and sabotage tactics which are carried out in many instances in form or manner successfully evasive of existing law.

(12) The Communist network in the United States is inspired and controlled in large part by foreign agents who are sent into the United States ostensibly as attachés of foreign legations, affiliates of international organizations, members of trading commissions, and in similar capacities, but who use their diplomatic or semi-diplomatic status as a shield behind which to engage in activities prejudicial to the public security.

(13) There are, under our present immigration laws, numerous aliens who have been found to be deportable, many of whom are in the subversive, criminal, or immoral classes who are free to roam the country at will without supervision or control.

(14) One device for infiltration by Communists is by procuring naturalization for disloyal aliens who use their citizenship as a badge for admission into the fabric of our society.

(15) The Communist movement in the United States is an organization numbering thousands of adherents, rigidly and ruthlessly disciplined. Awaiting and seeking to advance a moment when the United States may be so far extended by foreign engagements, so far divided in counsel, or so far in industrial or financial straits, that overthrow of the Government of the United States by force and violence may seem possible of achievement, it seeks converts far and wide by an extensive system of schooling and indoctrination. Such preparations by Communist organizations in other countries have aided in supplanting existing governments. The Communist organization in the United States, pursuing its stated objectives, the recent successes of Communist methods in other countries, and the nature and control of the world Communist movement itself, present a clear and present danger to the security of the United States and to the existence of free American institutions, and make it necessary that Congress, in order to provide for the common defense, to preserve the sovereignty of the United States as an independent nation, and to guarantee to each State a republican form of government, enact appropriate legislation recognizing the existence of such world-wide conspiracy and designed to prevent it from accomplishing its purpose in the United States.

Definitions

Sec. 3. For the purposes of this title . . .

(3) The term "Communist-action organization" means —

(a) any organization in the United States (other than a diplomatic representative or mission of a foreign government accredited as such by the Department of State) which (i) is substantially directed, dominated, or controlled by the foreign government or foreign organization controlling the world Communist movement referred to in section 2 of this title, and (ii) operates primarily to advance the objectives of such world Communist movement as referred to in section 2 of this title; and

(b) any section, branch, fraction, or cell of any organization defined in subparagraph (a) of this paragraph which has not complied with the registration requirements of this title.

(4) The term "Communist-front organization" means any organization in the United States (other than a Communist-action organization as defined in paragraph (3) of this section) which (A) is substantially directed, dominated, or controlled by a Communist-action organization, and (B) is primarily operated for the purpose of giving aid and support to a Communist-action organization, a Communist foreign government, or the world Communist movement referred to in section 2 of this title.

(4A) The term "Communist-infiltrated organization" means any organization in the United States (other than a Communist-action organization or a Communist-front organization) which (A) is substantially directed, dominated, or controlled by an individual or individuals who are, or who within three years have been actively engaged in, giving aid or support to a Communist-action organization, a Communist foreign government, or the world Communist movement referred to in section 2 of this title, and (B) is serving, or within three years has served, as a means for (i) the giving of aid or support to any such organization, government, or movement, or (ii) the impairment of the military strength of the United States or its industrial capacity to furnish logistical or other material support required by its Armed Forces: *Provided, however,* That any labor organization which is an affiliate in good standing of a national federation or other labor organization whose policies and activities have been directed to opposing Communist organizations, any Communist foreign government, or the world Communist movement, shall be presumed prima facie not to be a "Communist-infiltrated organization." [1]

(5) The term "Communist organization" means any Communist-action organization, Communist-front organization, or Communist-infiltrated organization. . . .

(14) The term "world communism" means a revolutionary movement, the purpose of which is to establish eventually a Communist totalitarian dictatorship in any or all of the countries of the world through the medium of an internationally coordinated Communist movement.

(15) The terms "totalitarian dictatorship" and "totalitarianism" mean and

---

[1] Section 4A and subsequent provisions dealing with "Communist-infiltrated organizations" were added by the Communist Control Act of 1954. 68 Stat. 775.

refer to systems of government not representative in fact, characterized by
(A) the existence of a single political party, organized on a dictatorial basis,
with so close an identity between such party and its policies and the governmental policies of the country in which it exists, that the party and the government constitute an indistinguishable unit, and (B) the forcible suppression of opposition to such party. . . .

Certain Prohibited Acts

Sec. 4 (a) It shall be unlawful for any person knowingly to combine, conspire, or agree with any other person to perform any act which would substantially contribute to the establishment within the United States of a totalitarian dictatorship, as defined in paragraph (15) of section 3 of this title, the
direction and control of which is to be vested in, or exercised by or under the
domination or control of, any foreign government, foreign organization, or
foreign individual: *Provided, however,* That this subsection shall not apply to
the proposal of a constitutional amendment. . . .

(d) Any person who violates any provision of this section shall, upon conviction thereof, be punished by a fine of not more than $10,000 or imprison-
ment for not more than ten years, or by both such fine and such imprisonment, and shall, moreover, be thereafter ineligible to hold any office, or place
of honor, profit, or trust created by the Constitution or laws of the United
States. . . .

(f) Neither the holding of office nor membership in any Communist organization by any person shall constitute per se a violation of subsection (a)
or subsection (c) of this section or of any other criminal statute. The fact of
the registration of any person under section 7 or section 8 of this title as an
officer or member of any Communist organization shall not be received in
evidence against such person in any prosecution for any alleged violation of
subsection (a) or subsection (c) of this section or for any alleged violation of
any other criminal statute.

[Section 5 provides, inter alia, that it is unlawful for a member of a registered "Communist organization" to hold any nonelective office or employment under the United States or any office or employment with any labor
organization, or represent any employer in a proceeding under the National
Labor Relations Act; or for any member of a registered "Communist-action"
organization to engage in any employment in any defense facility.[2]

Section 6 provides that it is unlawful for a member of a registered "Communist organization" to apply for or use a passport; or for a government
official to issue a passport to any individual knowing or having reason to

---

[2] In 1962 Congress amended this section to eliminate a requirement that the Secretary of Defense make public a list of the defense facilities to which this provision
applied. 76 Stat. 91; 50 U.S.C. §784(b).

believe that he is a member of a registered "Communist-action" organization.]

Registration and Annual Reports of Communist Organizations

Sec. 7. [Subsections (a) to (c) provide that a Communist organization shall register with the Attorney General within 30 days after (1) enactment of the Act, (2) the date it becomes a Communist organization, or (3) the date a Board order requiring registration becomes final.]

(d) The registration made under subsection (a) or (b) shall be accompanied by a registration statement, to be prepared and filed in such manner and form as the Attorney General shall by regulations prescribe, containing the following information:

(1) The name of the organization and the address of its principal office.

(2) The name and last-known address of each individual who is at the time of filing such registration statement, and of each individual who was at any time during the period of twelve full calendar months next preceding the filing of such statement, an officer of the organization, with the designation or title of the office so held, and with a brief statement of the duties and functions of such individual as such officer.

(3) An accounting, in such form and detail as the Attorney General shall by regulations prescribe, of all moneys received and expended (including the sources from which received and the purposes for which expended) by the organization during the period of twelve full calendar months next preceding the filing of such statement.

(4) In the case of a Communist-action organization, the name and last-known address of each individual who was a member of the organization at any time during the period of twelve full calendar months preceding the filing of such statement.

(5) In the case of any officer or member whose name is required to be shown in such statement, and who uses or has used or who is or has been known by more than one name, each name which such officer or member uses or has used or by which he is known or has been known.

(6) A listing, in such form and detail as the Attorney General shall by regulation prescribe, of all printing presses and machines including but not limited to rotary presses, flatbed cylinder presses, platen presses, lithographs, offsets, photo-offsets, mimeograph machines, multigraph machines, multilith machines, duplicating machines, ditto machines, linotype machines, intertype machines, monotype machines, and all other types of printing presses, typesetting machines or any mechanical devices used or intended to be used, or capable of being used to produce or publish printed matter or material, which are in the possession, custody, ownership, or control of the Communist-action or Communist-front or-

ganization or its officers, members, affiliates, associates, group, or groups in which the Communist-action or Communist-front organization, its officers or members have an interest.[3]

[Subsection (e) provides that each organization registered shall thereafter file with the Attorney General an annual report containing the same information as is required by subsection (d).]

(f) (1) It shall be the duty of each organization registered under this section to keep, in such manner and form as the Attorney General shall by regulations prescribe, accurate records and accounts of moneys received and expended (including the sources from which received and purposes for which expended) by such organization.

(2) It shall be the duty of each Communist-action organization registered under this section to keep, in such manner and form as the Attorney General shall by regulations prescribe, accurate records of the names and addresses of the members of such organization and of persons who actively participate in the activities of such organization. . . .

(h) In the case of failure on the part of any organization to register or to file any registration statement or annual report as required by this section, it shall be the duty of the executive officer (or individual performing the ordinary and usual duties of an executive officer) and of the secretary (or individual performing the ordinary and usual duties of a secretary) of such organization, and of such officer or officers of such organization as the Attorney General shall by regulations prescribe, to register for such organization, to file such registration statement, or to file such annual report, as the case may be.

Registration of Members of Communist-Action Organizations

Sec. 8 (a) Any individual who is or becomes a member of any organization concerning which (1) there is in effect a final order of the Board requiring such organization to register under section 7(a) of this title as a Communist-action organization, (2) more than thirty days have elapsed since such order has become final, and (3) such organization is not registered under section 7 of this title as a Communist-action organization, shall within sixty days after said order has become final or within thirty days after becoming a member of such organization, whichever is later, register with the Attorney General as a member of such organization.

(b) Each individual who is or becomes a member of any organization which he knows to be registered as a Communist-action organization under section 7(a) of this title, but to have failed to include his name upon the list of members thereof filed with the Attorney General, pursuant to the provisions of subsections (d) and (e) of section 7 of this title, shall, within sixty

[3] Subsection (6) was added by amendment in 1954. 68 Stat. 586, 50 U.S.C. §786(d)(6).

days after he shall have obtained such knowledge, register with the Attorney General as a member of such organization. . . .

[Section 9 provides that the Attorney General shall make the data filed with him open for public inspection and shall submit annual reports on such data to the President and to the Congress].

Use of the Mails and Instrumentalities of Interstate or Foreign Commerce

Sec. 10. It shall be unlawful for any organization which is registered under section 7, or for any organization with respect to which there is in effect a final order of the Board requiring it to register under section 7 or determining that it is a Communist-infiltrated organization, or for any person acting for or on behalf of any such organization —

(1) to transmit or cause to be transmitted, through the United States mails or by any means or instrumentality of interstate or foreign commerce, any publication which is intended to be, or which it is reasonable to believe is intended to be, circulated or disseminated among two or more persons, unless such publication, and any envelope, wrapper, or other container in which it is mailed or otherwise circulated or transmitted, bears the following, printed in such manner as may be provided in regulations prescribed by the Attorney General, with the name of the organization appearing in lieu of the blank: "Disseminated by _____, a Communist organization"; or

(2) to broadcast or cause to be broadcast any matter over any radio or television station in the United States, unless such matter is preceded by the following statement, with the name of the organization being stated in place of the blank: "The following program is sponsored by _____, a Communist organization."

[Section 11 provides that no tax deduction shall be allowed for contributions to any registered organization and no such organization shall be entitled to tax exemption.

Section 12 establishes a Subversive Activities Control Board of five members with power to determine, upon application by the Attorney General or any organization, whether an organization is a "Communist-action," "Communist-front" or "Communist-infiltrated" organization; and, upon application by the Attorney General or any individual to determine whether such individual is a member of a registered "Communist-action" organization.

Section 13 sets up an administrative procedure under which the Board may, upon petition by the Attorney General order organizations to register as "Communist-action" or "Communist-front" organizations, or individuals to register as members of "Communist-action" organizations under Section 8; and a procedure to review orders of the Attorney General denying petitions to cancel registration. It goes on to provide:]

(e) In determining whether any organization is a "Communist-action organization," the Board shall take into consideration —

(1) the extent to which its policies are formulated and carried out and its activities performed, pursuant to directives or to effectuate the policies of the foreign government or foreign organization in which is vested, or under the domination or control of which is exercised, the direction and control of the world Communist movement referred to in section 2 of this title; and

(2) the extent to which its views and policies do not deviate from those of such foreign government or foreign organization; and

(3) the extent to which it receives financial or other aid, directly or indirectly, from or at the direction of such foreign government or foreign organization; and

(4) the extent to which it sends members or representatives to any foreign country for instruction or training in the principles, policies, strategy, or tactics of such world Communist movement; and

(5) the extent to which it reports to such foreign government or foreign organization or to its representatives; and

(6) the extent to which its principal leaders or a substantial number of its members are subject to or recognize the disciplinary power of such foreign government or foreign organization or its representatives; and

(7) the extent to which, for the purpose of concealing foreign direction, domination, or control, or of expediting or promoting its objectives, (i) it fails to disclose, or resists efforts to obtain information as to, its membership (by keeping membership lists in code, by instructing members to refuse to acknowledge membership, or by any other method); (ii) its members refuse to acknowledge membership therein; (iii) it fails to disclose, or resists efforts to obtain information as to, records other than membership lists; (iv) its meetings are secret; and (v) it otherwise operates on a secret basis; and

(8) the extent to which its principal leaders or a substantial number of its members consider the allegiance they owe to the United States as subordinate to their obligations to such foreign government or foreign organization.

(f) In determining whether any organization is a "Communist-front organization," the Board shall take into consideration —

(1) the extent to which persons who are active in its management, direction, or supervision, whether or not holding office therein, are active in the management, direction, or supervision of, or as representatives of, any Communist-action organization, Communist foreign government, or the world Communist movement referred to in section 2; and

(2) the extent to which its support, financial or otherwise, is derived from any Communist-action organization, Communist foreign government, or the world Communist movement referred to in section 2; and

(3) the extent to which its funds, resources, or personnel are used to further or promote the objectives of any Communist-action organization, Communist foreign government, or the world Communist movement referred to in section 2; and

(4) the extent to which the positions taken or advanced by it from time to time on matters of policy do not deviate from those of any Communist-action organization, Communist-foreign government, or the world Communist movement referred to in section 2. . . .

[Section 13A establishes a similar procedure with respect to "Communist-infiltrated" organizations, establishes criteria for determining whether an organization is "Communist-infiltrated," and provides that a labor organization or employer so found shall be ineligible to exercise any "right or privilege or receive any other benefit" provided by the National Labor Relations Act.]

[Section 14 provides that any party aggrieved by an order of the Board may appeal to the Court of Appeals of the District of Columbia and, by certiorari, to the Supreme Court.]

Penalties

Sec. 15. (a) If there is in effect with respect to any organization or individual a final order of the Board requiring registration under section 7 or section 8 of this title —

(1) such organization shall, upon conviction of failure to register, to file any registration statement or annual report, or to keep records as required by section 7, be punished for each such offense by a fine of not more than $10,000, and

(2) each individual having a duty under subsection (h) of section 7 to register or to file any registration statement or annual report on behalf of such organization, and each individual having a duty to register under section 8, shall, upon conviction of failure to so register or to file any such registration statement or annual report, be punished for each such offense by a fine of not more than $10,000, or imprisonment for not more than five years, or by both such fine and imprisonment.

For the purposes of this subsection, each day of failure to register, whether on the part of the organization or any individual, shall constitute a separate offense.

(b) Any individual who, in a registration statement or annual report filed under section 7 or section 8, willfully makes any false statement or willfully omits to state any fact which is required to be stated, or which is necessary to make the statements made or information given not misleading, shall upon conviction thereof be punished for each such offense by a fine of not more than $10,000, or by imprisonment for not more than five years, or by both such fine and imprisonment. For the purposes of this subsection —

(1) each false statement willfully made, and each willful omission to

state any fact which is required to be stated, or which is necessary to make the statements made or information given not misleading, shall constitute a separate offense; and

(2) each listing of the name or address of any one individual shall be deemed to be a separate statement.

(c) Any organization which violates any provision of section 10 of this title shall, upon conviction thereof, be punished for each such violation by a fine or not more than $10,000. Any individual who violates any provision of sections 5, 6, or 10 of this title shall, upon conviction thereof, be punished for each such violation by a fine of not more than $10,000 or by imprisonment for not more than five years, or by both such fine and imprisonment.

TITLE II — EMERGENCY DETENTION

Short Title

Sec. 100. This title may be cited as the "Emergency Detention Act of 1950."

[Section 101 contains findings of fact similar to those made in Title I, with certain omissions and additions.]

Sec. 102. (a) In the event of any one of the following:

(1) Invasion of the territory of the United States or its possessions,

(2) Declaration of war by Congress, or

(3) Insurrection within the United States in aid of a foreign enemy, and if, upon the occurrence of one or more of the above, the President shall find that the proclamation of an emergency pursuant to this section is essential to the preservation, protection and defense of the Constitution, and to the common defense and safety of the territory and people of the United States, the President is authorized to make public proclamation of the existence of an "Internal Security Emergency."

(b) A state of "Internal Security Emergency" (hereinafter referred to as the "emergency") so declared shall continue in existence until terminated by proclamation of the President or by concurrent resolution of the Congress.

Sec. 103. (a) Whenever there shall be in existence such an emergency, the President, acting through the Attorney General, is hereby authorized to apprehend and by order detain, pursuant to the provisions of this title, each person as to whom there is reasonable ground to believe that such person probably will engage in, or probably will conspire with others to engage in, acts of espionage or of sabotage.

(b) Any person detained hereunder (hereinafter referred to as "the detainee") shall be released from such emergency detention upon —

(1) the termination of such emergency by proclamation of the President or by concurrent resolution of the Congress;

(2) an order of release by the Attorney General;

(3) a final order of release after hearing by the Board of Detention Review, hereinafter established;

(4) a final order of release by a United States court, after review of the action of the Board of Detention Review, or upon a writ of habeas corpus.

[Sections 104 to 111 provide the procedure for apprehension and detention. Any person apprehended has a right to a preliminary hearing before a hearing officer appointed by the President. "Such person may introduce evidence in his own behalf, and may cross-examine witnesses against him, except that the Attorney General or his representative shall not be required to furnish information the revelation of which would disclose the identity or evidence of Government agents or officers which he believes it would be dangerous to national safety and security to divulge." Thereafter the detainee may appeal to the Board of Detention Review, consisting of nine members appointed by the President, and from there to the Court of Appeals and, by certiorari, to the Supreme Court. Section 112 establishes criminal penalties for resisting or evading apprehension or advising or assisting others to do so.]

REFERENCES

1. For President Truman's veto of the bill, see 96 Cong. Rec. 15629-15632. The House immediately overrode the veto, 286 to 48. Id. 15632-15633. The Senate, after debating all night, likewise overrode the veto, by a vote of 57 to 10. Id. 15520-15726.

2. An exhaustive analysis of the Internal Security Act as originally passed may be found in Note, The Internal Security Act of 1950, 51 Colum. L. Rev. 606 (1951). A similar analysis of the amendment dealing with Communist-infiltrated organizations appears in Note, 55 Colum. L. Rev. 631, 674-701 (1955); Note, The Communist Control Act of 1954, 64 Yale L.J. 712, 752-764 (1955); see also Section D, infra. For other discussions see Sutherland, Freedom and Internal Security, 64 Harv. L. Rev. 383 (1951); McCarran, The Internal Security Act of 1950, 12 U. Pitt. L. Rev. 481 (1951); Frantz, Tooling Up For Mass Repression, The Nation, Dec. 12, 1953, p. 494; Chafee, The Blessings of Liberty, ch. V (1956); Notes, 39 Geo. L.J. 440 (1951); 46 Ill. L. Rev. 274 (1951); 25 St. John's L. Rev. 397 (1951); 24 Temple L.Q. 462 (1951). Discussion of the Mundt-Nixon bill may be found in Chafee, The Registration of "Communist-Front" Organizations in the Mundt-Nixon Bill, 63 Harv. L. Rev. 1382 (1950); Cohen and Fuchs, Communism's Challenge and the Constitution, 34 Cornell L.Q. 182, 352 (1948, 1949); Notes, 49 Colum. L. Rev. 363 (1949); 23 Notre Dame Law. 577 (1948). On the self-incrimination issue raised by the registration provisions, see Meltzer, Required Records, the McCarran Act and the Privilege Against Self-Incrimination, 18 U. Chi. L. Rev. 687 (1951); Notes, 1951 Wis. L. Rev. 704, 51 Colum. L. Rev. 206, 216-217 (1951); Fraser, The Privilege Against Self-Incrimination as Applied to Custodians of Organizational Records, 33 Wash. L. Rev. 435 (1958).

As to the impact of the Act upon freedom of association, see If in Doubt, Don't Join! U.S. News & World Report, Sept. 22, 1950, p. 20.

3. The appointment of the original Subversive Activities Control Board engendered some controversy. President Truman gave a recess appointment to the original five members on October 23, 1950. Upon the reassembling of Congress in November these names were submitted to the Senate for confirmation but no action was taken. The President again submitted the names for confirmation to the new Congress in February

1951 but action was delayed. On June 6, 1951, the Chairman, Seth Richardson, submitted his resignation on grounds of health. Three of the members were confirmed on August 9, 1951 but no action was taken on the fifth member, Charles M. LaFollette, who had become Acting Chairman. The LaFollette nomination lapsed with the adjournment of Congress in October. See 1st and 2d Annual Reports of the Subversive Activities Control Board 5 (1951 and 1952).

Later another controversy developed over the reappointment of Harry P. Cain, former Republican Senator. When Senator Cain became a frequent and articulate critic of the loyalty program his appointment was not renewed. N.Y. Times, July 26, 1956.

4. On October 20, 1950 the Attorney General issued regulations prescribing in detail the data to be filed by Communist organizations and officers and members of such organizations. 15 Fed. Reg. 7011. These regulations were elaborated and tightened by amendments on February 6, 1953 (18 Fed. Reg. 768), and further amended September 18, 1954 (19 Fed. Reg. 6035), and October 7, 1961 (26 Fed. Reg. 9509). See 28 Code of Fed. Regs. §§11.1 to 11.400. In their present form the Attorney General's regulations prescribe forms which require a full statement of every sum received, including "all moneys and other things of value received by the registrant from rents, sales, bazaars, benefits, socials, parties, entertainments, gifts, donations, contributions, subscriptions, subsidies, legacies, grants, or funds held in trust for the benefit of the registrant" (§§11.1(g), 11.203); and of all moneys expended, including "all moneys and other things of value which a registrant expends by way of purchase, barter, gift, donation, subscription, transfer, conveyance, lease, subsidy, assignment, endowment, or release" (§§11.1(h), 11.203). They also provide:

"(a) Each organization registered under the act shall make and keep current all bookkeeping and other financial records relating to registrant's activities, including can-celled checks, bank statements, and records of income and disbursements, showing names and addresses of all persons who have paid moneys to the registrant or who have received moneys from the registrant, the specific amounts so paid or received, the date on which each item was paid or received, and the purpose for which any item was expended.

"(b) Each Communist action organization in addition to keeping the books and records required by paragraph (a) of this section shall make and keep current such books and records as will disclose the names and addresses of the members of the registrant, the officers and employees of the registrant, and the names and addresses of persons, other than members, officers or employees, who actively participate in the activities of the registrant." §11.204.

The registration and statment forms required of individuals ordered to register under Section 8 of the Act are set forth in the Appendix to the Court's opinion in Albertson v. Subversive Activities Control Board, 382 U.S. 70, 86 S. Ct. 194, 15 L. Ed. 2d 165 (1965), noted infra.

NOTES

Following passage of the Internal Security Act no organizations registered vol-untarily. On November 22, 1950, the Attorney General filed a petition with the Subversive Activities Control Board for an order to compel the Communist Party to register as a Communist-action organization. N.Y. Times, Nov. 23, 1950 (carry-ing the text of the petition). A motion to dismiss the petition was denied, the Board stating it was not empowered to consider the constitutionality of the statute which created it. Thereupon the Communist Party filed suit to enjoin the Board from proceeding. The injunction was denied by a three-judge court on the ground that administrative remedies had not been exhausted, and the Supreme Court refused a stay. Communist Party v. McGrath, 96 F. Supp. 47 (D.D.C. 1951), petition for stay denied, 340 U.S. 950 (1951). After further motions the Communist Party filed an answer and hearings commenced before a panel of the Board on April 23, 1951.

When the Senate adjourned without confirming the appointment of Acting Chairman LaFollette, a member of the panel hearing the case, the Communist Party instituted a second suit to enjoin the proceedings. This was dismissed. Communist Party v. Brownell (D.D.C. Civil Action, 4648-51, unreported; see N.Y. Times, Feb. 6, 1952).

On June 9, 1952, the Attorney General finished the presentation of his case. The Communist Party defense commenced on that day and the taking of evidence was concluded on July 1, 1952. The record consisted of nearly 15,000 pages of testimony and 507 documentary exhibits. After the filing of briefs and proposed findings, and oral argument, the hearing panel issued its Recommended Decision, on October 20, 1952, finding against the Communist Party. Exceptions and briefs were filed and oral argument heard before the full Board. On April 20, 1953, the Board issued its Report, totaling 138 printed pages, finding the Communist Party a Communist-action organization and ordering it to register.

For summary of the above proceedings see Report of the Subversive Activities Control Board in Brownell v. Communist Party, No. 51-101, reprinted as Sen. Doc. No. 41, 83rd Cong., 1st Sess. (1953); see also the first three annual reports of the Subversive Activities Control Board (1951, 1952, 1953).

On June 17, 1953, the Communist Party petitioned the Court of Appeals for the District of Columbia for review. Subsequently it filed with the court a motion for leave to adduce additional evidence that three of the Attorney General's witnesses (Crouch, Johnson, and Matusow) had committed perjury in other proceedings.[1] The Court of Appeals heard argument on October 21, 1954, and rendered its decision on December 23, 1954. Communist Party v. Subversive Activities Control Board, 223 F.2d 531 (D.C. Cir. 1954).

The Court of Appeals overruled all objections made to the Act and the Board's proceedings and order, except that it struck two of the eight findings of the Board as unsupported by the evidence. It nevertheless affirmed the Board's order. The motion to reopen was denied at the same time without opinion. Judge Bazelon dissented on the ground that the registration violated the privilege against self-incrimination.

The Supreme Court granted a petition for certiorari and on April 30, 1956, reversed the case and remanded it to the Board on the ground that the Court of Appeals erred in not granting the Communist Party motion to reopen the case for consideration of the reliability of the evidence given by witnesses Crouch, Johnson, and Matusow. Justices Clark, Reed, and Minton dissented. Communist Party v. Subversive Activities Control Board, 351 U.S. 115, 76 S. Ct. 663, 100 L. Ed. 1003 (1956). Pointing out that the Government had not denied the allegations in the motion, and that the testimony of the three witnesses was extensive, the Court said:

"The untainted administration of justice is certainly one of the most cherished

---

[1] For the substance of the motion, see Communist Party v. Subversive Activities Control Board, 351 U.S. 115, 119-120, 76 S. Ct. 663, 665-666, 100 L. Ed. 1003, 1007-1008 (1956).

aspects of our institutions. Its observance is one of our proudest boasts. This Court is charged with supervisory functions in relation to proceedings in the federal courts. See McNabb v. United States, 318 U.S. 332. Therefore, fastidious regard for the honor of the administration of justice requires the Court to make certain that the doing of justice be made so manifest that only irrational or perverse claims of its disregard can be asserted.

"When uncontested challenge is made that a finding of subversive design by petitioner was in part the product of three perjurious witnesses, it does not remove the taint for a reviewing court to find that there is ample innocent testimony to support the Board's findings. If these witnesses in fact committed perjury in testifying in other cases on subject matter substantially like that of their testimony in the present proceedings, their testimony in this proceeding is inevitably discredited and the Board's determination must duly take this fact into account. We cannot pass upon a record containing such challenged testimony. We find it necessary to dispose of the case on the grounds we do, not in order to avoid a constitutional adjudication but because the fair administration of justice requires it. Since reversal is thus demanded, however, we do not reach the constitutional issues." 351 U.S. at 124-125.

On remand, the Attorney General not contradicting the allegations with respect to Crouch, Johnson and Matusow, the Board ordered their testimony expunged from the record. It rejected a Communist Party motion to reopen the case for additional evidence of events transpiring since the first hearing and proceeded to a reconsideration of the case on the basis of the expurgated record. None of the then current members of the Board had participated in the original decision. Following the remand the Communist Party also filed a motion with the Board for the production or inspection of reports made to the F.B.I. by four of the Attorney General's witnesses. This the Board denied. On December 18, 1956, the Board issued a revised report, again finding against the Communist Party and ordering it to register. See Modified Report of the Subversive Activities Control Board in Brownell v. Communist Party, No. 51-101 (G.P.O. 1956).

Upon appeal the Court of Appeals for the District of Columbia, in a decision rendered January 9, 1958, reversed and remanded the case to the Board. It ordered the Board to produce for inspection the reports of the four witnesses made to the F.B.I., applying to the proceeding the principle enunciated by the Supreme Court as to criminal proceedings in Jencks v. United States, 353 U.S. 657, 77 S. Ct. 1007, 1 L. Ed. 2d 1103 (1957). Communist Party v. Subversive Activities Control Board, 254 F.2d 314 (D.C. Cir. 1958).

After further administrative proceedings the Board on February 9, 1959, issued a modified report in which it readopted its first Modified Report with certain amendments, and reaffirmed its order to register. Modified Report of the Board on Second Remand in Rogers v. Communist Party, No. 51-101. The Court of Appeals on July 30, 1959, again affirmed, Judge Bazelon dissenting in part. Communist Party v. Subversive Activities Control Board, 277 F.2d 78 (D.C. Cir. 1959).

The Supreme Court granted certiorari February 5, 1960, and on June 5, 1961, nearly 11 years after passage of the statute, rendered its decision, set forth below.

COMMUNIST PARTY v. SUBVERSIVE ACTIVITIES
CONTROL BOARD
367 U.S. 1, 81 S. Ct. 1357, 6 L. Ed. 2d 625 (1961)

MR. JUSTICE FRANKFURTER delivered the opinion of the Court.

[The Court first summarizes the provisions of the Internal Security Act and the prior proceedings in the case.]

III

We come to the Communist Party's contentions that the Board and the Court of Appeals erred in their construction of the Act and in their application of it, on the facts of this record, to the Party. It is argued that both elements of the statutory definition of a Communist-action organization in §3(3) of the Act — what have come in the course of this litigation to be known as the "control" and "objectives" components — were misinterpreted below; that the Board misconceived the nature of each of the eight evidentiary considerations directed to its attention by §13(e) as pertinent to its determination whether an organization is or is not a Communist-action organization; that the Board misapplied the phrase "world Communist movement" in §2; and that the Board erred in taking account, as relevant to that determination, of conduct of the Party prior to the date of the Act. The Court of Appeals is said to have erred in failing to remand to the Board after striking one of its subsidiary findings as unsupported by the evidence. Finally, it is contended, the record as a whole does not support by the preponderance of the evidence, as required by §14(a), the conclusion that the Party is a Communist-action organization within the correct meaning of that phrase.

A. *The "Control Component."* Under §3(3) of the Act an organization cannot be found to be a Communist-action organization unless it is "substantially directed, dominated, or controlled by the foreign government or foreign organization controlling the world Communist movement. . . ." The Party asserts that this requirement is not satisfied by any lesser demonstration than that the foreign government or foreign organization controlling the world Communist movement exercises over the organization an enforceable, coercive power to exact compliance with its demands. The Court of Appeals disagreed, holding that in the circumstances of this record a consistent, undeviating dedication, over an extended period of time, to carrying out the programs of the foreign government or foreign organization, despite significant variations in direction of those programs, was sufficient. The Subversive Activities Control Board has not, in its reports, articulated any other understanding of the standard, and since its final factual determination was made after the Court of Appeals had put this definitive gloss on §3(3), we must attribute to it acceptance of the court's interpretation.

We agree that substantial direction, domination, or control of one entity by another may exist without the latter's having power, in the event of non-compliance, effectively to enforce obedience to its will. The issue which the Communist Party tenders as one of construction of statutory language is more sharply drawn in the abstract sphere of words than in the realm of fact. It is true that the Court of Appeals compendiously expressed its understanding of the Party's conduct over a course of thirty years, as revealed by this record and as found by the Board, in terms of "voluntary compliance." Opposing this phrase, the Party insists that the statute demands "enforceable control." But neither of these verbalisms was used by Congress, and neither has an invariant content. Nor has the language of the statute: "substantially directed, dominated, or controlled." Each of these notions carries meaning only as a situation in human relationships which arises and takes shape in different modes and patterns in the context of different circumstances. . . .

The subjection to foreign direction, domination, or control of which §3(3) speaks is a disposition unerringly to follow the dictates of a designated foreign country or foreign organization, not by the exercise of independent judgment on the intrinsic appeal that those dictates carry, but for the reason that they emanate from that country or organization. No more apt term than domination or control could be used to describe such a relationship. The nature of the circumstances which bind an organization to unwavering compliance may be diverse. They may consist, of course, of the sort of enforceable power over the organization's members which an employer has over an employee — the power to compel obedience by threat of discharge. But they may also consist of other incidents which assure that the organization will unquestioningly adhere to the line of conduct appointed for it. Some of these incidents are suggested by the evidentiary considerations which Congress has enumerated in §13(e) of the Act — foreign financial or other aid whose menaced withdrawal may serve as an instrument of influence, §13(e)(3); subjection to, or recognition of, personal disciplinary power of the designated foreign organs by the leaders or a substantial number of the members of an organization, §13(e)(6); obligations in the nature of allegiance owed to those foreign organs by an organization's leaders or a substantial number of its members. §13(e)(8). Other incidents may involve other forces felt by individuals or groups to be compelling: a recognition of mastery, for example, which makes criticism itself a severe sanction. The existence of direction, domination, or control in each instance is an issue of particular fact. The question whether in the case of a given organization such a compulsion or impulsion arises from the complex of ties which link it to a foreign government or organization that it will, because of those ties alone, adhere in its conduct to decisions made for it abroad, is one which Congress has committed, in the first instance, to an expert trier of fact. . . .

[The Court then summarizes the Board's findings.]

It is on the basis of these detailed findings that the Board and the court below predicated their conclusion that the Communist Party was substantially directed, dominated, or controlled by the Soviet Union. We cannot hold that they erred in the construction of the statute and in finding that the facts shown bring the Party within it.

B. *The "Objectives Component."* Section 3(3), defining a Communist-action organization, requires a finding that the organization "operates primarily to advance the objectives of [the] . . . world Communist movement as referred to in section 2 of this title." Although asserting that the reference to §2 is unclear, the Party offered in the Court of Appeals a construction of this requirement which defines the objectives of the world Communist movement as (a) overthrow of existing government by any means necessary, including force and violence, (b) establishment of a Communist totalitarian dictatorship, (c) which will be subservient to the Soviet Union. See §2(1), (2), (3), (6). We need not now determine whether this interpretation, insofar as it implies that an organization must operate to advance all of these objectives in order to come within the Act, is correct. Certainly, the elements which the Party has isolated are, singly or collectively, the major "objectives" described in §2. The Court of Appeals accepted the Party's analysis arguendo, and its judgment affirming the order of the Board rests on its conclusion that the Party operates to advance all three of these objectives. This conclusion is supported by the findings of the Board. It adopts the interpretation most favorable to the Party.

Within the framework of these definitions, the Court of Appeals held sufficient to demonstrate the Communist Party's objective to overthrow existing government the finding of the Board that the Party advocates the overthrow of the Government of the United States by force and violence if necessary. The Party argues that this finding is inadequate to satisfy the conception of overthrow embodied in §2(1) and (6); that under the compulsion of the First Amendment the Act must be read as reaching only organizations whose purpose to overthrow existing government is expressed in illegal action or incitement to illegal action; that advocacy of the use of violence "if necessary" amounts at most to the promulgation of abstract doctrine, not incitement. Section 2(1) recites that the purpose of the world Communist movement is "by treachery, deceit, infiltration . . . , espionage, sabotage, terrorism, and any other means deemed necessary, to establish a Communist totalitarian dictatorship in the countries throughout the world through the medium of a world-wide Communist organization." Section 2(6) recites that Communist-action organizations "endeavor to carry out the objectives of the world Communist movement by bringing about the overthrow of existing governments by any available means, including force if necessary. . . ." We think that an organization may be found to operate to advance objectives so defined although it does not incite the present use of force. Nor does the First Amendment compel any other construction. The Subversive Activities Control Act is a regulatory, not a prohibitory statute. It does not make unlawful pursuit of the objectives which §2 defines. In this context, the Party misapplies Yates v. United States, 354 U.S. 298, and Dennis v. United States, 341 U.S. 494, on which it relies. . . .

[The Court also rejected the other contentions of the Party with respect to the Board's application of the Act. It then held that, in this proceeding, its consideration of constitutional questions would be limited to the validity of the registration provisions of §7 of the Act.]

V

The constitutional contentions raised by the Party with respect to the registration requirement of §7 are (A) that that requirement, in the context of the Act, in effect "outlaws" the Party and is in the nature of a bill of attainder; (B) that compelling organizations to register and to list their members on a showing merely that they are foreign-dominated and operate primarily to advance the objectives of the world Communist movement constitutes a restraint on freedom of expression and association in violation of the First Amendment; (C) that requiring Party officers to file registration statements for the Party subjects them to self-incrimination forbidden by the Fifth Amendment; (D) that the Act violates due process by legislative predetermination of facts essential to bring the Communist Party within the definition of a Communist-action organization, and that the evidentiary elements prescribed for consideration by the Board bear no rational relation to that definition; (E) that in several aspects the Act is unconstitutionally vague; and (F) that the Subversive Activities Control Board is so necessarily biased against the Communist Party as to deprive it of a fair hearing.

A. *"Outlawry" and Attainder.* Our determination that in the present proceeding all questions are premature which regard only the constitutionality of the various particular consequences of a registration order to a registered organization and its members, does not foreclose the Party from arguing — and it does argue — that in light of the cumulative effect of those consequences the registration provisions of §7 are not what they seem, but represent a legislative attempt, by devious means, to "outlaw" the Party. The registration requirement, the Party contends, was designed not with the purpose of having Communist-action organizations register, but with a purpose to make it impossible to register, because of the onerous consequences of registration, and thus to establish a pretext for criminal prosecution of the organization and its members. The Act is said to be aimed particularly at the Communist Party as an identifiable entity, intending to punish it, and in this aspect to constitute a bill of attainder prohibited by Art. I, §9, cl. 3 of the Constitution.

Of course, "only the clearest proof could suffice to establish the unconstitutionality of a statute on such a ground." Flemming v. Nestor, 363 U.S. 603,

617. No such proof is offered here. The Act on its face gives no indication that the registration provisions were not intended to be complied with. None of the consequences which attach to registration, whatever may be their validity when weighed separately in the constitutional balance, is so devoid of rational relation to the purposes of the Act as expressed in its second section that it appears a mere pressuring device meant to catch an organization between two fires. . . . None of this is so lacking in consonance as to suggest a clandestine purpose behind the registration provisions. Nor does the legislative history contain any such suggestion. Rather, the Committee reports on the bills from which the Act derived express an object "to require the Communist movement in the United States to operate in the open rather than underground," and "to expose the Communist movement and protect the public against innocent and unwitting collaboration with it." . . .

The Act is not a bill of attainder. It attaches not to specified organizations but to described activities in which an organization may or may not engage. The singling out of an individual for legislatively prescribed punishment constitutes an attainder whether the individual is called by name or described in terms of conduct which, because it is past conduct, operates only as a designation of particular persons. See Cummings v. Missouri, 4 Wall. 277; Ex parte Garland, 4 Wall. 333. The Subversive Activities Control Act is not of that kind. It requires the registration only of organizations which, after the date of the Act, are found to be under the direction, domination, or control of certain foreign powers and to operate primarily to advance certain objectives. This finding must be made after full administrative hearing, subject to judicial review which opens the record for the reviewing court's determination whether the administrative findings as to fact are supported by the preponderance of the evidence. Present activity constitutes an operative element to which the statute attaches legal consequences, not merely a point of reference for the ascertainment of particular persons ineluctably designated by the legislature. . . .

Nor is the statute made an act of "outlawry" or of attainder by the fact that the conduct which it regulates is described with such particularity that, in probability, few organizations will come within the statutory terms. Legislatures may act to curb behavior which they regard as harmful to the public welfare, whether that conduct is found to be engaged in by many persons or by one. So long as the incidence of legislation is such that the persons who engage in the regulated conduct, be they many or few, can escape regulation merely by altering the course of their own present activities, there can be no complaint of an attainder. It would be ingenuous to refuse to recognize that the Subversive Activities Control Act of 1950 was designed to reach the Communist Party's operations as then reported to Congress — operations in which, the Board has found, the Party persists. But to base a determination of constitutionality on this design would be to confuse the occasion of legislation with its operative effect and consequently to mistake decisive constitutional determinants. No doubt, the activity whose regulation the Act seeks to achieve is activity historically associated with the Communist Party. From its legislative study of the Communist Party, Congress concluded that that kind of activity was potentially dangerous to the national interest and that it must be subjected to control. But whatever the source from which the legislative experience and instruction derived, the Act applies to a class of activity only, not to the Communist Party as such. Nothing in this offends the constitutional prohibition of attainder.

B. *The Freedoms of Expression and Association Protected by the First Amendment.* The Communist Party would have us hold that the First Amendment prohibits Congress from requiring the registration and filing of information, including membership lists, by organizations substantially dominated or controlled by the foreign powers controlling the world Communist movement and which operate primarily to advance the objectives of that movement: the overthrow of existing government by any means necessary and the establishment in its place of a Communist totalitarian dictatorship (§§3(3), 2(1) and (6)). We cannot find such a prohibition in the First Amendment. So to find would make a travesty of that Amendment and the great ends for the well-being of our democracy that it serves.

No doubt, a governmental regulation which requires registration as a condition upon the exercise of speech may in some circumstances affront the constitutional guarantee of free expression. Thomas v. Collins, 323 U.S. 516. In that case, the Court held that a State could not constitutionally punish for contempt a public speaker who had addressed a labor-organization meeting in violation of a restraining order prohibiting him from soliciting memberships in a labor union without having first registered as a paid labor organizer and secured an organizer's card. The decision was a narrow one, striking down the registration requirement only as applied to the particular circumstances of the case, id., at 541-542—that is, to an individual who, as the Court several times insisted, had come into the State "for one purpose and one only — to make the speech in question." Id., at 533; see also id., at 521, 526. Since this speech was the sole incident of Thomas' conduct upon which the State relied in asserting that he was an "organizer" and thus required to register as such, the Court regarded the statute, in this application, as basing the obligation to register upon speech activity alone. "So long as no more is involved than exercise of the rights of free speech and free assembly," the Court said, "it is immune to such a restriction." Id., at 540. The present statute does not, of course, attach the registration requirement to the incident of speech, but to the incidents of foreign domination and of operation to advance the objectives of the world Communist movement — operation which, the Board has found here, includes extensive, long-continuing organizational, as well as "speech," activity. Thus the *Thomas* case is applicable here only insofar as it establishes that subjection to registration requirements may be a sufficient restraint upon the exercise of liberties protected by the First Amendment to merit that it be weighed in the constitutional balance.

Similarly, we agree that compulsory disclosure of the names of an organization's members may in certain instances infringe constitutionally protected rights of association. N.A.A.C.P. v. Alabama, 357 U.S. 449; Bates v. Little Rock, 361 U.S. 516; Shelton v. Tucker, 364 U.S. 479. But to say this much is only to recognize one of the points of reference from which analysis must begin. To state that individual liberties may be affected is to establish the condition for, not to arrive at the conclusion of, constitutional decision. Against the impediments which particular governmental regulation causes to entire freedom of individual action, there must be weighed the value to the public of the ends which the regulation may achieve. Schenck v. United States, 249 U.S. 47; Dennis v. United States, 341 U.S. 494; American Communications Assn. v. Douds, 339 U.S. 382. . . .

[The Court here summarizes the N.A.A.C.P., Bates, and Shelton cases.]

The present case differs from Thomas v. Collins and from N.A.A.C.P., Bates, and Shelton in the magnitude of the public interests which the registration and disclosure provisions are designed to protect and in the pertinence which registration and disclosure bear to the protection of those interests. Congress itself has expressed in §2 of the Act both what those interests are and what, in its view, threatens them. . . .

It is not for the courts to re-examine the validity of these legislative findings and reject them. See Harisiades v. Shaughnessy, 342 U.S. 580, 590. They are the product of extensive investigation by Committees of Congress over more than a decade and a half. Cf. Nebbia v. New York, 291 U.S. 502, 516, 530. We certainly cannot dismiss them as unfounded or irrational imaginings. See Galvan v. Press, 347 U.S. 522, 529; American Communications Assn. v. Douds, 339 U.S. 382, 388-389. And if we accept them, as we must, as a not unentertainable appraisal by Congress of the threat which Communist organizations pose not only to existing government in the United States, but to the United States as a sovereign, independent nation — if we accept as not wholly unsupportable the conclusion that those organizations "are not free and independent organizations, but are sections of a world-wide Communist organization and are controlled, directed, and subject to the discipline of the Communist dictatorship of [a] . . . foreign country," §2(5) — we must recognize that the power of Congress to regulate Communist organizations of this nature is extensive. . . .

Of course, congressional power in this sphere, as in all spheres, is limited by the First Amendment. Individual liberties fundamental to American institutions are not to be destroyed under pretext of preserving those institutions, even from the gravest external dangers. But where the problems of accommodating the exigencies of self-preservation and the values of liberty are as complex and intricate as they are in the situation described in the findings of

§2 of the Subversive Activities Control Act — when existing government is menaced by a world-wide integrated movement which employs every combination of possible means, peaceful and violent, domestic and foreign, overt and clandestine, to destroy the government itself — the legislative judgment as to how that threat may best be met consistently with the safeguarding of personal freedom is not to be set aside merely because the judgment of judges would, in the first instance, have chosen other methods. Especially where Congress, in seeking to reconcile competing and urgently demanding values within our social institutions, legislates not to prohibit individuals from organizing for the effectuation of ends found to be menacing to the very existence of those institutions, but only to prescribe the conditions under which such organization is permitted, the legislative determination must be respected. . . .

[The Court then discusses other federal registration statutes, including the Foreign Agents Registration Act and the Voorhis Act.]

Congress, when it enacted the Subversive Activities Control Act, did attempt to cope with precisely such a danger [arising when secrecy itself is made an active instrument of public harm]. In light of its legislative findings, based on voluminous evidence collected during years of investigation, we cannot say that that danger is chimerical, or that the registration requirement of §7 is an ill-adjusted means of dealing with it. In saying this, we are not insensitive to the fact that the public opprobrium and obloquy which may attach to an individual listed with the Attorney General as a member of a Communist-action organization is no less considerable than that with which members of the National Association for the Advancement of Colored People were threatened in N.A.A.C.P. and Bates. But while an angry public opinion, and the evils which it may spawn, are relevant considerations in adjudging, in light of the totality of relevant considerations, the validity of legislation that, in effecting disclosure, may thereby entail some restraints on speech and association, the existence of an ugly public temper does not, as such and without more, incapacitate government to require publicity demanded by rational interests high in the scale of national concern. Where the mask of anonymity which an organization's members wear serves the double purpose of protecting them from popular prejudice and of enabling them to cover over a foreign-directed conspiracy, infiltrate into other groups, and enlist the support of persons who would not, if the truth were revealed, lend their support, see §2(1), (6), (7), it would be a distortion of the First Amendment to hold that it prohibits Congress from removing the mask. . . .

It is argued that if Congress may constitutionally enact legislation requiring the Communist Party to register, to list its members, to file financial statements, and to identify its printing presses, Congress may impose similar requirements upon any group which pursues unpopular political objectives or which expresses an unpopular political ideology. Nothing which we decide here remotely carries such an implication. The Subversive Activities Control

Act applies only to *foreign-dominated* organizations which work primarily to advance the objectives of a world movement controlled by the government of a *foreign* country. See §§3(3), 2(4). It applies only to organizations directed, dominated, or controlled by a *particular* foreign country, the leader of a movement which, Congress has found, is "in its origins, its development, and its present practice, . . . a world-wide revolutionary movement whose purpose it is, by treachery, deceit, infiltration into other groups . . . , espionage, sabotage, terrorism, and any other means deemed necessary, to establish a Communist totalitarian dictatorship in the countries throughout the world through the medium of a world-wide Communist organization." §2(1). This is the full purported reach of the statute, and its fullest effect. There is no attempt here to impose stifling obligations upon the proponents of a particular political creed as such, or even to check the importation of particular political ideas from abroad for propagation here. The Act compels the registration of organized groups which have been made the instruments of a long-continued, systematic, disciplined activity directed by a foreign power and purposing to overthrow existing government in this country. Organizations are subject to it only when shown, after administrative hearing subject to judicial review, to be dominated by the foreign power or its organs and to operate primarily to advance its purposes. That a portion of the evidence upon which such a showing is made may consist in the expression of political views by the organization does not alter the character of the Act or of the incidents to which it attaches. Such expressions are relevant only as probative of foreign control and of the purposes to which the organization's actions are directed. The Board, in the present proceeding, so understood the Act. The registration requirement of §7, on its face and as here applied, does not violate the First Amendment.

[The Court held that the self-incrimination challenge was premature and rejected the argument that Congress had predetermined the issues.]

The other constitutional questions raised by the Party have been carefully considered, but do not call for detailed discussion. And we must decline, of course, to enter into discussion of the wisdom of this legislation. The Constitution does not prohibit the requirement that the Communist Party register with the Attorney General as a Communist-action organization pursuant to §7.

The judgment of the Court of Appeals is
Affirmed.

[Mr. Chief Justice Warren dissented on the ground that "the record in this case presents four serious errors of a non-constitutional nature." Inter alia, he agreed with the Party's contention that "the objectives component of §3(3) should be construed in such a way that an organization could not be deemed to be advancing the first of the three cited objectives unless it engages in advocacy directed at prompting forceful overthrow of the Government, as distinguished from advocacy as an abstract doctrine; that the Board did not find that the Party engaged in illegal advocacy, but instead found that the petitioner merely engaged in the advocacy of force 'if necessary,' which is tantamount to the advocacy of forceful overthrow as an abstract doctrine; and that the absence of a finding of unlawful advocacy on the part of the petitioner renders the Board's order unsupportable."

Reaching the constitutional issues he agreed with Mr. Justice Brennan, whose opinion is also omitted, that the Act properly construed did not contravene the First Amendment but did violate the privilege against self-incrimination.]

Mr. Justice Black, dissenting.

I do not believe that it can be too often repeated that the freedoms of speech, press, petition and assembly guaranteed by the First Amendment must be accorded to the ideas we hate or sooner or later they will be denied to the ideas we cherish. The first banning of an association because it advocates hated ideas — whether that association be called a political party or not — marks a fateful moment in the history of a free country. That moment seems to have arrived for this country. . . .

The Court's opinion is devoted chiefly to the task of explaining why it will not decide any of the substantial issues raised by this attack upon the constitutionality of the Act as it is actually written and will actually operate and why it must decide the case just as though none of these other burdens existed and we were dealing with an Act that required nothing more than the registration of an organization. I cannot agree to decide the case on any such hypothetical basis. If registration were the only issue in the case, I would agree at once that Congress has power to require every "person" acting as an agent of a foreign principal to file registration statements comprehensively showing his agency activities as is required, for example, by the Foreign Agents Registration Act. . . .

[After pointing out that orders to register constituted "official legislative pronouncements as to the treasonable nature of those compelled to register," Mr. Justice Black continues:]

The plan of the Act is to make it impossible for an organization to continue to function once a registration order is issued against it. To this end, the Act first provides crushing penalties to insure complete compliance with the disclosure requirements of registration. . . .

In addition to these burdens imposed directly by the Act itself, the registration requirement must also be considered in the context of the other laws now existing which affect the Communist Party. The Act requires that the information obtained upon registration be given wide publicity thus insuring that those identified as members of the Party will be subjected to all the civil disabilities, criminal prosecutions and public harassments that have become common in recent years. I agree with Mr. Justice Douglas that this aspect of the Act is alone sufficient to establish its invalidity under the self-incrimination provision of the Fifth Amendment. But I think the interrelationship between the present Act and these other laws goes deeper than that, for I think that interrelationship establishes all but conclusively that the present Act cannot be upheld as a mere registration statute. The information elicited by the Act must be considered, not, as in the Viereck case [318 U.S. 236, dealing with the Foreign Agents Registration Act], an aid to the exercise of individual judgment by the people, but rather a part of a pattern of suppression by the Government, for that is certainly the inevitable effect of any system that requires registration on the one hand and imposes pains and penalties upon those registering on the other. . . .

In my judgment, the Act here under consideration is unconstitutional on at least three grounds in addition to its direct conflict with the self-incrimination provisions of the Fifth Amendment. It is, in the first instance, a classical bill of attainder which our Constitution in two places prohibits, for it is a legislative Act that inflicts pains, penalties and punishments in a number of ways without a judicial trial. The legislative fact-findings as to Communist activities, which the Court — despite the constitutional command for trial of such facts by a court and jury — accepts as facts, supply practically all of the proof needed to bring the Communist Party within the proscriptions of the Act. The Act points unerringly to the members of that Party as guilty people who must be penalized as the Act provides. At the same time, these legislative fact-findings fall little short of being adequate in themselves to justify a finding of guilt against any person who can be identified, however faintly, by any informer, as ever having been a member of the Communist Party. Most of whatever is lacking in the legislative fact-findings is later supplied by administrative fact-findings of an agency which is not a court, which is not manned by independent judges, and which does not have to observe the constitutional right to trial by jury and other trial safeguards unequivocally commanded by the Bill of Rights. Yet, after this agency has made its findings and its conclusions, neither its findings of fact nor the findings of fact of the legislative body can subsequently be challenged in court by any individual who may later be brought up on a charge that he failed to register as required by the Act and the Board. The Act thus not only is a legislative bill of attainder but also violates due process by short-cutting practically all of the Bill of Rights, leaving no hope for anyone entangled in this legislative-administrative web except what has proved in this case to be one of the most truncated judicial reviews that the history of this Court can afford.

I think also that this outlawry of the Communist Party and imprisonment of its members violate the First Amendment. The question under that Amendment is whether Congress has power to outlaw an association, group or party either on the ground that it advocates a policy of violent overthrow of the existing Government at some time in the distant future or on the ground that it is ideologically subservient to some foreign country. In my judgment, neither of these factors justifies an invasion of rights protected by the First Amendment. Talk about the desirability of revolution has a long and honorable history, not only in other parts of the world, but also in our own country. This kind of talk, like any other, can be used at the wrong time and for the wrong purpose. But, under our system of Government, the remedy for this danger must be the same remedy that is applied to the danger that comes from any other erroneous talk — education and contrary argument. If that remedy is not sufficient, the only meaning of free speech must be that the revolutionary ideas will be allowed to prevail.

This conclusion is not affected by the fact that those advocating a policy of revolution are in sympathy with a foreign government. If there is one thing certain about the First Amendment it is that this Amendment was designed to guarantee the freest interchange of ideas about all public matters and that, of course, means the interchange of *all* ideas, however such ideas may be viewed in other countries and whatever change in the existing structure of government it may be hoped that these ideas will bring about. Now, when this country is trying to spread the high ideals of democracy all over the world — ideals that are revolutionary in many countries — seems to be a particularly inappropriate time to stifle First Amendment freedoms in this country. The same arguments that are used to justify the outlawry of Communist ideas here could be used to justify an outlawry of the ideas of democracy in other countries.

The freedom to advocate ideas about public matters through associations of the nature of political parties and societies was contemplated and protected by the First Amendment. The existence of such groups is now, and for centuries has been, a necessary part of any effective promulgation of beliefs about governmental policies. And the destruction of such groups is now and always has been one of the first steps totalitarian governments take. . . .

[Mr. Justice Black then discusses various historical examples in England and the United States, including the Alien and Sedition Laws, of efforts to outlaw groups or associations.]

In the very face of the provisions of the First Amendment, however, the Court today upholds laws which ignore the wisdom of the Founders' decision to set up a limited Government and adopt the policy of force to crush views about public matters entertained by a small minority in this country. This, to me, marks a major break in the wall designed by the First Amendment to keep this country free by leaving the people free to talk about any kind of change in basic governmental policies they desire to talk about. I see no possible way to escape the fateful consequences of a return to the era in which all governmental critics had to face the probability of being sent to jail except for this Court to abandon what I consider to be the dangerous constitutional doctrine of "balancing" to which the Court is at present adhering. That doctrine is not a new one. In fact, history shows that it has been the excuse for practically every repressive measure that Government has ever seen fit to adopt. . . .

I realize that these laws are aimed only at the Communist Party. No one need console himself, however, that the policy of using governmental force to crush dissident groups upon which they are based can or will be stopped at that point. The weakening of constitutional safeguards in order to suppress one obnoxious group is a technique too easily available for the suppression of other obnoxious groups to expect its abandonment when the next generally hated group appears. Only eleven years ago, this Court upheld a governmental penalty directed at Communists on the ground that "only a relative handful" would be affected by the penalty involved in that case.[56] Today, it upholds statutes which I think totally outlaw that Party, claiming nonetheless that "[n]othing which we decide here remotely carries . . . [the] implication . . . [that] Congress may impose similar requirements upon any group which pursues unpopular political objectives or which expresses an unpopular political ideology." I am very much afraid that we will see the day when the very implication which the Court now denies is found. . . .

I believe with the Framers of the First Amendment that the internal security of a nation like ours does not and cannot be made to depend upon the use of force by Government to make all the beliefs and opinions of the people fit into a common mold on any single subject. Such enforced conformity of thought would tend only to deprive our people of the bold spirit of adventure and progress which has brought this Nation to its present greatness. The creation of public opinion by groups, organizations, societies, clubs, and parties has been and is a necessary part of our democratic society. Such groups, like the Sons of Liberty and the American Corresponding Societies, played a large part in creating sentiment in this country that led the people of the Colonies to want a nation of their own. The Father of the Constitution — James Madison — said, in speaking of the Sedition Act aimed at crushing the Jeffersonian Party, that had that law been in effect during the period before the Revolution, the United States might well have continued to be "miserable colonies, groaning under a foreign yoke." [57]

In my judgment, this country's internal security can better be served by depending upon the affection of the people than by attempting to instill them with fear and dread of the power of Government. The Communist Party has never been more than a small group in this country. And its numbers had been dwindling even before the Government began its campaign to destroy the Party by force of law. This was because a vast majority of the American people were against the Party's policies and overwhelmingly rejected its candidates year after year. That is the true American way of securing this Nation against dangerous ideas. Of course that is not the way to protect the Nation

[56] American Communications Assn. v. Douds, 339 U.S. 382, 404.
[57] Miller, Crisis in Freedom, 84.

against *actions* of violence and treason. The Founders drew a distinction in our Constitution which we would be wise to follow. They gave the Government the fullest power to prosecute overt actions in violation of valid laws but withheld any power to punish people for nothing more than advocacy of their views.

I am compelled to say in closing that I fear that all the arguments and urgings the Communists and their sympathizers can use in trying to convert Americans to an ideology wholly foreign to our habits and our instincts are far less dangerous to the security of this Nation than laws which embark us upon a policy of repression by the outlawry of minority parties because they advocate radical changes in the structure of Government. This widespread program for punishing ideas on the ground that they might impair the internal security of the Nation not only sadly fails to protect that security but also diverts our energies and thoughts from the many far more important problems that face us as a Nation in this troubled world.

I would reverse this case and leave the Communists free to advocate their beliefs in proletarian dictatorship publicly and openly among the people of this country with full confidence that the people will remain loyal to any democratic Government truly dedicated to freedom and justice — the kind of Government which some of us still think of as being "the last best hope of earth."

MR. JUSTICE DOUGLAS, dissenting. . . .

Freedom of association is included in the bundle of First Amendment rights. N.A.A.C.P. v. Alabama, 357 U.S. 449, 460. So if we had only the question whether those who band together to espouse a political, educational, literary, civic, or ideological cause could be made to register, I would protest. The late Zechariah Chafee spoke of the danger in limiting our freedoms under political pressures. "Universities," he wrote, "should not be transformed, as in Nazi Germany, into loud-speakers for the men who wield political power." The Blessings of Liberty (1956) 241. There have been attempts here to interfere by law in a myriad of ways with the shaping of public opinion through many groups, attacked because they were nonconformists of one kind or another. As we said recently, the identification of members of groups and fear of reprisal "might deter perfectly peaceful discussions of public matters of importance." Talley v. California, 362 U.S. 60, 65. There is, in my view, a disability on the part of government to probe the intimacies of relationships in the myriad of lawful societies and groups in this country. See, for example, United States v. Rumely, 345 U.S. 41, 48, 56-58 (concurring opinion); Bates v. Little Rock, 361 U.S. 516, 527 (concurring opinion); Uphaus v. Wyman, 364 U.S. 388, 401, 405-408 (dissenting opinion). From those precedents I would hopefully deduce two principles. First, no individual may be required to register before he makes a speech, for the First Amendment rights are not subject to any prior restraint. Second, a group engaged in lawful conduct may not be required to file with the Government a list of its members, no matter how unpopular it may be. For the disclosure of membership lists may cause harassment of members and seriously hamper their exercise of First Amendment rights. The more unpopular the group, the greater the likelihood of harassment. In logic then it might seem that the Communist Party, being at the low tide of popularity, might make out a better case of harassment than almost any other group on the contemporary scene.

We have, however, as I have said, findings that the Communist Party of the United States is "a disciplined organization" operating in this Nation "under Soviet Union control" with the aim of installing "a Soviet style dictatorship" here. These findings establish that more than debate, discourse, argumentation, propaganda, and other aspects of free speech and association are involved. An additional element enters, viz., espionage, business activities, or the formation of cells for subversion, as well as the use of speech, press, and association by a foreign power to produce on this continent a Soviet satellite. . . .

The Bill of Rights was designed to give fullest play to the exchange and dissemination of ideas that touch the politics, culture, and other aspects of our life. When an organization is used by a foreign power to make advances here, questions of security are raised beyond the ken of disputation and debate between the people resident here. Espionage, business activities, formation of cells for subversion, as well as the exercise of First Amendment rights, are then used to pry open our society and make intrusion of a foreign power easy. These machinations of a foreign power add additional elements to free speech just as marching up and down adds something to picketing that goes beyond free speech.

These are the reasons why, in my view, the bare requirement that the Communist Party register and disclose the names of its officers and directors is in line with the most exacting adjudications touching First Amendment activities. . . .

[Mr. Justice Douglas went on to say that the registration provisions should be held invalid as violating the privilege against self-incrimination.]

REFERENCES

1. For comment on the decision see, Note, The Supreme Court 1960 Term, 75 Harv. L. Rev. 40, 104-111 (1961); Koenigsberg, The Communist Party Registration Case, 21 Law in Trans. Q. 244 (1962); Note, 16 Miami L. Rev. 483 (1962).

2. Other federal statutes requiring registration of persons or organizations with foreign connections or engaged in "subversive" activities are:

(a) The Foreign Agents Registration Act (McCormack Act), requiring the registration of "any person who acts or agrees to act . . . as . . . a public-relations counsel, publicity agent, information-service employee, servant, agent, representative, or attorney for a foreign principal." 22 U.S.C. §611-621. The validity of the Act has not been seriously challenged. See Viereck v. United States, 318 U.S. 236, 63 S. Ct. 561, 87 L. Ed. 734 (1963); Rabinowitz v. Kennedy, 376 U.S. 605, 84 S. Ct. 919, 11 L. Ed. 2d 940 (1964). In 1951 the Peace Information Center, engaged in soliciting signatures for the so-called Stockholm Peace Pledge, and its officers were indicted for failure to register under the Foreign Agents Registration Act. A motion to dismiss the indictment was denied in United States v. Peace Information Center, 97 F. Supp. 255 (D.D.C. 1951), but the defendants were acquitted. N.Y. Times, Nov. 21, 1951. See generally, on the Foreign Agents Registration Act, Institute of Living Law, Combatting Totalitarian Propaganda: The Method of Exposure, 10 U. Chi. L. Rev. 107 (1943); Note, Disclosure Under the Foreign Agents Registration Act of 1938, As Amended, 14 W. Res. L. Rev. 579 (1963); McLaughlin, Foreign Agents Registration Act: Proposed Amendments, 40 N.Y.U.L. Rev. 311 (1965); Note, Attorneys Under the Foreign Agents Registration Act of 1938, 78 Harv. L. Rev. 619 (1965); O'Hara, The Foreign Agents Registration Act — "The Spotlight of Pitiless Publicity," 10 Vill. L. Rev. 435 (1965).

(b) The Voorhis Act, requiring registration with the Attorney General of every organization subject to foreign control which engages in political activity and every organization the purpose of which is to overthrow the government by force. 18 U.S.C. §2386. No prosecutions have been brought under this Act.

(c) The Alien Registration act, requiring annual registration of all aliens. 8 U.S.C. §§1301-1306.

3. In Bryant v. Zimmerman, 278 U.S. 63, 49 S. Ct. 61, 73 L. Ed. 184 (1928), mentioned in the Court's opinion, a New York statute requiring registration of oath-bound societies, N.Y. Civil Rights Law §§53-7, was upheld as to the Ku Klux Klan. The First Amendment issue, however, was not explored.

4. See also, in this connection, Lamont v. Postmaster General, 381 U.S. 301, 85 S. Ct. 1493, 14 L. Ed. 2d 398 (1965), considered in subsection 4. Other materials dealing with registration and disclosure, including the N.A.A.C.P. cases, are discussed in Chapter V. See also the materials on the right of assembly, Chapter IV, and the right of association, Chapter IX.

NOTE — PROCEEDINGS AGAINST THE COMMUNIST PARTY, ITS OFFICERS, AND MEMBERS FOR FAILURE TO REGISTER

1. The Supreme Court's mandate in Communist Party v. Subversive Activities Control Board was entered on October 20, 1961, thereby making the Board's order finally effective and giving the Communist Party 30 days to register. Shortly before then the Party sent a registered letter to the Attorney General on Party stationery, but signed only with the Party seal, stating that the Party's officers declined, for fear of self-incrimination, to submit registration forms or to authorize anyone to submit them. The Attorney General replied by telegram rejecting the claim of privilege. N.Y. Times, Nov. 19, 1961. On December 1 a grand jury indicted the Communist Party for failure to register. N.Y. Times, Dec. 2, 1961. The indictment contained 11 counts, each charging the Party with failure to register for one day from November 20 (the deadline) to November 30, as required by Section 7(a); and an additional count charging it with failure to file the supplementary registration statement required by Section 7(d). At the trial the Party was convicted on all 12 counts and the court imposed the maximum fine of $10,000 on each count, a total of $120,000.

On appeal the Court of Appeals reversed on self-incrimination grounds. Communist Party v. United States, 331 F.2d 807 (D.C. Cir. 1963), petition for rehearing en banc denied Feb. 21, 1964. The court said:

"The regulations accompanying §7 of the Act imposed a duty upon the Party to file certain forms signed by a natural person. To sustain a criminal charge for failure to comply, it must appear that someone was available who was either legally bound or willing to sign. Ordinarily, proof of this essential element may be supplied by presumptions that (1) an organization's legal obligation devolves upon its officers, whose failure to execute the obligation makes the organization liable; and (2) if an officer has legal justification for refusing to act, the organization can provide someone else who will act for it. The question before us is whether these presumptions apply in the circumstances of this case."

The court then reviewed existing laws, particularly the Smith Act, as a result of which membership in or association with the Communist Party "presents sufficient threat of criminal prosecution to support a claim of the privilege against self-incrimination." It went on:

"By assuming office in an organization one does not waive his privilege against self-incrimination, even in matters closely related to the organization's affairs. Curcio v. United States, 354 U.S. 118, 77 S. Ct. 1145, 1 L. Ed. 2d 1225 (1957). The privilege may be unavailable where the officer's representative duties are involved. Thus, under the 'required records' doctrine, an officer may not refuse to produce books and records *belonging to the organization* on the ground that the contents will incriminate *him*. United States v. Wilson, 221 U.S. 361, 31 S. Ct. 538, 55 L. Ed. 771 (1911); United States v. White, 322 U.S. 694, 64 S. Ct. 1248, 88 L. Ed. 1542 (1944). But in those cases, in sharp contrast to the present case, the mere act of producing the records was not incriminating. Wilson and White furnish no authority for compelling an officer to identify himself as such where, as here, such identification, without more, incriminates him. . . .

"We hold that the privilege against self-incrimination was available to the officers as legal justification for refusing to sign forms IS-51 and IS-51a. Since the officers could not identify themselves in claiming the privilege without surrendering its protection, . . . the November 10 letter was a sufficient assertion of their claim. It follows that the jury should have been instructed that the officers were privileged not to sign and that no liability attached to the Party by reason of their refusal.

"This does not exhaust the Party's responsibility. The regulations permit the forms to be signed by a 'member, employee, attorney, agent, or other person.' And it has been held in cases involving the duty of an organization to provide information that if the person selected by the organization to act on its behalf claims the privilege against self-incrimination, it must select someone else who can act without incriminating himself . . .

"These cases seem to support a legal presumption that an organization can always find someone willing, even if not legally bound, to act for it. But we think no such presumption can fairly be applied to the Communist Party. Since mere association with the Party incriminates, we cannot assume without proof that anyone is willing to submit data the possession of which implies an 'intimate knowledge of [the Party's] workings.' Whether or not such a volunteer was available is a question of fact which requires proof.

"We must therefore consider who has the burden of such proof. Ordinarily the government must prove beyond a reasonable doubt each element of the offense charged. But where the pertinent information is much more readily available to the defendant than to the government, the burden may be shifted to him, provided this can be done 'without subjecting the accused to hardship or oppression.' Morrison v. California, 291 U.S. 82, 87-89, 54 S. Ct. 281, 284, 78 L. Ed. 664 (1934). The proviso is required to safeguard the presumption of innocence. In the present case, we assume that the Party would be more likely than the government to know whether a willing volunteer was available. But to place the burden of proof on the Party would require it to prove, at the very least, that some person made reasonable efforts on its behalf to find a volunteer, and that such efforts failed. It is unlikely that the Party could make this proof unless someone waived his privilege and testified to his efforts on behalf of the Party in seeking a signer. If the burden were placed on the Party, unless someone waived his privilege the issue would be resolved against the Party by default. Thus the Party would be under duress to induce someone to waive. This is the sort of 'hardship or oppression' to which the defendant in a criminal case should not be subjected. Therefore the burden of proving that a willing volunteer was not available may not be assigned to the Party. The burden of proving that a volunteer *was* available remains with the government.

"The government presented no evidence that a volunteer was available. . . .

"The case is remanded to the District Court 'with instructions to grant a new trial if the Government shall request it; or, absent such request, to enter a judgment of acquittal.' Wright v. United States, 102 U.S. App. D.C. 36, 250 F.2d 4 (1957)."

The Supreme Court denied the Government's petition for certiorari. 377 U.S. 968 (1964).

On February 25, 1965, the Government obtained a second indictment. This also contained 12 counts, 11 alleging failure to register on each day from February 13 to 23, 1965, and the additional count charging failure to file the registration statement. The indictment also alleged that the Party "had knowledge of the identity and availability of someone willing to sign the registration form and statement" on behalf of the Party. N.Y. Times, Feb. 26, 1965. Trial on both the earlier and the new indictment opened on November 2, 1965 in the District of Columbia District Court. The Government undertook to prove that two F.B.I. informers in the Party were available and willing to register the Party. It also submitted evidence that a New York attorney, referred by the Legal Referral Service of the Association of the Bar of the City of New York at the request of the Department of Justice, was likewise available; but the trial judge ruled out this testimony on the ground that the offer was subject to agreement on a fee and other contingencies that might not have been met. The Party was again convicted and a fine of $230,000 assessed. N.Y. Times, Nov. 3, 4, 5, 16, 17, 18 and 20, 1965. The Party appealed.

2. The Department of Justice also undertook prosecution against individual officers of the Communist Party for failure to register the Party when the Party itself did not register, as required by Section 7(h) of the Act. Shortly after the decision in the main case, the Communist Party announced that it had reduced its national leadership to three officers. N.Y. Times, Dec. 1, 1961. Although the three officers were not identified by the Party, it was generally assumed that they were Eliza-

beth Gurley Flynn, chairman; Benjamin Davis, national secretary; and Gus Hall, general secretary. Ibid. In any event Davis and Hall were indicted in the District of Columbia on March 15, 1962, for failing to register under Section 7(h), each of several days being specified as individual violations (six as to Davis, five as to Hall). N.Y. Times, Mar. 17, 1962. Subsequently Davis died and the case as to him lapsed. N.Y. Times, Aug. 24, 1964. The proceedings against Hall were not pressed pending the outcome of the Government's efforts to require the Party to register. In May 1966 the court dismissed the indictment against Hall on request of the Government, "which said that a trial of Hall at that time would not serve the 'sound administration of justice.' " N.Y. Times, May 6, 1966.

3. Section 8 of the Internal Security Act provides that any person who is a member of a Communist-action organization ordered to register but failing to do so shall himself register with the Attorney General. The procedure for requiring such registration is by a proceeding before the Board similar to that involving registration of the organization. No individual registered under this provision. On May 31, 1962, the Attorney General petitioned the Board to order registration of 10 persons as members of the Communist Party. Thereafter similar petitions were filed with respect to 34 additional persons. By the end of 1965 the Board had issued decisions in all 44 cases, in each ordering the respondent to register. See Subversive Activities Control Board, Thirteenth Annual Report 6-7 (1963), Fourteenth Annual Report 6-7 (1964), and Fifteenth Annual Report 5-6 (1965).

Two of the individuals ordered to register appealed to the Court of Appeals as test cases. The court affirmed the Board's orders, refusing to rule on the self-incrimination issue, and refusing to review the 1953 determination of the character of the Communist Party in the "absence of any showing that circumstances have changed significantly." Albertson v. Subversive Activities Control Board, 332 F.2d 317 (D.C. Cir. 1964). The Supreme Court, Mr. Justice White not participating, reversed on self-incrimination grounds. Albertson v. Subversive Activities Control Board, 382 U.S. 70, 86 S. Ct. 194, 15 L. Ed. 2d 165 (1965). Rejecting the position that the claim of self-incrimination was premature, the Court reached the merits:

"The risks of incrimination which the petitioners take in registering are obvious. Form IS-52a requires an admission of membership in the Communist Party. Such an admission of membership may be used to prosecute the registrant under the membership clause of the Smith Act, 18 U.S.C. §2385 (1964 ed.), or under §4(a) of the Subversive Activities Control Act, 64 Stat. 991, 50 U.S.C. §783(a) (1964 ed.), to mention only two federal criminal statutes. Scales v. United States, 367 U.S. 203, 211. Accordingly, we have held that mere association with the Communist Party presents sufficient threat of prosecution to support a claim of privilege. Patricia Blau v. United States, 340 U.S. 159; Irving Blau v. United States, 340 U.S. 332; Brunner v. United States, 343 U.S. 918; Quinn v. United States, 349 U.S. 155. These cases involved questions to witnesses on the witness stand, but if the admission cannot be compelled in oral testimony, we do not see how compulsion in writing makes a difference for constitutional purposes. Cf. New York ex rel. Ferguson v. Reardon, 197 N.Y. 236, 243-244, 90 N.E. 829, 832. It follows that the requirement to accomplish registration by completing and filing Form IS-52a is inconsistent with the protection of the Self-Incrimination Clause. . . .

"Like the admission of Party membership demanded by Form IS-52a, the information called for by Form IS-52 — the organization of which the registrant is a member, his aliases, place and date of birth, a list of offices held in the Organization and duties thereof — might be used as evidence in or at least supply investigatory leads to a criminal prosecution." 382 U.S. at 77-78.

The Court then held that Section 4(f), "the purported immunity provision, does not save the registration orders" because "the immunity granted by §4(f) is not complete." In that connection it added:

"The Government does not contend that the shortcoming of §4(f) is remedied in regard to information called for on the registration statement, Form IS-52. With respect to Form IS-52a, however, the argument is made that, since an order to register is preceded by a Board finding of Party membership, the admission of membership required on that form would be of no investigatory value and thus is not 'incriminatory' within the meaning of the Fifth Amendment privilege. On this view the incompleteness of the §4(f) grant of immunity would be rendered immaterial and the admission of Party membership could be compelled without violating the privilege. We disagree. The judgment as to whether a disclosure would be 'incriminatory' has never been made dependent on an assessment of the information possessed by the Government at the time of interrogation; the protection of the privilege would be seriously impaired if the right to invoke it was dependent on such an assessment, with all its uncertainties." 382 U.S. at 81.

REFERENCES

For comment on the operation of the privilege against self-incrimination in the administration of the Internal Security Act see, in addition to the earlier materials cited above, Blake, Self-Incrimination, Registration Statutes, and George Washington's Cherry Tree, 23 Law in Trans. 197 (1963); Notes, 15 U. Fla. L. Rev. 435 (1962); 42 Texas L. Rev. 891 (1964); 16 W. Res. L. Rev. 206 (1964).

NOTE — PROCEEDINGS AGAINST ALLEGED COMMUNIST-FRONT AND COMMUNIST-INFILTRATED ORGANIZATIONS

Two days after the first decision of the Subversive Activities Control Board in the Communist Party case, on April 22, 1953, the Attorney General petitioned the Board for orders requiring 12 organizations to register as Communist-front organizations. Another petition was filed in 1954, five more in 1955 (including two directed against labor unions alleged to be Communist-infiltrated organizations), and five in 1956. After a lapse of some years an additional petition was filed in 1963, and one more in 1966. The 1966 petition, against the W.E.B. DuBois Clubs of America, had not been acted upon by the Board as of June 1966.[1] The disposition of the 24 other petitions is as follows:

Of the 22 petitions asking registration of alleged Communist-front organizations, eight cases were dismissed by the Board. These were the proceedings against

[1] On April 26, 1966, the DuBois clubs and various individuals brought suit in the District Court for the District of Columbia to enjoin the Attorney General and the Board from proceeding further in the matter. W.E.B. DuBois Clubs of America v. Katzenbach.

the International Workers Order, dismissed on order of the Court of Appeals for the District of Columbia on the ground that the New York courts had ordered its dissolution; the American Slav Congress and the Committee for a Democratic Far Eastern Policy, found by the Board to have dissolved prior to filing of the Attorney General's petition; and the Joint Anti-Fascist Refugee Committee, the Council on African Affairs, the National Negro Labor Council, the Save our Sons Committee, and the Committee to End Sedition Laws, dismissed on motion of the Attorney General. None of the last five continued to function either.

In the 14 remaining Communist-front cases the Board issued orders to register. In two of these cases — the Connecticut Volunteers for Civil Rights and the California Emergency Defense Committee — the organizations had ceased to operate and took no appeal to the courts. The Board's orders thus became final; but neither organization registered and no further action was taken. In the Advance and Burning Issues Youth Organizations case (the 1963 petition) the Board was informed in 1965 that the organization had dissolved and it issued an order "placing the case in the status of indefinite abeyance." The organization did not register.

In the remaining 11 cases appeals were filed in the Court of Appeals for the District of Columbia. In seven of these cases the organizations or their representatives filed motions to vacate the Board's order on the ground that the organization had dissolved and the proceedings became moot. The court remanded the cases to the Board for hearings and findings on the dissolution issue. On return of the proceedings to the Court of Appeals the court rejected the Board's contention that, even though the organization had dissolved, the Board's order should be affirmed and go into effect. The court reasoned that registration of non-existent organizations would be "meaningless exercises," and that "persons who once were members would live under heavy clouds of threats from which no relief would be available." It disposed of the seven cases as follows:

In three cases where the court found that the organization had in fact dissolved, it refused to vacate the order but remanded the proceedings to the Board "with instructions to place it in an indefinitely inactive status." Labor Youth League v. Subversive Activities Control Board, 322 F.2d 364 (D.C. Cir. 1963); Blau v. Subversive Activities Control Board, 322 F.2d 397 (D.C. Cir. 1963) (involving the Colorado Committee to Protect Civil Liberties); Haufrecht v. Subversive Activities Control Board, 322 F.2d 403 (D.C. Cir. 1963) (involving the American Peace Crusade). In a fourth case, involving a corporation which had formally dissolved, the court dismissed the petition to review the Board's order for lack of a party-petitioner. Washington Pension Union v. Subversive Activities Control Board, 322 F.2d 398 (D.C. Cir. 1963). In the remaining three cases the court found that the organizations, while inactive, had not proved dissolution. In two of these cases it denied the motion to dismiss, but allowed the organization further time to pursue its appeal. California Labor School v. Subversive Activities Control Board, 322 F.2d 393 (D.C. Cir. 1963); Patterson v. Subversive Activities Control Board, 322 F.2d 395 (D.C. Cir. 1963) (involving the Civil Rights Congress). In neither case was the appeal pursued. In the other case the court ruled on the merits and affirmed the Board's order, holding the registration provisions constitutional on the basis of the Supreme Court's decision in the main Communist Party registration case. Jefferson School of Social Science v. Subversive Activities Control Board, 331 F.2d

76 (D.C. Cir. 1963) (Judge Bazelon dissenting, on the dissolution issue). In none of these cases did the organization register; nor was any further action taken.

In the remaining four cases the issue of dissolution was not raised. In one the court set aside the Board's order on the ground that the Government had failed to establish that the organization was at the time of hearing "substantially directed, dominated or controlled" by a Communist-action organization. National Council of American-Soviet Friendship v. Subversive Activities Control Board, 322 F.2d 375 (D.C. Cir. 1963). In the three other cases it affirmed the Board's order. American Committee for Protection of Foreign Born v. Subversive Activities Control Board, 331 F.2d 53 (D.C. Cir. 1963) (Judge Bazelon dissenting); Veterans of the Abraham Lincoln Brigade v. Subversive Activities Control Board, 331 F.2d 64 (D.C. Cir. 1963) (Judge Bazelon dissenting); Weinstock v. Subversive Activities Control Board, 331 F.2d 75 (D.C. Cir. 1963) (Judge Bazelon concurring; involving the United May Day Committee). On the constitutional issues the court relied, without elaboration, on the Supreme Court's decision in the main Communist Party case.

The United May Day Committee had, in fact, become inactive and no further proceedings were taken in that case. The American Committee for Protection of Foreign Born and the Veterans of the Abraham Lincoln Brigade petitioned the Supreme Court for certiorari. The Supreme Court, per curiam, vacated the judgments of the Court of Appeals and remanded the cases to the Board on the ground that the records were "stale," Justices Douglas, Black, and Harlan dissenting. Without expressing any views on the constitutional issues, the per curiam opinion stated: "Our Communist Party decision on the Communist-action provisions did not necessarily foreclose petitioner's constitutional questions bearing on the Communist-front provisions." American Committee for Protection of Foreign Born v. Subversive Activities Control Board, 380 U.S. 503, 505, 85 S. Ct. 1148, 14 L. Ed. 2d 39 (1965); Veterans of the Abraham Lincoln Brigade v. Subversive Activities Control Board, 380 U.S. 513, 85 S. Ct. 1148, 14 L. Ed. 2d 46 (1965). In April 1966 the Subversive Activities Control Board, with the agreement of the Attorney General, vacated its earlier orders and dismissed the petitions as to both the American Committee for Protection of Foreign Born and the Veterans of the Abraham Lincoln Brigade. (S.A.C.B. orders of April 6 and 20, 1966.)

As noted above, two Communist-infiltrated proceedings were filed by the Attorney General. One, involving the United Electrical, Radio and Machine Workers of America, was dismissed by the Board, before hearing, on the Attorney General's motion. In the other case, against the International Union of Mine, Mill and Smelter Workers, the Board issued an order on May 4, 1962, finding that organization to be Communist-infiltrated. The Union filed a petition for review in the Court of Appeals. Thereafter it moved before the Board under Section 13 (A)(b) for a determination that the Union no longer was a Communist-infiltrated organization. The Board denied this motion on December 20, 1963, and the Union filed an appeal from that ruling also. In June 1966, however, the Board, with the agreement of the Attorney General, vacated its order and dismissed the petition. (S.A.C.B. order of June 16, 1966.)

In summary, no organization has been finally required to register as a Communist-front or Communist-infiltrated organization. Presumably issues of self-incrimination would be similar to those in the case of Communist-action organizations. Of the 23 alleged Communist-front organizations against which proceedings have been brought, 19 have ceased to function.

REFERENCES

The various proceedings in the registration cases are set forth in the annual reports of the Subversive Activities Control Board; the annual reports of the Attorney General to the President and the Congress of the United States; and the Civil Liberties Docket. For other comment see Subversive Activities Control Act of 1950, Report of the Subcommittee (of the Senate Judiciary Committee) to Investigate the Administration of the Internal Security Act and other Internal Security Laws, 84th Cong., 1st Sess. (1955); Note, Some Constitutional and Practical Problems of the Subversive Activities Control Act, 46 Geo. L.J. 299 (1957-1958); McKay, Review of Brownell v. Veterans of the Abraham Lincoln Brigade, 6 J. Pub. L. 236 (1957); Note, The Registration of Communist-Front Organizations: The Statutory Framework and the Constitutional Issue, 113 U. Pa. L. Rev. 1270 (1965); Note, 1965 Duke L.J. 369. A detailed analysis of the Court of Appeals decisions in the American Committee and Veterans cases appears in Note, Congress and the Communist Monolith: Communist Front Organizations under the Internal Security Act, 74 Yale L.J. 738 (1965).

An effort by the United Electrical Workers to enjoin the proceeding against it was rejected by the District Court and the Court of Appeals for the District of Columbia on the ground it had not exhausted its administrative remedies. U.E.R. & M.W. v. Brownell, 232 F.2d 687 (D.C. Cir. 1956).

NOTE — OTHER PROCEEDINGS UNDER THE INTERNAL SECURITY ACT

No prosecutions have been instituted under Section 4(a) of the Internal Security Act.

After the Supreme Court's decision in Communist Party v. Subversive Activities Control Board a number of proceedings were brought involving Section 6 of the Internal Security Act, which prohibits the granting or use of passports by members of organizations ordered to register. In Aptheker v. Secretary of State, 378 U.S. 500, 84 S. Ct. 1659, 12 L. Ed. 2d 992 (1964), the Supreme Court held Section 6 unconstitutional on the ground that it "too broadly and indiscriminately restricts the right to travel and thereby abridges the liberty guaranteed by the Fifth Amendment." 378 U.S. at 505. See also Mayer v. Rusk, 224 F. Supp. 929 (D. D.C. 1963), remanded in light of Aptheker, 378 U.S. 579 (1964); and Copeland v. Secretary of State, 226 F. Supp. 20 (S.D. N.Y. 1964), also remanded in light of Aptheker, 378 U.S. 588 (1964). The passport cases are considered in Chapter XI.

In United States v. Robel a shipyard worker was indicted under Section 5 of the Act for engaging in defense work while a member of the Communist Party and knowing the registration order was in effect. The indictment was dismissed by the District Court. 254 F. Supp. 291 (W.D. Wash. 1965). An appeal was taken to the Supreme Court and probable jurisdiction was noted, 384 U.S. 937 (1966).

As of June, 1966, there appear to be no other reported cases involving proceedings to apply other sanctions attaching to a final order of registration.

The detention provisions of Title II have never gone into operation. With funds provided in its 1951-1952 appropriations the Department of Justice rehabilitated six World War II installations to serve as detention camps in the event Title II came into effect. N.Y. Times, Jan. 1, 1962; American Civil Liberties Union Weekly Bulletin, Jan. 28, 1952; see also Hearings before Subcommittee of the House Committee on Appropriations on Department of Justice Appropriations Act for Fiscal Year 1952, 82nd Cong., 1st Sess. 483, 489 (1951); same hearings for 1953, 82nd Cong., 2d Sess., 219 (1952). The camps were maintained for a time on a standby basis by the Federal Bureau of Prisons of the Department of Justice. In December 1955 the New York Times, in an article describing the camps, reported: ". . . there are six camps needing only about as much work as would be required to make the beds and light the fires ready to receive those deemed dangerous to security if a national emergency rises." N.Y. Times, Dec. 27, 1955. In 1963 the Department of Justice stated that the camps had been abandoned or turned to other uses five years before. American Civil Liberties Union Weekly Bulletin, Feb. 11, 1963.

REFERENCES

On the detention provisions generally, see Note, The Internal Security Act of 1950, 51 Colum. L. Rev. 606, 646-657 (1951); Dunbar, Beyond Korematsu: The Emergency Detention Act of 1950, 13 U. Pitt. L. Rev. 221 (1952); O'Brian, Changing Attitudes Toward Freedom, 9 Wash. and Lee L. Rev. 157, 167-8 (1952); Note, The Constitution and the Emergency Detention Act of 1950, 13 Buffalo L. Rev. 477 (1964). See also Brecht, The Concentration Camp, 50 Colum. L. Rev. 761 (1950). For a discussion of British legislation interning enemy aliens during World War II (which served in part as a model for Title II of the Internal Security Act) see Cohn, Legal Aspects of Internment, 4 Modern L. Rev. 200 (1941); Cotter, Emergency Detention in War-Time: The British Experience, 6 Stan. L. Rev. 238 (1954). On India, see Tripathi, Preventive Detention: The Indian Experience, 9 Am. J. Comp. L. 219 (1960).

COMMUNIST CONTROL ACT OF 1954

Among a series of measures passed by Congress in 1954 dealing with national security, the most far-reaching was the Communist Control Act. Those provisions of the Act which amended the Internal Security Act have been set forth above. The remaining provisions follow.

COMMUNIST CONTROL ACT OF 1954
68 Stat. 775 (1954); 50 U.S.C. §§841-844

Findings of Fact

Sec. 2. The Congress hereby finds and declares that the Communist Party of the United States, although purportedly a political party, is in fact an instrumentality of a conspiracy to overthrow the Government of the United States. It constitutes an authoritarian dictatorship within a republic, demand-

ing for itself the rights and privileges accorded to political parties, but denying to all others the liberties guaranteed by the Constitution. Unlike political
parties, which evolve their policies and programs through public means, by
the reconciliation of a wide variety of individual views, and submit those
policies and programs to the electorate at large for approval or disapproval,
the policies and programs of the Communist Party are secretly prescribed for
it by the foreign leaders of the world Communist movement. Its members
have no part in determining its goals, and are not permitted to voice dissent
to party objectives. Unlike members of political parties, members of the
Communist Party are recruited for indoctrination with respect to its objectives and methods, and are organized, instructed, and disciplined to carry into
action slavishly the assignments given them by their hierarchical chieftains.
Unlike political parties, the Communist Party acknowledges no constitutional or statutory limitations upon its conduct or upon that of its members.
The Communist Party is relatively small numerically, and gives scant indication of capacity ever to attain its ends by lawful political means. The peril
inherent in its operation arises not from its numbers, but from its failure to
acknowledge any limitation as to the nature of its activities, and its dedication
to the proposition that the present constitutional Government of the United
States ultimately must be brought to ruin by any available means, including
resort to force and violence. Holding that doctrine, its role as the agency of a
hostile foreign power renders its existence a clear present and continuing
danger to the security of the United States. It is the means whereby individuals are seduced into the service of the world Communist movement, trained
to do its bidding, and directed and controlled in the conspiratorial performance of their revolutionary services. Therefore, the Communist Party should
be outlawed.

Proscribed Organizations

Sec. 3. The Communist Party of the United States, or any successors of
such party regardless of the assumed name, whose object or purpose is to
overthrow the Government of the United States, or the government of any
State, Territory, District, or possession thereof, or the government of any political subdivision therein by force and violence, are not entitled to any of the
rights, privileges, and immunities attendant upon legal bodies created under
the jurisdiction of the laws of the United States or any political subdivision
thereof; and whatever rights, privileges, and immunities which have heretofore been granted to said party or any subsidiary organization by reason of
the laws of the United States or any political subdivision thereof, are hereby
terminated: *Provided, however,* That nothing in this section shall be construed as amending the Internal Security Act of 1950, as amended.

Sec. 4. Whoever knowingly and willfully becomes or remains a member of
(1) the Communist Party, or (2) any other organization having for one of its

purposes or objectives the establishment, control, conduct, seizure, or over-throw of the Government of the United States, or the government of any State or political subdivision thereof, by the use of force or violence, with knowledge of the purpose or objective of such organization shall be subject to all the provisions and penalties of the Internal Security Act of 1950, as amended, as a member of a "Communist-action" organization.

(b) For the purposes of this section, the term "Communist Party" means the organization now known as the Communist Party of the United States of America, the Communist Party of any State or subdivision thereof, and any unit or subdivision of any such organization, whether or not any change is hereafter made in the name thereof.

Sec. 5. In determining membership or participation in the Communist Party or any other organization defined in this Act, or knowledge of the purpose or objective of such party or organization, the jury, under instructions from the court, shall consider evidence, if presented, as to whether the accused person:

(1) Has been listed to his knowledge as a member in any book or any of the lists, records, correspondence, or any other document of the organization;

(2) Has made financial contribution to the organization in dues, assessments, loans, or in any other form;

(3) Has made himself subject to the discipline of the organization in any form whatsoever;

(4) Has executed orders, plans, or directives of any kind of the organization;

(5) Has acted as an agent, courier, messenger, correspondent, organizer, or in any other capacity in behalf of the organization;

(6) Has conferred with officers or other members of the organization in behalf of any plan or enterprise of the organization;

(7) Has been accepted to his knowledge as an officer or member of the organization or as one to be called upon for services by other officers or members of the organization;

(8) Has written, spoken or in any other way communicated by signal, semaphore, sign, or in any other form of communication orders, directives, or plans of the organization;

(9) Has prepared documents, pamphlets, leaflets, books, or any other type of publication in behalf of the objectives and purposes of the organization;

(10) Has mailed, shipped, circulated, distributed, delivered, or in any other way sent or delivered to others material or propaganda of any kind in behalf of the organization;

(11) Has advised, counseled or in any other way imparted information, suggestions, recommendations to officers or members of the organization or to anyone else in behalf of the objectives of the organization;

(12) Has indicated by word, action, conduct, writing or in any other way a

willingness to carry out in any manner and to any degree the plans, designs, objectives, or purposes of the organization;

(13) Has in any other way participated in the activities, planning, actions, objectives, or purposes of the organization;

(14) The enumeration of the above subjects of evidence on membership or participation in the Communist Party or any other organization as above defined, shall not limit the inquiry into and consideration of any other subject of evidence on membership and participation as herein stated.

REFERENCES

1. The legislative history of the Act is described in Note, The Communist Control Act of 1954, 64 Yale L.J. 712, 713-714 (1955). See also Note, Federal Anti-Subversive Legislation of 1954, 55 Colum. L. Rev. 631, 701-703, 730-731 (1955); Note, Federal Anti-Subversive Legislation — The Communist Control Act of 1954, 53 Mich. L. Rev. 1153, 1154-1157 (1955).

2. For analysis and discussion, see Notes, supra, 64 Yale L.J. 712, 55 Colum. L. Rev. at 701-731, and 53 Mich. L. Rev. 1153; Auerbach, The Communist Control Act of 1954: A Proposed Legal-Political Theory of Free Speech, 23 U. Chi. L. Rev. 173 (1956); Chase, The Libertarian Case for Making It a Crime to Be a Communist, 29 Temple L.Q. 121 (1956).

NOTE

Only two cases appear to have been decided by the courts under the above provisions of the Communist Control Act. In Salwen v. Rees, 16 N.J. 216, 108 A. 2d 265 (1954), Section 3 was upheld as the basis for denying a candidate the right to appear on the ballot under the Communist Party label in a local election. See Auerbach, Note 2 supra, 23 U. Chi. L. Rev. at 175; Notes, supra, 55 Colum. L. Rev. at 707-708; 53 Mich. L. Rev. at 1159-1161. The case did not reach the Supreme Court. In 1964 the Attorney General of Connecticut ruled that the Communist Party could not be on the ballot in the November election. New Haven Journal Courier, Jan. 22, 1964. No legal action was taken. For further details on the Salwen case and materials dealing generally with the right of radical political parties to a place on the ballot see Section D, subsection 6, infra.

In 1957 the New York State Industrial Commissioner denied the claim of a Communist Party member to unemployment insurance based in part on his employment by the Communist Party. The Commissioner also suspended the registration of the United States and New York Communist Parties as "employers," and terminated their liability to state taxation, under the New York unemployment compensation laws. These actions were based upon Section 3 of the Communist Control Act. The New York courts reversed the Commissioner's ruling as to the individual claimant but upheld it as to the Parties. In the Matter of the Claim of Albertson, In re the Matter of the Claim of Communist Party, 8 N.Y.2d 77, 168 N.E.2d 242, 202 N.Y. S.2d 5 (1960). The decision relating to the Communist Parties was appealed and the Supreme Court reversed. The Court avoided decision on the constitutional issues, holding that the Act should not be construed to "require exclusion of the petitioners from New York's unemployment compensation system." Communist Party v. Catherwood, 367 U.S. 389, 395, 81 S. Ct. 1465, 6 L. Ed. 2d 919 (1961). For discussion of the case see Notes, 60 Colum. L. Rev. 1198 (1960); 36 N.Y.U.L. Rev. 1224 (1961); 22 Ohio St. L.J. 244 (1961); 23 Ohio St. L.J. 767 (1962).

4. Other Federal Legislation Directly Restricting Seditious or Subversive Activities

Other federal controls over activities considered seditious or subversive are contained in the postal and customs laws. Title XII of the Espionage Act of 1917, as noted previously, made non-mailable certain materials. See Section B, supra. In its present form, as 18 U.S.C. §1717, that provision makes it a criminal offense to mail anything in violation of the espionage or other specified laws, or "which contains any matter advocating or urging treason, insurrection, or forcible resistance to any law of the United States." In 1930 the customs laws were amended to prohibit the same matter from being imported into the United States. 46 Stat. 688, 19 U.S.C. §1305. In 1942 the Foreign Agents Registration Act was amended to require that any person required to register under the Act who disseminates "political propaganda" must file copies of such material with the Attorney General and must label the material as originating from the agent of a foreign principal. 56 Stat. 248, 255, 22 U.S.C. §614.

Beginning in 1951 the Government undertook a program to stop the flow of "foreign Communist propaganda" into the United States. At first the material was confiscated upon entry. In 1956 the policy was changed to allow persons who requested the material to receive it. The program was justified on the theory that persons abroad who sent propaganda into the United States could be treated as foreign agents under the Foreign Agents Registration Act. President Kennedy ordered the practice ended in March 1961. But the following year Congress passed legislation to reinstitute the system. 76 Stat. 840, 39 U.S.C. §4008. That legislation was invalidated by the Supreme Court in Lamont v. Postmaster General, 381 U.S. 301, 85 S. Ct. 1493, 14 L. Ed. 2d 398 (1965):

"Here the Congress — expressly restrained by the First Amendment from 'abridging' freedom of speech and of press — is the actor. The Act sets administrative officials astride the flow of mail to inspect it, appraise it, write the addressee about it, and await a response before dispatching the mail. Just as the licensing or taxing authorities in the Lovell, Thomas, and Murdock cases sought to control the flow of ideas to the public, so here federal agencies regulate the flow of mail. We do not have here, any more than we had in Hannegan v. Esquire, Inc., 327 U.S. 146, any question concerning the extent to which Congress may classify the mail and fix the charges for its carriage.

Nor do we reach the question whether the standard here applied could pass constitutional muster. Nor do we deal with the right of Customs to inspect material from abroad for contraband. We rest on the narrow ground that the addressee in order to receive his mail must request in writing that it be delivered. This amounts in our judgment to an unconstitutional abridgment of the addressee's First Amendment rights. The addressee carries an affirmative obligation which we do not think the Government may impose on him. This requirement is almost certain to have a deterrent effect, especially as respects those who have sensitive positions. Their livelihood may be dependent on a security clearance. Public officials, like schoolteachers who have no tenure, might think they would invite disaster if they read what the Federal Government says contains the seeds of treason. Apart from them, any addressee is likely to feel some inhibition in sending for literature which federal officials have condemned as 'communist political propaganda.' The regime of this Act is at war with the 'uninhibited, robust, and wide-open' debate and discussion that are contemplated by the First Amendment. New York Times Co. v. Sullivan, 376 U.S. 254, 270." 381 U.S. at 306-307.

REFERENCES

1. For detailed accounts of the Government's efforts to prohibit or curtail the flow of foreign Communist propaganda into the United States see Note, Government Exclusion of Foreign Political Propaganda, 68 Harv. L. Rev. 1393 (1955); Schwartz and Paul, Foreign Communist Propaganda in the Mails: A Report on Some Problems of Federal Censorship, 107 U. Pa. L. Rev. 621, 796 (1959). With respect to the 1962 statute and the legal issues involved, see Schwartz, The Mail Must Not Go Through — Propaganda and Pornography, 11 U.C.L.A.L. Rev. 805 (1964); Note, 77 Harv. L. Rev. 1165 (1964). For comment on the Lamont case, see Sigler, Freedom of the Mails: A Developing Right, 54 Geo. L.J. 30, 41-44 (1965); Note, 79 Harv. L. Rev. 103, 154-57 (1965).

2. Under 18 U.S.C. §871 it is an offense to send any document through the mails "containing any threat to take the life of or to inflict bodily harm upon the President of the United States, the President-elect, the Vice-President or other officer next in order of succession." A statute passed in 1965 punishes assassination, kidnapping or assault of the same officials. 79 Stat. 580 (1965), 18 U.S.C. §1751. See Forkosch, Presidential Murder — The Constitutionality of a Statute Making it a Federal Crime, 19 Sw. L.J. 229 (1965).

3. The series of measures passed by Congress in 1954 to deal with subversion, in addition to the Communist Control Act and the amendment of the espionage and sabotage laws (Section A, supra), included a bail-jumping statute, making it a crime to forfeit bail and wilfully fail to surrender within 30 days (68 Stat. 747, 18 U.S.C. §3146); and a harboring statute, increasing the penalty for harboring fugitives from justice (68 Stat. 747, amending 18 U.S.C. §1071). See Note, Federal Anti-Subversive Legislation of 1954, 55 Colum. L. Rev. 631, 666-668. Other legislation that year included the Expatriation Act, 68 Stat. 1146, 8 U.S.C. §1481 (a) (9), discussed infra; and the Compulsory Testimony Act, 68 Stat. 745, 18 U.S.C. §3486, discussed in Section F, infra. See generally Congressional Quarterly, Congress and the Nation, ch. 16 (1965).

4. Early in World War II Japanese living on the West Coast were removed from that area and confined in detention camps. The program, instituted originally under executive orders and later ratified by legislation, was upheld by the Supreme Court as justified by military requirements. Hirabayashi v. United States, 320 U.S. 81, 63 S. Ct. 1375, 87 L.

Ed. 1774 (1943); Korematzu v. United States, 323 U.S. 214, 65 S. Ct. 193, 89 L. Ed. 194 (1944); but cf. Ex parte Endo, 323 U.S. 283, 65 S. Ct. 208, 89 L. Ed. 243 (1944). For discussion see Leighton, The Governing of Man (1945); Thomas and Nishimoto, The Spoilage (1946); Thomas et al., The Salvage (1952); Bloom and Riemer, Removal and Return (1949); Grodzins, Americans Betrayed: Politics and the Japanese Evacuation (1949); Rostow, The Japanese American Cases — A Disaster, 54 Yale L.J. 489 (1945); Dembitz, Racial Discrimination and the Military Judgment: The Supreme Court's Korematsu and Endo Decisions, 45 Colum. L. Rev. 175 (1945); Freeman, Genesis, Exodus and Leviticus — Genealogy, Evacuation, and Law, 28 Cornell L.Q. 414 (1953); ten-Broek, Barnhart and Matson, Prejudice, War and the Constitution (1954); Murphy, Civil Liberties and the Japanese American Cases: A Study in the Uses of Stare Decisis, 11 Western Pol. Q. 3 (1958). But martial law in Hawaii was held invalid under the Hawaiian Organic Act in Duncan v. Kahanamoku, 327 U.S. 304, 66 S. Ct. 606, 90 L. Ed. 688 (1946). See Frank, Ex Parte Milligan v. The Five Companies: Martial Law in Hawaii, 44 Colum. L. Rev. 639 (1944); Fairman, The Supreme Court on Military Jurisdiction: Martial Rule in Hawaii and the Yamashita Case, 59 Harv. L. Rev. 833 (1946).

5. For discussion of anti-subversive legislation in other countries see Loewenstein, Militant Democracy and Fundamental Rights, 31 Am. Pol. Sci. Rev. 417, 638 (1937) (anti-fascist legislation), Legislative Control of Political Extremism in European Democracies, 38 Colum. L. Rev. 591, 725 (1938), Legislation Against Subversive Activities in Argentina, 56 Harv. L. Rev. 1261 (1943), and Political Power and the Governmental Process, ch. XI (1957); Antieau, "The Limitation of Liberty" — A Comparative Survey, 24 So. Cal. L. Rev. 238 (1951); Kirchheimer, Political Justice, ch. IV (1961); see also the discussion of this issue in the Columbia University symposium, Community Security v. Man's Right to Knowledge, 54 Colum. L. Rev. 667, 739-740 (Great Britain), 776-777 (France), 788-790 (Canada), 813-815 (Spain) (1954); for the British policy see also Wilson and Glickman, The Problem of Internal Security in Great Britain (1954). Legislation outlawing the Communist Party in Australia was declared unconstitutional by the Australian Supreme Court as not within the powers granted to the Federal Government by the Australian Constitution. Australian Communist Party v. Commonwealth [1951] Argus L.R. 129. For discussion see Beasley, Australia's Communist Party Dissolution Act, 29 Can. B. Rev. 490 (1951). For discussion of the outlawing of the Communist Party in West Germany, see McWhinney, The German Federal Constitutional Court and the Communist Party Decision, 32 Ind. L.J. 295 (1957).

5. State and Local Laws in the Period After World War II

By the time of World War II over two thirds of the states had enacted some type of anti-sedition law, prohibiting advocacy in some form. See Chapter II, Section F, supra. In the period following the war many states expanded these laws or adopted new ones to meet the dangers feared from Communism. At the present time 45 states have statutes of this nature on the books.

An example of the new legislation is the Maryland Ober Law, passed in 1949, which served as a model for a number of others. Md. Ann. Code art. 85A, §§1-9 (1957). Under this statute it is a felony, punishable by a fine of $20,000 or imprisonment for 20 years, or both, "for any person knowingly and wilfully to":

"(a) Commit, attempt to commit, or aid in the commission of any act intended to overthrow, destroy or alter, or to assist in the overthrow, destruction or alteration of, the constitutional form of the government of the United States, or of the State of Maryland, or any political subdivision of either of them, by revolution, force, or violence; or

"(b) Advocate, abet, advise, or teach by any means any person to commit, attempt to commit, or assist in the commission of any such act under such circumstances as to constitute a clear and present danger to the security of the United States, or of the State of Maryland or of any political subdivision of either of them; or

"(c) Conspire with one or more persons to commit any such act; or

"(d) Assist in the formation or participate in the management or to contribute to the support of any subversive organization or foreign subversive organization knowing said organization to be a subversive organization or a foreign subversive organization; or

"(e) Destroy any books, records or files, or secrete any funds in this State of a subversive organization or a foreign subversive organization, knowing said organization to be such."

It is also made a felony to become or remain a member of a subversive organization or a foreign subversive organization knowing the organization to be such. And it is unlawful for such organization "to exist or function in the State of Maryland," and any such organization found by a court to be functioning in Maryland "shall be dissolved" and "all funds, books, records and files of every kind and all other property . . . shall be seized by and for the State of Maryland."

The terms "subversive organization" and "foreign subversive organization" are defined as:

"*'Subversive organization'* means any organization which engages in or advocates, abets, advises, or teaches, or a purpose of which is to engage in or advocate, abet, advise, or teach activities intended to overthrow, destroy or alter, or to assist in the overthrow, destruction or alteration of, the constitutional form of the government of the United States, or of the State of Maryland, or of any political subdivision of either of them, by revolution, force, or violence.

"*'Foreign subversive organization'* means any organization directed, dominated or controlled directly or indirectly by a foreign government which engages in or advocates, abets, advises, or teaches, or a purpose of which is to engage in or to advocate, abet, advise, or teach, activities intended to overthrow, destroy or alter, or to assist in the overthrow, destruction or alteration of the constitutional form of the government of, the United States, or of the State of Maryland, or of any political subdivision of either of them, and to establish in place thereof any form of government the direction and control of which is to be vested in, or exercised by or under, the domination or control of any foreign government, organization, or individual; but does not and shall not be construed to mean an organization the bona fide purpose of which is to promote world peace by alliances or unions with other governments or world federations, unions or governments to be effected through constitutional means."

Eleven states — Alabama, Arkansas, California, Delaware, Louisiana, Michigan, Montana, New Mexico, South Carolina, Texas, and Wyoming — adopted registration laws, similar in many respects to the Federal Internal Security Act of 1950. Eight states — Arizona, Arkansas, Indiana, Massachusetts, Nebraska, Oklahoma, Pennsylvania, and Texas — enacted statutes outlawing the Communist Party by name or making membership in it a crime, comparable to the Federal Communist Control Act of 1954. Some of the other laws contain additional types of restrictions, such as the Louisiana Communist Propaganda Control Law. La. Rev. Stat. §§14:390-14:390.8 (Supp. 1962). See infra.

A large number of municipalities — estimated in 1951 at 150 — adopted municipal ordinances directed at subversive activities. These ordinances took a great variety of forms, in some instances adopting methods of restriction similar to the state statutes, in others adopting new variations. In one form, as in New Rochelle, N.Y., the ordinance required registration with the police of any member of a "communist organization" who "resides in, is employed in, has a regular place of business in, or who regularly enters or travels through any part of the City of New Rochelle." A "communist organization" is defined as one "organized, or which operates, primarily for the purposes of advancing the objectives of the world communist movement."

A second form, less common, is typified by the Birmingham, Ala., ordinance which provided a $100 fine and a maximum of 180 days in jail for each day that a known Communist remained in the City. The ordinance further provided that membership in the Communist Party would be presumed if a person "shall be found in any secret or non-public place in voluntary association or communication with any person or persons established to be or to have been members of the Communist Party." N.Y. Times, July 19, 1950.

An issue central to the validity of state and municipal legislation dealing with subversive activities is whether federal legislation in the same area has pre-empted the field. This problem came before the Supreme Court in Pennsylvania v. Nelson, set forth below.

REFERENCES

1. A digest of the state statutes and decisions may be found in Internal Security and Subversion: Principal State Laws and Cases, A Study Prepared for the Subcommittee to Investigate the Administration of the Internal Security Act and Other Internal Security Laws of the Senate Committee on the Judiciary, by Legislative Reference Service, Library of Congress (1965). An earlier compilation appears in Digest of the Public Record of Communism in the United States, Pt. II (Fund for the Republic 1955). See also Gellhorn, The States and Subversion, Apps. A and B (1952); Groner, State Control of Subversive Activities in the United States, 9 Fed. B.J. 61 (1947).

Two jurisdictions require registration or other identification of oath-bound or secret organizations. N.Y. Civ. Rights Law §§53-57, upheld in Bryant v. Zimmerman, 278 U.S. 63, 49 S. Ct. 61, 73 L. Ed. 184 (1928); N.C. Gen. Stat. §14-12.6.

2. Samples of municipal ordinances and a digest of the cases, up to 1955, appear in Digest, id. at 455-472. See also Sutherland, Freedom and Internal Security, 64 Harv. L. Rev. 383, 388 n.25 (1951). The estimate of 150 ordinances by 1951 was made by Marquis Child in New Haven Journal Courier, Feb. 16, 1951. Some of them have been declared unconstitutional by state and federal lower courts, including those in Birmingham, Jacksonville, Miami, Los Angeles, Erie, and McKeesport.

3. For discussion of the state laws prior to Pennsylvania v. Nelson, see Prendergast, State Legislatures and Communism: The Current Scene, 44 Am. Pol. Sci. Rev. 556 (1950); Note, State Control of Subversion: A Problem in Federalism, 66 Harv. L. Rev. 327 (1952); Note, Effectiveness of State Anti-Subversive Legislation, 28 Ind. L.J. 492 (1953); Hunt, Federal Supremacy and State Anti-Subversive Legislation, 53 Mich. L. Rev. 407 (1955); Note, State Sedition Laws: Their Scope and Misapplication, 31 Ind. L.J. 270 (1956). See also Governor Stevenson's veto of the Broyles bill in Busch, Adlai E. Stevenson of Illinois 136-144 (1952).

4. Decisions dealing with the pre-emption issue prior to Pennsylvania v. Nelson include Albertson v. Millard, 106 F. Supp. 635 (E.D. Mich. 1952), remanded, 345 U.S. 242 (1953); Nelson v. Wyman, 99 N.H. 33, 105 A.2d 756 (1954).

PENNSYLVANIA v. NELSON
350 U.S. 497, 76 S. Ct. 477, 100 L. Ed. 640 (1956)

MR. CHIEF JUSTICE WARREN delivered the opinion of the Court.

The respondent Steve Nelson, an acknowledged member of the Communist Party, was convicted in the Court of Quarter Sessions of Allegheny County, Pennsylvania, of a violation of the Pennsylvania Sedition Act and sentenced to imprisonment for twenty years and to a fine of $10,000 and to costs of prosecution in the sum of $13,000. The Superior Court affirmed the conviction. 172 Pa. Super. 125, 92 A.2d 431. The Supreme Court of Pennsylvania, recognizing but not reaching many alleged serious trial errors and conduct of the trial court infringing upon respondent's right to due process of law, decided the case on the narrow issue of supersession of the state law by the Federal Smith Act. In its opinion, the court stated:

"And, while the Pennsylvania statute proscribes sedition against either the Government of the United States or the Government of Pennsylvania, it is only alleged sedition against the United States with which the instant case is concerned. Out of all the voluminous testimony, we have not found, nor has anyone pointed to, a single word indicating a seditious act or even utterance directed against the Government of Pennsylvania."

The precise holding of the court, and all that is before us for review, is that the Smith Act of 1940, as amended in 1948, which prohibits the knowing advocacy of the overthrow of the Government of the United States by force and violence, supersedes the enforceability of the Pennsylvania Sedition Act which proscribes the same conduct.

Many State Attorneys General and the Solicitor General of the United

States appeared as amici curiae for petitioner, and several briefs were filed on behalf of the respondent. Because of the important question of federal-state relationship involved, we granted certiorari. 348 U.S. 814.

It should be said at the outset that the decision in this case does not affect the right of States to enforce their sedition laws at times when the Federal Government has not occupied the field and is not protecting the entire country from seditious conduct. The distinction between the two situations was clearly recognized by the court below. Nor does it limit the jurisdiction of the States where the Constitution and Congress have specifically given them concurrent jurisdiction, as was done under the Eighteenth Amendment and the Volstead Act. United States v. Lanza, 260 U.S. 377. Neither does it limit the right of the State to protect itself at any time against sabotage or attempted violence of all kinds. Nor does it prevent the State from prosecuting where the same act constitutes both a federal offense and a state offense under the police power, as was done in Fox v. Ohio, 5 How. 410, and Gilbert v. Minnesota, 254 U.S. 325, relied upon by petitioner as authority herein. In neither of those cases did the state statute impinge on federal jurisdiction. In the Fox case, the federal offense was counterfeiting. The state offense was defrauding the person to whom the spurious money was passed. In the Gilbert case this Court, in upholding the enforcement of a state statute, proscribing conduct which would "interfere with or discourage the enlistment of men in the military or naval forces of the United States or of the State of Minnesota," treated it not as an act relating to "the raising of armies for the national defense, nor to rules and regulations for the government of those under arms [a constitutionally exclusive federal power]. It [was] simply a local police measure . . . ."

Where, as in the instant case, Congress has not stated specifically whether a federal statute has occupied a field in which the States are otherwise free to legislate, different criteria have furnished touchstones for decision. Thus, "[t]his Court, in considering the validity of state laws in the light of . . . federal laws touching the same subject, has made use of the following expressions: conflicting; contrary to; occupying the field; repugnance; difference; irreconcilability; inconsistency; violation; curtailment; and interference. But none of these expressions provides an infallible constitutional test or an exclusive constitutional yardstick. In the final analysis, there can be no one crystal clear distinctly marked formula." Hines v. Davidowitz, 312 U.S. 52, 67.

And see Rice v. Santa Fe Elevator Corp., 331 U.S. 218, 230-231. In this case, we think that each of several tests of supersession is met.

First, "[t]he scheme of federal regulation [is] so pervasive as to make reasonable the inference that Congress left no room for the States to supplement it." Rice v. Santa Fe Elevator Corp., 331 U.S. at 230. The Congress determined in 1940 that it was necessary for it to re-enter the field of antisubversive legislation, which had been abandoned by it in 1921. In that year, it enacted the Smith Act which proscribes advocacy of the overthrow of any government—federal, state or local—by force and violence and organization of and knowing membership in a group which so advocates.[11] Conspiracy to commit any of these acts is punishable under the general criminal conspiracy provisions in 18 U.S.C. §371. The Internal Security Act of 1950 is aimed more directly at Communist organizations.

[The Court here summarizes the Internal Security Act and the Communist Control Act.]

We examine these Acts only to determine the congressional plan. Looking to all of them in the aggregate, the conclusion is inescapable that Congress has intended to occupy the field of sedition. Taken as a whole, they evince a congressional plan which makes it reasonable to determine that no room has been left for the States to supplement it. Therefore, a state sedition statute is superseded regardless of whether it purports to supplement the federal law. . . .

Second, the federal statutes "touch a field in which the federal interest is so dominant that the federal system [must] be assumed to preclude enforcement of state laws on the same subject." Rice v. Santa Fe Elevator Corp., 331 U.S. at 230, citing Hines v. Davidowitz, supra.[21] Congress has devised an all-embracing program for resistance to the various forms of totalitarian aggression. Our external defenses have been strengthened, and a plan to protect against internal subversion has been made by it. It has appropriated vast sums, not only for our own protection, but also to strengthen freedom throughout the world. It has charged the Federal Bureau of Investigation and the Central Intelligence Agency with responsibility for intelligence concerning Communist seditious activities against our Government, and has denominated such activities as part of a world conspiracy. It accordingly proscribed sedition against all government in the nation — national, state and local. Congress declared that these steps were taken "to provide for the common defense, to preserve the sovereignty of the United States as an independent nation, and to guarantee to each State a republican form of government . . . ."[22] Congress having thus treated seditious conduct as a matter of vital national concern, it is in no sense a local enforcement problem. . . .

Third, enforcement of state sedition acts present a serious danger of conflict with the administration of the federal program. Since 1939, in order to avoid a hampering of uniform enforcement of its program by sporadic local prosecutions, the Federal Government has urged local authorities not to in-

[11] . . . See also the Voorhis Act passed in 1940, now codified as 18 U.S.C. §2386, and the Foreign Agents Registration Act passed in 1938, 22 U.S.C. §611 et seq.

[21] It is worth observing that in Hines this Court held a Pennsylvania statute providing for alien registration was superseded by Title III of the same Act of which the commonly called Smith Act was Title I. Title II amended certain statutes dealing with the exclusion and deportation of aliens. The provisions of Title I involve a field of no less dominant federal interest than Titles II and III, in which Congress manifestly did not desire concurrent state action.

[22] 50 U.S.C. §781(15).

tervene in such matters, but to turn over to the federal authorities immediately and unevaluated all information concerning subversive activities. The President made such a request on September 6, 1939, when he placed the Federal Bureau of Investigation in charge of investigation in this field:

"The Attorney General has been requested by me to instruct the Federal Bureau of Investigation of the Department of Justice to take charge of investigative work in matters relating to espionage, sabotage, and violations of the neutrality regulations.

"This task must be conducted in a comprehensive and effective manner on a national basis, and all information must be carefully sifted out and correlated in order to avoid confusion and irresponsibility.

"To this end I request all police officers, sheriffs, and all other law enforcement officers in the United States promptly to turn over to the nearest representative of the Federal Bureau of Investigation any information obtained by them relating to espionage, counterespionage, sabotage, subversive activities and violations of the neutrality laws." [25]

And in addressing the Federal-State Conference on Law Enforcement Problems of National Defense, held on August 5 and 6, 1940, only a few weeks after the passage of the Smith Act, the Director of the Federal Bureau of Investigation said:

"The fact must not be overlooked that meeting the spy, the saboteur and the subverter is a problem that must be handled on a nation-wide basis. An isolated incident in the middle west may be of little significance, but when fitted into a national pattern of similar incidents, it may lead to an important revelation of subversive activity. It is for this reason that the President requested all of our citizens and law enforcing agencies to report directly to the Federal Bureau of Investigation any complaints or information dealing with espionage, sabotage or subversive activities. In such matters, time is of the essence. It is unfortunate that in a few States efforts have been made by individuals not fully acquainted with the far-flung ramifications of this problem to interject superstructures of agencies between local law enforcement and the FBI to sift what might be vital information, thus delaying its immediate reference to the FBI. This cannot be, if our internal security is to be best served. This is no time for red tape or amateur handling of such vital matters. There must be a direct and free flow of contact between the local law enforcement agencies and the FBI. The job of meeting the spy or saboteur is one for experienced men of law enforcement." [26]

Moreover, the Pennsylvania Statute presents a peculiar danger of interference with the federal program. For, as the court below observed:

"Unlike the Smith Act, which can be administered only by federal officers acting in their official capacities, indictment for sedition under the Pennsylva-

---

[25] The Public Papers and Addresses of Franklin D. Roosevelt, 1939 Volume, pp. 478-479 (1941).

[26] Proceedings, p. 23.

nia statute can be initiated upon an information made by a private individual. The opportunity thus present for the indulgence of personal spite and hatred or for furthering some selfish advantage or ambition need only be mentioned to be appreciated. Defense of the Nation by law, no less than by arms, should be a public and not a private undertaking. It is important that punitive sanctions for sedition *against the United States* be such as have been promulgated by the central governmental authority and administered under the supervision and review of that authority's judiciary. If that be done, sedition will be detected and punished, no less, wherever it may be found, and the right of the individual to speak freely and without fear, even in criticism of the government, will at the same time be protected."

In his brief, the Solicitor General states that forty-two States plus Alaska and Hawaii have statutes which in some form prohibit advocacy of the violent overthrow of established government. These statutes are entitled anti-sedition statutes, criminal anarchy laws, criminal syndicalist laws, etc. Although all of them are primarily directed against the overthrow of the United States Government, they are in no sense uniform. And our attention has not been called to any case where the prosecution has been successfully directed against an attempt to destroy state or local government. Some of these Acts are studiously drawn and purport to protect fundamental rights by appropriate definitions, standards of proof and orderly procedures in keeping with the avowed congressional purpose "to protect freedom from those who would destroy it, without infringing upon the freedom of all our people." Others are vague and are almost wholly without such safeguards. Some even purport to punish mere membership in subversive organizations which the federal statutes do not punish where federal registration requirements have been fulfilled.

When we were confronted with a like situation in the field of labor-management relations, Mr. Justice Jackson wrote:
"A multiplicity of tribunals and a diversity of procedures are quite as apt to produce incompatible or conflicting adjudications as are different rules of substantive law." [29]
Should the States be permitted to exercise a concurrent jurisdiction in this area, federal enforcement would encounter not only the difficulties mentioned by Mr. Justice Jackson, but the added conflict engendered by different criteria of substantive offenses.

Since we find that Congress has occupied the field to the exclusion of parallel state legislation, that the dominant interest of the Federal Government precludes state intervention, and that administration of state Acts would conflict with the operation of the federal plan, we are convinced that the decision of the Supreme Court of Pennsylvania is unassailable.

We are not unmindful of the risk of compounding punishments which would be created by finding concurrent state power. In our view of the case, we do not reach the question whether double or multiple punishment for the

[29] Garner v. Teamsters Union, 346 U.S. 485, 490-491.

same overt acts directed against the United States has constitutional sanction. Without compelling indication to the contrary, we will not assume that Congress intended to permit the possibility of double punishment. Cf. Houston v. Moore, 5 Wheat. 1, 31, 75; Jerome v. United States, 318 U.S. 101, 105.

The judgment of the Supreme Court of Pennsylvania is
Affirmed.

Mr. Justice Reed, with whom Mr. Justice Burton and Mr. Justice Minton join, dissenting. . . .

First, the Court relies upon the pervasiveness of the antisubversive legislation embodied in the Smith Act of 1940, 18 U.S.C. §2385, the Internal Security Act of 1950, 64 Stat. 987, and the Communist Control Act of 1954, 68 Stat. 775. It asserts that these Acts in the aggregate mean that Congress has occupied the "field of sedition" to the exclusion of the States. The "occupation of the field" argument has been developed by this Court for the Commerce Clause and legislation thereunder to prevent partitioning of this country by locally erected trade barriers. In those cases this Court has ruled that state legislation is superseded when it conflicts with the comprehensive regulatory scheme and purpose of a federal plan. Cloverleaf Butter Co. v. Patterson, 315 U.S. 148. . . .

But the federal sedition laws are distinct criminal statutes that punish willful advocacy of the use of force against "the government of the United States or the government of any State." These criminal laws proscribe certain local activity without creating any statutory or administrative regulation. There is, consequently, no question as to whether some general congressional regulatory scheme might be upset by a coinciding state plan. In these circumstances the conflict should be clear and direct before this Court reads a congressional intent to void state legislation into the federal sedition acts. . . . Moreover, it is quite apparent that since 1940 Congress has been keenly aware of the magnitude of existing state legislation proscribing sedition. It may be validly assumed that in these circumstances this Court should not void state legislation without a clear mandate from Congress.

We cannot agree that the federal criminal sanctions against sedition directed at the United States are of such a pervasive character as to indicate an intention to void state action.

Secondly, the Court states that the federal sedition statutes touch a field "in which the federal interest is so dominant" they must preclude state laws on the same subject. This concept is suggested in a comment on Hines v. Davidowitz, 312 U.S. 52, in the Rice case, at 230. The Court in Davidowitz ruled that federal statutes compelling alien registration preclude enforcement of state statutes requiring alien registration. We read Davidowitz to teach nothing more than that, when the Congress provided a single nation-wide integrated system of regulation so complete as that for aliens' registration (with fingerprinting, a scheduling of activities, and continuous information as to their residence), the Act bore so directly on our foreign relations as to make it evident that Congress intended only one uniform national alien registration system.

We look upon the Smith Act as a provision for controlling incitements to overthrow by force and violence the Nation, or any State, or any political subdivision of either. Such an exercise of federal police power carries, we think, no such dominancy over similar state powers as might be attributed to continuing federal regulations concerning foreign affairs or coinage, for example. In the responsibility of national and local governments to protect themselves against sedition, there is no "dominant interest."

We are citizens of the United States and of the State wherein we reside and are dependent upon the strength of both to preserve our rights and liberties. Both may enact criminal statutes for mutual protection unless Congress has otherwise provided. It was so held in Gilbert v. Minnesota, 254 U.S. 325. In Gilbert the federal interest in raising armies did not keep this Court from permitting Minnesota to punish persons who interfered with enlistments (id., at 326), even though a comprehensive federal criminal law proscribed identical activity. 40 Stat. 553. We do not understand that case as does the majority. In our view this Court treated the Minnesota statute only alternatively as a police measure, p. 331. Minnesota made it unlawful to advocate "that men should not enlist in the military or naval forces of the United States." It was contended, pp. 327-328, that the power to punish such advocacy was "conferred upon Congress and withheld from the States." This Court ruled against the contention, saying:

"An army, of course, can only be raised and directed by Congress, in neither has the State power, but it has power to regulate the conduct of its citizens and to restrain the exertion of baleful influences against the promptings of patriotic duty to the detriment of the welfare of the Nation and State. To do so is not to usurp a National power, it is only to render a service to its people, ..." Id., at 330-331.

Thirdly, the Court finds ground for abrogating Pennsylvania's antisedition statute because, in the Court's view, the State's administration of the Act may hamper the enforcement of the federal law. Quotations are inserted from statements of President Roosevelt and Mr. Hoover, the Director of the Federal Bureau of Investigation, to support the Court's position. But a reading of the quotations leads us to conclude that their purpose was to gain prompt knowledge of evidence of subversive activities so that the federal agency could be fully advised. We find no suggestion from any official source that state officials should be less alert to ferret out or punish subversion. The Court's attitude as to interference seems to us quite contrary to that of the Legislative and Executive Departments. Congress was advised of the existing state sedition legislation when the Smith Act was enacted and has been kept current with its spread. No declaration of exclusiveness followed. In this very case the Executive appears by brief of the Department of Justice, amicus curiae. The brief summarizes this point:

"The administration of the various state laws has not, in the course of the fifteen years that the federal and state sedition laws have existed side by side, in fact interfered with, embarrassed, or impeded the enforcement of the Smith Act. The significance of this absence of conflict in administration or enforcement of the federal and state sedition laws will be appreciated when it is realized that this period has included the stress of wartime security requirements and the federal investigation and prosecution under the Smith Act of the principal national and regional Communist leaders." Id., at 30-31.

Mere fear by courts of possible difficulties does not seem to us in these circumstances a valid reason for ousting a State from exercise of its police power. Those are matters for legislative determination. . . .

The law stands against any advocacy of violence to change established governments. Freedom of speech allows full play to the processes of reason. The state and national legislative bodies have legislated within constitutional limits so as to allow the widest participation by the law enforcement officers of the respective governments. The individual States were not told that they are powerless to punish local acts of sedition, nominally directed against the United States. Courts should not interfere. We would reverse the judgment of the Supreme Court of Pennsylvania.

REFERENCES

For discussion of the Nelson case see Hunt, State Control of Sedition: The Smith Act as the Supreme Law of the Land, 41 Minn. L. Rev. 287 (1957); Cramton, Pennsylvania v. Nelson: A Case Study in Federal Pre-emption, 26 U. Chi. L. Rev. 85 (1958); Notes, 70 Harv. L. Rev. 83, 116-120 (1956); 25 Fordham L. Rev. 522 (1956); 30 So. Cal. L. Rev. 101 (1956); 4 U.C.L.A.L. Rev. 118 (1956); 2 Vill. L. Rev. 127 (1956); 32 N.Y.U.L. Rev. 1302 (1957); 11 U. Fla. L. Rev. 224 (1958). For sample of the law review notes on the Pennsylvania court's decision see 44 Geo. L.J. 509 (1956); 67 Harv. L. Rev. 1419 (1954); 29 N.Y.U.L. Rev. 1293 (1954); 102 U. Pa. L. Rev. 1089 (1954).

NOTES

1. Following the Supreme Court's decision in Pennsylvania v. Nelson, the principal proceedings then pending under state anti-subversive laws were dismissed. Albertson v. Millard, 345 Mich. 519, 77 N.W.2d 104 (1956), noted in 2 Wayne L. Rev. 221 (1956); Commonwealth v. Gilbert, 334 Mass. 71, 134 N.E.2d 13 (1956) (involving Professor Dirk Struik of M.I.T.); Commonwealth v. Hood, 334 Mass. 76, 134 N.E.2d 12 (1956); Braden v. Commonwealth, 291 S.W.2d 843 (Ky. Ct. App. 1956); State v. Jenkins, 236 La. 300, 107 So. 2d 648 (1958).

2. The Supreme Court's decision in the Nelson case, together with a series of decisions the following term (including Yates and Jencks, noted in subsection 2,

supra), precipitated a bitter controversy over the powers of the Supreme Court to invalidate federal and state legislative action. Numerous bills were introduced in Congress to curb the Court. One of them, known as H.R. 3, was sponsored by Representative Howard W. Smith of Virginia, author of the Smith Act. As introduced in 1955 it provided:

"That no act of Congress shall be construed as indicating an intent on the part of Congress to occupy the field in which such act operates, to the exclusion of all State laws on the same subject matter, unless such act contains an express provision to that effect. No act of Congress shall be construed as invalidating a provision of State law which would be valid in the absence of such act, unless there is a direct and positive conflict between an express provision of such act and such provision of the State law so that the two cannot be reconciled or consistently stand together."

Modified to apply only to anti-subversive laws, H.R. 3 passed the House in 1956, but was not acted on by the Senate. In 1958 a similar bill was again enacted by the House but failed by a margin of one vote in the Senate. The legislation, in revised form, once more passed the House in 1959, but was not reported out of committee in the Senate.

A second piece of legislation, which was the subject of a long struggle in Congress, was the so-called Jenner bill. S. 2646, 85th Cong., 1st Sess. (1957). This proposal would have removed the jurisdiction of the Supreme Court to decide cases involving (1) contempt of Congress, (2) the federal loyalty-security program, (3) state anti-subversive laws, (4) regulations of employment and subversive activities in schools, and (5) admission to the practice of law. Somewhat watered down when it came before the Senate in 1958, the bill was tabled by a vote of 49 to 41.

REFERENCES

For full accounts of the controversy over the Supreme Court, including citation to voluminous materials and to the legislative history of the major bills, see Murphy, Congress and the Court (1962); Pritchett, Congress Versus the Supreme Court, 1957-1960 (1961) (bibliography at 160-162). See also Hyneman, The Supreme Court on Trial (1963); Nagel, Court-Curbing Periods in American History, 18 Vand. L. Rev. 925 (1965). Among the highlights of the controversy were reports and resolutions critical of the Supreme Court by the Conference of Chief Justices (of the state courts) and the American Bar Association. See Conference of Chief Justices, Report of the Committee on Federal-State Relationships as Affected by Judicial Decisions (Council of State Governments 1958); approved by Conference, Resolutions Adopted at the 10th Annual Meeting of the Conference of Chief Justices 1 (1958), reprinted 105 Cong. Rec. App. 44 (1959), and U.S. News and World Report, Aug. 29, 1958, p. 62. The Report was based upon monographs prepared by five members of the University of Chicago Law School faculty, which are printed in 8 U. Chi. Law School Record, No. 1, Spec. Supp. (1958). For a critical discussion see Lockhart, A Response to the Conference of State Chief Justices, 107 U. Pa. L. Rev. 802 (1959), reprinted in 105 Cong. Rec. 6771 (1959). For the American Bar Association action, see American Bar Association, Report of the Special Committee on Communist Tactics, Strategy and Objectives (1959), and resolutions adopted by the House of Delegates, 45 A.B.A.J. 360, 365, 406-410 (1959); see also 45 A.B.A.J. 343 (1959). For the hearings on S. 2646, see Senate Committee on the Judiciary, Subcommittee to

Investigate the Administration of the Internal Security Act and Other Internal Security Laws, Limitation on the Appellate Jurisdiction of the United States Supreme Court, Hearings on S. 2646, 86th Cong., 1st and 2nd Sess. (1957-1958).

NOTE

The extent to which the decision in Pennsylvania v. Nelson pre-empted state anti-subversive laws remained a disputed issue. In Uphaus v. Wyman, 360 U.S. 72, 79 S. Ct. 1040, 3 L. Ed. 2d 1090 (1959), a state legislative investigating case, the Court clarified its position:

"Appellant vigorously contends that the New Hampshire Subversive Activities Act of 1951 and the resolution creating the committee have been superseded by the Smith Act, as amended. In support of this position appellant cites Pennsylvania v. Nelson, supra. The argument is that Nelson, which involved a prosecution under a state sedition law, held that 'Congress has intended to occupy the field of sedition.' This rule of decision, it is contended, should embrace legislative investigations made pursuant to an effort by the Legislature to inform itself of the presence of subversives within the State and possibly to enact laws in the subversive field. The appellant's argument sweeps too broad. In Nelson itself we said that the 'precise holding of the court . . . is that the Smith Act . . . which prohibits the knowing advocacy of the overthrow of the Government of the United States by force and violence, supersedes the enforceability of the Pennsylvania Sedition Act which proscribed the *same conduct.*' (Italics supplied.) 350 U.S., at 499. The basis of Nelson thus rejects the notion that it stripped the States of the right to protect themselves. All the opinion proscribed was a race between federal and state prosecutors to the courthouse door. The opinion made clear that a State could proceed with prosecutions for sedition against the State itself; that it can legitimately investigate in this area follows a fortiori. In Sweezy v. New Hampshire [354 U.S. 234], where the same contention was made as to the identical state Act, it was denied sub silentio. Nor did our opinion in Nelson hold that the Smith Act had proscribed state activity in protection of itself either from actual or threatened 'sabotage or attempted violence of all kinds.' In footnote 8 of the opinion it is pointed out that the State had full power to deal with internal civil disturbances. Thus registration statutes, quo warranto proceedings as to subversive corporations, the subversive instigation of riots and a host of other subjects directly affecting state security furnish grist for the State's legislative mill. Moreover, the right of the State to require the production of corporate papers of a state-chartered corporation in an inquiry to determine whether corporate activity is violative of state policy is, of course, not touched upon in Nelson and today stands unimpaired, either by the Smith Act or the Nelson opinion." 360 U.S. at 76-77.

REFERENCES

For discussion of the Uphaus case and its impact on the pre-emption issue see Cramton, The Supreme Court and State Power to Deal With Subversion and Loyalty, 43 Minn. 1025 (1959); Note, State Access to Membership Lists: Legislative Investigation of Communism, 44 Minn. L. Rev. 555 (1960); Notes, 73 Harv. L. Rev. 124, 161-163 (1959); 33 So. Cal. L. Rev. 92 (1959); 28 Geo. Wash. L. Rev. 457 (1960); 38 Texas L. Rev.

330 (1960). See also the material on legislative investigating committees, Section F, infra.

For material dealing more generally with the pre-emption problem see Braden, Umpire to the Federal System, 10 U. Chi. L. Rev. 27 (1942); Note, "Occupation of the Field" in Commerce Clause Cases, 1936-1946: Ten Years of Federalism, 60 Harv. L. Rev. 262 (1946); Note, Pre-emption by Federal Criminal Statutes, 55 Colum. L. Rev. 83 (1955); Note, Pre-emption as a Preferential Ground: A New Canon of Construction, 12 Stan. L. Rev. 208 (1959).

NOTE

Proceedings under state anti-sedition laws have continued to be brought, though at a substantially reduced rate in comparison with the 1950's. In Louisiana ex rel. Gremillion v. N.A.A.C.P., 366 U.S. 293, 81 S. Ct. 1333, 6 L. Ed. 2d 301 (1961), the Supreme Court affirmed a district court injunction against the enforcement of two Louisiana statutes. One prohibited any "non-trading" association from doing business in Louisiana if it was affiliated with any "foreign or out of state non-trading" association "any of the officers or members of the board of directors of which are members of Communist, Communist-front or subversive organizations, as cited by the House of Congress [*sic*] Un-American Activities Committee or the United States Attorney." La. Rev. Stat. §14:386 (1958 Supp.). Moreover, every non-trading association affiliated with an out-of-state association was required to file annually with the Secretary of State an affidavit that "none of the officers" of the affiliate is "a member" of any such organization. Mr. Justice Douglas, speaking for the Court, held that the statute must be "struck down on account of vagueness." He said: "It is not consonant with due process to require a person to swear to a fact that he cannot be expected to know . . . or alternatively to refrain from a wholly lawful activity." 366 U.S. at 295. Justices Frankfurter, Clark, Harlan, and Stewart concurred.

In Dombrowski v. Pfister, set forth below, the Court dealt with the problem of federal injunction against prosecutions instituted under state anti-sedition legislation.

DOMBROWSKI v. PFISTER
380 U.S. 479, 85 S. Ct. 1116, 14 L. Ed. 2d 22 (1965)

Mr. Justice Brennan delivered the opinion of the Court.

Appellants filed a complaint in the District Court for the Eastern District of Louisiana, invoking the Civil Rights Act, Rev. Stat. §1979, 42 U.S.C. §1983 (1958 ed.), and seeking declaratory relief and an injunction restraining appellees — the Governor, police and law enforcement officers, and the Chairman of the Legislative Joint Committee on Un-American Activities in Louisiana — from prosecuting or threatening to prosecute appellants for alleged violations of the Louisiana Subversive Activities and Communist Control Law and the Communist Propaganda Control Law.[1] Appellant Southern Confer-

---

[1] The Subversive Activities and Communist Control Law is La. Rev. Stat. §§14:358 through 14:374 (Cum. Supp. 1962). The Communist Propaganda Control Law is La. Rev. Stat. §§14:390 through 14:390.8 (Cum. Supp. 1962).

ence Educational Fund, Inc. (SCEF), is active in fostering civil rights for Negroes in Louisiana and other States of the South. Appellant Dombrowski is its Executive Director; intervenor Smith, its Treasurer; and intervenor Waltzer, Smith's law partner and an attorney for SCEF. The complaint alleges that the statutes on their face violate the First and Fourteenth Amendment guarantees securing freedom of expression, because overbreadth makes them susceptible of sweeping and improper application abridging those rights. Supported by affidavits and a written offer of proof, the complaint further alleges that the threats to enforce the statutes against appellants are not made with any expectation of securing valid convictions, but rather are part of a plan to employ arrests, seizures, and threats of prosecution under color of the statutes to harass appellants and discourage them and their supporters from asserting and attempting to vindicate the constitutional rights of Negro citizens of Louisiana. . . .

[A three-judge District Court dismissed the complaint, one judge dissenting, on the ground that "this was an appropriate case for abstention." 227 F. Supp. 556.]

I

. . . It is generally to be assumed that state courts and prosecutors will observe constitutional limitations as expounded by this Court, and that the mere possibility of erroneous initial application of constitutional standards will usually not amount to the irreparable injury necessary to justify a disruption of orderly state proceedings. In Douglas v. City of Jeannette, 319 U.S. 157, for example, the Court upheld a district court's refusal to enjoin application of a city ordinance to religious solicitation, even though the ordinance was that very day held unconstitutional as so applied on review of a criminal conviction under it. . . .

But the allegations in this complaint depict a situation in which defense of the State's criminal prosecution will not assure adequate vindication of constitutional rights. They suggest that a substantial loss or impairment of freedoms of expression will occur if appellants must await the state courts' disposition and ultimate review in this Court of any adverse determination. These allegations, if true, clearly show irreparable injury.

A criminal prosecution under a statute regulating expression usually involves imponderables and contingencies that themselves may inhibit the full exercise of First Amendment freedoms. See, e.g., Smith v. California, 361 U.S. 147. When the statutes also have an overbroad sweep, as is here alleged, the hazard of loss or substantial impairment of those precious rights may be critical. For in such cases, the statutes lend themselves too readily to denial of those rights. The assumption that defense of a criminal prosecution will generally assure ample vindication of constitutional rights is unfounded in such cases. See Baggett v. Bullitt [377 U.S. 360, 379]. For "[t]he threat of sanctions may deter . . . almost as potently as the actual application of sanctions. . . ." NAACP v. Button, 371 U.S. 415, 433. Because of the sensitive nature of constitutionally protected expression, we have not required that all of those subject to overbroad regulations risk prosecution to test their rights. For free expression — of transcendent value to all society, and not merely to those exercising their rights — might be the loser. . . . Moreover, we have not thought that the improbability of successful prosecution makes the case different. The chilling effect upon the exercise of First Amendment rights may derive from the fact of the prosecution, unaffected by the prospects of its success or failure. . . .

Appellants' allegations and offers of proof outline the chilling effect on free expression of prosecutions initiated and threatened in this case. Early in October 1963 appellant Dombrowski and intervenors Smith and Waltzer were arrested by Louisiana state and local police and charged with violations of the two statutes. Their offices were raided and their files and records seized.[4] Later in October a state judge quashed the arrest warrants as not based on probable cause, and discharged the appellants. Subsequently, the court granted a motion to suppress the seized evidence on the ground that the raid was illegal. Louisiana officials continued, however, to threaten prosecution of the appellants, who thereupon filed this action in November. Shortly after the three-judge court was convened, a grand jury was summoned in the Parish of Orleans to hear evidence looking to indictments of the individual appellants. On appellants' application Judge Wisdom issued a temporary restraining order against prosecutions pending hearing and decision of the case in the District Court. Following a hearing the District Court, over Judge Wisdom's dissent, dissolved the temporary restraining order and, at the same time, handed down an order dismissing the complaint. Thereafter the grand jury returned indictments under the Subversive Activities and Communist Control Law against the individual appellants.

These events, together with repeated announcements by appellees that the appellant organization is a subversive or Communist-front organization, whose members must register or be prosecuted under the Louisiana statutes, have, appellants allege, frightened off potential members and contributors.

---

[4] The circumstances of the arrests are set forth in Judge Wisdom's dissenting opinion:

"At gunpoint their homes and offices were raided and ransacked by police officers and trustees from the House of Detention acting under the direct supervision of the staff director and the counsel for the State Un-American Activities Committee. The home and office of the director of Southern Conference Educational Fund were also raided. Among the dangerous articles removed was Thoreau's Journal. A truckload of files, membership lists, subscription lists to SCEF's newspaper, correspondence, and records were removed from SCEF's office, destroying its capacity to function. At the time of the arrests, Mr. Pfister, Chairman of the Committee, announced to the press that the raids and arrest resulted from 'racial agitation.'" 227 F. Supp., at 573.

Cf. Anti-Fascist Committee v. McGrath, 341 U.S. 123. Seizures of documents and records have paralyzed operations and threatened exposure of the identity of adherents to a locally unpopular cause. See NAACP v. Alabama, 357 U.S. 449. Although the particular seizure has been quashed in the state courts, the continuing threat of prosecution portends further arrests and seizures, some of which may be upheld and all of which will cause the organization inconvenience or worse. . . .

It follows that the District Court erred in holding that the complaint fails to allege sufficient irreparable injury to justify equitable relief.

The District Court also erred in holding that it should abstain pending authoritative interpretation of the statutes in the state courts, which might hold that they did not apply to SCEF, or that they were unconstitutional as applied to SCEF. We hold the abstention doctrine is inappropriate for cases such as the present one where, unlike Douglas v. City of Jeannette, statutes are justifiably attacked on their face as abridging free expression, or as applied for the purpose of discouraging protected activities.

. . . We believe that those affected by a statute are entitled to be free of the burdens of defending prosecutions, however expeditious, aimed at hammering out the structure of the statute piecemeal, with no likelihood of obviating similar uncertainty for others. Here, no readily apparent construction suggests itself as a vehicle for rehabilitating the statutes in a single prosecution, and appellants are entitled to an injunction. The State must, if it is to invoke the statutes after injunctive relief has been sought, assume the burden of obtaining a permissible narrow construction in a noncriminal proceeding[6] before it may seek modification of the injunction to permit future prosecutions. . . .

II

Each of the individual appellants was indicted for violating §364(7) of the Subversive Activities and Communist Control Law by failing to register as a member of a Communist-front organization. Smith and Waltzer were indicted for failing to register as members "of a Communist front organization known as the National Lawyers Guild, which said organization has been cited by committees and sub-committees of the United States Congress as a Communist front organization . . . ." Dombrowski and Smith were indicted for failing to register as members of "a Communist front organization known as the Southern Conference Educational Fund, which said organization is essentially the same as the Southern Conference for Human Welfare, which said Southern Conference for Human Welfare [has] . . . been cited by the committees of the United States Congress as a Communist front organization . . . ." Dombrowski and Smith were also indicted for violating

[6] Thirty-seven states, including Louisiana, have adopted the Uniform Declaratory Judgments Act. . . .

§364(4),[9] by acting as Executive Director and Treasurer respectively "of a subversive organization, to wit, the Southern Conference Educational Fund, said organization being essentially the same as the Southern Conference for Human Welfare, which said organization has been cited by committees of the United States Congress as a Communist front organization . . . ."

The statutory definition of "a subversive organization" in §359(5)[10] incorporated in the offense created by §364(4), is substantially identical to that of the Washington statute which we considered in Baggett v. Bullitt, supra, at 362, 363, n. 1. There the definition was used in a state statute requiring state employees to take an oath as a condition of employment. We held that the definition, as well as the oath based thereon, denied due process because it was unduly vague, uncertain and broad. Where, as here, protected freedoms of expression and association are similarly involved, we see no controlling distinction in the fact that the definition is used to provide a standard of criminality rather than the contents of a test oath. This overly broad statute also creates a "danger zone" within which protected expression may be inhibited. Cf. Speiser v. Randall, 357 U.S. 513, 526. So long as the statute remains available to the State the threat of prosecutions of protected expression is a real and substantial one. Even the prospect of ultimate failure of such prosecutions by no means dispels their chilling effect on protected expression. A Quantity of Copies of Books v. Kansas, 378 U.S. 205; Bantam Books, Inc. v. Sullivan, 372 U.S. 58; Marcus v. Search Warrant, 367 U.S. 717; Speiser v. Randall, supra. Since §364(4) is so intimately bound up with a definition invalid under the reasoning of Baggett v. Bullitt, we hold that it is invalid for the same reasons.

We also find the registration requirement of §364(7) invalid. That section creates an offense of failure to register as a member of a Communist-front organization, and, under §359(3),[11] "the fact that an organization has been officially cited or identified by the Attorney General of the United States, the Subversive Activities Control Board of the United States or any committee or

---

[9] Section 364(4) provides: "It shall be a felony for any person knowingly and willfully to . . . [a]ssist in the formation or participate in the management or to contribute to the support of any subversive organization or foreign subversive organization knowing said organization to be a subversive organization or a foreign subversive organization . . . ."

[10] Section 359(5) provides " 'Subversive organization' means any organization which engages in or advocates, abets, advises, or teaches, or a purpose of which is to engage in or advocate, abet, advise, or teach activities intended to overthrow, destroy, or to assist in the overthrow or destruction of the constitutional form of the government of the state of Louisiana, or of any political subdivision thereof by revolution, force, violence or other unlawful means, or any other organization which seeks by unconstitutional or illegal means to overthrow or destroy the government of the state of Louisiana or any political subdivision thereof and to establish in place thereof any form of government not responsible to the people of the state of Louisiana under the Constitution of the state of Louisiana."

[11] Section 359(3) provides: " 'Communist Front Organization' shall, for the purpose of this act include any communist action organization, communist front organization, communist infiltrated organization or communist controlled organization. . . ."

subcommittee of the United States Congress as a . . . communist front organization . . . shall be considered presumptive evidence of the factual status of any such organization." There is no requirement that the organization be so cited only after compliance with the procedural safeguards demanded by Anti-Fascist Committee v. McGrath, supra.

A designation resting on such safeguards is a minimum requirement to insure the rationality of the presumptions of the Louisiana statute and, in its absence, the presumptions cast an impermissible burden upon the appellants to show that the organizations are not Communist fronts. "Where the transcendent value of speech is involved, due process certainly requires . . . that the State bear the burden of persuasion to show that the appellants engaged in criminal speech." Speiser v. Randall, supra, at 526. It follows that §364(7), resting on the invalid presumption, is unconstitutional on its face. . . .

The judgment of the District Court is reversed and the cause is remanded for further proceedings consistent with this opinion. These shall include prompt framing of a decree restraining prosecution of the pending indictments against the individual appellants, ordering immediate return of all papers and documents seized, and prohibiting further acts enforcing the sections of the Subversive Activities and Communist Control Law here found void on their face. In addition, appellants are entitled to expeditious determination, without abstention, of the remaining issues raised in the complaint.

It is so ordered.

[Justices Black and Stewart did not participate in the decision. Mr. Justice Harlan, joined in his opinion by Mr. Justice Clark, dissented on the ground that the Court should have applied the abstention doctrine.]

REFERENCES

1. Legal discussion of the Dombrowski case has been primarily concerned with the use of federal power to enjoin state criminal proceedings. See Brewer, Dombrowski v. Pfister: Federal Injunctions Against State Prosecutions in Civil Rights Cases — A New Trend in Federal-State Judicial Relationships, 34 Fordham L. Rev. 71 (1965); Note, Federal Injunctions and State Enforcement of Invalid Criminal Statutes, 65 Colum. L. Rev. 647 (1965); Notes, 1965 Duke L.J. 813; 79 Harv. L. Rev. 103, 170-174 (1965); 114 U. Pa. L. Rev. 561 (1966). On this issue generally see also Note, Federal Power to Enjoin State Court Proceedings, 74 Harv. L. Rev. 726 (1961); Note, Developments in the Law — Injunctions, 78 Harv. L. Rev. 994 (1965); Amsterdam, Criminal Prosecutions Affecting Federally Guaranteed Civil Rights: Federal Removal and Habeas Corpus Jurisdiction to Abort State Court Trial, 113 U. Pa. L. Rev. 793 (1965).

2. In Cameron v. Johnson, 381 U.S. 741, 85 S. Ct. 1751, 14 L. Ed. 2d 715 (1965), the Court vacated per curiam, for consideration in light of Dombrowski, a District Court order dismissing a suit to enjoin enforcement of the Mississippi Anti-Picketing statute. 244 F. Supp. 846 (S.D. Miss. 1964). Justices Black, Harlan, Stewart, and White dissented, with Justices Black and White writing opinions. But in Wells v. Reynolds, 382 U.S. 39, 86 S. Ct. 160, 15 L. Ed. 2d 32 (1965), the Court affirmed per curiam a decision refusing

to enjoin a Georgia insurrection statute invoked against civil rights demonstrators in Albany, Georgia. Wells v. Hand, 238 F. Supp. 779 (M.D. Ga. 1965). Justices Douglas, Brennan, and Fortas dissented. See also Turner v. La Belle, 251 F. Supp. 443 (D. Conn. 1966).

NOTES

1. Shortly after the records of the Southern Conference Educational Fund were seized they were subpoenaed by the U.S. Senate Subcommittee on Internal Security from the Louisiana police. Dombrowski brought an action for damages and for an injunction against the Louisiana police to prevent removal of the records from Baton Rouge. At the hearing the defendants testified that the records had already been transferred to Mississippi at Senator Eastland's request and the injunction suit was dismissed as moot. Dombrowski v. Burbank, unreported (No. 13967, E.D. La., 1963). Later the S.C.E.F. and Dombrowski brought suit in the District of Columbia against Senator Eastland, the counsel for his Subcommittee, and certain Louisiana officials seeking an injunction against use of the records, their return, and damages in the amount of $500,000 for illegal seizure and false arrest. N.Y. Times, Nov. 2, 1963. The district court dismissed the injunction action and granted summary judgment for defendants as to the damage action. The court of appeals affirmed per curiam. Dombrowski v. Burbank, 358 F.2d 821 (D.C. Cir. 1966). Petition for certiorari, sub nom. Dombrowski v. Eastland, was filed in the Supreme Court. Meanwhile in the similar suit for $750,000 damages, brought in the federal district court in Louisiana against state officials, a motion for summary judgment by defendants was denied, interlocutory appeal was refused by the court of appeals, and the case was set for trial. Dombrowski v. Burbank (No. 13967, E.D. La.).

2. In Stanford v. Texas, 379 U.S. 476, 85 S. Ct. 506, 13 L. Ed. 2d 431 (1965), the Supreme Court considered the validity of a search warrant issued under Section 9 of the Texas Suppression Act, legislation which outlawed the Communist Party and created various individual criminal offenses. Tex. Rev. Civ. Stat., Art. 6889-3A. The warrant authorized the seizure of all "books, records, pamphlets, cards, receipts, lists, memoranda, pictures, recordings and other written instruments concerning the Communist Party of Texas, and the operations of the Communist Party in Texas."

Pursuant to the warrant state officials "went to the place described in the warrant, which was where the petitioner resided and carried on a mail order book business under the trade name 'All Points of View.' " As described by the Court: "Under the general supervision of one of the Assistant Attorneys General the officers spent more than four hours in gathering up about half the books they found in the house. Most of the material they took came from the stock in trade of the petitioner's business, but they took a number of books from his personal library as well. The books and pamphlets taken comprised approximately 300 separate titles, in addition to numerous issues of several different periodicals. Among the books taken were works by such diverse writers as Karl Marx, Jean Paul Sartre, Theodore Draper, Fidel Castro, Earl Browder, Pope John XXIII, and Mr. Justice Hugo L. Black. The officers also took possession of many of the petitioner's private documents and papers, including his marriage certificate, his insurance policies, his household bills and receipts, and files of his personal correspondence. All this material was packed into 14 cartons and hauled off to an investigator's office in the county courthouse. The officers did not find any 'records of the Communist Party' or any 'party lists and dues payments.'" 379 U.S. at 479-480.

Petitioner filed a motion with the magistrate who had issued the warrant, ask-ing him to annul the warrant and order return of all the property seized under it. The motion was denied. The Supreme Court reversed, without passing on the pre-emption problem, on the grounds that the Fourth Amendment as applicable to the states forbids "a general warrant."

3. Other recent cases of note involving proceedings under state anti-sedition laws include:

(a) On May 1, 1963, three students at the University of Indiana were indicted under the Indiana Anti-Communism Statute. Ind. Stat. Ann. §§10-5201 to 10-5209. The defendants were officers of the University chapter of the Young Socialist Alliance which had sponsored a campus meeting at which LeRoy McRae, a na-tional officer of the organization, had spoken on civil rights. They were charged with violation of a provision of the statute which stated: "Whenever two or more persons assemble for the purpose of advocating or teaching the doctrine that the government of the United States, or of the State of Indiana, should be overthrown by force, violence or any unlawful means, such an assembly is unlawful, and every person voluntarily participating therein by his presence, aid or instigation, shall be guilty of a felony." §10-5205. After the original indictment had been dismissed on a technicality, the defendants were reindicted. The new indictment added a charge under the same section based on a meeting in a private apartment of the defend-ants and their friends to discuss their defense against the first indictment, the proceedings having been tape-recorded by the landlord through a device attached to a heating duct.

The Indiana Supreme Court, overruling the trial court, upheld the indictment against pre-emption and First Amendment claims. State v. Levitt, — Ind. — , 203 N.E.2d 821 (1965). See N.Y. Times May 2, 3, and 4, 1963, and Mar. 21, 1964; Hanson, Hoosier Witch Hunt, The Nation, May 25, 1963.

(b) In August 1963 four civil rights leaders who had been engaged in a voter registration and desegregation campaign in Americus, Georgia, were arrested for violation of an insurrection statute of that state and a statute prohibiting unlawful assembly. Ga. Code §§26-902, 26-5301. The defendants were confined to jail with-out bail until November 1, when a three-judge federal court held the Georgia statutes unconstitutional and ordered their release. Aelony v. Pace (M.D. Ga. No. 530-1963); VIII Civil Liberties Docket 124 (1963); IX Civil Liberties Docket 4 (1963). For another aspect of this matter, see Allen v. State, 110 Ga. App. 56, 137 S.E.2d 711 (1964); X Civil Liberties Docket 9 (1964).

(c) In August 1964 William Epton was indicted under the New York criminal anarchy statute that had been involved in the Gitlow case. See Section C, subsection 1, supra. The charge grew out of a speech by Epton delivered at a street rally in Harlem on July 18, 1964. Two days before a white police officer had shot and killed a 15-year-old Negro boy. According to a tape recording of the speech, taken by a police agent in the crowd, Epton had said: "We will take our freedom. We will take it by any means necessary . . . we will create a new govern-ment . . . . And in the process of smashing the state we are going to have to kill a lot of these cops, a lot of these judges, and we'll have to go up against their army. We'll organize our own militia and our own army." N.Y. Times, Nov. 30, 1965. Epton was convicted, and sentenced to one year in jail. N.Y. Times, Dec. 21, 1965, and Jan. 28, 1966. For an account of the background of the indictment, see Donner, The Epton Anarchy Trial, The Nation, Nov. 15, 1965.

D. DENIAL OF PRIVILEGES OR POSITIONS OF INFLUENCE TO PERSONS DECLARED SUBVERSIVE

In the period following World War II there emerged a growing body of legislative and administrative measures which did not impose direct prohibitions upon conduct deemed detrimental to national security, but rather were designed to deny certain privileges, or eliminate from certain positions of influence, persons thought to pose such a threat. These restrictions do not normally involve, at least in the first instance, the use of criminal sanctions, and hence their administration and application are not confined by the traditional safeguards embodied in the criminal process. The proliferation of such measures, in the context of a society increasingly subject to manifold forms of social control, creates serious problems in maintaining a system of freedom of expression.

The most comprehensive of these restrictions, and in many ways the most significant, are the loyalty-security programs for employment, federal, state, and private. This phase of the problem is considered in the following section. At this point we are concerned with other types of restrictions, including those imposed upon holding office in labor organizations, the practice of law, the obtaining of tax or welfare benefits, access to the ballot, and citizenship. Freedom of movement is considered separately in Chapter XI.

REFERENCES

For discussion of this general development see O'Brian, National Security and Individual Freedom (1955); Chase, Security and Liberty: The Problem of Native Communists 1947-1955 (1955); Gellhorn, Individual Freedom and Governmental Restraints, chs. 1 and 3 (1956); Willcox, Invasions of the First Amendment Through Conditional Public Spending, 41 Cornell L.Q. 12 (1955); Konvitz, Fundamental Liberties of a Free People, chs. 22 and 23 (1957); Millis, Individual Freedom and the Common Defense 31-61 (1957); Brown, Loyalty and Security, especially chs. 3 and 15 (1958); Note, 28 Ind. L.J. 492 (1953); Ginzburg, Rededication to Freedom (1959); Cramton, The Supreme Court and State Power to Deal with Subversion and Loyalty, 43 Minn. L. Rev. 1025 (1959); Linde, Constitutional Rights in the Public Sector: Justice Douglas on Freedom in the Welfare State, 40 Wash. L. Rev. 10, 10-22 (1965).

On some of the broader aspects of the issues, see Franklin, Infamy and Constitutional Liberties, 14 Law. Guild Rev. 1 (1954); Cotter and Smith, Freedom and Authority in the Amphibial State, 1 Midwest J. Pol. Sci. 40 (1957); Jones, The Rule of Law and the Welfare State, 58 Colum. L. Rev. 143 (1958); Reich, The New Property, 73 Yale L.J.

733 (1964); Friedman, Freedom of Contract and Occupational Licensing 1890-1910: A Legal and Social Study, 53 Calif. L. Rev. 487 (1965).

With respect to the legal doctrine of unconstitutional conditions, see Merrill, Unconstitutional Conditions, 77 U. Pa. L. Rev. 879 (1920); Hale, Unconstitutional Conditions and Constitutional Rights, 35 Colum. L. Rev. 321 (1935); Note, Unconstitutional Conditions, 73 Harv. L. Rev. 1595 (1960); French, Unconstitutional Conditions: An Analysis, 50 Geo. L.J. 234 (1961).

1. Restrictions on Labor Organizations

The problems involved in denying privileges or positions to persons on the basis of political tests were posed initially by Section 9(h) of the Labor Management Relations Act (the Taft-Hartley Act), enacted in 1947. In the Douds case, set forth below, the Supreme Court for the first time addressed itself directly to these issues.

AMERICAN COMMUNICATIONS ASSOCIATION
v. DOUDS
339 U.S. 382, 70 S. Ct. 674, 94 L. Ed. 925 (1950)

Mr. Chief Justice Vinson delivered the opinion of the Court.

These cases present for decision the constitutionality of §9(h) of the National Labor Relations Act, as amended by the Labor Management Relations Act, 1947.[1] This section, commonly referred to as the non-Communist affidavit provision, reads as follows: "No investigation shall be made by the [National Labor Relations] Board of any question affecting commerce concerning the representation of employees, raised by a labor organization under subsection (c) of this section, no petition under section 9(e)(1) shall be entertained, and no complaint shall be issued pursuant to a charge made by a labor organization under subsection (b) of section 10, unless there is on file with the Board an affidavit executed contemporaneously or within the preceding twelve-month period by each officer of such labor organization and the officers of any national or international labor organization of which it is an affiliate or constituent unit that he is not a member of the Communist Party or affiliated with such party, and that he does not believe in, and is not a member of or supports any organization that believes in or teaches, the overthrow of the United States Government by force or by any illegal or unconstitutional methods. The provisions of section 35A of the Criminal Code shall be applicable in respect to such affidavits." . . .

[1] 61 Stat. 136, 146, 29 U.S.C. (Supp. III) §§141, 159(h), amending the National Labor Relations Act of 1935, 49 Stat. 449, 29 U.S.C. §151 et seq.

I

The constitutional justification for the National Labor Relations Act was the power of Congress to protect interstate commerce by removing obstructions to the free flow of commerce. National Labor Relations Board v. Jones & Laughlin Steel Corp., 301 U.S. 1 (1937). That Act was designed to remove obstructions caused by strikes and other forms of industrial unrest, which Congress found were attributable to the inequality of bargaining power between unorganized employees and their employers. It did so by strengthening employee groups, by restraining certain employer practices, and by encouraging the processes of collective bargaining.

When the Labor Management Relations Act was passed twelve years later, it was the view of Congress that additional impediments to the free flow of commerce made amendment of the original Act desirable. . . .

One such obstruction, which it was the purpose of §9(h) of the Act to remove, was the so-called "political strike." Substantial amounts of evidence were presented to various committees of Congress, including the committees immediately concerned with labor legislation, that Communist leaders of labor unions had in the past and would continue in the future to subordinate legitimate trade union objectives to obstructive strikes when dictated by Party leaders, often in support of the policies of a foreign government. And other evidence supports the view that some union leaders who hold to a belief in violent overthrow of the Government for reasons other than loyalty to the Communist Party likewise regard strikes and other forms of direct action designed to serve ultimate revolutionary goals as the primary objectives of labor unions which they control.[3] At the committee hearings, the incident most fully developed was a strike at the Milwaukee plant of the Allis-Chalmers Manufacturing Company in 1941, when that plant was producing vital materials for the national defense program. A full hearing was given not only to company officials, but also to leaders of the international and local unions involved. Congress heard testimony that the strike had been called solely in obedience to Party orders for the purpose of starting the "snowballing of strikes" in defense plants.[4]

No useful purpose would be served by setting out at length the evidence before Congress relating to the problem of political strikes, nor can we attempt to assess the validity of each item of evidence. It is sufficient to say that Congress had a great mass of material before it which tended to show that

[3] A detailed description of the aims and tactics of the Socialist Workers Party, for example, may be found in the transcript of record in Dunne v. United States, 320 U.S. 790 (1943), certiorari denied. We cite the record as evidence only and express no opinion whatever on the merits of the case. See record, pp. 267-271, 273-274, 330-332, 439, 475, 491-492, 495-496, 535, 606, 683-688, 693, 737, 804-805.

[4] See Hearings before House Committee on Education and Labor on Bills to Amend and Repeal the National Labor Relations Act, 80th Cong., 1st Sess. 3611-3615.

Communists and others proscribed by the statute had infiltrated union organizations not to support and further trade union objectives, including the advocacy of change by democratic methods, but to make them a device by which commerce and industry might be disrupted when the dictates of political policy required such action.

I I

. . . It cannot be denied that the practical effect of denial of access to the Board and the denial of a place on the ballot in representation proceedings is not merely to withhold benefits granted by the Government but to impose upon noncomplying unions a number of restrictions which would not exist if the Board had not been established.[6] The statute does not, however, specifically forbid persons who do not sign the affidavit from holding positions of union leadership nor require their discharge from office. The fact is that §9(h) may well make it difficult for unions to remain effective if their officers do not sign the affidavits. How difficult depends upon the circumstances of the industry, the strength of the union and its organizational discipline. We are, therefore, neither free to treat §9(h) as if it merely withdraws a privilege gratuitously granted by the Government, nor able to consider it a licensing statute prohibiting those persons who do not sign the affidavit from holding union office. The practicalities of the situation place the proscriptions of §9(h) somewhere between those two extremes. The difficult question that emerges is whether, consistently with the First Amendment, Congress, by statute, may exert these pressures upon labor unions to deny positions of leadership to certain persons who are identified by particular beliefs and political affiliations.

III

. . . The fact that the statute identifies persons by their political affiliations and beliefs, which are circumstances ordinarily irrelevant to permissible subjects of government action, does not lead to the conclusion that such circumstances are never relevant. In re Summers, 325 U.S. 561 (1945); Hamilton v. Regents, 293 U.S. 245 (1934). We have held that aliens may be barred from certain occupations because of a reasonable relation between that classification and the apprehended evil, Clarke v. Deckebach, 274 U.S. 392 (1927); Pearl Assurance Co. v. Harrington, 313 U.S. 549 (1941), even though the

[6] For example, a union whose officers do not file an affidavit in compliance with §9(h) may not enter into a union shop contract with an employer, as it was free to do before passage of the National Labor Relations Act. A noncomplying union is excluded from the ballot in representation proceedings. If another union is certified, the noncomplying union incurs the disabilities of §§8(b)4(C), and 303(a)(3), as it would not have done prior to 1935. Similarly, certain strikes and boycotts are prohibited to noncomplying unions by §§8(b)(4)(B), 8(b)(4)(C), 8(b)(4)(D) of the Act.

Constitution forbids arbitrary banning of aliens from the pursuit of lawful occupations. Truax v. Raich, 239 U.S. 33 (1915); Takahashi v. Fish and Game Commission, 334 U.S. 410 (1948). Even distinctions based solely on ancestry, which we declared "are by their very nature odious to a free people," have been upheld under the unusual circumstances of wartime. Hirabayashi v. United States, 320 U.S. 81 (1943). If accidents of birth and ancestry under some circumstances justify an inference concerning future conduct, it can hardly be doubted that voluntary affiliations and beliefs justify a similar inference when drawn by the legislature on the basis of its investigations.

This principle may be illustrated by reference to statutes denying positions of public importance to groups of persons identified by their business affiliations. One federal statute,[8] for example, provides that no partner or employee of a firm primarily engaged in underwriting securities may be a director of a national bank. . . . In this respect, §9(h) is not unlike a host of other statutes which prohibit specified groups of persons from holding positions of power and public interest because, in the legislative judgment, they threaten to abuse the trust that is a necessary concomitant of the power of office.

If no more were involved than possible loss of position, the foregoing would dispose of the case. But the more difficult problem here arises because, in drawing lines on the basis of beliefs and political affiliations, though it may be granted that the proscriptions of the statute bear a reasonable relation to the apprehended evil, Congress has undeniably discouraged the lawful exercise of political freedom as well. Stated otherwise, the problem is this: Communists, we may assume, carry on legitimate political activities. Beliefs are inviolate. Cantwell v. Connecticut, 310 U.S. 296, 303 (1940). Congress might reasonably find, however, that Communists, unlike members of other political parties, and persons who believe in overthrow of the Government by force, unlike persons of other beliefs, represent a continuing danger of disruptive political strikes when they hold positions of union leadership. By exerting pressures on unions to deny office to Communists and others identified therein, §9(h) undoubtedly lessens the threat to interstate commerce, but it has the further necessary effect of discouraging the exercise of political rights protected by the First Amendment. Men who hold union offices often have little choice but to renounce Communism or give up their offices. Unions which wish to do so are discouraged from electing Communists to office. To the grave and difficult problem thus presented we must now turn our attention.

IV

The unions contend that once it is determined that this is a free speech case, the "clear and present danger" test must apply. See Schenck v. United States,

---

[8] Sections 30 and 32 of the Banking Act of 1933, 48 Stat. 162, 193, 194, as amended, 49 Stat. 684, 709, 12 U.S.C. §§77, 78 [upheld in Board of Governors v. Agnew, 329 U.S. 441.]

249 U.S. 47 (1919). But they disagree as to how it should be applied. Appellant in No. 10 would require that joining the Communist Party or the expression of belief in overthrow of the Government by force be shown to be a clear and present danger of some substantive evil, since those are the doctrines affected by the statute. Petitioner in No. 13, on the other hand, would require a showing that political strikes, the substantive evil involved, are a clear and present danger to the security of the Nation or threaten widespread industrial unrest.

This confusion suggests that the attempt to apply the term, "clear and present danger," as a mechanical test in every case touching First Amendment freedoms, without regard to the context of its application, mistakes the form in which an idea was cast for the substance of the idea. . . .

[The] question with which we are here faced is not the same one that Justices Holmes and Brandeis found convenient to consider in terms of clear and present danger. Government's interest here is not in preventing the dissemination of Communist doctrine or the holding of particular beliefs because it is feared that unlawful action will result therefrom if free speech is practiced. Its interest is in protecting the free flow of commerce from what Congress considers to be substantial evils of conduct that are not the products of speech at all. Section 9(h), in other words, does not interfere with speech because Congress fears the consequences of speech; it regulates harmful conduct which Congress has determined is carried on by persons who may be identified by their political affiliations and beliefs. The Board does not contend that political strikes, the substantive evil at which §9(h) is aimed, are the present or impending products of advocacy of the doctrines of Communism or the expression of belief in overthrow of the Governmet by force. On the contrary, it points out that such strikes are called by persons who, so Congress has found, have the will and power to do so *without* advocacy or persuasion that seeks acceptance in the competition of the market. Speech may be fought with speech. Falsehoods and fallacies must be exposed, not suppressed, unless there is not sufficient time to avert the evil consequences of noxious doctrine by argument and education. That is the command of the First Amendment. But force may and must be met with force. Section 9(h) is designed to protect the public not against what Communists and others identified therein advocate or believe, but against what Congress has concluded they have done and are likely to do again.

The contention of petitioner in No. 13 that this Court must find that political strikes create a clear and present danger to the security of the Nation or of widespread industrial strife in order to sustain §9(h) similarly misconceives the purpose that phrase was intended to serve. In that view, not the relative certainty that evil conduct will result from speech in the immediate future, but the extent and gravity of the substantive evil must be measured by the "test" laid down in the Schenck case. But there the Court said that: "The question in every case is whether the *words* used are used in such circumstances and are of such a nature as to create a clear and present danger that they will bring about the substantive evils that Congress has a right to prevent." Schenck v. United States, supra at 52. (Emphasis supplied.)

So far as the Schenck case itself is concerned, imminent danger of any substantive evil that Congress may prevent justifies the restriction of speech. Since that time this Court has decided that however great the likelihood that a substantive evil will result, restrictions on speech and press cannot be sustained unless the evil itself is "substantial" and "relatively serious," Brandeis, J., concurring in Whitney v. California [274 U.S. at 374, 377], or sometimes "extremely serious," Bridges v. California, 314 U.S. 252, 263 (1941). And it follows therefrom that even harmful conduct cannot justify restrictions upon speech unless substantial interests of society are at stake. But in suggesting that the substantive evil must be serious and substantial, it was never the intention of this Court to lay down an absolutist test measured in terms of danger to the Nation. When the effect of a statute or ordinance upon the exercise of First Amendment freedoms is relatively small and the public interest to be protected is substantial, it is obvious that a rigid test requiring a showing of imminent danger to the security of the Nation is an absurdity. We recently dismissed for want of substantiality an appeal in which a church group contended that its First Amendment rights were violated by a municipal zoning ordinance preventing the building of churches in certain residential areas. Corporation of the Presiding Bishop of the Church of Jesus Christ of Latter-Day Saints v. Porterville, 338 U.S. 805 (1949). And recent cases in this Court involving contempt by publication likewise have no meaning if imminent danger of national peril is the criterion.[12] . . .

When particular conduct is regulated in the interest of public order, and the regulation results in an indirect, conditional, partial abridgment of speech, the duty of the courts is to determine which of these two conflicting interests demands the greater protection under the particular circumstances presented. The high place in which the right to speak, think, and assemble as you will was held by the Framers of the Bill of Rights and is held today by those who value liberty both as a means and an end indicates the solicitude with which we must view any assertion of personal freedoms. We must recognize, moreover, that regulation of "conduct" has all too frequently been employed by public authority as a cloak to hide censorship of unpopular ideas. We have been reminded that "It is not often in this country that we now meet with direct and candid efforts to stop speaking or publication as such. Modern inroads on these rights come from associating the speaking with some other factor which the state may regulate so as to bring the whole within official control." [13]

On the other hand, legitimate attempts to protect the public, not from the

[12] Bridges v. California, 314 U.S. 252 (1941); Pennekamp v. Florida, 328 U.S. 331 (1946); Craig v. Harney, 331 U.S. 367 (1947).
[13] Mr. Justice Jackson, concurring in Thomas v. Collins, 323 U.S. 516, 547 (1945).

remote possible effects of noxious ideologies, but from present excesses of direct, active conduct, are not presumptively bad because they interfere with and, in some of its manifestations, restrain the exercise of First Amendment rights. Reynolds v. United States [98 U.S. 145]; Prince v. Massachusetts [321 U.S. 158]; Cox v. New Hampshire [312 U.S. 569]; Giboney v. Empire Storage Co. [336 U.S. 490]. In essence the problem is one of weighing the probable effects of the statute upon the free exercise of the right of speech and assembly against the congressional determination that political strikes are evils of conduct which cause substantial harm to interstate commerce and that Communists and others identified by §9(h) pose continuing threats to that public interest when in positions of union leadership. We must, therefore, undertake the "delicate and difficult task . . . to weigh the circumstances and to appraise the substantiality of the reasons advanced in support of the regulation of the free enjoyment of the rights." Schneider v. State, 308 U.S. 147, 161 (1939).

V

The "reasons advanced in support of the regulation" are of considerable weight, as even the opponents of §9(h) agreed. They are far from being "[m]ere legislative preferences or beliefs respecting matters of public convenience [which] may well support regulation directed at other personal activities, but be insufficient to justify such as diminishes the exercise of rights so vital to the maintenance of democratic institutions." [14] It should be emphasized that Congress, not the courts, is primarily charged with determination of the need for regulation of activities affecting interstate commerce. This Court must, if such regulation unduly infringes personal freedoms, declare the statute invalid under the First Amendment's command that the opportunities for free public discussion be maintained. But insofar as the problem is one of drawing inferences concerning the need for regulation of particular forms of conduct from conflicting evidence, this Court is in no position to substitute its judgment as to the necessity or desirability of the statute for that of Congress. . . .

When compared with ordinances and regulations dealing with littering of the streets or disturbance of householders by itinerant preachers, the relative significance and complexity of the problem of political strikes and how to deal with their leaders becomes at once apparent. It must be remembered that §9(h) is not an isolated statute dealing with a subject divorced from the problems of labor peace generally. It is a part of some very complex machinery set up by the Federal Government for the purpose of encouraging the peaceful settlement of labor disputes. Under the statutory scheme, unions which become collective bargaining representatives for groups of employees often represent not only members of the union but nonunion workers or

[14] Schneider v. State, 308 U.S. 147, 161 (1939).

members of other unions as well. Because of the necessity to have strong unions to bargain on equal terms with strong employers, individual employees are required by law to sacrifice rights which, in some cases, are valuable to them. See J. I. Case Co. v. Labor Board, 321 U.S. 332 (1944). The loss of individual rights for the greater benefit of the group results in a tremendous increase in the power of the representative of the group — the union. But power is never without responsibility. And when authority derives in part from Government's thumb on the scales, the exercise of that power by private persons becomes closely akin, in some respects, to its exercise by Government itself. See Graham v. Brotherhood of Locomotive Firemen, 338 U.S. 232 (1949); Steele v. Louisville & N.R. Co., 323 U.S. 192 (1944); Tunstall v. Brotherhood of Locomotive Firemen, 323 U.S. 210 (1944); Railway Mail Association v. Corsi, 326 U.S. 88, 94 (1945).

We do not suggest that labor unions which utilize the facilities of the National Labor Relations Board become Government agencies or may be regulated as such. But it is plain that when Congress clothes the bargaining representative "with powers comparable to those possessed by a legislative body both to create and restrict the rights of those whom it represents," [15] the public interest in the good faith exercise of that power is very great.

What of the effects of §9(h) upon the rights of speech and assembly of those proscribed by its terms? The statute does not prevent or punish by criminal sanctions the making of a speech, the affiliation with any organization, or the holding of any belief. But as we have noted, the fact that no direct restraint or punishment is imposed upon speech or assembly does not determine the free speech question. Under some circumstances, indirect "discouragements" undoubtedly have the same coercive effect upon the exercise of First Amendment rights as imprisonment, fines, injunctions or taxes. A requirement that adherents of particular religious faiths or political parties wear identifying armbands, for example, is obviously of this nature.

But we have here no statute which is either frankly aimed at the suppression of dangerous ideas nor one which, although ostensibly aimed at the regulation of conduct, may actually "be made the instrument of arbitrary suppression of free expression of views." Hague v. Committee for Industrial Organization, 307 U.S. 496, 516 (1939). There are here involved none of the elements of censorship or prohibition of the dissemination of information that were present in the cases mainly relied upon by those attacking the statute. The "discouragements" of §9(h) proceed, not against the groups or beliefs identified therein, but only against the combination of those affiliations or beliefs with occupancy of a position of great power over the economy of the country. Congress has concluded that substantial harm, in the form of direct, positive action, may be expected from the combination. In this legislation, Congress did not restrain the activities of the Communist Party as a political organization; nor did it attempt to stifle beliefs. Compare West Virginia State

[15] Steele v. Louisville & N.R. Co., 323 U.S. 192, 202 (1944).

Board of Education v. Barnette, 319 U.S. 624 (1943). Section 9(h) touches only a relative handful of persons, leaving the great majority of persons of the identified affiliations and beliefs completely free from restraint. And it leaves those few who are affected free to maintain their affiliations and beliefs subject only to possible loss of positions which Congress has concluded are being abused to the injury of the public by members of the described groups. . . .

It is contended that the principle that statutes touching First Amendment freedoms must be narrowly drawn dictates that a statute aimed at political strikes should make the calling of such strikes unlawful but should not attempt to bring about the removal of union officers, with its attendant effect upon First Amendment rights. We think, however, that the legislative judgment that interstate commerce must be protected from a continuing threat of such strikes is a permissible one in this case. The fact that the injury to interstate commerce would be an accomplished fact before any sanctions could be applied, the possibility that a large number of such strikes might be called at a time of external or internal crisis, and the practical difficulties which would be encountered in detecting illegal activities of this kind are factors which are persuasive that Congress should not be powerless to remove the threat, not limited to punishing the act. . . .

VI

Previous discussion has considered the constitutional questions raised by §9(h) as they apply alike to members of the Communist Party and affiliated organizations and to persons who believe in overthrow of the Government by force. The breadth of the provision concerning belief in overthrow of the Government by force would raise additional questions, however, if it were read very literally to include all persons who might, under any conceivable circumstances, subscribe to that belief.

But we see no reason to construe the statute so broadly. . . . Its manifest purpose was to bring within the terms of the statute only those persons whose beliefs strongly indicate a will to engage in political strikes and other forms of direct action when, as officers, they direct union activities. The congressional purpose is therefore served if we construe the clause, "that he does not believe in, and is not a member of or supports any organization that believes in or teaches, the overthrow of the United States Government by force or by any illegal or unconstitutional methods," to apply to persons and organizations who believe in violent overthrow of the Government as it presently exists under the Constitution as an objective, not merely a prophecy. . . .

As thus construed, we think that the "belief" provision of the oath presents no different problem from that present in that part of the section having to do with membership in the Communist Party. Of course we agree that one may not be imprisoned or executed because he holds particular beliefs. But to attack the straw man of "thought control" is to ignore the fact that the sole effect of the statute upon one who believes in overthrow of the Government by force and violence — and does not deny his belief — is that he may be forced to relinquish his position as a union leader. That fact was crucial in our discussion of the statute as it relates to membership in the Communist Party. . . .

If the principle that one may under no circumstances be required to state his beliefs on any subject nor suffer the loss of any right or privilege because of his beliefs be a valid one, its application in other possible situations becomes relevant. Suppose, for example, that a federal statute provides that no person may become a member of the Secret Service force assigned to protect the President unless he swears that he does not believe in assassination of the President. Is this beyond the power of Congress, whatever the need revealed by its investigations? An affirmative answer hardly commends itself to reason unless, indeed, the Bill of Rights has been converted into a "suicide pact." Terminiello v. Chicago, 337 U.S. 1, 37 (1949) (dissenting opinion). Yet the example chosen is far-fetched only because of the manifest absurdity of reliance upon an oath in such a situation. One can have no doubt that the screening process in the selection of persons to occupy such positions probes far deeper than mere oath-taking can possibly do. . . .

Insofar as a distinction between beliefs and political affiliations is based upon absence of any "overt act" in the former case, it is relevant, if at all, in connection with problems of proof. In proving that one swore falsely that he is not a Communist, the act of joining the Party is crucial. Proof that one lied in swearing that he does not believe in overthrow of the Government by force, on the other hand, must consist in proof of his mental state. . . .

Considering the circumstances surrounding the problem — the deference due the congressional judgment concerning the need for regulation of conduct affecting interstate commerce and the effect of the statute upon rights of speech, assembly and belief — we conclude that §9(h) of the National Labor Relations Act, as amended by the Labor Management Relations Act, 1947, does not unduly infringe freedoms protected by the First Amendment. Those who, so Congress has found, would subvert the public interest cannot escape all regulation because, at the same time, they carry on legitimate political activities. Cf. Valentine v. Chrestensen, 316 U.S. 52 (1942). To encourage unions to displace them from positions of great power over the national economy, while at the same time leaving free the outlets by which they may pursue legitimate political activities of persuasion and advocacy, does not seem to us to contravene the purposes of the First Amendment. That Amendment requires that one be permitted to believe what he will. It requires that one be permitted to advocate what he will unless there is a clear and present danger that a substantial public evil will result therefrom. It does not require that he be permitted to be the keeper of the arsenal.

VII

There remain two contentions which merit discussion. One is that §9(h) is unconstitutionally vague. The other is that it violates the mandate of Art. I, §9 of the Constitution that "No Bill of Attainder or ex post facto Law shall be passed."

The argument as to vagueness stresses the breadth of such terms as "affiliated," "supports" and "illegal or unconstitutional methods." There is little doubt that imagination can conjure up hypothetical cases in which the meaning of these terms will be in nice question. The applicable standard, however, is not one of wholly consistent academic definition of abstract terms. It is, rather, the practical criterion of fair notice to those to whom the statute is directed. The particular context is all important.

The only criminal punishment specified is the application of §35(A) of the Criminal Code, 18 U.S.C. §1001, which covers only those false statements made "knowingly and willfully." The question in any criminal prosecution involving a non-Communist affidavit must therefore be whether the affiant acted in good faith or knowingly lied concerning his affiliations, beliefs, support of organizations, etc. And since the constitutional vice in a vague or indefinite statute is the injustice to the accused in placing him on trial for an offense, the nature of which he is given no fair warning, the fact that punishment is restricted to acts done with knowledge that they contravene the statute makes this objection untenable. As this Court pointed out in United States v. Ragen, 314 U.S. 513, 524 (1942), "A mind intent upon willful evasion is inconsistent with surprised innocence." Cf. Omaechevarria v. Idaho, 246 U.S. 343 (1918); Hygrade Provision Co. v. Sherman, 266 U.S. 497 (1925); Screws v. United States, 325 U.S. 91 (1945). Without considering, therefore, whether in other circumstances the words used in §9(h) would render a statute unconstitutionally vague and indefinite, we think that the fact that under §35(A) of the Criminal Code no honest, untainted interpretation of those words is punishable removes the possibility of constitutional infirmity.

The unions' argument as to bill of attainder cites the familiar cases, United States v. Lovett, 328 U.S. 303 (1946); Ex parte Garland, 4 Wall. 333 (1867); Cummings v. Missouri, 4 Wall. 277 (1867). Those cases and this also, according to the argument, involve the proscription of certain occupations to a group classified according to belief and loyalty. But there is a decisive distinction: in the previous decisions the individuals involved were in fact being punished for *past* actions; whereas in this case they are subject to possible loss of position only because there is substantial ground for the congressional judgment that their beliefs and loyalties will be transformed into *future* conduct. Of course, the history of the past conduct is the foundation for the judgment as to what the future conduct is likely to be; but that does not alter the conclusion that §9(h) is intended to prevent future action rather than to punish past action.

This distinction is emphasized by the fact that members of those groups identified in §9(h) are free to serve as union officers if at any time they renounce the allegiances which constituted a bar to signing the affidavit in the past. Past conduct, actual or threatened by their previous adherence to affiliations and beliefs mentioned in §9(h), is not a bar to resumption of the position. In the cases relied upon by the unions on the other hand, this Court has emphasized that, since the basis of disqualification was past action or loyalty, nothing that those persons proscribed by its terms could ever do would change the result. . . .

In their argument on this point, the unions seek some advantage from references to English history pertinent to a religious test oath. That experience is written into our Constitution in the following provision of Article VI: "The Senators and Representatives before mentioned, and the Members of the several State Legislatures, and all executive and judicial Officers, both of the United States and of the several States, shall be bound by Oath or Affirmation, to support this Constitution; but no religious Test shall ever be required as a Qualification to any Office or public Trust under the United States." It is obvious that not all oaths were abolished; the mere fact that §9(h) is in oath form hardly rises to the stature of a constitutional objection. All that was forbidden was a "religious Test." We do not think that the oath here involved can rightly be taken as falling within that category.

Clearly the Constitution permits the requirement of oaths by officeholders to uphold the Constitution itself. The obvious implication is that those unwilling to take such an oath are to be barred from public office. For the President, a specific oath was set forth in the Constitution itself. Art. II, §1. And Congress has detailed an oath for other Federal officers.[22] Obviously, the Framers of the Constitution thought that the exaction of an affirmation of minimal loyalty to the Government was worth the price of whatever deprivation of individual freedom of conscience was involved. All that we need hold here is that the casting of §9(h) into the mold of an oath does not invalidate it, if it is otherwise constitutional.

We conclude that §9(h) of the National Labor Relations Act, as amended by the Labor Management Relations Act, 1947, as herein construed, is compatible with the Federal Constitution and may stand. The judgments of the courts below are therefore

Affirmed.

Mr. Justice Douglas, Mr. Justice Clark, and Mr. Justice Minton took no part in the consideration or decision of these cases.

---

[22] 23 Stat. 22, 5 U.S.C. §16.

M<small>R</small>. J<small>USTICE</small> F<small>RANKFURTER</small> concurring in the Court's opinion except as to Part VII. . . .

In my view Congress has cast its net too indiscriminately in some of the provisions of §9(h). To ask avowal that one "does not believe in, and is not a member of or supports any organization that believes in . . . the overthrow of the United States Government . . . by any illegal or unconstitutional methods" is to ask assurances from men regarding matters that open the door too wide to mere speculation or uncertainty. It is asking more than rightfully may be asked of ordinary men to take oath that a method is not "unconstitutional" or "illegal" when constitutionality or legality is frequently determined by this Court by the chance of a single vote. It does not meet the difficulty to suggest that the hazard of a prosecution for perjury is not great since the convictions for perjury must be founded on willful falsity. To suggest that a judge might not be justified in allowing a case to go to a jury, or that a jury would not be justified in convicting, or that, on the possible happening of these events, an appellate court would be compelled to reverse, or, finally, that resort could be had to this Court for review on a petition for certiorari, affords safeguards too tenuous to neutralize the danger. See Musser v. Utah, 333 U.S. 95. The hazards that were found to be fatal to the legislation under review in Winters v. New York, 333 U.S. 507, appear trivial by comparison with what is here involved. . . .

I cannot deem it within the rightful authority of Congress to probe into opinions that involve only an argumentative demonstration of some coincidental parallelism of belief with some of the beliefs of those who direct the policy of the Communist Party, though without any allegiance to it. To require oaths as to matters that open up such possibilities invades the inner life of men whose compassionate thought or doctrinaire hopes may be as far removed from any dangerous kinship with the Communist creed as were those of the founders of the present orthodox political parties in this country.

The offensive provisions of §9(h) leave unaffected, however, the valid portions of the section. In §16, Congress has made express provision for such severance. Since the judgments below were based in part on what I deem unconstitutional requirements, I cannot affirm but would remand to give opportunity to obey merely the valid portions of §9(h).

M<small>R</small>. J<small>USTICE</small> J<small>ACKSON</small>, concurring and dissenting, each in part.

If the statute before us required labor union officers to forswear membership in the Republican Party, the Democratic Party or the Socialist Party, I suppose all agree that it would be unconstitutional. But why, if it is valid as to the Communist Party?

The answer, for me, is in the decisive differences between the Communist Party and every other party of any importance in the long experience of the United States with party government. In order that today's decision may not be useful as a precedent for suppression of any political opposition compatible with our free institutions, I limit concurrence to grounds and distinctions explicitly set forth herein, without which I should regard this Act as unconstitutional. . . .

From information before its several Committees and from facts of general knowledge, Congress could rationally conclude that, behind its political party façade, the Communist Party is a conspiratorial and revolutionary junta, organized to reach ends and to use methods which are incompatible with our constitutional system. A rough and compressed grouping of this data would permit Congress to draw these important conclusions as to its distinguishing characteristics.*

1. *The goal of the Communist Party is to seize powers of government by and for a minority rather than to acquire power through the vote of a free electorate.* It seeks not merely a change of administration, or of Congress, or reform legislation within the constitutional framework. Its program is not merely to socialize property more rapidly and extensively than the other parties are doing. While the difference between other parties in these matters is largely as to pace, the Communist Party's difference is one of direction. . . .

2. *The Communist Party alone among American parties past or present is dominated and controlled by a foreign government.* It is a satrap party which, to the threat of civil disorder, adds the threat of betrayal into alien hands. . . .

3. *Violent and undemocratic means are the calculated and indispensable methods to attain the Communist Party's goal.* It would be incredible naïveté to expect the American branch of this movement to forego the only methods by which a Communist Party has anywhere come into power. In not one of the countries it now dominates was the Communist Party chosen by a free or contestible election; in not one can it be evicted by any election. The international police state has crept over Eastern Europe by deception, coercion, coup d'etat, terrorism and assassination. Not only has it overpowered its critics and opponents; it has usually liquidated them. The American Communist Party has copied the organizational structure and its leaders have been schooled in the same technique and by the same tutors.

4. *The Communist Party has sought to gain this leverage and hold on the American population by acquiring control of the labor movement.* All political parties have wooed labor and its leaders. But what other parties seek is principally the vote of labor. The Communist Party, on the other hand, is not primarily interested in labor's vote, for it does not expect to win by votes. It strives for control of labor's coercive power — the sitdown, the slow-down, sabotage, or other means of producing industrial paralysis. . . .

5. *Every member of the Communist Party is an agent to execute the Communist program.* What constitutes a party? Major political parties in the United States have never been closely knit or secret organizations. Anyone

* [Mr. Justice Jackson's footnotes, citing the material upon which his conclusions are based, are omitted.]

who usually votes the party ticket is reckoned a member, although he has not applied for or been admitted to membership, pays no dues, has taken no pledge, and is free to vote, speak and act as he wills. . . .

Membership in the Communist Party is totally different. The Party is a secret conclave. Members are admitted only upon acceptance as reliable and after indoctrination in its policies, to which the member is fully committed. They are provided with cards or credentials, usually issued under false names so that the identification can only be made by officers of the Party who hold the code. Moreover, each pledges unconditional obedience to party authority. Adherents are known by secret or code names. They constitute "cells" in the factory, the office, the political society, or the labor union. For any deviation from the party line they are purged and excluded.

Inferences from membership in such an organization are justifiably different from those to be drawn from membership in the usual type of political party. Individuals who assume such obligations are chargeable, on ordinary conspiracy principles, with responsibility for and participation in all that makes up the Party's program. The conspiracy principle has traditionally been employed to protect society against all "ganging up" or concerted action in violation of its laws. No term passes that this Court does not sustain convictions based on that doctrine for violations of the antitrust laws or other statutes. However, there has recently entered the dialectic of politics a cliché used to condemn application of the conspiracy principle to Communists. "Guilt by association" is an epithet frequently used and little explained, except that it is generally accompanied by another slogan, "guilt is personal." Of course it is; but personal guilt may be incurred by joining a conspiracy. That act of association makes one responsible for the acts of others committed in pursuance of the association. It is wholly a question of the sufficiency of evidence of association to imply conspiracy. There is certainly sufficient evidence that all members owe allegiance to every detail of the Communist Party program and have assumed a duty actively to help execute it, so that Congress could, on familiar conspiracy principles, charge each member with responsibility for the goals and means of the Party. . . .

I conclude that we cannot deny Congress power to take these measures under the Commerce Clause to require labor union officers to disclose their membership in or affiliation with the Communist Party.

Congress has, however, required an additional disclaimer, which in my view does encounter serious constitutional objections. A union officer must also swear that "he does not believe in . . . the overthrow of the United States Government by force or by any illegal or unconstitutional methods."

If Congress has power to condition any right or privilege of an American citizen upon disclosure and disavowal of belief on any subject, it is obviously this one. But the serious issue is whether Congress has power to proscribe any opinion or belief which has not manifested itself in any overt act. While the forepart of the oath requires disclosure and disavowal of relationships which depend on overt acts of membership or affiliation, the afterpart demands revelation and denial of mere beliefs or opinions, even though they may never have matured into any act whatever or even been given utterance. In fact, the oath requires one to form and express a conviction on an abstract proposition which many good citizens, if they have thought of it at all, have considered too academic and remote to bother about.

That this difference is decisive on the question of power becomes unmistakable when we consider measures of enforcement. The only sanction prescribed, and probably the only one possible in dealing with a false affidavit, is punishment for perjury. If one is accused of falsely stating that he was not a member of, or affiliated with, the Communist Party, his conviction would depend upon proof of visible and knowable overt acts or courses of conduct sufficient to establish that relationship. But if one is accused of falsely swearing that he did not believe something that he really did believe, the trial must revolve around the conjecture as to whether he candidly exposed his state of mind.

The law sometimes does inquire as to mental state, but only so far as I recall when it is incidental to, and determines the quality of, some overt act in question. From its circumstances, courts sometimes must decide whether an act was committed intentionally or whether its results were intended, or whether the action taken was in malice, or after deliberation, or with knowledge of certain facts. But in such cases the law pries into the mind only to determine the nature and culpability of an act, as a mitigating or aggravating circumstance, and I know of no situation in which a citizen may incur civil or criminal liability or disability because a court infers an evil mental state where no act at all has occurred. Our trial processes are clumsy and unsatisfying for inferring cogitations which are incidental to actions, but they do not even pretend to ascertain the thought that has had no outward manifestation. Attempts of the courts to fathom modern political meditations of an accused would be as futile and mischievous as the efforts in the infamous heresy trials of old to fathom religious beliefs. . . .

I conclude that today's task can only be discharged by holding that all parts of this oath which require disclosure of overt acts of affiliation or membership in the Communist Party are within the competence of Congress to enact and that any parts of it that call for a disclosure of belief unconnected with any overt act are beyond its power.

Mr. Justice Black, dissenting.

We have said that "Freedom to think is absolute of its own nature; the most tyrannical government is powerless to control the inward workings of the mind."[1] But people can be, and in less democratic countries have been, made to suffer for their admitted or conjectured thoughts. Blackstone recalls

---

[1] Dissenting opinion in Jones v. Opelika, 316 U.S. 584, 618, adopted as the Court's opinion in 319 U.S. 103. See also Cantwell v. Connecticut, 310 U.S. 296, 303.

that Dionysius is "recorded to have executed a subject, barely for dreaming that he had killed him; which was held for a sufficient proof, that he had thought thereof in his waking hours."[2] Such a result, while too barbaric to be tolerated in our nation, is not illogical if a government can tamper in the realm of thought and penalize "belief" on the ground that it might lead to illegal conduct. Individual freedom and governmental thought-probing cannot live together. As the Court admits even today, under the First Amendment "Beliefs are inviolate."

Today's decision rejects that fundamental principle. The Court admits, as it must, that the "proscriptions" of §9(h) of the National Labor Relations Act as amended by the Taft-Hartley Act rest on "beliefs and political affiliations," and that "Congress has undeniably discouraged the lawful exercise of political freedoms" which are "protected by the First Amendment." These inescapable facts should compel a holding that §9(h) conflicts with the First Amendment.

Crucial to the Court's contrary holding is the premise that congressional power to regulate trade and traffic includes power to proscribe "beliefs and political affiliations." No case cited by the Court provides the least vestige of support for thus holding that the Commerce Clause restricts the right to think. On the contrary, the First Amendment was added after adoption of the Constitution for the express purpose of barring Congress from using previously granted powers to abridge belief or its expression. Freedom to think is inevitably abridged when beliefs are penalized by imposition of civil disabilities.

Since §9(h) was passed to exclude certain beliefs from one arena of the national economy, it was quite natural to utilize the test oath as a weapon. History attests the efficacy of that instrument for inflicting penalties and disabilities on obnoxious minorities. It was one of the major devices used against the Huguenots in France, and against "heretics" during the Spanish Inquisition. It helped English rulers identify and outlaw Catholics, Quakers, Baptists, and Congregationalists — groups considered dangerous for political as well as religious reasons. And wherever the test oath was in vogue, spies and informers found rewards far more tempting than truth. Painful awareness of the evils of thought espionage made such oaths "an abomination to the founders of this nation," In re Summers, 325 U.S. 561, 576, dissenting opinion. Whether religious, political, or both, test oaths are implacable foes of free thought. By approving their imposition, this Court has injected compromise into a field where the First Amendment forbids compromise.

The Court assures us that today's encroachment on liberty is just a small one, that this particular statutory provision "touches only a relative handful of persons, leaving the great majority of persons of the identified affiliations and beliefs completely free from restraint." But not the least of the virtues of the First Amendment is its protection of each member of the smallest and most unorthodox minority. Centuries of experience testify that laws aimed at

[2] 4 Blackstone, Commentaries 79 (6th ed. Dublin 1775).

one political or religious group, however rational these laws may be in their beginnings, generate hatreds and prejudices which rapidly spread beyond control. Too often it is fear which inspires such passions, and nothing is more reckless or contagious. In the resulting hysteria, popular indignation tars with the same brush all those who have ever been associated with any member of the group under attack or who hold a view which, though supported by revered Americans as essential to democracy, has been adopted by that group for its own purposes.

Under such circumstances, restrictions imposed on proscribed groups are seldom static, even though the rate of expansion may not move in geometric progression from discrimination to armband to ghetto and worse. Thus I cannot regard the Court's holding as one which merely bars Communists from holding union office and nothing more. For its reasoning would apply just as forcibly to statutes barring Communists and their suspected sympathizers from election to political office, mere membership in unions, and in fact from getting or holding any jobs whereby they could earn a living. . . .

Today the "political affiliation" happens to be the Communist Party: testimony of an ex-Communist that some Communist union officers had called "political strikes" is held sufficient to uphold a law coercing union members not to elect any Communist as an officer. Under this reasoning, affiliations with other political parties could be proscribed just as validly. Of course there is no practical possibility that either major political party would turn this weapon on the other, even though members of one party were accused of "political lockouts" a few years ago and members of the other are now charged with fostering a "welfare state" alien to our system. But with minor parties the possibility is not wholly fanciful. One, for instance, advocates socialism; another allegedly follows the Communist "line"; still another is repeatedly charged with a desire and purpose to deprive Negroes of equal job opportunities. Under today's opinion Congress could validly bar all members of these parties from officership in unions or industrial corporations; the only showing required would be testimony that some members in such positions had, by attempts to further their party's purposes, unjustifiably fostered industrial strife which hampered interstate commerce.

It is indicated, although the opinion is not thus limited and is based on threats to commerce rather than to national security, that members of the Communist Party or its "affiliates" can be individually attainted without danger to others because there is some evidence that as a group they act in obedience to the commands of a foreign power. This was the precise reason given in Sixteenth-Century England for attainting all Catholics unless they subscribed to test oaths wholly incompatible with their religion. Yet in the hour of crisis, an overwhelming majority of the English Catholics thus persecuted rallied loyally to defend their homeland against Spain and its Catholic troops. And in our own country Jefferson and his followers were earnestly accused of subversive allegiance to France. At the time, imposition of civil disability on all members of his political party must have seemed at least as desirable as does §9(h) today. For at stake, so many believed, was the survival of a newly-founded nation, not merely a few potential interruptions of commerce by strikes "political" rather than economic in origin.

These experiences underline the wisdom of the basic constitutional precept that penalties should be imposed only for a person's own conduct, not for his beliefs or for the conduct of others with whom he may associate. Guilt should not be imputed solely from association or affiliation with political parties or any other organization, however much we abhor the ideas which they advocate. Schneiderman v. United States, 320 U.S. 118, 136-139. Like anyone else, individual Communists who commit overt acts in violation of valid laws can and should be punished. But the postulate of the First Amendment is that our free institutions can be maintained without proscribing or penalizing political belief, speech, press, assembly, or party affiliation. This is a far bolder philosophy than despotic rulers can afford to follow. It is the heart of the system on which our freedom depends.

Fears of alien ideologies have frequently agitated the nation and inspired legislation aimed at suppressing advocacy of those ideologies. At such times the fog of public excitement obscures the ancient landmarks set up in our Bill of Rights. Yet then, of all times, should this Court adhere most closely to the course they mark. . . .

NOTES

1. The same issues were raised in Osman v. Douds, 339 U.S. 846, 70 S. Ct. 901, 94 L. Ed. 1328 (1950), decided per curiam a month later. Justices Douglas and Minton, who had not participated in the first case, voted in the Osman case. Mr. Justice Minton agreed with Chief Justice Vinson. Mr. Justice Douglas joined Justices Black, Frankfurter, and Jackson in holding the belief portion of the provision invalid, but found it unnecessary to pass on the remaining provisions. Mr. Justice Clark did not participate. The result was that the Court was equally divided on the belief portion of the affidavit and 6 to 1 in favor of the validity of the other provisions.

2. Prior to the repeal of Section 9(h) in 1959 (see infra), the overwhelming proportion of unions dealing with employers subject to the National Labor Relations Act maintained compliance with Section 9(h) through annual filing of the required affidavits. No official figures were published during most of these years but in a letter to the editors dated July 3, 1957 the National Labor Relations Board summarized the state of compliance as follows: "The number of international unions presently in compliance is about 250, and the number of affidavits filed by international union officers is approximately 2,750. The number of local unions in compliance is approximately 21,500, and the number of affidavits filed by local union officers is approximately 193,500. Although we have kept no running record of the number of affidavits filed with us during the years, we estimate that since 1947 there have been at least 1,500,000 individual affidavits filed." The only two major unions which refused to file affidavits, apart from transportation, govern-

mental and other unions dealing with employers not subject to the Act, appear to be the United Mine Workers and the International Typographical Union. Ibid.

3. The administration of Section 9(h) gave rise to a substantial volume of litigation involving the interpretation and application of the provision. The major issues related to what officials were required to file affidavits, the power of the National Labor Relations Board to find that a union was not in compliance by reason of alleged falsity of the affidavit, the effect of non-compliance upon the rights of the union, and various forms of evasion. The latter included questions of whether a resignation from the Communist Party was bona fide, whether an individual filing charges with the Board was "fronting" for a non-complying union, and whether the officials filing affidavits were actually the real officers of the union. For reference to material dealing with these matters, see below.

REFERENCES

1. For the legislative history of Section 9(h) of the Taft-Hartley Act see Lissaman, The Taft-Hartley Non-Communist Affidavit Provision, 5 Labor L.J. 697, 697-8 (1954). Discussion of the legal issues, written before the Douds decision, appears in Leonard Boudin, Supersedure and the Purgatory Oath Under the Taft-Hartley Law, 23 N.Y.U.L.Q. Rev. 72 (1948); Barnett, The Constitutionality of the Expurgatory Oath Requirement of the Labor Management Relations Act of 1947, 27 Ore. L. Rev. 85 (1948); Notes, 48 Colum. L. Rev. 253 (1948); 42 Ill. L. Rev. 487 (1947). For discussion after the Douds case, see Meiklejohn, The First Amendment and Evils That Congress Has a Right to Prevent, 26 Ind. L.J. 477 (1951); Louis Boudin, "Seditious Doctrines" and the "Clear and Present Danger" Rule, 38 Va. L. Rev. 143, 315, 315-324 (1952); Greenwald, Non-Communist Affidavits: Taft-Hartley Sound and Fury, 12 La. L. Rev. 407 (1952); Notes, 51 Colum. L. Rev. 130 (1951); 24 So. Cal. L. Rev. 197 (1951); 99 U. Pa. L. Rev. 409 (1950); Konvitz, Fundamental Liberties of a Free People, chs. 22 and 23 (1957). Compare Mr. Justice Jackson's analysis of the strategy and tactics of the Communist Party with that of Louis Boudin, id. at 181-186, 340-348.

In connection with Mr. Justice Black's discussion of the historical function of loyalty oaths, see Koenigsberg and Stavis, Test Oaths: Henry VIII to the American Bar Asociation, 11 Law. Guild Rev. 111 (1951); Dunham, Doctrines of Allegiance in Late Medieval English Law, 26 N.Y.U.L. Rev. 41 (1951). See also Jones, Do You Know the Nature of an Oath? 37 A.A.U.P. Bull. 442 (1951).

2. For discussion of N.L.R.B. and court decisions concerning the various problems of administration noted above, see Kearns, Non-Communist Affidavits Under the Taft-Hartley Act, 37 Geo. L.J. 297 (1949); Daykin, The Operation of the Taft-Hartley Act's Non-Communist Provisions, 36 Iowa L. Rev. 607 (1951); Note, 18 U. Chi. L. Rev. 783 (1951); Scanlan, The Communist-Dominated Union Problem, 28 Notre Dame Law. 458 (1953); Lissaman and Greenwald, supra; Note, Control of Communist Unions: A New Approach, 50 Nw. U.L. Rev. 396, 398-402 (1955); Note, Non-Communist Affidavits by Union "Officers" Under Taft-Hartley Section 9(h), 66 Yale L.J. 771 (1957); Morgan, Supreme Court and the Non-Communist Affidavit, 10 Lab. L.J. 28 (1959) (contains bibliography); Morgan, Supreme Court Interpretations vs. Congressional Intent, 21 U. Pitt. L. Rev. 507 (1960). The cases through 1954 are digested in Digest of the Public Record of Communism 89-95 (Fund for the Republic 1955); see also Notes, 95 L. Ed. 981, 97 L. Ed. 416, 100 L. Ed. 291, 2 L. Ed. 2d 1765. A summary of the decisions up to 1958 appears in the second edition of this book, at 469-471. See also the material cited below dealing with the repeal of Section 9(h).

NOTES

1. There would appear to have been a substantial number of cases in which government officials suspected union officers of filing false affidavits. Thus, in 1952 Department of Justice Officials testified that 68 cases had been referred to U.S. District Attorneys, and the Chairman of the N.L.R.B. said 55 cases had been referred by the Board to the Department of Justice. Hearings before Subcommittee on Labor and Labor-Management Relations of the Senate Committee on Labor and Public Welfare, 82d Cong., 2d Sess., pp. 58, 91 (1952). The number of prosecutions, however, was much smaller. As of July 1957 the Department of Justice reported that it had brought prosecutions against 16 union officers under 18 U.S.C. §1001 (penalizing false statements made to the Government) and two conspiracy cases under 18 U.S.C. §371 (general conspiracy statute). Letter from William F. Tompkins, Assistant Attorney General, July 24, 1957. No additional cases seem to have been brought. See Civil Liberties Docket, §291.

The Department of Justice was successful in obtaining convictions in these prosecutions, but a number of convictions were reversed on technical grounds. In only one case did the Supreme Court deal again with basic First Amendment issues:

In Killian v. United States, 368 U.S. 231, 82 S. Ct. 302, 7 L. Ed. 2d 256 (1961), the Court reversed a conviction for failure of the prosecution to produce certain documents, but went on to consider the validity of the trial court's instructions to the jury on the issues of membership in and affiliation with the Communist Party. The majority, in an opinion by Mr. Justice Whittaker, approved instructions defining membership as follows:

"Membership in the Communist Party, the same as membership in any other organization, constitutes the state of being one of those persons who belong to or comprise the Communist Party. It connotes a status of mutuality between the individual and the organization. That is to say, there must be present the desire on the part of the individual to belong to the Communist Party and a recognition by that Party that it considers him as a member." 368 U.S. at 247.

The instruction continued that membership could be shown by any acts or statements of the defendant, including conduct of the kind listed in the Communist Control Act of 1954 as indicia of membership. The majority overruled the defendant's contention "that the instruction respecting membership should have defined 'membership' as, and required a finding of, 'a definite objective factual phenomenon' or a 'specific formal act of joining' rather than, as was done, in the subjective terms of a state of mind." 368 U.S. at 246-247. It also stated:

"To petitioner's argument that the submitted criteria permitted the jury to find membership from statements and acts that were wholly innocent in themselves or even protected by the First Amendment, it is enough to recall that nothing in §9(h) or elsewhere in the National Labor Relations Act makes or purports to make criminal either membership in or affiliation with the Communist Party, American Communications Assn. v. Douds, supra, 339 U.S., at 402, and that petitioner was not charged with criminality for being a member of or affiliated with the Communist Party, nor with participating in any criminal activities of or for the Communist Party, but only with having made and submitted to the Government an affidavit falsely swearing that he was not a member of or affiliated with the Communist Party in violation of 18 U.S.C. §1001. It would be strange doctrine, indeed, to say that membership in the Communist Party — when, as here, a lawful status — cannot be proved by evidence of lawful acts and statements, but only by evidence of unlawful acts and statements." 368 U.S. at 254.

The majority likewise upheld the following instruction with respect to "affiliation":

"The verb 'affiliated,' as used in the Second Count of the indictment, means a relationship short of and less than membership in the Communist Party, but more than that of mere sympathy for the aims and objectives of the Communist Party.

"A person may be found to be 'affiliated' with an organization, even though not a member, when there is shown to be a close working alliance or association between him and the organization, together with a mutual understanding or recognition that the organization can rely and depend upon him to cooperate with it, and to work for its benefit, for an indefinite future period upon a fairly permanent basis."

Mr. Justice Douglas, in a dissenting opinion with which Mr. Chief Justice Warren and Mr. Justice Black concurred, said:

"Beliefs are as much in issue here as they were in the Douds case. If that case means anything, it means that one who was a member only to promote a lawful cause of the party should not be subjected to the legal odium that attaches to fullfledged members. The fact that one believes in peace, disarmament, a ban on nuclear testing, or the disbandment of NATO may put him out of step with the majority. But unless we toss to the winds the tolerance which a Free Society shows for unorthodox, as well as orthodox, views, the fact that a person embraces lawful views of the party should not establish that he is a 'member' of the party within the meaning of the Act. Membership, as that word is used in the Act, should be proved by facts which tie the accused to the illegal aims of the party. If beliefs are used to condemn the individual, we have ourselves gone a long way down the totalitarian path.

"Killian's association with the party appears to have been restricted to lawful purposes: he was against this country's policies in Indo-China; he was for the recognition of Red China; he was against colonialism; he was against war; he urged people to subscribe to The Daily Worker. He attended party meetings, promoted a united front, discussed current political events, recruited Negroes for party membership, and the like. If his attendance at the meetings was for an illegal purpose, I have failed to find it in the record. I find no evidence that Killian used his affiliation with the party to promote immediately or even at long range the overthrow of the government. I find no evidence that he organized violence, promoted sabotage, collected arms, or spied for a foreign power. If he lied in his affidavit, he lied about his beliefs. But insofar as the record shows, he had a right to promote those beliefs alone or in association with others. All the beliefs I find espoused by Killian in this record were protected by the First Amendment. He had a right to advocate them alone or in conjunction with others. Some causes espoused by the Communist Party may be wholly lawful. Such was the case in De Jonge v. Oregon, 299 U.S. 353, where speeches were made 'against illegal raids on workers' halls and homes and against the shooting of striking longshoremen' by the police and 'against conditions in the county jail,' id., at 359. The 'peaceable assembly' and that 'lawful public discussion' (id., at 365) were held not subject to punishment, even though the meeting was under the auspices of an organization that might have been prosecuted for other activities. If the De Jonge case means anything, it means there must be a separation of the lawful from the unlawful activities of a party when a 'member' is summoned to account for his actions." 368 U.S. at 263-265.

Mr. Justice Brennan also dissented on the ground that "membership" could not be taken "as signifying a subjective relationship of mutuality, provable by actions not particularly bespeaking an externally manifested tie." 368 U.S. at 270. He also thought that "affiliation" should be limited to proof of actual membership "in an organization that is in fact a controlled cover for [the Communist] . . . Party." 368 U.S. at 276.

2. There developed considerable criticism of Section 9(h) of the Taft-Hartley Act as inadequate and ineffective to deal with the problem of Communist influence in labor unions. See, e.g., Annual Report of the House Committee on Un-American Activities, 82d Cong., 2d Sess., p. 9 (1952); Hearings and Reports of Subcommittee on Labor and Labor-Management Relations of the Senate Committee on Labor and Public Welfare on Communist Domination of Unions and National Security, 82d Cong., 2d Sess. (1952); Staff Report to the above Subcommittee on the Problem of Delay in Administering the Labor Management Relations Act, 82d Cong., 2d Sess. (1952). See also the Greenwald, Scanlan, and Lissaman articles and other materials cited supra, and Shair, How Effective is the Non-Communist Affidavit, 1 Lab. L.J. 935 (1950); Chase, Security and Liberty: The Problem of Native Communists 1947-1955, ch. 5 (1955). For discussion of proposed alternatives see the Lissaman article, supra; Mayer, Labor's Responsibility to National Security — And Its Due, 7 N.Y.U. Annual Conference on Labor 473, 489-506 (1954); Public Policy Toward Communist Unions, America, April 25, 1953, p. 104; Should Labor Organizations be Subject to the General Techniques of the 1950 Internal Security Act? 33 Cong. Digest 148 (1954).

The first Congressional response to the operation of Section 9(h) came in the provisions of the Communist Control Act of 1954 dealing with "Communist-infiltrated organizations," set forth in Section C, subsection 3, supra. See the hearings and reports on that legislation. For analysis of these provisions see Notes, 64 Yale L.J. 712, 752-764 (1955); 55 Colum. L. Rev. 631, 674-701 (1955); 50 Nw. U.L. Rev. 396, 403-407 (1955); Brown, Loyalty and Security 73-76 (1958). Discussion of the contemplated impact of the provisions appears in Jolt for Communists in Unions, U.S. News and World Report, Aug. 27, 1954, p. 72; What Reds Are Up To In Unions, id., Mar. 4, 1955, p. 107; Curtains for the C.P., Fortune, March 1956, p. 206. See also Communists in Unions, Commonweal, Jan. 20, 1956, p. 395. As noted above, only two proceedings were brought against alleged "Communist-infiltrated organizations," both of which were dismissed by the Subversive Activities Control Board.

The Labor-Management Reporting and Disclosure Act of 1959 repealed Section 9(h) of the Taft-Hartley Act. §201(d), 73 Stat. 519, 525. In its place the new legislation provided, in Section 504, that "No person who is or has been a member of the Communist Party . . . shall serve . . . as an officer, director, trustee, member of any executive board or similar governing body, business agent, manager, organizer, or other employee (other than as an employee performing exclusively clerical or custodial duties) of any labor organization," or as an officer, employee or consultant to any association of employers dealing with any labor organization. Violation is punishable by a fine of not more than $10,000 or imprisonment for not more than a year, or both. 29 U.S.C. §504. The new provision came before the Supreme Court in United States v. Brown, set forth below.

UNITED STATES v. BROWN
381 U.S. 437, 85 S. Ct. 1707, 14 L. Ed. 2d 484 (1965)

MR. CHIEF JUSTICE WARREN delivered the opinion of the Court. . . .

Respondent has been a working longshoreman on the San Francisco docks, and an open and avowed Communist, for more than a quarter of a century. He was elected to the Executive Board of Local 10 of the International Longshoremen's and Warehousemen's Union for consecutive one-year terms in 1959, 1960, and 1961. On May 24, 1961, respondent was charged in a one-count indictment returned in the Northern District of California with "knowingly and wilfully serv[ing] as a member of an executive board of a labor organization . . . while a member of the Communist Party, in wilful violation of Title 29, United States Code, Section 504." It was neither charged nor proven that respondent at any time advocated or suggested illegal activity by the union, or proposed a political strike. The jury found respondent guilty, and he was sentenced to six months' imprisonment. The Court of Appeals for the Ninth Circuit, sitting en banc, reversed and remanded with instructions to set aside the conviction and dismiss the indictment, holding that §504 violates the First and Fifth Amendments to the Constitution. 334 F.2d 488. We granted certiorari, 379 U.S. 899.

Respondent urges — in addition to the grounds relied on by the court below — that the statute under which he was convicted is a bill of attainder, and therefore violates Art. I, §9, of the Constitution. We agree that §504 is void as a bill of attainder and affirm the decision of the Court of Appeals on that basis. We therefore find it unnecessary to consider the First and Fifth Amendment arguments.

The provisions outlawing bills of attainder were adopted by the Constitutional Convention unanimously, and without debate.

"No Bill of Attainder or ex post facto Law shall be passed [by the Congress]." Art. I, §9, cl. 3.

"No State shall . . . pass any Bill of Attainder, ex post facto Law, or Law impairing the Obligation of Contracts. . . ." Art. I, §10.

A logical starting place for an inquiry into the meaning of the prohibition is its historical background. The bill of attainder, a parliamentary act sentencing to death one or more specific persons, was a device often resorted to in sixteenth, seventeenth and eighteenth century England for dealing with persons who had attempted, or threatened to attempt, to overthrow the government. In addition to the death sentence, attainder generally carried with it a "corruption of blood," which meant that the attainted party's heirs could not inherit his property. The "bill of pains and penalties" was identical to the bill of attainder, except that it prescribed a penalty short of death, e.g., banishment, deprivation of the right to vote, or exclusion of the designated party's sons from Parliament. Most bills of attainder and bills of pains and penalties named the parties to whom they were to apply; a few, however, simply described them. While some left the designated parties a way of escaping the penalty, others did not. The use of bills of attainder and bills of pains and penalties was not limited to England. During the American Revolution, the legislatures of all thirteen States passed statutes directed against the Tories; among these statutes were a large number of bills of attainder and bills of pains and penalties.

While history thus provides some guidelines, the wide variation in form, purpose and effect of ante-constitutional bills of attainder indicates that the proper scope of the Bill of Attainder Clause, and its relevance to contemporary problems, must ultimately be sought by attempting to discern the reasons for its inclusion in the Constitution, and the evils it was designed to eliminate. The best available evidence, the writings of the architects of our constitutional system, indicates that the Bill of Attainder Clause was intended not as a narrow, technical (and therefore soon to be outmoded) prohibition, but rather as an implementation of the separation of powers, a general safeguard against legislative exercise of the judicial function, or more simply — trial by legislature. . . .

It is in this spirit that the Bill of Attainder Clause was consistently interpreted by this Court — until the decision in American Communications Assn. v. Douds. 339 U.S. 382, which we shall consider hereafter. . . .

[The Court then discusses Fletcher v. Peck, 6 Cranch 87; Cummings v. Missouri, 4 Wall. 277; Ex parte Garland, 4 Wall. 333; and United States v. Lovett, 328 U.S. 303.]

Under the line of cases just outlined, §504 of the Labor-Management Reporting and Disclosure Act plainly constitutes a bill of attainder. Congress undoubtedly possesses power under the Commerce Clause to enact legislation designed to keep from positions affecting interstate commerce persons who may use such positions to bring about political strikes. In §504, however, Congress has exceeded the authority granted it by the Constitution. The statute does not set forth a generally applicable rule decreeing that any person who commits certain acts or possesses certain characteristics (acts and characteristics which, in Congress' view, make them likely to initiate political strikes) shall not hold union office, and leave to courts and juries the job of deciding what persons have committed the specified acts or possess the specified characteristics. Instead, it designates in no uncertain terms the persons who possess the feared characteristics and therefore cannot hold union office without incurring criminal liability — members of the Communist Party.[24]

Communist Party v. Subversive Activities Control Board, 367 U.S. 1, lends support to our conclusion. . . . A majority of the Court rejected the argument that the Act was a bill of attainder, reasoning that §3 does not specify the persons or groups upon which the deprivations set forth in the Act are to be imposed, but instead sets forth a general definition. . . . The entire Court did not share the view of the majority that §3's definition constituted rule-making rather than specification. See also Garner v. Los Angeles Board, 341 U.S. 716, 723. However, language incorporated in the majority opinion indicates that there was agreement on one point: by focusing upon "the crucial constitutional significance of what Congress did when it rejected the approach of outlawing the Party by name and accepted instead a statutory program regulating not enumerated organizations but designated activities," 367 U.S., at 84-85, the majority clearly implied that if the Act had applied to the Communist Party by name, it would have been a bill of attainder. . . .

[The opinion then distinguishes Board of Governors v. Agnew, 329 U.S. 441, in which the Court had upheld §32 of the Banking Act of 1933, which provided that no officer, director, or employee of a corporation or association engaged in underwriting securities could serve at the same time as an officer, director, or employee of a member bank in the Federal Reserve System.]

It is argued, however, that in §504 Congress did no more than it did in enacting §32: it promulgated a general rule to the effect that persons possessing characteristics which make them likely to incite political strikes should not hold union office, and simply inserted in place of a list of those characteristics an alternative, shorthand criterion — membership in the Communist Party. Again, we cannot agree. The designation of Communists as those persons likely to cause political strikes is not the substitution of a semantically equivalent phrase; on the contrary, it rests, as the Court in Douds explicitly recognized, 339 U.S., at 389, upon an empirical investigation by Congress of the acts, characteristics and propensities of Communist Party members. In a number of decisions, this Court has pointed out the fallacy of the suggestion that membership in the Communist Party, or any other political organization, can be regarded as an alternative, but equivalent, expression for a list of undesirable characteristics. For, as the Court noted in Schneiderman v. United States, 320 U.S. 118, 136, "under our traditions beliefs are personal and not a matter of mere association, and . . . men in adhering to a political party or other organization notoriously do not subscribe unqualifiedly to all of its platforms or asserted principles." [30] Just last Term, in Aptheker v. Secretary of State, 378 U.S. 500, we held §6 of the Subversive Activities Control Act

---

[24] We of course take no position on whether or not members of the Communist Party are in fact likely to incite political strikes. The point we make is rather that the Constitution forbids Congress from making such determinations.

[30] To the same effect, see Noto v. United States, 367 U.S. 290, 299-300; Wieman v. Updegraff, 344 U.S. 183, 190.

to violate the Constitution because it "too broadly and indiscriminately" restricted constitutionally protected freedoms. One of the factors which compelled us to reach this conclusion was that §6 inflicted its deprivation upon all members of Communist organizations without regard to whether there existed any demonstrable relationship between the characteristics of the person involved and the evil Congress sought to eliminate. Id., at 509-511. These cases are relevant to the question before us. Even assuming that Congress had reason to conclude that some Communists would use union positions to bring about political strikes, "it cannot automatically be inferred that all members shar[e] their evil purposes or participat[e] in their illegal conduct." Schware v. Board of Bar Examiners, 353 U.S. 232, 246. In utilizing the term "members of the Communist Party" to designate those persons who are likely to incite political strikes, it plainly is not the case that Congress has merely substituted a convenient shorthand term for a list of the characteristics it was trying to reach.

The Solicitor General argues that §504 is not a bill of attainder because the prohibition it imposes does not constitute "punishment." In support of this conclusion, he urges that the statute was enacted for preventive rather than retributive reasons — that its aim is not to punish Communists for what they have done in the past, but rather to keep them from positions where they will in the future be able to bring about undesirable events. He relies on American Communications Assn. v. Douds, 339 U.S. 382, which upheld §9(h) of the National Labor Relations Act, the predecessor of the statute presently before us. . . .

This case is not necessarily controlled by Douds. For to prove its assertion that §9(h) was preventive rather than retributive in purpose, the Court in Douds focused on the fact that members of the Communist Party could escape from the class of persons specified by Congress simply by resigning from the Party . . .

. . . Section 504, unlike §9(h), disqualifies from the holding of union office not only present members of the Communist Party, but also anyone who has within the past five years been a member of the Party. However, even if we make the assumption that the five-year provision was inserted not out of desire to visit retribution but purely out of a belief that failure to include it would lead to pro forma resignations from the Party which would not decrease the threat of political strikes, it still clearly appears that §504 inflicts "punishment" within the meaning of the Bill of Attainder Clause. It would be archaic to limit the definition of "punishment" to "retribution." Punishment serves several purposes: retributive, rehabilitative, deterrent — and preventive. One of the reasons society imprisons those convicted of crimes is to keep them from inflicting future harm, but that does not make imprisonment any the less punishment. . . .

We do not hold today that Congress cannot weed dangerous persons out of the labor movement, any more than the Court held in Lovett that subversives must be permitted to hold sensitive government positions. Rather, we make again the point made in Lovett: that Congress must accomplish such results by rules of general applicability. It cannot specify the people upon whom the sanction it prescribes is to be levied. Under our Constitution, Congress possesses full legislative authority, but the task of adjudication must be left to other tribunals. . . .

The judgment of the Court of Appeals is
Affirmed.

Mr. Justice White, with whom Mr. Justice Clark, Mr. Justice Harlan, and Mr. Justice Stewart join, dissenting.

"A bill of attainder is a legislative act which inflicts punishment without a judicial trial." Cummings v. Missouri, 4 Wall. 277, 323. When an enactment is challenged as an attainder, the central inquiry must be whether the disability imposed by the act is "punishment" (i.e., is directed at an individual or a group of individuals) or is "regulation" (i.e., is directed at controlling future conduct). Flemming v. Nestor, 363 U.S. 603, at 613-614; accord, Trop v. Dulles, 356 U.S. 86, 95-96 (Warren, C. J., announcing judgment). Whether a punitive purpose would be inferred has depended in past cases on a number of circumstances, including the nature of the disability, whether it was traditionally regarded as punishment, whether it is rationally connected to a permissible legislative objective, as well as the specificity of the legislature's designation of the persons to be affected. See generally Kennedy v. Mendoza-Martinez, 372 U.S. 144, 168-169.

In this case, however, the Court discards this meticulous multifold analysis that has been deemed necessary in the past. . . .

It is not difficult to find some of the cases and statutes which the necessary implications of the Court's approach will overrule or invalidate. . . .

[The opinion then argues that the majority view would invalidate not only the provision involved in Douds, but §32 of the Banking Act, other conflict of interest statutes, and statutes disqualifying felons from practicing medicine or occupying certain other positions.]

And if the disqualification of Party members in the Subversive Activities Control Act is not a bill of attainder, neither is §504. If it is §504's specific designation of the Communist Party and its members which concerns the Court — if the Court would have the same concern if the statute in Agnew had disqualified the members of a particular underwriting firm — it seems to me that at this point this vice is no vice at all; for the Congress has provided in another statute, the Subversive Activities Control Act, for an adjudication about Communist-action organizations, the nature of the Party has now been adjudicated and an adequate probability about the future conduct of its members established to justify the disqualification which Congress has imposed. . . .

This, of course, is not the path the Court follows. Section 504 is said to impose punishment on specific individuals because it has disqualified all Communist Party members without providing for a judicial determination as to each member that he will call a political strike. A likelihood of doing so based on membership is not enough. By the same token, a statute disqualifying Communists (or authorizing the Executive Branch to do so) from holding sensitive positions in the Government would be automatically infirm, as would a requirement that employees of the Central Intelligence Agency or the National Security Agency disclaim membership in the Communist Party, unless in each case it is proved by evidence other than membership in the Communist Party, the nature of which has already been adjudicated, that the individual would commit acts of disloyalty or subordinate his official undertakings to the interests of the Party.

But how does one prove that a person would be disloyal? The Communist Party's illegal purpose and its domination by a foreign power have already been adjudicated, both administratively and judicially. If this does not in itself provide a sufficient probability with respect to the individual who persists in remaining a member of the Party, or if a probability is in any event insufficient, what evidence with regard to the individual will be sufficient to disqualify him? If he must be apprehended in the act of calling one political strike or in one act of disloyalty before steps can be taken to exclude him from office, there is little or nothing left of the preventive or prophylactic function of §504 or of the statutes such as the Court had before it in [Hawker v. New York, 170 U.S. 189, upholding a statute prohibiting convicted felons from practicing medicine] and Agnew. . . .

The basic flaw in the Court's reasoning, however, is its too narrow view of the legislative process. The Court is concerned to separate the legislative and judicial functions by ensuring that the legislature does not infringe the judicial function of applying general rules to specific circumstances. Congress is held to have violated the Bill of Attainder Clause here because, on the one hand, §504 does not encompass the whole class of persons having characteristics that would make them likely to call political strikes and, on the other hand, §504 does single out a particular group, members of the Communist Party, not all of whom possess such characteristics. Because of this combination of underinclusiveness and overinclusiveness the Court concludes that Communist Party members were singled out for punishment, thus rejecting the Government's contention that §504 has solely a regulatory aim.

The Court's conclusion that a statute which is both underinclusive and overinclusive must be deemed to have been adopted with a punitive purpose assumes that legislatures normally deal with broad categories and attack all of an evil at a time. Or if partial measures are undertaken, a legislature singles out a particular group for regulation only because the group label is a "shorthand phrase" for traits that are characteristic of the broader evil. But this Court has long recognized in equal protection cases that a legislature may prefer to deal with only part of an evil. . . . Admittedly the degree of specificity is a relevant factor — as when individuals are singled out by name — but because in many instances specificity of the degree here held impermissible may be wholly consistent with a regulatory, rather than a punitive purpose, the Court's per se approach cuts too broadly and invalidates legitimate legislative activity.

Putting aside the Court's per se approach based on the nature of the classification specified by the legislation, we must still test §504 against the traditional definition of the bill of attainder as legislative punishment of particular individuals. In my view, §504 does not impose punishment and is not a bill of attainder. . . .

Congress' concern with the possibility of political strikes is not simply a fictional concern advanced to mask a punitive purpose. . . . It was obviously reasonable for Congress to substitute §504 for §9(h), and no punitive purpose may be inferred from such congressional action.

Nor can it be denied that §504 is reasonably related to a permissible legislative objective. In American Communications Assn. v. Douds, we held that "Congress could rationally find that the Communist Party is not like other political parties in its utilization of positions of union leadership as means by which to bring about strikes. . . ," 339 U.S., at 391, and therefore Congress could rationally infer that members of the Communist Party were likely to call political strikes. See also Communist Party v. Subversive Activities Control Board, 367 U.S. 1, 93-94, 112. In 1956 the Subversive Activities Control Board found, after a trial-type hearing, that the Party's principal leaders and a substantial number of its members recognize the disciplinary power of the Soviet Union. Without question the findings previously made by Congress and the Subversive Activities Control Board afforded a rational basis in 1959 for Congress to conclude that Communists were likely to call political strikes, and sufficiently more likely than others to do so that special measures could appropriately be enacted to deal with the particular threat posed.

In view of Congress' demonstrated concern in preventing future conduct — political strikes — and the reasonableness of the means adopted to that end, I cannot conclude that §504 had a punitive purpose or that it constitutes a bill of attainder. I intimate no opinion on the issues that the Court does not reach.

REFERENCES

1. The legislative history of Section 504 of the Labor-Management Reporting and Disclosure Act of 1959 may be found in U.S. Code Congressional and Administrative News, 1959, 2318 at 2351, 2468, and 2508. For comment on the decision in the Court of Appeals, dealing with First Amendment rights of association, and due process, see Notes, 64 Colum. L. Rev. 1339 (1964); 53 Geo. L.J. 242 (1964); 10 Vill. L. Rev. 177 (1964); 50 Va. L. Rev. 1122 (1964); 43 Texas L. Rev. 575 (1965); 12 U.C.L.A.L. Rev. 597 (1965). On the Supreme Court's decision, see Notes, 79 Harv. L. Rev. 56, 120-123 (1965); 54 Calif. L. Rev. 212 (1966). See also Linehan v. Waterfront Commission of New York

Harbor, 116 F. Supp. 683 (S.D. N.Y. 1953), aff'd, 347 U.S. 439, 74 S. Ct. 623, 98 L. Ed. 826 (1954); Flemming v. Nestor, 363 U.S. 603, 80 S. Ct. 1367, 4 L. Ed. 2d 1435 (1960), discussed in subsection 4, infra.

2. Generally on the bill of attainder problem, see Wormuth, Legislative Disqualifications As Bills of Attainder, 4 Vand. L. Rev. 60 (1951); Note, The Constitutional Prohibition of Bills of Attainder, 63 Yale L.J. 844 (1954); Chafee, Three Human Rights in the Constitution of 1787, 90-161 (1956); Note, The Bounds of Legislative Specification: A Suggested Approach to the Bill of Attainder Clause, 72 Yale L.J. 330 (1962). See also, with respect to the general problem, Note, Retroactivity and First Amendment Rights, 110 U. Pa. L. Rev. 394 (1962).

NOTES

1. Other governmental action to eliminate subversive influences in labor unions includes various loyalty-security programs, such as the Industrial Security Program and the Port Security Program, considered in Section E, infra, and the activities of legislative investigating committees, considered in Section F, infra. In addition Section 703(f) of the Civil Rights Act of 1964 excludes from protection under the fair employment practices provisions of that legislation, any person "who is a member of the Communist Party of the United States or of any other organization required to register" under the Internal Security Act. 78 Stat. 241, 256; 42 U.S.C. §2000e-2.

In 1948 the Atomic Energy Commission instructed the General Electric Company to withdraw recognition from the United Electrical and Radio Workers Union (then C.I.O.) at the Knolls Atomic Power Laboratory because of "alleged Communist affiliation or association of various officers of UE taken together with the failure of UE officers to file non-Communist affidavits under the Labor Management Relations Act." N.Y. Times, Oct. 9, 1948. Since the union officers had not at that time filed non-Communist affidavits the union could not resort to the procedures of the National Labor Relations Board. A suit in the courts to nullify the action of the A.E.C. was unsuccessful. United Electrical Workers v. Lilienthal, 84 F. Supp. 640 (D. D.C. 1949); see Scanlan, The Communist-Dominated Union Problem, 28 Notre Dame Law. 458, 467-473 (1953). The National Labor Relations Board later held the matter was within the exclusive jurisdiction of the Atomic Energy Commission and that Board certification was conditional upon compliance with A.E.C. regulations. General Electric Co., 89 N.L.R.B. 726 (1950).

2. A number of measures have been taken by private parties — union or employer — to deal with Communist influences in the labor field. The constitutions of many unions exclude Communists from holding office or from membership. See Summers, The Right to Join a Union, 47 Colum. L. Rev. 33, 35 (1947), and Admission Policies of Labor Unions, 61 Q.J. Econ. 66, 75-76 (1946) (pointing out these provisions are not always rigorously administered); Paschell and Theodore, Anti-Communist Provisions in Union Constitutions, 77 Monthly Lab. Rev. 1097 (1954). The latter article analyzed 100 union constitutions and found that 59 of these, covering unions with a membership of 10,000,000, bar Communists from national office; and 40 with a membership of 6,000,000 apply anti-Communist restrictions to members, prospective members, and officers. The AFL-CIO Constitution states that "it is a basic principle of this Federation that it must be and

remain free from any and all corrupt influences and from the undermining efforts of communist, fascist or other totalitarian agencies who are opposed to the basic principles of our democracy and of free and democratic trade unionism." Art VIII, §7. And the AFL-CIO Code of Ethical Practices With Respect to Racketeers, Crooks, Communists and Fascists provides:

"1. The AFL-CIO and each of its affiliated unions should undertake the obligation, through appropriate constitutional or administrative measures and orderly procedures, to insure that no persons who constitute corrupt influences or practices or who represent or support communist, fascist or totalitarian agencies should hold office of any kind in such trade unions or organizations. . . .

"4. No person should hold or retain office or appointed position in the AFL-CIO or any of its affiliated national or international unions or subordinate bodies thereof who is a member, consistent supporter or who actively participates in the activities of the Communist Party or of any fascist or other totalitarian organization which opposes the democratic principles to which our country and the American trade union movement are dedicated."

The courts have declined to interfere where unions, either under a constitutional provision or in the absence of one, have removed officers or expelled members for Communist activity. See Shein v. Rose, 12 N.Y.S.2d 87 (Sup. Ct. N.Y. Co. 1939); Ames v. Dubinsky, 70 N.Y.S.2d 706 (Sup. Ct. N.Y. Co. 1947); Weinstock v. Ladisky, 197 Misc. 859, 98 N.Y.S.2d 85 (Sup. Ct. N.Y. Co. 1950); Garcia v. Ernst, 101 N.Y.S.2d 693 (Sup. Ct. N.Y. Co. 1950); Dakchoylous v. Ernst, 118 N.Y.S.2d 455 (Sup. Ct. Albany Co. 1952), aff'd, 282 App. Div. 1101, 126 N.Y.-S.2d 534 (Third Dept. 1953). Cf. Harmon v. United Mine Workers, 166 Ark. 255, 266 S.W. 84 (1924) (expulsion for membership in the Ku Klux Klan upheld). See Note, 96 U. Pa. L. Rev. 381, 398-400 (1948). For the controversy between two Pacific Coast maritime unions, involving in part charges of Communism, see Mahoney v. Sailors' Union of the Pacific, 43 Wash. 2d 874, 264 P.2d 1095 (1963), modified in 45 Wash. 2d 453, 275 P.2d 440 (1954), cert. den., 349 U.S. 915 (1955); Wollett and Lampman, The Law of Union Factionalism — The Case of the Sailors, 4 Stan. L. Rev. 177 (1952); Record, The Rise and Fall of a Maritime Union, 10 Ind. & Lab. Rel. Rev. 81 (1956).

In 1949 and 1950 the C.I.O. expelled ten unions on grounds they were dominated by Communists and consistently followed the Communist Party line. N.Y. Times, Nov. 3, 1949, Feb. 16, June 16, Aug. 30, 1950; see Fitch, The C.I.O. and Its Communists, The Survey, Dec. 1949, p. 642; Hearings and Reports of the Subcommittee on Labor and Labor-Management Relations of the Senate Committee on Labor and Public Welfare on Communist Domination of Unions and National Security, 82d Cong., 2d Sess. (1952); Communist Domination of Certain Unions, The Proceedings of the C.I.O. Executive Board in the Expulsion of Nine C.I.O. Unions, Sen. Doc. No. 89, 82d Cong., 2d Sess. (1952). Efforts to block the expulsion by legal proceedings proved futile. See Tisa v. Potofsky, 90 F. Supp. 175 (S.D. N.Y. 1950) and Chase v. Rieve, 90 F. Supp. 184 (S.D. N.Y. 1950) (motion to dismiss denied but motion for temporary injunction also denied); Durkin v. Murray, 90 F. Supp. 367 (D. D.C. 1950) (suit dismissed for failure to exhaust administrative remedies). Other purges of left-wing elements in the labor unions have also taken place. See Beck, Communism and American Labor Unions, Vital Speeches, Dec. 1, 1950; Eggleston, Labor and Civil Liberties, The Nation, June

28, 1952, p. 647; Mayer, Labor's Responsibility to National Security — And Its Due, 7 N.Y.U. Annual Conference on Labor 473, 486-488 (1954). Later accounts of these developments may be found in What Reds Are Up To In Unions, U.S. News and World Report, Mar. 4, 1955, p. 107; Curtains for the C.P., Fortune, March 1956, p. 206.

On the property and labor law consequences of the expulsion of the left-wing unions, see Note, Legal Consequences of Labor Union Schisms, 63 Harv. L. Rev. 1413 (1950); Petro, The UE-CIO Controversy in the Courts, 2 Labor L.J. 163 (1951); Mathews (ed.), Labor Relations and the Law 968-984 (1953).

For consideration of loyalty and security qualifications for employment imposed by private employers, and the problems arising under the National Labor Relations Act, see Section E, infra. For general discussion of management techniques for coping with left-wing unions, see Carey v. Boulware, Fortune, October 1952, p. 92; Subversives in Industry, Fortune, February 1954, p. 76.

3. Generally on the issue of Communist and left-wing influence in the labor movement see the various hearings and reports of Congressional Committees listed in Congressional Investigations of Communism and Subversive Activities, Sen. Doc. No. 148, 84th Cong. 2d Sess. (1956); Scanlan, The Communist-Dominated Union Problem, 28 Notre Dame Law. 458, 467-473 (1953); the Mayer article, supra; Note, 50 Nw. U.L. Rev. 396 (1955); Kampelman, The Communist Party v. the C.I.O. (1957), and Communists in the C.I.O., Kirkpatrick (ed.), The Strategy of Deception 343 (1963); Communists in Unions, Commonweal, Jan. 29, 1956, p. 395; Chase, Security and Liberty: The Problem of Native Communists, ch. 5 (1955); Brown, Loyalty and Security 211-215, 451-456 (1958).

2. Qualifications for the Practice of Law

A second area in which questions have been posed concerning the power of government to condition privileges or benefits upon political qualifications involves the right to practice law. Restrictions of this nature have been imposed both upon lawyers already admitted to practice and upon persons applying for admission. The major court decisions have dealt with the latter category.

In 1957 the Court decided two cases. In Schware v. Board of Bar Examiners of New Mexico, 353 U.S. 232, 77 S. Ct. 752, 1 L. Ed. 2d 796 (1957), New Mexico had denied Rudolph Schware admission to the bar on the ground that he had not demonstrated "good moral character" in that from 1934 to 1937 he had used certain aliases; that in 1934 he had been arrested in a labor dispute and in 1940 for alleged violation of the Neutrality Act, though not tried or convicted in either case; and that from 1932 to 1940 he had been a member of the Communist Party. The Court, in an opinion by Mr. Justice Black, examined in detail these events and the affirmative evidence of Schware's good character, and concluded: "There is no evidence in the record which rationally justifies a finding that Schware was morally unfit to practice law." 353 U.S. at 246-247. The Court therefore found that he had been denied due process of law.

In Konigsberg v. State Bar of California, 353 U.S. 252, 77 S. Ct. 722, 1 L. Ed. 2d 810 (1957), decided the same day, an applicant had been denied admission on the ground that he had failed to prove (1) that he was of good moral character, and (2) that he did not advocate overthrow of the government by unconstitutional means. In a series of hearings before the Committee of Bar Examiners Konigsberg had refused to answer questions about his political affiliations and beliefs, the questions being mainly directed at finding out whether he was or ever had been a member of the Communist Party. The majority of the Court found that Konigsberg had not been denied admission solely because of his refusal to answer the questions, an issue on which it reserved judgment, and went on to hold that, upon an examination of the record, "the evidence does not rationally support" the two grounds upon which admission was denied. 353 U.S. at 262.

On remand Konigsberg moved the California Supreme Court for immediate admission to the bar. The court vacated its previous order denying review and referred the matter to the Bar Committee for further consideration. At the ensuing Committee hearings Konigsberg introduced further evidence as to his good moral character (none of which was rebutted), reiterated unequivocally his disbelief in violent overthrow, and stated that he had never knowingly been a member of any organization which advocated such action. He persisted, however, in his refusals to answer any questions relating to his membership in the Communist Party. The Committee again declined to certify him, this time on the ground that his refusals to answer had obstructed a full investigation into his qualifications. The California Supreme Court, by a divided vote, refused review, and also denied Kongisberg's motion for direct admission to practice. 52 Cal. 2d 769, 344 P.2d 777. The United States Supreme Court affirmed. Konigsberg v. State Bar of California, 366 U.S. 36, 81 S. Ct. 997, 6 L. Ed. 2d 105 (1961). Writing for the majority, Mr. Justice Harlan said:

"At the outset we reject the view that freedom of speech and association (N.A.A.C.P. v. Alabama, 357 U.S. 449, 460), as protected by the First and Fourteenth Amendments, are 'absolutes,' not only in the undoubted sense that where the constitutional protection exists it must prevail, but also in the sense that the scope of that protection must be gathered solely from a literal reading of the First Amendment.[10] Throughout its history this Court has

---

[10] That view, which of course cannot be reconciled with the law relating to libel, slander, misrepresentation, obscenity, perjury, false advertising, solicitation of crime, complicity by encouragement, conspiracy, and the like, is said to be compelled by the fact that the commands of the First Amendment are stated in unqualified terms: "Congress shall make no law . . . abridging the freedom of speech, or of the press; or the right of the people peaceably to assemble . . . ." But as Mr. Justice Holmes once said: "[T]he provisions of the Constitution are not mathematical formulas having their essence in their form; they are organic institutions transplanted from English soil. Their significance is vital not formal; it is to be gathered not simply by taking the words and a dictionary, but by considering their origin and the line of their growth." Gompers v. United States, 233 U.S. 604, 610. In this connection also compare

consistently recognized at least two ways in which constitutionally protected freedom of speech is narrower than an unlimited license to talk. On the one hand, certain forms of speech, or speech in certain contexts, has been considered outside the scope of constitutional protection. See, e.g., Schenck v. United States, 249 U.S. 47; Chaplinsky, v. New Hampshire, 315 U.S. 568; Dennis v. United States, 341 U.S. 494; Beauharnais v. Illinois, 343 U.S. 250; Yates v. United States, 354 U.S. 298; Roth v. United States, 354 U.S. 476. On the other hand, general regulatory statutes, not intended to control the content of speech but incidentally limiting its unfettered exercise, have not been regarded as the type of law the First or Fourteenth Amendment forbade Congress or the States to pass, when they have been found justified by subordinating valid governmental interests, a prerequisite to constitutionality which has necessarily involved a weighing of the governmental interest involved. See, e.g., Schneider v. State, 308 U.S. 147, 161; Cox v. New Hampshire, 312 U.S. 569; Prince v. Massachusetts, 321 U.S. 158; Kovacs v. Cooper, 336 U.S. 77; American Communications Assn. v. Douds, 339 U.S. 382; Breard v. Alexandria, 341 U.S. 622. It is in the latter class of cases that this Court has always placed rules compelling disclosure of prior association as an incident of the informed exercise of a valid governmental function. Bates v. Little Rock, 361 U.S. 516, 524. Whenever, in such a context, these constitutional protections are asserted against the exercise of valid governmental powers a reconciliation must be effected, and that perforce requires an appropriate weighing of the respective interests involved. Watkins v. United States, 354 U.S. 178, 198; N.A.A.C.P. v. Alabama, supra; Barenblatt v. United States, 360 U.S. 109, 126-127; Bates v. Little Rock, supra; Wilkinson v. United States, 365 U.S. 399; Braden v. United States, 365 U.S. 431. With more particular reference to the present context of a state decision as to character qualifications, it is difficult, indeed, to imagine a view of the constitutional protections of speech and association which would automatically and without consideration of the extent of the deterrence of speech and association and of the importance of the state function, exclude all reference to prior speech or association on such issues as character, purpose, credibility, or intent." 366 U.S. at 49-51.

Mr. Chief Justice Warren and Justices Black, Douglas, and Brennan dissented. Mr. Justice Black said:

"The recognition that California has subjected 'speech and association to the deterrence of subsequent disclosure' is, under the First Amendment, sufficient in itself to render the action of the State unconstitutional unless one subscribes to the doctrine that permits constitutionally protected rights to be 'balanced' away whenever a majority of this Court thinks that a State might have interest sufficient to justify abridgment of those freedoms. As I have

---

the equally unqualified command of the Second Amendment: "the right of the people to keep and bear arms shall not be infringed." And see United States v. Miller, 307 U.S. 174.

indicated many times before,[10] I do not subscribe to that doctrine for I believe that the First Amendment's unequivocal command that there shall be no abridgment of the rights of free speech and assembly shows that the men who drafted our Bill of Rights did all the 'balancing' that was to be done in this field. The history of the First Amendment is too well known to require repeating here except to say that it certainly cannot be denied that the very object of adopting the First Amendment, as well as the other provisions of the Bill of Rights, was to put the freedoms protected there completely out of the area of any congressional control that may be attempted through the exercise of precisely those powers that are now being used to 'balance' the Bill of Rights out of existence." 366 U.S. at 60-61.

On the same day it decided the second Konigsberg case, the Supreme Court reached a similar conclusion in the case of George Anastaplo. In re Anastaplo, 366 U.S. 82, 81 S. Ct. 978, 6 L. Ed. 2d 135 (1961).

REFERENCES

1. In 1950 the American Bar Association urged that "all licensed to practice law in the United States of America" be required to attest to their "loyalty to our form of government by anti-communist oath." 36 A.B.A.J. 972 (1950). Similar proposals were advanced in 1951 and 1953. 37 A.B.A.J. 312-313 (1951); 39 A.B.A.J. 344-345 (1953). See also 39 A.B.A.J. 1028 (1953). Actual proceedings to disbar or discipline lawyers for Communist or other affiliation were, however, rare. Only three instances of an attempt at such action seem to have been made, and all were unsuccessful. Schlesinger Appeal, 404 Pa. 584, 172 A.2d 835 (1961); In re Steinberg, 7 Civil Liberties Docket 108 (Ct. Com. Pleas, Allegheny Co., Pa. 1962); Sheiner v. State, 82 So. 2d 657 (Fla. 1955), 112 So. 2d 571 (Fla. 1959).

2. In support of the American Bar Association proposals see editorials, 37 A.B.A.J. 128 (1951), 39 A.B.A.J. 1084 (1953); American Bar Association, Brief on Communism: Marxism-Leninism (Sept. 17, 1951); reports of A.B.A. Special Committee on Communist Tactics, Strategy and Objectives (originally appointed in 1950); Notes, 26 Notre Dame Law. 498 (1951); 2 U.C.L.A.L. Rev. 224, 228-233 (1955); Meredith, Communism and the British Columbia Bar, 28 Can. Bar Rev. 893 (1950); cf. Starrs, Considerations on Determination of Good Moral Character, 18 U. Det. L.J. 195, 219-220 (1955).

In opposition to the American Bar Association proposals see articles by Professor Chafee in the Harvard Law School Record, Nov. 1 and 8, 1950, reprinted in Chafee, The Blessings of Liberty, ch. 6 (1956); statement of 26 attorneys in opposition to the oath proposal, 37 A.B.A.J. 123 (1951); statements of National Lawyers Guild, 11 Law. Guild Rev. 42, 95 (1951); Koenigsberg and Stavis, Test Oaths: Henry VIII to the American Bar Association, 11 Law. Guild Rev. 111 (1951); Countryman, Loyalty Tests for Lawyers, 13 Law. Guild Rev. 149 (1953); National Lawyers Guild, The Independence of the Bar, 13 Law. Guild Rev. 158 (1953); Gellhorn, Individual Freedom and Governmental Restraints 131-140 (1956); Brown, Loyalty and Security, 109-116, 351-355 (1958).

See also Note, Constitutional Issues Raised by the Proposed Loyalty Oath for Lawyers,

---

[10] See, e.g., my dissenting opinions in Braden v. United States, 365 U.S. 431, 441-446; Wilkinson v. United States, 365 U.S. 399, 422-423; Uphaus v. Wyman, 364 U.S. 388, 392-393; Barenblatt v. United States, 360 U.S. 109, 140-144; American Communications Assn. v. Douds, 339 U.S. 382, 445-453.

36 Iowa L. Rev. 529 (1951); Brown and Fassett, Loyalty Tests for Admission to the Bar, 20 U. Chi. L. Rev. 480 (1953); Note, 65 Yale L.J. 873 (1956).

3. More specifically on the problem of disbarring lawyers who invoke the Fifth Amendment to inquiries on subversive activities see, in support of the American Bar Association position, Wright, The Lawyer's Responsibility and the Fifth Amendment, 34 Neb. L. Rev. 573 (1955); and in opposition, Brown, Lawyers and the Fifth Amendment: A Dissent, 40 A.B.A.J. 404 (1954); Countryman, Loyalty Tests for Lawyers, 13 Law. Guild Rev. 149 (1953); Weigel, The Fifth Amendment and the Lawyer's Responsibility, 34 Neb. L. Rev. 586 (1955). See also Notes, 41 Cornell L.Q. 304 (1956); 15 La. L. Rev. 577 (1956); 31 Notre Dame Law. 465 (1956); 56 Nw. U.L. Rev. 644 (1961). The amici briefs filed by the National Lawyers Guild (opposing disbarment) and the American Bar Association (urging disbarment) in the Sheiner case are reprinted in 15 Law. Guild Rev. 11 (1955). For an account of the Sheiner case see Weissman, Proceedings to Disbar Leo Sheiner, 16 Law. Guild Rev. 137 (1956).

Disbarment of a New York lawyer who claimed the state privilege against self-incrimination in a judicial inquiry into "ambulance chasing" was upheld in Cohen v. Hurley, 366 U.S. 117, 81 S. Ct. 954, 6 L. Ed. 2d 156 (1961). For earlier New York rulings to the contrary, see Matter of Grae, 282 N.Y. 428, 26 N.E.2d 963 (1940); Matter of Ellis, 282 N.Y. 435, 26 N.E.2d 967 (1940); discussed in Note, 41 Cornell L.Q. 304 (1956). For other cases, not involving lawyers, where invocation of the privilege against self-incrimination has led to loss of employment, see the materials on loyalty-security, Section E.

4. A more detailed account may be found in Brown and Fassett, Loyalty Tests for Admission to the Bar, 20 U. Chi. L. Rev. 480 (1953); Ginger and Koenigsberg, Report on Rules for Admission to the Bar: Tests of Applicants' "Loyalty" and "Good Moral Character," 18 Law. Guild Rev. 58 (1958). The applicable statutes and rules are collected in Internal Security and Subversion, Principal State Laws and Cases, A Study Prepared for the Subcommittee to Investigate the Administration of the Internal Security Act and Other Internal Security Laws of the Senate Committee on the Judiciary, by Legislative Reference Service, Library of Congress (1965). See also Digest of the Public Record of Communism in the United States 420-426 (Fund for the Republic 1955). Generally on the requirements for admission to the bar see West Publishing Co., Rules for Admission to the Bar (1955); Survey of the Legal Profession, Bar Examinations and Requirements for Admission to the Bar (1952); Starrs, Considerations on Determination of Good Moral Character, 18 U. Det. L.J. 195 (1955).

5. In In re Summers, 325 U.S. 561, 65 S. Ct. 1307, 89 L. Ed. 1795 (1945), The Supreme Court considered the right of the state of Illinois to refuse admission to the bar to a conscientious objector, and found no violation of the Fourteenth Amendment. See also In re Brooks, 57 Wash. 2d 66, 355 P.2d 840 (1960), cert. den., 365 U.S. 813 (1961). For a New York decision reaching the opposite result see Application of Steinbugler, 297 N.Y. 713, 77 N.E.2d 16 (1947).

6. On the Schware and first Konigsberg cases, see McCloskey, Useful Toil or the Paths of Glory? Civil Liberties in the 1956 Term of the Supreme Court, 43 Va. L. Rev. 803, 812-816 (1957); McTernan, Schware, Konigsberg and Independence of the Bar, 17 Law. Guild Rev. 48 (1957); Rehnquist, The Bar Admission Cases: A Strange Judicial Aberration, 44 A.B.A.J. 229 (1958); Notes, 71 Harv. L. Rev. 85, 154-158 (1957); 46 Geo. L.J. 344 (1957-1958); 26 Fordham L. Rev. 563 (1957); 56 Mich. L. Rev. 415 (1958); 5 U.C.L.A.L. Rev. 136 (1958); Cramton, The Supreme Court and State Power to Deal With Subversion and Loyalty, 43 Minn. L. Rev. 1025, 1059-1061, 1065-1068 (1959). According to Professor Cramton, "Schware apparently tired of the long vigil and did not press his application after the Supreme Court decision in his favor." 43 Minn. L. Rev. at 1067, n. 165.

7. The second Konigsberg and Anastaplo cases are discussed in Kalven and Steffen, The Bar Admission Cases: An Unfinished Debate Between Justice Harlan and Justice

Black, 21 Law in Trans. 155 (1961); Note, 75 Harv. L. Rev. 40, 130-131 (1961); 37 Notre Dame Law. 246 (1961); 15 Vand. L. Rev. 634 (1962). Materials on the Anastaplo case are collected in Anastaplo, Freedom of Speech and the First Amendment, 42 U. Det. L.J. 55, 73 (1964).

8. Generally on the role of the lawyer in a democratic society and the significance of an independent bar, see Stone, The Public Influence of the Bar, 48 Harv. L. Rev. 1 (1934); Jackson, The Advocate: Guardian of Our Traditional Liberties, 36 A.B.A.J. 607 (1950); Special Issue on Independence of the Bar, 18 Law. Guild Rev. 49 (1958); Symposium, The Right to Counsel and the "Unpopular Cause," 20 U. Pitt. L. Rev. 725 (1959); Jaworski, The Unpopular Cause, 47 A.B.A.J. 714 (1961); Kirchheimer, Political Justice 242-256, ch. VII (1961); Rostow, The Lawyer and His Client, 48 A.B.A.J. 25, 146 (1962). A collection of materials on these issues may be found in Alexander, The Right to Counsel for the Politically Unpopular, 22 Law in Trans. 19 (1962).

9. For material concerning the imposition of loyalty oaths and other restrictions on professional groups other than lawyers, see Countryman, The Bigots and the Professionals, The Nation, June 28, 1952, p. 641; Gellhorn, Individual Freedom and Governmental Restraints, ch. 3 (1956); Brown, Loyalty and Security 116-118, 164-176, 351-355 (1958). See also Barsky v. Board of Regents, 347 U.S. 442, 74 S. Ct. 650, 98 L. Ed. 829 (1954), discussed in 68 Harv. L. Rev. 96, 133 (1954) (upholding six months' suspension of physician after conviction of contempt for refusing to produce documents before Congressional committee, Justices Black, Douglas, and Frankfurter dissenting). See, generally, Barnett, Public Licenses and Private Rights, 33 Ore. L. Rev. 1 (1953).

3. *Taxation*

The taxing power, including the power to grant tax exemption, has served as the basis for restrictions upon political expression deemed subversive. The use of this power came before the Supreme Court in two cases involving the California loyalty requirements for tax exemption.

In Speiser v. Randall, 357 U.S. 513, 78 S. Ct. 1332, 2 L. Ed. 2d 1460 (1958), honorably discharged veterans of World War II who claimed the veterans property-tax exemption provided by the California Constitution were required to take an oath: "I do not advocate the overthrow of the Government of the United States or of the State of California by force or violence or other unlawful means, nor advocate the support of a foreign Government against the United States in event of hostilities." The Supreme Court, speaking through Mr. Justice Brennan, held the requirement invalid:

"The principle feature of the California procedure, as the appellees themselves point out, is that the appellants, 'as taxpayers under state law, have the affirmative burden of proof, in Court as well as before the Assessor. . . . [I]t is their burden to show that they are proper persons to qualify under the self-executing constitutional provision for the tax exemption in question — i.e., that they are not persons who advocate the overthrow of the government of the United States or the State by force or violence or other unlawful means or who advocate the support of a foreign government against the United States in the event of hostilities. . . . [T]he burden is on *them* to produce evidence justifying their claim of exemption.' Not only does the initial burden of bringing forth proof of nonadvocacy rest on the taxpayer, but throughout the judicial and administrative proceedings the burden lies on the taxpayer of persuading the assessor, or the court, that he falls outside the class denied the tax exemption. . . .

"The vice of the present procedure is that, where particular speech falls close to the line separating the lawful and the unlawful, the possibility of mistaken factfinding — inherent in all litigation — will create the danger that the legitimate utterance will be penalized. The man who knows that he must bring forth proof and persuade another of the lawfulness of his conduct necessarily must steer far wider of the unlawful zone, than if the State must bear these burdens. This is especially to be feared when the complexity of the proofs and the generality of the standards applied, cf. Dennis v. United States [341 U.S. 494], provide but shifting sands on which the litigant must maintain his position. How can a claimant whose declaration is rejected possibly sustain the burden of proving the negative of these complex factual elements? In practical operation, therefore, this procedural device must necessarily produce a result which the State could not command directly. It can only result in a deterrence of speech which the Constitution makes free. . . .

"[W]e hold that when the constitutional right to speak is sought to be deterred by a State's general taxing program due process demands that the speech be unencumbered until the State comes forward with sufficient proof to justify its inhibition. The State clearly has no such compelling interest at stake as to justify a short-cut procedure which must inevitably result in suppressing protected speech. Accordingly, though the validity of §19 of Art. XX of the State Constitution be conceded arguendo, its enforcement through procedures which place the burdens of proof and persuasion on the taxpayer is a violation of due process." 357 U.S. at 521-522, 526, 528-529.

Mr. Justice Clark dissented.

NOTES

1. At the same time the Court ruled the same way in First Unitarian Church v. County of Los Angeles, 357 U.S. 545, 78 S. Ct. 1350, 2 L. Ed. 2d 1484 (1958). Here a property-tax exemption had been denied to two churches under the California law because they had refused to subscribe to the oath. The majority found it unnecessary to pass upon the freedom of religion issue. Justices Douglas and Black, concurring, were of the opinion that the oath violated religious freedom. Mr. Justice Clark again dissented.

2. Speiser v. Randall was distinguished in Konigsberg v. State Bar of California, 366 U.S. 36, 81 S. Ct. 997, 6 L. Ed. 2d 105 (1961), noted in subsection 2, supra, on the ground that (1) "Speiser was explicitly limited so as not to reach cases where, as here, there is no showing of an intent to penalize political beliefs"; and (2) "[t]here is no unequivocal indication that California in this proceeding has placed upon petitioner the burden of proof of nonadvocacy of violent overthrow, as distinguished from its other requirement of 'good moral character.' " 366 U.S. at 54-

56. Mr. Justice Black, dissenting in Konigsberg, thought the decision "cut the heart out of" Speiser. 366 U.S. at 75. Mr. Justice Brennan's dissent rested solely on Speiser. 366 U.S. at 80-81. Both justices thought that California had put the burden of proof upon the applicant. The dissenters in In re Anastaplo, 366 U.S. 82, 81 S. Ct. 978, 6 L. Ed. 2d 135 (1961), also considered Speiser controlling.

REFERENCES

For discussion of the Speiser case, see Note, 72 Harv. L. Rev. 77, 185-188 (1958); Cramton, The Supreme Court and State Power to Deal With Subversion and Loyalty, 43 Minn. L. Rev. 1025, 1072-1075 (1959); Note, 28 U. Cinc. L. Rev. 346 (1959). See also Notes, 42 Marq. L. Rev. 560 (1959); 10 Syracuse L. Rev. 135 (1958); 36 U. Det. L.J. 341 (1959); 12 Vand. L. Rev. 275 (1958). Comment on the decisions of the Supreme Court of California appears in Notes, 10 Stan. L. Rev. 327 (1958); 31 Temple L.Q. 211 (1958); 106 U. Pa. L. Rev. 1060 (1958).

NOTES

1. In 1955 the Internal Revenue Service revoked the tax exempt status of the Institute of Pacific Relations and its affiliate the American Institute of Pacific Relations. The Institute had been under attack by the Senate Internal Security Subcommittee. The grounds for the revocation, as reported by the Institute, were that the Institute had "pursued its objectives through other than educational means" and had "to a substantial extent engaged in the dissemination of controversial and partisan propaganda"; and that it had "attempted to influence, directly and indirectly, the policies and/or actions of governments and government officials." See N.Y. Herald-Tribune, Oct. 13, 1955; N.Y. Times, Oct. 14, 1955; The Nation, Nov. 5, 1955, p. 373; mimeographed statement by William L. Holland, Ex. Sec., I.P.R., Oct. 26, 1955. Subsequently the Institute filed suit to recover taxes paid under the Internal Revenue Service ruling and, in 1960, the District Court ruled in its favor and ordered its tax exemption restored. Institute of Pacific Relations v. United States, 60-1 USTC ¶9404 (CCH); 5 AFTR 2d 1333 (P-H) (S.D. N.Y. 1960). Shortly afterwards the Institute moved from New York to the University of British Columbia: "the long loss of tax exemption seriously reduced gifts and contributions to the point where the institute had to seek a cheaper base of operations." N.Y. Times, Dec. 7, 1960.

Another controversy over tax exemption arose in connection with the Fellowship of Reconciliation. In January 1963 the Internal Revenue Service revoked the tax exemption of that organization on the ground that "your principal purpose is the prevention of war and the abolition of armaments"; and that, "Resolving international controversies is a political purpose, not a charitable or religious purpose." American Civil Liberties Union Bull., May 27, 1963. In June 1964 the Internal Revenue Service restored the Fellowship's tax-exempt status. Id., Oct. 5, 1964.

In 1965 Rev. Billy James Hargis, head of the Christian Crusade, charged that a proceeding by the Internal Revenue Service to remove tax exemption from that organization, on the ground that "a substantial part of your operations is directed at the accomplishment of political objectives," was an effort "to use the revenue code to harass conservatives who opposed Administration programs." Rev. Hargis added that, if tax exemption were withdrawn from the Christian Crusade, he would file citizen's suits challenging the exemption of such organizations as the National Council of Churches and the Southern Christian Leadership Conference. N.Y. Times, Aug. 9, 1965. In May, 1966, the New York Times reported that the Internal Revenue Service was studying the removal of tax exemption from the Christian Century and the Churchman, two liberal church magazines. N.Y. Times, May 16, 1966.

For discussion of the application of Section 501 of the Internal Revenue Code to political activity in general, see Note, Income Tax Disadvantages of Political Activities, 57 Colum. L. Rev. 273 (1957); Clark, The Limitation on Political Activities: A Discordant Note in the Law of Charities, 46 Va. L. Rev. 439 (1960).

2. In March 1956 the Internal Revenue Service asserted claims against the Communist Party for income and excess profits taxes, for the year 1951, in the sum of $261,058.33, plus penalties of $65,262.60 and interest of $62,952.48. Acting under its powers of jeopardy assessment the Service seized and padlocked the offices of the Party in New York, Philadelphia, San Francisco, Los Angeles, Chicago and Newark. It also seized the New York office of the Daily Worker, against which similar claims for non-payment of taxes were also made. The premises were returned a week later after an agreement had been reached for funds to be posted to cover the value of the seized properties. See N.Y. Times, March 28 to 31, April 2 to 5, 1956; American Civil Liberties Union Bull. April 9, 1956. Alleging the tax assessment was invalid and discriminatory, in that other political parties did not pay such taxes, the Party sought to enjoin the Internal Revenue Service from proceeding to collect the tax assessment, but failed. Communist Party v. Moysey, 141 F. Supp. 332 (S.D. N.Y. 1956); Publishers New Press v. Moysey, 141 F. Supp. 340 (S.D. N.Y. 1956). In August 1956 the Party petitioned in the Tax Court for redetermination of the tax deficiency. The Tax Court ruled, in 1962, that it was without jurisdiction to entertain the petition because of lack of showing that petitioner had authorized its attorney to act. 38 T.C. 862. The Court of Appeals reversed, saying "The obstacles placed in the way of this particular litigant seem to us as unusual in character as they are unfounded." Communist Party v. Commissioner of Internal Revenue, 332 F.2d 325, 329 (D.C. Cir. 1964). The matter went to trial before a judge of the Tax Court in March 1965. N.Y. Times, March 23, 1965. On October 6, 1965, the Tax Court sustained the Commissioner's determination of the deficiency; the Party appealed to the Court of Appeals. (No. 20,004). Meanwhile, in March 1962, the Government filed suit against the Communist Party and four of its officials to collect the taxes allegedly due for 1951, by now amounting to more than $500,000. N.Y. Times, March 20, 1962. The proceedings against the individual defendants were dismissed in United States v. Communist Party, 209 F. Supp. 132 (S.D. N.Y. 1962).

3. For other cases involving the impact of the taxing power upon First Amendment rights, see Chapter V.

4. Social Welfare Legislation

The development of social welfare legislation in the United States has given rise to a number of situations in which the legislature or administrative officials have undertaken to deny benefits under these laws to persons held to have engaged in conduct considered subversive or to belong to organizations alleged to be so. This subsection deals with these issues as they have arisen in connection with (a) welfare programs, (b) unemployment compensation, and (c) housing.

a. Welfare Programs

The Emergency Relief Act of 1941 prohibited relief employment of any "communist" or "member of any Nazi Bund organization." 54 Stat. 611, 620 (1941). This provision was held invalid by a federal district court in United States v. Schneider, 45 F. Supp. 848 (E.D. Wis. 1942), on the ground that there was no reasonable connection between political beliefs and financial distress. But the court did sustain that part of the indictment which charged falsification of facts in concealing Communist membership. See also United States v. Hautau, 43 F. Supp. 507 (D. N.J. 1942).

In 1943 Congress amended the veterans benefit laws to provide: "Any person shown by evidence satisfactory to the Administrator of Veterans' Affairs to be guilty of mutiny, treason, sabotage, or rendering assistance to an enemy of the United States or of its allies shall forfeit all accrued or future benefits under laws administered by the Veterans' Administration pertaining to gratuities for veterans and their dependents: Provided, however, That the Administrator of Veterans' Affairs, in his discretion, may apportion and pay any part of such benefits to the dependents of such person not exceeding the amount to which each dependent would be entitled if such person were dead." 57 Stat 554; 38 U.S.C. §728; now, in somewhat different form, 38 U.S.C. §3504. In 1954 the Veterans Administration announced the policy of suspending disability payments to veterans convicted under the Smith Act. Payments were suspended to two veterans — Saul Wellman and Robert Thompson — and refunds demanded. American Civil Liberties Union Bull., Sept. 17, 1956 and April 15, 1957. In Wellman's case it was decided, "on the basis of Wellman's conviction and on the evidence 'in its entirety,' that Wellman's participation in Communist Party activities in Michigan after 1946 and particularly during the period of the Korean conflict . . . rendered assistance to the enemy, 'the enemy being identified as the North Korean Government and the Communist Government of China.'" 259 F.2d at 165. The Court of Appeals reversed and remanded, noting that there was "no suggestion . . . that Wellman performed any overt act in behalf of the Communist Government of China or that of North Korea," and that his conviction under the Smith Act had meanwhile been reversed on appeal. Wellman v. Whittier, 259 F.2d 163 (D.C. Cir. 1958).

In Thompson's case the decision was predicated upon the finding that "during the Korean Conflict he made public utterances which were calculated by him to incite others to action beneficial to the North Korean Government and the Communist Government of China." 317 F.2d at 904-905. The Court of Appeals again reversed and remanded, holding that the Veterans Administrator had incorrectly interpreted the statute. The court said that the Administrator's interpretation raised serious First Amendment problems and that the correct construction of the statute was that "rendering assistance to an enemy" means conduct "defined by Congress as a crime and which does indeed render assistance to an enemy." Thompson v. Gleason, 317 F.2d 901, 906 (D.C. Cir. 1962). See also Thompson v. Whittier, 185 F. Supp. 306 (D. D.C. 1960), app. dis., 365 U.S. 465 (1961), noted in 6 Vill. L. Rev. 249 (1960-1961).

The Veterans Administration in 1955 also suspended payments to James Kutcher, a member of the Socialist Workers Party who had been discharged from his position with the Veterans Administration on loyalty grounds (see Section E, infra), but later restored them. N.Y. Times, Dec. 24, 1955; American Civil Liberties Union Bull. Jan. 9, 1956 and Feb. 20, 1956. See also 38 U.S.C. §§447, 812, 857.

In 1954, in a measure inspired by the Alger Hiss case, Congress prohibited the payment of retirement benefits earned by government employees convicted of various offenses, including espionage, treason, sedition, subversive activities or perjury relating to the above. 68 Stat. 1142 (1954); 5 U.S.C. §§2282-2288. See N.Y. Times, June 23 and 24, 1954. In Steinberg v. United States, 163 F. Supp. 590 (Ct. Cl. 1958), another provision of this Act, prohibiting payment of retirement benefits to government employees who invoked the privilege against self-incrimination in inquiries respecting their official duties, was declared unconstitutional.

The 1954 Act was felt to function too broadly in denying benefits to numerous employees guilty of minor infractions and was amended in 1961 to operate less restrictively. The provisions applicable to offenses against national security, however, remained substantially unchanged. 75 Stat. 640; 5 U.S.C. §§2281-2288. See also Garrott v. United States, 340 F.2d 615 (Ct. Cl. 1965).

In 1955 officials of the U.S. Department of Health, Education, and Welfare ruled that employees of the Communist Party were not eligible for old-age benefits based on such employment since the Communist Party was an agent of a foreign government. Payments were stopped to a number of persons and refunds demanded. N.Y. Times, Dec. 15 and 22, 1955, April 4, 1956, May 5 and 15, 1956. This ruling was reversed on appeal within the Department. N.Y. Times, June 22, 1956; American Civil Liberties Union Bull., Aug. 6, 1956. Later Congress passed a statute providing that upon conviction of espionage, treason. sedition, or other crime involving subversive activities the court could add to the penalty a requirement that prior wages or self-employment earnings could not be taken into account in determining the right to benefits under the old-age, survivorship, and disability provisions of the Social Security Act. 70 Stat. 807, 838-9 (1956); 42 U.S.C. §402(u). The statute also provided that wages paid by any organization registered or ordered to register under the Internal Security Act were similarly excluded from the Social Security Act. 42 U.S.C. §410(a)(17); 26 U.S.C. §3121(b)(17). No cases seem to have arisen under these provisions.

In Flemming v. Nestor, set forth below, the Supreme Court for the first time dealt with some of the issues raised by the denial of welfare benefits because of subversive conduct. The case involved the rights of an alien, but the principles discussed are more generally relevant.

FLEMMING v. NESTOR
363 U.S. 603, 80 S. Ct. 1367, 4 L. Ed. 2d 1435 (1960)

Mr. Justice Harlan delivered the opinion of the Court.

From a decision of the District Court for the District of Columbia holding §202(n) of the Social Security Act (68 Stat. 1083, as amended, 42 U.S.C. §402(n)) unconstitutional, the Secretary of Health, Education, and Welfare takes this direct appeal pursuant to 28 U.S.C. §1252. The challenged section . . . provides for the termination of old-age, survivor, and disability insurance benefits payable to, or in certain cases in respect of, an alien individual who, after September 1, 1954 (the date of enactment of the section), is deported under §241(a) of the Immigration and Nationality Act (8 U.S.C. §1251(a)) on any one of certain grounds specified in §202(n).

Appellee, an alien, immigrated to this country from Bulgaria in 1913, and became eligible for old-age benefits in November 1955. In July 1956 he was deported pursuant to §241(a)(6)(C)(i) of the Immigration and Nationality Act for having been a member of the Communist Party from 1933 to 1939. This being one of the benefit-termination deportation grounds specified in §202(n), appellee's benefits were terminated soon thereafter, and notice of the termination was given to his wife, who had remained in this country. Upon his failure to obtain administrative reversal of the decision, appellee commenced this action in the District Court, pursuant to §205(g) of the Social Security Act (53 Stat. 1370, as amended, 42 U.S.C. §405(g)), to secure judicial review. On cross-motions for summary judgment, the District Court ruled for appellee, holding §202(n) unconstitutional under the Due Process Clause of the Fifth Amendment in that it deprived appellee of an accrued property right. 169 F. Supp. 922. . . .

I

We think that the District Court erred in holding that §202(n) deprived appellee of an "accrued property right." 169 F. Supp., at 934. Appellee's right to Social Security benefits cannot properly be considered to have been of that order. . . .

The Social Security system may be accurately described as a form of social insurance, enacted pursuant to Congress' power to "spend money in aid of the 'general welfare,' " Helvering v. Davis [301 U.S. 619, 640], whereby persons gainfully employed, and those who employ them, are taxed to permit the payment of benefits to the retired and disabled, and their dependents. Plainly the expectation is that many members of the present productive work force will in turn become beneficiaries rather than supporters of the program. But each worker's benefits, though flowing from the contributions he made to the national economy while actively employed, are not dependent on the degree to which he was called upon to support the system by taxation. It is apparent that the noncontractual interest of an employee covered by the Act cannot be soundly analogized to that of the holder of an annuity, whose right to benefits is bottomed on his contractual premium payments. . . .

To engraft upon the Social Security system a concept of "accrued property rights" would deprive it of the flexibility and boldness in adjustment to ever-changing conditions which it demands. See Wollenberg, Vested Rights in Social-Security Benefits, 37 Ore. L. Rev. 299, 359. It was doubtless out of an awareness of the need for such flexibility that Congress included in the original Act, and has since retained, a clause expressly reserving to it "[t]he right to alter, amend, or repeal any provision" of the Act. §1104, 49 Stat. 648, 42 U.S.C. §1304. That provision makes express what is implicit in the institutional needs of the program. See Analysis of the Social Security System. Hearings before a Subcommittee of the Committee on Ways and Means, House of Representatives, 83d Cong., 1st Sess., pp. 920-921. It was pursuant to that provision that §202(n) was enacted.

We must conclude that a person covered by the Act has not such a right in benefit payments as would make every defeasance of "accrued" interests violative of the Due Process Clause of the Fifth Amendment.

II

This is not to say, however, that Congress may exercise its power to modify the statutory scheme free of all constitutional restraint. The interest of a covered employee under the Act is of sufficient substance to fall within the protection from arbitrary governmental action afforded by the Due Process Clause. In judging the permissibility of the cut-off provisions of §202(n) from this standpoint, it is not within our authority to determine whether the Congressional judgment expressed in that section is sound or equitable, or whether it comports well or ill with the purposes of the Act. . . . Particularly when we deal with a withholding of a noncontractual benefit under a social welfare program such as this, we must recognize that the Due Process Clause can be thought to interpose a bar only if the statute manifests a patently arbitrary classification, utterly lacking in rational justification.

Such is not the case here. The fact of a beneficiary's residence abroad — in the case of a deportee, a presumably permanent residence — can be of obvious relevance to the question of eligibility. One benefit which may be thought to accrue to the economy from the Social Security system is the increased over-all national purchasing power resulting from taxation of productive elements of the economy to provide payments to the retired and disabled, who might otherwise be destitute or nearly so, and who would generally spend a com-paratively large percentage of their benefit payments. This advantage would be lost as to payments made to one residing abroad. For these purposes, it is, of course, constitutionally irrelevant whether this reasoning in fact underlay the legislative decision, as it is irrelevant that the section does not extend to all to whom the postulated rationale might in logic apply. See United States v. Petrillo, 332 U.S. 1, 8-9; Steward Machine Co. v. Davis, 301 U.S. 548, 584-585; cf. Carmichael v. Southern Coal Co., 301 U.S. 495, 510-513. Nor, apart from this, can it be deemed irrational for Congress to have concluded that the public purse should not be utilized to contribute to the support of those de-ported on the grounds specified in the statute.

We need go no further to find support for our conclusion that this provi-sion of the Act cannot be condemned as so lacking in rational justification as to offend due process.

III

The remaining, and most insistently pressed, constitutional objections rest upon Art. I, §9, cl. 3, and Art. III, §2, cl. 3, of the Constitution, and the Sixth Amendment. It is said that the termination of appellee's benefits amounts to punishing him without a judicial trial, see Wong Wing v. United States, 163 U.S. 228; that the termination of benefits constitutes the imposition of pun-ishment by legislative act, rendering §202(n) a bill of attainder, see United States v. Lovett, 328 U.S. 303; Cummings v. Missouri, 4 Wall. 277; and that the punishment exacted is imposed for past conduct not unlawful when en-gaged in, thereby violating the constitutional prohibition on ex post facto laws, see Ex parte Garland, 4 Wall. 333.[7] Essential to the success of each of these contentions is the validity of characterizing as "punishment" in the constitutional sense the termination of benefits under §202(n).

In determining whether legislation which bases a disqualification on the happening of a certain past event imposes a punishment, the Court has sought to discern the objects on which the enactment in question was fo-cused. Where the source of legislative concern can be thought to be the activ-ity or status from which the individual is barred, the disqualification is not punishment even though it may bear harshly upon one affected. The contrary is the case where the statute in question is evidently aimed at the person or class of persons disqualified. In the earliest case on which appellee relies, a

---

[7] Appellee also adds, but hardly argues, the contention that he has been deprived of his rights under the First Amendment, since the adverse consequences stemmed from "mere past membership" in the Communist Party. This contention, which is no more than a collateral attack on appellee's deportation, is not open to him.

clergyman successfully challenged a state constitutional provision barring from that profession — and from many other professions and offices — all who would not swear that they had never manifested any sympathy or support for the cause of the Confederacy. Cummings v. Missouri, supra. . . .

[The Court then discusses Cummings, DeVeau v. Braisted, 363 U.S. 144, Ex parte Garland, Lovett, and Trop v. Dulles, 356 U.S. 86.]

It is thus apparent that, though the governing criterion may be readily stated, each case has turned on its own highly particularized context. Where no persuasive showing of a purpose "to reach the person, not the calling," Cummings v. Missouri, supra, at 320, has been made, the Court has not hampered legislative regulation of activities within its sphere of concern, despite the often-severe effects such regulation has had on the persons subject to it. Thus, deportation has been held to be not punishment, but an exercise of the plenary power of Congress to fix the conditions under which aliens are to be permitted to enter and remain in this country. Fong Yue Ting v. United States, 149 U.S. 698, 730; see Galvan v. Press, 347 U.S. 522, 530-531. Similarly, the setting by a State of qualifications for the practice of medicine, and their modification from time to time, is an incident of the State's power to protect the health and safety of its citizens, and its decision to bar from practice persons who commit or have committed a felony is taken as evidencing an intent to exercise that regulatory power, and not a purpose to add to the punishment of ex-felons. Hawker v. New York, 170 U.S. 189. See De Veau v. Braisted, supra (regulation of crime on the waterfront through disqualification of ex-felons from holding union office). Cf. Helvering v. Mitchell, 303 U.S. 391, 397-401, holding that, with respect to deficiencies due to fraud, a 50 percent addition to the tax imposed was not punishment so as to prevent, upon principles of double jeopardy, its assessment against one acquitted of tax evasion.

Turning, then, to the particular statutory provision before us, appellee cannot successfully contend that the language and structure of §202(n), or the nature of the deprivation, requires us to recognize a punitive design. Cf. Wong Wing v. United States, supra (imprisonment, at hard labor up to one year, of person found to be unlawfully in the country). Here the sanction is the mere denial of a noncontractual governmental benefit. No affirmative disability or restraint is imposed, and certainly nothing approaching the "infamous punishment" of imprisonment, as in Wong Wing, on which great reliance is mistakenly placed. Moreover, for reasons already given . . . , it cannot be said, as was said of the statute in Cummings v. Missouri, supra, at 319; see Dent v. West Virginia, 129 U.S. 114, 126, that the disqualification of certain deportees from receipt of Social Security benefits while they are not lawfully in this country bears no rational connection to the purposes of the legislation of which it is a part, and must without more therefore be taken as evidencing a Congressional desire to punish. Appellee argues, however, that the history and scope of §202(n) prove that no such postulated purpose can be thought to have motivated the legislature, and that they persuasively show that a punitive purpose in fact lay behind the statute. We do not agree.

[The Court then summarized the legislative history of Section 202(n).]

Appellee argues that this history demonstrates that Congress was not concerned with the *fact* of a beneficiary's deportation — which it is claimed alone would justify this legislation as being pursuant to a policy relevant to regulation of the Social Security system — but that it sought to reach certain *grounds* for deportation, thus evidencing a punitive intent. It is impossible to find in this meagre history the unmistakable evidence of punitive intent which, under principles already discussed, is required before a Congressional enactment of this kind may be struck down. Even were that history to be taken as evidencing Congress' concern with the grounds, rather than the fact, of deportation, we do not think that this, standing alone, would suffice to establish a punitive purpose. . . .

Reversed.

MR. JUSTICE BLACK, dissenting. . . .

In 1954, 15 years after Nestor had last been a Communist, and 18 years after he began to make payments into the old-age security fund, Congress passed a law providing, among other things, that any person who had been deported from this country because of past Communist membership under 66 Stat. 205, 8 U.S.C. §1251(a)(6)(C) should be wholly cut off from any benefits of the fund to which he had contributed under the law. 68 Stat. 1083, 42 U.S.C. §402(n). After the Government deported Nestor in 1956 it notified his wife, who had remained in this country, that he was cut off and no further payments would be made to him. This action, it seems to me, takes Nestor's insurance without just compensation and in violation of the Due Process Clause of the Fifth Amendment. Moreover, it imposes an ex post facto law and bill of attainder by stamping him, without a court trial, as unworthy to receive that for which he has paid and which the Government promised to pay him. The fact that the Court is sustaining this action indicates the extent to which people are willing to go these days to overlook violations of the Constitution perpetrated against anyone who has ever even innocently belonged to the Communist Party.

[Mr. Justice Black here summarizes the majority argument that Nestor had no "accrued property right."]

These are nice words but they cannot conceal the fact that they simply tell the contributors to this insurance fund that despite their own and their employers' payments the Government, in paying the beneficiaries out of the fund, is merely giving them something for nothing and can stop doing so when it pleases. This, in my judgment, reveals a complete misunderstanding of the purpose Congress and the country had in passing that law. It was then generally agreed, as it is today, that it is not desirable that aged people think of the Government as giving them something for nothing. An excellent statement of this view, quoted by Mr. Justice Douglas in another connection, was made by Senator George, the Chairman of the Finance Committee when the Social Security Act was passed, and one very familiar with the philosophy that brought it about:

"It comports better than any substitute we have discovered with the American concept that free men want to earn their security and not ask for doles — that what is due as a matter of earned right is far better than a gratuity. . . .

"Social Security is not a handout; it is not charity; it is not relief. It is an earned right based upon the contributions and earnings of the individual. As an earned right, the individual is eligible to receive his benefit in dignity and self-respect." 102 Cong. Rec. 15110.

The people covered by this Act are now able to rely with complete assurance on the fact that they will be compelled to contribute regularly to this fund whenever each contribution falls due. I believe they are entitled to rely with the same assurance on getting the benefits they have paid for and have been promised, when their disability or age makes their insurance payable under the terms of the law. . . .

Although not believing that the particular label "punishment" is of decisive importance, I think the Act does impose punishment even in a classic sense. The basic reason for Nestor's loss of his insurance payments is that he was once a Communist. This man, now 69 years old, has been driven out of the country where he has lived for 43 years to a land where he is practically a stranger, under an Act authorizing his deportation many years after his Communist membership. Cf. Galvan v. Press, 347 U.S. 522, 532, 533 (dissenting opinions). Now a similar ex post facto law deprives him of his insurance, which, while petty and insignificant in amount to this great Government, may well be this exile's daily bread, for the same reason and in accord with the general fashion of the day — that is, to punish in every way possible anyone who ever made the mistake of being a Communist in this country or who is supposed ever to have been associated with anyone who made that mistake. . . . Faithful observance of our holdings in [Lovett], in Ex parte Garland, 4 Wall. 333, and in Cummings v. Missouri, 4 Wall. 277, would, in my judgment, require us to hold that the 1954 Act is a bill of attainder. It is a congressional enactment aimed at an easily ascertainable group; it is certainly punishment in any normal sense of the word to take away from any person the benefits of an insurance system into which he and his employer have paid their moneys for almost two decades; and it does all this without a trial according to due process of law. . . .

A basic constitutional infirmity of this Act, in my judgment, is that it is a part of a pattern of laws all of which violate the First Amendment out of fear that this country is in grave danger if it lets a handful of Communist fanatics or some other extremist group make their arguments and discuss their ideas. This fear, I think, is baseless. It reflects a lack of faith in the sturdy patriotism of our people and does not give to the world a true picture of our abiding strength. It is an unworthy fear in a country that has a Bill of Rights containing provisions for fair trials, freedom of speech, press and religion, and other specific safeguards designed to keep men free. I repeat once more that I think this Nation's greatest security lies, not in trusting to a momentary majority of this Court's view at any particular time of what is "patently arbitrary," but in wholehearted devotion to and observance of our constitutional freedoms. See Wieman v. Updegraff, 344 U.S. 183, 192 (concurring opinion).

I would affirm the judgment of the District Court which held that Nestor is constitutionally entitled to collect his insurance.

[Mr. Justice Douglas' opinion, arguing that Section 202(n) constituted a bill of attainder, is omitted.]

MR. JUSTICE BRENNAN, with whom The Chief Justice and Mr. Justice Douglas join, dissenting. . . .

It seems to me that the statute itself shows that the sole legislative concern was with "the person or class of persons disqualified." Congress did not disqualify for benefits all beneficiaries residing abroad or even all dependents residing abroad who are aliens. If that had been the case I might agree that Congress' concern would have been with "the activity or status" and not with the "person or class of persons disqualified." The scales would then be tipped toward the conclusion that Congress desired to limit benefit payments to beneficiaries residing in the United States so that the American economy would be aided by expenditure of benefits here. Indeed a proposal along those lines was submitted to Congress in 1954, at the same time §202(n) was proposed, and it was rejected. . . .

This appraisal of the distinctions drawn by Congress between various kinds of conduct impels the conclusion, beyond peradventure that the distinctions can be understood only if the purpose of Congress was to strike at "the person or class of persons disqualified." The Court inveighs against invalidating a statute on "implication and vague conjecture." Rather I think the Court has strained to sustain the statute on "implication and vague conjecture," in holding that the congressional concern was "the activity or status from which the individual is barred." Today's decision sanctions the use of the spending power not to further the legitimate objectives of the Social Security program but to inflict hurt upon those who by their conduct have incurred the displeasure of Congress. The Framers ordained that even the worst of men should not be punished for their past acts or for any conduct without adherence to the procedural safeguards written into the Constitution. Today's decision is to me a regretful retreat from Lovett, Cummings and Garland.

Section 202(n) imposes punishment in violation of the prohibition against ex post facto laws and without a judicial trial. I therefore dissent.

REFERENCES

For comment on Flemming v. Nestor, see Notes, 73 Harv. L. Rev. 590 (1960); 21 Md. L. Rev. 331 (1961); 45 Minn. L. Rev. 1090 (1961); 40 Texas L. Rev. 276 (1961); 196 Wash. U.L.Q. 402 (1961); Reich, The New Property, 73 Yale L.J. 733, especially 768-771, 775-776 (1964); Linde, Constitutional Rights in the Public Sector: Justice Douglas on Liberty in the Welfare State, 40 Wash. L. Rev. 10, 14-22 (1965); O'Neil, Unconstitutional Conditions: Welfare Benefits with Strings Attached, 54 Calif. L. Rev. 443 (1966). On the problem of what is punishment, see Kennedy v. Mendoza-Martinez, 372 U.S. 144, 83 S. Ct. 554, 9 L. Ed. 2d 644 (1963); United States v. Brown, 381 U.S. 437, 85 S. Ct. 1707, 14 L. Ed. 2d 484 (1965), set forth in subsection 1, supra. See also the Supreme Court's decision in Sherbert v. Verner, discussed in the following materials on the unemployment compensation laws.

NOTES

1. In passing the Medicare law in 1965 Congress provided in Section 103(b)(1) that a person not already covered by federal social security programs could not qualify for hospital insurance benefits under the new program if "at the beginning of the first month in which he meets the requirements of subsection (a), [he is] a member of any organization" registered or ordered to register under the Internal Security Act. Pub. L. 89-97, 79 Stat. 286, 333; 42 U.S.C. §426 note. The Department of Health, Education, and Welfare, in the official form required for applying for such hospital insurance benefits, asks all applicants to answer the question: "Are you now, or have you been during the last 12 months, a member of any organization which is required to register under the Internal Security Act of 1950, as a communist-action organization, a communist-front organization, or a communist-infiltrated organization?" It was estimated that 2 million elderly persons would have to disclaim such membership in order to obtain benefits under the Medicare law. N.Y. Times, Dec. 17, 1965; American Civil Liberties Union Bull., Jan. 17, 1966. Suit to test the constitutionality of the provision was brought in the Southern District of New York in February 1966 by Mrs. Louis B. Weiss, 70, and her mother, Mrs. Sigmund K. Pollitzer, 95, well-known civic leaders in New York City. Weiss v. Gardner, Civil No. 66-498 (S.D. N.Y.); see American Civil Liberties Union Bull., Feb. 21, 1966. Similar suits were also brought in other areas. In April the Department of Health, Education, and Welfare announced that failure to answer the question on the form would not by itself disqualify applicants. American Civil Liberties Union, Civil Liberties, May 1966.

See also Sections 103(b)(2) and 104(b)(2) of the Medicare Act which deny benefits to persons convicted of the offenses listed in 42 U.S.C. §402(u), noted supra. 79 Stat. 333-335; 42 U.S.C. §§426 note, 1395o.

2. The loyalty provisions incorporated in the Economic Opportunity Act of 1964, establishing the anti-poverty program, are set out in Section E, infra.

b. Unemployment Compensation

The Ohio Unemployment Compensation Law was amended in 1949 to provide that no person is eligible for benefits who the administrator finds "advocates, or is a member of a party which advocates, the overthrow of our government by force"; and that every claimant for benefits must file an affidavit stating whether or not he advocates, or is a member of a party that advocates, overthrow of the government by force. Ohio G.C. §1345-6, par. c(4). The provision was upheld in Dworken v. Collopy, 91 N.E.2d 564 (Ct. C. P. Ohio 1950), noted in 29 Chi.-Kent L. Rev. 255 (1951). See also State v. Hamilton, 92 Ohio App. 285, 110 N.E.2d 37 (1951).

As noted above, the ruling of the State Industrial Commissioner excluding the Communist Party from the New York unemployment compensation system, on the ground that it was not a legal body under Section 3 of the Communist Control Act, was reversed in Communist Party v. Catherwood, 367 U.S. 389, 81 S. Ct. 1465, 6 L. Ed. 2d 919 (1961). See Section C, subsection 3, supra.

Questions concerning the denial of unemployment compensation to employees discharged for failure to answer questions relating to Communist Party membership have arisen in several states. In Connecticut such an employee who declined to answer questions before a Congressional investigating committee, relying on the First and Fifth Amendments, was held not to have engaged in "wilful misconduct" and to be entitled to compensation. Gilden v. Administrator, decision of Commissioner for Fourth District, June 25, 1957; accord, Re Robert Elkins, IX Civil Liberties Docket 17 (1963). In Maryland the Court of Appeals has ruled that a waitress who pleaded the privilege against self-incrimination before the House Un-American Activities Committee, and was therewith discharged, could not be disqualified from receiving benefits on the ground that she had engaged in "misconduct connected with [her] work." Fino v. Maryland Employment Security Board, 218 Md. 504, 147 A.2d 738 (1959). But the same court reached the opposite conclusion as to an employee of Bethlehem Steel Company who also refused to answer similar questions later propounded by his employer. Ostrofsky v. Maryland Employment Security Board, 218 Md. 509, 147 A.2d 741 (1959). In a Pennsylvania case another employee of Bethlehem Steel Company, after pleading the Fifth Amendment before a Congressional committee, testified before the grievance arbitrator under the collective bargaining contract that he was not a Communist Party member on the day before the committee hearing but again invoked the privilege as to prior membership. The Supreme Court of Pennsylvania upheld his claim to unemployment compensation, ruling that there was no proof that he was "subversive" and that he had not engaged in wilful misconduct connected with his work. Ault v. Unemployment Compensation Board of Review, 398 Pa. 250, 157 A.2d 375 (1960); for a similar ruling see Darin v. Unemployment Compensation Board of Review, 398 Pa. 259, 157 A.2d 407 (1960); Judge Bell dissented in both cases; lower court decisions noted in 20 U. Pitt. L. Rev. 884 (1959); 34 Notre Dame Law. 469 (1959).

In Syrek v. California Unemployment Insurance Appeals Board, 54 Cal. 2d

519, 354 P.2d 625 (1960), the applicant had refused to accept a civil service position on the ground that he was conscientiously opposed to taking the loyalty oath required by California law of such employees. The Supreme Court of California, in a 4 to 3 decision, held that this conduct did not constitute a refusal to accept employment without "good cause" and that the applicant was entitled to unemployment benefits. The decision rested on statutory interpretation grounds, but contained overtones of constitutional issues. For comment on the case, see Notes, 36 N.Y.U.L. Rev. 1052 (1961); 9 Kan. L. Rev. 346 (1961); 34 So. Cal. L. Rev. 367 (1961).

The Supreme Court of the United States touched on these issues, largely by way of dictum, in Sherbert v. Verner, 374 U.S. 398, 83 S. Ct. 1790, 10 L. Ed. 2d 965 (1963). In that case the claimant, a Seventh-day Adventist, had been denied unemployment compensation because she had refused to work on Saturday, the Sabbath Day of her faith. Holding that the disqualification imposed a "burden upon the free exercise of religion," the Court went on to say:

"Nor may the South Carolina court's construction of the statute be saved from constitutional infirmity on the ground that unemployment compensation benefits are not appellant's 'right' but merely a 'privilege.' It is too late in the day to doubt that the liberties of religion and expression may be infringed by the denial of or placing of conditions upon a benefit or privilege. American Communications Assn. v. Douds, 339 U.S. 382, 390; Wieman v. Updegraff, 344 U.S. 183, 191-192; Hannegan v. Esquire, Inc., 327 U.S. 146, 155-156. For example, in Flemming v. Nestor, 363 U.S. 603, 611, the Court recognized with respect to Federal Social Security benefits that '[t]he interest of a covered employee under the Act is of sufficient substance to fall within the protection from arbitrary governmental action afforded by the Due Process Clause.' In Speiser v. Randall, 357 U.S. 513, we emphasized that conditions upon public benefits cannot be sustained if they so operate, whatever their purpose, as to inhibit or deter the exercise of First Amendment freedoms." 374 U.S. at 404-405.

For further consideration of the case, see Chapter VIII. In general on these issues, see Note, Charity Versus Social Insurance in Unemployment Compensation Laws, 73 Yale L.J. 357 (1963).

c. Housing

In enacting the appropriation act for the Public Housing Administration in 1952 Congress incorporated a rider, known as the Gwinn Amendment, which read as follows:

"*Provided further,* That no housing unit constructed under the United States Housing Act of 1937 [42 U.S.C. §§1401 et seq.], as amended, shall be occupied by a person who is a member of an organization designated as subversive by the Attorney General: *Provided further,* That the foregoing prohibition shall be enforced by the local housing authority . . ." 66 Stat. 403 (1952), 42 U.S.C. §1411C (1952).

The Gwinn Amendment was re-enacted in 1953 (67 Stat. 307, 42 U.S.C. §1411C, Supp. 1953), but thereafter was dropped. Illinois in 1953 enacted somewhat similar legislation. Ill. Rev. Stat. c. 67½, §§25.01, 25.02.

The Gwinn Amendment was held unconstitutional by the Supreme Court of Wisconsin, on the ground that the harm from suppression of First Amendment freedoms outweighed the possible evils of occupancy by members of subversive organizations, and the United States Supreme Court denied certiorari. Lawson v. Housing Authority of the City of Milwaukee, 270 Wis. 269, 70 N.W.2d 605 (1955), cert. den., 350 U.S. 882 (1955). Attempts by local housing authorities to enforce the Gwinn Amendment were held invalid for various reasons in Rudder v. United States, 226 F.2d 51 (D.C. Cir. 1955); Kutcher v. Housing Authority of City of Newark, 20 N.J. 181, 119 A.2d 1 (1955); Peters v. N.Y.C. Housing Authority, 307 N.Y. 519, 121 N.E.2d 529 (1954), 1 App. Div. 2d 694, 147 N.Y.S.2d 859 (Second Dept. 1955); Weixel v. N.Y.C. Housing Authority, 1 App. Div. 2d 703, 147 N.Y.S.2d 467 (Second Dept. 1955); Chicago Housing Authority v. Clark, 4 Ill. 2d 319, 122 N.E.2d 522 (1954). See also Housing Authority of the City of Los Angeles v. Cordova, 130 Cal. App. 2d 883, 279 P.2d 215 (1955), cert. den., 350 U.S. 969 (1956). The Illinois statute was held invalid in Chicago Housing Authority v. Blackman, a companion case to the Clark case, on the ground that it penalized association regardless of knowledge of the aims of the organization.

For discussion see Williams, Tenant's Loyalty Oaths, 31 Notre Dame Law. 190 (1956); Note, Denial of Federally Aided Housing to Members of Organizations on the Attorney General's List, 69 Harv. L. Rev. 551 (1956); Note, The Gwinn Amendment: Practical and Constitutional Problems in its Enforcement, 104 U. Pa. L. Rev. 694 (1956). See also Notes, 53 Colum. L. Rev. 1166 (1953); 55 Colum. L. Rev. 1222 (1955); 44 Geo. L.J. 330 (1956); 2 Howard L.J. 136 (1956); 1 A.L.R.2d Supp. 1126.

5. Other Benefits or Privileges

a. Radio and Television Licensing

For many years the Federal Communications Commission has, in some instances, required an applicant for a broadcasting or operator's license, or for a renewal, to answer questions concerning past and present Communist Party membership and associations. In 1955 the Commission considered adoption of formal regulations on this subject, but eventually took no action. See Dockets No. 11060 and 11061; 1 P. & F. R.R. Pt. 2, p. 63/ix-xvi; Matter of Lafferty, 23 F.C.C. 761, 13 P. & F. R.R. 641 (1957). In 1960 its practice was upheld in Borrow v. Federal Communications Commission, 285 F.2d 666 (D.C. Cir. 1960), cert. den., 364 U.S. 892 (1960).

For comment on the Borrow case see Note, 59 Mich. L. Rev. 638 (1961). In accord with the Borrow case is Cronan v. Federal Communications Commission, 285 F.2d 288 (D.C. Cir. 1960), cert. den., 366 U.S. 904 (1960) (failure of F.C.C. to adopt formal regulations on the subject not material). See also Homer v. Richmond, 292 F.2d 719 (D.C. Cir. 1961) (denial of licenses as radio-telegraph officers in Merchant Marine, by Commandant of the United States Coast Guard, on similar grounds remanded for failure to grant hearing).

In Blumenthal v. Federal Communications Commission, 318 F.2d 276 (D.C. Cir. 1963), the court reached the same conclusions where the applicants had invoked the privilege against self-incrimination in refusing to answer the F.C.C. questions as to past membership.

The issues arose again in connection with the application for permanent licenses made by Pacifica Foundation, which operated three FM, listener-sponsored, stations in New York, Los Angeles and Berkeley. Pacifica, a non-profit educational foundation, presented "all points of view in its . . . broadcasts, from the extreme left to the extreme right," and the Communist point of view was not excluded. N.Y. Times, July 28, 1963. Although one of the applications was filed in 1959, the F.C.C. failed to take any action on the application.

In January, 1963, the Senate Internal Security Subcommittee held secret hearings to inquire into Pacifica's operations in order "to find out whether Communists had attempted to infiltrate" the Foundation. N.Y. Times, July 28, 1963. The transcript of the proceedings, released in July, indicated that Pacifica's executive vice-president invoked the Fifth Amendment when asked about prior communist affiliations. Pacifica Foundation, Hearings before the Subcommittee to Investigate Administration of the Internal Security and Other Internal Security Laws, of the Senate Committee on the Judiciary, 88th Cong., 1st Sess. (1963).

On October 7, the F.C.C. requested that Pacifica's officers, directors, and general managers file sworn responses to inquiries as to whether they had ever been members of the Communist Party or of any organization teaching or advocating the violent overthrow of the government. This request was refused. N.Y. Times, Nov. 11, 1963. The F.C.C.'s decision was announced on Jan. 22, 1964. The Commission granted Pacifica's applications, but in so doing devoted most of its opinion to discussion of obscenity charges made about certain of the Foundation's programs. As to the Communist issue the Commission said: "Under the public interest standard, it is relevant and important for the Commission to determine in certain cases whether its applicants, or the principals of its applicants, for broadcast licenses or radio operator licenses, are members of the Communist Party or of organizations which advocate or teach the overthrow of the Government by force or violence. . . . On the basis of information obtained from Government sources, the Foundation, and our own inquiry, we do not find any evidence warranting further inquiry into the qualifications in this respect of Pacifica Foundation." Matter of Pacifica Foundation, 36 F.C.C. 147, 151, 1 P.&F. R.R. 2d 747, 752-753 (1964).

b. *Occupational Licensing*

In a number of situations states and municipalities have imposed loyalty qualifications as a condition of obtaining an occupational license. Thus a 1951 Texas statute requires every person seeking a license as a pharmacist to take an oath "that he is not a member of the Communist Party or affiliated with such party, and that he does not believe in and is neither a member of nor supports any group or organization that believes in, furthers, or teaches the overthrow of the United States Government by force or by any illegal or unconstitutional methods." Tex. Rev. Civ. Stat. Ann. art. 4542a, §9. In the District of Columbia persons seeking a license to sell insurance are required to answer questions as to whether they are or ever have been members of the Communist Party or any organization on the Attorney General's list, or whether they have ever refused on constitutional grounds to give testimony before a court, grand jury or other duly authorized tribunal. American Civil Liberties Union Bull., Feb. 4, 1957, and Oct. 28, 1957. An extreme example of this type of restriction is the requirement in Indiana that professional wrestlers and boxers must take a loyalty oath. American Civil Liberties Union Annual Report 1954-1955, 39. See, for other examples, Gellhorn, Individual Freedom and Governmental Restraints 129-130 (1956); American Civil Liberties Union annual reports.

Since 1956 the Commissioner of Water Supply, Gas and Electricity has required a loyalty oath from applicants for permits to fish in New York City reservoirs. Permits were refused two Communists. N.Y. Times, May 7, 1957.

In 1960 the Commissioner of Motor Vehicles in New York denied renewal of a driving license to Benjamin Davis because of his conviction under the Smith Act. The action was reversed, on the ground that the Commissioner's action was without statutory authority. Matter of Davis v. Hults, 24 Misc. 2d 954, 204 N.Y.S.2d 865 (Sup. Ct. N.Y. Co. 1960). Thereafter the New York legislature enacted a law providing for mandatory revocation when the holder of the license had been convicted of advocating overthrow of the government by force or violence. N.Y. Laws 1961, ch. 962; Vehicle and Traffic Law §510 ¶2(b).

6. *Restrictions on Access to the Election Process*

Restrictions on access to the election process because of conduct or views raise similar, though not identical, problems as those presented in the previous subsections. These restrictions have taken two principal forms: (1) the exclusion of a party from the ballot; (2) the requirement that candidates for election to public office meet certain qualifications or take some form of oath.

The two forms of restriction are related, since refusal to allow a party to appear on the ballot may be construed as imposing qualifications upon the right to hold elective office.

In the first category the applicable federal legislation is Section 3 of the Communist Control Act of 1954, which provides that the Communist Party and its successors "are not entitled to any of the rights, privileges, and immunities attendant upon legal bodies created under the jurisdiction of the laws of the United States or any political subdivision thereof" and that all such rights, privileges and immunities "are terminated." 50 U.S.C. §842; see Section C, subsection 3, supra. This provision was clearly intended to restrict the right of the Communist Party to appear upon the ballot, although the exact extent of the limitation was not made clear. See Note, The Communist Control Act of 1954, 64 Yale L.J. 712, 738-744 (1955). In as much as the Communist Party has not run a candidate for President since 1940 and has rarely, if ever, sought a place on the ballot since 1948 the provisions of Section 3 have seldom been invoked. The only judicial decision involving Section 3, as noted above, is Salwen v. Rees, 16 N.J. 216, 108 A.2d 265 (1954). In that case a candidate sought to run for membership on the Board of Chosen Freeholders of Mercer County, New Jersey. The Communist Party not having polled 10 per cent of the votes in the previous election was not entitled to a place on the ballot automatically, but Salwen had obtained the requisite number of names on a nominating petition and requested that the designation "Communist Party" be printed on the ballot next to his name. The lower court upheld the action of the County Clerk in refusing to allow Salwen's name to appear on the ballot. Rejecting Salwen's contention that he was running as an individual, the court said: "It is the plaintiff's fault who insists upon identifying himself with the party and becoming its embodiment . . . [He] proclaims himself the candidate of the Communist Party, and proclaims to the electorate that a vote for him is a vote for the party enthronement." 16 N.J. at 217, 108 A.2d at 265. The New Jersey Supreme Court affirmed per curiam on the oral opinion below. Ibid. The constitutional basis for the provision, including its application to state elections, was not fully discussed. For comment see Notes, 55 Colum. L. Rev. 631, 707-708 (1955); 53 Mich. L. Rev. 1153, 1159-1161 (1955).

Some 24 states have legislation on the books excluding certain types of political parties from the ballot. Some of these exclude "subversive" organizations, variously defined; others specifically exclude the Communist Party; others outlaw the Communist Party or "subversive" organizations generally, thereby precluding them from a place on the ballot. Some state laws contain more than one of these provisions. Many of the legal problems arising under this type of legislation remain unresolved, due in part to the absence of efforts by the Communist Party in recent years to appear on the ballot. The more significant court decisions are the following:

In Communist Party v. Peek, 20 Cal. 2d 536, 127 P.2d 889 (1942), various provisions of an earlier California election law were involved. One provided that no party "shall be recognized or qualified to participate in any primary election which uses or adopts as any part of its party designation the word 'communist' or any derivative of the word 'communist.' " This provision the California Supreme Court held invalid as having no reasonable relation to the objective of eliminating subversive parties from the election process. Another portion of the law imposed the same limitation upon any party "which is directly or indirectly affiliated, by any means whatsoever, with the Communist Party of the United States, the Third Communist International, or any other foreign agency, political party, organization or government." This provision was also held invalid, the specific designation of the Communist Party being outlawed by the provision of the California Constitution prohibiting special legislation and the remainder being too broad in its sweep. A third prohibition against any party "which either directly or indirectly carries on, advocates, teaches, justifies, aids, or abets a program of sabotage, force and violence, sedition or treason against, the Government of the United States or this State" was held constitutional under the doctrine of Whitney v. California. But this third provision could be applied to any particular party only after opportunity for notice, hearing and judicial review.

An Arkansas statute, similar to the third provision of the California law, was held valid in Field v. Hall, 201 Ark. 77, 143 S.W.2d 567 (1940). The Arkansas court differed with the California court, however, in holding that the Communist Party could be excluded from the ballot under the statute without notice or hearing by the secretary of state, the trial in a mandamus proceeding affording sufficient due process. A similar provision, with the additional exclusion of a party "which has in any manner any connection with any foreign government or power," was upheld against attack by the Prohibition Party in State ex rel. Berry v. Hummel, 42 Ohio L. Abs. 40, 59 N.E.2d 238 (1944).

In Albertson v. Millard, 345 Mich. 519, 77 N.W.2d 104 (1956), the Michigan Supreme Court held that Section 7 of the Trucks Act, providing that no Communist's name may be printed on any ballot, was included among those provisions which were invalid as pre-empted by federal legislation under the United States Supreme Court's decision in Pennsylvania v. Nelson, 350 U.S. 497, 76 S. Ct. 477, 100 L. Ed. 640 (1956) (see Section C, subsection 5, supra).[1]

---

[1] In Feinglass v. Reinecke, 48 F. Supp. 438 (N.D. Ill. 1942), a federal court held invalid, as being too vague and uncertain, an Illinois statute excluding from the ballot any organization which was "associated, directly or indirectly, with Communist, Fascist, Nazi or other un-American principles and engages in activities or propaganda designed to teach subservience to the political principles and ideals of foreign nations or the overthrow by violence of the established constitutional form of government of the United States and the State of Illinois." Since the ballots had already been printed, however, the court refused to grant an injunction to Communist Party candidates restraining election officials from excluding them from the ballot. In Washington ex rel. Huff v. Reeves, 5 Wash. 2d 637, 106 P.2d 729 (1940), an attempt by election officials to bar the Communist Party from the ballot, in the absence of any statutory provision, was disallowed.

In practice the flexibilities of administration by election officials, as well as the difficulties and delays of judicial review, sometimes make it difficult for radical parties to secure their full privileges. See Ward, The Communist Party and the Ballot, 1 Bill of Rights Rev. 286 (1941); Note, 96 U. Pa. L. Rev. 381, 388-91 (1948); 16 U. Chi. L. Rev. 499 (1949); 51 Colum. L. Rev. 521 (1951); but cf. State ex rel. Beck v. Hummel, 150 Ohio St. 127, 80 N.E.2d 899 (1948) (reversing finding of Secretary of State that candidates for presidential electors supporting Henry Wallace should be excluded from ballot).

The other form of restriction — that requiring an oath or imposing other restrictions upon candidates — appears in the law of some 21 states. Among the decisions dealing with this problem are the following:

In Imbrie v. Marsh, 3 N.J. 578, 71 A.2d 352 (1950), the New Jersey statute required every candidate for public office to take an oath that he does not "believe in, advocate or advise the use of force, or violence, or other unlawful or unconstitutional means, to overthrow or make any change in the Government established in the United States or in this State," or belong to or is affiliated with any organization that does so. This provision was declared invalid on the ground that the oath to support the constitution required in the New Jersey constitution was exclusive. Similar holdings that such requirements for candidates for federal office cannot add to qualifications imposed by the Federal Constitution for United States Representatives were made in In re O'Connor, 173 Misc. 419, 17 N.Y.S.2d 758 (Sup. Ct. N.Y. Co. 1940); Danielson v. Fitzsimmons, 232 Minn. 149, 44 N.W.2d 484 (1950). But in Huntamer v. Coe, 40 Wash. 2d 767, 246 P.2d 489 (1952), the Supreme Court of Washington upheld the requirement that a candidate for state and federal office file an affidavit that he is not a "subversive person," on the ground that the provision did not add to the qualifications for office prescribed by the state and federal constitutions but merely implemented them.

The Maryland Ober law contained a similar provision, which was sustained as to candidates for state office but held invalid as to candidates for federal office in Shub v. Simpson, 196 Md. 177, 76 A.2d 332 (1950). This provision of the Ober law came before the United States Supreme Court in the Gerende case.

GERENDE v. BOARD OF SUPERVISORS OF ELECTIONS OF BALTIMORE
341 U.S. 56, 71 S. Ct. 565, 95 L. Ed. 745 (1951)

Per Curiam.

This is an appeal from a decision of the Court of Appeals of the State of Maryland the effect of which is to deny the appellant a place on the ballot for a municipal election in the City of Baltimore on the ground that she has refused to file an affidavit required by state law. Md. Laws 1949, c. 86, §15. 197 Md. 282, 78 A.2d 660. The scope of the state law was passed on in Shub v.

Simpson, 196 Md. 177, 76 A.2d 332. We read this decision to hold that to obtain a place on a Maryland ballot a candidate need only make oath that he is not a person who is engaged "in one way or another in the attempt to overthrow the government *by force or violence,"* and that he is not knowingly a member of an organization engaged in such an attempt. 196 Md. at 192, 76 A.2d at 338. At the bar of this Court the Attorney General of the State of Maryland declared that he would advise the proper authorities to accept an affidavit in these terms as satisfying in full the statutory requirement. Under these circumstances and with this understanding, the judgment of the Maryland Court of Appeals is

Affirmed.

MR. JUSTICE REED concurs in the result.

NOTES

1. A more extreme form of candidate's oath is that required in Texas (Tex. Election Code Ann. Art. 6.02, Supp. 1965): "I . . . do solemnly swear that I believe in and approve of our present representative form of government, and, if elected, I will support and defend our present representative form of government and will resist any effort or movement from any source which seeks to subvert or destroy the same or any part thereof . . ." The law further provides: "The name of no candidate or nominee of any political party whose principles include any thought or purpose of setting aside representative form of government and substituting therefor any other form of government shall be permitted on the official ballot."

2. Under a 1951 amendment to the Alabama Constitution no person may be registered to vote unless he subscribes to an oath "disavowing belief in or affiliation at any time with any group or party which advocated the overthrow of the Government of the United States or the state of Alabama by unlawful means." Ala. Con. Art. VIII, §181, Amend. XCI; see also Ala. Code Tit. 17, §31. This requirement was held constitutional by the Alabama Supreme Court in an advisory opinion rendered prior to submission of the amendment for ratification. Opinion of the Justices, 252 Ala. 351, 40 So. 2d 849 (1949).

REFERENCES

The state laws and decisions are collected in Internal Security and Subversion, Principal State Laws and Cases, A Study Prepared for the Subcommittee to Investigate the Administration of the Internal Security Act and Other Internal Security Laws of the Senate Committee on the Judiciary, by Legislative Reference Service, Library of Congress (1965). For the statistics on votes cast for Communist and Communist-supported minority candidates from 1924 to 1952, see Digest of the Public Record of Communism in the United States 324-343 (Fund for the Republic 1955). See generally on the subject Groner, State Control of Subversive Activities in the United States, 9 Fed. B.J. 61, 62-71 (1947); Notes, 96 U. Pa. L. Rev. 381, 388-391 (1948); 25 Notre Dame Law. 319 (1950); 24 Temple L.Q. 484 (1951); 64 Yale L.J. 712, 719-720, 738-744 (1955); 55 Colum. L. Rev. 631, 706-

708 (1955); Pfeffer, The Liberties of An American 212-218 (1956). See also Notes, 54 Harv. L. Rev. 155 (1940); 1 Stan. L. Rev. 85, 90-91 (1948); 34 Va. L. Rev. 450 (1948); 3 Vand. L. Rev. 811 (1950); 19 Geo. Wash. L. Rev. 552 (1951); 29 Wash. L. Rev. 63 (1954); Auerbach, The Communist Control Act of 1954, 23 U. Chi. L. Rev. 173, 204-211 (1956). For material on access to the ballot apart from issues of subversion, see Chapter XII.

See also Wilson v. Council of Highland Park, 284 Mich. 96, 278 S.W. 778 (1938) (court refused to remove city councilman for membership in Black Legion).

7. Expatriation

The Expatriation Act of 1954 amended Section 349(a)(9) of the Immigration and Nationality Act to read:

"(a) a person who is a national of the United States whether by birth or naturalization, shall lose his nationality by . . .

"(9) committing any act of treason against, or attempting by force to overthrow, or bearing arms against, the United States, violating or conspiring to violate any of the provisions of section 2383 of title 18, United States Code, or willfully performing any act in violation of section 2385 of title 18, United States Code, or violating section 2384 of said title by engaging in a conspiracy to overthrow, put down, or to destroy by force the Government of the United States, or to levy war against them, if and when he is convicted thereof by a court martial or by a court of competent jurisdiction . . ." 68 Stat. 1146 (1954), 8 U.S.C. §1481(a)(9).[1]

The amendment has not been tested in the courts but at the 1957 Term the Supreme Court considered a series of cases raising the issue in other connections of the power of Congress to revoke American citizenship. Perez v. Brownell, 356 U.S. 44, 78 S. Ct. 568, 2 L. Ed. 2d 603 (1958), involved the deportation of a person born in the United States who, the Government claimed, had lost his American citizenship under 8 U.S.C. §1481(a)(5) and (10) by voting in a Mexican election and remaining outside the United States in time of war to evade military service. The Supreme Court, by 5 to 4, upheld the Government's position that Perez had lost his citizenship. Mr. Justice Frankfurter, writing for the majority, held that the revocation of citizenship was valid under the power of Congress to regulate foreign relations:

"The first step in our inquiry must be to answer the question: what is the source of power on which Congress must be assumed to have drawn? Although there is in the Constitution no specific grant to Congress of power to enact legislation for the effective regulation of foreign affairs, there can be no doubt of the existence of this power in the law-making organ of the Nation. See United States v. Curtiss-Wright Export Corp., 299 U.S. 304, 318; Macken-

---

[1] The amendment added the provisions relating to Sections 2383, 2384, and 2385 of Title 18. Section 2383 deals with rebellion and insurrection, Section 2384 with seditious conspiracy, and Section 2385 is the Smith Act. See Chapter III, Section C. See also 75 Stat. 656 (1961), 8 U.S.C. §1481(c), putting burden on person claiming loss of nationality occurred to prove loss but creating rebuttable presumption that loss was voluntary.

zie v. Hare, 239 U.S. 299, 311-312. The States that joined together to form a single Nation and to create, through the Constitution, a Federal Government to conduct the affairs of that Nation must be held to have granted that Government the powers indispensable to its functioning effectively in the company of sovereign nations. The Government must be able not only to deal affirmatively with foreign nations, as it does through the maintenance of diplomatic relations with them and the protection of American citizens sojourning within their territories. It must also be able to reduce to a minimum the frictions that are unavoidable in a world of sovereigns sensitive in matters touching their dignity and interests.

"The inference is fairly to be drawn from the congressional history of the Nationality Act of 1940, read in light of the historical background of expatriation in this country, that, in making voting in foreign elections (among other behavior) an act of expatriation, Congress was seeking to effectuate its power to regulate foreign affairs. The legislators, counseled by those on whom they rightly relied for advice, were concerned about actions by citizens in foreign countries that create problems of protection and are inconsistent with American allegiance. Moreover, we cannot ignore the fact that embarrassments in the conduct of foreign relations were of primary concern in the consideration of the Act of 1907 of which the loss of nationality provisions of the 1940 Act are a codification and expansion.

"Broad as the power in the National Government to regulate foreign affairs must necessarily be, it is not without limitation. The restrictions confining Congress in the exercise of any of the powers expressly delegated to it in the Constitution apply with equal vigor when that body seeks to regulate our relations with other nations. Since Congress may not act arbitrarily, a rational nexus must exist between the content of a specific power in Congress and the action of Congress in carrying that power into execution. More simply stated, the means — in this case, withdrawal of citizenship — must be reasonably related to the end — here, regulation of foreign affairs. The inquiry — and, in the case before us, the sole inquiry — into which this Court must enter is whether or not Congress may have concluded not unreasonably that there is a relevant connection between this fundamental source of power and the ultimate legislative action." 356 U.S. at 57-58.

Mr. Justice Frankfurter went on to hold that the provision for revoking citizenship for voting in a foreign election was reasonably related to the Congressional power. 356 U.S. 59-62. He found it unnecessary to pass on the constitutionality of the other provision relied on by the Government.

Chief Justice Warren and Justices Black and Douglas dissented, asserting that citizenship could only be revoked by voluntary action on the part of the individual:

"What is this Government, whose power is here being asserted? And what is the source of that power? The answers are the foundation of our Republic. To secure the inalienable rights of the individual, 'Governments are instituted among Men, deriving their just powers from the consent of the governed.' I do not believe the passage of time has lessened the truth of this proposition. It is basic to our form of government. This Government was born of its citizens, it maintains itself in a continuing relationship with them, and, in my judgment, it is without power to sever the relationship that gives rise to its existence. I cannot believe that a government conceived in the spirit of ours was established with power to take from the people their most basic right.

"Citizenship *is* man's basic right for it is nothing less than the right to have rights. Remove this priceless possession and there remains a stateless person, disgraced and degraded in the eyes of his countrymen. He has no lawful claim to protection from any nation, and no nation may assert rights on his behalf. His very existence is at the sufferance of the state within whose borders he happens to be. In this country the expatriate would presumably enjoy, at most, only the limited rights and privileges of aliens, and like the alien he might even be subject to deportation and thereby deprived of the right to assert any rights. This government was not established with power to decree this fate.

"The people who created this government endowed it with broad powers. They created a sovereign state with power to function as a sovereignty. But the citizens themselves are sovereign, and their citizenship is not subject to the general powers of their government. Whatever may be the scope of its powers to regulate the conduct and affairs of all persons within its jurisdiction, a government *of* the people cannot take away their citizenship simply because one branch of that government can be said to have a conceivably rational basis for wanting to do so. . . .

"My conclusions are as follows. The Government is without power to take citizenship away from a native-born or lawfully naturalized American. The Fourteenth Amendment recognizes that this priceless right is immune from the exercise of governmental powers. If the Government determines that certain conduct by United States citizens should be prohibited because of anticipated injurious consequences to the conduct of foreign affairs or to some other legitimate governmental interest, it may within the limits of the Constitution proscribe such activity and assess appropriate punishment. But every exercise of governmental power must find its source in the Constitution. The power to denationalize is not within the letter or the spirit of the powers with which our Government was endowed. The citizen may elect to renounce his citizenship, and under some circumstances he may be found to have abandoned his status by voluntarily performing acts that compromise his undivided allegiance to his country. The mere act of voting in a foreign election, however, without regard to the circumstances attending the participation, is not sufficient to show a voluntary abandonment of citizenship. The record in this case does not disclose any of the circumstances under which this petitioner voted. We know only the bare fact that he cast a ballot. The basic right of American citizenship has been too dearly won to be so lightly lost." 356 U.S. at 64-65, 77-78.

Justices Douglas and Black, in a further opinion said:

". . . But if voting abroad is so pregnant with danger that Congress can penalize it by withdrawing the voter's American citizenship, all citizens should be filled with alarm. Some of the most heated political discussions in our history have concerned foreign policy. I had always assumed that the First Amendment, written in terms absolute, protected those utterances, no matter how extreme, no matter how unpopular they might be. Yet if the power to regulate foreign affairs can be used to deprive a person of his citizenship because he voted abroad, why may not it be used to deprive him of his citizenship because his views on foreign policy are unorthodox or because he disputed the position of the Secretary of State or denounced a Resolution of the Congress or the action of the Chief Executive in the field of foreign affairs?" 356 U.S. at 81.

Mr. Justice Whittaker, while agreeing "with the major premise of the majority's opinion," dissented on the ground that the statutory provision "is too broadly written." 356 U.S. at 84.

In Trop v. Dulles, 356 U.S. 86, 78 S. Ct. 590, 2 L. Ed. 2d 630 (1958), the issue was whether a native born citizen could be deprived of citizenship under 8 U.S.C. §1481(a)(8) for deserting the military forces in time of war. The Supreme Court held, 5 to 4, that, at least in this case he could not. Chief Justice Warren, in an opinion in which Justices Black, Douglas and Whittaker joined, ruled that the desertion law was a penal statute and constituted cruel and unusual punishment:

"At the outset, let us put to one side the death penalty as an index of the constitutional limit on punishment. Whatever the arguments may be against capital punishment, both on moral grounds and in terms of accomplishing the purposes of punishment — and they are forceful — the death penalty has been employed throughout our history, and in a day when it is still widely accepted, it cannot be said to violate the constitutional concept of cruelty. But it is equally plain that the existence of the death penalty is not a license to the Government to devise any punishment short of death within the limit of its imagination.

"The exact scope of the constitutional phrase 'cruel and unusual' has not been detailed by this Court. But the basic policy reflected in these words is firmly established in the Anglo-American tradition of criminal justice. The phrase in our Constitution was taken directly from the English Declaration of Rights of 1688, and the principle it represents can be traced back to the Magna Carta. The basic concept underlying the Eighth Amendment is nothing less than the dignity of man. While the State has the power to punish, the Amendment stands to assure that this power be exercised within the limits of civilized standards. Fines, imprisonment and even execution may be imposed depending upon the enormity of the crime, but any technique outside the bounds of these traditional penalties is constitutionally suspect. This Court has had little occasion to give precise content to the Eighth Amendment, and, in an enlightened democracy such as ours, this is not surprising. But when the Court was confronted with a punishment of 12 years in irons at hard and painful labor imposed for the crime of falsifying public records, it did not hesitate to declare that the penalty was cruel in its excessiveness and unusual in its character. Weems v. United States, 217 U.S. 349. The Court recognized in that case that the words of the Amendment are not precise, and that their scope is not static. The Amendment must draw its meaning from the evolving standards of decency that mark the progress of a maturing society.

"We believe, as did Chief Judge Clark in the court below, that use of denationalization as a punishment is barred by the Eighth Amendment. There may be involved no physical mistreatment, no primitive torture. There is instead the total destruction of the individual's status in organized society. It is a form of punishment more primitive than torture, for it destroys for the individual the political existence that was centuries in the development. The punishment strips the citizen of his status in the national and international political community. His very existence is at the sufferance of the country in which he happens to find himself. While any one country may accord him some rights, and presumably as long as he remained in this country he would enjoy the limited rights of an alien, no country need do so because he is stateless. Furthermore, his enjoyment of even the limited rights of an alien might be subject to termination at any time by reason of deportation. In short, the expatriate has lost the right to have rights.

"This punishment is offensive to cardinal principles for which the Constitution stands. It subjects the individual to a fate of ever-increasing fear and distress. He knows not what discriminations may be established against him, what proscriptions may be directed against him, and when and for what cause his existence in his native land may be terminated. He may be subject to banishment, a fate universally decried by civilized people. He is stateless, a condition deplored in the international community of democracies. It is no answer to suggest that all the disastrous consequences of this fate may not be brought to bear on a stateless person. The threat makes the punishment obnoxious.

"The civilized nations of the world are in virtual unanimity that statelessness is not to be imposed as punishment for crime. It is true that several countries prescribe expatriation in the event that their nationals engage in conduct in derogation of native allegiance. Even statutes of this sort are generally applicable primarily to naturalized citizens. But use of denationalization as punishment for crime is an entirely different matter. The United Nations' survey of the nationality laws of 84 nations of the world reveals that only two countries, the Philippines and Turkey, impose denationalization as a penalty for desertion. In this country the Eighth Amendment forbids this to be done." 356 U.S. at 99-103.

Mr. Justice Brennan concurred in the majority holding on the ground that, expatriation being intended as an additional punishment for desertion, "the requisite rational relation between this statute and the war power does not appear." 356 U.S. at 114.

Justices Frankfurter, Burton, Clark and Harlan dissented, believing the statute a reasonable exercise of the war power:

"Can it be said that there is no rational nexus between refusal to perform this ultimate duty of American citizenship and legislative withdrawal of that citizenship? Congress may well have thought that making loss of citizenship a consequence of wartime desertion would affect the ability of the military authorities to control the forces with which they were expected to fight and win a major world conflict. It is not for us to deny that Congress might reasonably have believed the morale and fighting efficiency of our troops would be impaired if our soldiers knew that their fellows who had abandoned them in their time of greatest need were to remain in the communion of our citizens." 356 U.S. at 122.

In Nishikawa v. Dulles, 356 U.S. 129, 78 S. Ct. 612, 2 L. Ed. 2d 659 (1958), the Court held, 7 to 2, that a native-born Japanese who had served in the Japanese army during the war had not lost his citizenship under 8 U.S.C. §1481(a)(3). The constitutional issues were not considered, the majority holding that the Government had not shown by "clear, convincing and unequivocal evidence" that the military service was voluntary. 356 U.S. at 138. Justices Harlan and Clark dissented.

A fourth case, raising the issue of whether a citizen had lost his citizenship by remaining outside the United States to avoid military service, was decided by the Supreme Court in Kennedy v. Mendoza-Martinez, 372 U.S. 144, 83 S. Ct. 554, 9 L. Ed. 2d 644 (1963). There the Court found, on the basis of a detailed study of the legislative history, that expatriation was intended by Congress as an additional punishment for draft evasion. As such, expatriation is subject in this instance to the safeguards of the Fifth and Sixth Amendments:

"As the Government concedes, §§401(j) and 349(a)(10) automatically strip an American of his citizenship, with concomitant deprivation 'of all that makes life worth living,' Ng Fung Ho v. White, 259 U.S. 276, 284-285, whenever a citizen departs from or remains outside the jurisdiction of this country for the purpose of evading his military obligations. Conviction for draft evasion, as Cort's case illustrates, is not prerequisite to the operation of this sanction. Independently of prosecution, forfeiture of citizenship attaches when the statutory set of facts develops. It is argued that the availability after the fact of administrative and judicial proceedings, including the machinery the Court approved last Term in Rusk v. Cort, 369 U.S. 367, to contest the validity of the sanction meets the measure of due process. But the legislative history and judicial expression with respect to every congressional enactment relating to the provisions in question dating back to 1865 establish that forfeiture of citizenship is a penalty for the act of leaving or staying outside the country to avoid the draft. This being so, the Fifth and Sixth Amendments mandate that this punishment cannot be imposed without a prior criminal trial and all its incidents, including indictment, notice, confrontation, jury trial, assistance of counsel, and compulsory process for obtaining witnesses. If the sanction these sections impose is punishment, and it plainly is, the procedural safe-guards required as incidents of a criminal prosecution are lacking. We need go no further." 372 U.S. at 166-167.

In United States ex rel. Marks v. Esperdy the District Court held that an American citizen did not become automatically expatriated upon serving in a foreign army and therefore was not excludable, and thus deportable, because not in possession of an immigrant visa at time of entry, since there had been no judicial proceeding or at least administrative proceeding on the issue of his citizenship. 203 F. Supp. 389, 396-397 (S.D. N.Y. 1962). The Circuit Court of Appeals, while conceding that generally "when an alleged alien claims United States citizenship and supports his claim by substantial evidence he is entitled by the due process clause of the Fifth Amendment to have his Amer-ican citizenship vel non determined by a judicial tribunal," nevertheless con-cluded that the equally clear Congressional intent to effect immediate expa-triation can be constitutionally enforced, since the deportation in Marks was not a punishment for entering without documents based upon a post-entry determination of alienage but "rather the delayed exercise of the congres-sional power to exclude aliens from entry into the United States." 315 F.2d 673, 675-676 (2d Cir. 1963). The Supreme Court affirmed by an equally di-vided bench. 377 U.S. 214 (1964).

For discussion and analysis of the Kennedy case, see Note, The Concept of Punitive Legislation and the Sixth Amendment: A New Look at Kennedy v. Mendoza-Martinez, 32 U. Chi. L. Rev. 290 (1966).

REFERENCES

For a full analysis of the Expatriation Act of 1954 see Note, The Expatriation Act of 1954, 64 Yale L.J. 1164 (1955); Note, Federal Anti-Subversive Legislation of 1954, 55 Colum. L. Rev. 631, 663-666 (1955).

On recent cases see, in addition to material cited supra, Roche, The Expatriation Decisions: A Study in Constitutional Improvisation and the Uses of History, 58 Am. Pol. Sci. Rev. 72 (1964), and The Expatriation Cases: "Breathes There The Man With Soul So Dead . . . ?" 1963 Sup. Ct. Rev. 325; Note, Expatriation: Demise of the "Rational Nexus," 12 U.C.L.A.L. Rev. 510 (1965); Kramer, The Restraints of Schneider v. Rusk Upon the Foreign Policy Powers of the "Political Branches": How Meaningful Are They? 38 Temple L.Q. 279 (1965); Note, 49 Cornell L.Q. 52 (1963); Provost and Rohner, Can Congress Denationalize? The Supreme Court's View in Kennedy v. Men-doza-Martinez, 12 Catholic U. L. Rev. 114 (1963); Note, 48 Iowa L. Rev. 815 (1963). On the subject of expatriation more generally see Boudin, Involuntary Loss of American Na-tionality, 73 Harv. L. Rev. 1510 (1960); Maxey, Loss of Nationality: Individual Choice or Government Fiat? 26 Albany L. Rev. 151 (1962); Note, Expatriating the Dual Na-tional, 68 Yale L.J. 1167 (1959); Klubock, Expatriation and the Constitution, 1 Law in Trans. Q. 25 (1964); Note, Expatriation — Its Origin and Meaning, 38 Notre Dame Law. 1 (1962); Gordon, The Citizen and the State: Power of Congress to Expatriate American Citizens, 53 Geo. L.J. 315 (1965); Appleman, The Supreme Court on Expatri-ation: An Historical Review, 23 Fed. B.J. 351 (1963); Scharf, A Study of the Law of Expatriation, 38 St. John's L. Rev. 251 (1964); Note, "Voluntary": A Concept in Expa-triation Law, 54 Colum. L. Rev. 932 (1954); Gathings, Loss of Citizenship and Civil

Rights for Conviction of Crime, 43 Am. Pol. Sci. Rev. 1228 (1949); Note, Developments in the Law of Immigration and Nationality, 66 Harv. L. Rev. 643, 731-745 (1953). See also Notes, 44 Ill. L. Rev. 106 (1949); 63 Harv. L. Rev. 885 (1950); 49 Mich. L. Rev. 595 (1951); 25 So. Cal. L. Rev. 196 (1952); 22 Geo. Wash. L. Rev. 493 (1954); 40 Cornell L.Q. 365 (1955); 6 J. Pub. L. 257 (1957).

For an historical note on outlawry see Taylor, Grand Inquest, App. III (1955). For other historical material see Tsiang, The Question of Expatriation in America Prior to 1907 (1942); Liddell, The U.S. Position in Regard to the "Right of Expatriation," 23 Temple L.Q. 325 (1950); Roche, The Loss of American Nationality — The Development of Statutory Expatriation, 99 U. Pa. L. Rev. 25 (1950); Flournoy, Naturalization and Expatriation, 31 Yale L.J. 702 (1922).

E. Loyalty-Security Qualifications for Employment

One of the most significant developments in freedom of political expression in the period since World War II has been the establishment of loyalty-security qualifications for employment. Major emphasis on these requirements has been in government employment and in defense plants, but programs have been established and proposed in a wider area of private employment as well.

Loyalty qualifications in employment have assumed two major forms. One is the requirement of taking a loyalty oath or completing a loyalty affidavit as a condition of employment. By constitution and statute public officials and employees have customarily been required to take oaths to support the constitution and laws. The main issue arises as to oaths and affidavits which carry beyond the traditional scope. The significance for freedom of political expression lies both in the restrictions imposed by the requirement of taking the oath and in the enforcement of the oath through perjury or similar proceedings. The other major form of loyalty qualification has been the requirement that persons meet certain standards of loyalty as a condition of obtaining or retaining employment. Characteristically, current federal loyalty programs have provided for comprehensive investigation of employees and applicants, and elaborate machinery for administering the program. Somewhere between the loyalty oath and the administrative screening of employee loyalty are the programs of many institutions which do not routinely investigate the politics of their personnel, but which hold hearings when an issue of employee loyalty is raised by charges of other persons, such as legislative investigating committees.

Loyalty requirements are justified primarily by the needs of "national security." And qualifications for employment necessary to satisfy the needs of national security may involve factors other than "loyalty." Hence, as the loyalty qualifications developed, especially in the federal programs, they came to merge with other facets of security, and the total program has come to be a "loyalty-security" program. We are concerned here primarily with the "loyalty" aspects of these programs, since it is this feature which impinges most upon freedom of political expression. But, of course, the two aspects of the problem cannot, at least in practice, be entirely separated.

BIBLIOGRAPHY ON LOYALTY–SECURITY QUALIFICATIONS FOR EMPLOYMENT

The material, legal and non-legal, dealing with the loyalty programs is voluminous. The most comprehensive and recent study is Brown, Loyalty and Security (1958), which contains references to the major literature up to 1958. The best source for current materials is the loose leaf service published by The Bureau of National Affairs, Inc. (Washington, D.C.), Government Security and Loyalty: A Manual of Laws, Regulations and Procedures, hereinafter referred to as BNA, Manual of Government Security and Loyalty or BNA Manual. Other source materials may be found in Digest of the Public Record of Communism in the United States (Fund for the Republic 1955); Internal Security Manual (rev.), Sen. Doc. No. 126, 86th Cong., 2d Sess. (1961).

There have been two studies of the federal loyalty program made by committees working through a staff. One was by the Special Committee on the Federal Loyalty-Security Program of the Association of the Bar of the City of New York, of which Dudley B. Bonsal was chairman. This study, financed by the Fund for the Republic, resulted in a report published under the title, The Federal Loyalty-Security Program (1956). The other study was made by the Commission on Government Security, created in 1955 pursuant to Public Law 304, 84th Cong., 1st Sess., 69 Stat. 595. The Commission was composed of six persons from each of the two major parties, selected equally by the President, the President of the Senate, and the Speaker of the House. The Chairman was Loyd Wright. Its report to the President and Congress has been published as Report of the Commission on Government Security (G.P.O., Wash. D.C., 1957).

Loyalty matters have come up frequently in legislative investigations. The major hearings on the operation of the program are (1) the hearings conducted in March 1955 under the chairmanship of Senator Humphrey on the proposal to establish the Commission on Government Security, Hearings before a Subcommittee on Reorganization of the Senate Committee on Government Operations, 84th Cong., 1st Sess. (1955); (2) the hearings conducted in 1955 and 1956 by a subcommittee headed by Senator Johnston, Hearings before a Subcommittee of the Senate Committee on Post Office and Civil Service, Administration of the Federal Employees' Security Program, 84th Cong., 1st and 2d Sess. (1955-1956), report issued in July 1956, Administration of the Federal Employees' Security Program, Sen. Rep. No. 2750, 84th Cong., 2d Sess. (1956); (3) hearings conducted by Senator Hennings in 1955 and 1956, and again in 1959, Hearings before the Subcommittee on Constitutional Rights of the Senate Committee on the Judiciary, Security and Constitutional Rights, 84th Cong., 1st and 2d Sess. (1955-1956), and 86th Cong., 1st and 2d Sess. (1959-1961); (4) hearings on the State Department security program held by the Subcommittee to Investigate the Administration of the Internal Security Act and Other Internal Security Laws of the Senate Committee on the Judiciary, 88th and 89th Cong. (1963-1965). For a full listing of Congressional investigations and reports through 1956, see Congressional Investigations of Communism and Subversive Activities, Sen. Doc. No. 148, 84th Cong., 2d Sess. (1956).

Individual studies prior to Professor Brown's book include Gellhorn, Security, Loyalty, and Science (1950); Bontecou, The Federal Loyalty-Security Program (1953). See also Emerson and Helfeld, Loyalty Among Government Employees, 58 Yale L.J. 1 (1948) (collecting materials up to the middle of 1948); Hoover, A Comment on the Article "Loyalty Among Government Employees," 58 Yale L.J. 401 (1949); Donovan and Jones, Program For a Democratic Counter Attack to Communist Penetration of Government

Service, 58 Yale L.J. 1211 (1949); Arnold, The Case Against the Federal Loyalty Program, and Sutherland, Additional Thoughts on the Federal Loyalty Program, both in The Strengthening of American Political Institutions, 53, 74 (Cornell U. Press 1949); Richardson (first Chairman of the Loyalty Review Board), The Federal Employee Loyalty Program, 51 Colum. L. Rev. 546 (1951); Barth, The Loyalty of Free Men, chs. V-VIII (1951); Public Affairs Pamphlet No. 179, Loyalty in a Democracy (1952); Westin, The Constitution and Loyalty Programs (published by the Carrie Chapman Catt Memorial Fund, 1954); Goldbloom, American Security and Freedom (1954); McLeod, American Political Democracy and the Problem of Personnel Security (U.S. Dept. of State Pub. No. 6106, Nov. 1955); O'Brian, National Security and Individual Freedom (1955); Garrison, Some Observations on the Loyalty-Security Program, 23 U. Chi. L. Rev. 1 (1955); Gellhorn, Individual Freedom and Governmental Restraints, ch. 3 (1956); Johnson, The Eisenhower Personnel Security Program, 18 J. of Politics 625 (1956); Fellman, The Loyalty Defendants, 1957 Wis. L. Rev. 4, reprinted in Fellman, The Defendant's Rights, ch. 12 (1958); Millis, Individual Freedom and the Common Defense 63-80 (1957); Morgan, Federal Loyalty-Security Removals 1946-1956, 36 Neb. L. Rev. 412 (1957); Rostow, Needed: A Rational Security Program, Harpers Magazine, July 1957, p. 33.

Symposia dealing with various aspects of the program include Secrecy, Security, and Loyalty, Bull. of the Atomic Scientists, April 1955; Internal Security and Civil Rights, 300 Annals 1 (July 1955); Problems of American Democracy: II. Security in a Free Society, Current History, October 1955; "Loyalty-Security" and the Law, 15 Law. Guild Rev. 119 (Winter 1955); People, Government and Security: An Analysis of Three Books and a Program, 51 Nw. U.L. Rev. 79 (1956); Federal Loyalty-Security Programs, 18 Ohio St. L.J. 283 (Summer 1957).

Material published after Professor Brown's study include Dykstra, "The Right Most Valued by Civilized Man," 6 Utah L. Rev. 305 (1959); Rackow, The Federal Loyalty Program: Politics and Civil Liberty, 12 W. Res. L. Rev. 701 (1961); Slotnick, Anathema of the Security Risk: Arbitrary Dismissals of Federal Government Civilian Employees and Civilian Employees of Private Contractors Doing Business With the Federal Government, 17 U. Miami L. Rev. 10 (1962). See also Latham, The Communist Controversy in Washington: From the New Deal to McCarthy (1966).

Studies of individual case histories include Yarmolinsky, Case Studies in Personnel Security (published by BNA 1955); Watts, The Draftee and Internal Security: A Study of the Army Military Personnel Security Program (published by Workers Defense League 1955; Supp. 1956); Department of Defense, Industrial Personnel Security Review Program, First Annual Report, App. C. (1956).

For historical studies of loyalty oaths, see Koenigsberg and Stavis, Test Oaths: Henry VIII to the American Bar Association, 11 Law. Guild Rev. 111 (1951); Hyman, To Try Men's Souls: Loyalty Tests in American History (1959). On the history of the judicial oath, see Silving, The Oath, 68 Yale L.J. 1329, 1529 (1959).

Studies from the political science and sociological point of view include Lasswell, National Security and Individual Freedom (1950); McWilliams, Witch Hunt: The Revival of Heresy (1950); Grodzins, The Loyal and the Disloyal: Social Boundaries of Patriotism and Treason (1956); Shils, The Torment of Secrecy, The Background and Consequences of American Security Policies (1956); Schaar, Loyalty in America (1957); Prestkus, The Organizational Society (1962). See also Commager, Freedom, Loyalty, Dissent (1954).

In the field of fiction, see Miller, The Sure Thing (1949); Dillon, Little Brother is Watching (1962).

State laws and decisions are collected in Internal Security and Subversion, Principal State Laws and Cases, A Study Prepared for the Subcommittee to Investigate the Administration of the Internal Security Act and Other Internal Security Laws, of the Senate

Committee on the Judiciary, by Legislative Reference Service, Library of Congress (1965). See also Gellhorn, The States and Subversion (1952); Note, 28 Ind. L.J. 492 (1953).

A bibliography of the material is Tompkins, Loyalty-Security Programs for Federal Employees: A Selected Bibliography (U. of Calif. 1955).

As to how other countries handle problems of loyalty among government employees, see Bontecou, The English Policy as to Communists and Fascists in the Civil Service, 51 Colum. L. Rev. 564 (1951); Wilson and Glickman, The Problem of Internal Security in Great Britain 1948-1953 (1954); Special Committee of the Association of the Bar of the City of New York, The Federal Loyalty-Security Program 199-202 (1956); Johnson, Individual Rights and National Security, 20 Modern L. Rev. 364 (1957); Emerson and Helfeld, Loyalty Among Government Employees, 58 Yale L.J. 1, 120-33 (1948); Decision of the Conseil d'Etat in the case of Barel et autres, 1954 Revue du Droit Public (Tome LXX), p. 509.

1. Federal Programs

a. Background and Structure

The modern loyalty-security programs originated in the Federal Government in the period following the establishment of the Committee on Un-American Activities in 1938. Prior to that time, there had been no loyalty program since the days of World War I. In fact, Civil Service Rule I, issued in 1884, required that no inquiry could be made of "the political or religious opinions or affiliations of any applicant." See 5 U.S.C. §633 (1946). The Lloyd-La Follette Act of 1912, and the Civil Service Regulations issued under it, did provide for the removal or discipline of employees "for such cause as will promote the efficiency of the service." 37 Stat. 555 (1912), 5 U.S.C. §652; Civil Service Rule XII, §1. But this provision does not appear to have been invoked for discharges on loyalty grounds prior to the World War II period.

In 1939 Congress passed the Hatch Act, which made it unlawful for any person employed by the Federal Government "to have membership in any political party or organization which advocates the overthrow of our constitutional form of government in the United States." 53 Stat. 1147, 1148 (1939), 5 U.S.C. §118j. Beginning in 1941 Congress incorporated in virtually all appropriation acts a provision that none of the funds could be used to pay the salary or wages of "any person who advocates, or who is a member of an organization that advocates, the overthrow of the Government of the United States by force or violence." See, e.g., 55 Stat. 5, 6 (1941). These provisions also made it a criminal offense for any such person to accept employment in the Federal Government. The Civil Service Commission interpreted the language of the Hatch Act and the appropriation riders to exclude from government employment members of "the Communist Party, the German Bund, or any other Communist, Nazi, or Fascist organization." Civil Service Circular No. 222, June 20, 1940, reprinted in Bontecou, The Federal Loyalty-Security Program 285-287 (1953). And in 1942 the Civil Service Commission amended its regulations to provide, as a ground for disqualification of an applicant or removal of an employee, "reasonable doubt as to the loyalty of the person involved to the Government of the United States." Civil Service War Regulations, §18.2(c)(7), 7 Fed. Reg. 7723.

Throughout the war years administration of loyalty measures remained largely uncoordinated and somewhat haphazard. In March 1947, however, President Truman promulgated Executive Order 9835 (12 Fed. Reg. 1935, Mar. 21, 1947), which served as the principal basis for the Federal employee loyalty program until it was superseded by Executive Order 10450, issued by President Eisenhower in April 1953. Executive Order 9835 provided for "a loyalty investigation of every person entering the civilian employment of any department or agency of the executive branch of the Federal Government." (Pt. I, §1). The basic standard for denial of employment or removal from employment was that, "on all the evidence, reasonable grounds exist for the belief that the person involved is disloyal to the Government of the United States" (Pt. V, §1). By an amendment issued April 28, 1951, designed to tighten the program, the standard became that "on all the evidence, there is a reasonable doubt as to the loyalty of the person involved to the Government of the United States." Executive Order 10241, 16 Fed. Reg. 3690. Executive Order 9835 went on to provide:

"Activities and associations of an applicant or employee which may be considered in connection with the determination of disloyalty may include one or more of the following:

"a. Sabotage, espionage, or attempts or preparations therefor, or knowingly associating with spies or saboteurs;

"b. Treason or sedition or advocacy thereof;

"c. Advocacy of revolution or force or violence to alter the constitutional form of government of the United States;

"d. Intentional, unauthorized disclosure to any person, under circumstances which may indicate disloyalty to the United States, of documents or information of a confidential or non-public character obtained by the person making the disclosure as a result of his employment by the Government of the United States;

"e. Performing or attempting to perform his duties, or otherwise acting, so as to serve the interests of another government in preference to the interests of the United States;

"f. Membership in, affiliation with or sympathetic association with any foreign or domestic organization, association, movement, group or combination of persons, designated by the Attorney General as totalitarian, fascist, communist, or subversive, or as having adopted a policy of advocating or approving the commission of acts of force or violence to deny other persons their rights under the Constitution of the United States, or as seeking to alter the form of government of the United States by unconstitutional means." Pt. I, §2.

Executive Order 9835 made the head of each agency "personally responsible" for administration of the program (Pt. II, §1). Each agency was required to appoint one or more loyalty boards, composed of not less than three representatives from the agency, to hear loyalty cases and make recommendations (Pt. II, §2). A recommendation by the agency loyalty board for dismissal could be appealed to the agency head, and from his decision the employee could take an appeal to a Loyalty Review Board, established in the Civil Service Commission (Pt. II, §§2, 3). But the decisions of the Loyalty Review Board were advisory only; final authority rested with the agency head (Pt. II, §3).

The employee had the right to written charges, "stated as specifically and completely as, in the discretion of the employing department or agency, security considerations permit" (Pt. II, §2). The employee was also entitled to a hearing, at which he could be represented by counsel, but there was no provision requiring the loyalty board to place on the record the evidence upon which it based its decision. Ibid.

In addition to the foregoing provisions, beginning in 1940 Congress passed a series of measures giving certain "sensitive agencies" the right of summary dismissal. See, e.g., 56 Stat. 1053 (1942). An example of these measures was the McCarran Rider, passed in 1946, which empowered the Secretary of State "in his absolute discretion . . . [to] terminate the employment of any officer or employee of the Department of State or of the Foreign Service of the United States whenever he shall deem such termination necessary or advisable in the interests of the United States." 60 Stat. 446, 458. These summary dismissal measures were made permanent in Public Law 733, passed in 1950, which is reprinted below. The machinery for administering these "security risk" programs was completely integrated with the loyalty program in those agencies operating under both. See Gellhorn, Security, Loyalty, and Science, ch. IV (1950).

PUBLIC LAW 733, 81st CONGRESS, 2d SESSION
64 Stat. 476 (1950), 5 U.S.C. §§22-1 to 22-3

Sec. 1. Notwithstanding the provisions of section 6 of the Act of August 24, 1912 (37 Stat. 555), as amended (5 USC 652), or the provisions of any other law, the Secretary of State; Secretary of Commerce; Attorney General; the Secretary of Defense; the Secretary of the Army; the Secretary of the Navy; the Secretary of the Air Force; the Secretary of the Treasury; Atomic Energy Commission; the Chairman, National Security Resources Board; or the Director, National Advisory Committee for Aeronautics, may, in his absolute discretion and when deemed necessary in the interest of national security, suspend, without pay, any civilian officer or employee of the Department of State (including the Foreign Service of the United States), Department of Commerce, Department of Justice, Department of Defense, Department of the Army, Department of the Navy, Department of the Air Force, Coast Guard, Atomic Energy Commission, National Security Resources Board, or National Advisory Committee for Aeronautics, respectively, or of their several field services: *Provided,* That to the extent that such agency head determines that the interests of the national security permit, the employee concerned shall be notified of the reasons for his suspension and within thirty days after such notification any such person shall have an opportunity to submit any statements or affidavits to the official designated by the head of the agency concerned to show why he should be reinstated or restored to duty. The agency head concerned may, following such investigation and review as he deems necessary, terminate the employment of such suspended civilian officer or employee whenever he shall determine such termination necessary or advisable in the interest of the national security of the United States, and such determination by the agency head concerned shall be conclusive and final: *Provided further,* That any employee having a permanent or indefinite appointment, and having completed his probationary or trial period, who is a citizen of the United States whose employment is suspended under the authority of this Act, shall be given after his suspension and before his employment is terminated under the authority of this Act, (1) a written statement within thirty days after his suspension of the charges against him, which shall be subject to amendment within thirty days thereafter and which shall be stated as specifically as security considerations permit; (2) an opportunity within thirty days thereafter (plus an additional thirty days if the charges are amended) to answer such charges and to submit affidavits; (3) a hearing, at the employee's request, by a duly constituted agency authority for this purpose; (4) a review of his case by the agency head, or some official designated by him, before a decision adverse to the employee is made final; and (5) a written statement of the decision of the agency head . . .

Sec. 3. The provisions of this Act shall apply to such other departments and agencies of the Government as the President may, from time to time, deem necessary in the best interests of national security. If any departments or agencies are included by the President, he shall so report to the Committees on the Armed Services of the Congress.

As noted above, the Internal Security Act of 1950, passed shortly after Public Law 733, contained provisions prohibiting members of registered Communist organizations from holding "any nonelective office or employment under the United States." 50 U.S.C. §784; see Section C, subsection 3, supra.

On its accession to office in 1953 the Eisenhower administration undertook a review of the loyalty program, with a view to making it more effective, and in April promulgated Executive Order 10450, set forth below. The new order transformed the program into a "loyalty-security" program.

EXECUTIVE ORDER 10450 [1]
18 Fed. Reg. 2489 (1953), 3 C.F.R.
1953 Supp. 72. 5 U.S.C. §631 note

WHEREAS the interests of the national security require that all persons privileged to be employed in the departments and agencies of the Government, shall be reliable, trustworthy, of good conduct and character, and of complete and unswerving loyalty to the United States; and

WHEREAS the American tradition that all persons should receive fair, impartial, and equitable treatment at the hands of the Government requires that all persons seeking the privilege of employment or privileged to be employed in the departments and agencies of the Government be adjudged by mutually consistent and no less than minimum standards and procedures among the departments and agencies governing the employment and retention in employment of persons in the Federal service:

Now, THEREFORE, by virtue of the authority vested in me by the Constitution and statutes of the United States, including section 1753 of the Revised Statutes of the United States (5 USC 631); the Civil Service Act of 1883 (22 Stat. 403; 5 USC 632, et seq.); section 9A of the act of August 2, 1939, 53 Stat. 1148 (5 USC 118j); and the act of August 26, 1950, 64 Stat. 476 (5 USC 22-1, et seq.), and as President of the United States, and deeming such action necessary in the best interests of the national security, it is hereby ordered as follows:

Sec. 1. In addition to the departments and agencies specified in the said act of August 26, 1950, and Executive Order No. 10237 of April 26, 1951, the provisions of that act shall apply to all other departments and agencies of the Government.

Sec. 2. The head of each department and agency of the Government shall be responsible for establishing and maintaining within his department or agency an effective program to insure that the employment and retention in employment of any civilian officer or employee within the department or agency is clearly consistent with the interests of the national security.

Sec. 3. (a) The appointment of each civilian officer or employee in any department or agency of the Government shall be made subject to investigation. The scope of the investigation shall be determined in the first instance according to the degree of adverse effect the occupant of the position sought to be filled could bring about, by virtue of the nature of the position, on the national security, but in no event shall the investigation include less than a national agency check (including a check of the fingerprint files of the Federal Bureau of Investigation), and written inquiries to appropriate local law-

---

[1] The Order as printed incorporates amendments made by Executive Orders 10491, 10531, 10548, and 10550.

enforcement agencies, former employers and supervisors, references, and schools attended by the person under investigation . . . Should there develop at any stage of investigation information indicating that the employment of any such person may not be clearly consistent with the interests of the national security, there shall be conducted with respect to such person a full field investigation, or such less investigation as shall be sufficient to enable the head of the department or agency concerned to determine whether retention of such person is clearly consistent with the interests of the national security.

[Section 4 provides for a re-adjudication, in accordance with the new standards, of all cases decided under the previous Executive Order.]

Sec. 6. Should there develop at any stage of investigation information indicating that the employment of any officer or employee of the Government may not be clearly consistent with the interests of the national security, the head of the department or agency concerned or his representative shall immediately suspend the employment of the person involved if he deems such suspension necessary in the interests of the national security and, following such investigation and review as he deems necessary, the head of the department or agency concerned shall terminate the employment of such suspended officer or employee whenever he shall determine such termination necessary or advisable in the interests of the national security, in accordance with the said act of August 26, 1950. . . .

Sec. 8. (a) The investigations conducted pursuant to this order shall be designed to develop information as to whether the employment or retention in employment in the Federal service of the person being investigated is clearly consistent with the interests of the national security. Such information shall relate, but shall not be limited, to the following:

(1) Depending on the relation of the Government employment to the national security:

(i) Any behavior, activities, or associations which tend to show that the individual is not reliable or trustworthy.

(ii) Any deliberate misrepresentations, falsifications, or omissions of material facts.

(iii) Any criminal, infamous, dishonest, immoral, or notoriously disgraceful conduct, habitual use of intoxicants to excess, drug addiction, or sexual perversion.

(iv) Any illness, including any mental condition, of a nature which in the opinion of competent medical authority may cause significant defect in the judgment or reliability of the employee, with due regard to the transient or continuing effect of the illness and the medical findings in such case.

(v) Any facts which furnish reason to believe that the individual may be subjected to coercion, influence, or pressure which may cause him to act contrary to the best interests of the national security.

(2) Commission of any act of sabotage, espionage, treason, or sedition, or

attempts thereat or preparation therefor, or conspiring with, or aiding or abetting, another to commit or attempt to commit any act of sabotage, espionage, treason or sedition.

(3) Establishing or continuing a sympathetic association with a saboteur, spy, traitor, seditionist, anarchist, or revolutionist, or with an espionage or other secret agent or representative of a foreign nation, or any representative of a foreign nation whose interests may be inimical to the interest of the United States, or with any person who advocates the use of force or violence to overthrow the government of the United States or the alteration of the form of government of the United States by unconstitutional means.

(4) Advocacy of use of force or violence to overthrow the government of the United States, or of the alteration of the form of government of the United States by unconstitutional means.

(5) Membership in, or affiliation or sympathetic association with, any foreign or domestic organization, association, movement, group, or combination of persons which is totalitarian, Fascist, Communist, or subversive, or which has adopted, or shows, a policy of advocating or approving the commission of acts of force or violence to deny other persons their rights under the Constitution of the United States, or which seeks to alter the form of Government of the United States by unconstitutional means.

(6) Intentional, unauthorized disclosure to any person of security information, or of other information disclosure of which is prohibited by law, or willful violation or disregard of security regulations.

(7) Performing or attempting to perform his duties, or otherwise acting, so as to serve the interests of another government in preference to the interests of the United States.

(8) Refusal by the individual, upon the ground of constitutional privilege against self-incrimination, to testify before a congressional committee regarding charges of his alleged disloyalty or other misconduct. . . .

Sec. 9 (a) There shall be established and maintained in the Civil Service Commission a security-investigations index covering all persons as to whom security investigations have been conducted by any department or agency of the Government under this order. . . .

(b) The heads of all departments and agencies shall furnish promptly to the Civil Service Commission information appropriate for the establishment and maintenance of the security-investigations index. . . .

Sec. 10. Nothing in this order shall be construed as eliminating or modifying in any way the requirement for any investigation or any determination as to security which may be required by law. . . .

NOTE

With the promulgation of Executive Order 10450 the Department of Justice issued a set of Sample Security Regulations to serve as a guide to other Government agencies. Following this model each agency issued its own set of regulations, setting forth its organization and procedures for dealing with loyalty-security cases. The Civil Service Commission also issued a Handbook as a guide for members of hearing boards. These documents in current form are reprinted in BNA, Manual of Government Security and Loyalty §15.

The Sample Security Regulations defined the term "national security," which was nowhere else defined, as relating "to the protection and preservation of the military, economic, and productive strength of the United States, including the security of the Government in domestic and foreign affairs, against or from espionage, sabotage, and subversion, and any and all other illegal acts designed to weaken or destroy the United States." §1(a). The Sample Regulations also defined the term "sensitive position," used in the Order to indicate jobs where extra investigation was appropriate, as "any position in the [department or agency] the occupant of which could bring about because of the nature of the position, a material adverse effect on the national security. Such positions shall include, but shall not be limited to, any position the occupant of which (1) may have access to security information or material classified as 'confidential,' 'secret,' or 'top secret,' or any other information or material having a direct bearing on the national security, and (2) may have opportunity to commit acts directly or indirectly adversely affecting the national security." §1(b); BNA, id. at 15:101.

In 1955 Congress passed a statute codifying the provisions of the Hatch Act and the appropriation acts by making it a criminal offense for any person "to accept or hold office or employment in the Government of the United States . . . who (1) advocates the overthrow of our constitutional form of government in the United States; [or] is a member of an organization that advocates the overthrow of our constitutional form of government in the United States, knowing that such organization so advocates." 69 Stat. 624 (1955); 5 U.S.C. §§118p, 118r. The act also provides that, with the exception of persons employed for less than 60 days for "sudden emergency work," every person "who accepts office or employment in the Government of the United States . . . shall . . . execute an affidavit that his acceptance and holding of such office or employment does not or . . . will not constitute a violation" of the above provisions. 5 U.S.C. §118q. With the passage of this law the appropriation provisions became unnecessary and were dropped.

Executive Order 10450, it will be noted, had applied the provisions and procedures of Public Law 733 (Act of 1950) to all applicants and employees in all departments and agencies of the Government (Sec. 1). The validity of this action came before the Supreme Court in 1956 in Cole v. Young, 351 U.S. 536, 76 S. Ct. 861, 100 L. Ed. 1396. The case involved the dismissal, under that Order, of a food and drug inspector employed in the New York District of the Food and Drug Administration by the Department of Health, Education, and Welfare. The Court held that Public Law 733 authorized dismissal of an employee under its provisions only where the dismissal is "necessary or advisable in the interest of national security"; that the term "national security" was intended to refer only to the protection of "sensitive" activities; and hence that an employee could be discharged under the Act only if he occupies a "sensitive" position. There being no finding by the Secretary of HEW that the employee in question held such a position, the Court found his discharge under Executive Order 10450 invalid. The Court took care to point out, however, that the general civil service laws (see infra) authorized dismissal on loyalty grounds: "Thus there was no want of substantive authority to dismiss employees on loyalty grounds, and the question for decision here is not whether an employee *can* be dismissed on such grounds but only the extent to which the summary *procedures* authorized by the 1950 Act are available in such a case." 351 U.S. at 544; italics in original. Justices Clark, Reed, and Minton dissented.

NOTES

Immediately after the Cole decision the Department of Justice advised all agencies that no further removal proceedings should be commenced against any employee in a non-sensitive position under Executive Order 10450, and that such employees under suspension should be reinstated. Subsequently the Department of Justice announced the policy that employees in non-sensitive positions who had been discharged under Executive Order 10450 should be reinstated and back pay granted, provided the claim was made within 18 months.[1] Altogether somewhat less than 100 employees seem to have been affected. For a full account see Report of the Commission on Government Security 35-40 (1957).

Following the Cole decision various proposals were made in Congress for legislation to establish a new basis for the loyalty-security program, but no action was taken. Ibid. Nor was the Executive Order revised. The only further legislative or presidential action dealing with civilian federal employment has been Public Law 88-290, approved March 26, 1964, amending the Internal Security Act to provide that no person shall be employed or given access to classified information in the National Security Agency unless such employment or access "is clearly consistent with the national security"; and giving the Secretary of Defense summary power to dismiss an officer or employee of that Agency "whenever he considers that action to be in the interest of the United States, and he determines that the procedures prescribed in other provisions of law that authorize the termination of the employment of that officer or employee cannot be invoked consistently with the national security." 78 Stat. 168 (1964), 50 U.S.C. §833.

The general civil service laws and regulations, to which the Court referred in the Cole case, currently include (1) the provisions of the Lloyd-LaFollette Act of 1912 (supra) and the Veterans Preference Acts (58 Stat. 390, as amended, 5 U.S.C. §863), authorizing dismissals for "such cause as will promote the efficiency of service"; (b) the 1955 Act codifying the Hatch Act and

[1] The 18-month limitation was held unreasonable, as to an employee who had waited two years and eight months pending the outcome of a similar case, in Duncan v. Summerfield, 251 F.2d 896 (D.C. Cir. 1957). In accord are Bernabei v. Summerfield and Tucker v. Brucker, 251 F.2d 898 (D.C. Cir. 1958).

the appropriations acts (supra), applying to any person who "advocates the overthrow of our constitutional form of government" or is a member of an organization which so advocates; and (3) the provisions of the Civil Service regulations, originally promulgated in 1942 under the "efficiency" clause, disqualifying or authorizing removal where there is "reasonable doubt as to the loyalty of the person involved to the Government of the United States" (5 C.F.R. 731.201(f)).

The present structure of the federal loyalty-security program therefore is:

(1) An applicant or employee in a "sensitive" position is subject to the provisions of Public Law 733 and Executive Order 10450, or in the case of the National Security Agency to Public Law 88-290.

(2) An applicant or employee under the civil service, whether or not a "sensitive" position is involved, is subject to the Hatch Act, the Lloyd-LaFollette suitability provision, and the Civil Service reasonable doubt regulation.

(3) An applicant or employee not under civil service is subject to rejection or removal without regard to statutory reasons, limited only by constitutional restrictions. See Vitarelli v. Seaton, 359 U.S. 535, 79 S. Ct. 968, 3 L. Ed. 2d 1012 (1959).

REFERENCES

1. On the background and development of the federal loyalty program as it applied to civilian employees, see Emerson and Helfeld, Loyalty Among Government Employees, 58 Yale L.J. 1, 8-26 (1948); Kammerer, Impact of War on Federal Personnel Administration, 1939-1945, ch. 6 (1951); Bontecou, The Federal Loyalty-Security Program, ch. 1 (1953); Report of the Commission on Government Security 5-17 (1957); Rackow, The Federal Loyalty Program: Politics and Civil Liberty, 12 W. Res. L. Rev. 701 (1961).

2. For discussion of the Cole decision and the problems raised by it see Morgan, Federal Loyalty-Security Removals 1946-1956, 36 Neb. L. Rev. 412, 433-42 (1957); Note, The Federal Employee Loyalty-Security Program and Cole v. Young, 51 Nw. L. Rev. 788 (1957); Note, Supreme Court, 1955 Term, 70 Harv. L. Rev. 83, 165-168 (1956); Bischoff, Constitutional Law and Civil Rights, in Annual Survey of American Law, 32 N.Y.U.L. Rev. 44, 51 (1957); Note, The Federal Employee Loyalty-Security Program: A Critique, 1956 Wash. U.L.Q. 353 (1956); Note, 36 B.U.L. Rev. 640 (1956).

3. The statutes, executive orders, and implementing regulations of the major federal agencies are set out in BNA, Manual of Government Security and Loyalty, ch. 15. The major provisions are also set forth in Part III of Internal Security Manual (rev.), Sen. Doc. 126, 86th Cong., 2d Sess. (1960). For a brief description of the program as it existed in 1956, largely unchanged to date, see Association of the Bar of the City of New York, The Federal Loyalty-Security Program, chs. IV and V (1956).

4. In addition to the program for civilian employees the Federal Government administers the industrial security program (for employees of government contractors), the port security program (for maritime workers), the program for military personnel, the Atomic Energy Commission program, the program for employees of international agencies, and others. Details are given in BNA Manual, supra.

As of 1958, the above federal programs subjected to loyalty qualifications about 8,500,000 persons, including about 2,300,000 in federal civilian employment, 3,000,000 in the armed forces, 3,000,000 under the industrial security program, several hundred thousand under the port security program, and a few U.N. employees. Professor Brown estimated the total number of persons covered by loyalty tests, including federal, state, local, and private, at around 13,500,000. His figures, broken down by occupation, are:

Professions	1,600,000
Managers	300,000
Government and military	7,200,000
Manufacturing, construction, transport, utilities	4,500,000
Total, round off to	13,500,000

He adds: "Taking the total labor force at around 65,000,000 this means that at least one person out of five, as a condition of his current employment, has taken a test oath, or completed a loyalty statement, or achieved official security clearance, or survived some undefined private scrutiny." Brown, Loyalty and Security 164-181 (1958).

Since 1958 there have been substantial increases in the number of federal, state and local employees, persons in the armed services, and workers covered by the industrial security program. Moreover, the above figures represent, of course, only the *current* number subject to loyalty tests. They do not take into account the turnover in employment. Thus, from the introduction of the Truman program in 1947 to its supercession by the Eisenhower program in 1953, some 4,756,705 federal employees were checked for loyalty under Executive Order 9835. Civil Service Commission, 1953 Annual Report 32; for further figures see Special Committee of the Association of the Bar of the City of New York, The Federal Loyalty-Security Program, App. A. (1956). From 1954 through 1962, over 2,500,000 persons were given loyalty checks for Federal Government employment and over 250,000 given full field investigations. Civil Service Commission, Annual Reports, 1954-1962. The figures do not take into account the impact of the exposure to loyalty tests upon members of the family, dependents, and the like.

For a summary of the situation see Morris, Academic Freedom and Loyalty Oaths, 28 Law & Contemp. Prob. 486, 496-497 (1963).

b. Standards of Loyalty and Security

The workings of the various federal loyalty programs are shrouded in some obscurity. The fact that the charges in a case are often lacking in specificity, that a substantial part of the evidence upon which the decision is reached is not revealed, that the deciding agency does not make available an opinion containing findings and reasoning, as well as the entire atmosphere of secrecy surrounding the whole process, make it difficult to obtain information upon which to determine what standards of loyalty or security are applied or otherwise to appraise the operation of the programs. See Brown, Loyalty and Security 33-34 (1958).

In a few cases the opinions of loyalty boards or deciding officials, or other relevant documents, have become available. The Chasanow case, set forth below, indicates the character of the proceeding.

In re ABRAHAM CHASANOW
Department of the Navy, 1953
BNA, *Manual of Government Security Loyalty,*
19:527-531

MEMORANDUM OF REASONING OF SECURITY
HEARING BOARD

. . . 4. The employee, prior to his suspension, was Director, Distribution Control Office, U. S. Navy Hydrographic Office, Suitland, Maryland.

5. Hearings were conducted on 21, 22 and 28 September 1953 in the U.S. Navy Hydrographic Office, Suitland, Maryland.

6. The employee, Abraham Chasanow, and his counsel, Mr. Joseph A. Fanelli, were present at the hearings. The employee testified and produced witnesses and affidavits in his behalf. The Government produced witnesses and certain investigative reports.

7. The evidence presented and considered by the Board did not establish, to any degree of certainty, that Mr. Chasanow was associated with Morris and Linda Solomon and Irving and Rose Rothchild.

8. The evidence presented and considered by the Board did not establish to any degree of certainty that Mr. Chasanow was associated with Mr. Henry C. Pearlman. There was evidence that Mr. Pearlman was a resident of Greenbelt and fairly well known to the residents of that community. Opinions of him varied. Mr. Chasanow's association with Mr. Pearlman, if any association did exist, was only in connection with civic enterprises and professionally as an attorney.

9. The evidence establishes that Mr. Chasanow was present at a social party of some description in the home of one Sherod East in Greenbelt sometime during the year 1941. This function was attended by many residents of Greenbelt, some of whom were reputed to have "radical" and "left-wing" tendencies and others whose reputation in the community was unquestioned. It was established that money was raised at this affair for the support of some Spanish Relief Organization, the exact name of which is not clear. The evidence indicates that the United States Spanish Aid Committee, which allegedly was the recipient of the money raised at the party, was not placed on the Attorney General's list of subversive organizations until eight (8) years subsequent to the party.

10. The evidence established that Mr. Chasanow did subscribe to a publica-

tion known as "In Fact" some twelve (12) years ago as a group subscriber at a reduced rate. There is no evidence to indicate that Mr. Chasanow ever renewed his subscription at the expiration thereof nor that he presently subscribes to this publication. The evidence does not indicate that the publishers of this periodical appear on the Attorney General's list of subversive activities.

11. The evidence establishes that in 1939 Mr. Chasanow became a member of the National Lawyers Guild for one (1) year. It does not appear that he subsequently renewed his membership nor is presently a member of this organization, nor is there any evidence to indicate that he actively participated in the affairs of this organization. Evidence received by the Board indicates that at the time Mr. Chasanow was a member of the National Lawyers Guild and prior thereto, lawyers of national prominence were members thereof and contributed articles to the "quarterly" published by the organization. There is no evidence to indicate that the National Lawyers Guild was considered a subversive organization when Mr. Chasanow was a member thereof.

12. Evidence establishes that Mr. Chasanow, as well as his wife, were connected in some minor capacity with the Greenbelt "Cooperator" as were numerous other residents of Greenbelt. His connection, like others, was on a voluntary basis for which no remuneration was received. Copies of this newspaper which were received in evidence and perused by the Board failed to reveal "radical" or "left-wing" tendencies on the part of the publisher thereof. Rather, these issues reflected an account of the activities of a "small town." No competent evidence was produced to establish that the "Cooperator" was ever a member of the "Washington Book Shop Association."

13. The evidence indicates that Mr. Chasanow's association with Mr. Albert E. Arent and Mr. Lewis I. Ziecheck was solely of a professional nature in connection with isolated legal matters.

14. There is a lack of credible evidence to establish beyond a reasonable doubt in the minds of the Board that Mr. Chasanow was a leader of or active in radical groups in Greenbelt. In fact, the weight of the evidence gleaned from numerous affiants prominent in that community and elsewhere and from witnesses is quite to the contrary. The weight of the evidence points to the non-existence of "radical" or "left-wing" groups as the words are loosely used.

15. The Board deems it advisable to comment on the association that did exist between one Max Salzman and Mr. Chasanow. The evidence indicates this association arose by virtue of mutual interest in cooperative housing affairs in Greenbelt, through attorney and client relationship, and by mutual employment in the Hydrographic Office. It appears that there was no close social relationship between them. The evidence is conclusive that Mr. Chasanow was not instrumental in Mr. Salzman's transfer from another office in the Hydrographic Office to the position of Deputy to Mr. Chasanow. The evidence establishes that Mr. Chasanow purposely refrained from making any decision in relationship to Mr. Salzman's transfer. The evidence discloses

that opinions of the residents of Greenbelt concerning Mr. Salzman varied to a considerable degree. He was liked by some and disliked by others mainly because of his connection with the Greenbelt housing activities which were exceedingly controversial.

16. The evidence presented to the Board by live witnesses and through numerous affidavits reveals an enlightening and interesting insight into the operations of an entirely cooperative city such as Greenbelt — one of three (3) in the United States.

 a. From its inception Greenbelt has been a subject of controversy.

 b. From without, it has been eyed suspiciously from the first as a "queer" experiment. Many believed the Government had no business starting it. The extent of the cooperative undertaking was viewed askance by many and associated with something apart from conventional private enterprise. The result has been that rumor and gossip has given Greenbelt a "radical" or "leftist" reputation.

 c. Within, considerations of how the various cooperatives should be organized, the terms under which they should be operated and the management of them have been characterized by frequent disagreements. The testimony shows that these disagreements in many cases have resulted in heated disputes that often developed into personal animosities. As a result, such terms as "crackpots," "long hairs," "radicals," "pinkos," and "Communists" have been bandied about loosely by disgruntled individuals.

 d. There can be little doubt that there have been and still are persons living in Greenbelt that have radical tendencies. This is true in any community and probably is true to a greater degree in such a town as Greenbelt where the novelty of the original experiment must have attracted many a "progressive" type. From the testimony, however, it appears that the more conservative elements have more and more predominated in the management of Greenbelt affairs.

 e. In this environment a civic-minded individual — whether conservative or otherwise — is bound to be exposed to criticism. In the case of Mr. Chasanow, who took part in many activities, the testimony showed that he was, if anything, a moderating, constructive and conservative influence.

17. In arriving at its decision, the Board was compelled to give credence to the numerous affidavits of individuals who have known Mr. Chasanow from college days. These affidavits came from persons who know him socially, professionally, and in connection with civic affairs in Greenbelt, as well as from persons acquainted with him in fraternal, church and other organizations and at his place of employment. Based on all the evidence heard by the Board and the reports of investigation furnished by the Government, the Board could reach no other conclusion but that Mr. Chasanow's employment is clearly consistent with the interests of national security.

Decision of the Department of the Navy
by J. H. Smith, Jr., Assistant Secretary
of the Navy for Air

. . . 2. The Navy Department Security Appeal Board has carefully reviewed the entire record in your case, including the findings of the Security Hearing Board and the comments and recommendations of the Hydrographer. On the basis of this record, the Navy Department Security Appeal Board has unanimously found that your employment is not clearly consistent with the interests of the national security. After such investigation and review as I deemed necessary in your case, I have concurred in the findings of the Navy Department Security Appeal Board. It is, therefore, my decision that your employment is not clearly consistent with the interests of the national security.

3. Accordingly, under authority of Executive Order 10450 and Public Law 733 (81st Congress) your employment is hereby terminated effective this date.

NOTES

1. After his dismissal, the N.Y. Times reported, Chasanow "took his fight for his job into the court of public opinion." N.Y. Times, April 16, 1954. The case received considerable publicity, including a series of articles in the Washington Daily News by Anthony Lewis, for which Lewis later received the Heywood Broun Award. After argument by Chasanow's counsel on May 3, Assistant Secretary Smith ordered a further hearing. On August 31 the Navy Department reinstated Chasanow, with back pay, stating that he had suffered a "grave injustice." N.Y. Times, Sept. 2, 1954. The N.Y. Times' report adds: "Mr. Smith condemned the unidentified informants who had accused Mr. Chasanow of Left-Wing associations, then on reinterrogation had 'either failed to corroborate their original testimony or were unable to produce specifics of earlier allegations' . . . However, he saw no solution in a requirement that all derogatory information be given under oath. Experts in the field of security investigation took the position, Mr. Smith said, that 'if you insist on sworn testimony you won't get any evidence at all.' " For an account of the case see Blank, This Man Was Nearly Destroyed by Lies, Look Magazine, May 17, 1955, p. 25; Forster and Epstein, Cross-Currents, ch. 3 (1956).

2. One of the best known cases of the 1950's was that of Dr. J. Robert Oppenheimer, nuclear physicist, who was declared a security risk by the Atomic Energy Commission in 1954. At the time Oppenheimer was Director of the Institute for Advanced Study in Princeton, N.J. The record of the hearing in the Oppenheimer case, except for deletions due to security considerations, has been published. U.S. Atomic Energy Commission, In the Matter of J. Robert Oppenheimer: Transcript of Hearing before Personnel Security Board (G.P.O., Wash. D.C. 1954). This is the only record of any loyalty-security hearing which has been so published.

For unfavorable comment on the Oppenheimer decision see Curtis, The Oppenheimer Case (1955) (reprinting substantial portions of the record); Kalven, The Case of J. Robert Oppenheimer before the Atomic Energy Commission, Bull. of the Atomic Scientists, September 1954, p. 259 (a summary of the evidence and critique of the decision); Frank, An American Tragedy, The Nation, Sept. 25, 1954, p. 245; Schlesinger, Oppenheimer Case, Atlantic Monthly, October 1954, p. 29, December 1954, p. 21; Alsop and Alsop, We Accuse! Harper's Magazine, Oct. 1954, p. 25; DeSantillana, Galileo and J. Robert Oppenheimer, The Reporter, Dec. 26, 1957, p. 10. In support of the decision see reply to the Alsop article by C. A. Rolander, Jr., Deputy Director of the Division of Security, A.E.C., printed in U.S. News & World Report, Dec. 24, 1954, pp. 88-103; address of Roger Robb, counsel for A.E.C. in the case, printed in U.S. News & World Report, April 1, 1955, pp. 92-95.

In 1963 Oppenheimer, with the approval of President Johnson, was given the Enrico Fermi Award by the Atomic Energy Commission. N.Y. Times, April 5, 1963, and Dec. 3, 1963.

3. Additional light is thrown on the standards applied in loyalty-security cases by the charges filed against employees, many of which are available. In one case, not atypical of the 1950's, a set of interrogatories addressed to an employee of a non-sensitive agency included the following (names and places in the first interrogatory changed to avoid identification):

"1. While a student at X University [one of the country's best known universities] did you associate with and do research work for Professor Y?

"a. If your answer is affirmative give full details on the extent of your association with this man in both a social as well as on a student-faculty relationship.

"b. Also, give the extent of your knowledge of the Communist sympathies of this man as evidenced by his membership in either the Communist Party or Communist Front organizations or otherwise.

"c. Further, give in detail the subject matter of the research work you performed, the purpose as understood by you of the work, and in what manner you were recruited and/or chosen to perform this work.

"2. Did you support the candidacy for the office of President of the United States of Henry A. Wallace on the Progressive Party platform in 1948?

"a. If so, give your reasons for this support and state the extent of your knowledge that his candidacy was supported by the Communist Party."

More extreme examples are not infrequent. In a case reported in Yarmolinsky, Case Studies in Personnel Security 32 (B.N.A. 1955), a civilian employee was charged with the following:

"5. [C] requested your release from the US Coast Guard and stated that you would be employed in the government agency with which he was then connected if you would be released from active duty in the US Coast Guard; information indicates that [C] was author of [title of book] which was advertised in a Louis Adamic publication; Louis Adamic has been listed as an official of the Progressive Party in Philadelphia in 1948 which has been cited as a Communist Front organization by the California Tenney Legislative Committee; [C] listed as references Robert E. Sherwood, Owen Lattimore, and [E] who have been identified as members of Communist Front groups."

In a military personnel case reported by Yarmolinsky, id. at 296, the charge was:

"Derogatory information has been received in this office which reveals the following:

"That you:

"(a) Exhibited a hypercritical attitude toward society that appeared to reflect home indoctrination."

REFERENCES

1. Other opinions of loyalty-security boards, including those involving John S. Service, John Carter Vincent, John Paton Davies, Jr., and James Kutcher, are reported in BNA, Manual of Government Security and Loyalty 19:501-538; 31:501-503; 41:77-82. In addition to the Oppenheimer case, the Atomic Energy Commission made public its findings and reasoning in two other cases, in both of which it cleared the persons involved: for the clearance of Edward U. Condon see N.Y. Times, July 16, 1948; on the clearance of Frank Graham see N.Y. Times, Dec. 21, 1948, and Gellhorn, Security, Loyalty, and Science, 90-91 (1950). An account of the proceedings in the case of William V. Vitarelli appears in Miller, Subversion and the Cold War, ch. 6 in Pritchett and Westin (eds.), The Third Branch of Government (1963).

For other materials which throw light upon the application of the standards in the loyalty program see the collections of case studies by Yarmolinsky and Watts, cited in the bibliographical note supra (giving primarily the employee's side of the story), and the First Annual Report of the Industrial Personnel Review Program, also supra (giving primarily the Government's side). A summary of some of the Yarmolinsky material appears in Lewis, Security: Interim Reports, The Reporter, Sept. 8, 1955, p. 27; Westin and Johnson, A Case-Study Report on the Eisenhower Security Program, The New Republic, Aug. 29, 1955, p. 16; Krash, Book Review 65 Yale L.J. 565 (1956). For another collection of cases see Scientists' Committee on Loyalty and Security, The Fort Monmouth Security Investigations, August 1953 — April 1954 (1954), summarized in Brown, Loyalty and Security 265-279 (1958); Some Individual Cases, Bull. of the Atomic Scientists, April 1955, p. 151.

See also Bontecou, The Federal Loyalty-Security Program 107-114 (1953); Acheson, A Democrat Looks at His Party 131-134 (1955) (on the Service case); Scott, The Letter Nobody Wrote, The Nation, Jan. 5, 1957 (on the William H. Taylor case).

2. For a discussion of the extent to which the employee's associations with other persons or groups came to be a significant factor in the application of loyalty standards, see O'Brian, Loyalty Tests and Guilt by Association, 61 Harv. L. Rev. 592 (1948); Cushman, Guilt by Association: The Game of Presumptions in White (ed.), The State of the Social Sciences 451 (1956). See also Commager, Guilt — and Innocence — by Association, N.Y. Times Magazine, Nov. 8, 1953. For light on the difficulties of applying loyalty standards with respect to conduct occurring in a past period and in a different context, see Willen, Who "Collaborated" With Russia? The Antioch Review, Fall 1954, p. 259; see also Schware v. Board of Bar Examiners, 353 U.S. 232, 77 S. Ct. 752 1 L. Ed. 2d 796 (1957), noted in Section D, supra.

3. Generally on the question of standards of loyalty, see Brown, id. at chs. 2, 11, 15, and 16; Fellman, The Loyalty Defendants, 1957 Wis. L. Rev. 4, 21-26; Association of the Bar of the City of New York, The Federal Loyalty-Security Program 149-157 (1956); Report of the Commission on Government Security 46-50, 130-133, 172-173, 214-220, 267-270, 353-356 (1957).

c. Court Review of Standards

At the advent of the loyalty program the right of government employees to judicial relief for dismissal, discipline, or refusal to hire was a very limited one. Doctrinally, judicial thinking was dominated by the famous formula of Justice Holmes: "petitioner may have a constitutional right to talk politics, but he has no constitutional right to be a policeman." McAuliffe v. New Bedford, 155 Mass. 216, 220, 29 N.E. 517 (1892). Under this doctrine of government employment as a "privilege" rather than a "right" the legal status of the public servant was much the same as a person in private employment, and such rights as he had were only those granted by statute. The most important statutory protection was that afforded by the Lloyd-LaFollette Act, which provided that "No person in the classified civil service of the United States shall be removed therefrom except for such cause as will promote the efficiency of said service." 37 Stat. 555 (1912), 5 U.S.C. §652. But the uniform rule of the courts was that judicial review of dismissals would be granted only to the extent of enforcing the statutory procedures, not for considering the merits of the dismissal. Keim v. United States, 177 U.S. 290, 20 S. Ct. 574, 44 L. Ed. 774 (1900); Eberlein v. United States, 257 U.S. 82, 42 S. Ct. 12, 66 L. Ed. 140 (1921); Levine v. Farley, 107 F.2d 186 (D.C. Cir. 1939), cert. den., 308 U.S. 622 (1940). By 1947, however, the Supreme Court had made clear that basic constitutional guarantees did apply to government employment. United Public Workers v. Mitchell, 330 U.S. 75, 67 S. Ct. 556, 91 L. Ed. 754 (1947).

The first loyalty case to reach the courts was Friedman v. Schwellenbach, 159 F.2d 22 (D.C. Cir. 1946), cert. den., 330 U.S. 838 (1947). Friedman, a temporary employee in the Labor Department, was denied permanent civil service status, and thereby dismissed from his position, on the ground that he failed to meet the requirements of the 1942 civil service regulation disqualifying an individual where there was "a reasonable doubt as to his loyalty." In a suit for injunction and reinstatement the court, dealing with the issue in the traditional fashion, held the regulation valid and refused to consider the merits of the discharge.

The expansion of the loyalty program, and its impact on government service and individual rights, forced a general reconsideration of accepted doctrines relating to the legal status of government employees. The issues were brought to the courts in this new context in Bailey v. Richardson, 182 F.2d 46 (D.C. Cir. 1950), arising under the Truman Order (Executive Order 9835). Miss Bailey, a training officer in the United States Employment Service, was dismissed after a finding by the loyalty board that "reasonable grounds exist for belief that [she] is disloyal to the Government of the United States." A hearing had been held, at which she appeared and presented evidence, but the evidence against her was not made available to her. In a suit for declaratory judgment and an order of reinstatement, a majority of the court, speaking through Judge Prettyman, held that "compliance with the Sixth Amendment is not a prerequisite to the dismissal of an employee from the Federal Government classified civil service"; that "Government employ is not 'property'" or "liberty" and hence "the due process clause does not apply to the holding of a Government office"; that there was no violation of the First Amendment since "so far as the Constitution is concerned there is no prohibition against the dismissal of Government employees because of their political beliefs, activities or affiliations"; that, in short, "The situation of the Government employee is not different in this respect from that of private employees." Judge Edgerton dissented, contending that dismissal for disloyalty is punishment and hence due process requires all the safeguards of a judicial trial; that the dismissal, based upon the holding of opinions, abridged freedom of speech; and that the attribution of guilt by association denied both freedom of assembly and due process.

The Bailey case was affirmed, without opinion, by an equally divided Supreme Court, Mr. Justice Clark not participating. 341 U.S. 918, 71 S. Ct. 669, 95 L. Ed. 1352 (1951). A similar result was reached in Washington v. McGrath, 182 F.2d 375 (D.C. Cir. 1950), aff'd without opinion by an equally divided vote, 341 U.S. 923, 71 S. Ct. 795, 95 L. Ed. 1356 (1951).

The substantive and procedural constitutional issues underlying the federal loyalty program were also presented to the Supreme Court in Joint Anti-Fascist Refugee Committee v. McGrath, 341 U.S. 123, 71 S. Ct. 624, 95 L. Ed. 817 (1951), decided the same day as the Bailey case. In this case three organizations brought suit against the Attorney General and the Loyalty Review Board for declaratory and injunctive relief, alleging that the Attorney General (acting under Executive Order 9835) had put them upon his list of subversive organizations (see infra), without notice or hearing, thereby causing them irreparable injury. A motion to dismiss was granted and the Court of Appeals affirmed. 177 F.2d 79 (D.C. Cir. 1949). The Supreme Court reversed by a vote of five to three, Mr. Justice Clark again not participating. The Court as a whole failed to reach the substantive constitutional issues, although most of the justices, in the course of the six separate opinions, expressed their views at length on these matters. All the participating Justices agreed that the organizations had standing to challenge the Attorney General's action. Mr. Justice Burton voted for reversal on narrow procedural grounds. Taking the allegations of the complaints as admitted by the motion to dismiss he held that the complaints in effect alleged that the Attorney General had included the organizations on the list without factual basis for finding them subversive. He therefore concluded that, on this state of the pleadings, the Attorney General had acted beyond the scope of his authority. Mr. Justice Black agreed with the Burton position on the procedural issue, and agreed with Mr. Justice Frankfurter that there had been a denial of procedural due process, but went on to hold that no constitutional power existed for the Attorney General to list organizations as subversive. Mr. Justice Frankfurter thought that the issue could not be disposed of by Mr. Justice Burton's interpretation of the pleadings and concluded that the procedure employed by the Attorney General violated due process. Mr. Justice Douglas, concurring with Mr. Justice Burton, wrote a separate opinion finding the

Loyalty Order as a whole unconstitutional. Mr. Justice Jackson took the view that a finding of disloyalty against an employee on the basis of membership in or affiliation with an organization, without a hearing on the nature of the organization, constituted a denial of due process, and that the organization could bring an action to vindicate its members' rights. Mr. Justice Reed, in an opinion in which Chief Justice Vinson and Mr. Justice Minton concurred, dissented on the ground that the Loyalty Order was valid.

In three later cases the unconstitutionality of the loyalty program on substantive and procedural grounds was extensively argued to the Supreme Court. Although it decided all three cases in favor of the employee, in none did the Court deal with basic constitutional issues:

Peters v. Hobby, 349 U.S. 331, 75 S. Ct. 790, 99 L. Ed. 1129 (1955), was a suit by Dr. John P. Peters of the Yale Medical School for a declaratory judgment that his removal and disbarment as Special Consultant in the U.S. Public Health Service on loyalty grounds was invalid. Dr. Peters had been cleared by the agency loyalty board but the Loyalty Review Board, considering the case on "post-audit," had determined that there was "reasonable doubt as to Dr. Peters' loyalty to the Government." Dr. Peters raised in court the same issues that were presented in the Bailey case, placing particular emphasis on the refusal to disclose to him evidence upon which the decision was based. The failure of Solicitor General Sobeloff to sign the Government's brief in the case was construed as indicating his disagreement with the Government's position on the issue. N.Y. Times, Apr. 5, 1955. The majority of the Court held that the Loyalty Review Board was not authorized by Executive Order 9835 to review on its own motion cases decided favorably to the employee by the agency loyalty board, and that its order was therefore invalid. It further ordered the Civil Service Commission "to expunge from its records" the Board's finding and the order of disbarment. Mr. Justice Douglas concurred in a vigorous opinion stating that the procedure of withholding evidence violated due process. Justices Reed and Burton dissented.

The second case was Cole v. Young, discussed above.

Service v. Dulles, 354 U.S. 363, 77 S. Ct. 1152, 1 L. Ed. 2d 1403 (1957), was a suit by John S. Service, discharged by the State Department on loyalty grounds. The Supreme Court found the discharge invalid because Secretary of State Acheson, in ordering the dismissal, had failed to follow the procedures set forth in the Department's regulations. Service was ordered reinstated. A few months later he returned to work in the State Department. N.Y. Times, Sept. 4, 1957.

Subsequent cases decided by the Supreme Court involved procedural issues and are considered at a later point. The net result is that the Court has never squarely addressed itself to the basic constitutional validity of the federal loyalty programs. But cf. Cafeteria Workers v. McElroy, 367 U.S. 886, 81 S. Ct. 1743, 6 L. Ed. 2d 1230 (1961), discussed in the materials dealing with loyalty procedures, infra. The Court's decisions relating to state loyalty programs, although concerned mostly with oath programs rather than screening programs, do of course bear on these issues. See subsection 2, infra.

The lower federal courts, after the Bailey decision, have uniformly considered the federal loyalty programs to be basically valid. See Jason v. Summerfield, 214 F.2d 273 (D.C. Cir. 1954), cert. den., 348 U.S. 840 (1954) (upholding dismissal of Post Office employee under standards of amended Truman Order despite his prior clearance under original order); Scher v. Weeks, 231 F.2d 494 (D.C. Cir. 1956), cert. den., 351 U.S. 973 (1956); McBride v. Roland, 248 F. Supp. 459 (S.D. N.Y. 1965) (upholding port security program). Most of their decisions have concerned procedural matters. See infra.

REFERENCES

1. On the right of Government employees to judicial review of dismissal or other adverse action by employing officials, see Westwood, The "Right" of an Employee of the United States Against Arbitrary Discharge, 7 Geo. Wash. L. Rev. 212 (1938); Note, 52 Colum. L. Rev. 787 (1952); Gardner, The Great Charter and the Case of Angilly v. United States, 67 Harv. L. Rev. 1 (1953); Richardson, Problems in the Removal of Federal Civil Servants, 54 Mich. L. Rev. 219 (1955); Morgan, Federal Loyalty-Security Removals, 1946-1956, 36 Neb. L. Rev. 412, 413-419 (1957); Murphy, Judicial Review of the Removal of Federal Employees: A Reexamination, 22 Fed. B.J. 25 (1962). On nongovernment employees, see Note, Security Clearance Revocation as a Justiciable Controversy, 16 Wash. & Lee L. Rev. 293 (1959). More generally on the legal aspects of government employment see Dotson, The Emerging Doctrine of Privilege in Public Employment, 15 Pub. Admin. Rev. 77 (1955); Richardson, Some Constitutional Issues Relating to Government Employment, 4 St. Louis L.J. 1, 101 (1956); Note, Due Process and the "Right" to a Job, 46 Va. L. Rev. 323 (1960); Note, 49 Iowa L. Rev. 891 (1964); Note, Dismissal of Federal Employees — The Emerging Judicial Role, 66 Colum. L. Rev. 719 (1966).

2. For an account of the Court decisions on the federal loyalty security program, see Slotnick, The Anathema of the Security Risk, 17 Miami L. Rev. 10 (1962). Discussion of the basic constitutional issues may be found in McCarran, The Supreme Court and the Loyalty Program: The Effect of Refugee Committee v. McGrath, 37 A.B.A.J. 434 (1951); Fraenkel, Law and Loyalty, 37 Iowa L. Rev. 153 (1952); Note, The "Right" to a Government Job, 6 Rutgers L. Rev. 451 (1952); Notes, 100 U. Pa. L. Rev. 274 (1951); 20 Geo. Wash. L. Rev. 294 (1952); 28 Ind. L.J. 520 (1953); Gardner, Bailey v. Richardson and the Constitution of the United States, 33 B.U.L. Rev. 177 (1953); Willcox, Invasions of the First Amendment Through Conditioned Public Spending, 41 Cornell L.Q. 12 (1955); the Richardson and Morgan articles, supra; Greenberg, Loyalty Oaths: An Appraisal of the Legal Issues, 20 J. Politics 487 (1958); Notes, 1962 Wash. U.L.Q. 432; 66 Colum. L. Rev. 719 (1966). For discussion published prior to the Bailey and Joint Anti-Fascist decisions see Emerson and Helfeld, Loyalty Among Government Employees 58 Yale L.J. 1, 79-120 (1948) (collecting materials up to middle of 1948); Notes, 36 Calif. L. Rev. 596 (1948); 48 Colum. L. Rev. 1050 (1948).

NOTE

The attempt by Congress in an appropriation rider to deny funds to three named individuals charged with subversive associations was held invalid as a bill of attainder in United States v. Lovett, 328 U.S. 303, 66 S. Ct. 1073, 90 L. Ed. 1252 (1946). The Lovett case is noted in 46 Colum. L. Rev. 849 (1946); 45 Mich. L. Rev. 98 (1946); 95 U. Pa. L. Rev. 80 (1946). Cf. Starkweather v. Blair, 245 Minn. 371, 71 N.W.2d 869 (1955), noted in 54 Mich. L. Rev. 849 (1956), where an appropriation rider providing no funds for a specified office was held not to constitute a bill of attainder. See Norville, Bill of Attainder — A Rediscovered Weapon Against Discriminatory Legislation, 26 Ore. L. Rev. 78 (1947); the Garner case, printed infra; and the materials on bill of attainder cited in Section D, subsection 1, supra.

d. Procedures

The procedural rights granted by statute to permanent employees in the classified civil service are set forth in the Lloyd-LaFollette Act of 1912: "No person in the classified civil service of the United States shall be removed therefrom except for such cause as will promote the efficiency of said service and for reasons given in writing, and the person whose removal is sought shall have notice of the same and of any charges preferred against him, and be furnished with a copy thereof, and also be allowed a reasonable time for personally answering the same in writing; and affidavits in support thereof; but no examination of witnesses nor any trial or hearing shall be required except in the discretion of the officer making the removal. . . ." 5 U.S.C. §652. Employees covered by the Veterans Preference Act have the additional right "to make a personal appearance, or an appearance through a designated representative." 5 U.S.C. §863. Employees in "sensitive" positions suspended or dismissed under Public Law 733 have only, so far as statutory provision is concerned, the procedural rights set forth in that law. See supra. Temporary or probational employees, or employers not in the classified civil service, have no procedural rights granted by statute. Nor do non-Government employees covered by the industrial security or port security programs.

The extent to which government or non-government employees dismissed or refused clearance under the loyalty-security programs have a constitutional right under the due process clause to notice and formal hearing has never been fully clarified by the Supreme Court. See the Bailey and Joint Anti-Fascist cases, supra, and the later cases discussed below; Note, Notice and Hearing in Government Exclusionary Action, 110 U. Pa. L. Rev. 1009 (1962) (collecting prior materials). As a matter of practice, the implementing regulations under the loyalty-security programs normally provide for notice and a hearing of some sort. Thus the Civil Service Commission regulations applicable to permanent employees in the classified service establish procedures in-

cluding the right to notice of charges; to file an answer and affidavits; to a
hearing on the adverse action "personally or through or accompanied by his
representative"; to a written decision which will "inform the employee of the
reasons for the action"; and to an appeal. But these rights do "not include the
right to a trial or formal hearing with examination of witnesses," except that
witnesses from the agency may in the discretion of the hearing officer be
called. 5 C.F.R. §§752, 771, 772. Somewhat similar rights are granted under
the other implementing regulations. See BNA, Manual of Government Security and Loyalty.

The chief procedural issues under the loyalty-security programs have been
concerned with the failure of the government to make confidential information upon which the decision is based available to the individual concerned
or to permit him to confront or cross-examine adverse witnesses. Objections
on these grounds were strongly presented in Bailey v. Richardson, discussed
supra, but were rejected by the majority of the Court of Appeals, 182 F.2d 46
(D.C. Cir. 1950). The Supreme Court, affirming by an equally divided vote,
did not render any opinion on the issues. 341 U.S. 918 (1951). The questions
were again briefed and argued elaborately in Peters v. Hobby, also considered
above, but the Supreme Court did not reach them in its decision. 349 U.S. 331,
75 S. Ct. 790, 99 L. Ed. 1129 (1955). See also Service v. Dulles, 354 U.S. 363, 77
S. Ct. 1152, 1 L. Ed. 2d 1403 (1957).

Meanwhile, the questions of secret evidence, confrontation and the right of
cross-examination reached the courts in connection with the port security
program, involving the rights of persons not employed by the government. In
United States v. Gray, a criminal prosecution for accepting employment on
merchant vessels without having received security clearance, the Court of
Appeals for the Ninth Circuit held that the procedures employed by the
Coast Guard in the security proceedings had not afforded the defendant adequate notice or opportunity to defend, and reversed the conviction. 207 F.2d
237 (9th Cir. 1953). And the same court in Parker v. Lester, after an elaborate discussion of the issues, ruled that the Coast Guard regulations, in not
affording the persons being screened the opportunity to know the evidence
against them, and in denying the right of confrontation and cross-examination, were invalid as a violation of due process. 227 F.2d 708 (9th Cir. 1955).
The court said:

"Under this screening system there is no provision whatever for notice and
an opportunity to be heard as generally understood to be required by the
provisions of the Fifth Amendment relating to due process. When it is proposed to take from a citizen through administrative proceedings some right
which he otherwise would have, it has always been held that the constitutional requirement is that he shall be afforded notice and an opportunity to be
heard." 227 F.2d at 716.

The procedural rights of government employees came before the Supreme
Court again in Vitarelli v. Seaton, 359 U.S. 535, 79 S. Ct. 968, 3 L. Ed. 2d 1012

(1959). But the Court again did not reach the constitutional issues. Shortly afterwards the Court handed down opinions in two further cases, both dealing with non-government employees, set forth below.

GREENE v. McELROY
360 U.S. 474, 79 S. Ct. 1400, 3 L. Ed. 2d 1377 (1959)

MR. CHIEF JUSTICE WARREN delivered the opinion of the Court.

This case involves the validity of the Government's revocation of security clearance granted to petitioner, an aeronautical engineer employed by a private manufacturer which produced goods for the armed services. Petitioner was discharged from his employment solely as a consequence of the revocation because his access to classified information was required by the nature of his job. After his discharge, petitioner was unable to secure employment as an aeronautical engineer and for all practical purposes that field of endeavor is now closed to him.

Petitioner was vice president and general manager of Engineering and Research Corporation (ERCO), a business devoted primarily to developing and manufacturing various mechanical and electronic products. . . .

[Hearings were held before the PSB and its successor, the Eastern Industrial Personnel Security Board. Petitioner appeared with counsel, answered questions, and presented evidence. The Government produced no witnesses. "It was obvious, however, . . . that the Board relied on confidential reports which were never made available to petitioner."]

Petitioner contends that the action of the Department of Defense in barring him from access to classified information on the basis of statements of confidential informants made to investigators was not authorized by either Congress or the President and has denied him "liberty" and "property" without "due process of law" in contravention of the Fifth Amendment. The alleged property is petitioner's employment; the alleged liberty is petitioner's freedom to practice his chosen profession. Respondents admit, as they must, that the revocation of security clearance caused petitioner to lose his job with ERCO and has seriously affected, if not destroyed, his ability to obtain employment in the aeronautics field. Although the right to hold specific private employment and to follow a chosen profession free from unreasonable governmental interference comes within the "liberty" and "property" concepts of the Fifth Amendment, Dent v. West Virginia, 129 U.S. 114; Schware v. Board of Bar Examiners, 353 U.S. 232; Peters v. Hobby, 349 U.S. 331, 352 (concurring opinion); cf. Slochower v. Board of Education, 350 U.S. 551; Truax v. Raich, 239 U.S. 33, 41; Allgeyer v. Louisiana, 165 U.S. 578, 589-590; Powell v. Pennsylvania, 127 U.S. 678, 684, respondents contend that the admitted interferences which have occurred are indirect by-products of necessary governmental action to protect the integrity of secret information and hence are not unreasonable and do not constitute deprivations within the meaning of the Amendment. Alternatively, respondents urge that even if petitioner has been restrained in the enjoyment of constitutionally protected rights, he was accorded due process of law in that he was permitted to utilize those procedural safeguards consonant with an effective clearance program, in the administration of which the identity of informants and their statements are kept secret to insure an unimpaired flow to the Government of information concerning subversive conduct. But in view of our conclusion that this case should be decided on the narrower ground of "authorization," we find that we need not determine the answers to these questions.

The issue, as we see it, is whether the Department of Defense has been authorized to create an industrial security clearance program under which affected persons may lose their jobs and may be restrained in following their chosen professions on the basis of fact determinations concerning their fitness for clearance made in proceedings in which they are denied the traditional procedural safeguards of confrontation and cross-examination. . . .

[The Court then summarizes the history of the industrial security program.]

Respondents maintain that congressional authorization to the President to fashion a program which denies security clearance to persons on the basis of confidential information which the individuals have no opportunity to confront and test is unnecessary because the President has inherent authority to maintain military secrets inviolate. And respondents argue that if a statutory grant of power is necessary, such a grant can readily by *inferred* "as a necessarily implicit authority from the generalized provisions" of legislation dealing with the armed services. But the question which must be decided in this case is not whether the President has inherent power to act or whether Congress has granted him such a power; rather, it is whether either the President or Congress exercised such a power and delegated to the Department of Defense the authority to fashion such a program.

Certain principles have remained relatively immutable in our jurisprudence. One of these is that where governmental action seriously injures an individual, and the reasonableness of the action depends on fact findings, the evidence used to prove the Government's case must be disclosed to the individual so that he has an opportunity to show that it is untrue. While this is important in the case of documentary evidence, it is even more important where the evidence consists of the testimony of individuals whose memory might be faulty or who, in fact, might be perjurers or persons motivated by malice, vindictiveness, intolerance, prejudice, or jealousy. We have formalized these protections in the requirements of confrontation and cross-examination. They have ancient roots. They find expression in the Sixth Amendment which provides that in all criminal cases the accused shall enjoy the right "to be confronted with the witnesses against him." This Court has been zealous to protect these rights from erosion. It has spoken out not only in criminal cases, e.g., Mattox v. United States, 156 U.S. 237, 242-244; Kirby v. United

States, 174 U.S. 47; Motes v. United States, 178 U.S. 458, 474; In re Oliver, 333 U.S. 257, 273, but also in all types of cases where administrative and regulatory actions were under scrutiny. E.g., Southern R. Co. v. Virginia, 290 U.S. 190; Ohio Bell Telephone Co. v. Public Utilities Commission, 301 U.S. 292; Morgan v. United States, 304 U.S. 1, 19; Carter v. Kubler, 320 U.S. 243; Reilly v. Pinkus, 338 U.S. 269. Nor, as it has been pointed out, has Congress ignored these fundamental requirements in enacting regulatory legislation. Joint Anti-Fascist Committee v. McGrath, 341 U.S. 168-169 (concurring opinion).

Professor Wigmore, commenting on the importance of cross-examination, states in his treatise, 5 Wigmore on Evidence (3d ed. 1940) §1367:

"For two centuries past, the policy of the Anglo-American system of Evidence has been to regard the necessity of testing by cross-examination as a vital feature of the law. The belief that no safeguard for testing the value of human statements is comparable to that furnished by cross-examination, and the conviction that no statement (unless by special exception) should be used as testimony until it has been probed and sublimated by that test, has found increasing strength in lengthening experience."

Little need be added to this incisive summary statement except to point out that under the present clearance procedures not only is the testimony of absent witnesses allowed to stand without the probing questions of the person under attack which often uncover inconsistencies, lapses of recollection, and bias, but, in addition, even the members of the clearance boards do not see the informants or know their identities, but normally rely on an investigator's summary report of what the informant said without even examining the investigator personally.

[The opinion then examines the relevant Executive Orders, statutes and appropriation acts.]

If acquiescence or implied ratification were enough to show delegation of authority to take actions within the area of questionable constitutionality, we might agree with respondents that delegation has been shown here. In many circumstances, where the Government's freedom to act is clear, and the Congress or the President has provided general standards of action and has acquiesced in administrative interpretation, delegation may be inferred. Thus, even in the absence of specific delegation, we have no difficulty in finding, as we do, that the Department of Defense has been authorized to fashion and apply an industrial clearance program which affords affected persons the safeguards of confrontation and cross-examination. But this case does not present that situation. We deal here with substantial restraints on employment opportunities of numerous persons imposed in a manner which is in conflict with our long-accepted notions of fair procedures. Before we are asked to judge whether, in the context of security clearance cases, a person may be deprived of the right to follow his chosen profession without full hearings where accusers may be confronted, it must be made clear that the President or Congress, within their respective constitutional powers, specifically has decided that the imposed procedures are necessary and warranted and has authorized their use. Cf. Watkins v. United States, 354 U.S. 178; Scull v. Virginia, 359 U.S. 344. Such decisions cannot be assumed by acquiescence or non-action. Kent v. Dulles, 357 U.S. 116; Peters v. Hobby, 349 U.S. 331; Ex parte Endo, 323 U.S. 283, 301-302. They must be made explicitly not only to assure that individuals are not deprived of cherished rights under procedures not actually authorized, see Peters v. Hobby, supra, but also because explicit action, especially in areas of doubtful constitutionality, requires careful and purposeful consideration by those responsible for enacting and implementing our laws. Without explicit action by lawmakers, decisions of great constitutional import and effect would be relegated by default to administrators who, under our system of government, are not endowed with authority to decide them. . . .

In the instant case, petitioner's work opportunities have been severely limited on the basis of a fact determination rendered after a hearing which failed to comport with our traditional ideas of fair procedure. The type of hearing was the product of administrative decision not explicitly authorized by either Congress or the President. Whether those procedures under the circumstances comport with the Constitution we do not decide. Nor do we decide whether the President has inherent authority to create such a program, whether congressional action is necessary, or what the limits on executive or legislative authority may be. We decide only that in the absence of explicit authorization from either the President or Congress the respondents were not empowered to deprive petitioner of his job in a proceeding in which he was not afforded the safeguards of confrontation and cross-examination.

Accordingly, the judgment is reversed and the case is remanded to the District Court for proceedings not inconsistent herewith.

It is so ordered.

Mr. Justice Frankfurter, Mr. Justice Harlan, and Mr. Justice Whittaker concur in the judgment on the ground that it has not been shown that either Congress or the President authorized the procedures whereby petitioner's security clearance was revoked, intimating no views as to the validity of those procedures.

Mr. Justice Harlan, concurring specially.

What has been written on both sides of this case makes appropriate a further word from one who concurs in the judgment of the Court, but cannot join its opinion.

Unlike my brother Clark who finds this case "both clear and simple," I consider the constitutional issue it presents most difficult and far-reaching. In my view the Court quite properly declined to decide it in the present posture of the case. My unwillingness to subscribe to the Court's opinion is due to the fact that it unnecessarily deals with the very issue it disclaims deciding. . . .

Mr. Justice Clark, dissenting. . . .

I believe that the Court is in error in holding, as it must, in order to reach this "authorization" issue, that Greene's "right to hold specific private employment and to follow a chosen profession free from unreasonable governmental interference" is protected by the Fifth Amendment. It cites four cases in support of this proposition and says compare four others. As I read those cases not one is in point. In fact, I cannot find a single case in support of the Court's position. . . .

In holding that the Fifth Amendment protects Greene the Court ignores the basic consideration in the case, namely, that no person, save the President, has a constitutional right to access to governmental secrets. Even though such access is necessary for one to keep a job in private industry, he is still not entitled to the secrets. It matters not if as a consequence he is unable to secure a specific job or loses one he presently enjoys. The simple reason for this conclusion is that he has no constitutional right to the secrets. If access to its secrets is granted by the Government it is entirely permissive and may be revoked at any time. That is all that the Cabinet officers did here. It is done every day in governmental operation. The Court seems to hold that the access granted Greene was for his benefit. It was not. Access was granted to secure for the Government the supplies or services it needed. . . .

The Court refuses to pass on the constitutionality of the procedures used in the hearings. It does say that the hearings provided for in the program permit the restraint of "employment opportunities through a denial of clearance without the safeguards of confrontation and cross-examination." I think the Court confuses administrative action with judicial trials. This Court has long ago and repeatedly approved administrative action where the rights of cross-examination and confrontation were not permitted. Chicago & Southern Air Lines v. Waterman Corp., 333 U.S. 103 (1948); Carlson v. Landon, 342 U.S. 524 (1952); United States v. Nugent, 346 U.S. 1 (1953); United States v. Reynolds, 345 U.S. 1 (1953); Knauff v. Shaughnessy, 338 U.S. 537 (1950); Shaughnessy v. Mezei, 345 U.S. 206 (1953); and Jay v. Boyd, 351 US. 345 (1956).

At no time since the programs now in vogue were established in 1942 have the rights of cross-examination and confrontation of witnesses been required. In fact the present regulations were patterned after the Employee Loyalty Program, first inaugurated upon the passage of the Hatch Act in 1939, in which the rights of confrontation and cross-examination have never been recognized. Every Attorney General since that time has approved these procedures, as has every President. And it should be noted, though several cases here have attacked the regulations on this ground, this Court has yet to strike them down.

I shall not labor the point further than to say that in my opinion the procedures here do comport with that fairness required of administrative action in the security field. A score of our cases, as I have cited, support me in this position. Not one is to the contrary. And the action of the Court in striking down the program for lack of specific authorization is indeed strange, and hard for me to understand at this critical time of national emergency. . . .

CAFETERIA & RESTAURANT WORKERS UNION
v. McELROY
367 U.S. 886, 81 S. Ct. 1743, 6 L. Ed. 2d 1230 (1961)

Mr. Justice Stewart delivered the opinion of the Court.

In 1956 the petitioner Rachel Brawner was a short-order cook at a cafeteria operated by her employer, M & M Restaurants, Inc., on the premises of the Naval Gun Factory in the city of Washington. She had worked there for more than six years, and from her employer's point of view her record was entirely satisfactory.

The Gun Factory was engaged in designing, producing, and inspecting naval ordnance, including the development of weapons systems of a highly classified nature. Located on property owned by the United States, the installation was under the command of Rear Admiral D. M. Tyree, Superintendent. Access to it was restricted, and guards were posted at all points of entry. Identification badges were issued to persons authorized to enter the premises by the Security Officer, a naval officer subordinate to the Superintendent. In 1956 the Security Officer was Lieutenant Commander H. C. Williams. Rachel Brawner had been issued such a badge.

The cafeteria where she worked was operated by M & M under a contract with the Board of Governors of the Gun Factory. Section 5(b) of the contract provided:

". . . In no event shall the Concessionaire engage, or continue to engage, for operations under this Agreement, personnel who

. . .

"(iii) fail to meet the security requirements or other requirements under applicable regulations of the Activity, as determined by the Security Officer of the Activity."

On November 15, 1956, Mrs. Brawner was required to turn in her identification badge because of Lieutenant Commander Williams' determination that she had failed to meet the security requirements of the installation. The Security Officer's determination was subsequently approved by Admiral Tyree, who cited §5(b)(iii) of the contract as the basis for his action. At the request of the petitioner Union, which represented the employees at the cafeteria, M & M sought to arrange a meeting with officials of the Gun Factory "for the purpose of a hearing regarding the denial of admittance to the Naval Gun Factory of Rachel Brawner." This request was denied by Admiral Tyree on the ground that such a meeting would "serve no useful purpose."

Since the day her identification badge was withdrawn Mrs. Brawner has not been permitted to enter the Gun Factory. M & M offered to employ her in another restaurant which the company operated in the suburban Washington area, but she refused on the ground that the location was inconvenient. . . .

[The opinion first reviews the relevant constitutional and statutory provisions, and regulations.]

Under the explicit authority of Article 0734 of the Navy Regulations, and in the light of the historically unquestioned power of a commanding officer summarily to exclude civilians from the area of his command, there can remain no serious doubt of Admiral Tyree's authority to exclude Rachel Brawner from the Gun Factory upon the Security Officer's determination that she failed to meet the "security requirements . . . of the Activity." . . .

The question remains whether Admiral Tyree's action in summarily denying Rachel Brawner access to the site of her former employment violated the requirements of the Due Process Clause of the Fifth Amendment. This question cannot be answered by easy assertion that, because she had no constitutional right to be there in the first place, she was not deprived of liberty or property by the Superintendent's action. "One may not have a constitutional right to go to Baghdad, but the Government may not prohibit one from going there unless by means consonant with due process of law." Homer v. Richmond, 110 U.S. App. D.C. 226, 229, 292 F.2d 719, 722. It is the petitioners' claim that due process in this case required that Rachel Brawner be advised of the specific grounds for her exclusion and be accorded a hearing at which she might refute them. We are satisfied, however, that under the circumstances of this case such a procedure was not constitutionally required.

The Fifth Amendment does not require a trial-type hearing in every conceivable case of government impairment of private interest. "For, though 'due process of law' generally implies and includes actor, reus, judex, regular allegations, opportunity to answer, and a trial according to some settled course of judicial proceedings, . . . yet, this is not universally true." Murray's Lessee v. Hoboken Land and Improvement Co., 18 How. 272, 280. The very nature of due process negates any concept of inflexible procedures universally applicable to every imaginable situation. Communications Comm'n v. WJR, 337 U.S. 265, 275-276; Hannah v. Larche, 363 U.S. 420, 440, 442; Hagar v. Reclamation District No. 108, 111 U.S. 701, 708-709. " '[D]ue process,' unlike some legal rules, is not a technical conception with a fixed content unrelated to time, place and circumstances." It is "compounded of history, reason, the past course of decisions. . . ." Joint Anti-Fascist Comm. v. McGrath, 341 U.S. 123, 162-163 (concurring opinion).

As these and other cases make clear, consideration of what procedures due process may require under any given set of circumstances must begin with a determination of the precise nature of the government function involved as well as of the private interest that has been affected by governmental action. Where it has been possible to characterize that private interest (perhaps in oversimplification) as a mere privilege subject to the Executive's plenary power, it has traditionally been held that notice and hearing are not constitutionally required. Oceanic Navigation Co. v. Stranahan, 214 U.S. 320, 340-343; Knauff v. Shaughnessy, 338 U.S. 537; Jay v. Boyd, 351 U.S. 345, 354-358; cf. Buttfield v. Stranahan, 192 U.S. 470, 497.

What, then, was the private interest affected by Admiral Tyree's action in the present case? It most assuredly was not the right to follow a chosen trade or profession. Cf. Dent v. West Virginia, 129 U.S. 114; Schware v. Board of Bar Examiners, 353 U.S. 232; Truax v. Raich, 239 U.S. 33. Rachel Brawner remained entirely free to obtain employment as a short-order cook or to get any other job, either with M & M or with any other employer. All that was denied her was the opportunity to work at one isolated and specific military installation.

Moreover, the governmental function operating here was not the power to regulate or license, as lawmaker, an entire trade or profession, or to control an entire branch of private business, but, rather, as proprietor, to manage the internal operation of an important federal military establishment. . . . In that proprietary military capacity, the Federal Government, as has been pointed out, has traditionally exercised unfettered control.

Thus, the nature both of the private interest which has been impaired and the governmental power which has been exercised makes this case quite different from that of the lawyer in Schware, supra, the physician in Dent, supra, and the cook in Raich, supra. This case, like Perkins v. Lukens Steel Co., 310 U.S. 113, involves the Federal Government's dispatch of its own internal affairs. The Court has consistently recognized that an interest closely analogous to Rachel Brawner's, the interest of a government employee in retaining his job, can be summarily denied. It has become a settled principle that government employment, in the absence of legislation, can be revoked at the will of the appointing officer. In the Matter of Hennen, 13 Pet. 230, 246, 259; Crenshaw v. United States, 134 U.S. 99, 108; Parsons v. United States, 167 U.S. 324, 331-334; Keim v. United States, 177 U.S. 290, 293-294; Taylor and Marshall v. Beckham (No. 1), 178 U.S. 548, 575-578. This principle was reaffirmed quite recently in Vitarelli v. Seaton, 359 U.S. 535. There we pointed out that Vitarelli, an Interior Department employee who had not qualified for statutory protection under the Civil Service Act, "could have been summarily discharged by the Secretary at any time without the giving of a reason. . . ." 359 U.S., at 539. . . .

Nothing that was said or decided in [United Public Workers v. Mitchell, 330 U.S. 75, or Wieman v. Updegraff, 344 U.S. 183] would lead to the conclusion that Rachel Brawner could not be denied access to the Gun Factory without notice and an opportunity to be heard. Those cases demonstrate only that the state and federal governments, even in the exercise of their internal operations, do not constitutionally have the complete freedom of action enjoyed by a private employer. But to acknowledge that there exist constitutional restraints upon state and federal governments in dealing with their employees is not to say that all such employees have a constitutional right to notice and a hearing before they can be removed. We may assume that Rachel Brawner could not constitutionally have been excluded from the Gun Factory if the announced grounds for her exclusion had been patently arbitrary or discriminatory — that she could not have been kept out because she was a Democrat or a Methodist. It does not follow, however, that she was entitled to notice and a hearing when the reason advanced for her exclusion was, as here, entirely rational and in accord with the contract with M & M.

Finally, it is to be noted that this is not a case where government action has operated to bestow a badge of disloyalty or infamy, with an attendant foreclosure from other employment opportunity. See Wieman v. Updegraff, 344 U.S. 183, 190-191; Joint Anti-Fascist Comm. v. McGrath, 341 U.S. 123, 140-141; cf. Bailey v. Richardson, 86 U.S. App. D.C. 248, 182 F.2d 46, affd by an equally divided Court, 341 U.S. 918. All this record shows is that, in the opinion of the Security Officer of the Gun Factory, concurred in by the Superintendent, Rachel Brawner failed to meet the particular security requirements of that specific military installation. There is nothing to indicate that this determination would in any way impair Rachel Brawner's employment opportunities anywhere else. As pointed out by Judge Prettyman, speaking for the Court of Appeals, "Nobody has said that Brawner is disloyal or is suspected of the slightest shadow of intentional wrongdoing. 'Security requirements' at such an installation, like such requirements under many other circumstances, cover many matters other than loyalty." 109 U.S. App. D.C., at 49, 284 F.2d, at 183. For all that appears, the Security Officer and the Superintendent may have simply thought that Rachel Brawner was garrulous, or careless with her identification badge.

For these reasons, we conclude that the Due Process Clause of the Fifth Amendment was not violated in this case.

Affirmed.

MR. JUSTICE BRENNAN, with whom The Chief Justice, Mr. Justice Black, and Mr. Justice Douglas join, dissenting. . . .

I read the Court's opinion to acknowledge that petitioner's status as an employee at the Gun Factory was an interest of sufficient definiteness to be protected by the Federal Constitution from some kinds of governmental injury. Indeed, this acknowledgment seems compelled by our cases. Wieman v. Updegraff, 344 U.S. 183 (1952); United Public Workers v. Mitchell, 330 U.S. 75, 100 (1947) (dictum); Torcaso v. Watkins [367 U.S. 488], decided today. In other words, if petitioner Brawner's badge had been lifted avowedly on grounds of her race, religion, or political opinions, the Court would concede that some constitutionally protected interest — whether "liberty" or "property" it is unnecessary to state — had been injured. But, as the Court says, there has been no such open discrimination here. The expressed ground of exclusion was the obscuring formulation that petitioner failed to meet the "security requirements" of the naval installation where she worked. I assume for present purposes that separation as a "security risk," if the charge is properly established, is not unconstitutional. But the Court goes beyond that. It holds that the mere assertion by government that exclusion is for a valid reason forecloses further inquiry. That is, unless the government official is foolish enough to admit what he is doing — and few will be so foolish after today's decision — he may employ "security requirements" as a blind behind which to dismiss at will for the most discriminatory of causes.

Such a result in effect nullifies the substantive right — not to be arbitrarily injured by Government — which the Court purports to recognize. What sort of right is it which enjoys absolutely no procedural protection? I do not mean to imply that petitioner could not have been excluded from the installation without the full procedural panoply of first having been subjected to a trial, with cross-examination and confrontation of accusers, and proof of guilt beyond a reasonable doubt. I need not go so far in this case. For under today's holding petitioner is entitled to no process at all. She is not told what she did wrong; she is not given a chance to defend herself. She may be the victim of the basest calumny, perhaps even the caprice of the government officials in whose power her status rested completely. In such a case, I cannot believe that she is not entitled to some procedures. . . .

One further circumstance makes this particularly a case where procedural requirements of fairness are essential. Petitioner was not simply excluded from the base summarily, without a notice and chance to defend herself. She was excluded as a "security risk," that designation most odious in our times. The Court consoles itself with the speculation that she may have been merely garrulous, or careless with her identification badge, and indeed she might, although she will never find out. But, in the common understanding of the public with whom petitioner must hereafter live and work, the term "security risk" carries a much more sinister meaning. See Beilan v. Board of Public Education, 357 U.S. 399, 421-423 (1958) (dissenting opinion). It is far more likely to be taken as an accusation of communism or disloyalty than imputation of some small personal fault. Perhaps the Government has reasons for lumping such a multitude of sins under a misleading term. But it ought not to affix a "badge of infamy," Wieman v. Updegraff, supra, at 191, to a person without some statement of charges, and some opportunity to speak in reply. . . .

REFERENCES

1. For discussion of the secret evidence and confrontation issues in loyalty-security cases see, in support of the policy, Richardson, The Federal Employee Loyalty Program, 51 Colum. L. Rev. 546, 549-551 (1951); Hoover, The Confidential Nature of FBI Reports, 8 Syracuse L. Rev. 2 (1956); Report of the Commission on Government Security 657-664 (1957) (including statement by J. Edgar Hoover). In criticism of the policy see Emerson and Helfeld, Loyalty Among Government Employees, 58 Yale L.J. 1, 101-109

(1948); O'Brian, Changing Attitudes Toward Freedom, 9 Wash. and Lee L. Rev. 157 (1952); Brown and Fassett, Security Tests for Maritime Workers: Due Process Under the Port Security Program, 62 Yale L.J. 1163 (1953); Chafee, The Blessings of Liberty 34-37 (1956); Brown, Loyalty and Security 394-397 (1958); McKay, The Right of Confrontation, 1959 Wash. U.L.Q. 122 (1959); Pollitt, The Right of Confrontation: Its History and Modern Dress, 8 J. Pub. L. 831 (1959); Rauh, Nonconfrontation in Security Cases: The Greene Decision, 45 Va. L. Rev. 1175 (1959). See also Haydock, Some Evidentiary Problems Posed by the Atomic Energy Security Requirements, 61 Harv. L. Rev. 468 (1948); Association of the Bar of the City of New York, The Federal-Loyalty Security Program 174-180 (1956); Krasnowiecki, Confrontation by Witness in Government Employee Security Proceedings, 33 Notre Dame Law. 180 (1958); Subcommittee on Constitutional Rights of the Senate Committee on the Judiciary, Hearings on Security and Constitutional Rights, Parts 3 and 4, 86th Cong., 1st and 2d Sess. (1959); Notes, 104 U. Pa. L. Rev. 703 (1956); 45 Calif. L. Rev. 524 (1957); 19 Mont. L. Rev. 121 (1958); 10 Stan. L. Rev. 335 (1958); 73 Harv. L. Rev. 84, 196-200 (1959); 48 Geo. L.J. 576 (1960); 44 Minn. L. Rev. 771 (1960).

For particular discussion of the Cafeteria Workers case see Bickel, Foreword: The Passive Virtues, 75 Harv. L. Rev. 40, 71-74 (1961); Notes, 36 N.Y.U.L. Rev. 506 (1961); 36 Notre Dame Law. 576 (1961).

2. Other cases in which the Supreme Court has considered the problem of undisclosed evidence and lack of confrontation in situations involving national security include Knauff v. Shaughnessy, 338 U.S. 537, 70 S. Ct. 309, 94 L. Ed. 317 (1950) (upholding non-disclosure of evidence to alien seeking entry), Justices Jackson, Black, and Frankfurter dissenting; Shaughnessy v. Mezei, 345 U.S. 206, 73 S. Ct. 625, 97 L. Ed. 956 (1953) (same), Justices Black, Jackson, Frankfurter, and Douglas dissenting; Jay v. Boyd, 351 U.S. 345, 76 S. Ct. 919, 100 L. Ed. 1242 (1956) (upholding non-disclosure on issue of suspension of deportation), Mr. Chief Justice Warren and Justices Black, Frankfurter, and Douglas dissenting. See also the passport cases cited in Chapter XI. With respect to the problem of disclosing F.B.I. reports upon which Selective Service Boards act in determining the draft status of persons claiming to be conscientious objectors, see United States v. Nugent, 346 U.S. 1, 73 S. Ct. 991, 97 L. Ed. 1417 (1953) (Board must give draftee a fair résumé of the report); Simmons v. United States, 348 U.S. 397, 75 S. Ct. 397, 99 L. Ed. 453 (1955); Gonzales v. United States, 348 U.S. 407, 75 S. Ct. 409, 99 L. Ed. 467 (1955); Gonzales v. United States, 364 U.S. 59, 80 S. Ct. 1554, 4 L. Ed. 2d 1569 (1960). See Notes, 50 Nw. U.L. Rev. 660, 669-676 (1955); 24 Ind. L.J. 441, 445-451 (1959).

In Garrott v. United States, 340 F.2d 615 (Ct. Cl. 1965), the Court of Claims held that a former employee, discharged on loyalty grounds, was entitled to a trial type hearing in proceedings under 5 U.S.C. §2283 to terminate his annuity rights on grounds of false statements and concealment of material facts relating to his affiliation with the Communist Party. The decision was based on the ground that the statute required such a hearing; the court did not reach the constitutional issues. But cf. Bennett v. United States, 356 F.2d 525 (Ct. Cl. 1966).

Cases raising the issue as to dismissal of government employees, but where the ground for withholding the evidence or confrontation was not national security, include Money v. Anderson, 208 F.2d 34 (D.C. Cir. 1953); Ellmore v. Brucker, 236 F.2d 734 (D.C. Cir. 1956); Beard v. Stahr, 200 F. Supp. 766 (D. D.C. 1961), complaint dismissed on ground suit was premature, 370 U.S. 41, 82 S. Ct. 1105, 8 L. Ed. 2d 321 (1962); see also Williams v. Zuckert, 296 F.2d 416 (D.C. Cir. 1961), aff'd, 371 U.S. 531, 83 S. Ct. 403, 9 L. Ed. 2d 486 (1963), rev'd on petition for rehearing, 372 U.S. 765, 83 S. Ct. 1102, 10 L. Ed. 136 (1963).

For discussion of the secret evidence and confrontation issues in areas beyond that of national security see, in addition to the McKay and Pollitt articles, cited above, Davis,

Administrative Law Treatise, ch. 7 (1958); Carrow, Governmental Nondisclosure in Judicial Proceedings, 107 U. Pa. L. Rev. 166 (1958); Newman, The Process of Prescribing "Due Process," 49 Calif. L. Rev. 215 (1961); Notes, 48 Geo. L.J. 576 (1960); 12 Syracuse L. Rev. 206 (1961).

3. The Democratic Party Platform in the 1960 election stated: "We shall provide full and fair hearing including confrontation of the accuser to any person whose public or private employment or reputation is jeopardized by a loyalty or security proceeding."

4. For a recent case, in which the court held the Government to strict standards of procedure in dismissing an employee, see Scott v. Macy, 349 F.2d 182 (D.C. Cir. 1965), discussed in Note, 66 Colum. L. Rev. 719 (1966).

NOTES

1. Some months after the Supreme Court's decision in Greene v. McElroy, President Eisenhower issued Executive Order 10865 prescribing more detailed standards and procedures in the industrial security program. 25 Fed. Reg. 1583 (1960), amended by Executive Order 10909, 26 Fed. Reg. 508 (1961), set forth as amended in BNA, Manual of Government Security and Loyalty 24:11. The procedural provisions of the order specify that the applicant for clearance must be given (1) a written statement of the reasons for denying clearance "as comprehensive and detailed as the national security permits"; (2) "a reasonable opportunity to reply in writing"; (3) an opportunity to appear personally and "to present evidence in his behalf"; (4) a reasonable time to prepare; (5) an opportunity to be represented by counsel; (6) "an opportunity to cross-examine persons either orally or through written interrogatories in accordance with Section 4 on matters not relating to the characterization in the statement of reasons of any organization or individual other than the applicant"; (7) a written notice of the final decision which, if adverse, "shall specify whether [the deciding official] found for or against him with respect to each allegation in the statement of reasons." §3. Section 4 provides:

"(A) An applicant shall be afforded an opportunity to cross-examine persons who have made oral or written statements adverse to the applicant relating to a controverted issue except that any such statement may be received and considered without affording such opportunity in the circumstances described in either of the following paragraphs:

"(1) The head of the department supplying the statement certifies that the person who furnished the information is a confidential informant who has been engaged in obtaining intelligence information for the government and that disclosure of his identity would be substantially harmful to the national interest.

"(2) The head of the department concerned or his special designee for that particular purpose has preliminarily determined, after considering information furnished by the investigative agency involved as to the reliability of the person and the accuracy of the statement concerned, that the statement concerned appears to be reliable and material, and the head of the department or such special designee has determined that failure to receive and consider such statement would, in view of the level of access sought, be substantially harmful to the national security and that the person who furnished the information cannot appear to testify:

"(a) due to death, severe illness, or similar cause, in which case the identity of the person and the information to be considered shall be made
available to the applicant, or

"(b) due to some other cause determined by the head of the department to
be good and sufficient.

"(B) Whenever procedures under paragraphs (1) or (2) of subsection (A) of
this section are used:

"(1) The applicant shall be given a summary of the information which shall be
as comprehensive and detailed as the national security permits,

"(2) Appropriate consideration shall be accorded to the fact that the applicant
did not have an opportunity to cross-examine such persons or person, and

"(3) A final determination adverse to the applicant shall be made only by the
head of the department based upon his personal review of the case."

Section 5 provides for making available to the applicant "a summary or description" of classified records, other than investigative reports, "to the extent that
national security permits." And Section 6 requires the agency, "so far as national
security permits," to identify persons who have made adverse statements and assist
the applicant in making such persons available for cross-examination.

Qualifying the above procedures, Section 9 provides:

"Nothing contained in this order shall be deemed to limit or affect the responsibility and powers of the head of a department to deny or revoke access to a specific
classification category if the security of the nation so requires. Such authority may
not be delegated and may be exercised only when the head of a department determines that the procedures prescribed in Sections 3, 4, and 5 cannot be invoked
consistently with the national security and such determination shall be conclusive."

No cases challenging the constitutionality of the new procedures have reached
the Supreme Court or apparently been the subject of lower court decision. For
discussion of Executive Order 10865, see Subcommittee on Constitutional Rights
of the Senate Committee on the Judiciary, Hearings on Security and Constitutional Rights, Pt. 4, 1998-2007, 2228-2242 (86th Cong., 2d Sess., 1959); Note,
New Procedures for Industrial Security Hearings, 28 Geo. Wash. L. Rev. 886
(1960).

2. Following Parker v. Lester the Coast Guard also amended its regulations,
both as to service on vessels and access to waterfront facilities. 33 C.F.R. pts. 121
and 125; BNA, Manual of Government Security and Loyalty 51:41 and 51:51. The
new regulations contain detailed provisions giving the right to notice, answer,
representation by counsel, presentation of evidence, and cross-examination. The
Government is required to make "every effort" to produce adverse witnesses for
confrontation and cross-examination. However, the use of secret evidence and nonconfrontation is not excluded: "The Board shall reach its conclusion and base its
determination on information presented at the hearing, together with such information as may have been developed through investigations and inquiries or made
available by the applicant or holder." 33 C.F.R. §§121:19 and 125:43.

In McBride v. Roland, 248 F. Supp. 459 (S.D. N.Y. 1965), a case where the
court found no indication that evidence outside the record had been used in
denying clearance to a seaman, constitutional objections to the Coast Guard regulations were rejected, as was the contention that the program was not based on
statutory authority. Other cases decided under the port security program after

Greene v. McElroy have ruled against the Coast Guard on the ground no hearing was afforded. Graham v. Richmond, 272 F.2d 517 (D.C. Cir. 1959), and Homer v. Richmond, 292 F.2d 719 (D.C. Cir. 1961).

3. There were also some changes, after Greene v. McElroy, in the loyalty-security programs affecting government employees. Thus the Atomic Energy Commission amended its regulations on April 30, 1962, to grant employees and applicants for employment rights similar to those embodied in Executive Order 10865, the first federal agency to do so. 27 Fed. Reg. 4324; N.Y. Times, May 1, 1962. And the Court of Appeals of the District of Columbia, in two cases involving naval reservists given less than honorable discharges on security grounds, without passing on constitutional issues, invalidated proceedings which did not afford confrontation and cross-examination. Bland v. Connally, 293 F.2d 852 (D.C. Cir. 1961); Davis v. Stahr, 293 F.2d 860 (D.C. Cir. 1961).

4. Apart from issues of secret evidence, confrontation and cross-examination, the courts have from the beginning of the loyalty program frequently ruled in favor of the employee or applicant on non-constitutional procedural grounds. See the Peters, Service, Vitarelli, and Kutcher cases, supra. See also Deak v. Pace, 185 F.2d 997 (D.C. Cir. 1950) (charges not sufficiently specific to satisfy requirements of applicable statute); Burrell v. Martin, 232 F.2d 33 (D.C. Cir. 1955) (discharge after protracted proceedings reversed for inadequate findings); Haynes v. Thomas, 232 F.2d 688 (D.C. Cir. 1956) (failure to follow statutory procedure); Coleman v. Brucker, 257 F.2d 661 (D.C. Cir. 1958) (discharge of six employees at Fort Monmouth, growing out of McCarthy hearings, reversed for failure of Army to follow its own regulations); Spector v. McElroy, 269 F.2d 242 (D.C. Cir. 1959) (failure to furnish employee copy of hearing board's conclusion, contrary to regulations).

REFERENCES

1. On the lack of procedural protections for temporary or probationary employees, or employees not in the classified civil service see, in addition to the Vitarelli case, supra, Nadelhaft v. United States, 131 F. Supp. 930 (Ct. Cl. 1955); Harrison v. McNamara, 228 F. Supp. 406 (D. Conn. 1964), aff'd, 360 U.S. 261 (1965); Bennett v. United States, 356 F.2d 525 (Ct. Cl. 1966). Cf. Haynes v. Thomas, supra.

2. The Attorney General's list of subversive organizations, prepared in connection with the loyalty program, may be found in BNA, Manual of Government Security and Loyalty 15:112-119; House Committee on Un-American Activities, Guide to Subversive Organizations and Publications, App. II (1961). For the background and development of the Attorney General's list see Bontecou, The Federal Loyalty-Security Program, ch. V (1953); Report of the Commission on Government Security 645-652 (1957). Generally, see Gellhorn, Security, Loyalty, and Science 134-143 (1950); Hearings before the Subcommittee on Constitutional Rights, supra, 252-296; Report of the Senate Committee on Post Office and Civil Service, Administration of the Federal Employees' Security Program, Sen. Rep. No. 2750, 84th Cong., 2d Sess., pp. 221-229 (1956); Notes, 44 Calif. L. Rev. 748; 29 Temple L.Q. 95 (1955); 42 Geo. L.J. 401 (1954).

e. Administration

The results of the loyalty-security programs, in terms of the number of employees dismissed or denied clearance and the number of applicants rejected, are difficult of determination. The figures on the operation of the loyalty program for federal employees under the Truman Order (Executive Order 9835) from its inception in March 1947 to the issuance of the Eisenhower Order in April 1953 have been given by the Civil Service Commission as follows:

"In the course of the program, 4,756,705 loyalty forms on individuals were checked with the files of the Federal Bureau of Investigation and with other records and sources as appropriate. Of the total, 1,787,188 forms related to 'incumbent' employees, i.e., persons on the rolls October 1, 1947, and 2,969,517 forms related to persons subsequently appointed or considered for appointment.

"Whenever a question of loyalty was revealed by these checks, an investigation was scheduled. In all, reports of investigation on 26,236 persons were referred to appropriate boards for consideration — the cases of 101 persons under investigation when the program began and 26,135 investigated thereafter by the Federal Bureau of Investigation. During the consideration of these cases, loyalty boards issued 12,859 interrogatories and letters of charges and held 4,119 hearings.

"The results of action by agencies, by regional boards of the Commission, and by the Loyalty Review Board on the cases of the 26,236 employees, new appointees, and applicants were as follows: 16,503 persons were cleared by favorable decisions on loyalty, including 252 on appeal; 560 persons were removed or denied Federal employment on grounds relating to loyalty; proceeding were discontinued in 6,828 cases because these persons left the service or withdrew their applications — 1,192 after they had been sent interrogatories or charges; and the cases of 569 persons were considered by the Department of the Army solely under security laws. Loyalty proceedings involving the remaining 1,776 persons were incomplete when the program was terminated; these cases were therefore to be decided under the provisions of the President's security order." Civil Service Commission, 1953 Annual Report 32.

Other statistics are less available or less helpful. Professor Brown estimates that the number of dismissals on security grounds during the same period, by agencies operating under summary dismissal statutes similar to P.L. 733 was, at "a very rough guess," twice as many as the loyalty dismissals. Brown, Loyalty and Security 57 (1958).

Under the Eisenhower loyalty-security program the figures were clouded by political controversy, and the publication of statistics became known as "the numbers game." The Civil Service Commission announced a total of

8008 dismissals of federal employees for the period May 1953 to October 1954; but these included resignations of employees who happened to have some "derogatory information" in their files, dismissals for security reasons not involving loyalty, and terminations under regular civil service procedures for other causes not under Order 10450. The Johnston Subcommittee, after lengthy investigation, reported that through June 30, 1955 only 343 persons had been dismissed "pursuant to Executive Order 10450." Sen. Rep. No. 2750, 84th Cong., 2d Sess. 371-2. As to applicants, Professor Brown found "little meaningful information." See Brown, id. at 54-60.

With respect to the operation up to 1958 of all the loyalty-security programs — federal, state and private — Professor Brown made a "very rough" estimate of "dismissals, plus denials of clearance or exclusions from a calling that are equivalent to dismissals," as follows:

All federal employees, including military	3,900
Private employees subject to federal programs	5,400
State and local government employees	1,000
Self- and privately employed	1,200
	11,500

See Brown, id. at 181-182, 487-488.

Beginning in 1955 there was a noticeable relaxation of the loyalty-security programs, at least at the higher levels. See Oakes, The Security Issue: A Changing Atmosphere, N.Y. Times Magazine, Aug. 14, 1955, p. 9; Lewis, Security Law Losing Some of Its Rigidity, N.Y. Times, May 13, 1956. On the other hand the Wright Commission, reporting in 1957, recommended adherence to the main features of the program, an extension of its scope in some respects, and greater centralization through the creation of a Central Security Office. See Brown, Regression in the Wright Report, Bull. of the Atomic Scientists, Sept. 1957, p. 253. In substance, the loyalty-security programs have remained relatively unchanged since 1956. However, there have been some modifications in the direction of affording individuals under investigation greater procedural protections, particularly, as noted above, after the Supreme Court's decision in Greene v. McElroy. Statistics on the number of persons disqualified under the programs since 1958 do not appear available.

The effect of the loyalty-security programs in terms of their value for national security, impact upon the morale of the government service, influence upon scientific advancement, effect upon freedom of political expression generally, and other ramifications, has been the subject of much controversy. The programs have been held necessary and justified by the executive branch of the government, by various legislative committees, and by individuals or groups such as the Commission on Government Security. They have been criticized in some aspects by observers, such as the Special Committee of the Association of the Bar of the City of New York. And they have been severely criticized by other individuals and groups. Some of the literature appraising the programs and discussing various aspects of their administration is set forth below.

REFERENCES

1. For other analyses of the statistical results of the loyalty-security programs, see Report of the Senate Committee on Post Office and Civil Service, Administration of the Federal Employees' Security Program, Sen. Rep. No. 2750, 84th Cong., 2d Sess. 364-386 (1956); Association of the Bar of the City of New York, The Federal Loyalty-Security Program 114-117, 219-226 (1956); Rackow, The Federal Loyalty Program: Politics and Civil Liberty, 12 W. Res. L. Rev. 701, 718-722 (1961); Green, Q-Clearance: The Development of a Personnel Security Program, Bull. of the Atomic Scientists, May 1964, p. 9 (summarizing the results of the Atomic Energy Program through 1963).

2. On the question of investigations and initial evaluation of data, see Brown, Loyalty and Security 24-30 (1958); Brown, The Operation of Personnel Security Programs, 300 Annals of the Am. Acad. of Pol. and Soc. Sci. 94 (1955); Bontecou, The Federal Loyalty-Security Program, ch. III (1953); Bontecou, Due Process in Security Dismissals, 300 Annals of the Am. Acad. of Pol. and Soc. Sci. 102 (1955); Association of the Bar of the City of New York, The Federal Loyalty-Security Program 85-94 (1956); Goudsmit, The Task of the Security Officer, Bull. of the Atomic Scientists, April 1955, p. 145; Fellman, The Loyalty Defendants, 1957 Wis. L. Rev. 4, 19-21; BNA, Manual of Government Security and Loyalty 11:8-28, 15:701-712, 71:2-3.

3. For discussion of the procedure at hearings and appeals see Brown, id. at 41-8; Civil Service Handbook, Guides for Members of Security Hearing Boards Under Executive Order 10450, printed in BNA, id. at 15:569-584; Trial of a Loyalty or Security Case, id. at 71:1-17; Association of the Bar of the City of New York, id. at 94-103; Gressman, So You're Having a Loyalty Hearing, The New Republic, April 14, 1952, p. 10; Bontecou, The Federal Loyalty-Security Program, ch. II (1953); Bontecou, Due Process in Security Dismissals, 300 Annals of the Am. Acad. of Pol. and Soc. Sci. 102 (1955); Yarmolinsky, How a Lawyer Conducts a Security Case, The Reporter, Mar. 2, 1954, p. 18; Garrison, Some Observations on the Loyalty-Security Program, 23 U. Chi. L. Rev. 1 (1955); Stein, The Defense of Army Security Risk Cases, 4 St. Louis U.L.J. 34 (1956); Symposium, Federal Loyalty-Security Programs, 18 Ohio St. L.J. 283 (1957), especially Day, Problems of Trial Practice in Loyalty and Security Cases, 18 Ohio St. L.J. 359.

On the work of the Loyalty Review Board, which functioned under the Truman Order, see Seasongood and Strecker, The Loyalty Review Board, 25 U. Cinc. L. Rev. 1 (1956). Mr. Seasongood was a member of the Loyalty Review Board.

Accounts of actual hearings, including a recital of some of the questions asked, may be found in the case studies cited above; Emerson and Helfeld, Loyalty Among Government Employees, 58 Yale L.J. 1, 73-75; Arnold, The Case Against the Federal Loyalty Program in The Strengthening of American Political Institutions 62-70 (Cornell U. Press, 1949); Rogge, Our Vanishing Civil Liberties (1949); Gellhorn, Security, Loyalty, and Science, ch. VI (1950); Barth, The Loyalty of Free Men, ch. V (1951); Biddle, The Fear of Freedom 219-235 (1951); Bontecou, The Loyalty-Security Program, ch. IV (1953). See also the description by Edward U. Condon, former Director of the Bureau of Standards, of the various proceedings involving him. Time to Stop Baiting Scientists, Bull. of the Atomic Scientists, Feb. 1958, p. 80.

With respect to the problem of repeated investigations and hearings concerning the same emp'oyee, see Note, Res Judicata in the Federal Loyalty Program, 20 U. Chi. L. Rev. 570 (1953); Blumrosen, Repeated Federal Employee Security Adjudications, 1 Wayne L. Rev. 77 (1955).

4. With respect to the role of the F.B.I. in loyalty investigations see, for a favorable view, Hoover, A Comment on the Article "Loyalty Among Government Employees," 58 Yale L.J. 401 (1949); Hoover, Civil Liberties and Law Enforcement: The Role of the FBI, 37 Iowa L. Rev. 175 (1952); Hoover, Role of the F.B.I. in the Federal Employee Security Program, 49 Nw. U. L. Rev. 333 (1954); Hoover, The Confidential Nature of FBI Reports, 8 Syracuse L. Rev. 2 (1956); Whitehead, The FBI Story, ch. 30 (1956). For criticism of the FBI see Emerson and Helfeld, Loyalty Among Government Employees, 58 Yale L.J. 1, 70-72 (1948); Rauh, Informers, G-Men, and Free Men, The Progressive, May 1950, p. 9; Report on Certain Alleged Practices of the FBI, 10 Law. Guild Rev. 185 (1950); Barth, The Loyalty of Free Men, ch. VII (1951); Barth, How Good is an FBI Report? Harper's Magazine, March 1954, p. 25; McKay, The Right of Confrontation, 1959 Wash. U.L.Q. 122, 148-155.

On the history and operation of the F.B.I. generally see, for favorable materials, Whitehead, The FBI Story (1956); Hoover, Masters of Deceit (1958), articles in 44 A.B.A.J. 1155 (1958), 46 A.B.A.J. 835 (1960), 12 Syracuse L. Rev. 1 (1960), 36 Notre Dame Law. 158 (1961), 48 A.B.A.J. 117 (1962), and interview in U.S. News & World Report, Dec. 21, 1964, p. 36; Mowery, War on the G-Man, Newark Star-Ledger, Feb. 1-9, 1959, reprinted as Sen. Doc. 23, 86th Cong., 1st Session (1959); Tully, The FBI's Most Famous Cases (1965). Materials from a more critical viewpoint include Lowenthal, The Federal Bureau of Investigation (1950); Cook, The FBI, The Nation, Oct. 18, 1958, p. 221, and The FBI Nobody Knows (1964); New York Post, J. Edgar Hoover and the FBI, originally published Oct. 7-20, 1959, and reprinted in slightly different form in The Progressive, Dec. 1959, p. 26, Jan. 1960, p. 20, and Feb. 1960, p. 24; Levine, Hoover and the Red Scare, The Nation, Oct. 20, 1962, p. 232 (by a former F.B.I. agent); Wechsler, The Decline of J. Edgar Hoover, The Progressive, Jan. 1965, p. 12. See also Phelan, Hoover of the FBI, Saturday Evening Post, Sept. 25, 1965, p. 23.

5. On the use of informers in the loyalty program, and in the administration of other security measures, see Bontecou, The Federal Loyalty-Security Program 131-135 (1953); Donner, The Informer, The Nation, April 10, 1954, p. 298; Hoover, The Confidential Nature of FBI Reports, 8 Syracuse L. Rev. 2 (1956); Paid Informers in the U.S. — They're Used All the Time, U.S. News and World Report, Feb. 18, 1955; Packer, Ex-Communist Witnesses: Four Studies in Fact Finding (1962) (dealing with Whittaker Chambers, Elizabeth Bentley, Louis F. Budenz and John Lautner).

In August, 1955, the Department of Justice stated that it had paid 47 undercover informants a total of $43,000 in fees and expenses from July 1, 1953 through April 15, 1955. The highest paid individual was John Lautner, former Communist, who had received $16,000. Paul Crouch received $1,579.65 and Harvey Matusow $2,100 for the fiscal year 1954. N.Y. Times, Aug. 24, 1955.

In 1962, Jack Levine, former Special Agent in the F.B.I., asserted: "Today, the FBI has nearly 1,500 informants in the Communist Party — a ratio of one informant for every 5.7 members." Levine, Hoover and the Red Scare, The Nation, Oct. 20, 1962, p. 232 at 233.

A number of the informers used by the Government in political cases subsequently recanted or were otherwise discredited. The best known of these — Harvey Matusow — has recorded his story in False Witness (1955). For a different version see Report of the Internal Security Subcommittee of the Senate Committee on the Judiciary, Strategy and Tactics of World Communism (Significance of the Matusow Case), 84th Cong., 1st Sess. (1955), reprinted in part in U.S. News and World Report, Jan. 13, 1956, p. 114. In 1955 Matusow, after signing an affidavit that his testimony in the Jencks case was false, was sentenced to three years in prison by the trial judge for contempt of court. N.Y. Times, Mar. 13 and 17, 1955. This was reversed by the Court of Appeals. Matusow v. United States, 229 F.2d 335 (5th Cir. 1956). In 1956 Matusow was convicted of perjury in New York for stating that Roy Cohn, one of the prosecuting attorneys in the Flynn case under the Smith Act, had suborned him to testify falsely in the case; he was sentenced to five years in prison. N.Y. Times, Sept. 29, 1956. This conviction was affirmed. United States v. Matusow, 244 F.2d 532 (2d Cir. 1957), cert. den., 354 U.S. 942 (1957). As a result of the Matusow recantation, however, the conviction of two defendants in the Flynn case was set aside. 130 F. Supp. 412 (S.D. N.Y. 1955), Section C, subsection 2, supra. See also on the Matusow affair, Goodman, Who Promoted Matusow? The New Republic, Mar. 7, 1955, p. 12; Weissman, Harvey Matusow and the Role of the Prosecutors in United States v. Flynn, 15 Law. Guild Rev. 103 (1955).

On the case of Paul Crouch, another turnabout witness, see N.Y. Times, July 9, 1954; Shelton, Paul Crouch, Informer, The New Republic, July 19, 1954. With respect to Joseph D. Mazzei, see Mesarosh v. United States, 352 U.S. 1, 77 S. Ct. 1, 1 L. Ed. 2d 1 (1956), discussed in Section C, subsection 2, supra. On Manning Johnson, as well as Matusow and Crouch, see the reversal in Communist Party v. Subversive Activities Control Board, 351 U.S. 115, 76 S. Ct. 663, 100 L. Ed. 1003 (1956), and subsequent proceedings, Section C, subsection 3, supra.

In support of the use of informers see Krasilovsky, Elevating the Role of the Informer: The Value of Secret Information, 40 A.B.A.J. 603 (1954); Interview with Herbert Brownell, Jr., Shall Doors Be Opened To Spies and Subversives? U.S. News and World Report, April 29, 1955, p. 54; report of speech by Assistant Attorney General Warren Olney 3d, N.Y. Times, July 24, 1954; extracts of speeches by F.B.I. Director J. Edgar Hoover and Assistant Attorney General William F. Tompkins, U.S. News and World Report, Oct. 14, 1955, pp. 106, 107; Malachi and Cross, The Informer in Law Enforcement (1960). For criticism of the manner in which informers were being used in political cases see Chafee, Spies into Heroes, The Nation, June 28, 1952, p. 618, reprinted in part in The Blessings of Liberty, 95-97 (1956); Rovere, The Kept Witness, Harper's Magazine, May 1955, p. 25.

On the legal aspects of the problem see Donnelly, Judicial Control of Informants, Spies, Stool Pigeons, and Agents Provocateurs, 60 Yale L.J. 1091 (1951); Note, An Informer's Tale: Its Use in Judicial and Administrative Proceedings, 63 Yale L.J. 206 (1953); Note, Concealment of an Informant's Identity — A Governmental Privilege, 1959 Wash. U.L.Q. 296; Dubin, The Informer's Privilege Versus the Constitution: A Doctrinal Dilemma, 50 J. Crim. L. 554 (1960).

6. With respect to the use of mail covers, lie detector tests, and similar practices by Government agencies, see the materials on the right of privacy, Chapter X.

7. On the quality of security personnel see Fellman, The Loyalty Defendants, 1957 Wis. L. Rev. 4, 32-33; Brown, Loyalty and Security 27-28 (1958).

8. False statements made by applicants in connection with loyalty-security proceedings have been held to be valid grounds for dismissal or refusal of clearance. See, e.g., Garvin v. Gilliland, 141 F. Supp. 394 (D. D.C. 1956); Harrison v. McNamara, 228 F. Supp. 406 (D. Conn. 1964), aff'd, 380 U.S. 261 (1965). Note also the proceedings before the Atomic Energy Commission involving Dr. J. Robert Oppenheimer, referred to above.

Alleged false statements have also been grounds for prosecution under the False Claims Act, 18 U.S.C. §1001. See, e.g., Marzani v. United States, 168 F.2d 133, 141 (D.C. Cir. 1948), aff'd by an equally divided court, 335 U.S. 895 (1948), 336 U.S. 922 (1949); United States v. Mamber, 127 F. Supp. 925 (D. Mass. 1955); United States v. Giarraputo, 140 F. Supp. 831 (E.D. N.Y. 1965); Pitts v. United States, 263 F.2d 353 (9th Cir. 1959), cert. den., 360 U.S. 935 (1960); Ogden v. United States, 303 F.2d 724 (9th Cir. 1962), 323 F.2d 818 (9th Cir. 1963), cert. den., 376 U.S. 973 (1964). See also Digest of the Public Record of Communism in the United States (Fund for the Republic 1955), 78-79, 88; the Johnston report, Administration of the Federal Employees' Security Program, Sen. Rep. No. 2750, 84th Cong. 2d Sess. (1956), 99-104. With respect to the indictment of Val Lorwin, later dismissed by the Department of Justice as having been obtained by misrepresentation, see N.Y. Times, Dec. 5, 1953 and May 26, 1954.

9. Employees improperly dismissed or refused clearance under the loyalty security

programs have normally succeeded in recovering back salary. See, e.g., Leiner v. United States, 181 F. Supp. 400 (Ct. Cl. 1958); Greene v. United States, 376 U.S. 149, 84 S. Ct. 615, 11 L. Ed. 2d 576 (1964), noted supra. But cf. Dupree v. United States, 247 F.2d 819 (3d Cir. 1957), 264 F.2d 140 (3d Cir. 1959), cert. den., 361 U.S. 823 (1959) (suits under Federal Tort Claims Act unsuccessful). For additional cases, see BNA, Manual of Government Security and Loyalty, ch. 19.

With respect to suits by employees for alleged defamatory statements made to government investigators, see Foltz v. Moore McCormack Lines, 189 F.2d 537 (2d Cir. 1951), cert. den., 342 U.S. 871 (1951), lower court decision noted in 51 Colum. L. Rev. 244 (1951); Jackson v. Allen Industries, 250 F.2d 629 (6th Cir. 1958), cert. den., 356 U.S. 972 (1958).

10. For one comment on the political pressures that affected the administration of the loyalty-security programs in the 1950's, see the address of President Truman to the National Civil Service League, N.Y. Times, May 3, 1952:

"The loyalty program was designed to protect innocent employes as well as the Government. When I set it up, I intended it to expose the guilty and at the same time to safeguard the rights and the reputations of those who were innocent. But I have become increasingly concerned in recent months by attempts to use the loyalty program as a club with which to beat Government employes over the head.

"Political gangsters are attempting to pervert the program into an instrument of intimidation and blackmail, to coerce or destroy any who dare oppose them. These men and those who abet them have besmirched the reputations of decent, loyal public servants. They have not hesitated to lie, under cover of Congressional immunity, of course, and to repeat the lies again and again.

"This is a matter for great concern. These tactics contain the seeds of tyranny. Can we be sure that people who employ such tactics are really loyal to our form of Government, with its Bill of Rights and its tradition of individual liberty? The fact is that they are breaking these things down. They are undermining the foundation stones of our Constitution. I believe such men betray our country and all it stands for. I believe they are as grave a menace as the Communists."

Other material which gives some insight into the atmosphere of the loyalty program in the 1950's includes the remarks of Chairman Bingham of the Loyalty Review Board, reported in State Department Lax on Loyalty Cases? U.S. News and World Report, Feb. 8, 1952, p. 18; Marder, The Fort Monmouth Story, Bull. of the Atomic Scientists, January 1954, p. 21; McLeod, We're Cleaning Up "The Mess" in the State Department, U.S. News and World Report, Feb. 12, 1954, p. 62; Goudsmit, The Task of the Security Officer, Bull. of the Atomic Scientists, April 1955, p. 145; Morgenthau, Government Administration and Security, Current History, October 1955, p. 210; Brown, id. at ch. 15. For further material, in addition to the major studies already cited, see Richardson, The Federal Employee Loyalty Program, 51 Colum. L. Rev. 546, 553-554 (1951); Interview with Hiram Bingham: Catching the Disloyal, U.S. News and World Report, Nov. 23, 1951, p. 22; a series of three articles in the N.Y. Times by W. H. Lawrence, beginning April 13, 1953; Jahoda, Morale in the Federal Service, 300 Annals of the Am. Acad. of Pol. and Soc. Sci. 110 (1955); and materials cited in Fellman, The Loyalty Defendants, 1957 Wis. L. Rev. 4, 33-35. A recent appraisal of the industrial security program may be found in Miller, The Economics of Industrial Security: A Legal Analysis, 22 Fed. B.J. 242 (1962).

With respect to the problems of the State Department see the statement by five former diplomats, N.Y. Times, Jan. 17, 1954; statement by George F. Kennan, N.Y. Times, Feb. 22, 1953; reply by Secretary of State Dulles, N.Y. Times, Feb. 28, 1953; Clubb, National Security and Our Foreign Service, The Nation, Dec. 25, 1954, p. 544; Morgenthau, The Impact of Loyalty-Security Measures on the State Department, Bull. of the Atomic Scientists, April 1955, p. 134; Fosdick, For the Foreign Service — Help Wanted,

N.Y. Times Magazine, Nov. 20, 1955, p. 13; Hearings before the Subcommittee on Constitutional Rights of the Senate Committee on the Judiciary, Security and Constitutional Rights, 86th Cong., 1st Sess. 983-985 (1959).

Concerning the effect of the loyalty-security programs on science, see Gellhorn, Security, Loyalty, and Science (1950); Mather, Scientist in the Doghouse, The Nation, June 28, 1952. p. 638; Bush, If We Alienate Our Scientist, N.Y. Times Magazine, June 13, 1954, p. 9; statement of Dr. Bush, N.Y. Times, Oct. 19, 1954; Shils, Security and Science Sacrificed to Loyalty, Bull. of the Atomic Scientists, April 1955, p. 106; Beckerly, The Impact of Government Information and Security Controls on Competitive Industry, Bull. of the Atomic Scientists, April 1955, p. 123; Livingston, Science and Security, 300 Annals of the Am. Acad. of Pol. and Soc. Sci. 4 (1955); letters of 16 American scientists who had received Nobel prizes, reported in N.Y. Times, June 15, 1959; statement of Dr. J. Robert Oppenheimer upon receiving the Enrico Fermi award, N.Y. Times, Apr. 6, 1963.

For social science studies of the impact of the loyalty programs see Jahoda and Cook, Security Measures and Freedom of Thought: An Exploratory Study of the Impact of Loyalty and Security Programs, 61 Yale L.J. 295 (1952); Committee on Social Issues of the Group for the Advancement of Psychiatry, Considerations Regarding the Loyalty Oath as a Manifestation of Current Social Tension and Anxiety (Oct. 1954); Kaufman and Kaufman, Some Problems of Treatment Arising from the Federal Loyalty and Security Program, 25 Am. J. of Orthopsychiatry 813 (1955).

11. Numerous proposals for reform of the federal loyalty programs have been advanced from time to time. See the major studies and other articles cited above. See also the proposals made by the Sixth American Assembly at Arden House, N.Y. Times, Oct. 11, 1954; Mankiewicz, Mangum and Moody, Federal Loyalty-Security Program: A Proposed Statute, 44 Calif. L. Rev. 72 (1956); proposals made by the League of Women Voters, reported in American Civil Liberties Weekly Bull., April 21, 1958.

2. *State and Local Loyalty Programs*

Prior to the Second World War state legislation imposing loyalty qualifications as a condition of state employment took the form mainly of teachers' oath laws. After the war, however, there was a rapid development in state laws requiring loyalty oaths or tests for state employees generally. At the present time such laws exist in 32 states: Alabama, Alaska, Arizona, Arkansas, California, Florida, Georgia, Hawaii, Idaho, Illinois, Indiana, Kansas, Louisiana, Maryland, Massachusetts, Michigan, Minnesota, Mississippi, Nebraska, New Hampshire, New Jersey, New Mexico, New York, Ohio, Oklahoma, Oregon, Pennsylvania, South Dakota, Texas, Utah, Washington, and Wyoming. Five other states — Colorado, Montana, South Carolina, Tennessee, and Vermont — have loyalty requirements applicable only to teachers. In 43 states there are loyalty qualifications for Civil Defense Workers.

These laws may take the form of test oaths or administative programs, or a combination of the two. The oaths imposed usually require the employee to swear that he does not advocate the overthrow of government by force or belong to an organization that does. Sometimes they cover past and often future conduct. Others go further. Thus the Georgia oath includes the statement "that I am not a member of the Communist Party and that I have no sympathy for the doctrines of communism and will not lend my aid, my support, my advice, my counsel nor my influence to the Communist Party or to the teachings of communism." Geo. Code Ann. §89-313. The Texas law includes in the oath a statement that "the affiant is not, and, during the preceding five year period, has not been, a member of any organization" on the Attorney General's list or registered under the Internal Security Act of 1950. Tex. Ann. Stat. tit. 110A, art. 6252-7, §1.

The statutes providing for an administrative program vary. Some laws contain little detail and no machinery. The Maryland Ober law, typical of others, has an elaborate definition of the "subversive persons" excluded and provides that the appointing authorities shall establish rules to ascertain, before persons are appointed, that "there are no reasonable grounds to believe such persons are subversive persons." Md. Ann. Code Gen. Laws, art. 85A, §§1, 11.

The sanctions provided by these statutes, in addition to ineligibility for obtaining or retaining government employment, normally include perjury and sometimes additional criminal penalties. Some statutes, such as in Florida (Fla. Stat. §876.08), also provide criminal penalties for any state official who "knowingly or carelessly" allows a subordinate to retain a position in violation of law. With some exceptions, however, the state programs do not include the general check and intensive investigations that characterize the federal program.

The first cases in which the state loyalty programs were considered by the Supreme Court were Gerende v. Board of Supervisors, printed in Section D, subsection 6, supra, and the Garner case, printed below.

REFERENCES

1. A digest of the state laws as they existed in 1964 is contained in Internal Security and Subversion: Principal State Laws and Cases, A Study prepared for the Subcommittee to Investigate the Administration of the Internal Security Act and Other Internal Security Laws of the Senate Committee on the Judiciary, by the Legislative Reference Service, Library of Congress, 89th Cong., 1st Sess. (1965). For an earlier compilation see Digest of the Public Record of Communism in the United States 347-382 (Fund for the Republic 1955). See also Prendergast, State Legislatures and Communism: The Current Scene, 44 Am. Pol. Sci. Rev. 556 (1950); Gellhorn, The States and Subversion, Apps. A and B (1952).

2. For a good summary of the state laws see Brown, Loyalty and Security 92-109, 405-408 (1958). An account of the operation of the Pennsylvania Pechan Act may be found in Byse, A Report on the Pennsylvania Loyalty Act, 101 U. Pa. L. Rev. 480 (1953); and of the Los Angeles program in Horowitz, Report on the Los Angeles City and County Loyalty Programs, 5 Stan. L. Rev. 233 (1953). See also, for an analysis of the Pennsylvania legislation, Note, 14 U. Pitt. L. Rev. 90 (1952); and of the Ohio legislation, Hill, A Critique of Recent Ohio Anti-Subversive Legislation, 14 Ohio St. L.J. 439 (1953).

The New York Security Risk Law, enacted in 1951 during the Korean War as a temporary measure and renewed yearly, was the subject of an investigation by the Committee on Public Employee Security Procedures, appointed by Governor Harriman in 1956 with Whitelaw Reid as chairman. In the final report issued in January 1958 the Committee stated that of 179,059 persons checked for state employment under the law, 24 were removed, resigned, or were disqualified; and of 165,169 New York City employees investigated, 61 resigned, retired or were dismissed. N.Y. Times, Jan. 16, 1958. The Committee's interim report for 1957 is printed in McKinney's 1957 Session Laws of New York, pp. 1519-1521. In 1960 the law was allowed to expire. N.Y. Times, June 28, 1960.

GARNER v. BOARD OF PUBLIC WORKS
OF LOS ANGELES
341 U.S. 716, 71 S. Ct. 909, 95 L. Ed. 1317 (1951)

Mr. Justice Clark delivered the opinion of the Court.

In 1941 the California Legislature amended the Charter of the City of Los Angeles to provide in part as follows:

". . . no person shall hold or retain or be eligible for any public office or employment in the service of the City of Los Angeles, in any office or department thereof, either elective or appointive, who has within five (5) years prior to the effective date of this section advised, advocated or taught, or who may, after this section becomes effective [April 28, 1941], advise, advocate or teach, or who is now or has been within five (5) years prior to the effective date of this section, or who may, after this section becomes effective, become a member of or affiliated with any group, society, association, organization or party which advises, advocates or teaches, or has, within said period of five (5) years, advised, advocated or taught the overthrow by force or violence of the government of the United States of America or of the State of California.

"In so far as this section may be held by any court of competent jurisdiction not to be self-executing, the City Council is hereby given power and authority to adopt appropriate legislation for the purpose of effectuating the objects hereof." Calif. Stat. 1941, c. 67.

Pursuant to the authority thus conferred the City of Los Angeles in 1948 passed ordinance No. 94,004 requiring every person who held an office or position in the service of the city to take an oath prior to January 6, 1949. In relevant part the oath was as follows: "I further swear (or affirm) that I do not advise, advocate or teach, and have not within the period beginning five (5) years prior to the effective date of the ordinance requiring the making of this oath or affirmation, advised, advocated or taught, the overthrow by force, violence or other unlawful means, of the Government of the United States of America or of the State of California and that I am not now and have not, within said period, been or become a member of or affiliated with any group, society, association, organization or party which advises, advocates or teaches, or has, within said period, advised, advocated or taught, the overthrow by force, violence or other unlawful means of the Government of the United States, or of the State of California. I further swear (or affirm) that I will not, while I am in the service of the City of Los Angeles, advise, advocate or teach, or be or become a member of or affiliated with any group, association, society, organization or party which advises, advocates or teaches, or has within said period, advised, advocated or taught, the overthrow by force, violence or other unlawful means, of the Government of the United States of America or of the State of California . . ."

The ordinance also required every employee to execute an affidavit "stating whether or not he is or ever was a member of the Communist Party of the United States of America or of the Communist Political Association, and if he is or was such a member, stating the dates when he became, and the periods during which he was, such a member. . . ."

On the final date for filing of the oath and affidavit petitioners were civil service employees of the City of Los Angeles. Petitioners Pacifico and Schwartz took the oath but refused to execute the affidavit. The remaining fifteen petitioners refused to do either. All were discharged for such cause, after administrative hearing, as of January 6, 1949. In this action they sue for reinstatement and unpaid salaries. The District Court of Appeal denied relief. 98 Cal. App. 2d 493, 220 P.2d 958 (1950). We granted certiorari, 340 U.S 941 (1951).

Petitioners attack the ordinance as violative of the provision of Art. I, §10 of the Federal Constitution that "No State shall . . . pass any Bill of Attainder [or] ex post facto Law. . . ." They also contend that the ordinance deprives them of freedom of speech and assembly and of the right to petition for redress of grievances.

Petitioners have assumed that the oath and affidavit provisions of the ordinance present similar constitutional considerations and stand or fall together. We think, however, that separate disposition is indicated.

1. The affidavit raises the issue whether the City of Los Angeles is constitutionally forbidden to require that its employees disclose their past or present membership in the Communist Party or the Communist Political Association. Not before us is the question whether the city may determine that an employee's disclosure of such political affiliation justifies his discharge.

We think that a municipal employer is not disabled because it is an agency of the State from inquiring of its employees as to matters that may prove relevant to their fitness and suitability for the public service. Past conduct may well relate to present fitness; past loyalty may have a reasonable relationship to present and future trust. Both are commonly inquired into in determining fitness for both high and low positions in private industry and are not less relevant in public employment. The affidavit requirement is valid.

2. In our view the validity of the oath turns upon the nature of the Charter amendment (1941) and the relation of the ordinance (1948) to this amendment. Immaterial here is any opinion we might have as to the Chapter provision insofar as it purported to apply retrospectively for a five-year period prior to its effective date. We assume that under the Federal Constitution the Charter amendment is valid to the extent that it bars from the city's public service

persons who, subsequent to its adoption in 1941, advise, advocate, or teach the violent overthrow of the Government or who are or become affiliated with any group doing so. The provisions operating thus prospectively were a reasonable regulation to protect the municipal service by establishing an employment qualification of loyalty to the State and the United States. Cf. Gerende v. Board of Supervisors of Elections, 341 U.S. 56 (1951). Likewise, as a regulation of political activity of municipal employees, the amendment was reasonably designed to protect the integrity and competency of the service. This Court has held that Congress may reasonably restrict the political activity of federal civil service employees for such a purpose, United Public Workers v. Mitchell, 330 U.S. 75, 102-103 (1947), and a State is not without power to do as much. . . .

The ordinance would be ex post facto if it imposed punishment for past conduct lawful at the time it was engaged in. Passing for the moment the question whether separation of petitioners from their employment must be considered as punishment, the ordinance clearly is not ex post facto. The activity covered by the oath had been proscribed by the Charter in the same terms, for the same purpose, and to the same effect over seven years before, and two years prior to the period embraced in the oath. Not the law but the fact was posterior.

Bills of attainder are "legislative acts . . . that apply either to named individuals or to easily ascertainable members of a group in such a way as to inflict punishment on them without a judicial trial. . . ." United States v. Lovett, 328 U.S. 303, 315 (1946). Punishment is a prerequisite. See concurring opinion in Lovett, supra, at 318, 324. Whether legislative action curtailing a privilege previously enjoyed amounts to punishment depends upon "the circumstances attending and the causes of the deprivation." Cummings v. Missouri, 4 Wall. 277, 320 (1867). We are unable to conclude that punishment is imposed by a general regulation which merely provides standards of qualification and eligibility for employment.

Cummings v. Missouri, 4 Wall. 277 (1867), and Ex parte Garland, 4 Wall. 333 (1867), the leading cases in this Court applying the federal constitutional prohibitions against bills of attainder, recognized that the guarantees against such legislation have never been intended to preclude legislative definition of standards of qualification for public or professional employment. Carefully distinguishing an instance of legislative "infliction of punishment" from the exercise of "the power of Congress to prescribe qualifications," the Court said in Garland's case: "The legislature may undoubtedly prescribe qualifications for the office, to which he must conform, as it may, where it has exclusive jurisdiction, prescribe qualifications for the pursuit of any of the ordinary avocations of life." 4 Wall. at pages 379-380. See also, Cummings v. Missouri, supra, at 318-319. This doctrine was reaffirmed in Dent v. West Virginia, 129 U.S. 114 (1889), in which Mr. Justice Field, who had written the Cummings and Garland opinions, wrote for a unanimous Court upholding a statute elevating standards of qualification to practice medicine. And in Hawker v. New York, 170 U.S. 189 (1898), the Court upheld a statute forbidding the practice of medicine by any person who had been convicted of a felony. Both Dent and Hawker distinguished the Cummings and Garland cases as inapplicable when the legislature establishes reasonable qualifications for a vocational pursuit with the necessary effect of disqualifying some persons presently engaged in it.

Petitioners rely heavily upon United States v. Lovett, 328 U.S. 303 (1946), in which a legislative act effectively separating certain public servants from their positions was held to be a bill of attainder. Unlike the provisions of the Charter and ordinance under which petitioners were removed, the statute in the Lovett case did not declare general and prospectively operative standards of qualification and eligibility for public employment. Rather, by its terms it prohibited any further payment of compensation to named individual employees. Under these circumstances, viewed against the legislative background, the statute was held to have imposed penalties without judicial trial.

Nor are we impressed by the contention that the oath denies due process because its negation is not limited to affiliations with organizations known to the employee to be in the proscribed class. We have no reason to suppose that the oath is or will be construed by the City of Los Angeles or by California courts as affecting adversely those persons who during their affiliation with a proscribed organization were innocent of its purpose, or those who severed their relations with any such organization when its character became apparent, or those who were affiliated with organizations which at one time or another during the period covered by the ordinance were engaged in proscribed activity but not at the time of affiant's affiliation. We assume that scienter is implicit in each clause of the oath. As the city has done nothing to negative this interpretation, we take for granted that the ordinance will be so read to avoid raising difficult constitutional problems which any other application would present. Fox v. Washington, 236 U.S. 273, 277 (1915). It appears from correspondence of record between the city and petitioners that although the city welcomed inquiry as to its construction of the oath, the interpretation upon which we have proceeded may not have been explicitly called to the attention of petitioners before their refusal. We assume that if our interpretation of the oath is correct, the City of Los Angeles will give those petitioners who heretofore refused to take the oath an opportunity to take it as interpreted and resume their employment.

The judgment as to Pacifico and Schwartz is affirmed. The judgment as to the remaining petitioners is affirmed on the basis of the interpretation of the ordinance which we have felt justified in assuming.

Affirmed.

MR. JUSTICE FRANKFURTER, concurring in part and dissenting in part. . . .
A municipality like Los Angeles ought to be allowed adequate scope in

seeking to elicit information about its employees and from them. It would give to the Due Process Clause an unwarranted power of intrusion into local affairs to hold that a city may not require its employees to disclose whether they have been members of the Communist Party or the Communist Political Association. In the context of our time, such membership is sufficiently relevant to effective and dependable government, and to the confidence of the electorate in its government. I think the precise Madison would have been surprised even to hear it suggested that the requirement of this affidavit was an "Attainder" under Art. I, §10, of the Constitution. For reasons outlined in the concurring opinion in United States v. Lovett, 328 U.S. 303, 318, I cannot so regard it. This kind of inquiry into political affiliation may in the long run do more harm than good. But the two employees who were dismissed solely because they refused to file an affidavit stating whether or when they had been members of the Communist Party or the Communist Political Association cannot successfully appeal to the Constitution of the United States.

A very different issue is presented by the fifteen employees who were discharged because they refused to take [that part of the oath relating to membership in or affiliation with organizations].

The validity of an oath must be judged on the assumption that it will be taken conscientiously. This ordinance does not ask the employee to swear that he "knowingly" or "to the best of his knowledge" had no proscribed affiliation. Certainty is implied in the disavowal exacted. The oath thus excludes from city employment all persons who are not certain that every organization to which they belonged or with which they were affiliated (with all the uncertainties of the meaning of "affiliated") at any time since 1943 has not since that date advocated the overthrow by "unlawful means" of the Government of the United States or of the State of California. . . .

If this ordinance is sustained, sanction is given to like oaths for every governmental unit in the United States. Not only does the oath make an irrational demand. It is bound to operate as a real deterrent to people contemplating even innocent associations. How can anyone be sure that an organization with which he affiliates will not at some time in the future be found by a State or National official to advocate overthrow of government by "unlawful means"? All but the hardiest may well hesitate to join organizations if they know that by such a proscription they will be permanently disqualified from public employment. These are considerations that cut deep into the traditions of our people. Gregariousness and friendliness are among the most characteristic of American attitudes. Throughout our history they have been manifested in "joining." See Arthur M. Schlesinger, Sr., Biography of a Nation of Joiners, published in 50 American Historical Review 1, reprinted in Schlesinger, Paths to the Present 23.

Giving full scope to the selective processes open to our municipalities and States in securing competent and reliable functionaries free from allegiance to any alien political authority, I do not think that it is consonant with the Due

Process Clause for men to be asked, on pain of giving up public employment, to swear to something they cannot be expected to know. Such a demand is at war with individual integrity; it can no more be justified than the inquiry into belief which MR. JUSTICE BLACK, MR. JUSTICE JACKSON, and I deemed invalid in American Communications Ass'n v. Douds, 339 U.S. 382.

The needs of security do not require such curbs on what may well be innocuous feelings and associations. Such curbs are indeed self-defeating. They are not merely unjustifiable restraints on individuals. They are not merely productive of an atmosphere of repression uncongenial to the spiritual vitality of a democratic society. The inhibitions which they engender are hostile to the best conditions for securing a high-minded and high-spirited public service. . . .

[Mr. Justice Burton took the view that the oath was retrospective and hence invalid under the Lovett, Garland and Cummings cases, but that the affidavit requirement was valid.]

MR. JUSTICE DOUGLAS, with whom Mr. Justice Black joins, dissenting. . . .

The case is governed by Cummings v. Missouri, 4 Wall. 277, and Ex parte Garland, 4 Wall. 333, which struck down test oaths adopted at the close of the Civil War. The Cummings case involved provisions of the Missouri constitution requiring public officials and certain classes of professional people, including clergymen, to take an oath that, inter alia, they had never been "in armed hostility" to the United States; that they had never "by act or word" manifested their "adherence to the cause" of enemies of the country or their "desire" for the triumph of its enemies; that they had never "knowingly and willingly harbored, aided, or countenanced" an enemy; that they had never been a "member of, or connected with, any order, society, or organization inimical to the government of the United States" or engaged "in guerrila warfare" against its inhabitants; that they had never left Missouri "for the purpose of avoiding enrollment for or draft into the military service of the United States" or become enrolled as a southern sympathizer.

The Garland case involved certain Acts of Congress requiring public officials and attorneys practicing before the federal courts to take an oath that they had "voluntarily given no aid, countenance, counsel, or encouragement to persons engaged in armed hostility" against the United States and that they had "neither sought nor accepted, nor attempted to exercise the functions of any office whatever, under any authority or pretended authority in hostility to the United States." The Court amended its rules of admission to require this oath.

Cummings, a Catholic priest, was indicted and convicted for teaching and preaching without having first taken the oath.

Garland, a member of the Bar of the Court, had served in the Confederate Government, for which he had received a pardon from the President conditioned on his taking the customary oath of loyalty. He applied for permission to practice before the Court without taking the new oath.

Article I, §10 of the Constitution forbids any state to "pass any Bill of Attainder" or any "ex post facto Law." Article I, §9 curtails the power of Congress by providing that "No Bill of Attainder or ex post facto Law shall be passed." The Court ruled that the test oaths in the Cummings and Garland cases were bills of attainder and ex post facto laws within the meaning of the Constitution. "A bill of attainder," wrote Mr. Justice Field for the Court, "is a legislative act which inflicts punishment without a judicial trial." Cummings v. Missouri, supra, p. 323, and see United States v. Lovett, 328 U.S. 303, 317, 318. The Court held that deprivation of the right to follow one's profession is punishment. A bill of attainder, though generally directed against named individuals, may be directed against a whole class. Bills of attainder usually declared the guilt; here they assumed the guilt and adjudged the punishment conditionally, i.e., they deprived the parties of their right to preach and to practice law unless the presumption were removed by the expurgatory oath. That was held to be as much a bill of attainder as if the guilt had been irrevocably pronounced. The laws were also held to be ex post facto since they imposed a penalty for an act not so punishable at the time it was committed.

There are, of course, differences between the present case and the Cummings and Garland cases. Those condemned by the Los Angeles ordinance are municipal employees; those condemned in the others were professional people. Here the past conduct for which punishment is exacted is single — advocacy within the past five years of the overthrow of the Government by force and violence. In the other cases the acts for which Cummings and Garland stood condemned covered a wider range and involved some conduct which might be vague and uncertain. But those differences, seized on here in hostility to the constitutional provisions, are wholly irrelevant. Deprivation of a man's means of livelihood by reason of past conduct, not subject to this penalty when committed, is punishment whether he is a professional man, a day laborer who works for private industry, or a government employee. The deprivation is nonetheless unconstitutional whether it be for one single past act or a series of past acts. The degree of particularity with which the past act is defined is not the criterion. We are not dealing here with the problem of vagueness in criminal statutes. No amount of certainty would have cured the laws in the Cummings and Garland cases. They were stricken down because of the mode in which punishment was inflicted.

Petitioners were disqualified from office not for what they are today, not because of any program they currently espouse (cf. Gerende v. Board of Supervisors, 341 U.S. 56), not because of standards related to fitness for the office, cf. Dent v. West Virginia, 129 U.S. 114; Hawker v. New York, 170 U.S. 189, but for what they once advocated. They are deprived of their livelihood by legislative act, not by judicial processes. We put the case in the aspect most invidious to petitioners. Whether they actually advocated the violent overthrow of Government does not appear. But here, as in the Cummings case, the vice is in the presumption of guilt which can only be removed by the expurgatory oath. That punishment, albeit conditional, violates here as it did in the Cummings case the constitutional prohibition against bills of attainder. Whether the ordinance also amounts to an ex post facto law is a question we do not reach.

[Mr. Justice Black's separate opinion is omitted].

NOTES

1. In the following term the Supreme Court upheld the New York Feinberg Law, designed to eliminate "subversive persons from the public school system." Justices Black and Douglas dissented on substantive constitutional grounds, and Mr. Justice Frankfurter dissented on standing grounds. Adler v. Board of Education, 342 U.S. 485, 72 S. Ct. 380, 96 L. Ed. 517 (1952).

2. In Wieman v. Updegraff, 344 U.S. 183, 73 S. Ct. 215, 97 L. Ed. 216 (1952), the Supreme Court considered the validity of an Oklahoma loyalty oath, required of all state officers and employees including faculty and staff of the state's universities, which provided, inter alia, that the employee swear that within the past five years "I have not been a member of the Communist Party, the Third Communist International, or of any agency, party, organization, association, or group whatever which has been officially determined by the United States Attorney General or other authorized public agency of the United States to be a communist front or subversive organization, or of any party or organization, political or otherwise, that advocated the overthrow of the Government of the United States or of the State of Oklahoma by force or violence or other unlawful means." The Oklahoma Supreme Court had interpreted the oath as excluding from government service persons "solely on the basis of organizational membership, regardless of their knowledge concerning the organizations to which they had belonged." The United States Supreme Court held the oath requirement invalid:

"But membership may be innocent. A state servant may have joined a proscribed organization unaware of its activities and purposes. In recent years, many completely loyal persons have severed organizational ties after learning for the first time of the character of groups to which they had belonged. 'They had joined, [but] did not know what it was; they were good, fine young men and women, loyal Americans, but they had been trapped into it — because one of the great weaknesses of all Americans, whether adult or youth, is to join something.' [3] At the time of affiliation, a group itself may be innocent, only later coming under the influence of those who would turn it toward illegitimate ends. Conversely, an organization formerly subversive and therefore designated as such may have subsequently freed itself from the influences which originally led to its listing.

[3] Testimony of J. Edgar Hoover, Hearings before House Committee on Un-American Activities on H.R. 1884 and H.R. 2122, 80th Cong., 1st Sess. 46.

"There can be no dispute about the consequences visited upon a person excluded from public employment on disloyalty grounds. In the view of the community, the stain is a deep one; indeed, it has become a badge of infamy. Especially is this so in time of cold war and hot emotions when 'each man begins to eye his neighbor as a possible enemy.' [4] Yet under the Oklahoma Act, the fact of association alone determines disloyalty and disqualification; it matters not whether association existed innocently or knowingly. To thus inhibit individual freedom of movement is to stifle the flow of democratic expression and controversy at one of its chief sources. We hold that the distinction observed between the case at bar and Garner, Adler and Gerende is decisive. Indiscriminate classification of innocent with knowing activity must fall as an assertion of arbitrary power. The oath offends due process." 344 U.S. at 190-191.

Justices Black, Douglas, Frankfurter, and Burton concurred.

REFERENCES

1. For prior litigation over the Los Angeles County loyalty program see Steiner v. Darby, 88 Cal. App. 2d 481, 199 P. 2d 429 (1948), dismissed as not ripe for review sub nom. Parker v. Los Angeles, 338 U.S. 327, 70 S. Ct. 161, 94 L. Ed. 144 (1949). The Garner case is noted in 50 Mich. L. Rev. 467 (1952); 20 U. Cinc. L. Rev. 514 (1951); 40 Geo. L.J. 127 (1951).

Materials on the bill of attainder problem are collected in the references following United States v. Brown, Section D, subsection 1, supra.

2. The Updegraff case is noted in 39 Cornell L.Q. 118 (1953); 7 Miami L.Q. 578 (1953); 51 Mich. L. Rev. 1076 (1953); 1953 U. Ill. L.F. 281 (1953). For the background of the Oklahoma law and subsequent developments see Robinson, Anti-Sedition Legislation and Loyalty Investigations in Oklahoma (U. Okla. 1956); Bickel, The Least Dangerous Branch 40-42 (1962).

NOTES

1. In a number of cases the issues arising under the state loyalty programs involved, not a dismissal based directly upon failure to meet the loyalty requirements, but one based upon a refusal to answer questions concerning such matters. The first case to reach the Supreme Court in this context was Slochower v. Board of Higher Education of New York City, 350 U.S. 551, 76 S. Ct. 637, 100 L. Ed. 692 (1956). Slochower had invoked the privilege against self-incrimination under the Fifth Amendment before an investigating committee of the United States Senate, and was summarily discharged from his position as associate professor at Brooklyn College, an institution maintained by the City of New York. The dismissal was based upon §903 of the New York City Charter which provides that whenever an employee of the City utilizes the privilege against self-incrimination to avoid answering a question relating to his official conduct, "his term or tenure of office or employment shall terminate and such office or employment shall be vacant, and he shall not be eligible to election or appointment to any office or employment under the city or any agency." The Court held the discharge invalid:

[4] Address by Judge Learned Hand at the 86th Convocation of the University of the State of New York, delivered October 24, 1952, at Albany, New York.

"As interpreted and applied by the state courts, [Section 903] operates to discharge every city employee who invokes the Fifth Amendment. In practical effect the questions asked are taken as confessed and made the basis of the discharge. No consideration is given to such factors as the subject matter of the questions, remoteness of the period to which they are directed, or justification for exercise of the privilege. It matters not whether the plea resulted from mistake, inadvertence or legal advice conscientiously given, whether wisely or unwisely. The heavy hand of the statute falls alike on all who exercise their constitutional privilege, the full enjoyment of which every person is entitled to receive. Such action falls squarely within the prohibition of Wieman v. Updegraff. . . .

"This is not to say that Slochower has a constitutional right to be an associate professor of German at Brooklyn College. The State has broad powers in the selection and discharge of its employees, and it may be that proper inquiry would show Slochower's continued employment to be inconsistent with a real interest of the State. But there has been no such inquiry here. We hold that the summary dismissal of appellant violates due process of law." 350 U.S. at 558-559.

Justices Black and Douglas concurred. Justices Reed, Burton, Minton, and Harlan dissented.

For comment on the Slochower case see Notes, 35 N.C.L. Rev. 90 (1956); 70 Harv. L. Rev. 83, 120 (1956); 45 Ill. B.J. 182 (1956); 41 Minn. L. Rev. 128 (1956); 10 Vand. L. Rev. 139 (1956).

2. However, Lerner v. Casey and Beilan v. Board of Public Instruction, 357 U.S. 468, 399, 78 S. Ct. 1311, 1317, 2 L. Ed. 2d 1423, 1414 (1958), upheld the discharges of a subway conductor and a teacher who refused to answer questions of their employers concerning Communist Party affiliations. Mr. Chief Justice Warren and Justices Black, Douglas, and Brennan dissented. For comment on the Lerner and Beilan cases, see Notes, 74 Harv. L. Rev. 77, 188-193 (1958); 27 Geo. Wash. L. Rev. 581 (1959). The cases from Garner through Beilan are discussed in Cramton, The Supreme Court and State Power to Deal With Subversion and Loyalty, 43 Minn. L. Rev. 1025, 1053-1057, 1061-1078 (1959).

3. In Nelson v. County of Los Angeles, 362 U.S. 1, 80 S. Ct. 527, 4 L. Ed. 2d 494 (1960), two employees of Los Angeles County were dismissed for refusing, on self-incrimination and First Amendment grounds, to answer questions before the House Committee on Un-American Activities concerning alleged Communist affiliations. A California statute made it the duty of any public employee to give testimony relating to such matters on pain of discharge. One of the employees, Nelson, held a permanent position as social worker; he was given a hearing and then dismissed. The other employee, Globe, was a temporary employee in the same department; under the state's civil service rules he was not entitled to a hearing and was summarily discharged. The California courts affirmed both dismissals. 163 Cal. App. 2d 595, 607, 329 P.2d 971, 978 (1958), petition for review denied, three judges dissenting, 163 Cal. App. 2d 606, 614, 329 P.2d 978, 983 (1958). The United States Supreme Court affirmed the Nelson case by an equally divided vote, no opinion being rendered. The Court affirmed the Globe case, distinguishing the Slochower case and relying upon Lerner and Beilan. Justices Black, Douglas, and Brennan dissented. Mr. Chief Justice Warren did not participate in either decision. For comment, see Note, 74 Harv. L. Rev. 81, 123-126 (1960).

In Malloy v. Hogan, 378 U.S. 1, 84 S. Ct. 1489, 12 L. Ed. 2d 653 (1964), the Supreme Court, reversing its prior position, held that the Fifth Amendment privilege against self-incrimination was applicable to the states under the Fourteenth Amendment. For other materials on the effect which may be given to the refusal to answer questions, including invocation of the privilege against self-incrimination, see Section D, subsection 2, supra. See also Stevens v. Marks, 383 U.S. 234, 86 S. Ct. 788, 15 L. Ed. 2d 724 (1966).

4. The extent to which state loyalty programs are vulnerable to challenge on grounds of undue breadth or vagueness was raised again before the Supreme Court in a series of cases beginning in 1960. In Shelton v. Tucker, 364 U.S. 479, 81 S. Ct. 247, 5 L. Ed 2d 231 (1960), the Court by a five-to-four vote invalidated an Arkansas statute which required every teacher to file annually an affidavit listing each organization to which he had belonged or contributed regularly during the past five years. The majority ruled the statute invalid because of its "unlimited and indiscriminate sweep."

Cramp v. Board of Public Instruction, 368 U.S. 278, 82 S. Ct. 275, 7 L. Ed. 2d 285 (1961), involved a Florida statute which required all state employees to execute a written oath that, among other things, specified, "I have not and will not lend my aid, support, advice, counsel or influence to the Communist Party." In a unanimous decision the Supreme Court held the statute invalid under the rule against undue vagueness. After cataloguing some of the ambiguities he found in the oath, Mr. Justice Stewart went on to say:

"The very absurdity of these possibilities brings into focus the extraordinary ambiguity of the statutory language. With such vagaries in mind, it is not unrealistic to suggest that the compulsion of this oath provision might weigh most heavily upon those whose conscientious scruples were the most sensitive. While it is perhaps fanciful to suppose that a perjury prosecution would ever be instituted for past conduct of the kind suggested, it requires no strain of the imagination to envision the possibility of prosecution for other types of equally guiltless knowing behaviour. It would be blinking reality not to acknowledge that there are some among us always ready to affix a Communist label upon those whose ideas they violently oppose. And experience teaches that prosecutors too are human." 368 U.S. at 286-287.

For comment on the case see Notes, 76 Harv. L. Rev. 54, 147-150 (1962); 34 Rocky Mt. L. Rev. 548 (1962).

On motion for entry of judgment pursuant to the mandate of the Supreme Court, the Florida Supreme Court ordered stricken from the oath that portion (quoted above) which was the subject of the United States Supreme Court's decision, and held the remainder valid. Those provisions which remained included: "that I am not a member of the Communist Party; that I do not believe in the overthrow of the Government of the United States or the State of Florida by force or violence; that I am not a member of any organization or party which believes in or teaches, directly or indirectly, the overthrow of the Government of the United States or of Florida by force or violence." The court concluded that "appellant Cramp is bound by the statute to execute the oath with the objectionable language eliminated." 137 So. 2d 828 (1962).

BAGGETT v. BULLITT
377 *U.S. 360, 84 S. Ct. 1316, 12 L. Ed. 2d 377 (1964)*

MR. JUSTICE WHITE delivered the opinion of the Court.

Appellants, approximately 64 in number, are members of the faculty, staff and student body of the University of Washington who brought this class action asking for a judgment declaring unconstitutional two Washington statutes requiring the execution of two different oaths by state employees and for an injunction against the enforcement of these statutes by appellees, the President of the University, members of the Washington State Board of Regents and the State Attorney General.

The statutes under attack are Chapter 377, Laws of 1955, and Chapter 103, Laws of 1931, both of which require employees of the State of Washington to take the oaths prescribed in the statutes as a condition of their employment. The 1931 legislation applies only to teachers, who, upon applying for a license to teach or renewing an existing contract, are required to subscribe to the following:

"I solemnly swear (or affirm) that I will support the constitution and laws of the United States of America and of the State of Washington, and will by precept and example promote respect for the flag and the institutions of the United States of America and the State of Washington, reverence for law and order and undivided allegiance to the government of the United States." Wash. Laws 1931, c. 103.

The oath requirements of the 1955 Act, Wash. Laws 1955, c. 377, applicable to all state employees, incorporate various provisions of the Washington Subversive Activities Act of 1951, which provides generally that "[n]o subversive person, as defined in this act, shall be eligible for employment in, or appointment to any office, or any position of trust or profit in the government, or in the administration of the business, of this state, or of any county, municipality, or other political subdivision of this state." Wash. Rev. Code §9.81.060. The term "subversive person" is defined as follows:

" 'Subversive person' means any person who commits, attempts to commit, or aids in the commission, or advocates, abets, advises or teaches by any means any person to commit, attempt to commit, or aid in the commission of any act intended to overthrow, destroy or alter, or to assist in the overthrow, destruction or alteration of, the constitutional form of the government of the United States, or of the state of Washington, or any political subdivision of either of them by revolution, force, or violence; or who with knowledge that the organization is an organization as described in subsections (2) and (3) hereof, becomes or remains a member of a subversive organization or a foreign subversive organization." Wash. Rev. Code §9.81.010(5).

The Act goes on to define at similar length and in similar terms "subversive organization" and "foreign subversive organization" and to declare the Communist Party a subversive organization and membership therein a subversive activity. . . .

Appellants contend in this Court that the oath requirements and the statutory provisions on which they are based are invalid on their face because their language is unduly vague, uncertain and broad. We agree with this contention and therefore, without reaching the numerous other contentions pressed upon us, confine our considerations to that particular question. . . .

The oath required by the 1955 statute suffers from similar infirmities [as in the Cramp case]. A teacher must swear that he is not a subversive person: that he is not one who commits an act or who advises, teaches, abets or advocates by any means another person to commit or aid in the commission of any act intended to overthrow or alter, or to assist the overthrow or alteration, of the constitutional form of government by revolution, force or violence. A subversive organization is defined as one which engages in or assists activities intended to alter or overthrow the Government by force or violence or which has as a purpose the commission of such acts. The Communist Party is declared in the statute to be a subversive organization, that is, it is presumed that the Party does and will engage in activities intended to overthrow the Government. Persons required to swear they understand this oath may quite reasonably conclude that any person who aids the Communist Party or teaches or advises known members of the Party is a subversive person because such teaching or advice may now or at some future date aid the activities of the Party. Teaching and advising are clearly acts, and one cannot confidently assert that his counsel, aid, influence or support which adds to the resources, rights and knowledge of the Communist Party or its members does not aid the Party in its activities, activities which the statute tells us are all in furtherance of the stated purpose of overthrowing the Government by revolution, force, or violence. The questions put by the Court in Cramp may with equal force be asked here. Does the statute reach endorsement or support for Communist candidates for office? Does it reach a lawyer who represents the Communist Party or its members or a journalist who defends constitutional rights of the Communist Party or its members or anyone who supports any cause which is likewise supported by Communists or the Communist Party? The susceptibility of the statutory language to require forswearing of an undefined variety of "guiltless knowing behavior" is what the Court condemned in Cramp. This statute, like the one at issue in Cramp, is unconstitutionally vague.

The Washington statute suffers from additional difficulties on vagueness grounds. A person is subversive not only if he himself commits the specified acts but if he abets or advises another in aiding a third person to commit an act which will assist yet a fourth person in the overthrow or alteration of constitutional government. The Washington Supreme Court has said that knowledge is to be read into every provision and we accept this construction. Nostrand v. Balmer, 53 Wash. 2d 460, 483-484, 335 P.2d 10, 24; Nostrand v.

Little, 58 Wash. 2d 111, 123-124, 361 P.2d 551, 559. But what is it that the Washington professor must "know"? Must he know that his aid or teaching will be used by another and that the person aided has the requisite guilty intent or is it sufficient that he know that his aid or teaching would or might be useful to others in the commission of acts intended to overthrow the Government? Is it subversive activity, for example, to attend and participate in international conventions of mathematicians and exchange views with scholars from Communist countries? What about the editor of a scholarly journal who analyzes and criticizes the manuscripts of Communist scholars submitted for publication? Is selecting outstanding scholars from Communist countries as visiting professors and advising, teaching, or consulting with them at the University of Washington a subversive activity if such scholars are known to be Communists, or regardless of their affiliations, regularly teach students who are members of the Communist Party, which by statutory definition is subversive and dedicated to the overthrow of the Government?

The Washington oath goes beyond otherthrow or alteration by force or violence. It extends to alteration by "revolution" which, unless wholly redundant and its ordinary meaning distorted, includes any rapid or fundamental change. Would, therefore, any organization or any person supporting, advocating or teaching peaceful but far-reaching constitutional amendments be engaged in subversive activity? Could one support the repeal of the Twenty-second Amendment or participation by this country in a world government?

We also conclude that the 1931 oath offends due process because of vagueness. The oath exacts a promise that the affiant will, by precept and example, promote respect for the flag and the institutions of the United States and the State of Washington. The range of activities which are or might be deemed inconsistent with the required promise is very wide indeed. The teacher who refused to salute the flag or advocated refusal because of religious beliefs might well be accused of breaching his promise. Cf. West Virginia State Board of Education v. Barnette, 319 U.S. 624. Even criticism of the design or color scheme of the state flag or unfavorable comparison of it with that of a sister State or foreign country could be deemed disrespectful and therefore violative of the oath. And what are "institutions" for the purposes of this oath? Is it every "practice, law, custom, etc., which is a material and persistent element in the life or culture of an organized social group" or every "established society or corporation," every "establishment, esp[ecially] one of a public character"? [9] The oath may prevent a professor from criticizing his state judicial system or the Supreme Court or the institution of judicial review. Or it might be deemed to proscribe advocating the abolition, for example, of the Civil Rights Commission, the House Committee on Un-American Activities, or foreign aid.

It is likewise difficult to ascertain what might be done without transgressing the promise to "promote . . . undivided allegiance to the government of

[9] Webster's New Int. Dictionary (2d ed.), at 1288.

the United States." It would not be unreasonable for the serious-minded oath taker to conclude that he should dispense with lectures voicing far-reaching criticism of any old or new policy followed by the Government of the United States. He could find it questionable under this language to ally himself with any interest group dedicated to opposing any current public policy or law of the Federal Government, for if he did, he might well be accused of placing loyalty to the group above allegiance to the United States.

Indulging every presumption of a narrow construction of the provisions of the 1931 oath, consistent, however, with a proper respect for the English language, we cannot say that this oath provides an ascertainable standard of conduct or that it does not require more than a State may command under the guarantees of the First and Fourteenth Amendments.

As in Cramp v. Board of Public Instruction, "[t]he vice of unconstitutional vagueness is further aggravated where, as here, the statute in question operates to inhibit the exercise of individual freedoms affirmatively protected by the Constitution." 368 U.S. 278, 287. We are dealing with indefinite statutes whose terms, even narrowly construed, abut upon sensitive areas of basic First Amendment freedoms. The uncertain meanings of the oaths require the oath-taker — teachers and public servants — to "steer far wider of the unlawful zone," Speiser v. Randall, 357 U.S. 513, 526, than if the boundaries of the forbidden areas were clearly marked. Those with a conscientious regard for what they solemnly swear or affirm, sensitive to the perils posed by the oath's indefinite language, avoid the risk of loss of employment, and perhaps profession, only by restricting their conduct to that which is unquestionably safe. Free speech may not be so inhibited. . . .

The State labels as wholly fanciful the suggested possible coverage of the two oaths. It may well be correct, but the contention only emphasizes the difficulties with the two statutes; for if the oaths do not reach some or any of the behavior suggested, what specific conduct do the oaths cover? Where does fanciful possibility end and intended coverage begin?

It will not do to say that a prosecutor's sense of fairness and the Constitution would prevent a successful perjury prosecution for some of the activities seemingly embraced within the sweeping statutory definitions. The hazard of being prosecuted for knowing but guiltless behavior nevertheless remains. . . . Well-intentioned prosecutors and judicial safeguards do not neutralize the vice of a vague law. Nor should we encourage the casual taking of oaths by upholding the discharge or exclusion from public employment of those with a conscientious and scrupulous regard for such undertakings.

It is further argued, however, that, notwithstanding the uncertainties of the 1931 oath and the statute on which it is based, the oath does not offend due process because the vagaries are contained in a promise of future conduct, the breach of which would not support a conviction for perjury. Without the criminal sanctions, it is said, one need not fear taking this oath, regardless of whether he understands it and can comply with its mandate, however understood. This contention ignores not only the effect of the oath on those who will not solemnly swear unless they can do so honestly and without prevarication and reservation, but also its effect on those who believe the written law means what it says. . . .

Mr. Justice Clark, with whom Mr. Justice Harlan joins, dissenting. . . .

[Those] factors which caused the Court to find the Cramp oath unconstitutionally vague are clearly not present in the Washington oath. Washington's oath proscribes only the commission of an *act* of overthrow or alteration of the constitutional form of government by revolution, force or violence; or advising, teaching, abetting or advocating by any means another person to commit or aid in the commission of any act intended to overthrow or alter or to assist the overthrow or alteration of the constitutional form of government by revolution, force or violence. The defects noted by the Court when it passed on the Cramp oath have been cured in the Washington statute.

. . . It is, of course, absurd to say that, under the words of the Washington Act, a professor risks violation when he teaches German, English, history or any other subject included in the curriculum for a college degree, to a class in which a Communist Party member might sit. To so interpret the language of the Act is to extract more sunbeams from cucumbers than did Gulliver's mad scientist. And to conjure up such ridiculous questions, the answers to which we all know or should know are in the negative, is to build up a whimsical and farcical straw man which is not only grim but Grimm. . . .

REFERENCES

1. Earlier stages of the litigation over the Washington loyalty oaths are reported in Nostrand v. Balmer, 53 Wash. 2d 460, 335 P.2d 10 (1959), remanded in Nostrand v. Little, 362 U.S. 474, 80 S. Ct. 840, 4 L. Ed. 2d 892 (1960); Nostrand v. Little, 58 Wash. 2d 111, 361 P.2d 551 (1961), app. dis., 368 U.S. 436, 82 S. Ct. 464, 7 L. Ed. 2d 426 (1962). See Lycette, Standing to Challenge Constitutionality of Loyalty Oath, 37 Wash. L. Rev. 106 (1962).

For comment on the Baggett case, see Morris, Washington's Loyalty Oath and "Guiltless Knowing Behavior," 39 Wash. L. Rev. 734 (1964), also printed in 1 Law in Trans. Q. 185 (1964) (Morris was counsel for appellants in Baggett v. Bullitt); Notes, 78 Harv. L. Rev. 143, 230-233 (1964); 25 Md. L. Rev. 64 (1965); 26 U. Pitt. L. Rev. 621 (1965).

2. Following Baggett v. Bullitt, loyalty requirements in a number of states were challenged in the federal courts. In Heckler v. Shepard, 243 F. Supp. 841 (D. Idaho 1965), a three-judge court, while finding the Idaho oath valid under Garner, Cramp, and Baggett, held that the procedure whereby an employee refusing to take the oath was automatically discharged without hearing violated due process. In New York a further attack upon the Feinberg law was made by a group of teachers from the State University of New York. The District Court refused to convene a three-judge court on the ground that no substantial federal question was presented, but the Court of Appeals reversed. Keyishian v. Board of Regents, 233 F. Supp. 752 (W.D. N.Y. 1964), rev'd, 345 F.2d 236 (2d Cir. 1965). Subsequently the three-judge court upheld the statute. — F. Supp. — (W.D. N.Y. 1966). The Supreme Court granted certiorari. 384 U.S. 998 (1966).

The Georgia teachers' oath was held invalid in part and upheld in part in Georgia Conference of the American Assn. of University Professors v. Board of Regents, 246 F. Supp. 553 (N.D. Ga. 1965). Meanwhile the Supreme Court decided the Arizona case, set forth below.

ELFBRANDT v. RUSSELL
384 U.S. 11, 86 S. Ct. 1238, 16 L. Ed. 2d 321 (1966)

MR. JUSTICE DOUGLAS delivered the opinion of the Court. . . .

The oath reads in conventional fashion as follows:

"I, (type or print name) do solemnly swear (or affirm) that I will support the Constitution of the United States and the Constitution and laws of the State of Arizona; that I will bear true faith and allegiance to the same, and defend them against all enemies, foreign and domestic, and that I will faithfully and impartially discharge the duties of the office of (name of office) according to the best of my ability, so help me God (or so I do affirm)."

The Legislature put a gloss on the oath by subjecting to a prosecution for perjury and for discharge from public office anyone who took the oath and who "knowingly and wilfully becomes or remains a member of the communist party of the United States or its successors or any of its subordinate organizations" or "any other organization" having for "one of its purposes" the overthrow of the government of Arizona or any of its political subdivisions where the employee had knowledge of the unlawful purpose. Petitioner, a teacher and a Quaker, decided she could not in good conscience take the oath, not knowing what it meant and not having any chance to get a hearing at which its precise scope and meaning could be determined. This suit for declaratory relief followed. . . .

We recognized in Scales v. United States, 367 U.S. 203, 229, that "quasi-political parties or other groups . . . may embrace both legal and illegal aims." We noted that a "blanket prohibition of association with a group having both legal and illegal aims" would pose "a real danger that legitimate political expression or association would be impaired." The statute with which we dealt in Scales, the so-called "membership clause" of the Smith Act (18 U.S.C. §2385), was found not to suffer from this constitutional infirmity because, as the Court construed it, the statute reached only "active" membership (id., at 222) with the "specific intent" of assisting in achieving the unlawful ends of the organization (id., at 229-230). The importance of this limiting construction from a constitutional standpoint was emphasized in Noto v. United States, 367 U.S. 290, 299-300, decided the same day:

"[I]t should also be said that this element of the membership crime [the defendant's 'personal criminal purpose to bring about the overthrow of the Government by force and violence'], like its others, must be judged strictissimi juris, for otherwise there is a danger that one in sympathy with the legitimate aims of such an organization, but not specifically intending to accomplish them by resort to violence, might be punished for his adherence to lawful and constitutionally protected purposes, because of other and unprotected purposes which he does not necessarily share."

Any lingering doubt that proscription of mere knowing membership, without any showing of "specific intent," would run afoul of the Constitution was set at rest by our decision in Aptheker v. Secretary of State, 378 U.S. 500. We dealt there with a statute which provided that no member of a Communist organization ordered by the Subversive Activities Control Board to register shall apply for or use a passport. We concluded that the statute would not permit a narrow reading of the sort we gave §2385 in Scales. See 378 U.S., at 511, n. 9. The statute, as we read it, covered membership which was not accompanied by a specific intent to further the unlawful aims of the organization, and we held it unconstitutional.

The oath and accompanying statutory gloss challenged here suffer from an identical constitutional infirmity. One who subscribes to this Arizona oath and who is, or thereafter becomes, a knowing member of an organization which has as "one of its purposes" the violent overthrow of the government, is subject to immediate discharge and criminal penalties. Nothing in the oath, the statutory gloss, or the construction of the oath and statutes given by the Arizona Supreme Court, purports to exclude association by one who does not subscribe to the organization's unlawful ends. Here as in Baggett v. Bullitt, supra, the "hazard of being prosecuted for knowing but guiltless behavior" (id., at 373) is a reality. People often label as "communist" ideas which they oppose; and they often make up our juries. "[P]rosecutors too are human." Cramp v. Board of Public Instruction, 368 U.S. 278, 287. Would a teacher be safe and secure in going to a Pugwash Conference? Would it be legal to join a seminar group predominantly Communist and therefore subject to control by those who are said to believe in the overthrow of the government by force and violence? Juries might convict though the teacher did not subscribe to the wrongful aims of the organization. And there is apparently no machinery provided for getting clearance in advance.

Those who join an organization but do not share its unlawful purposes and who do not participate in its unlawful activities surely pose no threat, either as citizens or as public employees. Laws such as this which are not restricted in scope to those who join with the "specific intent" to further illegal action impose, in effect, a conclusive presumption that the member shares the unlawful aims of the organization. See Aptheker v. Secretary of State, supra, at 511. The constitutionality of this Act follows a fortiori from Speiser v. Randall, 357 U.S. 513, where we held that a State may not even place on an applicant for a tax exemption the burden of proving that he has not engaged in criminal advocacy.

This Act threatens the cherished freedom of association protected by the First Amendment, made applicable to the States through the Fourteenth Amendment. . . . A statute touching those protected rights must be "narrowly drawn to define and punish specific conduct as constituting a clear and present danger to a substantial interest of the State." Cantwell v. Connecticut,

310 U.S. 296, 311. Legitimate legislative goals "cannot be pursued by means that broadly stifle fundamental personal liberties when the end can be more narrowly achieved." Shelton v. Tucker, 364 U.S. 479, 488. . . . A law which applies to membership without the "specific intent" to further the illegal aims of the organization infringes unnecessarily on protected freedoms. It rests on the doctrine of "guilt by association" which has no place here. See Schneiderman v. United States, 320 U.S. 118, 136; Schware v. Board of Bar Examiners, 353 U.S. 232, 246. Such a law cannot stand.

Reversed.

MR. JUSTICE WHITE, with whom Mr. Justice Clark, Mr. Justice Harlan, and Mr. Justice Stewart concur, dissenting.

According to unequivocal prior holdings of this Court, a state is entitled to condition public employment upon its employees abstaining from knowing membership in the Communist Party and other organizations advocating the violent overthrow of the government which employs them; the state is constitutionally authorized to inquire into such affiliations and it may discharge those who refuse to affirm or deny them [citing Gerende, Garner, Adler, Beilan, Lerner and Nelson]. The Court does not mention or purport to overrule these cases; nor does it expressly hold that a state must retain, even in its most sensitive positions, those who lend such support as knowing membership entails to those organizations, such as the Communist Party, whose purposes include the violent destruction of democratic government.

Under existing constitutional law, then, Arizona is free to require its teachers to refrain from knowing membership in the designated organizations and to bar from employment all knowing members as well as those who refuse to establish their qualifications to teach by executing the oath prescribed by the statute. Arizona need not retain those employees on the governor's staff, in the Phoenix police department or in its schools who insist on holding membership in and lending their name and influence to those organizations aiming at violent overthrow. Adler v. Board of Education, 342 U.S. 485.

It would seem, therefore, that the Court's judgment is aimed at the criminal provisions of the Arizona law which expose an employee to a perjury prosecution if he swears falsely about membership when he signs the oath or if he later becomes a knowing member while remaining in public employment. But the State is entitled to condition employment on the absence of knowing membership; and if an employee obtains employment by falsifying his present qualifications, there is no sound constitutional reason for denying the State the power to treat such false swearing as perjury. Alire v. United States, 313 F.2d 31; Ogden v. United States, 303 F.2d 724.[1] By the same token,

[1] These cases uphold the constitutionality of 18 U.S.C. §1001 (1964), which makes it a crime to make false statements with regard to any matter within the jurisdiction of any department or agency of the United States. Many States have comparable statutes, e.g., Cal. Govt. Code §§1368, 3108; Mass. Laws Ann., c. 264, §§14, 15; Okla. Stat. Ann., Tit. 51, §§36.5, 36.6.

since knowing membership in specified organizations is a valid disqualification, Arizona cannot sensibly be forbidden to make it a crime for a person, while a state employee, to join an organization knowing of its dedication to the forceful overthrow of his employer and knowing that membership disqualifies him for state employment. The crime provided by the Arizona law is not just the act of becoming a member of an organization but it is that membership plus concurrent public employment. If a State may disqualify for knowing membership and impose criminal penalties for falsifying employment applications, it is likewise within its powers to move criminally against the employee who knowingly engages in disqualifying acts during his employment. If a government may remove from office, 5 U.S.C. §118(i) (1964 ed.), United Public Workers of America v. Mitchell, 330 U.S. 75, and criminally punish, 18 U.S.C. §607 (1964 ed.), its employees who engage in certain political activities, it is unsound to hold that it may not, on pain of criminal penalties, prevent its employees from affiliating with the Communist Party or other organizations prepared to employ violent means to overthrow constitutional government. Our Constitution does not require this kind of protection for the secret proselyting of government employees into the Communist Party, an organization which has been found to be controlled by a foreign power and to be dedicated to the overthrow of the government by any illegal means necessary to achieve this end. Communist Party of the United States v. Subversive Activities Control Board, 367 U.S. 1. . . .

Even if Arizona may not take criminal action against its law enforcement officers or its teachers who become Communists knowing of the purposes of the Party, the Court's judgment overreaches itself in invalidating this Arizona statute. Whether or not Arizona may make knowing membership a crime, it need not retain the member as an employee and is entitled to insist that its employees disclaim, under oath, knowing membership in the designated organizations and to condition future employment upon future abstention from membership. It is, therefore, improper to invalidate the entire statute in this declaratory judgment action. If the imposition of criminal penalties under the present act is invalid, the Court should so limit its holding and remand the case to the Arizona courts to determine the severability of the criminal provisions under the severability provisions of the act itself. Arizona Communist Control Act of 1961, Ariz. Laws 1961, c. 108, §8.

REFERENCES

1. For discussion of the Elfbrandt case in the Arizona courts, see Beggs, Loyalty Oaths, Conscience, and the Constitution, 5 Ariz. L. Rev. 254 (1964).

2. The state loyalty laws for public employees have been consistently upheld by the state courts. In addition to the cases set forth above which reached the United States Supreme Court, see Bowen v. Los Angeles County, 39 Cal. 2d 714, 249 P.2d 285 (1952), cert. den., 345 U.S. 1002 (1953); Hirschman v. Los Angeles County, 39 Cal. 2d 698, 249 P.2d 287 (1952), cert. den. sub nom. Petherbridge v. Los Angeles County, 345 U.S. 1002

(1953); Fitzgerald v. Philadelphia, 376 Pa. 379, 102 A.2d 887 (1954); Gottlieb v. City of New Orleans, 101 So. 2d 242 (Ct. App., Orleans Parish, cert. den., by Louisiana Supreme Court 1958); Wirin v. Ostly, 191 Cal. App. 2d 710, 13 Cal. Rptr. 31 (1961), cert. den., 368 U.S. 952 (1962) (Levering Act oath held valid as to notary public); Crowe v. County of Wayne, 365 Mich. 656, 114 N.W.2d 240 (1962). After Baggett, suits were brought in the state courts attacking the loyalty oaths in Massachusetts and Oregon.

The state courts have also upheld discharges for refusal to answer questions. In addition to the cases on this issue reaching the Supreme Court, see Callender v. San Diego Co., 161 Cal. App. 2d 481, 327 P.2d 74 (1958) (hearing denied by California Supreme Court); Wolstenholme v. Oakland Library Board, 191 Cal. App. 2d 710, 13 Cal. Rptr. 31 (1961), cert. den., 368 U.S. 952 (1952).

The giving of false answers to questions concerning alleged subversive activities was held ground for dismissal in Pawell v. Unemployment Compensation Board of Review, 146 Pa. Super. 147, 22 A.2d 43 (1941); Calvert v. City of Pontiac and companion cases, 288 Mich. 401, 396, 404, 284 N.W.2d 921, 924, 923 (1939); Rubenstein v. Monaghan, 124 N.Y.S.2d 76 (Sup. Ct. N.Y. Co. 1953). But see Kaminsky v. Kennedy, 9 App. Div. 2d 541, 196 N.Y.S.2d 520 (1st Dept. 1960). For a perjury conviction growing out of the loyalty program, see New York v. Carman, 7 App. Div. 2d 633, 180 N.Y.S.2d 246 (First Dept. 1959), aff'd, 6 N.Y.2d 241, 160 N.E.2d 484, 189 N.Y.S.2d 188 (1959).

For a case in which the court reversed the dismissal of an employee on non-constitutional grounds, see Nagin v. Zurmuhlen, 6 App. Div. 2d 677, 173 N.Y.S.2d 899 (First Dept. 1958). For other cases in which the employee was successful, see Hamilton v. Brennan, 203 Misc. 536, 119 N.Y.S.2d 83 (Sup. Ct. N.Y. Co. 1953); State ex rel. Martin v. Burnquist, 141 Minn. 308, 170 N.W. 201 (1918); Rabouine v. McNamara, 275 App. Div. 1052, 92 N.Y.S.2d 110 (Second Dept. 1949), aff'd, 301 N.Y. 785, 96 N.E.2d 91 (1950); Matson v. Jackson, 368 Pa. 283, 83 A.2d 134 (1951). See also Wilson v. City of Los Angeles, 54 Cal. 2d 61, 351 P.2d 761, 4 Cal. Rptr. 489 (1960).

A digest of the important cases through 1964 may be found in Internal Security and Subversion: Principal Laws and Cases, A Study prepared for the Subcommittee to Investigate the Administration of the Internal Security Act and Other Internal Security Laws of the Senate Committee on the Judiciary, by Legislative Reference Service, Library of Congress, 89th Cong., 1st Sess. (1965). The cases up to 1955 are summarized in Digest of the Public Record of Communism in the United States 347-382 (Fund for the Republic 1955). See also Notes, 18 A.L.R.2d 268 (1951); 44 A.L.R.2d 789 (1955), and supplements to date. For discussion see, in addition to the materials cited above, Swanstrom, The Scienter Requirement and Retrospective Clauses in Loyalty Oaths, 3 Duke B.J. 94 (1953); Notes, 49 Mich. L. Rev. 1219 (1951); 25 Temple L.Q. 207 (1951); 2 De Paul L. Rev. 274 (1952); 28 Ind. L.J. 520 (1953); 28 Notre Dame Law. 406 (1953); 4 Syracuse L. Rev. 325 (1953); 34 Chi.-Kent L. Rev. 144 (1956); 32 Notre Dame Law. 524 (1957); 2 Vill. L. Rev. 418 (1957); Bryson, Legality of Loyalty Oath and Non-Oath Requirements for Public School Teachers (1963).

3. Loyalty programs for municipal or county employees exist in a number of areas, including, in addition to Los Angeles County, New York, Newark, Columbus, Detroit, Topeka, Kansas City, and Dade County, Florida. For an account of one of the most elaborate — the Detroit program — see Mowitz, Michigan: State and Local Attack on Subversion in Gellhorn, The States and Subversion, ch. IV (1952). For other local programs see Security and Constitutional Rights, Hearings before the Subcommittee on Constitutional Rights of the Senate Committee on the Judiciary, 84th Cong., 2d Sess. 252-296 (1955).

4. With respect to the more recent controversy over whether members of the John Birch Society should be permitted to serve on the police forces, see N.Y. Times, Feb. 23 and 24, 1966, Mar. 19, 1966, and May 27, 1966; American Civil Liberties Union Bull., Feb. 15, 1965; Foster, John Birch on the Police Force, The Progressive, October 1965, p.

15. In New York City a social worker in the Welfare Department was dismissed because of his membership in the Ku Klux Klan. N.Y. Times, Nov. 11, 1965.

5. The most comprehensive treatment of private loyalty programs, including both a description of the programs and an analysis of legal rights, is Brown, Loyalty and Security, chs. 5, 18 (1958). For other general discussions of the legal issues, see Note, Loyalty and Private Employment: The Right of Employers to Discharge Suspected Subversives, 62 Yale L.J. 954 (1953); Note, The Right to Discharge a Private Employee Because of His Political Beliefs, 31 Temple L.Q. 291 (1958).

F. LEGISLATIVE INVESTIGATIONS

Legislative investigations are by no means a novel feature of American political life. Not more than three years after the first Congress met, the House of Representatives created a committee to investigate the reasons for General St. Clair's defeat at the hands of the Indians. Annals of Congress, 2d Cong., 1st Sess. (1792), col. 490-493. Since then there have been hundreds of federal, state, and local legislative investigations, and their frequency and intensity have progressively increased. At the present time, at least in terms of Congressional effort and public attention, the investigating activities of Congress rank almost on a par with its law-making activities.

Until the last three decades the investigatory powers of Congress were primarily employed by reformist and politically progressive groups. The investigations were largely, though not exclusively, directed at unearthing inefficiency or corruption in government or at exposing to public view the social abuses emerging from the rapid industrialization of the country. Beginning in 1933 the New Deal Administration used the legislative investigating powers of Congress extensively and a series of well-known investigations took place under its auspices. These included inquiries into financial practices on the security markets, into operations of public utility holding companies, into the activities of labor spies and professional strikebreakers, into lobbying, into concentration of economic power, and into many other areas where the New Deal sought reform. These New Deal investigations marked an advance in the techniques of investigation and revealed some of the broader implications of the investigating power.

As the New Deal political fortunes began to wane, beginning with its defeat in the 1938 mid-term elections, Congressional investigations commenced to take a new direction. They became less concerned with social reform and were directed more into methods of government administration and into alleged subversive activities in government and in other sectors of American life. Beginning with the Dies Committee in 1938 a continuous series of investigations have taken place in the field of political expression. The most active committees in this area have been the House Committee on Un-American Activities, authorized to investigate "the extent, character, and objects of un-American propaganda activities in the United States"; the Subcommittee on Internal Security of the Senate Judiciary Committee, which functioned under the chairmanship of Senators McCarran, Jenner, and Eastland; and, for a time, the Subcommittee on Investigations of the Senate Committee on Government Operations under Senator McCarthy. These committees and others have directed their inquiries in the first instance at Communist activities and influences, but the range of investigation has frequently extended beyond this area. State and local legislative investigations have followed the same pattern.

Within recent years important investigations have also taken place in the area of government corruption, lobbying, interstate crime, labor racketeering, and other problems. These also raise serious issues of individual rights. Our concern here, however, is primarily with legislative investigations in the field of political expression.

Along with the expansion of the scope of legislative investigation there have occurred important advances in the techniques of investigation. Modern committees normally have more funds available, employ larger staffs of investigators, and utilize publicity more skillfully. Moreover, the major committees have tended to become "institutionalized," with permanent staffs, an accumulation of files, longer experience, and a continuous operation over a period of years.

The effect of these developments in scope and technique has been reinforced by the social, economic, and political forces characteristic of a highly industrialized modern society. Thus the growing influence of the mass media of communication, the greater dependence of the individual on government, and the many other pressures toward conformity in thought and action, have combined to give the legislative investigating committee an unprecedented influence.

As a result of all these factors the modern legislative committee has become one of the most potent forces in American political life today. The operation of the committees in the area of political expression has perhaps been the single most significant force in shaping public attitudes and influencing governmental and private action toward radical and unorthodox political thought and activity during the past two decades.

This section will consider some of the major problems that have emerged from the current growth of the legislative investigation, dealing with (1) the basic powers and limitations of investigating committees, (2) the privilege against self-incrimination and other specific constitutional limitations, (3) various non-constitutional limitations, and (4) the procedural rights of persons called before or attacked before legislative committees.

REFERENCES

Historical accounts of the development of legislative investigating committees may be found in Eberling, Congressional Investigations (1928); Dimock, Congressional Investigating Committees (1929); McGeary, The Developments of Congressional Investigative Power (1940) (dealing mostly with the investigations of the 1930's); Taylor, Grand Inquest: The Story of Congressional Investigations, chs. I-IV (1955). See also McGeary,

Congressional Investigations: Historical Development, 18 U. Chi. L. Rev. 425 (1951); Gillmor, Fear, The Accuser, chs. 2-4 (1954); Smelser, The Grand Inquest of the Nation 1792-1948, 29 Notre Dame Law. 163 (1954).

For samples of liberal writing during the 1920's in support of vigorous use of the legislative investigating power, see Frankfurter, Hands Off The Investigations, The New Republic, May 21, 1924, p. 329; Landis, Constitutional Limitations on the Congressional Power of Investigation, 40 Harv. L. Rev. 153 (1926); Potts, Power of Legislative Bodies to Punish For Contempt, 74 U. Pa. L. Rev. 691 (1926). For critical material, seeking to limit legislative inquiry in behalf of individual rights, see Coudert, Congressional Inquisition vs. Individual Liberty, 15 Va. L. Rev. 537 (1929). See also Wigmore, Comment, 19 Ill. L. Rev. 452 (1925). For further reference to some of the earlier material, see Barsky v. United States, 167 F.2d 241, 244 n. 5 (D.C. Cir. 1948).

A summary-index of Congressional hearings and reports dealing with subversive activities, which includes lists of witnesses and exhibits, and tables of contents of reports, is Congressional Investigations of Communism and Subversive Activities, Summary-Index, 1918 to 1956, Sen. Doc. No. 148, 84th Cong., 2d Sess. (1956). The applicable statutes, the resolutions authorizing inquiries, and a listing of the hearings and reports are included in Internal Security Manual (rev.), Sen. Doc. No. 126, 86th Cong., 2d Sess. (1961). The Committee on Un-American Activities issues periodically an index to its publications, which also contains an index of all witnesses who have testified before the Committee. A digest of the hearings and reports of federal, state, and local investigating committees, together with a topical guide, appears in Digest of the Public Record of Communism in the United States pt. III (Fund for the Republic 1955). A summary account of all Congressional investigations from 1945 through 1964 is set forth in Congressional Quarterly, Congress and the Nation, ch. 17 (1965). In Beck, Contempt of Congress (1959), Appendix A contains a synopsis of all contempt citations from 1787 through 1943, and Appendix B tabulates all contempt citations (with references to the legislative history and court decisions) from 1944 through 1958. A collection of original materials and of references may be found in Newman and Surrey, Legislation: Cases and Materials 250-563 (1955). Two general studies on the subject are Barth, Government by Investigation (1955), and Taylor, Grand Inquest: The Story of Congressional Investigations (1955). Other general discussions include the symposium, Congressional Investigations, 18 U. Chi. L. Rev. 421 (Spring Issue 1951); the symposium, Legislative Investigations: Safeguards for Witnesses, 29 Notre Dame Law. 157 (Winter Issue 1954); symposium, Congressional Hearings and Investigations, 14 Fed. B.J. 5, 91 (1954); Carr, The Constitution and Congressional Investigating Committees (published by the Carrie Chapman Catt Memorial Fund 1954); Congressional Power of Investigation, Sen. Doc. No. 99, 83d Cong., 2d Sess. (1954) (a study prepared for the Senate Judiciary Committee by the Legislative Reference Service of the Library of Congress). See also Johnsen, The Investigating Powers of Congress (1951) (with bibliography).

The operation of the Committee on Un-American Activities from its origin in 1938 to the end of 1944 is described in Ogden, The Dies Committee (2d ed. 1945); and from 1945 through 1950 in Carr, The House Committee on Un-American Activities (1952). See also Gellermann, Martin Dies (1944). More recent appraisals, from opposing viewpoints, are Donner, The Un-Americans (1961), and Buckley (ed.), The Committee and Its Critics (1962). See also comment on the Buckley book in Auerbach, Some Comments on the Case for the House Un-American Activities Committee, 47 Minn. L. Rev. 593 (1963). For criticism of particular reports of the Committee, see Gellhorn, Report on a Report of the House Committee on Un-American Activities, 60 Harv. L. Rev. 1193 (1947), criticizing the Committee's report on the Southern Conference for Human Welfare, H.R. Rep. No. 592, 80th Cong., 1st Sess. (1947); Emerson, The National Lawyers Guild: Legal Bulwark of Democracy, 10 Law Guild Rev. 93 (1950), a reply to the

Committee's report The National Lawyers Guild: Legal Bulwark of the Communist Party, Sept. 17, 1950.

On the McCarthy Committee see the material cited in the bibliography following Section C, subsection 1, supra. The hearings and reports leading to the censure of Senator McCarthy are Hearings before Special Subcommittee on Investigations of the Senate Committee on Government Operations pursuant to S. Res. 189, 83d Cong., 2d Sess. (1954); report of the Subcommittee, Sen. Rep. No. 2507, 83d Cong., 2d Sess. (1954), reprinted in part in U.S. News and World Report, Sept. 10, 1954, p. 76; Report of the Select Committee to Study Censure Charges, Sen. Rep. No. 2508, 83d Cong., 2d Sess. (1954), reprinted in U.S. News and World Report, Oct. 8, 1954, p. 60. See also Straight, Trial by Television (1954); deFuria, The McCarthy Censure Case, 42 A.B.A.J. 329 (1956); Dorsen and Simon, McCarthy and the Army: A Fight on the Wrong Front, 7 Colum. U. Forum 21 (1964).

Material dealing with other well-known investigations includes Newman, The Supreme Court, Congressional Investigations, and Influence Peddling, 33 N.Y.U.L. Rev. 796 (1958) (House Subcommittee on Legislative Oversight); Schwartz, The Professor and the Commissions (1959) (same); Kalven, Congressional Testing of Linus Pauling, Bull. of the Atomic Scientists, December 1960, p. 383, and January 1961, p. 12 (Internal Security Subcommittee); Jacobs, Extracurricular Activities of the McClellan Committee, 51 Calif. L. Rev. 296 (1963).

For accounts of individual experiences with legislative investigating committees see Lattimore, Ordeal by Slander (1950); Welborn, The Ordeal of Dr. Condon, Harper's Magazine, January 1950, p. 46; Wechsler, The Age of Suspicion, chs. 13 and 14 (1953); Gillmore, Fear, The Accuser (1954); Oxnam, I Protest (1954); Wittenberg (ed.), The Lamont Case (1957); Hiss, In the Court of Public Opinion, chs. 1-6 (1957); Tynan, Command Performance: A British Critic's Report on His Interrogation by a Senate Committee, Harper's Magazine, October 1960, p. 39; Bessie, Inquisition in Eden (1965).

Descriptions of the operation of state legislative committees may be found in the following books published as part of the Cornell Studies in Civil Liberties, Prof. Robert E. Cushman, Editor: Gellhorn, The States and Subversion (1952); Barrett, The Tenney Committee: Legislative Investigation of Subversive Activities in California (1951); Chamberlain, Loyalty and Legislative Action: A Survey of Activity by the New York State Legislature, 1919-1949 (1951); Countryman, Un-American Activities in the State of Washington (1951). See also Harper, Legislative Investigation of Un-American Activities, Exhibit A: The Tenney Committee, 39 Calif. L. Rev. 502 (1951); Donner, The Miami Formula: Grass-Roots McCarthyism, The Nation, Jan. 22, 1955, p. 65; Council of State Governments, Handbook for Legislative Committees (1963).

Among the voluminous legal discussions on the powers of legislative investigating committees and review of their actions in the courts, see Note, Constitutional Limitations on the Un-American Activities Committee, 47 Colum. L. Rev. 416 (1947); Nutting, Freedom of Silence: Constitutional Protection Against Government Intrusions in Political Affairs, 47 Mich. L. Rev. 181, 200-202 (1948); Boudin, Congressional and Agency Investigations, 35 Va. L.R. 143 (1949); Morgan, Congressional Investigations and Judicial Review: Kilbourn v. Thompson Revisited, 37 Calif. L. Rev. 556 (1949); Note, 45 Ill. L. Rev. 633 (1950); Driver, Constitutional Limitations on the Power of Congress to Punish Contempts of Its Investigating Committees, 38 Va. L. Rev. 887, 1011 (1952); Lashley, The Investigating Power of Congress: Its Scope and Limitations, 40 A.B.A.J. 763 (1954); articles with the same title by Merry, 40 A.B.A.J. 1073 (1954), and by Tunstall, 40 Va. L. Rev. 875 (1954); Note, 29 Ind. L.J. 162 (1954); Taylor, Judicial Review of Legislative Investigations, 29 Notre Dame Law. 242 (1954); Taylor, Grand Inquest, chs. V and VI (1955); Note, Legislative Inquiry Into Political Activity: First Amendment Immunity from Committee Interrogation, 65 Yale L.J. 1159 (1956); Dembitz, Congressional Investigation of Newspapermen, Authors, and Others in the Opinion Field — Its Legality Under the First Amendment, 40 Minn. L. Rev. 517 (1956); Note, The Power of Congress to Investigate and to Compel Testimony, 70 Harv. L. Rev. 671 (1957); Beck, Contempt of Congress (1959); Summers, The First Amendment as a Restraint on the Power of Congress to Investigate, 43 Marq. L. Rev. 459 (1960); Alfange, Congressional Investigations and the Fickle Court, 30 U. Cinc. L. Rev. 113 (1961); Redlich, Rights of Witnesses Before Congressional Committees, 36 N.Y.U.L. Rev. 1126 (1961); Note, 7 Vill. L. Rev. 84 (1961); Goldfarb, The Contempt Power, ch. IV (1963); Symposium, 51 Calif. L. Rev. 267 (1963); Shapiro, Law and Politics in the Supreme Court, ch. 2 (1964). See also Franklin, Infamy and Constitutional Civil Liberties, 14 Law. Guild Rev. 1 (1954). A popular analysis of the legal issues in Arthur Miller's case is Kalven, A View From the Law, The New Republic, May 27, 1957, p. 8.

For discussion of the legal powers of state and local committees see Herwitz and Mulligan, The Legislative Investigating Committee — A Survey and Critique, 33 Colum. L. Rev. 4 (1933); Cousens, The Purposes and Scope of Investigations Under Legislative Authority, 26 Geo. L.J. 905 (1938); Ebel, Investigatory Powers of City Councils, 38 Marq. L. Rev. 223 (1955); Note, 9 Rutgers L. Rev. 576 (1955).

With respect to limitations on investigations by administrative commissions, see Hannah v. Larche, 363 U.S. 420, 80 S. Ct. 1502, 4 L. Ed. 2d 1307 (1960); Newman, Due Process, Investigations and Civil Rights, 8 U.C.L.A.L. Rev. 735 (1961).

Other materials commenting on particular decisions are cited infra, as are materials dealing with self-incrimination, other specific limitations, and committee procedures.

There are numerous discussions of the policy issues involved in modern legislative investigations. In addition to the above material see, for a sample of the debate, White, An Inquiry Into Congressional Inquiries, N.Y. Times Magazine. March 23, 1952, p. 11; Gossett, Are We Neglecting Constitutional Liberty? 38 A.B.A.J. 817 (1952); Williams, The Duty to Investigate, 3 Freeman, 1953, p. 917; Morris, Should Congress Investigate? The Case for the Senate Subcommittee on Internal Security, Saturday Review, Feb. 19, 1955, p. 9; Angell, Should Congress Investigate? A New Procedure for the Congressional Committee, Saturday Review, Feb. 26, 1955, p. 9; Clardy, Congressional Investigations of Subversion, 35 Mich. St. B.J. No. 4 (April 1956), p. 37, answering Kauper, Government of Laws — Not of Men, 33 Mich. St. B.J. No. 8 (Aug. 1954), p. 9.

For a more complete bibliography see Tompkins, Investigating Procedures of Congressional Committees: A Bibliography (U. of Calif., 1954); Beck, Contempt of Congress 252-258 (1959).

On the British use of the power of inquiry see Finer, Congressional Investigations: The British System, 18 U. Chi. L. Rev. 521 (1951); Hailsham, Parliamentary Inquiry and Congressional Investigation Compared, 40 A.B.A.J. 787 (1954); Robson, Public Inquiries as an Instrument of Government, 1 Brit. J. Ad. L. 71 (1954); Clokie and Robinson, Royal Commissions of Inquiry (1937); Taylor, Grand Inquest, App. I (1955). See also Campbell, Parliamentary Investigations: The Australian Experience, 9 J. Pub. L. 382 (1960).

1. Basic Powers and Limitations

Issues relating to the powers of Congressional investigating committees had come before the Supreme Court in a number of cases, beginning with Kilbourn v. Thompson in 1881. 103 U.S. 168, 26 L. Ed. 377. In a series of decisions during the 1920's, of which the most important was McGrain v. Daugherty, 273 U.S. 135, 47 S. Ct. 319, 71 L. Ed. 580 (1927), the Court had broadly upheld the power of Congress to investigate and obtain information in aid of its legislative or other functions. The problem in its present context, involving the modern legislative committee investigation in the field of political expression, arose in an increasing volume of cases in the years following World War II.

The first decisions of the appellate courts were in United States v. Josephson, 165 F.2d 82 (2d Cir. 1947) and Barsky v. United States, 167 F.2d 241 (D.C. Cir. 1948). In these cases the Court of Appeals for the Second Circuit (Judge Clark dissenting) and the Court of Appeals for the District of Columbia Circuit (Judge Edgerton dissenting) held that the Committee on Un-American Activities was not exceeding constitutional powers or acting in violation of the First Amendment, in questioning witnesses about Communist Party membership or associations. The opinions, majority and minority, dealt with the constitutional issues at length. The Supreme Court, however, denied certiorari in both cases. 333 U.S. 838 (1948) (Justices Douglas, Murphy, and Rutledge dissenting); 334 U.S. 843 (1948). Other cases raising similar issues were disposed of in the same fashion, thus leaving the Josephson and Barsky cases as the controlling law.

Following these decisions and the indictment of the Communist Party leaders under the Smith Act in July 1948, a number of witnesses began to invoke the privilege against self-incrimination in refusing to answer questions on alleged subversive activities before Congressional committees. The use of the privilege was sustained by the courts, and came to be widely employed. Some witnesses, however, continued to challenge the committees as lacking affirmative power or violating the First Amendment in making such inquiries. No decision of the lower federal courts upheld these contentions. But in a substantial proportion of the cases the courts did uphold the witness on non-constitutional objections to the committee's authority or procedure.

The Supreme Court did not take occasion to express its views on the power of legislative committees to inquire into the area of political expression until its decision in 1953 in the Rumely case, and then only indirectly. That case involved an investigation by the House Select Committee on Lobbying Activities (the Buchanan Committee), operating under a resolution authorizing it to investigate "all lobbying activities intended to influence, encourage, promote, or retard legislation." Rumely, executive secretary of the Committee for Constitutional Government, was found guilty of contempt for refusing to reveal to the Buchanan Committee the names of individuals making bulk purchases of The Road Ahead (by John Flynn) and other books for distribution by Rumely's organization. A majority of the Supreme Court avoided a direct decision on the constitutional issues by construing the resolution as not authorizing the Buchanan Committee to inquire into the matters about which Rumely refused to answer. Otherwise, the Court said, it would be confronted with "grave constitutional questions": "Surely it cannot be denied that giving the scope to the resolution for which the Government contends, that is, deriving from it the power to inquire into all efforts of private individuals to influence public opinion through books and periodicals, however remote the radiations of influence which they may exert upon the ultimate legislative process, raises doubts of constitutionality in view of the prohibition of the First Amendment." United States v. Rumely, 345 U.S. 41, 46, 73 S. Ct. 543, 97 L. Ed. 770 (1953). See also United States v. Harriss, 347 U.S. 612, 74 S. Ct. 808, 98 L. Ed. 989 (1954).

In the following term the Supreme Court again touched on the issue, by way of dictum, in a Fifth Amendment case. Quinn v. United States, 349 U.S. 155, 161, 75 S. Ct. 668, 672, 99 L. Ed. 964, 971 (1955). Finally in the spring of 1957 the Supreme Court came to grips with some of the issues in major decisions in the Watkins and Sweezy cases.

REFERENCES

Other cases in which the lower federal courts, following the Josephson and Barsky decisions, upheld the basic power of Congressional committees to investigate alleged subversive activities include Dennis v. United States, 171 F.2d 986 (D.C. Cir. 1948), considered by the Supreme Court on the jury issue, 339 U.S. 162, 70 S. Ct. 519, 94 L. Ed. 734 (1950); Lawson v. United States and Trumbo v. United States, 176 F.2d 49 (D.C. Cir. 1949), cert. den., 339 U.S. 934 (1950) (the "Hollywood Ten" cases); Marshall v. United States, 176 F.2d 473 (D.C. Cir. 1949), cert. den., 339 U.S. 933 (1950); Morford v. United States, 184 F.2d 864 (D.C. Cir. 1950), cert. den., 340 U.S. 878 (1950). See also Eisler v. United States, 170 F.2d 273 (D.C. Cir. 1948), in which the witness was convicted of contempt when he refused to be sworn until he had read a statement. The Supreme Court granted certiorari, 335 U.S. 857 (1948), but later dismissed the case as moot after Eisler had fled the country. 338 U.S. 189 (1949).

See also Kamp v. United States, 176 F.2d 618 (D.C. Cir. 1948), cert. den., 339 U.S. 957 (1950).

WATKINS v. UNITED STATES
354 U.S. 178, 77 S. Ct. 1173, 1 L. Ed. 2d 1273 (1957)

Mr. Chief Justice Warren delivered the opinion of the Court.

[Petitioner Watkins was convicted of "contempt of Congress" under 2 U.S.C. §192 for refusing to answer questions before a Subcommittee of the House Committee on Un-American Activities investigating Communist activities in the Chicago area. Watkins, who had been a union official for many years, answered all questions about himself, denying that he had been a member of the Communist Party but stating that he had "cooperated with the Communist Party and participated in Communist activities." When asked to identify a group of persons (whom he had known) as members of the Communist Party, he took the position: "I will also answer questions about those persons whom I knew to be members of the Communist Party and whom I believe still are. I will not, however, answer any questions with respect to others with whom I associated in the past."]

We start with several basic premises on which there is general agreement.

The power of the Congress to conduct investigations is inherent in the legislative process. That power is broad. It encompasses inquiries concerning the administration of existing laws as well as proposed or possibly needed statutes. It includes surveys of defects in our social, economic or political system for the purpose of enabling the Congress to remedy them. It comprehends probes into departments of the Federal Government to expose corruption, inefficiency or waste. But, broad as is this power of inquiry, it is not unlimited. There is no general authority to expose the private affairs of individuals without justification in terms of the functions of the Congress. This was freely conceded by the Solicitor General in his argument of this case.[8] Nor is the Congress a law enforcement or trial agency. These are functions of the executive and judicial departments of government. No inquiry is an end in itself; it must be related to, and in furtherance of, a legitimate task of the Congress. Investigations conducted solely for the personal aggrandizement of the investigators or to "punish" those investigated are indefensible.

It is unquestionably the duty of all citizens to cooperate with the Congress in its efforts to obtain the facts needed for intelligent legislative action. It is their unremitting obligation to respond to subpoenas, to respect the dignity of the Congress and its committees and to testify fully with respect to matters within the province of proper investigation. This, of course, assumes that the constitutional rights of witnesses will be respected by the Congress as they are in a court of justice. The Bill of Rights is applicable to investigations as to all forms of governmental action. Witnesses cannot be compelled to give evidence against themselves. They cannot be subjected to unreasonable search and seizure. Nor can the First Amendment freedoms of speech, press, religion, or political belief and association be abridged. . . .

[The opinion then discusses the history of the legislative contempt power in England and the United States, and notes the applicability of the Fifth Amendment privilege against self-incrimination to legislative committees, as recognized in the Quinn case.]

A far more difficult task evolved from the claim by witnesses that the committees' interrogations were infringements upon the freedoms of the First Amendment. Clearly, an investigation is subject to the command that the Congress shall make no law abridging freedom of speech or press or assembly. While it is true that there is no statute to be reviewed, and that an investigation is not a law, nevertheless an investigation is part of law-making. It is justified solely as an adjunct to the legislative process. The First Amendment may be invoked against infringement of the protected freedoms by law or by law-making.

Abuses of the investigative process may imperceptibly lead to abridgment

---

[8] "Now, we don't claim on behalf of the Government that there is any right to expose for the purposes of exposure. And I don't know that Congress has ever claimed any such right. But we do say, in the same breath, that there is a right to inform the public at the same time you inform the Congress."

of protected freedoms. The mere summoning of a witness and compelling him to testify, against his will, about his beliefs, expressions or associations is a measure of governmental interference. And when those forced revelations concern matters that are unorthodox, unpopular, or even hateful to the general public, the reaction in the life of the witness may be disastrous. This effect is even more harsh when it is past beliefs, expressions or associations that are disclosed and judged by current standards rather than those contemporary with the matters exposed. Nor does the witness alone suffer the consequences. Those who are identified by witnesses and thereby placed in the same glare of publicity are equally subject to public stigma, scorn and obloquy. Beyond that, there is the more subtle and immeasureable effect upon those who tend to adhere to the most orthodox and uncontroversial views and associations in order to avoid a similar fate at some future time. That this impact is partly the result of non-governmental activity by private persons cannot relieve the investigators of their responsibility for initiating the reaction. . . .

Accommodation of the congressional need for particular information with the individual and personal interest in privacy is an arduous and delicate task for any court. We do not underestimate the difficulties that would attend such an undertaking. It is manifest that despite the adverse effects which follow upon compelled disclosure of private matters, not all such inquiries are barred. Kilbourn v. Thompson teaches that such an investigation into individual affairs is invalid if unrelated to any legislative purpose. That is beyond the powers conferred upon the Congress in the Constitution. United States v. Rumely makes it plain that the mere semblance of legislative purpose would not justify an inquiry in the face of the Bill of Rights. The critical element is the existence of, and the weight to be ascribed to, the interest of the Congress in demanding disclosures from an unwilling witness. We cannot simply assume, however, that every congressional investigation is justified by a public need that overbalances any private rights affected. To do so would be to abdicate the responsibility placed by the Constitution upon the judiciary to insure that the Congress does not unjustifiably encroach upon an individual's right to privacy nor abridge his liberty of speech, press, religion or assembly.

Petitioner has earnestly suggested that the difficult questions of protecting these rights from infringement by legislative inquiries can be surmounted in this case because there was no public purpose served in his interrogation. His conclusion is based upon the thesis that the Subcommittee was engaged in a program of exposure for the sake of exposure. The sole purpose of the inquiry, he contends, was to bring down upon himself and others the violence of public reaction because of their past beliefs, expressions and associations. In support of this argument, petitioner has marshalled an impressive array of evidence that some Congressmen have believed that such was their duty, or part of it.[32]

---

[32] In a report to the House, the Committee declared:

"While Congress does not have the power to deny to citizens the right to believe in,

We have no doubt that there is no congressional power to expose for the sake of exposure. The public is, of course, entitled to be informed concerning the workings of its government.[33] That cannot be inflated into a general power to expose where the predominant result can only be an invasion of the private rights of individuals. But a solution to our problem is not to be found in testing the motives of committee members for this purpose. Such is not our function. Their motives alone would not vitiate an investigation which had been instituted by a House of Congress if that assembly's legislative purpose is being served.

Petitioner's contentions do point to a situation of particular significance from the standpoint of the constitutional limitations upon congressional investigations. The theory of a committee inquiry is that the committee members are serving as the representatives of the parent assembly in collecting information for a legislative purpose. Their function is to act as the eyes and ears of the Congress in obtaining facts upon which the full legislature can act. To carry out this mission, committees and subcommittees, sometimes one Congressman, are endowed with the full power of the Congress to compel testimony. In this case, only two men exercised that authority in demanding information over petitioner's protest.

An essential premise in this situation is that the House or Senate shall have instructed the committee members on what they are to do with the power delegated to them. It is the responsibility of the Congress, in the first instance, to insure that compulsory process is used only in furtherance of a legislative

---

teach, or advocate, communism, fascism, and naziism, it does have the right to focus the spotlight of publicity upon their activities. . . ." H.R. Rep. No. 2, 76th Cong., 1st Sess. 13.

A year later, the Committee reported that ". . . investigation to inform the American people . . . is the real purpose of the House Committee." H.R. Rep. No. 1476, 76th Cong., 3d Sess. 1-2.

A pamphlet issued by the Committee in 1951 stated that: "Exposure in a systematic way began with the formation of the House Committee on Un-American Activities, May 26, 1938." The Committee believed itself commanded ". . . to expose people and organizations attempting to destroy this country. That is still its job and to that job it sticks." 100 Things You Should Know About Communism, H.R. Doc. No. 136, 82d Cong., 1st Sess. 19, 67.

In its annual reports, the Committee has devoted a large part of its information to a public listing of names along with a summary of their activities. ". . . [T]he committee feels that the Congress and the American people will have a much clearer and fuller picture of the success and scope of communism in the United States by having set forth the names and, where possible, the positions occupied by individuals who have been identified as Communists, or former Communists, during the past year." H.R. Rep. No. 2516, 82d Cong., 2d Sess. 6-7.

[33] We are not concerned with the power of the Congress to inquire into and publicize corruption, maladministration or inefficiency in agencies of the Government. That was the only kind of activity described by Woodrow Wilson in Congressional Government when he wrote: "The informing function of Congress should be preferred even to its legislative function." Id., at 303. From the earliest times in its history, the Congress has assiduously performed an "informing function" of this nature. See Landis, Constitutional Limitations on the Congressional Power of Investigation, 40 Harv. L. Rev. 153, 168-194.

purpose. That requires that the instructions to an investigating committee spell out that group's jurisdiction and purpose with sufficient particularity. Those instructions are embodied in the authorizing resolution. That document is the committee's charter. Broadly drafted and loosely worded, however, such resolutions can leave tremendous latitude to the discretion of the investigators. The more vague the committee's charter is, the greater becomes the possibility that the committee's specific actions are not in conformity with the will of the parent House of Congress.

The authorizing resolution of the Un-American Activities Committee was adopted in 1938 when a select committee, under the chairmanship of Representative Dies, was created.[35] Several years later, the Committee was made a standing organ of the House with the same mandate.[36] It defines the Committee's authority as follows:

"The Committee on Un-American Activities, as a whole or by subcommittee, is authorized to make from time to time investigations of (1) the extent, character, and objects of un-American propaganda activities in the United States, (2) the diffusion within the United States of subversive and un-American propaganda that is instigated from foreign countries or of a domestic origin and attacks the principle of the form of government as guaranteed by our Constitution, and (3) all other questions in relation thereto that would aid Congress in any necessary remedial legislation." [37]

It would be difficult to imagine a less explicit authorizing resolution. Who can define the meaning of "un-American"? What is that single, solitary "principle of the form of government as guaranteed by our Constitution"? [38] There is no need to dwell upon the language, however. At one time, perhaps, the resolution might have been read narrowly to confine the Committee to the subject of propaganda.[39] The events that have transpired in the fifteen years before the interrogation of petitioner make such a construction impossible at this date.

The members of the Committee have clearly demonstrated that they did not feel themselves restricted in any way to propaganda in the narrow sense of the word.[40] Unquestionably the Committee conceived of its task in the

[35] H. Res. 282, 75th Cong., 3d Sess., 83 Cong. Rec. 7568, 7586.

[36] H. Res. 5, 79th Cong., 1st Sess., 91 Cong. Rec. 10, 15.

[37] H. Res. 5, 83d Cong., 1st Sess., 99 Cong. Rec. 18, 24.

[38] For contrasting views, see Morford v. United States, 176 F.2d 54, 57-58, and Barsky v. United States, 167 F.2d 241, 247-248.

[39] The language of the resolution was obviously taken from the Dickstein resolution, which established the McCormack Committee in 1934 to study Nazi and other propaganda sent into the United States from foreign countries. H. Res. 198, 73d Cong., 2d Sess., 78 Cong. Rec. 4934, 4949.

[40] In 1947, Judge Charles E. Clark, now Chief Judge of the Court of Appeals for the Second Circuit, wrote about the Committee:

"Suffice it to say here that its range of activity has covered all varieties of organizations, including the American Civil Liberties Union, the C.I.O., the National Catholic Welfare Conference, the Farmer-Labor party, the Federal Theatre Project, consumers' organizations, various publications from the magazine 'Time' to the 'Daily Worker,'

grand view of its name. Un-American activities were its target, no matter how or where manifested. Notwithstanding the broad purview of the Committee's experience, the House of Representatives repeatedly approved its continuation. Five times it extended the life of the special committee. Then it made the group a standing committee of the House. A year later, the Committee's charter was embodied in the Legislative Reorganization Act. On five occasions, at the beginning of sessions of Congress, it has made the authorizing resolution part of the rules of the House. On innumerable occasions, it has passed appropriation bills to allow the Committee to continue its efforts.

Combining the language of the resolution with the construction it has been given, it is evident that the preliminary control of the Committee exercised by the House of Representatives is slight or non-existent. No one could reasonably deduce from the charter the kind of investigation that the Committee was directed to make. As a result, we are asked to engage in a process of retroactive rationalization. Looking backward from the events that transpired, we are asked to uphold the Committee's actions unless it appears that they were clearly not authorized by the charter. As a corollary to this inverse approach, the Government urges that we must view the matter hospitably to the power of the Congress — that if there is any legislative purpose which might have been furthered by the kind of disclosure sought, the witness must be punished for withholding it. No doubt every reasonable indulgence of legality must be accorded to the actions of a coordinate branch of our Government. But such deference cannot yield to an unnecessary and unreasonable dissipation of precious constitutional freedoms.

The Government contends that the public interest at the core of the investigations of the Un-American Activities Committee is the need by the Congress to be informed of efforts to overthrow the Government by force and violence so that adequate legislative safeguards can be erected. From this core, however, the Committee can radiate outward infinitely to any topic thought to be related in some way to armed insurrection. The outer reaches of this domain are known only by the content of "un-American activities." Remoteness of subject can be aggravated by a probe for a depth of detail even farther removed from any basis of legislative action. A third dimension is added when the investigators turn their attention to the past to collect minutiae on remote topics, on the hypothesis that the past may reflect upon the present.

The consequences that flow from this situation are manifold. In the first place, a reviewing court is unable to make the kind of judgment made by the Court in United States v. Rumely, supra. The Committee is allowed, in es-

---

and varying forms and types of industry, of which the recent investigation of the movie industry is fresh in the public mind. While it has avoided specific definition of what it is seeking, it has repeatedly inquired as to membership in the Communist party and in other organizations which it regards as communist controlled or affected." United States v. Josephson, 165 F.2d 82, 95 (dissent).

sence, to define its own authority, to choose the direction and focus of its activities. In deciding what to do with the power that has been conferred upon them, members of the Committee may act pursuant to motives that seem to them to be the highest. Their decisions, nevertheless, can lead to ruthless exposure of private lives in order to gather data that is neither desired by the Congress nor useful to it. Yet it is impossible in this circumstance, with constitutional freedoms in jeopardy, to declare that the Committee has ranged beyond the area committed to it by its parent assembly because the boundaries are so nebulous.

More important and more fundamental than that, however, it insulates the House that has authorized the investigation from the witnesses who are subjected to the sanctions of compulsory process. There is a wide gulf between the responsibility for the use of investigative power and the actual exercise of that power. This is an especially vital consideration in assuring respect for constitutional liberties. Protected freedoms should not be placed in danger in the absence of a clear determination by the House or the Senate that a particular inquiry is justified by a specific legislative need.

It is, of course, not the function of this Court to prescribe rigid rules for the Congress to follow in drafting resolutions establishing investigating committees. That is a matter peculiarly within the realm of the legislature, and its decisions will be accepted by the courts up to the point where their own duty to enforce the constitutionally protected rights of individuals is affected. An excessively broad charter, like that of the House Un-American Activities Committee, places the courts in an untenable position if they are to strike a balance between the public need for a particular interrogation and the right of citizens to carry on their affairs free from unnecessary governmental interference. It is impossible in such a situation to ascertain whether any legislative purpose justifies the disclosures sought and, if so, the importance of that information to the Congress in furtherance of its legislative function. The reason no court can make this critical judgment is that the House of Representatives itself has never made it. Only the legislative assembly initiating an investigation can assay the relative necessity of specific disclosures.

Absence of the qualitative consideration of petitioner's questioning by the House of Representatives aggravates a serious problem, revealed in this case, in the relationship of congressional investigating committees and the witnesses who appear before them. Plainly these committees are restricted to the missions delegated to them, i.e., to acquire certain data to be used by the House or the Senate in coping with a problem that falls within its legislative sphere. No witness can be compelled to make disclosures on matters outside that area. This is a jurisdictional concept of pertinency drawn from the nature of a congressional committee's source of authority. It is not wholly different from nor unrelated to the element of pertinency embodied in the criminal statute under which petitioner was prosecuted. When the definition of jurisdictional pertinency is as uncertain and wavering as in the case of the Un-American Activities Committee, it becomes extremely difficult for the Committee to limit its inquiries to statutory pertinency.

Since World War II, the Congress has practically abandoned its original practice of utilizing the coercive sanction of contempt proceedings at the bar of the House. The sanction there imposed is imprisonment by the House until the recalcitrant witness agrees to testify or disclose the matters sought, provided that the incarceration does not extend beyond adjournment. The Congress has instead invoked the aid of the federal judicial system in protecting itself against contumacious conduct. It has become customary to refer these matters to the United States Attorneys for prosecution under criminal law.

The appropriate statute is found in 2 U.S.C. §192. It provides:

"Every person who having been summoned as a witness by the authority of either House of Congress to give testimony or to produce papers upon any matter under inquiry before either House, or any joint committee established by a joint or concurrent resolution of the two Houses of Congress, or any committee of either House of Congress, willfully makes default, or who, having appeared, refuses to answer any question pertinent to the question under inquiry, shall be deemed guilty of a misdemeanor, punishable by a fine of not more than $1,000 nor less than $100 and imprisonment in a common jail for not less than one month nor more than twelve months." [45]

In fulfillment of their obligation under this statute, the courts must accord to the defendants every right which is guaranteed to defendants in all other criminal cases. Among these is the right to have available, through a sufficiently precise statute, information revealing the standard of criminality before the commission of the alleged offense.[46] Applied to persons prosecuted under §192, this raises a special problem in that the statute defines the crime as refusal to answer "any question pertinent to the question under inquiry." Part of the standard of criminality, therefore, is the pertinency of the questions propounded to the witness.

The problem attains proportion when viewed from the standpoint of the witness who appears before a congressional committee. He must decide at the time the questions are propounded whether or not to answer. As the Court said in Sinclair v. United States, 279 U.S. 263, the witness acts at his peril. He

---

[45] This statute was passed in 1857 as a direct result of an incident which caused the Congress to feel that it needed more severe sanctions to compel disclosures than were available in the historical procedure of summoning the recalcitrant witness before the bar of either House of Congress and ordering him held in custody until he agreed to testify. Such imprisonment is valid only so long as the House remains in session. See Anderson v. Dunn, 6 Wheat. 204, 231; Eberling, Congressional Investigations, 180-184. . . .

[46] United States v. Harriss, 347 U.S. 612; United States v. Cardiff, 344 U.S. 174; Winters v. New York, 333 U.S. 507; Musser v. Utah, 333 U.S. 95; Lanzetta v. New Jersey, 306 U.S. 451.

is ". . . bound rightly to construe the statute." Id., at 299. An erroneous determination on his part, even if made in the utmost good faith, does not exculpate him if the court should later rule that the questions were pertinent to the question under inquiry.

It is obvious that a person compelled to make this choice is entitled to have knowledge of the subject to which the interrogation is deemed pertinent. That knowledge must be available with the same degree of explicitness and clarity that the Due Process Clause requires in the expression of any element of a criminal offense. The "vice of vagueness" must be avoided here as in all other crimes. There are several sources that can outline the "question under inquiry" in such a way that the rules against vagueness are satisfied. The authorizing resolution, the remarks of the chairman or members of the committee, or even the nature of the proceedings themselves, might sometimes make the topic clear. This case demonstrates, however, that these sources often leave the matter in grave doubt.

[The Court then holds that neither the authorizing resolution, the delegation from the full Committee to the Subcommittee, nor the opening statements of the Chairman, made clear the topic of the inquiry.]

The Government believes that the topic of inquiry before the Subcommittee concerned Communist infiltration in labor. In his introductory remarks, the Chairman made reference to a bill, then pending before the Committee, which would have penalized labor unions controlled or dominated by persons who were, or had been, members of a "Communist-action" organization, as defined in the Internal Security Act of 1950. The Subcommittee, it is contended, might have been endeavoring to determine the extent of such a problem.

This view is corroborated somewhat by the witnesses who preceded and followed petitioner before the Subcommittee. Looking at the entire hearings, however, there is strong reason to doubt that the subject revolved about labor matters. The published transcript is entitled: Investigation of Communist Activities in the Chicago Area, and six of the nine witnesses had no connection with labor at all.

The most serious doubts as to the Subcommittee's "question under inquiry," however, stem from the precise questions that petitioner has been charged with refusing to answer. Under the terms of the statute, after all, it is these which must be proved pertinent. Petitioner is charged with refusing to tell the Subcommittee whether or not he knew that certain named persons had been members of the Communist Party in the past. The Subcommittee's counsel read the list from the testimony of a previous witness who had identified them as Communists. Although this former witness was identified with labor, he had not stated that the persons he named were involved in union affairs. Of the thirty names propounded to petitioner, seven were completely unconnected with organized labor. One operated a beauty parlor. Another was a watchmaker. Several were identified as "just citizens" or "only Communists." When almost a quarter of the persons on the list are not labor people, the inference becomes strong that the subject before the Subcommittee was not defined in terms of Communism in labor.

The final source of evidence as to the "question under inquiry" is the Chairman's response when petitioner objected to the questions on the grounds of lack of pertinency. The Chairman then announced that the Subcommittee was investigating "subversion and subversive propaganda." This is a subject at least as broad and indefinite as the authorizing resolution of the Committee, if not more so.

Having exhausted the several possible indicia of the "question under inquiry," we remain unenlightened as to the subject to which the questions asked petitioner were pertinent. Certainly, if the point is that obscure after trial and appeal, it was not adequately revealed to petitioner when he had to decide at his peril whether or not to answer. Fundamental fairness demands that no witness be compelled to make such a determination with so little guidance. Unless the subject matter has been made to appear with undisputable clarity, it is the duty of the investigative body, upon objection of the witness on grounds of pertinency, to state for the record the subject under inquiry at that time and the manner in which the propounded questions are pertinent thereto. To be meaningful, the explanation must describe what the topic under inquiry is and the connective reasoning whereby the precise questions asked relate to it.

The statement of the Committee Chairman in this case, in response to petitioner's protest, was woefully inadequate to convey sufficient information as to the pertinency of the questions to the subject under inquiry. Petitioner was thus not accorded a fair opportunity to determine whether he was within his rights in refusing to answer, and his conviction is necessarily invalid under the Due Process Clause of the Fifth Amendment.

We are mindful of the complexities of modern government and the ample scope that must be left to the Congress as the sole constitutional depository of legislative power. Equally mindful are we of the indispensable function, in the exercise of that power, of congressional investigations. The conclusions we have reached in this case will not prevent the Congress, through its committees, from obtaining any information it needs for the proper fulfillment of its role in our scheme of government. The legislature is free to determine the kinds of data that should be collected. It is only those investigations that are conducted by use of compulsory process that give rise to a need to protect the rights of individuals against illegal encroachment. That protection can be readily achieved through procedures which prevent the separation of power from responsibility and which provide the constitutional requisites of fairness for witnesses. A measure of added care on the part of the House and the Senate in authorizing the use of compulsory process and by their committees in exercising that power would suffice. That is a small price to pay if it serves to uphold the principles of limited, constitutional government without constricting the power of the Congress to inform itself.

The judgment of the Court of Appeals is reversed, and the case is remanded to the District Court with instructions to dismiss the indictment.

It is so ordered.

Mr. Justice Burton and Mr. Justice Whittaker took no part in the consideration or decision of this case.

Mr. Justice Frankfurter, concurring.

I deem it important to state what I understand to be the Court's holding. Agreeing with its holding, I join its opinion. . . .

To turn to the immediate problem before us, the scope of inquiry that a committee is authorized to pursue must be defined with sufficiently unambiguous clarity to safeguard a witness from the hazards of vagueness in the enforcement of the criminal process against which the Due Process Clause protects. The questions must be put with relevance and definiteness sufficient to enable the witness to know whether his refusal to answer may lead to conviction for criminal contempt and to enable both the trial and the appellate courts readily to determine whether the particular circumstances justify a finding of guilt.

While implied authority for the questioning by the Committee, sweeping as was its inquiry, may be squeezed out of the repeated acquiescence by Congress in the Committee's inquiries, the basis for determining petitioner's guilt is not thereby laid. Prosecution for contempt of Congress presupposes an adequate opportunity for the defendant to have awareness of the pertinency of the information that he has denied to Congress. And the basis of such awareness must be contemporaneous with the witness' refusal to answer and not at the trial for it. Accordingly, the actual scope of the inquiry that the Committee was authorized to conduct and the relevance of the questions to that inquiry must be shown to have been luminous at the time when asked and not left, at best, in cloudiness. The circumstances of this case were wanting in these essentials.

Mr. Justice Clark, dissenting.

As I see it the chief fault in the majority opinion is its mischievous curbing of the informing function of the Congress. While I am not versed in its procedures, my experience in the Executive Branch of the Government leads me to believe that the requirements laid down in the opinion for the operation of the committee system of inquiry are both unnecessary and unworkable. It is my purpose to first discuss this phase of the opinion and then record my views on the merits of Watkins' case.

It may be that at times the House Committee on Un-American Activities has, as the Court says, "conceived of its task in the grand view of its name."

And, perhaps, as the Court indicates, the rules of conduct placed upon the Committee by the House admit of individual abuse and unfairness. But that is none of our affair. So long as the object of a legislative inquiry is legitimate and the questions propounded are pertinent thereto, it is not for the courts to interfere with the committee system of inquiry. To hold otherwise would be an infringement on the power given the Congress to inform itself, and thus a trespass upon the fundamental American principle of separation of powers. The majority has substituted the judiciary as the grand inquisitor and supervisor of congressional investigations. It has never been so. . . .

Permanent or standing committees of both Houses have been given power in exceedingly broad terms. For example, the Committees on the Armed Services have jurisdiction over "Common defense generally"; the Committees on Interstate and Foreign Commerce have jurisdiction over "Interstate and foreign commerce generally"; and the Committees on Appropriation have jurisdiction over "Appropriation of the revenue for the support of the Government." Perhaps even more important for purposes of comparison are the broad authorizations given to select or special committees established by the Congress from time to time. Such committees have been "authorized and directed" to make full and complete studies "of whether *organized crime* utilizes the facilities of interstate commerce or otherwise operates in interstate commerce"; "of . . . *all lobbying activities* intended to influence, encourage, promote, or retard legislation"; "to determine the extent to which current literature . . . containing *immoral,* [or] *obscene* . . . matter, or placing *improper* emphasis on crime . . . are being made available to the people of the United States . . ."; and "of the extent to which criminal or other *improper* practices . . . are, or have been, engaged in *in the field of labor-management relations* . . . to the *detriment* of the *interests* of the public. . . ." (Emphasis added in each example.) Surely these authorizations permit the committees even more "tremendous latitude" than the "charter" of the Un-American Activities Committee. Yet no one has suggested that the powers granted were too broad. To restrain and limit the breadth of investigative power of this Committee necessitates the similar handling of all other committees. The resulting restraint imposed on the committee system appears to cripple the system beyond workability. . . .

While ambiguity prevents exactness (and there is "vice in vagueness" the majority reminds), the sweep of the opinion seems to be that "preliminary control" of the Committee must be exercised. The Court says a witness' protected freedoms cannot "be placed in danger in the absence of a clear determination by the House or the Senate that a particular inquiry is justified by a specific legislative need." Frankly I do not see how any such procedure as "preliminary control" can be effected in either House of the Congress. What will be controlled preliminarily? The plans of the investigation, the necessity of calling certain witnesses, the questions to be asked, the details of subpoenas duces tecum, etc? As it is now, Congress is hard pressed to find sufficient time to fully debate and adopt all needed legislation. . . . In contempt prosecutions before a court, . . . the majority places an investigative hearing on a par with a criminal trial, requiring that "knowledge of the subject to which the interrogation is deemed pertinent . . . must be available [to the witness] with the same degree of explictness and clarity that the Due Process Clause requires in the expression of any element of a criminal offense." I know of no such claim ever being made before. Such a requirement has never been thought applicable to investigations and is wholly out of place when related to the informing function of the Congress. See Frankfurter, Hands Off The Investigations, 38 New Republic, May 21, 1924, p. 329, 65 Cong. Rec. 9080-9082. The Congress does not have the facts at the time of the investigation for it is the facts that are being sought. In a criminal trial the investigation has been completed and all of the facts are at hand. The informing function of the Congress is in effect "a study by the government of circumstances which seem to call for study in the public interest." See Black, Inside a Senate Investigation, 172 Harpers Magazine, Feb. 1936, pp. 275, 278. In the conduct of such a proceeding it is impossible to be as explicit and exact as in a criminal prosecution. If the Court is saying that its new rule does not apply to contempt cases tried before the bar of the House affected, it may well lead to trial of all contempt cases before the bar of the whole House in order to avoid the restrictions of the rule. But this will not promote the result desired by the majority. Summary treatment, at best, could be provided before the whole House because of the time factor, and such treatment would necessarily deprive the witness of many of the safeguards in the present procedures. On review here the majority might then find fault with that procedure.

Coming to the merits of Watkins' case, the Court reverses the judgment because: (1) The subject matter of the inquiry was not "made to appear with undisputable clarity" either through its "charter" or by the Chairman at the time of the hearing and, therefore, Watkins was deprived of a clear understanding of "the manner in which the propounded questions [were] pertinent thereto"; and (2) the present committee system of inquiry of the House, as practiced by the Un-American Activities Committee, does not provide adequate safeguards for the protection of the constitutional right of free speech. I subscribe to neither conclusion.

Watkins had been an active leader in the labor movement for many years and had been identified by two previous witnesses at the Committee's hearing in Chicago as a member of the Communist Party. There can be no question that he was fully informed of the subject matter of the inquiry. His testimony reveals a complete knowledge and understanding of the hearings at Chicago. . . .

I think the Committee here was acting entirely within its scope and that the purpose of its inquiry was set out with "undisputable clarity." In the first place, the authorizing language of the Reorganization Act must be read as a whole, not dissected. It authorized investigation into subversive activity, its

extent, character, objects, and diffusion. While the language might have been
more explicit than using such words as "un-American," or phrases like "principle of the form of government," still these are fairly well understood terms.
We must construe them to give them meaning if we can. Our cases indicate
that rather than finding fault with the use of words or phrases, we are bound
to presume that the action of the legislative body in granting authority to the
Commitee was with a legitimate object "if [the action] is *capable* of being so
construed." (Emphasis added.) People ex rel. McDonald v. Keeler, 99 N.Y.
463, 487, 2 N.E. 615, 627-628 (1885), as quoted and approved in McGrain v.
Daugherty, supra, at 178. Before we can deny the authority "it must be obvious that" the Committee has "exceeded the bounds of legislative power."
Tenney v. Brandhove, 341 U.S. 367, 378 (1951). The fact that the Committee
has often been attacked has caused close scrutiny of its acts by the House as a
whole and the House has repeatedly given the Committee its approval.
"Power" and "responsibility" have not been separated. . . .

The Court makes much of petitioner's claim of "exposure for exposure's
sake" and strikes at the purposes of the Committee through this catch phrase.
But we are bound to accept as the purpose of the Committee that stated in
the Reorganization Act together with the statements of the Chairman at the
hearings involved here. Nothing was said of exposure. The statements of a
single Congressman cannot transform the real purpose of the Committee into
something not authorized by the parent resolution. See United States v.
Rumely, 345 U.S. 41 (1953); Sinclair v. United States, 279 U.S. 263, 290, 295
(1929). The Court indicates that the questions propounded were asked for
exposure's sake and had no pertinency to the inquiry. It appears to me that
they were entirely pertinent to the announced purpose of the Committee's
inquiry. Undoubtedly Congress has the power to inquire into the subjects of
communism and the Communist Party. American Communications Assn. v.
Douds, 339 U.S. 382 (1950). As a corollary of the congressional power to
inquire into such subject matter, the Congress, through its committees, can
legitimately seek to identify individual members of the Party. Barsky v.
United States, 167 F.2d 241 (1948), cert. denied, 334 U.S. 843. See also Lawson
v. United States, 176 F.2d 49, 52-53 (1949), cert. denied, 339 U.S. 934; United
States v. Josephson, 165 F.2d 82, 90-92 (1947), cert. denied, 333 U.S. 838.

The pertinency of the questions is highlighted by the need for the Congress
to know the extent of infiltration of communism in labor unions. This technique of infiltration was that used in bringing the downfall of countries formerly free but now still remaining behind the Iron Curtain. The Douds case
illustrates that the Party is not an ordinary political party and has not been at
least since 1945. Association with its officials is not an ordinary association.
Nor does it matter that the questions related to the past. Influences of past
associations often linger on as was clearly shown in the instance of the witness Matusow and others. The techniques used in the infiltration which admittedly existed here might well be used again in the future. If the parties

about whom Watkins was interrogated were Communists and collaborated with him, as a prior witness indicated, an entirely new area of investigation might have been opened up. Watkins' silence prevented the Committee from learning this information which could have been vital to its future investigation. The Committee was likewise entitled to elicit testimony showing the truth or falsity of the prior testimony of the witnesses who had involved Watkins and the union with collaboration with the Party. If the testimony was untrue a false picture of the relationship between the union and the Party leaders would have resulted. For these reasons there were ample indications of the pertinency of the questions. . . .

I do not see how any First Amendment rights were endangered here. There is nothing in the First Amendment that provides the guarantees Watkins claims. That Amendment was designed to prevent attempts by law to curtail freedom of speech. Whitney v. California, 274 U.S. 357, 375 (1927). It forbids Congress from making any law "abridging the freedom of speech, or of the press." It guarantees Watkins' right to join any organization and make any speech that does not have an intent to incite to crime. Dennis v. United States, 341 U.S. 494 (1951). But Watkins was asked whether he knew named individuals and whether they were Communists. He refused to answer on the ground that his rights were being abridged. What he was actually seeking to do was to protect his former associates, not himself, from embarrassment. He had already admitted his own involvement. He sought to vindicate the rights, if any, of his associates. It is settled that one cannot invoke the constitutional rights of another. Tileston v. Ullman, 318 U.S. 44, 46 (1943).

As already indicated, even if Watkins' associates were on the stand they could not decline to disclose their Communist connections on First Amendment grounds. While there may be no restraint by the Government of one's beliefs, the right of free belief has never been extended to include the withholding of knowledge of past events or transactions. There is no general privilege of silence. The First Amendment does not make speech or silence permissible to a person in such measure as he chooses. Watkins has here exercised his own choice as to when he talks, what questions he answers, and when he remains silent. A witness is not given such a choice by the Amendment. Remote and indirect disadvantages such as "public stigma, scorn and obloquy" may be related to the First Amendment, but they are not enough to block investigation. . . .

NOTES

1. In Sweezy v. New Hampshire, 354 U.S. 234, 77 S. Ct. 1203, 1 L. Ed. 2d 1311 (1957), decided the same day, the Supreme Court set aside a conviction for contempt of a one-man legislative committee in New Hampshire, saying that the committee had been "given such a sweeping and uncertain mandate" that the courts could not "have any assurance that the questions petitioner refused to

answer fall into a category of matters upon which the legislature wanted to be informed." 354 U.S. at 253-254. Justices Clark and Burton dissented.

2. Following Watkins and Sweezy the Supreme Court remanded, for reconsideration in the light of those decisions, a number of other cases pending before it, involving both federal and state legislative investigating committees. Substantial doubt existed, however, as to the significance of the decisions. The Committee on Un-American Activities did not accept the argument that the Watkins case had held its authorizing resolution invalid and continued to conduct its inquiries as before. See N.Y. Times, Aug. 24, 1957, and Aug. 6, 1958. A panel of the Court of Appeals for the District of Columbia reversed per curiam, on the basis of Watkins, a conviction of a witness, a member of the Cornell faculty, who had refused to answer questions concerning his associates before the Committee on Un-American Activities. Singer v. United States, 247 F.2d 535 (D.C. Cir. 1957). But shortly afterwards, in Barenblatt v. United States, the Court of Appeals sitting en banc rejected Barenblatt's contention that the Supreme Court in the Watkins case had struck down the resolution creating the Committee on Un-American Activities as too vague to meet the requirements of due process, as well as that the pertinency of the questions had not been made clear to him. 252 F.2d 129 (D.C. Cir. 1958). Judges Edgerton and Bazelon dissented on the ground that the Watkins case had invalidated the resolution creating the Committee on Un-American Activities and that, even if this were not so, the resolution should not be construed as authorizing an investigation into the field of education, an investigation which would raise serious constitutional questions under the Sweezy case. Judges Fahy and Washington dissented on the latter ground, not passing on the general authority of the committee.

3. Similar issues arose in connection with two cases growing out of investigations by the Subcommittee on Internal Security of the Senate Judiciary Committee. The Subcommittee operates under a Senate resolution, passed in 1950, which provides:

"That the Committee on the Judiciary, or any duly authorized subcommittee thereof is authorized and directed to make a complete and continuing study and investigation of (1) the administration, operation, and enforcement of the Internal Security Act of 1950; (2) the administration, operation, and enforcement of other laws relating to espionage, sabotage, and the protection of the internal security of the United States; and (3) the extent, nature and effects of subversive activities in the United States, its Territories and possessions, including, but not limited to, espionage, sabotage, and infiltration by persons who are or may be under the domination of the foreign government or organizations controlling the world Communist movement or any other movement seeking to overthrow the Government of the United States by force and violence." Sen. Res. 366, 81st Cong., 2d Sess. (1950), 96 Cong. Rec. 16872.

In Sacher v. United States, 356 U.S. 576, 78 S. Ct. 842, 2 L. Ed. 2d 987 (1958), the Supreme Court reversed a contempt conviction, per curiam, on the ground that the questions did not relate to a subject "within the subcommittee's scope of inquiry as authorized by its parent committee." And in Flaxer v. United States, 358 U.S. 147, 79 S. Ct. 191, 3 L. Ed. 2d 183 (1958), the Court reversed a conviction of a union official for refusal to produce membership lists, on the ground that "there was ambiguity in [the subcommittee's] ruling on the time of performance."

4. A third case decided by the Supreme Court in the period after Watkins and Sweezy, and prior to its decision in Barenblatt (see infra), was Scull v. Virginia, 359 U.S. 344, 79 S. Ct. 838, 3 L. Ed. 2d 865 (1959). Scull was called to testify before the Virginia Committee on Law Reform and Racial Activities, a committee set up as part of Virginia's program of "massive resistance" to the school segregation decisions of 1954. He refused to answer a series of questions dealing with membership and activity in various civil liberties and other organizations. Without reaching First Amendment issues the Court unanimously held that "Scull did not have an opportunity of understanding the basis for the questions or any justification on the part of the Committee for seeking the information he refused to give."

5. A number of other cases pending in the lower federal courts at the time of the Watkins case were dismissed. These included cases involving Seymour Peck of the New York Times, United States v. Peck, 154 F. Supp. 603 (D. D.C. 1957); Dr. Otto Nathan, N.Y. Times, Nov. 23, 1957; and Lee Lorch, instructor at Philander and Smith College, N.Y. Times, Nov. 28, 1957. In the case of Arthur Miller, the playwright, the District Court dismissed one count of the indictment but sustained another, fining Miller $500 and giving him a suspended one-month jail sentence. N.Y. Times, June 29 and July 26, 1957. The Court of Appeals reversed and ordered the indictment dismissed, on the ground that the Committee had not unequivocally demanded an answer. Miller v. United States, 259 F.2d 187 (D.C. Cir. 1958).

6. Following the Watkins and Sweezy decisions legislation was introduced in Congress which would withdraw the jurisdiction of the Supreme Court in any case, inter alia, "where there is drawn into question the validity of (1) any function or practice of, or the jurisdiction of, any committee or subcommittee of the United States Congress, or any action or proceeding against a witness charged with contempt of Congress;" or (3) "any statute or executive regulation of any State the general purpose of which is to control subversive activities within such State." S. 2646 (introduced by Senator Jenner), 85th Cong., 1st Sess. (1957). As noted previously, the Jenner bill was eventually defeated. See Section C, subsection 5, of this chapter.

REFERENCES

For discussion of the Watkins case and post-Watkins developments, see Alfange, Congressional Investigations and the Fickle Court, 30 U. Cinc. L. Rev. 113, 135-150 (1061); Notes, 5 U.C.L.A.L. Rev. 645 (1958); 7 Vill. L. Rev. 84, 90-94 (1961). See also Note, 24 U. Chi. L. Rev. 740 (1957), and the material, cited infra, dealing with the Barenblatt case.

BARENBLATT v. UNITED STATES
360 U.S. 109, 79 S. Ct. 1081, 3 L. Ed. 2d 1115 (1959)

Mr. Justice Harlan delivered the opinion of the Court.

Once more the Court is required to resolve the conflicting constitutional claims of congressional power and of an individual's right to resist its exercise. The congressional power in question concerns the internal process of

Congress in moving within its legislative domain; it involves the utilization of its committees to secure "testimony needed to enable it efficiently to exercise a legislative function belonging to it under the Constitution." McGrain v. Daugherty, 273 U.S. 135, 160. The power of inquiry has been employed by Congress throughout our history, over the whole range of the national interests concerning which Congress might legislate or decide upon due investigation not to legislate; it has similarly been utilized in determining what to appropriate from the national purse, or whether to appropriate. The scope of the power of inquiry, in short, is as penetrating and far-reaching as the potential power to enact and appropriate under the Constitution.

Broad as it is, the power is not, however, without limitations. Since Congress may only investigate into those areas in which it may potentially legislate or appropriate, it cannot inquire into matters which are within the exclusive province of one of the other branches of the Government. Lacking the judicial power given to the Judiciary, it cannot inquire into matters that are exclusively the concern of the Judiciary. Neither can it supplant the Executive in what exclusively belongs to the Executive. And the Congress, in common with all branches of the Government, must exercise its powers subject to the limitations placed by the Constitution on governmental action, more particularly in the context of this case the relevant limitations of the Bill of Rights.

The congressional power of inquiry, its range and scope, and an individual's duty in relation to it, must be viewed in proper perspective. McGrain v. Daugherty, supra; Landis, Constitutional Limitations on the Congressional Power of Investigation, 40 Harv. L. Rev. 153, 214; Black, Inside a Senate Investigation, 172 Harpers Monthly 275 (February 1936). The power and the right of resistance to it are to be judged in the concrete, not on the basis of abstractions. In the present case congressional efforts to learn the extent of a nation-wide, indeed world-wide, problem have brought one of its investigaing committees into the field of education. Of course, broadly viewed, inquiries cannot be made into the teaching that is pursued in any of our educational institutions. When academic teaching-freedom and its corollary learning-freedom, so essential to the well-being of the Nation, are claimed, this Court will always be on the alert against intrusion by Congress into this constitutionally protected domain. But this does not mean that the Congress is precluded from interrogating a witness merely because he is a teacher. An educational institution is not a constitutional sanctuary from inquiry into matters that may otherwise be within the constitutional legislative domain merely for the reason that inquiry is made of someone within its walls. . . .

Pursuant to a subpoena, and accompanied by counsel, petitioner on June 28, 1954, appeared as a witness before this congressional Subcommittee. After answering a few preliminary questions and testifying that he had been a graduate student and teaching fellow at the University of Michigan from 1947 to 1950 and an instructor in psychology at Vassar College from 1950 to shortly before his appearance before the Subcommittee, petitioner objected generally to the right of the Subcommittee to inquire into his "political" and "religious" beliefs or any "other personal and private affairs" or "associational activities," upon grounds set forth in a previously prepared memorandum which he was allowed to file with the Subcommittee. Thereafter petitioner specifically declined to answer each of the following five questions:

"Are you now a member of the Communist Party? [Count One.]

"Have you ever been a member of the Communist Party? [Count Two.]

"Now, you have stated that you knew Francis Crowley. Did you know Francis Crowley as a member of the Communist Party? [Count Three.]

"Were you ever a member of the Haldane Club of the Communist Party while at the University of Michigan? [Count Four.]

"Were you a member while a student of the University of Michigan Council of Arts, Sciences, and Professions?" [Count Five.]

In each instance the grounds of refusal were those set forth in the prepared statement. Petitioner expressly disclaimed reliance upon "the Fifth Amendment." . . .

As we conceive the ultimate issue in this case to be whether petitioner could properly be convicted of contempt for refusing to answer questions relating to his participation in or knowledge of alleged Communist Party activities at educational institutions in this country, we find it unnecessary to consider the validity of his conviction under the Third and Fifth Counts, the only ones involving questions which on their face do not directly relate to such participation or knowledge.

Petitioner's various contentions resolve themselves into three propositions: First, the compelling of testimony by the Subcommittee was neither legislatively authorized nor constitutionally permissible because of the vagueness of Rule XI of the House of Representatives, Eighty-third Congress, the charter of authority of the parent Committee. Second, petitioner was not adequately apprised of the pertinency of the Subcommittee's questions to the subject matter of the inquiry. Third, the questions petitioner refused to answer infringed rights protected by the First Amendment.

Subcommittee's Authority to Compel Testimony

At the outset it should be noted that Rule XI authorized this Subcommittee to compel testimony within the framework of the investigative authority conferred on the Un-American Activities Committee. Petitioner contends that Watkins v. United States [354 U.S. 178] nevertheless held the grant of this power in all circumstances ineffective because of the vagueness of Rule XI in delineating the Committee jurisdiction to which its exercise was to be appurtenant. This view of Watkins was accepted by two of the dissenting judges below. 102 U.S. App. D.C., at 124, 252 F.2d, at 136.

The Watkins case cannot properly be read as standing for such a proposition. A principal contention in Watkins was that the refusals to answer were justified because the requirement of 2 U.S.C. §192 that the questions asked be "pertinent to the question under inquiry" had not been satisfied. 354 U.S., at 208-209. This Court reversed the conviction solely on that ground, holding that Watkins had not been adequately apprised of the subject matter of the Subcommittee's investigation or the pertinency thereto of the questions he refused to answer. Id., at 206-209, 214-215; and see the concurring opinion in that case, id., at 216. In so deciding the Court drew upon Rule XI only as one of the facets in the total mise en scène in its search for the "question under inquiry" in that particular investigation. Id., at 209-215. The Court, in other words, was not dealing with Rule XI at large, and indeed in effect stated that no such issue was before it, id., at 209. That the vagueness of Rule XI was not alone determinative is also shown by the Court's further statement that aside from the Rule "the remarks of the chairman or members of the committee, or even the nature of the proceedings themselves, might sometimes make the topic [under inquiry] clear." Ibid. In short, while Watkins was critical of Rule XI, it did not involve the broad and inflexible holding petitioner now attributes to it.

Petitioner also contends, independently of Watkins, that the vagueness of Rule XI deprived the Subcommittee of the right to compel testimony in this investigation into Communist activity. We cannot agree with this contention, which in its furthest reach would mean that the House Un-American Activities Committee under its existing authority has no right to compel testimony in any circumstances. Granting the vagueness of the Rule, we may not read it in isolation from its long history in the House of Representatives. Just as legislation is often given meaning by the gloss of legislative reports, administrative interpretation, and long usage, so the proper meaning of an authorization to a congressional committee is not to be derived alone from its abstract terms unrelated to the definite content furnished them by the course of congressional actions. The Rule comes to us with a "persuasive gloss of legislative history," United States v. Witkovich, 353 U.S. 194, 199, which shows beyond doubt that in pursuance of its legislative concerns in the domain of "national security" the House has clothed the Un-American Activities Committee with pervasive authority to investigate Communist activities in this country.

The essence of that history can be briefly stated. The Un-American Activities Committee, originally known as the Dies Committee, was first established by the House in 1938. The Committee was principally a consequence of concern over the activities of the German-American Bund, whose members were suspected of allegiance to Hitler Germany, and of the Communist Party, supposed by many to be under the domination of the Soviet Union. From the beginning, without interruption to the present time, and with the undoubted knowledge and approval of the House, the Committee has devoted a major part of its energies to the investigation of Communist activities. More particularly, in 1947 the Committee announced a wide-range program in this field, pursuant to which during the years 1948 to 1952 it conducted diverse inquiries into such alleged Communist activities as espionage; efforts to learn atom bomb secrets; infiltration into labor, farmer, veteran, professional, youth, and motion picture groups; and in addition held a number of hearings upon various legislative proposals to curb Communist activities.

In the context of these unremitting pursuits, the House has steadily continued the life of the Committee at the commencement of each new Congress; it has never narrowed the powers of the Committee, whose authority has remained throughout identical with that contained in Rule XI; and it has continuingly supported the Committee's activities with substantial appropriations. Beyond this, the Committee was raised to the level of a standing committee of the House in 1945, it having been but a special committee prior to that time.

In light of this long and illuminating history it can hardly be seriously argued that the investigation of Communist activities generally, and the attendant use of compulsory process, was beyond the purview of the Committee's intended authority under Rule XI. . . .

PERTINENCY CLAIM

Undeniably a conviction for contempt under 2 U.S.C. §192 cannot stand unless the questions asked are pertinent to the subject matter of the investigation. Watkins v. United States, supra, at 214-215. But the factors which led us to rest decision on this ground in Watkins were very different from those involved here.

In Watkins the petitioner had made specific objection to the Subcommittee's questions on the ground of pertinency; the question under inquiry had not been disclosed in any illuminating manner; and the questions asked the petitioner were not only amorphous on their face, but in some instances clearly foreign to the alleged subject matter of the investigation — "Communism in labor." Id., at 185, 209-215.

In contrast, petitioner in the case before us raised no objections on the ground of pertinency at the time any of the questions were put to him. . . .

We need not, however, rest decision on petitioner's failure to object on this score, for here "pertinency" was made to appear "with undisputable clarity." Id., at 214. First of all, it goes without saying that the scope of the Committee's authority was for the House, not a witness, to determine, subject to the ultimate reviewing responsibility of this Court. What we deal with here is whether petitioner was sufficiently apprised of "the topic under inquiry" thus authorized "and the connective reasoning whereby the precise questions asked relate[d] to it." Id., at 215. In light of his prepared memorandum of constitutional objections there can be no doubt that this petitioner was well aware of the Subcommittee's authority and purpose to question him as it did.

See p. 123, supra. In addition the other sources of this information which we recognized in Watkins, supra, at 209-215, leave no room for a "pertinency" objection on this record. The subject matter of the inquiry had been identified at the commencement of the investigation as Communist infiltration into the field of education. Just prior to petitioner's appearance before the Subcommittee, the scope of the day's hearings had been announced as "in the main communism in education and the experiences and background in the party by Francis X. T. Crowley. It will deal with activities in Michigan, Boston, and in some small degree, New York." Petitioner had heard the Subcommittee interrogate the witness Crowley along the same lines as he, petitioner, was evidently to be questioned, and had listened to Crowley's testimony identifying him as a former member of an alleged Communist student organization at the University of Michigan while they both were in attendance there. Further, petitioner had stood mute in the face of the Chairman's statement as to why he had been called as a witness by the Subcommittee. And, lastly, unlike Watkins, id., at 182-185, petitioner refused to answer questions as to his own Communist Party affiliations, whose pertinency of course was clear beyond doubt.

Petitioner's contentions on this aspect of the case cannot be sustained.

CONSTITUTIONAL CONTENTIONS

Our function, at this point, is purely one of constitutional adjudication in the particular case and upon the particular record before us, not to pass judgment upon the general wisdom or efficacy of the activities of this Committee in a vexing and complicated field.

The precise constitutional issue confronting us is whether the Subcommittee's inquiry into petitioner's past or present membership in the Communist Party transgressed the provisions of the First Amendment, which of course reach and limit congressional investigations. Watkins, supra, at 197.

The Court's past cases establish sure guides to decision. Undeniably, the First Amendment in some circumstances protects an individual from being compelled to disclose his associational relationships. However, the protections of the First Amendment, unlike a proper claim of the privilege against self-incrimination under the Fifth Amendment, do not afford a witness the right to resist inquiry in all circumstances. Where First Amendment rights are asserted to bar governmental interrogation resolution of the issue always involves a balancing by the courts of the competing private and public interests at stake in the particular circumstances shown. These principles were recognized in the Watkins case, where, in speaking of the First Amendment in relation to congressional inquiries, we said (at p. 198): "It is manifest that despite the adverse effects which follow upon compelled disclosure of private matters, not all such inquiries are barred. . . . The critical element is the existence of, and the weight to be ascribed to, the interest of the Congress in demanding disclosures from an unwilling witness." See also American Communications Assn. v. Douds, 339 U.S. 382, 399-400; United States v. Rumely, supra, at 43-44. More recently in National Association for the Advancement of Colored People v. Alabama, 357 U.S. 449, 463-466, we applied the same principles in judging state action claimed to infringe rights of association assured by the Due Process Clause of the Fourteenth Amendment, and stated that the " 'subordinating interest of the State must be compelling' " in order to overcome the individual constitutional rights at stake. See Sweezy v. New Hampshire, 354 U.S. 234, 255, 265 (concurring opinion). In light of these principles we now consider petitioner's First Amendment claims.

The first question is whether this investigation was related to a valid legislative purpose, for Congress may not constitutionally require an individual to disclose his political relationships or other private affairs except in relation to such a purpose. See Watkins v. United States, supra, at 198.

That Congress has wide power to legislate in the field of Communist activity in this Country, and to conduct appropriate investigations in aid thereof, is hardly debatable. The existence of such power has never been questioned by this Court, and it is sufficient to say, without particularization, that Congress has enacted or considered in this field a wide range of legislative measures, not a few of which have stemmed from recommendations of the very Committee whose actions have been drawn in question here.[27] In the last analysis this power rests on the right of self-preservation, "the ultimate value of any society," Dennis v. United States, 341 U.S. 494, 509. Justification for its exercise in turn rests on the long and widely accepted view that the tenets of the Communist Party include the ultimate overthrow of the Government of the United States by force and violence, a view which has been given formal expression by the Congress.[28]

On these premises, this Court in its constitutional adjudications has consistently refused to view the Communist Party as an ordinary political party, and has upheld federal legislation aimed at the Communist problem which in a different context would certainly have raised constitutional issues of the gravest character. See, e.g., Carlson v. Landon, 342 U.S. 524; Galvan v. Press, 347 U.S. 522. On the same premises this Court has upheld under the Fourteenth Amendment state legislation requiring those occupying or seeking public office to disclaim knowing membership in any organization advocating overthrow of the Government by force and violence, which legislation none can avoid seeing was aimed at membership in the Communist Party. See Gerende v. Board of Supervisors, 341 U.S. 56; Garner v. Board of Public Works, 341 U.S. 716. See also Beilan v. Board of Public Education, 357 U.S. 399; Lerner v. Casey, 357 U.S. 468; Adler v. Board of Education, 342 U.S. 485.

[27] See, Legislative Recommendations by House Committee on Un-American Activities, Subsequent Action Taken by Congress or Executive Agencies (A Research Study by Legislative Reference Service of the Library of Congress), Committee on Un-American Activities, House of Representatives, 85th Cong., 2d Sess., June 1958.

[28] See, Subversive Activities Control Act of 1950, Title I of the Internal Security Act of 1950, §2, 64 Stat. 987-989. See also Carlson v. Landon, 342 U.S. 524, 535, n. 21.

Similarly, in other areas, this Court has recognized the close nexus between the Communist Party and violent overthrow of government. See Dennis v. United States, supra; American Communications Assn. v. Douds, supra. To suggest that because the Communist Party may also sponsor peaceable political reforms the constitutional issues before us should now be judged as if that Party were just an ordinary political party from the standpoint of national security, is to ask this Court to blind itself to world affairs which have determined the whole course of our national policy since the close of World War II, affairs to which Judge Learned Hand gave vivid expression in his opinion in United States v. Dennis, 183 F.2d 201, 213, and to the vast burdens which these conditions have entailed for the entire Nation.

We think that investigatory power in this domain is not to be denied Congress solely because the field of education is involved. . . . Indeed we do not understand petitioner here to suggest that Congress in no circumstances may inquire into Communist activity in the field of education. Rather, his position is in effect that this particular investigation was aimed not at the revolutionary aspects but at the theoretical classroom discussion of communism.

In our opinion this position rests on a too constricted view of the nature of the investigatory process, and is not supported by a fair assessment of the record before us. An investigation of advocacy of or preparation for overthrow certainly embraces the right to identify a witness as a member of the Communist Party, see Barsky v. United States, 83 U.S. App. D.C. 127, 167 F.2d 241, and to inquire into the various manifestations of the Party's tenets. The strict requirements of a prosecution under the Smith Act, see Dennis v. United States, supra, and Yates v. United States, 354 U.S. 298, are not the measure of the permissible scope of a congressional investigation into "overthrow," for of necessity the investigatory process must proceed step by step. Nor can it fairly be concluded that this investigation was directed at controlling what is being taught at our universities rather than at overthrow. The statement of the Subcommittee Chairman at the opening of the investigation evinces no such intention, and so far as this record reveals nothing thereafter transpired which would justify our holding that the thrust of the investigation later changed. The record discloses considerable testimony concerning the foreign domination and revolutionary purposes and efforts of the Communist Party. That there was also testimony on the abstract philosophical level does not detract from the dominant theme of this investigation — Communist infiltration furthering the alleged ultimate purpose of overthrow. And certainly the conclusion would not be justified that the questioning of petitioner would have exceeded permissible bounds had he not shut off the Subcommittee at the threshold.

Nor can we accept the further contention that this investigation should not be deemed to have been in furtherance of a legislative purpose because the true objective of the Committee and of the Congress was purely "exposure." So long as Congress acts in pursuance of its constitutional power, the Judiciary lacks authority to intervene on the basis of the motives which spurred the exercise of that power. Arizona v. California, 283 U.S. 423, 455, and cases there cited. "It is, of course, true," as was said in McCray v. United States, 195 U.S. 27, 55, "that if there be no authority in the judiciary to restrain a lawful exercise of power by another department of the government, where a wrong motive or purpose has impelled to the exertion of the power, that abuses of a power conferred may be temporarily effectual. The remedy for this, however, lies, not in the abuse by the judicial authority of its functions, but in the people, upon whom, after all, under our institutions, reliance must be placed for the correction of abuses committed in the exercise of a lawful power." These principles of course apply as well to committee investigations into the need for legislation as to the enactments which such investigations may produce. Cf. Tenney v. Brandhove, 341 U.S. 367, 377-378. Thus, in stating in the Watkins case, p. 200, that "there is no congressional power to expose for the sake of exposure," we at the same time declined to inquire into the "motives of committee members," and recognized that their "motives alone would not vitiate an investigation which had been instituted by a House of Congress if that assembly's legislative purpose is being served." Having scrutinized this record we cannot say that the unanimous panel of the Court of Appeals which first considered this case was wrong in concluding that "the primary purposes of the inquiry were in aid of legislative processes." 240 F.2d, at 881. Certainly this is not a case like Kilbourn v. Thompson, 103 U.S. 168, 192, where "the House of Representatives not only exceeded the limit of its own authority, but assumed a power which could only be properly exercised by another branch of the government, because it was in its nature clearly judicial." See McGrain v. Daugherty, 273 U.S. 135, 171. The constitutional legislative power of Congress in this instance is beyond question.

Finally, the record is barren of other factors which in themselves might sometimes lead to the conclusion that the individual interests at stake were not subordinate to those of the state. There is no indication in this record that the Subcommittee was attempting to pillory witnesses. Nor did petitioner's appearance as a witness follow from indiscriminate dragnet procedures, lacking in probable cause for belief that he possessed information which might be helpful to the Subcommittee. And the relevancy of the questions put to him by the Subcommittee is not open to doubt.

We conclude that the balance between the individual and the governmental interests here at stake must be struck in favor of the latter, and that therefore the provisions of the First Amendment have not been offended.

We hold that petitioner's conviction for contempt of Congress discloses no infirmity, and that the judgment of the Court of Appeals must be

Affirmed.

MR. JUSTICE BLACK, with whom The Chief Justice and Mr. Justice Douglas concur, dissenting.

On May 28, 1954, petitioner Lloyd Barenblatt, then 31 years old, and a teacher of psychology at Vassar College, was summoned to appear before a Subcommittee of the House Committee on Un-American Activities. After service of the summons, but before Barenblatt appeared on June 28, his four-year contract with Vassar expired and was not renewed. He, therefore, came to the Committee as a private citizen without a job. Earlier that day, the Committee's interest in Barenblatt had been aroused by the testimony of an ex-Communist named Crowley. When Crowley had first appeared before the Un-American Activities Committee he had steadfastly refused to admit or deny Communist affiliations or to identify others as Communists. After the House reported this refusal to the United States Attorney for prosecution, Crowley "voluntarily" returned and asked to testify. He was sworn in and interrogated, but not before he was made aware by various Committee members of Committee policy to "make an appropriate recommendation" to protect any witness who "fully cooperates with the committee." He then talked at length, identifying by name, address and occupation, whenever possible, people he claimed had been Communists. One of these was Barenblatt, who, according to Crowley, had been a Communist during 1947-1950 while a graduate student and teaching fellow at the University of Michigan. Though Crowley testified in great detail about the small group of Communists who had been at Michigan at that time and though the Committee was very satisfied with his testimony, it sought repetition of much of the information from Barenblatt. Barenblatt, however, refused to answer their questions and filed a long statement outlining his constitutional objections. . . .

I cannot agree with this disposition of the case for I believe that the resolution establishing the House Un-American Activities Committee and the questions that Committee asked Barenblatt violate the Constitution in several respects. (1) Rule XI creating the Committee authorizes such a sweeping, unlimited, all-inclusive and undiscriminating compulsory examination of witnesses in the field of speech, press, petition and assembly that it violates the procedural requirements of the Due Process Clause of the Fifth Amendment. (2) Compelling an answer to the questions asked Barenblatt abridges freedom of speech and association in contravention of the First Amendment. (3) The Committee proceedings were part of a legislative program to stigmatize and punish by public identification and exposure all witnesses considered by the Committee to be guilty of Communist affiliations, as well as all witnesses who refused to answer Committee questions on constitutional grounds; the Committee was thus improperly seeking to try, convict, and punish suspects, a task which the Constitution expressly denies to Congress and grants exclusively to the courts, to be exercised by them only after indictment and in full compliance with all the safeguards provided by the Bill of Rights.

[Mr. Justice Black's argument that Rule XI is too broad and vague is omitted.]

The First Amendment says in no equivocal language that Congress shall pass no law abridging freedom of speech, press, assembly or petition. The activities of this Committee, authorized by Congress, do precisely that, through exposure, obloquy and public scorn. See Watkins v. United States, 354 U.S. 178, 197-198. The Court does not really deny this fact but relies on a combination of three reasons for permitting the infringement: (A) The notion that despite the First Amendment's command Congress can abridge speech and association if this Court decides that the governmental interest in abridging speech is greater than an individual's interest in exercising that freedom, (B) the Government's right to "preserve itself," (C) the fact that the Committee is only after Communists or suspected Communists in this investigation.

(A) I do not agree that laws directly abridging First Amendment freedoms can be justified by a congressional or judicial balancing process. There are, of course, cases suggesting that a law which primarily regulates conduct but which might also indirectly affect speech can be upheld if the effect on speech is minor in relation to the need for control of the conduct. With these cases I agree. Typical of them are Cantwell v. Connecticut, 310 U.S. 296, and Schneider v. Irvington, 308 U.S. 147. Both of these involved the right of a city to control its streets. . . . But we did not in Schneider, any more than in Cantwell, even remotely suggest that a law directly aimed at curtailing speech and political persuasion could be saved through a balancing process. Neither these cases, nor any others, can be read as allowing legislative bodies to pass laws abridging freedom of speech, press and association merely because of hostility to views peacefully expressed in a place where the speaker had a right to be. Rule XI, on its face and as here applied, since it attempts inquiry into beliefs, not action — ideas and associations, not conduct — does just that.

To apply the Court's balancing test under such circumstances is to read the First Amendment to say "Congress shall pass no law abridging freedom of speech, press, assembly and petition, unless Congress and the Supreme Court reach the joint conclusion that on balance the interest of the Government in stifling these freedoms is greater than the interest of the people in having them exercised." This is closely akin to the notion that neither the First Amendment nor any other provision of the Bill of Rights should be enforced unless the Court believes it is *reasonable* to do so. Not only does this violate the genius of our *written* Constitution, but it runs expressly counter to the injunction to Court and Congress made by Madison when he introduced the Bill of Rights. "If they [the first ten amendments] are incorporated into the Constitution, independent tribunals of justice will consider themselves in a peculiar manner the guardians of those rights; they will be an impenetrable bulwark against *every* assumption of power in the Legislative or Executive; they will be naturally led to resist *every* encroachment upon rights expressly stipulated for in the Constitution by the declaration of rights." [11] Unless we return to this view of our judicial function, unless we once again accept the notion that the Bill of Rights means what it says and that this Court must

[11] 1 Annals of Cong. 439 (1789). (Italics supplied.)

enforce that meaning, I am of the opinion that our great charter of liberty will be more honored in the breach than in the observance.

But even assuming what I cannot assume, that some balancing is proper in this case, I feel that the Court after stating the test ignores it completely. At most it balances the right of the Government to preserve itself, against Barenblatt's right to refrain from revealing Communist affiliations. Such a balance, however, mistakes the factors to be weighed. In the first place, it completely leaves out the real interest in Barenblatt's silence, the interest of the people as a whole in being able to join organizations, advocate causes and make political "mistakes" without later being subjected to governmental penalties for having dared to think for themselves. It is this right, the right to err politically, which keeps us strong as a Nation. For no number of laws against communism can have as much effect as the personal conviction which comes from having heard its arguments and rejected them, or from having once accepted its tenets and later recognized their worthlessness. Instead, the obloquy which results from investigations such as this not only stifles "mistakes" but prevents all but the most courageous from hazarding any views which might at some later time become disfavored. This result, whose importance cannot be overestimated, is doubly crucial when it affects the universities, on which we must largely rely for the experimentation and development of new ideas essential to our country's welfare. It is these interests of society, rather than Barenblatt's own right to silence, which I think the Court should put on the balance against the demands of the Government, if any balancing process is to be tolerated. Instead they are not mentioned, while on the other side the demands of the Government are vastly overstated and called "self preservation." It is admitted that this Committee can only seek information for the purpose of suggesting laws, and that Congress' power to make laws in the realm of speech and association is quite limited, even on the Court's test. Its interest in making such laws in the field of education, primarily a state function, is clearly narrower still. Yet the Court styles this attenuated interest self-preservation and allows it to overcome the need our country has to let us all think, speak, and associate politically as we like and without fear of reprisal. Such a result reduces "balancing" to a mere play on words and is completely inconsistent with the rules this Court has previously given for applying a "balancing test," where it is proper: "[T]he courts should be *astute* to examine the *effect* of the challenged legislation. Mere *legislative preferences* or *beliefs* . . . may well support regulation directed at other personal activities, but be insufficient to justify such as diminishes the exercise of rights so vital to the maintenance of democratic institutions." Schneider v. Irvington, 308 U.S. 147, 161. (Italics supplied.)

(B) Moreover, I cannot agree with the Court's notion that First Amendment freedoms must be abridged in order to "preserve" our country. That notion rests on the unarticulated premise that this Nation's security hangs upon its power to punish people because of what they think, speak or write about, or because of those with whom they associate for political purposes. The Government, in its brief, virtually admits this position when it speaks of the "communication of unlawful ideas." I challenge this premise, and deny that ideas can be proscribed under our Constitution. I agree that despotic governments cannot exist without stifling the voice of opposition to their oppressive practices. The First Amendment means to me, however, that the only constitutional way our Government can preserve itself is to leave its people the fullest possible freedom to praise, criticize or discuss, as they see fit, all governmental policies and to suggest, if they desire, that even its most fundamental postulates are bad and should be changed; "Therein lies the security of the Republic, the very foundation of constitutional government." [De Jonge v. Oregon, 299 U.S. 353, 365.] On that premise this land was created, and on that premise it has grown to greatness. Our Constitution assumes that the common sense of the people and their attachment to our country will enable them, after free discussion, to withstand ideas that are wrong. To say that our patriotism must be protected against false ideas by means other than these is, I think, to make a baseless charge. Unless we can rely on these qualities — if, in short, we begin to punish speech — we cannot honestly proclaim ourselves to be a free Nation and we have lost what the Founders of this land risked their lives and their sacred honor to defend.

(C) The Court implies, however, that the ordinary rules and requirements of the Constitution do not apply because the Committee is merely after Communists and they do not constitute a political party but only a criminal gang. "[T]he long and widely accepted view," the Court says, is "that the tenets of the Communist Party include the ultimate overthrow of the Government of the United States by force and violence." This justifies the investigation undertaken. By accepting this charge and allowing it to support treatment of the Communist Party and its members which would violate the Constitution if applied to other groups, the Court, in effect, declares that Party outlawed. It has been only a few years since there was a practically unanimous feeling throughout the country and in our courts that this could not be done in our free land. Of course it has always been recognized that members of the Party who, either individually or in combination, commit acts in violation of valid laws can be prosecuted. But the Party as a whole and innocent members of it could not be attainted merely because it had some illegal aims and because some of its members were lawbreakers.

[Mr. Justice Black then cites the De Jonge case and the statements of public figures opposing outlawry of the Communist Party.]

All these statements indicate quite clearly that no matter how often or how quickly we repeat the claim that the Communist Party is not a political party, we cannot outlaw it, as a group, without endangering the liberty of all of us. The reason is not hard to find, for mixed among those aims of communism which are illegal are perfectly normal political and social goals. And muddled with its revolutionary tenets is a drive to achieve power through the ballot, if it can be done. These things necessarily make it a political party whatever other, illegal, aims it may have. Cf. Gerende v. Board of Supervisors, 341 U.S. 56. Significantly until recently the Communist Party was on the ballot in many States. When that was so, many Communists undoubtedly hoped to accomplish its lawful goals through support of Communist candidates. Even now some such may still remain. To attribute to them, and to those who have left the Party, the taint of the group is to ignore both our traditions that guilt like belief is "personal and not a matter of mere association" and the obvious fact that "men adhering to a political party or other organization notoriously do not subscribe unqualifiedly to all of its platforms or asserted principles." Schneiderman v. United States, 320 U.S. 118, 136. See also Dennis v. United States, 341 U.S. 494, 579, 581 (dissenting opinions).

The fact is that once we allow any group which has some political aims or ideas to be driven from the ballot and from the battle for men's minds because some of its members are bad and some of its tenets are illegal, no group is safe. Today we deal with Communists or suspected Communists. In 1920, instead, the New York Assembly suspended duly elected legislators on the ground that, being Socialists, they were disloyal to the country's principles. In the 1830's the Masons were hunted as outlaws and subversives, and abolitionists were considered revolutionaries of the most dangerous kind in both North and South. Earlier still, at the time of the universally unlamented alien and sedition laws, Thomas Jefferson's party was attacked and its members were derisively called "Jacobins." Fisher Ames described the party as a "French faction" guilty of "subversion" and "officered, regimented and formed to subordination." Its members, he claimed, intended to "take arms against the laws as soon as they dare." History should teach us then, that in times of high emotional excitement minority parties and groups which advocate extremely unpopular social or governmental innovations will always be typed as criminal gangs and attempts will always be made to drive them out. It was knowledge of this fact, and of its great dangers, that caused the Founders of our land to enact the First Amendment as a guarantee that neither Congress nor the people would do anything to hinder or destroy the capacity of individuals and groups to seek converts and votes for any cause, however radical or unpalatable their principles might seem under the accepted notions of the time. Whatever the States were left free to do, the First Amendment sought to leave Congress devoid of any kind or quality of power to direct any type of national laws against the freedom of individuals to think what they please, advocate whatever policy they choose, and join with others to bring about the social, religious, political and governmental changes which seem best to them. Today's holding, in my judgment, marks another major step in the progressively increasing retreat from the safeguards of the First Amendment.

[Mr. Justice Black's argument that the chief purpose of the Un-American Activities Committee is to expose and punish, and that this is not a legislative function, is omitted.]

Ultimately all the questions in this case really boil down to one — whether we as a people will try fearfully and futilely to preserve democracy by adopting totalitarian methods, or whether in accordance with our traditions and our Constitution we will have the confidence and courage to be free.

I would reverse this conviction.

MR. JUSTICE BRENNAN, dissenting.

I would reverse this conviction. It is sufficient that I state my complete agreement with my Brother Black that no purpose for the investigation of Barenblatt is revealed by the record except exposure purely for the sake of exposure. This is not a purpose to which Barenblatt's rights under the First Amendment can validly be subordinated. An investigation in which the process of law-making and law-evaluating are submerged entirely in exposure of individual behavior — in adjudication, of a sort, through the exposure process — is outside the constitutional pale of congressional inquiry. . . .

NOTES

1. On the same day it decided Barenblatt the Supreme Court handed down its decision in Uphaus v. Wyman, 360 U.S. 72, 79 S. Ct. 1040, 3 L. Ed. 2d 1090 (1959), upholding the contempt conviction of Dr. Willard Uphaus, Executive Director of World Fellowship, Inc., for refusing to produce the names of all persons who in 1954 and 1955 had attended a summer camp in New Hampshire maintained by World Fellowship. Mr. Justice Brennan, in an opinion joined by Mr. Chief Justice Warren and Justices Black and Douglas, dissented.

After further proceedings in the New Hampshire courts Dr. Uphaus again sought review by the Supreme Court, but was again unsuccessful, Mr. Chief Justice Warren and Justices Black and Douglas dissenting. 364 U.S. 388, 81 S. Ct. 153, 5 L. Ed. 2d 148 (1960). Dr. Uphaus served a year in jail.

In another phase of the New Hampshire investigation, the Supreme Court upheld the right of that state to confer immunity upon a witness who had pleaded self-incrimination, Wyman v. DeGregory, 101 N.H. 171, 137 A.2d 512 (1957), app. dis., 360 U.S. 717 (1959), two justices dissenting, and to compel him to answer the question: "Are you presently a member of the Communist Party?" 103 N.H. 214, 169 A.2d 1 (1961), aff'd per curiam, 368 U.S. 19 (1961), four Justices dissenting. After the second decision the witness, Hugh DeGregory, purged himself of contempt by answering the question in the negative. For the further proceedings against DeGregory, see infra.

2. The Supreme Court followed Barenblatt in two later cases decided in 1961. Both grew out of hearings held by a subcommittee of the Un-American Activities Committee in Atlanta for the purpose of investigating "Communist infiltration into basic industry in the South" and "Communist Party propaganda in the

South." In Wilkinson v. United States, 365 U.S. 399, 81 S. Ct. 567, 5 L. Ed. 2d 633 (1961), the Court, by the same vote as in Barenblatt, upheld the conviction of Frank Wilkinson. Wilkinson had gone to Atlanta on behalf of the Emergency Civil Liberties Committee to mobilize opposition to the Committee's hearings. He was subpoenaed by the Committee and asked, ". . . are you now a member of the Communist Party?" The majority of the Court, in an opinion by Mr. Justice Stewart, held that the subcommittee's investigation was authorized by Congress, that the subcommittee was pursuing a valid legislative purpose, that the question was pertinent to the subject matter of the investigation, that Wilkinson was apprised of the pertinency of the question, and that the subcommittee's interrogation did not violate the First Amendment. On the last issue the Court said that Barenblatt was controlling, but added: "It is sought to differentiate this case upon the basis that 'the activities in which petitioner was believed to be participating consisted of public criticism of the Committee and attempts to influence public opinion to petition Congress for redress — to abolish the Committee.' But we cannot say that, simply because the petitioner at the moment may have been engaged in lawful conduct, his Communist activities in connection therewith could not be investigated. The subcommittee had reasonable ground to suppose that the petitioner was an active Communist Party member, and that as such he possessed information that would substantially aid it in its legislative investigation. As the Barenblatt opinion makes clear, it is the nature of the Communist activity involved, whether the momentary conduct is legitimate or illegitimate politically, that establishes the Government's overbalancing interest." 365 U.S. at 414.

Mr. Justice Black, in an opinion with which Mr. Chief Justice Warren and Mr. Justice Douglas concurred, urged that Barenblatt be overruled. The same justices, in an opinion by Mr. Justice Douglas, also contended that the Committee's authorization should be construed narrowly so as to exclude "an investigation whose central aim was finding out what criticism a citizen was making" of the Committee. 365 U.S. at 428. Mr. Justice Brennan dissented on the ground that the Committee had "failed to lay an adequate foundation at the hearing" for the question; and that, since the Committee knew from a prior hearing that Wilkinson would refuse to answer the question, "the Committee's purpose could not have been the legitimate one of fact gathering." 365 U.S. at 429-430.

In Braden v. United States, 365 U.S. 431, 81 S. Ct. 584, 5 L. Ed. 2d 653 (1961), the witness, Carl Braden, a field secretary of the Southern Conference Educational Fund, was called to testify about his conduct in organizing opposition to the Atlanta hearings and to pending legislation in Congress which would overturn Pennsylvania v. Nelson. In connection with the latter issue, Braden had prepared a letter urging opposition to the bill. The subcommittee asked him, "Were you a member of the Communist Party the instant you affixed your signature to that letter?" The majority of the Court considered the issues to be the same as in Wilkinson. To the contention that the sending of the letter was "not only legitimate but constitutionally protected activity," the Court said: "But Barenblatt did not confine congressional committee investigation to overt criminal activity, nor did that case determine that Congress can only investigate the Communist Party itself. Rather, the decision upheld an investigation of Communist activity in education. Education, too, is legitimate and protected activity. Communist infiltration and propaganda in a given area of the country, which were the subjects of the subcommittee investigation here, are surely as much within its pervasive authority as Communist activity in educational institutions. The subcommittee had reason to believe that the petitioner was a member of the Communist Party, and that he had been actively engaged in propaganda efforts. It was making a legislative inquiry into Communist Party propaganda activities in the southern States. Information as to the extent to which the Communist Party was utilizing legitimate organizations and causes in its propaganda efforts in that region was surely not constitutionally beyond the reach of the subcommittee's inquiry." 365 U.S. at 435.

The majority also rejected contentions that the jury, rather than the court, should have determined whether the question was pertinent to the subject under inquiry; and that since Braden had in good faith relied upon the Watkins decision there was no intentional violation of the statute. The four dissenters, in an opinion by Mr. Justice Douglas, disagreed on the latter point, emphasizing that no "foundation was ever laid here," which would "justify an investigation into matters that on their face seemed well within the First Amendment." "Otherwise," the dissent concluded, "the Committee may roam at will, requiring any individual to disclose his association with any group or with any publication which is unpopular with the Committee and which it can discredit by calling it communistic." 365 U.S. at 456-457.

Mr. Justice Black, joined by Mr. Chief Justice Warren and Mr. Justice Douglas, also dissented on First Amendment grounds, reiterating his objections to the balancing test: "For the presently prevailing constitutional doctrine, which treats the First Amendment as a mere admonition, leaves the liberty-giving freedoms which were intended to be protected by that Amendment completely at the mercy of Congress and this Court whenever a majority of this Court concludes, on the basis of any of the several judicially created 'tests' now in vogue, that abridgment of these freedoms is more desirable than freedom itself." 365 U.S. at 442-443.

3. In the same term as the Wilkinson and Braden decisions the Supreme Court upheld, by a five-to-four vote, the conviction of a witness who had refused to produce records of the Civil Rights Congress before the Committee on Un-American Activities. McPhaul v. United States, 364 U.S. 372, 81 S. Ct. 138, 5 L. Ed. 2d 136 (1960). In two other cases it reversed contempt convictions. Deutch v. United States, 367 U.S. 456, 81 S. Ct. 1587, 6 L. Ed. 2d 963 (1961); Slagle v. Ohio, 366 U.S. 259, 81 S. Ct. 1076, 6 L. Ed. 2d 277 (1961). In none of these cases did the Court deal with basic constitutional issues. Up to the Gibson case in 1963 (see infra) the Court ruled on various legislative committee matters, in all cases reversing convictions, without passing on issues of basic power. These decisions are summarized in subsection 3, infra.

REFERENCES

1. For discussion of the Barenblatt, Uphaus, Wilkinson, and Braden cases see, in addition to the material cited above in the general bibliography, Meiklejohn, The Barenblatt Opinion, 27 U. Chi. L. Rev. 329 (1960); Kalven, Mr. Alexander Meiklejohn and the Barenblatt Opinion, 27 U. Chi. L. Rev. 315 (1960); Slotnick, The Congressional Investigating Power: Ramifications of the Watkins-Barenblatt Enigma, 14 U. Miami L. Rev. 381 (1960); Alfange, Congressional Investigations and the Fickle Court, 30 U. Cinc. L. Rev. 113 (1961); Meiklejohn, The Balancing of Self-Preservation Against Political Freedom, 49 Calif. L. Rev. 4 (1961); Frantz, Wilkinson, Braden, and Deutch: The Legisla-

tive Investigation Cases, 21 Law in Trans. 219 (1962); McKay, Congressional Investigations and the Supreme Court, 51 Calif. L. Rev. 267 (1963); Notes, 47 Calif. L. Rev. 930 (1959); 73 Harv. L. Rev. 84, 159-163 (1959); 45 Cornell L.Q. 354 (1960); 28 Geo. Wash. L. Rev. 779 (1960); 58 Mich. L. Rev. 406 (1960); 75 Harv. L. Rev. 40, 65-71, 117-125 (1961); 45 Marq. L. Rev. 294 (1961). More particularly on the Uphaus case, see Cramton, The Supreme Court and State Power to Deal with Subversion and Loyalty, 43 Minn. L. Rev. 1025, 1037-1053 (1959); Note, The Application of the Law of Contempt to the Uphaus Case, 61 Colum. L. Rev. 725 (1961); Notes, 1959 U. Ill. L.F. 869; 21 Ohio St. L.J. 117 (1960). For an account by New Hampshire Attorney General Wyman of the Uphaus case, see Wyman, Fact and Fiction in the Uphaus Case, 3 N.H. Bar J. 174 (1961); for the other side see Bownes, Willard Uphaus — Prisoner of Conscience, 3 N.H. Bar J. 159 (1961), and Dr. Uphaus' own story in Uphaus, Commitment (1963).

2. A collection of material undertaking to show that the Committee on Un-American Activities operates for purposes of exposure appears in Appendix B of Petitioner's Brief in the Braden case. The Court also rejected an exposure argument in Hutcheson v. United States, 369 U.S. 599, 82 S. Ct. 1005, 8 L. Ed. 2d 137 (1962) (an investigation of labor union activities). An effort by defense counsel to introduce expert testimony on the factual issues raised by the Barenblatt balancing test was rejected in United States v. Yellin, 287 F.2d 292 (7th Cir. 1961), rev'd on other grounds, 374 U.S. 109, 83 S. Ct. 1828, 10 L. Ed. 2d 778 (1963). The testimony is reprinted in The First Amendment: What Factors Should be Considered in Striking the Balance Under Barenblatt? 20 Law. Guild Rev. 41 (1960). See also Frantz, The First Amendment in the Balance, 71 Yale L.J. 1424, 1443-1444 (1962); McKay, supra, 51 Calif. L. Rev. at 293-295.

3. Lower federal court decisions following the Barenblatt case include Davis v. United States, 269 F.2d 357 (6th Cir. 1959), cert. den., 361 U.S. 919 (1959), Justices Black and Douglas dissenting; and others reversed by the Supreme Court on non-constitutional grounds (see infra).

4. State cases upholding the power of state legislative committees to investigate alleged subversive activities include In re Coon, 44 Cal. App. 2d 531, 112 P.2d 767 (1941); State ex rel. Benemovsky v. Sullivan, 37 So. 2d 907 (Fla., 1948); State v. James, 36 Wash. 2d 882, 221 P.2d 482 (1950), cert. den., 341 U.S. 911 (1951); and the cases which reached the United States Supreme Court, supra. For the cases up to 1955 see Digest of the Public Record of Communism in the United States 444-451 (Fund for the Republic 1955).

GIBSON v. FLORIDA LEGISLATIVE INVESTIGATION COMMITTEE
372 U.S. 539, 83 S. Ct. 889, 9 L. Ed. 2d 929 (1963)

Mr. Justice Goldberg delivered the opinion of the Court.

This case is the culmination of protracted litigation involving legislative investigating committees of the State of Florida and the Miami branch of the National Association for the Advancement of Colored People.

The origins of the controversy date from 1956, when a committee of the Florida Legislature commenced an investigation of the N.A.A.C.P. Upon expiration of this committee's authority, a new committee was established to pursue the inquiry. The new committee, created in 1957, held hearings and sought by subpoena to obtain the entire membership list of the Miami branch of the N.A.A.C.P.; production was refused and the committee obtained a court order requiring that the list be submitted. On appeal, the Florida Supreme Court held that the committee could not require production and disclosure of the entire membership list of the organization, but that it could compel the custodian of the records to bring them to the hearings and to refer to them to determine whether specific individuals, otherwise identified as, or "suspected of being," Communists, were N.A.A.C.P. members. 108 So. 2d 729, cert. denied, 360 U.S. 919.

Because of the impending expiration of the authority of the 1957 committee, the Florida Legislature in 1959 established the respondent Legislative Investigation Committee to resume the investigation of the N.A.A.C.P. The authorizing statute, c. 59-207, Fla. Laws 1959, defining the purpose and operations of the respondent, declared:

"It shall be the duty of the committee to make as complete an investigation as time permits of all organizations whose principles or activities include a course of conduct on the part of any person or group which would constitute violence, or a violation of the laws of the state, or would be inimical to the well-being and orderly pursuit of their personal and business activities by the majority of the citizens of this state. . . ."

The petitioner, then president of the Miami branch of the N.A.A.C.P., was ordered to appear before the respondent Committee on November 4, 1959, and, in accordance with the prior decision of the Florida Supreme Court, to bring with him records of the association which were in his possession or custody and which pertained to the identity of members of, and contributors to, the Miami and state N.A.A.C.P. organizations. Prior to interrogation of any witnesses the Committee chairman read the text of the statute creating the Committee and declared that the hearings would be "concerned with the activities of various organizations which have been or are presently operating in this State in the fields of, first, race relations; second, the coercive reform of social and educational practices and mores by litigation and pressured administrative action; third, of labor; fourth, of education; fifth, and other vital phases of life in this State." The chairman also stated that the inquiry would be directed to Communists and Communist activities, including infiltration of Communists into organizations operating in the described fields.

Upon being called to the stand, the petitioner admitted that he was custodian of his organization's membership records and testified that the local group had about 1,000 members, that individual membership was renewed annually, and that the only membership lists maintained were those for the then current year.

The petitioner told the Committee that he had not brought these records with him to the hearing and announced that he would not produce them for the purpose of answering questions concerning membership in the N.A.A.C.P. He did, however, volunteer to answer such questions on the basis of his own personal knowledge; when given the names and shown photographs of 14 persons previously identified as Communists or members of Communist front or affiliated organizations, the petitioner said that he could associate none of them with the N.A.A.C.P.

The petitioner's refusal to produce his organization's membership lists was based on the ground that to bring the lists to the hearing and to utilize them as the basis of his testimony would interfere with the free exercise of Fourteenth Amendment associational rights of members and prospective members of the N.A.A.C.P.

In accordance with Florida procedure, the petitioner was brought before a state court and, after a hearing, was adjudged in contempt, and sentenced to six months' imprisonment and fined $1,200, or, in default in payment thereof, sentenced to an additional six months' imprisonment. The Florida Supreme Court sustained the judgment below, 126 So. 2d 129, and this Court granted certiorari, 366 U.S. 917; the case was argued last Term and restored to the calendar for reargument this Term, 369 U.S. 834.

I

We are here called upon once again to resolve a conflict between individual rights of free speech and association and governmental interest in conducting legislative investigations. Prior decisions illumine the contending principles.

This Court has repeatedly held that rights of association are within the ambit of the constitutional protections afforded by the First and Fourteenth Amendments. . . .

The First and Fourteenth Amendment rights of free speech and free association are fundamental and highly prized, and "need breathing space to survive." NAACP v. Button, 371 U.S. 415, 433. . . .

At the same time, however, this Court's prior holdings demonstrate that there can be no question that the State has power adequately to inform itself — through legislative investigation, if it so desires — in order to act and protect its legitimate and vital interests. . . . It is no less obvious, however, that the legislative power to investigate, broad as it may be, is not without limit. The fact that the general scope of the inquiry is authorized and permissible does not compel the conclusion that the investigatory body is free to inquire into or demand all forms of information. Validation of the broad subject matter under investigation does not necessarily carry with it automatic and wholesale validation of all individual questions, subpoenas, and documentary demands. See, e.g., Watkins v. United States, supra, 354 U.S., at 197-199. See also Barenblatt v. United States, supra, 360 U.S., at 127-130. When, as in this case, the claim is made that particular legislative inquiries and demands infringe substantially upon First and Fourteenth Amendment associational rights of individuals, the courts are called upon to, and must, determine the permissibility of the challenged actions, Watkins v. United States, supra, 354 U.S., at 198-199; "[T]he delicate and difficult task falls upon the courts to weigh the circumstances and to appraise the substantiality of the reasons advanced in support of the regulation of the free enjoyment of the rights," Schneider v. State, 308 U.S. 147, 161. The interests here at stake are of significant magnitude, and neither their resolution nor impact is limited to, or dependent upon, the particular parties here involved. Freedom and viable government are both, for this purpose, indivisible concepts; whatever affects the rights of the parties here, affects all.

II

Significantly, the parties are in substantial agreement as to the proper test to be applied to reconcile the competing claims of government and individual and to determine the propriety of the Committee's demands. As declared by the respondent Committee in its brief to this Court, "Basically, this case hinges entirely on the question of whether the evidence before the Committee [was] . . . sufficient to show probable cause or nexus between the N.A.A.C.P. Miami Branch, and Communist activities." We understand this to mean — regardless of the label applied, be it "nexus," "foundation," or whatever — that it is an essential prerequisite to the validity of an investigation which intrudes into the area of constitutionally protected rights of speech, press, association and petition that the State convincingly show a substantial relation between the information sought and a subject of overriding and compelling state interest. Absent such a relation between the N.A.A.C.P. and conduct in which the State may have a compelling regulatory concern, the Committee has not "demonstrated so cogent an interest in obtaining and making public" the membership information sought to be obtained as to "justify the substantial abridgment of associational freedom which such disclosures will effect." Bates v. Little Rock, supra, 361 U.S., at 524. "Where there is a significant encroachment upon personal liberty, the State may prevail only upon showing a subordinating interest which is compelling." Ibid.

Applying these principles to the facts of this case, the respondent Committee contends that the prior decisions of this Court in Uphaus v. Wyman, 360 U.S. 72; Barenblatt v. United States, 360 U.S. 109; Wilkinson v. United States, 365 U.S. 399; and Braden v. United States, 365 U.S. 431, compel a result here upholding the legislative right of inquiry. In Barenblatt, Wilkinson, and Braden, however, it was a refusal to answer a question or questions concerning the witness' *own* past or present membership *in the Communist Party* which supported his conviction. It is apparent that the necessary preponderating governmental interest and, in fact, the very result in those cases were founded on the holding that the Communist Party is not an ordinary or legitimate political party, as known in this country, and that, because of its particular nature, membership therein is *itself* a permissible subject of regulation and legislative scrutiny. Assuming the correctness of the premises on which those cases were decided, no further demonstration of compelling governmental interest was deemed necessary, since the direct object of the challenged questions there was discovery of membership in the Communist Party, a matter held pertinent to a proper subject then under inquiry.

Here, however, it is not alleged Communists who are the witnesses before the Committee and it is not discovery of their membership in that party which is the object of the challenged inquiries. Rather, it is the N.A.A.C.P. itself which is the subject of the investigation, and it is its local president, the petitioner, who was called before the Committee and held in contempt because he refused to divulge the contents of its membership records. There is no suggestion that the Miami branch of the N.A.A.C.P. or the national organization with which it is affiliated was, or is, itself a subversive organization. Nor is there any indication that the activities or policies of the N.A.A.C.P. were either Communist dominated or influenced. In fact, this very record indicates that the association was and is against communism and has voluntarily taken steps to keep Communists from being members. Each year since 1950, the N.A.A.C.P. has adopted resolutions barring Communists from membership in the organization. Moreover, the petitioner testified that all prospective officers of the local organization are thoroughly investigated for Communist or subversive connections and, though subversive activities constitute grounds for termination of association membership, no such expulsions from the branch occurred during the five years preceding the investigation.

Thus, unlike the situation in Barenblatt, Wilkinson and Braden, supra, the Committee was not here seeking from the petitioner or the records of which he was custodian any information as to whether he, himself, or even other persons were members of the Communist Party, Communist front or affiliated organizations, or other allegedly subversive groups; instead, the entire thrust of the demands on the petitioner was that he disclose whether other persons were members of the N.A.A.C.P., itself a concededly legitimate and nonsubversive organization. Compelling such an organization, engaged in the exercise of First and Fourteenth Amendment rights, to disclose its membership presents, under our cases, a question wholly different from compelling the Communist Party to disclose its own membership. Moreover, even to say, as in Barenblatt, supra, 360 U.S., at 129, that it is permissible to inquire into the subject of Communist infiltration of educational or other organizations does not mean that it is permissible to demand or require from such other groups disclosure of their membership by inquiry into their records when such disclosure will seriously inhibit or impair the exercise of constitutional rights and has not itself been demonstrated to bear a crucial relation to a proper governmental interest or to be essential to fulfillment of a proper governmental purpose. The prior holdings that governmental interest in controlling subversion and the particular character of the Communist Party and its objectives outweigh the right of individual Communists to conceal party membership or affiliations by no means require the wholly different conclusion that other groups — concededly legitimate — automatically forfeit their rights to privacy of association simply because the general subject matter of the legislative inquiry is Communist subversion or infiltration. The fact that governmental interest was deemed compelling in Barenblatt, Wilkinson, and Braden and held to support the inquiries there made into membership in the Communist Party does not resolve the issues here, where the challenged questions go to membership in an admittedly lawful organization.

Respondent's reliance on Uphaus v. Wyman, supra, as controlling is similarly misplaced. There, this Court upheld the right of the State of New Hampshire, in connection with an investigation of whether "subversive" persons were within the State, to obtain a list of guests who attended a World Fellowship summer camp located in the State. In Uphaus this Court found that there was demonstrated a sufficient connection between subversive activity — held there to be a proper subject of governmental concern — and the World Fellowship, itself, to justify discovery of the guest list; no semblance of such a nexus between the N.A.A.C.P. and subversive *activities* has been shown here. See III, infra. Moreover, contrary to the facts in this case, the claim to associational privacy in Uphaus was held to be "tenuous at best," 360 U.S., at 80, since the disputed list was already a matter of public record by virtue of a generally applicable New Hampshire law requiring that places of accommodation, including the camp in question, maintain a guest register open to public authorities. Thus, this Court noted that the registration statute "made public at the inception the association they [the guests] now wish to keep private." 360 U.S., at 81. Finally, in Uphaus, the State was investigating whether subversive persons were within its boundaries and whether their presence constituted a threat to the State. No such purpose or need is evident here. The Florida Committee is not seeking to identify subversives by questioning the petitioner; apparently it is satisfied that it already knows who they are.

III

In the absence of directly determinative authority, we turn, then, to consideration of the facts now before us. Obviously, if the respondent were still seeking discovery of the entire membership list, we could readily dispose of this case on the authority of Bates v. Little Rock [361 U.S. 516] and NAACP v. Alabama [357 U.S. 449]; a like result would follow if it were merely attempting to do piecemeal what could not be done in a single step. Though there are indications that the respondent Committee intended to inquire broadly into the N.A.A.C.P. membership records, there is no need to base our decision today upon a prediction as to the course which the Committee might have pursued if initially unopposed by the petitioner. Instead, we rest our result on the fact that the record in this case is insufficient to show a substantial connection between the Miami branch of the N.A.A.C.P. and Communist *activities* which the respondent Committee itself concedes is an essential prerequisite to demonstrating the immediate, substantial, and subordinating state interest necessary to sustain its right of inquiry into the membership lists of the association.

[The Court's analysis of the evidence is omitted.]

This summary of the evidence discloses the utter failure to demonstrate the existence of any substantial relationship between the N.A.A.C.P. and subversive or Communist activities. In essence, there is here merely indirect, less than unequivocal, and mostly hearsay testimony that in years past some 14 people who were asserted to be, or to have been, Communists or members of Communist front or "affiliated organizations" attended occasional meetings of the Miami branch of the N.A.A.C.P. "and/or" were members of that branch, which had a total membership of about 1,000.

On the other hand, there was no claim made at the hearings, or since, that the N.A.A.C.P. or its Miami branch was engaged in any subversive activities or that its legitimate activities have been dominated or influenced by Communists. Without any indication or present subversive infiltration in, or influence on, the Miami branch of the N.A.A.C.P., and without any reasonable, demonstrated factual basis to believe that such infiltration or influence existed in the past, or was actively attempted or sought in the present — in short without any showing of a meaningful relationship between the N.A.A.C.P., Miami branch, and subversives or subversive or other illegal activities — we are asked to find the compelling and subordinating state interest which must exist if essential freedoms are to be curtailed or inhibited. This we cannot do. The respondent Committee has laid no adequate foundation for its direct demands upon the officers and records of a wholly legitimate organization for disclosure of its membership; the Committee has neither demonstrated nor pointed out any threat to the State by virtue of the existence of the N.A.A.C.P. or the pursuit of its activities or the minimal associational ties of the 14 asserted Communists. The strong associational interest in maintaining the privacy of membership lists of groups engaged in the constitutionally protected free trade in ideas and beliefs may not be substantially infringed upon such a slender showing as here made by the respondent. While, of course, all legitimate organizations are the beneficiaries of these protections, they are all the more essential here, where the challenged privacy is that of persons espousing beliefs already unpopular with their neighbors and the deterrent and "chilling" effect on the free exercise of constitutionally enshrined rights of free speech, expression, and association is consequently the more immediate and substantial. . . .

Of course, a legislative investigation — as any investigation — must proceed "step by step," Barenblatt v. United States, supra, 360 U.S., at 130, but step by step or in totality, an adequate foundation for inquiry must be laid before proceeding in such a manner as will substantially intrude upon and severely curtail or inhibit constitutionally protected activities or seriously interfere with similarly protected associational rights. No such foundation has been laid here. The respondent Committee has failed to demonstrate the compelling and subordinating governmental interest essential to support direct inquiry into the membership records of the N.A.A.C.P.

Nothing we say here impairs or denies the existence of the underlying legislative right to investigate or legislate with respect to subversive activities by Communists or anyone else; our decision today deals only with the manner in which such power may be exercised and we hold simply that groups which themselves are neither engaged in subversive or other illegal or improper activities nor demonstrated to have any substantial connections with such activities are to be protected in their rights of free and private association. . . .

To permit legislative inquiry to proceed on less than an adequate foundation would be to sanction unjustified and unwarranted intrusions into the very heart of the constitutional privilege to be secure in associations in legitimate organizations engaged in the exercise of First and Fourteenth Amendment rights; to impose a lesser standard than we here do would be inconsistent with the maintenance of those essential conditions basic to the preservation of our democracy.

The judgment below must be and is
Reversed.

Mr. Justice Black, concurring. . . .

In my view the constitutional right of association includes the privilege of any person to associate with Communists or anti-Communists, Socialists or anti-Socialists, or, for that matter, with people of all kinds of beliefs, popular or unpopular. I have expressed these views in many other cases and I adhere to them now. Since, as I believe, the National Association for the Advancement of Colored People and its members have a constitutional right to choose their own associates, I cannot understand by what constitutional authority Florida can compel answers to questions which abridge that right. Accordingly, I would reverse here on the ground that there has been a direct abridgment of the right of association of the National Association for the Advancement of Colored People and its members. But, since the Court assumes for purposes of this case that there was no direct abridgment of First Amendment freedoms, I concur in the Court's opinion, which is based on constitutional principles laid down in Schneider v. Irvington, 308 U.S. 147, 161 (1939), and later cases of this Court following Schneider.

Mr. Justice Douglas, concurring.

I join the opinion of the Court, because it is carefully written within the framework of our current decisions. But since the matters involved touch constitutional rights and since I see the Constitution in somewhat different dimensions than are reflected in our decisions, it seems appropriate to set out my views. . . .

When the State or Federal Government is prohibited from dealing with a subject, it has no constitutional privilege to investigate it. An investigation to permit a legislature properly to perform its powers of internal management is of course allowed. See Barry v. Cunningham, 279 U.S. 597, 613. But otherwise the power to investigate is only an adjunct of the power to legislate — an auxiliary power "necessary and appropriate to that end." McGrain v. Daugherty, 273 U.S. 135, 175. Investigation to determine how constitutional laws are being administered marks one limitation. The other is an investigation to determine what constitutional laws should be passed. When the constitutional limits of lawmaking are passed, investigation is out of bounds, apart from the exception noted. See Kilbourn v. Thompson, 103 U.S. 168, 194-200; McGrain v. Daugherty, supra, 171-175. That is to say, investigations by a legislative committee which "could result in no valid legislation on the subject" are beyond the pale. Kilbourn v. Thompson, supra, p. 195. For it misses the whole point of our constitutional history to assume that "government," or any branch of government, somehow has rights and powers of its own apart from those necessarily attending the proper performance of its constitutional functions.

Joining a lawful organization, like attending a church, is an associational activity that comes within the purview of the First Amendment . . . "Peaceably to assemble" as used in the First Amendment necessarily involves a coming together, whether regularly or spasmodically. Historically the right to assemble was secondary to the right to petition, the latter being the primary right. But today, as the Court stated in De Jonge v. Oregon, 299 U.S. 353, 364, "The right of peaceable assembly is a right cognate to those of free speech and free press and is equally fundamental." Assembly, like speech, is indeed essential "in order to maintain the opportunity for free political discussion, to the end that government may be responsive to the will of the people and that changes, if desired, may be obtained by peaceful means." Id., p. 365. "The holding of meetings for peaceable political action cannot be proscribed." Ibid. A Free Society is made up of almost innumerable institutions through which views and opinions are expressed, opinion is mobilized, and social, economic, religious, educational, and political programs are formulated. . . .

In my view, government is not only powerless to legislate with respect to membership in a lawful organization; it is also precluded from probing the intimacies of spiritual and intellectual relationships in the myriad of such societies and groups that exist in this country, regardless of the legislative purpose sought to be served. "[T]he provisions of the First Amendment . . . of course reach and limit . . . investigations." Barenblatt v. United States, 360 U.S. 109, 126. If that is not true, I see no barrier to investigation of newspapers, churches, political parties, clubs, societies, unions, and any other association for their political, economic, social, philosophical, or religious views. If, in its quest to determine whether existing laws are being enforced or new laws are needed, an investigating committee can ascertain whether known Communists or criminals are members of an organization not shown to be engaged in conduct properly subject to regulation, it is but a short and inexorable step to the conclusion that it may also probe to ascertain what effect they have had on the other members. For how much more "necessary and appropriate" this information is to the legislative purpose being pursued! . . .

The right of association has become a part of the bundle of rights protected by the First Amendment (see, e.g., NAACP v. Alabama, supra), and the need for a pervasive right of privacy against government intrusion has been recognized, though not always given the recognition it deserves. Unpopular groups (NAACP v. Alabama, supra) like popular ones are protected. Unpopular groups if forced to disclose their membership lists may suffer reprisals or other forms of public hostility. NAACP v. Alabama, supra, p. 462. But whether a group is popular or unpopular, the right of privacy implicit in the First Amendment creates an area into which the Government may not enter. . . .

There is no other course consistent with the Free Society envisioned by the First Amendment. For the views a citizen entertains, the beliefs he harbors, the utterances he makes, the ideology he embraces and the people he associates with are no concern of government. That article of faith marks indeed the main difference between the Free Society which we espouse and the dictatorships both on the Left and on the Right. . . .

Mr. Justice Harlan, whom Mr. Justice Clark, Mr. Justice Stewart, and Mr. Justice White join, dissenting. . . .

The Court's reasoning is difficult to grasp. I read its opinion as basically proceeding on the premise that the governmental interest in investigating Communist infiltration into admittedly nonsubversive organizations, as distinguished from investigating organizations themselves suspected of subversive activities, is not sufficient to overcome the countervailing right to freedom of association. . . . On this basis "nexus" is seemingly found lacking because it was never claimed that the N.A.A.C.P. Miami Branch had itself engaged in subversive activity, . . . and because none of the Committee's evidence relating to any of the 52 alleged Communist Party members was sufficient to attribute such activity to the local branch or to show that it was dominated, influenced, or used "by Communists." . . .

But, until today, I had never supposed that any of our decisions relating to state or federal power to investigate in the field of Communist subversion could possibly be taken as suggesting any difference in the degree of governmental investigatory interest as between Communist infiltration *of* organizations and Communist activity *by* organizations. See, e.g., Barenblatt v. United States, 360 U.S. 109 (infiltration into education); Wilkinson v. United States, 365 U.S. 399, and Braden v. United States, 365 U.S. 431 (infiltration into basic industries); Russell v. United States, 369 U.S. 749, 773 (infiltration of newspaper business).

Considering the number of congressional inquiries that have been conducted in the field of "Communist infiltration" since the close of World War II, affecting such diverse interests as "labor, farmer, veteran, professional, youth, and motion picture groups" (Barenblatt, supra, at 119), it is indeed strange to find the strength of state interest in the same type of investigation now impugned. And it is not amiss to recall that government evidence in Smith Act prosecutions has shown that the sensitive area of race relations has long been a prime target of Communist efforts at infiltration. See Scales v. United States, 367 U.S. 203, 235, 245, 249 n. 26, 251, 255-256.

Given the unsoundness of the basic premise underlying the Court's holding as to the absence of "nexus," this decision surely falls of its own weight. For unless "nexus" requires an investigating agency to prove in advance the very things it is trying to find out, I do not understand how it can be said that the information preliminarily developed by the Committee's investigator was not sufficient to satisfy, under any reasonable test, the requirement of "nexus." . . .

I also find it difficult to see how this case really presents any serious question as to interference with freedom of association. Given the willingness of the petitioner to testify from recollection as to individual memberships in the local branch of the N.A.A.C.P., the germaneness of the membership records to the subject matter of the Committee's investigation, and the limited purpose for which their use was sought — as an aid to refreshing the witness' recollection, involving their divulgence only to the petitioner himself . . . — this case of course bears no resemblance whatever to NAACP v. Alabama, 357 U.S. 449, or Bates v. Little Rock, 361 U.S. 516. In both of those cases the State had sought general divulgence of local N.A.A.C.P. membership lists without any showing of a justifying state interest. In effect what we are asked to hold here is that the petitioner had a constitutional right to give only partial or inaccurate testimony, and that indeed seems to me the true effect of the Court's holding today. . . .

Mr. Justice White, dissenting.

In my view, the opinion of the Court represents a serious limitation upon the Court's previous cases dealing with this subject matter and upon the right of the legislature to investigate the Communist Party and its activities. Although one of the classic and recurring activities of the Communist Party is the infiltration and subversion of other organizations, either openly or in a clandestine manner, the Court holds that even where a legislature has evidence that a legitimate organization is under assault and even though that organization is itself sounding open and public alarm, an investigating committee is nevertheless forbidden to compel the organization or its members to reveal the fact, or not, of membership in that organization of named Communists assigned to the infiltrating task.

While the Court purports to be saving such a case for later consideration, it is difficult for me to understand how under today's decision a Communist in the process of performing his assigned job could be required to divulge not only his membership in the Communist Party but his membership or activities in the target organization as well. The Court fails to articulate why the State's interest is any the more compelling or the associational rights any the less endangered when a known Communist is asked whether he belongs to a protected association than here when the organization is asked to confirm or deny that membership. As I read the Court's opinion the exposed Communist might well, in the name of the associational freedom of the legitimate organization and of its members including himself, successfully shield his activities from legislative inquiry. Thus to me the decision today represents a marked departure from the principles of Barenblatt v. United States, 360 U.S. 109, and like cases. . . .

I would have thought that the freedom of association which is and should be entitled to constitutional protection would be promoted, not hindered, by disclosure which permits members of an organization to know with whom they are associating and affords them the opportunity to make an intelligent choice as to whether certain of their associates who are Communists should be allowed to continue their membership. In these circumstances, I cannot join the Court in attaching great weight to the organization's interest in concealing the presence of infiltrating Communists, if such be the case.

The net effect of the Court's decision is, of course, to insulate from effective legislative inquiry and preventive legislation the time-proven skills of the Communist Party in subverting and eventually controlling legitimate organizations. Until such a group, chosen as an object of Communist Party action, has been effectively reduced to vassalage, legislative bodies may seek no information from the organization under attack by duty-bound Communists. When the job has been done and the legislative committee can prove it, it then has the hollow privilege of recording another victory for the Communist Party, which both Congress and this Court have found to be an organization under the direction of a foreign power, dedicated to the overthrow of the Government if necessary by force and violence. I respectfully dissent.

REFERENCES

For comment on the Gibson case see Notes, 32 Geo. Wash. L. Rev. 139 (1963); 77 Harv. L. Rev. 62, 119-122 (1963); 1963 U. Ill. L.F. 293 (1963).

Other decisions involving investigation by state legislative committees of civil rights organizations and activities include N.A.A.C.P. v. Committee on Offenses Against Administration of Justice, 199 Va. 665, 101 S.E.2d 631 (1958) (court ordered enforcement of Committee subpoenas), remanded as moot, 358 U.S. 40, 79 S. Ct. 24, 3 L. Ed. 2d 46 (1958); 201 Va. 890, 114 S.E.2d 721 (1960) (suit by N.A.A.C.P. to recover records unsuccessful); 204 Va. 693, 133 S.E.2d 540 (1963) (N.A.A.C.P. need not give Committee list of donors of $25 or more).

In DeGregory v. Attorney General of New Hampshire, 383 U.S. 825, 86 S. Ct. 1148, 16 L. Ed. 2d 292 (1966), the Supreme Court, distinguishing Uphaus, invalidated a conviction of Hugh DeGregory for refusal to answer questions relating to Communist activities prior to 1957. Justices Harlan, Stewart, and White dissented.

2. *The Privilege Against Self-Incrimination and Other Constitutional Limitations*

As noted above, following the Josephson and Barsky cases and the indictment of the Communist Party leaders under the Smith Act, a number of witnesses before legislative investigating committees began to invoke the Fifth Amendment as a basis for refusing to answer questions pertaining to alleged subversive activities. Reliance upon the constitutional privilege in this situation was uniformly upheld by the courts. In the first cases to reach the Supreme Court — the Quinn, Emspak and Bart cases — the issue was not the basic right to rely upon the privilege but the manner and extent of its application.

QUINN v. UNITED STATES
349 U.S. 155, 75 S. Ct. 668, 99 L. Ed. 964 (1955)

Mr. Chief Justice Warren delivered the opinion of the Court.

Petitioner was convicted of contempt of Congress under 2 U.S.C. §192 in the District Court for the District of Columbia. Section 192 provides for the punishment of any witness before a congressional committee "who . . . refuses to answer any question pertinent to the question under inquiry. . . ." On appeal, the Court of Appeals for the District of Columbia Circuit reversed the conviction and remanded the case for a new trial. Claiming that the Court of Appeals should have directed an acquittal, petitioner applied to this Court for certiorari. We granted the writ because of the fundamental and recurrent character of the questions presented.

Pursuant to subpoena, petitioner appeared on August 10, 1949, before a subcommittee of the Committee on Un-American Activities of the House of Representatives. Petitioner was then a member and field representative of the United Electrical, Radio and Machine Workers of America. Also subpoenaed to appear on that day were Thomas J. Fitzpatrick and Frank Panzino, two officers of the same union. At the outset of the hearings, counsel for the committee announced that the purpose of the investigation was to inquire into "the question of Communist affiliation or association of certain members" of the union and "the advisability of tightening present security requirements in industrial plants working on certain Government contracts." All three witnesses were asked questions concerning alleged membership in the Communist Party. All three declined to answer.

Fitzpatrick was the first to be called to testify. He based his refusal to answer on "the first and fifth amendments" as well as "the first amendment to the Constitution, supplemented by the fifth amendment." Immediately following Fitzpatrick's testimony, Panzino was called to the stand. In response to the identical questions put to Fitzpatrick, Panzino specifically adopted as his own the grounds relied upon by Fitzpatrick. In addition, at one point in his testimony, Panzino stated that "I think again, Mr. Chairman, under the fifth amendment, that is my own personal belief." On the following day, petitioner, unaccompanied by counsel, was called to the stand and was also asked whether he had ever been a member of the Communist Party. Like Panzino before him, he declined to answer, specifically adopting as his own the grounds relied upon by Fitzpatrick. . . .

The privilege against self-incrimination is a right that was hard-earned by our forefathers. The reasons for its inclusion in the Constitution — and the necessities for its preservation — are to be found in the lessons of history. As early as 1650, remembrance of the horror of Star Chamber proceedings a decade before had firmly established the privilege in the common law of England. Transplanted to this country as part of our legal heritage, it soon made its way into various state constitutions and ultimately in 1791 into the federal Bill of Rights. The privilege, this Court has stated, "was generally regarded then, as now, as a privilege of great value, a protection to the innocent though a shelter to the guilty, and a safeguard against heedless, unfounded or tyrannical prosecutions." [27] Co-equally with our other constitutional guarantees, the Self-Incrimination Clause "must be accorded liberal construction in favor of the right it was intended to secure." [28] Such liberal construction is particularly warranted in a prosecution of a witness for a refusal to answer, since the respect normally accorded the privilege is then buttressed by the presumption of innocence accorded a defendant in a criminal trial. To apply the privilege narrowly or begrudgingly — to treat it as an historical relic, at most merely to be tolerated — is to ignore its development and purpose.

In the instant case petitioner was convicted for refusing to answer the committee's question as to his alleged membership in the Communist Party. Clearly an answer to the question might have tended to incriminate him.[29] As a consequence, petitioner was entitled to claim the privilege. The principal issue here is whether or not he did.

It is agreed by all that a claim of the privilege does not require any special combination of words. Plainly a witness need not have the skill of a lawyer to invoke the protection of the Self-Incrimination Clause. If an objection to a question is made in any language that a committee may reasonably be expected to understand as an attempt to invoke the privilege, it must be re-

---

[27] Twining v. New Jersey, 211 U.S. 78, 91. See also Boyd v. United States, 116 U.S. 616, 631-632.

[28] Hoffman v. United States, 341 U.S. 479, 486. Cf. Counselman v. Hitchcock, 142 U.S. 547, 562.

[29] Blau v. United States, 340 U.S. 159, specifically holding that such a question is protected by the privilege; Brunner v. United States, 343 U.S. 918, reversing 190 F.2d 167 (C.A. 9th Cir.). See also Hoffman v. United States, 341 U.S. 479.

spected both by the committee and by a court in a prosecution under §192.

Here petitioner, by adopting the grounds relied upon by Fitzpatrick, based his refusal to answer on "the first and fifth amendments" and "the first amendment to the Constitution, supplemented by the fifth amendment." The Government concedes — as we think it must — that a witness may invoke the privilege by stating "I refuse to testify on the ground of the Fifth Amendment." Surely, in popular parlance and even in legal literature, the term "Fifth Amendment" in the context of our time is commonly regarded as being synonymous with the privilege against self-incrimination. The Government argues, however, that the references to the Fifth Amendment in the instant case were inadequate to invoke the privilege because Fitzpatrick's statements are more reasonably understood as invoking rights under the First Amendment. We find the Government's argument untenable. The mere fact that Fitzpatrick and petitioner also relied on the First Amendment does not preclude their reliance on the Fifth Amendment as well. If a witness urges two constitutional objections to a committee's line of questioning, he is not bound at his peril to choose between them. By pressing both objections, he does not lose a privilege which would have been valid if he had only relied on one.

The Government, moreover, apparently concedes that petitioner *intended* to invoke the privilege. In its brief the Government points out "the probability that petitioner's ambiguous references to the Fifth Amendment . . . were phrased deliberately in such vague terms so as to enable petitioner . . . to obtain the benefit of the privilege without incurring the popular opprobrium which often attaches to its exercise." But the fact that a witness expresses his intention in vague terms is immaterial so long as the claim is sufficiently definite to apprise the committee of his intention. As everyone agrees, no ritualistic formula is necessary in order to invoke the privilege. In the instant case, Quinn's references to the Fifth Amendment were clearly sufficient to put the committee on notice of an apparent claim of the privilege. It then became incumbent on the committee either to accept the claim or to ask petitioner whether he was in fact invoking the privilege. Particularly is this so if it is true, as the Government contends, that petitioner feared the stigma that might result from a forthright claim of his constitutional right to refuse to testify. It is precisely at such times — when the privilege is under attack by those who wrongly conceive of it as merely a shield for the guilty — that governmental bodies must be most scrupulous in protecting its exercise.

This ruling by no means leaves a congressional committee defenseless at the hands of a scheming witness intent on deception. When a witness declines to answer a question because of constitutional objections and the language used is not free from doubt, the way is always open for the committee to inquire into the nature of the claim before making a ruling. If the witness unequivocally and intelligently waives any objection based on the Self-Incrimination Clause, or if the witness refuses a committee request to state whether he relies on the Self-Incrimination Clause, he cannot later invoke its protection in a prosecution for contempt for refusing to answer that question. Here the committee made no attempt to have petitioner particularize his objection. Under these circumstances, we must hold that petitioner's references to the Fifth Amendment were sufficient to invoke the privilege and that the court below erred in failing to direct a judgment of acquittal. . . .

[The dissenting opinion of Mr. Justice Reed is omitted.]

NOTES

1. In Emspak v. United States, 349 U.S. 190, 75 S. Ct. 687, 99 L. Ed. 997 (1955), and Bart v. United States, 349 U.S. 219, 75 S. Ct. 712, 99 L. Ed. 1016 (1955), the Court also concluded that the Committee had not clearly overruled the claim of privilege and directed an answer. For later cases applying the same rule see Fagerhaugh v. United States, 232 F.2d 803 (9th Cir. 1956); Jackins v. United States, 231 F.2d 405 (9th Cir. 1956).

Other cases in which the Supreme Court dealt with the privilege against self-incrimination in legislative inquiries are Raley v. Ohio, 360 U.S. 423, 79 S. Ct. 1257, 3 L. Ed. 2d 1344 (1959) (due process clause held to prevent conviction of persons for refusing to answer questions of Ohio Un-American Activities Commission where they relied upon assurance of Commission that privilege was available to them although in fact, because of Ohio immunity law, it was not); McPhaul v. United States, 364 U.S. 372, 81 S. Ct. 138, 5 L. Ed. 2d 136 (1960) (privilege not available to Executive Secretary of Civil Rights Congress ordered to produce records of that organization); Hutcheson v. United States, 369 U.S. 599, 82 S. Ct. 1005, 8 L. Ed. 2d 137 (1962) (possible self-incrimination under state law not ground for refusing to answer questions before federal (McClellan) committee).

2. The leading case on the necessity and manner of establishing the incriminating effect of an answer where the witness invokes the privilege against self-incrimination is Hoffman v. United States, 341 U.S. 479, 71 S. Ct. 814, L. Ed. 1118 (1951). There the Court stated the test as follows:

"This guarantee against testimonial compulsion . . . must be accorded liberal construction in favor of the right it was intended to secure. . . . To sustain the privilege, it need only be evident from the implication of the question, in the setting in which it is asked, that a responsive answer to the question or an explanation of why it cannot be answered might be dangerous because injurious disclosure could result. The trial judge in appraising the claim 'must be governed as much by his personal perception of the peculiarities of the case as by the facts actually in evidence.' . . . In this setting it was not *'perfectly clear,* from a careful consideration of all the circumstances in the case, that the witness is mistaken, and that the answer[s] *cannot possibly* have such tendency' to incriminate." 341 U.S. at 486-488. (Italics in original.)

Professor Barrows Dunham, professor of philosophy at Temple University, when called as a witness before the Committee on Un-American Activities, gave his name and date of birth but refused to answer other questions, even his place of employment and education. His reliance on the privilege was sustained. United States v. Dunham, Crim. No. 1148-54 (D. D.C. Oct. 19, 1955), unreported; see

N.Y. Times, Oct. 20, 1955. See also Aiuppa v. United States, 201 F.2d 287 (6th Cir. 1952) (blanket refusal to answer sustained); Marcello v. United States, 196 F.2d 437 (5th Cir. 1952) (same); Simpson v. United States, 355 U.S. 7, 78 S. Ct. 14, 2 L. Ed. 2d 22 (1957) (same).

In Brunner v. United States, 190 F.2d 167 (9th Cir. 1951), the Court of Appeals upheld the District Court in refusing to allow a witness to invoke the privilege against self-incrimination as to questions concerning his membership in the Communist Party in 1937 and 1938, before passage of the Smith Act in 1940. The Supreme Court reversed per curiam, citing Blau v. United States, 340 U.S. 159, 71 S. Ct. 223, 95 L. Ed. 170 (1950). 343 U.S. 918, 72 S. Ct. 674, 96 L. Ed. 1332 (1952). See also the second Blau case, 340 U.S. 332, 71 S. Ct. 301, 95 L. Ed. 306 (1951).

The state courts have also consistently upheld the privilege with respect to questions about alleged subversive activities. See, e.g., State v. Kelley, 76 So. 2d 798 (Fla. 1954); Jones v. Commonwealth, 327 Mass. 491, 99 N.E.2d 456 (1951).

3. One of the chief problems with respect to the use of the Fifth Amendment has been the doctrine of waiver. In Rogers v. United States, 340 U.S. 367, 71 S. Ct. 438, 95 L. Ed. 344 (1951), the defendant testified before a grand jury that she was Treasurer of the Communist Party of Denver and that she had been in possession of the membership lists and dues records of the Party, but had turned them over to another person. Upon demand of the Grand Jury to identify the person who had received the books the defendant refused, giving as her reason, "I don't feel that I should subject a person or persons to the same thing that I'm going through." The Court upheld her conviction for contempt. It ruled that, having voluntarily testified to her status as an officer of the Communist Party, "response to the specific question in issue here would not further incriminate her" and hence she could no longer invoke the privilege: "To uphold a claim of privilege in this case would open the way to distortion of facts by permitting a witness to select any stopping place in the testimony." 340 U.S. at 369, 373, 371. The Court further held that the defendant could not claim the privilege as grounds for refusing to produce organizational records she held in her capacity as officer of an association.

Justices Black, Frankfurter, and Douglas, dissenting in an opinion by the first, said:

"Apparently, the Court's holding is that at some uncertain point in petitioner's testimony, regardless of her intention, admission of associations with the Communist Party automatically effected a 'waiver' of her constitutional protection as to all related questions. To adopt such a rule for the privilege against self-incrimination, when other constitutional safeguards must be knowingly waived, relegates the Fifth Amendment's privilege to a second-rate position. Moreover, today's holding creates this dilemma for witnesses: On the one hand, they risk imprisonment for contempt by asserting the privilege prematurely; on the other, they might lose the privilege if they answer a single question. The Court's view makes the protection depend on timing so refined that lawyers, let alone laymen, will have difficulty in knowing when to claim it." 340 U.S. at 377-378.

The Rogers case has given rise to some confusion. Generally the Government's efforts to rely upon the waiver doctrine have been unsuccessful. See Jackins v. United States, 231 F.2d 405 (9th Cir. 1956); Starkovitch v. United States, 231 F.2d 411 (9th Cir. 1956); United States v. Cohen, 101 F. Supp. 906 (N.D. Cal. 1952);

United States v. Raley, 96 F. Supp. 495 (D. D.C. 1951). The only conviction based upon the waiver doctrine in a subversive activities case appears to be United States v. Singer, 139 F. Supp. 847 (D. D.C. 1956), aff'd, 244 F.2d 349 (D.C. Cir. 1957), in which the witness testified with respect to his own Communist affiliation but refused to give the names of associates. Singer's conviction was ultimately reversed after the Watkins decision. 247 F.2d 535; see supra. See also the Bart case in the lower court, 203 F.2d 45 (D.C. Cir. 1952); George v. Lindberg, 138 F. Supp. 77 (D. Minn. 1956). And see Brown v. United States, 356 U.S. 148, 78 S. Ct. 622, 2 L. Ed. 2d 589 (1958); Presser v. United States, 284 F.2d 233 (D.C. Cir. 1960), cert. den., 365 U.S. 816 (1961).

The courts have consistently held that testimony before another tribunal or on another occasion does not constitute a waiver of the privilege. See Marcello v. United States, 196 F.2d 437 (5th Cir. 1952); Poretto v. United States, 196 F.2d 392 (5th Cir. 1952); In re Neff, 206 F.2d 149 (3d Cir. 1953); United States v. Malone, 111 F. Supp. 37 (N.D. Cal. 1953); Krogmann v. United States, 225 F.2d 220 (6th Cir. 1955); United States v. Steffen, 103 F. Supp. 415 (N.D. Cal. 1951). But cf. United States v. Shibley, 112 F. Supp. 734 (S.D. Cal. 1953); Communist Party v. Subversive Activities Control Board, 223 F.2d 531, 549 (D.C. Cir. 1954) (dictum).

United States v. Field, 193 F.2d 92 (2d Cir. 1951), cert. den., 342 U.S. 894 (1951), held that the trustees of the Civil Rights Congress Bail Fund, which posted bail for convicted Dennis case defendants pending appeal, had thereby waived the privilege as to questions concerning the whereabouts of the defendants who jumped bail, and as to questions about the names of contributors to the Fund. The trustees were examined in a special proceeding in the District Court to determine the whereabouts of the missing defendants. The same result was reached when the trustees invoked the privilege to similar questions before a grand jury. United States v. Field, 193 F.2d 109 (2d Cir. 1951). The cases are noted in 65 Harv. L. Rev. 691 (1952); 32 Neb. L. Rev. 577 (1953).

For discussion of the waiver issue see Note, The Privilege Against Self-Incrimination: The Doctrine of Waiver, 61 Yale L.J. 105 (1952); Boudin, The Constitutional Privilege in Operation, 12 Law. Guild Rev. 128 (1952); Notes, 18 Brooklyn L. Rev. 287 (1952); 52 Nw. U.L. Rev. 542 (1957); Redlich, Rights of Witnesses Before Congressional Committees: Effects of Recent Supreme Court Decisions, 36 N.Y.U.L. Rev. 1126, 1131-1136 (1961).

The rule of the Rogers case has proved an important factor in limiting testimony before legislative investigating committees. Thus Miss Lillian Hellman, called before the Committee on Un-American Activities, wrote the Committee as follows:

". . . I am ready and willing to testify before the representatives of our Government as to my own opinions and my own actions, regardless of any risks or consequences to myself.

"But I am advised by counsel that if I answer the committee's questions about myself, I must also answer questions about other people, and that if I refuse to do so, I can be cited for contempt. My counsel tells me that if I answer questions about myself, I will have waived my rights under the Fifth Amendment and could be forced legally to answer questions about others.

"This is very difficult for a layman to understand. But there is one principle that I do understand: I am not willing, now or in the future, to bring bad trouble to people who, in my past association with them, were completely innocent of any talk or any action that was disloyal or subversive.

"I do not like subversion or disloyalty in any form, and if I had ever seen any I would have considered it my duty to have reported it to the proper authorities. But to hurt innocent people whom I knew many years ago in order to save myself is, to me, inhuman and indecent and dishonorable.

"I cannot and will not cut my conscience to fit this year's fashions, even though I long ago came to the conclusion that I was not a political person and could have no comfortable place in any political group. . . .

"I am prepared to waive the privilege against self-incrimination and to tell you anything you wish to know about my views or actions, if your committee will agree to refrain from asking me to name other people. If the committee is unwilling to give me this assurance, I will be forced to plead the privilege of the Fifth Amendment at the hearing."

Committee Chairman Wood refused the offer, saying that the Committee could not permit a witness to set forth terms for testifying or be "placed in the position of trading with a witness." N.Y. Times, May 22, 1952.

4. With respect to the doctrine that the privilege against self-incrimination is a personal right and does not protect officers of organizations insofar as organization records are concerned, mentioned in the Rogers case, see also McPhaul v. United States, 364 U.S. 372, 81 S. Ct. 138, 5 L. Ed. 2d 136 (1960). But cf. Curcio v. United States, 354 U.S. 118, 77 S. Ct. 1145, 1 L. Ed. 2d 1225 (1957). Note also Presser v. United States, 284 F.2d 233 (D.C. Cir. 1960), cert. den., 365 U.S. 816 (1961). For discussion of the doctrine see the material cited in connection with the Internal Security Act of 1950, Section C, subsection 3.

5. Until 1964, the Supreme Court had held that a person could not refuse to answer questions before a federal authority on the ground that the answer would tend to incriminate him under state law, United States v. Murdock, 284 U.S. 141, 52 S. Ct. 63, 76 L. Ed. 210 (1931), or before a state authority on the ground the answer would tend to incriminate him under federal law, Knapp v. Schweitzer, 357 U.S. 371, 78 S. Ct. 1302, 2 L. Ed. 2d 1393 (1958). See also Feldman v. United States, 322 U.S. 487, 64 S. Ct. 1082, 88 L. Ed. 1408 (1944). For discussion, see Grant, Federalism and Self-Incrimination, 4 U.C.L.A.L. Rev. 549, 5 U.C.L.A.L. Rev. 1 (1957-1958); Parsons, State-Federal Crossfire in Search and Seizure and Self Incrimination, 42 Cornell L.Q. 346 (1957); Kroner, Self Incrimination: The External Reach of the Privilege, 60 Colum. L. Rev. 816 (1960). But in Murphy v. Waterfront Commission, 378 U.S. 52, 84 S. Ct. 1594, 12 L. Ed. 2d 678 (1964), the Court reversed the prior decisions, saying: "We hold that the constitutional privilege against self-incrimination protects a state witness against incrimination under federal as well as state law and a federal witness against incrimination under state as well as federal law." 378 U.S. at 77-78. See also Malloy v. Hogan, 378 U.S. 1, 84 S. Ct. 1489, 12 L. Ed. 2d 653 (1964), decided the same day, holding that the privilege against self-incrimination in the Fifth Amendment is applicable to the states under the Fourteenth Amendment. For the effect of the new doctrine on the operation of immunity statutes see infra. For comment on the Murphy and Malloy cases, see Note, 78 Harv. L. Rev. 143, 223-230 (1964). See also Notes, 31 Brooklyn L. Rev. 157, 166 (1964); 33 Fordham L. Rev. 77 (1964); 36 Miss. L.J. 103 (1964); 43 N.C.L. Rev. 161 (1964); 43 Texas L. Rev. 239 (1964); 15 W. Res. L. Rev. 797

(1964); 7 Ariz. L. Rev. 124 (1965); 11 How. L.J. 237 (1965); 18 Vand. L. Rev. 744 (1965).

REFERENCES

1. On the historical background and general development of the privilege against self-incrimination, see Corwin, The Supreme Court's Construction of the Self-Incrimination Clause, 29 Mich. L. Rev. 1, 191 (1930); Pittman, The Colonial and Constitutional History of the Privilege Against Self-Incrimination in America, 21 Va. L. Rev. 763 (1935); 8 Wigmore, Evidence §§2250-2284 (3d ed. 1940); Morgan, The Privilege Against Self-Incrimination, 34 Minn. L. Rev. 1 (1949); Inbau, Self-Incrimination (1950); Wolfram, John Lilburne: Democracy's Pillar of Fire, 3 Syracuse L. Rev. 213 (1952); Huard, The Fifth Amendment — An Evaluation, 42 Geo. L.J. 345 (1954); Franklin, The Encyclopédiste Origin and Meaning of the Fifth Amendment, 15 Law. Guild Rev. 41 (1955); Graper, The Origins of the Privilege Against Self Accusation — An Introduction, 16 U. Pitt. L. Rev. 339 (1955); Pittman, The Fifth Amendment: Yesterday, Today and Tomorrow, 42 A.B.A.J. 509 (1956); Randall, Sir Edward Coke and the Privilege Against Self-Incrimination, 8 S.C.L.Q. 417 (1956); Horowitz, The Privilege Against Self-Incrimination — How Did It Originate? 31 Temple L.Q. 121 (1958); Kemp, The Background of the Fifth Amendment in English Law, 1 Wm. & Mary L. Rev. 247 (1958); Mayers, Shall We Amend the Fifth Amendment? (1959); Griswold, The Right To Be Let Alone, 55 Nw. U.L. Rev. 216 (1960).

2. For material on the problem of self-incrimination as it pertains to legislative investigating committees and other areas involving freedom of political expression, see Boudin, The Constitutional Privilege in Operation, 12 Law. Guild Rev. 128 (1952); Griswold, The Fifth Amendment Today (1955); O'Conor, The Fifth Amendment: Should a Good Friend Be Abused? 41 A.B.A.J. 307 (1955); Taylor, Grand Inquest, ch. VII (1955); Williams, Problems of the Fifth Amendment, 24 Ford. L. Rev. 19 (1955); Chafee, The Blessings of Liberty, ch. VII (1956); Hook, Common Sense and the Fifth Amendment (1957); Nutting, The Fifth Amendment and Privacy, 18 U. Pitt. L. Rev. 533 (1957); Pollitt, The Fifth Amendment Plea Before Congressional Committees Investigating Subversion: Motives and Justifiable Presumptions — A Survey of 120 Witnesses, 106 U. Pa. L. Rev. 1117 (1958); Beck, Contempt of Congress, chs. IV and V (1959) (reviewing all federal legislative committee cases from 1948 to 1957); Redlich, Rights of Witnesses Before Congressional Committees; Effects of Recent Supreme Court Decisions, 36 N.Y.U.L. Rev. 1126, 1127-1136 (1961). See also Note, Applicability of Privilege Against Self-Incrimination to Legislative Investigations, 49 Colum. L. Rev. 87 (1949); Note, Self-Incrimination and Federal Anti-Communist Measures, 51 Colum. L. Rev. 206 (1951); Falknor, Self-Incrimination Privilege: Links in The Chain, 5 Vand. L. Rev. 479 (1952); Noonan, Inferences From the Invocation of the Privilege Against Self-Incrimination, 41 Va. L. Rev. 311 (1955); Pollitt, Pleading the Fifth Amendment Before a Congressional Committee: A Study and Explanation, 32 Notre Dame Law. 43 (1956); Note, Privilege Against Self-Incrimination in the Federal Courts, 70 Harv. L. Rev. 1454 (1957). For collection of the cases see Notes, 38 A.L.R.2d 225, 239 (1954); 19 A.L.R. 2d 388 (1951).

3. With regard to the practical consequences of pleading the Fifth Amendment, so far as concerns private employment, public employment, professional career, and teaching, see Ratner, Consequences of Exercising the Privilege Against Self-Incrimination, 24 U. Chi. L. Rev. 472 (1957); Beck, Contempt of Congress 122-125 (1959).

4. For discussion of some of the broader questions of policy involved in an individual's decision as to whether to invoke the Fifth Amendment, see Meltzer, Invoking the Fifth Amendment — Some Legal and Practical Considerations, Bull. of the Atomic Scientists,

June 1953, p. 176; Kalven, Invoking the Fifth Amendment — Some Legal and Impractical Considerations, id. at 181; Frantz and Redlich, Does Silence Mean Guilt? The Nation, June 6, 1953, p. 471; Westin, Do Silent Witnesses Defend Civil Liberties, Commentary, June 1953, p. 537; The Use and Meaning of the Fifth Amendment, U. Chi. Round
Table, Aug. 23, 1953, p. 1; Symposium, Problems of the Fifth Amendment in Modern
Times, 39 Marq. L. Rev. 179 (1956); Hunt and Lacey, Friends and the Use of the Fifth
Amendment (published by the Civil Liberties Committee of Philadelphia Yearly Meeting of Friends, 1957); Kenealy, Fifth Amendment Morals, 3 Catholic Law. 340 (1957).

5. For a survey of the law relating to the privilege against self-incrimination in various
countries of Western Europe see Appendix II to the dissenting opinion of Judge Frank
in United States v. Grunewald, 233 F.2d 556, 587-592 (2d Cir. 1956), rev'd, 353 U.S. 391,
77 S. Ct. 963, 1 L. Ed. 2d 931 (1957).

NOTE — OTHER CONSTITUTIONAL LIMITATIONS

1. The Supreme Court has consistently stated that legislative investigating
committees are subject to the requirements of the Fourth Amendment prohibiting
unreasonable searches and seizures. See, e.g., Watkins v. United States, 354 U.S.
178, 188, 77 S. Ct. 1173, 1179, 1 L. Ed. 2d 1273, 1284 (1957). But the courts have
sustained legislative subpoenas, as in the case of administrative and judicial subpoenas, which call for extensive production of documents. Thus in McPhaul v.
United States, 364 U.S. 372, 81 S. Ct. 138, 5 L. Ed. 2d 136 (1960), the Court
upheld against Fourth Amendment objection a subpoena of the Committee on Un-
American Activities directing the Executive Secretary of the Civil Rights Congress
to produce "all records, correspondence and memoranda pertaining to the organization of, the affiliation with other organizations and all monies received or expended by the Civil Rights Congress." See also United States v. Bryan, 72 F.
Supp. 58 (D. D.C. 1947) (denial of motion to dismiss indictment), 339 U.S. 323,
70 S. Ct. 724, 94 L. Ed. 884 (1950) (affirming conviction); cf. United States v.
Groves, 18 F. Supp. 3 (W.D. Pa. 1937).

Where a legislative committee has seized documents in violation of the Fourth
Amendment such documents may not be used in a criminal prosecution. Nelson v.
United States, 208 F.2d 505 (D.C. Cir. 1953), cert. den., 346 U.S. 827 (1953).
Whether a witness before the committee could refuse to answer questions relating
to such documents was left unanswered in Lanza v. New York, 370 U.S. 139, 82 S.
Ct. 1218, 8 L. Ed. 2d 384 (1962). But where the illegally seized evidence was in
the possession of the committee an attempt to enjoin its use by the committee has
failed, on the theory that the courts will not enjoin the contemplated action of the
legislature. Hearst v. Black, 87 F.2d 68 (D.C. Cir. 1936). See also Lanza v. New
York State Joint Legislative Committee, 3 N.Y.2d 92, 164 N.Y.S.2d 9, 143 N.E.2d
722 (1957), cert. den., 355 U.S. 856 (1957); and cases cited infra dealing with
attempts to enjoin legislative committees.

On the seizure of the records of the Southern Conference Educational Fund, its
Director and attorneys by the Louisiana Joint Committee on Un-American Activities, see the account in Dombrowski v. Pfister, 380 U.S. 479, 85 S. Ct. 1116, 14 L.
Ed. 2d 22 (1965), and the discussion in Section C, subsection 5. In its decision in
Dombrowski the Supreme Court held not only that prosecutions in the case
should be restrained but the Louisiana officials ordered to make "immediate return
of all papers and documents seized." 380 U.S. at 497. But the effort to enjoin

Senator Eastland, Chairman of the Internal Security Subcommittee, and the Subcommittee's counsel, from using the records was rejected by the Court of Appeals in the District of Columbia. Dombrowski v. Burbank, 358 F.2d 821 (D.C. Cir. 1966), pet. for cert. filed sub nom. Dombrowski v. Eastland.

For discussion of Fourth Amendment limitations on legislative committees, see Driver, Constitutional Limitations on the Power of Congress to Punish Contempts of Its Investigating Committees, 38 Va. L. Rev. 887, 898-902 (1952); Note, 29 Fordham L. Rev. 357, 360-362 (1960); Goldfarb, The Contempt Power 224-230 (1963).

2. The Supreme Court has stated on a number of occasions that the legislative investigating power does not extend to matters exclusively within the judicial or executive branches of government. See, e.g., the Watkins and Barenblatt cases, supra. In Kilbourn v. Thompson, 103 U.S. 168, 26 L. Ed. 377 (1881), the Court reversed a contempt citation on the ground that the matter under inquiry — the bankruptcy of Jay Cooke & Co. — was "in its nature clearly judicial" and therefore one "confided by the Constitution to the judicial and not to the legislative department of the government." 103 U.S. at 192, 193. And in United States v. Icardi, 140 F. Supp. 383 (D. D.C. 1956), the District Court dismissed a perjury indictment of a witness called before the Committee on Armed Services to give his version of the alleged murder of Major Holohan in Italy during the war. The court held that the committee was in effect functioning as an adjudicatory tribunal rather than as a bona fide investigating agency, and further that the questions did not relate to a "material matter" since the committee already had all the information on which to base its report. The claim that the legislative committee was interfering with judicial functions has, however, otherwise not been successful. See Sinclair v. United States, 279 U.S. 263, 49 S. Ct. 268, 73 L. Ed. 692 (1929); Hutcheson v. United States, 369 U.S. 599, 82 S. Ct. 1005, 8 L. Ed. 2d 137 (1962).

Issues relating to legislative interference with executive functions have tended to be resolved outside the judicial system. For discussion of the problem, see Ginnane, The Control of Federal Administrative Action by Congressional Resolutions and Committees, 66 Harv. L. Rev. 569 (1953); Bishop, The Executive's Right of Privacy, 66 Yale L.J. 477 (1957); Younger, Congressional Investigations and Executive Secrecy: A Study in the Separation of Powers, 20 U. Pitt. L. Rev. 755 (1959): Rourke, Administrative Secrecy: A Congressional Dilemma, 54 Am. Pol. Sci. Rev. 684 (1960); Kramer and Marcuse, Executive Privilege — A Study of the Period 1953-1960, 29 Geo. Wash. L. Rev. 623, 827 (1961); Senate Judiciary Committee, Subcommittee on Constitutional Rights, Withholding Information from the Congress (86 Cong., 2d Sess. 1961); Harris, Congressional Control of Administration (1964); Berger, Executive Privilege v. Congressional Inquiry, 12 U.C.L.A. L. Rev. 1044, 1288 (1965).

3. The power of a federal legislative committee to investigate the operations of state government agencies was raised in Tobin v. United States, 195 F. Supp. 588 (D. D.C. 1961), rev'd, 306 F.2d 270 (D.C. Cir. 1962), cert. den., 371 U.S. 902 (1962). There the House Judiciary Committee undertook an investigation of the Port of New York Authority, a bi-state agency established under an interstate compact between New Jersey and New York. Tobin, Executive Director of the Authority, refused to produce certain documents claimed to relate to the internal

administration of the Authority and was cited for contempt. The District Court found him guilty, overruling constitutional claims, inter alia, that the investigation invaded the reserved powers of the states under the Tenth Amendment, that the documents were protected under executive privilege, and that non-compliance resulted from the orders of superiors. The Court of Appeals, however, reversed on the ground that the committee's authorizing resolution should be construed as not empowering it to seek the information demanded; hence constitutional issues were avoided. See Notes, 30 Geo. Wash. L. Rev. 536 (1962); 31 Geo. Wash. L. Rev. 842 (1963).

4. For the argument that legislative investigations may constitute a bill of attainder, see Brant, The Bill of Rights, ch. 37 (1965). See also Note, 34 Ind. L.J. 231, 234-249 (1959).

3. Non-Constitutional Issues

In addition to the constitutional limitations, the courts have imposed upon legislative investigating committees a variety of non-constitutional requirements. These have, in some respects, operated as a more limiting factor than the constitutional doctrines. From the Supreme Court decisions already set forth the following principles may be noted: that the inquiry must be authorized by the legislature, or that House conducting the investigation (Rumely, Watkins, Barenblatt); that the question asked must be pertinent to the matter under investigation (Sinclair, Watkins, cf. Scull); that the matter under inquiry and the pertinency of the question to the matter under inquiry must be made clear to the witness (Watkins, Barenblatt, cf. Scull); that the questions asked by a subcommittee must be within the scope of the inquiry authorized by the full committee (Sacher); and that the committee must unambiguously require the question to be answered at the time the contempt is alleged (Quinn, Emspak, Bart, Flaxer). In addition the following decisions of the Supreme Court involved non-constitutional requirements:

In Christoffel v. United States, 338 U.S. 84, 69 S. Ct. 1447, 93 L. Ed. 1826 (1949), the Court held that a witness before a legislative committee can be found guilty of perjury only where a quorum of the committee is present at the time the perjury is committed; and that in a prosecution for perjury it is not enough to prove that a quorum was present when the hearing began but it must be shown affirmatively that a quorum existed at the time of the offense. Chief Justice Vinson and Justices Jackson, Reed, and Burton dissented. But this decision was qualified in United States v. Bryan, 339 U.S. 323, 70 S. Ct. 724, 94 L. Ed. 884 (1950). Here it was held that a witness subpoenaed to produce records and failing to produce them at a committee hearing could not raise the issue of a lack of quorum, particularly where it had not been raised at the hearing. Justices Black and Frankfurter dissented on grounds not involving the quorum point. See also Meyers v. United States, 181 F.2d 802 (D.C. Cir. 1950), cert. den., 339 U.S. 983 (1950), refusing to vacate the judgment in the case of Gen. Bennett Meyers for perjury in testimony concerning fraud in government contracts. See Note, 11 Law. Guild Rev. 36 (1951).

In United States v. Fleischman, 339 U.S. 349, 70 S. Ct. 739, 94 L. Ed. 906 (1950), the Court, reversing the Court of Appeals of the District of Columbia, held that the defendant, a member of the executive board of the Joint Anti-Fascist Committee, had not made such efforts to produce the organization's records as would absolve her of contempt for failure of the board to produce them. For the remand see 183 F.2d 996, cert. den., 340 U.S. 866 (1950). See also McPhaul v. United States, 364 U.S. 372, 81 S. Ct. 138, 5 L. Ed. 2d 136 (1960), noted supra.

In Deutch v. United States, 367 U.S. 456, 81 S. Ct. 1587, 6 L. Ed. 2d 963 (1961), a subcommittee of the House Un-American Activities Committee conducted hearings on "Communist Party activities in the Albany (New York) area," particularly "within the field of labor." The witness testified freely about his Communist Party activities at Cornell University but refused to answer questions concerning other persons with whom he was associated at the time. The Court reversed a conviction for contempt on the ground that "the Government at the trial failed to carry its burden of proving the pertinence of the questions," which "had nothing to do with the Albany area or with Communist infiltration into labor unions." 367 U.S. at 469, 470. Justices Harlan, Frankfurter, Whittaker, and Clark dissented.

In Slagle v. Ohio, 366 U.S. 259, 81 S. Ct. 1076, 6 L. Ed. 2d 277 (1961), a unanimous Court, Mr. Justice Frankfurter not participating, reversed contempt convictions of two witnesses before the Ohio Un-American Activities Committee for the reason that the committee had not pressed for answers, but affirmed by evenly divided vote the conviction of three others who relied upon arguments of lack of pertinency, absence of legislative purpose, and invalidity of an immunity statute.

Nine convictions were reversed by the Supreme Court in 1962 because "in each case the indictment returned by the grand jury failed to identify the subject under congressional subcommittee inquiry at the time the witness was interrogated." Justices Clark and Harlan dissented; Justices Frankfurter and White did not participate. Russell v. United States, 369 U.S. 749, 82 S. Ct. 1038, 8 L. Ed. 2d 240 (1962) (involving Norton Anthony Russell, Robert Shelton, Alden Whitman, Herman Liveright, William A. Price, and John T. Gojack); Silber v. United States, 370 U.S. 717, 82 S. Ct. 1287, 8 L. Ed. 2d 798 (1962); Grumman v. United States, 370 U.S. 288, 82 S. Ct. 1560, 8 L. Ed. 2d 501 (1962); Hartman v. United States, 370 U.S. 724, 82 S. Ct. 1574, 8 L. Ed. 2d 801 (1962). In the Silber case the issue, while raised in the trial court, had not been urged in the Court of Appeals or the Supreme Court.

In Yellin v. United States, 374 U.S. 109, 83 S. Ct. 1828, 10 L. Ed. 2d 778 (1963), a contempt conviction was reversed because the House Committee on Un-American Activities had failed to observe its own rules. A committee rule provided that if a majority of the committee or subcommittee "believes that the interrogation of a witness in a public hearing might . . . unjustly injure his reputation . . . the Committee shall interrogate such witness in Executive Session for the purpose of determining the necessity or advisability of conducting such interrogation thereafter in a public hearing." After Yellin had been served with a subpoena, his counsel sent a telegram to the Committee requesting an executive session, but the request was summarily denied by the Staff Director. The Court found the Committee had violated its rule by not considering injury to the witness when it originally subpoenaed Yellin to appear at a public hearing, and by failing to act (as a committee) on the request for an executive session. This failure to comply with its rules excused the witness' refusal to answer questions, and the witness was entitled to prove the defense when he discovered at his contempt trial that his rights under the executive session rule had been violated. Justices Clark, Harlan, Stewart, and White dissented.

The Gojack case, one of those involved in the Russell decisions, came back to the Supreme Court in 1966. Gojack v. United States, 384 U.S. 702, 86 S. Ct. 1689, 16 L. Ed. 2d 870 (1966).

Gojack had been reindicted and again convicted for refusal to answer before the House Committee on Un-American Activities in 1955 questions concerning his affiliation with the Communist Party, the affiliation of others, and his connection with the "Peace Crusade." The Supreme Court unanimously reversed. Gojack's counsel had asked the Court to reconsider Barenblatt, but the Court said: "Since we decide the present case on other grounds, it is not necessary nor would it be appropriate to reach the constitutional question." The "other grounds" were (1) the committee had failed to follow its own rules requiring that "no major investigation shall be initiated without approval of a majority of the Committee"; and (2) the authorization from the full Committee to the Subcommittee "failed to specify the subject of inquiry that the Subcommittee was to undertake."

The Court, speaking through Mr. Justice Fortas, emphasized: "We are not here dealing with the justification for an investigation by a committee of the Congress as a matter of congressional administration. That is a legislative matter. We are here concerned with a criminal proceeding. It is clear as a matter of law that the usual standards of the criminal law must be observed, including proper allegation and proof of all the essential elements of the offense." 384 U.S. at 707. Mr. Justice Black concurred in the opinion, although he "would prefer" to reverse on the grounds of his Barenblatt dissent.

NOTES

1. The lower federal courts have also frequently refused to hold witnesses guilty of contempt, relying upon various non-constitutional and often highly technical grounds. The major cases of this nature are: United States v. Browder (D. D.C.

Mar. 14, 1951, unreported), discussed in 40 Geo. L.J. 137 (1951) (committee did not press for an answer); Bowers v. United States, 202 F.2d 447 (D.C. Cir. 1953) (Government did not sustain burden of proving pertinency), noted in 41 Geo. L.J. 568 (1953), 39 Va. L. Rev. 532 (1953), but cf. United States v. Orman, 207 F.2d 148 (3d Cir. 1953); Kenney v. United States, 218 F.2d 843 (D.C. Cir. 1954) (receipt of evidence on issue of pertinency in presence of jury held prejudicial); United States v. Kamin, 135 F. Supp. 382, 136 F. Supp. 791 (D. Mass. 1955 and 1956) (questions outside scope of committee's authority); United States v. Lamont, 18 F.R.D. 27 (S.D. N.Y. 1955), aff'd, 236 F.2d 312 (2d Cir. 1956) (indictment failed to specify subcommittee's authority from full committee); O'Connor v. United States, 240 F.2d 404 (D.C. Cir. 1956) (question "whether he was a member of the Communist conspiracy" too "imprecise and ambiguous"); Brewster v. United States, 255 F.2d 899 (D.C. Cir. 1958), cert. den., 358 U.S. 842 (1958) (Congress did not give authorization for investigation "with sufficient clarity and certainty"); Watson v. United States, 280 F.2d 689 (D.C. Cir. 1960) (subject of inquiry and pertinency of questions not made clear to witness); Knowles v. United States, 280 F.2d 696 (D.C. Cir. 1960) (same); United States v. Turoff, 291 F.2d 864 (2d Cir. 1961) (defendant prejudiced at trial by reading of irrelevant portions of committee transcript); United States v. Yarus, 198 F. Supp. 425 (S.D. N.Y. 1961) (failure to prove authorizing resolution); United States v. Seeger, 303 F.2d 478 (2d Cir. 1962) (indictment failed to allege subcommittee's authority from full committee); Popper v. United States, 306 F.2d 290 (D.C. Cir. 1962) (indictment failed to set forth question under inquiry).

In all of the nine cases reversed by the Supreme Court in 1962 (see supra), the Government obtained new indictments. All but Gojack were dimissed at the trial: United States v. Russell, Crim. No. 820-62 (D. D.C. unreported); United States v. Whitman, Crim. No. 826-62 (D. D.C. unreported); United States v. Grumman and United States v. Silber, 227 F. Supp. 227 (D. D.C. 1964) (similar to Yellin); United States v. Hartman, 8 Civil Liberties Docket 100, 131 (1963); or reversed by the Court of Appeals: Shelton v. United States, 327 F.2d 601 (D.C. Cir. 1963) (failure to follow committee rules in issuing subpoena); Liveright v. United States, 347 F.2d 473 (D.C. Cir. 1965) (same); Price v. United States (D.C. Cir. unreported). The Gojack case was reversed again by the Supreme Court. See supra.

Where the witness subpoenaed has failed to appear before the committee, contempt convictions have been sustained. Wheeldin v. United States, 283 F.2d 535 (9th Cir. 1960), cert. den., 366 U.S. 977 (1961); Licavoli v. United States, 294 F.2d 207 (D.C. Cir. 1961), cert. den., 366 U.S. 936 (1961).

See also United States v. Cuesta, 8 Civil Liberties Docket 21 (1962) (jurisdiction of House Committee on Un-American Activities does not extend to Puerto Rico).

From a compilation made by Carl Beck it would appear that, out of 226 contempt citations voted by Congress during 1944-1957, only 44 resulted in court decisions upholding the contempt. There were 122 cases of acquittal or dismissal in the courts, 35 cases never brought to court, and 25 cases still pending. Beck, Contempt of Congress 243 (1959). Thus most of the contempt citations resulting from the hearings of the Kefauver Committee (investigating organized crime) ended in acquittals or reversals. See Boudin, The Immunity Bill, 42 Geo. L.J. 497, 504 n. 31 (1954) (collecting the cases). And none of the seven prosecutions for contempt in refusing to answer questions of the McCarthy Committee (Permanent Subcommittee on Investigations of the Senate Committee on Government Operations) was successful.

2. In United States v. Kleinman, 107 F. Supp. 407 (D. D.C. 1962), the court upheld the refusal of a witness to testify when "there were, in close proximity to the witness, television cameras, newsreel cameras, news photographers with their concomitant flashbulbs, radio microphones, a large and crowded hearing room with spectators standing along the walls, etc." See Notes, 26 Temple L.Q. 70 (1952); 51 Mich. L. Rev. 1072 (1953); 37 Minn. L. Rev. 297 (1953). But in United States v. Hintz, 193 F. Supp. 325 (N.D. Ill. 1961), where the issue arose on a motion to dismiss the indictment, the court refused to follow the Kleinman case.

The obverse situation arose in the contempt citations of Dagmar Wilson, Donna Allen, and Russell Nixon in 1964. These witnesses refused to testify before a subcommittee of the House Un-American Activities Committee in executive session, but asserted their willingness to testify at a public hearing. They were found guilty of contempt. N.Y. Times, April 9, 1965. The court of appeals reversed, but based its decision on the ground that the Speaker of the House, who transmitted the Committee's citation to the United States attorney for criminal prosecution while the House was not in session, had erred in believing that he had no discretion in the matter. Wilson v. United States, — F.2d — (D.C. Cir. 1966).

3. On the question of the right of witnesses to invoke such common law privileges as attorney-client, clergyman-penitent, and physician-patient relations, see Notes, 45 Calif, L. Rev. 347 (1957); 70 Harv. L. Rev. 671, 682-684 (1957). See also United States v. Kenney, 111 F. Supp. 233 (D. D.C. 1953), rev'd, 218 F.2d 843 (D.C. Cir. 1954).

REFERENCES

For a collection of the cases see, in addition to Beck, notes in 97 L. Ed. 782 (1953), 99 L. Ed. 985 (1955), 3 L. Ed. 2d 1647 (1959), and 10 L. Ed. 2d 1329 (1963). The cases up to 1955 are digested in Digest of the Public Record of Communism in the United States 218-231 (Fund for the Republic 1955). For legal discussion see Redlich, Rights of Witnesses Before Congressional Committees: Effects of Recent Supreme Court Decisions, 36 N.Y.U.L. Rev. 1126 (1961); Notes, 29 Fordham L. Rev. 357 (1960); 8 N.Y.L.F. 133 (1962).

A well-known case, not involving civil liberties issues but the investigation of influence peddling, is Goldfine v. United States, 268 F.2d 941 (1st Cir. 1959), cert. den., 363 U.S. 842 (1960), affirming contempt conviction reported at 169 F. Supp. 93 (D. Mass. 1958). For another phase of the case see Goldfine v. Pastore, 261 F.2d 519 (1st Cir. 1958).

NOTE — PERJURY

Witnesses before legislative investigating committees are subject to prosecution under the perjury laws for willfully false testimony. Prosecutions have been rare. A key case during the height of Senator McCarthy's influence was that of Owen Lattimore. Lattimore was called before the Internal Security Subcommittee of the Senate Judiciary Committee in the course of its investigation of the Institute of Pacific Relations and examined for 12 days. Later he was indicted for perjury on seven counts, the principal one being that he had testified falsely when he said that he had "never been a sympathizer or any other kind of promoter of Communism or Communist interests." The District Court dismissed this count and was upheld by the Court of Appeals, on the ground that the word "sympathizer" was too vague to satisfy the Sixth Amendment. United States v. Lattimore, 112 F. Supp. 507 (D. D.C. 1953), 215 F.2d 847 (D.C. Cir. 1954). The Government subsequently re-indicted Lattimore on two counts: that he perjured himself when he denied he was a "follower of the Communist line" and when he testified he had never been "a promoter of Communist interests." Both counts were dismissed on the ground of vagueness, 127 F. Supp. 405 (D. D.C. 1955), Judge Youngdahl saying, "The Court cannot escape the conclusion that 'follower of the Communist line' is not a phrase with a meaning about which men of ordinary intellect could agree, nor one which could be used with mutual understanding by a questioner and answerer unless it were defined at the time it were sought and offered as testimony. This count, even with its apparent definition, is an open invitation to the jury to substitute, by conjecture, their understanding of the phrase for that of the defendant." 127 F. Supp. at 410. The decision was affirmed by an evenly divided Court of Appeals. 232 F.2d 334 (D.C. Cir. 1955); see N.Y. Times, June 15, 1955. The Government subsequently dropped the case. N.Y. Times, June 29, 1955.

The Lattimore case is discussed in Boudin, Immunity Bill, 42 Geo. L.J. 497 (1954); Notes, 49 Nw. U.L. Rev. 77 (1954); 43 Geo. L.J. 111 (1954); 32 Texas L. Rev. 450 (1954); 102 U. Pa. L. Rev. 251 (1953); and see Lattimore's own account, Ordeal by Slander (1950); Gilbert, New Light on the Lattimore Case, The New Republic, Dec. 27, 1954, p. 7, and reply by Sol Stein, Executive Director of the American Committee for Cultural Freedom, The New Republic, Feb. 14, 1955, p. 20.

See also the Hiss and Remington cases, noted in Section C, subsection 1, and the Icardi case, noted in subsection 2 of this section. Other cases of perjury before Congressional committees investigating other matters than subversion are digested in Note, Perjury Committed by False Testimony Before a Congressional Committee, 98 L. Ed. 98 (1955). For a prosecution for obstruction of justice through mutilating and concealing records sought by a legislative committee, see Presser v. United States, 292 F.2d 171 (6th Cir. 1961), aff'd by equally divided court, 371 U.S. 71 (1962).

NOTE — METHODS OF OBTAINING JUDICIAL REVIEW

Judicial review of the action of federal legislative committees is obtainable through habeas corpus, where the legislature attempts to enforce its contempt citation directly, or through regular court procedures where criminal prosecution is brought under 2 U.S.C. §192. In both proceedings the witness obtains judicial scrutiny of the legislative action only at the risk of incurring penalties for contempt unless the court decision is in his favor. Attempts to obtain review by injunction or declaratory judgment have been unsuccessful. See Hearst v. Black, 87 F.2d 68 (D.C. Cir. 1936), noted above; but the court indicated that it would enjoin agents of the committee from seizing documents if the action were brought before the seizure took place, 87 F.2d at 71; Mins v. McCarthy, 209 F.2d 307 (D.C.

Cir. 1953) (attempt to enjoin enforcement of subpoena and holding of hearing); Fischler v. McCarthy, 117 F. Supp. 643 (S.D. N.Y. 1954), aff'd for lack of venue, 218 F.2d 164 (2d Cir. 1954) (attempt to enjoin Senator McCarthy from forcing production of documents and to obtain declaratory judgment); In re Motion to Quash Subpoenas and Vacate Service, 146 F. Supp. 792 (W.D. Pa. 1956) (attempt to quash subpoena duces tecum); Pauling v. Eastland, 288 F.2d 126 (D.C. Cir. 1960), cert. den., 364 U.S. 900 (1960) (attempt by Linus Pauling to obtain declaratory judgment and injunction against order of Senate Internal Security Subcommittee to produce correspondence relating to petition to United Nations); Randolph v. Willis, 220 F. Supp. 355 (S.D. Cal. 1963) (proceeding for declaratory judgment and injunction against members and staff of House Un-American Activities Committee); Stamler v. Hall (N.D. Ill. 1965) (unreported; on appeal to 7th Cir.) (same). In Yellin v. United States, 374 U.S. 109, 83 S. Ct. 1828, 10 L. Ed. 2d 778 (1963), the Court remarked: "If the Committee ignores [petitioner's] request for an executive session, it is highly improbable that petitioner could obtain an injunction against the Committee that would protect him from public exposure," citing the Pauling case. 374 U.S. at 121.

In August, 1966, when the House Committee on Un-American Activities subpoenaed a number of witnesses to testify upon opposition to the Viet Nam war, two of the witnesses brought suit in the District of Columbia to enjoin the Committee from holding the hearings and enforcing the subpoenas. Judge Corcoran granted a temporary restraining order, but this was dissolved the following day by a three-judge court and the matter set for hearing. Krebs v. Ashbrook (Civ. Action No. 2157-66, D.D.C. 1966); see N.Y. Times, Aug. 16 and 17, 1966.

An action to enjoin the Senate Internal Security Subcommittee from publishing a report in which it found, without hearing, that the Methodist Federation for Social Action was a Communist front was unsuccessful in Methodist Federation for Social Action v. Eastland, 141 F. Supp. 729 (D. D.C. 1956). The case is noted in 43 Cornell L.Q. 103 (1957); 70 Harv. L. Rev. 723 (1957); 43 Iowa L. Rev. 132 (1957); 4 U.C.L.A.L. Rev. 466 (1957).

On the other hand in Jordan v. Hutcheson, 323 F.2d 597 (4th Cir. 1963), the court took jurisdiction over a suit to enjoin members and staff of Virginia's Legislative Committee on Offenses from attempting through its investigatory powers to "intimidate, discourage and impede the plaintiffs and all Negro citizens of Virginia from using the courts as a means of ending the practices of racial segregation in that state." See also United States v. Owlett, 15 F. Supp. 736 (M.D. Pa. 1936) (enjoining state legislative committee from investigating activities of the Works Progress Administration, a federal agency). See also the Dombrowski litigation, Section C, subsection 5. And state courts, under some circumstances, have given injunctive relief against state legislative investigations. Gilbreath v. Willett, 148 Tenn. 92, 251 S.W. 910, 28 A.L.R. 1147 (1923); Annenberg v. Roberts, 333 Pa. 203, 2 A.2d 612 (1938); McGinley v. Scott, 401 Pa. 310, 164 A.2d 424 (1960); see also Greenfield v. Russel, 292 Ill. 392, 127 N.E. 102, 9 A.L.R. 1334 (1920); Luscomb v. Bowker, 334 Mass. 468, 136 N.E.2d 192 (1956). But see Lanza v. New York State Joint Legislative Committee, 3 N.Y.2d 92, 164 N.Y.S.2d 9, 143 N.E.2d 772 (1957), cert. den., 355 U.S. 856 (1957); N.A.A.C.P. v. Committee on Offenses Against Administration of Justice, 201 Va. 890, 114 S.E.2d 721 (1960). Cf. the Julian Bond case, noted in Chapter V, Section B.

Some of the state legislative committees operate under a procedure by which, when the witness refuses to produce or answer, the committee may take the matter to a court and obtain a court order requiring the witness to give the evidence; if the witness then refuses he is punishable as in contempt of court. See N.Y. Civil Practice Act §406; and the procedure employed in the Sweezy case. This method of compelling evidence gives the witness an opportunity for judicial review before incurring a penalty.

REFERENCES

For discussion of the above matters, see Morgan, Congressional Investigations and Judicial Review: Kilbourn v. Thompson Revisited, 37 Calif. L. Rev. 556 (1949); Maslow, Fair Procedures in Congressional Investigations: A Proposed Code, 54 Colum. L. Rev. 839, 882-885 (1954); Note, Rights of Witness Threatened With Congressional Contempt Citation Held Nonjusticiable in Declaratory Judgment Action, 61 Colum. L. Rev. 1159 (1961) (note on the Pauling case); Sky, Judicial Review of Congressional Investigations: Is There an Alternative to Contempt? 31 Geo. Wash. L. Rev. 399 (1962); Note, Alternative to Contempt Sought in Congressional Investigations, 31 Geo. Wash. L. Rev. 842 (1963).

NOTE — RELIEF THROUGH ACTIONS FOR DAMAGES

Members of legislative committees enjoy legislative immunity and are not subject to suits in damages or otherwise for their actions in connection with the functioning of the committee. See Kilbourn v. Thompson, 103 U.S. 168, 26 L. Ed. 377 (1880); Tenney v. Brandhove, 341 U.S. 367, 71 S. Ct. 783, 95 L. Ed. 1019 (1951); Hancock v. Burns, 158 Cal. App. 2d 785, 323 P.2d 456 (Cal. App., 1958); United States v. Johnson, 383 U.S. 169, 86 S. Ct. 749, 15 L. Ed. 2d 681 (1966). But agents of the legislature do not enjoy legislative immunity. See Kilbourn v. Thompson, supra. In Wheeldin v. Wheeler, 373 U.S. 647, 83 S. Ct. 1441, 10 L. Ed. 2d 605 (1963), however, the Supreme Court held that no cause of action under federal law lay against an investigator of the House Committee on Un-American Activities who allegedly served a subpoena upon the plaintiff without authority of the committee in a malicious effort to injure him. Mr. Chief Justice Warren and Justices Black and Brennan dissented. See also Barr v. Matteo, 360 U.S. 564, 79 S. Ct. 1335, 3 L. Ed. 2d 1434 (1959). For discussion of the Wheeldin case (in the lower court) see Note, Absolute Privilege as Applied to Investigators for Congressional Committees, 63 Colum. L. Rev. 326 (1963). On this issue see also Dombrowski v. Burbank, 358 F.2d 821 (D.C. Cir. 1966), pet. for cert. filed sub nom. Dombrowski v. Eastland, noted supra.

Witnesses compelled to testify and fair and accurate press reports of legislative proceedings are privileged by common law decision. See Note, 16 U. Chi. L. Rev. 544, 552-554 (1949); Nelson, Libel in News of Congressional Investigating Committees (1961). See also Chapter VI.

4. *Procedural Rights of Persons Called Before or Attacked Before Legislative Committees*

Some of the most severe criticism of legislative investigating committees has been directed toward the absence of adequate procedural safeguards or effective remedy against damaging but unwarranted charges. Eric Johnston, then head of the Motion Picture Association, expressed forcefully the dilemma facing persons attacked before a legislative committee:

"With no vested right to be heard and no vested right to challenge accusations against him, the innocent citizen is helpless. He can be indicted and convicted in the public mind on the unchallenged say-so of a witness who may be completely sincere, but can be either misinformed or riddled with prejudice. Without fear of reprisal, a prejudiced witness can exercise venom as well as veracity." [1]

A number of proposals for affording greater protection to persons attacked by or before legislative committees have been put forward. Thus it has been proposed that the immunity provisions of Article I, Section 6, of the Constitution be repealed. It has also been suggested that all "investigations" as distinct from "legislative hearings" be conducted by impartial commissions on the order of the British Royal Commissions. Another proposal has been that a suit for libel or slander be allowed against the government. These measures, however, have never been seriously considered by Congress.

Many proposals have been advanced for legislation or committee rules to afford greater procedural protections. Lindsay Rogers has proposed that the provisions of the Administrative Procedure Act be made applicable to legislative committee proceedings. See Rogers, Congressional Investigations: The Problem and its Solution, 18 U. Chi. L. Rev. 464 (1951). Other proposals, embodied in various bills, include affording persons attacked the right to be advised in advance, to present evidence, to appear with counsel and cross-examine (usually to a limited extent) adverse witnesses, to file statements, to subpoena favorable witnesses, and the like. Additional proposals would require that committee reports be approved by a majority of the whole committee before issuance, that minority reports be issued simultaneously with the majority report, and that members of committees be prohibited from lecturing or writing about investigations for compensation.

While no radical changes in committee procedures have been adopted, there has been a gradual modification in the direction of extending more rights to witnesses and persons adversely affected. In 1955 the House adopted general rules applicable to all its investigating committees. Amendment to Rule XI (26) of the Rules of the House of Representatives, 101 Cong. Rec.

---

[1] Motion Picture Association Press Release for Oct. 26, 1947, quoted in Glassie and Cooley, Congressional Investigations — Salvation in Self Regulation, 38 Geo. L.J. 343, 356 (1950).

3569-3585. In addition each committee has its own rules, those of the Committee on Un-American Activities being set forth below. The Senate has not adopted general rules but each committee is governed by its own.

HOUSE COMMITTEE ON UN-AMERICAN ACTIVITIES — COMMITTEE RULES OF PROCEDURE
Revised September 14, 1965, 89th Cong., 1st Sess.

I — INITIATION OF INVESTIGATIONS

No major investigation shall be initiated without approval of a majority of the Committee. Preliminary inquiries, however, may be initiated by the Committee's staff with the approval of the Chairman of the Committee.

II — SUBJECTS OF INVESTIGATION

The subject of any investigation in connection with which witnesses are summoned or shall otherwise appear shall be announced in an opening statement to the Committee or Subcommittee before the commencement of any hearings; and the information sought to be elicited at the hearings shall be relevant and germane to the subject as so stated. . . .

IV — EXECUTIVE AND PUBLIC HEARINGS

(1) If the Committee or a Subcommittee believes that the interrogation of a witness in a public hearing might endanger national security, it shall interrogate such witness in an Executive Session for the purpose of determining the necessity or advisability of conducting such interrogation thereafter in a public hearing.

(2) Attendance at Executive Sessions shall be limited to Members of the Committee, its staff, and other persons whose presence is requested, or consented to, by the Committee or Subcommittee.

(3) No testimony taken or material presented in an Executive Session, or any summary thereof, shall be made public either in whole or in part, unless authorized by a majority of the Committee.

V — TESTIMONY UNDER OATH

All witnesses at public or executive hearings who testify as to matters of fact shall give all testimony under oath or affirmation. Only the Chairman or a Member of the Committee shall be empowered to administer said oath or affirmation. . . .

VII — Advice of Counsel

A — At every hearing, public or executive, every witness shall be accorded the privilege of having counsel of his own choosing.

B — The participation of counsel during the course of any hearing and while the witness is testifying shall be limited to advising said witness as to his legal rights. Counsel shall not be permitted to engage in oral argument with the Committee, but shall confine his activity to the area of legal advice to his client.

VIII — Conduct of Counsel

Counsel for a witness shall conduct himself in a professional, ethical, and proper manner. His failure to do so shall, upon a finding to that effect by a majority of the Committee or Subcommittee before which the witness is appearing, subject such counsel to disciplinary action which may include warning, censure, removal of counsel from the hearing room, or a recommendation of contempt proceedings.[2]

In case of such removal of counsel, the witness shall have a reasonable time to obtain other counsel, said time to be determined by the Committee or Subcommittee. Should the witness deliberately or capriciously fail or refuse to obtain the services of other counsel within such reasonable time, the hearing shall continue and the testimony of such witness shall be heard without benefit of counsel.

IX — Statement by Witness

A — Any witness desiring to make a prepared or written statement for the record of the proceedings, in Executive or Public Sessions, shall file a copy of such statement with the counsel of the Committee not less than 48 hours in advance of the hearing at which the statement is to be presented.[3]

B — All such statements or portions thereof so received which are relevant and germane to the subject of the investigation may, at the conclusion of the testimony of the witness, upon approval by a majority vote of the Committee or Subcommittee Members present, be inserted in the official transcript of the proceedings.

---

[2] The Committee seeks factual testimony within the personal knowledge of the witness and such testimony and answers must be given by the witness himself and not suggested to witness by counsel.

[3] Statements which take the form of personal attacks by the witness upon the motives of the Committee, the personal characters of any Members of the Congress or of the Committee staff, and statements clearly in the nature of accusation are not deemed to be either relevant or germane.

X — Rights of Persons Affected by a Hearing

A — Where practicable, any person named in a public hearing, or in the released testimony of an executive hearing, as subversive, Fascist, Communist, or affiliated with one or more subversive-front organizations, who has not been previously so named, shall, within a reasonable time thereafter, be notified by registered letter, return receipt requested, to the address last known to the Committee, of such fact, including:

(1) A statement that he has been so named;

(2) The date and place of said hearing;

(3) The name of the person who so testified;

(4) The name of the subversive, Fascist, Communist, or front organization with which he has been identified; and

(5) A copy of the printed Rules of Procedure of the Committee.

B — Any person, so notified, who believes that his character or reputation has been adversely affected or to whom has been imputed subversive activity, may within 15 days after receipt of said notice:

(1) Communicate with the Counsel of the Committee;[4] and/or

(2) Request to appear at his own expense in person before the Committee or any Subcommittee thereof in Public Session and give testimony, in denial or affirmation, relevant and germane to the subject of the investigation.

C — Any such person testifying under the provisions of B(2) above shall be accorded the same privileges as any other witness appearing before the Committee, and may be questioned concerning any matter relevant and germane to the subject of the investigation.

XI — Admissibility of Testimony

A witness shall be limited to giving information relevant and germane to the subject under investigation. The Committee or Subcommittee, through its presiding member, shall rule upon the admissibility of all testimony or information presented by the witness.[5] . . .

[4] All witnesses are invited at any time to confer with Committee Counsel or investigators for the Committee prior to hearings.

[5] The rules of legislative bodies and their committees differ from those of courts. The procedures of any body must be geared to its purpose. Courts have one purpose, Congressional Committees another. Courts conduct trials to determine guilt or innocence, or to adjudicate private rights. Court proceedings are adversary in nature; committee proceedings are not. Committees hold hearings to develop information that will assist in the enactment of legislation. Courtroom procedures are not followed in Congressional hearings or vice versa, because any attempt to apply the rules of one to the other would tend to frustrate the attainment of the different purposes for which they were created.

The Congress has given careful consideration to this subject and has determined that, in order to carry out the responsibilities imposed on it by the Constitution, court procedures governing the reception of evidence and the examination of witnesses are not binding on the Committees of the Congress.

XVI — PUBLICATION OF NAMES OF SUBPENAED WITNESSES

No Member of the Committee or staff shall make public the name of any witness subpenaed before the Committee or Subcommittee prior to the date of his appearance. . . .

REFERENCES

1. The proposal for ending Congressional immunity was embodied in Sen. Joint Res. 203, 81st Cong., 2d Sess., introduced by Senator Hunt in 1950. His argument for the amendment may be found in Hunt, Dangers in Congressional Immunity, N.Y. Times Magazine, June 24, 1951, p. 14. The suggestion for impartial commissions is advanced in Ives, In Place of Congressional "Circuses," N.Y. Times Magazine, Aug. 27, 1950, p. 20. The remedy by way of a damage suit against the government is considered in Paul and Mandel, A Remedy for Smear-by-Congress, The New Republic, Feb. 27, 1950, p. 14; Note, 3 Stan. L. Rev. 486 (1951); Green, Public Destruction of Private Reputation — A Remedy? 38 Minn. L. Rev. 567 (1954). See also Cutler and Packer, Make Them Tell Congress the Truth, Harper's Magazine, March 1952, p. 82, advocating that a person injured by false testimony be allowed to bring a suit for damages against the witness.

2. In 1954 both Houses of Congress held extensive hearings on the matter of committee procedures. Hearings before the Subcommittee on Legislative Procedure of the House Rules Committee, Legislative Procedure, 83d Cong., 2d Sess. (1954); Hearings before the Subcommittee on Rules of the Senate Rules and Administration Committee, Rules of Procedure for Senate Investigating Committees, 83d Cong., 2d Sess. (1954). See also Report of Senate Committee on Rules and Administration to accompany S. Res. 17, Rules of Procedure for Senate Investigating Committees, 84th Cong., 1955. Changes in committee procedures were also considered by the Joint Committee on the Organization of the Congress, established under S. Con. Res. 2, 89th Cong., 1st Sess. (1965), which conducted extensive hearings under the chairmanship of Senator Monroney and Congressman Madden. See, e.g., the proposals advanced by the American Civil Liberties Union. Hearings 2014-2025. For a summary of legislative consideration of the problem, see Congressional Quarterly Service, Congress and the Nation: 1945-1964 1683-1685 (1965).

For the code of procedure for legislative and executive investigations, adopted by New York in 1954, see N.Y. Civil Rights Law, §73.

3. On issues of committee procedures the most comprehensive treatment, citing the prior material, is Maslow, Fair Procedure in Congressional Investigations: A Proposed Code, 54 Colum. L. Rev. 839 (1954). See also Fortas, Methods of Committees Investigating Subversion — A Critique, 29 Notre Dame Law. 192 (1954); Garrison, Congressional Investigations: Are They a Threat to Civil Liberties? 40 A.B.A.J. 125 (1954); Scott and King, Rules for Congressional Committees: An Analysis of House Resolution 447, 40 Va. L. Rev. 249 (1954); Buckley and Bozell, McCarthy and His Enemies, ch. XIII (1954); Rauh and Pollitt, Right to and Nature of Representation Before Congressional Committees, 45 Minn. L. Rev. 853 (1961).

On proposals for procedural changes see Galloway, Congressional Investigations: Proposed Reforms, 18 U. Chi. L. Rev. 478 (1951); Maslow, supra (formulating a detailed code and also discussing many other proposals, including those advanced by the Association of the Bar of the City of New York, the New York State Bar Association, the Bar Association of the District of Columbia, the Senate Republican Policy Committee, and the New York Legislature); Note, An Act to Establish Rules for Legislative Investigating Committees, 1 Harv. J. on Legis. 175 (1964). See also Liacos, Rights of Witnesses

Before Congressional Committees, 33 B.U.L. Rev. 337 (1953); Symposium, Legislative Investigations: Safeguards for Witnesses, 29 Notre Dame Law. 157 (1954); Dulaney, The "Trilemma" of the Congressional Committee Witness, 26 Miss. L.J. 69 (1954); Keating, The Investigating Powers of Congress, 14 Fed. B.J. 171 (1954); Kefauver, A Code of Conduct for Congressional Investigations, 8 Ark. L. Rev. 369 (1954); Civil Rights in Legislative Probes, 11 N.Y. County Lawyers Assn. Bar Bull. 217 (1954); Chase, Improving Congressional Investigations: A No-Progress Report, 30 Temple L.Q. 126 (1957). For drafts of codes suggested by the American Bar Association, see 40 A.B.A.J. 900 (1954); Report of American Bar Association Special Committee on Individual Rights as Affected by National Security, 86 Reps. of the A.B.A. 677 (1961).

CHAPTER IV

Internal Order

Maintenance of law and order within the local community is, of course, an elementary requirement of any society. Reconciliation of this basic social interest with freedom of expression has always posed some difficult problems. Most of the legal issues have centered around questions arising in connection with public assemblies of some sort — meetings, parades, demonstrations — or public distribution of pamphlets and other literature. The participants, at least those involved in the legal controversies, have tended to be persons without substantial access to more general forms of communication, such as the mass media. In the past the major issues have usually been associated with the current political and social movements of the period, including the abolitionist, labor, socialist, and women's suffrage movements. In recent years the problems have related primarily to the civil rights and peace movements.

This chapter deals mostly with questions of assembly, petition, and canvassing. The first section considers the basic rights to engage in such activities (Section A). Then follows material on the problem of reconciling these rights of expression with the community's interest in protecting itself against violence or similar forms of public disorder (Section B). The ensuing section takes up issues of reconciliation with other community interests (Section C). A final section deals with permit systems, injunctions against communication, and administrative problems (Section D).

A. Basic Rights of Assembly, Petitioning, and Canvassing

The initial question concerned the right of the public to use the streets, parks, and other open places for assembling, petitioning, and canvassing. In Davis v. Massachusetts, 167 U.S. 43, 17 S. Ct. 731, 42 L. Ed. 71 (1897), where the plaintiff in error had been convicted of violating an ordinance which prohibited making a public address on Boston Common, the Supreme Court quoted with approval the statement of the Massachusetts Supreme Judicial Court: "For the legislature absolutely or conditionally to forbid public speaking in a highway or public park is no more an infringement of the rights of a member of the public than for the owner of a private house to forbid it in his house." It went on: "It is, therefore, conclusively determined there was no right in the plaintiff in error to use the common except in such mode and subject to such regulations as the legislature in its wisdom may have deemed proper to prescribe." 167 U.S. at 47.

Some years later, however, in Hague v. Committee for Industrial Organization, 307 U.S. 496, 59 S. Ct. 954, 83 L. Ed. 1423 (1939), the prevailing opinion of the Court expressed a different view:

"We have no occasion to determine whether, on the facts disclosed, the Davis case was rightly decided, but we cannot agree that it rules the instant case. Wherever the title of streets and parks may rest, they have immemorially been held in trust for the use of the public and, time out of mind, have been used for purposes of assembly, communicating thoughts between citizens, and discussing public questions. Such use of the streets and public places has, from ancient times, been a part of the privileges, immunities, rights, and liberties of citizens. The privilege of a citizen of the United States to use the streets and parks for communication of views on national questions may be regulated in the interest of all; it is not absolute, but relative, and must be exercised in subordination to the general comfort and convenience, and in consonance with peace and good order; but it must not, in the guise of regulation, be abridged or denied." 307 U.S. at 515-516.

NOTES

1. While there was no majority holding in Hague, it was assumed in later decisions and by commentators that the public did have a basic constitutional right to use the streets, parks, and public places in the exercise of First Amendment rights. See, e.g., Cox v. New Hampshire, 312 U.S. 569, 61 S. Ct. 762, 85 L. Ed. 1049 (1941); Kunz v. New York, 340 U.S. 290, 71 S. Ct. 312, 95 L. Ed. 280 (1951); Edwards v. South Carolina, 372 U.S. 229, 83 S. Ct. 680, 9 L. Ed. 2d 697 (1963); and materials cited at the end of these notes. But the issue seems to have been reopened in the opinions of Mr. Justice Goldberg and Mr. Justice Black in the Cox v. Louisiana cases, set out infra.

2. As a practical matter the existence of a basic constitutional right may not be as significant as it otherwise would be, because of the rulings of the courts that there can be no discrimination in the exercise of the right to expression between different users of the streets, parks, and open places. See Fowler v. Rhode Island, 345 U.S. 67, 73 S. Ct. 526, 97 L. Ed. 828 (1953) (refusal to allow Jehovah's Witnesses to conduct religious services in a park, although other religious groups were permitted to do so, held to violate First Amendment); People v. Amdur, 123 Cal. App. 2d Supp. 951, 267 P.2d 445 (1954). See also Ellis v. Dixon, summarized in note 5 below; Notes, 38 Va. L. Rev. 1075 (1952); 51 Mich. L. Rev. 1234 (1953).

3. In Murdock v. Pennsylvania, 319 U.S. 105, 63 S. Ct. 870, 87 L. Ed. 1292 (1943), and Jones v. Opelika, 319 U.S. 103, 63 S. Ct. 890, 87 L. Ed. 1290 (1943), vacating its prior decision in 316 U.S. 584, 62 S. Ct. 1231, 86 L. Ed. 1691 (1942), the Court held invalid a license tax as applied to Jehovah's Witnesses who were engaged in door-to-door sales of religious literature. And in Follett v. McCormick, 321 U.S. 573, 64 S. Ct. 717, 88 L. Ed. 938 (1944), the Court extended the ruling to invalidate a tax on book agents as applied to a Jehovah's Witness who was a resident of the town making his living from the sale of religious books. But cf. Cox v. New Hampshire, noted in Section D, infra.

4. In Valentine v. Chrestensen, 316 U.S. 52, 62 S. Ct. 920, 86 L. Ed. 1262 (1942), the Court upheld a municipal ordinance which prohibited the distribution upon any public street or in any public place of commercial handbills or advertising matter. In that case the handbills contained advertising on one side and a religious message on the other. A similar distinction between the distribution of literature primarily for commercial rather than religious purposes was made in Breard v. Alexandria, 341 U.S. 622, 71 S. Ct. 920, 15 L. Ed. 1233 (1951), where the Court upheld an ordinance prohibiting all uninvited door-to-door solicitation as a public nuisance. The defendant, a magazine subscription solicitor, objected on the grounds that he was arbitrarily deprived of his occupation, that the ordinance was an unreasonable burden on interstate commerce, and that it violated guarantees of freedom of speech. Mr. Justice Reed, distinguishing Martin v. Struthers, 319 U.S. 141, 63 S. Ct. 862, 87 L. Ed. 1313 (1943), which had upheld door-to-door religious canvassing (see Section C, infra), said for the majority: "There was dissent even to this carefully phrased application of the principles of the First Amendment. As no element of the commercial entered into this free solicitation and the opinion was narrowly limited to the precise fact of the free distribution of an invitation to religious services, we feel that it is not necessarily inconsistent with the conclusion reached in this case." 341 U.S. at 643. For discussion, see Gardner, Free Speech in Public Places, 36 B.U.L. Rev. 239 (1956). On the application of First Amendment rights to commercial activity generally, see Chapter V, Section A.

5. With respect to the use of public auditoriums or other facilities for meetings or similar activities, there would appear to be no cases holding that the public authorities had any affirmative obligation to make such facilities available. But the rule against discrimination as between different users (and, to some degree at least, against discrimination between different uses) would appear applicable. In Ellis v. Dixon, 349 U.S. 458, 75 S. Ct. 850, 99 L. Ed. 1231 (1955), the Yonkers Committee for Peace requested the state court to direct the Board of Education, which had denied a permit, to issue one for the use of school buildings for a forum on peace and war. The complaint alleged that "permission is freely granted to others applying [for the use of school buildings] . . . for the purpose of public assembly and discussion." 349 U.S. at 460. After adverse rulings by the state courts the Supreme Court first granted certiorari (347 U.S. 926), and then held that it had been improvidently granted because the record was "vague" and "empty" especially in that the complaint failed to allege that "other organizations of a similar character have been allowed to use the Yonkers' schools." Justices Warren, Black, Douglas, and Clark dissented on the ground that the complaint sufficiently alleged discrimination under the equal protection clause. See Note, 69 Harv. L. Rev. 128 (1955). See also Hooker v. Conte, 208 Misc. 188, 143 N.Y.S.2d 750 (Sup. Ct. Westchester Co., 1955) (denial of permit to use firehouse auditorium by Nationalist Party not a violation of equal protection in view of "inconclusive" evidence that other political organizations had been granted permission). See also the materials in Section C of this chapter.

6. Meetings or other forms of expression utilizing privately owned property do not, of course, give rise to any problem of the basic right to use the facilities where the owner consents to such use. Various issues have been presented, however, where the owner does not give permission or where his consent is ambiguous. The major questions have arisen over whether the property can be considered "dedicated to public use" and therefore treated as public property for First Amendment

purposes. In Marsh v. Alabama, 326 U.S. 501, 66 S. Ct. 276, 90 L. Ed. 265 (1946), the Court, reversing a criminal conviction, upheld the right of a Jehovah's Witness to distribute religious literature on the streets of a company town despite company regulations prohibiting such activity. Mr. Justice Black, writing the majority opinion, said: "The State urges in effect that the corporation's right to control the inhabitants of Chickasaw is coextensive with the right of a homeowner to regulate the conduct of his guests. We cannot accept that contention. . . . Whether a corporation or a municipality owns or possesses the town the public in either case has an identical interest in the functioning of the community in such manner that the channels of communication remain free." 326 U.S. at 505-506, 507. In a decision the same day the Court applied the same principle to a village built by the Federal Government as a defense housing project. Tucker v. Texas, 326 U.S. 517, 66 S. Ct. 274, 90 L. Ed. 274 (1946). See also Farmer v. Moses, 232 F. Supp. 154 (S.D. N.Y. 1964) (upholding the right of the N.A.A.C.P. to picket and distribute leaflets on World's Fair grounds). Cf. Good v. Dow Chemical Co., 247 S.W.2d 608 (Tex. Civ. App. 1952), cert. den., 344 U.S. 805 (1952) (privately owned park held not dedicated to public and not available for Jehovah's Witnesses' meetings).

The exercise of First Amendment rights on privately owned property has also arisen in connection with door-to-door canvassing in houses, apartment houses, and business districts. See Section C, infra. As to the civil rights sit-in cases, also see Section C and Chapter XX. Compare the problem of the right to carry on union activity on company property under the National Labor Relations Act. See Republic Aviation Corp. v. N.L.R.B., 324 U.S. 793, 65 S. Ct. 982, 89 L. Ed. 1372 (1945). See also Nolan, The Unions, Free Speech, and the Shopping Center, 37 So. Cal. L. Rev. 573 (1964).

REFERENCES

Materials dealing generally with the right of assembly, petition, and canvassing include: Jarrett and Mund, The Right of Assembly, 9 N.Y.U.L.Q. Rev. 1 (1931); Note, Limitations on the Right of Assembly, 23 Calif. L. Rev. 180 (1935); Note, Public Order and the Right of Assembly in England and the United States, 47 Yale L.J. 404 (1938); Murphy, Free Speech and the Interest in Local Law and Order, 1 J. Pub. Law 40 (1952); Gardner, Free Speech in Public Places, 36 B.U.L. Rev. 239 (1956); Gellhorn, American Rights, ch. 3 (1960); Stewart, Public Speech and Public Order in Britain and the United States, 13 Vand. L. Rev. 625 (1960); Abernathy, The Right of Assembly and Association (1961); Ervin, Freedom of Assembly and Racial Demonstrations, 10 Clev.-Mar. L. Rev. 88 (1961); Fellman, The Constitutional Right of Association (1963); Van Alstyne, Political Speakers at State Universities: Some Constitutional Considerations, 111 U. Pa. L. Rev. 328 (1963).

Materials dealing more specifically with the problems as they concern the civil rights movement include: Kalven, The Negro and the First Amendment, chs. III, IV (1960); Marshall, The Protest Movement and the Law, 51 Va. L. Rev. 785 (1965); Pollitt, Legal Problems in Southern Desegregation, 43 N.C.L. Rev. 689 (1965); Symposium, Violence in the Streets, 40 Notre Dame Law. 497 (1965); Sibley, Direct Action and the Struggle for Integration, 16 Hastings L.J. 351 (1965). See also, American Civil Liberties Union, How Americans Protest (1963); Towler, The Police Role in Racial Conflicts (1964); Oppenheimer and Lakey, A Manual for Direct Action: Strategy and Tactics for Civil Rights and All Other Non-Violent Protest Movements (1965).

For some of the historical background see Smith, A Dangerous Freedom (1954); Radzinowicz, New Departures in Maintaining Public Order in the Face of Chartist Disturbances, 1960 Camb. L.J. 51; Rudé, The Crowd in History, 1730-1848 (1964).

B. MAINTAINING THE PUBLIC PEACE

In recognizing and assuring the basic rights of assembly, petition, and canvassing the initial questions of concern to society are those that arise when the communication leads or may lead to conduct involving violence, use of physical force, or similar disorder in violation of existing laws. This, generally speaking, is the problem of maintaining the public peace. While total absence of violence in a community can only be obtained at the price of total repression, if then, the problem of reconciling these interests is one of major concern to society and has been the cause of most of the controversies over exercise of the rights here under consideration.

The legal controls designed to protect society against communication thought to endanger the public peace take three major forms. In one form they are directed to the punishment of communication which has already taken place. The principal tools here are the unlawful assembly, inciting to riot, breach of the peace, disorderly conduct, and similar laws. In the second form the government undertakes to prevent in advance communication or other conduct which it fears may lead to public disorder. The usual devices for this are licensing or permit systems and court injunctions. And in a third form, in some ways a combination of the other two, the government attempts to halt communication while it is still in progress, as where the police order a speaker to desist or a crowd to disperse. The problems raised by these varying forms of legal restriction are, in important respects, different. We deal in this section with the first and third. The second is treated in Section D.

One further preliminary distinction needs to be made. With respect to each form of governmental control, the issues may arise in two contexts. The threat to public order may come from persons who support the communicator or his views. Or it may emanate from those who are hostile to him and oppose the views being expressed. While different considerations are present in each, the two situations are not always clearly distinct, and the problem may involve elements of both. In any event, in the materials below no attempt has been made to separate the two kinds of issues.

The Supreme Court first addressed itself to these problems in two cases decided during the 1940's. In Cantwell v. Connecticut, 310 U.S. 296, 60 S. Ct. 900, 84 L. Ed. 1213 (1940), a member of the Jehovah's Witnesses was charged with inciting a breach of the peace: "[Cantwell] stopped two men in the street, asked, and received, permission to play a phonograph record, and played the record 'Enemies,' which attacked the religion and church of the two men, who were Catholics. Both were incensed by the contents of the record and were tempted to strike Cantwell unless he went away. On being told to be on his way he left their presence. There was no evidence that he was personally offensive or entered into any argument with those he interviewed." 310 U.S. at 302-303. The Court set aside the conviction, Mr. Justice Roberts saying:

". . . Decision as to the lawfulness of the conviction demands the weighing of two conflicting interests. The fundamental law declares the interest of the United States that the free exercise of religion be not prohibited and that freedom to communicate information and opinion be not abridged. The State of Connecticut has an obvious interest in the preservation and protection of peace and good order within her borders. We must determine whether the alleged protection of the State's interest, means to which end would, in the absence of limitation by the Federal Constitution, lie wholly within the State's discretion, has been pressed, in this instance, to a point where it has come into fatal collision with the overriding interest protected by the federal compact. . . .

"The offense known as breach of the peace embraces a great variety of conduct destroying or menacing public order and tranquility. It includes not only violent acts but acts and words likely to produce violence in others. No one would have the hardihood to suggest that the principle of freedom of speech sanctions incitement to riot or that religious liberty connotes the privilege to exhort others to physical attack upon those belonging to another sect. When clear and present danger of riot, disorder, interference with traffic upon the public streets, or other immediate threat to public safety, peace, or order, appears, the power of the State to prevent or punish is obvious. Equally obvious is it that a State may not unduly suppress free communication of views, religious or other, under the guise of conserving desirable conditions. Here we have a situation analogous to a conviction under a statute sweeping in a great variety of conduct under a general and indefinite characterization, and leaving to the executive and judicial branches too wide a discretion in its application. . . .

"Although the contents of the record not unnaturally aroused animosity, we think that, in the absence of a statute narrowly drawn to define and punish specific conduct as constituting a clear and present danger to a substantial interest of the State, the petitioner's communication, considered in the light of the constitutional guarantees, raised no such clear and present menace to public peace and order as to render him liable to conviction of the common law offense in question." 310 U.S. at 307, 308, 311.

In Chaplinsky v. New Hampshire, 315 U.S. 568, 62 S. Ct. 766, 86 L. Ed. 1031 (1942), another Jehovah's Witness was distributing religious literature on the street, was taken into custody by a police officer, and "addressed to complainant" (the city marshal) the following words: "You are a God damned racketeer" and "a damned Fascist and the whole government of Rochester are Fascists or agents of Fascists." The Court sustained the conviction, Mr. Justice Murphy saying:

"Allowing the broadest scope to the language and purpose of the Fourteenth Amendment, it is well understood that the right of free speech is not absolute at all times and under all circumstances. There are certain well-defined and narrowly limited classes of speech, the prevention and punishment of which have never been thought to raise any Constitutional problem. These include the lewd and obscene, the profane, the libelous, and the insulting or "fighting" words — those which by their very utterance inflict injury or tend to incite an immediate breach of the peace. It has been well observed that such utterances are no essential part of any exposition of ideas, and are of such slight social value as a step to truth that any benefit that may be derived from them is clearly out-weighed by the social interest in order and morality. . . .

"We are unable to say that the limited scope of the statute as thus construed contravenes the Constitutional right of free expression. It is a statute narrowly drawn and limited to define and punish specific conduct lying within the domain of state power, the use in a public place of words likely to cause a breach of the peace. . . . A statute punishing verbal acts, carefully drawn so as not unduly to impair liberty of expression, is not too vague for a criminal law." 315 U.S. at 571-574.

The issues were again raised in Terminiello v. City of Chicago, 337 U.S. 1, 69 S. Ct. 894, 93 L. Ed. 1131 (1949), in which the speaker, a suspended Catholic priest, had addressed a public meeting in Chicago, attacking "Communistic Zionistic Jews." A crowd had gathered outside the auditorium to protest the meeting. Both groups were "angry and turbulent" and there were "several disturbances." Terminiello was convicted of disorderly conduct. The majority of the Court did not pass on the basic issues, finding error in the trial court's charge to the jury which had construed "breach of the peace" to include speech that "stirs the public to anger, invites dispute, brings about a condition of unrest, or creates a disturbance." Mr. Justice Douglas, writing for the majority, said: "[A] function of free speech under our system of government is to invite dispute. It may indeed best serve its high purpose when it induces a condition of unrest, creates dissatisfaction with conditions as they are, or even stirs people to anger. Speech is often provocative and challenging. It may strike at prejudices and preconceptions and have profound unsettling effects as it presses for acceptance of an idea. That is why freedom of speech, though not absolute [Chaplinsky v. New Hampshire] is nevertheless protected against censorship or punishment, unless shown likely to produce a clear and present danger of a serious substantive evil that rises far above public inconvenience, annoyance, or unrest. . . . There is no room under our Constitution for a more restrictive view. For the alternative would lead to standardization of ideas either by legislatures, courts, or dominant political or community groups." 337 U.S. at 4-5.

Four justices dissented on the ground that the issue of the trial court's charge to the jury had never been raised below. Mr. Justice Jackson in a long dissent, joined by Mr. Justice Burton, discussed the merits and vigorously contended that the conviction should be upheld.

The problems next received the attention of the Supreme Court in the Kunz and Feiner cases, set forth below.

REFERENCES

1. For discussion of the "fighting words" doctrine, see Wade, Tort Liability for Abusive and Insulting Language, 4 Vand. L. Rev. 63, 102-110 (1950); Note, 26 N.Y.U.L. Rev. 489, 497-498 (1951); Konvitz, Fundamental Liberties of a Free People, ch. 17 (1957); Stewart, Public Speech and Public Order in Britain and the United States, 13 Vand. L. Rev. 625, 634 (1960). On the Terminiello case, see Murphy, Free Speech and Atom Bombs, 2 Ala. L. Rev. 24 (1949); Note, Verbal Acts and Ideas — The Common Sense of Free Speech, 16 U. Chi. L. Rev. 328 (1949); Rosenwein, The Supreme Court and Freedom of Speech — Terminiello v. City of Chicago, 9 Law. Guild Rev. 70 (1949); Notes, 61 Harv. L. Rev. 537 (1948); 49 Colum. L. Rev. 1118 (1949); 24 N.Y.U.L.Q. Rev. 885 (1949); 25 Notre Dame Law. 99 (1949); 23 Temple L.Q. 393 (1950). On the propriety of deciding the case on the jury instruction issue when it had not been raised before, see Note, 59 Yale L.J. 971 (1950).

2. Although the United States Supreme Court has not squarely ruled on a clear-cut issue involving a conviction for speech where the fear of violence was based on conduct of the speaker or his supporters, rather than the opposition, there are a number of state cases dealing with this matter. Cases upholding convictions include People v. Most, 128 N.Y. 108, 27 N.E. 970 (1891); State v. Quinlan, 86 N.J. L. 120, 91 Atl. 111 (1914); State v. Schleifer, 99 Conn. 432, 121 Atl. 805 (1923); People ex rel. Neiman v. McWilliams, 22 N.Y.S.2d 571 (Magis. Ct. 5th Dist. 1940), rev'd on other grounds, 31 N.Y.S.2d 37 (1941); Commonwealth v. Albert, 169 Pa. Super. 318, 82 A.2d 695 (1951). See also American League of Friends of the New Germany of Hudson Co. v. Eastwood, 174 Atl. 156 (N.J. Ch. 1934) (refusal to enjoin police from preventing meeting). Cases upholding the speaker or demonstrators include Shields v. State, 187 Wis. 448, 204 N.W. 486 (1925); State v. Butterworth, 104 N.J. L. 579, 142 Atl. 57 (1928); People v. Downer, 6 N.Y.S.2d 566 (Magis. Ct. 8th Dist. 1938); People v. Kieran, 26 N.Y.S.2d 291 (Nassau Co. 1940); Flores v. Denver, 122 Colo. 71, 220 P.2d 373 (1950); Garcia Dominicci v. District Court, 71 Puerto Rico 122 (1950).

FEINER v. NEW YORK
340 U.S. 315, 71 S. Ct. 303, 95 L. Ed. 295 (1951)

Mr. Chief Justice Vinson delivered the opinion of the Court.

Petitioner was convicted of the offense of disorderly conduct, a misdemeanor under the New York penal laws, in the Court of Special Sessions of the City of Syracuse and was sentenced to thirty days in the county penitentiary. The conviction was affirmed by the Onondaga County Court and the New York Court of Appeals, 300 N.Y. 391, 91 N.E.2d 316 (1950). The case is here on certiorari, 339 U.S. 962 (1950), petitioner having claimed that the conviction is in violation of his right of free speech under the Fourteenth Amendment.

In the review of state decisions where First Amendment rights are drawn in question, we of course make an examination of the evidence to ascertain independently whether the right has been violated. Here, the trial judge, who heard the case without jury, rendered an oral decision at the end of the trial, setting forth his determination of the facts upon which he found the petitioner guilty. His decision indicated generally that he believed the state's witnesses, and his summation of the testimony was used by the two New York courts on review in stating the facts. Our appraisal of the facts is, therefore, based upon the uncontroverted facts and, where controversy exists, upon that testimony which the trial judge did reasonably conclude to be true.

On the evening of March 8, 1949, petitioner Irving Feiner was addressing an open-air meeting at the corner of South McBride and Harrison Streets in the City of Syracuse. At approximately 6:30 P.M., the police received a telephone complaint concerning the meeting, and two officers were detailed to investigate. One of these officers went to the scene immediately, the other arriving some twelve minutes later. They found a crowd of about seventy-five or eighty people, both Negro and white, filling the sidewalk and spreading out into the street. Petitioner, standing on a large wooden box on the sidewalk, was addressing the crowd through a loud-speaker system attached to an automobile. Although the purpose of his speech was to urge his listeners to attend a meeting to be held that night in the Syracuse Hotel, in its course he was making derogatory remarks concerning President Truman, the American Legion, the Mayor of Syracuse, and other local political officials.

The police officers made no effort to interfere with petitioner's speech, but were first concerned with the effect of the crowd on both pedestrian and vehicular traffic. They observed the situation from the opposite side of the street, noting that some pedestrians were forced to walk in the street to avoid the crowd. Since traffic was passing at the time, the officers attempted to get the people listening to petitioner back on the sidewalk. The crowd was restless and there was some pushing, shoving and milling around. One of the officers telephoned the police station from a nearby store, and then both policemen crossed the street and mingled with the crowd without any intention of arresting the speaker.

At this time, petitioner was speaking in a "loud, high-pitched voice." He gave the impression that he was endeavoring to arouse the Negro people against the whites, urging that they rise up in arms and fight for equal rights. The statements before such a mixed audience "stirred up a little excitement." Some of the onlookers made remarks to the police about their inability to handle the crowd and at least one threatened violence if the police did not act. There were others who appeared to be favoring petitioner's arguments. Because of the feeling that existed in the crowd both for and against the speaker, the officers finally "stepped in to prevent it from resulting in a fight." One of the officers approached the petitioner, not for the purpose of arresting him, but to get him to break up the crowd. He asked petitioner to get down off the box, but the latter refused to accede to his request and continued talking. The officer waited for a minute and then demanded that he cease talking. Although the officer had thus twice requested petitioner to stop over the course of several minutes, petitioner not only ignored him but continued talking. During all this time, the crowd was pressing closer around petitioner and the officer. Finally, the officer told petitioner he was under arrest and ordered him to get down from the box, reaching up to grab him. Petitioner stepped down, announcing over the microphone that "the law has arrived, and I suppose they will take over now." In all, the officer had asked petitioner to get down off the box three times over a space of four or five minutes. Petitioner had been speaking for over a half hour.

On these facts, petitioner was specifically charged with violation of §722 of the Penal Law of New York, the pertinent part of which is set out in the margin.[1] The bill of particulars, demanded by petitioner and furnished by the state, gave in detail the facts upon which the prosecution relied to support the charge of disorderly conduct. Paragraph C is particularly pertinent here: "By ignoring and refusing to heed and obey reasonable police orders issued at the time and place mentioned in the Information to regulate and control said crowd and to prevent a breach or breaches of the peace and to prevent injury to pedestrians attempting to use said walk, and being forced into the highway adjacent to the place in question, and prevent injury to the public generally."

We are not faced here with blind condonation by a state court of arbitrary police action. Petitioner was accorded a full, fair trial. The trial judge heard testimony supporting and contradicting the judgment of the police officers that a clear danger of disorder was threatened. After weighing this contradictory evidence, the trial judge reached the conclusion that the police officers were justified in taking action to prevent a breach of the peace. The exercise of the police officers' proper discretionary power to prevent a breach of the peace was thus approved by the trial court and later by two courts on review.[2] The courts below recognized petitioner's right to hold a street meeting

---

[1] Section 722. "Any person who with intent to provoke a breach of the peace, or whereby a breach of the peace may be occasioned, commits any of the following acts shall be deemed to have committed the offense of disorderly conduct:

"1. Uses offensive, disorderly, threatening, abusive or insulting language, conduct or behavior;

"2. Acts in such a manner as to annoy, disturb, interfere with, obstruct, or be offensive to others;

"3. Congregates with others on a public street and refuses to move on when ordered by the police; . . ."

[2] The New York Court of Appeals said: "An imminent danger of a breach of the peace, of a disturbance of public order, perhaps even of riot, was threatened . . . the defendant, as indicated above, disrupted pedestrian and vehicular traffic on the sidewalk and street, and, with intent to provoke a breach of the peace and with knowledge of the consequences, so inflamed and agitated a mixed audience of sympathizers and opponents that, in the judgment of the police officers present, a clear danger of disorder and violence was threatened. Defendant then deliberately refused to accede to the reasonable request of the officer, made within the lawful scope of his authority, that the defendant desist in the interest of public welfare and safety." 300 N.Y. 391, 400, 402, 91 N.E.2d 316, 319, 321.

at this locality, to make use of loud-speaking equipment in giving his speech, and to make derogatory remarks concerning public officials and the American Legion. They found that the officers in making the arrest were motivated solely by a proper concern for the preservation of order and protection of the general welfare, and that there was no evidence which could lend color to a claim that the acts of the police were a cover for suppression of petitioner's views and opinions. Petitioner was thus neither arrested nor convicted for the making or the content of his speech. Rather, it was the reaction which it actually engendered.

The language of Cantwell v. Connecticut, 310 U.S. 296 (1940), is appropriate here. [The Court then quotes the passage on breach of the peace set forth above.] The findings of the New York courts as to the condition of the crowd and the refusal of petitioner to obey the police requests, supported as they are by the record of this case, are persuasive that the conviction of petitioner for violation of public peace, order and authority does not exceed the bounds of proper state police action. This Court respects, as it must, the interest of the community in maintaining peace and order on its streets. Schneider v. State, 308 U.S. 147, 160 (1939); Kovacs v. Cooper, 336 U.S. 77, 82 (1949). We cannot say that the preservation of that interest here encroaches on the constitutional rights of this petitioner.

We are well aware that the ordinary murmurings and objections of a hostile audience cannot be allowed to silence a speaker, and are also mindful of the possible danger of giving overzealous police officials complete discretion to break up otherwise lawful public meetings. "A State may not unduly suppress free communication of views, religious or other, under the guise of conserving desirable conditions." Cantwell v. Connecticut, supra, at 308. But we are not faced here with such a situation. It is one thing to say that the police cannot be used as an instrument for the oppression of unpopular views, and another to say that, when as here the speaker passes the bounds of argument or persuasion and undertakes incitement to riot, they are powerless to prevent a breach of the peace. Nor in this case can we condemn the considered judgment of three New York courts approving the means which the police, faced with a crisis, used in the exercise of their power and duty to preserve peace and order. The findings of the state courts as to the existing situation and the imminence of greater disorder coupled with petitioner's deliberate defiance of the police officers convince us that we should not reverse this conviction in the name of free speech.

Affirmed.

[Mr. Justice Frankfurter, concurring in a separate opinion dealing with this case and the Kunz and Niemotko cases (see following Note) together:]

. . . Feiner forced pedestrians to walk in the street by collecting a crowd on the public sidewalk, he attracted additional attention by using sound amplifiers, he indulged in name-calling, he told part of his audience that it should rise up in arms. In the crowd of 75 to 80 persons, there was angry muttering and pushing. Under these circumstances, and in order to prevent a disturbance of the peace, an officer asked Feiner to stop speaking. When he had twice ignored the request, Feiner was arrested. The trial judge concluded that "the officers were fully justified in feeling that a situation was developing which could very, very easily result in a serious disorder." His view was sustained by an intermediate appellate court and by a unanimous decision of the New York Court of Appeals. 300 N.Y. 391, 91 N.E.2d 316. The estimate of a particular local situation thus comes here with the momentum of the weightiest judicial authority of New York.

This Court has often emphasized that in the exercise of our authority over state court decisions the Due Process Clause must not be construed in an abstract and doctrinaire way by disregarding local conditions. In considering the degree of respect to be given findings by the highest court of a State in cases involving the Due Process Clause, the course of decisions by that court should be taken into account. Particularly within the area of due process colloquially called "civil liberties," it is important whether such a course of decisions reflects a cavalier attitude toward civil liberties or real regard for them. Only unfamiliarity with its decisions and the outlook of its judges could generate a notion that the Court of Appeals of New York is inhospitable to claims of civil liberties or is wanting in respect for this Court's decisions in support of them. It is pertinent, therefore, to note that all members of the New York Court accepted the finding that Feiner was stopped not because the listeners or police officers disagreed with his views but because these officers were honestly concerned with preventing a breach of the peace. This unanimity is all the more persuasive since three membrs of the Court had dissented, only three months earlier, in favor of Kunz, a man whose vituperative utterances must have been highly offensive to them.

As was said in Hague v. C.I.O., supra, uncontrolled official suppression of the speaker "cannot be made a substitute for the duty to maintain order." 307 U.S. at 516. Where conduct is within the allowable limits of free speech, the police are peace officers for the speaker as well as for his hearers. But the power effectively to preserve order cannot be displaced by giving a speaker complete immunity. Here, there were two police officers present for 20 minutes. They interfered only when they apprehended imminence of violence. It is not a constitutional principle that, in acting to preserve order, the police must proceed against the crowd, whatever its size and temper, and not against the speaker.

It is true that breach-of-peace statutes, like most tools of government, may be misused. Enforcement of these statutes calls for public tolerance and intelligent police administration. These, in the long run, must give substance to whatever this Court may say about free speech. But the possibility of misuse is not alone a sufficient reason to deny New York the power here asserted or so limit it by constitutional construction as to deny its practical exercise.

[MR. JUSTICE JACKSON, concurring in a separate opinion dealing with this case and the Kunz and Niemotko cases together:]

. . . I join in Feiner v. New York. When in a colored neighborhood Feiner urged the colored people to rise up in arms and fight, he was using words which may have been "rhetorical," but it was the rhetoric of violence. Of course, we cannot tell, from a cold record, whether the action taken was the wisest way of dealing with the situation. But some latitude for honest judgment must be left to the locality. It is a startling proposition to me that serious public utterance which advises, encourages, or incites to a crime may not be made a crime because within constitutional protection. . . .

MR. JUSTICE BLACK, dissenting.

The record before us convinces me that petitioner, a young college student, has been sentenced to the penitentiary for the unpopular views he expressed[1] on matters of public interest while lawfully making a street-corner speech in Syracuse, New York.[2] Today's decision, however, indicates that we must blind ourselves to this fact because the trial judge fully accepted the testimony of the prosecution witnesses on all important points.[3] Many times in the past this Court has said that despite findings below, we will examine the evidence for ourselves to ascertain whether federally protected rights have been denied; otherwise review here would fail of its purpose in safeguarding constitutional guarantees. Even a partial abandonment of this rule marks a dark day for civil liberties in our Nation.

But still more has been lost today. Even accepting every "finding of fact" below, I think this conviction makes a mockery of the free speech guarantees of the First and Fourteenth Amendments. The end result of the affirmance here is to approve a simple and readily available technique by which cities and states can with impunity subject all speeches, political or otherwise, on streets or elsewhere, to the supervision and censorship of the local police. I

---

[1] The trial judge framed the question for decision as follows: "The question here, is what was said and what was done? And it doesn't make any difference whether whatever was said, was said with a loud speaker or not. There are acts and conduct an individual can engage in when you don't even have to have a crowd gathered around which would justify a charge of disorderly conduct. The question is, what did this defendant say and do at that particular time and the Court must determine whether those facts, concerning what the defendant did or said, are sufficient to support the charge." There is no suggestion in the record that petitioner "did" anything other than (1) speak and (2) continue for a short time to invite people to a public meeting after a policeman had requested him to stop speaking.

[2] There was no charge that any city or state law prohibited such a meeting at the place or time it was held. Evidence showed that it was customary to hold public gatherings on that same corner every Friday night, and the trial judge who convicted petitioner admitted that he understood the meeting was a lawful one. Nor did the judge treat the lawful meeting as unlawful because a crowd congregated on the sidewalk. Consequently, any discussion of disrupted pedestrian and vehicular traffic, while suggestive coloration, is immaterial under the charge and conviction here. . . .

[3] The trial court made no findings of fact as such. A decision was rendered from the bench in which, among other things, the trial judge expressed some views on the evidence. See note 11, infra.

will have no part or parcel in this holding which I view as a long step toward totalitarian authority.

Considering only the evidence which the state courts appear to have accepted, the pertinent "facts" are: Syracuse city authorities granted a permit for O. John Rogge, a former Assistant Attorney General, to speak in a public school building on March 8, 1948 on the subject of racial discrimination and civil liberties. On March 8th, however, the authorities cancelled the permit. The Young Progressives under whose auspices the meeting was scheduled then arranged for Mr. Rogge to speak at the Hotel Syracuse. The gathering on the street where petitioner spoke was held to protest the cancellation and to publicize the meeting at the hotel. In this connection, petitioner used derogatory but not profane language with reference to the city authorities, President Truman and the American Legion. After hearing some of these remarks, a policeman, who had been sent to the meeting by his superiors, reported to Police Headquarters by telephone. To whom he reported or what was said does not appear in the record, but after returning from the call, he and another policeman started through the crowd toward petitioner. Both officers swore they did not intend to make an arrest when they started, and the trial court accepted their statements. They also said, and the court believed, that they heard and saw "angry mutterings," "pushing," "shoving and milling around" and "restlessness." Petitioner spoke in a "loud, high pitched voice." He said that "colored people don't have equal rights and they should rise up *in arms* and fight for them." One man who heard this told the officers that if they did not take that "S...O...B..." off the box, he would. The officers then approached petitioner for the first time. One of them first "asked" petitioner to get off the box, but petitioner continued urging his audience to attend Rogge's speech. The officer next "told" petitioner to get down, but he did not. The officer finally "demanded" that petitioner get down, telling him he was under arrest. Petitioner then told the crowd that "the law would take over" and asked why he was arrested. The officer first replied that the charge was "unlawful assembly" but later changed the ground to "disorderly conduct." [6]

The Court's opinion apparently rests on this reasoning: The policeman, under the circumstances detailed, could reasonably conclude that serious fighting or even riot was imminent; therefore he could stop petitioner's speech to prevent a breach of peace; accordingly, it was "disorderly conduct" for petitioner to continue speaking in disobedience of the officer's request. As

---

[6] "A charge of using language likely to cause a breach of the peace is a convenient catchall to hold unpopular soapbox orators." Chafee, Free Speech in the United States, 524. The related charge of conducting a "disorderly house" has also been used to suppress and punish minority views. For example, an English statute of 1799 classified as disorderly houses certain unlicensed places ("House, Room, Field, or other Place") in which "any Lecture or Discourse shall be publickly delivered, or any publick Debate shall be had on any Subject . . ." or which was used "for the Purpose of reading Books, Pamphlets, Newspapers or other Publications . . . ." 39 Geo. III, c. 79, §15.

to the existence of a dangerous situation on the street corner, it seems far-fetched to suggest that the "facts" show any imminent threat of riot or uncontrollable disorder.[7] It is neither unusual nor unexpected that some people at public street meetings mutter, mill about, push, shove, or disagree, even violently, with the speaker. Indeed, it is rare where controversial topics are discussed that an outdoor crowd does not do some or all of these things. Nor does one isolated threat to assault the speaker forbode disorder. Especially should the danger be discounted where, as here, the person threatening was a man whose wife and two small children accompanied him and who, so far as the record shows, was never close enough to petitioner to carry out the threat.

Moreover, assuming that the "facts" did indicate a critical situation, I reject the implication of the Court's opinion that the police had no obligation to protect petitioner's constitutional right to talk. The police of course have power to prevent breaches of the peace. But if, in the name of preserving order, they ever can interfere with a lawful public speaker, they first must make all reasonable efforts to protect him.[8] Here the policemen did not even pretend to try to protect petitioner. According to the officers' testimony, the crowd was restless but there is no showing of any attempt to quiet it; pedestrians were forced to walk into the street, but there was no effort to clear a path on the sidewalk; one person threatened to assault petitioner but the officers did nothing to discourage this when even a word might have sufficed. Their duty was to protect petitioner's right to talk, even to the extent of arresting the man who threatened to interfere.[9] Instead, they shirked that duty and acted only to suppress the right to speak.

---

[7] The belief of the New York Court of Appeals that the situation on the street corner was critical is not supported by the record and accordingly should not be given much weight here. Two illustrations will suffice: The Court of Appeals relied upon a specific statement of one policeman that he interfered with Feiner at a time when the crowd was "getting to the point where they would be unruly." But this testimony was so patently inadmissible that it was excluded by the trial judge in one of the rare instances where the defendant received a favorable ruling. Secondly, the Court of Appeals stated that after Feiner had been warned by the police, he continued to "blare out his provocative utterances over loud speakers to a milling, restless throng . . . ." I am unable to find anything in the record to support this statement unless the unsworn arguments of the assistant district attorney are accepted as evidence. The principal prosecution witness testified that after he asked Feiner to get down from the box, Feiner merely "kept telling [the audience] to go to the Syracuse Hotel and hear John Rogge." And this same witness even answered "No" to the highly suggestive question which immediately followed, "Did he say anything more about arming and fighting at that time?"

[8] Cf. Hague v. C.I.O., 307 U.S. 496; Terminiello v. Chicago, 337 U.S. 1; Sellers v. Johnson, 163 F.2d 877; see also, summary of Brief for Committee on the Bill of Rights of the American Bar Association as amicus curiae, Hague v. C.I O., supra, reprinted at 307 U.S. 678-682.

[9] In Schneider v. State, 308 U.S. 147, we held that a purpose to prevent littering of the streets was insufficient to justify an ordinance which prohibited a person lawfully on the street from handing literature to one willing to receive it. We said at page 162, "There are obvious methods of preventing littering. Amongst these is the punishment of those who actually throw papers on the streets." In the present case as well, the

Finally, I cannot agree with the Court's statement that petitioner's disregard of the policeman's unexplained request amounted to such "deliberate defiance" as would justify an arrest or conviction for disorderly conduct. On the contrary, I think that the policeman's action was a "deliberate defiance" of ordinary official duty as well as of the constitutional right of free speech. For at least where time allows, courtesy and explanation of commands are basic elements of good official conduct in a democratic society. Here petitioner was "asked" then "told" then "commanded" to stop speaking, but a man making a lawful address is certainly not required to be silent merely because an officer directs it. Petitioner was entitled to know why he should cease doing a lawful act. Not once was he told. I understand that people in authoritarian countries must obey arbitrary orders. I had hoped that there was no such duty in the United States.

In my judgment, today's holding means that as a practical matter, minority speakers can be silenced in any city. Hereafter, despite the First and Fourteenth Amendments, the policeman's club can take heavy toll of a current administration's public critics.[10] Criticism of public officials will be too dangerous for all but the most courageous.[11] This is true regardless of the fact that in two other cases decided this day, Kunz v. New York, 340 U.S. 290; Niemotko v. Maryland, 340 U.S. 268, a majority, in obedience to past decisions of this Court, provides a theoretical safeguard for freedom of speech.

---

threat of one person to assault a speaker does not justify suppression of the speech. There are obvious available alternative methods of preserving public order. One of these is to arrest the person who threatens an assault. Cf. Dean Milk Co. v. Madison, 340 U.S. 349, decided today, in which the Court invalidates a municipal health ordinance under the Commerce Clause because of a belief that the city could have accomplished its purposes by reasonably adequate alternatives. The Court certainly should not be less alert to protect freedom of speech than it is to protect freedom of trade.

[10] Today the Court characterizes petitioner's speech as one designed to incite riot and approves suppression of his views. There is an alarming similarity between the power thus possessed by the Syracuse (or any other) police and that possessed by English officials under an act passed by Parliament in 1795. In that year Justices of the Peace were authorized to arrest persons who spoke in a manner which could be characterized as "inciting and stirring up the People to Hatred or Contempt . . ." of the King or the Government. 36 Geo. III, c. 8, §7. This statute "was manifestly intended to put an end for ever to all popular dicussion either on political or religious matters." 1 Buckle, History of Civilization in England (2d London ed.) 350.

[11] That petitioner and the philosophy he espoused were objects of local antagonism appears clearly from the printed record in this case. Even the trial judge in his decision made no attempt to conceal his contempt for petitioner's views. He seemed outraged by petitioner's criticism of public officials and the American Legion. Moreover, the judge gratuitously expressed disapproval of O. John Rogge by quoting derogatory statements concerning Mr. Rogge which had appeared in the Syracuse press. The court approved the view that freedom of speech should be denied those who pit "class against class . . . and religion against religion." And after announcing its decision, the court persistently refused to grant bail pending sentence.

Although it is unnecessary for me to reach the question of whether the trial below met procedural due process standards, I cannot agree with the opinion of the Court that "Petitioner was accorded a full, fair trial."

For whatever is thought to be guaranteed in Kunz and Niemotko is taken away by what is done here. The three cases read together mean that while previous restraints probably cannot be imposed on an unpopular speaker, the police have discretion to silence him as soon as the customary hostility to his views develops.

In this case I would reverse the conviction, thereby adhering to the great principles of the First and Fourteenth Amendments . . .

Mr. Justice Douglas, with whom Mr. Justice Minton concurs, dissenting.

Feiner, a university student, made a speech on a street corner in Syracuse, New York, on March 8, 1949. The purpose of the speech was to publicize a meeting of the Young Progressives of America to be held that evening. A permit authorizing the meeting to be held in a public school auditorium had been revoked and the meeting shifted to a local hotel.

Feiner delivered his speech in a small shopping area in a predominantly colored residential section of Syracuse. He stood on a large box and spoke over loudspeakers mounted on a car. His audience was composed of about 75 people, colored and white. A few minutes after he started two police officers arrived.

The speech was mainly devoted to publicizing the evening's meeting and protesting the revocation of the permit. It also touched on various public issues. The following are the only excerpts revealed by the record:

"Mayor Costello (of Syracuse) is a champagne-sipping bum; he does not speak for the negro people."

"The 15th Ward is run by corrupt politicians, and there are horse rooms operating there."

"President Truman is a bum."

"Mayor O'Dwyer is a bum."

"The American Legion is a Nazi Gestapo."

"The negroes don't have equal rights; they should rise up in arms and fight for their rights."

There was some pushing and shoving in the crowd and some angry muttering. That is the testimony of the police. But there were no fights and no "disorder" even by the standards of the police. There was not even any heckling of the speaker.

But after Feiner had been speaking about 20 minutes a man said to the police officers, "If you don't get that son of a bitch off, I will go over and get him off there myself." It was then that the police ordered Feiner to stop speaking; when he refused, they arrested him.

Public assemblies and public speech occupy an important role in American life. One high function of the police is to protect these lawful gatherings so that the speakers may exercise their constitutional rights. When unpopular causes are sponsored from the public platform there will commonly be mutterings and unrest and heckling from the crowd. When a speaker mounts a platform it is not unusual to find him resorting to exaggeration, to vilification of ideas and men, to the making of false charges. But those extravagances, as we emphasized in Cantwell v. Connecticut, 310 U.S. 296, do not justify penalizing the speaker by depriving him of the platform or by punishing him for his conduct.

A speaker may not, of course, incite a riot any more than he may invite a breach of the peace by the use of "fighting words." See Chaplinsky v. New Hampshire, 315 U.S. 568. But this record shows no such extremes. It shows an unsympathetic audience and the threat of one man to haul the speaker from the stage. It is against that kind of threat that speakers need police protection. If they do not receive it and instead the police throw their weight on the side of those who would break up the meetings, the police become the new censors of speech. Police censorship has all the vices of the censorship from city halls which we have repeatedly struck down. See Lovell v. City of Griffin, 303 U.S. 444; Hague v. C.I.O., 307 U.S. 496; Cantwell v. Connecticut, supra; Murdock v. Pennsylvania, 319 U.S. 105; Saia v. New York, 334 U.S. 558.

REFERENCES

For comment on the Feiner case see Notes, 46 Ill. L. Rev. 489 (1951); 49 Mich. L. Rev. 1185 (1951); 26 N.Y.U.L. Rev. 489 (1951); Murphy, Free Speech and the Interest in Local Law and Order, 1 J. Pub. Law 40 (1952); Abernathy, The Right of Assembly and Association 73-80 (1961). See also Dembitz, Free Speech vs. Free-for-All, The Nation, July 14, 1951, p. 29; Countryman, Freedom for Insulting Speech — A Reply, The Nation, July 21, 1951, p. 50. Other materials discussing the problems of the Feiner case are cited following the Cox case, infra.

NOTES

The Court handed down, on the same day as Feiner, its decisions in Kunz v. New York, 340 U.S. 290, 71 S. Ct. 312, 95 L. Ed. 280 (1951), and Niemotko v. Maryland, 340 U.S. 268, 71 S. Ct. 325, 95 L. Ed. 267 (1951). These cases dealt with permit systems and are considered in Section D.

In the 1960's the major cases grew out of the civil rights movement. The first case to receive the attention of the Supreme Court was Edwards v. South Carolina, 372 U.S. 229, 83 S. Ct. 680, 9 L. Ed. 2d 297 (1963). In that case a group of nearly 200 Negro high school and college students walked single file or two abreast through the grounds of the State Capitol in Columbia, South Carolina, carrying signs protesting segregation. A crowd of 200 to 300 onlookers gathered in the adjacent area. After the demonstration had lasted 30 to 45 minutes the police told the marchers that if they did not disperse in 15 minutes they would be arrested. "Instead of dispersing, the petitioners engaged in what the City Manager described as 'boisterous,' 'loud,' and 'flamboyant' conduct, which, as his later testimony made clear, consisted of listening to a 'religious harangue' by one of their leaders, and loudly singing 'The Star Spangled Banner' and other patriotic and religious songs, while stamping their feet and clapping their hands. After 15 minutes had passed, the police arrested the petitioners and marched them off to jail." Convictions for breach of the peace were set aside. Mr. Justice Stewart, speaking for the Court, said:

"The circumstances in this case reflect an exercise of these basic constitutional rights in their most pristine and classic form. The petitioners felt aggrieved by laws of South Carolina which allegedly 'prohibited Negro privileges in this State.' They peaceably assembled at the site of the State Government and there peaceably expressed their grievances 'to the citizens of South Carolina, along with the Legislative Bodies of South Carolina.' Not until they were told by police officials that they must disperse on pain of arrest did they do more. Even then, they but sang patriotic and religious songs after one of their leaders had delivered a 'religious harangue.' There was no violence or threat of violence on their part, or on the part of any member of the crowd watching them. Police protection was 'ample.' . . .

"The Fourteenth Amendment does not permit a State to make criminal the peaceful expression of unpopular views. . . . As in the Terminiello case [337 U.S. 1], the courts of South Carolina have defined a criminal offense so as to permit conviction of the petitioners if their speech 'stirred people to anger, invited public dispute, or brought about a condition of unrest. A conviction resting on any of those grounds may not stand.' Id., at 5." 372 U.S. at 235-238.

Mr. Justice Clark dissented:

"Here 200 youthful Negro demonstrators were being aroused to a 'fever pitch' before a crowd of some 300 people who undoubtedly were hostile. Perhaps their speech was not so animated but in this setting their actions, their placards reading 'You may jail our bodies but not our souls' and their chanting of 'I Shall Not Be Moved,' accompanied by stamping feet and clapping hands, created a much greater danger of riot and disorder. It is my belief that anyone conversant with the almost spontaneous combustion in some Southern communities in such a situation will agree that the City Manager's action may well have averted a major catastrophe." 372 U.S. at 244.

In two other cases, decided the next term, the Supreme Court reversed per curiam, citing the Edwards decision, convictions under the South Carolina breach of the peace statute involving somewhat similar circumstances. Fields v. South Carolina, 375 U.S. 44, 84 S. Ct. 149, 11 L. Ed. 2d 107 (1963); Henry v. City of Rock Hill, 376 U.S. 776, 84 S. Ct. 1042, 12 L. Ed. 2d 79 (1964).

COX v. LOUISIANA

379 U.S. 536, 85 S. Ct. 453, 13 L. Ed. 2d 471 (1965)

Mr. Justice Goldberg delivered the opinion of the Court.

Appellant, the Reverend Mr. B. Elton Cox, the leader of a civil rights demonstration, was arrested and charged with four offenses under Louisiana law — criminal conspiracy, disturbing the peace, obstructing public passages, and picketing before a courthouse. In a consolidated trial before a judge without a jury, and on the same set of facts, he was acquitted of criminal conspiracy but convicted of the other three offenses. He was sentenced to serve four months in jail and pay a $200 fine for disturbing the peace, to serve five months in jail and pay a $500 fine for obstructing public passages, and to serve one year in jail and pay a $500 fine for picketing before a courthouse. The sentences were cumulative. . . .

Appellant filed two separate appeals to this Court from these judgments contending that the three statutes under which he was convicted were unconstitutional on their face and as applied. We noted probable jurisdiction of both appeals, 377 U.S. 921. This case, No. 24, involves the convictions for disturbing the peace and obstructing public passages, and No. 49 concerns the conviction for picketing before a courthouse.

I

THE FACTS

On December 14, 1961, 23 students from Southern University, a Negro college, were arrested in downtown Baton Rouge, Louisiana, for picketing stores that maintained segregated lunch counters. This picketing, urging a boycott of those stores, was part of a general protest movment against racial segregation, directed by the local chapter of the Congress of Racial Equality, a civil rights organization. The appellant, an ordained Congregational minister, the Reverend Mr. B. Elton Cox, a Field Secretary of CORE, was an advisor to this movement. On the evening of December 14, appellant and Ronnie Moore, student president of the local CORE chapter, spoke at a mass meeting at the college. The students resolved to demonstrate the next day in front of the courthouse in protest of segregation and the arrest and imprisonment of the picketers who were being held in the parish jail located on the upper floor of the courthouse building.

The next morning about 2,000 students left the campus, which was located approximately five miles from downtown Baton Rouge. Most of them had to walk into the city since the drivers of their busses were arrested. Moore was also arrested at the entrance to the campus while parked in a car equipped with a loudspeaker, and charged with violation of an antinoise statute. Because Moore was immediately taken off to jail and the vice president of the CORE chapter was already in jail for picketing, Cox felt it his duty to take over the demonstration and see that it was carried out as planned. He quickly drove to the city "to pick up this leadership and keep things orderly."

When Cox arrived, 1,500 of the 2,000 students were assembling at the site of the old State Capitol building, two and one-half blocks from the courthouse. Cox walked up and down cautioning the students to keep to one side of the sidewalk while getting ready for their march to the courthouse. The students circled the block in a file two or three abreast occupying about half of the sidewalk. The police had learned of the proposed demonstration the night before from news media and other sources. Captain Font of the City Police Department and Chief Kling of the Sheriff's office, two high-ranking subordinate officials, approached the group and spoke to Cox at the northeast corner of the capitol grounds. Cox identified himself as the group's leader, and, according to Font and Kling, he explained that the students were demonstrating to protest "the illegal arrest of some of their people who were being held in jail." The version of Cox and his witnesses throughout was that they came not "to protest just the arrest but . . . [also] to protest the evil of discrimination." Kling asked Cox to disband the group and "take them back from whence they came." Cox did not acquiesce in this request but told the officers that they would march by the courthouse, say prayers, sing hymns, and conduct a peaceful program of protest. The officer repeated his request to disband, and Cox again refused. Kling and Font then returned to their car in order to report by radio to the Sheriff and Chief of Police who were in the immediate vicinity; while this was going on, the students, led by Cox, began their walk toward the courthouse.

They walked in an orderly and peaceful file, two or three abreast, one block east, stopping on the way for a red traffic light. In the center of this block they were joined by another group of students. The augmented group now totaling about 2,000 turned the corner and proceeded south, coming to a halt in the next block opposite the courthouse.

As Cox, still at the head of the group, approached the vicinity of the courthouse, he was stopped by Captain Font and Inspector Trigg and brought to Police Chief Wingate White, who was standing in the middle of St. Louis Street. The Chief then inquired as to the purpose of the demonstration. Cox, reading from a prepared paper, outlined his program to White, stating that it would include a singing of the Star Spangled Banner and a "freedom song," recitation of the Lord's Prayer and the Pledge of Allegiance, and a short speech. White testified that he told Cox that "he must confine" the demonstration "to the west side of the street." White added, "This, of course, was not — I didn't mean it in the import that I was giving him any permission to do it, but I was presented with a situation that was accomplished, and I had to make a decision." Cox testified that the officials agreed to permit the meeting. James Erwin, news director of radio station WIBR, a witness for the State, was present and overheard the conversation. He testified that "My understanding was that they would be allowed to demonstrate if they stayed on the west side of the street and stayed within the recognized time," and that this was "agreed to" by White.

The students were then directed by Cox to the west sidewalk, across the street from the courthouse, 101 feet from its steps. They were lined up on this sidewalk about five feet deep and spread almost the entire length of the block. The group did not obstruct the street. It was close to noon and, being lunch time, a small crowd of 100 to 300 curious white people, mostly courthouse personnel, gathered on the east sidewalk and courthouse steps, about

100 feet from the demonstrators. Seventy-five to eighty policemen, including city and state patrolmen and members of the Sheriff's staff, as well as members of the fire department and a fire truck were stationed in the street between the two groups. Rain fell throughout the demonstration.

Several of the students took from beneath their coats picket signs similar to those which had been used the day before. These signs bore legends such as "Don't buy discrimination for Christmas," "Sacrifice for Christ, don't buy," and named stores which were proclaimed "unfair." They then sang "God Bless America," pledged allegiance to the flag, prayed briefly, and sang one or two hymns, including "We Shall Overcome." The 23 students, who were locked in jail cells in the courthouse building out of the sight of the demonstrators, responded by themselves singing; this in turn was greeted with cheers and applause by the demonstrators. Appellant gave a speech, described by a State's witness as follows:

"He said that in effect that it was a protest against the illegal arrest of some of their members and that other people were allowed to picket . . . and he said that they were not going to commit any violence, that if anyone spit on them, they would not spit back on the person that did it."

Cox then said:

"All right. It's lunch time. Let's go eat. There are twelve stores we are protesting. A number of these stores have twenty counters; they accept your money from nineteen. They won't accept it from the twentieth counter. This is an act of racial discrimination. These stores are open to the public. You are members of the public. We pay taxes to the Federal Government and you who live here pay taxes to the State."

In apparent reaction to these last remarks, there was what state witnesses described as "muttering" and "grumbling" by the white onlookers.

The Sheriff, deeming, as he testified, Cox's appeal to the students to sit in at the lunch counters to be "inflammatory," then took a power microphone and said, "Now, you have been allowed to demonstrate. Up until now your demonstration has been more or less peaceful, but what you are doing now is a direct violation of the law, a disturbance of the peace, and it has got to be broken up immediately." The testimony as to what then happened is disputed. Some of the State's witnesses testified that Cox said, "don't move"; others stated that he made a "gesture of defiance." It is clear from the record, however, that Cox and the demonstrators did not then and there break up the demonstration. Two of the Sheriff's deputies immediately started across the street and told the group, "You have heard what the Sheriff said, now, do what he said." A state witness testified that they put their hands on the shoulders of some of the students "as though to shove them away."

Almost immediately thereafter — within a time estimated variously at two to five minutes — one of the policemen exploded a tear gas shell at the crowd. This was followed by several other shells. The demonstrators quickly dispersed, running back towards the State Capitol and the downtown area; Cox tried to calm them as they ran and was himself one of the last to leave.

No Negroes participating in the demonstration were arrested on that day. The only person then arrested was a young white man, not a part of the demonstration, who was arrested "because he was causing a disturbance." The next day appellant was arrested and charged with the four offenses above described.

II

THE BREACH OF THE PEACE CONVICTION

Appellant was convicted of violating a Louisiana "disturbing the peace" statute, which provides:

"Whoever with intent to provoke a breach of the peace, or under circumstances such that a breach of the peace may be occasioned thereby . . . crowds or congregates with others . . . in or upon . . . a public street or public highway, or upon a public sidewalk, or any other public place or building . . . and who fails or refuses to disperse and move on . . . when ordered so to do by any law enforcement officer of any municipality, or parish, in which such act or acts are committed, or by any law enforcement officer of the state of Louisiana, or any other authorized person . . . shall be guilty of disturbing the peace." La. Rev. Stat. §14:103.1 (Cum. Supp. 1962).

It is clear to us that on the facts of this case, which are strikingly similar to those present in Edwards v. South Carolina, 372 U.S. 229, and Fields v. South Carolina, 375 U.S. 44, Louisiana infringed appellant's rights of free speech and free assembly by convicting him under this statute. As in Edwards, we do not find it necessary to pass upon appellant's contention that there was a complete absence of evidence so that his conviction deprived him of liberty without due process of law. Cf. Thompson v. Louisville, 362 U.S. 199. We hold that Louisiana may not constitutionally punish appellant under this statute for engaging in the type of conduct which this record reveals, and also that the statute as authoritatively interpreted by the Louisiana Supreme Court is unconstitutionally broad in scope.

The Louisiana courts have held that appellant's conduct constituted a breach of the peace under state law, and, as in Edwards, "we may accept their decision as binding upon us to that extent," Edwards v. South Carolina, supra, at 235; but our independent examination of the record, which we are required to make, shows no conduct which the State had a right to prohibit as a breach of the peace.

Appellant led a group of young college students who wished "to protest segregation" and discrimination against Negroes and the arrest of 23 fellow students. They assembled peaceably at the State Capitol building and marched to the courthouse where they sang, prayed and listened to a speech. A reading of the record reveals agreement on the part of the State's witnesses that Cox had the demonstration "very well controlled," and until the end of Cox's speech, the group was perfectly "orderly." Sheriff Clemmons testified that the crowd's activities were not "objectionable" before that time. They became objectionable, according to the Sheriff himself, when Cox, concluding his speech, urged the students to go uptown and sit in at lunch counters. The Sheriff testified that the sole aspect of the program to which he objected was "[t]he inflammatory manner in which he [Cox] addressed that crowd and told them to go on up town, go to four places on the protest list, sit down and if they don't feed you, sit there for one hour." Yet this part of Cox's speech obviously did not deprive the demonstration of its protected character under the Constitution as free speech and assembly. See Edwards v. South Carolina, supra; Cantwell v. Connecticut, 310 U.S. 296: Thornhill v. Alabama, 310 U.S. 88: Garner v. Louisiana, 368 U.S. 157, 185 (concurring opinion of Mr. Justice Harlan).

The state argues, however, that while the demonstrators started out to be orderly, the loud cheering and clapping by the students in response to the singing from the jail converted the peaceful assembly into a riotous one.[9] The record, however, does not support this assertion. It is true that the students, in response to the singing of their fellows who were in custody, cheered and applauded. However, the meeting was an outdoor meeting and a key state witness testified that while the singing was loud, it was not disorderly. There is, moreover, no indication that the mood of the students was ever hostile, aggressive, or unfriendly. Our conclusion that the entire meeting from the beginning until its dispersal by tear gas was orderly and not riotous is confirmed by a film of events taken by a television news photographer, which was offered in evidence as a state exhibit. We have viewed the film, and it reveals that the students, though they undoubtedly cheered and clapped, were well-behaved throughout. . . .

Our conclusion that the record does not support the contention that the students' cheering, clapping and singing constituted a breach of the peace is confirmed by the fact that these were not relied on as a basis for conviction by the trial judge, who, rather, stated as his reason for convicting Cox of disturbing the peace that "[i]t must be recognized to be inherently dangerous and a breach of the peace to bring 1,500 people, colored people, down in the predominantly white business district in the City of Baton Rouge and congregate across the street from the courthouse and sing songs as described to me

[9] The cheering and shouting were described differently by different witnesses, but the most extravagant descriptions were the following: "a jumbled roar like people cheering at a football game," "loud cheering and spontaneous clapping and screaming and a great hullabaloo," "a great outburst," a cheer of "conquest . . . much wilder than a football game," "a loud reaction, not disorderly, loud," "a shout, a roar," and an emotional response "in jubilation and exhortation." Appellant agreed that some of the group "became emotional" and "tears flowed from young ladies' eyes."

by the defendant as the CORE national anthem carrying lines such as 'black and white together' and to urge those 1,500 people to descend upon our lunch counters and sit there until they are served. That has to be an inherent breach of the peace, and our statute 14:103.1 has made it so."

Finally, the State contends that the conviction should be sustained because of fear expressed by some of the state witnesses that "violence was about to erupt" because of the demonstration. It is virtually undisputed, however, that the students themselves were not violent and threatened no violence. The fear of violence seems to have been based upon the reaction of the group of white citizens looking on from across the street. One state witness testified that "he felt the situation was getting out of hand" as on the courthouse side of St. Louis Street "were small knots or groups of white citizens who were muttering words, who seemed a little bit agitated." A police officer stated that the reaction of the white crowd was not violent, but "was rumblings." Others felt the atmosphere became "tense" because of "mutterings," "grumbling," and "jeering" from the white group. There is no indication, however, that any member of the white group threatened violence. And this small crowd estimated at between 100 and 300 was separated from the students by "seventy-five to eighty" armed policemen, including "every available shift of the City Police," the "Sheriff's Office in full complement," and "additional help from the State Police," along with a "fire truck and the Fire Department." As Inspector Trigg testified, they could have handled the crowd.

This situation, like that in Edwards, is "a far cry from the situation in Feiner v. New York, 340 U.S. 315." See Edwards v. South Carolina, supra, at 236. Nor is there any evidence here of "fighting words." See Chaplinsky v. New Hampshire, 315 U.S. 568. Here again, as in Edwards, this evidence "showed no more than that the opinions which . . . [the students] were peaceably expressing were sufficiently opposed to the views of the majority of the community to attract a crowd and necessitate police protection." Edwards v. South Carolina, supra, at 237. Conceding this was so, the "compelling answer . . . is that constitutional rights may not be denied simply because of hostility to their assertion or exercise." Watson v. Memphis, 373 U.S. 526, 535.

There is an additional reason why this conviction cannot be sustained. The statute at issue in this case, as authoritatively interpreted by the Louisiana Supreme Court, is unconstitutionally vague in its overly broad scope. The statutory crime consists of two elements: (1) congregating with others "with intent to provoke a breach of the peace, or under circumstances such that a breach of the peace may be occasioned," and (2) a refusal to move on after having been ordered to do so by a law enforcement officer. While the second part of this offense is narrow and specific, the first element is not. The Louisiana Supreme Court in this case defined the term "breach of the peace" as "to agitate, to arouse from a state of repose, to molest, to interrupt, to hinder, to disquiet." 244 La., at 1105, 156 So. 2d, at 455. In Edwards, defendants had been convicted of a common-law crime similarly defined by the South Carolina Supreme Court. Both definitions would allow persons to be punished merely for peacefully expressing unpopular views. . . .

In Terminiello [337 U.S. 1] convictions were not allowed to stand because the trial judge charged that speech of the defendants could be punished as a breach of the peace "if it stirs the public to anger, invites dispute, or creates a disturbance, or if it molests the inhabitants in the enjoyment of peace and quiet by arousing alarm.'" Id., at 3. The Louisiana statute, as interpreted by the Louisiana court, is at least as likely to allow conviction for innocent speech as was the charge of the trial judge in Terminiello. Therefore, as in Terminiello and Edwards the conviction under this statute must be reversed as the statute is unconstitutional in that it sweeps within its broad scope activities that are constitutionally protected free speech and assembly. Maintenance of the opportunity for free political discussion is a basic tenet of our constitutional democracy. As Chief Justice Hughes stated in Stromberg v. California, 283 U.S. 359, 369: "A statute which upon its face, and as authoritatively construed, is so vague and indefinite as to permit the punishment of the fair use of this opportunity is repugnant to the guaranty of liberty contained in the Fourteenth Amendment."

For all these reasons we hold that appellant's freedoms of speech and assembly, secured to him by the First Amendment, as applied to the States by the Fourteenth Amendment, were denied by his conviction for disturbing the peace. The conviction on this charge cannot stand.

[The portion of Mr. Justice Goldberg's opinion dealing with the obstructing public passages conviction and the Court's decision in No. 49 on picketing the court house (379 U.S. 559), are set forth in Section C.

Justices Black, Clark, and White wrote separate opinions, reported in No. 49, concurring in the breach of the peace aspect of the case. Mr. Justice Harlan joined in Mr. Justice White's opinion.]

MR. JUSTICE BLACK, concurring in No. 24. . . .

I agree with that part of the Court's opinion holding that the Louisiana breach-of-the-peace statute on its face and as construed by the State Supreme Court is so broad as to be unconstitutionally vague under the First and Fourteenth Amendments. See Winters v. New York, 333 U.S. 507, 509-510. The statute does not itself define the conditions upon which people who want to express views may be allowed to use the public streets and highways, but leaves this to be defined by law enforcement officers. The statute therefore neither forbids all crowds to congregate and picket on streets, nor is it narrowly drawn to prohibit congregating or patrolling under certain clearly defined conditions while preserving the freedom to speak of those who are using the streets as streets in the ordinary way that the State permits. A state statute of either of the two types just mentioned, regulating *conduct* — patrolling and marching — as distinguished from *speech,* would in my judgment be constitutional, subject only to the condition that if such a law had the effect of indirectly impinging on freedom of speech, press, or religion, it would be unconstitutional if under the circumstances it appeared that the State's interest in suppressing the conduct was not sufficient to outweigh the individual's interest in engaging in conduct closely involving his First Amendment freedoms. As this Court held in Schneider v. State, 308 U.S. 147, 161:

"Mere legislative preferences or beliefs respecting matters of public convenience may well support regulation directed at other personal activities, but be insufficient to justify such as diminishes the exercise of rights so vital to the maintenance of democratic institutions. And so, as cases arise, the delicate and difficult task falls upon the courts to weigh the circumstances and to appraise the substantiality of the reasons advanced in support of the regulation of the free enjoyment of the rights." . . .

As I discussed at length in my dissenting opinion in Barenblatt v. United States, 360 U.S. 109, 141-142, when passing on the validity of a regulation of conduct, which may *indirectly* infringe on free speech, this Court does, and I agree that it should, "weigh the circumstances" in order to protect, not to destroy, freedom of speech, press, and religion.

The First and Fourteenth Amendments, I think, take away from government, state and federal, all power to restrict freedom of speech, press, and assembly *where people have a right to be for such purposes.* This does not mean, however, that these amendments also grant a constitutional right to engage in the conduct of picketing or patrolling, whether on publicly owned streets or on privately owned property. See Labor Board v. Fruit & Vegetable Packers & Warehousemen, 377 U.S. 58, 76 (concurring opinion). Were the law otherwise, people on the streets, in their homes and anywhere else could be compelled to listen against their will to speakers they did not want to hear. Picketing, though it may be utilized to communicate ideas, is not speech, and therefore is not of itself protected by the First Amendment. Hughes v. Superior Court, 339 U.S. 460, 464-466; Giboney v. Empire Storage & Ice Co., 336 U.S. 490; Bakery & Pastry Drivers & Helpers v. Wohl, 315 U.S. 769, 775-777 (DOUGAS, J., concurring).

However, because Louisiana's breach-of-peace statute is not narrowly drawn to assure nondiscriminatory application, I think it is constitutionally invalid under our holding in Edwards v. South Carolina, 372 U.S. 229. See also Musser v. Utah, 333 U.S. 95, 96-97. . . . In the case before us Louisiana has by a broad, vague statute given policemen an unlimited power to order people off the streets, not to enforce a specific, nondiscriminatory state statute forbidding patrolling and picketing, but rather whenever a policeman makes a decision on his own personal judgment that views being expressed on the street are provoking or might provoke a breach of the peace. Such a statute does not provide for government by clearly defined laws, but rather for government by the moment-to-moment opinions of a policeman on his beat.

Compare Yick Wo v. Hopkins, 118 U.S. 356, 369-370. This kind of statute provides a perfect device to arrest people whose views do not suit the policeman or his superiors, while leaving free to talk anyone with whose views the police agree. See Feiner v. New York, 340 U.S. 315, 321 (dissenting opinion); cf. Peters v. Hobby, 349 U.S. 331, 349-350 (concurring opinion); Barsky v. Board of Regents, 347 U.S. 442, 463-464 (dissenting opinion); Shaughnessy v. United States ex rel. Mezei, 345 U.S. 206, 217-218 (dissenting opinion); Ludecke v. Watkins, 335 U.S. 160, 173 (dissenting opinion). In this situation I think Edwards v. South Carolina and other such cases invalidating statutes for vagueness are controlling. . . .

[Mr. Justice Clark disagreed that the statute was unconstitutionally vague: "Certainly the language in the present statute is no more vague than that in the New York statute which was challenged on vagueness grounds in Feiner v. New York, 340 U.S. 315." 379 U.S. at 589. But he concurred in the result: ". . . because this statute contains an express exclusion for the activities of labor unions, I would hold the statute unconstitutional on the equal protection ground." 379 U.S. at 591. Mr. Justice White, with whom Mr. Justice Harlan joined, concurred on the ground that "the conviction for breach of peace is governed by Edwards v. South Carolina." 379 U.S. at 591.]

REFERENCES

1. For discussion of the Edwards and Cox cases see Heyman, Civil Rights 1964 Term: Responses to Direct Action, 1965 Sup. Ct. Rev. 159; Note, 30 Brooklyn L. Rev. 116 (1963).

On the problem of the hostile audience, see Note, Freedom of Speech and Assembly: The Problem of the Hostile Audience, 49 Colum. L. Rev. 1118 (1949); Note, Free Speech and the Hostile Audience, 26 N.Y.U.L. Rev. 489 (1951); Murphy, Free Speech and the Interest in Local Law and Order, 1 J. Pub. L. 40 (1952). Cases in which the Court has held that the constitutional right of equal protection may not be denied because of violent opposition or the possibility of disorder include Cooper v. Aaron, 358 U.S. 1, 78 S. Ct. 1401, 3 L. Ed. 2d 5 (1958); Wright v. Georgia, 373 U.S. 284, 83 S. Ct. 1240, 10 L. Ed. 2d 349 (1963).

2. Issues similar to those considered in Edwards and Cox have been raised in a number of cases where injunctions have been sought by civil rights demonstrators against interference by the police or other officials. Injunctions were granted, sometimes with conditions attached, in Young v. Davis, 9 Race Rel. L. Rep. 590 (M.D. Fla. 1964) (St. Augustine); Farmer v. Moses, 232 F. Supp. 154 (S.D. N.Y. 1964) (World's Fair); Williams v. Wallace, 240 F. Supp. 100 (M.D. Ala. 1965) (Selma to Montgomery march), discussed in Marshall, The Protest Movement and the Law, 51 Va. L. Rev. 785, 787-792 (1965); United States v. U.S. Klans et al., 6 Race Rel. L. Rep. 528 (N.D. Ala. 1961) (temporary restraining order obtained by Federal Government against Klan interference with Freedom Riders). See also Kelly v. Page, 335 F.2d 114 (5th Cir. 1964) (Albany, Ga.; complaint held sufficient and case remanded). Injunctions were denied in Wells v. Hand, 238 F. Supp. 779 (M.D. Ga. 1965) (Albany, Ga.); Barnum v. Chambliss, 247 F. Supp. 794 (M.D. Ga. 1965) (Americus, Ga.). See also Zellner v. Lingo, 218 F. Supp. 513 (N.D. Ala. 1963), aff'd per curiam, 334 F.2d 620 (5th Cir. 1964); Baines v. City of Danville, 337 F.2d 579 (4th Cir. 1964). For an injunction granted prohibiting city officials from interfering with a protest march against the Viet Nam war, see Hurwitt v.

City of Oakland, 247 F. Supp. 995 (N.D. Cal. 1965). See also Smith v. Cremins, 308 F.2d 187 (9th Cir. 1962). See Beranek, Prior Restraint of Racial Picketing, 17 U. Fla. L. Rev. 453 (1964).

3. State cases upholding convictions for speech uttered in connection with meetings or demonstrations include Kasper v. State, 206 Tenn. 434, 326 S.W.2d 664 (1959), cert. den., 361 U.S. 930 (1960); City of Chicago v. Lambert, 47 Ill. App. 2d 151, 197 N.E.2d 448 (App. Ct. of Ill., 1st Dist. 1964). See also People v. Penn, 48 Misc. 2d 634, 265 N.Y.S.2d 155 (App. Term 1st Dept. 1964), 16 N.Y.2d 581, 260 N.Y.S.2d 847, 208 N.E.2d 789 (1965), cert. den. 383 U.S. 969 (1966) (obstructing trucks in protest against racial discrimination). See Note, Mass Demonstrations and Criminal Conspiracies, 16 Hastings L.J. 465 (1965).

4. With respect to laws prohibiting the wearing of masks, hoods, and uniforms in public assemblies, see Note, Public Order and the Right of Assembly in England and the United States, 47 Yale L.J. 404, 423-427 (1938); Note, 53 Harv. L. Rev. 150 (1939); Note, Anti-Mask and Anti-Klan Laws, 1 J. Pub. L. 182 (1952). See also West v. Commonwealth, 208 Ky. 735, 271 S.W. 1079 (1925). The red flag laws, enacted in part on the theory that the display of such symbols would provoke disorder, are discussed in Chapter III, Section C. On criminal libel see Chapter VI.

NOTES

The denial of use of public buildings to groups alleged to be subversive has been the cause of litigation in several states, particularly in California. In 1946 the California Supreme Court, in Danskin v. San Diego Unified School District, 28 Cal. 2d 536, 171 P.2d 885 (1946), held invalid a regulation denying use of a school auditorium to a "subversive element" and requiring prospective users to file affidavits stating facts to show whether or not they were subversive. The term "subversive element" was defined as a group "which advocates or has for its object . . . the overthrow of the present government . . . by force or violence or other unlawful means." Holding that such activity could not be made unlawful in the absence of a clear and present danger, the court reasoned: "The state is under no duty to make school buildings available for public meetings. See Merryman v. School Dist., 43 Wyo. 376, 5 P.2d 267, 86 A.L.R. 1195, 47 Am. Jur. 344. If it elects to do so, however, it cannot arbitrarily prevent any members of the public from holding such meetings. State of Missouri ex rel. Gaines v. Canada, 305 U.S. 337, 349, 59 S. Ct. 232, 83 L. Ed. 208, see Marsh v. Alabama [326 U.S. 501]. . . . Nor can it make the privilege of holding them dependent on conditions that would deprive any members of the public of their constitutional rights. A state is without power to impose an unconstitutional requirement as a condition for granting a privilege even though the privilege is the use of state property. . . ."

In 1951 the California legislature enacted a new "auditorium oath" requirement (Cal. Ed. Code §§16564-16565) attempting to overcome objections to the statute held unconstitutional in the Danskin case by adopting Internal Security Act language. The new statute forbade school districts to permit use of school property by groups advocating overthrow of the government by force and violence and required applicants to sign a statement that the property would not be used for such a purpose. The Supreme Court of California held the law unconstitutional on the ground that the test oath requirement abridged freedom of speech and assembly as guaranteed by the First and Fourteenth Amendments. American Civil Liberties Union of Southern California v. Board of Education of City of Los Angeles, 55 Cal. 2d 167, 359 P.2d 45 (1961), cert. den., 368 U.S. 819 (1961), and American Civil Liberties Union of Southern California v. Board of Education of City of San Diego, 55 Cal. 2d 906, 359 P.2d 57 (1961).

The city of San Diego thereupon adopted, as its own regulation, language almost identical with the outlawed provisions of the State Education Code. In American Civil Liberties Union of Southern California v. Board of Education of the San Diego Unified School District, 59 Cal. 2d 224, 379 P.2d 16 (1963), these regulations were held unconstitutional.

The Los Angeles Board, however, adopted regulations requiring an applicant for use of a school auditorium to file a statement that to the best of his knowledge the property would not be used for commission of any act prohibited by law or commission of any crime including, but not limited to, criminal syndicalism. In American Civil Liberties Union of Southern California v. Board of Education of City of Los Angeles, 59 Cal. 2d 203, 379 P.2d 4 (1963), the California Supreme Court held (on the same day as the San Diego case) that this regulation did not abridge freedom of speech and assembly. The court declared that the state law had been intended to bar certain organizations on account of their political beliefs, while in this case the city had "simply conditioned its consent upon a statement that the applicant does not intend to put the property to an illegal use." 59 Cal. 2d at 213, 379 P.2d at 9. The court also rejected arguments of vagueness. The United States Supreme Court denied certiorari, 375 U.S. 823 (1963).

REFERENCES

1. For other laws dealing with the use of public buildings, see Digest of the Public Record of Commission in the United States 487-488 (Fund for the Republic 1955). For denials of privately owned halls and meeting places because of pressure by private groups or public officials, see the annual reports of the American Civil Liberties Union.

2. With respect to the English laws and cases dealing with violence or the possibility of violence in public assemblies, see Beatty v. Gillbanks, 9 Q.B.D. 308 (1882); Wise v. Dunning, [1902] K.B. 167; Duncan v. Jones, [1936] 1 K.B. 218; Jordan v. Burgoyne, [1963] 2 All E.R. 225. For discussion see Note, Public Order and the Right of Assembly in England and the United States, 47 Yale L.J. 404 (1938); Stewart, Public Speech and Public Order in Britain and the United States, 13 Vand. L. Rev. 625 (1960); Abernathy, The Right of Assembly and Association 35-38, 77-79 (1961).

C. PROTECTING OTHER COMMUNITY INTERESTS

Exercise of the right to freedom of expression through assembly, petitioning, or canvassing may come into conflict with various social interests other than the maintenance of the public peace. The Supreme Court has dealt with these problems in a variety of situations. The earlier cases are summarized by Mr. Justice Frankfurter in his opinion in the Niemotko case, set forth in part below.

NIEMOTKO v. MARYLAND
340 U.S. 268, 71 S. Ct. 325, 95 L. Ed. 267 (1951)

MR. JUSTICE FRANKFURTER, concurring in the result. . . .

The cases more exclusively concerned with restrictions upon expression in its divers forms in public places have answered problems varying greatly in content and difficulty.

1. The easiest cases have been those in which the only interest opposing free communication was that of keeping the streets of the community clean. This could scarcely justify prohibiting the dissemination of information by handbills or censoring their contents. In Lovell v. Griffin, 303 U.S. 444, an ordinance requiring a permit to distribute pamphlets was held invalid where the licensing standard was "not limited to ways which might be regarded as inconsistent with the maintenance of public order or as involving disorderly conduct, the molestation of the inhabitants, or the misuse or littering of the streets." Id., at 451. In Hague v. C.I.O. 307 U.S. 496, a portion of the ordinance declared invalid prohibited the distribution of pamphlets. In Schneider v. State, 308 U.S. 147, three of the four ordinances declared invalid by the Court prohibited the distribution of pamphlets. In Jamison v. Texas, 318 U.S. 413, the Court again declared invalid a municipal ordinance prohibiting the distribution of all handbills.

2. In a group of related cases, regulation of solicitation has been the issue. Here the opposing interest is more substantial — protection of the public from fraud and from criminals who use solicitation as a device to enter homes. The fourth ordinance considered in Schneider v. State, supra, allowed the chief of police to refuse a permit if he found, in his discretion, that the canvasser was not of good character or was canvassing for a project not free from fraud. The ordinance was found invalid because the officer who could, in his discretion, make the determinations concerning "good character" and "project not free from fraud" in effect held the power of censorship. In Cantwell v. Connecticut, 310 U.S. 296, conviction was, in part, under a State statute requiring a permit for religious solicitation. The statute was declared invalid because the licensing official could determine what causes were religious, allowing a "censorship of religion." Id., at 305. Again, in Largent v. Texas, 318 U.S. 418, an ordinance requiring a permit from the mayor, who was to issue the permit only if he deemed it "proper or advisable," was declared invalid as creating an administrative censorship. The Court has also denied the right of those in control of a company town or Government housing project to prohibit solicitation by Jehovah's Witnesses. Marsh v. Alabama, 326 U.S. 501; Tucker v. Texas, 326 U.S. 517. In Thomas v. Collins, 323 U.S. 516, the solicitation was in the interest of labor rather than religion. There a State statute requiring registration of labor organizers was found unconstitutional when invoked to enjoin a speech in a public hall. The inter-

est of the State in protecting its citizens through the regulation of vocations was deemed insufficient to support the statute. . . .

4. Martin v. Struthers, 319 U.S. 141, represents another situation. An ordinance of the City of Struthers, Ohio, forbade knocking on the door or ringing the doorbell of a residence in order to deliver a handbill. Prevention of crime and assuring privacy in an industrial community where many worked on night shifts, and had to obtain their sleep during the day, were held insufficient to justify the ordinance in the case of handbills distributed on behalf of Jehovah's Witnesses.

5. In contrast to these decisions, the Court held in Prince v. Massachusetts, 321 U.S. 158, that the application to Jehovah's Witnesses of a State statute providing that no boy under 12 or girl under 18 should sell periodicals on the street was constitutional. Claims of immunity from regulation of religious activities were subordinated to the interest of the State in protecting its children. . . .

(b) Two cases have involved the additional considerations incident to the use of sound trucks. In Saia v. New York, 334 U.S. 558, the ordinance required a license from the chief of police for use of sound amplification devices in public places. The ordinance was construed not to prescribe standards to be applied in passing upon a license application. In the particular case, a license to use a sound truck in a small city park had been denied because of complaints about the noise which resulted when sound amplifiers had previously been used in the park. There was no indication that the license had been refused because of the content of the speeches. Nevertheless, the Court held the ordinance unconstitutional. In Kovacs v. Cooper, 336 U.S. 77, part of the Court construed the ordinance as allowing conviction for operation of any sound truck emitting "loud and raucous" noises, and part construed the ordinance to ban all sound trucks. The limits of the decision of the Court upholding the ordinance are therefore not clear, but the result in any event does not leave the Saia decision intact. . . .

NOTES

1. In Watchtower Bible and Tract Soc. v. Metropolitan Life Ins. Co., 297 N.Y. 339, 79 N.E.2d 433 (1948), cert. den., 335 U.S. 886 (1948), the regulation of a privately owned housing development prohibited canvassing and similar actions except with the consent of the manager or upon written consent or invitation of one of the tenants. The court held that the exception was reasonable since it did not keep plaintiffs, the Jehovah's Witnesses, off streets and sidewalks and permitted them to enter the buildings upon invitation of the tenants. The court felt, therefore, that it did not need to reach the larger constitutional question of whether the Constitution of the United States and that of New York "have anything to do with rules made by any dwelling proprietors governing conduct inside other edifices." Cf. Commonwealth v. Richardson, 313 Mass. 632, 48 N.E.2d 678

(1943), in which the court held that tenants have an easement over the common passageways of the apartment house which extends to all other guests and invitees including Jehovah's Witnesses who had persuaded tenants to release the lock on the inner vestibule door. Once tenants extended their permission the landlord could not keep the Witnesses out. Their entering after his warning in these circumstances did not violate a "trespass after warning" law. For comment see Note, 48 Colum. L. Rev. 1105 (1948).

See also State v. Korich, 219 Minn. 268, 17 N.W.2d 497 (1945) (Jehovah's Witness' quiet and orderly solicitation in apartment house, though annoying, does not violate Minneapolis "disorderly conduct" ordinance); Ex parte Luehr, 159 Tex. Crim. App. 566, 266 S.W.2d 375 (1954) (holding unconstitutional an ordinance prohibiting all uninvited solicitors from going in or upon any private residence); People v. Framer, 139 N.Y. S.2d 331 (Mag. Ct. N.Y.C., 1954) (upholding New York City ordinance making it unlawful "to solicit money," etc. "upon the streets, in office or business buildings, by house to house canvass, or in public places in the city, except upon a license" as designed to prevent fraudulent solicitation and not involving the right to free speech).

See, generally, Notes, 37 Iowa L. Rev. 261 (1952); 75 Harv. L. Rev. 1649 (1962).

2. A problem somewhat similar to that arising from the use of soundtrucks may result when programs are broadcasted to a captive audience on public transportation systems. In Washington, D.C., the Capital Transit Company had installed FM receivers in buses and streetcars to play music and make commercial announcements. The Public Utility Commission held a hearing at which passengers objected to the programs. In Public Utilities Commission v. Pollak, 343 U.S. 451, 72 S. Ct. 813, 96 L. Ed. 1068 (1952), the Supreme Court held there was no infringement of the First and Fifth Amendments. The First Amendment was not violated because there was no showing that ordinary conversations could not take place due to the broadcasts, and the broadcasts did not involve objectionable propaganda. The Fifth Amendment was held not to guarantee a right to privacy on buses. Mr. Justice Douglas dissented.

REFERENCES

1. Generally on controls over the distribution of literature and canvassing, see Lindsay, Council and Court: The Handbill Ordinances, 1889-1939, 39 Mich. L. Rev. 561 (1941).

2. For discussion of the soundtruck cases, see 34 A.B.A.J. 589, 591 (1948); 58 Yale L.J. 335 (1949); 34 Cornell L.Q. 626 (1949); 3 Rutgers L. Rev. 250 (1949); 22 So. Calif. L. Rev. 416 (1949); 2 U. Fla. L. Rev. 103 (1949). A model ordinance, drafted prior to the Kovacs case, is printed in National Institute of Municipal Law Officers, Report No. 123 (1948). For discussion of developments since the Saia and Kovacs cases, see Notes, 31 Notre Dame Law. 493 (1956); 49 Iowa L. Rev. 567 (1964).

3. For studies of the effect of noise in general, see Bartlett, The Problem of Noise (1934); McLachlan, Noise (1935). On the legal aspects see Spater, Noise and the Law, 63 Mich. L. Rev. 1373 (1965).

4. On the captive audience problem considered in the Pollak case, see Black, He Cannot Choose But Hear: The Plight of the Captive Auditor, 53 Colum. L. Rev. 960 (1953); Notes, 1 J. Pub. L. 507 (1952); 100 U. Pa. L. Rev. 271 (1951); Shipley, Some Constitutional Aspects of Transit Radio, 11 Fed. Com. B.J. 150 (1950).

TALLEY v. CALIFORNIA
362 U.S. 60, 80 S. Ct. 536, 4 L. Ed. 2d 559 (1960)

Mr. Justice Black delivered the opinion of the Court.

The question presented here is whether the provisions of a Los Angeles City ordinance restricting the distribution of handbills "abridge the freedom of speech and of the press secured against state invasion by the Fourteenth Amendment of the Constitution." The ordinance, §28.06 of the Municipal Code of the City of Los Angeles, provides:

"No person shall distribute any hand-bill in any place under any circumstances, which does not have printed on the cover, or the face thereof, the name and address of the following:

"(a) The person who printed, wrote, compiled or manufactured the same.

"(b) The person who caused the same to be distributed; provided, however, that in the case of a fictitious person or club, in addition to such fictitious name, the true names and addresses of the owners, managers or agents of the person sponsoring said handbill shall also appear thereon."

The petitioner was arrested and tried in a Los Angeles Municipal Court for violating this ordinance. It was stipulated that the petitioner had distributed handbills in Los Angeles, and two of them were presented in evidence. Each had printed on it the following:

National Consumers Mobilization
Box 6533
Los Angeles 55, Calif.
Pleasant 9-1576

The handbills urged readers to help the organization carry on a boycott against certain merchants and businessmen, whose names were given, on the ground that, as one set of handbills said, they carried products of "manufacturers who will not offer equal employment opportunities to Negroes, Mexicans, and Orientals." There also appeared a blank, which, if signed, would request enrollment of the signer as a "member of National Consumers Mobilization," and which was preceded by a statement that "I believe that every man should have an equal opportunity for employment no matter what his race, religion, or place of birth."

The Municipal Court held that the information printed on the handbills did not meet the requirements of the ordinance, found the petitioner guilty as charged, and fined him $10. . . .

In Lovell v. Griffin, 303 U.S. 444, we held void on its face an ordinance that comprehensively forbade any distribution of literature at any time or place in Griffin, Georgia, without a license. Pamphlets and leaflets, it was pointed out, "have been historic weapons in the defense of liberty"[3] and enforcement of the Griffin ordinance "would restore the system of license and censorship in its baldest form." Id., at 452. A year later we had before us four ordinances each forbidding distribution of leaflets — one in Irvington, New Jersey, one in Los Angeles, California, one in Milwaukee, Wisconsin, and one in Worcester, Massachusetts. Schneider v. State, 308 U.S. 147. Efforts were made to distinguish these four ordinances from the one held void in the Griffin case. The chief grounds urged for distinction were that the four ordinances had been passed to prevent either frauds, disorder, or littering, according to the records in these cases, and another ground urged was that two of the ordinances applied only to certain city areas. This Court refused to uphold the four ordinances on those grounds pointing out that there were other ways to accomplish these legitimate aims without abridging freedom of speech and press. Frauds, street littering and disorderly conduct could be denounced and punished as offenses, the Court said. Several years later we followed the Griffin and Schneider cases in striking down a Dallas, Texas, ordinance which was applied to prohibit the dissemination of information by the distribution of handbills. We said that although a city could punish any person for conduct on the streets if he violates a valid law, "one who is rightfully on a street . . . carries with him there as elsewhere the constitutional right to express his views in an orderly fashion . . . by handbills and literature as well as by the spoken word." Jamison v. Texas, 318 U.S. 413, 416.

The broad ordinance now before us, barring distribution of "any hand-bill in any place under any circumstances," falls precisely under the ban of our prior cases unless this ordinance is saved by the qualification that handbills can be distributed if they have printed on them the names and addresses of the persons who prepared, distributed or sponsored them. For, as in Griffin, the ordinance here is not limited to handbills whose content is "obscene or offensive to public morals or that advocates unlawful conduct."[5] Counsel has urged that this ordinance is aimed at providing a way to identify those responsible for fraud, false advertising and libel. Yet the ordinance is in no manner so limited, nor have we been referred to any legislative history indicating such a purpose. Therefore we do not pass on the validity of an ordinance limited to prevent these or any other supposed evils. This ordinance simply bars all handbills under all circumstances anywhere that do not have the names and addresses printed on them in the place the ordinance requires.

---

[3] The Court's entire sentence was: "These [pamphlets and leaflets] indeed have been historic weapons in the defense of liberty, as the pamphlets of Thomas Paine and others in our own history abundantly attest." It has been noted that some of Thomas Paine's pamphlets were signed with pseudonyms. See Bleyer, Main Currents in the History of American Journalism 90-93 (1927). Illustrations of other anonymous and pseudonymous pamphlets and other writings used to discuss important public questions can be found in this same volume.

[5] Lovell v. Griffin, 303 U.S., at 451.

There can be no doubt that such an identification requirement would tend to restrict freedom to distribute information and thereby freedom of expression. "Liberty of circulating is as essential to that freedom as liberty of publishing; indeed, without the circulation, the publication would be of little value." Lovell v. Griffin, 303 U.S., at 452.

Anonymous pamphlets, leaflets, brochures and even books have played an important role in the progress of mankind. Persecuted groups and sects from time to time throughout history have been able to criticize oppressive practices and laws either anonymously or not at all. The obnoxious press licensing law of England, which was also enforced on the Colonies was due in part to the knowledge that exposure of the names of printers, writers and distributors would lessen the circulation of literature critical of the government. The old seditious libel cases in England show the lengths to which government had to go to find out who was responsible for books that were obnoxious to the rulers. John Lilburne was whipped, pilloried and fined for refusing to answer questions designed to get evidence to convict him or someone else for the secret distribution of books in England. Two Puritan Ministers, John Penry and John Udal, were sentenced to death on charges that they were responsible for writing, printing or publishing books.[6] Before the Revolutionary War colonial patriots frequently had to conceal their authorship or distribution of literature that easily could have brought down on them prosecutions by English-controlled courts. Along about that time the Letters of Junius were written and the identity of their author is unknown to this day.[7] Even the Federalist Papers, written in favor of the adoption of our Constitution, were published under fictitious names. It is plain that anonymity has sometimes been assumed for the most constructive purposes.

We have recently had occasion to hold in two cases that there are times and circumstances when States may not compel members of groups engaged in the dissemination of ideas to be publicly identified. Bates v. Little Rock, 361 U.S. 516; N.A.A.C.P. v. Alabama, 357 U.S. 449, 462. The reason for those holdings was that identification and fear of reprisal might deter perfectly peaceful discussions of public matters of importance. This broad Los Angeles ordinance is subject to the same infirmity. We hold that it, like the Griffin, Georgia, ordinance, is void on its face. . . .

Mr. Justice Harlan, concurring.

In judging the validity of municipal action affecting rights of speech or

---

[6] Penry was executed and Udal died as a result of his confinement. 1 Hallam, The Constitutional History of England (1855), 205-206, 232.

[7] In one of the letters written May 28, 1770, the author asked the following question about the tea tax imposed on this country, a question which he could hardly have asked but for his anonymity:

"What is it then, but an odious, unprofitable exertion of a speculative right, and fixing a badge of slavery upon the Americans, without service to their masters?" 2 Letters of Junius (1821) 39.

association protected against invasion by the Fourteenth Amendment, I do not believe that we can escape, as Mr. Justice Roberts said in Schneider v. State, 308 U.S. 147, 161, "the delicate and difficult task" of weighing "the circumstances" and appraising "the substantiality of the reasons advanced in support of the regulation of the free enjoyment of" speech. More recently we have said that state action impinging on free speech and association will not be sustained unless the governmental interest asserted to support such impingement is compelling. See N.A.A.C.P. v. Alabama, 357 U.S. 449, 463, 464; Sweezy v. New Hampshire, 354 U.S. 234, 265 (concurring opinion); see also Bates v. Little Rock, 361 U.S. 516.

Here the State says that this ordinance is aimed at the prevention of "fraud, deceit, false advertising, negligent use of words, obscenity, and libel," in that it will aid in the detection of those responsible for spreading material of that character. But the ordinance is not so limited, and I think it will not do for the State simply to say that the circulation of all anonymous handbills must be suppressed in order to identify the distributors of those that may be of an obnoxious character. In the absence of a more substantial showing as to Los Angeles' actual experience with the distribution of obnoxious handbills, such a generality is for me too remote to furnish a constitutionally acceptable justification for the deterrent effect on free speech which this all-embracing ordinance is likely to have.

On these grounds I concur in the judgment of the Court.

Mr. Justice Clark, whom Mr. Justice Frankfurter and Mr. Justice Whittaker join, dissenting.

To me, Los Angeles' ordinance cannot be read as being void on its face. Certainly a fair reading of it does not permit a conclusion that it prohibits the distribution of handbills "of any kind at any time, at any place, and in any manner," Lovell v. Griffin, 303 U.S. 444, 451 (1938), as the Court seems to conclude. In Griffin, the ordinance completely prohibited the unlicensed distribution of any handbills. As I read it, the ordinance here merely prohibits the distribution of a handbill which does not carry the identification of the name of the person who "printed, wrote, compiled . . . manufactured [or] . . . caused" the distribution of it. There could well be a compelling reason for such a requirement. The Court implies as much when it observes that Los Angeles has not "referred to any legislative history indicating" that the ordinance was adopted for the purpose of preventing "fraud, false advertising and libel." But even as to its legislative background there is pertinent material which the Court overlooks. At oral argument, the City's chief law enforcement officer stated that the ordinance was originally suggested in 1931 by the Los Angeles Chamber of Commerce in a complaint to the City Council urging it to "do something about these handbills and advertising matters which were false and misleading." Upon inquiry by the Council, he said, the matter was referred to his office, and the Council was advised that such an ordinance as the present one would be valid. He further stated that this ordinance, relating to the original inquiry of the Chamber of Commerce, was thereafter drafted and submitted to the Council. It was adopted in 1932. In the face of this and the presumption of validity that the ordinance enjoys, the Court nevertheless strikes it down, stating that it "falls precisely under the ban of our prior cases." This cannot follow, for in each of the three cases cited, the ordinances either "forbade any distribution of literature . . . without a license," Lovell v. Griffin, supra, or forbade, without exception, any distribution of handbills on the streets, Jamison v. Texas, 318 U.S. 413 (1943); or, as in Schneider v. State, 308 U.S. 147 (1939), which covered different ordinances in four cities, they were either outright bans or prior restraints upon the distribution of handbills. I, therefore, cannot see how the Court can conclude that the Los Angeles ordinance here "falls precisely" under any of these cases. On the contrary, to my mind, they neither control this case nor are apposite to it. In fact, in Schneider, depended upon by the Court, it was held, through Mr. Justice Roberts, that, "In every case . . . where legislative abridgment of the rights is asserted, the courts should be astute to examine the effect of the challenged legislation . . . weigh the circumstances and . . . appraise the substantiality of the reasons advanced. . . ." Id., at 161. The Court here, however, makes no appraisal of *the circumstances,* or *the substantiality* of the claims of the litigants, but strikes down the ordinance as being "void on its face." I cannot be a party to using such a device as an escape from the requirements of our cases, the latest of which was handed down only last month. Bates v. Little Rock, 361 U.S. 516.[1]

Therefore, before passing upon the validity of the ordinance, I would weigh the interests of the public in its enforcement against the claimed right of Talley. The record is barren of any claim, much less proof, that he will suffer any injury whatever by identifying the handbill with his name. Unlike N.A.A.C.P. v. Alabama, 357 U.S. 449 (1958), which is relied upon, there is neither allegation nor proof that Talley or any group sponsoring him would suffer "economic reprisal, loss of employment, threat of physical coercion [or] other manifestations of public hostility." Id., at 462. Talley makes no showing whatever to support his contention that a restraint upon his freedom of speech will result from the enforcement of the ordinance. The existence of such a restraint is necessary before we can strike the ordinance down.

But even if the State had this burden, which it does not, the substantiality of Los Angeles' interest in the enforcement of the ordinance sustains its validity. Its chief law enforcement officer says that the enforcement of the ordinance prevents "fraud, deceit, false advertising, negligent use of words, obscenity, and libel," and, as we have said, that such was its purpose. In the

---

[1] "When it is shown that state action threatens significantly to impinge upon constitutionally protected freedom it becomes the duty of this Court to determine whether the action bears a reasonable relationship to the achievement of the governmental purpose asserted as its justification." 361 U.S., at 525.

absence of any showing to the contrary by Talley, this appears to me entirely sufficient.

I stand second to none in supporting Talley's right of free speech — but not his freedom of anonymity. The Constitution says nothing about freedom of anonymous speech. In fact, this Court has approved laws requiring no less than Los Angeles' ordinance. I submit that they control this case and require its approval under the attack made here. First, Lewis Publishing Co. v. Morgan, 229 U.S. 288 (1913), upheld an Act of Congress requiring any newspaper using the second-class mails to publish the names of its editor, publisher, owner, and stockholders. 39 U.S.C. §233. Second, in the Federal Regulation of Lobbying Act, 2 U.S.C. §267, Congress requires those engaged in lobbying to divulge their identities and give "a modicum of information" to Congress. United States v. Harriss, 347 U.S. 612, 625 (1954). Third, the several States have corrupt practices acts outlawing, inter alia, the distribution of anonymous publications with reference to political candidates. While these statutes are leveled at political campaign and election practices, the underlying ground sustaining their validity applies with equal force here.

No civil right has a greater claim to constitutional protection or calls for more rigorous safeguarding than voting rights. In this area the danger of coercion and reprisals — economic and otherwise — is a matter of common knowledge. Yet these statutes, disallowing anonymity in promoting one's views in election campaigns, have expressed the overwhelming public policy of the Nation. Nevertheless the Court is silent about this impressive authority relevant to the disposition of this case.

All three of the types of statutes mentioned are designed to prevent the same abuses — libel, slander, false accusations, etc. The fact that some of these statutes are aimed at elections, lobbying, and the mails makes their restraint no more palatable, nor the abuses they prevent less deleterious to the public interest, than the present ordinance.

All that Los Angeles requires is that one who exercises his right of free speech through writing or distributing handbills identify himself just as does one who speaks from the platform. The ordinance makes for the responsibility in writing that is present in public utterance. When and if the application of such an ordinance in a given case encroaches on First Amendment freedoms, then will be soon enough to strike that application down. But no such restraint has been shown here. After all, the public has some rights against which the enforcement of freedom of speech would be "harsh and arbitrary in itself." Kovacs v. Cooper, 336 U.S. 77, 88 (1949). We have upheld complete proscription of uninvited door-to-door canvassing as an invasion of privacy. Breard v. Alexandria, 341 U.S. 622 (1951). Is this less restrictive than complete freedom of distribution — regardless of content — of a signed handbill? And commercial handbills may be declared verboten, Valentine v. Chrestensen, 316 U.S. 52 (1942), regardless of content or identification. Is Talley's anonymous handbill, designed to destroy the business of a commercial establishment, passed out at its very front door, and attacking its then lawful commercial practices, more comportable with First Amendment freedoms? I think not. Before we may expect international responsibility among nations, might not it be well to require individual responsibility at home? Los Angeles' ordinance does no more.

REFERENCES

1. For extensive discussion of the Talley case and its implications, see Notes, Anonymity: An Emerging Fundamental Right, 36 Ind. L.J. 306 (1961); The Constitutional Right to Anonymity: Free Speech, Disclosure and the Devil, 70 Yale L.J. 1084 (1961); Disclosure as a Legislative Device, 76 Harv. L. Rev. 1273 (1963). See also Notes, 60 Colum. L. Rev. 1173 (1960); 7 U.C.L.A.L. Rev. 786 (1960); 14 Vand. L. Rev. 392 (1960); 22 Ohio St. L.J. 220 (1961).

2. Issues as to the role of disclosure in facilitating or hampering freedom of expression, and the First Amendment limitations on requiring disclosure, have been much debated. President Truman's Committee on Civil Rights in its 1947 Report recommended: "The enactment by Congress and the state legislatures of legislation requiring all groups, which attempt to influence public opinion, to disclose the pertinent facts about themselves through systematic registration procedures." To Secure These Rights 164, 51-53 (G.P.O. 1947). The argument for disclosure is made in Smith, Democratic Control of Propaganda Through Registration and Disclosure, 6 Pub. Opin. Q. 27 (1942); Institute of Living Law, Combatting Totalitarian Propaganda, 10 U. Chi. L. Rev. 107 (1943); Fly, Full Disclosure: Public Safeguard, The Nation, Mar. 12, 1949; Ernst and Katz, Speech: Public and Private, 53 Colum. L. Rev. 620 (1953); Mendelson, Clandestine Speech and the First Amendment — A Reappraisal of the Dennis Case, 51 Mich. L. Rev. 553 (1953). For a different point of view see Hays, "Full Disclosure": Dangerous Precedent, The Nation, Jan. 29, 1949; Chafee, The Blessings of Liberty, ch. V (1956); Franklin, The Encyclopédiste Origin and Meaning of the Fifth Amendment, 15 Law. Guild Rev. 41 (1955); Note, Registration of Groups Tending to Influence Public Opinion, 48 Colum. L. Rev. 589 (1948). Other discussions of the ramifications of the problem in various areas of freedom of expression, in addition to those cited in paragraph 1 above, are Nutting, Freedom of Silence: Constitutional Protection Against Governmental Intrusions in Political Affairs, 47 Mich. L. Rev. 181 (1948); Robison, Protection of Associations From Compulsory Disclosure of Membership, 58 Colum. L. Rev. 614 (1958); Fellman, The Constitutional Right of Association, ch. IV (1963); Kent, Compulsory Disclosure and the First Amendment — The Scope of Judicial Review, 41 B.U.L. Rev. 443 (1961); Kalven, The Negro and the First Amendment, ch. II (1965). See also Lasswell, The Threat to Privacy, in MacIver (ed.), Conflict of Loyalties, ch. XI (1952).

The issues arise in many connections. See, e.g., the materials on the Foreign Agents Registration Act and the Internal Security Act in Chapter III; on the N.A.A.C.P. right of association cases, the corrupt practices acts, and lobbying acts in Chapter IV; on defamation in Chapter VI.

COX v. LOUISIANA
379 U.S. 559, 85 S. Ct. 476, 13 L. Ed. 2d 487 (1965)

[The facts are set forth in the related case, No. 24, printed in part in Section B, supra.]

Mr. Justice Goldberg delivered the opinion of the Court.

Appellant was convicted of violating a Louisiana statute which provides:

"Whoever, with the intent of interfering with, obstructing, or impeding the administration of justice, or with the intent of influencing any judge, juror, witness, or court officer, in the discharge of his duty pickets or parades in or near a building housing a court of the State of Louisiana . . . shall be fined not more than five thousand dollars or imprisoned not more than one year, or both." La. Rev. Stat. §14:401 (Cum. Supp. 1962). . . .

This statute was passed by Louisiana in 1950 and was modeled after a bill pertaining to the federal judiciary, which Congress enacted later in 1950, 64 Stat. 1018, 18 U.S.C. §1507 (1958 ed.). Since that time, Massachusetts and Pennsylvania have passed similar statutes. Mass. Ann. Laws, c. 268, §13A; Purdon's Pa. Stat. Ann., Tit. 18, §4327. The federal statute resulted from the picketing of federal courthouses by partisans of the defendants during trials involving leaders of the Communist Party. . . .

This statute, unlike the two previously considered, is a precise, narrowly drawn regulatory statute which proscribes certain specific behavior. Cf. Edwards v. South Carolina, 372 U.S. 229, 236. It prohibits a particular type of conduct, namely, picketing and parading, in a few specified locations, in or near courthouses. . . .

Nor does such a statute infringe upon the constitutionally protected rights of free speech and free assembly. The conduct which is the subject of this statute — picketing and parading — is subject to regulation even though intertwined with expression and association. The examples are many of the application by this Court of the principle that certain forms of conduct mixed with speech may be regulated or prohibited. The most classic of these was pointed out long ago by Mr. Justice Holmes: "The most stringent protection of free speech would not protect a man in falsely shouting fire in a theatre and causing a panic." Schenck v. United States, 249 U.S. 47, 52. A man may be punished for encouraging the commission of a crime, Fox v. Washington, 236 U.S. 273, or for uttering "fighting words," Chaplinsky v. New Hampshire, 315 U.S. 568. This principle has been applied to picketing and parading in labor disputes. See Hughes v. Superior Court, 339 U.S. 460; Giboney v. Empire Storage & Ice Co., 336 U.S. 490; Building Service Employees v. Gazzam, 339 U.S. 532. But cf. Thornhill v. Alabama, 310 U.S. 88. These authorities make it clear, as the Court said in Giboney, that "it has never been deemed an abridgment of freedom of speech or press to make a course of conduct illegal merely because the conduct was in part initiated, evidenced, or carried out by means of language, either spoken, written, or printed." Giboney v. Empire Storage & Ice Co., supra, at 502.

Bridges v. California, 314 U.S. 252, and Pennekamp v. Florida, 328 U.S. 331, do not hold to the contrary. Both these cases dealt with the power of a judge to sentence for contempt persons who published or caused to be published writings commenting on judicial proceedings. They involved newspaper editorials, an editorial cartoon, and a telegram sent by a labor leader to the Secretary of Labor. Here we deal not with the contempt power — a power which is "based on a common law concept of the most general and undefined nature." Bridges v. California, supra, at 260. Rather, we are reviewing a statute narrowly drawn to punish specific conduct that infringes a substantial state interest in protecting the judicial process. See Cantwell v. Connecticut, 310 U.S. 296, 307-308; Giboney v. Empire Storage & Ice Co., supra. We are not concerned here with such a pure form of expression as newspaper comment or a telegram by a citizen to a public official. We deal in this case not with free speech alone, but with expression mixed with particular conduct. . . .

We hold that this statute on its face is a valid law dealing with conduct subject to regulation so as to vindicate important interests of society and that the fact that free speech is intermingled with such conduct does not bring with it constitutional protection. . . .

Appellant invokes the clear and present danger doctrine in support of his argument that the statute cannot constitutionally be applied to the conduct involved here. He says, relying upon Pennekamp and Bridges, that "[n]o reason exists to apply a different standard to the case of a criminal penalty for a peaceful demonstration in front of a courthouse than the standard of clear and present danger applied in the contempt cases." (Appellant's Br., p. 22.) He defines the standard to be applied to both situations to be whether the expression of opinion presents a clear and present danger to the administration of justice.

We have already pointed out the important differences between the contempt cases and the present one, supra, at 563-564. Here we deal not with the contempt power but with a narrowly drafted statute and not with speech in its pristine form but with conduct of a totally different character. Even assuming the applicability of a general clear and present danger test, it is one thing to conclude that the mere publication of a newspaper editorial or a telegram to a Secretary of Labor, however critical of a court, presents no clear and present danger to the administration of justice and quite another thing to conclude that crowds, such as this, demonstrating before a courthouse may not be prohibited by a legislative determination based on experience that such conduct inherently threatens the judicial process. We therefore reject the clear and present danger argument of appellant.

[The Court then rejected appellant's contention that his conviction violated due process because there was no evidence of intent as required by the statute. In the final portion of its opinion, however, the Court reversed the conviction on the ground that the officials present gave permission to hold the demonstration across the street from the courthouse and thus, in effect, advised appellant that a demonstration at that place would not be "near" the courthouse within the terms of the statute. This grant of permission was not withdrawn by the sheriff's order to disperse since that order was given, not because the demonstration was too near the court house, "but because officials erroneously concluded that what he said threatened a breach of the peace."]

Nothing we have said here or in No. 24, *ante*, is to be interpreted as sanctioning riotous conduct in any form or demonstrations, however peaceful their conduct or commendable their motives, which conflict with properly drawn statutes and ordinances designed to promote law and order, protect the community against disorder, regulate traffic, safeguard legitimate interests in private and public property, or protect the administration of justice and other essential governmental functions.

Liberty can only be exercised in a system of law which safeguards order. We reaffirm the repeated holdings of this Court that our constitutional command of free speech and assembly is basic and fundamental and encompasses peaceful social protest, so important to the preservation of the freedoms treasured in a democratic society. We also reaffirm the repeated decisions of this Court that there is no place for violence in a democratic society dedicated to liberty under law, and that the right of peaceful protest does not mean that everyone with opinions or beliefs to express may do so at any time and at any place. There is a proper time and place for even the most peaceful protest and a plain duty and responsibility on the part of all citizens to obey all valid laws and regulations. There is an equally plain requirement for laws and regulations to be drawn so as to give citizens fair warning as to what is illegal; for regulation of conduct that involves freedom of speech and assembly not to be so broad in scope as to stifle First Amendment freedoms, which "need breathing space to survive," NAACP v. Button, 371 U.S. 415, 433; for appropriate limitations on the discretion of public officials where speech and assembly are intertwined with regulated conduct; and for all such laws and regulations to be applied with an equal hand. We believe that all of these requirements can be met in an ordered society dedicated to liberty. We reaffirm our conviction that "[f]reedom and viable government are . . . indivisible concepts." Gibson v. Florida Legislative Comm., 372 U.S. 539, 546.

The application of these principles requires us to reverse the judgment of the Supreme Court of Louisiana.

Reversed.

MR. JUSTICE BLACK . . . dissenting in No. 49. . . .

While I agree that the record does not show boisterous or violent conduct or indecent language on the part of the "demonstrators," the ample evidence that this group planned the march on the courthouse and carried it out for the express purpose of influencing the courthouse officials in the performance of their official duties brings this case squarely within the prohibitions of the Louisiana statute and I think leaves us with no alternative but to sustain the conviction unless the statute itself is unconstitutional, and I do not believe that this statute is unconstitutional, either on its face or as applied.

This statute, like the federal one which it closely resembles, was enacted to protect courts and court officials from the intimidation and dangers that inhere in huge gatherings at courthouse doors and jail doors to protest arrests and to influence court officials in performing their duties. The very purpose of a court system is to adjudicate controversies, both criminal and civil, in the calmness and solemnity of the courtroom according to legal procedures. Justice cannot be rightly administered, nor are the lives and safety of prisoners secure, where throngs of people clamor against the processes of justice right outside the courthouse or jailhouse doors. The streets are not now and never have been the proper place to administer justice. Use of the streets for such purposes has always proved disastrous to individual liberty in the long run, whatever fleeting benefits may have appeared to have been achieved. And minority groups, I venture to suggest, are the ones who always have suffered and always will suffer most when street multitudes are allowed to substitute their pressures for the less glamorous but more dependable and temperate processes of the law. Experience demonstrates that it is not a far step from what to many seems the earnest, honest, patriotic, kind-spirited multitude of today, to the fanatical, threatening, lawless mob of tomorrow. And the crowds that press in the streets for noble goals today can be supplanted tomorrow by street mobs pressuring the courts for precisely opposite ends.

Minority groups in particular need always to bear in mind that the Constitution, while it requires States to treat all citizens equally and protect them in the exercise of rights granted by the Federal Constitution and laws, does not take away the State's power, indeed its duty, to keep order and to do justice according to law. Those who encourage minority groups to believe that the United States Constitution and federal laws give them a right to patrol and picket in the streets whenever they choose, in order to advance what they think to be a just and noble end, do no service to those minority groups, their cause, or their country. I am confident from this record that this appellant violated the Louisiana statute because of a mistaken belief that he and his followers had a constitutional right to do so, because of what they believed were just grievances. But the history of the past 25 years if it shows nothing else shows that his group's constitutional and statutory rights have to be protected by the courts, which must be kept free from intimidation and coercive pressures of any kind. Government under law as ordained by our Constitution is too precious, too sacred, to be jeopardized by subjecting the courts to intimidatory practices that have been fatal to individual liberty and minority rights wherever and whenever such practices have been allowed to poison the streams of justice. I would be wholly unwilling to join in moving this country a single step in that direction.

[Justices Clark, Harlan, and White also dissented.]

NOTES

1. After the convictions of Cox were set aside by the Supreme Court, the Louisiana authorities sought to prosecute him on charges of "attempting" to obstruct justice, based on the same conduct. Removal to the federal court was granted on the ground of a denial of federal rights involving a "planned prosecutional abuse of a state criminal statue." Cox v. Louisiana, 348 F.2d 750 (5th Cir. 1965).

2. Numerous decisions of the Supreme Court have dealt with the question of to what extent labor picketing constitutes freedom of expression protected by the First Amendment. The story begins with Thornhill v. Alabama, 310 U.S. 88, 60 S. Ct. 736, 84 L. Ed. 1093 (1940), involving an Alabama statute which in effect prohibited all labor picketing. The Supreme Court, in an opinion by Mr. Justice Murphy, held the statute invalid on its face: "In the circumstances of our times the dissemination of information concerning the facts of a labor dispute must be regarded as within that area of free disussion that is guaranteed by the Constitution . . . . Abridgement of the liberty of such discussion can be justified only where the clear danger of substantive evils arises under circumstances affording no opportunity to test the merits of ideas by competition for acceptance in the market of public opinion. We hold that the danger of injury to an industrial concern is neither so serious nor so imminent as to justify the sweeping proscription of freedom of discussion embodied in §3448." 310 U.S. at 102, 104-105. See also Carlson v. California, 310 U.S. 106, 60 S. Ct. 746, 84 L. Ed. 1104 (1940).

The following year the Court held that picketing can be enjoined when it is "enmeshed with contemporaneously violent conduct which is concededly outlawed," but noted that a state may not "enjoin peaceful picketing merely because it may provoke violence in others." Milk Wagon Drivers Union v. Meadowmoor Dairies, Inc., 312 U.S. 287, 292, 296, 61 S. Ct. 552, 85 L. Ed. 836 (1941).

In Giboney v. Empire Storage Co., 336 U.S. 490, 69 S. Ct. 684, 93 L. Ed. 834 (1949), the Court, in an opinion by Mr. Justice Black, adopted the view that peaceful picketing in a labor dispute "may include conduct other than speech, conduct which can be made the subject of restrictive legislation" (336 U.S. at 501), and hence such picketing can be enjoined where it is being used to effectuate an unlawful purpose. In that case the Court upheld an injunction against picketing that was part of a course of conduct in violation of the state's anti-trust laws. The Court quoted from a Douglas concurring opinion in an earlier case: "Picketing by an organized group is more than free speech, since it involves patrol of a particular locality and since the very presence of a picket line may induce action of one kind or another, quite irrespective of the nature of the ideas which are being disseminated." Bakery Drivers Local v. Wohl, 315 U.S. 769, 776, 62 S. Ct. 816, 86 L. Ed. 1178 (1942). And it added: "[It] is clear that appellants were doing more than exercising a right of free speech or press. . . . They were exercising their economic power together with that of their allies to compel Empire to abide by union rather than by state regulation of trade." 336 U.S. at 503.

Thereafter the Court extended the Giboney doctrine to permit the prohibition of any labor picketing which was being carried on in support of conduct that violated the public policy of a state. The development is recorded in International

Brotherhood of Teamsters, Local 695 v. Vogt, 354 U.S. 284, 77 S. Ct. 1166, 1 L. Ed. 2d 1347 (1957), Mr. Chief Justice Warren and Justices Black and Douglas dissenting. That the Thornhill doctrine still has some life, however, is indicated by Youngdahl v. Rainfair, Inc., 355 U.S. 131, 78 S. Ct. 206, 2 L. Ed. 2d 151 (1957), where the Court, though dealing with the federal pre-emption problem, indicated that where violence "was scattered in time and much of it was unconnected with the picketing," an injunction should be directed against the violence rather than the picketing. 355 U.S. at 139.

The unlawful-purpose rule of labor picketing was applied by the Court to picketing by a non-labor organization against an employer's discriminatory hiring policy in Hughes v. Superior Court of California, 339 U.S. 460, 70 S. Ct. 718, 94 L. Ed. 985 (1950). In that case the Progressive Citizens of America picketed a grocery store in support of its demands that, as white clerks quit or were transferred, the store hire Negroes until the proportion of Negro clerks to white clerks approximated the proportion of Negro to white customers. Mr. Justice Frankfurter, writing for the majority, found that California's public policy, as expressed by its courts in this case, condemned such conduct because it "would encourage discriminatory hiring to give constitutional protection to petitioners' efforts to subject the opportunity of getting a job to a quota system." 339 U.S. at 463. Upholding the injunction against the picketing the Court said: "[While] picketing is a mode of communication it is inseparably something more and different. . . . Publication in a newspaper, or by distribution of circulars, may convey the same information or make the same charge as do those patrolling a picket line. But the very purpose of a picket line is to exert influences, and it produces consequences, different from other modes of communication. The loyalties and responses evoked and enacted by picket lines are unlike those flowing from appeals by printed word." 339 U.S. at 464-465. Cf. New Negro Alliance v. Sanitary Grocery Co., 303 U.S. 552, 58 S. Ct. 703, 82 L. Ed. 1012 (1938) (picketing by a Negro organization against an employer to protest discriminatory employment policies is a labor dispute within the Norris-LaGuardia Act and hence the District Court of the District of Columbia was without jurisdiction to issue an injunction).

REFERENCES

1. For comment on the "entrapment" aspect of the Cox case see Notes, 79 Harv. L. Rev. 56, 152-154 (1965); 40 Tulane L. Rev. 185 (1965).

2. For a case similar to Hughes, enjoining picketing to compel hiring of Negroes in proportion to population, see Fair Share Organization v. Mitnick, 188 N.E.2d 840, 8 Race Rel. L. Rep. 165 (Ind. App. Div. 1963).

3. There is a voluminous literature on the constitutional aspects of picketing, mostly concerned with labor picketing. Material which discusses whether and when picketing should be considered as speech or coercion includes Cox, Strikes, Picketing and the Constitution, 4 Vand. L. Rev. 574 (1951); Jones, Picketing and Coercion: A Jurisprudence of Epithets, 39 Va. L. Rev. 1023 (1953); Gregory, Picketing and Coercion: A Defense, id. at 1053; Jones, Picketing and Coercion: A Reply, id. at 1063; Gregory, Picketing and Coercion: A Conclusion, id. at 1067; Jones, The Right to Picket — Twilight Zone of the Constitution, 102 U. Pa. L. Rev. 995 (1954); Jones, Free Speech: Pickets on the Grass, Alas! Amidst Confusion, A Consistent Principle, 29 So. Calif. L. Rev. 137 (1959); Picketing and the Communication of Ideas, 2 U.C.L.A.L. Rev.

212 (1955); Burstein, Picketing and Speech, 4 Labor Law J. 791 (1953); Forkosch, An Analysis and Re-evaluation of Picketing in Labor Relations, 26 Fordham L. Rev. 391 (1957); Drinker, Some Observations on the Four Freedoms of the First Amendment, ch. II (1957); Mueller, The Current Legal Status of Peaceful and Truthful Picketing, 48 A.B.A.J. 624 (1962).

On the history of the judicial treatment of picketing, see Tanenhaus, Picketing as a Tort: The Development of the Law of Picketing From 1880 to 1940, 14 U. Pitt. L. Rev. 170 (1953); Tanenhaus, Picketing as Free Speech: Early Stages in the Growth of the New Law of Picketing, 14 U. Pitt. L. Rev. 397 (1953); Tanenhaus, Picketing-Free Speech: The Growth of the New Law of Picketing From 1940 to 1952, 38 Cornell L.Q. 1 (1952).

4. For discussion of boycotts and similar conduct associated with picketing and other forms of group action, see Notes, The Common-Law and Constitutional Status of Anti-Discrimination Boycotts, 66 Yale L.J. 397 (1957); Group Action: Civil Rights and Freedom of Association, 54 Nw. U.L. Rev. 390, 399-404 (1959); Legal Responsibility for Extra-Legal Censure, 62 Colum. L. Rev. 475 (1962); Sibley, Direct Action and the Struggle for Integration, 16 Hastings L.J. 351 (1965). See also the materials on private group action in the obscenity area, noted in Chapter VII.

NOTES

1. Sit-in demonstrations or similar forms of "direct action" may come into conflict with community interests where they take place on property being used for government purposes or on private property. The legal issues in these cases have been formed primarily in terms of equal protection and the Court as a whole has not ruled on First Amendment problems. In two cases, however, individual justices addressed themselves to the question:

In Bell v. Maryland, 378 U.S. 226, 84 S. Ct. 1814, 12 L. Ed. 2d 822 (1964), involving a sit-in at Hooper's restaurant in Baltimore, Mr. Justice Black said:

"Petitioners, but not the Solicitor General, contend that their convictions for trespass deny them the right of freedom of expression guaranteed by the Constitution. . . . Their argument comes down to this: that since petitioners did not shout, obstruct Hooper's business (which the record refutes), make speeches, or display picket signs, handbills, or other means of communication, they had a perfect constitutional right to assemble and remain in the restaurant, over the owner's continuing objections, for the purpose of expressing themselves by language and 'demonstrations' bespeaking their hostility to Hooper's refusal to serve Negroes. This Court's prior cases do not support such a privilege growing out of the constitutional rights of speech and assembly. Unquestionably petitioners had a constitutional right to express these views wherever they had an unquestioned legal right to be. Cf. Marsh v. Alabama [326 U.S. 501]. But there is the rub in this case. The contention that petitioners had a constitutional right to enter or to stay on Hooper's premises against his will because, if there, they would have had a constitutional right to express their desire to have restaurant service over Hooper's protest, is a boot-strap argument. The right to freedom of expression is a right to express views — not a right to force other people to supply a platform or a pulpit. It is argued that this supposed constitutional right to invade other people's property would not mean that a man's home, his private club, or his church could be forcibly entered or used against his will — only his store or place of business which he has himself 'opened to the public' by selling goods or services for money. In the first place, that argument assumes that Hooper's restaurant *had* been opened to the public. But the whole quarrel of petitioners with Hooper was that instead of being open to all, the restaurant refused service to Negroes. Furthermore, legislative bodies with power to act could of course draw lines like this, but if the Constitution itself fixes its own lines, as is argued, legislative bodies are powerless to change them, and home-owners, churches, private clubs, and other property owners would have to await case-by-case determination by this Court before they knew who had a constitutional right to trespass on their property. And even if the supposed constitutional right is confined to places where goods and services are offered for sale, it must be realized that such a constitutional rule would apply to all businesses and professions alike. A statute can be drafted to create such exceptions as legislators think wise, but a constitutional rule could as well be applied to the smallest business as to the largest, to the most personal professional relationship as to the most impersonal business, to a family business conducted on a man's farm or in his home as to businesses carried on elsewhere.

"A great purpose of freedom of speech and press is to provide a forum for settlement of acrimonious disputes peaceably, without resort to intimidation, force, or violence. The experience of ages points to the inexorable fact that people are frequently stirred to violence when property which the law recognizes as theirs is forcibly invaded or occupied by others. Trespass laws are born of this experience. They have been, and doubtless still are, important features of any government dedicated, as this country is, to a rule of law. Whatever power it may allow the States or grant to the Congress to regulate the use of private property, the Constitution does not confer upon any group the right to substitute rule by force for rule by law. Force leads to violence, violence to mob conflicts, and these to rule by the strongest groups with control of the most deadly weapons. Our Constitution, noble work of wise men, was designed — all of it — to chart a quite different course: to 'establish Justice, insure domestic Tranquility . . . and secure the Blessings of Liberty to ourselves and our Posterity.' At times the rule of law seems too slow to some for the settlement of their grievances. But it is the plan our Nation has chosen to preserve both 'Liberty' and equality for all. On that plan we have put our trust and staked our future. This constitutional rule of law has served us well. Maryland's trespass law does not depart from it. Nor shall we." 378 U.S. at 344-346.

The First Amendment aspects of sit-in demonstrations on public property were also considered by some of the justices in Brown v. Louisiana, 383 U.S. 131, 86 S. Ct. 719, 15 L. Ed. 2d 637 (1966). That case involved a public library which operated on a segregated plan under which Negroes were not permitted to use the reading room. A group of Negroes went to the library, asking for a book, and then remained sitting or standing in the reading room. They were convicted of breach of the peace under the same statute that was involved in Cox v. Louisiana. The Supreme Court reversed. Mr. Justice Fortas, joined by Mr. Chief Justice Warren and Mr. Justice Douglas, took the position that there was no evidence to support the conviction of breach of the peace, and added:

"We are here dealing with an aspect of a basic constitutional right — the right under the First and Fourteenth Amendments guaranteeing freedom of speech and of assembly, and freedom to petition the Government for a redress of grievances.

The Constitution of the State of Louisiana reiterates these guaranties. See Art. I, §§3,5. As this Court has repeatedly stated,[6] these rights are not confined to verbal expression. They embrace appropriate types of action which certainly include the right in a peaceable and orderly manner to protest by silent and reproachful presence, in a place where the protestant has every right to be, the unconstitutional segregation of public facilities. Accordingly, even if the accused action were within the scope of the statutory instrument, we would be required to assess the constitutional impact of its application, and we would have to hold that the statute cannot constitutionally be applied to punish petitioners' actions in the circumstances of this case. See Edwards v. South Carolina, [372 U.S. 229] at 235. The statute was deliberately and purposefully applied solely to terminate the reasonable, orderly, and limited exercise of the right to protest the unconstitutional segregation of a public facility. Interference with this right, so exercised, by state action is intolerable under our Constitution. Wright v. Georgia, [373 U.S. 284] at 292." 383 U.S. at 141-142.

Mr. Justice Brennan concurred, on grounds that the statute was overbroad, and Mr. Justice White concurred, for the reason that the Negroes "were making only a normal and authorized use" of the library. 383 U.S. at 151.

Mr. Justice Black, with whom Justices Clark, Harlan, and Stewart agreed, dissented. On the First Amendment issue he said:

"The constitutional doctrine that actually prevails in this Court today for the first time in its history rests at least in great part on the Court's interpretation of the First Amendment as carried into the States by the Fourteenth. This is the First Amendment which, as I have said in the past, is to me the very heart of our free government without which liberty and equality cannot exist. But I have never thought and do not now think that the First Amendment can sustain the startling doctrine the prevailing opinion here creates. The First Amendment, I think, protects speech, writings, and expression of views in any manner in which they can be legitimately and validly communicated. But I have never believed that it gives any person or group of persons the constitutional right to go wherever they want, whenever they please, without regard to the rights of private or public property or to state law. Indeed a majority of this Court said as much in Cox v. Louisiana, 379 U.S. 559, 574. Though the First Amendment guarantees the right of assembly and the right of petition along with the rights of speech, press, and religion, it does not guarantee to any person the right to use someone else's property, even that owned by government and dedicated to other purposes, as a stage to express dissident ideas. The novel constitutional doctrine of the prevailing opinion nevertheless exalts the power of private nongovernmental groups to determine what use shall be made of governmental property over the power of the elected governmental officials of the States and the Nation. . . .

"The prevailing opinion laments the fact that the place where these events took place was 'a public library — a place dedicated to quiet, to knowledge, and to beauty.' I too lament this fact, and for this reason I am deeply troubled with the fear that powerful private groups throughout the Nation will read the Court's

[6] See, e.g., NAACP v. Button, 371 U.S. 415, 428-431; Garner v. Louisiana, [368 U.S. 157], at 201 (separate opinion of Mr. Justice Harlan); NAACP v. Alabama, 357 U.S. 449, 460-463; Stromberg v. California, 283 U.S. 359, 369. See Kalven, [The Negro and the First Amendment] 129-138.

action, as I do — that is, as granting them a license to invade the tranquillity and beauty of our libraries whenever they have quarrel with some state policy which may or may not exist. It is an unhappy circumstance in my judgment that the group, which more than any other has needed a government of equal laws and equal justice, is now encouraged to believe that the best way for it to advance its cause, which is a worthy one, is by taking the law into its own hands from place to place and from time to time. Governments like ours were formed to substitute the rule of law for the rule of force. Illustrations may be given where crowds have gathered together peaceably by reason of extraordinarily good discipline reinforced by vigilant officers. 'Demonstrations' have taken place without any manifestations of force at the time. But I say once more that the crowd moved by noble ideals today can become the mob ruled by hate and passion and greed and violence tomorrow. If we ever doubted that, we know it now. The peaceful songs of love can become as stirring and provocative as the Marseillaise did in the days when a noble revolution gave way to rule by successive mobs until chaos set in. The holding in this case today makes it more necessary than ever that we stop and look more closely at where we are going." 383 U.S. at 166-168.

See also Wright v. Georgia, 373 U.S. 284, 83 S. Ct. 1240, 10 L. Ed. 2d 349 (1963) (breach of peace conviction of Negroes for playing basketball in segregated park reversed).

2. Other courts have held, where equal protection and state action issues were not present, that sit-ins, lie-ins, and similar conduct on private or public premises was prohibitable. See Curtis v. Tozer, 374 S.W.2d 557 (Ct. App. Mo. 1964), habeas corpus denied sub nom. Ford v. Boeger, 236 F. Supp. 831 (E.D. Mo. 1964) (criminal contempt of court conviction upheld for violation of temporary order restraining members of CORE from barring entry and exit from a bank by sit-in and lie-in demonstrations); People v. Martin, 43 Misc. 2d 355, 251 N.Y.S.2d 66 (App. Term 1964), aff'd (3 judges dissenting), 15 N.Y.2d 933, 259 N.Y.S.2d 152, 207 N.E.2d 197 (1965), cert. den., 382 U.S. 828 (1965) (disorderly conduct conviction for sit-in at close of evening school board meeting held in Malverne Jr. High School, Long Island, by parents protesting school segregation). See also Ford v. State, 210 Tenn. 105 and 114, 355 S.W.2d 102, 356 S.W.2d 726 (1962), cert. den., 377 U.S. 994 (1964), habeas corpus denied, 236 F. Supp. 780 (W.D. Tenn. 1965) (conviction for disturbing a religious rally held in a public park where Negroes were admitted and told to take first available empty seats in the rear but then "scattered out" causing commotion and causing some participants to leave). Cf. Potomac Electric Power Co. v. Washington Chapter of CORE, 209 F. Supp. 559 and 210 F. Supp. 418 (D. D.C. 1962) (injunction granted against campaign to distribute stamps stating "We Believe in Merit Hiring" and asking customers to paste stamps on electric bills, which interfered with processing of bills through computing machines).

For discussion of the sit-in cases so far as equal protection issues are concerned, see Chapter XX.

3. The remaining major areas of potential conflict between freedom of expression through assembly, petition, and canvassing and other community interests involve controls designed to (1) assure that streets and playgrounds will be available for various purposes, such as transportation and recreation as well as speech,

and assure that such facilities are kept clean and otherwise in usable condition, and (2) assure that competing communicators do not drown each other out or seek to use the same space at the same time. These problems are largely solved through permit systems, dealt with in Section D, but certain aspects raise important issues which are considered below.

COX v. LOUISIANA
379 U.S. 536, 85 S. Ct. 453, 13 L. Ed. 2d 471 (1965)

[The first part of this case, giving the facts, is printed in Section B, supra, and the companion case, No. 49, is printed above.]

Mr. Justice Goldberg delivered the opinion of the Court. . . .

We now turn to the issue of the validity of appellant's conviction for violating the Louisiana statute, La. Rev. Stat. §14:100.1 (Cum. Supp. 1962), which provides:

"Obstructing Public Passages

"No person shall wilfully obstruct the free, convenient and normal use of any public sidewalk, street, highway, bridge, alley, road, or other passageway, or the entrance, corridor or passage of any public building, structure, watercraft or ferry, by impeding, hindering, stifling, retarding or restraining traffic or passage thereon or therein.

"Providing however nothing herein contained shall apply to a bona fide legitimate labor organization or to any of its legal activities such as picketing, lawful assembly or concerted activity in the interest of its members for the purpose of accomplishing or securing more favorable wage standards, hours of employment and working conditions."

Appellant was convicted under this statute, not for leading the march to the vicinity of the courthouse, which the Louisiana Supreme Court stated to have been "orderly," 244 La., at 1096, 156 So. 2d, at 451, but for leading the meeting on the sidewalk across the street from the courthouse. Id., at 1094, 1106-1107, 156 So. 2d, at 451, 455. In upholding appellant's conviction under this statute, the Louisiana Supreme Court thus construed the statute so as to apply to public assemblies which do not have as their specific purpose the obstruction of traffic. There is no doubt from the record in this case that this far sidewalk was obstructed, and thus, as so construed, appellant violated the statute.

Appellant, however, contends that as so construed and applied in this case, the statute is an unconstitutional infringement on freedom of speech and assembly. This contention on the facts here presented raises an issue with which this Court has dealt in many decisions, that is, the right of a State or municipality to regulate the use of city streets and other facilities to assure the safety and convenience of the people in their use and the concomitant right of the people of free speech and assembly. See Lovell v. Griffin, 303 U.S. 444; Hague v. CIO, 307 U.S. 496; Schneider v. State, 308 U.S. 147; Thornhill v. Alabama, 310 U.S. 88; Cantwell v. Connecticut, 310 U.S. 296; Cox v. New Hampshire, 312 U.S. 569; Largent v. Texas, 318 U.S. 418; Saia v. New York, 334 U.S. 558; Kovacs v. Cooper, 336 U.S. 77; Niemotko v. Maryland, 340 U.S. 268; Kunz v. New York, 340 U.S. 290; Poulos v. New Hampshire, 345 U.S. 395.

From these decisions certain clear principles emerge. The rights of free speech and assembly, while fundamental in our democratic society, still do not mean that everyone with opinions or beliefs to express may address a group at any public place and at any time. The constitutional guarantee of liberty implies the existence of an organized society maintaining public order, without which liberty itself would be lost in the excesses of anarchy. The control of travel on the streets is a clear example of governmental responsibility to insure this necessary order. A restriction in that relation, designed to promote the public convenience in the interest of all, and not susceptible to abuses of discriminatory application, cannot be disregarded by the attempted exercise of some civil right which, in other circumstances, would be entitled to protection. One would not be justified in ignoring the familiar red light because this was thought to be a means of social protest. Nor could one, contrary to traffic regulations, insist upon a street meeting in the middle of Times Square at the rush hour as a form of freedom of speech or assembly. Governmental authorities have the duty and responsibility to keep their streets open and available for movement. A group of demonstrators could not insist upon the right to cordon off a street, or entrance to a public or private building, and allow no one to pass who did not agree to listen to their exhortations. See Lovell v. Griffin, supra, at 451; Cox v. New Hampshire, supra, at 574; Schneider v. State, supra, at 160-161; Cantwell v. Connecticut, supra, at 306-307; Giboney v. Empire Storage & Ice Co., 336 U.S. 490; Poulos v. New Hampshire, supra, at 405-408; see also, Edwards v. South Carolina, supra, at 236.

We emphatically reject the notion urged by appellant that the First and Fourteenth Amendments afford the same kind of freedom to those who would communicate ideas by conduct such as patrolling, marching, and picketing on streets and highways, as these amendments afford to those who communicate ideas by pure speech. See the discussion and cases cited in No. 49 [379 U.S. at 563]. We reaffirm the statement of the Court in Giboney v. Empire Storage & Ice Co., supra, at 502, that "it has never been deemed an abridgment of freedom of speech or press to make a course of conduct illegal merely because the conduct was in part initiated, evidenced, or carried out by means of language, either spoken, written, or printed."

We have no occasion in this case to consider the constitutionality of the uniform, consistent, and nondiscriminatory application of a statute forbidding all access to streets and other public facilities for parades and meetings.[13] Although the statute here involved on its face precludes all street assemblies and parades,[14] it has not been so applied and enforced by the Baton Rouge authorities. City officials who testified for the State clearly indicated that certain meetings and parades are permitted in Baton Rouge, even though they have the effect of obstructing traffic, provided prior approval is obtained. This was confirmed in oral argument before this Court by counsel for the State. He stated that parades and meetings are permitted, based on "arrangements . . . made with officials." The statute itself provides no standards for the determination of local officials as to which assemblies to permit or which to prohibit. Nor are there any administrative regulations on this subject which have been called to our attention. From all the evidence before us it appears that the authorities in Baton Rouge permit or prohibit parades or street meetings in their completely uncontrolled discretion.

The situation is thus the same as if the statute itself expressly provided that there could only be peaceful parades or demonstrations in the unbridled discretion of the local officials. The pervasive restraint on freedom of discussion by the practice of the authorities under the statute is not any less effective than a statute expressly permitting such selective enforcement. A long line of cases in this Court makes it clear that a State or municipality cannot "require all who wish to disseminate ideas to present them first to police authorities for their consideration and approval, with a discretion in the police to say some ideas may, while others may not, be . . . disseminate[d]. . . ." Schneider v. State, supra, at 164. See Lovell v. Griffin, supra; Hague v. CIO, supra; Largent v. Texas, supra; Saia v. New York, supra; Niemotko v. Maryland, supra; Kunz v. New York, supra.

This Court has recognized that the lodging of such broad discretion in a public official allows him to determine which expressions of view will be permitted and which will not. This thus sanctions a device for the suppression of the communication of ideas and permits the official to act as a censor. See Saia v. New York, supra, at 562. Also inherent in such a system allowing parades or meetings only with the prior permission of an official is the obvious danger to the right of a person or group not to be denied equal protection of the laws. See Niemotko v. Maryland, supra, at 272, 284; cf. Yick Wo v.

---

[13] It has been argued that, in the exercise of its regulatory power over streets and other public facilities, a State or municipality could reserve the streets completely for traffic and other facilities for rest and relaxation of the citizenry. See Kovacs v. Cooper, supra, at 98 (opinion of Mr. Justice Jackson); Kunz v. New York, supra, at 298 (Mr. Justice Jackson, dissenting). The contrary, however, has been indicated, at least to the point that some open area must be preserved for outdoor assemblies. See Hague v. CIO, supra, at 515-516 (opinion of Mr. Justice Roberts); Kunz v. New York, supra, at 293; Niemotko v. Maryland, supra, at 283 (Mr. Justice Frankfurter, concurring). See generally, Poulos v. New Hampshire, supra, at 403; Niemotko v. Maryland, supra, at 272-273.

[14] With the express exception, of course, of labor picketing. This exception points up the fact that the statute reaches beyond mere traffic regulation to restrictions on expression.

Hopkins, 118 U.S. 356. It is clearly unconstitutional to enable a public official to determine which expressions of view will be permitted and which will not or to engage in invidious discrimination among persons or groups either by use of a statute providing a system of broad discretionary licensing power or, as in this case, the equivalent of such a system by selective enforcement of an extremely broad prohibitory statute.

It is, of course, undisputed that appropriate, limited discretion, under properly drawn statutes or ordinances, concerning the time, place, duration, or manner of use of the streets for public assemblies may be vested in administrative officials, provided that such limited discretion is "exercised with 'uniformity of method of treatment upon the facts of each application, free from improper or inappropriate considerations and from unfair discrimination' . . . [and with] a 'systematic, consistent and just order of treatment, with reference to the convenience of public use of the highways. . . .'" Cox v. New Hampshire, supra, at 576. See Poulos v. New Hampshire, supra.

But here it is clear that the practice in Baton Rouge allowing unfettered discretion in local officials in the regulation of the use of the streets for peaceful parades and meetings is an unwarranted abridgment of appellant's freedom of speech and assembly secured to him by the First Amendment, as applied to the States by the Fourteenth Amendment. It follows, therefore, that appellant's conviction for violating the statute as so applied and enforced must be reversed.

Mr. Justice Black, concurring [in No. 29]. . . .

The Louisiana law against obstructing the streets and sidewalks, while applied here so as to convict Negroes for assembling and picketing on streets and sidewalks for the purpose of publicly protesting racial discrimination, expressly provides that the statute shall not bar picketing and assembly by labor unions protesting unfair treatment of union members. I believe that the First and Fourteenth Amendments require that if the streets of a town are open to some views, they must be open to all. It is worth noting in passing that the objectives of labor unions and of the group led by Cox here may have much in common. Both frequently protest discrimination against their members in the matter of employment. Compare New Negro Alliance v. Sanitary Grocery Co., 303 U.S. 552, 561. This Louisiana law opens the streets for union assembly, picketing, and public advocacy, while denying that opportunity to groups protesting against racial discrimination. As I said above, I have no doubt about the general power of Louisiana to bar all picketing on its streets and highways. Standing, patrolling, or marching back and forth on streets is conduct, not speech, and as conduct can be regulated or prohibited. But by specifically permitting picketing for the publication of labor union views, Louisiana is attempting to pick and choose among the views it is willing to have discussed on its streets. It thus is trying to prescribe by law what matters of public interest people whom it allows to assemble on its streets may and may not discuss. This seems to me to be censorship in a most odious form, unconstitutional under the First and Fourteenth Amendments. And to deny this appellant and his group use of the streets because of their views against racial discrimination, while allowing other groups to use the streets to voice opinions on other subjects, also amounts, I think, to an invidious discrimination forbidden by the Equal Protection Clause of the Fourteenth Amendment. Moreover, as the Court points out, city officials despite this statute apparently have permitted favored groups other than labor unions to block the streets with their gatherings. For these reasons I concur in reversing the conviction based on this law.

[Mr. Justice Clark concurred with Mr. Justice Black.]

Mr. Justice White, with whom Mr. Justice Harlan joins, dissenting. . . .

Regretfully, I . . . dissent from the reversal of the conviction for obstruction of public passages. The Louisiana statute is not invalidated on its face but only in its application. But this remarkable emasculation of a prohibitory statute is based on only very vague evidence that other meetings and parades have been allowed by the authorities. The sole indication in the record from the state court that such has occurred was contained in the testimony of the Chief of Police who, in the process of pointing out that Cox and his group had not announced the fact or purpose of their meeting, said "most organizations that want to hold a parade or a meeting of any kind, they have no reluctance to evidence their desires at the start." There is no evidence in the record that other meetings of this magnitude had been allowed on the city streets, had been allowed in the vicinity of the courthouse or had been permitted completely to obstruct the sidewalk and to block access to abutting buildings. Indeed, the sheriff testified that "we have never had such a demonstration since I have been in law enforcement in this parish." He also testified that "any other organization" would have received the same treatment if it "had conducted such a demonstration in front of the Parish Courthouse," whether it had been "colored or white, Protestant, Catholic, Jewish, any kind of organization, if they had conducted this same type of demonstration. . . ." Similarly the trial judge noted that although Louisiana respects freedom of speech and the right to picket, Louisiana courts "have held that picketing is unlawful when it is mass picketing."

At the oral argument in response to Mr. Justice Goldberg's question as to whether parades and demonstrations are allowed in Baton Rouge, counsel said, "arrangements are usually made depending on the size of the demonstration, of course, arrangements are made with the officials and their cooperation is not only required it is needed where you have such a large crowd." In my view, however, all of this evidence together falls far short of justification for converting this prohibitory state statute into an open-ended licensing statute invalid under prior decisions of this Court as applied to this case. This is particularly true since the Court's approach is its own invention and has not been urged or litigated by the parties either in this Court or the courts below. Certainly the parties have had no opportunity to develop or to refute the factual basis underlying the Court's rationale.

Under the Court's broad, rather uncritical approach it would seem unavoidable that these same demonstrators could have met in the middle of any street during the rush hour or could have extended their meeting at any location hour after hour, day after day, without risking any action under this statute for interfering with the normal use of the streets and sidewalks. I doubt that this bizarre intrusion into local management of public streets is either required or justified by the prior cases in this Court.

Furthermore, even if the obstruction statute, because of prior permission granted to others, could not be applied in this case so as to prevent the demonstration, it does not necessarily follow that the federal license to use the streets is unlimited as to time and circumstance. Two thousand people took possession of the sidewalk in an entire city block. Building entrances were blocked and normal use of the sidewalk was impossible. If the crowd was entitled to obstruct in order to demonstrate as the Court holds, it is nevertheless unnecessary to hold that the demonstration and the obstruction could continue *ad infinitum*. Here the demonstration was permitted to proceed for the period of time that the demonstrators had requested. When they were asked to disband, Cox twice refused. If he could refuse at this point I think he could refuse at any later time as well. But in my view at some point the authorities were entitled to apply the statute and to clear the streets. That point was reached here. To reverse the conviction under these circumstances makes it only rhetoric to talk of local power to control the streets under a properly drawn ordinance.

NOTES

1. In Cameron v. Johnson, 381 U.S. 741, 85 S. Ct. 1751, 14 L. Ed. 2d 715 (1965), an action was brought under 42 U.S.C. §1983 to enjoin enforcement of the Mississippi anti-picketing statute on the ground that it was an unconstitutionally broad regulation of speech, and that it was being applied for the purpose of discouraging appellants' civil rights activities. The statute provided:

"It shall be unlawful for any person, singly or in concert with others, to engage in picketing or mass demonstrations in such a manner as to obstruct or interfere with free ingress or egress to and from any public premises, State property, country or municipal courthouses, city halls, office buildings, jails, or other public buildings or property owned by the State of Mississippi or any county or municipal government located therein or with the transaction of public business or administration of justice therein or thereon conducted or so as to obstruct or interfere with free use of public streets, sidewalks or other public ways adjacent or contiguous thereto."

A three-judge district court, without passing on the constitutional issues, dismissed the complaint on abstention grounds, Judge Rives dissenting. The Supreme Court, per curiam, vacated the judgment and remanded the case for consideration in the light of Dombrowski v. Pfister, 380 U.S. 479, 85 S. Ct. 1116, 14 L. Ed. 2d 22 (1965) (see Chapter III, Section C). Justices Black, Harlan, Stewart, and White dissented. In a long opinion, joined by Justices Harlan and Stewart, Mr. Justice Black found the statute valid on its face.

2. In Shuttlesworth v. City of Birmingham, 382 U.S. 87, 86 S. Ct. 211, 15 L. Ed. 2d 176 (1965), Rev. F. L. Shuttlesworth, a well-known civil rights leader, was charged with violation of two Birmingham, Alabama, ordinances. Section 1142 of the City Code provided: "It shall be unlawful for any person or any number of persons to so stand, loiter or walk upon any street or sidewalk in the city as to obstruct free passage over, on or along said street or sidewalk. It shall also be unlawful for any person to stand or loiter upon any street or sidewalk of the city after having been requested by any police officer to move on." The other ordinance, Section 1231, provided: "It shall be unlawful for any person to refuse or fail to comply with any lawful order, signal or direction of a police officer." The facts were described by Mr. Justice Stewart, writing for the Court, as follows:

"The evidence was in conflict, but the prosecution's version of the facts can be briefly summarized. On April 4, 1962, at about 10:30 A.M., Patrolman Byars of the Birmingham Police Department observed Shuttlesworth standing on a sidewalk with 10 or 12 companions outside a department store near the intersection of 2d Ave. and 19th St. in the City of Birmingham. After observing the group for a minute or so, Byars walked up and 'told them they would have to move on and clear the sidewalk and not obstruct it for the pedestrians.' After some, but not all, of the group began to disperse, Byars repeated this request twice. In response to the second request, Shuttlesworth said, 'You mean to say we can't stand here on the sidewalk?' After the third request he replied, 'Do you mean to tell me we can't stand here in front of this store?' By this time everybody in the group but Shuttlesworth had begun to walk away, and Patrolman Byars told him he was under arrest. Shuttlesworth then responded, 'Well, I will go into the store,' and walked into the entrance of the adjacent department store. Byars followed and took him into custody just inside the store's entrance." [3] 382 U.S. at 89-91.

Shuttlesworth was found guilty and sentenced to imprisonment for 180 days at hard labor and an additional 61 days at hard labor in default of a $100 fine and costs. The Supreme Court reversed. As to the conviction under Section 1142, the Court said: "Literally read, therefore, the second part of this ordinance says that a person can stand on a public sidewalk in Birmingham only at the whim of any police officer of that city. The constitutional vice of so broad a provision needs no demonstration." 382 U.S. at 90. It then pointed out that the Alabama Court of Appeals, in a case decided two years after Shuttlesworth's conviction, had given the statute a narrower construction, ruling that it "applies only when a person who stands, loiters, or walks on a street or sidewalk so as to obstruct free passage refuses to obey a request by an officer to move on. . . . As so construed, we cannot say

[3] "The record contains many references to a so-called 'selective buying campaign' in which Birmingham Negroes were engaged at that time. There was no showing, however, of any connection between this campaign and the presence of petitioner and his companions outside the department store on the morning of his arrest."

that the ordinance is unconstitutional, though it requires no great feat of imagination to envisage situations in which such an ordinance might be unconstitutionally applied." 382 U.S. at 91. The Court went on to hold that since the limiting construction was not available to the court at the time of Shuttlesworth's trial, and because "we are unable to say that the Alabama courts in this case did not judge the petitioner by an unconstitutional construction of the ordinance, the petitioner's conviction . . . cannot stand." 382 U.S. at 92.

As to Section 1231, the Court held that the provision was intended to apply to the regulation of vehicular traffic and there was no evidence under the doctrine of Thompson v. City of Louisville, 362 U.S. 199, 80 S. Ct. 624, 4 L. Ed. 2d 654 (1960), to support the conviction.

Mr. Justice Douglas concurred, on the ground that the Louisville doctrine applied to the conviction under Section 1142. Mr. Justice Fortas, also concurring, said that "on the facts here presented" any conviction "would violate basic constitutional guarantees" and that he "would make this clear now." 382 U.S. at 99.

3. Lower federal court decisions dealing with the obstruction problem include Whaley v. Cavanagh, 237 F. Supp. 900 (N.D. Cal. 1963), aff'd, 341 F.2d 295 (9th Cir. 1965), cert. den., 382 U.S. 872 (1965) (suit under 42 U.S.C. §1983 for deprivation of constitutional rights against police officer who ordered picketer with placard containing over 200 words to keep moving; judgment for defendant); United States v. Jones, 244 F. Supp. 181 (S.D. N. Y.1965) (disorderly conduct prosecution sustained for blocking entrances to courthouse by chain-in).

4. Materials concerned with allocation of facilities between several individuals or groups seeking to hold meetings, parades, or demonstrations are set forth in Section D, dealing with permit systems.

REFERENCES

For discussion of the problems, see Thompson, Police Controls over Citizen Use of the Public Streets, 49 J. Crim. L. 562 (1959); Note, The Enforcement of the Right of Access in Mass Picketing Situations, 113 U. Pa. L. Rev. 111 (1964) (dealing with labor picketing); Pollitt, Legal Problems in Southern Desegregation, The Chapel Hill Story, 43 N.C.L. Rev. 689, 745-754 (1965).

D. Permit Systems, Injunctions, and Administration

As noted previously, legal controls designed to reconcile freedom of assembly, petition, and canvassing with other social interests may take the form of regulations designed to prevent a conflict, or potential conflict, from ever developing. The most common device for this purpose is a permit or licensing system, under which the communication cannot take place until official approval has been granted. Court injunctions, although essentially negative in their impact, serve the same purpose. These forms of regulation, together with problems in the practical administration of controls, form the subject matter of this section.

Two major legal principles are particularly relevant. One is the doctrine against prior restraint which, broadly speaking, holds that the First Amendment is intended to prohibit advance censorship of expression. The other is the rule against vagueness, undue breadth of restriction, or unfettered discretion, which is a requirement of due process but has special application in areas involving First Amendment rights.

REFERENCES

The doctrine of prior restraint was first enunciated in Near v. Minnesota, 283 U.S. 697, 51 S. Ct. 625, 75 L. Ed. 1357 (1931), set forth in Chapter VII. For general discussion see Emerson, The Doctrine of Prior Restraint, 20 Law & Contemp. Prob. 648 (1955). On the rule against vagueness, see Amsterdam, The Void for Vagueness Doctrine, 109 U. Pa. L. Rev. 67 (1960). Other materials on vagueness are cited in Chapter III, Section C. The earlier Supreme Court decisions applying these doctrines are summarized in Mr. Justice Frankfurter's opinion in Niemotko v. Maryland, set out in Section C, and in Kunz v. New York, printed below. Discussion of these decisions and the general problems may be found in the materials collected at the end of Section A.

KUNZ v. NEW YORK
340 U.S. 290, 71 S. Ct. 312, 95 L. Ed. 280 (1951)

Mr. CHIEF JUSTICE VINSON delivered the opinion of the Court.

New York City has adopted an ordinance which makes it unlawful to hold public worship meetings on the streets without first obtaining a permit from the city police commissioner. Appellant, Carl Jacob Kunz, was convicted and fined $10 for violating this ordinance by holding a religious meeting without a permit. The conviction was affirmed by the Appellate Part of the Court of Special Sessions, and by the New York Court of Appeals, three judges dissenting, 300 N.Y. 273, 90 N.E.2d 455 (1950). The case is here on appeal, it having been urged that the ordinance is invalid under the Fourteenth Amendment.

Appellant is an ordained Baptist minister who speaks under the auspices of the "Outdoor Gospel Work," of which he is the director. He has been preaching for about six years, and states that it is his conviction and duty to "go out on the highways and byways and preach the word of God." In 1946, he applied for and received a permit under the ordinance in question, there being no question that appellant comes within the classes of persons entitled to receive permits under the ordinance. This permit, like all others, was good only for the calendar year in which issued. In November, 1946, his permit was revoked after a hearing by the police commissioner. The revocation was based on evidence that he had ridiculed and denounced other religious beliefs in his meetings.

Although the penalties of the ordinance apply to anyone who "ridicules and denounces other religious beliefs," the ordinance does not specify this as a ground for permit revocation. Indeed, there is no mention in the ordinance of any power of revocation. However, appellant did not seek judicial or administrative review of the revocation proceedings, and any question as to the propriety of the revocation is not before us in this case. In any event, the revocation affected appellant's rights to speak in 1946 only. Appellant applied for another permit in 1947, and again in 1948, but was notified each time that his application was "disapproved," with no reason for the disapproval being given. On September 11, 1948, appellant was arrested for speaking at Columbus Circle in New York City without a permit. It is from the conviction which resulted that this appeal has been taken.

Appellant's conviction was thus based upon his failure to possess a permit for 1948. We are here concerned only with the propriety of the action of the police commissioner in refusing to issue that permit. Disapproval of the 1948 permit application by the police commissioner was justified by the New York courts on the ground that a permit had previously been revoked "for good reasons." [3] It is noteworthy that there is no mention in the ordinance of reasons for which such a permit application can be refused. This interpretation allows the police commissioner, an administrative official, to exercise discretion in denying subsequent permit applications on the basis of his interpretation, at that time, of what is deemed to be conduct condemned by the ordinance. We have here, then, an ordinance which gives an administrative official discretionary power to control in advance the right of citizens to speak on religious matters on the streets of New York. As such, the ordinance is clearly invalid as a prior restraint on the exercise of First Amendment rights.

In considering the right of a municipality to control the use of public streets for the expression of religious views, we start with the words of Mr. Justice Roberts that "Wherever the title of streets and parks may rest, they have immemorially been held in trust for the use of the public and, time out of mind, have been used for purposes of assembly, communicating thoughts between citizens, and discussing public questions." Hague v. C.I.O., 307 U.S. 496, 515 (1939). Although this Court has recognized that a statute may be enacted which prevents serious interference with normal usage of streets and parks, Cox v. New Hampshire, 312 U.S. 569 (1941), we have consistently condemned licensing systems which vest in an administrative official discretion to grant or withhold a permit upon broad criteria unrelated to proper regulation of public places. In Cantwell v. Connecticut, 310 U.S. 296 (1940), this Court held invalid an ordinance which required a license for soliciting money for religious causes. Speaking for a unanimous Court, Mr. Justice Roberts said: "But to condition the solicitation of aid for the perpetuation of religious views or systems upon a license, the grant of which rests in the exercise of a determination by state authority as to what is a religious cause, is

---

[3] The New York Court of Appeals said: "The commissioner had no reason to assume, and no promise was made, that defendant wanted a new permit for any uses different from the disorderly ones he had been guilty of before." 300 N.Y. at 278, 90 N.E.2d at 457.

to lay a forbidden burden upon the exercise of liberty protected by the Constitution." 310 U.S. at 307. To the same effect are Lovell v. Griffin, 303 U.S. 444 (1938); Hague v. C.I.O., 307 U.S. 496 (1939); Largent v. Texas, 318 U.S. 418 (1943). In Saia v. New York, 334 U.S. 558 (1948), we reaffirmed the invalidity of such prior restraints upon the right to speak: "We hold that §3 of this ordinance is unconstitutional on its face, for it establishes a previous restraint on the right of free speech in violation of the First Amendment which is protected by the Fourteenth Amendment against State action. To use a loudspeaker or amplifier one has to get a permit from the Chief of Police. There are no standards prescribed for the exercise of his discretion." 334 U.S. at 559-560.

The court below has mistakenly derived support for its conclusion from the evidence produced at the trial that appellant's religious meetings had, in the past, caused some disorder. There are appropriate public remedies to protect the peace and order of the community if appellant's speeches should result in disorder or violence. "In the present case, we have no occasion to inquire as to the permissible scope of subsequent punishment." Near v. Minnesota, 283 U.S. 697, 715 (1931). We do not express any opinion on the propriety of punitive remedies which the New York authorities may utilize. We are here concerned with suppression — not punishment. It is sufficient to say that New York cannot vest restraining control over the right to speak on religious subjects in an administrative official where there are no appropriate standards to guide his action.

Reversed.

Mr. Justice Black concurs in the result.

[Mr. Justice Frankfurter concurred in this case and the Niemotko case, infra, in a single opinion, reprinted in part supra.]

Mr. Justice Jackson, dissenting.

Essential freedoms are today threatened from without and within. It may become difficult to preserve here what a large part of the world has lost — the right to speak, even temperately, on matters vital to spirit and body. In such a setting, to blanket hateful and hate-stirring attacks on races and faiths under the protections for freedom of speech may be a noble innovation. On the other hand, it may be a quixotic tilt at windmills which belittles great principles of liberty. Only time can tell. But I incline to the latter view and cannot assent to the decision.

I

. . . At these meetings, Kunz preached, among many other things of like tenor, that "The Catholic Church makes merchandise out of souls," that Catholicism is "a religion of the devil," and that the Pope is "the anti-Christ."

The Jews he denounced as "Christ-killers," and he said of them, "All the garbage that didn't believe in Christ should have been burnt in the incinerators. It's a shame they all weren't."

These utterances, as one might expect, stirred strife and threatened violence. Testifying in his own behalf, Kunz stated that he "became acquainted with" one of the complaining witnesses, whom he thought to be a Jew, "when he happened to sock one of my Christian boys in the puss." Kunz himself complained to the authorities, charging a woman interrupter with disorderly conduct. He also testified that when an officer is not present at his meetings "I have trouble then," but "with an officer, no trouble."

The contention which Kunz brings here and which this Court sustains is that such speeches on the streets are within his constitutional freedom and therefore New York City has no power to require a permit. He does not deny that this has been and will continue to be his line of talk. He does not claim that he should have been granted a permit; he attacks the whole system of control of street meetings and says the Constitution gives him permission to speak and he needs none from the City. . . .

This Court today initiates the doctrine that language such as this, in the environment of the street meeting, is immune from prior municipal control. We would have a very different question if New York had presumed to say that Kunz could not speak his piece in his own pulpit or hall. But it has undertaken to restrain him only if he chooses to speak at street meetings. There is a world of difference. The street preacher takes advantage of people's presence on the streets to impose his message upon what, in a sense, is a captive audience. A meeting on private property is made up of an audience that has volunteered to listen. The question, therefore, is not whether New York could, if it tried, silence Kunz, but whether it must place its streets at his service to hurl insults at the passer-by. . . .

[Mr. Justice Jackson then discusses Chaplinsky v. New Hampshire, 315 U.S. 568, noted in Section A.]

There held to be "insulting or 'fighting' words" were calling one a "God damned racketeer" and a "damned Fascist." Equally inciting and more clearly "fighting words," when thrown at Catholics and Jews who are rightfully on the streets of New York, are statements that "The Pope is the anti-Christ" and the Jews are "Christ-killers." These terse epithets come down to our generation weighted with hatreds accumulated through centuries of bloodshed. They are recognized words of art in the profession of defamation. They are not the kind of insult that men bandy and laugh off when the spirits are high and the flagons are low. They are not in that class of epithets whose literal sting will be drawn if the speaker smiles when he uses them. They are always, and in every context, insults which do not spring from reason and can be answered by none. Their historical associations with violence are well understood, both by those who hurl and those who are struck by these missiles. Jews, many of whose families perished in extermination furnaces of Dachau and Auschwitz, are more than tolerant if they pass off lightly the suggestion that unbelievers in Christ should all have been burned. Of course, people might pass this speaker by as a mental case, and so they might file out of a theatre in good order at the cry of "fire." But in both cases there is genuine likelihood that someone will get hurt.

This Court's prior decisions, as well as its decisions today, will be searched in vain for clear standards by which it does, or lower courts should, distinguish legitimate speaking from that acknowledged to be outside of constitutional protection. One reason for this absence is that this Court has had little experience in deciding controversies over city control of street meetings. . . .

What evidences that a street speech is so provocative, insulting or inciting as to be outside of constitutional immunity from community interference? Is it determined by the actual reaction of the hearers? Or is it a judicial appraisal of the inherent quality of the language used? Or both? . . .

It is peculiar that today's opinion makes no reference to the "clear and present danger" test which for years has played some part in free-speech cases. . . .

A hostile reception of his subject certainly does not alone destroy one's right to speak. A temperate and reasoned criticism of Roman Catholicism or Judaism might, and probably would, cause some resentment and protest. But in a free society all sects and factions, as the price of their own freedom to preach their views, must suffer that freedom in others. Tolerance of unwelcome, unorthodox ideas or information is a constitutionally protected policy not to be defeated by persons who would break up meetings they do not relish.

But emergencies may arise on streets which would become catastrophes if there was not immediate police action. The crowd which should be tolerant may be prejudiced and angry or malicious. If the situation threatens to get out of hand for the force present, I think the police may require the speaker, even if within his rights, to yield his right temporarily to the greater interest of peace. Of course, the threat must be judged in good faith to be real, immediate and serious. But silencing a speaker by authorities as a measure of mob control is like dynamiting a house to stop the spread of a conflagration. It may be justified by the overwhelming community interest that flames not be fed as compared with the little interest to be served by continuing to feed them. But this kind of disorder does not abridge the right to speak except for the emergency and, since the speaker was within his constitutional right to speak, it could not be grounds for revoking or refusing him a permit or convicting him of any offense because of his utterance. If he resisted an officer's reasonable demand to cease, he might incur penalties.

And so the matter eventually comes down to the question whether the "words used are used in such circumstances and are of such a nature" that we can say a reasonable man would anticipate the evil result. In this case the Court does not justify, excuse, or deny the inciting and provocative character of the language, and it does not, and on this record could not, deny that when Kunz speaks he poses a "clear and present" danger to peace and order. Why, then, does New York have to put up with it? . . .

The question remains whether the Constitution prohibits a city from control of its streets by a permit system which takes into account dangers to public peace and order. I am persuaded that it does not do so, provided, of course, that the city does not so discriminate as to deny equal protection of the law or undertake a censorship of utterances that are not so defamatory, insulting, inciting, or provocative as to be reasonably likely to cause disorder and violence.

The Court does not hold that New York has abused the permit system by discrimination or actual censorship, nor does it deny the abuses on Kunz's part. But neither, says the Court, matters, holding that any prior restraint is bad, regardless of how fairly administered or what abuses it seeks to prevent.

It strikes rather blindly at permit systems which indirectly may affect First Amendment freedoms. Cities throughout the country have adopted permit requirements to control private activities on public streets and for other purposes. The universality of this type of regulation demonstrates a need and indicates widespread opinion in the profession that it is not necessarily incompatible with our constitutional freedoms. Is everybody out of step but this Court?

In the Chaplinsky case, *prevention* as well as *punishment* of "limited classes of speech . . . have never been thought to raise *any* Constitutional problem." (Emphasis supplied.) Mr. Justice Holmes pointed out in the Schenck case that the Constitution would not protect one from an injunction against uttering words that lead to riot. In Cox v. New Hampshire, 312 U.S. 569, 577-578, Chief Justice Hughes, for a unanimous Court, distinguished the requirement of a license for a parade or procession from other cases now relied on by this Court. He found requirement of a permit there constitutional and observed that such authority "has never been regarded as inconsistent with civil liberties but rather as one of the means of safeguarding the good order upon which they ultimately depend." Id., at 574. The concept of civil liberty without order is the contribution of later-day jurists.

The Court, as authority for stripping New York City of control of street meetings, resurrects Saia v. New York, supra, which I, like some who now rely on it, had supposed was given decent burial by Kovacs v. Cooper, supra. Must New York, if it is to avoid chaos in its streets, resort to the sweeping prohibitions sanctioned in Kovacs, instead of the milder restraints of this permit system? Compelling a choice between allowing all meetings or no meetings is a dubious service to civil liberties.

Of course, as to the press, there are the best of reasons against any licensing or prior restraint. Decisions such as Near v. Minnesota, supra, hold any licensing or prior restraint of the press unconstitutional, and I heartily agree. But precedents from that field cannot reasonably be transposed to the street-meeting field. The impact of publishing on public order has no similarity with that of a street meeting. Publishing does not make private use of public property. It reaches only those who choose to read, and, in that way, is analogous to a meeting held in a hall where those who come do so by choice. Written words are less apt to incite or provoke to mass action than spoken words, speech being the primitive and direct communication with the emotions. Few are the riots caused by publication alone, few are the mobs that have not had their immediate origin in harangue. The vulnerability of various forms of communication to community control must be proportioned to their impact upon other community interests.

It is suggested that a permit for a street meeting could be required if the ordinance would prescribe precise standards for its grant or denial. . . .

Of course, standards for administrative action are always desirable, and the more exact the better. But I do not see how this Court can condemn municipal ordinances for not setting forth comprehensive First Amendment standards. This Court never has announced what those standards must be, it does not now say what they are, and it is not clear that any majority could agree on them. In no field are there more numerous individual opinions among the Justices. The Court as an institution not infrequently disagrees with its former self or relies on distinctions that are not very substantial. . . . It seems hypercritical to strike down local laws on their faces for want of standards when we have no standard. And I do not find it required by existing authority. I think that where speech is outside of constitutional immunity the local community or the State is left a large measure of discretion as to the means for dealing with it. . . .

If the Court is deciding that the permit system for street meetings is so unreasonable as to deny due process of law, it would seem appropriate to point out respects in which it is unreasonable. This I am unable to learn, from this or any former decision. The Court holds, however, that Kunz must not be required to get permission, the City must sit by until some incident, perhaps a sanguinary one, occurs and then there are unspecified "appropriate public remedies." We may assume reference is to the procedure of the Feiner case which, with one-third of the Court dissenting, is upheld. This invites comparison of the merits of the two methods both as to impact on civil liberties and as to achieving the ends of public order. . . .

Turning then to the permit system as applied by the Court of Appeals, whose construction binds us, we find that issuance the first time is required. Denial is warranted only in such unusual cases as where an applicant has had a permit which has been revoked for cause and he asserts the right to continue the conduct which was cause for revocation. If anything less than a reasonable certainty of disorder was shown, denial of a permit would be improper. The procedure by which that decision is reached commends itself to the orderly mind — complaints are filed, witnesses are heard, opportunity to cross-examine is given, and decision is reached by what we must assume to be an impartial and reasonable administrative officer, and, if he denies the permit, the applicant may carry his cause to the courts. He may thus have a civil test of his rights without the personal humiliation of being arrested as presenting a menace to public order. It seems to me that this procedure better protects freedom of speech than to let everyone speak without leave, but subject to surveillance and to being ordered to stop in the discretion of the police.

It is obvious that a permit is a source of security and protection for the civil liberties of the great number who are entitled to receive them. It informs the police of the time and place one intends to speak, which allows necessary steps to insure him a place to speak where overzealous police officers will not order everyone who stops to listen to move on, and to have officers present to insure an orderly meeting. Moreover, disorder is less likely, for the speaker knows that if he provokes disorder his permit may be revoked, and the objector may be told that he has a remedy by filing a complaint and does not need to take the law in his own hands. Kunz was not arrested in 1946,when his speeches caused serious objections, nor was he set upon by the crowd. Instead, they did the orderly thing and made complaints which resulted in the revocation of his permit. This is the method that the Court frustrates today.

Of course, emergencies may arise either with or without the permit system. A speaker with a permit may go beyond bounds and incite violence, or a mob may undertake to break up an authorized and properly conducted meeting. In either case, the policeman on the spot must make the judgment as to what measures will most likely avoid violent disorders. But these emergencies seem less likely to occur with the permit system than if every man and his adversary take the law in their own hands.

The law of New York does not segregate, according to their diverse nationalities, races, religions, or political associations, the vast hordes of people living in its narrow confines. Every individual in this frightening aggregation is legally free to live, to labor, to travel, when and where he chooses. In streets and public places, all races and nationalities and all sorts and conditions of men walk, linger and mingle. Is it not reasonable that the City protect the dignity of these persons against fanatics who take possession of its streets to hurl into its crowds defamatory epithets that hurt like rocks?

If any two subjects are intrinsically incendiary and divisive, they are race and religion. Racial fears and hatreds have been at the root of the most terrible riots that have disgraced American civilization. They are ugly possibilities that overhang every great American city. The "consecrated hatreds of sect" account for more than a few of the world's bloody disorders. These are the explosives which the Court says Kunz may play with in the public streets, and the community must not only tolerate but aid him. I find no such doctrine in the Constitution.

NOTES

1. A companion case, Niemotko v. Maryland, 340 U.S. 268, 71 S. Ct. 325, 95 L. Ed. 267 (1951), involved a conviction of two members of Jehovah's Witnesses for holding a meeting in a public park in Havre de Grace without a permit. Although there was no ordinance prohibiting or regulating the use of the park it had been the custom for organizations and individuals desiring to use it for meetings and celebrations of various kinds to obtain a permit from the Park Commissioner. The Jehovah's Witnesses applied to the Park Commissioner for a permit but permission was refused. An appeal was taken to the City Council but it also denied the request. On the next Sunday the Jehovah's Witnesses commenced to hold the meeting anyway but were arrested. "There was no evidence of disorder, threats of violence or riot. . . . The conclusion is inescapable that the use of the park was denied because of the City Council's dislike for or disagreement with the Witnesses or their views." 340 U.S. at 271-272. The Supreme Court reversed, Mr. Chief Justice Vinson saying: "No standards appear anywhere; no narrowly drawn limitations; no circumscribing of this absolute power; no substantial interest of the community to be served. . . . It thus becomes apparent that the lack of standards in the license-issuing 'practice' renders that 'practice' a prior restraint in contravention of the Fourteenth Amendment, and that the completely arbitrary and discriminatory refusal to grant the permit was a denial of equal protection." 340 U.S. at 272-273. Justices Black and Frankfurter concurred in the result.

2. The Kunz and Niemotko cases were followed in Staub v. City of Baxley, 355 U.S. 313, 78 S. Ct. 277, 2 L. Ed. 2d 302 (1958). Here a city ordinance required a permit before soliciting membership in an organization requiring dues. "In passing upon such application [for the permit] the Mayor and Council shall consider the character of the applicant, the nature of the business of the organization for which members are desired to be solicited, and its effects upon the general welfare of citizens of the City of Baxley." 355 U.S. at 315. An organizer for the International Ladies Garment Workers Union, without applying for a permit, began to organize factory workers in Baxley and was arrested. The Supreme Court set aside her conviction: "It is undeniable that the ordinance authorized the Mayor and Council of the City of Baxley to grant 'or refuse to grant' the required permit in their uncontrolled discretion. It thus makes enjoyment of speech contingent upon the will of the Mayor and Council of the City. . . . For these reasons, the ordinance, on its face, imposes an unconstitutional prior restraint upon the enjoyment of First Amendment freedoms. . . ." 355 U.S. at 325. Justices Frankfurter and Clark dissented on procedural grounds. See, on the regulation of union organizers, Note, Validity of Statutes and Ordinances Requiring the Licensing of Union Organizers, 70 Harv. L. Rev. 1271 (1957).

3. The state cases have normally followed the Kunz and Niemotko decisions. See, e.g., American Cancer Society v. City of Dayton, 160 Ohio St. 114, 114 N.E.2d 219 (1953) (an ordinance charging the licensing authority to grant permits, where it finds that "the cause for which the solicitation is made is in fact charitable, educational, civic, patriotic, religious, or philanthropic" and "is not incompatible with the public welfare," held lacking in adequate standards), noted in 15 Ohio St. L.J. 216 (1954); 5 W. Res. L. Rev. 212 (1954); Commonwealth v. Jacobs, 333

Mass. 204, 129 N.E.2d 620 (1955) (holding too vague an ordinance requiring discretionary license to "publicly address the people on or passing over any public street or ground in the city").

One of the major state cases grew out of the refusal of the New York City Commissioner of Parks to grant a permit to George Lincoln Rockwell, self-styled American Nazi, to make a political speech in Union Square in 1960. The New York Supreme Court upheld the Commissioner, saying: "Petitioner Rockwell, in words recorded and concededly accurate, as well as in signed pamphlets circulated freely by him and his followers, has accused more than two million New York City residents of Jewish faith and another half-million or more Negro and Puerto Rican residents of this city of being traitors. He has complimented Adolph Hitler as a great Christian crusader and openly advocates Hitlerian actions in this country. . . . This court cannot agree that the constitutional guarantee of free speech encompasses such an invitation to public disorder, violence and even incitement to murder." Rockwell v. Morris, 26 Misc. 2d 229, 208 N.Y.S.2d 154 (Sup. Ct., N.Y. Co. 1960). The Appellate Division reversed. 12 App. Div. 2d 272, 211 N.Y.S.2d 25 (App. Div., 1st Dept. 1960). Justice Breitel, in a long opinion reviewing the cases, concluded: ". . . there is no power in government under our Constitution to exercise prior restraint of the expression of views, unless it is demonstrable on a record that such expression will immediately and irreparably create injury to the public weal — not that such expression, without itself being unlawful, will incite criminal acts in others." 12 App. Div. 2d at 277-278, 211 N.Y.S.2d at 32. Justice Eager, also after a long review of the cases, dissented. The Court of Appeals affirmed the Appellate Division, 9 N.Y.2d 791, 215 N.Y.S.2d 502, 175 N.E.2d 162 (1961); 10 N.Y.2d 721, 219 N.Y.S.2d 268, 176 N.E.2d 836 (1961); 10 N.Y.2d 749, 219 N.Y.S.2d 605, 177 N.E.2d 48 (1961), and the United States Supreme Court denied certiorari. 368 U.S. 913 (1961). For an account of the matter, see McReynolds, Hitler in New York, The Progressive, Dec. 1960, p. 24. Cf. Coughlin v. Chicago Park District, 364 Ill. 90, 4 N.E.2d 1 (1936).

4. Issues of prior restraint also arise in situations where an injunction is sought to prevent the holding of a meeting, demonstration, or other form of communication in public. In recent years these questions have been presented primarily in the civil rights area:

In connection with the desegregation of the public schools under a decree of the federal district court in Clinton, Tennessee, in 1956, school officials filed a petition in the district court alleging that one John Kasper had come to Clinton and was attempting to prevent the execution of the court's order by forming picket lines, causing large crowds to assemble at the school, and intimidating Negro children and their parents. On the basis of this petition Judge Taylor issued a temporary restraining order, ex parte, enjoining Kasper, other named persons, and "all other persons who are acting or may act in concert with them" from "further hindering, obstructing, or any wise interfering with the carrying out of the aforesaid order of this Court, or from picketing Clinton High School, either by words or acts or otherwise." 1 Race Rel. L. Rep. at 876.

After being served with a copy of this restraining order Kasper announced his intention before a crowd of 1000 to 1500 people of continuing his activities. Thereupon he was summoned to court, found guilty of criminal contempt by the court without a jury, and sentenced to a year in jail. 1 Race Rel. Rep. 872, 1045. On appeal Kasper contended, inter alia, that the contempt conviction violated the First Amendment. Rejecting the defense, the Court of Appeals stated:

"The First Amendment does not confer the right to persuade others to violate the law. . . . The speech here enjoined was clearly calculated to cause a violation of law and speech of that character is not within the protection of the First Amendment . . . Appellant had urged the crowd to disregard the orders of the court and to continue pressure upon the school officials until Negroes were eliminated from the Clinton High School. This clearly was not a mere exposition of ideas. It was advocacy of immediate action to accomplish an illegal result, sought to be avoided by the restraining order. The clear and present danger test, as applied by Judge Learned Hand, and adopted by the Supreme Court in the Dennis case, is here met by the mob violence that followed the urgings of the appellant. Danger that calls for the presence of the State Patrol and the National Guard, with the use of bayonets and tear gas, is, we think, within the narrowest limits of the concept and cries aloud for such court action as was here taken." Kasper v. Brittain, 245 F.2d 92, 95-96 (6th Cir. 1957), cert. den., 355 U.S. 834 (1957). See discussion in Stewart, Public Speech and Public Order in Britain and the United States, 13 Vand. L. Rev. 625, 629-630 (1960).

In Congress of Racial Equality v. Burt, 318 F.2d 95 (5th Cir .1963), cert. den., 375 U.S. 829 (1963), the Mayor of McComb, Mississippi, and owners of a restaurant in a bus station brought suit to enjoin CORE from sponsoring, encouraging, or financing persons to utilize the terminal facilities in that city "for the purpose of fomenting violence or provoking breaches of the peace . . . or for the purpose of testing the tempers and reactions of the local citizens. . . ." The trial court granted a preliminary injunction. The Court of Appeals found that "the record is completely bare of any evidence of an intent by CORE to provoke breaches of the peace, to incite violence, to disturb the domestic tranquility for CORE's own financial gain, to bring violence upon themselves, or to taunt and tantalize the community." 318 F.2d at 100. Relying upon Edwards v. South Carolina, set forth in Section B, and the Kunz case the court, with Judge Gewin dissenting, reversed and set aside the injunction:

"The posture of this case in particular is even more favorable to the defendants than was the Edwards case to the defendants therein, in that an injunction is involved here which prohibits the exercise of constitutionally guaranteed rights. It is a prior restraint. As the Court said in Kunz v. New York, 340 U.S. 290, 295, 71 S. Ct. 312, 315, 95 L. Ed. 280, 'We are here concerned with suppression — not punishment,' and so are we here in this case. Although the protection against previous restraints on the liberties guaranteed by the First Amendment is not unlimited, it takes on an even more guarded protection than punishment after the exercise thereof. . . . We find that the injunction below is an unconstitutional abridgement of the First Amendment rights, as protected by the Fourteenth Amendment, as a prior restraint on the freedom of speech." 318 F.2d at 102.

Injunctions against civil rights demonstrators were also set aside or denied in CORE v. Clemmons, 323 F.2d 54 (5th Cir. 1963) (on ground plaintiffs had failed to show a federal cause of action, without passing on constitutional issues); Kelly v. Page, 335 F.2d 114 (5th Cir. 1964) (Albany, Ga.; see Section B); Florence v. Myers, 9 Race Rel. L. Rep. 144 (M.D. Fla. 1964) (Ocala, Fla.); Barnum v. Chambliss, 247 F. Supp. 794 (M.D. Ga. 1965) (Americus, Ga.). But cf. Griffin v. Congress of Racial Equality, 221 F. Supp. 899 (E.D. La. 1963) (Plaquemine, La.).

In Nichols v. Philadelphia Chapter of CORE, 9 Race Rel. L. Rep. 326 (Ct. C. P. Pa. 1964), the court enjoined the Murray Club, Purel Club, Liberty Clowns Club, Philip J. Hammond Club, and "all persons, whether affiliated or not with any group, from marching in [the Philadelphia annual] Mummers' Parade in 'black-face.' " It also enjoined CORE and "all other persons connected in any way therewith, from attempting through violence, coercion or any other pressure from interfering with the conduct of said Mummers' Parade."

See, generally, Note, Prior Restraint in Racial Picketing, 17 U. Fla. L. Rev. 453 (1964).

ADMINISTRATION OF PERMIT SYSTEMS

Where a permit system is unconstitutional on its face, and a speaker is denied a permit, the speaker may nevertheless proceed with the speech and raise the constitutional issues in any subsequent prosecution for speaking without a permit. See the Kunz and Niemotko cases. Indeed, under Staub v. City of Baxley, he does not even have to apply for a permit. But if the permit system is not invalid on its face, and a permit is denied, critical questions arise as to whether the person seeking to speak must first exhaust his administrative or other remedies, or whether he may proceed with the speech and still raise the invalidity of the permit denial in a subsequent prosecution. Where the initial restraint is imposed by court injunction, violation of which constitutes contempt, special problems arise. These issues have never been fully resolved by the Supreme Court.

In Poulos v. New Hampshire, 345 U.S. 395, 73 S. Ct. 760, 97 L. Ed. 1105 (1953), Jehovah's Witnesses had been denied a permit to conduct religious meetings in a park as required by an ordinance providing that ". . . no open air public meeting shall be permitted unless a license therefor shall first be obtained from the City Council." 345 U.S. at 397. Defendants held the meeting and were convicted for violating the ordinance. New Hampshire courts held that the ordinance was valid on its face, though arbitrarily applied in this instance. However, the proper remedy was by way of certiorari to review the unlawful denial of a permit, not by holding public religious services in the park without a license and then defending on the ground of the arbitrary refusal. State v. Poulos, 97 N.H. 352, 88 A.2d 860 (1952). In upholding the conviction Mr. Justice Reed relied in part on the New Hampshire court's interpretation of the ordinance in another case, State v. Cox, 91 N.H. 137, 143, 16 A.2d 508, 513 (1940), which was as follows: "The discretion thus vested in the authority . . . is limited in its exercise by the bounds of reason, in uniformity of method of treatment upon the facts of each application, free from improper or inappropriate considerations and from unfair discrimination. A systematic, consistent and just order of treatment, with reference to the convenience of public use of the highways, is the statutory mandate." Mr. Justice Reed agreed that the ordinance was valid on its face: "By its construction of

the ordinance the state left to the licensing officials no discretion as to granting permits, no power to discriminate, no control over speech." 345 U.S. at
404. Addressing himself to the question of whether the arbitrary refusal of a
permit must be regarded by the state as a proper defense in a criminal prosecution, Mr. Justice Reed went on to say: ". . . to allow applicants to proceed
without the required permits to run businesses, erect structures, purchase fire-
arms, transport or store explosives or inflammatory products, hold public
meetings without prior safety arrangements or take other unauthorized action is apt to cause breaches of the peace or create public dangers. The valid
requirements of license are for the good of the applicants and the public. It
would be unreal to say that such official failures to act in accordance with state
law, redressable by state judicial procedures, are state acts violative of the . . .
Constitution. . . ." 345 U.S. at 409.

Mr. Justice Reed then distinguished Cantwell v. Connecticut and Thomas
v. Collins as well as Royall v. Virginia, 116 U.S. 572, as involving invalid state
statutes: "In the Royall case, the statute requiring payment of the license fee
in money was unconstitutional. In the Cantwell case, the statute had not been
construed by the state court 'to impose a mere ministerial duty on the secretary of the welfare council.' The right to solicit depended on his decision as to
a 'religious cause.' . . . Therefore we held that a statute authorizing this previous restraint was unconstitutional even though an error might be corrected
after trial. In the Thomas case, the section of the Texas act was held prohibitory of labor speeches anywhere on private or public property without registration. This made §5 unconstitutional. The statutes were as though they did
not exist. Therefore there were no offenses in violation of a valid law. In the
present prosecution there was a valid ordinance. . . . The state had authority
to determine, in the public interest, the reasonable method for correction of
the error, that is, by certiorari. . . ." 345 U.S. at 413-414.

In his dissent Mr. Justice Douglas stated in part: "An unconstitutional
statute is not necessarily a nullity; it may have intermediate consequences
binding upon people. . . . But when a legislature undertakes to proscribe the
exercise of a citizen's constitutional right to free speech, it acts lawlessly; and
the citizen can take matters in his own hands and proceed on the basis that
such a law is no law at all. . . . The reason is the preferred position granted
freedom of speech, freedom of press, freedom of assembly, and freedom of
religion by the First Amendment. . . . The case is therefore quite different
from a legislative program in the field of business, labor, housing, and the
like where regulation is permissible and the claim of unconstitutionality usually can be determined only by the manner or degree of application of the
statute to an aggrieved person. . . . If the citizen can flout the legislature
when it undertakes to tamper with his First Amendment rights, I fail to see
why he may not flout the official or agency who administers a licensing law
designed to regulate the exercise of the right of speech. Defiance of a statute is
hardly less harmful to an orderly society than defiance of an administrative

order. . . . Of course, a state could deny the use of a park to one religious group if a prior application had been granted to another group and the meetings would conflict. But there is no suggestion by New Hampshire that its system of regulation vests the licensing authority with only that limited power. The gloss which the New Hampshire court has placed on the statute grants a power reasonably to regulate free speech. That unfortunately is a doctrine that has been slowly creeping into our constitutional law. It has no place there. It is a doctrine dangerous to liberty and destructive of the great rights guaranteed by the First Amendment.

"So, one answer to the Court's holding that appellant should have gone into court to compel the issuance of a license is that the licensing power was discretionary not ministerial and that a discretionary power to license free speech is unconstitutional.

"There is another answer which is found in Cantwell v. Connecticut. . . . In that case it was argued that a licensing power in a state statute be construed so as to limit the power of the licensing authority to ministerial acts. We rejected that offer on two grounds. In the first place, the statute had not been so narrowly construed by the state court. In the second place, the availability of judicial relief would not *in any event* save the statute. . . . Those who wrote the First Amendment conceived of the right to free speech as wholly independent of the prior restraint of anyone. The judiciary was not granted a privilege of restraint withheld from other officials. For history proved that judges too were sometimes tyrants." 345 U.S. at 422-426.

Mr. Justice Black's dissent was on the ground that the "First Amendment . . . prohibits a state from convicting a man of crime whose only offense is that he makes an orderly religious appeal after he has been illegally, 'arbitrarily and unreasonably' denied a 'license' to talk." 345 U.S. at 422. Mr. Justice Frankfurter wrote a concurring opinion.

NOTES

1. The question whether, in a contempt proceeding for violation of an injunction restraining the holding of a meeting, the defendant can raise the invalidity of the permit statute upon which the injunction was based, was answered negatively by the Alabama Supreme Court in Fields v. City of Fairfield, 273 Ala. 588, 143 So. 2d 177 (1962). The issues were argued in the United States Supreme Court, but the case was reversed per curiam, for lack of evidence, under the Thompson v. City of Louisville doctrine. 375 U.S. 248, 84 S. Ct. 360, 11 L. Ed. 2d 311 (1963). The leading case holding that violation of an invalid injunction is nevertheless contempt is United States v. United Mine Workers of America, 330 U.S. 258, 67 S. Ct. 677, 91 L. Ed. 844 (1947), a labor injunction case noted in Chapter XIII, Section G.

For discussion of the issues in First Amendment cases, see Abernathy, The Right of Assembly and Association 64-73 (1961); Notes, 53 Colum. L. Rev. 1013 (1953); 38 Minn. L. Rev. 168 (1954).

2. The imposition of a fee as a condition of obtaining a permit, ranging from a nominal sum to $300 depending on the size of the parade and the cost of policing it, was upheld in Cox v. New Hampshire, 312 U.S. 569, 61 S. Ct. 762, 85 L. Ed. 1049 (1941). But see United Steel Workers v. Fuqua, 40 L.R.R.M. 2241 (W.D. Ky. 1957) (requirement of annual $25 fee held unconstitutional as an interference with the Labor Management Relations Act).

3. In City of Richmond Heights v. Richmond Heights Memorial Post Benevolent Assn., 358 Mo. 70, 213 S.W.2d 479 (1948), plaintiff city sued to enjoin defendant American Legion post from maintaining a meeting place and recreation building in an area zoned as "Single Family Dwelling District." The court ruled for the plaintiff. It rejected the allegation that the zoning ordinance as applied here was unconstitutional, declaring that "the right to peaceably assemble [is] subject to the legitimate exercise of the police power of the state . . . The facts . . . of this case do not demonstrate that the power was so arbitrarily or unreasonably used as to violate due process."

4. On indirect controls that can be exercised by the police through licensing of public halls or by withdrawing licenses from those who rent such halls to dangerous groups, see Note, 47 Yale L.J. 404, 421 (1938); Jarrett and Mund, The Right of Assembly, 9 N.Y.U.L.Q. Rev. 1, 29 (1931). In Local 309, U.F.W. v. Gates, 75 F. Supp. 620 (N.D. Ind. 1948), the Indiana state police attended a membership meetings of the union and took notes. Evidence showed that this activity had the same effect on freedom of discussion as more direct interference. The court granted an injunction upon the request of a number of individual members.

But in Mohammad v. Sommers, 238 F. Supp. 806 (E.D. Mich. 1964), Elijah Mohammad, the leader of The Nation of Islam (the so-called "Black Muslims"), brought a suit under the Civil Rights Acts for damages against three police officers and the City Attorney of Flint, Michigan. The complaint alleged that, while the plaintiff was conducting a religious meeting at an auditorium in Flint, the police entered the meeting and, although requested to do so, refused to surrender their weapons; that one of the tenets of The Nation of Islam forbids the holding of any meeting where weapons are present; and that when the police officers refused either to leave or disarm, it was necessary to terminate the meeting. The complaint was dismissed.

5. In Moses v. Kennedy, 219 F. Supp. 762 (D.D.C. 1963), an action against the Attorney General and the Director of the Federal Bureau of Investigation for mandamus to compel them to protect Negroes and others in Mississippi engaged in civil rights activities, and to bring prosecutions against persons infringing their rights, was unsuccessful.

6. With respect to the possibility of relief by federal injunction against state prosecution of persons exercising rights of assembly, petition, and canvassing, see Dombrowski v. Pfister, 380 U.S. 479, 85 S. Ct. 1116, 14 L. Ed. 2d 22 (1965), discussed in Chapter III, Section C. Efforts prior to Dombrowski were unsuccessful in Chase v. McCain, 220 F. Supp. 407 (W.D. Va. 1963) (Danville ordinance); Baines v. City of Danville, 321 F.2d 643 (4th Cir. 1963) (temporary injunction granted), 337 F.2d 579 (4th Cir. 1964) (temporary injunction dissolved); People of the State of Michigan v. Barnard, 239 F. Supp. 306 (E.D. Mich. 1965). See Note, 114 U. Pa. L. Rev. 561 (1966). On relief by way of removal from state to federal courts, see Chapter XVII.

7. The ultimate resort of the government, in situations where internal order has broken down, is martial law. The major materials are collected in Chapter XIII, Section G.

REFERENCES

For discussion of police techniques in controlling public assemblies, see Wilson, Police Planning (2d ed. 1957); Towler, The Police Role in Racial Conflicts (1964) (the author is a captain in the police department of Danville, Va.); Edwards, Order and Civil Liberties: A Complex Role for the Police, 64 Mich. L. Rev. 47 (1965); Leary, The Role of the Police in Riotous Demonstrations, 40 Notre Dame Law. 499 (1965). See also, in addition to the reports of the United States Commission on Civil Rights, cited in Chapter XV, 4 National Commission on Law Observance and Enforcement, Police (1931); Wiard, Chemical Warfare Munitions for Law Enforcement Agencies, 26 J. Crim. L. & Crim. 438 (1935); The Use of Tear Smoke by Police, 21 Police J. 208 (1948), 26 Police J. 217 (1953). Cf. Oppenheimer and Lakey, A Manual for Direct Action: Strategy and Tactics for Civil Rights and All Other Non-Violent Protest Movements (1965) (the authors are civil rights workers). For a British view, see Royal Commission on the Police, Final Report (1962).

NOTES

1. Other problems in maintaining internal order and freedom of expression move into the area of counselling a crime, solicitation, and attempts. The courts have never fully reconciled this ancient branch of the law with modern doctrines of the First Amendment. See, for samples of the problem, Keegan v. United tates, 325 U.S. 478, 65 S. Ct. 1203, 89 L. Ed. 1745 (1945) (members of the German-American Bund counselling resistance to the draft); Musser v. Utah, 333 U.S. 95, 68 S. Ct. 397, 92 L. Ed. 562 (1948) (Mormons counselling plural marriage); the Gara and other cases under the Universal Military Training and Service Act, noted in Chapter III, Section B. See also State v. McLaughlin, 4 Ohio App. 2d 327, 212 N.E.2d 635 (Ct. App. 1965) (mother counselling unmarried daughter on birth control methods). See, generally, Note, 16 U. Chi. L. Rev. 328, 332-334 (1949); Curran, Solicitation: A Substantive Crime, 17 Minn. L. Rev. 499 (1933); Wechsler, Jones, and Korn, The Treatment of Inchoate Crimes in the Model Penal Code of the American Law Institute: Attempt, Solicitation and Conspiracy, 61 Colum. L. Rev. 571, 957 (1961); Emerson, Toward a General Theory of the First Amendment, 72 Yale L.J. 877, 932-933 (1963).

2. On issues of civil disobedience, material written by lawyers includes: Wasserstrom, The Obligation to Obey the Law, 10 U.C.L.A.L. Rev. 780 (1963); Tweed, Segal and Packer, Civil Rights and Disobedience to Law, 36 N.Y. St. B.J 290 (1964); Civil Disobedience and the Law: A Symposium, 3 Am. Crim. L.Q. 11 (1964); McKay, Racial Protest, Civil Disobedience, and the Rule of Law, Arts and Sciences (Winter 1964-1965); Black, The Problem of the Compatibility of Civil Disobedience with American Institutions of Government, 43 Texas L. Rev. 492 (1965); Liebman, Civil Disobedience: A Threat to Our Law Society, 51 A.B.A.J. 645 (1965); MacGuigan, Civil Disobedience and Natural Law, 11 Catholic Law. 118 (1965); Marshall, The Protest Movement and the Law, 51 Va. L. Rev. 785

(1965); Taylor, Civil Disobedience, in King and Quick (eds.), Legal Aspects of the Civil Rights Movement 227 (1965).

Among the discussions by non-lawyers are: King, Letter From Birmingham Jail, in Westin (ed.), Freedom Now! (1964); Frankel, Is It Ever Right to Break the Law? N.Y. Times Magazine, Jan. 12, 1964, p. 17; Cohen, Essence and Ethics of Civil Disobedience, The Nation, Mar. 16, 1964, p. 257; Keeton, The Morality of Civil Disobedience, 43 Texas L. Rev. 507 (1965); Templin, Democracy and Non-violence (1965); Civil Disobedience (Center for the Study of Democratic Institutions 1966).

For collections of material, see Sibley, Quiet Battle: Writings on the Theory and Practice of Non-violent Resistance (1963); Urquhart, A Matter of Life (1963) (views of 23 leading world citizens); Lynd, Nonviolence in America: A Documentary History (1966).

CHAPTER V

Other Social Interests

This chapter deals with reconciliation of the right to freedom of expression with social interests other than national security and internal order. The main issues have arisen in connection with taxation and business regulation (Section A), regulation of political activities (Section B), and the administration of justice (Section C). Problems in the field of defamation and obscenity are treated in Chapters VI and VII, respectively.

A. Taxation and Business Regulation

First Amendment protection in the area of taxation rests upon the decision in Grosjean v. American Press Co., 297 U.S. 233, 56 S. Ct. 444, 80 L. Ed. 660 (1936). In that case Louisiana had imposed a license tax of 2 per cent on gross receipts derived from advertising, the tax being applicable only to publications with a circulation of more than 200,000 copies a week. Reviewing the history of "taxes on knowledge," the Court struck down the tax "because, in the light of its history and of its present setting, it is seen to be a deliberate and calculated device in the guise of a tax to limit the circulation of information to which the public is entitled in virtue of the constitutional guaranties." 297 U.S. at 250. Following the Grosjean decision the Court of Appeals of Maryland invalidated a tax of 4 per cent upon the gross sales price paid by purchasers of advertising in newspapers, other publications, on radio and TV, and by billboards, and a tax of 2 per cent of gross receipts upon the sellers of such advertising. Mayor of Baltimore v. A. S. Abell Co., 218 Md. 273, 145 A.2d 111 (1958). But in City of Corona v. Corona Daily Independent, 115 Cal. App. 2d 382, 252 P.2d 56 (Ct. App. 1953), the court upheld a general license tax on business enterprises, including newspapers. The United States Supreme Court denied certiorari, Justices Black and Douglas dissenting. 346 U.S. 833 (1953).

In Cammarano v. United States, 358 U.S. 498, 79 S. Ct. 524, 3 L. Ed. 2d 462 (1959), a tax regulation providing that money expended by persons or corporations for the defeat of legislation could not be deducted from gross income for income tax purposes was unanimously upheld. Mr. Justice Douglas, concurring, found it more difficult than the majority to draw the line between legitimate and illegitimate forms of control over commercial enterprises. See also Southwestern Electric Power Co. v. United States, 312 F.2d 437 (Ct. Cl. 1963).

General economic regulations, part of a broader scheme of control not discriminating against the media of communication, have regularly been upheld over First Amendment objections. See, e.g., Associated Press v. N.L.R.B., 301 U.S. 103, 57 S. Ct. 650, 81 L. Ed. 953 (1937) (application of National Labor Relations Act to Associated Press); Lincoln Federal Labor Union v. Northwestern Iron and Metal Co., 335 U.S. 525, 69 S. Ct. 251, 93 L. Ed. 212 (1949) (right-to-work laws not a violation of the First Amendment); Lorain Journal Co. v. United States, 342 U.S. 143, 72 S. Ct. 181, 96 L. Ed. 162 (1951) (application of anti-trust laws to newspapers). But particular applications of economic regulation have raised more difficult issues under the First Amendment.

The most controversial of these has been the extent to which labor controls under the National Labor Relations Act and its amendments infringe upon the freedom of expression of employers or employees. In the leading case, N.L.R.B. v. Virginia Electric and Power Co., 314 U.S. 469, 62 S. Ct. 344, 86 L. Ed. 348 (1941), the Court upheld the prohibition against employer interference with union activity through forms of speech to the extent that such speech involved "coercion." But the application of the rule, as well as restrictions on expression in other aspects of labor relations, continue to present troublesome questions.

In Eastern R.R. Presidents Conference v. Noerr Motor Freight, Inc., 365 U.S. 127, 81 S. Ct. 523, 5 L. Ed. 2d 464 (1961), a group of motor carriers brought suit under the anti-trust laws against an organization of railroads, alleging that the latter had combined with others to obtain the passage and enforcement of laws detrimental to the motor carriers. Mr. Justice Black, writing for a unanimous Court, held that the anti-trust laws could not be interpreted to forbid such conduct for the reason, among others, that "such a construction of the Sherman Act would raise important constitutional questions" under the First Amendment. 365 U.S. at 138.

Recently, First Amendment issues have been raised in this area by the attempts of some states to impose restrictions on civil rights organizations, under the guise of tax or business regulation. These cases, which are important also as the origin of the new constitutional "right of association," are set forth below.

REFERENCES

1. A general discussion of this whole field (other than the "right of association" cases) may be found in Note, Freedom of Expression in a Commercial Context, 78 Harv. L. Rev. 1191 (1965). See also Note, 4 Vill. L. Rev. 377 (1959).

2. On the background of the taxation problem, see Collett, History of Taxes on Knowledge (1903); Chafee, Free Speech in the United States 381-384 (1941); Note, Use of Taxation and Licensing in the Suppression of Freedom of Religion and the Press, 52

Yale L.J. 168 (1942). For discussion of the Grosjean and Abell problem, see Silverstein, To What Extent Should Freedom of the Press Limit Municipal Taxation of the Sale of Advertising? 20 U. Pitt. L. Rev. 607 (1959); Notes, 59 Colum. L. Rev. 359 (1959); 27 Ford L. Rev. 615 (1958-1959); 4 Vill. L. Rev. 442 (1959). On the Cammarano problem, see Sunderland, Taxation of Free Speech, 26 U. Chi. L. Rev. 109 (1958); Sharp, Reflection on the Disallowance of Income Tax Deduction for Lobbying Expenditures, 39 B.U.L. Rev. 365 (1959); Notes, 46 Va. L. Rev. 112 (1960); 69 Yale L.J. 1017 (1960). See also the discussion of Murdock v. Pennsylvania, 319 U.S. 105, 63 S. Ct. 870, 87 L. Ed. 1292 (1943); Breard v. City of Alexandria, 341 U.S. 622, 71 S. Ct. 920, 95 L. Ed. 1233 (1951); and Valentine v. Chrestensen, 316 U.S. 52, 62 S. Ct. 920, 86 L. Ed. 1262 (1942), in Chapter IV, Section A.

3. There is a large body of literature on the free speech rights of employers and employees as affected by labor relations legislation. For a recent article which cites some of the earlier material, see Pokempner, Employer Free Speech Under the National Labor Relations Act, 25 Md. L. Rev. 111 (1965). Other material includes Daykin, The Employers' Right of Free Speech Under the Taft-Hartley Act, 37 Iowa L. Rev. 212 (1952); Rose, Is the NLRB Tampering with Freedom of Speech? 15 U. Pitt. L. Rev. 462 (1954); Wirtz, The New NLRB: Herein of "Employer Persuasion," 49 Nw. U.L. Rev. 594 (1954); Woolett and Rowen, Employer Speech and Related Issues, 16 Ohio St. L.J. 380 (1955); Burke, Employer Free Speech, 26 Ford. L. Rev. 266 (1957); Note, Labor Union Free Speech and Unlawful Economic Coercion Under Section 8(b)(1)(A) of Taft-Hartley, 67 Yale L.J. 1462 (1958); Note, 34 Notre Dame Law. 384 (1959); Koretz, Employer Interference with Union Organization Versus Employer Free Speech, 29 Geo. Wash. L. Rev. 399 (1960); Williams, Freedom to Speak — But Only Ineffectively, 38 Texas L. Rev. 373 (1960); Affeldt, The Right of Association and Labor Law, 7 Vill. L. Rev. 27 (1961); Aaron, Employer Free Speech: The Search for a Policy, in Aaron, Shister and Summers (eds.), Public Policy and Collective Bargaining (1962); Bok, The Regulation of Campaign Tactics in Representation Elections Under the National Labor Relations Act, 78 Harv. L. Rev. 38 (1964); Pollitt, The National Labor Relations Board and Race Hate Propaganda in Union Organization Drives, 17 Stan. L. Rev. 373 (1965).

4. With respect to the Noerr problem, see Note, Does the First Amendment Protect the Use of Lobbying Activities and Mass Communication to Obtain an Illegal Monopoly? 19 U. Pitt. L. Rev. 777 (1958); Note, Appeals to the Electorate by Private Businesses: Injury to Competitors and the Right to Petition, 70 Yale L.J. 135 (1960); Handler, Recent Antitrust Developments, 71 Yale L.J. 75, 88-89 (1961). See also the materials in Section B of this chapter.

5. In People v. Stover et vir, 12 N.Y.2d 462, 240 N.Y.S.2d 734, 191 N.E.2d 272 (1963), app. dis., 375 U.S. 42 (1963), the defendants hung a clothesline, "filled with old clothes and rags" in their front yard, and each year added another similar line, as a form of "peaceful protest" against the high taxes imposed by the city. The city enacted an ordinance prohibiting the erection and maintenance of clotheslines in a front or side yard abutting a street, except in cases of "practical difficulty or unnecessary hardship," in which event a permit was required. The defendants were convicted of violating the ordinance and the Court of Appeals upheld the conviction over First Amendment objections. The court, assuming the conduct of defendants was a "form of nonverbal expression," held the ordinance a permissible regulation in the interests of aesthetics. Judge Van Voorhis dissented. See, generally, on regulation for aesthetic purposes, Dukeminier, Zoning for Aesthetic Objectives: A Reappraisal, 20 Law & Contemp. Prob. 218 (1955); Note, Zoning, Aesthetics, and the First Amendment, 64 Colum. L. Rev. 81 (1964).

NATIONAL ASSOCIATION FOR THE ADVANCE-
MENT OF COLORED PEOPLE v. ALABAMA ex rel.
PATTERSON, ATTORNEY GENERAL
357 U.S. 449, 78 S. Ct. 1163, 2 L. Ed. 2d 1488 (1958)

Mr. Justice Harlan delivered the opinion of the Court.

We review from the standpoint of its validity under the Federal Constitution a judgment of civil contempt entered against petitioner, the National Association for the Advancement of Colored People, in the courts of Alabama. The question presented is whether Alabama, consistently with the Due Process Clause of the Fourteenth Amendment, can compel petitioner to reveal to the State's Attorney General the names and addresses of all its Alabama members and agents, without regard to their positions or functions in the Association. The judgment of contempt was based upon petitioner's refusal to comply fully with a court order requiring in part the production of membership lists. Petitioner's claim is that the order, in the circumstances shown by this record, violated rights assured to petitioner and its members under the Constitution.

Alabama has a statute similar to those of many other States which requires a foreign corporation, except as exempted, to qualify before doing business by filing its corporate charter with the Secretary of State and designating a place of business and an agent to receive service of process. The statute imposes a fine on a corporation transacting intrastate business before qualifying and provides for criminal prosecution of officers of such a corporation. Ala. Code, 1940, Tit. 10, §§192-198. The National Association for the Advancement of Colored People is a nonprofit membership corporation organized under the laws of New York. Its purposes, fostered on a nationwide basis, are those indicated by its name, and it operates through chartered affiliates which are independent unincorporated associations, with membership therein equivalent to membership in petitioner. The first Alabama affiliates were chartered in 1918. Since that time the aims of the Association have been advanced through activities of its affiliates, and in 1951 the Association itself opened a regional office in Alabama, at which it employed two supervisory persons and one clerical worker. The Association has never complied with the qualification statute, from which it considered itself exempt.

In 1956 the Attorney General of Alabama brought an equity suit in the State Circuit Court, Montgomery County, to enjoin the Association from conducting further activities within, and to oust it from, the State. . . . On the day the complaint was filed, the Circuit Court issued ex parte an order restraining the Association, pendente lite, from engaging in further activities within the State and forbidding it to take any steps to qualify itself to do business therein.

Petitioner demurred to the allegations of the bill and moved to dissolve the restraining order. It contended that its activities did not subject it to the qualification requirements of the statute and that in any event what the State sought to accomplish by its suit would violate rights to freedom of speech and assembly guaranteed under the Fourteenth Amendment to the Constitution of the United States. Before the date set for a hearing on this motion, the State moved for the production of a large number of the Association's records and papers, including bank statements, leases, deeds, and records containing the names and addresses of all Alabama "members" and "agents" of the Association. It alleged that all such documents were necessary for adequate preparation for the hearing, in view of petitioner's denial of the conduct of intrastate business within the meaning of the qualification statute. Over petitioner's objections, the court ordered the production of a substantial part of the requested records, including the membership lists, and postponed the hearing on the restraining order to a date later than the time ordered for production.

Thereafter petitioner filed its answer to the bill in equity. It admitted its Alabama activities substantially as alleged in the complaint and that it had not qualified to do business in the State. Although still disclaiming the statute's application to it, petitioner offered to qualify if the bar from qualification made part of the restraining order were lifted, and it submitted with the answer an executed set of the forms required by the statute. However petitioner did not comply with the production order, and for this failure was adjudged in civil contempt and fined $10,000. The contempt judgment provided that the fine would be subject to reduction or remission if compliance were forthcoming within five days but otherwise would be increased to $100,000.

At the end of the five-day period petitioner produced substantially all the data called for by the production order except its membership lists, as to which it contended that Alabama could not constitutionally compel disclosure, and moved to modify or vacate the contempt judgment, or stay its execution pending appellate review. This motion was denied. While a similar stay application, which was later denied, was pending before the Supreme Court of Alabama, the Circuit Court made a further order adjudging petitioner in continuing contempt and increasing the fine already imposed to $100,000. Under Alabama law, see Jacoby v. Goetter, Weil & Co., 74 Ala. 427, the effect of the contempt adjudication was to foreclose petitioner from obtaining a hearing on the merits of the underlying ouster action, or from taking any steps to dissolve the temporary restraining order which had been issued ex parte, until it purged itself of contempt. . . .

The Association both urges that it is constitutionally entitled to resist official inquiry into its membership lists, and that it may assert, on behalf of its members, a right personal to them to be protected from compelled disclosure by the State of their affiliation with the Association as revealed by the membership lists. We think that petitioner argues more appropriately the rights of its members, and that its nexus with them is sufficient to permit that it act as their representative before this Court. In so concluding, we reject respondent's argument that the Association lacks standing to assert here constitutional rights pertaining to the members, who are not of course parties to the litigation. . . .

If petitioner's rank-and-file members are constitutionally entitled to withhold their connection with the Association despite the production order, it is manifest that this right is properly assertable by the Association. To require that it be claimed by the members themselves would result in nullification of the right at the very moment of its assertion. Petitioner is the appropriate party to assert these rights, because it and its members are in every practical sense identical. The Association, which provides in its constitution that "[a]ny person who is in accordance with [its] principles and policies . . ." may become a member, is but the medium through which its individual members seek to make more effective the expression of their own views. The reasonable likelihood that the Association itself through diminished financial support and membership may be adversely affected if production is compelled is a further factor pointing towards our holding that petitioner has standing to complain of the production order on behalf of its members. Cf. Pierce v. Society of Sisters, 268 U.S. 510, 534-536.

We thus reach petitioner's claim that the production order in the state litigation trespasses upon fundamental freedoms protected by the Due Process Clause of the Fourteenth Amendment. Petitioner argues that in view of the facts and circumstances shown in the record, the effect of compelled disclosure of the membership lists will be to abridge the rights of its rank-and-file members to engage in lawful association in support of their common beliefs. It contends that governmental action which, although not directly suppressing association, nevertheless carries this consequence, can be justified only upon some overriding valid interest of the State.

Effective advocacy of both public and private points of view, particularly controversial ones, is undeniably enhanced by group association, as this Court has more than once recognized by remarking upon the close nexus between the freedoms of speech and assembly. De Jonge v. Oregon, 299 U.S. 353, 364; Thomas v. Collins, 323 U.S. 516, 530. It is beyond debate that freedom to engage in association for the advancement of beliefs and ideas is an inseparable aspect of the "liberty" assured by the Due Process Clause of the Fourteenth Amendment, which embraces freedom of speech. See Gitlow v. New York, 268 U.S. 652, 666; Palko v. Connecticut, 302 U.S. 319, 324; Cantwell v. Connecticut, 310 U.S. 296, 303; Staub v. City of Baxley, 355 U.S. 313, 321. Of course, it is immaterial whether the beliefs sought to be advanced by association pertain to political, economic, religious or cultural matters, and state action which may have the effect of curtailing the freedom to associate is subject to the closest scrutiny.

The fact that Alabama, so far as is relevant to the validity of the contempt judgment presently under review, has taken no direct action, cf. De Jonge v. Oregon, supra; Near v. Minnesota, 283 U.S. 697, to restrict the right of petitioner's members to associate freely, does not end inquiry into the effect of the production order. See American Communications Assn. v Douds, 339 U.S. 382, 402. In the domain of these indispensable liberties, whether of speech, press, or association, the decisions of this Court recognize that abridgment of such rights, even though unintended, may inevitably follow from varied forms of governmental action. Thus in Douds, the Court stressed that the legislation there challenged, which on its face sought to regulate labor unions and to secure stability in interstate commerce, would have the practical effect "of discouraging" the exercise of constitutionally protected political rights, 339 U.S., at 393, and it upheld the statute only after concluding that the reasons advanced for its enactment were constitutionally sufficient to justify its possible deterrent effect upon such freedoms. Similar recognition of possible unconstitutional intimidation of the free exercise of the right to advocate underlay this Court's narrow construction of the authority of a congressional committee investigating lobbying and of an Act regulating lobbying, although in neither case was there an effort to suppress speech. United States v. Rumely, 345 U.S. 41, 46-47; United States v. Harriss, 347 U.S. 612, 625-626. The governmental action challenged may appear to be totally unrelated to protected liberties. Statutes imposing taxes upon rather than prohibiting particular activity have been struck down when perceived to have the consequence of unduly curtailing the liberty of freedom of press assured under the Fourteenth Amendment. Grosjean v. American Press Co., 297 U.S. 233; Murdock v. Pennsylvania, 319 U.S. 105.

It is hardly a novel perception that compelled disclosure of affiliation with groups engaged in advocacy may constitute as effective a restraint on freedom of association as the forms of governmental action in the cases above were thought likely to produce upon the particular constitutional rights there involved. This Court has recognized the vital relationship between freedom to associate and privacy in one's associations. When referring to the varied forms of governmental action which might interfere with freedom of assembly, it said in American Communications Assn. v. Douds, supra, at 402: "A requirement that adherents of particular religious faiths or political parties wear identifying arm-bands, for example, is obviously of this nature." Compelled disclosure of membership in an organization engaged in advocacy of particular beliefs is of the same order. Inviolability of privacy in group association may in many circumstances be indispensable to preservation of freedom of association, particularly where a group espouses dissident beliefs. Cf. United States v. Rumely, supra, at 56-58 (concurring opinion).

We think that the production order, in the respects here drawn in question, must be regarded as entailing the likelihood of a substantial restraint upon the exercise by petitioner's members of their right to freedom of association. Petitioner has made an uncontroverted showing that on past occasions revelation of the identity of its rank-and-file members has exposed these members to economic reprisal, loss of employment, threat of physical coercion, and other manifestations of public hostility. Under these circumstances, we think it apparent that compelled disclosure of petitioner's Alabama membership is likely to affect adversely the ability of petitioner and its members to pursue their collective effort to foster beliefs which they admittedly have the right to advocate, in that it may induce members to withdraw from the Association and dissuade others from joining it because of fear of exposure of their beliefs shown through their associations and of the consequences of this exposure.

It is not sufficient to answer, as the State does here, that whatever repressive effect compulsory disclosure of names of petitioner's members may have upon participation by Alabama citizens in petitioner's activities follows not from *state* action but from *private* community pressures. The crucial factor is the interplay of governmental and private action, for it is only after the initial exertion of state power represented by the production order that private action takes hold.

We turn to the final question whether Alabama has demonstrated an interest in obtaining the disclosures it seeks from petitioner which is sufficient to justify the deterrent effect which we have concluded these disclosures may well have on the free exercise by petitioner's members of their constitutionally protected right of association. See American Communications Assn. v. Douds, supra, at 400; Schneider v. State, 308 U.S. 147, 161. Such a ". . . subordinating interest of the State must be compelling," Sweezy v. New Hampshire, 354 U.S. 234, 265 (concurring opinion). It is not of moment that the State has here acted solely through its judicial branch, for whether legislative or judicial, it is still the application of state power which we are asked to scrutinize. . . .

Whether there was "justification" in this instance turns solely on the substantiality of Alabama's interest in obtaining the membership lists. During the course of a hearing before the Alabama Circuit Court on a motion of petitioner to set aside the production order, the State Attorney General presented at length, under examination by petitioner, the State's reason for requesting the membership lists. The exclusive purpose was to determine whether petitioner was conducting intrastate business in violation of the Alabama foreign corporation registration statute, and the membership lists were expected to help resolve this question. The issues in the litigation commenced by Alabama by its bill in equity were whether the character of petitioner and its activities in Alabama had been such as to make petitioner subject to the registration statute, and whether the extent of petitioner's activities without qualifying suggested its permanent ouster from the State. Without intimating the slightest view upon the merits of these issues, we are unable to perceive that the disclosure of the names of petitioner's rank-and-file members has a substantial bearing on either of them. As matters stand in the state court, petitioner (1) has admitted its presence and conduct of activities in

Alabama since 1918; (2) has offered to comply in all respects with the state qualification statute, although preserving its contention that the statute does not apply to it; and (3) has apparently complied satisfactorily with the production order, except for the membership lists, by furnishing the Attorney General with varied business records, its charter and statement of purposes, the names of all of its directors and officers, and with the total number of its Alabama members and the amount of their dues. These last items would not on this record appear subject to constitutional challenge and have been furnished, but whatever interest the State may have in obtaining names of ordinary members has not been shown to be sufficient to overcome petitioner's constitutional objections to the production order.

From what has already been said, we think it apparent that Bryant v. Zimmerman, 278 U.S. 63, cannot be relied on in support of the State's position, for that case involved markedly different considerations in terms of the interest of the State in obtaining disclosure. There, this Court upheld, as applied to a member of a local chapter of the Ku Klux Klan, a New York statute requiring any unincorporated association which demanded an oath as a condition to membership to file with state officials copies of its ". . . constitution, by-laws, rules, regulations and oath of membership, together with a roster of its membership and a list of its officers for the current year." N. Y. Laws 1923, c. 664, §§53, 56. In its opinion, the Court took care to emphasize the nature of the organization which New York sought to regulate. The decision was based on the particular character of the Klan's activities, involving acts of unlawful intimidation and violence, which the Court assumed was before the state legislature when it enacted the statute, and of which the Court itself took judicial notice. Furthermore, the situation before us is significantly different from that in Bryant, because the organization there had made no effort to comply with any of the requirements of New York's statute but rather had refused to furnish the State with *any* information as to its local activities.

We hold that the immunity from state scrutiny of membership lists which the Association claims on behalf of its members is here so related to the right of the members to pursue their lawful private interests privately and to associate freely with others in so doing as to come within the protection of the Fourteenth Amendment. And we conclude that Alabama has fallen short of showing a controlling justification for the deterrent effect on the free enjoyment of the right to associate which disclosure of membership lists is likely to have. Accordingly, the judgment of civil contempt and the $100,000 fine which resulted from petitioner's refusal to comply with the production order in this respect must fall. . . .

Reversed.

NOTE

Bates v. City of Little Rock, 361 U.S. 516, 80 S. Ct. 412, 4 L. Ed. 2d 480 (1960), involved two municipal ordinances imposing a license tax upon persons, firms, or corporations engaging in any "trade, business, profession, vocation or calling" within the city limits. In 1957 the two cities adopted amendments requiring organizations subject to the tax to supply the city clerk with certain information, including "dues, assessments, and contributions paid, by whom and when paid." This information was open to public inspection. Petitioners, custodians of the records of two local branches of the N.A.A.C.P., supplied all the data demanded except the names of members who had paid dues. They were convicted of violating the ordinance. The Supreme Court, in an opinion by Mr. Justice Stewart, reversed:

"On this record it sufficiently appears that compulsory disclosure of the membership lists of the local branches of the National Association for the Advancement of Colored People would work a significant interference with the freedom of association of their members. There was substantial uncontroverted evidence that public identification of persons in the community as members of the organizations had been followed by harassment and threats of bodily harm. There was also evidence that fear of community hostility and economic reprisals that would follow public disclosure of the membership lists had discouraged new members from joining the organizations and induced former members to withdraw. This repressive effect, while in part the result of private attitudes and pressures, was brought to bear only after the exercise of governmental power had threatened to force disclosure of the members' names. N.A.A.C.P. v. Alabama, 357 U.S., at 463. Thus, the threat of substantial government encroachment upon important and traditional aspects of individual freedom is neither speculative nor remote.

"Decision in this case must finally turn, therefore, on whether the cities as instrumentalities of the State have demonstrated so cogent an interest in obtaining and making public the membership lists of these organizations as to justify the substantial abridgment of associational freedom which such disclosures will effect. Where there is a significant encroachment upon personal liberty, the State may prevail only upon showing a subordinating interest which is compelling. . . .

"In this record we can find no relevant correlation between the power of the municipalities to impose occupational license taxes and the compulsory disclosure and publication of the membership lists of the local branches of the National Association for the Advancement of Colored People. The occupational license tax ordinances of the municipalities are squarely aimed at reaching all the commercial, professional, and business occupations within the communities. The taxes are not, and as a matter of state law cannot be, based on earnings or income, but upon the nature of the occupation or enterprise conducted.

"Inquiry of organizations within the communities as to the purpose and nature of their activities would thus appear to be entirely relevant to enforcement of the ordinances. . . .

"We conclude that the municipalities have failed to demonstrate a controlling justification for the deterrence of free association which compulsory disclosure of the membership lists would cause. The petitioners cannot be punished for refusing to produce information which the municipalities could not constitutionally require. The judgments cannot stand." 361 U.S. at 523-527.

Justices Black and Douglas concurred, saying:

"[We] believe, as we indicated in United States v. Rumely, 345 U.S. 41, 48, at 56 (concurring opinion), that First Amendment rights are beyond abridgment either by legislation that directly restrains their exercise or by suppression or impairment through harassment, humiliation, or exposure by government. One of those rights, freedom of assembly, includes of course freedom of association; and it is entitled to no less protection than any other First Amendment rights as N.A.A.C.P. v. Alabama, 357 U.S. 449, at 460, and De Jonge v. Oregon, 299 U.S. 353, at 363, hold. These are principles applicable to all people under our Constitution irrespective of their race, color, politics, or religion. That is, for us, the essence of the present opinion of the Court." 361 U.S. at 528.

NATIONAL ASSOCIATION FOR THE ADVANCE-MENT OF COLORED PEOPLE v. BUTTON
371 U.S. 415, 83 S. Ct. 328, 9 L. Ed. 2d 405 (1963)

Mr. Justice Brennan delivered the opinion of the Court. . . .

There is no substantial dispute as to the facts: the dispute centers about the constitutionality under the Fourteenth Amendment of Chapter 33, as construed and applied by the Virginia Supreme Court of Appeals to include NAACP's activities within the statute's ban against "the improper solicitation of any legal or professional business." . . .

Petitioner challenges the decisions of the Supreme Court of Appeals on many grounds. But we reach only one: that Chapter 33 as construed and applied abridges the freedoms of the First Amendment, protected against state action by the Fourteenth. More specifically, petitioner claims that the chapter infringes the right of the NAACP and its members and lawyers to associate for the purpose of assisting persons who seek legal redress for infringements of their constitutionally guaranteed and other rights. We think petitioner may assert this right on its own behalf, because, though a corporation, it is directly engaged in those activities, claimed to be constitutionally protected, which the statute would curtail. Cf. Grosjean v. American Press Co., 297 U.S. 233. We also think petitioner has standing to assert the corresponding rights of its members. See N.A.A.C.P v. Alabama ex rel. Patterson, 357 U.S. 449, 458-460; Bates v. City of Little Rock, 361 U.S. 516, 523, n.9; Louisiana ex rel. Gremillion v. N.A.A.C.P., 366 U.S. 293, 296.

We reverse the judgment of the Virginia Supreme Court of Appeals. We hold that the activities of the NAACP, its affiliates and legal staff shown on this record are modes of expression and association protected by the First and Fourteenth Amendments, which Virginia may not prohibit, under its power to regulate the legal profession, as improper solicitation of legal business violative of Chapter 33 and the Canons of Professional Ethics.

We meet at the outset the contention that "solicitation" is wholly outside the area of procedure protected by the First Amendment. To this contention there are two answers. The first is that a State cannot foreclose the exercise of constitutional rights by mere labels. The second is that abstract discussion is not the only species of communication which the Constitution protects; the First Amendment also protects vigorous advocacy, certainly of lawful ends, against governmental intrusion. Thomas v. Collins, 323 U.S. 516, 537; Herndon v. Lowry, 301 U.S. 242, 259-264. Cf. Cantwell v. Connecticut, 310 U.S. 296; Stromberg v. California, 283 U.S. 359, 369; Terminiello v. Chicago, 337 U.S. 1, 4. In the context of NAACP objectives, litigation is not a technique of resolving private differences; it is a means for achieving the lawful objectives of equality of treatment by all government, federal, state and local, for the members of the Negro community in this country. It is thus a form of political expression. Groups which find themselves unable to achieve their objectives through the ballot frequently turn to the courts. Just as it was true of the opponents of New Deal legislation during the 1930's, for example, no less is it true of the Negro minority today. And under the conditions of modern government, litigation may well be the sole practicable avenue open to a minority to petition for redress of grievances.

We need not, in order to find constitutional protection for the kind of cooperative, organizational activity disclosed by this record, whereby Negroes seek through lawful means to achieve legitimate political ends, subsume such activity under a narrow, literal conception of freedom of speech, petition or assembly. For there is no longer any doubt that the First and Fourteenth Amendments protect certain forms of orderly group activity. Thus we have affirmed the right "to engage in association for the advancement of beliefs and ideas." N.A.A.C.P. v. Alabama, supra, at 460. We have deemed privileged, under certain circumstances, the efforts of a union official to organize workers. Thomas v. Collins, supra. We have said that the Sherman Act does not apply to certain concerted activities of railroads "at least insofar as those activities comprised mere solicitation of governmental action with respect to the passage and enforcement of laws" because "such a construction of the Sherman Act would raise important constitutional questions," specifically, First Amendment questions. Eastern R. Presidents Conference v. Noerr Motor Freight, Inc., 365 U.S. 127, 138. And we have refused to countenance compelled disclosure of a person's political associations in language closely applicable to the instant case [quoting Sweezy v. New Hampshire, 354 U.S. 234.]

The NACP is not a conventional political party; but the litigation it assists, while serving to vindicate the legal rights of members of the American Negro community, at the same time and perhaps more importantly, makes possible the distinctive contribution of a minority group to the ideas and beliefs of our society. For such a group, association for litigation may be the most effective form of political association. . . .

We conclude that under Chapter 33, as authoritatively construed by the Supreme Court of Appeals, a person who advises another that his legal rights have been infringed and refers him to a particular attorney or group of attorneys (for example, to the Virginia Conference's legal staff) for assistance has committed a crime, as has the attorney who knowingly renders assistance under such circumstances. There thus inheres in the statute the gravest danger of smothering all discussion looking to the eventual institution of litigation on behalf of the rights of members of an unpopular minority. Lawyers on the legal staff or even mere NAACP members or sympathizers would understandably hesitate, at an NAACP meeting or on any other occasion, to do what the decree purports to allow, namely, acquaint "persons with what they believe to be their legal rights and . . . [advise] them to assert their rights by commencing or further prosecuting a suit. . . ." For if the lawyers, members or sympathizers also appeared in or had any connection with any litigation supported with NAACP funds contributed under the provision of the decree by which the NAACP is not prohibited "from contributing money to persons to assist them in commencing or further prosecuting such suits," they plainly would risk (if lawyers) disbarment proceedings and, lawyers and nonlawyers alike, criminal prosecution for the offense of "solicitation," to which the Virginia court gave so broad and uncertain a meaning. It makes no difference whether such prosecutions or proceedings would actually be commenced. It is enough that a vague and broad statute lends itself to selective enforcement against unpopular causes. We cannot close our eyes to the fact that the militant Negro civil rights movement has engendered the intense resentment and opposition of the politically dominant white community of Virginia; litigation assisted by the NAACP has been bitterly fought. In such circumstances, a statute broadly curtailing group activity leading to litigation may easily become a weapon of oppression, however even-handed its terms appear. Its mere existence could well freeze out of existence all such activity on behalf of the civil rights of Negro citizens. . . .

However valid may be Virginia's interest in regulating the traditionally illegal practices of barratry, maintenance and champerty, that interest does not justify the prohibition of the NAACP activities disclosed by this record. Malicious intent was of the essence of the common-law offenses of fomenting or stirring up litigation. And whatever may be or may have been true of suits against government in other countries, the exercise in our own, as in this case, of First Amendment rights to enforce constitutional rights through litigation, as a matter of law, cannot be deemed malicious. Even more modern, subtler regulations of unprofessional conduct or interference with professional relations, not involving malice, would not touch the activities at bar; regulations which reflect hostility to stirring up litigation have been aimed chiefly at those who urge recourse to the courts for private gain, serving no public interest. . . .

We conclude that although the petitioner has amply shown that its activities fall within the First Amendment's protections, the State has failed to advance any substantial regulatory interest, in the form of substantive evils flowing from petitioner's activities, which can justify the broad prohibitions which it has imposed. Nothing that this record shows as to the nature and purpose of NAACP activities permits an inference of any injurious intervention in or control of litigation which would constitutionally authorize the application of Chapter 33 to those activities. A fortiori, nothing in this record justifies the breadth and vagueness of the Virginia Supreme Court of Appeals' decree. . . .

Reversed.

[Mr. Justice Douglas concurred. Mr. Justice White concurred in part and dissented in part.]

Mr. Justice Harlan, whom Mr. Justice Clark, and Mr. Justice Stewart join, dissenting. . . .

Freedom of expression embraces more than the right of an individual to speak his mind. It includes also his right to advocate and his right to join with his fellows in an effort to make that advocacy effective. Thomas v. Collins, 323 U.S. 516; N.A.A.C.P. v. Alabama, 357 U.S. 449; Bates v. Little Rock, 361 U.S. 516. And just as it includes the right jointly to petition the legislature for redress of grievances, see Eastern R. Presidents Conference v. Noerr Motor Freight, Inc., 365 U.S. 127, 137-138, so it must include the right to join together for purposes of obtaining judicial redress. We have passed the point where litigation is regarded as an evil that must be avoided if some accommodation short of a lawsuit can possibly be worked out. Litigation is often the desirable and orderly way of resolving disputes of broad public significance, and of obtaining vindication of fundamental rights. This is particularly so in the sensitive area of racial relationships.

But to declare that litigation is a form of conduct that may be associated with political expression does not resolve this case. Neither the First Amendment nor the Fourteenth constitutes an absolute bar to government regulation in the fields of free expression and association. This Court has repeatedly held that certain forms of speech are outside the scope of the protection of those Amendments, and that, in addition, "general regulatory statutes, not intended to control the content of speech but incidentally limiting its unfettered exercise," are permissible "when they have been found justified by subordinating valid governmental interests." [1] The problem in each such case is to weigh the legitimate interest of the State against the effect of the regulation on individual rights.

An analogy may be drawn between the present case and the rights of workingmen in labor disputes. At the heart of these rights are those of a laborer or a labor representative to speak: to inform the public of his disputes and to

---

[1] Konigsberg v. State Bar, 366 U.S. 36, 50-51; and see cases cited therein, including Cox v. New Hampshire, 312 U.S. 569; Chaplinsky v. New Hampshire, 315 U.S. 568; Breard v. Alexandria, 341 U.S. 622; Roth v. United States, 354 U.S. 476; Bates v. Little Rock, 361 U.S. 516, 524; Wilkinson v. United States, 365 U.S. 399.

urge his fellow workers to join together for mutual aid and protection. So important are these particular rights that absent a clear and present danger of the gravest evil, the State not only is without power to impose a blanket prohibition on their exercise, Thornhill v. Alabama, 310 U.S. 88, but also may not place any significant obstacle in their path, Thomas v. Collins, 323 U.S. 516.

But as we move away from speech alone and into the sphere of conduct — even conduct associated with speech or resulting from it — the area of legitimate governmental interest expands. A regulation not directly suppressing speech or peaceable assembly, but having some impact on the form or manner of their exercise will be sustained if the regulation has a reasonable relationship to a proper governmental objective and does not unduly interfere with such individual rights. Thus, although the State may not prohibit all informational picketing, it may prevent mass picketing, Allen-Bradley Local v. Wisconsin Board, 315 U.S. 740, and picketing for an unlawful objective, Giboney v. Empire Storage & Ice Co., 336 U.S. 490. Although it may not prevent advocacy of union membership, it can to some degree inquire into and define the qualifications of those who solicit funds from prospective members or who hold other positions of responsibility. A legislature may not wholly eliminate the right of collective action by workingmen, but it may to a significant extent dictate the form their organization shall take and may limit the demands that the organization may make on employers and others, see, e.g., International Brotherhood of Electrical Workers v. Labor Board, 341 U.S. 694, 705.

Turning to the present case, I think it evident that the basic rights in issue are those of the petitioner's members to associate, to discuss, and to advocate. Absent the gravest danger to the community, these rights must remain free from frontal attack or suppression, and the state court has recognized this in striking down Chapter 36 and in carefully limiting the impact of Chapter 33. But litigation, whether or not associated with the attempt to vindicate constitutional rights, is *conduct;* it is speech *plus*. Although the State surely may not broadly prohibit individuals with a common interest from joining together to petition a court for redress of their grievances, it is equally certain that the State may impose reasonable regulations limiting the permissible form of litigation and the manner of legal representation within its borders. Thus the State may, without violating protected rights, restrict those undertaking to represent others in legal proceedings to properly qualified practitioners. And it may determine that a corporation or association does not itself have standing to litigate the interests of its shareholders or members — that only individuals with a direct interest of their own may join to press their claims in its courts. Both kinds of regulation are undeniably matters of legitimate concern to the State and their possible impact on the rights of expression and association is far too remote to cause any doubt as to their validity.

So here, the question is whether the particular regulation of conduct concerning litigation has a reasonable relation to the furtherance of a proper state interest, and whether that interest outweighs any foreseeable harm to the furtherance of protected freedoms.

[Mr. Justice Harlan then goes on to argue that Virginia's interest "in maintaining high professional standards among those who practice law within its borders" outweighs the "rights of petitioner and its members to free expres· sion and association." This portion of the opinion is omitted.]

NATIONAL ASSOCIATION FOR THE ADVANCE-
MENT OF COLORED PEOPLE v. ALABAMA ex rel.
FLOWERS, ATTORNEY GENERAL
377 U.S. 288, 84 S. Ct. 1302, 12 L. Ed. 2d 325 (1964)

[After the reversal and remand in the prior NAACP case the Supreme Court of Alabama reaffirmed its judgment of contempt, on the ground that the judgment of the United States Supreme Court had rested on a "mistaken premise." 268 Ala. 531, 532, 109 So. 2d 138, 139. The United States Supreme Court again reversed and remanded. 360 U.S. 240. No hearing on the issues having been held by the Alabama courts for a year, the NAACP commenced proceedings in the United States District Court to obtain a hearing there. The District Court dismissed the action (190 F. Supp. 583), the Court of Appeals affirmed (290 F.2d 337), and the case reached the United States Supreme Court for the third time. That Court vacated the judgment and remanded the case to the Court of Appeals with instructions to direct the District Court to proceed with the trial "unless within a reasonable time, no later than January 2, 1962, the State of Alabama shall have accorded to petitioner an opportunity to be heard to dissolve the state restraining order of June 1, 1956, and upon the merits of the action in which such order was issued." 368 U.S. 16.

In December, 1961, more than five years after issuance of the initial restraining order, the Alabama court heard the case and entered a final decree finding that the NAACP had continued to do business in Alabama "in violation of the Constitution and laws of the state relating to foreign corporations" and that the Association's activities in the state were "in violation of other laws of the State of Alabama and are and have been a usurpation and abuse of its corporate functions and detrimental to the State of Alabama. . . ." The decree permanently enjoined the Association and those affiliated with it from doing "any further business of any description or kind" in Alabama and from attempting to qualify to do business there.]

Mr. Justice Harlan delivered the opinion of the Court. . . .

The complaint against the Association, as finally amended, alleged that it was a New York corporation maintaining an office and doing business in Alabama. The acts charged against the Association were:

(1) that it had "employed or otherwise paid money" to Authurine Lucy

and Polly Meyers Hudson to encourage them to enroll as students in the University of Alabama in order to test the legality of its policy against admitting Negroes;

(2) that it had furnished legal counsel to represent Authurine Lucy in proceedings to obtain admission to the University;

(3) that it had "engaged in organizing, supporting and financing an illegal boycott" to compel a bus line in Montgomery, Alabama, not to segregate passengers according to race;

(4) that it had "falsely charged" officials of the State and the University of Alabama with acts in violation of state and federal law;

(5) that it had "falsely charged" the Attorney General of Alabama and the Alabama courts with "arbitrary, vindictive, and collusive" acts intended to prevent it from contesting its ouster from the State "before an impartial judicial forum," and had "falsely charged" the Circuit Court and Supreme Court of the State with deliberately denying it a hearing on the merits of its ouster;

(6) that it had "falsely charged" the State and its Attorney General with filing contempt proceedings against it, knowing the charges therein to be false;

(7) that it had "willfully violated" the order restraining it from carrying on activities in the State;

(8) that it attempted to "pressure" the mayor of Philadelphia, the Governor of Pennsylvania, and the Penn State football team into "a boycott of the Alabama football team" when the two teams were to play each other in the Liberty Bowl;

(9) that it had "encouraged, aided, and abetted the unlawful breach of the peace in many cities in Alabama for the purpose of gaining national notoriety and attention to enable it to raise funds under a false claim that it is for the protection of alleged constitutional rights";

(10) that it had "encouraged, aided, and abetted a course of conduct within the State of Alabama, seeking to deny to the citizens of Alabama the constitutional right to voluntarily segregate"; and

(11) that it had carried on its activities in Alabama without complying with state laws requiring foreign corporations to register and perform other acts in order to do business within the State.

All of these acts were alleged to be "causing irreparable injury to the property and civil rights of the residents and citizens of the State of Alabama for which criminal prosecution and civil actions at law afford no adequate relief. . . ." The complaint stated also that "the said conduct, procedure, false allegations, and methods used by Respondent render totally unacceptable to the State of Alabama and its people the said Respondent corporation and the activities and business it transacts in this State."

The last allegation, that the Association has failed to comply with the statutory requirements for a foreign corporation to do business in Alabama, furnishes no basis under Alabama law for its ouster. . . .

There is nothing in [the Alabama statutes] which attaches the consequence of permanent ouster to a foreign corporation which fails to register. . . .

The other asserted grounds for excluding the petitioner from Alabama furnish no better foundation for the action below. The first two grounds relied on are manifestly untenable. Before these proceedings were commenced, this Court had upheld the right of Authurine Lucy and Polly Anne Meyers to enroll at the University of Alabama. Lucy v. Adams, 350 U.S. 1. Neither furnishing them with financial assistance, in effect a scholarship, to attend the University, nor providing them with legal counsel to assist their efforts to gain admission was unlawful or could, consistently with the decisions of this Court, be inhibited because contrary to the University's policy against admitting Negroes. N.A.A.C.P. v. Button, 371 U.S. 415.

The third charge listed above is scarcely more substantial. Even if we were to indulge the doubtful assumption that an organized refusal to ride on Montgomery's buses in protest against a policy of racial segregation might, without more, in some circumstances violate a valid state law, such a violation could not constitutionally be the basis for a permanent denial of the right to associate for the advocacy of ideas by lawful means. As we said at a prior stage in this litigation:

"It is beyond debate that freedom to engage in association for the advancement of beliefs and ideas is an inseparable aspect of the 'liberty' assured by the Due Process Clause of the Fourteenth Amendment, which embraces freedom of speech." 357 U.S., at 460.

This Court has repeatedly held that a governmental purpose to control or prevent activities constitutionally subject to state regulation may not be achieved by means which sweep unnecessarily broadly and thereby invade the area of protected freedoms. See id., at 463-464. ". . . [T]he power to regulate must be so exercised as not, in attaining a permissible end, unduly to infringe the protected freedom." Cantwell v. Connecticut, 310 U.S. 296, 304. ". . . [E]ven though the governmental purpose be legitimate and substantial, that purpose cannot be pursued by means that broadly stifle fundamental personal liberties when the end can be more narrowly achieved." Shelton v. Tucker, 364 U.S. 479, 488 (footnote omitted). For other cases elaborating this principle, see Lovell v. Griffin, 303 U.S. 444, 451; Schneider v. State, 308 U.S. 147, 161, 165; Martin v. Struthers, 319 U.S. 141, 146-149; Saia v. New York, 334 U.S. 558; American Communications Assn. v. Douds, 339 U.S. 382; Kunz v. New York, 340 U.S. 290, 294-295; Louisiana ex rel. Gremillion v. N.A.A.C.P., 366 U.S. 293. This principle is applicable here even though the ouster of the petitioner from Alabama has been accomplished solely by judicial act; "whether legislative or judicial, it is still the application of state power which we are asked to scrutinize." 357 U.S., at 463.

In the first proceedings in this case, we held that the compelled disclosure of the names of the petitioner's members would entail "the likelihood of a substantial restraint upon the exercise by petitioner's members of their right to freedom of association." 357 U.S., at 462. It is obvious that the complete suppression of the Association's activities in Alabama which was accomplished by the order below is an even more serious abridgment of that right. The allegations of illegal conduct contained in the third charge against the petitioner suggest no legitimate governmental objective which requires such restraint. Compare Kunz v. New York, supra, at 294-295.

The fourth, fifth, and sixth charges against the petitioner all involve alleged "false charges" made by the Association or its representatives against state officials.[13] Without speculating on other possible constitutional infirmities to which these allegations may be subject, cf. New York Times Co. v. Sullivan, 376 U.S. 254, we conclude that, for the reasons discussed above, they furnish no basis for the restriction of the right of the petitioner's members to associate in Alabama. So too with the seventh charge, which alleges violation of the "temporary" restraining order in effect from 1956 to 1961 (when it was made permanent). We dispose of this charge on the same basis as the others, without considering the sufficiency of the evidence to support the finding that there was a violation of the order or the serious constitutional questions raised by an order which restrained for so long a time the exercise of unquestionable constitutional rights on the grounds involved here. We pass the eighth charge without comment; by no stretch can it be considered germane to the present controversy. The ninth charge, involving alleged breaches of the peace, falls with the third. "There are appropriate public remedies to protect the peace and order of the community . . . ," Kunz, supra, at 294, which do not infringe constitutional rights. The tenth charge, if it adds anything to those which have gone before, simply challenges the right of the petitioner and its members to express their views, by words and lawful conduct, on a subject of vital constitutional concern. Such a challenge cannot stand.

There is no occasion in this case for us to consider how much survives of the principle that a State can impose such conditions as it chooses on the right of a foreign corporation to do business within the State, or can exclude it from the State altogether. E.g., Crescent Cotton Oil Co. v. Mississippi, 257 U.S. 129, 137. This case, in truth, involves not the privilege of a corporation to do business in a State, but rather the freedom of individuals to associate for the collective advocacy of ideas. . . .

---

[13] The "false charges" with which the fourth charge against the Association is concerned were made (and later withdrawn) by Authurine Lucy, in proceedings in the Federal District Court to compel officials in the University of Alabama to vacate an order suspending her from attendance at classes. See Lucy v. Adams, Civ. No. 652, decided in the United States District Court for the Northern District of Alabama on January 24, 1957.

The fifth and sixth charges against the Association concern the proceedings in this case, and were added to the complaint, along with the fourth charge, by amendment in 1961.

NOTES

The above line of "right of association" cases, all invalidating state regulation, includes also Shelton v. Tucker, 364 U.S. 479, 81 S. Ct. 247, 5 L. Ed. 2d 231 (1960), holding unconstitutional an Arkansas statute requiring all teachers to list all organizations to which they belong; Louisiana ex rel. Gremillion v. N.A.A.C.P., 366 U.S. 293, 81 S. Ct. 1333, 6 L. Ed. 2d 301 (1961), striking down two Louisiana statutes, one noted in Chapter III, the other requiring "benevolent" associations to file a list of all officers and members; and Brotherhood of R.R. Trainmen v. Virginia ex rel. Virginia State Bar, 377 U.S. 1, 84 S. Ct. 1113, 12 L. Ed. 2d 89 (1964), following the Button case in upholding the Brotherhood's legal assistance plan for its members.

REFERENCES

1. For an account of the N.A.A.C.P. litigation in Alabama, see Osborne, Freedom of Association: The NAACP in Alabama, in Pritchett and Westin (eds.), The Third Branch of Government (1963).

General discussion of restrictions imposed on civil rights organizations may be found in Note, State Control over Political Organizations: First Amendment Checks on Powers of Regulation, 66 Yale L.J. 545 (1957); Robison, Protection of Associations from Compulsory Disclosure of Membership, 58 Colum. L. Rev. 614 (1958); McKay, The Repression of Civil Rights as an Aftermath of the School Segregation Cases, 4 How. L.J. 9 (1958); Kalven, The Negro and the First Amendment, ch. II (1965). See also Note, 20 Ohio St. L.J. 123 (1959).

The right of a dissenting group to incorporate under the laws of New York arose in the case of the Association for the Preservation of Freedom of Choice. The proposed certificate of incorporation listed as one of the purposes of the organization: "to promote the right to individual freedom of choice and association, constituting the right of the individual to associate with only those persons with whom he desires to associate." The organization, charged with being a "hate group," was denied the right to incorporate on the ground that the purposes of the proposed corporation must be "in accord with public policy and not injurious to the community." The ruling was affirmed by the Appellate Division, but reversed by the Court of Appeals. In the Matter of the Association for the Preservation of Freedom of Choice v. Shapiro, 9 N.Y.2d 376, 214 N.Y.S.2d 388, 174 N.E.2d 487 (1961). For comment on the case in the lower courts, see McAulay and Brewster, In re Application of the Association for the Preservation of Freedom of Choice, 6 How. L.J. 169 (1960); Vance, Freedom of Association and Freedom of Choice in New York State, 46 Cornell L.Q. 290 (1961); Note, 6 N.Y.L.F. 69 (1960). For related litigation, see Association for the Preservation of Freedom of Choice v. Simon, 299 F.2d 212 (2d Cir. 1962).

2. There is a growing literature on the constitutional right of association, first enunciated in the 1958 Alabama case. It includes Solter, Freedom of Association — A New and Fundamental Civil Right, 27 Geo. Wash. L. Rev. 653 (1959); Note, Freedom of Association, 4 Race Rel. L. Rep. 207 (1959); Note, Freedom of Association: Constitutional Right or Judicial Technique? 46 Va. L. Rev. 730 (1960); Abernathy, The Right of Assembly and Association (1961); Hotes and Hotes, Freedom of Association, 10 Clev.-Mar. L. Rev. 104 (1961); Kauper, Civil Liberties and the Constitution, ch. III (1962); Rice, Freedom of Association (1962); Douglas, The Right of Association, 63 Colum. L. Rev. 1361 (1963); Fellman, The Constitutional Right of Association (1963); Develop-

ments in the Law — Judicial Control of Actions of Private Associations, 76 Harv. L. Rev. 983 (1963); Emerson, Freedom of Association and Freedom of Expression, 74 Yale L.J. 1 (1964); Rice, The Constitutional Right of Association, 16 Hastings L.J. 491 (1965). See also Horn, Groups and the Constitution (1956).

3. With respect to the Button and R.R. Brotherhood problem, see Birkby and Murphy, Interest Group Conflict in the Judicial Arena: The First Amendment and Group Access to the Courts, 42 Texas L. Rev. 1018 (1964); Bodle, Group Legal Services: The Case for BRT, 12 U.C.L.A.L. Rev. 306 (1965); Note, Group Legal Services and the Right of Association, 63 Mich. L. Rev. 1089 (1965). See also Notes, 32 U. Cinc. L. Rev. 550 (1963); 40 U. Det. L.J. 531 (1963); 43 Texas L. Rev. 254 (1964); 25 U. Pitt. L. Rev. 142 (1964); 25 La. L. Rev. 558 (1965).

B. Regulation of the Political Process

Extensive federal and state legislation undertakes to regulate the political process. The major controls are the corrupt practices acts and laws pertaining to lobbying. Certain other aspects of elections and the operations of the legislature, which involve questions of reconciliation with freedom of expression, have also arisen. Issues concerned with obstruction of the right to vote on racial grounds are dealt with in Chapter XIV. Reapportionment, the rights of minority parties, and similar aspects of the right of franchise are considered in Chapter XII.

1. Corrupt Practices Legislation

Corrupt practices legislation, setting limits to the amount of political contributions, requiring disclosure, and imposing similar restrictions, has been generally considered to raise no serious constitutional issues. The basic validity of such legislation was upheld in Burroughs v. United States, 290 U.S. 534, 54 S. Ct. 287, 78 L. Ed. 484 (1934). While the legislation, both federal and state, has been subject to vigorous criticism for its inadequacy and ineffectiveness, there has been no further disposition to challenge it broadly on constitutional grounds. But two particular aspects of the legislation have given rise to constitutional controversy. One is the prohibition against election contributions and expenditures by corporations and labor organizations; the other is the proscription of political activity by government employees.

SECTION 304 OF THE TAFT-HARTLEY ACT
18 U.S.C. §610

It is unlawful for any national bank, or any corporation organized by authority of any law of Congress, to make a contribution or expenditure in connection with any election to any political office, or in connection with any primary election or political convention or caucus held to select candidates for any political office, or for any corporation whatever, or any labor organization to make a contribution or expenditure in connection with any election at which Presidential and Vice Presidential electors or a Senator or Representative in, or a Delegate or Resident Commissioner to Congress are to be voted for, or in connection with any primary election or political convention or caucus held to select candidates for any of the foregoing offices, or for any candidate, political committee, or other person to accept or receive any contribution prohibited by this section.

Every corporation or labor organization which makes any contribution or expenditure in violation of this section shall be fined not more than $5,000; and every officer or director of any corporation, or officer of any labor organization, who consents to any contribution or expenditure by the corporation or labor organization, as the case may be, and any person who accepts or receives any contribution, in violation of this section shall be fined not more than $1,000 or imprisoned not more than one year, or both; and if the violation was willful, shall be fined not more than $10,000 or imprisoned not more than two years, or both.

NOTES

The Congress of Industrial Organizations sought to test the constitutionality of Section 304 in United States v. Congress of Industrial Organizations, 335 U.S. 106, 68 S. Ct. 1349, 92 L. Ed. 1849 (1948). The indictment charged that the C.I.O. and its president published with union funds a regular periodical containing an editorial favoring one candidate in a Maryland Congressional election, and expended union funds to print and distribute extra copies in the election district. The defendants contended that Section 304 violated, among other constitutional provisions, the rights to freedom of speech, press, and assembly and to petition the Government for redress of grievances, as guaranteed by the First Amendment. But the Supreme Court side-stepped the constitutional issues, holding that the indictment failed to state an offense under the statute: "We are unwilling to say that Congress by its prohibition against corporations or labor organizations making an 'expenditure in connection with any election' of candidates for federal office intended to outlaw such a publication. We do not think [§304] reaches such a use of corporate or labor organization funds." 335 U.S. at 123-124. Mr. Justice Rutledge concurred in the result, with Justices Black, Douglas, and Murphy joining him, arguing that the case came squarely within the prohibition of Section 304, but that the statute constituted a prior restraint on freedom of expression and assembly and violated the First Amendment.

Two other efforts to challenge Section 304 likewise resulted in dismissal of the indictments on grounds that the conduct of the defendants was not prohibited by the statute. United States v. Painters Local Union No. 481, 172 F.2d 854 (2d Cir. 1949) (indictment charged union with making expenditures to purchase political advertisements in a newspaper and on the radio); United States v. Construction and General Laborers Local Union No. 264, 101 F. Supp. 869 (W.D. Mo. 1951) (three employees of the union devoted a considerable portion of their time to political campaign).

The question again reached the Supreme Court in United States v. International

Union United Automobile, Aircraft and Agricultural Implement Workers of America, 138 F. Supp. 53 (E.D. Mich. 1956), rev'd, 352 U.S. 567, 77 S. Ct. 529, 1 L. Ed. 2d 563 (1957). Here the indictment charged that the U.A.W. had spent some $6000 from its general funds to pay for a series of television broadcasts during the 1954 primary and general election campaigns in Michigan. These broadcasts, it was alleged, "urged and endorsed selection of certain persons to be candidates for representatives and senator to the Congress of the United States and included expressions of political advocacy intended by defendant to influence the electorate and to affect the results of the election." 138 F. Supp. at 54; N.Y. Times, July 21, 1955. The district court dismissed the indictment on the ground that "Congress did not intend to write an unconstitutional law" and that the "'expenditures' charged in this indictment are not expenditures prohibited by the Act." 138 F. Supp. at 59. Reversing, the Supreme Court held that "§304 was understood to proscribe the expenditure of union dues to pay for commercial broadcasts that are designed to urge the public to elect a certain candidate or party." 352 U.S. at 586-587. The C.I.O. case was distinguished on the ground that the communication there involved "was neither directed nor delivered to the public at large." 352 U.S. at 589. The Court remanded the case for trial, refusing to pass on the constitutional issues at that point. Mr. Justice Douglas, joined by Chief Justice Warren and Justice Black, dissented on the ground that Section 304 as construed by the majority violated the First Amendment. At the trial the U.A.W. was found not guilty by the jury. N.Y. Times, Nov. 7, 1957.

The various loopholes in the legislation have made the constitutional issues somewhat academic, and they have never been resolved.

REFERENCES

1. Since the Supreme Court's decision in the Automobile Workers case, prosecutions under 18 U.S.C. §610 have been rare.

2. For discussion of Section 304 and the earlier cases, see Note, Section 304, Taft-Hartley Act: Validity of Restrictions on Union Political Activity, 57 Yale L.J. 806 (1948); Kallenbach, The Taft-Hartley Act and Union Political Contributions and Expenditures, 33 Minn. L. Rev. 1 (1948); Note, Regulation of Labor's Political Contributions and Expenditures: The British and American Experience, 19 U. Chi. L. Rev. 371 (1952); Bicks and Friedman, Regulation of Federal Election Finance: A Case of Misguided Morality, 28 N.Y.U.L. Rev. 975, 992-996 (1953); Chang, Labor Political Action and the Taft-Hartley Act, 33 Neb. L. Rev. 554 (1954); Notes, 34 Va. L. Rev. 461 (1948); 27 Texas L. Rev. 565 (1949); 7 Wash. & Lee L. Rev. 87 (1950); 48 Nw. U.L. Rev. 64 (1953). The U.A.W. case is discussed in Notes, 46 Geo. L.J. 176 (1957); 71 Harv. L. Rev. 120 (1957); 42 Iowa L. Rev. 609 (1957); 31 Temple L.Q. 71 (1957); 1957 U. Ill. L.F. 319.

Later material includes Note, Control of Corporate and Union Political Expenditures: A Constitutional Analysis, 27 Ford. L. Rev. 559 (1959); Fillenwarth, Politics and Labor Unions, 37 Notre Dame Law. 172 (1961); Rauh, Legality of Union Political Expenditures, 34 So. Cal. L. Rev. 152 (1961); Woll, Unions in Politics: A Study in Law and the Workers' Needs, 34 So. Cal. L. Rev. 130 (1961); Note, Corporate Political Affairs Programs, 70 Yale L.J. 821 (1961); King, Corporate Political Spending and the First Amendment, 23 U. Pitt. L. Rev. 847 (1962); Zon, Labor in Politics, 27 Law & Contemp. Prob. 234 (1962); Hacker and Aberbach, Businessmen in Politics, 27 Law &

Contemp. Prob. 252 (1962); Haley, Limitations on Political Activities of Corporations, 9 Vill. L. Rev. 593 (1964).

As to comparable state legislation, see Kallenbach, supra, at 9-11; Brown, State Regulation of Union Political Action, 6 Lab. L.J. 769 (1955); Bowe v. Secretary of the Commonwealth, 320 Mass. 230, 69 N.E.2d 115 (1946); Note, 2 Wyo. L.J. 124 (1948).

3. With respect to the general problem of corrupt practices legislation, see Clark, Federal Regulation of Election Campaign Activities, 6 Fed. B.J. 5 (1944); Lederle, Political Committee Expenditures and the Hatch Act, 44 Mich. L. Rev. 294 (1945); Bicks and Friedman, supra; Note, Statutory Regulation of Political Campaign Funds, 66 Harv. L. Rev. 1259 (1953); McKesson and Dickey, Financing of Political Campaigns: Abuses and Suggested Controls, 34 So. Cal. L. Rev. 165 (1961); Roady, Ten years of Florida's "Who Gave It — Who Got It" Law, 27 Law & Contemp. Prob. 434 (1962). The chief federal legislation is 18 U.S.C. §§591-612, and 2 U.S.C. §§241-256. For a collection of the state laws and a discussion of the English experience, see Bottomly, Corrupt Practices in Political Campaigns, 30 B.U.L. Rev. 331 (1950).

More generally on the problem, see Overacker, Presidential Campaign Funds, 39 Am. Pol. Sci. Rev. 899 (1945); Overacker, Presidential Campaign Funds (1946); Key, Politics, Parties, and Pressure Groups, ch. 18 (3d ed. 1952); Heard, The Costs of Democracy (1960); Report of President's Commission on Campaign Costs, Financing Presidential Campaigns (1962); Alexander, Financing the 1960 Election (1962); Alexander, Studies in Money in Politics (1965); Congressional Quarterly Service, Congress and the Nation, ch. 13 (1965).

On May 26, 1966, President Johnson sent a special message to Congress asking for tightening of existing controls and proposing that small contributors be encouraged by allowing a tax deduction up to $100 for political contributions. 112 Cong. Rec. 11003, 11123 (daily ed., May 26, 1966), reprinted in 1966 U.S. Code Congressional and Administrative News 1654. For discussion of tax incentive proposals see, Peters, Political Campaign Financing: Tax Incentives for Small Contributors, 18 La. L. Rev. 414 (1958); Goldman, Income Tax Incentives for Political Contributions: A Study of the 1963 Proposals, 11 U.C.L.A.L. Rev. 212 (1964).

4. In United States v. Scott, 195 F. Supp. 440 (D.N.D. 1961), the court upheld 18 U.S.C. §612, which makes it a criminal offense to publish pamphlets concerning candidates for federal office without disclosing the names of those responsible for publication and distribution. See Note, 60 Mich. L. Rev. 506 (1962). See also Canon v. Justice Court for Lake Valley Judicial District, 61 Cal. 2d 446, 39 Cal. Rptr. 228, 393 P.2d 428 (1964).

5. In Mills v. Alabama, 384 U.S. 214, 86 S. Ct. 1434, 16 L. Ed. 2d 484 (1966), the editor of a daily newspaper was charged with violation of a provision of the Alabama Corrupt Practices Act which made it a crime "to do any electioneering or to solicit any votes . . . in support of or in opposition to any proposition that is being voted on on the day on which the election affecting such candidates or proposition is being held." The Supreme Court held the law to be in violation of the First Amendment.

SECTION 9 OF THE HATCH ACT
5 U.S.C. §118i

(a) It shall be unlawful for any person employed in the executive branch of the Federal Government, or any agency or department thereof, to use his official authority or influence for the purpose of interfering with an election or affecting the result thereof. No officer or employee in the executive branch of the Federal Government, or any agency or department thereof, shall take any active part in political management or in political campaigns. All such persons shall retain the right to vote as they may choose and to express their opinions on all political subjects and candidates. For the purposes of this section the term "officer" or "employee" shall not be construed to include (1) the President and Vice President of the United States; (2) persons whose compensation is paid from the appropriation for the office of the President; (3) heads and assistant heads of executive departments; (4) officers who are appointed by the President, by and with the advice and consent of the Senate, and who determine policies to be pursued by the United States in its relations with foreign powers or in the Nation-wide administration of Federal laws.

(b) Any person violating the provisions of this section shall be removed immediately from the position or office held by him . . . *Provided, however,* That the United States Civil Service Commission finds by unanimous vote that the violation does not warrant removal, a lesser penalty shall be imposed by direction of the Commission: *Provided further,* That in no case shall the penalty be less than ninety days' suspension without pay . . .

UNITED PUBLIC WORKERS v. MITCHELL
330 U.S. 75, 67 S. Ct. 556, 91 L. Ed. 754 (1947)

Mr. Justice Reed delivered the opinion of the Court.

[Certain employees in the executive branch of the Federal Government and a union of such employees sued to enjoin members of the Civil Service Commission from enforcing the provisions of Section 9(a) of the Hatch Act. The Court holds first that only Poole, a roller in the Philadelphia mint, has standing to bring the action.]

This brings us to consider the narrow but important point involved in Poole's situation. Poole's stated offense is taking an "active part in political management or in political campaigns." He was a ward executive committeeman of a political party and was politically active on election day as a worker at the polls and a paymaster for the services of other party workers. The issue for decision and the only one we decide is whether such a breach of the Hatch Act and Rule 1 of the Commission can, without violating the Constitution, be made the basis for disciplinary action.

When the issue is thus narrowed, the interference with free expression is seen in better proportion as compared with the requirements of orderly management of administrative personnel. Only while the employee is politically active, in the sense of Rule 1, must he withhold expression of opinion on public subjects. See note 6. We assume that Mr. Poole would be expected to comment publicly as committeeman on political matters, so that indirectly there is an attenuated interference. We accept appellants' contention that the nature of political rights reserved to the people by the Ninth and Tenth Amendments are involved. The right claimed as inviolate may be stated as the right of a citizen to act as a party official or worker to further his own political views. Thus we have a measure of interference by the Hatch Act and the Rules with what otherwise would be the freedom of the civil servant under the First, Ninth and Tenth Amendments. And, if we look upon due process as a guarantee of freedom in those fields, there is a corresponding impairment of that right under the Fifth Amendment. Appellants' objections under the Amendments are basically the same.

We do not find persuasion in appellants' argument that such activities during free time are not subject to regulation even though admittedly political activities cannot be indulged in during working hours. The influence of political activity by government employees, if evil in its effects on the service, the employees or people dealing with them, is hardly less so because that activity takes place after hours. Of course, the question of the need for this regulation is for other branches of government rather than the courts. Our duty in this case ends if the Hatch Act provision under examination is constitutional.

Of course, it is accepted constitutional doctrine that these fundamental human rights are not absolutes. The requirements of residence and age must be met. The essential rights of the First Amendment in some instances are subject to the elemental need for order without which the guarantees of civil rights to others would be a mockery. The powers granted by the Constitution to the Federal Government are subtracted from the totality of sovereignty originally in the states and the people. Therefore, when objection is made that the exercise of a federal power infringes upon rights reserved by the Ninth and Tenth Amendments, the inquiry must be directed toward the granted power under which the action of the Union was taken. If granted power is found, necessarily the objection of invasion of those rights, reserved by the Ninth and Tenth Amendments, must fail. Again this Court must balance the extent of the guarantees of freedom against a congressional enactment to protect a democratic society against the supposed evil of political partisanship by classified employees of government. . . .

The provisions of §9 of the Hatch Act and the Civil Service Rule 1 are not dissimilar in purpose from the statutes against political contributions of money. The prohibitions now under discussion are directed at political contributions of energy by government employees. These contributions, too, have a long background of disapproval. Congress and the President are responsible for an efficient public service. If, in their judgment, efficiency may be best obtained by prohibiting active participation by classified employees in politics as party officers or workers, we see no constitutional objection.

Another Congress may determine that, on the whole, limitations on active political management by federal personnel are unwise. The teaching of experience has evidently led Congress to enact the Hatch Act provisions. To declare that the present supposed evils of political activity are beyond the power of Congress to redress would leave the nation impotent to deal with what many sincere men believe is a material threat to the democratic system. Congress is not politically naive or regardless of public welfare or that of the employees. It leaves untouched full participation by employees in political decisions at the ballot box and forbids only the partisan activity of federal personnel deemed offensive to efficiency. With that limitation only, employees may make their contributions to public affairs or protect their own interests, as before the passage of the Act.

The argument that political neutrality is not indispensable to a merit system for federal employees may be accepted. But because it is not indispensable does not mean that it is not desirable or permissible. Modern American politics involves organized political parties. Many classifications of government employees have been accustomed to work in politics — national, state and local — as a matter of principle or to assure their tenure. Congress may reasonably desire to limit party activity of federal employees so as to avoid a tendency toward a one-party system. It may have considered that parties would be more truly devoted to the public welfare if public servants were not overactive politically.

Appellants urge that federal employees are protected by the Bill of Rights and that Congress may not "enact a regulation providing that no Republican, Jew or Negro shall be appointed to federal office, or that no federal employee shall attend Mass or take any active part in missionary work." None would deny such limitations on congressional power but, because there are some limitations, it does not follow that a prohibition against acting as ward leader or worker at the polls is invalid. A reading of the Act and Rule 1, notes 2 and 6, supra, together with the Commission's determination shows the wide range of public activities with which there is no interference by the legislation. It is only partisan political activity that is interdicted. It is active participation in political management and political campaigns. Expressions, public or private, on public affairs, personalities and matters of public interest, not an objective of party action, are unrestricted by law so long as the government employee does not direct his activities toward party success.

It is urged, however, that Congress has gone further than necessary in prohibiting political activity to all types of classified employees. It is pointed out by appellants "that the impartiality of many of these is a matter of complete indifference to the effective performance" of their duties. Mr. Poole would appear to be a good illustration for appellants' argument. The complaint states that he is a roller in the mint. We take it this is a job calling for the qualities of a skilled mechanic and that it does not involve contact with the public. Nevertheless, if in free time he is engaged in political activity, Congress may have concluded that the activity may promote or retard his advancement or preferment with his superiors. Congress may have thought that government employees are handy elements for leaders in political policy to use in building a political machine. For regulation of employees it is not necessary that the act regulated be anything more than an act reasonably deemed by Congress to interfere with the efficiency of the public service. There are hundreds of thousands of United States employees with positions no more influential upon policy determination than that of Mr. Poole. Evidently what Congress feared was the cumulative effect on employee morale of political activity by all employees who could be induced to participate actively. It does not seem to us an unconstitutional basis for legislation. . . .

We have said that Congress may regulate the political conduct of government employees "within reasonable limits," even though the regulation trenches to some extent upon unfettered political action. The determination of the extent to which political activities of governmental employees shall be regulated lies primarily with Congress. Courts will interfere only when such regulation passes beyond the generally existing conception of governmental power. That conception develops from practice, history, and changing educational, social and economic conditions. The regulation of such activities as Poole carried on has the approval of long practice by the Commission, court decisions upon similar problems and a large body of informed public opinion. Congress and the administrative agencies have authority over the discipline and efficiency of the public service. When actions of civil servants in the judgment of Congress menace the integrity and the competency of the service, legislation to forestall such danger and adequate to maintain its usefulness is required. The Hatch Act is the answer of Congress to this need. We cannot say with such a background that these restrictions are unconstitutional. . . .

[Mr. Justice Frankfurter concurred. Justices Murphy and Jackson did not participate.]

Mr. Justice Black, dissenting.

. . . The number of federal employees thus barred from political action is approximately three million. Section 12 of the same Act affects the participation in political campaigns of many thousands of state employees. No one of all these millions of citizens can, without violating this law, "take any active part" in any campaign for a cause or for a candidate if the cause or candidate is "specifically identified with any National or State political party." Since under our common political practices most causes and candidates are espoused by political parties, the result is that, because they are paid out of the public treasury, all these citizens who engage in public work can take no really effective part in campaigns that may bring about changes in their lives, their fortunes, and their happiness.

. . . The result is that the sum of political privilege left to government and state employees, and their families, to take part in political campaigns seems to be this: They may vote in silence; they may carefully and quietly express a political view at their peril; and they may become "spectators" (this is the Commission's word) at campaign gatherings, though it may be highly dangerous for them to "second a motion" or let it be known that they agree or disagree with a speaker. . . .

Had this measure deprived five million farmers or a million businessmen of all right to participate in elections, because Congress thought that federal farm or business subsidies might prompt some of them to exercise, or be susceptible to, a corrupting influence on politics or government, I would not sustain such an Act on the ground that it could be interpreted so as to apply only to some of them. Certainly laws which restrict the liberties guaranteed by the First Amendment should be narrowly drawn to meet the evil aimed at and to affect only the minimum number of people imperatively necessary to prevent a grave and imminent danger to the public. Furthermore, what federal employees can or cannot do, consistently with the various civil service regulations, rules, warnings, etc., is a matter of so great uncertainty that no person can even make an intelligent guess. This was demonstrated by the government's briefs and oral arguments in this case. I would hold that the provision here attacked is too broad, ambiguous, and uncertain in its consequences to be made the basis of removing deserving employees from their jobs. See dissenting opinion, Williams v. North Carolina, 325 U.S. 226, 261, 276-278 and cases collected, note 16.

The right to vote and privately to express an opinion on political matters, important though they be, are but parts of the broad freedoms which our Constitution has provided as the bulwark of our free political institutions. Popular government, to be effective, must permit and encourage much wider political activity by all the people. Real popular government means "that men may speak as they think on matters vital to them and that falsehoods may be exposed through the processes of education and discussion . . . Those who won our independence had confidence in the power of free and fearless reasoning and communication of ideas to discover and spread political and economic truth." Thornhill v. Alabama, 310 U.S. 88, 95. Legislation which muzzles several million citizens threatens popular government, not only because it injures the individuals muzzled, but also because of its harmful effect on the body politic in depriving it of the political participation and interest of such a large segment of our citizens. Forcing public employees to contribute money and influence can well be proscribed in the interest of "clean politics" and public administration. But I think the Constitution prohibits legislation which prevents millions of citizens from contributing their arguments, complaints, and suggestions to the political debates which are the essence of our democracy; prevents them from engaging in organizational activity to urge others to vote and take an interest in political affairs; bars them from performing the interested citizen's duty of insuring that his and his fellow citizens' votes are counted. Such drastic limitations on the right of all the people to express political opinions and take political action would be inconsistent with the First Amendment's guaranty of freedom of speech, press, assembly and petition. And it would violate, or come dangerously close to violating, Article I and the Seventeenth Amendment of the Constitution, which protect the right of the people to vote for their Congressmen and their United States Senators and to have their votes counted. See Ex parte Yarbrough, 110 U.S.

651; United States v. Mosley, 238 U.S. 383; United States v. Classic, 313 U.S. 299, 314. . . .

Our political system, different from many others, rests on the foundation of a belief in rule by the people — not some, but all the people. Education has been fostered better to fit people for self-expression and good citizenship. In a country whose people elect their leaders and decide great public issues, the voice of none should be suppressed — at least such is the assumption of the First Amendment. That Amendment, unless I misunderstand its meaning, includes a command that the Government must, in order to promote its own interest, leave the people at liberty to speak their own thoughts about government, advocate their own favored governmental causes, and work for their own political candidates and parties.

The section of the Act here held valid reduces the constitutionally protected liberty of several million citizens to less than a shadow of its substance. It relegates millions of federal, state, and municipal employees to the role of mere spectators of events upon which hinge the safety and welfare of all the people, including public employees. It removes a sizable proportion of our electorate from full participation in affairs destined to mould the fortunes of the nation. It makes honest participation in essential political activities an offense punishable by proscription from public employment. It endows a governmental board with the awesome power to censor the thoughts, expressions, and activities of law-abiding citizens in the field of free expression, from which no person should be barred by a government which boasts that it is a government of, for, and by the people — all the people. Laudable as its purpose may be, it seems to me to hack at the roots of a Government by the people themselves; and consequently I cannot agree to sustain its validity.

Mr. Justice Douglas, dissenting in part.

. . . In other situations where the balance was between constitutional rights of individuals and a community interest which sought to qualify those rights, we have insisted that the statute be "narrowly drawn to define and punish specific conduct as constituting a clear and present danger to a substantial interest" of government. Cantwell v. Connecticut, 310 U.S. 296, 311. And see Murdock v. Pennsylvania, 319 U.S. 105, 116; Thornhill v. Alabama, 310 U.S. 88, 104-105.

That seems to me the proper course to follow here. The prohibition in §9(a) of the Hatch Act against government employees taking an "active part in political management or in political campaigns" applies without discrimination to all employees whether industrial or administrative. The same is true of the Civil Service Rules. See Rules I, §1, XV, 5 C.F.R. Cum. Supp., §§1.1, 15.1. But the supposed evils are both different and narrower in case of industrial workers than they are in the case of the administrative group. The public interest in the political activity of a machinist or elevator operator or charwoman is a distinct and different problem. In those cases the public concern is in the preservation of an unregimented industrial group, in a group free from political pressures of superiors who use their official power for a partisan purpose. Then official power is misused, perverted. The Government is corrupted by making its industrial workers political captives, victims of bureaucratic power, agents for perpetuating one party in power.

Offset against that public concern are the interests of the employees in the exercise of cherished constitutional rights. The nature and importance of those rights have been fully expounded in Mr. Justice Black's opinion. If those rights are to be qualified by the larger requirements of modern democratic government, the restrictions should be narrowly and selectively drawn to define and punish the specific conduct which constitutes a clear and present danger to the operations of government. It seems plain to me that that evil has its roots in the coercive activity of those in the hierarchy who have the power to regiment the industrial group or who undertake to do so. To sacrifice the political rights of the industrial workers goes far beyond any demonstrated or demonstrable need. Those rights are too basic and fundamental in our democratic political society to be sacrificed or qualified for anything short of a clear and present danger to the civil service system. No such showing has been made in the case of these industrial workers which justifies their political sterilization as distinguished from selective measures aimed at the coercive practices on which the spoils system feeds.

[Mr. Justice Rutledge concurred with Mr. Justice Black insofar as Poole was concerned, but did not pass on constitutional questions as to other employees.]

NOTES

1. Another provision of the Hatch Act applies the same restrictions to state employees "whose principal employment is in connection with any activity which is financed in whole or in part by loans or grants made by the United States or by any Federal agency." 5 U.S.C. §118k (1952). This provision was upheld in Oklahoma v. United States Civil Service Commission, 330 U.S. 127, 67 S. Ct. 544, 91 L. Ed. 794 (1947). Justices Black and Rutledge dissented and Justices Murphy and Jackson did not participate. See also Illinois v. United States Civil Service Commission, 297 F.2d 450 (7th Cir. 1962), cert. den., 369 U.S. 849 (1962). For a decision holding a county charter provision restricting the political activities of county employees to be too broadly drawn and hence in violation of free speech protections, see Fort v. Civil Service Commission of County of Alameda, 61 Cal. 2d 331, 38 Cal. Rptr. 625, 392 P.2d 385 (1964).

2. Decisions of the Civil Service Commission interpreting Section 9 of the Hatch Act are collected in Hatch Act Decisions of the U.S. Civil Service Commission, prepared by James W. Irwin, Chief Hearing Examiner, U.S. Civil Service Commission (G.P.O. 1949). In Wilson v. U.S. Civil Service Com., 136 F. Supp. 104 (D.C. 1955), a decision of the Commission, suspending a Post Office employee

for writing a letter to a newspaper urging defeat of a candidate, was reversed. The court held that the letter "did not fairly indicate active participation in organized political affairs." Further on the interpretation of the Hatch Act, see United States Civil Service Commission, Political Activity of Federal Officers and Employees (Pamphlet 20, 1961); Rose, A Critical Look at the Hatch Act, 75 Harv. L. Rev. 510 (1962).

3. Federal employees who circulate petitions addressed to members of Congress or otherwise communicate with them are protected by 5 U.S.C. §652(d), which provides: "The right of persons employed in the civil service of the United States, either individually or collectively, to petition Congress, or any member thereof, or to furnish information to either House of Congress, or to any Committee or member thereof, shall not be denied or interfered with." See Steck v. Connally, 199 F. Supp. 104 (D.D.C. 1961). But in Turner v. Kennedy, 332 F.2d 304 (D.C. Cir. 1964), cert. den., 379 U.S. 901 (1964), the court upheld the discharge of an F.B.I. agent for making "false, irresponsible, and unjustified" statements in letters to Congressmen. Judge Fahy dissented on First Amendment grounds, arguing that the employee should be protected unless actual malice was shown. The case is discussed in Note, Dismissals of Public Employees for Petitioning Congress: Administrative Discipline and 5 U.S.C. Section 652(d), 74 Yale L.J. 1156 (1965).

REFERENCES

For discussion of the Hatch Act and the Mitchell and Oklahoma decisions, see Kirchheimer, The Historical and Comparative Background of the Hatch Law, II Public Policy 341 (1941); Howard, Federal Restrictions on Political Activity of Government Employees, 35 Am. Pol. Sci. Rev. 470 (1941); Friedman and Klinger, The Hatch Act: Regulation by Administrative Action of Political Activities of Governmental Employees, 7 Fed. Bar J. 5, 138 (1945-1946); Note, Political Sterilization of Government Employees, 47 Colum. L. Rev. 295 (1947); Mosher, Government Employees Under the Hatch Act, 22 N.Y.U.L.Q Rev. 233 (1947); Notes, 33 Cornell L.Q. 133 (1947); 15 Geo. Wash. L. Rev. 443 (1947); 32 Minn. L. Rev. 176, 301 (1948); Esman, The Hatch Act — A Reappraisal, 60 Yale L.J. 986 (1951); Nelson, Public Employees and the Right to Engage in Political Activity, 9 Vand. L. Rev. 27 (1955); Irwin, Public Employees and the Hatch Act, 9 Vand. L. Rev. 527 (1956); Still, The Hatch Act — Political Immaturity? 45 Geo. L.J. 233 (1957); Ford, Political Activities and Public Service: A Continuing Problem (Institute of Government Studies, Berkeley 1963). See also Report of the Special Committee to Investigate and Study the Operation and Enforcement of the Hatch Political Activity Act, H.R. Rep. 2707, 85th Cong., 2d Sess. (1958).

With respect to the treatment of the problem in other countries, see White et al., Civil Service Abroad (1935); Kingsley, Representative Bureaucracy (1944); Morstein Marx, Comparative Administrative Law: Political Activity of Civil Servants, 29 Va. L. Rev. 52 (1942); Emerson and Helfeld, Loyalty Among Government Employees, 58 Yale L.J. 1, 120, 133 (1948); Report of the Committee on Political Activities of Civil Servants (Masterman Report), H.M. Stationery Office, London, Cmd. 7718 (1949); Political Activities of Civil Servants, H.M. Stationery Office, London, Cmd. 8783 (1953); Campbell, The Civil Service in Britain 305-310 (1955); Christoph, Political Rights and Impartiality in the British Civil Service, 51 Am. Pol. Sci. Rev. 67 (1957).

2. *Regulation of Lobbying Activities*

Legislation regulating lobbying activities, largely by way of registration and disclosure, has been on the statute books, federal and state, for many years. The Supreme Court considered the constitutional issues, somewhat indirectly, in United States v. Rumely, 345 U.S. 41, 73 S. Ct. 543, 97 L. Ed. 770 (1953), noted in Chapter III, Section F. The issues were squarely presented to the Court in the Harriss case, set forth below.

UNITED STATES v. HARRISS
347 U.S. 612, 74 S. Ct. 808, 98 L. Ed. 989 (1954)

MR. CHIEF JUSTICE WARREN delivered the opinion of the Court.

The appellees were charged by information with violation of the Federal Regulation of Lobbying Act, 60 Stat. 812, 839, 2 U.S.C. §§261-270. Relying on its previous decision in National Association of Manufacturers v. McGrath, 103 F. Supp. 510, vacated as moot, 344 U.S. 804, the District Court dismissed the information on the ground that the Act is unconstitutional. 109 F. Supp. 641. The case is here on direct appeal under the Criminal Appeals Act, 18 U.S.C. §3731.

Seven counts of the information are laid under §305, which requires designated reports to Congress from every person "receiving any contributions or expending any money" for the purpose of influencing the passage or defeat of any legislation by Congress.[1] One such count charges the National Farm

---

[1] Section 305 provides:

"(a) Every person receiving any contributions or expending any money for the purposes designated in subparagraph (a) or (b) of section 307 shall file with the Clerk between the first and tenth day of each calendar quarter, a statement containing complete as of the day next preceding the date of filing —

"(1) the name and address of each person who has made a contribution of $500 or more not mentioned in the preceding report; except that the first report filed pursuant to this title shall contain the name and address of each person who has made any contribution of $500 or more to such person since the effective date of this title;

"(2) the total sum of the contributions made to or for such person during the calendar year and not stated under paragraph (1);

"(3) the total sum of all contributions made to or for such person during the calendar year;

"(4) the name and address of each person to whom an expenditure in one or more items of the aggregate amount or value, within the calendar year, of $10 or more has been made by or on behalf of such person, and the amount, date, and purpose of such expenditure;

"(5) the total sum of all expenditures made by or on behalf of such person during the calendar year and not stated under paragraph (4);

"(6) the total sum of expenditures made by or on behalf of such person during the calendar year.

"(b) The statements required to be filed by subsection (a) shall be cumulative during the calendar year to which they relate, but where there has been no change in an item reported in a previous statement only the amount need be carried forward." . . .

Committee, a Texas corporation, with failure to report the solicitation and receipt of contributions to influence the passage of legislation which would cause a rise in the price of agricultural commodities and commodity futures and the defeat of legislation which would cause a decline in those prices. The remaining six counts under §305 charge defendants Moore and Harriss with failure to report expenditures having the same single purpose. Some of the alleged expenditures consist of the payment of compensation to others to communicate face-to-face with members of Congress, at public functions and committee hearings, concerning legislation affecting agricultural prices; the other alleged expenditures relate largely to the costs of a campaign to induce various interested groups and individuals to communicate by letter with members of Congress on such legislation.

The other two counts in the information are laid under §308, which requires any person "who shall engage himself for pay or for any consideration for the purpose of attempting to influence the passage or defeat of any legislation" to register with Congress and to make specified disclosures.[2] These two counts allege in considerable detail that defendants Moore and Linder were hired to express certain views to Congress as to agricultural prices or to cause others to do so, for the purpose of attempting to influence the passage of legislation which would cause a rise in the price of agricultural commodi-

---

[2] Section 308 provides:

"(a) Any person who shall engage himself for pay or for any consideration for the purpose of attempting to influence the passage or defeat of any legislation by the Congress of the United States shall, before doing anything in furtherance of such object, register with the Clerk of the House of Representatives and the Secretary of the Senate and shall give to those officers in writing and under oath, his name and business address, the name and address of the person by whom he is employed, and in whose interest he appears or works, the duration of such employment, how much he is paid and is to receive, by whom he is paid, how much he is to be paid for expenses, and what expenses are to be included. Each such person so registering shall, between the first and tenth day of each calendar quarter, so long as his activity continues, file with the Clerk and Secretary a detailed report under oath of all money received and expended by him during the preceding calendar quarter in carrying on his work; to whom paid; for what purposes; and the names of any papers, periodicals, magazines, or other publications in which he has caused to be published any articles or editorials; and the proposed legislation he is employed to support or oppose. The provisions of this section shall not apply to any person who merely appears before a committee of the Congress of the United States in support of or opposition to legislation; nor to any public official acting in his official capacity; nor in the case of any newspaper or other regularly published periodical (including any individual who owns, publishes, or is employed by any such newspaper or periodical) which in the ordinary course of business publishes news items, editorials, or other comments, or paid advertisements, which directly or indirectly urge the passage or defeat of legislation, if such newspaper, periodical, or individual, engages in no further or other activities in connection with the passage or defeat of such legislation, other than to appear before a committee of the Congress of the United States in support of or in opposition to such legislation.

"(b) All information required to be filed under the provisions of this section with the Clerk of the House of Representatives and the Secretary of the Senate shall be compiled by said Clerk and Secretary, acting jointly, as soon as practicable after the close of the calendar quarter with respect to which such information is filed and shall be printed in the Congressional Record."

ties and commodity futures and a defeat of legislation which would cause a decline in such prices; and that pursuant to this undertaking, without having registered as required by §308, they arranged to have members of Congress contacted on behalf of these views, either directly by their own emissaries or through an artificially stimulated letter campaign.

. . . The key section of the Lobbying Act is §307, entitled "Persons to Whom Applicable." Section 307 provides:

"The provisions of this title shall apply to any person (except a political committee as defined in the Federal Corrupt Practices Act, and duly organized State or local committees of a political party), who by himself, or through any agent or employee or other persons in any manner whatsoever, directly or indirectly, solicits, collects, or receives money or any other thing of value to be used principally to aid, or the principal purpose of which person is to aid, in the accomplishment of any of the following purposes:

"(a) The passage or defeat of any legislation by the Congress of the United States.

"(b) To influence, directly or indirectly, the passage or defeat of any legislation by the Congress of the United States."

This section modifies the substantive provisions of the Act, including §305 and §308. In other words, unless a "person" falls within the category established by §307, the disclosure requirements of §305 and §308 are inapplicable. Thus coverage under the Act is limited to those persons (except for the specified political committees) who solicit, collect, or receive contributions of money or other thing of value, and then only if "the principal purpose" of either the persons or the contributions is to aid in the accomplishment of the aims set forth in §307(a) and (b). In any event, the solicitation, collection, or receipt of money or other thing of value is a prerequisite to coverage under the Act.

[The Court then discusses the interpretation to be given the Act.]

To summarize, therefore, there are three prerequisites to coverage under §307: (1) the "person" must have solicited, collected, or received contributions; (2) one of the main purposes of such "person," or one of the main purposes of such contributions, must have been to influence the passage or defeat of legislation by Congress; (3) the intended method of accomplishing this purpose must have been through direct communication with members of Congress. And since §307 modifies the substantive provisions of the Act, our construction of §307 will of necessity also narrow the scope of §305 and §308, the substantive provisions underlying the information in this case. Thus §305 is limited to those persons who are covered by §307; and when so covered, they must report all contributions and expenditures having the purpose of attempting to influence legislation through direct communication with Congress. Similarly, §308 is limited to those persons (with the stated exceptions) who are covered by §307 and who, in addition, engage themselves for pay or for any other valuable consideration for the purpose of attempting to influence legislation through direct communication with Congress. Construed in this way, the Lobbying Act meets the constitutional requirement of definiteness.

Thus construed, §§305 and 308 also do not violate the freedoms guaranteed by the First Amendment — freedom to speak, publish, and petition the Government.

Present-day legislative complexities are such that individual members of Congress cannot be expected to explore the myriad pressures to which they are regularly subjected. Yet full realization of the American ideal of government by elected representatives depends to no small extent on their ability to properly evaluate such pressures. Otherwise the voice of the people may all too easily be drowned out by the voice of special interest groups seeking favored treatment while masquerading as proponents of the public weal. This is the evil which the Lobbying Act was designed to help prevent.

Toward that end, Congress has not sought to prohibit these pressures. It has merely provided for a modicum of information from those who for hire attempt to influence legislation or who collect or spend funds for that purpose. It wants only to know who is being hired, who is putting up the money, and how much. It acted in the same spirit and for a similar purpose in passing the Federal Corrupt Practices Act — to maintain the integrity of a basic governmental process. See Burroughs and Cannon v. United States, 290 U.S. 534, 545.

Under these circumstances, we believe that Congress, at least within the bounds of the Act as we have construed it, is not constitutionally forbidden to require the disclosure of lobbying activities. To do so would be to deny Congress in large measure the power of self-protection. And here Congress has used that power in a manner restricted to its appropriate end. We conclude that §§305 and 308, as applied to persons defined in §307, do not offend the First Amendment.

It is suggested, however, that the Lobbying Act, with respect to persons other than those defined in §307, may as a practical matter act as a deterrent to their exercise of First Amendment rights. Hypothetical borderline situations are conjured up in which such persons choose to remain silent because of fear of possible prosecution for failure to comply with the Act. Our narrow construction of the Act, precluding as it does reasonable fears, is calculated to avoid such restraint. But, even assuming some such deterrent effect, the restraint is at most an indirect one resulting from self-censorship, comparable in many ways to the restraint resulting from criminal libel laws.[17] The hazard of such restraint is too remote to require striking down a statute which on its face is otherwise plainly within the area of congressional power and is designed to safeguard a vital national interest.

---

[17] Similarly, the Hatch Act probably deters some federal employees from political activity permitted by that statute, but yet was sustained because of the national interest in a nonpolitical civil service. United Public Workers v. Mitchell, 330 U.S. 75.

[The Court found it unnecessary to pass on the contention that the penalty provisions violated the First Amendment in prescribing that any person convicted under the Act "is prohibited, for a period of three years from the date of such conviction, from attempting to influence, directly or indirectly, the passage or defeat of any proposed legislation or from appearing before a committee of the Congress in support of or opposition to proposed legislation."]

MR. JUSTICE DOUGLAS, with whom MR. JUSTICE BLACK concurs, dissenting.

I am in sympathy with the effort of the Court to save this statute from the charge that it is so vague and indefinite as to be unconstitutional. My inclinations were that way at the end of the oral argument. But further study changed my mind. I am now convinced that the formula adopted to save this Act is too dangerous for use. It can easily ensnare people who have done no more than exercise their constitutional rights of speech, assembly, and press. . . .

Can Congress require one to register before he writes an article, makes a speech, files an advertisement, appears on radio or television, or writes a letter seeking to influence existing, pending, or proposed legislation? That would pose a considerable question under the First Amendment, as Thomas v. Collins, 323 U.S. 516, indicates. I do not mean to intimate that Congress is without power to require disclosure of the real principals behind those who come to Congress (or get others to do so) and speak as though they represent the public interest, when in fact they are undisclosed agents of special groups. I mention the First Amendment to emphasize why statutes touching this field should be "narrowly drawn to prevent the supposed evil" (see Cantwell v. Connecticut, 310 U.S. 296, 307) and not be cast in such vague and indefinite terms as to cast a cloud on the exercise of constitutional rights. . . .

If that rule were relaxed, if Congress could impose registration requirements on the exercise of First Amendment rights, saving to the courts the salvage of the good from the bad, and meanwhile causing all who might possibly be covered to act at their peril, the law would in practical effect be a deterrent to the exercise of First Amendment rights. The Court seeks to avoid that consequence by construing the law narrowly as applying only to those who are paid to "buttonhole" Congressmen or who collect and expend moneys to get others to do so. It may be appropriate in some cases to read a statute with the gloss a court has placed on it in order to save it from the charge of vagueness. See Fox v. Washington, 236 U.S. 273, 277. But I do not think that course is appropriate here.

The language of the Act is so broad that one who writes a letter or makes a speech or publishes an article or distributes literature or does many of the other things with which appellees are charged has no fair notice when he is close to the prohibited line. No construction we give it today will make clear retroactively the vague standards that confronted appelles when they did the acts now charged against them as criminal. Cf. Pierce v. United States, 314

U.S. 306, 311. Since the Act touches on the exercise of First Amendment rights, and is not narrowly drawn to meet precise evils, its vagueness has some of the evils of a continuous and effective restraint.

[Mr. Justice Jackson also dissented. His opinion is omitted. Mr. Justice Clark did not participate.]

REFERENCES

For a full discussion of the Federal Lobbying Act and similar state legislation, see Notes, Improving the Legislative Process, 56 Yale L.J. 304 (1947); The Federal Lobbying Act of 1946, 47 Colum. L. Rev. 98 (1947). A later discussion of the Federal Act appears in Walter, Federal Regulation of Lobbying, 34 So. Calif. L. Rev. 111 (1961). See also Note, 49 Nw. U.L. Rev. 807 (1955). An extensive investigation of the Federal Act was made by a special House committee in 1950-1951. See House Select Committee on Lobbying Activities, General Interim Report (H.R. Rep. 3138), and Report and Recommendations on Federal Lobbying Act (H.R. Rep. 3239) 81st Cong., 2d Sess. (1950, 1951). For material on the operations of the Act, see Congressional Quarterly Service, Congress and the Nation, ch. XIV (1965).

On the general question of lobbying and its regulation, see Schriftgeisser, The Lobbyists (1951); Truman, The Governmental Process (1951); Bailey and Samuel, Congress at Work (1952); Key, Politics, Parties and Pressure Groups (3d ed. 1952); Latham, The Group Basis of Politics (1952); Gross, The Legislative Struggle (1953); Unofficial Government: Pressure Groups and Lobbies, 319 Annals of the Am. Acad. of Pol. and Soc. Sci. (Sept. 1958); Ehrmann, Interest Groups on Four Continents (1958); Wahlke et al., The Legislative System, ch. 14 (1962); Lane, Lobbying and the Law (1964).

See also Cammarano v. United States, 358 U.S. 498, 79 S. Ct. 524, 3 L. Ed. 2d 462 (1959), and Eastern Railroad Presidents Conference v. Noerr Motor Freight, Inc., 365 U.S. 127, 81 S. Ct. 523, 5 L. Ed. 2d 464 (1961), both noted in Section A above.

NOTE

In June, 1965, Julian Bond, a Negro, was elected to the Georgia House of Representatives. Subsequently he publicly endorsed a statement issued by SNCC (of which Bond was communications director) concerning the Viet Nam war. The statement said in part:

"The Student Nonviolent Coordinating Committee has a right and a responsibility to dissent with United States foreign policy on any issue when it sees fit. The Student Nonviolent Coordinating Committee now states its opposition to United States' involvement in Vietnam on these grounds:

"We believe the United States government has been deceptive in its claims of concern for the freedom of the Vietnamese people, just as the government has been deceptive in such other countries as the Dominican Republic, the Congo, South Africa, Rhodesia, and in the United States itself. . . .

"We question, then, the ability and even the desire of the United States government to guarantee free elections abroad. We maintain that our country's cry of 'preserve freedom in the world' is a hypocritical mask behind which it squashes liberation movements which are not bound, and refuse to be bound, by the expediencies of United States cold war policies.

"We are in sympathy with, and support, the men in this country who are unwilling to respond to a military draft which would compel them to contribute their lives to United States aggression in Vietnam in the name of the 'freedom' we find so false in this country.

"We recoil with horror at the inconsistency of a supposedly 'free' society where responsibility to freedom is equated with the responsibility to lend oneself to military aggression. We take note of the fact that 16% of the draftees from this country are Negroes called on to stifle the liberation of Vietnam, to preserve a 'democracy' which does not exist for them at home.

"We ask, where is the draft for the freedom fight in the United States?

"We therefore encourage those Americans who prefer to use their energy in building, democratic forms within this country. We believe that work in the civil rights movement and with other human relations organizations is a valid alternative to the draft. We urge all Americans to seek this alternative, knowing full well that it may cost them their lives — as painfully as in Vietnam."

When asked for his views on the burning of draft cards Bond stated that he would not burn his own but admired the courage of those who did; that he was a pacifist and supported the opposition of others to the war.

When Bond appeared to take his seat in the legislature, proceedings were instituted to exclude him, on the ground that "Mr. Bond's actions and statements gave aid and comfort to the enemies of the United States, and also violated the Selective Service Laws . . . and tended to bring discredit and disrespect upon the House of Representatives." Bond was refused his seat. N.Y. Times, Jan. 11, 1966. At a second election to fill the vacancy he was re-elected, N.Y. Times, Feb. 24, 1966, and again barred. N.Y. Times, May 25, 1966.

Bond and others brought an action in the federal district court to enjoin the legislature from excluding him. A three-judge court dismissed the complaint. Bond v. Floyd, 251 F. Supp. 333 (N.D. Ga. 1966).

The Supreme Court noted probable jurisdiction. 384 U.S. 997 (1966).

REFERENCES

1. For the federal precedents in excluding persons from taking a seat in the legislature, see Senate Election, Expulsion and Censure Cases From 1789 to 1960, compiled by Richard D. Hupman (G.P.O. 1962). For the refusals to seat Victor Berger and the five New York Socialists, see Chapter II, Section F. Cf. Application of Esther James, 241 F. Supp. 858 (S.D. N.Y. 1965).

2. With respect to state pay-while-voting statutes, see Day-Brite Lighting, Inc. v. Missouri, 342 U.S. 421, 72 S. Ct. 405 96 L. Ed. 469 (1952); Heimgaertnor v. Benjamin Electric Manufacturing Co., 6 Ill. 2d 152, 128 N.E.2d 691 (1955); Note, Pay While Voting, 47 Colum. L. Rev. 135 (1947); Notes, 47 Nw. U. L. Rev. 252 (1952); 27 Notre Dame Law. 456 (1952); 22 Geo. Wash. L. Rev. 108 (1953); 33 Chi-Kent L. Rev. 267 (1955).

3. On proposed controls over broadcasts of early election returns, see Note, Tom Swift and His Electric Electorate: Legislation to Restrict Election Coverage, 40 Notre Dame Law. 191 (1965).

C. Administration of Justice

Reconciliation of the right to expression with the social interest in the fair and effective administration of justice has presented problems in two forms. One arises where the expression constitutes a criticism of the court itself. The other is where the expression has an influence upon jurors, witnesses, prosecutors, or others involved in the judicial process, which may result in unfairness to the accused or one of the parties before the court.

In a series of cases beginning in 1941, the Supreme Court has considered the question of the extent to which the First Amendment limits the judicial power to punish as contempt of court publications criticising the court or its handling of matters pending before it. In these cases the Court has consistently applied the clear and present danger test, and in each case has found that no clear and present danger to the administration of justice was presented by the communications in question. The earlier cases are: Bridges v. California, 314 U.S. 252, 62 S. Ct. 190, 86 L. Ed. 192 (1941) (Mr. Chief Justice Stone and Justices Frankfurter, Roberts, and Byrnes dissenting) (publication of telegram and editorials to influence judge in fixing a sentence); Pennekamp v. Florida, 328 U.S. 331, 66 S. Ct. 1029, 90 L. Ed. 1295 (1946) (criticism for dismissing indictment); Craig v. Harney, 331 U.S. 367, 67 S. Ct. 1249, 91 L. Ed. 1546 (1947) (Mr. Chief Justice Vinson and Justices Frankfurter and Jackson dissenting) (criticism of judge during frequent refusals to accept jury verdict.) In a more recent decision, Wood v. Georgia, 370 U.S. 375, 82 S. Ct. 1364, 8 L. Ed. 2d 569 (1962), a majority of the Court reached the same conclusions.

The more common problem in reconciling freedom of expression and the fair administration of justice has arisen where newspaper or other publicity has jeopardized, or possibly jeopardized, the right of an accused to a fair trial. There are several avenues open to the courts in this situation. Those which do not attempt to impose controls upon the participants in the publicity process include change of venue or a setting aside of the trial. For a number of years the contention that a defendant had been deprived of due process by inflammatory publicity was urged unsuccessfully on the Supreme Court. See Sheppard v. Florida, 341 U.S. 50, 71 S. Ct. 549, 95 L. Ed. 740 (1951); Stroble v. California, 343 U.S. 181, 72 S. Ct. 599, 96 L. Ed. 872 (1952); Beck v. Washington, 369 U.S. 541, 82 S. Ct. 955, 8 L. Ed. 2d 98 (1962). But in Irvin v. Dowd, 366 U.S. 717, 81 S. Ct. 639, 6 L. Ed. 2d 751 (1961), the Court for the first time accepted the contention and reversed a conviction. Since then the Court has set aside convictions for prejudicial publicity in Rideau v. Louisiana, 373 U.S. 723, 83 S. Ct. 1417, 10 L. Ed. 2d 663 (1963); and Sheppard v. Maxwell, 384 U.S. 333, 86 S. Ct. 1507, 16 L. Ed. 2d 600 (1966). Cf. Marshall v. United States, 360 U.S. 310, 79 S. Ct. 1171, 3 L. Ed. 2d 1250 (1959). In Estes v. Texas, set forth below, the Court considered the problem in the context of radio and TV in the courtroom.

ESTES v. TEXAS
381 U.S. 532, 85 S. Ct. 1628, 14 L. Ed. 2d 543 (1965)

Mr. Justice Clark delivered the opinion of the Court.

The question presented here is whether the petitioner, who stands convicted in the District Court for the Seventh Judicial District of Texas at Tyler for swindling,[1] was deprived of his right under the Fourteenth Amendment to due process by the televising and broadcasting of his trial. Both the trial court and the Texas Court of Criminal Appeals found against the petitioner. We hold to the contrary and reverse his conviction.

I.

While petitioner recites his claim in the framework of Canon 35 of the Judicial Canons of the American Bar Association he does not contend that we should enshrine Canon 35 in the Fourteenth Amendment, but only that the time-honored principles of a fair trial were not followed in his case and that he was thus convicted without due process of law. Canon 35, of course, has of itself no binding effect on the courts but merely expresses the view of the Association in opposition to the broadcasting, televising and photographing of court proceedings. Likewise, Judicial Canon 28 of the Integrated State Bar of Texas, 27 Tex. B.J. 102 (1964), which leaves to the trial judge's sound discretion the telecasting and photographing of court proceedings, is of itself not law. In short, the question here is not the validity of either Canon 35 of the American Bar Association or Canon 28 of the State Bar of Texas, but only whether petitioner was tried in a manner which comports with the due process requirement of the Fourteenth Amendment.

Petitioner's case was originally called for trial on September 24, 1962, in Smith County after a change of venue from Reeves County, some 500 miles west. Massive pretrial publicity totaling 11 volumes of press clippings, which are on file with the Clerk, had given it national notoriety. All available seats in the courtroom were taken and some 30 persons stood in the aisles. However, at that time a defense motion to prevent telecasting, broadcasting by radio and news photography and a defense motion for continuance were presented, and after a two-day hearing the former was denied and the latter granted.

These initial hearings were carried live by both radio and television, and

---

[1] The evidence indicated that petitioner, through false pretenses and fraudulent representations, induced certain farmers to purchase fertilizer tanks and accompanying equipment, which in fact did not exist, and to sign and deliver to him chattel mortgages on the fictitious property.

news photography was permitted throughout. The videotapes of these hearings clearly illustrate that the picture presented was not one of that judicial serenity and calm to which petitioner was entitled. Cf. Wood v. Georgia, 370 U.S. 375, 383 (1962); Turner v. Louisiana, 379 U.S. 466, 472 (1965); Cox v. Louisiana, 379 U.S. 559, 562 (1965). Indeed, at least 12 cameramen were engaged in the courtroom throughout the hearing taking motion and still pictures and televising the proceedings. Cables and wires were snaked across the courtroom floor, three microphones were on the judge's bench and others were beamed at the jury box and the counsel table. It is conceded that the activities of the television crews and news photographers led to considerable disruption of the hearings. Moreover, veniremen had been summoned and were present in the courtroom during the entire hearing but were later released after petitioner's motion for continuance had been granted. The court also had the names of the witnesses called; some answered but the absence of others led to a continuance of the case until October 22, 1962. It is contended that this two-day pretrial hearing cannot be considered in determining the question before us. We cannot agree. Pretrial can create a major problem for the defendant in a criminal case. Indeed, it may be more harmful than publicity during the trial for it may well set the community opinion as to guilt or innocence. Though the September hearings dealt with motions to prohibit television coverage and to postpone the trial, they are unquestionably relevant to the issue before us. All of this two-day affair was highly publicized and could only have impressed those present, and also the community at large, with the notorious character of the petitioner as well as the proceeding. The trial witnesses present at the hearing, as well as the original jury panel, were undoubtedly made aware of the peculiar public importance of the case by the press and television coverage being provided, and by the fact that they themselves were televised live and their pictures rebroadcast on the evening show.

When the case was called for trial on October 22 the scene had been altered. A booth had been constructed at the back of the courtroom which was painted to blend with the permanent structure of the room. It had an aperture to allow the lens of the cameras an unrestricted view of the courtroom. All television cameras and newsreel photographers were restricted to the area of the booth when shooting film or telecasting.

Because of continual objection, the rules governing live telecasting, as well as radio and still photos, were changed as the exigencies of the situation seemed to require. As a result, live telecasting was prohibited during a great portion of the actual trial. Only the opening[2] and closing arguments of the State, the return of the jury's verdict and its receipt by the trial judge were carried live with sound. Although the order allowed videotapes of the entire proceeding without sound, the cameras operated only intermittently, recording various portions of the trial for broadcast on regularly scheduled newscasts later in the day and evening. At the request of the petitioner, the trial

---

[2] Due to mechanical difficulty there was no picture during the opening argument.

judge prohibited coverage of any kind, still or television, of the defense counsel during their summations to the jury.

Because of the varying restrictions placed on sound and live telecasting the telecasts of the trial were confined largely to film clips shown on the stations' regularly scheduled news programs. The news commentators would use the film of a particular part of the day's trial activities as a backdrop for their reports. Their commentary included excerpts from testimony and the usual reportorial remarks. On one occasion the videotapes of the September hearings were rebroadcast in place of the "late movie."

II

In Rideau v. Louisiana, 373 U.S. 723 (1963), this Court constructed a rule that the televising of a defendant in the act of confessing to a crime was inherently invalid under the Due Process Clause of the Fourteenth Amendment even without a showing of prejudice or a demonstration of the nexus between the televised confession and the trial. See id., at 729 (dissenting opinion of Clark, J.). Here, although there was nothing so dramatic as a home-viewed confession, there had been a bombardment of the community with the sights and sounds of a two-day hearing during which the original jury panel, the petitioner, the lawyers and the judge were highly publicized. The petitioner was subjected to characterization and minute electronic scrutiny to such an extent that at one point the photographers were found attempting to picture the page of the paper from which he was reading while sitting at the counsel table. The two-day hearing and the order permitting television at the actual trial were widely known throughout the community. This emphasized the notorious character that the trial would take and, therefore, set it apart in the public mind as an extraordinary case or, as Shaw would say, something "not conventionally unconventional." When the new jury was empaneled at the trial four of the jurors selected had seen and heard all or part of the broadcasts of the earlier proceedings.

III

We start with the proposition that it is a "public trial" that the Sixth Amendment guarantees to the "accused." The purpose of the requirement of a public trial was to guarantee that the accused would be fairly dealt with and not unjustly condemned. History had proven that secret tribunals were effective instruments of oppression. . . . It is said, however, that the freedoms granted in the First Amendment extend a right to the news media to televise from the courtroom, and that to refuse to honor this privilege is to discriminate between the newspapers and television. This is a misconception of the rights of the press.

The free press has been a mighty catalyst in awakening public interest in governmental affairs, exposing corruption among public officers and employes and generally informing the citizenry of public events and occurrences, including court proceedings. While maximum freedom must be allowed the press in carrying on this important function in a democratic society its exercise must necessarily be subject to the maintenance of absolute fairness in the judicial process. . . .

Nor can the courts be said to discriminate where they permit the newspaper reporter access to the courtroom. The television and radio reporter has the same privilege. All are entitled to the same rights as the general public. The news reporter is not permitted to bring his typewriter or printing press. When the advances in these arts permit reporting by printing press or by television without their present hazards to a fair trial we will have another case.

IV

Court proceedings are held for the solemn purpose of endeavoring to ascertain the truth which is the sine qua non of a fair trial. Over the centuries Anglo-American courts have devised careful safeguards by rule and otherwise to protect and facilitate the performance of this high function. As a result, at this time those safeguards do not permit the televising and photographing of a criminal trial, save in two States and there only under restrictions. The federal courts prohibit it by specific rule. This is weighty evidence that our concepts of a fair trial do not tolerate such an indulgence. We have always held that the atmosphere essential to the preservation of a fair trial — the most fundamental of all freedoms — must be maintained at all costs. Our approach has been through rules, contempt proceedings and reversal of convictions obtained under unfair conditions. Here the remedy is clear and certain of application and it is our duty to continue to enforce the principles that from time immemorial have proven efficacious and necessary to a fair trial.

V

The State contends that the televising of portions of a criminal trial does not constitute a denial of due process. Its position is that because no prejudice has been shown by the petitioner as resulting from the televising, it is permissible; that claims of "distractions" during the trial due to the physical presence of television are wholly unfounded; and that psychological considerations are for psychologists, not courts, because they are purely hypothetical. It argues further that the public has a right to know what goes on in the courts; that the court has no power to "suppress, edit, or censor events which transpire in proceedings before it," citing Craig v. Harney, 331 U.S. 367, 374 (1947); and that the televising of criminal trials would be enlightening to the public and would promote greater respect for the courts.

At the outset the notion should be dispelled that telecasting is dangerous because it is new. It is true that our empirical knowledge of its full effect on the public, the jury or the participants in a trial, including the judge, witnesses and lawyers, is limited. However, the nub of the question is not its newness but, as Mr. Justice Douglas says, "the insidious influences which it puts to work in the administration of justice." Douglas, The Public Trial and the Free Press, 33 Rocky Mt. L. Rev. 1 (1960). These influences will be detailed below, but before turning to them the State's argument that the public has a right to know what goes on in the courtroom should be dealt with.

It is true that the public has the right to be informed as to what occurs in its courts, but reporters of all media, including television, are always present if they wish to be and are plainly free to report whatever occurs in open court through their respective media. This was settled in Bridges v. California, 314 U.S. 252 (1941), and Pennekamp v. Florida, 328 U.S. 331 (1946), which we reaffirm. These reportorial privileges of the press were stated years ago:

"The law, however, favors publicity in legal proceedings, so far as that object can be attained without injustice to the persons immediately concerned. The public are permitted to attend nearly all judicial inquiries, and there appears to be no sufficient reason why they should not also be allowed to see in print the reports of trials, if they can thus have them presented as fully as they are exhibited in court, or at least all the material portion of the proceedings impartially stated, so that one shall not, by means of them, derive erroneous impressions, which he would not have been likely to receive from hearing the trial itself." 2 Cooley's Constitutional Limitations 931-932 (Carrington ed. 1927).

The State, however, says that the use of television in the instant case was "without injustice to the person immediately concerned," basing its position on the fact that the petitioner has established no isolatable prejudice and that this must be shown in order to invalidate a conviction in these circumstances. The State paints too broadly in this contention, for this Court itself has found instances in which a showing of actual prejudice is not a prerequisite to reversal. This is such a case. It is true that in most cases involving claims of due process deprivations we require a showing of identifiable prejudice to the accused. Nevertheless, at times a procedure employed by the State involves such a probability that prejudice will result that it is deemed inherently lacking in due process. . . .

This rule was followed in Rideau, supra, and in Turner v. Louisiana, 379 U.S. 466 (1965). In each of these cases the Court departed from the approach it charted in Stroble v. California, 343 U.S. 181 (1952), and in Irvin v. Dowd, 366 U.S. 717 (1961), where we made a careful examination of the facts in order to determine whether prejudice resulted. In Rideau and Turner the Court did not stop to consider the actual effect of the practice but struck down the conviction on the ground that prejudice was inherent in it. Likewise in Gideon v. Wainwright, 372 U.S. 335 (1963), and White v. Maryland,

373 U.S. 59 (1963), we applied the same rule, although in different contexts.

In this case it is even clearer that such a rule must be applied. In Rideau, Irvin and Stroble, the pretrial publicity occurred outside the courtroom and could not be effectively curtailed. The only recourse other than reversal was by contempt proceedings. In Turner the probability of prejudice was present through the use of deputy sheriffs, who were also witnesses in the case, as shepherds for the jury. No prejudice was shown but the circumstances were held to be inherently suspect, and, therefore, such a showing was not held to be a requisite to reversal. Likewise in this case the application of this principle is especially appropriate. Television in its present state and by its very nature, reaches into a variety of areas in which it may cause prejudice to an accused. Still one cannot put his finger on its specific mischief and prove with particularity wherein he was prejudiced. This was found true in Murchison, Tumey, Rideau and Turner. Such untoward circumstances as were found in those cases are inherently bad and prejudice to the accused was presumed. Forty-eight of our States and the Federal Rules have deemed the use of television improper in the courtroom. This fact is most telling in buttressing our conclusion that any change in procedure which would permit its use would be inconsistent with our concepts of due process in this field.

V I

As has been said, the chief function of our judicial machinery is to ascertain the truth. The use of television, however, cannot be said to contribute materially to this objective. Rather its use amounts to the injection of an irrelevant factor into court proceedings. In addition experience teaches that there are numerous situations in which it might cause actual unfairness — some so subtle as to defy detection by the accused or control by the judge. We enumerate some in summary:

1. The potential impact of television on the jurors is perhaps of the greatest significance. They are the nerve center of the fact-finding process. It is true that in States like Texas where they are required to be sequestered in trials of this nature the jurors will probably not see any of the proceedings as televised from the courtroom. But the inquiry cannot end here. From the moment the trial judge announces that a case will be televised it becomes a *cause célèbre*. The whole community, including prospective jurors, becomes interested in all the morbid details surrounding it. The approaching trial immediately assumes an important status in the public press and the accused is highly publicized along with the offense with which he is charged. Every juror carries with him into the jury box these solemn facts and thus increases the chance of prejudice that is present in every criminal case. And we must remember that realistically it is only the notorious trial which will be broadcast, because of the necessity for paid sponsorship. The conscious or unconscious effect that this may have on the juror's judgment cannot be evaluated, but experience

indicates that it is not only possible but highly probable that it will have a direct bearing on his vote as to guilt or innocence. Where pretrial publicity of all kinds has created intense public feeling which is aggravated by the telecasting or picturing of the trial the televised jurors cannot help but feel the pressures of knowing that friends and neighbors have their eyes upon them. If the community be hostile to an accused a televised juror, realizing that he must return to neighbors who saw the trial themselves, may well be led "not to hold the balance nice, clear and true between the State and the accused. . . ."

Moreover, while it is practically impossible to assess the effect of television on jury attentiveness, those of us who know juries realize the problem of jury "distraction." The State argues this is de minimis since the physical disturbances have been eliminated. But we know that distractions are not caused solely by the physical presence of the camera and its telltale red lights. It is the awareness of the fact of telecasting that is felt by the juror throughout the trial. We are all self-conscious and uneasy when being televised. Human nature being what it is, not only will a juror's eyes be fixed on the camera, but also his mind will be preoccupied with the telecasting rather than with the testimony.

Furthermore, in many States the jurors serving in the trial may see the broadcasts of the trial proceedings. Admittedly, the Texas sequestration rule would prevent this occurring there. In other States following no such practice jurors would return home and turn on the TV if only to see how they appeared upon it. They would also be subjected to re-enactment and emphasis of the selected parts of the proceedings which the requirements of the broadcasters determined would be telecast and would be subconsciously influenced the more by that testimony. Moreover, they would be subjected to the broadest commentary and criticism and perhaps the well-meant advice of friends, relatives and inquiring strangers who recognized them on the streets.

Finally, new trials plainly would be jeopardized in that potential jurors will often have seen and heard the original trial when it was telecast. Yet viewers may later be called upon to sit in the jury box during the new trial. These very dangers are illustrated in this case where the court, due to the defendant's objections, permitted only the State's opening and closing arguments to be broadcast with sound to the public.

2. The quality of the testimony in criminal trials will often be impaired. The impact upon a witness of the knowledge that he is being viewed by a vast audience is simply incalculable. Some may be demoralized and frightened, some cocky and given to overstatement; memories may falter, as with anyone speaking publicly, and accuracy of statement may be severely undermined. Embarrassment may impede the search for the truth, as may a natural tendency toward overdramatization. Furthermore, inquisitive strangers and "cranks" might approach witnesses on the street with jibes, advice or demands for explanation of testimony. There is little wonder that the defendant

cannot "prove" the existence of such factors. Yet we all know from experience that they exist.

In addition the invocation of the rule against witnesses is frustrated. In most instances witnesses would be able to go to their homes and view broadcasts of the day's trial proceedings, notwithstanding the fact that they had been admonished not to do so. They could view and hear the testimony of preceding witnesses, and so shape their own testimony as to make its impact crucial. And even in the absence of sound, the influences of such viewing on the attitude of the witness toward testifying, his frame of mind upon taking the stand or his apprehension of withering cross-examination defy objective assessment. Indeed, the mere fact that the trial is to be televised might render witnesses reluctant to appear and thereby impede the trial as well as the discovery of the truth.

While some of the dangers mentioned above are present as well in newspaper coverage of any important trial, the circumstances and extraneous influences intruding upon the solemn decorum of court procedure in the televised trial are far more serious than in cases involving only newspaper coverage.

3. A major aspect of the problem is the additional responsibilities the presence of television places on the trial judge. His job is to make certain that the accused receives a fair trial. This most difficult task requires his undivided attention. Still when television comes into the courtroom he must also supervise it. In this trial, for example, the judge on several different occasions — aside from the two days of pretrial — was obliged to have a hearing or enter an order made necessary solely because of the presence of television. Thus, where telecasting is restricted as it was here, and as even the State concedes it must be, his task is made much more difficult and exacting. And, as happened here, such rulings may unfortunately militate against the fairness of the trial. In addition, laying physical interruptions aside, there is the ever-present distraction that the mere awareness of television's presence prompts. Judges are human beings also and are subject to the same psychological reactions as laymen. Telecasting is particularly bad where the judge is elected, as is the case in all save a half dozen of our States. The telecasting of a trial becomes a political weapon, which, along with other distractions inherent in broadcasting, diverts his attention from the task at hand — the fair trial of the accused.

But this is not all. There is the initial decision that must be made as to whether the use of television will be permitted. This is perhaps an even more crucial consideration. Our judges are high-minded men and women. But it is difficult to remain oblivious to the pressures that the news media can bring to bear on them both directly and through the shaping of public opinion. Moreover, where one judge in a district or even in a State permits telecasting, the requirement that the others do the same is almost mandatory. Especially is this true where the judge is selected at the ballot box.

4. Finally, we cannot ignore the impact of courtroom television on the defendant. Its presence is a form of mental — if not physical — harassment,

resembling a police line-up or the third degree. The inevitable close-ups of his gestures and expressions during the ordeal of his trial might well transgress his personal sensibilities, his dignity, and his ability to concentrate on the proceedings before him — sometimes the difference between life and death — dispassionately, freely and without the distraction of wide public surveillance. A defendant on trial for a specific crime is entitled to his day in court, not in a stadium, or a city or nationwide arena. The heightened public clamor resulting from radio and television coverage will inevitably result in prejudice. Trial by television is, therefore, foreign to our system. Furthermore, telecasting may also deprive an accused of effective counsel. The distractions, intrusions into confidential attorney-client relationships and the temptation offered by television to play to the public audience might often have a direct effect not only upon the lawyers, but the judge, the jury and the witnesses. See Pye, The Lessons of Dallas — Threats to Fair Trial and Free Press, National Civil Liberties Clearing House, 16th Annual Conference.

The television camera is a powerful weapon. Intentionally or inadvertently it can destroy an accused and his case in the eyes of the public. While our telecasters are honorable men, they too are human. The necessity for sponsorship weighs heavily in favor of the televising of only notorious cases, such as this one, and invariably focuses the lens upon the unpopular or infamous accused. Such a selection is necessary in order to obtain a sponsor willing to pay a sufficient fee to cover the costs and return a profit. We have already examined the ways in which public sentiment can affect the trial participants. To the extent that television shapes that sentiment, it can strip the accused of a fair trial. . . .

VII

The facts in this case demonstrate clearly the necessity for the application of the rule announced in Rideau. The sole issue before the court for two days of pretrial hearing was the question now before us. The hearing was televised live and repeated on tape in the same evening, reaching approximately 100,000 viewers. In addition, the courtroom was a mass of wires, television cameras, microphones and photographers. The petitioner, the panel of prospective jurors, who were sworn the second day, the witnesses and the lawyers were all exposed to this untoward situation. The judge decided that the trial proceedings would be telecast. He announced no restrictions at the time. This emphasized the notorious nature of the coming trial, increased the intensity of the publicity on the petitioner and together with the subsequent televising of the trial beginning 30 days later inherently prevented a sober search for the truth. This is underscored by the fact that the selection of the jury took an entire week. As might be expected, a substantial amount of that time was devoted to ascertaining the impact of the pretrial televising on the prospective jurors.

As we have noted, four of the jurors selected had seen all or part of those broadcasts. The trial, on the other hand, lasted only three days.

Moreover, the trial judge was himself harassed. After the initial decision to permit telecasting he apparently decided that a booth should be built at the broadcasters expense to confine its operations; he then decided to limit the parts of the trial that might be televised live; then he decided to film the testimony of the witnesses without sound in an attempt to protect those under the rule; and finally he ordered that defense counsel and their argument not be televised, in the light of their objection. Plagued by his original error — recurring each day of the trial — his day-to-day orders made the trial more confusing to the jury, the participants and to the viewers. Indeed, it resulted in a public presentation of only the State's side of the case. . . .

It is said that the ever-advancing techniques of public communication and the adjustment of the public to its presence may bring about a change in the effect of telecasting upon the fairness of criminal trials. But we are not dealing here with future developments in the field of electronics. Our judgment cannot be rested on the hypothesis of tomorrow but must take the facts as they are presented today.

The judgment is therefore

Reversed.

Mr. Chief Justice Warren, whom Mr. Justice Douglas, and Mr. Justice Goldberg join, concurring.

While I join the Court's opinion and agree that the television of criminal trials is inherently a denial of due process, I desire to express additional views on why this is so. In doing this, I wish to emphasize that our condemnation of televised criminal trials is not based on generalities or abstract fears. The record in this case presents a vivid illustration of the inherent prejudice of televised criminal trials and supports our conclusion that this is the appropriate time to make a definitive appraisal of television in the courtroom. . . .

I believe that it violates the Sixth Amendment for federal courts and the Fourteenth Amendment for state courts to allow criminal trials to be televised to the public at large. I base this conclusion on three grounds: (1) that the televising of trials diverts the trial from its proper purpose in that it has an inevitable impact on all the trial participants; (2) that it gives the public the wrong impression about the purpose of trials, thereby detracting from the dignity of court proceedings and lessening the reliability of trials; and (3) that it singles out certain defendants and subjects them to trials under prejudicial conditions not experienced by others. . . .

Nothing in this opinion is inconsistent with the constitutional guarantees of a public trial and the freedoms of speech and the press. . . .

To satisfy the constitutional requirement that trials be public it is not necessary to provide facilities large enough for all who might like to attend a particular trial, since to do so would interfere with the integrity of the trial process and make the publicity of trial proceedings an end in itself. Nor does the requirement that trials be public mean that observers are free to act as they please in the courtroom, for persons who attend trials cannot act in such a way as to interfere with the trial process . . . When representatives of the communications media attend trials they have no greater rights than other members of the public. Just as an ordinary citizen might be prohibited from using field glasses or a motion picture camera in the courthouse because by so doing he would interfere with the conduct of the trial, representatives of the press and broadcasting industries are subject to similar limitations when they attend court. Since the televising of criminal trials diverts the trial process from its proper end it must be prohibited. This prohibition does not conflict with the constitutional guarantee of a public trial, because a trial is public, in the constitutional sense, when a courtroom has facilities for a reasonable number of the public to observe the proceedings, which facilities are not so small as to render the openness negligible and not so large as to distract the trial participants from their proper function, when the public is free to use those facilities, and when all those who attend the trial are free to report what they observed at the proceedings.

Nor does the exclusion of television cameras from the courtroom in any way impinge upon the freedoms of speech and the press. Court proceedings, as well as other public matters, are proper subjects for press coverage. . . . So long as the television industry, like the other communications media, is free to send representatives to trials and to report on those trials to its viewers, there is no abridgment of the freedom of press. The right of the communications media to comment on court proceedings does not bring with it the right to inject themselves into the fabric of the trial process to alter the purpose of that process.

In summary, television is one of the great inventions of all time and can perform a large and useful role in society. But the television camera, like other technological innovations, is not entitled to pervade the lives of everyone in disregard of constitutionally protected rights. The television industry, like other institutions, has a proper area of activities and limitations beyond which it cannot go with its cameras. That area does not extend into an American courtroom. On entering that hallowed sanctuary, where the lives, liberty and property of people are in jeopardy, television representatives have only the rights of the general public, namely, to be present, to observe the proceedings, and thereafter, if they choose, to report them.

[Mr. Justice Harlan, in a concurring opinion, took the position that, "at least as to a notorious criminal trial such as this one, the considerations against allowing television in the courtroom so far outweigh the countervailing factors advanced in its support as to require a holding that what was done in this case infringed the fundamental right to a fair trial assured by the Due Process Clause of the Fourteenth Amendment."]

MR. JUSTICE STEWART, whom Mr. Justice Black, Mr. Justice Brennan, and Mr. Justice White join, dissenting.

I cannot agree with the Court's decision that the circumstances of this trial led to a denial of the petitioner's Fourteenth Amendment rights. I think that the introduction of television into a courtroom is, at least in the present state of the art, an extremely unwise policy. It invites many constitutional risks, and it detracts from the inherent dignity of a courtroom. But I am unable to escalate this personal view into a per se constitutional rule. And I am unable to find, on the specific record of this case, that the circumstances attending the limited televising of the petitioner's trial resulted in the denial of any right guaranteed to him by the United States Constitution. . . .

What ultimately emerges from this record, therefore, is one bald question — whether the Fourteenth Amendment of the United States Constitution prohibits all television cameras from a state courtroom whenever a criminal trial is in progress. In the light of this record and what we now know about the impact of television on a criminal trial, I can find no such prohibition in the Fourteenth Amendment or in any other provision of the Constitution. If what occurred did not deprive the petitioner of his constitutional right to a fair trial, then the fact that the public could view the proceeding on television has no constitutional significance. The Constitution does not make us arbiters of the image that a televised state criminal trial projects to the public.

While no First Amendment claim is made in this case, there are intimations in the opinions filed by my Brethren in the majority which strike me as disturbingly alien to the First and Fourteenth Amendments' guarantees against federal or state interference with the free communication of information and ideas. The suggestion that there are limits upon the public's right to know what goes on in the courts causes me deep concern. The idea of imposing upon any medium of communications the burden of justifying its presence is contrary to where I had always thought the presumption must lie in the area of First Amendment freedoms. See Speiser v. Randall, 357 U.S. 513, 525. And the proposition that nonparticipants in a trial might get the "wrong impression" from unfettered reporting and commentary contains an invitation to censorship which I cannot accept. Where there is no disruption of the "essential requirement of the fair and orderly administration of justice," "[f]reedom of discussion should be given the widest range." Pennekamp v. Florida, 328 U.S. 331, 347: Bridges v. California, 314 U.S. 252. Cf. Cox v. Louisiana, 379 U.S. 559, 563.

I do not think that the Constitution denies to the State or to individual trial judges all discretion to conduct criminal trials with television cameras present, no matter how unobtrusive the cameras may be. I cannot say at this time that it is impossible to have a constitutional trial whenever any part of the proceedings is televised or recorded on television film. I cannot now hold that the Constitution absolutely bars television cameras from every criminal courtroom, even if they have no impact upon the jury, no effect upon any witness, and no influence upon the conduct of the judge.

For these reasons I would affirm the judgment.

Mr. Justice White, with whom Mr. Justice Brennan joins, dissenting.

I agree with Mr. Justice Stewart that a finding of constitutional prejudice on this record entails erecting a flat ban on the use of cameras in the courtroom and believe that it is premature to promulgate such a broad constitutional principle at the present time. . . .

———

When a solution to the problem is sought through imposing restrictions upon persons participating in the publicity process outside the courtroom, other issues arise. Insofar as the government — whether through legislative, executive, or judicial measures — undertakes to restrict its own agents, no substantial constitutional issues would seem to be raised. There is, of course, much debate on the policy aspects of such controls. An example of this approach is set forth below in the guidelines issued by the United States Attorney General.

The Supreme Court has not passed upon the basic issues involved in an attempt to impose general restrictions upon news media, or persons other than its agents. In Baltimore Radio Show, Inc. v. Maryland, 193 Md. 300, 67 A.2d 497 (1949), it declined the opportunity. In that case a broadcasting company had been convicted of contempt for broadcasting statements that an accused had a long criminal record, that he had confessed, and similar matters. The Maryland Court of Appeals reversed, on First Amendment grounds, and the United States Supreme Court denied certiorari. 338 U.S. 912 (1950).

ATTORNEY GENERAL KATZENBACH,
STATEMENT OF POLICY
CONCERNING THE RELEASE OF INFORMATION
BY PERSONNEL OF THE DEPARTMENT OF JUSTICE
RELATING TO CRIMINAL PROCEEDINGS
28 C.F.R. §50.2 (April 16, 1965)

The availability to news media of information in criminal cases is a matter which has become increasingly a subject of concern in the administration of criminal justice. The purpose of this statement is to formulate specific guidelines for the release of such information by personnel of the Department of Justice.

While the release of information for the purpose of influencing a trial is, of course, always improper, there are valid reasons for making available to the public information about the administration of the criminal laws. The task of striking a fair balance between the protection of individuals accused of crime and public understanding of the problems of controlling crime depends largely on the exercise of sound judgment by those responsible for administering the criminal laws and by representatives of the press and other media.

Inasmuch as the Department of Justice has generally fulfilled its responsibilities with awareness and understanding of the competing needs in this area, this statement, to a considerable extent, reflects and formalizes the standards to which representatives of the Department have adhered in the past. Nonetheless, it will be helpful in ensuring uniformity of practice to set forth the following guidelines for all personnel of the Department of Justice.

Because of the difficulty and importance of the questions they raise, it is felt that some portions of the matters covered by this statement, such as the authorization to make available federal conviction records and a description of items seized at the time of arrest, should be the subject of continuing review and consideration by the Department on the basis of experience and suggestions from those within and outside the Department.

1. These guidelines shall apply to the release of information to news media from the time a person is arrested or is charged with a criminal offense until the proceeding has been terminated by trial or otherwise.

2. At no time shall personnel of the Department of Justice furnish any statement or information for the purpose of influencing the outcome of a defendant's trial.

3. Personnel of the Department of Justice, subject to specific limitations imposed by law or court rule or order, may make public the following information:

(a) The defendant's name, age, residence, employment, marital status, and similar background information.

(b) The substance or text of the charge, such as a complaint, indictment, or information.

(c) The identity of the investigating and arresting agency and the length of the investigation.

(d) The circumstances immediately surrounding an arrest, including the time and place of arrest, resistance, pursuit, possession and use of weapons, and a description of items seized at the time of arrest.

Disclosures should include only incontrovertible, factual matters, and should not include subjective observations. In addition, where background information or information relating to the circumstances of an arrest would be highly prejudicial and where the release thereof would serve no law enforcement function, such information should not be made public.

4. Personnel of the Department shall not volunteer for publication any information concerning a defendant's prior criminal record. However, this is not intended to alter the Department's present policy that, since federal criminal conviction records are matters of public record permanently maintained in the Department, this information may be made available upon specific inquiry.

5. Because of the particular danger of prejudice resulting from statements in the period approaching and during trial, they ought strenuously to be avoided during that period. Any such statement or release shall be made only on the infrequent occasion when circumstances absolutely demand a disclosure of information and shall include only information which is clearly not prejudicial.

6. The release of certain types of information generally tends to create dangers of prejudice without serving a significant law enforcement function. Therefore, personnel of the Department should refrain from making available the following:

(a) Observations about a defendant's character.

(b) Statements, admissions, confessions, or alibis attributable to a defendant.

(c) References to investigative procedures, such as fingerprints, polygraph examinations, ballistic tests, or laboratory tests.

(d) Statements concerning the identity, credibility, or testimony of prospective witnesses.

(e) Statements concerning evidence or argument in the case, whether or not it is anticipated that such evidence or argument will be used at trial.

7. Personnel of the Department of Justice should take no action to encourage or assist news media in photographing or televising a defendant or accused person being held or transported in federal custody. Departmental representatives should not make available photographs of a defendant unless a law enforcement function is served thereby.

8. This statement of policy is not intended to restrict the release of information concerning a defendant who is a fugitive from justice.

9. Since the purpose of this statement is to set forth generally applicable guidelines, there will, of course, be situations in which it will limit release of information which would not be prejudicial under the particular circumstances. If a representative of the Department believes that in the interest of the fair administration of justice and the law enforcement process information beyond these guidelines should be released in a particular case, he shall request the permission of the Attorney General or the Deputy Attorney General to do so.

REFERENCES

The problems raised in the above materials have been widely discussed, in the law journals and elsewhere. For a recent general survey of the contempt power see Goldfarb, The Contempt Power (1963). On the issue of contempt by publication, see Nelles and King, Contempt by Publication in the United States, 28 Colum. L. Rev. 525 (1928); Hanson, The Supreme Court on Freedom of the Press and Contempt by Publication, 27 Cornell L.Q. 165 (1942); Radin, Freedom of Speech and Contempt of Court, 36 Ill. L. Rev. 599 (1942); Note, Contempt by Publication, 59 Yale L.J. 534 (1950); Notes, 23 Ind. L.J. 192 (1948); 1948 Wis. L. Rev. 125; 63 Harv. L. Rev. 840 (1950); Donnelly and

Goldfarb, Contempt by Publication in the United States, 24 Mod. L. Rev. 239 (1961); Oliver, Contempt by Publication and the First Amendment, 27 Mo. L. Rev. 171(1962); Note, Contempt by Publication, 60 Nw. U.L. Rev. 531 (1965).

On the fair trial–free press issue see, in addition, Panel Discussion, Fair Trial and Freedom of the Press, 19 F.R.D. 16 (1956); Note, Free Press: Fair Trial — Rights in Collision, 34 N.Y.U.L. Rev. 1278 (1959); Douglas, The Public Trial and the Free Press, 46 A.B.A.J. 840 (1960); Mueller, Problems Posed by Publicity to Crime and Criminal Proceedings, 110 U. Pa. L. Rev. 1 (1961); Kutner, Unfair Comment: A Warning to News Media, 17 U. Miami L. Rev. 51 (1962); Note, The Case Against Trial by Newspaper: Analysis and Proposal, 57 Nw. U.L. Rev. 217 (1962); Note, Fair Trial v. Freedom of the Press in Criminal Cases, 35 Temp. L.Q. 412 (1962); Will, Free Press vs. Fair Trial, 12 De Paul L. Rev. 197 (1963); Gelb, Fair Trials and Free Speech, 31 Geo. Wash. L. Rev. 607 (1963); Daly, Ensuring Fair Trials and a Free Press: A Task for the Press and the Bar Alike, 50 A.B.A.J. 1037 (1964); Meyer, Free v. Fair Trial: The Judge's View, 41 N.D.L. Rev. 14 (1964); Stanton, Free Press v. Fair Trial: The Broadcaster's View, 41 N.D.L. Rev. 8 (1964); Gillmor and Barron, Free Press v. Fair Trial: A Continuing Dialogue, 41 N.D.L. Rev. 156 (1965); Haimbaugh, Free Press Versus Fair Trial: The Contribution of Mr. Justice Frankfurter, 26 U. Pitt. L. Rev. 491 (1965); Royster, The Free Press and Fair Trial, 43 N.C.L. Rev. 364 (1965); Note, Fair Trial v. Free Press: The Psychological Effect of Pre-Trial Publicity on the Juror's Ability to be Impartial: A Plea for Reform, 38 So. Cal. L. Rev. 672 (1965); Note, "Free Press — Fair Trial" Revisited: Defendant-Centered Remedies as a Publicity Policy, 33 U. Chi. L. Rev. 512 (1966); Note, The Impartial Jury — Twentieth Century Dilemma: Some Solutions to the Conflict Between Free Press and Fair Trial, 51 Cornell L.Q. 306 (1966).

For collections of other materials, see Association of the Bar of the City of New York, Special Committee on Radio and Television, Radio, Television, and the Administration of Justice: A Documented Survey of Materials (1965); Hearings before the Subcommittee on Constitutional Rights and the Subcommittee on Improvements in Judicial Machinery of the Senate Committee on the Judiciary on S. 290, Free Press and Fair Trial, 89th Cong., 1st Sess. (1965).

See also Kaplan and Waltz, The Trial of Jack Ruby (1965); Felsher and Rosen, The Press in the Jury Box (1966).

More specifically on cameras, radio and television in the courtroom, see Note, The New Star Chamber — TV in the Courtroom, 32 So. Cal. L. Rev. 281 (1959); Skinner, Constitutional Aspects of Television in the Courtroom, 35 U. Cinc. L. Rev. 48 (1966). See also Lewis, Cameras in Court? — A Growing Debate, N.Y. Times Magazine, Oct. 2, 1960, p. 22; Rodell, TV or No TV in Court? N.Y. Times Magazine, April 12, 1964, p. 16. For notes on the Estes case, see 79 Harv. L. Rev. 56, 146 (1965); 27 U. Pitt. L. Rev. 141 (1965); 18 Vand. L. Rev. 204 (1965).

On the practice in England, see Notes 17 U. Chi. L. Rev. 540 (1950); 13 W. Res. L. Rev. 147 (1961); McGuigan, Crime Reporting: The British and American Approaches, 50 A.B.A.J. 442 (1964); Gillmor, Free Press and Fair Trial in English Law, 22 Wash. & Lee L. Rev. 17 (1965).

CHAPTER VI

Defamation

BEAUHARNAIS v. ILLINOIS
343 U.S. 250, 72 S. Ct. 725, 96 L. Ed. 919 (1952)

MR. JUSTICE FRANKFURTER delivered the opinion of the Court.

The petitioner was convicted upon information in the Municipal Court of Chicago of violating §224a of Division 1 of the Illinois Penal Code, Ill. Rev. Stat. 1949, c. 38, §471. He was fined $200. The section provides:

"It shall be unlawful for any person, firm or corporation to manufacture, sell, or offer for sale, advertise or publish, present or exhibit in any public place in this state any lithograph, moving picture, play, drama or sketch, which publication or exhibition portrays depravity, criminality, unchastity, or lack of virtue of a class of citizens, of any race, color, creed or religion which said publication or exhibition exposes the citizens of any race, color, creed or religion to contempt, derision, or obloquy or which is productive of breach of the peace or riots. . . ."

Beauharnais challenged the statute as violating the liberty of speech and of the press guaranteed as against the States by the Due Process Clause of the Fourteenth Amendment, and as too vague, under the restrictions implicit in the same Clause, to support conviction for crime. The Illinois courts rejected these contentions and sustained defendant's conviction. 408 Ill. 512. We granted certiorari in view of the serious questions raised concerning the limitations imposed by the Fourteenth Amendment on the power of a State to punish utterances promoting friction among racial and religious groups. 342 U.S. 809.

The information, cast generally in the terms of the statute, charged that Beauharnais "did unlawfully . . . exhibit in public places lithographs, which publications portray depravity, criminality, unchastity or lack of virtue of citizens of Negro race and color and which exposes [*sic*] citizens of Illinois of the Negro race and color to contempt, derision, or obloquy. . . ." The lithograph complained of was a leaflet setting forth a petition calling on the Mayor and City Council of Chicago "to halt the further encroachment, harassment and invasion of white people, their property, neighborhoods and persons, by the Negro. . . ." Below was a call for "One million self respecting white people in Chicago to unite . . ." with the statement added that "If persuasion and the need to prevent the white race from becoming mongrelized by the negro will not unite us, then the aggressions . . . rapes, robberies, knives, guns and marijuana of the negro, surely will." This, with more language, similar if not so violent, concluded with an attached application for membership in the White Circle League of America, Inc.

The testimony at the trial was substantially undisputed. From it the jury could find that Beauharnais was president of the White Circle League; that, at a meeting on January 6, 1950, he passed out bundles of the lithographs in question, together with other literature, to volunteers for distribution on downtown Chicago street corners the following day; that he carefully organized that distribution, giving detailed instructions for it; and that the leaflets were in fact distributed on January 7 in accordance with his plan and instructions. The court, together with other charges on burden of proof and the like, told the jury "if you find . . . that the defendant, Joseph Beauharnais, did . . . manufacture, sell, or offer for sale, advertise or publish, present or exhibit in any public place the lithograph . . . then you are to find the defendant guilty. . . ." He refused to charge the jury, as requested by the defendant, that in order to convict they must find "that the article complained of was likely to produce a clear and present danger of a serious substantive evil that rises far above public inconvenience, annoyance or unrest." Upon this evidence and these instructions, the jury brought in the conviction here for review.

The statute before us is not a catchall enactment left at large by the State court which applied it. Cf. Thornhill v. Alabama, 310 U.S. 88; Cantwell v. Connecticut, 310 U.S. 296, 307. It is a law specifically directed at a defined evil, its language drawing from history and practice in Illinois and in more than a score of other jurisdictions a meaning confirmed by the Supreme Court of that State in upholding this conviction. We do not, therefore, parse the statute as grammarians or treat it as an abstract exercise in lexicography. We read it in the animating context of well-defined usage, Nash v. United States, 229 U.S. 373, and State court construction which determines its meaning for us. Cox v. New Hampshire, 312 U.S. 569; Chaplinsky v. New Hampshire, 315 U.S. 568.

The Illinois Supreme Court tells us that §224a "is a form of criminal libel law." 408 Ill. 512, 517. The defendant, the trial court and the Supreme Court consistently treated it as such. The defendant offered evidence tending to prove the truth of parts of the utterance, and the courts below considered and disposed of this offer in terms of ordinary criminal libel precedents.[1] Section 224a does not deal with the defense of truth, but by the Illinois Constitution, Art. II, §4, "in all trials for libel, both civil and criminal, the truth, when published with good motives and for justifiable ends, shall be a sufficient

---

[1] 408 Ill. 512, 518. Illinois law requires that for the defense to prevail, the truth of all facts in the utterance must be shown together with good motive for publication. People v. Strauch, 247 Ill. 220; People v. Fuller, 238 Ill. 116; cf. Ogren v. Rockford Star Printing Co., 288 Ill. 405.

defense." See also Ill. Rev. Stat., 1949, c. 38, §404. Similarly, the action of the trial court in deciding as a matter of law the libelous character of the utterance, leaving to the jury only the question of publication, follows the settled rule in prosecutions for libel in Illinois and other States.[2] Moreover, the Supreme Court's characterization of the words prohibited by the statute as those "liable to cause violence and disorder" paraphrases the traditional justification for punishing libels criminally, namely their "tendency to cause breach of the peace." [3]

Libel of an individual was a common-law crime, and thus criminal in the colonies. Indeed, at common law, truth or good motives was no defense. In the first decades after the adoption of the Constitution, this was changed by judicial decision, statute or constitution in most States, but nowhere was there any suggestion that the crime of libel be abolished.[4] Today, every American jurisdiction — the forty-eight States, the District of Columbia, Alaska, Hawaii and Puerto Rico — punish libels directed at individuals.[5]

[2] See, e.g., State v. Sterman, 199 Iowa 569; State v. Howard, 169 N.C. 312, 313; cf. Ogren v. Rockford Star Printing Co., supra.

[3] See, e.g., People v. Speilman, 318 Ill. 482, 489; Odgers, Libel and Slander (6th ed.), 368; 19 A.L.R. 1470. Some States hold, however, that injury to reputation, as in civil libel, and not tendency to breach of the peace, is the gravamen of the offense. See Tanenhaus, Group Libel, 35 Cornell L.Q. 261, 273 and n.67.

[4] For a brief account of this development see Warren, History of the American Bar, 236-239. See also correspondence between Chief Justice Cushing of Massachusetts and John Adams, published in 27 Mass. L.Q. 11-16 (Oct. 1942). Jefferson explained in a letter to Abigail Adams, dated September 11, 1804, that to strike down the Alien and Sedition Act would not "remove all restraint from the overwhelming torrent of slander which is confounding all vice and virtue, all truth and falsehood in the US. The power to do that is fully possessed by the several state legislatures." See Dennis v. United States, 341 U.S. 494, 522, n.4. See Miller, Crisis in Freedom, 168-169, 231-232. See also provisions as to criminal libel in Edward Livingston's famous draft System of Penal Law for Louisiana, 2 Works of Edward Livingston 100-108.

[5] In eight States the offense is punished as at common law, without legislative enactment. State v. Roberts, 2 Marv. 450, 43 A. 252 (Del.); Cole v. Commonwealth, 222 Ky. 350, 300 S.W. 907; Robinson v. State, 108 Md. 644, 71 A. 433; Commonwealth v. Canter, 269 Mass. 359, 168 N.E. 790; State v. Burnham, 9 N.H. 34; State v. Spear, 13 R.I. 324; State v. Sutton, 74 Vt. 12, 52 A. 116; State v. Payne, 87 W. Va. 102, 104 S.E. 288. Twelve other jurisdictions made "libel" a crime by statute, without defining the term. Ala. Code, 1940, Tit. 14, §347; Alaska Comp. Laws Ann., 1949, §65-4-28; D.C. Code, 1940, §22-2301; Fla. Stat. Ann., 1943, §836.01; Burns Ind. Stat., 1933, §10-3201; Miss. Code, 1942, §2268; Neb. Rev. Stat., 1943, §28-440; N.J. Stat. Ann., 1939, §2:146-1; N.C. Gen. Stat., 1943, §14-47; Page's Ohio Gen. Code, 1939, §13383; Wis. Stat., 1949, §348-41; Wyo. Comp. Stat., 1945, §9-1601. Thus, twenty American jurisdictions punish "libel" as defined by the case-by-case common-law development.

The remaining jurisdictions have sought to cast the common-law definition in a statutory form of words. Two formulas have been popular. Eleven jurisdictions, Illinois among them, have accepted with minor variations the following:

"A libel is a malicious defamation, expressed either by printing, or by signs or pictures, or the like, tending to blacken the memory of one who is dead, or to impeach the honesty, integrity, virtue or reputation or publish the natural defects of one who is alive, and thereby to expose him to public hatred, contempt, ridicule, or financial injury." Ariz. Code Ann., 1939, §43.3501; Ark. Stat., 1947, §41-2401; Deering's Cal. Penal Code, 1949, §248; Colo. Stat. Ann., 1935, c. 48, §199; Ga. Code Ann., 1936, §26-2101; Idaho Code, 1947, §18-4801; Smith-Hurd's Ill. Ann. Stat., 1936, c. 38, §402; Mont.

"There are certain well-defined and narrowly limited classes of speech, the prevention and punishment of which have never been thought to raise any constitutional problem. These include the lewd and obscene, the profane, the libelous, and the insulting or 'fighting' words — those which by their very utterance inflict injury or tend to incite to an immediate breach of the peace. It has been well observed that such utterances are no essential part of any exposition of ideas, and are of such slight social value as a step to truth that any benefit that may be derived from them is clearly outweighed by the social interest in order and morality. 'Resort to epithets or personal abuse is not in any proper sense communication of information or opinion safe-guarded by the Constitution, and its punishment as a criminal act would raise no question under that instrument.' Cantwell v. Connecticut, 310 U.S. 296, 309-310." Such were the views of a unanimous Court in Chaplinsky v. New Hampshire, supra, at 571-572.[6]

Rev. Codes, 1947, §94-2801; Nev. Comp. Laws, 1929, §10110; P.R. Codiga Penal, 1937, §243; Utah Code Ann., 1943, §103-38-1; cf. Virgin Islands Code, Tit. IV, c. 5, §36.

The other version, again with minor variations, has found favor in twelve jurisdictions.

"A libel is a malicious defamation of a person, made public by any printing, writing, sign, picture, representation or effigy, tending to provoke him to wrath or expose him to public hatred, contempt or ridicule, or to deprive him of the benefits of public confidence and social intercourse; or any malicious defamation, made public as aforesaid, designed to blacken and vilify the memory of one who is dead, and tending to scandalize or provoke his surviving relatives or friends."

Iowa Code Ann., 1949, §737.1; Kan. Gen. Stat., 1935; §21-2401; Dart's La. Crim. Code, 1943, Art. 740-47; Me. Rev. Stat., 1944, c. 117, §30; Minn. Stat., 1949, §619.51; Mo. Rev. Stat., 1949, §559.410; McKinney's N.Y. Laws, Penal Code, §1340; N.D. Rev. Code, 1943, §12-2801; Okla. Stat. Ann., 1936, Tit. 21, §771; Purdon's Pa. Stat. Ann., 1945, Tit. 18, §4412; William's Tenn. Code, 1934, §§11021, 11022; Remington's Wash. Rev. Stat., 1932, §2424.

The remaining nine jurisdictions have definitions of criminal libel which fall into no common pattern. See Conn. Gen. Stat., 1949, §8518; Hawaii Rev. Laws, 1945, §11450; Mich. Comp. Laws, 1948, §750-370; N.M. Stat., 1941, §§41-2701, 41-2708; Ore. Comp. Laws, 1940, §23-437; S.C. Code, 1942, §1395; S.D. Code, 1939, §13-3401; Vernon's Tex. Stat. 1948, Art. 1269, 1275; Va. Code, 1950, §18-133.

Our examination of the homogeneity of these statutory definitions of criminal libel might well begin and end with the words "virtue" and "ridicule." Of thirty-two jurisdictions, twelve outlaw statements impeaching the "virtue" of another; eleven of these, and fifteen more — twenty-six in all — prohibit utterances tending to bring another into "public ridicule."

For the common-law definition, applicable in the twenty jurisdictions first noted above, see L. Hand, J., in Grant v. Reader's Digest Assn., 151 F.2d 733, 735, where he speaks of defining libel "in accordance with the usual rubric, as consisting of utterances which arouse 'hatred, contempt, scorn, obloquy or shame,' and the like." Cf. Restatement, Torts, §559, comment (b); Odgers, Libel and Slander (6th ed.), 16-17; Newell, Slander and Libel (4th ed.), 1-2.

Even a cursory examination of these enactments and common-law pronouncements demonstrates that Illinois, in §224a, was using a form of words which invoked the familiar common law of libel to define the prohibited utterances. The defendant and the Illinois courts, as we have seen, understood this and acted upon it.

[6] In all but five States, the constitutional guarantee of free speech to every person is explicitly qualified by holding him "responsible for the abuse of that right." See Pennekamp v. Florida, 328 U.S. 331, 356, n.5. See Jefferson in Kentucky Resolutions

No one will gainsay that it is libelous falsely to charge another with being a rapist, robber, carrier of knives and guns, and user of marijuana. The precise question before us, then, is whether the protection of "liberty" in the Due Process Clause of the Fourteenth Amendment prevents a State from punishing such libels — as criminal libel has been defined, limited and constitutionally recognized time out of mind — directed at designated collectivities and flagrantly disseminated. There is even authority, however dubious, that such utterances were also crimes at common law.[7] It is certainly clear that some American jurisdictions have sanctioned their punishment under ordinary criminal libel statutes.[8] We cannot say, however, that the question is concluded by history and practice. But if an utterance directed at an individual may be the object of criminal sanctions, we cannot deny to a State power to punish the same utterance directed at a defined group, unless we can say that this is a wilful and purposeless restriction unrelated to the peace and well-being of the State.

Illinois did not have to look beyond her own borders or await the tragic experience of the last three decades[9] to conclude that wilful purveyors of falsehood concerning racial and religious groups promote strife and tend powerfully to obstruct the manifold adjustments required for free, ordered life in a metropolitan, polyglot community. From the murder of the abolitionist Lovejoy in 1837 to the Cicero riots of 1951, Illinois has been the scene of exacerbated tension between races, often flaring into violence and destruction.[10] In many of these outbreaks, utterances of the character here in question, so the Illinois legislature could conclude, played a significant part.[11] The

---

of 1798 and 1799, 4 Elliot's Debates 540-541, and in an undated draft prepared, but not used, for his December 8, 1801, Message to Congress, Library of Congress Jefferson Papers, Vol. 119, Leaf 20569. In Carlson v. California, 310 U.S. 106, 112, we noted that the statute there invalidated made "no exceptions with respect to the truthfulness and restraint of the information conveyed . . . ."

[7] Compare reports of King v. Osborne in 2 Barn. K.B. 138, 166, 94 Eng. Rep. 406, 425; 2 Swans. 503, n.(c), 36 Eng. 705, 717; W. Kel. 230, 25 Eng. Rep. 584 (1732). The present Attorney General of England asserted that this case obviated the need of special group libel legislation for Great Britain. See The [London] Times, March 26, 1952, p. 2, col. 4. See also Odgers, Libel and Slander (6th ed.), 369; Tanenhaus, Group Libel, 35 Cornell L.Q. 261, 267-269.

[8] One of the leading cases arose in Illinois. People v. Spielman, 318 Ill. 482 (1925) sustaining a conviction for libel on the members of the American Legion. The authorities are collected and discussed in Tanenhaus, Group Libel, 35 Cornell L.Q. 261, 269-276.

[9] See, e.g., Loewenstein, Legislative Control of Political Extremism in European Democracies, 38 Col. L. Rev. 591 and 725; Riesman, Democracy and Defamation, 42 Col. L. Rev. 727, 1085 and 1282; Public Order Act, 1936, 1 Edw. VIII and 1 Geo. VI, c. 6, and 317 H.C. Deb. 1350-1474 (5th ser. 1936); 318 H.C. Deb. 50-194, 582-710, 1659-1786, 2782-2784 (5th ser. 1936); 103 H. L. Deb. 742-774, 962-971 (5th ser. 1936).

[10] See generally The Chicago Commission on Race Relations, The Negro in Chicago, 1-78, and passim (University of Chicago Press, 1922); Research Memorandum No. 5, First Annual Rep. Ill. Inter-Racial Comm'n (1944).

[11] The May 28, 1917, riot in East St. Louis, Illinois, was preceded by a violently inflammatory speech to unemployed workmen by a prominent lawyer of the town. Re-

law was passed on June 29, 1917, at a time when the State was struggling to assimilate vast numbers of new inhabitants, as yet concentrated in discrete racial or national or religious groups — foreign-born brought to it by the crest of the great wave of immigration, and Negroes attracted by jobs in war plants and the allurements of Northern claims.[12] Nine years earlier, in the very city where the legislature sat, what is said to be the first northern race riot had cost the lives of six people, left hundreds of Negroes homeless and shocked citizens into action far beyond the borders of the State.[13] Less than a month before the bill was enacted, East St. Louis had seen a day's rioting, prelude to an outbreak, only four days after the bill became law, so bloody that it led to Congressional investigation.[14] A series of bombings had begun which was to culminate two years later in the awful race riot which held Chicago in its grip for seven days in the summer of 1919.[15] Nor has tension and violence between the groups defined in the statute been limited in Illinois to clashes between whites and Negroes.

In the face of this history and its frequent obligato of extreme racial and religious propaganda, we would deny experience to say that the Illinois leg-

---

port of the Special Committee Authorized by Congress to Investigate the East St. Louis Riots, H.R. Doc. No. 1231, 65th Cong., 2d Sess. 11; Chicago Commission on Race Relations, The Negro in Chicago, 75. And see id., at 118-122 for literature circulated by real estate associations and other groups during the series of bombings leading up to the Chicago riots of 1919. For the Commission's comments on the role of propaganda in promoting race frictions, see id., at 589, 638-639.

[12] Tables in Drake and Cayton, Black Metropolis, 8, show that between 1900 and 1920 the number of foreign born in Chicago increased by over ⅓ and the Negro population trebled. United States census figures show the following population growth for the State as a whole and selected counties:

	Illinois		*Cook County* *(Chicago)*		*St. Clair County* *(East St. Louis)*	
	Total	*Negro*	*Total*	*Negro*	*Total*	*Negro*
1900	4,821,550	85,078	1,838,735	31,838	86,685	3,987
1910	5,638,591	109,049	2,405,233	46,627	119,870	8,110
1920	6,485,280	182,274	3,053,017	115,238	136,520	10,136
1930	7,630,654	328,972	3,982,123	246,992	157,775	15,550
1940	7,897,241	387,446	4,063,342	249,157	166,899	21,567
1950	8,712,176	645,989	4,508,792	521.007	205,995	34,566

For an account of these vast population movements entailing great social maladjustments, see Drake and Cayton, Black Metropolis, 8-18, 31-65; Chicago Commission on Race Relations, The Negro in Chicago, 79-105; Carl Sandburg, The Chicago Race Riots, 9-30.

[13] See Walling, Race War in the North, 65 The Independent 529 (1908). This article apparently led to the founding of the National Association for the Advancement of Colored People. Ovington, How the National Association for the Advancement of Colored People Began, 8 Crisis 184 (1914). See also Chicago Commission on Race Relations, The Negro in Chicago 67-71.

[14] Report of the Special Committee Authorized by Congress to Investigate the East St. Louis Riots, H.R. Doc. No. 1231, 65th Cong., 2d Sess. See also The Massacre of East St. Louis, 14 Crisis 219 (1917).

[15] Chicago Commission on Race Relations, The Negro in Chicago 122-133.

islature was without reason in seeking ways to curb false or malicious defamation of racial and religious groups, made in public places and by means calculated to have a powerful emotional impact on those to whom it was presented. "There are limits to the exercise of these liberties [of speech and of the press]. The danger in these times from the coercive activities of those who in the delusion of racial or religious conceit would incite violence and breaches of the peace in order to deprive others of their equal right to the exercise of their liberties, is emphasized by events familiar to all. These and other transgressions of those limits the States appropriately may punish." [16] This was the conclusion, again of a unanimous Court, in 1940. Cantwell v. Connecticut, supra, at 310.

It may be argued, and weightily, that this legislation will not help matters; that tension and on occasion violence between racial and religious groups must be traced to causes more deeply embedded in our society than the rantings of modern Know-Nothings.[17] Only those lacking responsible humility will have a confident solution for problems as intractable as the frictions attributable to differences of race, color or religion. This being so, it would be out of bounds for the judiciary to deny the legislature a choice of policy, provided it is not unrelated to the problem and not forbidden by some explicit limitation on the State's power. That the legislative remedy might not in practice mitigate the evil, or might itself raise new problems, would only manifest once more the paradox of reform. It is the price to be paid for the trial-and-error inherent in legislative efforts to deal with obstinate social issues. "The science of government is the most abstruse of all sciences; if, indeed, that can be called a science which has but few fixed principles, and practically consists in little more than the exercise of a sound discretion, applied to the exigencies of the state as they arise. It is the science of experiment." Anderson v. Dunn, 6 Wheat. 204, 226. Certainly the Due Process Clause does not require the legislature to be in the vanguard of science — especially sciences as young as human ecology and cultural anthropology. See Tigner v. Texas, 310 U.S. 141, 148.

Long ago this Court recognized that the economic rights of an individual may depend for the effectiveness of their enforcement on rights in the group, even though not formally corporate, to which he belongs. American Foun-

---

[16] The utterances here in question "are not," as a detached student of the problem has noted, "the daily grist of vituperative political debate. Nor do they represent the frothy imaginings of lunatics, or the 'idle' gossip of a country town. Rather, they indicate the systematic avalanche of falsehoods which are circulated concerning the various groups, classes and races which make up the countries of the western world." Riesman, Democracy and Defamation; Control of Group Libel, 42 Col. L. Rev. at 727. Professor Riesman continues: "Such purposeful attacks are nothing new, of course. . . . What is new, however, is the existence of a mobile public opinion as the controlling force in politics, and the systematic manipulation of that opinion by the use of calculated falsehood and vilification." Id., at 728.

[17] See, e.g., L. Hand, J., in a symposium in The Saturday Review of Literature, Mar. 15, 1947, pp. 23-24; Report of the Committee on the Law of Defamation, Cmd. 7536, 11 (1948).

dries v. Tri-City Council, 257 U.S. 189. Such group-protection on behalf of the individual may, for all we know, be a need not confined to the part that a trade union plays in effectuating rights abstractly recognized as belonging to its members. It is not within our competence to confirm or deny claims of social scientists as to the dependence of the individual on the position of his racial or religious group in the community. It would, however, be arrant dogmatism, quite outside the scope of our authority in passing on the powers of a State, for us to deny that the Illinois legislature may warrantably believe that a man's job and his educational opportunities and the dignity accorded him may depend as much on the reputation of the racial and religious group to which he willy-nilly belongs, as it does on his own merits. This being so, we are precluded from saying that speech concededly punishable when immediately directed at individuals cannot be outlawed if directed at groups with whose position and esteem in society the affiliated individual may be inextricably involved.

We are warned that the choice we permit the Illinois legislature here may be abused, that the law may be discriminatorily enforced; prohibiting libel of a creed or of a racial group, we are told, is but a step from prohibiting libel of a political party.[18] Every power may be abused, but the possibility of abuse is a poor reason for denying Illinois the power to adopt measures against criminal libels sanctioned by centuries of Anglo-American law. "While this Court sits" it retains and exercises authority to nullify action which encroaches on freedom of utterance under the guise of punishing libel. Of course discussion cannot be denied and the right, as well as the duty, of criticism must not be stifled.

The scope of the statute before us, as construed by the Illinois court, disposes of the contention that the conduct prohibited by the law is so ill-defined that judges and juries in applying the statute and men in acting cannot draw from it adequate standards to guide them. The clarifying construction and fixed usage which govern the meaning of the enactment before us were not present, so the Court found, in the New York law held invalid in Winters v. New York, 333 U.S. 507. Nor, thus construed and limited, is the act so broad that the general verdict of guilty on an indictment drawn in the statutory language might have been predicated on constitutionally protected conduct. On this score, the conviction here reviewed differs from those upset in Stromberg v. California, 283 U.S. 359, Thornhill v. Alabama, supra, and Terminiello v. Chicago, 337 U.S. 1. Even the latter case did not hold that the unconsti-

---

[18] It deserves emphasis that there is no such attempt in this statute. The rubric "race, color, creed or religion" which describes the type of group libel which is punishable, has attained too fixed a meaning to permit political groups to be brought within it. If a statute sought to outlaw libels of political parties, quite different problems not now before us would be raised. For one thing, the whole doctrine of fair comment as indispensable to the democratic political process would come into play. See People v. Fuller, supra, at 125; Commonwealth v. Pratt, 208 Mass. 553, 559. Political parties, like public men, are, as it were, public property.

tutionality of a statute is established *because* the speech prohibited by it raises a ruckus.

[Here Mr. Justice Frankfurter takes up the further contention that the statute violates Due Process by not permitting "(1) the defense of truth; (2) justification of the utterance as 'fair comment'; and (3) its privilege as a means for redressing grievances." He disposes of privilege and "fair comment" on the basis that these were not raised by "proffer of evidence, requests for instructions, nor motion before or after verdict" or as a ground for reversal urged to the Supreme Court. As to the defense of truth, Illinois requires, in common with many other States, "not only that the utterance state the facts, but also that the publication be made 'with good motives and for justifiable ends.'" Defendant offered to show that in Negro districts there were more crimes than in those where whites predominated, "three specific crimes allegedly committed by Negroes, and . . . that property values declined when Negroes moved into a neighborhood." Even if one assumes that this offer was adequate as to the defense of truth it did not meet the additional requirement of "good motives for justifiable ends."]

Libellous utterances, not being within the area of constitutionally protected speech, it is unnecessary, either for us or for the State courts, to consider the issue behind the phrase "clear and present danger." Certainly no one would contend that obscene speech, for example, may be punished only upon a showing of such circumstances. Libel, as we have seen, is in the same class.

We find no warrant in the Constitution for denying to Illinois the power to pass the law here under attack.[23] But it bears repeating — although it should not — that our finding that the law is not constitutionally objectionable carries no implication of approval of the wisdom of the legislation or of its efficacy. These questions may raise doubts in our minds as well as in others. It is not for us, however, to make the legislative judgment. We are not at liberty to erect those doubts into fundamental law.

Affirmed.

[Mr. Justice Reed's dissenting opinion in which Mr. Justice Douglas joined, after reiterating that the Fourteenth Amendment makes the First applicable to the states, concluded that the statutory language was so broad as to include "punishment of incidents fairly within the protection of the guarantee of free speech." The language of the statute did not limit the meaning of words like "virtue," "derision" or "obloquy." The fact that the statute is described as a criminal libel law, or that the word "virtue" is found in an individual libel statute does not clarify the meaning of these words. No cases are cited to support the majority's notion of an existing "clarifying construction" and "fixed usage."

---

[23] The law struck down by the New Jersey court in Klapprott v. New Jersey, 127 N.J.L. 395, was quite different than the one before us and was not limited, as is the Illinois statute, by construction or usage. Indeed, in that case the court emphasized that "It is not a case of libel," and contrasted the history at common law of criminal prosecutions for written and spoken defamation.

Mr. Justice Douglas' separate dissenting opinion deplored what he felt was the Court's recent tendency to engraft "the right of regulation onto the First Amendment by placing in the hands of the legislative branch the right to regulate 'within reasonable limits' the right of free speech." The law that today convicts a white man for "protesting in unseemly language against our decisions invalidating restrictive covenants" may tomorrow convict a Negro for denouncing "lynch law in heated terms." Shouting and raving, intemperate speech, "exaggerating weaknesses, magnifying error, viewing with alarm" were well known to the framers of the Constitution who, though they lived in dangerous days, chose liberty against restrictions which might result in the abuse of liberty. The Court's opinion "is notice to the legislatures that they have the power to control unpopular blocs" and "a warning to every minority that when the Constitution guarantees free speech it does not mean what it says."

Mr. Justice Jackson's dissenting opinion primarily expounds the thesis "that the Fourteenth Amendment did not 'incorporate' the First," and that the restrictions on the states are not of the same dimensions as those imposed on Congress. While the Court has never sustained a federal criminal libel law and the validity of such a law would be "extremely doubtful" the validity of ordinary state criminal libel statutes is well established. Indeed, they were tolerated by "the very authors and partisans of the Fourteenth Amendment." The power of the states is limited by the "concept of ordered liberty." This includes restrictions on libel prosecutions generally accepted by states, such as defenses of truth and good motives, fair comment and privilege. And where expression "is punished, although it has not actually caused injuries or disorders but is thought to have a tendency to do so" the Supreme Court has imposed the "clear and present danger test" in addition to the above safeguards which the states have "voluntarily taken upon themselves." Here the traditional defenses were not entertained by the courts below. Moreover "no actual violence and no specific injury was charged or proved. . . . The conviction rests on judicial attribution of a likelihood of evil results." Yet the "trial court . . . refused to charge the jury that it must find some clear and present danger. . . ."]

Mr. Justice Black, with whom Mr. Justice Douglas concurs, dissenting . . .

Today's case degrades First Amendment freedoms to the "rational basis" level. It is now a certainty that the new "due process" coverall offers far less protection to liberty than would adherence to our former cases compelling states to abide by the unequivocal First Amendment command that its defined freedoms shall not be abridged.

The Court's holding here and the constitutional doctrine behind it leave the rights of assembly, petition, speech and press almost completely at the mercy of state legislative, executive, and judicial agencies. I say "almost" because state curtailment of these freedoms may still be invalidated if a majority of this Court conclude that a particular infringement is "without reason," or is "a wilful and purposeless restriction unrelated to the peace and well being of the State." But lest this encouragement should give too much hope as to how and when this Court might protect these basic freedoms from state invasion, we are cautioned that state legislatures must be left free to "experiment" and to make "legislative" judgments. We are told that mistakes may be made during the legislative process of curbing public opinion. In such event the Court fortunately does not leave those mistakenly curbed, or any of us for that matter, unadvised. Consolation can be sought and must be found in the philosophical reflection that state legislative error in stifling speech and press "is the price to be paid for the trial-and-error inherent in legislative efforts to deal with obstinate social issues." My own belief is that no legislature is charged with the duty or vested with the power to decide what public issues Americans can discuss. In a free country that is the individual's choice, not the state's. State experimentation in curbing freedom of expression is startling and frightening doctrine in a country dedicated to self-government by its people. I reject the holding that either state or nation can punish people for having their say in matters of public concern. . . .

This statute imposes state censorship over the theater, moving pictures, radio, television, leaflets, magazines, books and newspapers. No doubt the statute is broad enough to make criminal the "publication, sale, presentation or exhibition" of many of the world's great classics, both secular and religious.

The Court condones this expansive state censorship by painstakingly analogizing it to the law of criminal libel. As a result of this refined analysis, the Illinois statute emerges labeled a "group libel law." This label may make the Court's holding more palatable for those who sustain it, but the sugar-coating does not make the censorship less deadly. However tagged, the Illinois law is not that criminal libel which has been "defined, limited and constitutionally recognized time out of mind." [4] For as "constitutionally recognized" that crime has provided for punishment of false, malicious, scurrilous charges against individuals, not against huge groups. This limited scope of the law of criminal libel is of no small importance. It has confined state punishment of

---

[4] The Court's finding of a close kinship between "criminal libel" and "group-libel" because both contain the word "libel" and have some factors in common is reminiscent of what Earl Stanhope said in 1792 in discussing Mr. Fox's Libel Bill. He was arguing that a jury of laymen might more likely protect liberty than judges, because judges were prone to rely too heavily on word books. "He put the case, that an action for a libel was brought for using a modern word, not to be found in any grammar or glossary, viz. for saying that a man was 'a great bore;' a jury would laugh at such a ground of prosecution, but the judges would turn to their grammars and glossaries, and not being able to meet with it, would say they could not find such a phrase as 'a great bore,' but they had found a wild boar, which no doubt it meant; and yet it could not be, as a wild boar had four legs, and a man was a two legged animal; then it must mean, that the plaintiff was like a wild boar in disposition, which was a wicked libel, and therefore let the defendant be hanged." 29 Hansard, Parliamentary History of England, p. 1411.

speech and expression to the narrowest of areas involving nothing more than purely private feuds. Every expansion of the law of criminal libel so as to punish discussions of matters of public concern means a corresponding invasion of the area dedicated to free expression by the First Amendment.

Prior efforts to expand the scope of criminal libel beyond its traditional boundaries have not usually met with widespread popular acclaim. "Seditious libel" was such an expansion and it did have its day, particularly in the English Court of Star Chamber. But the First Amendment repudiated seditious libel for this country. And one need only glance through the parliamentary discussion of Fox's Libel Law passed in England in 1792, to sense the bad odor of criminal libel in that country even when confined to charges against individuals only.

The Court's reliance on Chaplinsky v. New Hampshire, 315 U.S. 568, is also misplaced. New Hampshire had a state law making it an offense to direct insulting words at an *individual* on a public street. Chaplinsky had violated that law by calling a man vile names "face-to-face." We pointed out in that context that the use of such "fighting words" was not an essential part of exposition of ideas. Whether the words used in their context here are "fighting words" in the same sense is doubtful, but whether so or not they are not addressed to or about *individuals*. Moreover, the leaflet used here was also the means adopted by an assembled group to enlist interest in their efforts to have legislation enacted. And the "fighting" words were but a part of arguments on questions of wide public interest and importance. Freedom of petition, assembly, speech and press could be greatly abridged by a practice of meticulously scrutinizing every editiorial, speech, sermon or other printed matter to extract two or three naughty words on which to hang charges of "group libel." The Chaplinsky case makes no such broad inroads on First Amendment freedoms. Nothing Mr. Justice Murphy wrote for the Court in that case or in any other case justifies any such inference.

Unless I misread history the majority is giving libel a more expansive scope and more respectable status than it was ever accorded even in the Star Chamber. For here it is held to be punishable to give publicity to any picture, moving picture, play, drama or sketch, or any printed matter which a judge may find unduly offensive to any race, color, creed or religion. In other words, in arguing for or against the enactment of laws that may differently affect huge groups, it is now very dangerous indeed to say something critical of one of the groups. And any "person, firm or corporation" can be tried for this crime. "Person, firm or corporation" certainly includes a book publisher, newspaper, radio or television station, candidate or even a preacher.

It is easy enough to say that none of this latter group have been proceeded against under the Illinois Act. And they have not — yet. But emotions bubble and tempers flare in racial and religious controversies, the kind here involved. It would not be easy for any court, in good conscience, to narrow this Act so as to exclude from it any of those I have mentioned. Furthermore, persons tried under the Act could not even get a jury trial except as to the bare fact of publication. Here, the court simply charged the jury that Beauharnais was guilty if he had caused distribution of the leaflet. Such trial by judge rather than by jury was outlawed in England in 1792 by Fox's Libel Law. . . .

We are told that freedom of petition and discussion are in no danger "while this Court sits." This case raises considerable doubt. Since those who peacefully petition for changes in the law are not to be protected "while this Court sits," who is? I do not agree that the Constitution leaves freedom of petition, assembly, speech, press or worship at the mercy of a case-by-case, day-by-day majority of this Court. I had supposed that our people could rely for their freedom on the Constitution's commands, rather than on the grace of this Court on an individual case basis. To say that a legislative body can, with this Court's approval, make it a crime to petition for and publicly discuss proposed legislation seems as farfetched to me as it would be to say that a valid law could be enacted to punish a candidate for President for telling the people his views. I think the First Amendment, with the Fourteenth, "absolutely" forbids such laws without any "ifs" or "buts" or "whereases." Whatever the danger, if any, in such public discussions, it is a danger the Founders deemed outweighed by the danger incident to the stifling of thought and speech. The Court does not act on this view of the Founders. It calculates what it deems to be the danger of public discussion, holds the scales are tipped on the side of state suppression, and upholds state censorship. This method of decision offers little protection to First Amendment liberties "while this Court sits."

If there be minority groups who hail this holding as their victory, they might consider the possible relevancy of this ancient remark:

"Another such victory and I am undone."

[The appendix containing a copy of the brochure involved is omitted.]

NOTES

1. In the Klapprott case, 127 N.J.L. 395, 22 A.2d 877 (1941), distinguished in the Beauharnais opinion, the New Jersey statute provided:

"Any person who shall, in the presence of two or more persons, in any language, make or utter any speech, statement or declaration, which in any way incites, counsels, promotes, or advocates hatred, abuse, violence or hostility against any group or groups of persons residing or being in this state by reason of race, color, religion or manner of worship, shall be guilty of a misdemeanor."

The court's opinion, holding the statute unconstitutional, reads in part as follows:

"It is our view that the statute, supra, by punitive sanction, tends to restrict what one may say lest by one's utterances there be incited or advocated hatred, hostility or violence against a group 'by reason of race, color, religion or manner of worship.' But additionally and looking now to strict statutory construction, is the statute definite, clear and precise so as to be free from the constitutional infirmity of the vague and indefinite? That the terms 'hatred,' 'abuse,' 'hostility,' are abstract and indefinite admits of no contradiction. When do they arise? Is it to be left to a jury to conclude beyond reasonable doubt when the emotion of hatred or hostility is aroused in the mind of the listener as a result of what a speaker has said? Nothing in our criminal law can be invoked to justify so wide a discretion. The criminal code must be definite and informative so that there may be no doubt in the mind of the citizenry that the interdicted act or conduct is illicit. The element of 'violence,' mentioned in the statute, is universally understood to connote the unlawful exercise of force, i.e., a breach of the peace, but in the indictments before us neither breach of the peace nor resulting violence are alleged. Unbridled license in the matter of speech has no absolute immunity either in the federal courts or the courts of the states generally (cf. Gitlow v. New York [268 U.S. 652]); but in the matter of free speech the utterances subject to punishment must be of the class that bring injury to society as such or are intended so to do. The cases cited above make this abundantly clear." 127 N.J.L. at 401.

The Supreme Court quoted this opinion with approval in Winters v. New York, 333 U.S. 507, 68 S. Ct. 665, 92 L. Ed. 840 (1948).

Other group libel statutes are Ind. Stat. Ann. §§10-904 to 10-914 (Burns 1956) (contains also a provision for a civil suit for an injunction); Conn. Gen. Stat. §53-37 (1958) (limited to advertisements); West Va. Code §6109 (1961) (limited to picture and theater performances); Mass. Gen. Laws c. 272, §98c (1956) (provides that any person who publishes ". . . any false, written or printed material with the intent to maliciously promote hatred of any group of persons in the commonwealth because of race, color or religion shall be guilty of libel . . .").

The Illinois statute was repealed in 1961, Ill. Ann. Stat. ch. 38, §§27-1, 27-2 (1961). See the Lambert case below.

See discussion in Kalven, The Negro and the First Amendment, ch. 1 (1965). See also Note, 28 Mass. L.Q. 104 (Dec. 1943); Perlman and Ploscowe, False, Defamatory, Anti-racial and Anti-religious Propaganda and the Use of the Mails, 4 Law. Guild Rev. 13 (1944). For a collection of local group libel ordinances, see Tanenhaus, Group Libel, 35 Cornell L.Q. 261, 283-285 (1950); Brown and Stern, Group Defamation in the U.S.A., 13 Clev.-Mar. L. Rev. 7 (1964).

2. In City of Chicago v. Lambert, 47 Ill. App. 2d 151, 197 N.E.2d 448 (1964), defendants wearing uniforms who picketed and distributed leaflets attacking Jews and Negroes in front of a theater showing a Sammy Davis, Jr., motion picture were convicted of violating state and municipal breach of peace laws and a state criminal defamation statute which provided: "A person commits criminal defamation when, with intent to defame another, living or dead, he communicates by any means to any person matter which tends to provoke a breach of the peace." Ill. Rev. Stat. 1961, ch. 38, §27-1. The statute also provided that truth "when communicated with good motives, and for justifiable ends, shall be an affirmative defense." Id. §27-2. Part of a leaflet showed an arrow pointing to a book entitled How to be a Jew. The arrow was pointing from a balloon stating "Sammy-the-Kosher-Coon shows you how . . . in ten easy lessons!!" In commenting on the defense that the reference to "Kosher-Coon" was true and did not show bad motives, the court stated in part: "They explained 'Kosher' meant pure; 'coon' was and is used in songs and literature without any offensive imputations. Even if we were to accept this explanation, it does not account for the deliberate hyphenating

of these words with intent to erase any honest or good motives or for justifiable means. We need not reiterate the signs and the leaflets to establish the defamation of two races and a religion. No one can impute good motives or justifiable means in defendants' conduct even if by a wide stretch of the imagination one could find truth in the statements and legends. The defendants banded, wore special type of attire, and expressed distinct convictions establishing motives unwholesome and contrary to the laws and constitution of our land." 47 Ill. App. 2d at 163, 197 N.E.2d at 455. The opinion in dealing with the defamation charge spoke of the need for such prosecution today relying in part on the Beauharnais case.

AN ACT TO MAKE UNLAWFUL THE DEFAMATION OF RACIAL, RELIGIOUS OR NATIONAL GROUPS
Proposed model statute suggested in Note,
47 Colum. L. Rev. 595, 609-612 (1947)

Section I. Findings.

The State has a special interest in the preservation of harmonious relations among its people. In order that the people be permitted to reach decisions on matters of public concern on the basis of free choice among conflicting doctrines, freedom of speech must be guarded jealously, not only from governmental interference but from private restraint and obstruction as well. Where such doctrines involve discussion of racial, religious and national groups, special problems arise. False representations of fact about these groups made in support of a course of action impede the free interchange and wise choice of ideas because the enormity and repetition of such falsehoods have been shown to increase their acceptance. Free interchange and wise choice are also impeded when resort is had to violence, or when threats or insults are uttered for the purpose of intimidation. Experience has shown that substitution of such conduct for free and frank discussion endangers the peace of the community by engendering unrest, anger, violent resentment and a clear and present danger of grave evil in the community.

Section II. Definitions. As used in this Act:

A. *Public place* means any publicly owned place, any public conveyance, any place where at the time of the offense the public is present by invitation or sufferance with or without the payment of a fee, or any place where 20 or more persons are present;

B. *Utter* means to communicate, cause to be communicated, or assist in communicating, by the spoken or written word or by any sign, picture, or symbol including, but not limited to, communication by any electrical or mechanical means;

C. *Person* means any individual, partnership, corporation, unincorporated association, or organization;

D. *Defamatory statement* means any utterance which, directly or by innuendo, holds up the group, person or persons concerning whom it is uttered, to public contempt, hatred, shame, disgrace, or obloquy, or causes him or them to be shunned, avoided or injured in his or their business, profession, or occupation;

   E. *Racial, religious or national group* means any racial, religious or national group, a portion thereof, or a person because of his belonging to such group or portion thereof;

   F. *Authorized corporation* means a non-profit corporation, chartered by the United States or any state thereof, authorized to do business in this State and which has as its purpose, or among its purposes, the protection of the civil or political liberties or other rights of the aggrieved group.

   [G. *Breach of the peace* means an utterance which, when judged by the probable reactions of a person of normal self-control, tends to provoke violence, or incites to violence, or which tends to stir anger, unrest or violent resentment on the part of those abused or on the part of others against those abused, or tends to create a disturbance.]*

Section III. Group libel and slander prohibited.

   A. No person shall utter in a public place any false and defamatory statement of fact concerning a racial, religious or national group.

   B. An action authorized by this section may be commenced by:

      (1) a representative number of individuals who are members of an aggrieved racial, religious or national group,

      (2) an authorized corporation,

      (3) the Attorney General, or

      (4) the district attorney of any county.

   C. Any person who has violated subsection A of this section shall be ordered to retract, in a manner deemed appropriate by the court, the false and defamatory statement which he uttered, and may be ordered (1) to refrain from repeating the false and defamatory statement which he uttered or its substantial equivalent, and (2) to post a bond in a reasonable amount and for a reasonable period of time conditioned upon his not violating this section; *provided* that after a person has had three judgments rendered against him under this section, an order to post such a bond shall be mandatory. No money damages shall be awarded to a plaintiff in an action brought under this section.

   D. An action commenced under this section may be discontinued only with the court's permission.

   E. If an action under this section is commenced by a plaintiff or plaintiffs authorized by paragraph (1), subsection B of this section, the defendant may move to dismiss the action on the ground that the plaintiff or plaintiffs are not representative of the defamed group, but such motion may be made only before answering. If the court finds for the defendant on the motion, the

---

* The criminal provisions of the proposed statute are bracketed; removal of the bracketed portions would leave a complete civil statute.

court, before dismissing such action, shall afford the plaintiff or plaintiffs a reasonable period in which to join as parties plaintiff additional members of the group. A dismissal of an action upon such a motion shall not be deemed or stated by the defendant to have been upon the merits. Such a statement is a defamatory statement.

F. Actions brought under this section must be commenced within one year after the occurrence of the defamatory conduct complained of.

G. An action under this section may be brought in any court of general jurisdiction in this State.

H. Upon motion of the defendant in an action commenced by a plaintiff or plaintiffs authorized under paragraphs (1) or (2) of subsection B of this section, an undertaking shall be provided by such plaintiff or plaintiffs in the amount of $300 conditioned upon the action's being carried forward and upon the payment of costs should the action be unsuccessful.

I. Any judgment on the merits rendered in an action authorized by this section shall constitute a defense in any subsequent suit brought under this section based on the same utterance.

[*Section IV. Breach of peace prohibited.*

A. It shall be unlawful for any person to utter, in a public place, concerning a racial, religious or national group under circumstances tending to a breach of the peace:

    (1) any threat of violence,

    (2) any offensive, abusive, insulting or derogatory words except when used in the course of and as part of an exposition primarily directed to the advocacy of ideas on matters of public concern, or

    (3) any false and defamatory statement of fact.

B. Any person violating this section shall, upon the first conviction thereof, be fined not less than $25 nor more than $250, or imprisoned for not more than 3 months, or both and upon the second or subsequent conviction, be fined not less than $50 nor more than $1000 or imprisoned for not more than 6 months, or both. In addition to such punishment the Court may order the defendant to post a bond in a reasonable amount and for a reasonable period of time conditioned upon his not violating this section. An order to post such a bond shall be mandatory upon the third conviction for violating this section.]

Section V. Burden of proof.

Whenever in an action under section 3 [or in a prosecution under paragraph (3), subsection A of section 4] the plaintiff [or prosecution] has shown that the utterance is defamatory, the burden shall be upon the defendant to come forward with evidence of its truth until, but only until, a prima facie case of its truth has been established.

Section VI. Separability of provisions.

If any provision of this Act, or the application thereof to any person or circumstances, is held invalid, the remainder of this Act and the application of such provisions to other persons or circumstances shall not be affected thereby.

NOTES

1. For federal group libel bills which would make it unlawful to bring defamatory literature into the country or ship it across state lines, see H.R. 535 and H.R. 1104, 88th Cong., 1st Sess. (1963), and other bills in Legislative Reference Service, Proposed Federal Group Libel Legislation, House Committee on the Judiciary, Staff Report 15-18 (Feb. 1963). H.R. 535 reads: "That . . . all papers [etc.] . . . containing any defamatory and false statements which tend to expose persons designated, identified or characterized therein by race or religion, any of whom reside in the United States, to hatred, contempt, ridicule or obloquy or tend to cause such persons to be shunned or avoided or to be injured in their business or occupation are hereby declared nonmailable matter. . . ." The only proposals which have become law are 62 Stat. 782 (1948), 18 U.S.C. §1718, making it a crime to knowingly deposit for mailing an envelope, post card or outside mail cover containing libelous, scurrilous or defamatory material; and 62 Stat. 768 (1948), 18 U.S.C. §1461, making it an offense to mail "indecent" articles or matter "tending to incite arson, murder, or assassination." See, Comment, Class Defamation — Scurrilous Matters in the Mail, 6 Vill. L. Rev. 525 (1961).

2. In some situations actions against group libel have been attempted under the general libel laws:

(a) In some states the criminal libel laws seem broad enough to cover aspects of group defamation. See Nev. Rev. Stat. §§200.510 et seq.; Cal. Pen. Code, c. 11 §258 (Dering 1960) (defines "slander"). In some cases, as in the Spielman case cited by Mr. Justice Frankfurter, prosecutions against defamers of groups have been upheld even though there is no showing that particular individuals have been affected. See, e.g., People v. Turner, 28 Cal. App. 766, 154 Pac. 34 (1915); Crane v. State, 14 Okla. Crim. 30, 166 Pac. 1110 (1917); People v. Gordon, 63 Cal. App. 627, 219 Pac. 486 (1923); Alumbaugh v. State, 39 Ga. App. 559, 147 S.E. 714 (1929) (defamatory remarks about Knights of Columbus). For cases holding that harm to individuals must be shown, see Drozda v. State, 86 Tex. Crim. 614, 218 S.W. 765 (1920); People v. Edmondson, 168 Misc. 142, 4 N.Y.2d 257 (1938). Despite the possibility of prosecution in many jurisdictions, action against group defamers is rarely taken under criminal libel statutes. See Tanenhaus, Group Libel, 35 Cornell L.Q. 261, 263-276 (1950); Note, 61 Yale L.J. 252 (1955); Leflar, The Social Utility of the Criminal Law of Defamation, 34 Texas L. Rev. 984 (1956); Brown and Stern, Group Defamation in the U.S.A., 13 Clev.-Mar. L. Rev. 7, 18 (1964); Note, Group Defamation: Is the Cure Too Costly? 1 Manitoba L. Sch. J. 255 (1964-1965); Gropper, Hate Literature — The Problem of Control, 30 Sask. B. Rev. 181 (1965).

(b) A civil action can generally not be brought for defamation of a large group (sometimes designated a "class") unless the individual can show that the communication applies to him in a special way. In case of a small group, individuals may sue if the definition clearly applies to every single member or if the group is so small that there can be no doubt that it covers all belonging to it. Groups also have been allowed to sue. Partnerships and corporations, though not in a position to claim mental anguish, can show pecuniary harm because of disparagement of business reputation or credit standing. Unincorporated groups face considerable procedural obstacles. For a successful suit brought by a union, see Kirkwood v. Westchester Newspapers, 287 N.Y. 373, 39 N.E.2d 919 (1942) (under N.Y. Gen. Assoc. Law §12 (1942), permitting suit by president or treasurer). For a more typical case, however, see Fowler v. Curtis Publishing Co., 182 F.2d 377 (D.C. Cir. 1950). Here the court described an article in a popular magazine as a "caustic, merciless diatribe depicting taxicab drivers in the Nation's capital as ill-mannered, brazen, and contemptuous of their patrons . . . cheating their customers when opportunity arose." The article was illustrated by a picture which showed one of the cabs of the company for which the plaintiff driver was working in such a way that the name could be clearly identified by the reader. The court nevertheless affirmed the lower court's dismissal of the complaint of one of the drivers, for failure to state a cause of action. See also Macaulay v. Bryan, 75 Nev. 278, 339 P.2d 377 (1959) (defamation of an association and its sympathizers, consisting of 12,500 and 20,000 persons respectively, held not actionable on the part of a member not singled out or pointed to; the plaintiff claimed he was present at a public hearing where the alleged slander occurred and that he was representing the association); Note, 70 A.L.R.2d 1382 (1960).

According to Tanenhaus, supra, 35 Cornell L.Q. at 263-265:

"Courts have held that actions could not be maintained by individuals when the 'Stivers clan,' 'wine-joint' owners, insurance agents, correspondence schools, trading-stamp concerns, the officials of a labor union, and antique dealers were libeled. Plaintiffs were permitted to sustain actions when the 'Fenstermaker family,' the members of a partnership, a staff of young doctors at a particular hospital, a court-martial, the occupants of a house, a jury, a county commission, a board of town trustees, an election board, the administrative board of a university, a group of coroner's physicians, and a group of harness-makers in a fire department were defamed. Actions by individuals were unsuccessful against publications alleging that most of the persons at a donation party were there for the liquor, part of a particular hose company had committed a theft, one of a man's sons was a thief, and that several of a group of six witnesses would be indicted for perjury. The courts did, on the other hand, find that 'subordinate engineers of a construction company or some of them,' and 'all radio editors save one' were sufficiently narrow categories to permit suits."

See also Bloomfield, Defamation of Corporations, 13 Clev.-Mar. L. Rev. 95 (1964).

3. In addition to ethnic and religious minorities, political groups and parties are of course frequent objects of vilification. The question has been raised whether libel actions should be available to these groups. For the view that all such groups, except official parties, should be protected, provided the justification of "fair comment" is retained and the range of actionable words is limited, see Leflar, supra, 34 Texas L. Rev. 984 (1956); Note, 98 U. Pa. L. Rev. 865 (1950).

On the question of whether a public official has standing to sue where the government or a government agency has been libeled, see N.Y. Times v. Sullivan, reprinted infra.

4. The effectiveness of group libel laws has been seriously questioned. Some of the objections are: (a) Prosecuting attorneys would be reluctant to prosecute and juries would rarely represent the point of view of minority groups. (b) Because of their necessarily vague language group libel laws might be used to suppress legitimate controversial opinions, contrary to their original purpose. (c) Such laws might make the courtroom a soundingboard for professional propagandists who would attempt to benefit from the prosecution by representing themselves as martyrs. (d) In the case of statutes permitting civil suits one libel might destroy a publisher who was sued separately by every member of a group. (e) Such a situation might also result in the clogging of court calendars. (f) Damages would be difficult to assess. (g) One member of an injured group might jeopardize its reputation by submitting what might be delicate and controversial issues to the official judgment of the jury. See 1 Chafee, Government and Mass Communications 122-130 (1947); Note, 61 Yale L.J. 252, 259-261; Tanenhaus, supra, 35 Cornell L.Q. at 297-302; Belton, The Control of Group Defamation: A Comparative Study of Law and Its Limitations, 34 Tulane L. Rev. 469 (1960).

5. Generally, on the subject of group libel laws see in addition to Riesman and Loewenstein cited in the Beauharnais opinion, Chafee, Free Speech in the United States 174 (1941); 1 Chafee, Government and Mass Communications 116-130 (1947); Fraenkel, Our Civil Liberties 18-20, 73, 87-88 (1944); American Civil Liberties Union, The Case Against Legal Restraints on Racial Libels and Anonymous Publications (1946); Fineberg, Can Anti-Semitism Be Outlawed? 6 Contemporary Jewish Record 619 (1943); Vishniak, An International Convention Against Anti-Semitism (1946); Pekelis, Law and Social Action 187-203 (1950); Note, Group Libel Laws: Abortive Efforts to Combat Hate Propaganda, 61 Yale L.J. 252 (1952); Beth, Group Libel and Free Speech, 39 Minn. L. Rev. 167 (1955) (a political science–philosophical approach to the subject); Group Libel, 7 Decalogue J. 10 (1956); Konvitz, Fundamental Liberties of a Free People, ch. 16 (1957); Lewis, The Individual Member's Right to Recover for a Defamation Leveled at the Group, 17 U. Miami L. Rev. 519 (1963); Group Defamation Symposium, 13 Clev.-Mar. L. Rev. 1 (1964) (contains, among others, articles on the Dutch, English, French, and West German experience); Cahn, The Predicament of Democratic Man 135-139 (1961).

6. Alternative proposals that have been suggested for combatting hate propaganda include:

(1) "Compulsory reply" statutes requiring publishers to print a rebuttal. Under one such proposal an Advisory Committee composed of members of minority groups is to decide whether to reply and to designate a writer. See Rothenberg, The Right of Reply to Libels in the Press, 23 J. Comp. Legis. & Int. L. 38 (1941).

(2) "Disclosure" measures which forbid anonymously published defamation and compel groups that "attempt to influence public opinion" to register. See, Report of the President's Committee on Civil Rights, To Secure These Rights 164-165 (1947); and other materials cited in Chapter III, Section C. Florida has a statute requiring disclosure with respect to libels of religious groups. Fla. Stat. Ann. §836.11. Federal legislation has been proposed which would deny use of the mails to anonymous hate propaganda. S. 990, 77th Cong., 1st Sess. (1941).

(3) The suggestion that the concept of intentional or negligent infliction of mental injury might be used to establish civil liability for group defamation. See Brown and Stern, Group Defamation in the U.S.A., 13 Clev.-Mar. L. Rev. 7, 29 (1964). See also Note, 15 A.L.R.2d 108, 111 (1951).

For a partial collection of materials on whether legal means are appropriate to counteract hate propaganda and on the effectiveness of counterpropaganda, see the second edition of this book at 836-837. On the effect of mass communication designed to reduce race prejudice see Rose, Studies in the Reduction of Prejudice (Am. Council of Race Relations, 2d ed. 1948).

NEW YORK TIMES CO. v. SULLIVAN
376 U.S. 254, 84 S. Ct. 710, 11 L. Ed. 2d 686 (1964)

Mr. Justice Brennan delivered the opinion of the Court.

We are required in this case to determine for the first time the extent to which the constitutional protections for speech and press limit a State's power to award damages in a libel action brought by a public official against critics of his official conduct.

Respondent L. B. Sullivan is one of the three elected Commissioners of the City of Montgomery, Alabama. He testified that he was "Commissioner of Public Affairs and the duties are supervision of the Police Department, Fire Department, Department of Cemetery and Department of Scales." He brought this civil libel action against the four individual petitioners, who are Negroes and Alabama clergymen, and against petitioner the New York Times Company, a New York corporation which publishes the New York Times, a daily newspaper. A jury in the Circuit Court of Montgomery County awarded him damages of $500,000, the full amount claimed, against all the petitioners, and the Supreme Court of Alabama affirmed. 273 Ala. 656, 144 So. 2d 25.

Respondent's complaint alleged that he had been libeled by statements in a full-page advertisement that was carried in the New York Times on March 29, 1960.[1] Entitled "Heed Their Rising Voices," the advertisement began by stating that "As the whole world knows by now, thousands of Southern Negro students are engaged in widespread non-violent demonstrations in positive affirmation of the right to live in human dignity as guaranteed by the U.S. Constitution and the Bill of Rights." It went on to charge that "in their efforts to uphold these guarantees, they are being met by an unprecedented wave of terror by those who would deny and negate that document which the whole world looks upon as setting the pattern for modern freedom. . . ." Succeeding paragraphs purported to illustrate the "wave of terror" by describing certain alleged events. The text concluded with an appeal for funds for three purposes: support of the student movement, "the struggle for the right-

[1] A copy of the advertisement is printed in the Appendix.

to-vote," and the legal defense of Dr. Martin Luther King, Jr., leader of the movement, against a perjury indictment then pending in Montgomery.

The text appeared over the names of 64 persons, many widely known for their activities in public affairs, religion, trade unions, and the performing arts. Below these names, and under a line reading "We in the south who are struggling daily for dignity and freedom warmly endorse this appeal," appeared the names of the four individual petitioners and of 16 other persons, all but two of whom were identified as clergymen in various Southern cities. The advertisement was signed at the bottom of the page by the "Committee to Defend Martin Luther King and the Struggle for Freedom in the South," and the officers of the Committee were listed.

Of the 10 paragraphs of text in the advertisement, the third and a portion of the sixth were the basis of respondent's claim of libel. They read as follows:

Third paragraph:

"In Montgomery, Alabama, after students sang 'My Country, 'Tis of Thee' on the State Capitol steps, their leaders were expelled from school, and truck-loads of police armed with shotguns and tear-gas ringed the Alabama State College Campus. When the entire student body protested to state authorities by refusing to re-register, their dining hall was padlocked in an attempt to starve them into submission."

Sixth paragraph:

"Again and again the Southern violators have answered Dr. King's peaceful protests with intimidation and violence. They have bombed his home almost killing his wife and child. They have assaulted his person. They have arrested him seven times — for 'speeding,' 'loitering' and similar 'offenses.' And now they have charged him with 'perjury' — a *felony* under which they could imprison him for *ten years.* . . ."

Although neither of these statements mentions respondent by name, he contended that the word "police" in the third paragraph referred to him as the Montgomery Commissioner who supervised the Police Department, so that he was being accused of "ringing" the campus with police. He further claimed that the paragraph would be read as imputing to the police, and hence to him, the padlocking of the dining hall in order to starve the students into submission.[2] As to the sixth paragraph, he contended that since arrests are ordinarily made by the police, the statement "They have arrested [Dr. King] seven times" would be read as referring to him; he further contended that the "They" who did the arresting would be equated with the "They" who committed the other described acts and with the "Southern violators." Thus, he argued, the paragraph would be read as accusing the Montgomery police, and hence him, of answering Dr. King's protests with "intimidation

---

[2] Respondent did not consider the charge of expelling the students to be applicable to him, since "that responsibility rests with the State Department of Education."

and violence," bombing his home, assaulting his person, and charging him with perjury. Respondent and six other Montgomery residents testified that they read some or all of the statements as referring to him in his capacity as Commissioner.

It is uncontroverted that some of the statements contained in the two paragraphs were not accurate descriptions of events which occurred in Montgomery. Although Negro students staged a demonstration on the State Capitol steps, they sang the National Anthem and not "My Country, 'Tis of Thee." Although nine students were expelled by the State Board of Education, this was not for leading the demonstration at the Capitol, but for demanding service at a lunch counter in the Montgomery County Courthouse on another day. Not the entire student body, but most of it, had protested the expulsion, not by refusing to register, but by boycotting classes on a single day; virtually all the students did register for the ensuing semester. The campus dining hall was not padlocked on any occasion, and the only students who may have been barred from eating there were the few who had neither signed a preregistration application nor requested temporary meal tickets. Although the police were deployed near the campus in large numbers on three occasions, they did not at any time "ring" the campus and they were not called to the campus in connection with the demonstration on the State Capitol steps, as the third paragraph implied. Dr. King had not been arrested seven times, but only four; and although he claimed to have been assaulted some years earlier in connection with his arrest for loitering outside a courtroom, one of the officers who made the arrest denied that there was such an assault.

On the premise that the charges in the sixth paragraph could be read as referring to him, respondent was allowed to prove that he had not participated in the events described. Although Dr. King's home had in fact been bombed twice when his wife and child were there, both of these occasions antedated respondent's tenure as Commissioner, and the police were not only not implicated in the bombings, but had made every effort to apprehend those who were. Three of Dr. King's four arrests took place before respondent became Commissioner. Although Dr. King had in fact been indicted (he was subsequently acquitted) on two counts of perjury, each of which carried a possible five-year sentence, respondent had nothing to do with procuring the indictment.

Respondent made no effort to prove that he suffered actual pecuniary loss as a result of the alleged libel.[3] One of his witnesses, a former employer, testified that if he had believed the statements, he doubted whether he "would want to be associated with anybody who would be a party to such things that

[3] Approximately 394 copies of the edition of the Times containing the advertisement were circulated in Alabama. Of these, about 35 copies were distributed in Montgomery County. The total circulation of the Times for that day was approximately 650,000 copies.

are stated in that ad," and that he would not re-employ respondent if he believed "that he allowed the Police Department to do the things that the paper say he did." But neither this witness nor any of the others testified that he had actually believed the statements in their supposed reference to respondent.

The cost of the advertisement was approximately $4800, and it was published by the Times upon an order from a New York advertising agency acting for the signatory Committee. The agency submitted the advertisement with a letter from A. Philip Randolph, Chairman of the Committee, certifying that the persons whose names appeared on the advertisement had given their permission. Mr. Randolph was known to the Times' Advertising Acceptability Department as a responsible person, and in accepting the letter as sufficient proof of authorization it followed its established practice. There was testimony that the copy of the advertisement which accompanied the letter listed only the 64 names appearing under the text, and that the statement, "We in the south . . . warmly endorse this appeal," and the list of names thereunder, which included those of the individual petitioners, were subsequently added when the first proof of the advertisement was received. Each of the individual petitioners testified that he had not authorized the use of his name, and that he had been unaware of its use until receipt of respondent's demand for a retraction. The manager of the Advertising Acceptability Department testified that he had approved the advertisement for publication because he knew nothing to cause him to believe that anything in it was false, and because it bore the endorsement of "a number of people who are well known and whose reputation" he "had no reason to question." Neither he nor anyone else at the Times made an effort to confirm the accuracy of the advertisement, either by checking it against recent Times news stories relating to some of the described events or by any other means.

Alabama law denies a public officer recovery of punitive damages in a libel action brought on account of a publication concerning his official conduct unless he first makes a written demand for a public retraction and the defendant fails or refuses to comply. Alabama Code, Tit. 7, §914. Respondent served such a demand upon each of the petitioners. None of the individual petitioners responded to the demand, primarily because each took the position that he had not authorized the use of his name on the advertisement and therefore had not published the statements that respondent alleged had libeled him. The Times did not publish a retraction in response to the demand, but wrote respondent a letter stating, among other things, that "we . . . are somewhat puzzled as to how you think the statements in any way reflect on you," and "you might, if you desire, let us know in what respect you claim that the statements in the advertisement reflect on you." Respondent filed this suit a few days later without answering the letter. The Times did, however, subsequently publish a retraction of the advertisement upon the demand of Governor John Patterson of Alabama, who asserted that the publication charged him with "grave misconduct and . . . improper actions and omissions as Governor of Alabama and Ex-Officio Chairman of the State Board of Education of Alabama." When asked to explain why there had been a retraction for the Governor but not for respondent, the Secretary of the Times testified: "We did that because we didn't want anything that was published by The Times to be a reflection on the State of Alabama and the Governor was, as far as we could see, the embodiment of the State of Alabama and the proper representative of the State and, furthermore, we had by that time learned more of the actual facts which the ad purported to recite and, finally, the ad did refer to the action of the State authorities and the Board of Education presumably of which the Governor is the ex-officio chairman. . . ." On the other hand, he testified that he did not think that "any of the language in there referred to Mr. Sullivan."

The trial judge submitted the case to the jury under instructions that the statements in the advertisement were "libelous per se" and were not privileged, so that petitioners might be held liable if the jury found that they had published the advertisement and that the statements were made "of and concerning" respondent. The jury was instructed that, because the statements were libelous per se, "the law . . . implies legal injury from the bare fact of publication itself," "falsity and malice are presumed," "general damages need not be alleged or proved but are presumed," and "punitive damages may be awarded by the jury even though the amount of actual damages is neither found nor shown." An award of punitive damages — as distinguished from "general" damages, which are compensatory in nature — apparently requires proof of actual malice under Alabama law, and the judge charged that "mere negligence or carelessness is not evidence of actual malice or malice in fact, and does not justify an award of exemplary or punitive damages." He refused to charge, however, that the jury must be "convinced" of malice, in the sense of "actual intent" to harm or "gross negligence and recklessness," to make such an award, and he also refused to require that a verdict for respondent differentiate between compensatory and punitive damages. The judge rejected petitioners' contention that his rulings abridged the freedoms of speech and of the press that are guaranteed by the First and Fourteenth Amendments.

In affirming the judgment, the Supreme Court of Alabama sustained the trial judge's rulings and instructions in all respects. 273 Ala. 656, 144 So. 2d 25. It held that "where the words published tend to injure a person libeled by them in his reputation, profession, trade or business, or charge him with an indictable offense, or tend to bring the individual into public contempt," they are "libelous per se"; that "the matter complained of is, under the above doctrine, libelous per se, if it was published of and concerning the plaintiff"; and that it was actionable without "proof of pecuniary injury . . . , such injury being implied." Id., at 673, 676, 144 So. 2d, at 37, 41. It approved the trial court's ruling that the jury could find the statements to have been made "of and concerning" respondent, stating: "We think it common knowledge that the average person knows that municipal agents, such as police and firemen, and others, are under the control and direction of the city governing body, and more particularly under the direction and control of a single commissioner. In measuring the performance or deficiencies of such groups, praise or criticism is usually attached to the official in complete control of the body." Id., at 674-675, 144 So. 2d, at 39. In sustaining the trial court's determination that the verdict was not excessive, the court said that malice could be inferred from the Times' "irresponsibility" in printing the advertisement while "the Times in its own files had articles already published which would have demonstrated the falsity of the allegations in the advertisement"; from the Times' failure to retract for respondent while retracting for the Governor, whereas the falsity of some of the allegations was then known to the Times and "the matter contained in the advertisement was equally false as to both parties"; and from the testimony of the Times' Secretary that, apart from the statement that the dining hall was padlocked, he thought the two paragraphs were "substantially correct." Id., at 686-687, 144 So. 2d, at 50-51. The court reaffirmed a statement in an earlier opinion that "There is no legal measure of damages in cases of this character." Id., at 686, 144 So. 2d, at 50. It rejected petitioners' constitutional contentions with the brief statements that "The First Amendment of the U.S. Constitution does not protect libelous publications" and "The Fourteenth Amendment is directed against State action and not private action." Id., at 676, 144 So. 2d, at 40.

Because of the importance of the constitutional issues involved, we granted the separate petitions for certiorari of the individual petitioners and of the Times. 371 U.S. 946. We reverse the judgment. We hold that the rule of law applied by the Alabama courts is constitutionally deficient for failure to provide the safeguards for freedom of speech and of the press that are required by the First and Fourteenth Amendments in a libel action brought by a public official against critics of his official conduct.[4] We further hold that under the proper safeguards the evidence presented in this case is constitutionally insufficient to support the judgment for respondent.

[4] Since we sustain the contentions of all the petitioners under the First Amendment's guarantees of freedom of speech and of the press as applied to the States by the Fourteenth Amendment, we do not decide the questions presented by the other claims of violation of the Fourteenth Amendment. The individual petitioners contend that the judgment against them offends the Due Process Clause because there was no evidence to show that they had published or authorized the publication of the alleged libel, and that the Due Process and Equal Protection Clauses were violated by racial segregation and racial bias in the courtroom. The Times contends that the assumption of jurisdiction over its corporate person by the Alabama courts overreaches the territorial limits of the Due Process Clause. The latter claim is foreclosed from our review by the ruling of the Alabama courts that the Times entered a general appearance in the action and thus waived its jurisdictional objection; we cannot say that this ruling lacks "fair or substantial support" in prior Alabama decisions. See Thompson v. Wilson, 224 Ala. 299, 140 So. 439 (1932); compare N.A.A.C.P. v. Alabama, 357 U.S. 449, 454-458.

I

We may dispose at the outset of two grounds asserted to insulate the judgment of the Alabama courts from constitutional scrutiny. The first is the proposition relied on by the State Supreme Court — that "The Fourteenth Amendment is directed against State action and not private action." That proposition has no application to this case. Although this is a civil lawsuit between private parties, the Alabama courts have applied a state rule of law which petitioners claim to impose invalid restrictions on their constitutional freedoms of speech and press. It matters not that that law has been applied in a civil action and that it is common law only, though supplemented by statute. See, e.g., Alabama Code, Tit. 7, §§908-917. The test is not the form in which state power has been applied but, whatever the form, whether such power has in fact been exercised. See Ex parte Virginia, 100 U.S. 339, 346-347; American Federation of Labor v. Swing, 312 U.S. 321.

The second contention is that the constitutional guarantees of freedom of speech and of the press are inapplicable here, at least so far as the Times is concerned, because the allegedly libelous statements were published as part of a paid, "commercial" advertisement. The argument relies on Valentine v. Chrestensen, 316 U.S. 52, where the Court held that a city ordinance forbidding street distribution of commercial and business advertising matter did not abridge the First Amendment freedoms, even as applied to a handbill having a commercial message on one side but a protest against certain official action on the other. The reliance is wholly misplaced. The Court in Chrestensen reaffirmed the constitutional protection for "the freedom of communicating information and disseminating opinion"; its holding was based upon the factual conclusions that the handbill was "purely commercial advertising" and that the protest against official action had been added only to evade the ordinance.

The publication here was not a "commercial" advertisement in the sense in which the word was used in Chrestensen. It communicated information, expressed opinion, recited grievances, protested claimed abuses, and sought financial support on behalf of a movement whose existence and objectives are matters of the highest public interest and concern. See N.A.A.C.P. v. Button, 371 U.S. 415, 435. That the Times was paid for publishing the advertisement is as immaterial in this connection as is the fact that newspapers and books are sold. Smith v. California, 361 U.S. 147, 150; cf. Bantam Books, Inc., v. Sullivan, 372 U.S. 58, 64, n.6. Any other conclusion would discourage newspapers from carrying "editorial advertisements" of this type, and so might shut off an important outlet for the promulgation of information and ideas by persons who do not themselves have access to publishing facilities — who wish to exercise their freedom of speech even though they are not members of the press. Cf. Lovell v. Griffin, 303 U.S. 444, 452; Schneider v. State, 308

U.S. 147, 164. The effect would be to shackle the First Amendment in its attempt to secure "the widest possible dissemination of information from diverse and antagonistic sources." Associated Press v. United States, 326 U.S. 1, 20. To avoid placing such a handicap upon the freedoms of expression, we hold that if the allegedly libelous statements would otherwise be constitutionally protected from the present judgment, they do not forfeit that protection because they were published in the form of a paid advertisement.[5]

II

Under Alabama law as applied in this case, a publication is "libelous per se" if the words "tend to injure a person . . . in his reputation" or to "bring [him] into public contempt"; the trial court stated that the standard was met if the words are such as to "injure him in his public office, or impute misconduct to him in his office, or want of official integrity, or want of fidelity to a public trust. . . ." The jury must find that the words were published "of and concerning" the plaintiff, but where the plaintiff is a public official his place in the governmental hierarchy is sufficient evidence to support a finding that his reputation has been affected by statements that reflect upon the agency of which he is in charge. Once "libel per se" has been established, the defendant has no defense as to stated facts unless he can persuade the jury that they were true in all their particulars. Alabama Ride Co. v. Vance, 235 Ala. 263, 178 So. 438 (1938); Johnson Publishing Co. v. Davis, 271 Ala. 474, 494-495, 124 So. 2d 441, 457-58 (1960). His privilege of "fair comment" for expressions of opinion depends on the truth of the facts upon which the comment is based. Parsons v. Age-Herald Publishing Co., 181 Ala. 439, 450, 61 So. 345, 350 (1913). Unless he can discharge the burden of proving truth, general damages are presumed, and may be awarded without proof of pecuniary injury. A showing of actual malice is apparently a prerequisite to recovery of punitive damages, and the defendant may in any event forestall a punitive award by a retraction meeting the statutory requirements. Good motives and belief in truth do not negate an inference of malice, but are relevant only in mitigation of punitive damages if the jury chooses to accord them weight. Johnson Publishing Co. v. Davis, supra, 271 Ala., at 495, 124 So. 2d, at 458.

The question before us is whether this rule of liability, as applied to an action brought by a public official against critics of his official conduct, abridges the freedom of speech and of the press that is guaranteed by the First and Fourteenth Amendments.

Respondent relies heavily, as did the Alabama courts, on statements of this Court to the effect that the Constitution does not protect libelous publications.[6] Those statements do not foreclose our inquiry here. None of the cases

---

[5] See American Law Institute, Restatement of Torts, §593, Comment b (1938).
[6] Konigsberg v. State Bar of California, 366 U.S. 36, 49, and n.10; Times Film Corp. v. City of Chicago, 365 U.S. 43, 48; Roth v. United States, 354 U.S. 476, 486-487;

sustained the use of libel laws to impose sanctions upon expression critical of the official conduct of public officials. The dictum in Pennekamp v. Florida, 328 U.S. 331, 348-349, that "when the statements amount to defamation, a judge has such remedy in damages for libel as do other public servants," implied no view as to what remedy might constitutionally be afforded to public officials. In Beauharnais v. Illinois, 343 U.S. 250, the Court sustained an Illinois criminal libel statute as applied to a publication held to be both defamatory of a racial group and "liable to cause violence and disorder." But the Court was careful to note that it "retains and exercises authority to nullify action which encroaches on freedom of utterance under the guise of punishing libel"; for "public men, are, as it were, public property," and "discussion cannot be denied and the right, as well as the duty, of criticism must not be stifled." Id., at 263-264, and n.18. In the only previous case that did present the question of constitutional limitations upon the power to award damages for libel of a public official, the Court was equally divided and the question was not decided. Schenectady Union Pub. Co. v. Sweeney, 316 U.S. 642. In deciding the question now, we are compelled by neither precedent nor policy to give any more weight to the epithet "libel" than we have to other "mere labels" of state law. N.A.A.C.P. v. Button, 371 U.S. 415, 429. Like insurrection,[7] contempt,[8] advocacy of unlawful acts,[9] breach of the peace,[10] obscenity,[11] solicitation of legal business,[12] and the various other formulae for the repression of expression that have been challenged in this Court, libel can claim no talismanic immunity from constitutional limitations. It must be measured by standards that satisfy the First Amendment.

The general proposition that freedom of expression upon public questions is secured by the First Amendment has long been settled by our decisions. . . .

The present advertisement, as an expression of grievance and protest on one of the major public issues of our time, would seem clearly to qualify for the constitutional protection. The question is whether it forfeits that protection by the falsity of some of its factual statements and by its alleged defamation of respondent.

Authoritative interpretations of the First Amendment guarantees have consistently refused to recognize an exception for any test of truth — whether administered by judges, juries, or administrative officials — and especially one that puts the burden of proving truth on the speaker. . . .

Injury to official reputation affords no more warrant for repressing speech

---

Beauharnais v. Illinois, 343 U.S. 250, 266; Pennekamp v. Florida, 328 U.S. 331, 348-349; Chaplinsky v. New Hampshire, 315 U.S. 568, 572; Near v. Minnesota, 283 U.S. 697, 715.

[7] Herndon v. Lowry, 301 U.S. 242.

[8] Bridges v. California, 314 U.S. 252; Pennekamp v. Florida, 328 U.S. 331.

[9] De Jonge v. Oregon, 299 U.S. 353.

[10] Edwards v. South Carolina, 372 U.S. 229.

[11] Roth v. United States, 354 U.S. 476.

[12] N.A.A.C.P. v. Button, 371 U.S. 415.

that would otherwise be free than does factual error. . . . Criticism of . . . official conduct does not lose its constitutional protection merely because it is effective criticism and hence diminishes . . . official reputations.

If neither factual error nor defamatory content suffices to remove the constitutional shield from criticism of official conduct, the combination of the two elements is no less inadequate. This is the lesson to be drawn from the great controversy over the Sedition Act of 1798, 1 Stat. 596, which first crystallized a national awareness of the central meaning of the First Amendment. See Levy, Legacy of Suppression (1960), at 258 et seq.; Smith, Freedom's Fetters (1956), at 426, 431, and passim. That statute made it a crime, punishable by a $5,000 fine and five years in prison, "if any person shall write, print, utter or publish . . . any false, scandalous and malicious writing or writings against the government of the United States, or either house of the Congress . . . , or the President . . . , with intent to defame . . . or to bring them, or either of them, into contempt or disrepute; or to excite against them, or either or any of them, the hatred of the good people of the United States." The Act allowed the defendant the defense of truth, and provided that the jury were to be judges both of the law and the facts. Despite these qualifications, the Act was vigorously condemned as unconstitutional in an attack joined in by Jefferson and Madison. In the famous Virginia Resolutions of 1798, the General Assembly of Virginia resolved that it

"doth particularly protest against the palpable and alarming infractions of the Constitution, in the two late cases of the 'Alien and Sedition Acts,' passed at the last session of Congress. . . . [The Sedition Act] exercises . . . a power not delegated by the Constitution, but, on the contrary, expressly and positively forbidden by one of the amendments thereto — a power which, more than any other, ought to produce universal alarm, because it is levelled against the right of freely examining public characters and measures, and of free communication among the people thereon, which has ever been justly deemed the only effectual guardian of every other right." 4 Elliot's Debates, supra, pp. 553-554.

Madison prepared the Report in support of the protest. His premise was that the Constitution created a form of government under which "The people, not the government, possess the absolute sovereignty." The structure of the government dispersed power in reflection of the people's distrust of concentrated power, and of power itself at all levels. This form of government was "altogether different" from the British form, under which the Crown was sovereign and the people were subjects. "Is it not natural and necessary, under such different circumstances," he asked, "that a different degree of freedom in the use of the press should be contemplated?" Id., pp. 569-570. Earlier, in a debate in the House of Representatives, Madison had said: "If we advert to the nature of Republican Government, we shall find that the censorial power is in the people over the Government, and not in the Government over the people." 4 Annals of Congress, p. 934 (1794). Of the exercise of that power by the press, his Report said: "In every state, probably, in the Union, the press has exerted a freedom in canvassing the merits and measures of public men, of every description, which has not been confined to the strict limits of the common law. On this footing the freedom of the press has stood; on this foundation it yet stands. . . ." 4 Elliot's Debates, supra, p. 570. The right of free public discussion of the stewardship of public officials was thus, in Madison's view, a fundamental principle of the American form of government.[15]

Although the Sedition Act was never tested in this Court,[16] the attack upon its validity has carried the day in the court of history. Fines levied in its prosecution were repaid by Act of Congress on the ground that it was unconstitutional. See, e.g., Act of July 4, 1840, c. 45, 6 Stat. 802, accompanied by H.R. Rep. No. 86, 26th Cong., 1st Sess. (1840). Calhoun, reporting to the Senate on February 4, 1836, assumed that its invalidity was a matter "which no one now doubts." Report with Senate bill No. 122, 24th Cong., 1st Sess., p. 3. Jefferson, as President, pardoned those who had been convicted and sentenced under the Act and remitted their fines, stating: "I discharged every person under punishment or prosecution under the sedition law, because I considered, and now consider, that law to be a nullity, as absolute and as palpable as if Congress had ordered us to fall down and worship a golden image." Letter to Mrs. Adams, July 22, 1804, 4 Jefferson's Works (Washington ed.), pp. 555, 556. The invalidity of the Act has also been assumed by Justices of this Court. . . .

There is no force in respondent's argument that the constitutional limitations implicit in the history of the Sedition Act apply only to Congress and not to the States. It is true that the First Amendment was originally addressed only to action by the Federal Government, and that Jefferson, for one, while denying the power of Congress "to control the freedom of the press," recognized such a power in the States. See the 1804 Letter to Abigail Adams quoted in Dennis v. United States, 341 U.S. 494, 522, n.4 (concurring opin-

---

[15] The Report on the Virginia Resolutions further stated:

"[I]t is manifestly impossible to punish the intent to bring those who administer the government into disrepute or contempt, without striking at the right of freely discussing public characters and measures; . . . which, again, is equivalent to a protection of those who administer the government, if they should at any time deserve the contempt or hatred of the people, against being exposed to it, by free animadversions on their characters and conduct. Nor can there be a doubt . . . that a government thus intrenched in penal statutes against the just and natural effects of a culpable administration, will easily evade the responsibility which is essential to a faithful discharge of its duty.

"Let it be recollected, lastly, that the right of electing the members of the government constitutes more particularly the essence of a free and responsible government. The value and efficacy of this right depends on the knowledge of the comparative merits of the candidates for public trust, and on the equal freedom, consequently, of examining and discussing these merits and demerits of the candidates respectively." 4 Elliot's Debates, supra, p. 575.

[16] The Act expired by its terms in 1801.

ion). But this distinction was eliminated with the adoption of the Fourteenth Amendment and the application to the States of the First Amendment's restrictions. . . .

What a State may not constitutionally bring about by means of a criminal statute is likewise beyond the reach of its civil law of libel.[17] The fear of damage awards under a rule such as that invoked by the Alabama courts here may be markedly more inhibiting than the fear of prosecution under a criminal statute. See City of Chicago v. Tribune Co., 307 Ill. 595, 607, 139 N.E. 86, 90 (1923). Alabama, for example, has a criminal libel law which subjects to prosecution "any person who speaks, writes, or prints of and concerning another any accusation falsely and maliciously importing the commission by such person of a felony, or any other indictable offense involving moral turpitude," and which allows as punishment upon conviction a fine not exceeding $500 and a prison sentence of six months. Alabama Code, Tit. 14, §350. Presumably a person charged with violation of this statute enjoys ordinary criminal-law safeguards such as the requirements of an indictment and of proof beyond a reasonable doubt. These safeguards are not available to the defendant in a civil action. The judgment awarded in this case — without the need for any proof of actual pecuniary loss — was one thousand times greater than the maximum fine provided by the Alabama criminal statute, and one hundred times greater than that provided by the Sedition Act. And since there is no double-jeopardy limitation applicable to civil lawsuits, this is not the only judgment that may be awarded against petitioners for the same publication.[18] Whether or not a newspaper can survive a succession of such judgments, the pall of fear and timidity imposed upon those who would give voice to public criticism is an atmosphere in which the First Amendment freedoms cannot survive. Plainly the Alabama law of civil libel is "a form of regulation that creates hazards to protected freedoms markedly greater than those that attend reliance upon the criminal law." Bantam Books, Inc., v. Sullivan, 372 U.S. 58, 70.

The state rule of law is not saved by its allowance of the defense of truth. A defense for erroneous statements honestly made is no less essential here than was the requirement of proof of guilty knowledge which, in Smith v. California, 361 U.S. 147, we held indispensable to a valid conviction of a bookseller for possessing obscene writings for sale. . . . A rule compelling the critic of official conduct to guarantee the truth of all his factual assertions — and to do so on pain of libel judgments virtually unlimited in amount — leads to a comparable "self-censorship." Allowance of the defense of truth, with the burden of proving it on the defendant, does not mean that only false speech

[17] Cf. Farmers Union v. WDAY, 360 U.S. 525, 535.

[18] The Times states that four other libel suits based on the advertisement have been filed against it by others who have served as Montgomery City Commissioners and by the Governor of Alabama; that another $500,000 verdict has been awarded in the only one of these cases that has yet gone to trial; and that the damages sought in the other three total $2,000,000.

will be deterred.[19] Even courts accepting this defense as an adequate safeguard have recognized the difficulties of adducing legal proofs that the alleged libel was true in all its factual particulars. See, e.g., Post Publishing Co. v. Hallam, 59 F. 530, 540 (C.A. 6th Cir. 1893); see also Noel, Defamation of Public Officers and Candidates, 49 Col. L. Rev. 875, 892 (1949). Under such a rule, would-be critics of official conduct may be deterred from voicing their criticism, even though it is believed to be true and even though it is in fact true, because of doubt whether it can be proved in court or fear of the expense of having to do so. They tend to make only statements which "steer far wider of the unlawful zone." Speiser v. Randall, supra, 357 U.S., at 526. The rule thus dampens the vigor and limits the variety of public debate. It is inconsistent with the First and Fourteenth Amendments.

The constitutional guarantees require, we think, a federal rule that prohibits a public official from recovering damages for a defamatory falsehood relating to his official conduct unless he proves that the statement was made with "actual malice" — that is, with knowledge that it was false or with reckless disregard of whether it was false or not. An oft-cited statement of a like rule, which has been adopted by a number of state courts,[20] is found in the Kansas case of Coleman v. MacLennan, 78 Kan. 711, 98 P. 281 (1908). The State Attorney General, a candidate for re-election and a member of the commission charged with the management and control of the state school fund, sued a newspaper publisher for alleged libel in an article purporting to state facts relating to his official conduct in connection with a school-fund transaction. The defendant pleaded privilege and the trial judge, over the plaintiff's objection, instructed the jury that

"where an article is published and circulated among voters for the sole pur-

---

[19] Even a false statement may be deemed to make a valuable contribution to public debate, since it brings about "the clearer perception and livelier impression of truth, produced by its collision with error." Mill, On Liberty (Oxford: Blackwell, 1947), at 15; see also Milton, Areopagitica, in Prose Works (Yale, 1959), Vol. II, at 561.

[20] E.g., Ponder v. Cobb, 257 N.C. 281, 299, 126 S.E.2d 67, 80 (1962); Lawrence v. Fox, 357 Mich. 134, 146, 97 N.W.2d 719, 725 (1959); Stice v. Beacon Newspaper Corp., 185 Kan. 61, 65-67, 340 P.2d 396, 400-401 (1959); Bailey v. Charleston Mail Assn., 126 W. Va. 292, 307, 27 S.E.2d 837, 844 (1943); Salinger v. Cowles, 195 Iowa 873, 889, 191 N.W. 167, 174 (1922); Snively v. Record Publishing Co., 185 Cal. 565, 571-576, 198 P. 1 (1921); McLean v. Merriman, 42 S.D. 394, 175 N.W. 878 (1920). Applying the same rule to candidates for public office, see, e.g., Phoenix Newspapers v. Choisser, 82 Ariz. 271, 276-277, 312 P.2d 150, 154 (1957); Friedell v. Blakely Printing Co., 163 Minn. 226, 230, 203 N.W. 974, 975 (1925). And see Chagnon v. Union-Leader Corp., 103 N.H. 426, 438, 174 A.2d 825, 833 (1961), cert. denied, 369 U.S. 830.

The consensus of scholarly opinion apparently favors the rule that is here adopted. E.g., 1 Harper and James, Torts, §5.26, at 449-450 (1956); Noel, Defamation of Public Officers and Candidates, 49 Col. L. Rev. 875, 891-895, 897, 903 (1949); Hallen, Fair Comment, 8 Tex. L. Rev. 41, 61 (1929); Smith, Charges Against Candidates, 18 Mich. L. Rev. 1, 115 (1919); Chase, Criticism of Public Officers and Candidates for Office, 23 Am. L. Rev. 346, 367-371 (1889); Cooley, Constitutional Limitations (7th ed., Lane, 1903), at 604, 616-628. But see, e.g., American Law Institute, Restatement of Torts, §598, Comment a (1938) (reversing the position taken in Tentative Draft 13, §1041 (2) (1936)); Veeder, Freedom of Public Discussion, 23 Harv. L. Rev. 413, 419 (1910).

pose of giving what the defendant believes to be truthful information concerning a candidate for public office and for the purpose of enabling such voters to cast their ballot more intelligently, and the whole thing is done in good faith and without malice, the article is privileged, although the principal matters contained in the article may be untrue in fact and derogatory to the character of the plaintiff; and in such a case the burden is on the plaintiff to show actual malice in the publication of the article."

In answer to a special question, the jury found that the plaintiff had not proved actual malice, and a general verdict was returned for the defendant. On appeal the Supreme Court of Kansas, in an opinion by Justice Burch, reasoned as follows (78 Kan., at 724, 98 P., at 286):

"It is of the utmost consequence that the people should discuss the character and qualifications of candidates for their suffrages. The importance to the state and to society of such discussions is so vast, and the advantages derived are so great, that they more than counterbalance the inconvenience of private persons whose conduct may be involved, and occasional injury to the reputations of individuals must yield to the public welfare, although at times such injury may be great. The public benefit from publicity is so great, and the chance of injury to private character so small, that such discussion must be privileged."

The court thus sustained the trial court's instruction as a correct statement of the law, saying:

"In such a case the occasion gives rise to a privilege, qualified to this extent: any one claiming to be defamed by the communication must show actual malice or go remediless. This privilege extends to a great variety of subjects, and includes matters of public concern, public men, and candidates for office." 78 Kan., at 723, 98 P., at 285.

Such a privilege for criticism of official conduct [21] is appropriately analogous to the protection accorded a public official when *he* is sued for libel by a private citizen. In Barr v. Matteo, 360 U.S. 564, 575, this Court held the utterance of a federal official to be absolutely privileged if made "within the outer perimeter" of his duties. The States accord the same immunity to statements of their highest officers, although some differentiate their lesser officials and qualify the privilege they enjoy.[22] But all hold that all officials are protected unless actual malice can be proved. The reason for the official privilege is said to be that the threat of damage suits would otherwise "inhibit the fearless, vigorous, and effective administration of policies of government" and "dampen the ardor of all but the most resolute, or the most irresponsible, in the unflinching discharge of their duties." Barr v. Matteo, supra, 360 U.S., at

---

[21] The privilege immunizing honest misstatements of fact is often referred to as a "conditional" privilege to distinguish it from the "absolute" privilege recognized in judicial, legislative, administrative and executive proceedings. See, e.g., Prosser, Torts (2d ed., 1955), §95.

[22] See 1 Harper and James, Torts, §5.23, at 429-430 (1956); Prosser, Torts (2d ed., 1955), at 612-613; American Law Institute, Restatement of Torts (1938), §591.

571. Analogous considerations support the privilege for the citizen-critic of government. It is as much his duty to criticize as it is the official's duty to administer. See Whitney v. California, 274 U.S. 357, 375 (concurring opinion of Mr. Justice Brandeis), quoted supra, p. 270. As Madison said, see supra, p. 275, "the censorial power is in the people over the Government, and not in the Government over the people." It would give public servants an unjustified preference over the public they serve, if critics of official conduct did not have a fair equivalent of the immunity granted to the officials themselves.

We conclude that such a privilege is required by the First and Fourteenth Amendments.

III

We hold today that the Constitution delimits a State's power to award damages for libel in actions brought by public officials against critics of their official conduct. Since this is such an action,[23] the rule requiring proof of actual malice is applicable. While Alabama law apparently requires proof of actual malice for an award of punitive damages,[24] where general damages are

---

[23] We have no occasion here to determine how far down into the lower ranks of government employees the "public official" designation would extend for purposes of this rule, or otherwise to specify categories of persons who would or would not be included. Cf. Barr v. Matteo, 360 U.S. 564, 573-575. Nor need we here determine the boundaries of the "official conduct" concept. It is enough for the present case that respondent's position as an elected city commissioner clearly made him a public official, and that the allegations in the advertisement concerned what was allegedly his official conduct as Commissioner in charge of the Police Department. As to the statements alleging the assaulting of Dr. King and the bombing of his home, it is immaterial that they might not be considered to involve respondent's official conduct if he himself had been accused of perpetrating the assault and the bombing. Respondent does not claim that the statements charged him personally with these acts; his contention is that the advertisement connects him with them only in his official capacity as the Commissioner supervising the police, on the theory that the police might be equated with the "They" who did the bombing and assaulting. Thus, if these allegations can be read as referring to respondent at all, they must be read as describing his performance of his official duties.

[24] Johnson Publishing Co. v. Davis, 271 Ala. 474, 487, 124 So.2d 441, 450 (1960). Thus, the trial judge here instructed the jury that "mere negligence or carelessness is not evidence of actual malice or malice in fact, and does not justify an award of exemplary or punitive damages in an action for libel." The court refused, however, to give the following instruction which had been requested by the Times:
"I charge you . . . that punitive damages, as the name indicates, are designed to punish the defendant, the New York Times Company, a corporation, and the other defendants in this case, . . . and I further charge you that such punitive damages may be awarded only in the event that you, the jury, are convinced by a fair preponderance of the evidence that the defendant . . . was motivated by personal ill will, that is actual intent to do the plaintiff harm, or that the defendant . . . was guilty of gross negligence and recklessness and not of just ordinary negligence or carelessness in publishing the matter complained of so as to indicate a wanton disregard of plaintiff's rights."
The trial court's error in failing to require any finding of actual malice for an award of general damages makes it unnecessary for us to consider the sufficiency under the federal standard of the instructions regarding actual malice that were given as to punitive damages.

concerned malice is "presumed." Such a presumption is inconsistent with the federal rule. "The power to create presumptions is not a means of escape from constitutional restrictions," Bailey v. Alabama, 219 U.S. 219, 239; "the showing of malice required for the forfeiture of the privilege is not presumed but is a matter for proof by the plaintiff. . . ." Lawrence v. Fox, 357 Mich. 134, 146, 97 N.W.2d 719, 725 (1959). Since the trial judge did not instruct the jury to differentiate between general and punitive damages, it may be that the verdict was wholly an award of one or the other. But is it impossible to know, in view of the general verdict returned. Because of this uncertainty, the judgment must be reversed and the case remanded. . . .

Since respondent may seek a new trial, we deem that considerations of effective judicial administration require us to review the evidence in the present record to determine whether it could constitutionally support a judgment for respondent. This Court's duty is not limited to the elaboration of constitutional principles; we must also in proper cases review the evidence to make certain that those principles have been constitutionally applied. This is such a case, particularly since the question is one of alleged trespass across "the line between speech unconditionally guaranteed and speech which may legitimately be regulated." Speiser v. Randall, 357 U.S. 513, 525. In cases where that line must be drawn, the rule is that we "examine for ourselves the statements in issue and the circumstances under which they were made to see . . . whether they are of a character which the principles of the First Amendment, as adopted by the Due Process Clause of the Fourteenth Amendment, protect." Pennekamp v. Florida, 328 U.S. 331, 335; see also One, Inc., v. Olesen, 355 U.S. 371; Sunshine Book Co. v. Summerfield, 355 U.S. 372. We must "make an independent examination of the whole record," Edwards v. South Carolina, 372 U.S. 229, 235, so as to assure ourselves that the judgment does not constitute a forbidden intrusion on the field of free expression.[26]

Applying these standards, we consider that the proof presented to show actual malice lacks the convincing clarity which the constitutional standard demands, and hence that it would not constitutionally sustain the judgment for respondent under the proper rule of law. The case of the individual petitioners requires little discussion. Even assuming that they could constitutionally be found to have authorized the use of their names on the advertisement, there was no evidence whatever that they were aware of any erroneous state-

---

[26] The Seventh Amendment does not, as respondent contends, preclude such an examination by this Court. That Amendment, providing that "no fact tried by a jury, shall be otherwise reexamined in any Court of the United States, than according to the rules of the common law," is applicable to state cases coming here. Chicago, B. &. Q. R. Co. v. Chicago, 166 U.S. 226, 242-243; cf. The Justices v. Murray, 9 Wall. 274. But its ban on re-examination of facts does not preclude us from determining whether governing rules of federal law have been properly applied to the facts. "[T]his Court will review the finding of facts by a State court . . . where a conclusion of law as to a Federal right and a finding of fact are so intermingled as to make it necessary, in order to pass upon the Federal question, to analyze the facts." Fiske v. Kansas, 274 U.S. 380, 385-386. See also Haynes v. Washington, 373 U.S. 503, 515-516.

ments or were in any way reckless in that regard. The judgment against them is thus without constitutional support.

As to the Times, we similarly conclude that the facts do not support a finding of actual malice. The statement by the Times' Secretary that, apart from the padlocking allegation, he thought the advertisement was "substantially correct," affords no constitutional warrant for the Alabama Supreme Court's conclusion that it was a "cavalier ignoring of the falsity of the advertisement [from which] the jury could not have but been impressed with the bad faith of The Times, and its maliciousness inferable therefrom." The statement does not indicate malice at the time of the publication; even if the advertisement was not "substantially correct" — although respondent's own proofs tend to show that it was — that opinion was at least a reasonable one, and there was no evidence to impeach the witness' good faith in holding it. The Times' failure to retract upon respondent's demand, although it later retracted upon the demand of Governor Patterson, is likewise not adequate evidence of malice for constitutional purposes. Whether or not a failure to retract may ever constitute such evidence, there are two reasons why it does not here. *First,* the letter written by the Times reflected a reasonable doubt on its part as to whether the advertisement could reasonably be taken to refer to respondent at all. *Second,* it was not a final refusal, since it asked for an explanation on this point — a request that respondent chose to ignore. Nor does the retraction upon the demand of the Governor supply the necessary proof. It may be doubted that a failure to retract which is not itself evidence of malice can retroactively become such by virtue of a retraction subsequently made to another party. But in any event that did not happen here, since the explanation given by the Times' Secretary for the distinction drawn between respondent and the Governor was a reasonable one, the good faith of which was not impeached.

Finally, there is evidence that the Times published the advertisement without checking its accuracy against the news stories in the Times' own files. The mere presence of the stories in the files does not, of course, establish that the Times "knew" the advertisement was false, since the state of mind required for actual malice would have to be brought home to the persons in the Times' organization having responsibility for the publication of the advertisement. With respect to the failure of those persons to make the check, the record shows that they relied upon their knowledge of the good reputation of many of those whose names were listed as sponsors of the advertisement, and upon the letter from A. Philip Randolph, known to them as a responsible individual, certifying that the use of the names was authorized. There was testimony that the persons handling the advertisement saw nothing in it that would render it unacceptable under the Times' policy of rejecting advertisements containing "attacks of a personal character"; [27] their failure to reject it

[27] The Times has set forth in a booklet its "Advertising Acceptability Standards." Listed among the classes of advertising that the newspaper does not accept are advertisements that are "fraudulent or deceptive," that are "ambiguous in wording and . . .

on this ground was not unreasonable. We think the evidence against the Times supports at most a finding of negligence in failing to discover the misstatements, and is constitutionally insufficient to show the recklessness that is required for a finding of actual malice. Cf. Charles Parker Co. v. Silver City Crystal Co., 142 Conn. 605, 618, 116 A.2d 440, 446 (1955); Phoenix Newspapers, Inc., v. Choisser, 82 Ariz. 271, 277-278, 312 P.2d 150, 154-155 (1957).

We also think the evidence was constitutionally defective in another respect: it was incapable of supporting the jury's finding that the allegedly libelous statements were made "of and concerning" respondent. Respondent relies on the words of the advertisement and the testimony of six witnesses to establish a connection between it and himself. Thus, in his brief to this Court, he states:

"The reference to respondent as police commissioner is clear from the ad. In addition, the jury heard the testimony of a newspaper editor . . . ; a real estate and insurance man . . . ; the sales manager of a men's clothing store . . . ; a food equipment man . . . ; a service station operator . . . ; and the operator of a truck line for whom respondent had formerly worked. . . . Each of these witnesses stated that he associated the statements with respondent. . . ." (Citations to record omitted.)

There was no reference to respondent in the advertisement, either by name or official position. A number of the allegedly libelous statements — the charges that the dining hall was padlocked and that Dr. King's home was bombed, his person assaulted, and a perjury prosecution instituted against him — did not even concern the police; despite the ingenuity of the arguments which would attach this significance to the word "They," it is plain that these statements could not reasonably be read as accusing respondent of personal involvement in the acts in question. The statements upon which respondent principally relies as referring to him are the two allegations that did concern the police or police functions: that "truckloads of police . . . ringed the Alabama State College Campus" after the demonstration on the State Capitol steps, and that Dr. King had been "arrested . . . seven times." These statements were false only in that the police had been "deployed near" the campus but had not actually "ringed" it and had not gone there in connection with the State Capitol demonstration, and in that Dr. King had been arrested only four times. The ruling that these discrepancies between what was true and what was asserted were sufficient to injure respondent's reputation may itself raise constitutional problems, but we need not consider them here. Although the statements may be taken as referring to the police, they did not on their face make even an oblique reference to respondent as an individual. Support for the asserted reference must, therefore, be sought in the testimony of re-

may mislead," and that contain "attacks of a personal character." In replying to respondent's interrogatories before the trial, the Secretary of the Times stated that "as the advertisement made no attacks of a personal character upon any individual and otherwise met the advertising acceptability standards promulgated," it had been approved for publication.

spondent's witnesses. But none of them suggested any basis for the belief that respondent himself was attacked in the advertisement beyond the bare fact that he was in overall charge of the Police Department and thus bore official responsibility for police conduct; to the extent that some of the witnesses thought respondent to have been charged with ordering or approving the conduct or otherwise being personally involved in it, they based this notion not on any statements in the advertisement, and not on any evidence that he had in fact been so involved, but solely on the unsupported assumption that, because of his official position, he must have been.[28] This reliance on the bare

---

[28] Respondent's own testimony was that "as Commissioner of Public Affairs it is part of my duty to supervise the Police Department and I certainly feel like it [a statement] is associated with me when it describes police activities." He thought that "by virtue of being Police Commissioner and Commissioner of Public Affairs," he was charged with "any activity on the part of the Police Department." "When it describes police action, certainly I feel it reflects on me as an individual." He added that "It is my feeling that it reflects not only on me but on the other Commissioners and the community."

Grover C. Hall testified that to him the third paragraph of the advertisement called to mind "the City government — the Commissioners," and that "now that you ask it I would naturally think a little more about the police Commissioner because his responsibility is exclusively with the constabulary." It was "the phrase about starvation" that led to the association; "the other didn't hit me with any particular force."

Arnold D. Blackwell testified that the third paragraph was associated in his mind with "the Police Commissioner and the police force. The people on the police force." If he had believed the statement about the padlocking of the dining hall, he would have thought "that the people on our police force or the heads of our police force were acting without their jurisdiction and would not be competent for the position." "I would assume that the Commissioner had ordered the police force to do that and therefore it would be his responsibility."

Harry W. Kaminsky associated the statement about "truckloads of police" with respondent "because he is the Police Commissioner." He thought that the reference to arrests in the sixth paragraph "implicates the Police Department, I think, or the authorities that would do that — arrest folks for speeding and loitering and such as that." Asked whether he would associate with respondent a newspaper report that the police had "beat somebody up or assaulted them on the streets of Montgomery," he replied: "I still say he is the Police Commissioner and those men are working directly under him and therefore I would think that he would have something to do with it." In general, he said, "I look at Mr. Sullivan when I see the Police Department."

H. M. Price, Sr., testified that he associated the first sentence of the third paragraph with respondent because: "I would just automatically consider that the Police Commissioner in Montgomery would have to put his approval on those kind of things as an individual."

William M. Parker, Jr., testified that he associated the statements in the two paragraphs with "the Commissioners of the City of Montgomery," and since respondent was the Police Commissioner," he "thought of him first." He told the examining counsel: "I think if you were the Police Commissioner I would have thought it was speaking of you."

Horace W. White, respondent's former employer, testified that the statement about "truck-loads of police" made him think of respondent "as being the head of the Police Department." Asked whether he read the statement as charging respondent himself with ringing the campus or having shotguns and tear-gas, he replied: "Well, I thought of his department being charged with it, yes, sir. He is the head of the Police Department as I understand it." He further said that the reason he would have been unwilling to re-employ respondent if he had believed the advertisement was "the fact that he allowed the Police Department to do the things that the paper say he did."

fact of respondent's official position[29] was made explicit by the Supreme Court of Alabama. That court, in holding that the trial court "did not err in over-ruling the demurrer [of the Times] in the aspect that the libelous matter was not of and concerning the [plaintiff,]" based its ruling on the proposition that:

"We think it common knowledge that the average person knows that mu-nicipal agents, such as police and firemen, and others, are under the control and direction of the city governing body, and more particularly under the direction and control of a single commissioner. In measuring the perform-ance or deficiencies of such groups, praise or criticism is usually attached to the official in complete control of the body." 273 Ala., at 674-675, 144 So. 2d, at 39.

This proposition has disquieting implications for criticism of governmental conduct. For good reason, "no court of last resort in this country has ever held, or even suggested, that prosecutions for libel on government have any place in the American system of jurisprudence." City of Chicago v. Tribune Co., 307 Ill. 595, 601, 139 N.E. 86, 88 (1923). The present proposition would sidestep this obstacle by transmuting criticism of government, however im-personal it may seem on its face, into personal criticism, and hence potential libel, of the officials of whom the government is composed. There is no legal alchemy by which a State may thus create the cause of action that would otherwise be denied for a publication which, as respondent himself said of the advertisement, "reflects not only on me but on the other Commissioners and the community." Raising as it does the possibility that a good-faith critic of government will be penalized for his criticism, the proposition relied on by the Alabama courts strikes at the very center of the constitutionally protected area of free expression.[30] We hold that such a proposition may not constitu-tionally be utilized to establish that an otherwise impersonal attack on gov-ernmental operations was a libel of an official responsible for those operations. Since it was relied on exclusively here, and there was no other evidence to connect the statements with respondent, the evidence was constitutionally insufficient to support a finding that the statements referred to respondent.

The judgment of the Supreme Court of Alabama is reversed and the case is remanded to that court for further proceedings not inconsistent with this opinion.

Reversed and remanded.

---

[29] Compare Ponder v. Cobb, 257 N.C. 281, 126 S.E.2d 67 (1962).

[30] Insofar as the proposition means only that the statements about police conduct libeled respondent by implicitly criticizing his ability to run the Police Department, recovery is also precluded in this case by the doctrine of fair comment. See American Law Institute, Restatement of Torts (1938), §607. Since the Fourteenth Amendment requires recognition of the conditional privilege for honest misstatements of fact, it follows that a defense of fair comment must be afforded for honest expression of opinion based upon privileged, as well as true, statements of fact. Both defenses are of course defeasible if the public official proves actual malice, as was not done here.

NOTES

1. Mr. Justice Black, with whom Mr. Justice Douglas joined, concurred in the result on the basis that the First and Fourteenth Amendments do "not merely 'delimit' a State's power to award damages to 'public officials against critics of their official conduct' but completely prohibit a State from exercising such a power." 376 U.S. at 293. Their opinion would extend this prohibition not only to public officials but at the very least to the discussion of all "public affairs." 376 U.S. at 296. Mr. Justice Goldberg's concurrence, in which Mr. Justice Douglas also joined, was in a similar vein, but Mr. Justice Goldberg carefully asserted that private libel is not covered by the First Amendment.

2. In another decision the Supreme Court denied certiorari in a libel suit brought by public officials against the New York Times where the circuit court had ruled that because of the joinder of four Alabama individuals as co-defendants with the Times the case could not be removed to the federal courts on diversity grounds. New York Times v. Parks, 376 U.S. 949, 84 S. Ct. 964, 11 L. Ed. 2d 969 (1964), denying cert. from 308 F.2d 474 (5th Cir. 1962). In still another case decided by a federal jury since the Sullivan decision, the former Police Commissioner of Birmingham, T. Eugene Connor, won a $40,000 damage award against the New York Times. N.Y. Times, Sept. 25, 1964.

3. In Garrison v. Louisiana, 379 U.S. 64, 85 S. Ct. 209, 13 L. Ed. 2d 125 (1964), the Supreme Court reversed the conviction for criminal libel of a district attorney who at a press conference had blamed the backlog of criminal cases on the excessive vacations, laziness, and inefficiency of the judges and had also alleged that they had hampered enforcement of the vice laws by refusing to authorize expenses for investigation and closing down of "clip joints," thus making it "eloquently clear where their sympathies lie in regard to aggressive vice investigations. . . ." The Court stated that, at least where criticism of public officials is concerned, criminal libel laws are not free from the limitations established in the Sullivan case because whatever may have been their function in the age of dueling, they no longer, unless obviously so limited, serve any special function of preserving the public peace. After mentioning with approval the Model Penal Code, Tent. Draft No. 13, 1961, §250.7, Comments, at 44, recommending only narrowly drawn statutes such as that involved in Chaplinsky v. New Hampshire, 315 U.S. 568, 62 S. Ct. 766, 86 L. Ed. 1031 (1942), "designed to reach words tending to cause a breach of the peace," or statutes such as the one in the Beauharnais case, supra, "designed to reach speech, such as group vilification 'especially likely to lead to public disorders,'" the Court, in referring to the Louisiana law, stated: "But Louisiana's rejection of the clear-and-present-danger standard as irrelevant to the application of its statute . . . coupled with the absence of any limitation in the statute itself to speech calculated to cause breaches of the peace, leads us to conclude that the Louisiana statute is not this sort of narrowly drawn statute." 379 U.S. at 70. The Court then applied the principles of the Sullivan case as follows: "[We] hold that the Louisiana statute, as authoritatively interpreted by the Supreme Court of Louisiana, incorporates constitutionally invalid standards in the context of criticism of the official conduct of public officials. For, contrary to the New York Times rule, which absolutely prohibits punishment of truthful criticism, the statute directs

punishment for true statements made with 'actual malice,' see LSA — R.S. §14:48; State v. Cox, 246 La. 748, 756, 167 So. 352, 355 (1964), handed down after the New York Times decision; Bennett, The Louisiana Criminal Code, 5 La. L. Rev. 6, 34 (1942). And 'actual malice' is defined in the decisions below to mean 'hatred, ill will or enmity or a wanton desire to injure. . . .' 244 La., at 851, 154 So. 2d, at 423. The statute is also unconstitutional, as interpreted to cover false statements against public officials. The New York Times standard forbids the punishment of false statements, unless made with knowledge of their falsity or in reckless disregard of whether they are true or false. But the Louisiana statute punishes false statements without regard to that test if made with ill-will; even if ill-will is not established, a false statement concerning public officials can be punished if not made in the reasonable belief of its truth. The Louisiana Supreme Court affirmed the conviction solely on the ground that the evidence sufficed to support the trial court's finding of ill-will, enmity, or a wanton desire to injure. But the trial court also rested the conviction on additional findings that the statement was false and not made in the reasonable belief of its truth. The judge said:

" 'It is inconceivable to me that the Defendant could have had a reasonable belief, which could be defined as an honest belief, that not one but all eight of these Judges of the Criminal District Court were guilty of what he charged them with in the defamatory statement. These men have been honored . . . with very high offices. . . . It is inconceivable to me that all of them could have been guilty of all of the accusations made against them. Therefore, I do not believe that the qualified privilege under LSA — R.S., Title 14, Section 49, is applicable. . . .'

"This is not a holding applying the New York Times test. The reasonable-belief standard applied by the trial judge is not the same as the reckless-disregard-of-truth standard. According to the trial court's opinion, a reasonable belief is one which 'an ordinarily prudent man might be able to assign a just and fair reason for'; the suggestion is that under this test the immunity from criminal responsibility in the absence of ill-will disappears on proof that the exercise of ordinary care would have revealed that the statement was false. The test which we laid down in New York Times is not keyed to ordinary care; defeasance of the privilege is conditioned, not on mere negligence, but on reckless disregard for the truth." 379 U.S. at 77-79. See also Moity v. Louisiana, 379 U.S. 201, 85 S. Ct. 323, 13 L. Ed. 2d 339 (1964).

Ashton v. Kentucky, 384 U.S. 195, 86 S. Ct. 1407, 16 L. Ed. 2d 469 (1966), involved a criminal libel conviction for defaming the sheriff, a chief of police, and a newspaper owner in connection with their conduct and background in relation to a labor dispute. The indictment charged "the offense of criminal libel" committed "by publishing a false and malicious publication which tends to degrade or injure" the three individuals. The charge to the jury stated: ". . . criminal libel is defined as any writing calculated to create disturbances of the peace, corrupt the public morals, or lead to any act, which, when done, is indictable." The trial court added that falsity and malice are essential elements of the offense. The Kentucky Court of Appeals though affirming the conviction, defined libel differently, stating that the element of breach of the peace was no longer a constitutional basis for imposing criminal liability. Its definition was, "the publication of a defamatory statement about another which is false, with malice." Mr. Justice Douglas, for the Court, referring to Shuttlesworth v. Birmingham, 382 U.S. 87, 86 S. Ct. 211, 15

L. Ed. 2d 176 (1965), indicated first that the Court of Appeals' narrow construction to save the statute could not sustain a conviction based on a broader construction under which the law is unconstitutional. He held the law, in so far as it was based on breach of the peace, too vague on the basis of Cantwell v. Connecticut, 310 U.S. 296, 60 S. Ct. 900, 84 L. Ed. 1213 (1940); Terminiello v. Chicago, 337 U.S. 1, 69 S. Ct. 894, 93 L. Ed. 1131 (1949); Edwards v. South Carolina, 372 U.S. 229, 83 S. Ct. 680, 9 L. Ed. 2d 697 (1963); Cox v. Louisiana, 379 U.S. 536, 85 S. Ct. 453, 13 L. Ed. 2d 471 (1965), all considered in Chapter IV. Mr. Justice Harlan concurred in the result without opinion.

See also State v. Browne, 86 N.J. Super. 217, 206 A.2d 591 (1965). For discussion of criminal libel, see Kelly, Criminal Libel and Free Speech, 6 Kan. L. Rev. 295 (1958); Note, Constitutionality of the Law of Criminal Libel, 52 Colum. L. Rev. 521 (1952).

4. In Henry v. Collins, 380 U.S. 356, 85 S. Ct. 992, 13 L. Ed. 2d 892 (1965), the Supreme Court reversed a libel award against Aaron A. Henry, a Mississippi civil rights leader, who had charged that his arrest was the result of "a diabolical plot" by the county attorney and city police chief. The Supreme Court made the following observation about the trial court's charge on malice:

"The following instructions requested by the respondents, approved by the trial judge, were read to the jury:

" 'The court instructs the jury for the plaintiff that malice does not necessarily mean hatred or ill will, but that malice may consist merely of culpable recklessness or a wilful and wanton disregard of the rights and interests of the person defamed.'

"The jury, was also instructed, at respondents' request, that

" '. . . [I]f you believe from the evidence that defendant published a false statement charging that his arrest . . . was the result of a diabolical plot . . . , you may infer malice, as defined in these instructions, from the falsity and libelous nature of the statement, although malice as a legal presumption does not arise from the fact that the statement in question is false and libelous. It is for you to determine as a fact, if you have first determined from the evidence that defendant published the statement in question and that it is false, whether or not the statement in question was actually made with malice.'

"The jury might well have understood these instructions to allow recovery on a showing of intent to inflict harm, rather than intent to inflict harm through falsehood. See Garrison v. Louisiana, 379 U.S. 64, 73. 'The constitutional guarantees . . . [prohibit] a public official from recovering damages for a defamatory falsehood relating to his official conduct unless he proves that the statement was made . . . with knowledge that it was false or with reckless disregard of whether it was false or not.' New York Times Co. v. Sullivan, 376 U.S. 254, 279-280." 380 U.S. at 357.

5. In Rosenblatt v. Baer, 383 U.S. 75, 86 S. Ct. 669, 15 L. Ed. 2d 597 (1966), the allegedly libelous statement read:

"Been doing a little listening and checking at Belknap Recreation Area and am thunderstruck by what am learning.

"This year, a year without snow till very late, a year with actually few very major changes in procedure; the difference in cash income simply fantastic, almost unbelievable.

"On any sort of comparative basis, the Area this year is doing literally hundreds of per cent BETTER than last year.

"When consider that last year was excellent snow year, that season started because of more snow, months earlier last year, one can only ponder following question:

"What happened to all the money last year? and every other year? What magic has Dana Beane [Chairman of the new commission] and rest of commission, and Mr. Warner [respondent's replacement as Supervisor] wrought to make such tremendous difference in net cash results?"

The respondent had been the supervisor of the Belknap recreation area. The opinion by Mr. Justice Brennan, reversing a libel judgment in favor of the respondent, commented on plaintiff's theories of recovery in part as follows:

"The first was that the jury could award him damages if it found that the column cast suspicion indiscriminately on the small number of persons who comprised the former management group, whether or not it found that the imputation of misconduct was specifically made of and concerning him. This theory of recovery was open to respondent under New Hampshire law; the trial judge explicitly instructed the jury that 'an imputation of impropriety or a crime to one or some of a small group that casts suspicion upon all is actionable.' The question is presented, however, whether that theory of recovery is precluded by our holding in New York Times that, in the absence of sufficient evidence that the attack focused on the plaintiff, an otherwise impersonal attack on governmental operations cannot be utilized to establish a libel of those administering the operations. 376 U.S., at 290-292. . . .

"Were the statement at issue in this case an explicit charge that the Commissioners and Baer or the entire Area management were corrupt, we assume without deciding that any member of the identified group might recover.[5] The statement itself might be sufficient evidence that the attack was specifically directed at each individual. Even if a charge and reference were merely implicit, as is alleged here, but a plaintiff could show by extrinsic proofs that the statement referred to him, it would be no defense to a suit by one member of an identifiable group engaged in governmental activity that another was also attacked. These situations are distinguishable from the present case; here, the jury was permitted to infer both defamatory content and reference from the challenged statement itself, although the statement on its face is only an impersonal discussion of government activity. To the extent the trial judge authorized the jury to award respondent a recovery without regard to evidence that the asserted implication of the column was made specifically of and concerning him, we hold that the instruction was erroneous.[6]

---

[5] Such recovery would, of course, be subject to a showing of actual malice if the individual were a "public official" within the meaning of New York Times.

[6] It might be argued that the charge instructed the jury to award recovery only if it found that the libel was aimed at Mr. Baer or if it found the libel aimed at Mr. Baer, along with a few others. Such a charge might not be objectionable; we do not mean to suggest that the fact that more than one person is libeled by a statement is a defense to suit by a member of the group. However, we cannot read the charge as being so limited. The jury was told:

"an imputation of impropriety or a crime to one or some of a small group that casts suspicion upon all is actionable. It is sufficient if Mr. Baer . . . proves . . . that he was one of a group upon whom *suspicion was cast* . . . ; but Mr. Baer has the burden of

Here, no explicit charge of peculation was made; no assault on the previous management appears. The jury was permitted to award damages upon a finding merely that respondent was one of a small group acting for an organ of government, only some of whom were implicated, but all of whom were tinged with suspicion. In effect, this permitted the jury to find liability merely on the basis of his relationship to the government agency, the operations of which were the subject of discussion. It is plain that the elected Commissioners, also members of that group, would have been barred from suit on this theory under New York Times. They would be required to show specific reference. Whether or not respondent was a public official, as a member of the group he bears the same burden.[7] A theory that the column cast indiscriminate suspicion on the members of the group responsible for the conduct of this governmental operation is tantamount to a demand for recovery based on libel of government, and therefore is constitutionally insufficient. Since the trial judge's instructions were erroneous in this respect, the judgment must be reversed.

"Respondent's second theory, supported by testimony of several witnesses, was that the column was read as referring specifically to him, as the 'man in charge' at the Area, personally responsible for its financial affairs. Even accepting respondent's reading, the column manifestly discusses the conduct of operations of government.[8] The subject matter may have been only of local interest, but at least here, where publication was addressed primarily to the interested community, that fact is constitutionally irrelevant. The question is squarely presented whether the 'public official' designation under New York Times applies.

"If it does, it is clear that the jury instructions were improper. Under the instructions, the jury was permitted to find that negligent misstatement of fact would defeat petitioner's privilege. That test was rejected in Garrison, 379 U.S., at 79, where we said, 'The test which we laid down in New York Times is not keyed to ordinary care; defeasance of the privilege is conditioned, not on mere negligence, but on reckless disregard for the truth.' The trial court also charged that '[d]efamatory matter which constitutes comment rather than fact is justified if made without malice and represented fair comment on matters of public interest,' and defined malice to include 'ill will, evil motive, intention to injure. . . .' This definition of malice is constitutionally insufficient where discussion of public affairs is concerned; '[w]e held in New York Times that a public official might be allowed the civil remedy only if he establishes that the utterance was false and that it was made with knowledge of its falsity or in reckless disregard of whether it was false or true.' Garrison, 379 U.S., at 74.

---

showing that the defamation, if you find that there was one, either was directed to him or *could have been* as one of a small group." (Emphasis supplied.)
The latitude allowed the jury to find defamatory reference in this apparently impersonal discussion of government affairs was thus too broad.

[7] See Gilberg v. Goffi, 21 App. Div. 2d 517, 251 N.Y.S.2d 823 (1964), aff'd, 15 N.Y.2d 1023, 207 N.E.2d 620 (1965); Comment, 114 U. Pa. L. Rev. 241 (1965).

[8] The New Hampshire court fully recognized that this was the subject of the column. It instructed the jury:

"You are entitled, I think, to find that the public had a right to be informed about any difficulties or discrepancies in income or thievery at this public area. It's in the public domain. It's public property . . . Keep in mind that the public has a right to know how their public affairs are being conducted. . . ."

"Turning, then, to the question whether respondent was a 'public official' within New York Times, we reject at the outset his suggestion that it should be answered by reference to state-law standards. States have developed definitions of 'public official' for local administrative purposes, not the purposes of a national constitutional protection.[9] If existing state-law standards reflect the purposes of New York Times, this is at best accidental. Our decision in New York Times, moreover, draws its force from the constitutional protections afforded free expression. The standards that set the scope of its principles cannot therefore be such that 'the constitutional limits of free expression in the Nation would vary with state lines.' Pennekamp v. Florida, 328 U.S. 331, 335.[10]

"We remarked in New York Times that we had no occasion 'to determine how far down into the lower ranks of government employees the "public official" designation would extend for purposes of this rule, or otherwise to specify categories of persons who would or would not be included.' 376 U.S., at 283, n.23. No precise lines need be drawn for the purposes of this case. The motivating force for the decision in New York Times was twofold. We expressed 'a profound national commitment to the principle that debate on public issues should be uninhibited, robust, and wide-open *and* that [such debate] may well include vehement, caustic, and sometimes unpleasantly sharp attacks on government and public officials.' 376 U.S., at 270. (Emphasis supplied.) There is, first, a strong interest in debate on public issues, and, second, a strong interest in debate about those persons who are in a position significantly to influence the resolution of those issues. Criticism of government is at the very center of the constitutionally protected area of free discussion. Criticism of those responsible for government operations must be free, lest criticism of government itself be penalized. It is clear, therefore, that the 'public official' designation applies at the very least to those among the hierarchy of government employees who have, or appear to the public to have, substantial responsibility for or control over the conduct of governmental affairs.[11]

"This conclusion does not ignore the important social values which underlie the law of defamation. Society has a pervasive and strong interest in preventing and redressing attacks upon reputation. But in cases like the present, there is tension between this interest and the values nurtured by the First and Fourteenth Amendments. The thrust of New York Times is that when interests in public discussion are particularly strong, as they were in that case, the Constitution limits the protec-

---

[9] See, e.g., Opinion of the Justices, 73 N.H. 621, 62 A. 969 (1906).

[10] For similar reasons, we reject any suggestion that our references in New York Times, 376 U.S., at 282, 283, n.23, and Garrison, 379 U.S., at 74, to Barr v. Matteo, 360 U.S. 564, mean that we have tied the New York Times rule to the rule of official privilege. The public interests protected by the New York Times rule are interests in discussion, not retaliation, and our reference to Barr should be taken to mean no more than that the scope of the privilege is to be determined by reference to the functions it serves. See Pedrick, Freedom of the Press and the Law of Libel: The Modern Revised Translation, 49 Cornell L.Q. 581, 590-591 (1964).

[11] Compare, e.g., Clancy v. Daily News Corp., 202 Minn. 1, 277 N.W. 264 (1938); Tanzer v. Crowley Publishing Corp., 240 App. Div. 203, 268 N.Y. Supp. 620 (1934); Poleski v. Polish Am. Publishing Co., 254 Mich. 15, 235 N.W. 841 (1931); 1 Harper & James, Torts §5.26, pp. 449-450 (1956); Prosser, Torts §110, p. 815 (3d ed. 1964); Noel, Defamation of Public Officers and Candidates, 49 Col. L. Rev. 875, 896-897, 901-902 (1949); Comment, 113 U. Pa. L. Rev. 284, 288 (1964); Note, 18 Vand. L. Rev. 1429, 1445 (1965).

tions afforded by the law of defamation. Where a position in government has such apparent importance that the public has an independent interest in the qualifications and performance of the person who holds it, beyond the general public interest in the qualifications and performance of all government employees, both elements we identified in New York Times are present[12] and the New York Times malice standards apply.[13]

"As respondent framed his case, he may have held such a position. Since New York Times had not been decided when his case went to trial, his presentation was not shaped to the 'public official' issue. He did, however, seek to show that the article referred particularly to him. His theory was that his role in the management of the Area was so prominent and important that the public regarded him as the man responsible for its operations, chargeable with its failures and to be credited with its successes. Thus, to prove the article referred to him, he showed the importance of his role; the same showing, at the least, raises a substantial argument that he was a 'public official.' [14]

"The record here, however, leaves open the possibility that respondent could have adduced proofs to bring his claim outside the New York Times rule. Moreover, even if the claim falls within New York Times, the record suggests respondent may be able to present a jury question of malice as there defined. Because the trial here was had before New York Times, we have concluded that we should not foreclose him from attempting retrial of his action. We remark only that, as is the case with questions of privilege generally, it is for the trial judge in the first instance to determine whether the proofs show respondent to be a 'public official.' [15]

---

[12] We are treating here only the element of public position, since that is all that has been argued and briefed. We intimate no view whatever whether there are other bases for applying the New York Times standards — for example, that in a particular case the interests in reputation are relatively insubstantial, because the subject of discussion has thrust himself into the vortex of the discussion of a question of pressing public concern. Cf. Salinger v. Cowles, 195 Iowa 873, 889, 191 N.W. 167, 173-174 (1922); Peck v. Coos Bay Times Publishing Co., 122 Ore. 408, 420-421, 259 P. 307, 311-312 (1927); Coleman v. MacLennan, 78 Kan. 711, 723-724, 98 P. 281, 285-286 (1908); Pauling v. News Syndicate Co., 335 F.2d 659, 671 (C.A.2d Cir. 1964).

[13] It is suggested that this test might apply to a night watchman accused of stealing state secrets. But a conclusion that the New York Times malice standards apply could not be reached merely because a statement defamatory of some person in government employ catches the public's interest; that conclusion would virtually disregard society's interest in protecting reputation. The employee's position must be one which would invite public scrutiny and discussion of the person holding it, entirely apart from the scrutiny and discussion occasioned by the particular charges in controversy.

[14] It is not seriously contended, and could not be, that the fact respondent no longer supervised the Area when the column appeared has decisional significance here. To be sure, there may be cases where a person is so far removed from a former position of authority that comment on the manner in which he performed his responsibilities no longer has the interest necessary to justify the New York Times rule. But here the management of the Area was still a matter of lively public interest; propositions for further change were abroad, and public interest in the way in which the prior administration had done its task continued strong. The comment, if it referred to respondent, referred to his performance of duty as a county employee.

[15] 1 Harper & James, Torts §5.29 (1956); Prosser, Torts §110, p. 823 (3d ed. 1964); Restatement, Torts, §619. Such a course will both lessen the possibility that a jury will use the cloak of a general verdict to punish unpopular ideas or speakers, and it would assure an appellate court the record and findings required for review of constitutional decision. Cf. Speiser v. Randall, 357 U.S. 513, 525; New York Times, 376 U.S., at 285.

"The judgment is reversed and the case remanded to the New Hampshire Supreme Court for further proceedings not inconsistent with this opinion."

In his concurrence, Mr. Justice Douglas asked: "But since freedom of speech is now the guideline, do state libel laws have any place at all in our constitutional system, at least when it comes to public issues?" He added: "The case is therefore for me in a different posture than the one discussed by the Court." He regarded the writ as improvidently granted in view of the fact that the trial occurred prior to the Sullivan case, but joined in the second part of Mr. Justice Brennan's opinion and in Mr. Justice Black's separate opinion "to facilitate" the work of the Court.

Mr. Justice Stewart's concurrence regarded as a "misleading" euphemism the Court's characterization of the Sullivan rule as involving "uninhibited, robust and wide-open" debate. "What the New York Times rule ultimately protects is defamatory falsehood. . . . That rule should not be applied except where a State's law of defamation has been unconstitutionally converted into a law of seditious libel. . . . Surely if the 1950's taught us anything, they taught us that the poisonous atmosphere of the easy lie can infect and degrade a whole society."

Mr. Justice Harlan concurred in all respects except the second part of Mr. Justice Brennan's opinion. In his view the Sullivan case did not mean to do away with the conventional tort law which is to the effect that where the "group is small enough numerically or sufficiently restricted geographically so that people reasonably think the defamatory utterance was directed to or intended to include the plaintiff, there may be recovery." Sullivan in this respect only sought to prevent the conversion of an attack on a general governmental activity into a cause of action for personal libel. The trial judge's charge was well within the ordinary limits of the tort law.

Mr. Justice Black concurred but dissented from that part of the opinion which left room for a new trial since in his view the First Amendment bars actions for criticizing public agents engaged in public activities whether or not they are labeled as "public officials" or belong to the higher or lower echelons. He reiterated his view in Sullivan: "An unconditional right to say what one pleases about public affairs is what I consider to be the minimum guarantee of the First Amendment." He also deplored the ruling that the judge was to decide "in the first instance" whether the respondent is a "public official." "I regret to see the Court take a single step in the direction of holding that a judge rather than the jury is to have the determination of any fact in libel cases."

Mr. Justice Fortas dissented, thinking the writ improvidently granted because the pre-Sullivan record "was not shaped in light of the principles" there announced.

6. In Linn v. United Plant Guard Workers of America, 383 U.S. 53, 86 S. Ct. 657, 15 L. Ed 2d 582 (1966), the Court, with the Chief Justice and Justices Black, Douglas, and Fortas dissenting, held that Section 8(b) of the National Labor Relations Act, 61 Stat. 136, 29 U.S.C. §§141 et seq., dealing with unfair labor practices, did not on pre-emption grounds bar a civil libel action by the employer's official for statements published by the union and its officers during a union organizing campaign. The opinion by Mr. Justice Clark read in part:

"We acknowledge that the enactment of §8(c) manifests a congressional intent to encourage free debate on issues dividing labor and management.[5] And, as we

[5] The wording of the statute indicates, however, that §8(c) was not designed to serve this interest by immunizing all statements made in the course of a labor controversy.

stated in another context, cases involving speech are to be considered 'against the background of a profound . . . commitment to the principle that debate . . . should be uninhibited, robust, and wide open, and that it may well include vehement, caustic, and sometimes unpleasantly sharp attacks.' New York Times v. Sullivan, 376 U.S. 254, 270 (1964). Such considerations likewise weigh heavily here; the most repulsive speech enjoys immunity provided it falls short of a deliberate or reckless untruth. But it must be emphasized that malicious libel enjoys no constitutional protection in any context. After all the labor movement has grown up and must assume ordinary responsibilities. The malicious utterance of defamatory statements in any form cannot be condoned, and unions should adopt procedures calculated to prevent such abuses.

". . . In order that the recognition of legitimate state interests does not interfere with effective administration of national labor policy the possibility of such consequences must be minimized. We therefore limit the availability of state remedies for libel to those instances in which the complainant can show that the defamatory statements were circulated with malice and caused him damage."

7. In McCrossen v. United States, 339 F.2d 810 (10th Cir. 1965), the defendant in a criminal prosecution for marking upon the envelope material which was libelous, defamatory, or intended to reflect injuriously upon the character and conduct of another, claimed that since the statements were about public figures they were privileged on the authority of the Garrison and Sullivan cases. The court declared the case governed by the Postal powers rather than by "any First Amendment limitation" and then distinguished Sullivan by stating that Congress in the Postal laws did not merely prohibit libelous matter but also prohibited defamatory and other scurrilous matter which may not be strictly libelous. The court concluded: "Whatever may be said about the libelous nature of the writings in question and any claim of privilege in connection therewith, it is clear that a jury could reasonably conclude that they were defamatory or calculated and intended to reflect injuriously upon the character and conduct of the persons referred to." 339 F.2d at 813.

8. For the view that the Sullivan rule extends beyond public officials in connection with matters of public concern, see Pauling v. News Syndicate Co., 335 F.2d 659 (2d Cir. 1964); Clark v. Allen, 415 Pa. 484, 204 A.2d 42 (1964); Walker v. Courier-Journal, 246 F. Supp. 231 (W.D. Ky. 1965); Pauling v. Globe-Democrat Publishing Co., 362 F.2d 188 (8th Cir. 1966) (public figure acting on matters of public concern). See also Nusbaum v. Newark Morning Ledger Co., 86 N.J. Super. 132, 206 A.2d 185 (1965); Pauling v. National Review, Inc., 269 N.Y.S.2d 11 (Sup. Ct. N.Y. Co. 1966). But cf. Afro-American Publishing Co. v. Jaffee, — F.2d — (D.C. Cir. 1966) (not applicable to private person who has not mounted

---

Rather, §8(c) provides that the "expressing of any views, argument, or opinion . . . shall not constitute or be evidence of an unfair labor practice . . . if such expression contains no threat of reprisal or force or promise of benefit." 61 Stat. 142 (1947), 29 U.S.C. §158(c) (1964 ed.). It is more likely that Congress adopted this section for a narrower purpose, i.e., to prevent the Board from attributing anti-union motive to an employer on the basis of his past statements. See H.R. Rep. No. 510, 80th Cong., 1st Sess., 45 (1947). Comparison with the express protection given union members to criticize the management of their unions and the conduct of their officers, 73 Stat. 523 (1959), 29 U.S.C. §411 (a)(2) (1964 ed.), strengthens this interpretation of congressional intent.

public rostrum even though the subject matter of race relations is of high public interest). For a collection of lower court cases showing the range of rank of officials, both elected and appointed, candidates for official positions, and people in business relationships to officials to whom the Sullivan doctrine has been applied, see Pauling v. Globe-Democrat Publishing Co., supra, at 196-197.

REFERENCES

For discussion of the Sullivan case see Pedrick, Freedom of the Press and The Law of Libel: The Modern Revised Translation, 49 Cornell L.Q. 581 (1964); Kalven, The New York Times Case: A Note on "The Central Meaning of the First Amendment," 1964 Sup. Ct. Rev. 191 (this article suggests that perhaps the Court, at least with respect to many free speech problems, has substituted for the clear and present danger, the ad hoc balancing test, or other tests, an is-it-like-seditious-libel test of First Amendment validity; cf. Garrison v. Louisiana and Mr. Justice Stewart's view in Rosenblatt, supra); Berney, Libel and the First Amendment — A New Constitutional Privilege, 51 Va. L. Rev. 1 (1965) (this article discusses among other things the constitutional relevance of the malice qualification as well as the constitutional relevance of other existing or proposed qualifications, such as (a) existence of special damages, (b) special damages unless libel per se, and (c) substantial truth); Note, Defamation of Public Officials — Coleman v. MacLennan Revisited, 13 Kan. L. Rev. 399 (1965); Pierce, The Anatomy of an Historic Decision: New York Times Co. v. Sullivan, 43 N. C. L. Rev. 315 (1965). See also Note, 95 A.LR..2d 1450 (1964) (listing state cases which are of doubtful authority in light of the Sullivan decision); Notes 113 U. Pa. L. Rev. 284 (1964); 10 N.Y.L.F. 249 (1964); 44 B.U.L. Rev. 563 (1964); Defamation of Public Officials — Free Speech and the New Constitutional Standard, 12 U.C.L.A.L. Rev. 1420 (1965); Constitutional Limitations on the Defenses of Fair Comment and Conditional Privilege, 30 Mo. L. Rev. 467 (1965); 51 Va. L. Rev. 106 (1965); 75 Yale L.J. 642 (1966). Cf. Cahn, Defamation Control vs. Press Freedom: A Current Chapter in Israel, 13 J. Pub. L. 3 (1964).

For discussion of the relation of the law of defamation to the First Amendment prior to the Sullivan case, see Kalven, The Law of Defamation and the First Amendment, in University of Chicago Law School, Conference on the Arts, Publishing and the Law 3 (1952); Cahn, Justice Black and First Amendment "Absolutes": A Public Interview, 37 N.Y.U.L. Rev. 549 (1962). Compare the critical remarks on the Black position in Hook, Book Review, The New Leader, May 13, 1963, pp. 11, 15; Emerson, Toward a General Theory of the First Amendment, 72 Yale L.J. 877, 922-924 (1963). And compare the distinction between private and public speech in Meiklejohn, Political Freedom 39-42 (1960).

For the position that the Constitution intended to leave the law of seditious libel intact, see materials cited in Chapter II, Section A. The view that the First Amendment did not affect the general libel law, since it was not an "abridgement" within the protection afforded individual reputation at the time of the First Amendment's adoption, was of course widespread prior to the Sullivan case. See Pedrick, supra, 49 Cornell L.Q. at 586-587, nn.20-21 (1964).

NOTES

1. The total number of libel actions in the South pending at the time of the Sullivan case and growing out of the racial issue were 17 according to the New York Times, April 4, 1963. The total damages sought were $288 million.

For recent examples of large damage awards see Butts v. Curtis Publishing Co., 225 F. Supp. 916, 242 F. Supp. 390 (N.D. Ga. 1964), aff'd, 351 F.2d 702 (5th Cir. 1965) (charge that college athletic director was involved in fixing football games; verdict of $3 million reduced to $460,000 in lieu of new trial); Faulk v. Aware, Inc., 19 A.D.2d 464, 244 N.Y.S.2d 259 (1st Dept. 1963), 14 N.Y.2d 899, 252 N.Y.S.2d 95, 200 N.E.2d 778, amended, 14 N.Y.2d 954, 253 N.Y.S.2d 990, 202 N.E.2d 372 (1964), cert. den., 380 U.S. 916 (1965) (award of $3.5 million reduced to $400,000 compensation plus $150,000 in punitive damages). See also Reynolds v. Pegler, 123 F. Supp. 36 (S.D. N.Y. 1964) aff'd, 223 F.2d 429 (2d Cir. 1955), cert. den., 350 U.S. 846 (1955) ($1.00 compensatory damages from each defendant plus $175,000 total punitive damages). For collection of cases indicating scrupulous review of libel awards see 35 A.L.R.2d 218 (1954). The suggestion that the Court in the Sullivan case might have reversed on the ground that grossly excessive damages burden the freedom of press is made by Pedrick, Freedom of the Press and the Law of Libel: The Modern Revised Translation, supra, 49 Cornell L.Q. 581, 587 (1964), alluding also to Crowell-Collier Pub. Co. v. Caldwell, 170 F.2d 941 (5th Cir. 1948) (large verdict in favor of governor reversed because "spectacle of a sectional row" unleashed passions prejudicing trial).

Prior to the Sullivan case the highest damages awarded for defamation in Alabama since 1900 had been $67,500, reduced to $45,000. Brief of American Civil Liberties Union as Amicus Curiae, App. 1a-2a, in New York Times Co. v. Sullivan.

For an analysis of libel in terms of the risk-bearing capability of the press, see Morris, Inadvertent Newspaper Libel and Retraction, 32 Ill. L. Rev. 36 (1937).

2. Among questions left unanswered by the Supreme Court in the libel cases are: Is the privilege there established limited to public officials or does it extend beyond to other areas of public concern? Correlatively, what area is still left in the majority jurisdictions for the operation of their previously developed fair comment rule and related privileges? Do the cases raise constitutional issues concerning other governmental regulation to assure dissemination of truthful information such as Federal Trade Commission and Securities Exchange Commission regulations? See McCrossen v. United States, 339 F.2d 819 (10th Cir. 1965), noted above. At what point does the communication become so commercial as not to come within the compass of the First Amendment under Valentine v. Chrestensen? See Chapter IV, Section A. To what extent does the more extensive privilege open the possibility that the press like radio, see infra, will be treated as a common carrier not empowered to censor advertisements in the area covered by the Sullivan case or even the statements of responsible news sources? To what extent do the court's opinions leave open alternative remedies to the victim of an alleged libel such as those listed under "suggested reform," infra? See Pedrick, supra, 49 Cornell L.Q. at 589-595.

3. Fair comment and other bases for defendants' protection prior to Sullivan: Prior to the Sullivan case the majority jurisdictions did not extend the fair comment defense to misstatements of fact, but only to comment or opinion based on facts truly stated. Though the truth requirement is now eliminated with respect to public officials (either on the theory of fair comment or conditional privilege), it might remain applicable in certain jurisdictions to libel of others engaged in matters of public concern such as musicians, actors, teachers, authors, athletes, and

persons engaging in public controversy. See Note, Fair Comment, 62 Harv. L. Rev. 1207, 1208-1209, nn.10-25 (1949). Earlier cases denied the defense to statements related to a person's "private character" or "opinion and motives." Noel, Defamation of Public Officers and Candidates, 49 Colum. L. Rev. 875, 887-888 (1949). Later authority permitted the defense but required that the criticism be one "with which a man of reasonable intelligence and judgment might agree." Restatement of Torts §607, Comment i (1938). Where the statement was not about "private character" but about the conduct of public affairs the comment did not need to be fair in the aforementioned sense but could also be foolish and prejudicial. See Noel, supra, 49 Colum. L. Rev. at 880; Restatement of Torts §606, Comment c (1938).

While the "fair comment" defense was said to apply to statements of opinion only and not to statements of fact (at least in the majority of jurisdictions), this line at times was not easy to draw. Thus, where the facts upon which the criticism was based were not stated, the defense of fair comment was denied because of the possibility that the statement might have various factual implications. Truth (which was virtually impossible to prove under these circumstances; but cf. Note, 18 Vand. L. Rev. 1429, 1438 (1965)), became the only defense. Eikhoff v. Gilbert, 124 Mich. 353 (1900); Hogan v. New York Times Co., 313 F.2d 354 (2d Cir. 1963). On the other hand the Sullivan case and especially Mr. Justice Brennan's comments in the Rosenblatt case on the trial judge's attempted separation of fact and comment would suggest that today, in a "pure" comment situation covered by Sullivan, the plaintiff rather than the defendant would have the impossible burden of proving that the comment was related knowingly to false "facts" or to "facts" gathered with reckless disregard of the truth. See also Mr. Justice Brennan's reference to "privileged" facts in footnote 30 of the Sullivan opinion.

Prior to Sullivan the fair comment defense has been said to be available if the facts on which the opinion is based are "otherwise known or available to the recipient as a member of the public." Restatement of Torts §606 (1938); Pauling v. News Syndicate Co., 335 F.2d 659 (2d Cir. 1964) (case also allows introduction of hearsay in connection with "fair comment" defense and on question of extent of damages where existing reputation of plaintiff is relevant); Kenna v. Daily Mirror, 250 App. Div. 625, 295 N.Y. Supp. 219 (1st Dept. 1937), aff'd per curiam, 276 N.Y. 483 (1937); Hoan v. Journal Co., 238 Wis. 311, 298 N.W. 228 (1941). But cf. A. S. Abell Co. v. Kirby, 227, Md. 267, 176 A.2d 340 (1961) (facts though not fully stated must at least be recognizably referred to). See also Note, 90 A.L.R.2d 1279 (1963).

Among other rules which even prior to the Sullivan case limited the impact of the libel law where public officials or matters of public concern were involved are: (1) The libel per se doctrine and the so-called "public officials" rule. See Carpenter, Libel Per Se in California and Some Other States, 17 So. Cal. L. Rev. 347 (1944); Berney, Libel and the First Amendment — A New Constitutional Privilege, 51 W. Va. L. Rev. 1, 13-15 (1965); Cotulla v. Kerr, 74 Tex. 89, 11 S.W. 1058 (1889); Sweeney v. Caller-Times Pub. Co., 41 F. Supp. 163 (S.D. Tex. 1941); Sweeney v. Patterson, 128 F.2d 457 (D.C. Cir. 1942), cert. den., 317 U.S. 678 (1942) (public official cannot recover unless crime, gross immorality, or gross incompetence charged and special damage results); cf. Afro-American Publishing Co. v. Jaffee, — F.2d — (D.C. Cir. 1966); contra, Jenkins v. Taylor, 4 S.W.2d 656 (Tex. Civ.

App. 1928); Tanzer v. Crowley Pub. Corp., 240 App. Div. 203, 268 N.Y. Supp. 620 (4th Dept. 1934); Note, 51 Yale L.J. 693, 695 n.11 (1942). (2) Privilege in relation to communications addressed to participants in an election or in the removal of officials. See Weinstein v. Rhorer, 240 Ky. 679, 42 S.W.2d 892 (1931); Note, 92 A.L.R. 1029 (1934) (nonpolitical situations). (3) Rule that in case of public officials and candidates plaintiff has burden of proving statements false. Kleinschmidt v. Johnson, 183 S.W.2d 82 (Mo. 1944); Note, 18 Vand. L. Rev. 1429, 1441 (1965). For the view that the flexibility of the "fair comment" doctrine, as well as the availability of other bases for avoiding liability for false statements set out above, may mean that the court in the Sullivan case did not functionally bring about as important a change of law as would at first appear, see Berney, supra, 51 Va. L. Rev. at 9-15.

Perhaps the most important area where the Sullivan case may have brought about a change is in the definition of "malice," or abuse of privilege. To make a statement not primarily for the purpose of furthering the interest protected by the privilege, or to make a statement from motives such as hatred or ill will, or to state something other than one's honest opinion, or in the case of a privileged misstatement of fact, to state it without belief in its truth or without reasonable ground for belief in its truth, or at least without good faith, all have been held at times to be bases for loss of privilege. The Sullivan case and the cases following it, in requiring a showing of either knowledge of the falsehood or "reckless disregard for the truth" and in their implied imposition of a heavy burden of proof, seem to narrow considerably the area of loss of privilege that previously existed, at least with respect to situations to which the Sullivan rule is held to apply. Cf. Keogh v. Pearson, 244 F. Supp. 482 (D.D.C. 1965) (holding recklessness may at times be implied from obviously defamatory material, at least to the extent that mere ignorance on the part of the publisher is no excuse). Prior to Rosenblatt there was some basis for arguing that Sullivan required that any comment as distinguished from a statement of fact be an "honest expression" of the writer's opinion, New York Times v. Sullivan, supra, n.30. But even under such a requirement it would have been unlikely, once the jury found the fact statement (in other than the "pure" comment situations) to be privileged, that any comment related to these facts would be found to have been made in bad faith. See Note, 18 Vand. L. Rev. 1429, 1441-1442, 1451-1453 (1965). At any rate Mr. Justice Brennan's opinion in the Rosenblatt case now seems to allow a comment (where the facts were not knowingly false or based on reckless disregard) when made with "ill will, evil motive," or "intention to injure." While these words are not necessarily synonymous with "bad faith" Mr. Justice Brennan's statement in context seems to tend strongly in the direction of eliminating a separate consideration of the libelous nature of the "comment."

REFERENCES

For discussion of "fair comment" as applied by the states prior to the Sullivan case, see A.S. Abell Co. v. Kirby, 227 Md. 267, 273, 176 A.2d 340, 342-343 (1962); Restatement of Torts §§598 et seq. (1938); Noel, Defamation of Public Officers and Candidates, 49 Colum. L. Rev. 875 (1949); Riesman, Democracy and Defamation: Fair Game and Fair Comment, 42 Colum. L. Rev. 1085, 1282 (1942); Veeder, Freedom of Public Discussion, 23

Harv. L. Rev. 413 (1910). See also Yankwich, The Protection of Newspaper Comment on Public Men and Public Matters, 11 La. L. Rev. 327 (1951); Notes, 37 Geo. L.J. 404 (1949); 62 Harv. L. Rev. 1207 (1949); 110 A.L.R. 412 (1937); 150 A.L.R. 358 (1944). For critical appraisal see Boyer, Fair Comment, 15 Ohio St. L.J. 280 (1954); Hallen, Fair Comment, 8 Texas L. Rev. 41 (1929); Thayer, Fair Comment as a Defense, 1950 Wis. L. Rev. 288; Titus, Statement of Fact versus Statement of Opinion — A Spurious Dispute in Fair Comment, 15 Vand. L. Rev. 1203 (1962).

NOTES

1. Other doctrines recognized at times which gave the press a certain amount of freedom related to the republication of material that did not originate with the newspublisher or its employees. Examples are: (1) Republication from another source admitted in evidence on the question of malice in nonprivileged situations. See Note, 74 A.L.R. at 738 (1931). (2) Good faith privilege for fair and accurate reports of public statements made by a responsible person. See cases and statutes in Pedrick, Freedom of the Press and the Law of Libel: The Modern Revised Translation, 49 Cornell L.Q. 581, 599 n.63. (3) Privilege accorded to stories supplied by news services. See Layne v. Tribune Co., 108 Fla. 177, 146 So. 234 (1933), noted in 46 Harv. L. Rev. 1032 (1933); 1 U. Chi. L. Rev. 156 (1933); 33 Colum. L. Rev. 373 (1933); majority view, contra, 1 Harper & James, Torts §5.18 at 404 (1956). (4) Publication of reports of privileged proceedings. See infra, and Pauling v. News Syndicate Co., 335 F.2d 659, 665 (2d Cir. 1964) (combining this privilege with "fair comment").

2. The privilege extended to public statements by public officials involved in the Barr v. Matteo case, mentioned in the principal case, and to statements of official proceedings and reports of those proceedings, presents most dramatically the issue of whether lifting restrictions on speech resulting from the law of defamation always serves the cause of free speech. Especially in the case of legislative investigations of political activities, an important impediment to the expression of unpopular views is that persons who are falsely accused not merely of holding such views but of other activities are left virtually defenseless against possible harm done to their reputations and the ensuing social and economic consequences. See, in addition to Barr v. Matteo and Howard v. Lyons, 360 U.S. 593, 79 S. Ct. 1331, 3 L. Ed. 2d 1454 (1959), Tenney v. Brandhove, 341 U.S. 367, 71 S. Ct. 783, 95 L. Ed. 1019 (1951); Sauber v. Gliedman, 283 F.2d 941 (7th Cir. 1960); Steinberg v. O'Connor, 200 F. Supp. 737 (D. Conn. 1961); Methodist Federation for Social Action v. Eastland, 141 F. Supp. 729 (D.D.C. 1956); Logan's Super Markets, Inc., v. McCalla, 208 Tenn. 68, 343 S.W.2d 892 (1961); Pauling v. News Syndicate Co., 335 F.2d 659 (2d Cir. 1964). See also Vigoda v. Barton, 348 Mass. 478, 204 N.E.2d 441 (1965), showing influence of Sullivan dicta about reciprocity on this branch of state libel law in states where utterances made by public officials are still granted only a qualified privilege. Cf. Joint Anti-Fascist Refugee Committee v. McGrath, 341 U.S. 123, 71 S. Ct. 624, 95 L. Ed. 817 (1951), discussed in Chapter III, Section E. Cf. also Pape v. Time Inc., 318 F.2d 653 (7th Cir. 1963) (rewording of Civil Rights Commission report concerning a detective's alleged mistreatment of a Negro presents a question for the jury of whether the rewording exceeded fair

comment bounds). As to privilege of witnesses informing the F.B.I. about government employees, see Chapter III, Section E.

REFERENCES

See generally Nelson, Libel in News of Congressional Investigating Committees (1961); Becht, The Absolute Privilege of the Executive in Defamation, 15 Vand. L. Rev. 1127 (1962); Handler and Klein, The Defense of Privilege in Defamation Suits Against Government Executive Officials, 74 Harv. L. Rev. 44 (1960); Note, 55 Nw. U.L. Rev. 228 (1960); Pedrick, Senator McCarthy and the Law of Libel: A Study of Two Campaign Speeches, 48 Nw. U.L. Rev. 135 (1953); Yankwich, The Immunity of Congressional Speech — Its Origin, Meaning and Scope, 99 U. Pa. L. Rev. 960 (1951); Barnett, The Privilege of Defamation by Private Report of Public Official Proceedings, 31 Ore. L. Rev. 185 (1952); Note, Libel and Slander — Absolute Privilege Before Administrative Agencies, 5 Vill. L.R. 121 (1959); Gilbert, Privileged Publications in Labor Disputes Under California Libel Laws, 30 So. Cal. L. Rev. 35 (1956).

Compare on the related problem of a claimed press privilege not to disclose the source of information: Garland v. Torre, 259 F.2d 545 (2d Cir. 1958) (contempt for failure on the part of columnist to disclose in the course of taking her deposition the name of a "network executive" who made allegedly defamatory statements concerning an actress; neither evidentiary privilege nor First Amendment privilege granted); In Re Goodfader, 45 Haw. 317 (1961); but see Taylor and Selby Appeals, 412 Pa. 32 (1963); Application of Howard, 289 P.2d 537 (Cal. App. 1955) (privilege granted by statute). See further 8 Wigmore, Evidence §2286 (3d ed. 1940); New York State Law Revision Commission Rept. 23-168 (1949); Smith, The Reporter's Right to Shield His "Reliable" Source, 16 N.Y.U. Intra. L.R. 23 (1960); Carter, The Journalist, His Informant and Testimonial Privilege, 35 N.Y.U.L. Rev. 1111 (1960); Notes, 8 J. Pub. L. 596 (1959); 54 Nw. U.L. Rev. 243 (1959); 34 Notre Dame Law. 259 (1959); 11 Stan. L. Rev. 541 (1959).

NOTE — MISCELLANEOUS PROBLEMS

1. *The standard.* Some of the difficulties in formulating a standard with respect to group libel that concerned the dissenters in the Beauharnais case apply to all types of defamation actions. An interesting problem, focusing attention on the difficulties of regulating communications according to majority rule, arises in certain cases where the courts attempt to decide what constitutes defamation per se (whether the issue of the defamatory nature of the statement is removed from the jury). In the case of utterances that some segments of the community would consider laudatory and other segments would think defamatory, which segment of the community should set the standard for the case? Suppose what is involved is a false accusation that the plaintiff obeyed a certain law and suppose that segment of the community to which the plaintiff belongs considers such obedience of the law disreputable? Would granting relief to one falsely accused of obeying the law mean that the courts encourage illegality by (a) not discouraging law breakers in denying recovery and (b) lending their prestige to values of a minority strongly opposed to the law? See Connelly v. McKay, 176 Misc. 685, 28 N.Y.S.2d 327 (Sup. Ct. Broome Co., 1941); Note, 58 Yale L.J. 1387 (1949). A somewhat similar problem arises where a person is falsely accused of being a member of an unpopular political minority. Compare Garriga v. Richfield, 174 Misc. 315, 20 N.Y.S.2d 544 (Sup. Ct. N.Y. Co. 1940) (as long as party is legal, accusation of membership not

defamatory per se; case brought prior to Russo-German non-aggression pact), with Levy v. Gelber, 175 Misc. 746, 25 N.Y.S.2d 148 (Sup. Ct. Bronx Co. 1941), Spanel v. Pegler, 160 F.2d 619 (7th Cir. 1947), and Wright v. Farm Journal Inc., 158 F.2d 976 (2d Cir. 1947) (libel per se).

See also Keefe v. O'Brien, 116 N.Y.S.2d 286 (Sup. Ct. Kings Co., 1952) and Gutler v. Union Parts Manufacturing Co., 285 App. Div. 643, 140 N.Y.S.2d 254 (1st Dept. 1955), aff'd, 1 N.Y.2d 5, 150 N.Y.S.2d 4 (1956). In the Keefe case the opinion reads in part: "To hold that calling one a communist is slander would unwittingly entrap the unwary, for nothing would please communists better than to enable them to institute suits for damages promiscuously, regardless of the ultimate outcome. It has been amply demonstrated that it is part of communist doctrine and strategy to make the courtroom its forum for propaganda purposes . . . [T]he court will take judicial notice of the cold war now existing between our form of government and communism. Our safety is therefore best served by an exposure of communists and communism. It is far better, therefore, to allow free play of our emotions in dealing with persons whom we believe to be communists rather than seal the lips of people who might be frightened into silence and suppression lest use of the word 'communist' should per se force upon them costly litigation." For collection of cases see Note, 33 A.L.R.2d 1196 (1954). See also Beaman, Slander — And The Epithet "Communist," 18 U. Det. L.J. 189 (1955).

Where the allegation falls short of clearly charging communism it has been held not libelous. See Julian v. American Business Consultants, Inc., 2 N.Y.2d 1, 155 N.Y.S.2d 1 (1956) (suit against publisher of Red Channels). But cf. Faulk v. Aware, Inc., 155 N.Y.S.2d 726 (Sup. Ct. N.Y.Co. 1956), aff'd 160 N.Y.S.2d 621 (App. Div. 1st Dept. 1957), where the opinion distinguishes the Julian case as follows: "In that case, the only references to the plaintiff therein were found on one page of a book of 213 pages. Plaintiff was listed as having spoken, in 1942, at a meeting of Artists' Front to Win the War, and as having attended a meeting, many years later, whose purpose was to abolish the House Un-American Activities Committee. The Court of Appeals declared that 'The listing of attendance of Julian at only two meetings widely separated . . . in itself does not support the plaintiff's charge that it was the intention of the book to cast him as a "sympathizer," "dupe," "tool" or "sucker," "colonist" or other so-called objectionable terms. This participation at Communist front meetings fell far short of that activity necessary to be classified as a "sympathizer," "dupe," "tool," "sucker" or "fellow-traveler." The terms "dupe," "sucker," "sympathizer," "tool," or "fellow-traveler" and other so-called objectionable terms as used in this book clearly connote a regular and continuous use of the presence and talents of an individual. The references to plaintiff, when read together with the introduction and purpose statement of Part II, are not susceptible of a libelous interpretation.' The last sentence of the foregoing quotation related to the statement in Part II of the book that 'many prominent actors and artists have been *inveigled* to lend their names . . . to organizations espousing Communists causes . . . *regardless of whether they actually believe in, sympathize with, or even recognize the cause advanced.'* (Italics supplied.) The 'purpose statement of Part II mentions "innocents," "well-intentioned liberals," persons who "advanced Communist objectives with complete unconsciousness," "genuine liberals." ' The court pointed out 'There is no allusion in the book, containing 151 names, to indicate in which, if any, of the categories the plaintiff belongs. It does show he was *not* in the category of a member of the Communist party.' In the instant case, there are many more references to participation by the plaintiff in Communist front activities and functions then there were in the cited case, and there is absent a statement, similar to that containeed in Part II of the book involved in the cited case, indicating that the references to plaintiff might have been intended to refer to him as a person who advanced the Communist cause innocently and without realizing it. On the contrary, Exhibit A is expressly directed against plaintiff, by name, as one whose record of participation in Communist front functions and affairs is such as to discredit his statement that he is opposed to Communism." 155 N.Y. Supp. at 730-731.

For further litigation in this case see citations in the prior Note.

Compare Pauling v. News Syndicate Co., 335 F.2d 659, 663 (2d Cir. 1964), where the court distinguished the implied accusations against Pauling in an editorial from outright accusations of Communism or even Communist sympathy as follows:

"But the editorial here did not unambiguously accuse Dr. Pauling of being a Communist or pro-Communist or disloyal, although it could be so understood. The passages particularly relied on by the plaintiff are the references to Premier Khrushchev as Dr. Pauling's 'friend in the Kremlin' and the statement about now having Dr. Pauling 'on the American side for once.' But these must be read against the editorial's opening sentence truthfully stating that Dr. Pauling had long been 'agitating against nuclear weapons and weapon tests' which the writer regarded as 'the best defense the West has against Soviet Russian and Chinese Red manpower.' The statements could carry at least two interpretations which were not defamatory: one that Dr. Pauling's public agitations, although not motivated by disloyalty, had unwittingly resulted in helping the Russian cause and harming the American; the other, even more innocuous, that Dr. Pauling was Khrushchev's 'friend' in the sense that their opinions were often in agreement and that he was 'on the American side for once' in that his views had usually been opposed to the official American Government position on disputed questions. The case was thus one where, under New York law, a jury might find the editorial defamatory."

For a recent case where a defeated encumbent political candidate, John Goldmark, won a jury verdict in the state of Washington against defendants who, among other things, had charged him with belonging to the American Civil Liberties Union, which in turn was called a Communist front and "an organization closely affiliated with the Communist movement," see American Civil Liberties Union Weekly Bull., Feb. 24, 1964. The Union was jubilant over this victory. Ironically a retrial has since been granted on the ground that the Sullivan case governed the situation, N.Y. Times, Dec. 10, 1964. The Union was an amicus curiae for the defendant in the Sullivan case and has, since the retrial order in the Goldmark case, issued a statement of policy taking the same position as the Supreme Court on civil libel actions involving public officials. A.C.L.U. Position on Libel, adopted April 4, 1965. This paper also opposed all criminal libel prosecutions and all group libel laws, since prosecutions under such laws generally involve political life or political and social issues.

2. *Additional difficulties with common law remedies for defamation.* Some

of the additional problems involved in common law remedies for defamation are: (a) Great risks in bringing suit because of: (1) Vagueness of the standard alluded to above (i.e., has the plaintiff been held up to contempt and ridicule) varies from time to time, area to area, and group to group. (2) It is a defense that the accusation is substantially true. In mitigation of damages the defendant can prove that plaintiff's reputation is already tarnished. The result of the suit may be a greater injury to the plaintiff's reputation than existed before. (3) Damages are highly uncertain. A small award may mean to the public that plaintiff's reputation is not worth much. (4) Victory in court may not be sufficiently publicized to overcome the effect of defamatory publication. On the contrary the type of publicity given the case may further impair the plaintiff's reputation.

(b) Great risk in publishing because of: (1) Newspaper's strict liability for libelous material it publishes unless it is privileged, and the possible award of punitive damages. (2) The common law considered each copy sold a new libel. Newspapers could thus be subjected to chain libel suits for a single libelous statement in a single issue. (Recent decisions do not generally follow the common law on this point).[1] (3) Time and expense of libel suit to publisher is very great. (4) Pre-publication censorship by publisher's own lawyers does not on the whole prevent suits. These arise largely because of errors in fact that could not be discovered by censors. Moreover censorship tends to interfere with the smooth workings of a newspaper. Other techniques for controlling some of the risks of publishing are a contract with the syndicate supplying a story to save the newspaper or radio station harmless, and libel insurance. These, of course, still increase the over-all cost of publishing.

On the risk because of the uncertainty of outcome and the particular role of the jury, see, further, Green, Relational Interest, 30 Ill. L. Rev. 314 (1935); Wellman, Luck and Opportunity (1938). Consider the possibilities of content analysis for the development of a more scientific approach. On punitive damages see Reynolds v. Pegler, 123 F. Supp. 36 (S.D. N.Y. 1954), noted in 64 Yale L.J. 610 (1955). On the general unavailability of an injunction to prevent personal defamation see Note, 47 A.L.R.2d 715 (1956).

3. *Suggested reforms.* Reforms that have been suggested include:

(a) Optional retraction: Under the common law a retraction does not excuse a publisher from liability but may go to show no malice and thus eliminate or reduce punitive damages. Statutes to this effect exist in many states. In some others, especially where the statutes have been broader in scope, they have been declared unconstitutional. But other states, such as Minnesota and California, have

---

[1] An example of a chain libel suit is that of Annie Oakley who in 48 proceedings recovered against 50 newspapers. Awards varied from $500 to as much as $2500. See Ernst and Lindey, Hold Your Tongue 190 (rev. ed. 1950). See also suits brought by Congressman Sweeny because of an article charging him with opposing the appointment of a federal judge because he was a Jew. Plaintiff brought 68 suits seeking a total of $7,500,000 in damages. See Donnelly, The Law of Defamation: Proposals for Reform, 33 Minn. L. Rev. 609, 627 (1949). For a ruling that would not permit such suits see Hartmann v. Time, Inc., 166 F.2d 127 (3d Cir. 1948), cert. den., 334 U.S. 838 (1948). For a recent discussion see Warner, Multistate Publication in Radio and Television, 23 Law & Contemp. Prob. 14 (1958); Leflar, The Single Publication Rule, 25 Rocky Mt. L. Rev. 263 (1953); Prosser, Interstate Publication, 51 Mich. L. Rev. 959 (1953); Note, 32 U. Cinc. L. Rev. 520 (1963).

upheld them. California, which has a very liberal statute, provides for the elimination of all but special damages if a retraction is published, without regard to whether the original item was published with malice. In Minnesota the retraction has this effect only where the original publication was inadvertently libelous.

(b) Compulsory retraction: The judgment requires the defendant to print a revised version of the facts.

(c) The right of reply: This would provide that newspapers or other media must give space for a reply within a short time to an adversely affected group or individual. If they fail to do so, a speedy judgment compelling publication of the reply may be obtained.

(d) Provision for judicial hearing for anyone defamed by a public official.

REFERENCES

1. See generally Donnelly, The Right of Reply: An Alternative to an Action for Libel, 34 Va. L. Rev. 867 (1948); 1 Chafee, Government and Mass Communications, ch. 4 (1947); Leflar, Legal Remedies for Defamation, 6 Ark. L. Rev. 423, 450-454 (1952). On judicial hearing for those libeled by public officials see Pedrick, Freedom of the Press and the Law of Libel, 49 Cornell L. Rev. 581, 602-603 (1964); Becht, The Absolute Privilege of the Executive in Defamation, 15 Vand. L. Rev. 1127 (1962). On retraction statutes see Notes, 38 Calif. L. Rev. 951 (1950); 64 Harv. L. Rev. 678 (1951); and cases upholding state laws such as Allen v. Pioneer-Press Co., 40 Minn. 117, 41 N.W. 936 (1889); Werner v. Southern California Associated Newspapers, 206 P.2d 952 (Cal. App. 1949), aff'd, 35 Cal. 2d 121, 216 P.2d 825, 13 A.L.R.2d 252 (1950), app. dis. on motion of counsel for appellant, 340 U.S. 910 (1951). For a summary of the law, see 3 Restatement of Torts §§558-623 (1958); 1 Harper and James, The Law of Torts, ch. V (1956); Thomas, Libel and Slander and Related Actions (1963); O'Sullivan and Brown, The Law of Defamation (1958) (English law); Note, Developments in the Law of Defamation, 69 Harv. L. Rev. 875 (1956); Yankwich, Recent Development in the Law of Creation, Expression, and Communication of Ideas, 48 Nw. U.L. Rev. 543 (1953). See also Ashley, Say It Safely (1959); Ernst and Lindey, Hold Your Tongue (rev. ed. 1950).

2. For a historical discussion, see Veeder, The History and Theory of the Law of Defamation, 3 Colum. L. Rev. 546 (1903), 4 Colum. L. Rev. 33 (1904). For a broadly oriented discussion, see Riesman, Democracy and Defamation, 42 Colum. L. Rev. 727, 1282 (1942); Green, The Right to Communicate, 35 N.Y.U.L. Rev. 903 (1960) (stressing the minority view in the Sullivan case); Leflar, The Free-ness of Free Speech, 15 Vand. L. Rev. 1073 (1962). See also Prosser, Injurious Falsehood: The Basis of Liability, 59 Colum. L. Rev. 425 (1959).

3. On defamation by radio, see Farmers Educational and Cooperative Union of America v. WDAY, Inc., 360 U.S. 525, 79 S. Ct. 1302, 3 L. Ed. 2d 1407 (1959), holding that Section 315 of the Federal Communications Act, 48 Stat. 1088, as amended, 47 U.S.C. §315(a), which provides for equal time for political candidates and prohibits censorship, forbids the station to delete libelous material and immunizes the station from libel actions under state law.

See also, Friedenthal and Medalie, The Impact of Federal Regula·ion on Political Broadcasting: Section 315 of the Communications Act, 72 Harv. L. Rev. 445 (1959); Note, Broadcasters' Immunity from Liability for Political Defamation, 48 Geo. L.J. 544 (1960). See also Smead, Freedom of Speech by Radio and Television (1959).

4. On the division among the states on the question of whether broadcasters are strictly liable for defamation occurring on the air (at times put as the distinction between libel and slander), compare with Sorensen v. Wood (cited in the principal opinion

which supported strict liability), Summit Hotel Company v. National Broadcasting Co., 336 Pa. 182, 8 A.2d 302 (1939) (taking a different point of view: broadcasting has characteristics halfway between libel and slander). See also Hartmann v. Winchell, 296 N.Y. 296, 73 N.E.2d 30 (1947); Gibler v. Houston Post Co., 310 S.W.2d 377 (Tex. Civ. App. 1958) (statement read from a script constitutes libel). Cf. Meldrum v. Australian Broadcasting Co. Ltd., [1932] Vict. L.R. 425 (statement read from script is slander because listener does not know it is being read). See also Youssoupoff v. Metro-Goldwyn-Mayer Pictures, Inc., 50 Times L. Rep. 581 (C.A. 1934), and Brown v. Paramount Publix Corp., 240 App. Div. 520, 270 N.Y. Supp. 544 (1934) (motion picture defamation constitutes libel). To the effect that television defamation is libel even though made in an ad-lib remark, see Shor v. Billingsley, 4 Misc. 2d 857, 158 N.Y.S.2d 476 (Sup. Ct. 1956, 1957). See also American Broadcasting-Paramount Theatres v. Simpson, 106 Ga. App. 230, 126 S.E.2d 873 (1962) (case involving "The Untouchables"; new tort "defamacast" actionable per se). For recent collection of state statutes and general discussion of the subject see Gwin, The Ad-Lib Statement on Television — Libel or Slander, 33 Miss. L.J. 115, especially 126 n.85 (1961). See also Remmers, Recent Legislative Trends in Defamation by Radio, 64 Harv. L. Rev. 727 (1951); Leflar, Radio and TV Defamation: "Fault" or Strict Laibility? 15 Ohio St. L.J. 252 (1954); Note, 71 Harv. L. Rev. 384 (1957).

5. In situations to which Section 315 is not applicable, censorship is not prohibited and Section 315 is not available in defense. See Felix v. Westinghouse Radio Stations, 186 F. 2d 1 (3d Cir. 1950), cert. den., 341 U.S. 909 (1951); cf. Lamb v. Sutton, 274 F.2d 705 6th Cir. 1960). On the general principles governing federal pre-emption of broadcast regulation, see Mr. Justice Brennan's concurring opinion in Head v. New Mexico Board of Examiners, 374 U.S. 424, 433, 83 S. Ct. 1759, 1765, 10 L. Ed. 2d 983, 990 (1963); Note, State Regulation of Radio and Television, 73 Harv. L. Rev. 386 (1959).

CHAPTER VII

Obscenity

A. STANDARDS

ROTH v. UNITED STATES
ALBERTS v. CALIFORNIA
354 U.S. 476, 77 S. Ct. 1304, 1 L. Ed. 2d 1498 (1957)

MR. JUSTICE BRENNAN delivered the opinion of the Court.

The constitutionality of a criminal obscenity statute is the question in each of these cases. In Roth, the primary constitutional question is whether the federal obscenity statute[1] violates the provision of the First Amendment that "Congress shall make no law . . . abridging the freedom of speech, or of the press. . . ." In Alberts, the primary constitutional question is whether the obscenity provisions of the California Penal Code[2] invade the freedoms of speech and press as they may be incorporated in the liberty protected from state action by the Due Process Clause of the Fourteenth Amendment.

---

[1] The federal obscenity statute provided, in pertinent part:

"Every obscene, lewd, lascivious, or filthy book, pamphlet, picture, paper, letter, writing, print or other publication of an indecent character; and —

"Every written or printed card, letter, circular, book, pamphlet, advertisement, or notice of any kind giving information, directly or indirectly, where, or how, or from whom, or by what means any of such mentioned matters, articles, or things may be obtained or made, . . . whether sealed or unsealed . . .

"Is declared to be nonmailable matter and shall not be conveyed in the mails or delivered from any post office or by any letter carrier.

"Whoever knowingly deposits for mailing or delivery, anything declared by this section to be nonmailable, or knowingly takes the same from the mails for the purpose of circulating or disposing thereof, or of aiding in the circulation or disposition thereof, shall be fined not more than $5,000 or imprisoned not more than five years, or both." 18 U.S.C. §1461.

The 1955 amendment of this statute, 69 Stat. 183, is not applicable to this case.

[2] The California Penal Code provides, in pertinent part:

"Every person who wilfully and lewdly, either:

. . .

"3. Writes, composes, stereotypes, prints, publishes, sells, distributes, keeps for sale, or exhibits any obscene or indecent writing, paper, or book; or designs, copies, draws, engraves, paints, or otherwise prepares any obscene or indecent picture or print; or molds, cuts, casts, or otherwise makes any obscene or indecent figure; or,

"4. Writes, composes, or publishes any notice or advertisement of any such writing, paper, book, picture, print or figure; . . .

. . .

"6. . . . is guilty of a misdemeanor. . . ." West's Cal. Penal Code Ann., 1955, §311.

Other constitutional questions are: whether these statutes violate due process,[3] because too vague to support conviction for crime; whether power to punish speech and press offensive to decency and morality is in the States alone, so that the federal obscenity statute violates the Ninth and Tenth Amendments (raised in Roth); and whether Congress, by enacting the federal obscenity statute, under the power delegated by Art. I, §8, cl. 7, to establish post offices and post roads, pre-empted the regulation of the subject matter (raised in Alberts).

Roth conducted a business in New York in the publication and sale of books, photographs and magazines. He used circulars and advertising matter to solicit sales. He was convicted by a jury in the District Court for the Southern District of New York upon 4 counts of a 26-count indictment charging him with mailing obscene circulars and advertising, and an obscene book, in violation of the federal obscenity statute. His conviction was affirmed by the Court of Appeals for the Second Circuit.[4] We granted certiorari.

Alberts conducted a mail-order business from Los Angeles. He was convicted by the Judge of the Municipal Court of the Beverly Hills Judicial District (having waived a jury trial) under a misdemeanor complaint which charged him with lewdly keeping for sale obscene and indecent books, and with writing, composing and publishing an obscene advertisement of them, in violation of the California Penal Code. The conviction was affirmed by the Appellate Department of the Superior Court of the State of California in and for the County of Los Angeles.[6] We noted probable jurisdiction.

The dispositive question is whether obscenity is utterance within the area of protected speech and press.[8] Although this is the first time the question has been squarely presented to this Court, either under the First Amendment or under the Fourteenth Amendment, expressions found in numerous opinions indicate that this Court has always assumed that obscenity is not protected by the freedoms of speech and press. Ex parte Jackson, 96 U.S. 727, 736-737; United States v. Chase, 135 U.S. 255, 261; Robertson v. Baldwin, 165 U.S. 275, 281; Public Clearing House v. Coyne, 194 U.S. 497, 508; Hoke v. United States, 227 U.S. 308, 322; Near v. Minnesota, 283 U.S. 697, 716; Chaplinsky v. New Hampshire, 315 U.S. 568, 571-572; Hannegan v. Esquire, Inc., 327 U.S. 146, 158; Winters v. New York, 333 U.S. 507, 510; Beauharnais v. Illinois, 343 U.S. 250, 266.[9]

---

[3] In Roth, reliance is placed on the Due Process Clause of the Fifth Amendment, and in Alberts, reliance is place upon the Due Process Clause of the Fourteenth Amendment.

[4] 237 F.2d 796.

[6] 138 Cal. App. 2d Supp. 909, 292 P.2d 90. This is the highest state appellate court available to the appellant. Cal. Const., Art VI, §5; see Edwards v. California, 314 U.S. 160.

[8] No issue is presented in either case concerning the obscenity of the material involved.

[9] See also the following cases in which convictions under obscenity statutes have

The guaranties of freedom of expression in effect in 10 of the 14 States which by 1792 had ratified the Constitution, gave no absolute protection for every utterance. Thirteen of the 14 States provided for the prosecution of libel, and all of those States made either blasphemy or profanity, or both, statutory crimes. As early as 1712, Massachusetts made it criminal to publish "any filthy, obscene, or profane song, pamphlet, libel or mock sermon" in imitation or mimicking of religious services. Acts and Laws of the Province of Mass. Bay, c. CV, §8 (1712), Mass. Bay Colony Charters & Laws 399 (1814). Thus, profanity and obscenity were related offenses.

In light of this history, it is apparent that the unconditional phrasing of the First Amendment was not intended to protect every utterance. This phrasing did not prevent this Court from concluding that libelous utterances are not within the area of constitutionally protected speech. Beauharnais v. Illinois, 343 U.S. 250, 266. At the time of the adoption of the First Amendment, obscenity law was not as fully developed as libel law, but there is sufficiently contemporaneous evidence to show that obscenity, too, was outside the protection intended for speech and press.[13]

The protection given speech and press was fashioned to assure unfettered interchange of ideas for the bringing about of political and social changes desired by the people. This objective was made explicit as early as 1774, in a letter of the Continental Congress to the inhabitants of Quebec:

"This last right we shall mention, regards the freedom of the press. The importance of this consists, besides the advancement of truth, science, morality, and arts in general, in its diffusion of liberal sentiments on the administration of Government, its ready communication of thoughts between subjects, and its consequential promotion of union among them, whereby oppressive officers are shamed or intimidated, into more honourable and just modes of conducting affairs." 1 Journals of the Continental Congress 108 (1774).

All ideas having even the slightest redeeming social importance — unorthodox ideas, controversial ideas, even ideas hateful to the prevailing climate of opinion — have the full protection of the guaranties, unless excludable because they encroach upon the limited area of more important interests.[14] But

---

been reviewed: Grimm v. United States, 156 U.S. 604; Rosen v. United States, 161 U.S. 29; Swearingen v. United States, 161 U.S. 446; Andrews v. United States, 162 U.S. 420; Price v. United States, 165 U.S. 311; Dunlop v. United States, 165 U.S. 486; Bartell v. United States, 227 U.S. 427; United States v. Limehouse, 285 U.S. 424.

[13] Act Concerning Crimes and Punishments, §69 (1821), Stat. Laws of Conn. 109 (1824); Knowles v. State, 3 Day (Conn.) 103 (1808); Rev. Stat. of 1835, c. 130, §10, Rev. Stat. of Mass. 740 (1836); Commonwealth v. Holmes, 17 Mass. 335 (1821); Rev. Stat. of 1842, c. 113, §2, Rev. Stat. of N.H. 221 (1843); Act for Suppressing Vice and Immorality, §XII (1798), N.J. Rev. Laws 329, 331 (1800); Commonwealth v. Sharpless, 2 S. & R. (Pa.) 91 (1815).

[14] E.g., United States v. Harriss, 347 U.S. 612; Breard v. Alexandria, 341 U.S. 622; Teamsters Union v. Hanke, 339 U.S. 470; Kovacs v. Cooper, 336 U.S. 77; Prince v. Massachusetts, 321 U.S. 158; Labor Board v. Virginia Elec. & Power Co., 314 U.S. 469; Cox v. New Hampshire, 312 U.S. 569; Schenck v. United States, 249 U.S. 47.

implicit in the history of the First Amendment is the rejection of obscenity as utterly without redeeming social importance. This rejection for that reason is mirrored in the universal judgment that obscenity should be restrained, reflected in the international agreement of over 50 nations,[15] in the obscenity laws of all of the 48 States,[16] and in the 20 obscenity laws enacted by the Congress from 1842 to 1956. This is the same judgment expressed by this Court in Chaplinsky v. New Hampshire, 315 U.S. 568, 571-572:

". . . There are certain well-defined and narrowly limited classes of speech, the prevention and punishment of which have never been thought to raise any Constitutional problem. *These include the lewd and obscene . . . It has been well observed that such utterances are no essential part of any exposition of ideas, and are of such slight social value as a step to truth that any benefit that may be derived from them is clearly outweighed by the social interest in order and morality. . . .*" (Emphasis added.)

We hold that obscenity is not within the area of constitutionally protected speech or press.

It is strenuously urged that these obscenity statutes offend the constitutional guaranties because they punish incitation to impure sexual *thoughts,* not shown to be related to any overt antisocial conduct which is or may be incited in the persons stimulated to such *thoughts.* In Roth, the trial judge instructed the jury: "The words 'obscene, lewd and lascivious' as used in the law, signify that form of immorality which has relation to sexual impurity and has a tendency to excite lustful *thoughts.*" (Emphasis added.) In Alberts, the trial judge applied the test laid down in People v. Wepplo, 78 Cal. App. 2d Supp. 959, 178 P.2d 853, namely, whether the material has "a substantial tendency to deprave or corrupt its readers by inciting lascivious *thoughts* or arousing lustful desires." (Emphasis added.) It is insisted that the constitutional guaranties are violated because convictions may be had without proof either that obscene material will perceptibly create a clear and present danger of antisocial conduct,[18] or will probably induce its recipients to such conduct.[19] But, in light of our holding that obscenity is not protected speech, the complete answer to this argument is in the holding of this Court in Beauharnais v. Illinois, supra, at 266:

---

[15]Agreement for the Suppression of the Circulation of Obscene Publications, 37 Stat. 1511; Treaties in Force 209 (U.S. Dept. State, October 31, 1956).

[16] Hearings before Subcommittee to Investigate Juvenile Delinquency of the Senate Committee on the Judiciary, pursuant to S. Res. 62, 84th Cong., 1st Sess. 49-52 (May 24, 1955).

Although New Mexico has no general obscenity statute, it does have a statute giving to municipalities the power "to prohibit the sale or exhibiting of obscene or immoral publications, prints, pictures, or illustrations." N.M. Stat. Ann., 1953, §§14-21-3, 14-21-12.

[18] Schenck v. United States, 249 U.S. 47. This approach is typified by the opinion of Judge Bok (written prior to this court's opinion in Dennis v. United States, 341 U.S. 494) in Commonwealth v. Gordon, 66 Pa. D. & C. 101, aff'd, sub nom. Commonwealth v. Feigenbaum, 166 Pa. Super. 120, 70 A.2d 389.

[19] Dennis v. United States, 341 U.S. 494. This approach is typified by the concurring opinion of Judge Frank in the Roth case, 237 F.2d, at 801. See also Lockhart & McClure, Literature, The Law of Obscenity, and the Constitution, 38 Minn. L. Rev. 295 (1954).

"Libelous utterances not being within the area of constitutionally protected speech, it is unnecessary, either for us or for the State courts, to consider the issues behind the phrase 'clear and present danger.' Certainly no one would contend that obscene speech, for example, may be punished only upon a showing of such circumstances. Libel, as we have seen, is in the same class."

However, sex and obscenity are not synonymous. Obscene material is material which deals with sex in a manner appealing to prurient interest.[20] The portrayal of sex, e.g., in art, literature and scientific works,[21] is not itself sufficient reason to deny material the constitutional protection of freedom of speech and press. Sex, a great and mysterious motive force in human life, has indisputably been a subject of absorbing interest to mankind through the ages; it is one of the vital problems of human interest and public concern. As to all such problems, this Court said in Thornhill v. Alabama, 310 U.S. 88, 101-102:

"The freedom of speech and of the press guaranteed by the Constitution embraces at the least the liberty to discuss publicly and truthfully *all matters of public concern* without previous restraint or fear of subsequent punishment. The exigencies of the colonial period and the efforts to secure freedom from oppressive administration developed a broadened conception of these liberties as adequate to supply the public need for *information and education with respect to the significant issues of the times*. . . . Freedom of discussion, if it would fulfill its historic function in this nation, must embrace *all issues about which information is needed or appropriate to enable the members of society to cope with the exigencies of their period*." (Emphasis added.)

The fundamental freedoms of speech and press have contributed greatly to the development and well-being of our free society and are indispensable to its continued growth.[22] Ceaseless vigilance is the watchword to prevent their erosion by Congress or by the States. The door barring federal and state

---

[20] I.e., material having a tendency to excite lustful thoughts. Webster's New International Dictionary (Unabridged, 2d ed., 1949) defines *prurient,* in pertinent part, as follows:

". . . Itching; longing; uneasy with desire or longing; of persons, having itching, morbid, or lascivious longings; of desire, curiosity, or propensity, lewd. . . ."

Pruriency is defined, in pertinent part, as follows:

". . . Quality of being prurient; lascivious desire or thought. . . ."

See also Mutual Film Corp. v. Industrial Comm'n, 236 U.S. 230, 242, where this Court said as to motion pictures: ". . . They take their attraction from the general interest, eager and wholesome it may be, in their subjects, but a *prurient interest may be excited and appealed to*. . . ." (Emphasis added.)

We perceive no significant difference between the meaning of obscenity developed in the case law and the definition of the A.L.I., Model Penal Code, §207.10(2) (Tent. Draft No. 6 1957), viz.:

". . . A thing is obscene if, considered as a whole, its predominant appeal is to prurient interest, i.e., a shameful or morbid interest in nudity, sex, or excretion, and if it goes substantially beyond customary limits of candor in description or representation of such matters. . . ." See Comment, id., at 10, and the discussion at page 29 et seq.

[21] See, e.g., United States v. Dennett, 39 F.2d 564.

[22] Madison's Report on the Virginia Resolutions, 4 Elliot's Debates 571.

intrusion into this area cannot be left ajar; it must be kept tightly closed and opened only the slightest crack necessary to prevent encroachment upon more important interests.[23] It is therefore vital that the standards for judging obscenity safeguard the protection of freedom of speech and press for material which does not treat sex in a manner appealing to prurient interest.

The early leading standard of obscenity allowed material to be judged merely by the effect of an isolated excerpt upon particularly susceptible persons. Regina v. Hicklin, [1868] L.R. 3 Q.B. 360.[24] Some American courts adopted this standard [25] but later decisions have rejected it and substituted this test: whether to the average person, applying contemporary community standards, the dominant theme of the material taken as a whole appeals to prurient interest.[26] The Hicklin test, judging obscenity by the effect of isolated passages upon the most susceptible persons, might well encompass material legitimately treating with sex, and so it must be rejected as unconstitutionally restrictive of the freedoms of speech and press. On the other hand, the substituted standard provides safeguards adequate to withstand the charge of constitutional infirmity.

Both trial courts below sufficiently followed the proper standard. Both courts used the proper definition of obscenity. In addition, in the Alberts case, in ruling on a motion to dismiss, the trial judge indicated that, as the trier of facts, he was judging each item as a whole as it would affect the normal person,[27] and in Roth, the trial judge instructed the jury as follows:

". . . The test is not whether it would arouse sexual desires or sexual impure thoughts in those comprising a particular segment of the community, the young, the immature or the highly prudish or would leave another segment, the scientific or highly educated or the so-called worldly-wise and sophisticated indifferent and unmoved. . . .

"The test in each case is the effect of the book, picture or publication considered as a whole, not upon any particular class, but upon all those whom it

---

[23] See note 14, supra.

[24] But see the instructions given to the jury by Mr. Justice Stable in Regina v. Martin Secker & Warburg, [1954] 2 All Eng. 683 (C.C.C.).

[25] United States v. Kennerley, 209 F. 119; MacFadden v. United States, 165 F. 51; United States v. Bennett, 24 Fed. Cas. 1093; United States v. Clarke, 38 F. 500; Commonwealth v. Buckley, 200 Mass. 346, 86 N.E. 910.

[26] E.g., Walker v. Popenoe, 80 U.S. App. D.C. 129, 149 F.2d 511; Parmelee v. United States, 72 App. D.C. 203, 113 F.2d 729; United States v. Levine, 83 F.2d 156; United States v. Dennett, 39 F.2d 564; Khan v. Feist, Inc., 70 F. Supp. 450, aff'd, 165 F.2d 188; United States v. One Book Called "Ulysses," 5 F. Supp. 182, aff'd, 72 F.2d 705; American Civil Liberties Union v. Chicago, 3 Ill. 2d 334, 121 N.E.2d 585; Commonwealth v. Isentadt, 318 Mass. 543, 62 N.E.2d 840; Missouri v. Becker, 364 Mo. 1079, 272 S.W.2d 283; Adams Theatre Co. v. Keenan, 12 N.J. 267, 96 A.2d 519; Bantam Books, Inc. v. Melko, 25 N.J. Super. 292, 96 A.2d 47; Commonwealth v. Gordon, 66 Pa. D. & C. 101, aff'd, sub nom. Commonwealth v. Feigenbaum, 166 Pa. Super. 120, 70 A.2d 389; cf. Roth v. Goldman, 172 F.2d 788, 794-795 (concurrence).

[27] In Alberts, the contention that the trial judge did not read the materials in their entirety is not before us because not fairly comprised within the questions presented. U.S. Sup. Ct. Rules, 15(1)(c)(1).

is likely to reach. In other words, you determine its impact upon the average person in the community. The books, pictures and circulars must be judged as a whole, in their entire context, and you are not to consider detached or separate portions in reaching a conclusion. You judge the circulars, pictures and publications which have been put in evidence by present-day standards of the community. You may ask yourselves does it offend the common conscience of the community by present-day standards.

. . .

"In this case, ladies and gentlemen of the jury, you and you alone are the exclusive judges of what the common conscience of the community is, and in determining that conscience you are to consider the community as a whole, young and old, educated and uneducated, the religious and the irreligious — men, women and children."

It is argued that the statutes do not provide reasonably ascertainable standards of guilt and therefore violate the constitutional requirements of due process. Winters v. New York, 333 U.S. 507. The federal obscenity statute makes punishable the mailing of material that is "obscene, lewd, lascivious, or filthy . . . or other publication of an indecent character." [28] The California statute makes punishable, inter alia, the keeping for sale or advertising material that is "obscene or indecent." The thrust of the argument is that these words are not sufficiently precise because they do not mean the same thing to all people, all the time, everywhere.

Many decisions have recognized that these terms of obscenity statutes are not precise.[29] This Court, however, has consistently held that lack of precision is not itself offensive to the requirements of due process. ". . . [T]he Constitution does not require impossible standards"; all that is required is that the language "conveys sufficiently definite warning as to the proscribed conduct when measured by common understanding and practices. . . ." United States v. Petrillo, 332 U.S. 1, 7-8. These words, applied according to the proper standard for judging obscenity, already discussed, give adequate warning of the conduct proscribed and mark ". . . boundaries sufficiently distinct for judges and juries fairly to administer the law. . . . That there may be marginal cases in which it is difficult to determine the side of the line on which a particular fact situation falls is no sufficient reason to hold the language too ambiguous to define a criminal offense. . . ." Id., at 7. See also United States v. Harriss, 347 U.S. 612, 624, n.15; Boyce Motor Lines, Inc. v. United States, 342 U.S. 337, 340; United States v. Ragen, 314 U.S. 513, 523-524; United States

[28] This Court, as early as 1896, said of the federal obscenity statute:

". . . Every one who uses the mails of the United States for carrying papers or publications must take notice of what, in this enlightened age, is meant by decency, purity, and chastity in social life, and what must be deemed obscene, lewd, and lascivious." Rosen v. United States, 161 U.S. 29, 42.

[29] E.g., Roth v. Goldman, 172 F.2d 788, 789; Parmelee v. United States, 72 App. D.C. 203, 204, 113 F.2d 729, 730; United States v. 4200 Copies International Journal, 134 F. Supp. 490, 493; United States v. One Unbound Volume, 128 F. Supp. 280, 281.

v. Wurzbach, 280 U.S. 396; Hygrade Provision Co. v. Sherman, 266 U.S. 497; Fox v. Washington, 236 U.S. 273; Nash v. United States, 229 U.S. 373.[30]

In summary, then, we hold that these statutes, applied according to the proper standard for judging obscenity, do not offend constitutional safeguards against convictions based upon protected material, or fail to give men in acting adequate notice of what is prohibited.

Roth's argument that the federal obscenity statute unconstitutionally encroaches upon the powers reserved by the Ninth and Tenth Amendments to the States and to the people to punish speech and press where offensive to decency and morality is hinged upon his contention that obscenity is expression not excepted from the sweep of the provision of the First Amendment that *"Congress* shall make *no law* . . . abridging the freedom of speech, or of the press. . . ." (Emphasis added.) That argument falls in light of our holding that obscenity is not expression protected by the First Amendment.[31] We therefore hold that the federal obscenity statute punishing the use of the mails for obscene material is a proper exercise of the postal power delegated to Congress by Art. I, §8, cl. 7.[32] In United Public Workers v. Mitchell, 330 U.S. 75, 95-96, this Court said:

". . . The powers granted by the Constitution to the Federal Government are subtracted from the totality of sovereignty originally in the states and the people. Therefore, when objection is made that the exercise of a federal power infringes upon rights reserved by the Ninth and Tenth Amendments, the inquiry must be directed toward the granted power under which the action of the Union was taken. If granted power is found, necessarily the objection of invasion of those rights, reserved by the Ninth and Tenth Amendments, must fail. . . ."

Alberts argues that because his was a mail-order business, the California statute is repugnant to Art. I, §8, cl. 7, under which the Congress allegedly preempted the regulatory field by enacting the federal obscenity statute punish-

---

[30] It is argued that because juries may reach different conclusions as to the same material, the statutes must be held to be insufficiently precise to satisfy due process requirements. But, it is common experience that different juries may reach different results under any criminal statute. That is one of the consequences we accept under our jury system. Cf. Dunlop v. United States, 165 U.S. 486, 499-500.

[31] For the same reason, we reject, in this case, the argument that there is greater latitude for state action under the word "liberty" under the Fourteenth Amendment than is allowed to Congress by the language of the First Amendment.

[32] In Public Clearing House v. Coyne, 194 U.S. 497, 506-508, this Court said: "The constitutional principles underlying the administration of the Post Office Department were discussed in the opinion of the court in Ex parte Jackson, 96 U.S. 727, in which we held that the power vested to establish post offices and post roads embraced the regulation of the entire postal system of the country; that Congress might designate what might be carried in the mails and what excluded . . . . It may . . . refuse to include in its mails such printed matter or merchandise as may seem objectionable to it upon the ground of public policy . . . . For more than thirty years not only has the transmission of obscene matter been prohibited, but it has been made a crime, punishable by fine or imprisonment, for a person to deposit such matter in the mails. The constitutionality of this law we believe has never been attacked. . . ."

ing the mailing or advertising by mail of obscene material. The federal statute deals only with actual mailing; it does not eliminate the power of the state to punish "keeping for sale" or "advertising" obscene material. The state statute in no way imposes a burden or interferes with the federal postal functions. ". . . The decided cases which indicate the limits of state regulatory power in relation to the federal mail service involve situations where state regulation involved a direct, physical interference with federal activities under the postal power or some direct, immediate burden on the performance of the postal functions. . . ." Railway Mail Assn. v. Corsi, 326 U.S. 88, 96.

The judgments are

Affirmed.

MR. CHIEF JUSTICE WARREN, concurring in the result.

I agree with the result reached by the Court in these cases, but, because we are operating in a field of expression and because broad language used here may eventually be applied to the arts and sciences and freedom of communication generally, I would limit our decision to the facts before us and to the validity of the statutes in question as applied. . . .

The line dividing the salacious or pornographic from literature or science is not straight and unwavering. Present laws depend largely upon the effect that the materials may have upon those who receive them. It is manifest that the same object may have a different impact, varying according to the part of the community it reached. But there is more to these cases. It is not the book that is on trial; it is a person. The conduct of the defendant is the central issue, not the obscenity of a book or picture. The nature of the materials is, of course, relevant as an attribute of the defendant's conduct, but the materials are thus placed in context from which they draw color and character. A wholly different result might be reached in a different setting. . . .

The defendants in both these cases were engaged in the business of purveying textual or graphic matter openly advertised to appeal to the erotic interest of their customers. They were plainly engaged in the commerical exploitation of the morbid and shameful craving for materials with prurient effect. I believe that the State and Federal Governments can constitutionally punish such conduct. That is all that these cases present to us, and that is all we need to decide.

I agree with the Court's decision in its rejection of the other contentions raised by these defendants.

MR. JUSTICE HARLAN, concurring in the result in No. 61 [Alberts], and dissenting in No. 582 [Roth].

I regret not to be able to join the Court's opinion. I cannot do so because I find lurking beneath its disarming generalizations a number of problems which not only leave me with serious misgivings as to the future effect of today's decisions, but which also, in my view, call for different results in these two cases.

I

My basic difficulties with the Court's opinion are threefold. First, the opinion paints with such a broad brush that I fear it may result in a loosening of the tight reins which state and federal courts should hold upon the enforcement of obscenity statutes. Second, the Court fails to discriminate between the different factors which, in my opinion, are involved in the constitutional adjudication of state and federal obscenity cases. Third, relevant distinctions between the two obscenity statutes here involved, and the Court's own definition of "obscenity," are ignored. . . .

The Court seems to assume that "obscenity" is a peculiar *genus* of "speech and press," which is as distinct, recognizable, and classifiable as poison ivy is among other plants. On this basis the *constitutional* question before us simply becomes, as the Court says, whether "obscenity," as an abstraction, is protected by the First and Fourteenth Amendments, and the question whether a *particular* book may be suppressed becomes a mere matter of classification, of "fact," to be entrusted to a fact-finder and insulated from independent constitutional judgment. But surely the problem cannot be solved in such a generalized fashion. Every communication has an individuality and "value" of its own. The suppression of a particular writing or other tangible form of expression is, therefore, an *individual* matter, and in the nature of things every such suppression raises an individual constitutional problem, in which a reviewing court must determine for *itself* whether the attacked expression is suppressable within constitutional standards. Since those standards do not readily lend themselves to generalized definitions, the constitutional problem in the last analysis becomes one of particularized judgments which appellate courts must make for themselves. . . .

My second reason for dissatisfaction with the Court's opinion is that the broad strides with which the Court has proceeded has led it to brush aside with perfunctory ease the vital constitutional considerations which, in my opinion, differentiate these two cases. It does not seem to matter to the Court that in one case we balance the power of a State in this field against the restrictions of the Fourteenth Amendment, and in the other the power of the Federal Government against the limitations of the First Amendment. I deal with this subject more particularly later.

Thirdly, the Court has not been bothered by the fact that the two cases involve different statutes. In California the book must have a "tendency to deprave or corrupt its readers"; under the federal statute it must tend "to stir sexual impulses and lead to sexually impure thoughts." [1] The two statutes do

[1] In Alberts v. California, the state definition of "obscenity" is, of course, binding on us. The definition there used derives from People v. Wepplo, 78 Cal. App. 2d Supp. 959, 178 P.2d 853, the question being whether the material has "a substantive tendency to deprave or corrupt its readers by exciting lascivious thoughts or arousing lustful desire."

not seem to me to present the same problems. Yet the Court compounds confusion when it superimposes on these two statutory definitions a third, drawn from the American Law Institute's Model Penal Code, Tentative Draft No. 6: "A thing is obscene if, considered as a whole, its predominant appeal is to prurient interest." The bland assurance that this definition is the same as the ones with which we deal flies in the face of the authors' express rejection of the "deprave and corrupt" and "sexual thoughts" tests:

"Obscenity [in the Tentative Draft] is defined in terms of material which appeals predominantly to prurient interest in sexual matters and which goes beyond customary freedom of expression in these matters. We reject the prevailing test of tendency to arouse lustful thoughts or desires because it is unrealistically broad for a society that plainly tolerates a great deal of erotic interest in literature, advertising, and art, and because regulation of thought or desire, unconnected with overt misbehavior, raises the most acute constitutional as well as practical difficulties. We likewise reject the common definition of obscene as that which 'tends to corrupt or debase.' If this means anything different from tendency to arouse lustful thought and desire, it suggests that change of character or actual misbehavior follows from contact with obscenity. Evidence of such consequences is lacking. . . . On the other hand, 'appeal to prurient interest' refers to qualities of the material itself: the capacity to attract individuals eager for a forbidden look. . . ." [2]

As this passage makes clear, there is a significant distinction between the definitions used in the prosecutions before us, and the American Law Institute formula. If, therefore, the latter is the correct standard, as my Brother BRENNAN elsewhere intimates,[3] then these convictions should surely be reversed. Instead, the Court merely assimilates the various tests into one indiscriminate potpourri.

I now pass to the consideration of the two cases before us.

II

I concur in the judgment of the Court in No. 61, Alberts v. California.

The question in this case is whether the defendant was deprived of liberty

---

In *Roth v. United States*, our grant of certiorari was limited to the question of the constitutionality of the statute, and did not encompass the correctness of the definition of "obscenity" adopted by the trial judge as a matter of statutory construction. We must therefore assume that the trial judge correctly defined that term, and deal with the constitutionality of the statute as construed and applied in this case.

The two definitions do not seem to me synonymous. Under the federal definition it is enough if the jury finds that the book as a whole leads to certain thoughts. In California, the further inference must be drawn that such thoughts will have a substantive "tendency to deprave or corrupt" — i.e., that the thoughts induced by the material will affect character and action. See American Law Institute, Model Penal Code, Tentative Draft No. 6, §207.10(2), Comments, p.10.

[2] Ibid.

[3] See dissenting opinion of Mr. Justice Brennan in Kingsley Books, Inc. v. Brown, [354 U.S. 436]. . . .

without due process of law when he was convicted for selling certain materials found by the judge to be obscene because they would have a "tendency to deprave or corrupt its readers by exciting lascivious thoughts or arousing lustful desire."

In judging the constitutionality of this conviction, we should remember that our function in reviewing state judgments under the Fourteenth Amendment is a narrow one. We do not decide whether the policy of the State is wise, or whether it is based on assumptions scientifically substantiated. We can inquire only whether the state action so subverts the fundamental liberties implicit in the Due Process Clause that it cannot be sustained as a rational exercise of power. See Jackson, J., dissenting in Beauharnais v. Illinois, 343 U.S. 250, 287. The States' power to make printed words criminal is, of course, confined by the Fourteenth Amendment, but only insofar as such power is inconsistent with our concepts of "ordered liberty." Palko v. Connecticut, 302 U.S. 319, 324-325.

What, then, is the purpose of this California statute? Clearly the state legislature has made the judgment that printed words *can* "deprave or corrupt" the reader — that words can incite to antisocial or immoral action. The assumption seems to be that the distribution of certain types of literature will induce criminal or immoral sexual conduct. It is well known, of course, that the validity of this assumption is a matter of dispute among critics, sociologists, psychiatrists, and penologists. There is a large school of thought, particularly in the scientific community, which denies any causal connection between the reading of pornography and immorality, crime, or delinquency. Others disagree. Clearly it is not our function to decide this question. That function belongs to the state legislature. Nothing in the Constitution requires California to accept as truth the most advanced and sophisticated psychiatric opinion. It seems to me clear that it is not irrational, in our present state of knowledge, to consider that pornography can induce a type of sexual conduct which a State may deem obnoxious to the moral fabric of society. In fact the very division of opinion on the subject counsels us to respect the choice made by the State.

Furthermore, even assuming that pornography cannot be deemed ever to cause, in an immediate sense, criminal sexual conduct, other interests within the proper cognizance of the States may be protected by the prohibition placed on such materials. The State can reasonably draw the inference that over a long period of time the indiscriminate dissemination of materials, the essential character of which is to degrade sex, will have an eroding effect on moral standards. And the State has a legitimate interest in protecting the privacy of the home against invasion of unsolicited obscenity.

Above all stands the realization that we deal here with an area where knowledge is small, data are insufficient, and experts are divided. Since the domain of sexual morality is pre-eminently a matter of state concern, this Court should be slow to interfere with state legislation calculated to protect that morality. It seems to me that nothing in the broad and flexible command of the Due Process Clause forbids California to prosecute one who sells books whose dominant tendency might be to "deprave or corrupt" a reader. I agree with the Court, of course, that the books must be judged as a whole and in relation to the normal adult reader.

What has been said, however, does not dispose of the case. It still remains for us to decide whether the state court's determination that this material should be suppressed is consistent with the Fourteenth Amendment; and that, of course, presents a federal question as to which we, and not the state court, have the ultimate responsibility. And so, in the final analysis, I concur in the judgment because, upon an independent perusal of the material involved, and in light of the considerations discussed above, I cannot say that its suppression would so interfere with the communication of "ideas" in any proper sense of that term that it would offend the Due Process Clause. I therefore agree with the Court that appellant's conviction must be affirmed.

III

I dissent in No. 582, Roth v. United States.

We are faced here with the question whether the federal obscenity statute, as construed and applied in this case, violates the First Amendment to the Constitution. To me, this question is of quite a different order than one where we are dealing with state legislation under the Fourteenth Amendment. I do not think it follows that state and federal powers in this area are the same, and that just because the State may suppress a particular utterance, it is automatically permissible for the Federal Government to do the same. I agree with Mr. Justice Jackson that the historical evidence does not bear out the claim that the Fourteenth Amendment "incorporates" the First in any literal sense. See Beauharnais v. Illinois, supra. But laying aside any consequences which might flow from that conclusion, cf. Mr. Justice Holmes in Gitlow v. New York, 268 U.S. 652, 672,[4] I prefer to rest my views about this case on broader and less abstract grounds. . . .

The Federal Government has, for example, power to restrict seditious speech directed against it, because that Government certainly has the substantive authority to protect itself against revolution. Cf. Pennsylvania v. Nelson, 350 U.S. 497. But in dealing with obscenity we are faced with the converse situation, for the interests which obscenity statutes purportedly protect are primarily entrusted to the care, not of the Federal Government, but of the States. Congress has no substantive power over sexual morality. Such powers as the Federal Government has in this field are but incidental to its other

---

[4] "The general principle of free speech, it seems to me, must be taken to be included in the Fourteenth Amendment, in view of the scope that has been given to the word 'liberty' as there used, although perhaps it may be accepted with a somewhat larger latitude of interpretation than is allowed to Congress by the sweeping language that governs or ought to govern the laws of the United States."

powers, here the postal power, and are not of the same nature as those possessed by the States, which bear direct responsibility for the protection of the local moral fabric.[5] . . .

Not only is the federal interest in protecting the Nation against pornography attenuated, but the dangers of federal censorship in this field are far greater than anything the States may do. It has often been said that one of the great strengths of our federal system is that we have, in the forty-eight States, forty-eight experimental social laboratories. "State statutory law reflects predominantly this capacity of a legislature to introduce novel techniques of social control. The federal system has the immense advantage of providing forty-eight separate centers for such experimentation."[6] Different States will have different attitudes toward the same work of literature. The same book which is freely read in one State might be classed as obscene in another.[7] And it seems to me that no overwhelming danger to our freedom to experiment and to gratify our tastes in literature is likely to result from the suppression of a borderline book in one of the States, so long as there is no uniform nationwide suppression of the book, and so long as other States are free to experiment with the same or bolder books.

Quite a different situation is presented, however, where the Federal Government imposes the ban. The danger is perhaps not great if the people of one State, through their legislature, decide that "Lady Chatterley's Lover" goes so far beyond the acceptable standards of candor that it will be deemed offensive and nonsellable, for the State next door is still free to make its own choice. At least we do not have one uniform standard. But the dangers to free thought and expression are truly great if the Federal Government imposes a blanket ban over the Nation on such a book. The prerogative of the States to differ on their ideas of morality will be destroyed, the ability of States to experiment will be stunted. The fact that the people of one State cannot read some of the works of D. H. Lawrence seems to me, if not wise or desirable, at least acceptable. But that no person in the United States should be allowed to do so seems to me to be intolerable, and violative of both the letter and spirit of the First Amendment.

I judge this case, then, in view of what I think is the attenuated federal interest in this field, in view of the very real danger of a deadening uniform-

[5] The hoary dogma of Ex parte Jackson, 96 U.S. 727, and Public Clearing House v. Coyne, 194 U.S. 497, that the use of the mails is a privilege on which the Government may impose such conditions as it chooses, has long since evaporated. See Brandeis, J., dissenting, in Milwaukee Social Democratic Publishing Co. v. Burleson, 255 U.S. 407, 430-433; Holmes, J., dissenting, in Leach v. Carlile, 258 U.S. 138, 140; Cates v. Haderline, 342 U.S. 804, reversing 189 F.2d 369; Door v. Donaldson, 90 U.S. App. D.C. 188, 195 F.2d 764.

[6] Hart, The Relations Between State and Federal Law, 54 Col. L. Rev. 489, 493.

[7] To give only a few examples: Edmund Wilson's "Memoirs of Hecate County" was found obscene in New York, see Doubleday & Co. v. New York, 335 U.S. 848; a bookseller indicted for selling the same book was acquitted in California. "God's Little Acre" was held to be obscene in Massachusetts, not obscene in New York and Pennsylvania.

ity which can result from nation-wide federal censorship, and in view of the fact that the constitutionality of this conviction must be weighed against the First and not the Fourteenth Amendment. So viewed, I do not think that this conviction can be upheld. The petitioner was convicted under a statute which, under the judge's charge,[8] makes it criminal to sell books which "tend to stir sexual impulses and lead to sexually impure thoughts." I cannot agree that any book which tends to stir sexual impulses and lead to sexually impure thoughts necessarily is "utterly without redeeming social importance." Not only did this charge fail to measure up to the standards which I understand the Court to approve, but as far as I can see, much of the great literature of the world could lead to conviction under such a view of the statute. Moreover, in no event do I think that the limited federal interest in this area can extend to mere "thoughts." The Federal Government has no business, whether under the postal or commerce power, to bar the sale of books because they might lead to any kind of "thoughts." [9]

It is no answer to say, as the Court does, that obscenity is not protected speech. The point is that this statute, as here construed, defines obscenity so widely that it encompasses matters which might very well be protected speech. I do not think that the federal statute can be constitutionally construed to reach other than what the Government has termed as "hard-core" pornography. Nor do I think the statute can fairly be read as directed only at *persons* who are engaged in the business of catering to the prurient minded, even though their wares fall short of hard-core pornography. Such a statute would raise constitutional questions of a different order. That being so, and since in my opinion the material here involved cannot be said to be hard-core pornography, I would reverse this case with instructions to dismiss the indictment.

Mr. Justice Douglas, with whom Mr. Justice Black concurs, dissenting.

When we sustain these convictions, we make the legality of a publication turn on the purity of thought which a book or tract instills in the mind of the reader. I do not think we can approve that standard and be faithful to the command of the First Amendment, which by its terms is a restraint on Congress and which by the Fourteenth is a restraint on the States.

In the Roth case the trial judge charged the jury that the statutory words "obscene, lewd and lascivious" describe "that form of immorality which has relation to sexual impurity and has a tendency to excite lustful thoughts." He stated that the term "filthy" in the statute pertains "to that sort of treatment of sexual matters in such a vulgar and indecent way, so that it tends to arouse

---

[8] While the correctness of the judge's charge is not before us, the question is necessarily subsumed in the broader question involving the constitutionality of the statute as applied in this case.

[9] See American Law Institute, Model Penal Code, Tentative Draft No. 6, §207.10, Comments, p. 20: "As an independent goal of penal legislation, repression of sexual thoughts and desires is hard to support. Thoughts and desires not manifested in overt antisocial behavior are generally regarded as the exclusive concern of the individual and his spiritual advisors."

a feeling of disgust and revulsion." He went on to say that the material "must be calculated to corrupt and debauch the minds and morals" of "the average person in the community," not those of any particular class. "You judge the circulars, pictures and publications which have been put in evidence by present-day standards of the community. You may ask yourselves does it offend the common conscience of the community by present-day standards."

The trial judge who, sitting without a jury, heard the Alberts case and the appellate court that sustained the judgment of conviction, took California's definition of "obscenity" from People v. Wepplo, 78 Cal. App. 2d Supp. 959, 961, 178 P.2d 853, 855. That case held that a book is obscene "if it has a substantial tendency to deprave or corrupt its readers by inciting lascivious thoughts or arousing lustful desire."

By these standards punishment is inflicted for thoughts provoked, not for overt acts nor antisocial conduct. This test cannot be squared with our decisions under the First Amendment. Even the ill-starred Dennis case conceded that speech to be punishable must have some relation to action which could be penalized by government. Dennis v. United States, 341 U.S. 494, 502-511. Cf. Chafee, The Blessings of Liberty (1956), p. 69. This issue cannot be avoided by saying that obscenity is not protected by the First Amendment. The question remains, what is the constitutional test of obscenity?

The tests by which these convictions were obtained require only the arousing of sexual thoughts. Yet the arousing of sexual thoughts and desires happens every day in normal life in dozens of ways. Nearly 30 years ago a questionnaire sent to college and normal school women graduates asked what things were most stimulating sexually. Of 409 replies, 9 said "music"; 18 said "pictures"; 29 said "dancing"; 40 said "drama"; 95 said "books"; and 218 said "man." Alpert, Judicial Censorship of Obscene Literature, 52 Harv. L. Rev. 40, 73.

The test of obscenity the Court endorses today gives the censor free range over a vast domain. To allow the State to step in and punish mere speech or publication that the judge or the jury thinks has an *undesirable* impact on thoughts but that is not shown to be a part of unlawful action is drastically to curtail the First Amendment. As recently stated by two of our outstanding authorities on obscenity, "The danger of influencing a change in the current moral standards of the community, or of shocking or offending readers, or of stimulating sex thoughts or desires apart from objective conduct, can never justify the losses to society that result from interference with literary freedom." Lockhart & McClure, Literature, The Law of Obscenity, and the Constitution, 38 Minn. L. Rev. 295, 387.

If we were certain that impurity of sexual thoughts impelled to action, we would be on less dangerous ground in punishing the distributors of this sex literature. But it is by no means clear that obscene literature, as so defined, is a significant factor in influencing substantial deviations from the community standards.

"There are a number of reasons for real and substantial doubts as to the soundness of that hypothesis. (1) Scientific studies of juvenile delinquency demonstrate that those who get into trouble, and are the greatest concern of the advocates of censorship, are far less inclined to read than those who do not become delinquent. The delinquents are generally the adventurous type, who have little use for reading and other non-active entertainment. Thus, even assuming that reading sometimes has an adverse effect upon moral conduct, the effect is not likely to be substantial, for those who are susceptible seldom read. (2) Sheldon and Eleanor Glueck, who are among the country's leading authorities on the treatment and causes of juvenile delinquency, have recently published the results of a ten year study of its causes. They exhaustively studied approximately 90 factors and influences that might lead to or explain juvenile delinquency, but the Gluecks gave no consideration to the type of reading material, if any, read by the delinquents. This is, of course, consistent with their finding that delinquents read very little. When those who know so much about the problem of delinquency among youth — the very group about whom the advocates of censorship are most concerned — conclude that what delinquents read has so little effect upon their conduct that it is not worth investigating in an exhaustive study of cases, there is good reason for serious doubt concerning the basic hypothesis on which obscenity censorship is defended. (3) The many other influences in society that stimulate sexual desire are so much more frequent in their influence, and so much more potent in their effect, that the influence of reading is likely, at most, to be relatively insignificant in the composite of forces that lead an individual into conduct deviating from the community sex standards. The Kinsey studies show the minor degree to which literature serves as a potent sexual stimulant. And the studies demonstrating that sex knowledge seldom results from reading indicates [*sic*] the relative unimportance of literature in sex thoughts as compared with other factors in society." Lockhart & McClure, op. cit. supra, pp. 385-386.

The absence of dependable information on the effect of obscene literature on human conduct should make us wary. It should put us on the side of protecting society's interest in literature, except and unless it can be said that the particular publication has an impact on action that the government can control.

As noted, the trial judge in the Roth case charged the jury in the alternative that the federal obscenity statute outlaws literature dealing with sex which offends "the common conscience of the community." That standard is, in my view, more inimical still to freedom of expression.

The standard of what offends "the common conscience of the community" conflicts, in my judgment, with the command of the First Amendment that "Congress shall make no law . . . abridging the freedom of speech, or of the press." Certainly that standard would not be an acceptable one if religion, economics, politics or philosophy were involved. How does it become a constitutional standard when literature treating with sex is concerned?

Any test that turns on what is offensive to the community's standards is too loose, too capricious, too destructive of freedom of expression to be squared with the First Amendment. Under that test, juries can censor, suppress, and punish what they don't like, provided the matter relates to "sexual impurity" or has a tendency "to excite lustful thoughts." This is community censorship in one of its worst forms. It creates a regime where in the battle between the literati and the Philistines, the Philistines are certain to win. If experience in this field teaches anything, it is that "censorship of obscenity has almost always been both irrational and indiscriminate." Lockhart & McClure, op. cit. supra, at 371. The test adopted here accentuates that trend.

I assume there is nothing in the Constitution which forbids Congress from using its power over the mails to proscribe *conduct* on the grounds of good morals. No one would suggest that the First Amendment permits nudity in public places, adultery, and other phases of sexual misconduct.

I can understand (and at times even sympathize) with programs of civic groups and church groups to protect and defend the existing moral standards of the community. I can understand the motives of the Anthony Comstocks who would impose Victorian standards on the community. When speech alone is involved, I do not think that government, consistently with the First Amendment, can throw its weight behind one school or another. Government should be concerned with antisocial conduct, not with utterances. Thus, if the First Amendment guarantee of freedom of speech and press is to mean anything in this field, it must allow protests even against the moral code that the standard of the day sets for the community. In other words, literature should not be suppressed merely because it offends the moral code of the censor.

The legality of a publication in this country should never be allowed to turn either on the purity of thought which it instills in the mind of the reader or on the degree to which it offends the community conscience. By either test the role of the censor is exalted, and society's values in literary freedom are sacrificed.

The Court today suggests a third standard. It defines obscene material as that "which deals with sex in a manner appealing to prurient interest." * Like the standards applied by the trial judges below, that standard does not require any nexus between the literature which is prohibited and action which the legislature can regulate or prohibit. Under the First Amendment, that standard is no more valid than those which the courts below adopted.

I do not think that the problem can be resolved by the Court's statement that "obscenity is not expression protected by the First Amendment." With the exception of Beauharnais v. Illinois, 343 U.S. 250, none of our cases have resolved problems of free speech and free press by placing any form of expres-

---

* The definition of obscenity which the Court adopts seems in substance to be that adopted by those who drafted the A.L.I., Model Penal Code. §207.10(2) (Tentative Draft No. 6, 1957). . . .

sion beyond the pale of the absolute prohibition of the First Amendment. Unlike the law of libel, wrongfully relied on in Beauharnais, there is no special historical evidence that literature dealing with sex was intended to be treated in a special manner by those who drafted the First Amendment. In fact, the first reported court decision in this country involving obscene literature was in 1821. Lockhart & McClure, op. cit. supra, at 324, n.200. I reject too the implication that problems of freedom of speech and of the press are to be resolved by weighing against the values of free expression, the judgment of the Court that a particular form of that expression has "no redeeming social importance." The First Amendment, its prohibition in terms absolute, was designed to preclude courts as well as legislatures from weighing the values of speech against silence. The First Amendment puts free speech in the preferred position.

Freedom of expression can be suppressed if, and to the extent that, it is so closely brigaded with illegal action as to be an inseparable part of it. Giboney v. Empire Storage Co., 336 U.S. 490, 498; Labor Board v. Virginia Power Co., 314 U.S. 469, 477-478. As a people, we cannot afford to relax that standard. For the test that suppresses a cheap tract today can suppress a literary gem tomorrow. All it need do is to incite a lascivious thought or arouse a lustful desire. The list of books that judges or juries can place in that category is endless.

I would give the broad sweep of the First Amendment full support. I have the same confidence in the ability of our people to reject noxious literature as I have in their capacity to sort out the true from the false in theology, economics, politics, or any other field.

JACOBELLIS v. OHIO
378 U.S. 184, 84 S. Ct. 1676, 12 L. Ed. 2d 793 (1964)

Mr. Justice Brennan announced the judgment of the Court and delivered an opinion in which Mr. Justice Goldberg joins.

Appellant, Nico Jacobellis, manager of a motion picture theater in Cleveland Heights, Ohio, was convicted on two counts of possessing and exhibiting an obscene film in violation of Ohio Revised Code (1963 Supp.), §2905.34.[1] He was fined $500 on the first count and $2,000 on the second, and

---

[1] *"Selling, exhibiting, and possessing obscene literature or drugs, for criminal purposes.*

"No person shall knowingly sell, lend, give away, exhibit, or offer to sell, lend, give away, or exhibit, or publish or offer to publish or have in his possession or under his control an obscene, lewd, or lascivious book, magazine, pamphlet, paper, writing, advertisement, circular, print, picture, photograph, motion picture film, or book, pamphlet, paper, magazine not wholly obscene but containing lewd or lascivious articles, advertisements, photographs, or drawing, representation, figure, image, cast, instrument, or article of an indecent or immoral nature, or a drug, medicine, article, or thing intended for the prevention of conception or for causing an abortion, or advertise any of them for sale, or write, print, or cause to be written or printed a card, book, pamphlet, advertisement, or notice giving information when, where, how, of whom, or by what means any of such articles or things can be purchased or obtained, or

was sentenced to the workhouse if the fines were not paid. His conviction, by a court of three judges upon waiver of trial by jury, was affirmed by an intermediate appellate court, 115 Ohio App. 226, 175 N.E.2d 123, and by the Supreme Court of Ohio, 173 Ohio St. 22, 179 N.E.2d 777. We noted probable jurisdiction of the appeal, 371 U.S. 808, and subsequently restored the case to the calendar for reargument, 373 U.S. 901. The dispositive question is whether the state courts properly found that the motion picture involved, a French film called "Les Amants" ("The Lovers"), was obscene and hence not entitled to the protection for free expression that is guaranteed by the First and Fourteenth Amendments. We conclude that the film is not obscene and that the judgment must accordingly be reversed.

Motion pictures are within the ambit of the constitutional guarantees of freedom of speech and of the press. Joseph Burstyn, Inc., v. Wilson, 343 U.S. 495. But in Roth v. United States and Alberts v. California, 354 U.S. 476, we held that obscenity is not subject to those guarantees. Application of an obscenity law to suppress a motion picture thus requires ascertainment of the "dim and uncertain line" that often separates obscenity from constitutionally protected expression. Bantam Books, Inc., v. Sullivan, 372 U.S. 58, 66; see Speiser v. Randall, 357 U.S. 513, 525.[2] It has been suggested that this is a task in which our Court need not involve itself. We are told that the determination whether a particular motion picture, book, or other work of expression is obscene can be treated as a purely factual judgment on which a jury's verdict is all but conclusive, or that in any event the decision can be left essentially to state and lower federal courts, with this Court exercising only a limited review such as that needed to determine whether the ruling below is supported by "sufficient evidence." The suggestion is appealing, since it would lift from our shoulders a difficult, recurring, and unpleasant task. But we cannot accept it. Such an abnegation of judicial supervision in this field would be inconsistent with our duty to uphold the constitutional guarantees. Since it is only "obscenity" that is excluded from the constitutional protection, the question whether a particular work is obscene necessarily implicates an issue of consti-

---

manufacture, draw, print, or make such articles or things, or sell, give away, or show to a minor, a book, pamphlet, magazine, newspaper, story paper, or other paper devoted to the publication, or principally made up, of criminal news, police reports, or accounts of criminal deeds, or pictures and stories of immoral deeds, lust, or crime, or exhibit upon a street or highway or in a place which may be within the view of a minor, any of such books, papers, magazines, or pictures.

"Whoever violates this section shall be fined not less than two hundred nor more than two thousand dollars or imprisoned not less than one nor more than seven years, or both."

[2] It is too late in the day to argue that the location of the line is different, and the task of ascertaining it easier, when a state rather than a federal obscenity law is involved. The view that the constitutional guarantees of free expression do not apply as fully to the States as they do to the Federal Government was rejected in Roth-Alberts, supra, where the Court's single opinion applied the same standards to both a state and a federal conviction. Cf. Ker v. California, 374 U.S. 23, 33; Malloy v. Hogan, [378 US. 1], 10-11.

tutional law. See Roth v. United States, supra, 354 U.S., at 497-498 (separate opinion). Such an issue, we think, must ultimately be decided by this Court. Our duty admits of no "substitute for facing up to the tough individual problems of constitutional judgment involved in every obscenity case." Id., at 498; see Manual Enterprises, Inc., v. Day, 370 U.S. 478, 488 (opinion of Harlan, J.).[3]

In other areas involving constitutional rights under the Due Process Clause, the Court has consistently recognized its duty to apply the applicable rules of law upon the basis of an independent review of the facts of each case. . . . We cannot understand why the Court's duty should be any different in the present case, where Jacobellis has been subjected to a criminal conviction for disseminating a work of expression and is challenging that conviction as a deprivation of rights guaranteed by the First and Fourteenth Amendments. Nor can we understand why the Court's performance of its constitutional and judicial function in this sort of case should be denigrated by such epithets as "censor" or "super-censor." In judging alleged obscenity the Court is no more "censoring" expression than it has in other cases "censored" criticism of judges and public officials, advocacy of governmental overthrow, or speech alleged to constitute a breach of the peace. Use of an opprobrious label can neither obscure nor impugn the Court's performance of its obligation to test challenged judgments against the guarantees of the First and Fourteenth Amendments and, in doing so, to delineate the scope of constitutionally protected speech. Hence we reaffirm the principle that, in "obscenity" cases as in all others involving rights derived from the First Amendment guarantees of free expression, this Court cannot avoid making an independ-

[3] See Kingsley Int'l Pictures Corp. v. Regents, 360 U.S. 684, 708 (separate opinion): "It is sometimes said that this court should shun considering the particularities of individual cases in this difficult field lest the Court become a final 'board of censorship.' But I cannot understand why it should be thought that the process of constitutional judgment in this realm somehow stands apart from that involved in other fields, particularly those presenting questions of due process. . . ."

See also Lockhart and McClure, Censorship of Obscenity: The Developing Constitutional Standards, 45 Minn. L. Rev. 5, 116 (1960): "This obligation — to reach an independent judgment in applying constitutional standards and criteria to constitutional issues that may be cast by lower courts 'in the form of determinations of fact' — appears fully applicable to findings of obscenity by juries, trial courts, and administrative agencies. The Supreme Court is subject to that obligation, as is every court before which the constitutional issue is raised."

And see id., at 119:

"It may be true . . . that judges 'possess no special expertise' qualifying them 'to supervise the private morals of the Nation' or to decide 'what movies are good or bad for local communities.' But they do have a far keener understanding of the importance of free expression than do most government administrators or jurors, and they have had considerable experience in making value judgments of the type required by the constitutional standards for obscenity. If freedom is to be preserved, neither government censorship experts nor juries can be left to make the final effective decisions restraining free expression. Their decisions must be subject to effective, independent review, and we know of no group better qualified for that review than the appellate judges of this country under the guidance of the Supreme Court."

ent constitutional judgment on the facts of the case as to whether the material involved is constitutionally protected.[6]

The question of the proper standard for making this determination has been the subject of much discussion and controversy since our decision in Roth seven years ago. Recognizing that the test for obscenity enunciated there — "whether to the average person, applying contemporary community standards, the dominant theme of the material taken as a whole appeals to prurient interest," 354 U.S., at 489 — is not perfect, we think any substitute would raise equally difficult problems, and we therefore adhere to that standard. We would reiterate, however, our recognition in Roth that obscenity is excluded from the constitutional protection only because it is "utterly without redeeming social importance," and that "the portrayal of sex, e.g., in art, literature and scientific works, is not itself sufficient reason to deny material the constitutional protection of freedom of speech and press." Id., at 484, 487. It follows that material dealing with sex in a manner that advocates ideas, Kingsley Int'l Pictures Corp. v. Regents, 360 U.S. 684, or that has literary or scientific or artistic value or any other form of social importance, may not be branded as obscenity and denied the constitutional protection.[7] Nor may the constitutional status of the material be made to turn on a "weighing" of its social importance against its prurient appeal, for a work cannot be proscribed unless it is "utterly" without social importance. See Zeitlin v. Arnebergh, 59 Cal. 2d 901, 920, 383 P.2d 152, 165, 31 Cal. Rptr. 800, 813 (1963). It should also be recognized that the Roth standard requires in the first instance a finding that the material "goes substantially beyond customary limits of candor in description or representation of such matters." This was a requirement of the Model Penal Code test that we approved in Roth, 354 U.S., at 487, n.20, and it is explicitly reaffirmed in the more recent Proposed Official Draft of the Code.[8] In the absence of such a deviation from society's standards of decency,

[6] This is precisely what the Court did in Times Film Corp. v. City of Chicago, 355 U.S. 35; One, Inc., v. Olesen, 355 U.S. 371; and Sunshine Book Co. v. Summerfield, 355 U.S. 372. The obligation has been recognized by state courts as well. See, e.g., State v. Hudson County News Co., 41 N.J. 247, 256-257, 196 A.2d 225, 230 (1963); Zeitlin v. Arnebergh, 59 Cal. 2d 901, 909-911, 383 P.2d 152, 157-158, 31 Cal. Rptr. 800, 805-806 (1963); People v. Richmond County News, Inc., 9 N.Y.2d 578, 580-581, 175 N.E.2d 681, 681-682, 216 N.Y.S.2d 369, 370 (1961). See also American Law Institute, Model Penal Code, Proposed Official Draft (May 4, 1962), §251.4(4).

Nor do we think our duty of constitutional adjudication in this area can properly be relaxed by reliance on a "sufficient evidence" standard of review. Even in judicial review of administrative agency determinations, questions of "constitutional fact" have been held to require de novo review. Ng Fung Ho v. White, 259 U.S. 276, 284-285; Crowell v. Benson, 285 U.S. 22, 54-65.

[7] See, e.g., Attorney General v. Book Named "Tropic of Cancer," 345 Mass. 11, 184 N.E.2d 328 (Mass. 1962); Zeitlin v. Arnebergh, 59 Cal. 2d 901, 383 P.2d 152, 31 Cal. Rptr. 800 (1963).

[8] American Law Institute, Model Penal Code, Proposed Official Draft (May 4, 1962), §251.4(1):

"Material is obscene if, considered as a whole, its predominant appeal is to prurient interest . . . and if *in addition* it goes substantially beyond customary limits of candor in describing or representing such matters." (Italics added.)

we do not see how any official inquiry into the allegedly prurient appeal of a work of expression can be squared with the guarantees of the First and Fourteenth Amendments. See Manual Enterprises, Inc., v. Day, 370 U.S. 478, 482-488 (opinion of Harlan, J.).

It has been suggested that the "contemporary community standards" aspect of the Roth test implies a determination of the constitutional question of obscenity in each case by the standards of the particular local community from which the case arises. This is an incorrect reading of Roth. The concept of "contemporary community standards" was first expressed by Judge Learned Hand in United States v. Kennerley, 209 F. 119, 121 (D.C.S.D.N.Y. 1913), where he said:

"Yet, if the time is not yet when men think innocent all that which is honestly germane to a pure subject, however little it may mince its words, still I scarcely think that they would forbid all which might corrupt the most corruptible, or that society is prepared to accept for its own limitations those which may perhaps be necessary to the weakest of its members. If there be no abstract definition, such as I have suggested, should not the word 'obscene' be allowed to indicate the present critical point in the compromise between candor and shame at which *the community may have arrived here and now?* . . . To put thought in leash to the *average conscience of the time* is perhaps tolerable, but to fetter it by the necessities of the lowest and least capable seems a fatal policy.

"Nor is it an objection, I think, that such an interpretation gives to the words of the statute a varying meaning from time to time. Such words as these do not embalm the precise morals of an age or place; while they presuppose that some things will always be shocking to the public taste, the vague subject matter is left to the gradual development of general notions about what is decent. . . ." (Italics added.)

It seems clear that in this passage Judge Hand was referring not to state and local "communities," but rather to "the community" in the sense of "society at large; . . . the public, or people in general." [9] Thus, he recognized that under his standard the concept of obscenity would have a "varying meaning from time to time" — not from county to county, or town to town.

We do not see how any "local" definition of the "community" could properly be employed in delineating the area of expression that is protected by the Federal Constitution. Mr. Justice Harlan pointed out in Manual Enterprises, Inc., v. Day, supra, 370 U.S., at 488, that a standard based on a particular local community would have "the intolerable consequence of denying some sections of the country access to material, there deemed acceptable, which in others might be considered offensive to prevailing community standards of decency. Cf. Butler v. Michigan, 352 U.S. 380." It is true that Manual Enterprises dealt with the federal statute banning obscenity from the mails. But the mails are not the only means by which works of expression cross local-

[9] Webster's New International Dictionary (2d ed. 1949), at 542.

community lines in this country. It can hardly be assumed that all the patrons of a particular library, bookstand, or motion picture theater are residents of the smallest local "community" that can be drawn around that establishment. Furthermore, to sustain the suppression of a particular book or film in one locality would deter its dissemination in other localities where it might be held not obscene, since sellers and exhibitors would be reluctant to risk criminal conviction in testing the variation between the two places. It would be a hardy person who would sell a book or exhibit a film anywhere in the land after this Court had sustained the judgment of one "community" holding it to be outside the constitutional protection. The result would thus be "to restrict the public's access to forms of the printed word which the State could not constitutionally suppress directly." Smith v. California, 361 U.S. 147, 154.

It is true that local communities throughout the land are in fact diverse, and that in cases such as this one the Court is confronted with the task of reconciling the rights of such communities with the rights of individuals. Communities vary, however, in many respects other than their toleration of alleged obscenity, and such variances have never been considered to require or justify a varying standard for application of the Federal Constitution. The Court has regularly been compelled, in reviewing criminal convictions challenged under the Due Process Clause of the Fourteenth Amendment, to reconcile the conflicting rights of the local community which brought the prosecution and of the individual defendant. Such a task is admittedly difficult and delicate, but it is inherent in the Court's duty of determining whether a particular conviction worked a deprivation of rights guaranteed by the Federal Constitution. The Court has not shrunk from discharging that duty in other areas, and we see no reason why it should do so here. The Court has explicitly refused to tolerate a result whereby "the constitutional limits of free expression in the Nation would vary with state lines," Pennekamp v. Florida, supra, 328 U.S., at 335; we see even less justification for allowing such limits to vary with town or county lines. We thus reaffirm the position taken in Roth to the effect that the constitutional status of an allegedly obscene work must be determined on the basis of a national standard.[10] It is, after all, a national Constitution we are expounding.

We recognize the legitimate and indeed exigent interest of States and localities throughout the Nation in preventing the dissemination of material deemed harmful to children. But that interest does not justify a total suppression of such material, the effect of which would be to "reduce the adult population . . . to reading only what is fit for children." Butler v. Michigan, 352 U.S. 380, 383. State and local authorities might well consider whether their objectives in this area would be better served by laws aimed specifically at

---

[10] See State v. Hudson County News Co., 41 N.J. 247, 266, 196 A.2d 225, 235 (1963). Lockhart and McClure, note 3, supra, 45 Minn. L. Rev., at 108-112; American Law Institute, Model Penal Code, Tentative Draft No. 6 (May 6, 1957), at 45; Proposed Official Draft (May 4, 1962), §251.4(4)(d).

preventing distribution of objectionable material to children, rather than at totally prohibiting its dissemination.[11] Since the present conviction is based upon exhibition of the film to the public at large and not upon its exhibition to children, the judgment must be reviewed under the strict standard applicable in determining the scope of the expression that is protected by the Constitution.

We have applied that standard to the motion picture in question. "The Lovers" involves a woman bored with her life and marriage who abandons her husband and family for a young archaeologist with whom she has suddenly fallen in love. There is an explicit love scene in the last reel of the film, and the State's objections are based almost entirely upon that scene. The film was favorably reviewed in a number of national publications, although disparaged in others, and was rated by at least two critics of national stature among the best films of the year in which it was produced. It was shown in approximately 100 of the larger cities in the United States, including Columbus and Toledo, Ohio. We have viewed the film, in the light of the record made in the trial court, and we conclude that it is not obscene within the standards enunciated in Roth v. United States and Alberts v. California, which we reaffirm here.

Reversed.

NOTES

1. Mr. Justice White concurred in the judgment without opinion. Justices Black and Douglas concurred on the ground that "conviction of appellant or anyone else for exhibiting a motion picture abridges freedom of press . . . ." 378 U.S. at 196. Mr. Justice Stewart's short concurrence stated:

". . . I have reached the conclusion, which I think is confirmed at least by negative implication in the Court's decisions since Roth and Alberts, that under the First and Fourteenth Amendments criminal laws in this area are constitutionally limited to hard-core pornography. I shall not today attempt further to define the kinds of material I understand to be embraced within that shorthand description; and perhaps I could never succeed in intelligibly doing so. But I know it when I see it, and the motion picture involved in this case is not that." 378 U.S. at 197.

Mr. Justice Goldberg's concurrence reiterated the protection afforded motion pictures in Burstyn v. Wilson, cited in the principal opinion, and stressed the fleeting character of the questioned scene. The Chief Justice, with whom Mr. Justice Clark joined, would use the Roth test applying local community standards and review cases applying the Roth rule only on the question of the "sufficiency" of the evidence. Mr. Justice Harlan dissented, reiterating his position in the Roth case that a federal test such as that developed in Roth, which he here accepted, be limited to federal cases:

"As to the States, I would make the federal test one of rationality. I would not prohibit them from banning any material which, taken as a whole, has been rea-

[11] See State v. Settle, 90 R.I. 195, 156 A.2d 921 (1959).

sonably found in state judicial proceedings to treat with sex in a fundamentally offensive manner, under rationally established criteria for judging such material." 378 U.S. at 204.

2. In 1966 the Supreme Court held "Fanny Hill" was not obscene under the Roth-Jacobellis test. A Book Named "John Cleland's Memoirs of a Woman of Pleasure" v. Attorney General of Massachusetts, 383 U.S. 413, 86 S. Ct. 975, 16 L. Ed. 2d 1 (1966). Mr. Justice Brennan, with whom the Chief Justice and Mr. Justice Fortas joined, stated:

"The Supreme Judicial Court erred in holding that a book need not be 'unqualifiedly worthless before it can be deemed obscene.' A book cannot be proscribed unless it is found to be *utterly* without redeeming social value. This is so even though the book is found to possess the requisite prurient appeal and to be patently offensive. Each of the three federal constitutional criteria is to be applied independently; the social value of the book can neither be weighed against nor canceled by its prurient appeal or patent offensiveness. Hence, even on the view of the court below that Memoirs possessed only a modicum of social value, its judgment must be reversed as being founded on an erroneous interpretation of a federal constitutional standard." 383 U.S. at 419-420.

Mr. Justice Douglas concurred, noting the lack of proof of harm stemming from obscenity, and stressed the absoluteness of the First Amendment, as did Mr. Justice Black, who also pointed out the impossibility of administering the Court's standard except on a highly subjective basis. He indicated that he preferred prior censorship to criminal punishment based on uncertain standards and censorship policy made by governmental institutions other than the Court, if censorship there must be. Mr. Justice Stewart concurred on the ground that "Fanny Hill" is not "hard core pornography" which he stated to be "a distinct and easily identifiable class of material." [1] 383 U.S. at 499. Mr. Justice Clark's dissent read in part as follows:

"Let me first pinpoint the effect of today's holding in the obscenity field. While there is no majority opinion in this case, there are three Justices who import a new test into that laid down in Roth v. United States, 354 U.S. 476 (1957), namely, that '[a] book cannot be proscribed unless it is found to be *utterly* without redeeming social value.' I agree with my Brother White that such a condition rejects the basic holding of Roth and gives the smut artist free rein to carry on his dirty business.

[1] In footnote 3 the opinion quotes with approval a description from the Solicitor General's brief:

". . . Such materials include photographs, both still and motion picture, with no pretense of artistic value, graphically depicting acts of sexual intercourse, including various acts of sodomy and sadism, and sometimes involving several participants in scenes of orgy-like character. They also include strips of drawings in comic-book format grossly depicting similar activities in an exaggerated fashion. There are, in addition, pamphlets and booklets, sometimes with photographic illustrations, verbally describing such activities in a bizarre manner with no attempt whatsoever to afford portrayals of character or situation and with no pretense to literary value. All of this material . . . cannot conceivably be characterized as embodying communication of ideas or artistic values inviolate under the First Amendment. . . ."

The opinion also notes in footnote 4 that government counsel during oral argument stated that the vast majority of prosecutions under the federal statute involve this type of material, result in guilty pleas, and never are seen by the Supreme Court.

The Stewart opinion is written as a dissent in the Ginzburg case, infra, but is applicable also to the "Fanny Hill" case. See 383 U.S. at 421.

My vote in that case — which was the deciding one for the majority opinion — was cast solely because the Court declared the test of obscenity to be: 'whether to the average person, applying contemporary community standards, the dominant theme of the material taken as a whole appeals to prurient interest.' I understood that test to include only two constitutional requirements: (1) the book must be judged as a whole, not by its parts; and (2) it must be judged in terms of its appeal to the prurient interest of the average person, applying contemporary community standards. Indeed, obscenity was denoted in Roth as having *'such slight social value as a step to truth that any benefit that may be derived . . . is clearly outweighed by the social interest in order and morality. . . .'* At 485 (quoting Chaplinsky v. New Hampshire, 315 U.S. 568, 572 (1942). Moreover, in no subsequent decision of this Court has any 'utterly without redeeming social value' test been suggested, much less expounded. . . . The first reference to such a test was made by my Brother Brennan in Jacobellis v. Ohio, 378 U.S. 184, 191 (1964), seven years after Roth. . . . Significantly no opinion in Jacobellis, other than that of my Brother Brennan, mentioned the 'utterly without redeeming social importance' test which he there introduced into our many and varied previous opinions in obscenity cases. Indeed, rather than recognizing the 'utterly without social importance' test The Chief Justice in his dissent in Jacobellis, which I joined, specifically stated:

'In light of the foregoing, I would reiterate my acceptance of the rule of the Roth case: *Material is obscene and not constitutionally protected against regulation and proscription* if "to the average person, applying contemporary community standards the dominant theme of the material taken as a whole appeals to prurient interest." ' (Emphasis added). At 202.

The Chief Justice and I further asserted that the enforcement of this rule should be committed to the state and federal courts whose judgments made pursuant to the Roth rule we would accept, limiting our review to a consideration of whether there is 'sufficient evidence' in the record to support a finding of obscenity. At 202.

"Three members of the majority hold that reversal here is necessary solely because their novel 'utterly without redeeming social value' test was not properly interpreted or applied by the Supreme Judicial Court of Massachusetts. Massachusetts now has to retry the case although the 'Findings of Fact, Rulings of Law and Order for Final Decree' of the trial court specifically held that 'this book is "utterly without redeeming social importance" in the fields of art, literature, science, news or ideas of any social importance and that it is obscene, indecent and impure.' . . . None of these findings of the trial court were overturned on appeal, although the Supreme Judicial Court of Massachusetts observed in addition that 'the fact that the testimony may indicate this book has some minimal literary value does not mean it is of any social importance. We do not interpret the "social importance" test as requiring that a book which appeals to prurient interest and is patently offensive must be unqualifiedly worthless before it can be deemed obscene.' My Brother Brennan reverses on the basis of this casual statement, despite the specific findings of the trial court. Why, if the statement is erroneous, Brother Brennan does not affirm the holding of the trial court which beyond question is correct, one cannot tell. This course has often been followed in other cases." 383 U.S. at 441-445.

After summarizing the facts on the basis of which Mr. Justice Clark believed the book's whole purpose was to arouse the prurient interest and on the basis of which he regarded the book as "patently offensive," facts which "weigh heavily in any appraisal of the book's claims to 'redeeming social importance,' " the opinion continues:

"Let us now turn to evidence of the book's alleged social value. While unfortunately the State offered little testimony,[2] the defense called several experts to attest that the book has literary merit and historical value. A careful reading of testimony, however, reveals that it has no substance. For example, the first witness testified:

'I think it is a work of art . . . it asks for and receives a literary response . . . presented in an orderly and organized fashion, with a fictional central character, and with a literary style . . . . I think the central character is . . . what I call an intellectual . . . someone who is extremely curious about life and who seeks . . . to record with accuracy the details of the external world, physical sensations, psychological responses . . . an empiricist . . . . I find that this tells me things . . . about the 18th century I might not otherwise know.'

If a book of art is one that asks for and receives a literary response, Memoirs is no work of art. The sole response evoked by the book is sensual. Nor does the orderly presentation of Memoirs make a difference; it presents nothing but lascivious scenes organized solely to arouse prurient interest and produce sustained erotic tension.[3] Certainly the book's baroque style cannot vitiate the determination of obscenity. From a legal standpoint, we must remember that obscenity is no less obscene though it be expressed in 'elaborate language.' Indeed, the more meticulous its presentation, the more it appeals to the prurient interest. To say that Fanny is an 'intellectual' is an insult to those who travel under that tag. She was nothing but a harlot — a sensualist — exploiting her sexual attractions which she sold for fun, for money, for lodging and keep, for an inheritance, and finally for a husband. If she was curious about life, her curiosity extended only to the pursuit of sexual delight wherever she found it. The book describes nothing in the 'external world' except bawdy houses and debaucheries. As an empiricist, Fanny confines her observations and 'experiments' to sex, with primary attention to depraved, lewd, and deviant practices.

"Other experts produced by the defense testified that the book emphasizes the profound 'idea that a sensual passion is only truly experienced when it is associated with the emotion of love' and that the sexual relationship 'can be a wholesome, healthy, experience itself,' whereas in certain modern novels 'the relationship between the sexes is seen as another manifestation of modern decadence, insterility or perversion.' In my view this proves nothing as to social value. The state court properly gave such testimony no probative weight. A review offered by the defense noted that 'where "pornography" does not brutalize, it idealizes. The book is, in

---

[2] In a preface to the paperback edition, "A Note on the American History of Memoirs of a Woman of Pleasure," the publisher itself mentions several critics who denied the book had any literary merit and found it totally undistinguished. These critics included Ralph Thompson and Clifton Fadiman. P. xviii.

[3] As one review stated: "Yet all these pangs of defloration are in the service of erotic pleasure — Fanny's and the reader's. Postponing the culmination of Fanny's deflowering is equivalent to postponing the point where the reader has a mental orgasm."

this sense, an erotic fantasy — and a male fantasy, at that, put into the mind of a woman. The male organ is phenomenal to the point of absurdity.' Finally, it saw the book as 'a minor fantasy, deluding as a guide to conduct, but respectful of our delight in the body . . . an interesting footnote in the history of the English novel.' These unrelated assertions reveal to me nothing whatever of literary, historical, or social value. Another review called the book 'a great novel . . . one which turns its convention upside down . . . .' Admittedly Cleland did not attempt 'high art' because he was writing 'an erotic novel. He can skip the elevation and get on with the erections.' Fanny's 'downfall' is seen as 'one long delightful swoon into the depths of pleasurable sensation.' Rather than indicating social value in the book, this evidence reveals just the contrary. Another item offered by the defense described Memoirs as being 'widely accredited as the first deliberately dirty novel in English.' However, the reviewer found Fanny to be 'no common harlot. Her "Memoirs" combine literary grace with a disarming enthusiasm for an activity which is, after all, only human. What is more, she never uses a dirty word.' The short answer to such 'expertise' is that none of these so-called attributes have any value to society. On the contrary, they accentuate the prurient appeal.

"Another expert described the book as having 'detectable literary merit' since it reflects 'an effort to interpret a rather complex character . . . going through a number of very different adventures.' To illustrate his assertion that the 'writing is very skillfully done' this expert pointed to the description of a whore, 'Phoebe, who is "red-faced, fat and in her early 50's, who waddles into a room." She doesn't walk in, she waddles in.' Given this standard for 'skillful writing,' it is not surprising that he found the book to have merit.

"The remaining experts testified in the same manner, claiming the book to be a 'record of the historical, psychological, [and] social events of the period.' One has but to read the history of the 18th century to disprove this assertion. The story depicts nothing besides the brothels that are present in metropolitan cities in every period of history. One expert noticed 'in this book a tendency away from nakedness during the sexual act which I find an interesting sort of sociological observation' on tastes different from contemporary ones. As additional proof, he marvels that Fanney 'refers constantly to the male sexual organ as an engine . . . which is pulling you away from the way these events would be described in the 19th or 20th century.' How this adds social value to the book is beyond my comprehension. It only indicates the lengths to which these experts go in their effort to give the book some semblance of value. For example, the ubiquitous descriptions of sexual acts are excused as being necessary in tracing the 'moral progress' of the heroine, and the giving of a silver watch to a servant is found to be 'an odd and interesting custom that I would like to know more about.' This only points up the bankruptcy of Memoirs in both purpose and content, adequately justifying the trial court's finding that it had absolutely no social value.

"It is, of course, the duty of the judge or the jury to determine the question of obscenity, viewing the book by contemporary community standards. It can accept the appraisal of experts or discount their testimony in the light of the material itself or other relevant testimony. So-called 'literary obscenity,' *i.e.,* the use of erotic fantasies of the hard-core type clothed in an engaging literary style has no constitutional protection. If a book deals solely with erotic material in a manner calculated to appeal to the prurient interest, it matters not that it may be expressed in beautiful prose. There are obviously dynamic connections between art and sex — the emotional, intellectual, and physical — but where the former is used solely to promote prurient appeal, it cannot claim constitutional immunity. Cleland uses this technique to promote the prurient appeal of Memoirs. It is true that Fanny's perverse experiences finally bring from her the observation that 'the heights of [sexual] enjoyment cannot be achieved until true affection prepares the bed of passion.' But this merely emphasizes that sex, wherever and however found, remains the sole theme of Memoirs. In my view, the book's repeated and unrelieved appeals to the prurient interest of the average person leave it utterly without redeeming social importance." 383 U.S. at 446-450.

Mr. Justice Harlan dissented on the basis of the rationality test he had stated before with respect to state proceedings as contrasted with federal proceedings, which he would, like Mr. Justice Stewart, restrict to the "hard-core pornography" category:

"From my standpoint, the Fourteenth Amendment requires of a State only that it apply criteria rationally related to the accepted notion of obscenity and that it reach results not wholly out of step with current American standards. As to criteria, it should be adequate if the court or jury considers such elements as offensiveness, pruriency, social value and the like. . . . I think it more satisfactory to acknowledge that on this record the book has been shown to have some quantum of social value, that it may at the same time be deemed offensive and salacious, and that the State's decision to weigh these elements and to ban this particular work does not exceed constitutional limits." 383 U.S. at 458-459. The Harlan dissent concludes with the following allusion to the problem of judicial administration:

"A final aspect of the obscenity problem is the role this Court is to play in administering its standards, a matter that engendered justified concern at the oral argument of the cases now decided. Short of saying that no material relating to sex may be banned, or that all of it may be, I do not see how this Court can escape the task of reviewing obscenity decisions on a case-by-case basis. The views of literary or other experts could be made controlling, but those experts had their say in 'Fanny Hill' and apparently the majority is no more willing than I to say that Massachusetts must abide by their verdict. Yet I venture to say that the Court's burden of decision would be ameliorated under the constitutional principles that I have advocated. 'Hard-core pornography' for judging federal cases is one of the more tangible concepts in the field. As to the States, the due latitude my approach would leave them ensures that only the unusual case would require plenary review and correction by this Court." 383 U.S. at 459-460.

Mr. Justice White's dissent, as indicated in Mr. Justice Clark's opinion, was based on the rejection of the "social importance" criterion as an independent test.

With Mr. Justice Clark's dissent compare excerpts from the book review by Gore Vidal, reprinted in section 4 of this Note, and the book review of Story of O, reprinted in section 7.

3. (a) In another case decided on the same day as the "Fanny Hill" case, Mishkin v. New York, 383 U.S. 502, 86 S. Ct. 958, 16 L. Ed. 2d 56 (1966), Mr. Justice Brennan, in an opinion affirming a conviction under the New York obscenity law, further attempted to clarify the Roth-Jacobellis standard:

"The New York courts have interpreted obscenity in §1141 to cover only so-called 'hard-core pornography,' see People v. Richmond County News, Inc., 9

N.Y.2d 78, 586-587, 175 N.E.2d 681, 685-686 (1961). . . . Since that definition of obscenity is more stringent than the Roth definition, the judgment that the constitutional criteria are satisfied is implicit in the application of §1141 below. Indeed, appellant's sole contention regarding the nature of the material is that some of the books involved in this prosecution,[6] those depicting various deviant sexual practices, such as flagellation, fetishism, and lesbianism, do not satisfy the prurient-appeal requirement because they do not appeal to a prurient interest of the 'average person' in sex, that 'instead of stimulating the erotic, they disgust and sicken.' We reject this argument as being founded on an unrealistic interpretation of the prurient-appeal requirement.

"Where the material is designed for and primarily disseminated to a clearly defined deviant sexual group, rather than the public at large, the prurient-appeal requirement of the Roth test is satisfied if the dominant theme of the material taken as a whole appeals to the prurient interest in sex of the members of that group. The reference to the 'average' or 'normal' person in Roth, 354 U.S., at 489-490, does not foreclose this holding.[7] In regard to the prurient-appeal requirement, the concept of the 'average' or 'normal' person was employed in Roth to serve the essentially negative purpose of expressing our rejection of that aspect of the Hicklin test, Regina v. Hicklin, [1868] L.R. 3 Q.B. 360, that made the impact on the most susceptible person determinative. We adjust the prurient-appeal requirement to social realities by permitting the appeal of this type of material to be assessed in terms of the sexual interests of its intended and probable recipient group; and since our holding requires that the recipient group be defined with more specificity than in terms of sexually immature persons,[8] it also avoids the inadequacy of the most-susceptible-person facet of the Hicklin test." 383 U.S. at 508-509.

Justices Black, Stewart, and Douglas dissented, and Mr. Justice Harlan noted that on the issue of obscenity he affirmed on the basis of his dissent in the "Fanny Hill" case.

(b) For an earlier modification of the Roth "average person" test by a lower federal court to allow importation of material by the Institute for Sex Research of Indiana (Kinsey Institute), see United States v. 31 Photographs, 156 F. Supp. 350 (S.D. N.Y. 1957). Cf. also United States v. Klaw, 350 F.2d 155 (2d Cir. 1965) (noting possibility of variable standard for "deviate" audiences).

(c) A.L.I. Model Penal Code §251.4(1)(1962) reads in part as follows:

"Predominant appeal shall be judged with reference to ordinary adults unless it

---

[6] It could not be plausibly maintained that all of the appellant's books, including those dominated by descriptions of relatively normal heterosexual relationships, are devoid of the requisite prurient appeal.

[7] See Manual Enterprises, Inc. v. Day, 370 U.S. 478, 482 (opinion of Harlan, J.); Lockhart and McClure, Censorship of Obscenity: The Developing Constitutional Standards, 45 Minn. L. Rev. 5, 72-73 (1960).

It is true that some of the material in Alberts v. California, decided with Roth, resembled the deviant material involved here. But no issue involving the obscenity of the material was before us in either case. 354 U.S., at 481, n.8. The basic question for decision there was whether the publication and sale of obscenity, however defined, could be criminally punished in light of First Amendment guarantees. Our discussion of definition was not intended to develop all the nuances of a definition required by the constitutional guarantees.

[8] See generally, 1 American Handbook of Psychiatry (Arieti ed. 1959) 593-604, for a description of the pertinent types of deviant sexual groups.

appears from the character of the material or the circumstances of its dissemination to be designed for children or other specially susceptible audience." The Code also exempts dissemination to institutions or individuals having scientific or other special justification for possessing such material. Ibid. See also Mr. Chief Justice Warren's concurring opinion in the Roth case, supra; the Court of Appeals opinion in Manual Enterprises, Inc. v. Day, 289 F.2d 455 (D.C. Cir. 1961); Lockhart and McLure, Censorship of Obscenity: The Developing Constitutional Standards, 45 Minn. L. Rev. at 68-88 (1960), cited in the Mishkin opinion, generally advocating a standard of "variable obscenity"; and Emerson, Toward a General Theory of the First Amendment, 72 Yale L.J. 877, 939 (1963).

Statutory attempts to define as obscene for minors that which is not obscene for adults are also discussed in Note, "For Adults Only": The Constitutionality of Governmental Film Censorship by Age Classification, 69 Yale L.J. 141 (1959), commenting on Paramount Film Distributing Corp. v. City of Chicago, 172 F. Supp. 69 (N.D. Ill. 1959); Gerber, A Suggested Solution to the Riddle of Obscenity, 112 U. Pa. L. Rev. 834, 847-852 (1964); Rice, The Youth-Obscenity Problem — A Proposal, 52 Ky. L.J. 429 (1964). For foreign experience see St. John-Stevas, Obscenity and the Law 212-213, 221-231, 243, 247-250, 256 (1956); Green, Obscenity, Censorship, and Juvenile Delinquency, 14 U. Toronto L.J. 229 (1962).

(d) Butler v. Michigan, 352 U.S. 380, 77 S. Ct. 524, 1 L. Ed. 2d 412 (1957), referred to in Mr. Justice Brennan's Jacobellis opinion, involved a statute which prohibited the distribution to the general reading public of material "containing obscene, immoral, lewd or lascivious language, or . . . prints, pictures . . . [etc.] . . . tending to incite minors to violent or depraved or immoral acts, manifestly tending to the corruption of the morals of youth. . . ." Mr. Justice Frankfurter's opinion read in part:

"[W]e are free to put aside the claim that the Michigan law falls within the doctrine whereby a New York obscenity statute was found invalid in Winters v. New York, 333 U.S. 507. . . .

"The State insists that, by thus quarantining the general reading public against books not too rugged for grown men and women in order to shield juvenile innocence, it is exercising its power to promote the general welfare. Surely, this is to burn the house to roast the pig. Indeed, the Solicitor General of Michigan has, with characteristic candor, advised the Court that Michigan has a statute specifically designed to protect its children against obscene matter 'tending to the corruption of the morals of youth.' But the appellant was not convicted for violating this statute.

"We have before us legislation not reasonably restricted to the evil with which it is said to deal. The incidence of this enactment is to reduce the adult population of Michigan to reading only what is fit for children. It thereby arbitrarily curtails one of those liberties of the individual, now enshrined in the Due Process Clause of the Fourteenth Amendment, that history has attested as the indispensable conditions for the maintenance and progress of a free society. We are constrained to reverse this conviction." 352 U.S. at 382-384.

(e) In State v. Locks, 94 Ariz. 134, 382 P.2d 241 (1963), the Supreme Court of Arizona reversed the conviction of a bookseller for selling "Girlie" magazines to a 17-year-old boy under a statute punishing any "person who by any act, causes, encourages, or contributes to the . . . delinquency of a child . . . or who for any cause is responsible therefor. A.R.S. §13-822, subd. A." The conviction was reversed because the jury was read the statute's provision concerning liberal construction. In the course of the opinion, however, the court found the statute constitutional and applicable:

" 'Delinquency' is defined by A.R.S. §13-821, subd. C as 'Any act which tends to debase or injure the morals, health or welfare of a child.' Since one of the principal purposes of the statute is to prevent the delinquency of children, acts or omissions which tend to cause or contribute to a minor's delinquency are made crimes and punishable as such. Under the statute it was and is unnecessary for the prosecution to establish that defendant's acts actually debased or injured the morals of the child . . . but only that they may tend to do so. Moreover, the statute is comprehensive enough to include acts leading to unacceptable social patterns in later adult life. . . .

"It is to be noticed the information specifies the act of selling obscene or indecent writings, papers, books and pictures as tending to debase and injure the morals, health and welfare of the child. The prosecution categorically classified the publications as obscene but whether they are so in fact is a matter unrelated to the inquiry here. It can not be doubted but that the jury could find that the sale of publications or material which would tend to corrupt a child's mind would contribute in some measure to debase and injure his morals. It could have believed that to the immature the suggestion that meretricious sexual relations are acceptable social conduct may be more injurious to the welfare of the child than an act of physical ravishment. Hence, we do not find it necessary to reach the question whether these publications are obscene so as to be without the protection of the First Amendment to the Constitution of the United States. E.g. Manual Enterprises v. Day, 370 U.S. 478, 82 S. Ct. 1432, 8 L. Ed. 2d 639; Roth v. United States, 354 U.S. 476, 77 S. Ct. 1304, 1 L. Ed. 2d 1498.

"Defendant has assigned as error that there was no showing he encouraged or contributed to the delinquency of a minor. The short answer is the testimony established that the original purchases on February 25th, 1951 were induced by the defendant directing the minor's attention to the magazines. If this were not enough, we would still be of the view that one whose choice of business is that of defendant's has the responsibility of seeing that this type of publication does not reach the hands of the emotionally immature. If knowledge of content were necessary, the covers alone in the instant case would be sufficient to alert the vendor thereof." 94 Ariz. at 136-137, 382 P.2d at 242-243.

4. With Mr. Justice Brennan's discussion in the Mishkin case of "deviant sexual practices" as appealing to a special audience and Mr. Justice Clark's discussion in the "Fanny Hill" case of the lack of social value of a rather joyful account of prostitution, compare Gore Vidal, On Pornography, New York Review of Books, March 31, 1966, which reads in part:

"Our tribal standards are those of Moses combined with that military sense of caste which characterized those savage tribesmen who did indeed engulf the world of cities. The contempt for people in trade one still finds amongst the WASP aristocracy, the sense of honor (furtive but gnawing), the pride in family, the loyalty to class and (though covert) the admiration for the military virtues and physical strength are all inherited not from our civilized predecessors who lived in the great cities but from their conquerors, the wandering tribesmen, who planted no grain, built no cities, conducted no trade yet preyed successfully upon those who did these contemptible, unmanly things. Today of course we are all as mixed in values as in blood, but the unstated assumptions that it is better to be physically strong than wise, violent than gentle, continent than sensual, land-owner or coupon-clipper than shopkeeper linger on, a memorial to those marauding tribes who broke into history at the start of the Bronze Age and whose values are with us still, as the Gallup Poll attested recently, when it revealed that the President's war in Vietnam is most popular in the South, the most 'tribal' part of the United States. Yet the city is the glory of our race and today in the West, though we are all city-dwellers, we still accept as the true virtue the code of our wild conquerors, even though our actual lives do not conform to their laws, nor should they, nor should we feel guilty because they don't.

"In ten thousand years we have learned how to lengthen human lives but we have found no way to delay human puberty. As a result, between the economics of the city and the tabus of the tribe we have created a monstrous sexual ethic. To mention the most notorious paradox: It is not economically convenient for the adolescent to marry; it is not tribally correct for him to have sex outside of marriage. Solutions to this man-made problem range from insistence upon total chastity to a vague permissiveness which, worriedly, allows some sexuality if those involved are 'sincere' and 'mature' and 'loving.' Until this generation, tribal moralists could argue with perfect conviction that there was only one correct sexual equation: man plus woman equals baby; anything else is wrong. But now that half the world lives with famine and all the world by the year 2000 if Pope Paul's as yet unborn guests are allowed to attend the 'banquet of life,' the old equation has been changed to read: man plus woman equals baby equals famine. If the human race is to survive, population will have to be reduced drastically, if not by atomic war, by law, an unhappy prospect for civil liberties but better than starving to death. In any case, it is no longer possible to maintain that those sexual acts which do not create (or simulate the creation of) a child are unnatural; unless, to strike the eschatological note, it is indeed Nature's will that we perish through overpopulation, in which case reliable hands again clutch the keys of Peter.

"Fortunately, the pornographers appear to be on the side of survival. They make nothing of virginity deflowered, an important theme for two thousand years; they make nothing of it for the simple reason we make little of it. Straightforward adultery no longer fascinates the pornographer; the scarlet letter has faded. Incest, mysteriously, figures not at all in current pornographies. . . . The decline of incest as a marketable theme is probably due to today's inadequate middle-class housing. . . .

"Homosexuality is now taken entirely for granted by the pornographers because we take it for granted. Yet though there is considerable awareness nowadays of what people actually do, the ancient somewhat ambivalent hostility of the tribe persists, witness Time magazine's recent diagnosis of homosexuality as a 'pernicious sickness' like influenza or opposing the war in Vietnam. . . .

"Happily, in a single generation, science has changed many old assumptions. Economics has changed others. A woman can now easily support herself, independent of a man. With the slamming of Nora's door, the family ceased to be the inevitable social unit. Also, the newly affluent middle class can now pursue other pleasures. In the film 'The Collector,' a lower-class boy captures an educated girl and after alternately tormenting and boring her, he says balefully, 'If more people had more time and money, there would be a lot more of this.' This got an unintended laugh in the theater but he is probably right. Sexual experiment is becoming more open. A placid mid-Western town was recently appalled to learn that its young married set was systematically swapping wives. In the cities, group sex is popular, particularly among the young. Yet despite the new freedoms which the pornographers reflect (sadly for them since their craft may ultimately wither away) the world they show, though closer to human reality than that of the tribalists, reveals a new illness: the powerlessness that most people feel in an over-populated and over-organized society. The sado-masochist books that dominate this year's pornography are not the result of a new enthusiasm for the vice anglaise so much as a symptom of helplessness in a society where most of the male's aggressive-creative drive is thwarted. The will to prevail is a powerful one, and if it cannot be fulfilled in work or battle, it may find an outlet in sex. The man who wants to act out fantasies of tying up or being tied up is imposing upon his sex life a power drive which became socially undesirable once he got onto that escalator at IBM which, by predictable stages, will take him to early retirement and the long boredom of sunset years, medically prolonged. Solution of this problem will not be easy, to say the least.

"Meanwhile, effort must be made to bring what we think about sex and what we say about sex and what we do about sex into some kind of realistic relationship. Indirectly, the pornographers do this. They recognize that the only sexual norm is that there is none. Therefore, in a civilized society law should not function at all in the area of sex except to protect people from being 'interfered with' against their will. Unfortunately, even the most enlightened of the American state codes (Illinois) still assumes that since adultery is a tribal sin it must be regarded as a civil crime. It is not, and neither is prostitution, that most useful of human institutions. Traditionally, liberals have opposed prostitution on the ground that no one ought to be forced to sell his body because of poverty. Yet in the affluent society, prostitution continues to flourish for the simple reason that it is needed. If most men and women were forced to rely upon physical charm to attract lovers, their sexual lives would be not only meagre but in a youth-worshipping country like America painfully brief. Recognizing this state of affairs, a Swedish psychologist recently proposed state brothels for women as well as for men, in recognition of the sad biological fact that the middle-aged woman is at her sexual peak at a time when she is no longer able to compete successfully with younger women. As for the prostitutes themselves, they practice an art as legitimate as any other, somewhere between that of masseur and psychiatrist. The best are natural healers and, contrary to tribal superstition, they often enjoy their work. It is to the credit of today's pornographer that intentionally or not he is the one who tells us most about the extraordinary variety of human sexual response and in his way he shows us as we are, rather like those Fun House mirrors which even as they distort and mock the human figure never cease to reflect the real thing."

See also Address by Rev. John Graham, reprinted as an appendix to Mr. Justice Douglas' opinion in the "Fanny Hill" case, which reads in part:

"There is real irony in the fact that Fanny Hill, a rather naive young girl who becomes a prostitute, finds warmth, understanding and the meaning of love and faithfulness amid surroundings and situations which the society, as a whole, condemns as debased and depraved. The world outside the brothel affirms its faith in the dignity of man, but people are often treated as worthless and unimportant creatures. However, within the world of prostitution, Fanny Hill finds friendship, understanding, respect and is treated as a person of value. When her absent lover returns, she is not a lost girl of the gutter. One perceives that she is a whole and healthy person who has discovered the ability to love and be loved in a brothel.

"I think Cleland is suggesting that one must be cautious about what is condemned and what is held in honor. From Dr. Peale's viewpoint, the story of Fanny Hill is a tragedy because she did not demonstrate self-control. She refused to internalize the values inherent in the Judeo-Christian tradition and the catalog of sexual scenes in the book, fifty-two in all, are a symbol of the debased individual and the society in which he lives.

"Dr. Peale and others, would be correct in saying that Fanny Hill did not demonstrate self-control. She did, however, come to appreciate the value of self-expression. At no time were her 'clients' looked upon as a means to an end. She tried and did understand them and she was concerned about them as persons. When her lover, Charles, returned she was not filled with guilt and remorse. She accepted herself as she was and was able to offer him her love and devotion.

"I have a feeling that many people fear the book Fanny Hill, not because of its sexual scenes, but because the author raises serious questions with the issue of what is moral and what is immoral. He takes exception to the idea that repression and restraint create moral individuals. He develops the thought that self-expression is more human than self-control. And he dares to suggest that, in a situation which society calls immoral and debased, a genuine love and respect for life and for people, as human beings, can develop. Far from glorifying vice, John Cleland points an accusing finger at the individual who is so certain as to what it means to be a moral man." 383 U.S. at 436-438.

5. In a third case, decided on the same day as the "Fanny Hill" case, Ginzburg v. United States, 383 U.S. 463, 86 S. Ct. 942, 16 L. Ed. 2d 31 (1966), affirming a conviction under the mail obscenity statute, Mr. Justice Brennan added a fourth element to the Roth-Jacobellis test. The opinion reads in part as follows:

"The three publications were EROS, a hard-cover magazine of expensive format; Liaison, a bi-weekly newsletter; and The Housewife's Handbook on Selective Promiscuity (hereinafter the Handbook), a short book. The issue of EROS specified in the indictment, Vol. 1, No. 4, contains 15 articles and photo-essays on the subject of love, sex, and sexual relations. The specified issue of Liaison, Vol. 1, No. 1, contains a prefatory 'Letter from the Editors' announcing its dedication to 'keeping sex an art and preventing it from becoming a science.' The remainder of the issue consists of digests of two articles concerning sex and sexual relations which had earlier appeared in professional journals and a report of an interview with a psychotherapist who favors the broadest license in sexual relationships. As the trial judge noted, '[w]hile the treatment is largely superficial, it is presented entirely without restraint of any kind. According to defendants' own expert, it is entirely without literary merit.' 224 F. Supp., at 134. The Handbook purports to be a sexual autobiography detailing with complete candor the author's sexual experiences from age 3 to 36. The text includes, and prefatory and concluding sections of the book elaborate, her views on such subjects as sex education of children, laws regulating private consensual adult sexual practices, and the equality of women in sexual relationships. It was claimed at trial that women would find the book valuable, for example as a marriage manual or as an aid to the sex education of their children.

"Besides testimony as to the merit of the material, there was abundant evidence to show that each of the accused publications was originated or sold as stock in trade of the sordid business of pandering — 'the business of purveying textual or graphic matter openly advertised to appeal to the erotic interest of their customers.' [7] EROS early sought mailing privileges from the postmasters of Intercourse and Blue Ball, Pennsylvania. The trial court found the obvious, that these hamlets were chosen only for the value their names would have in furthering petitioners' efforts to sell their publications on the basis of salacious appeal;[8] the facilities of the post offices were inadequate to handle the anticipated volume of mail, and the privileges were denied. Mailing privileges were then obtained from the postmaster of Middlesex, New Jersey. EROS and Liaison thereafter mailed several million circulars soliciting subscriptions from that post office; over 5,500 copies of the Handbook were mailed.

"The 'leer of the sensualist' also permeates the advertising for the three publications. The circulars sent for EROS and Liaison stressed the sexual candor of the respective publications, and openly boasted that the publishers would take full advantage of what they regarded as an unrestricted license allowed by law in the expression of sex and sexual matters.[9] The advertising for the Handbook, appar-

[7] Roth v. United States, supra, 354 U.S., at 495-496 (Warren, C.J., concurring).

[8] Evidence relating to petitioners' efforts to secure mailing privileges from these post offices was, contrary to the suggestion of Mr. Justice Harlan in dissent, introduced for the purpose of supporting such a finding. Scienter had been stipulated prior to trial. The Government's position was revealed in the following colloquy, which occurred when it sought to introduce a letter to the postmaster of Blue Ball, Pennsylvania:

"The COURT. Who signed the letter?

"Mr. CREAMER. It is signed by Frank R. Brady, Associate Publisher of Mr. Ginzburg. It is on Eros Magazine, Incorporated's stationery.

"The COURT. And your objection is —

"Mr. SHAPIRO. It is in no way relevant to the particular issue or publication upon which the defendant has been indicted and in my view, even if there was an identification with respect to a particular issue, it would be of doubtful relevance in that event.

"The COURT. Anything else to say?

"Mr. CREAMER. If Your Honor pleases, there is a statement in this letter indicating that it would be advantageous to this publication to have it disseminated through Blue Ball, Pennsylvania, post office. I think this clearly goes to intent, as to what the purpose of publishing these magazines was. At least, it clearly establishes one of the reasons why they were disseminating this material.

"The COURT. Admitted."

[9] Thus, one EROS advertisement claimed:

"Eros is a child of its times. . . . [It] is the result of recent court decisions that have realistically interpreted America's obscenity laws and that have given to this country a new breadth of freedom of expression. . . . EROS takes full advantage of this new freedom of expression. It is *the* magazine of sexual candor."

In another, more lavish spread:

"EROS is a new quarterly devoted to the subjects of Love and Sex. In the few short weeks since its birth, EROS has established itself as the rave of the American intellectual community — and the rage of prudes everywhere! And it's no wonder: EROS handles the subjects of Love and Sex with complete candor. The publication of this magazine — which is frankly and avowedly concerned with erotica — has been enabled by recent court decisions ruling that a literary piece or painting, though explicitly sexual in content, has a right to be published if it is a genuine work of art.

ently mailed from New York, consisted almost entirely of a reproduction of the introduction of the book, written by one Dr. Albert Ellis. Although he alludes to the book's informational value and its putative therapeutic usefulness, his remarks are preoccupied with the book's sexual imagery. The solicitation was indiscriminate, not limited to those, such as physicians or psychiatrists, who might independently discern the book's therapeutic worth.[10] Inserted in each advertisement was a slip labeled 'GUARANTEE' and reading, 'Documentary Books, Inc. unconditionally guarantees full refund of the price of THE HOUSEWIFE'S HANDBOOK ON SELECTIVE PROMISCUITY if the book fails to reach you because of U.S. Post Office censorship interference.' Similar slips appeared in the advertising for EROS and Liaison; they highlighted the gloss petitioners put on the publications, eliminating any doubt what the purchaser was being asked to buy.[11]

"This evidence, in our view, was relevant in determining the ultimate question of obscenity and, in the context of this record, serves to resolve all ambiguity and doubt. The deliberate representation of petitioners' publications as erotically arousing, for example, stimulated the reader to accept them as prurient; he looks for titillation, not for saving intellectual content. Similarly, such representation would tend to force public confrontation with the potentially offensive aspects of the work; the brazenness of such an appeal heightens the offensiveness of the publications to those who are offended by such material. And the circumstances of presentation and dissemination of material are equally relevant to determining whether social importance claimed for material in the courtroom was, in the circumstances, pretense or reality — whether it was the basis upon which it was traded in the marketplace or a spurious claim for litigation purposes. Where the purveyor's sole emphasis is on the sexually provocative aspects of his publications, that fact may be decisive in the determination of obscenity. Certainly in a prosecution which, as here, does not necessarily imply suppression of the materials involved, the fact that they originate or are used as a subject of pandering is relevant to the application of the Roth test.

"EROS is a genuine work of art. . . ."

An undisclosed number of advertisements for Liaison were mailed. The outer envelopes of these ads ask, "Are you among the chosen few?" The first line of the advertisement eliminates the ambiguity: "Are you a member of the sexual elite?" It continues:

"That is, are you among the few happy and enlightened individuals who believe that a man and woman can make love without feeling pangs of conscience? Can you read about love and sex and discuss them without blushing and stammering?

"If so, you ought to know an important new periodical called Liasion.

. . .

"In short, Liason is Cupid's Chronicle. . . .

"Though Liason handles the subjects of love and sex with complete candor, I wish to make it clear that it is not a scandal sheet and it is not written for the man in the street. Liason is aimed at intelligent, educated adults who can accept love and sex as part of life.

". . . I'll venture to say that after you've read your first biweekly issue, Liason will be your most eagerly awaited piece of mail."

[10] Note 13, infra.

[11] There is much additional evidence supporting the conclusion of petitioners' pandering. One of petitioners' former writers for Liaison, for example, testified about the editorial goals and practices of that publication.

"A proposition argued as to EROS, for example, is that the trial judge improperly found the magazine to be obscene as a whole, since he concluded that only four of the 15 articles predominantly appealed to prurient interest and substantially exceeded community standards of candor, while the other articles were admittedly non-offensive. But the trial judge found that '[t]he deliberate and studied arrangement of EROS is editorialized for the purpose of appealing predominantly to prurient interest and to insulate through the inclusion of non-offensive material.' 224 F. Supp., at 131. However erroneous such a conclusion might be if unsupported by the evidence of pandering, the record here supports it. EROS was created, represented and sold solely as a claimed instrument of the sexual stimulation it would bring. Like the other publications, its pervasive treatment of sex and sexual matters rendered it available to exploitation by those who would make a business of pandering to the 'widespread weakness for titillation by pornography.' [12] Petitioners' own expert agreed, correctly we think, that '[i]f the object [of a work] is material gain for the creator through an appeal to the sexual curiosity and appetite,' the work is pornographic. In other words, by animating sensual detail to give the publication a salacious cast, petitioners reinforced what is conceded by the Government to be an otherwise debatable conclusion.

"A similar analysis applies to the judgment regarding the Handbook. The bulk of the proofs directed to social importance concerned this publication. Before selling publication rights to petitioners, its author had printed it privately; she sent circulars to persons whose names appeared on membership lists of medical and psychiatric associations, asserting its value as an adjunct in therapy. Over 12,000 sales resulted from this solicitation, and a number of witnesses testified that they found the work useful in their professional practice. The Government does not seriously contest the claim that the book has worth in such a controlled, or even neutral, environment. Petitioners, however, did not sell the book to such a limited audience, or focus their claims for it on its supposed therapeutic or educational value; rather, they deliberately emphasized the sexually provocative aspects of the work, in order to catch the salaciously disposed. They proclaimed its obscenity; and we cannot conclude that the court below erred in taking their own evaluation at its face value and declaring the book as a whole obscene despite the other evidence.[13]

"The decision in United States v. Rebhuhn, 109 F.2d 512, is persuasive authority for our conclusion.[14] That was a prosecution under the predecessor to §1461,

---

[12] Schwartz, Morals Offenses and the Model Penal Code, 63 Col. L. Rev. 669, 677 (1963).

[13] The Government drew a distinction between the author's and petitioners' solicitation. At the sentencing proceeding the United States Attorney stated:
". . . [the author] was distributing . . . only to physicians; she never had widespread, indiscriminate distribution of the Handbook, and, consequently, the Post Office Department did not interfere . . . . If Mr. Ginzburg had distributed and sold and advertised these books solely to . . . physicians . . . we, of course, would not be here this morning with regard to The Housewife's Handbook . . . ."

[14] The Proposed Official Draft of the ALI Model Penal Code likewise recognizes the question of pandering as relevant to the obscenity issue, §251.4(4); Tentative Draft No. 6 (May 6, 1957), at pp. 1-3, 13-17, 45-46, 53; Schwartz, supra, n.12; see Craig, Suppressed Books, 195-206 (1963). Compare Grove Press, Inc. v. Christenberry, 175 F. Supp. 488, 496-497 (D.C.S.D.N.Y. 1959), aff'd 276 F.2d 433 (C.A. 2d Cir. 1960); United States v. One Book Entitled Ulysses, 72 F.2d 705, 707 (C.A. 2d Cir. 1934),

brought in the context of pandering of publications assumed useful to scholars and members of learned professions. The books involved were written by authors proved in many instances to have been men of scientific standing, as anthropologists or psychiatrists. The Court of Appeals for the Second Circuit therefore assumed that many of the books were entitled to the protection of the First Amendment, and 'could lawfully have passed through the mails, if directed to those who would be likely to use them for the purposes for which they were written. . . .' 109 F.2d, at 514. But the evidence, as here, was that the defendants had not disseminated them for their 'proper use, but . . . woefully misused them, and it was that misuse which constituted the gravamen of the crime.' Id., at 515. Speaking for the Court in affirming the conviction, Judge Learned Hand said:

" '. . . [T]he works themselves had a place, though a limited one, in anthropology and in psychotherapy. They might also have been lawfully sold to laymen who wished seriously to study the sexual practices of savage or barbarous peoples, or sexual aberrations; in other words, most of them were not obscene per se. In several decisions we have held that the statute does not in all circumstances forbid the dissemination of such publications. . . . However, in the case at bar, the prosecution succeeded . . . when it showed that the defendants had indiscriminately flooded the mails with advertisements, plainly designed merely to catch the prurient, though under the guise of distributing works of scientific or literary merit. We do not mean that the distributor of such works is charged with a duty to insure that they shall reach only proper hands, nor need we say what care he must use, for these defendants exceeded any possible limit; the circulars were no more than appeals to the salaciously disposed, and no [fact finder] could have failed to pierce the fragile screen, set up to cover that purpose.' 109 F.2d, at 514-515.

"We perceive no threat to First Amendment guarantees in thus holding that in close cases evidence of pandering may be probative with respect to the nature of the material in question and thus satisfy the Roth test.[15] No weight is ascribed to the fact that petitioners have profited from the sale of publications which we have assumed but do not hold cannot themselves be adjudged obscene in the abstract; to sanction consideration of this fact might indeed induce self-censorship, and offend the frequently stated principle that commercial activity, in itself, is no justification for narrowing the protection of expression secured by the First Amendment.[16] Rather, the fact that each of these publications was created or exploited entirely on the basis of its appeal to prurient interests[17] strengthens the conclusion

---

affirming 5 F. Supp. 182 (D.C.S.D.N.Y. 1933). See also The Trial of Lady Chatterly — Regina v. Penguin Books, Ltd. (Rolph. ed. 1961).

[15] Our conclusion is consistent with the statutory scheme. Although §1461, in referring to "obscene . . . matter" may appear to deal with the qualities of material in the abstract, it is settled that the mode of distribution may be a significant part in the determination of the obscenity of the material involved. United States v. Rebhuhn, supra. Because the statute creates a criminal remedy, cf. Manual Enterprises v. Day, 370 U.S. 478, 495 (opinion of Brennan, J.), it readily admits such an interpretation, compare United States v. 31 Photographs, etc., 156 F. Supp. 350 (D.C.S.D. N.Y. 1957).

[16] See New York Times v. Sullivan, 376 U.S. 254, 265-266; Smith v. California, 361, U.S. 147, 150.

[17] See Valentine v. Chrestensen, 316 U.S. 52, where the Court viewed handbills purporting to contain protected expression as merely commercial advertising. Compare that decision with Jamison v. Texas, 318 U.S. 413, and Murdock v. Pennsylvania, 319 U.S. 105, where speech having the characteristics of advertising was held to be an in-

that the transactions here were sales of illicit merchandise, not sales of constitutionally protected matter.[18] A conviction for mailing obscene publications, but explained in part by the presence of this element, does not necessarily suppress the materials in question, nor chill their proper distribution for a proper use. Nor should it inhibit the enterprise of others seeking through serious endeavor to advance human knowledge or understanding in science, literature, or art. All that will have been determined is that questionable publications are obscene in a context which brands them as obscene as that term is defined in Roth — a use inconsistent with any claim to the shelter of the First Amendment.[19] 'The nature of the materials is, of course, relevant as an attribute of the defendant's conduct, but the materials are thus placed in context from which they draw color and character. A wholly different result might be reached in a different setting.' Roth v. United States, 354 U.S., at 495 (Warren, C.J., concurring).

"It is important to stress that this analysis simply elaborates the test by which the obscenity vel non of the material must be judged. Where an exploitation of interests in titillation by pornography is shown with respect to material lending itself to such exploitation through pervasive treatment or description of sexual matters, such evidence may support the determination that the material is obscene even though in other contexts the material would escape such condemnation." 383 U.S. at 466-476.

Justices Black, Douglas, Harlan, and Stewart dissented. Reasons in addition to those mentioned in connection with the "Fanny Hill" and Mishkin cases supra were: (1) In the opinion of Justices Black and Harlan, the fact that the Court may have rewritten the federal statute and then applied it retroactively to Ginzburg. (2) In Mr. Justice Harlan's opinion, that Ginzburg should be given a day in court to disprove the new "pandering" charge which was not the theory of the prosecution below nor the basis of the lower court discussions. (3) Mr. Justice Douglas' dissent, which also applied to the Mishkin case, stressed the elusiveness of all the standards which have been proposed, and the fact that they amount at best to a rationale for suppressing minority views and tastes, as further reasons for honoring the absoluteness of the First Amendment.

6. "Predominant theme." (a) *Advocacy of socially disapproved or illegal practices:* While, since Kingsley International Pictures Corp. v. Regents, 360 U.S. 684, 79 S. Ct. 1362, 3 L. Ed. 2d 1512 (1959), discussed in the Jacobellis opinion, the Constitution seems to extend protection to the advocacy of socially frowned on or even illegal practices, such as adultery, the question has been raised whether it also

---

tegral part of religious discussions and hence protected. Material sold solely to produce sexual arousal, like commercial advertising, does not escape regulation because it has been dressed up as speech, or in other contexts might be recognized as speech.

[18] Compare Breard v. Alexandria, 341 U.S. 622, with Martin v. Struthers, 319 U.S. 141. Cf. Kovacs v. Cooper, 336 U.S. 77; Giboney v. Empire Storage Co., 336 U.S. 490; Cox v. Louisiana, 379 U.S. 536, 559.

[19] One who advertises and sells a work on the basis of its prurient appeal is not threatened by the perhaps inherent residual vagueness of the Roth test, cf. Dombrowski v. Pfister, 380 U.S. 479, 486-487, 491-492; such behavior is central to the objectives of criminal obscenity laws. ALI Model Penal Code, Tentative Draft No. 6 (May 6, 1957), pp. 1-3, 13-17; Comments to the Proposed Official Draft §251.4, supra; Schwartz, Morals Offenses and the Model Penal Code, 63 Col. L. Rev. 669, 677-681 (1963); Paul & Schwartz, Federal Censorship — Obscenity in the Mail, 212-219 (1961); see Mishkin v. New York, post, p. 502, at 507, n.5.

protects "the circulation of detailed instructions on how to accomplish adultery, fornication or seduction." See Kahm v. United States, 300 F.2d 78 (5th Cir. 1962), cert. den., 369 U.S. 859 (1962) (the opinion found the material obscene without reaching this issue). Cf. Haldeman v. United States, 340 F.2d 59 (10th Cir. 1965), where the court in holding not obscene pamphlets written by a doctor giving medical answers for the layman on subjects such as "Orogenital Contacts," "Cunnilingus" and "Undinism" remarked: "All the booklets discuss revolting, nauseating, filthy and disgusting incidents, but they are no more repulsive than any discussion on the same subjects for medical, scientific, educational or general information purposes. . . . The guarantee of the Constitution is not confined to conventional material or to the expression of views shared by a majority of citizens [citing Kingsley v. Regents]." 340 F.2d at 60-62. Cf. Ginzburg v. United States, supra.

(b) *The packaging unit:* In addition to the previously excerpted text of Mr. Justice Brennan's opinion in the Ginzburg case, see footnote 5, previously omitted, which states: "Our affirmance of the conviction for mailing EROS and Liaison is based upon their characteristics as a whole, including their editorial formats, and not upon particular articles contained, digested, or excerpted in them. Thus we do not decide whether particular articles, for example in EROS, although identified by the trial judge as offensive, should be condemned as obscene whatever their setting." 383 U.S. at 466. Cf. Kahm v. United States, supra, commenting on an excerpt from Peyton Place in a collection of excerpts. The passage contained "a vivid description of the accomplishment of sexual intercourse between a boy and a girl.":

"Had the appellant undertaken to send through the mail the book 'Peyton Place' a different problem would be presented, for then inquiry would have to be made as to whether notwithstanding the fact that the book contained passages of the kind here referred to, 'to the average person, applying contemporary community standards, the dominant theme of the material taken as a whole appeals to prurient interest.' No such question is presented to us here for the appellant in merely selecting the most obscene passages from various books has seen to it that his readers are not subjected to any book as a whole."[5] 300 F.2d at 82-83.

See further 300 F.2d at 83-84 rejecting the claim that non-obscene excerpts placed in the same package with obscene material save the obscene material from prosecution. See also Flying Eagle Publications, Inc. v. United States, 285 F.2d 307 (1st Cir. 1961). But cf. People v. Bruce, 31 Ill. 2d 459, 202 N.E.2d 497 (1964), following Jacobellis in reversing own ruling because "some of the topics commented on by [the] defendant [a night club entertainer] are of social importance." 31 Ill. 2d at 461, 202 N.E.2d at 498. The Bruce case was quoted with approval in footnote 7 of Mr. Justice Brennan's opinion in the "Fanny Hill" case. See also Murphy, The Value of Pornography, 10 Wayne L. Rev. 655 (1964); Burgess, Obscenity Prosecution: Artistic Value and the Concept of Immunity, 39 N.Y.U.L. Rev. 1063 (1964); Vidal, On Pornography, New York Review of Books, March 31, 1966, supra.

7. Effect: In 1962, after a three-year study, the American Civil Liberties Union, while advocating a non-censorship position as ideal, stated that where censorship

---

[5] The entire book such as "Peyton Place" might serve a useful purpose and have value in portraying the life of a community whose people have become obsessed with sex; or it might be a useful study in the psychology and mental processes of the author.

or punishment is employed because of obscenity there must be "proof beyond a reasonable doubt that such an expression would directly cause in a normal adult, behavior which has validly been made criminal by statute." Where there is "proof beyond a reasonable doubt that the target group of a particular distribution charged to be obscene is composed of other than average adults (e.g., children or savants) then the test should be the effect established beyond a reasonable doubt on that group." American Civil Liberties Union Bull., June 11, 1962.

Cf. also Judge Frank's concurring opinion when the Roth case was before the Second Circuit, 237 F.2d 796 (1956):

"In Commonwealth v. Gordon, 66 Pa. D&C 101 (1949), Judge Bok said: 'A book, however sexually impure and pornographic . . . cannot be a present danger unless its reader closes it, lays it aside, and transmutes its erotic allurement into overt action. That such action must inevitably follow as a direct consequence of reading the book does not bear analysis, nor is it borne out by general human experience; too much can intervene and too many diversions take place. . . . The only clear and present danger . . . that will satisfy . . . the Constitution . . . is the commission or the imminence of the commission of criminal behavior resulting from the reading of a book. Publication alone can have no such automatic effect.' The constitutional operation of 'the statute,' Judge Bok continued, thus 'rests on narrow ground . . . I hold that (the statute) may constitutionally be applied . . . only where there is a reasonable and demonstrable cause to believe that a crime or misdemeanor has been committed or is about to be committed as the perceptible result of the publication and distribution of the writing in question: the opinion of anyone that a tendency thereto exists or that such a result is self-evident is insufficient and irrelevant. The causal connection between the book and the criminal behavior must appear beyond a reasonable doubt.'

"I confess that I incline to agree with Judge Bok's opinion. But I think it should be modified in a few respects: (a) Because of the Supreme Court's opinion in the Dennis case, 341 U.S. 494 (1951), decided since Judge Bok wrote, I would stress the element of probability in speaking of a 'clear danger.' (b) I think the danger need not be that of probably inducing behavior which has already been made criminal at common law or by statute, but rather of probably inducing any seriously anti-social conduct (*i.e.,* conduct which, by statute, could validly be made a state or federal crime). (c) I think that the causal relation need not be between such anti-social conduct and a particular book involved in the case on trial, but rather between such conduct and a book of the kind or type involved in the case.[70] " 237 F.2d at 825-826.

See also Lockhart and McClure, Obscenity Censorship: The Core Constitutional Issue — What is Obscene? 7 Utah L. Rev. 289, 302 (1961), suggesting that laws dealing with material that is not obscene, thus bringing the material within the free speech category, may still be constitutional if they meet the "clear and present" danger test.

On the inconclusiveness of findings of studies of the effect of literature or films

---

[70] According to Judge Bok, an obscenity statute may be validly enforced when there is proof of a causal relation between a particular book and undesirable conduct. Almost surely, such proof cannot ever be adduced. In the instant case, the government did not attempt to prove it.

on attitudes, states of mental stimulation, and overt behavior, see Cairns, Paul, and
Wishner, Sex Censorship: The Assumptions of Anti-Obscenity Laws and the Empirical Evidence, 46 Minn. L. Rev. 1009 (1962). Among the studies critically analyzed or the critical analysis of which by others is summarized are (1) Questionnaire test: Blumer and Hauser, Movies, Delinquency and Crime (1963) (subjects
stated they were stimulated and wanted to engage in overt behaviour); Haines,
Juvenile Delinquency and TV, 1 J. Social Therapy (1955) (among youthful prisoners similar result but of smaller percentage); Ramsey, The Sexual Development
of Boys, 56 Amer. J. Psychology 217 (1943) (subjects asked to rank sexual stimuli:
obscene pictures, female nudity, sex conversation variously ranked depending on
age); Lorang, The Effect of Reading on Moral Conduct and Emotional Experience, Studies in Psychology and Psychiatry, March 1945; Kinsey, Pomeroy, and
Martin, Sexual Behavior in the Human Male 510 (1948) (males more stimulated
by direct material, females by indirect material); see also their study on the female
662 (1953). (2) Indirect techniques of testing preferences for sexual stimuli: An
unpublished study by Buchwald reported in the principal article. 46 Minn. L. Rev.
at 1022. (3) Phantasy productions as a result of sexual stimuli: Mussen and Scodel,
The Effects of Sexual Stimulation Under Varying Conditions on TAT Sexual
Responsiveness, 19 J. Consulting Psychology 90 (1955) (sexual phantasy inhibited
when stimuli presented in presence of authority figure); Clark, The Projective
Measurement of Experimentally Induced Levels of Sexual Motivation, 12 J. Exp.
Psychology 44 (1952) (greater sexual content in story invention in party situation
than classroom). (4) Tests of physiological response: Dysinger and Ruckmick,
The Emotional Responses of Children to the Motion Picture Situation (1933);
Clark and Triechler, Psychic Stimulation of Prostatic Secretion, 12 Psychosomatic
Medicine 261 (1950).

See also Gebhard, Gagnon, Pomeroy, and Christenson, Sex Offenders (1965) (a
Kinsey study concluding that there is little connection between pornography and
sexual offenses); Murphy, The Value of Pornography, 10 Wayne L. Rev. 655
(1964) (collecting material on various factual assumptions behind obscenity laws);
Jahoda et al., The Impact of Literature: A Psychological Discussion of Some Assumptions in the Censorship Debate, Research Center for Human Relations, New
York University (1954); Kronhausen and Kronhausen, Pornography and the Law
(rev. ed. 1964); Levy, Lippsitt, and Rosenbluth, Brown University Psychologists
Report on Censorship, Censorship Bull., Aug. 1958, p. 1.

For the strong conclusion, based on interviews, that reading is an important
causal link to overt criminal behavior, see Wertham, Seduction of the Innocent
(1953). On the effect of studies dealing with other than sexual communication, see
Schramm, Mass Media and National Development: The Role of Information in the
Developing Countries (1964); Klapper, The Effects of Mass Communication
(1960); Hovland, Janis, and Kelly, Communication and Persuasion (1953); Berk-
owitz, The Effects of Observing Violence, Scientific American, Feb. 1964, p. 35,
and bibliography p. 152; Bandura and Ross, Imitation of Film-Mediated Agressive
Models, 66 J. Abnormal Soc. Psychol. 3 (1963); Himmelweit, Oppenheim, and
Vince, Television and the Child (1958); Siegel, The Influence of Violence in the
Mass Media Upon Children's Role Expectations, 29 Child Development 35 (1958).
See further the collection of communication studies, including effect and content
analysis studies, in the second edition of this book 964-971. For a brief theoretical

summary of effect studies see Rose, The Study of the Influence of the Mass Media on Public Opinion, 15 Kyklos 465 (1962).

For general expressions of the opinion that obscenity causes anti-social conduct and/or attitudes, see the collection of legislative committee reports in Mr. Justice Clark's dissenting opinion in the "Fanny Hill" case, supra, 383 U.S. at 452-453; Subcommittee on Juvenile Delinquency of the Senate Committee on the Judiciary, Rep. No. 1608, 88th Cong., 1st Sess., Oct. 2, 1964. See further Cairns, Paul, and Wishner, supra, 46 Minn. L. Rev. at 1013-1014; Hayes, A Position on the Control of Obscenity, 51 Ky. L.J. 641, 647 (1963); Schmidt, A Justification of Statutes Barring Pornography from the Mail, 26 Ford. L. Rev. 70 (1957); Murphy, Censorship: Government and Obscenity 131-151 (1963); Gardiner, Moral Principles Towards a Definition of the Obscene, 20 Law and Contemp. Prob. 560 (1955); Gardiner, Catholic Viewpoint on Censorship (1958); Kyle-Keith, The High Price of Pornography (1961); Hewitt, Does Pornography Matter? (1961).

Compare the following book review of Pauline Réage's Story of O, by Eliot Fremont-Smith, which appeared in the New York Times, March 2, 1966, and was reprinted in advertisements by the Grove Press subsequent to the Ginzburg decision:

"The free publication of 'Story of O' in this country is an event of considerable importance — not because the book has more than limited artistic or literary merit (it probably doesn't) or because it is in some way attractive (it isn't), but because it marks the end of any coherent restrictive application of the concept of pornography to books.

"What 'Story of O' does is to fracture the last rationale of censorship, our late and somewhat desperate distinction between 'literary' pornography and 'hard-core' pornography. It uses — or anyway is a serious attempt to use — erotic fantasies of the most perverted 'hard-core' sort to elicit erotic responses in the reader as means to traditional literary ends: the delineation of character, the exploration of motivation, the elucidation of, in this case, a somewhat mystical philosophy of life and love.

"In this way 'Story of O' differs both from erotic romances (for want of a better word) in which the response is intended to be erotic and nothing more, and from startlers like 'Last Exit to Brooklyn,' in which the response is anti-erotic, shock for a moral purpose. Of course the differences are only matters of degree, and 'Story of O,' which was originally published in Paris in 1954, certainly has its French forebears — most obviously, the works of Jean Genet, the Surrealists, Beaudelaire and (most obviously of all) that old workhorse of libertinage, the Marquis de Sade.

"In brief, 'Story of O' relates the progressive, willful debasement of a young and beautiful Parisian fashion photographer, O, who wants nothing more than to be a slave to her lover, René. The test is severe — sexual in method, psychological in substance. She is subjected to every imaginable form of sadistic humiliation, each of which she must learn to like not for its own sake, but because her lover wishes it. And beyond this — beyond the whips and chains and other paraphernalia of sadism, the impeccable rules of 'discipline' and fetishistic dress, the carefully staged orgies and tableaux — she must learn to give up René and love his friend Sir Stephen instead, because René wishes it.

"At the end, O is literally a mannequin of perversion. By her own choice, her own exercise of ego, she has rid herself of ego because that is her lover's request. Moreover, she has done so not knowing whether or not René cares or is even aware that she has done so. Only death awaits her, at Sir Stephen's whim.

"All of this is told against two sets of scenery, one of modern Paris and one right out of Sade ('The 120 Days of Sodom'), and in a tone of earnest, precise, anonymous matter-of-factness. Both the relentless, straight-line logic of the story and the pristine manner of its telling are profoundly French, and the result is certainly surreal.

"It is also, for this American reader, revolting, haunting, somewhat erotic, rather more emetic, ludicrous, boring, unbelievable and quite unsettling. Yet it does have a note of 'tragic grandeur' (as one French critic put it) and its style is 'irreproachable.' Its artistic merit is debatable, but as a technical experiment at least, 'Story of O' is of undeniable artistic interest.

"But one returns to the matter of pornography, for the artistic interest here has precisely to do with the use not only of erotic materials but also erotic methods, the deliberate stimulation of the reader as a part of and means to a total, authentic literary experience. It has been argued that sensual arousal and valid artistic responses are antithetical; 'Story of O' suggests that the argument is faulty. It is a curious argument in any case, once one stops to think about it: who would deny the dynamic connections between sex and art or between the emotional, the intellectual and the physical? It's the definition of these relationships, not their existence, that eludes us.

"Yet the whole matter is profoundly disturbing to most people for many reasons. Even the antiseptic discussion of it here will disturb some people. (It is noteworthy that Grove Press has published 'Story of O' in plain white wrappers showing nothing but the title and a 'limited to adults' legend, has priced it at a high $6 and has pulled in much respectable introductory material with emphasis on the book's supposed purity and the possible real identity of the pseudononymous 'Pauline Réage.')

"Perhaps most disturbing is the idea, recently put forth by the critic Leslie Fiedler, that pornography as a concept may soon disappear. (The legal concept has been so chipped away there is almost nothing left.) We have considerable stake in our taboos, and the existence of something we can call pornographic serves many purposes. One of these, Fiedler has suggested, is the preservation of social distinctions: high-class erotica is okay, the rest is smut. One might call this the system of privileged prurience. In fact, it works both ways: many people who don't mind men's smokers and bathroom jokes are furious when the same material gets into things called books. And there are other non-qualitative distinctions pornography helps to maintain — between men and women (or ladies), between generations, and so on — all of them somewhat false, all of them partial devices for not seeing ourselves in candid relation to each other.

"Perhaps some of this is necessary. But what art is about is *seeing,* which is why art is always at war with those who would righteously restrict the scope or manner of its vision. 'Story of O' may not be a post-pornographic work — its use of extreme perversion in obtaining its effects suggests it is not — but it is a significant measure of how far we have come in lifting the restrictions on art and our responses to it. For some this will be terrible news. But it is art's gain, and I would suggest that what art gains we all gain."

Compare also Eliasberg, Art: Immoral or Immortal, 45 J. Crim. L.C. & P.S. 274 (1954), reprinted in the second edition of this book 911-914; and Psychiatric Viewpoints on Indecency, Obscenity, and Pornography in Literature and the Arts, 16 Am. J. of Psychotherapy 477 (1962); Eliasberg and Stuart, Authoritarian Personality and the Obscenity Threshold, 55 J. Soc. Psychology 143 (1961).

8. Expert testimony and comparative material: (a) Expert testimony on the issue of "obscenity" or "appeal to prurient interest" is generally not allowed. But cf. United States v. Klaw, 350 F.2d 155 (2d Cir. 1965), where the court reversed a conviction for mailing stories, photographs, and drawing of the "bondage" genre because of the Government's failure to present any witnesses on the issue of "prurient appeal":

"And if proof of prurient stimulation and response is generally important, it is particularly necessary when the prurient interest may be that of a deviant segment of society whose reactions are hardly a matter of common knowledge. . . .

"Furthermore, nothing in the record shows that the material even has prurient appeal to the average man. The parent witnesses did not react to Junior's new literary and pictorial delights in a prurient manner, nor did the other recipient witnesses. Junior was not called upon to describe the appeal (if any) to his prurient interest; he probably would not have understood what 'prurient' meant any more than do his elders. Most of the witnesses testified that they found the material disgusting or revolting, but that lascivious and lecherous thoughts had not been aroused in them. . . .

"If the witnesses presented in this case provide any sampling, these pamphlets and pictures stimulated no one's prurient interest. Although it may be difficult to find expert and other witnesses properly qualified to inform the jury about what does or does not appeal to the prurient interest of the average person, cf. Klaw v. Schaffer, supra, 151 F. Supp. at 539-540, it would not seem impossible. On the other hand, it is clear that jurors should not consider their own personal reactions as setting the standard; there is too much truth in the observation that 'what is pornography for one man is the laughter of genius to another.' Cf. Ass'n of the Bar of the City of New York, Comm. on the Bill of Rights, Report on H.R. 319 88th Cong., 2d Sess. (1964), on "Morally Offensive Mail," in Reports of the Ass'n of the Bar Concerned with Federal Legislation 54, 56 (1965). . . .

"Whatever the value of mere 'autoptical' evidence in other contexts, it should not be countenanced in this area. Otherwise, too easily the Government's test might allow a jury to equate patent offensiveness to prurient appeal, thus obliterating the conjunction that has been thought indispensable. See e.g., Manual Enterprises, Inc. v. Day, supra, 370 U.S. at 482, 82 S. Ct. 1432; Jacobellis v. State of Ohio, supra, 378 U.S. at 191-192, 84 S. Ct. 1676. Too easily the jury could aid suppression simply on the basis of speculations and suspicions about the prurient appeal of material of some unknown, undefined person whose psyche is not known. With the First Amendment in the background, this cannot be abided. . . . .

"In this case, the jury had insufficient evidence even to 'recognize' that the material appealed to the prurient interest of the average person. It had absolutely no evidentiary basis from which to 'recognize' any appeal to the prurient interest of the deviate or the typical recipient — a class never really defined in the record. Because there was insufficient evidence for the jury to consider Nutrix material 'obscene' under any proper view of the Roth test, the motion for directed verdict of acquittal should have been granted.[14] " 350 F.2d at 165-168.

Cf. also Yudkin v. State, 229 Md. 223, 182 A.2d 798 (1962).

(b) Expert testimony on literary value has frequently been admitted with the literary experts almost inevitably testifying as well on the issue of "obscenity." As to "community standards" there seems to be a greater tendency to disallow such testimony in a jury case and to allow it where the case is tried by a judge. See United States v. West Coast News Co., 228 F. Supp. 171 (W.D. Mich. 1964), and the cases there cited and discussed, including United States v. Levine, 83 F.2d 156 (2d Cir. 1963), and Parmelee v. United States, 113 F.2d 729 (D.C. Cir. 1940); but cf. United States v. Klaw supra. Cf. also Mr. Justice Frankfurter's opinion in Smith v. California, 361 U.S. 147, 160-161, 80 S. Ct. 215, 4 L. Ed. 2d 205 (1959). See also Mr. Justice Harlan's opinion concurring in part and dissenting in part, 361 U.S. at 228. For a case allowing the testimony of two nudists and two average housewives for the defense and the Government, respectively, see United States v. 4200 Copies International Journal, 134 F. Supp. 490 (E.D. Wash. 1955). Even where expert testimony on an issue is held to be admissible, it is not always clear how the expert's qualification is to be established. See Womack v. United States, 294 F.2d 204 (D.C. Cir. 1961).

(c) On the question of "dominant theme" at least one trial judge has ruled that the dominant theme of the book in question may not be established through experts but they may testify on the similarity of the dominant theme of other books in circulation in the community. United States v. West Coast News Co., supra, 228 F. Supp. at 189. Such comparative material has in a number of cases in the past not been admitted. See People v. Finkelstein, 11 N.Y.2d 300, 183 N.E.2d 661, 229 N.Y.S.2d 367 (1962), cert. den., 371 U.S. 863 (1962) (where offensiveness obvious); Commonwealth v. Donaducy, 167 Pa. Super. 611, 76 A.2d 440 (1950), cert. den., 341 U.S. 949 (1951). But especially since Mr. Justice Harlan's concurrence in Smith v. California, supra, exclusion comes less easy. See in addition to Yudkin v. State, supra, In re Harris, 56 Cal. 2d 879, 366 P.2d 305, 16 Cal. Rptr. 889 (1961); People v. Brooklyn News Co., 12 Misc. 2d 768, 174 N.Y.S.2d 813 (Kings Co. 1958). See Note, 76 Harv. L. Rev. 1498 (1963), for suggestion that differing treatment of comparative material may be based on whether such material has been cleared of obscenity. In a number of cases judges have not permitted comparison books to be presented to the jury until it is proved to the judge's satisfaction that "the book enjoys substantial acceptability in the community," and until a qualified expert convinces the judge "as a matter of law" through testimony "that the books are substantially similar to the challenged books." United States v. West Coast

---

[14] Even with adequate proof under the average man test, there might still be problems, for the jury was charged to consider the material from the standpoint of the average man in the nation as a whole. We very much doubt whether twelve random New Yorkers can make such a judgment without being further informed about "the common conscience of the nation," if there be such a thing. In any case, we do not read the Court's plurality opinions in Jacobellis as unequivocal authority for the proposition. In announcing the Court's judgment, Justice Brennan was speaking only for himself and Justice Goldberg. Justices White, Black and Douglas concurred only in the judgment. Justice Stewart concurred without indicating adoption of the national community standard. As for the dissenters, the Chief Justice explicitly rejected the national standard, as did Justice Harlan, presumably in light of his views in Roth. See Gent v. State, Ark., 393 S.W.2d 219 (1965) . . .

News Co., supra, 228 F. Supp. at 195. See also Womack v. United States, supra.

It is of course too early to establish the full extent to which the Supreme Court's continuing role as the ultimate trier of fact, its treatment of expert testimony, and the Court's insistence on a national community standard will affect lower federal and state court treatment of expert testimony and comparative material.

9. Standards other than obscenity — Vagueness: In Winters v. New York, 333 U.S. 507 68 S. Ct. 665, 92 L. Ed. 840 (1948), mentioned in the principal opinions, the Court stated that statutes using typical terms like "obscene," "lewd," "lascivious," "filthy," "indecent" and "disgusting" have that "permissible uncertainty . . . caused by describing crimes by words well understood through long use in the criminal law." 333 U.S. at 518. In that case the defendant attacked the constitutionality of a section of the New York Penal Code which made it a misdemeanor to publish or distribute in any way any publication "devoted to . . . and principally made up of criminal news, police reports, or accounts of criminal deeds, or pictures, or stories of deeds of bloodshed, lust or crime. . . ." The New York Court of Appeals had by construction limited the meaning of the section so as "not to outlaw all commentaries on crime from detective tales to scientific treatises." It held that so far as applicable in the Winters case the statute merely extended the meaning of "indecent or obscene" which in New York previously had been construed to refer only to matters of sexual impurity. The extended notion of obscenity and indecency was designed to include only criminal deeds of bloodshed and lust "so massed as to become vehicles for inciting violent and depraved crimes against a person." 294 N.Y. 545, 63 N.E.2d 98, 294 N.Y. 979, 63 N.E.2d 713 (1945). In holding the statute unconstitutional the Supreme Court stated:

"Even though all detective tales and treatises on criminology are not forbidden, and though publications made up of criminal deeds not characterized by bloodshed or lust are omitted from the interpretation of the Court of Appeals, we think fair use of collections of pictures and stories would be interdicted because of the utter impossibility of the actor or the trier to know where this new standard of guilt would draw the line between the allowable and the forbidden publications. No intent or purpose is required — no indecency or obscenity in any sense heretofore known to the law. 'So massed as to incite to crime' can become meaningful only by concrete instances. This one example is not enough. The clause proposes to punish the printing and circulation of publications that courts or juries may think influence generally persons to commit crimes of violence against the person. No conspiracy to commit a crime is required. . . . It is not an effective notice of new crime. The clause has no technical or common law meaning. Nor can light as to the meaning be gained from the section as a whole or the Article of the Penal Law under which it appears." 333 U.S. at 519.

Mr. Justice Frankfurter dissented, characterizing the dilemma facing the legislature as follows:

"If a law is framed with narrow particularity, too easy opportunities are afforded to nullify the purposes of the legislation. If the legislation is drafted in terms so vague that no ascertainable line is drawn in advance between innocent and condemned conduct, the purpose of the legislation cannot be enforced because no purpose is defined. . . . The reconciliation of these two contradictories is necessarily an empiric enterprise largely depending on the nature of the particular legislative problem. . . .

"Not to make the magazines with which this case is concerned part of the Court's opinion is to play 'Hamlet' without Hamlet. But the Court sufficiently summarizes one aspect of what the State of New York here condemned when it says 'we can see nothing of any possible value to society in these magazines.' From which it jumps to the conclusion that, nevertheless, 'they are as much entitled to the protection of free speech as the best of literature.' Wholly neutral futilities, of course, come under the protection of free speech as fully as do Keats' poems or Donne's sermons. But to say that these magazines have 'nothing of any possible value to society' is only half the truth. This merely denies them goodness. It disregards their mischief. As a result of appropriate judicial determination, these magazines were found to come within the prohibition of the law against inciting 'violent and depraved crimes against the person,' and the defendant was convicted because he exposed for sale such materials. The essence of the Court's decision is that it gives publications which have 'nothing of any possible value to society' constitutional protection but denies to the States the power to prevent the grave evils to which, in their rational judgment, such publications give rise. The legislatures of New York and the other States were concerned with these evils and not with neutral abstractions of harmlessness. Nor was the New York Court of Appeals merely resting, as it might have done, on a deep-seated conviction as to the existence of an evil and as to the appropriate means for checking it. That court drew on its experience, as revealed by 'many recent records' of criminal convictions before it, for its understanding of the practical concrete reasons that led the legislatures of a score of States to pass the enactments now here struck down." 333 U.S. at 525, 527-528.

In Burstyn v. Wilson, 343 U.S. 495, 72 S. Ct. 777, 96 L. Ed. 1098 (1952), Mr. Justice Clark, in declaring invalid the denial of a license by the New York State Board of Regents for the showing of the film "The Miracle" on the ground that it was "sacrilegious," had this to say after first declaring that motion pictures are protected by the First Amendment:

"New York's highest court says there is 'nothing mysterious' about the statutory provision applied in this case: 'It is simply this: that no religion, as that word is understood by the ordinary, reasonable person, shall be treated with contempt, mockery, scorn and ridicule . . . .' [15] This is far from the kind of narrow exception of freedom of expression which a state may carve out to satisfy the adverse demands of other interests of society. In seeking to apply the broad and all-inclusive

---

[15] 303 N.Y. 242, 258, 101 N.E.2d 665, 672. At another point the Court of Appeals gave "sacrilegious" the following definition: "the act of violating or profaning anything sacred." Id., at 255, 101 N.E.2d at 670. The Court of Appeals also approved the Appellate Division's interpretation: "As the court below said of the statute in question, 'All it purports to do is to bar a visual caricature of religious beliefs held sacred by one sect or another . . .'" Id., at 258, 101 N.E.2d at 672. Judge Fuld, dissenting, concluded from all the statements in the majority opinion that "the basic criterion appears to be whether the film treats a religious theme in such a manner as to offend the religious beliefs of any group of persons. If the film does have that effect, and it is 'offered as a form of entertainment,' it apparently falls within the statutory ban regardless of the sincerity and good faith of the producer of the film, no matter how temperate the treatment of the theme, and no matter how unlikely a public disturbance or breach of the peace. The drastic nature of such a ban is highlighted by the fact that the film in question makes no direct attack on, or criticism of, any religious dogma or principle, and it is not claimed to be obscene, scurrilous, intemperate or abusive." Id., at 271-272, 101 N.E.2d at 680.

definition of 'sacrilegious' given by the New York courts, the censor is set adrift upon a boundless sea amid a myriad of conflicting currents of religious views, with no charts but those provided by the most vocal and powerful orthodoxies. New York cannot vest such unlimited restraining control over motion pictures in a censor. Cf. Kunz v. New York, 340 U.S. 290 (1951). Under such a standard the most careful and tolerant censor would find it virtually impossible to avoid favoring one religion over another, and he would be subject to an inevitable tendency to ban the expression of unpopular sentiments sacred to a religious minority. Application of the 'sacrilegious' test, in these or other respects, might raise substantial questions under the First Amendment's guaranty of separate church and state with freedom of worship for all. However, from the standpoint of freedom of speech and the press, it is enough to point out that the state has no legitimate interest in protecting any or all religions from views distasteful to them which is sufficient to justify prior restraints upon the expression of those views. It is not the business of government in our nation to suppress real or imagined attacks upon a particular religious doctrine, whether they appear in publications, speeches, or motion pictures.

"Since the term 'sacrilegious' is the sole standard under attack here, it is not necessary for us to decide, for example, whether a state may censor motion pictures under a clearly-drawn statute designed and applied to prevent the showing of obscene films. That is a very different question from the one now before us. We hold only that under the First and Fourteenth Amendments a state may not ban a film on the basis of a censor's conclusion that it is 'sacrilegious.' " 343 U.S. at 504-506.

Mr. Justice Frankfurter's concurring opinion did not reach the free speech issue. In his view "sacrilegious" lacked "the necessary precision of meaning which the Due Process clause enjoins for statutes regulating men's activities." After a thorough history of the origin and various meanings of the word "sacrilege" he concluded that it had no single meaning and that none of its various meanings include the one attributed to it by the New York court.

In People v. Bookcase, Inc., 14 N.Y.2d 409, 201 N.E.2d 14 (1964), the statute in question prohibited the sale to a minor under 18 years of age of "any book . . . [etc.] . . . the cover or content of which exploits, is devoted to or is principally made up of descriptions of illicit sex or sexual immorality." N.Y. Penal Law §484-h. In declaring the statute unconstitutional the New York Court of Appeals stated in part:

"The decisions of the United States Supreme Court leave no doubt that legislation designed to restrict the sale or other distribution to adults of material principally devoted to, or even advocating, illicit sex or sexual immorality would be unconstitutional, both upon the grounds of vagueness, in case of criminal statutes, and of abridgment of freedom of speech or of the press in case of all statutes (Winters v. New York, supra; Joseph Burstyn, Inc., v. Wilson, 343 U.S. 495, 72 S. Ct. 777, 96 L. Ed. 1098; Superior Films Inc. v. Department of Educ. of State of Ohio, Division of Film Censorship, 346 U.S. 587, 74 S. Ct. 286, 98 L. Ed. 329; Commercial Pictures Corp. v. Regents of University of State of New York, 346 U.S. 587, 74 S. Ct. 286, 98 L. Ed. 329, revg. 305 N.Y. 336, 113 N.E.2d 502, where a motion picture had been censored under Education Law, Consol. Laws c. 16 §122 as immoral and tending to corrupt morals; Gelling v. Texas, 343 U.S. 960, 72 S,

Ct. 1002, 96 L. Ed. 1359; Holmby Prods. v. Vaughn, 350 U.S. 870, 76 S. Ct. 117, 100 L. Ed. 770, where the statute prohibited productions tending to debase or corrupt morals; One, Inc. v. Olesen, 355 U.S. 371, 78 S. Ct. 364, 2 L. Ed. 352, revg. 9 Cir., 241 F.2d 772; Times Film Corp. v. City of Chicago, 355 U.S. 35, 78 S. Ct. 115, 2 L. Ed. 2d 72, revg. 7 Cir., 244 F.2d 432; Sunshine Book Co. v. Summerfield, 355 U.S. 372, 78 S. Ct. 365, 2 L. Ed. 352, revg. 101 U.S. App. D.C. 358, 249 F.2d 114; Kingsley International Pictures Corp. v. Regents of University of State of New York, 360 U.S. 684, 79 S. Ct. 1362, 3 L. Ed. 2d 1512, upholding the right to portray or advocate other standards of sexual conduct than those approved by the community.)

"The question remains whether the constitutionality of section 484-h of the Penal Law is saved by the circumstances that it relates only to minors under 18 years of age. . . .

"No question is here presented concerning how the Legislature might constitutionally provide different standards of obscenity as applicable to different age groups. . . .

"The issue shapes itself into whether the Legislature can constitutionally restrict the sale, circulation or exhibition of pictures or printed material to minors under 18 years, for the reason that it is principally devoted to the subjects of illicit sex or sexual immorality. These words are either too vague to apprise possible defendants of what they mean, or, if they are to be interpreted as referring exclusively to extra-marital sex or sexual perversion, then they would forbid all publications or pictures mainly devoted to those subjects, regardless of the manner in which they are presented, whether by way of fiction, sociological discussion, moralizing or otherwise. The Oedipus legend in classic Greek drama would be forbidden because it is principally devoted to incest, the Tristan and Isolde legend and Hawthorne's 'Scarlet Letter' would be illicit reading for the young because it is principally made up of adultery, Bernard Shaw's 'Mrs. Warren's Profession' would be outlawed for obvious reasons, as well as all writings dealing with homosexuality. Such a list could be extended almost indefinitely. It is not suggested that these or other parallel works of literature are likely to be offered for sale at the same newsstands where the type of comic books are purchased which was the main reason for the adoption of this legislation, but the constitutionality of a statute governing publications is to be tested by what can be done under it and not by the particular violation which is charged with having occurred. It seems to us that this statute is drawn so broadly as to render criminal sales or other exhibition to the young of pictures and publications of all kinds which are principally devoted to these subjects, in however serious or dignified a manner, and, in our view, it is so broad and so obscure in its coverage as to abridge the constitutionally protected freedom of speech and of the press as well as the due process clauses in the Federal and State Constitutions." 14 N.Y.2d at 415-418, 201 N.E.2d at 17-19.

Compare the Mishkin case, supra, where §1141 of the New York Penal Law applied to "any obscene, loud, lascivious, filthy, indecent, sadistic, masochistic and disgusting book . . ." Mr. Justice Brennan refused to consider the merits of the contention that the terms "sadistic" and "masochistic" are impermissibly vague because "the New York Courts held in this case that the terms 'sadistic' and 'masochistic' as well as the other adjectives used in §1141 . . . are 'synonymous with "obscene," ' 26 Misc. 2d at 154, 207 N.Y.S.2d at 393." 383 U.S. at 506.

10. Scienter and vagueness: In Smith v. California, 361 U.S. 147, 80 S. Ct. 215, 4 L. Ed. 2d 205 (1959), the Court held unconstitutional an ordinance which imposed criminal liability on a seller for possession or selling obscene material even though no knowledge of the book's content on his part was proved. The Court commented:

"By dispensing with any requirement of knowledge of the contents of the book on the part of the seller, the ordinance tends to impose a severe limitation on the public's access to constitutionally protected matter. For if the bookseller is criminally liable without knowledge of the contents, and the ordinance fulfills its purpose,[8] he will tend to restrict the books he sells to those he has inspected; and thus the State will have imposed a restriction upon the distribution of constitutionally protected as well as obscene literature. It has been well observed of a statute construed as dispensing with any requirement of scienter that: 'Every bookseller would be placed under an obligation to make himself aware of the contents of every book in his shop. It would be altogether unreasonable to demand so near an approach to omniscience.'[9] The King v. Ewart, 25 N.Z.L.R. 709, 729 (C.A.). And the bookseller's burden would become the public's burden, for by restricting him the public's access to reading matter would be restricted. If the contents of bookshops and periodical stands were restricted to material of which their proprietors had made an inspection, they might be depleted indeed. The bookseller's limitation in the amount of reading material with which he could familiarize himself and his timidity in the face of his absolute criminal liability, thus would tend to restrict the public's access to forms of the printed word which the State could not constitutionally suppress directly. The bookseller's self-censorship, compelled by the State, would be a censorship affecting the whole public hardly less virulent for being privately administered. Through it, the distribution of all books, both obscene and not obscene, would be impeded.

"It is argued that unless the scienter requirement is dispensed with, regulation of the distribution of obscene material will be ineffective, as booksellers will falsely disclaim knowledge of their books' contents or falsely deny reason to suspect their obscenity. We might observe that it has been some time now since the law viewed itself as impotent to explore the actual state of a man's mind. See Pound, The Role of the Will in Law, 68 Harv. L. Rev. 1. Cf. American Communications Assn. v. Douds, 339 U.S. 382, 411. Eyewitness testimony of a bookseller's perusal of a book hardly need be a necessary element in proving his awareness of its contents. The circumstances may warrant the inference that he was aware of what a book contained, despite his denial.

"We need not and most definitely do not pass today on what sort of mental

---

[8] The effectiveness of absolute criminal liability laws in promoting caution has been subjected to criticism. See Hall, General Principles of Criminal Law, pp. 300-301. See generally Williams, Criminal Law — The General Part, pp. 267-274; Sayre, Public Welfare Offenses, 33 Col. L. Rev. 55; Mueller, On Common Law Mens Rea, 42 Minn. L. Rev. 1043; Morissette v. United States, 342 U.S. 246.

[9] Common-law prosecutions for the dissemination of obscene matter strictly adhered to the requirement of scienter. See the discussion in Attorney General v. Simpson, 93 Irish L.T. 33, 37-38 (Dist. Ct.). Cf. Obscene Publications Act, 1959, 7 & 8 Eliz. 2, c. 66, §2(5); American Law Institute Model Penal Code §207.10(7) (Tentative Draft No. 6, May 1957), and Comments, pp. 49-51.

The general California obscenity statute, Penal Code §311, requires scienter . . . and was of course sustained by us in Roth v. United States, supra. . . .

element is requisite to a constitutionally permissible prosecution of a bookseller for carrying an obscene book in stock; whether honest mistake as to whether its contents in fact constituted obscenity need be an excuse; whether there might be circumstances under which the State constitutionally might require that a bookseller investigate further, or might put on him the burden of explaining why he did not, and what such circumstances might be. Doubtless any form of criminal obscenity statute applicable to a bookseller will induce some tendency to self-censorship and have some inhibitory effect on the dissemination of material not obscene, but we consider today only one which goes to the extent of eliminating all mental elements from the crime." 361 U.S. at 153-155.

Since the Smith case many jurisdictions have construed existing statutes as requiring scienter though they contained no specific language. See e.g., Demetropolos v. Commonwealth, 342 Mass. 658, 175 N.E.2d 259 (1961); State v. Andrews, 150 Conn. 92, 186 A.2d 546 (1962), and cases cited there. But cf. State v. Gump, 57 Wash. 2d 224, 356 P.2d 289 (1960); State v. Griffith, 174 Ohio St. 553, 190 N.E.2d 907 (1963); State v. Warth, 173 Ohio St. 15, 179 N.E.2d 772 (1962); City of Cincinnati v. Marshall, 172 Ohio St. 280, 175 N.E.2d 178 (1961). Cf. further State v. Coleman, 240 Ohio Op. 2d 179, 193 N.E.2d 198 (Lucas Co. 1963) (construing statute as not prohibiting mere private possession). On how knowledge of content may be proved and on whether knowledge of the obscene nature of the material must also be shown and if so how such knowledge may be proved, see the comment in State v. Andrews, supra, following a quote from the Smith case on the lack of need for eyewitnesses to the seller's perusal of the book:

"Knowledge by a bookseller of the obscene or indecent character of the magazines possessed by him can ordinarily be proved only by circumstantial evidence. State v. Sul, 146 Conn. 78, 87, 147 A.2d 686; see State v. Heno, 119 Conn. 29, 32, 174 A. 181, 94 A.L.R. 696; State v. Weiner, 84 Conn. 411, 417, 80 A. 198. The defendant admitted to the police officer who confiscated the thirteen magazines that they did not come to the store through normal channels but by railway express and personal delivery. The magazines here involved and those of similar character were displayed separately from other magazines. The two magazines purchased by a police officer on June 17, 1960 — 'Modern Man — 1960 Yearbook of Queens' and 'Modern Man' July, 1960, issue — were delivered to him in a paper bag. Two cartons of magazines of the same general kind were found in the back room of the store. The pictures on the covers of these magazines, as well as the titles of articles and the prices listed thereon, were such as would put the defendant on notice concerning the kind of magazines they were. These facts, considered cumulatively, reasonably warrant an inference that the defendant knew the kind of magazines he had for sale. See State v. Chobot, supra, 12 Wis. 2d 119; Alexander v. United States, 271 F.2d 140, 145 (8th Cir.); United States v. Hochman, 175 F. Supp. 881, 882 (E.D. Wis.), aff'd 277 F.2d 631 (7th Cir.), cert. denied 364 U.S. 837, 81 S. Ct. 70, 5 L. Ed. 2d 61; People v. Zucker, 15 A.D.2d 883, 225 N.Y.S.2d 154, cert. denied 83 S. Ct. 116; People v. Finkelstein, 11 N.Y.S.2d 300, 304, 229 N.Y.S.2d 367, 183 N.E.2d 661, cert. denied 83 S. Ct. 116. The facts were sufficient reasonably to support a finding, at least prima facie, that the defendant was aware of the nature of the contents of the magazines. State v. Del Vecchio, 145 Conn. 549, 553, 145 A.2d 199; State v. Rich, 129 Conn. 537, 540, 29 A.2d 771." 150 Conn. at 103-104, 186 A.2d at 552.

Compare Mr. Justice Black's statement in the Ginzburg case:

"My conclusion is that certainly after the fourteen separate opinions handed down in these three cases today no person, not even the most learned judge much less a layman, is capable of knowing in advance of an ultimate decision in his particular case by this Court whether certain material comes within the area of 'obscenity' as that term is confused by the Court today. For this reason even if, as appears from the result of the three cases today, this country is far along the way to a censorship of the subjects about which the people can talk or write, we need not commit further constitutional transgressions by leaving people in the dark as to what literature or what words or what symbols if distributed through the mails make a man a criminal. As bad and obnoxious as I believe governmental censorship is in a Nation that has accepted the First Amendment as its basic ideal for freedom, I am compelled to say that censorship that would stamp certain books and literature as illegal in advance of publication or conviction would in some ways be preferable to the unpredictable book-by-book censorship into which we have now drifted." 343 U.S. at 480-481.

See also State v. Onorato, 2 Conn. Cir. 428, 199 A.2d 715 (1963); City of Chicago v. Doe, 47 Ill. App. 2d 460, 197 N.E.2d 711 (1964) (high price, stapling, and location of book next to cash register all indication of defendant's knowledge of nature of contents); State v. Witzel, 173 Ohio St. 16, 179 N.E.2d 773 (1962). Cf. People v. Harris, 192 Cal. App. 2d Supp. 887, 13 Cal. Reptr. 642 (1961) (proof of knowledge of content and not the nature of the content is all that is required). But cf. State v. Locks, 97 Ariz. 148, 397 P.2d 949 (1964) (a statute which speaks merely of obscene matter without further definition is too vague because the ordinary layman could not know whether the character of this material was obscene). The court had previously held that the scienter requirement was implied. 91 Ariz. 394, 372 P.2d 724 (1962).

On the question of the need for actual eyewitness evidence of the seller's perusal of the book, see further United States v. Mishkin, 317 F.2d 634 (2d Cir. 1963); State v. Hudson County News Co., 41 N.J. 247, 196 A.2d 225 (1963). See also presumption of knowledge from commercial use of obscene material in A.L.I. Model Penal Code, §251.4 (2).

In the most recent expression by the Supreme Court, Mishkin v. New York, 383 U.S. 502, 86 S. Ct. 958, 16 L. Ed. 2d 56 (1966), Mr. Justice Brennan stated:

"In People v. Finkelstein, 9 N.Y.2d 342, 344-345, 174 N.E.2d 470, 472 (1961), the New York Court of Appeals authoritatively interpreted §1141 to require the 'vital element of scienter,' and it defined the required mental element in these terms:

" 'A reading of the statute [§1141] as a whole clearly indicates that only those who are in some manner aware of the *character* of the material they attempt to distribute should be punished. It is not innocent but *calculated purveyance* of filth which is exorcised. . . .' (Emphasis added.)

Appellant's challenge to the validity of §1141 founded on Smith v. California, 361 U.S. 147, is thus foreclosed,[10] and this construction of §1141 makes it unnecessary

[10] The scienter requirement set out in the text would seem to be, as a matter of state law, as applicable to publishers as it is to booksellers; both types of activities are encompassed within subdivision 1 of §1141. Moreover, there is no need for us to speculate as to whether this scienter requirement is also present in subdivision 2 of §1141 (making

for us to define today 'what sort of mental element is requisite to a constitutionally permissible prosecution.' Id., at 154. The Constitution requires proof of scienter to avoid the hazard of self-censorship of constitutionally protected material and to compensate for the ambiguities inherent in the definition of obscenity. The New York definition of the scienter required by §1141 amply serves those ends, and therefore fully meets the demands of the Constitution. Cf. Roth v. United States, 354 U.S. at 495-496 (Warren, C.J., concurring).

"Appellant's principal argument is that there was insufficient proof of scienter. This argument is without merit. The evidence of scienter in this record consists, in part, of appellant's instructions to his artists and writers; his efforts to disguise his role in the enterprise that published and sold the books; the transparency of the character of the material in question, highlighted by the titles, covers, and illustrations; the massive number of obscene books appellant published, hired others to prepare, and possessed for sale; the repetitive quality of the sequences and formats of the books; and the exorbitant prices marked on the books. This evidence amply shows that appellant 'was aware of the character of the material' and that his activity was 'not innocent but calculated purveyance of filth.' " 380 U.S. at 510-512.

11. Obscene "communication" — its relation to prohibited "action" which is "communicative": In Trans-Lux Dist. Corp. v. Board of Regents, 14 N.Y.2d 88, 248 N.Y.S.2d 857 (1964), reversed on the basis of Freedman v. Maryland, 380 U.S. 259, 85 S. Ct. 952, 13 L. Ed. 2d 959 (1965), reprinted infra, Judge Burke in the course of the majority opinion holding that depiction of sexual intercourse on the screen is obscene, stated:

"It is my view that a filmed presentation of sexual intercourse, whether real or simulated, is just as subject to State prohibition as similar conduct if engaged in on the street. I believe the nature of films is sufficiently different from books to justify the conclusion that the critical difference between advocacy and actual perform-ance of the forbidden act is reached when simulated sexual intercourse is portrayed on the sceen. I take it to be conceded that New York may constitutionally prohibit sexual intercourse in public. As Mr. Justice Douglas acknowledged, dissenting in Roth v. United States, 354 U.S. 476, 512, 77 S. Ct. 1304, 1323, 1 L. Ed. 2d 1498, in contrasting books with conduct: 'I assume there is nothing in the Constitution which forbids Congress from using its power over the mails to proscribe *conduct* on the grounds of good morals. No one would suggest that the First Amendment permits nudity in public places, adultery, and other phases of sexual misconduct' (emphasis in text).

"This observation is equally pertinent, of course, whether the sexual exhibition-ism is done spontaneously in the street or in theatres for money (e.g., Penal Law, Consol. Laws, c. 40, §§43, 1140, 1140-a, 1140-b.) There have been many cases dealing with what sort of behavior was covered by statutes against sexual exhibi-tionism and the like, but they were solely concerned with statutory interpretation, never, obviously, the First Amendment. (Miller v. People, 5 Barb. 203; People v. Burke, 243 App. Div. 83, 276 N.Y.S. 402, affd. 267 N.Y. 571, 196 N.E. 585; People

---

it a crime to hire others to prepare obscene books); for appellant's convictions for that offense involved books of which he was also convicted of publishing.

No constitutional claim was asserted below or in this Court as to the possible dupli-cative character of the hiring and publishing counts.

v. Mitchell, 296 N.Y. 672, 70 N.E.2d 168; People v. Dash, 282 N.Y. 632, 25 N.E.2d 979).

"This comparison between the acknowledged competence of the State to forbid public or semipublic sex displays and its power to exert similar control over similar conduct depicted on the screen is not intended to imply any broad theory of legal equivalence between real conduct and a filmed imitation. Indeed, the meaningful comparison exists only in a narrow range of cases. In most instances, the real conduct is illegal because of what is accomplished by the person, as in murder, forgery, or adultery. In such cases, the filmed dramatization obviously does not share the evil aimed at in the law applicable to the real thing. Where, however, the real conduct is illegal, not because of what is accomplished by those involved, but simply because what is done is shocking, offensive to see, and generally believed destructive of the general level of morality, then a filmed simulation fully shares, it seems to me, the evil of the original. In such cases the free expression protection of the First Amendment must apply to both or neither. It makes no sense at all to say that the conduct can be forbidden but not the play or film.

"The pattern of statutory regulation in New York aims at offensive — more properly, obscene — *displays of conduct* whether in the street (Penal Law, §§43, 1140, 1140-b), on the stage (Penal Law, §1140-a; People v. Vickers, 259 App. Div. 841, 19 N.Y.S.2d 165 — lewd dance) or on the screen (Penal Law, §§1140-a, 1141; Education Law, §122). These laws care not about the communication of ideas (see Stromberg v. California, 283 U.S. 359, 51 S. Ct. 532, 75 L. Ed. 1117); they are aimed at certain narrow sorts of conduct. It seems to me, therefore, that if the defendants in People v. Stover, [12 N.Y.2d 462], could constitutionally be prohibited from selecting the forbidden form of conduct as the vehicle for the communication of their protest, then this petitioner cannot choose acted-out intercourse as the vehicle for its art (see, also, People v. Vickers, supra, where a performer was prohibited from choosing a certain sort of dance as her vehicle and the 'nude gymnasium' prohibited by Penal Law, §1140-b). Numerous other instances also suggest themselves.

"If we can accept the obvious — that sexual intercourse whether performed in the park or simulated on the stage or screen is in itself a form of conduct (in which the public have an interest[1]), it is apparent that when this defendant

---

[1] The police or general powers of government extend to "the preservation of good order and the public morals." (Beer Co. v. Massachusetts, 97 U.S. 25, 33, 24 L. Ed. 989.) As Mr. Justice Harlan recently stated on the State's authority to legislate in support of moral standards: "Yet the very inclusion of the category of morality among state concerns indicates that society is not limited in its objects only to the physical well-being of the community, but has traditionally concerned itself with the moral soundness of its people as well. Indeed to attempt a line between public behavior and that which is purely consensual or solitary would be to withdraw from community concern a range of subjects with which every society in civilized times has found it necessary to deal. The laws regarding marriage which provide both when the sexual powers may be used and the legal and societal context in which children are born and brought up, as well as laws forbidding adultery, fornication and homosexual practices which express the negative of the proposition, confining sexuality to lawful marriage, form a pattern so deeply pressed into the substance of our social life that any Constitutional doctrine in this area must build upon that basis. Compare McGowan v. Maryland, 366 U.S. 420, 81 S. Ct. 1101, 1153, 1213 [6 L. Ed. 2d 393]." (Harlan, J., dissenting in Poe v. Ullman, 367 U.S. 497, 545-546, 81 S. Ct. 1752, 1778, 6 L. Ed. 2d 989.)

chooses to use it as a vehicle for the expression of art it has "brigaded" the communication (to the extent that it is "communication") with conduct completely. In so doing the petitioner has subjected itself to such regulations as are appropriate to the conduct when engaged in for reasons having nothing to do with expression. There is otherwise no difference between advocacy and action. (Compare Thornhill v. Alabama, 310 U.S. 88, 60 S. Ct. 736, 84 L. Ed. 1093, with Local Union No. 10, etc., Plumbers Union v. Graham, 345 U.S. 192, 73 S. Ct. 585, 97 L. Ed. 946). 'Freedom of expression can be suppressed if, and to the extent that, it it so closely brigaded with illegal action as to be an inseparable part of it' (Douglas, J., dissenting in Roth v. United States, 354 U.S. 476, 514, 77 S. Ct. 1304, 1324, 1 L. Ed. 2d 1498).

"Just what regulations are appropriate regarding displays of sexual intimacy in public or semipublic places may be a matter for debate. The debate is most profitably conducted, however, in the malleable forum of public policy rather than within the rigidities of constitutional law. In regard to conduct which has been legislatively declared to be against public policy, we are reminded by Mr. Justice Holmes that 'There is nothing that I more deprecate than the use of the Fourteenth Amendment beyond the absolute compulsion of its words to prevent the making of social experiments that an important part of the community desires, in the insulated chambers afforded by the several states, even though the experiments may seem futile or even noxious to me and to those whose judgment I most respect' (dissenting opinion in Truax v. Corrigan, 257 U.S. 312, 344, 42 S. Ct. 124, 134, 66 L. Ed. 254). The sole exception to this tolerance of experimentation is legislation hostile to that freedom of expression necessary to the healthy functioning of an open democratic society. It is after careful consideration that I conclude that, far from hostility to any idea, even hateful ideas that undermine social morality, section 122 of the Education Law merely proscribes certain behavior, which, when viewed by the public, is deemed offensive and destructive of moral standards historically protected by the State and which 'bears no necessary relationship to the freedom to speak, write, print or distribute information or opinion' (Schneider v. State, 308 U.S. 147, 161, 60 S. Ct. 146, 150, 84 L. Ed. 155).

"The scenes referred to by the State are obscene within the meaning of section 122 of the Education Law as I understand it in light of the Fourteenth Amendment. The issue of obscenity as a constitutional standard applicable to speech proper, or whether the conduct here depicted can even be meaningfully thought of as speech in this context, need not be decided.

"Lastly, because the material assigned as obscene in this case is not, in my view, speech, as opposed to conduct, it need not come within the test laid down in Roth v. United States, 354 U.S. 476, 77 S. Ct. 1304, 1 L. Ed. 2d 1498, supra, that, in speech cases, obscenity must be the dominant theme of the work as a whole." 14 N.Y.2d at 92-96, 248 N.Y.S.2d at 861-863.

REFERENCES

Generally, on the above problems, see Lockhart and McClure, Censorship of Obscenity: The Developing Constitutional Standard, 45 Minn. L. Rev. 5 (1960), and Obscenity Censorship; The Core Constitutional Issue — What is Obscene? 7 Utah L. Rev. 289

(1961); Specter et al., Censorship and Obscenity: A Panel Discussion, 66 Dick. L. Rev. 421 (1962); Slough and McAnany, Obscenity and Constitutional Freedom, 8 St. Louis U. L.J. 279, 449 (1964); Schwartz, Morals Offenses and the Model Penal Code, 63 Colum. L. Rev. 669 (1963); Kalven, The Metaphysics of the Law of Obscenity, 1960 Sup. Ct. Rev. 11; Murphy, The Value of Pornography 655 (1964); Fleishman, Obscenity: The Exquisitely Vague Crime, 2 Law in Trans. Q. 97 (1965); Seaton, Obscenity: The Search for A Standard, 13 Kan. L. Rev. 117 (1964); Krash, Book Review of Rolph, the Trial of Lady Chatterley (1961), 71 Yale L.J. 1351 (1962); Coleman, Obscenity, Blasphemy, Sedition: Censorship in Australia (1962); Whitmore, Obscenity In Literature: Crime or Free Speech, 4 Sydney L. Rev. 179 (1963); Elias, Obscenity: The Law, a Dissenting Voice, 15 Baylor L. Rev. 1 (1963); Lacy, Freedom and Communication (1961); Leigh, Aspects of the Control of Obscene Literature in Canada, 27 Mod. L. Rev. 669 (1964); Kronhausen and Kronhausen, Pornography and the Law (2d ed. 1964); Ernst and Schwartz, Censorship: The Search for the Obscene (1964); Haney, Comstockery in America (1960); Gardiner, Catholic Viewpoint on Censorship (1958); Chandos (ed.), "To Deprave and Corrupt . . .": Original Studies in the Nature and Definition of 'Obscenity' (1962); Emerson, Toward a General Theory of the First Amendment, 72 Yale L.J. 877, 937-939 (1963); Henkin, Morals and the Constitution, 63 Colum. L. Rev. 391 (1963); Zuckman, The Law of Obscenity and Military Practice, 20 Mil. L. Rev. 43 (1963); Craig, Suppressed Books (1963), and The Banned Books of England and Other Countries (1962); St. John-Stevas, Obscenity and the Law (1956); Dibble, Obscenity: A State Quarantine to Protect Children, 39 So. Cal. L. Rev. 345 (1966).

B. Procedures

1. *Prior Restraint–Due Process*

NEAR v. MINNESOTA
283 U.S. 697, 51 S. Ct. 625, 75 L. Ed. 1357 (1931)

[Chapter 285 of the Session Laws of Minnesota for the year 1925 provided in Section 1:

"Any person who, as an individual, or as a member or employee of a firm, or association or organization, or as an officer, director, member or employee of a corporation, shall be engaged in the business of regularly or customarily producing, publishing or circulating, having in possession, selling or giving away

　　(a) an obscene, lewd and lascivious newspaper, magazine, or other periodical, or

　　(b) a malicious, scandalous and defamatory newspaper, magazine or other periodical,

is guilty of a nuisance, and all persons guilty of such nuisance may be enjoined, as hereinafter provided."

Under clause (b) of the above statute the County Attorney of Hennepin County brought suit to enjoin the defendants from publishing a newspaper known as The Saturday Press. The lower court, after trial, granted a permanent injunction and this was upheld by the Supreme Court of Minnesota. The defendants then appealed to the United States Supreme Court.]

Mr. Chief Justice Hughes delivered the opinion of the Court. . . .

Without attempting to summarize the contents of the voluminous exhibits attached to the complaint, we deem it sufficient to say that the articles charged in substance that a Jewish gangster was in control of gambling, bootlegging and racketeering in Minneapolis, and that law enforcing officers and agencies were not energetically performing their duties. Most of the charges were directed against the Chief of Police; he was charged with gross neglect of duty, illicit relations with gangsters, and with participation in graft. The County Attorney was charged with knowing the existing conditions and with failure to take adequate measures to remedy them. The Mayor was accused of inefficiency and dereliction. One member of the grand jury was stated to be in sympathy with the gangsters. A special grand jury and a special prosecutor were demanded to deal with the situation in general, and, in particular, to investigate an attempt to assassinate one Guilford, one of the original defendants, who, it appears from the articles, was shot by gangsters after the first issue of the periodical had been published. There is no question but that the articles made serious accusations against the public officers named and others in connection with the prevalence of crimes and the failure to expose and punish them. . . .

This statute, for the suppression as a public nuisance of a newspaper or periodical, is unusual, if not unique, and raises questions of grave importance transcending the local interests involved in the particular action. It is no longer open to doubt that the liberty of the press, and of speech, is within the liberty safeguarded by the due process clause of the Fourteenth Amendment from invasion by state action. . . .

If we cut through mere details of procedure, the operation and effect of the statute in substance is that public authorities may bring the owner or publisher of a newspaper or periodical before a judge upon a charge of conducting a business of publishing scandalous and defamatory matter — in particular that the matter consists of charges against public officers of official dereliction — and, unless the owner or publisher is able and disposed to bring competent evidence to satisfy the judge that the charges are true and are published with good motives and for justifiable ends, his newspaper or periodical is suppressed and further publication is made punishable as a contempt. This is of the essence of censorship.

The question is whether a statute authorizing such proceedings in restraint of publication is consistent with the conception of the liberty of the press as historically conceived and guaranteed. In determining the extent of the constitutional protection, it has been generally, if not universally, considered that it is the chief purpose of the guaranty to prevent previous restraints upon publication. The struggle in England, directed against the legislative power of the licenser, resulted in renunciation of the censorship of the press. . . .

[It] is recognized that punishment for the abuse of the liberty accorded to the press is essential to the protection of the public, and that the common law rules that subject the libeler to responsibility for the public offense, as well as for the private injury, are not abolished by the protection extended in our constitution. [2 Cooley, Const. Lim., 8th ed., pp. 883, 884.] The law of criminal libel rests upon that secure foundation. There is also the conceded authority of courts to punish for contempt when publications directly tend to prevent the proper discharge of judicial functions. Patterson v. Colorado [205 U.S. 454]; Toledo Newspaper Co. v. United States, 247 U.S. 402, 419. In the present case, we have no occasion to inquire as to the permissible scope of subsequent punishment. For whatever wrong the appellant has committed or may commit, by his publications, the State appropriately affords both public and private redress by its libel laws. As has been noted, the statute in question does not deal with punishments; it provides for no punishment, except in case of contempt for violation of the court's order, but for suppression and injunction, that is, for restraint upon publication.

The objection has also been made that the principle as to immunity from previous restraint is stated too broadly, if every such restraint is deemed to be prohibited. That is undoubtedly true; the protection even as to the previous restraint is not absolutely unlimited. But the limitation has been recognized only in exceptional cases: "When a nation is at war many things that might be said in time of peace are such a hindrance to its efforts that their utterance will not be endured so long as men fight and that no Court could regard them as protected by any constitutional right." Schenck v. United States, 249 U.S. 47, 52. No one would question but that a government might prevent actual obstruction to its recruiting service or the publication of the sailing dates of transports or the number and location of troops. On similar grounds, the primary requirements of decency may be enforced against obscene publications. The security of the community life may be protected against incitements to acts of violence and the overthrow by force of orderly government. The constitutional guaranty of free speech does not "protect a man from an injunction against uttering words that may have all the effect of force. Gompers v. Buck's Stove & Range Co., 221 U.S. 418, 439." Schenck v. United States, supra. These limitations are not applicable here. Nor are we now concerned with questions as to the extent of authority to prevent publications in order to protect private rights according to the principles governing the exercise of the jurisdiction of courts of equity.

The exceptional nature of its limitations places in a strong light the general conception that liberty of the press, historically considered and taken up by the Federal Constitution, has meant, principally although not exclusively, immunity from previous restraints or censorship. The conception of the liberty of the press in this country had broadened with the exigencies of the colonial period and with the efforts to secure freedom from oppressive administration. That liberty was especially cherished for the immunity it afforded from previous restraint of the publication of censure of public officers and charges of official misconduct. . . .

The fact that for approximately one hundred and fifty years there has been almost an entire absence of attempts to impose previous restraints upon publications relating to the malfeasance of public officers is significant of the deep-seated conviction that such restraints would violate constitutional right. Public officers, whose character and conduct remain open to debate and free discussion in the press, find their remedies for false accusations in actions under libel laws providing for redress and punishment, and not in proceedings to restrain the publication of newspapers and periodicals. The general principle that the constitutional guaranty of the liberty of the press gives immunity from previous restraints has been approved in many decisions under the provisions of state constitutions.[11]

The importance of this immunity has not lessened. While reckless assaults upon public men, and efforts to bring obloquy upon those who are endeavoring faithfully to discharge official duties, exert a baleful influence and deserve the severest condemnation in public opinion, it cannot be said that this abuse is greater, and it is believed to be less, than that which characterized the period in which our institutions took shape. Meanwhile, the administration of government has become more complex, the opportunities for malfeasance and corruption have multiplied, crime has grown to most serious proportions, and the danger of its protection by unfaithful officials and of the impairment of the fundamental security of life and property by criminal alliances and official neglect, emphasizes the primary need of a vigilant and courageous press, especially in great cities. The fact that the liberty of the press may be abused by miscreant purveyors of scandal does not make any the less necessary the immunity of the press from previous restraint in dealing with official misconduct. Subsequent punishment for such abuses as may exist is the appropriate remedy, consistent with constitutional privilege. . . .

Nor can it be said that the constitutional freedom from previous restraint is lost because charges are made of derelictions which constitute crimes. With the multiplying provisions of penal codes, and of municipal charters and ordinances carrying penal sanctions, the conduct of public officers is very largely within the purview of criminal statutes. The freedom of the press from previous restraint has never been regarded as limited to such animadversions as lay outside the range of penal enactments. Historically, there is no such limitation; it is inconsistent with the reason which underlies the privilege, as the privilege so limited would be of slight value for the purposes for which it came to be established.

The statute in question cannot be justified by reason of the fact that the publisher is permitted to show, before injunction issues, that the matter published is true and is published with good motives and for justifiable ends. If

---

[11] [The footnote, collecting numerous state cases, is omitted.]

such a statute, authorizing suppression and injunction on such a basis, is constitutionally valid, it would be equally permissible for the legislature to provide that at any time the publisher of any newspaper could be brought before a court, or even an administrative officer (as the constitutional protection may not be regarded as resting on mere procedural details) and required to produce proof of the truth of his publication, or of what he intended to publish, and of his motives, or stand enjoined. If this can be done, the legislature may provide machinery for determining in the complete exercise of its discretion what are justifiable ends and restrain publication accordingly. And it would be but a step to a complete system of censorship. The recognition of authority to impose previous restraint upon publication in order to protect the community against the circulation of charges of misconduct, and especially of official misconduct, necessarily would carry with it the admission of the authority of the censor against which the constitutional barrier was erected. The preliminary freedom, by virtue of the very reason for its existence, does not depend, as this Court has said, on proof of truth. Patterson v. Colorado, supra.

Equally unavailing is the insistence that the statute is designed to prevent the circulation of scandal which tends to disturb the public peace and to provoke assaults and the commission of crime. Charges of reprehensible conduct, and in particular of official malfeasance, unquestionably create a public scandal, but the theory of the constitutional guaranty is that even a more serious public evil would be caused by authority to prevent publication. "To prohibit the intent to excite those unfavorable sentiments against those who administer the Government, is equivalent to a prohibition of the actual excitement of them; and to prohibit the actual excitement of them is equivalent to a prohibition of discussions having that tendency and effect; which, again, is equivalent to a protection of those who administer the Government, if they should at any time deserve the contempt or hatred of the people, against being exposed to it by free animadversions on their characters and conduct." [12] . . . The danger of violent reactions becomes greater with effective organization of defiant groups resenting exposure, and, if this consideration warranted legislative interference with the initial freedom of publication, the constitutional protection would be reduced to a mere form of words.

For these reasons we hold the statute, so far as it authorized the proceedings in this action under clause (b) of section one, to be an infringement of the liberty of the press guaranteed by the Fourteenth Amendment. . . .

Judgment reversed.

Mr. Justice Butler, dissenting.

The decision of the Court in this case declared Minnesota and every other State powerless to restrain by injunction the business of publishing and circulating among the people malicious, scandalous and defamatory periodicals that in due course of judicial procedure has been adjudged to be a public

[12] [Madison, Report on the Virginia Resolutions, Madison's Works, vol. iv. 549.]

nuisance. It gives to freedom of the press a meaning and a scope not heretofore recognized and construes "liberty" in the due process clause of the Fourteenth Amendment to put upon the States a federal restriction that is without precedent. . . .

The Minnesota statute does not operate as a *previous* restraint on publication within the proper meaning of that phrase. It does not authorize administrative control in advance such as was formerly exercised by the licensers and censors, but prescribes a remedy to be enforced by a suit in equity. In this case there was previous publication made in the course of the business of regularly producing malicious, scandalous, and defamatory periodicals. The business and publications unquestionably constitute an abuse of the right of free press. The statute denounces the things done as a nuisance on the ground, as stated by the state supreme court, that they threaten morals, peace, and good order. There is no question of the power of the State to denounce such transgressions. The restraint authorized is only in respect of continuing to do what has been duly adjudged to constitute a nuisance. . . . There is nothing in the statute purporting to prohibit publications that have not been adjudged to constitute a nuisance. It is fanciful to suggest similarity between the granting or enforcement of the decree authorized by this statute to prevent *further* publication of malicious, scandalous, and defamatory articles and the *previous restraint* upon the press by licensers as referred to by Blackstone and described in the history of the times to which he alludes.

The opinion seems to concede that under clause (a) of the Minnesota law the business of regularly publishing and circulating an obscene periodical may be enjoined as a nuisance. It is difficult to perceive any distinction, having any relation to constitutionality, between clause (a) and clause (b) under which this action was brought. Both nuisances are offensive to morals, order, and good government. As that resulting from lewd publications constitutionally may be enjoined, it is hard to understand why the one resulting from a regular business of malicious defamation may not.

It is well known, as found by the state supreme court, that existing libel laws are inadequate effectively to suppress evils resulting from the kind of business and publications that are shown in this case. The doctrine that measures such as the one before us are invalid because they operate as previous restraints to infringe freedom of press exposes the peace and good order of every community and the business and private affairs of every individual to the constant and protracted false and malicious assaults of any insolvent publisher who may have purpose and sufficient capacity to contrive and put into effect a scheme or program for oppression, blackmail or extortion.

The judgment should be affirmed.

Mr. Justice Van Devanter, Mr. Justice McReynolds, and Mr. Justice Sutherland concur in this opinion.*

* The case is discussed in Notes, 31 Colum. L. Rev. 1148 (1931); 9 N.Y.U.L.Q. Rev. 64 (1931); 41 Yale L.J. 262 (1931); Emerson, The Doctrine of Prior Restraint, 20 Law & Contemp. Prob. 648, 652-655 (1955). — Ed.

FREEDMAN v. MARYLAND
380 U.S. 51, 85 S. Ct. 734, 13 L. Ed. 2d 649 (1965)

MR. JUSTICE BRENNAN delivered the opinion of the Court.

Appellant sought to challenge the constitutionality of the Maryland motion picture censorship statute, Md. Ann. Code, 1957, Art. 66A, and exhibited the film "Revenge at Daybreak" at his Baltimore theatre without first submitting the picture to the State Board of Censors as required by §2 thereof.[1] The State concedes that the picture does not violate the statutory standards[2] and would have received a license if properly submitted, but the appellant was convicted of a §2 violation despite his contention that the statute in its entirety unconstitutionally impaired freedom of expression. The Court of Appeals of Maryland affirmed, 233 Md. 498, 197 A.2d 232, and we noted probable jurisdiction, 377 U.S. 987. We reverse.

I

In Times Film Corp. v. City of Chicago, 365 U.S. 43, we considered and upheld a requirement of submission of motion pictures in advance of exhibition. The Court of Appeals held, on the authority of that decision, that "the Maryland censorship law must be held to be not void on its face as violative

---

[1] Md. Ann. Code, 1957, Art. 66A, §2:

"It shall be unlawful to sell, lease, lend, exhibit or use any motion picture film or view in the State of Maryland unless the said film or view has been submitted by the exchange, owner or lessee of the film or view and duly approved and licensed by the Maryland State Board of Censors, hereinafter in this article called the Board."

[2] Md. Ann. Code, 1957, Art. 66A, §6:

"(a) *Board to examine, approve or disapprove films* — The Board shall examine or supervise the examination of all films or views to be exhibited or used in the State of Maryland and shall approve and license such films or views which are moral and proper, and shall disapprove such as are obscene, or such as tend, in the judgment of the Board, to debase or corrupt morals or incite to crimes. All films exclusively portraying current events or pictorial news of the day, commonly called news reels, may be exhibited without examination and no license or fees shall be required therefor.

"(b) *What films considered obscene.* — For the purposes of this article, a motion picture film or view shall be considered to be obscene if, when considered as a whole, its calculated purpose or dominant effect is substantially to arouse sexual desires, and if the probability of this effect is so great as to outweigh whatever other merits the film may possess.

"(c) *What films tend to debase or corrupt morals.* — For the purposes of this article, a motion picture film or view shall be considered to be of such a character that its exhibition would tend to debase or corrupt morals if its dominant purpose or effect is erotic or pornographic; or if it portrays acts of sexual immorality, lust or lewdness, or if it expressly or impliedly presents such acts as desirable, acceptable or proper patterns of behavior.

"(d) *What films tend to incite to crime.* — For the purposes of this article, a motion picture film or view shall be considered of such a character that its exhibition would tend to incite to crime if the theme or the manner of its presentation presents the commission of criminal acts or contempt for law as constituting profitable, desirable, acceptable, respectable or commonly accepted behavior, or if it advocates or teaches the use of, or the methods of use of, narcotics or habit-forming drugs."

of the freedoms protected against State action by the First and Fourteenth Amendments." 233 Md., at 505, 197 A.2d, at 235. This reliance on Times Film was misplaced. The only question tendered for decision in that case was "whether a prior restraint was necessarily unconstitutional *under all circumstances.*" Bantam Books, Inc. v. Sullivan, 372 U.S. 58, 70, n.10 (emphasis in original). The exhibitor's argument that the requirement of submission without more amounted to a constitutionally prohibited prior restraint was interpreted by the Court in Times Film as a contention that the "constitutional protection includes complete and absolute freedom to exhibit, at least once, any and every kind of motion picture . . . even if this film contains the basest type of pornography, or incitement to riot, or forceful overthrow of orderly government. . . ." 365 U.S., at 46, 47. The Court held that on this "narrow" question, id., at 46, the argument stated the principle against prior restraints too broadly; citing a number of our decisions, the Court quoted the statement from Near v. Minnesota, 283 U.S. 697, 716, that "the protection even as to previous restraint is not absolutely unlimited." In rejecting the proffered proposition in Times Film the Court emphasized, however, that "[i]t is that question alone which we decide," 365 U.S., at 46, and it would therefore be inaccurate to say that Times Film upheld the specific features of the Chicago censorship ordinance.

Unlike the petitioner in Times Film, appellant does not argue that §2 is unconstitutional simply because it may prevent even the first showing of a film whose exhibition may legitimately be the subject of an obscenity prosecution. He presents a question quite distinct from that passed on in Times Film; accepting the rule in Times Film, he argues that §2 constitutes an invalid prior restraint because, in the context of the remainder of the statute, it presents a danger of unduly suppressing protected expression. He focuses particularly on the procedure for an initial decision by the censorship board, which, without any judicial participation, effectively bars exhibition of any disapproved film, unless and until the exhibitor undertakes a time-consuming appeal to the Maryland courts and succeeds in having the Board's decision reversed. Under the statute, the exhibitor is required to submit the film to the Board for examination, but no time limit is imposed for completion of Board action, §17. If the film is disapproved, or any elimination ordered, §19 provides that

"the person submitting such film or view for examination will receive immediate notice of such elimination or disapproval, and if appealed from, such film or view will be promptly re-examined, in the presence of such person, by two or more members of the Board, and the same finally approved or disapproved promptly after such re-examination, with the right of appeal from the decision of the Board to the Baltimore City Court of Baltimore City. There shall be a further right of appeal from the decision of the Baltimore City Court to the Court of Appeals of Maryland, subject generally to the time and manner provided for taking appeal to the Court of Appeals."

Thus there is no statutory provision for judicial participation in the procedure which bars a film, nor even assurance of prompt judicial review. Risk of delay is built into the Maryland procedure, as is borne out by experience; in the only reported case indicating the length of time required to complete an appeal, the initial judicial determination has taken four months and final vindication of the film on appellate review, six months. United Artists Corp. v. Maryland State Board of Censors, 210 Md. 586, 124 A.2d 292.

In the light of the difference between the issues presented here and in Times Film, the Court of Appeals erred in saying that, since appellant's refusal to submit the film to the Board was a violation only of §2, "he has restricted himself to an attack on that section alone, and lacks standing to challenge any of the other provisions (or alleged shortcomings) of the statute." 233 Md., at 505, 197 A.2d, at 236. Appellant has not challenged the submission requirement in a vacuum but in a concrete statutory context. His contention is that §2 effects an invalid prior restraint because the structure of the other provisions of the statute contributes to the infirmity of §2; he does not assert that the other provisions are independently invalid.

In the area of freedom of expression it is well established that one has standing to challenge a statute on the ground that it delegates overly broad licensing discretion to an administrative office, whether or not his conduct could be proscribed by a properly drawn statute, and whether or not he applied for a license. "One who might have had a license for the asking may . . . call into question the whole scheme of licensing when he is prosecuted for failure to procure it." Thornhill v. Alabama, 310 U.S. 88, 97; see Staub v. City of Baxley, 355 U.S. 313, 319; Saia v. New York, 334 U.S. 558; Thomas v. Collins, 323 U.S. 516; Hague v. CIO, 307 U.S. 496; Lovell v. City of Griffin, 303 U.S. 444, 452-453. Standing is recognized in such cases because of the ". . . danger of tolerating, in the area of First Amendment freedoms, the existence of a penal statute susceptible of sweeping and improper application." N.A.A.C.P. v. Button, 371 U.S. 415, 433; see also Amsterdam, Note, The Void-for-Vagueness Doctrine in the Supreme Court, 109 U. Pa. L. Rev. 67, 75-76, 80-81, 96-104 (1960). Although we have no occasion to decide whether the vice of overbroadness infects the Maryland statute,[3] we think that appellant's assertion of a similar danger in the Maryland apparatus of censorship — one always fraught with danger and viewed with suspicion — gives him standing to make that challenge. In substance his argument is that, because the apparatus operates in a statutory context in which judicial review may be too little and too late, the Maryland statute lacks sufficient safeguards for confining the censor's action to judicially determined constitutional limits, and therefore contains the same vice as a statute delegating excessive administrative discretion.

[3] Appellant also challenges the constitutionality of §6, establishing standards, as invalid for vagueness under the Due Process Clause; §11, imposing fees for the inspection and licensing of a film, as constituting an invalid tax upon the exercise of freedom of speech; and §23, allowing exemptions to various classes of exhibitors, as denying him the equal protection of the laws. In view of our result, we express no views upon these claims.

I I

Although the Court has said that motion pictures are not "necessarily sub-ject to the precise rules governing any other particular method of expression," Joseph Burstyn, Inc. v. Wilson, 343 U.S. 495, 503, it is as true here as of other forms of expression that "[a]ny system of prior restraints of expression comes to this Court bearing a heavy presumption against its constitutional validity." Bantam Books, Inc. v. Sullivan, supra, at 70. ". . . [U]nder the Fourteenth Amendment, a State is not free to adopt whatever procedures it pleases for dealing with obscenity . . . without regard to the possible consequences for constitutionally protected speech." Marcus v. Search Warrant, 367 U.S. 717, 731. The administration of a censorship system for motion pictures presents peculiar dangers to constitutionally protected speech. Unlike a prosecution for obscenity, a censorship proceeding puts the initial burden on the exhibitor or distributor. Because the censor's business is to censor, there inheres the danger that he may well be less responsive than a court — part of an inde-pendent branch of government — to the constitutionally protected interests in free expression.[4] And if it is made unduly onerous, by reason of delay or otherwise, to seek judicial review, the censor's determination may in practice be final.

Applying the settled rule of our cases, we hold that a noncriminal process which requires the prior submission of a film to a censor avoids constitutional infirmity only if it takes place under procedural safeguards designed to obvi-ate the dangers of a censorship system. First, the burden of proving that the film is unprotected expression must rest on the censor. As we said in Speiser v. Randall, 357 U.S. 513, 526, "Where the transcendent value of speech is involved, due process certainly requires . . . that the State bear the burden of persuasion to show that the appellants engaged in criminal speech." Second, while the State may require advance submission of all films, in order to pro-ceed effectively to bar all showings of unprotected films, the requirement cannot be administered in a manner which would lend an effect of finality to the censor's determination whether a film constitutes protected expression. The teaching of our cases is that, because only a judicial determination in an adversary proceeding ensures the necessary sensitivity to freedom of expres-sion, only a procedure requiring a judicial determination suffices to impose a valid final restraint. See Bantam Books, Inc. v. Sullivan, supra; A Quantity of Books v. Kansas, 378 U.S. 205; Marcus v. Search Warrant, supra; Manual Enterprises, Inc. v. Day, 370 U.S. 478, 518-519. To this end, the exhibitor must be assured, by statute or authoritative judicial construction, that the censor

---

[4] See Emerson, The Doctrine of Prior Restraint, 20 Law & Contemp. Prob. 648, 656-659 (1955). This is well illustrated by the fact that the Maryland Court of Appeals has reversed the Board's disapproval in every reported case. United Artists Corp. v. Mary-land State Board of Censors, supra; Maryland State Board of Censors v. Times Film Corp., 212 Md. 454, 129 A.2d 833; Fanfare Films, Inc. v. Motion Picture Censor Board, 234 Md. 10, 197 A.2d 839.

will, within a specified brief period, either issue a license or go to court to restrain showing the film. Any restraint imposed in advance of a final judicial determination on the merits must similarly be limited to preservation of the status quo for the shortest fixed period compatible with sound judicial resolution. Moreover, we are well aware that, even after expiration of a temporary restraint, an administrative refusal to license, signifying the censor's view that the film is unprotected, may have a discouraging effect on the exhibitor. See Bantam Books, Inc. v. Sullivan, supra. Therefore, the procedure must also assure a prompt final judicial decision, to minimize the deterrent effect of an interim and possibly erroneous denial of a license.

Without these safeguards, it may prove too burdensome to seek review of the censor's determination. Particularly in the case of motion pictures, it may take very little to deter exhibition in a given locality. The exhibitor's stake in any one picture may be insufficient to warrant a protracted and onerous course of litigation. The distributor, on the other hand, may be equally unwilling to accept the burdens and delays of litigation in a particular area when, without such difficulties, he can freely exhibit his film in most of the rest of the country; for we are told that only four States and a handful of municipalities have active censorship laws.[5]

It is readily apparent that the Maryland scheme does not satisfy these criteria. First, once the censor disapproves the film, the exhibitor must assume the burden of instituting judicial proceedings and of persuading the courts that the film is protected expression. Second, once the Board has acted against a film, exhibition is prohibited pending judicial review, however protracted. Under the statute, appellant could have been convicted if he had shown the film after unsuccessfully seeking a license, even though no court had ever ruled on the obscenity of the film. Third, it is abundantly clear that the Maryland statute provides no assurance of prompt judicial determination. We hold, therefore, that appellant's conviction must be reversed. The Maryland scheme fails to provide adequate safeguards against undue inhibition of protected expression, and this renders the §2 requirement of prior submission of films to the Board an invalid previous restraint.

III

How or whether Maryland is to incorporate the required procedural safeguards in the statutory scheme is, of course, for the State to decide. But a model is not lacking: In Kingsley Books, Inc. v. Brown, 354 U.S. 436, we upheld a New York injunctive procedure designed to prevent the sale of obscene books. That procedure postpones any restraint against sale until a

---

[5] An appendix to the brief amici curiae of the American Civil Liberties Union and its Maryland Branch lists New York, Virginia and Kansas as the three States having statutes similar to the Maryland statute, and the cities of Chicago, Detroit, Fort Worth and Providence as having similar ordinances. Twenty-eight of the remaining 39 municipal ordinances and codes are listed as "inactive."

judicial determination of obscenity following notice and an adversary hearing. The statute provides for a hearing one day after joinder of issue; the judge must hand down his decision within two days after termination of the hearing. The New York procedure operates without prior submission to a censor, but the chilling effect of a censorship order, even one which requires judicial action for its enforcement, suggests all the more reason for expeditious determination of the question whether a particular film is constitutionally protected.

The requirement of prior submission to a censor sustained in Times Film is consistent with our recognition that films differ from other forms of expression. Similarly, we think that the nature of the motion picture industry may suggest different time limits for a judicial determination. It is common knowledge that films are scheduled well before actual exhibition, and the requirement of advance submission in §2 recognizes this. One possible scheme would be to allow the exhibitor or distributor to submit his film early enough to ensure an orderly final disposition of the case before the scheduled exhibition date — far enough in advance so that the exhibitor could safely advertise the opening on a normal basis. Failing such a scheme or sufficiently early submission under such a scheme, the statute would have to require adjudication considerably more prompt than has been the case under the Maryland statute. Otherwise, litigation might be unduly expensive and protracted, or the victorious exhibitor might find the most propitious opportunity for exhibition past. We do not mean to lay down rigid time limits or procedures, but to suggest considerations in drafting legislation to accord with local exhibition practices, and in doing so to avoid the potentially chilling effect of the Maryland statute on protected expression.

Reversed.

Mr. Justice Douglas, whom Mr. Justice Black joins, concurring.

On several occasions I have indicated my view that movies are entitled to the same degree and kind of protection under the First Amendment as other forms of expression. Superior Films v. Department of Education, 346 U.S. 587, 588; Kingsley Pictures Corp. v. Regents, 360 U.S. 684, 697; Times Film Corp. v. Chicago, 365 U.S. 43, 78.* For the reasons there stated, I do not believe any form of censorship — no matter how speedy or prolonged it may be — is permissible. As I see it, a pictorial presentation occupies as preferred a position as any other form of expression. If censors are banned from the publishing business, from the pulpit, from the public platform — as they are

---

* The Court today holds that a system of movie censorship must contain at least three procedural safeguards if it is not to run afoul of the First Amendment: (1) the censor must have the burden of instituting judicial proceedings; (2) any restraint prior to judicial review can be imposed only briefly in order to preserve the status quo; and (3) a prompt judicial determination of obscenity must be assured. Thus the Chicago censorship system, upheld by the narrowest of margins in Times Film Corp. v. Chicago, 365 U.S. 43, could not survive under today's standards, for it provided not one of these safeguards, as the dissenters there expressly pointed out. Id., at 73-75.

— they should be banned from the theatre. I would not admit the censor even for the limited role accorded him in Kingsley Books, Inc. v. Brown, 354 U.S. 436. I adhere to my dissent in that case. Id., at 446-447. Any authority to obtain a temporary injunction gives the State "the paralyzing power of a censor." Id., at 446. The regime of Kingsley Books "substitutes punishment by contempt for punishment by jury trial." Id., at 447. I would put an end to all forms and types of censorship and give full literal meaning to the command of the First Amendment.

NOTES

1. In Bantam Books, Inc. v. Sullivan, 372 U.S. 58, 83 S. Ct. 631, 9 L. Ed. 2d 584 (1963), referred to in the principal case, Rhode Island created a Commission "to educate the public concerning any book . . . or other thing containing obscene, indecent or impure language, or manifestly tending to the corruption of youth as defined [in other sections] and to investigate and recommend the prosecution of all violations of said sections." The commission in practice sent notices to distributors informing them of books found objectionable for distribution or sale or display to those under eighteen. The notices indicated that they were sent to local police departments, that the commission had the duty to recommend prosecution, and that the distributors were requested to cooperate. In holding (at the request of out of state publishers for declaratory relief and injunction) that the law and its administration were unconstitutional, the Court stated in part:

"[The] Fourteenth Amendment requires that regulation by the Sates of obscenity conform to procedures that will ensure against the curtailment of constitutionally protected expression, which is often separated from obscenity only by a dim and uncertain line. It is characteristic of the freedoms of expression in general that they are vulnerable to gravely damaging yet barely visible encroachments. Our insistence that regulations of obscenity scrupulously embody the most rigorous procedural safeguards, Smith v. California, 361 U.S. 147; Marcus v. Search Warrant, [367 U.S. 717], is therefore but a special instance of the larger principle that the freedoms of expression must be ringed about with adequate bulwarks. See e.g., Thornhill v. Alabama, 310 U.S. 88; Winters v. New York, 333 U.S. 507; NAACP v. Button, 371 U.S. 415. '[T]he line between speech unconditionally guaranteed and speech which may legitimately be regulated . . . is finely drawn. . . . The separation of legitimate from illegitimate speech calls for . . . sensitive tools . . . .' Speiser v. Randall, 357 U.S. 513, 525.

"But, it is contended, these salutary principles have no application to the activities of the Rhode Island Commission because it does not regulate or suppress obscenity but simply exhorts booksellers and advises them of their legal rights. This contention, premised on the Commission's want of power to apply formal legal sanctions, is untenable. It is true that appellants' books have not been seized or banned by the State, and that no one has been prosecuted for their possession or sale. But though the Commission is limited to informal sanctions — the threat of invoking legal sanctions and other means of coercion, persuasion, and intimidation — the record amply demonstrates that the Commission deliberately set about to achieve the suppression of publications deemed 'objectionable' and succeeded in its aim.[7] We are not the first court to look through forms to the substance and recognize that informal censorship may sufficiently inhibit the circulation of publications to warrant injunctive relief.[8]

"It is not as if this were not regulation by the State of Rhode Island. The acts and practices of the members and Executive Secretary of the Commission disclosed on this record were performed under color of state law and so constituted acts of the State within the meaning of the Fourteenth Amendment. Ex parte Young, 209 U.S. 123. Cf. Terry v. Adams, 345 U.S. 461. These acts and practices directly and designedly stopped the circulation of publications in many parts of Rhode Island. It is true, as noted by the Supreme Court of Rhode Island, that Silverstein was 'free' to ignore the Commission's notices, in the sense that his refusal to 'cooperate' would have violated no law. But it was found as a fact — and the finding, being amply supported by the record, binds us — that Silverstein's compliance with the Commission's directives was not voluntary. People do not lightly disregard public officers' thinly veiled threats to institute criminal proceedings against them if they do not come around, and Silverstein's reaction, according to uncontroverted testimony, was no exception to this general rule. The Commission's notices, phrased virtually as orders, reasonably understood to be such by the distributor, invariably followed up by police visitations, in fact stopped the circulation of the listed publications ex proprio vigore. It would be naive to credit the State's assertion that these blacklists are in the nature of mere legal advice, when they plainly serve as instruments of regulation independent of the laws against obscenity.[9] Cf. Joint Anti-Fascist Refugee Committee v. McGrath, 341 U.S. 123.

[7] For discussions of the problem of "informal censorship," see Lockhart and McClure, Censorship of Obscenity: The Developing Constitutional Standards, 45 Minn. L. Rev. 5, 6-9 and n. 7-22 (1960); Note, Extralegal Censorship of Literature, 33 N.Y.U.L. Rev. 989 (1958); Note, Entertainment: Public Pressures and the Law, 71 Harv. L. Rev. 326, 344-347 (1957); Note, Regulation of Comic Books, 68 Harv. L. Rev. 489, 494-499 (1955); Comment, Censorship of Obscene Literature by Informal Governmental Action, 22 Univ. of Chi. L. Rev. 216 (1954); Lockhart and McClure, Literature, the Law of Obscenity, and the Constitution, 38 Minn. L. Rev. 295, 309-316 (1954).

[8] Threats of prosecution or of license revocation, or listings or notifications of supposedly obscene or objectionable publications or motion pictures, on the part of chiefs of police or prosecutors, have been enjoined in a number of cases. See Kingsley International Pictures Corp. v. Blanc, 396 Pa. 448, 153 A.2d 243 (1959); Bunis v. Conway, 17 App. Div. 2d 207, 234 N.Y.S.2d 435 (1962) (dictum); Sunshine Book Co. v. McCaffrey, 4 App. Div. 2d 643, 168 N.Y.S.2d 268 (1957); Random House, Inc., v. Detroit, No. 555684 Chancery, Cir. Ct., Wayne County, Mich., March 29, 1957; HMH Publishing Co. v. Garrett, 151 F. Supp. 903 (D.C.N.D. Ind. 1957); New American Library of World Literature v. Allen, 114 F. Supp. 823 (D.C.N.D. Ohio 1953); Bantam Books, Inc., v. Melko, 25 N.J. Super. 292, 96 A.2d 47 (Chancery 1953), modified on other grounds, 14 N.J. 524, 103 A.2d 256 (1954); Dearborn Publishing Co. v. Fitzgerald, 271 F. 479 (D.C.N.D. Ohio 1921); Epoch Producing Corp. v. Davis, 19 Ohio N.P. (N.S.) 465 (C.P. 1917). Cf. In re Louisiana News Co., 187 F. Supp. 241 (D.C.E.D. La. 1960); Roper v. Winner, 244 S.W.2d 355, 357 (Tex. Civ. App. 1951); American Mercury, Inc., v. Chase, 13 F.2d 224 (D.C.D. Mass. 1926). Relief has been denied in the following cases: Pocket Books, Inc., v. Walsh, 204 F. Supp. 297 (D.C.D. Conn. 1962); Dell Publishing Co. v. Beggans, 110 N.J. Eq. 72, 158 A. 765 (Chancery 1932). See also Magtab Publishing Corp. v. Howard, 169 F. Supp. 65 (D.C.W.D. La. 1959). None of the foregoing cases presents the precise factual situation at bar, and we intimate no view one way or the other as to their correctness.

[9] We note that the Commission itself appears to have understood its function as the proscribing of objectionable publications, and not merely the giving of legal advice to

"Herein lies the vice of the system. The Commissioner's operation is a form of effective state regulation superimposed upon the State's criminal regulation of obscenity and making such regulation largely unnecessary. In thus obviating the need to employ criminal sanctions, the State has at the same time eliminated the safeguards of the criminal process. Criminal sanctions may be applied only after a determination of obscenity has been made in a criminal trial hedged about with the procedural safeguards of the criminal process. The Commission's practice is in striking contrast, in that it provides no safeguards whatever against the suppression of nonobscene, and therefore constitutionally protected, matter. It is a form of regulation that creates hazards to protected freedoms markedly greater than those that attend reliance upon the criminal law.

"What Rhode Island has done, in fact, has been to subject the distribution of publications to a system of prior administrative restraints, since the Commission is not a judicial body and its decisions to list particular publications as objectionable do not follow judicial determinations that such publications may lawfully be banned. Any system of prior restraints of expression comes to this Court bearing a heavy presumption against its constitutional validity. See Near v. Minnesota, 283 U.S. 697; Lovell v. Griffin, 303 U.S. 444, 451; Schneider v. State, 308 U.S. 147, 164; Cantwell v. Connecticut, 310 U.S. 296, 306; Niemotko v. Maryland, 340 U.S. 268, 273; Kunz v. New York, 340 U.S. 290, 293; Staub v. Baxley, 355 U.S. 313, 321. We have tolerated such a system only where it operated under judicial superintendence and assured an almost immediate judicial determination of the validity of the restraint.[10] Kingsley Books, Inc., v. Brown, 354 U.S. 436. The system at bar in-

---

distributors. See the first notice received by Silverstein, quoted in note 5, supra. The minutes of one of the Commission's meetings read in part:

". . . Father Flannery [a member of the Commission] noted that he had been called about magazines proscribed by the Commission remaining on sale after lists had been *scent* [*sic*] to distributors and police, to which Mr. McAloon suggested that it could be that the same magazines were seen, but that it probably was not the same edition proscribed by the Commission.

"Father Flannery questioned the state-wide compliance by the police, or anyone else, to get the proscribed magazines off the stands. Mr. McAloon showed the Commissioners the questionnaires sent to the chiefs of police from this office and returned to us."

The minutes of another meeting read in part:

". . . Mr. Sullivan [member of the Commission] suggested calling the Cranston Chief of Police to inquire the reason Peyton Place was still being sold, distributed and displayed since the Police departments had been advised of the Commission's vote."

Of course, it is immaterial whether in carrying on the function of censor, the Commission may have been exceeding its statutory authority. Its acts would still constitute state action. Ex parte Young, 209 U.S. 123. The issue of statutory authority was not raised or argued in this litigation.

Our holding that the scheme of informal censorship here constitutes state action is in no way inconsistent with Standard Computing Scale Co. v. Farrell, 249 U.S. 571. In that case it was held that a bulletin of specifications issued by the State Superintendent of Weights and Measures could not be deemed state action for Fourteenth Amendment purposes because the bulletin was purely advisory; the decision turned on the fact that the bulletin was not coercive in purport.

[10] Nothing in the Court's opinion in Times Film Corp. v. Chicago, 365 U.S. 43, is inconsistent with the Court's traditional attitude of disfavor toward prior retraints of expression. The only question tendered to the Court in that case was whether a prior restraint was necessarily unconstitutional *under all circumstances*. In declining to hold

cludes no such saving features. On the contrary, its capacity for suppression of constitutionally protected publications is far in excess of that of the typical licensing scheme held constitutionally invalid by this Court. There is no provision whatever for judicial superintendence before notices issue or even for judicial review of the Commission's determinations of objectionableness. The publisher or distributor is not even entitled to notice and hearing before his publications are listed by the Commission as objectionable. Moreover, the Commission's statutory mandate is vague and uninformative, and the Commission has done nothing to make it more precise. Publications are listed as "objectionable" without further elucidation. The distributor is left to speculate whether the Commission considers his publication obscene or simply harmful to juvenile morality. For the Commission's domain is the whole of youthful morals. Finally, we note that although the Commission's supposed concern is limited to youthful readers, the "cooperation" it seeks from distributors invariably entails the complete suppression of the listed publications; adult readers are equally deprived of the opportunity to purchase the publications in the State. Cf. Butler v. Michigan, 353 U.S. 380.

"The procedures of the Commission are radically deficient. They fall far short of the constitutional requirements of governmental regulation of obscenity. We hold that the system of informal censorship disclosed by this record violates the Fourteenth Amendment.

"In holding that the activities disclosed on this record are constitutionally proscribed, we do not mean to suggest that private consultation between law enforcement officers and distributors prior to the institution of a judicial proceeding can never be constitutionally permissible. We do not hold that law enforcement officers must renounce all informal contacts with persons suspected of violating valid laws prohibiting obscenity. Where such consultation is genuinely undertaken with the purpose of aiding the distributor to comply with such laws and avoid prosecution under them, it need not retard the full enjoyment of First Amendment freedoms." 372 U.S. at 66-72.

2. In A Quantity of Copies of Books v. Kansas, 378 U.S. 205, 84 S. Ct. 1723, 12 L. Ed. 2d 809 (1964), referred to in the principal case, a state criminal obscenity statute was held unconstitutional in so far as it authorized the seizure of books before an adversary determination that they were obscene and authorized their destruction thereafter. The statute provided for a filing of a verified information prior to seizure stating no more than that "upon information and belief . . . there is [an] . . . obscene book . . . located within [the] county." The actual information in the case, however, went further to name allegedly obscene novels published under the same caption. A number of these were submitted with the information and were scrutinized ex parte by the judge prior to ordering seizure of all the named books. The Supreme Court's opinion read in part, as follows:

"The steps taken beyond the express requirements of the statute were thought by the Attorney General to be necessary under our decision in Marcus v. Search Warrant, 367 U.S. 717, decided a few weeks before the Information was filed. Marcus involved a proceeding under a strikingly similar Missouri search and seizure statute and implementing rule of court. See 367 U.S. 719, at notes 2, 3. In

---

prior restraints unconstitutional per se, the Court did not uphold the constitutionality of any specific such restraint. Furthermore, the holding was expressly confined to motion pictures.

Marcus the warrant gave the police virtually unlimited authority to seize any publications which they considered to be obscene, and was issued on a verified complaint lacking any specific description of the publications to be seized, and without prior submission of any publications whatever to the judge issuing the warrant. We reversed a judgment directing the destruction of the copies of 100 publications held to be obscene, holding that, even assuming that they were obscene, the procedures leading to their condemnation were constitutionally deficient for lack of safeguards to prevent suppression of nonobscene publications protected by the Constitution.

"It is our view that since the warrant here authorized the sheriff to seize all copies of the specified titles, and since P-K was not afforded a hearing on the question of the obscenity even of the seven novels before the warrant issued, the procedure was likewise constitutionally deficient.[2] This is the teaching of Kingsley Books, Inc., v. Brown, 354 U.S. 436. See Marcus, at pp. 734-738. The New York injunctive procedure there sustained does not afford ex parte relief but postpones all injunctive relief until 'both sides have had an opportunity to be heard.' Tenney v. Liberty News Distributors, 13 App. Div. 2d 770, 215 N.Y.S.2d 663, 664. In Marcus we explicitly said that Kingsley Books 'does not support the proposition that the State may impose the extensive restraints imposed here on the distribution of these publications prior to an adversary proceeding on the issue of obscenity, irrespective of whether or not the material is legally obscene.' 367 U.S., at 735-736. A seizure of all copies of the named titles is indeed more repressive than an injunction preventing further sale of the books. State regulation of obscenity must 'conform to procedures that will ensure against the curtailment of constitutionally protected expression, which is often separated from obscenity only by a dim and uncertain line.' Bantam Books, Inc., v. Sullivan, 372 U.S. 58, 66; the Constitution requires a procedure 'designed to focus searchingly on the question of obscenity,' Marcus, p. 732. We therefore conclude that in not first affording P-K an adversary hearing, the procedure leading to the seizure order was constitutionally deficient. What we said of the Missouri procedure, id., 736-737, also fits the Kansas procedure employed to remove these books from circulation:

" '. . . there is no doubt that an effective restraint — indeed the most effective restraint possible — was imposed prior to hearing on the circulation of the publications in this case, because all copies on which the [sheriff] could lay [his] hands were physically removed . . . from the premises of the wholesale distributor. An opportunity . . . to circulate the [books] . . . and then raise the claim of nonobscenity by way of defense to a prosecution for doing so was never afforded these appellants because the copies they possessed were taken away. Their ability to circulate their publications was left to the chance of securing other copies, themselves subject to mass seizure under other such warrants. The public's opportunity to obtain the publications was thus determined by the distributor's readiness and ability to outwit the police by obtaining and selling other copies before they in turn could be seized. In addition to its unseemliness, we do not believe that this kind of enforced competition affords a reasonable likelihood that nonobscene publications, entitled to constitutional protection, will reach the public. A distributor

---

[2] P-K News Service also asserts that its constitutional right against unreasonable searches and seizures was violated. The result here makes it unnecessary to pass upon this contention.

may have every reason to believe that a publication is constitutionally protected and will be so held after judicial hearing, but his belief is unavailing as against the contrary [ex parte] judgment [pursuant to which the sheriff] . . . seizes it from him.'

"It is no answer to say that obscene books are contraband, and that consequently the standards governing searches and seizures of allegedly obscene books should not differ from those applied with respect to narcotics, gambling paraphernalia and other contraband. We rejected that proposition in Marcus. We said, 367 U.S., at 730-731:

" 'The Missouri Supreme Court's assimilation of obscene literature to gambling paraphernalia or other contraband for purposes of search and seizure does not therefore answer the appellants' constitutional claim, but merely restates the issue whether obscenity may be treated in the same way. The authority to the police officers under the warrants issued in this case, broadly to seize "obscene . . . publications," poses problems not raised by the warrants to seize "gambling implements" and "all intoxicating liquors" involved in the cases cited by the Missouri Supreme Court. 334 S.W.2d, at 125. For the use of these warrants implicates questions whether the procedures leading to their issuance and surrounding their execution were adequate to avoid suppression of constitutionally protected publications. ". . . [T]he line between speech unconditionally guaranteed and speech which may legitimately be regulated, suppressed, or punished is finely drawn. . . . The separation of legitimate from illegitimate speech calls for . . . sensitive tools. . . ." Speiser v. Randall. 357 U.S. 513, 525. It follows that, under the Fourteenth Amendment, a State is not free to adopt whatever procedures it pleases for dealing with obscenity as here involved without regard to the possible consequences for constitutionally protected speech.'
See also Smith v. California, 361 U.S. 147, 152-153.

"Nor is the order under review saved because, after all 1,715 copies were seized and removed from circulation, P-K News Service was afforded a full hearing on the question of the obscenity of the novels. For if seizure of books precedes an adversary determination of their obscenity, there is danger of abridgment of the right of the public in a free society to unobstructed circulation of non-obscene books. Bantam Books v. Sullivan, supra; Roth v. United States, 354 U.S. 476; Marcus v. Search Warrant, supra; Smith v. California, supra. Here, as in Marcus, 'since a violation of the Fourteenth Amendment infected the proceedings, in order to vindicate appellants' constitutional rights' 367 U.S., at 738, the judgment resting on a finding of obscenity must be reversed." 278 U.S. at 209-213.

3. In Mishkin v. New York, 383 U.S. 502, 86 S. Ct. 958, 16 L. Ed. 2d 56 (1966), printed in part in Section A, the issue of the improper seizure of books introduced into evidence was raised before the Supreme Court. Mr. Justice Brennan stated:

"The far-reaching and important questions tendered by this claim are not presented by the record with sufficient clarity to require or justify their decision. Appellant's standing to assert the claim in regard to all the seizures is not entirely clear; there is no finding on the extent or nature of his interest in two book stores, the Main Stem Book Shop and Midget Book Shop, from which some of the books were seized. The State seeks to justify the basement storeroom seizure, in part, on the basis of the consent of the printer-accomplice; but there were no findings as to the authority of the printer over the access to the storeroom, or as to the voluntariness of his alleged consent. It is also maintained that the seizure in the storeroom was made on the authority of a search warrant; yet neither the affidavit upon which the warrant issued nor the warrant itself is in the record. Finally, while the search and seizure issue has a First Amendment aspect because of the alleged massive quality of the seizures, see A Quantity of Copies of Books v. Kansas, 378 U.S. 205, 206 (opinion of Brennan, J.); Marcus v. Search Warrant, 367 U.S. 717, the record in this regard is inadequate. There is neither evidence nor finding as to how many of the total available copies of the books in the various book stores were seized and it is impossible to determine whether the books seized in the basement storeroom were on the threshold of dissemination. Indeed, this First Amendment aspect apparently was not presented or considered by the state courts, nor was it raised in appellant's jurisdictional statement; it appeared for the first time in his brief on the merits.

"In light of these circumstances, which were not fully apprehended at the time we took the case, we decline to reach the merits of the search and seizure claim; insofar as notation of probable jurisdiction may be regarded as a grant of the certiorari writ on the search and seizure issue, that writ is dismissed as improvidently granted. . . ." 383 U.S. at 512-513.

See also Evergreen Review, Inc. v. Cahn, 230 F. Supp. 498 (E.D. N.Y. 1964) (ordering return of books to publisher and injunction against further interference with distribution in suit based on federal civil rights provision, 42 U.S.C. §1983); Louisiana News Co. v. Dayries, 187 F. Supp. 241 (E.D. La. 1960) (ordering return to publishers and newsstands of material not needed for the criminal prosecution). But cf. Outdoor American Corporation v. City of Philadelphia, 333 F.2d 963 (3d Cir. 1964), cert. den., 379 U.S. 903 (1964), and Dale Book Co. v. Leary, 233 F. Supp. 754 (E.D. Pa. 1964) (denying such a remedy especially where it is sought by publishers or distributors who are themselves not being prosecuted under the state obscenity law but whose publications have been seized in connection with prosecution of others such as magazine dealers).

For a case granting an injunction against interference by the police with the distribution of a book at the request of a prospective purchaser, see Chicago Sunday Star, April 1, 1962 (full reprint of Judge Epstein's opinion involving Tropic of Cancer). The court also ruled the book was not obscene, presumably to reassure booksellers against later prosecution. However, the injunction was stayed when the city of Chicago filed an appeal. Ibid. For another similar ruling by another Illinois lower court, see American Civil Liberties Union Bull., Aug. 13, 1962.

4. Subsequent to the Freedman case, supra, the Maryland statute was amended. Md. Laws 1965, c. 598. Under the new provisions, a film submitted to the board must be reviewed within five days. If disapproved the board must seek a judicial determination within three days and the court must act within the next seven days. An appeal by the exhibitor may be taken to the Maryland Court of Appeals which is to hear such appeal at "the earliest practicable date." See Trans-Lux Dist. Corp. v. Maryland State Board of Censors, 240 Md. 98, 213 A.2d 235 (1965).

5. After the Supreme Court of Georgia held unconstitutional, as a prior restraint, a state statute and an ordinance of the city of Atlanta requiring, before a picture could be exhibited, a permit following a review by a board of censorship, K. Gordon Murray Productions, Inc. v. Floyd, 217 Ga. 784, 125 S.E.2d 207 (1962), the city provided that a "Motion Picture Reviewer" shall screen and classify all

movies prior to exhibition as "approved," "unsuitable for the young," or "objectionable," and that if the picture falls in the latter two categories all advertisements of the picture must reveal that fact. The Georgia Supreme Court in a short opinion invalidated these provisions on the ground that they too constituted the type of prior resraint declared invalid by its prior ruling. City of Atlanta v. Twentieth Century-Fox Film Corp., 219 Ga. 271, 133 S.E.2d 12 (1963). To the same effect, see Interstate Circuit, Inc. v. City of Dallas, 247 F. Supp. 906 (N.D. Tex. 1965).

REFERENCES

See Note, A Blueprint for Censorship of Obscene Material: Standards for Procedural Due Process, 11 Vill. L. Rev. 125 (1965); Giglio, Prior Restraint of Motion Pictures, 69 Dick. L. Rev. 379 (1965); Verani, Motion Picture Censorship and the Doctrine of Prior Restraint, 3 Houston L. Rev. 11 (1965); Note, Legal Responsibility for Extra-Legal Censure, 62 Colum. L. Rev. 475 (1962).

On actual enforcement practices see Note, Obscenity Regulation and Enforcement in St. Louis and St. Louis County, 1964 Wash. U.L.Q. 98; Cook, Candy Comes to Chicago, The Nation, Sept. 19, 1964, p. 125; cf. Wasby, Public Law, Politics and the Local Courts: Obscene Literature in Chicago, 14 J. Pub. L. 105 (1965).

2. *Post Office*

Use of the mails is not controlled only by criminal sanctions such as those invoked in the Roth case or by the provisions concerning foreign propaganda declared unconstitutional in Lamont v. Postmaster General, 381 U.S. 301, 85 S. Ct. 1493, 14 L. Ed. 2d 398 (1965), noted in Chapter III, Section C, subsection 4. Based partly on implications[1] drawn from criminal statutes, the Postmaster excludes from the mails material which is seditious, threatening, amounts to a preparation of a lottery, is obscene, tends to incite a crime, or contains indecent or libelous matter on the wrapper. Though the legality of this procedure with respect to mail with obscene content which is not on the wrapper or on a postcard has long been questioned on the basis of lack of sufficient statutory authority, see Paul and Schwartz, Federal Censorship: Obscenity in the Mail 28, 252-262 (1961); Paul, The Post Office and Nonmailability of Obscenity: An Historical Note, 8 U.C.L.A.L. Rev. 44 (1961), a major statement of judicial skepticism about the Postmaster's powers to exclude such mail did not occur until 1962. In Manual Enterprises, Inc. v. Day, 370 U.S. 478, 82 S. Ct. 1432, 8 L. Ed. 2d 639 (1962), only Mr. Justice Clark unequivocally decided in favor of the Postmaster's authority; the Chief Justice and Justices Brennan and Douglas stated that despite one hundred years of a practice of exclusion the legislative history of the Comstock Act did not support the Postmaster's position. Mr. Justice Brennan's opinion added: "I imply no doubt that Congress could constitutionally authorize a noncriminal process in the nature of a judicial proceeding under closely defined proce-

---

[1] For specific authority in some instances see References, infra.

dural safeguards. But the suggestion that Congress may constitutionally authorize any process other than a fully judicial one immediately raises the gravest doubts." 370 U.S. at 518-519. Justices Harlan and Stewart did not see any need to reach the issue and they declined to rule in the absence of a "full-dress argument and briefing." Mr. Justice Black concurred in the result (ruling in favor of the mailer in part on the ground that the material was not obscene) without writing an opinion.

As indicated by Paul and Schwartz, supra, procedures for exclusion were for many years quite informal. The original discovery of obscenity, except for a somewhat more systematic scrutiny of "girlie" and similar magazines, would usually result from an offhand remark by a sender or from the coming open of a wrapper. A postal employee might then on the basis of "common sense" decide that the contents were not "fit for the home" and send the material to lawyers in the Fraud and Mailability Division. If they decided that the material was obscene they would issue a ruling that such material was non-mailable in the name of the Solicitor, who rarely reviewed these cases. The local postmaster would then notify the sender, who had recourse to an informal conference in Washington or to a challenge of the ruling in the courts. Prior to the conference the mail was stopped, and at the conference the argument was before the same lawyers who had issued the order. Expert witnesses and comparative material were generally not considered relevant and an original ruling was seldom revised. See Paul and Schwartz, id. at 91-96. These summary procedures were declared violative of the Due Process Clause of the Fifth Amendment in Walker v. Popenoe, 149 F.2d 511 (D.C. Cir. 1945); cf. Sunshine Book Co. v. Summerfield, 249 F.2d 114 (D.C. Cir. 1957) (upholding Post Office powers against broad attack), reversed per curiam on the basis of the Roth case, 355 U.S. 372, 78 S. Ct. 365, 2 L. Ed. 2d 352 (1958). The Post Office ignored the Walker case but there were some later court rulings and dicta which indicated that the Administrative Procedure Act would apply to all Post Office censorship proceedings. See unpublished district court rulings involving Rogue, Playboy, and Confidential magazines, ordering an Administrative Procedure Act hearing and ruling that mail could not be intercepted until such a hearing was held and a finding of obscenity made, in Paul and Schwartz, id. at 97. See further Door v. Donaldson, 195 F.2d 764 (D.C. Cir. 1952) (Administrative Procedure Act applies to mail block proceedings, see infra) see also Stanard v. Olesen, 74 S. Ct. 768, 98 L. Ed. 1151 (1954) (Mr. Justice Douglas's opinion in stay proceedings indicating interim mail blocks prior to hearing are illegal in absence of clear statutory authority); Cates v. Haderlein, 342 U.S. 804, 72 S. Ct. 47, 96 L. Ed. 609 (1951), affirming 189 F.2d 369 (7th Cir. 1951); Pinkus v. Reilly, 178 F. Supp. 399 (D.N.J. 1959); Borg-Johnson v. Christenberry, 169 F. Supp. 746 (S.D. N.Y. 1959) (Administrative Procedure Act and postal fraud proceedings); Wong Yang Sung v. McGrath, 339 U.S. 33, 70 S. Ct. 445, 94 L. Ed. 616

(1950) (leading case holding that the Administrative Procedure Act applies where there is no specific exemption).

In 1958, 1959 and 1961 the Post Office regulations were changed. A General Counsel, instead of the former Solicitor, was required to serve a complaint. A notice of hearing was sent to the sender of the questionable mail, who could request a hearing meeting the requirements of the Administrative Procedure Act. A prompt proceeding and prompt delivery of mail when found not obscene was prescribed. A "Judicial Officer," who was not connected with the prosecuting function, was appointed within the department. Subject to final authority in the Postmaster General, this officer was given the power to review the work of the Hearing Examiners. All decisions were required to be in writing and were to be based on a written record. See 39 C.F.R. Pt. 203 (1966). See also 39 C.F.R. Pt. 201 (1966) (rules pursuant to Administrative Procedure Act); 39 C.F.R. Pt. 204 (1966) (procedures with respect to second class mail privilege, see infra).

In addition to excluding certain mail, the Post Office may order local postmasters not to deliver any incoming mail to commercial distributors of offending materials. 39 U.S.C. §4006. One issue raised by this sanction was the question of whether interim mail blocks could be instituted prior to an administrative hearing resulting in a finding of obscenity. Until 1956 this was done by the Post Office without specific authority. A 1956 statute permitted interim mail blocks for a twenty-day period. Extensions had to be obtained by petitioning a district court. No such order could be obtained against holders of second class permits. Though the interim order was not subject to the Administrative Procedure Act, the person whose mail was blocked had to be fully notified. Former 39 U.S.C. §259(b) and (c) (1959). In 1960 this statute was amended so as to require the Post Office to apply to a district court from the very beginning for a temporary mail block order. The district court was empowered to issue such an order — this time for as long as the formal administrative hearing took — only after a full judicial hearing and a finding of "probable cause to believe" that the "statute is being violated." The district court could order that detained mail be opened for examination by the respondent and the respondent could take mail "clearly not connected with the alleged unlawful activity." Publications with second class mail privileges were again exempted from interim mail block orders. 39 U.S.C. 4007, amending former 39 U.S.C. §§259(b) and (c).

REFERENCES

For description and analysis, with examples from post office cases, of the above procedures, see Schwartz, The Mail Must Not Go Through — Propaganda and Pornography, 11 U.C.L.A.L. Rev. 805, 845 (1964); Note, Obscenity in the Mails: Post Office Department Procedures and the First Amendment, 58 Nw. U.L. Rev. 664 (1963); Fleishman, Obscenity and Post Office Censorship, 22 Law in Trans. 222 (1963); Note, Obscenity and the Post Office: Removal from the Mail Under Section 1461, 27 U. Chi. L. Rev. 354 (1960); Zuckman, Obscenity in the Mails, 33 So. Cal. L. Rev. 171 (1960); Paul and Schwartz, Federal Censorship: Obscenity in the Mail 91-116, 173-188, 274-281, 287-290, 344-347, 349-357 (1961), and the many Congressional Hearings and Reports there cited. See also Sigler, Freedom of the Mails: A Developing Right, 54 Geo. L.J. 30 (1965); Note, Mootness and Ripeness: The Postman Always Rings Twice, 65 Colum. L. Rev. 867 (1965); Paul, The Post Office and Non-Mailability of Obscenity: An Historical Note, 8 U.C.L.A.L. Rev. 44 (1961); De Grazia, Obscenity and the Mail: A Study of Administrative Restraint, 20 Law & Contemp. Prob. 608 (1955); Note, Postal Sanctions: A Study of the Summary Use of Administrative Power, 31 Ind. L.J. 257 (1956); Cutler, The Post Office Department and the Administrative Procedure Act, 47 Nw. U.L. Rev. 72 (1952).

For statutes specifically authorizing withdrawal from the mails, see e.g. 18 U.S.C. §1463, 25 Stat. 496 (obscene writings on envelopes or postcards); 18 U.S.C. §1718, 62 Stat. 782 (1948) (mailing matter libelous on its face); 39 U.S.C. (Supp. II) §§4003, 4005, 74 Stat. 654 (1960) (mail fraud and lottery); and others cited by Mr. Justice Brennan, 370 U.S. at 511 n. 20.

NOTES

1. Another issue raised by the mail block power concerns the scope of this authority. Does the fact that some issues of a magazine are obscene entitle the Post Office to stop all incoming mail to the publisher indefinitely. In Summerfield v. Sunshine Book Co., 221 F.2d 42 (D.C. Cir. 1954), cert. den., 349 U.S. 921 (1955), and Tourlanes Publishing Co. v. Summerfield, 231 F.2d 773 (D.C. Cir. 1956), cert. den., 352 U.S. 912 (1956), the circuit court held that the mail block order must be confined to incoming mail connected with "materials already published and duly found unlawful." Since this mail is not easy to identify, a mail block became difficult to impose on a publisher of both obscene and nonobscene material. For example, in the Tourlanes case, supra, the offending material was a booklet of nudes called "Studio Art" and the defense against an unlimited mail block was the publication of other material such as a "tax guide." In 1958 the Post Office adopted the procedure of permitting persons whose mail is blocked to open their impounded mail under supervision in the local post office and to take that mail which is not related to the obscene publication. See Paul and Schwartz, Federal Censorship: Obscenity in the Mail 28, 174 (1961). See also 39 U.S.C. §4007, noted supra.

2. Another provision of the postal laws, Pub. L. 87-793 §307, 76 Stat. 841 (1962), printed in note to 39 U.S.C. §4001, directs the Postmaster General to publicize the fact that obscene matter is being introduced from abroad, authorizes recipients to return such matter sent to them through the mails to local post offices, and, with the qualification that no mail may be inspected or censored unless the Post Office is so authorized by the addressee, provides that persons may request a local post office to detain and dispose of obscene mail from abroad addressed to them. See Regulations of Post Office Department §44.1 (Postal Manual §154.11), 28 Fed. Reg. 6537 (June 26, 1963) (addressee may request two-year detention). Cf. material in the Note infra on customs practices, subsection 3. Recent bills would expand this power by providing that when an addressee notifies the Post Office that specific mail is "morally offensive" to him the sender is notified to stop mailing such material to the addressee or his child. Noncompliance results in various sanctions,

such as loss of permits. Procedural safeguards vary in the different bills. See the discussion in Sigler, Freedom of the Mails: A Developing Right, 54 Geo. L.J. 30, 44-46 (1965).

3. The Postmaster also grants second class mail privileges to printed publications issued at stated intervals. One of the statutory prerequisites for receiving these privileges is that the publication must be for "the dissemination of information of a public character or devoted to literature, the sciences, arts or some special industry." In United States ex rel. Milwaukee Social Democratic Publishing Co. v. Burleson, 255 U.S. 407, 41 S. Ct. 352, 65 L. Ed. 704 (1921), the Supreme Court, without referring to any specific condition in the second class mail statute, upheld a determination by the Postmaster that where past issues were non-mailable because of seditious matter second class mailing privileges may be withdrawn from future issues. The Postmaster sought more extensive powers in Hannegan v. Esquire, 327 U.S. 146, 66 S. Ct. 456, 90 L. Ed. 586 (1946). There he had denied second class mailing privileges to Esquire because it had not met the statutory requirement quoted above. On the basis of general language in the Milwaukee case, he had construed the requirement to mean at least that the magazine must contribute to the public good and the public welfare, which, in his opinion, Esquire failed to do. The Supreme Court held that the Postmaster's power does not extend that far:

"But grave constitutional questions are immediately raised once it is said that the use of the mails is a privilege which may be extended or withheld on any grounds whatsoever. See the dissents of Mr. Justice Brandeis and Mr. Justice Holmes in Milwaukee Publishing Co. v. Burleson, 255 U.S. 407, 421-423, 430-432, 437-438. Under that view the second class rate could be granted on condition that certain economic and political ideas not be disseminated. The provisions of the Fourth condition would have to be far more explicit for us to assume that Congress made such a radical departure from our traditions and undertook to clothe the Postmaster-General with the power to supervise the tastes of the reading public of the country.

"It is plain, as we have said, that the favorable second class rates were granted periodicals meeting the requirements of the Fourth condition, so that the public good might be served through a dissemination of the class of periodicals described. But that is a far cry from assuming that Congress had any idea that each applicant for the second class rate must convince the Postmaster-General that his publication positively contributes to the public good or public welfare." 327 U.S. at 156-158.

See also Sunshine Publishing Co. v. Summerfield, 184 F. Supp. 767 (D.D.C. 1960).

For doubts about the power to revoke established second class mailing permits expressed by the Department's Judicial Officer, see In re Greenleaf Publishing Co., P.O.D. 4/202 (1958). For procedural safeguards see 39 C.F.R. §204.6 (1966) (issuance of ruling of suspension or revocation); id. §204.8(b) (petition that revocation is "erroneous"); id. §204.5 (hearing); id. §204.13 (counsel).

4. The Post Office also at times orders a mail watch or mail cover, consisting of a recording of data obtained from envelopes or the packaging of incoming mail in connection with investigations of possible criminal misconduct. First class mail is not opened. Recently this practice came to general public attention in connection with a perjury trial against Roy M. Cohn where the United States Attorney had

requested and obtained a mail cover on the mail of defendants after an indictment had been filed, in order to uncover possible tampering with government witnesses. The trial judge, though critical of the Government, refused to dismiss the indictment since the mail was never opened, no evidence was obtained as a result of the mail watch, and the use of a mail watch does not violate any constitutional rights. N.Y. Times, March 6, 1964. Since then it has become known as a result of a Senate investigation that 24,000 persons had been under surveillance by mail cover during 1963 and 1964. N.Y. Times, Feb. 24, 1965. For a case upholding a mail watch see also United States v. Costello, 157 F. Supp. 461 (S.D.N.Y. 1957), aff'd, 255 F.2d 876 (2d Cir. 1958); cf. United States v. Schwartz, 176 F. Supp. 613 (E.D. Pa. 1959) (though particular cover violated Post Office regulations, evidence obtained not excluded). On opening of first class mail as a violation of the Fourth Amendment, see Ex parte Jackson, 96 U.S. 727, 24 L. Ed. 877 (1878). See also Oliver v. United States, 239 F.2d 818 (8th Cir. 1957), cert. den., 353 U.S. 952 (1957). On the propriety of opening a prisoner's mail, see Stroud v. United States, 251 U.S. 15, 40 S. Ct. 50, 64 L. Ed. 103 (1919). See also Commonwealth v. Goodwin, 186 Pa. 218, 40 A. 412 (1898); State v. Booker, 68 W. Va. 8, 69 S.E. 295 (1910). It has been held that evidence obtained through opening mail sent to a prisoner may be used against the sender. In re Bull, 123 F. Supp. 389 (D.C. Nev. 1954).

3. Customs

The United States Government also controls circulation of obscene matter through the customs. The applicable statute provides for seizure by the Collector of (1) any obscene book "or any cast, instrument or other article which is obscene or immoral"; (2) books which contain matter "advocating or urging treason or insurrection" or "forcible resistance to any law" or "containing any threat to take the life of or inflict bodily harm upon any person"; (3) contraceptive devices; and (4) any lottery ticket or any advertisement of any lottery. 19 U.S.C. §1305. The statute also gives the Secretary of the Treasury discretionary authority to "admit the so-called classics or books of recognized and established literary or scientific merit . . . when imported for noncommercial purposes." See 18 U.S.C. §1462, for criminal penalties once the articles are seized and a District Attorney proceeds against them in the district court. While in theory the prescribed procedures suggest largely judicial rather than administrative censorship, the practice frequently means that there is a good deal of authority exercised by the agency without there being even an administrative hearing. According to Paul and Schwartz, when inspectors discover offending material it is submitted to a deputy collector who may decide to release it or condemn it when there is a clear ruling covering the matter. Or he may send it to Washington, which is usually the case. In Washington when the officials in charge were still in doubt, Mr. Huntington Cairns, who acted as Under Secretary of the Treasury and special adviser to the Department, would in effect make a final decision. Once there is a decision to seize the articles a form letter is sent to the recipient asking assent to the seizure. Where the importer protests there might occasionally be a review in Washington, but most of the time his remedy is a contest in the libel or condemnation case. Where the recipient does not reply to the notice the Department treats it as an indication of assent to the seizure. The seized articles are stored in a warehouse and on an average of once a year a local United States Attorney will file a libel petition or complaint to condemn the articles. Where the importer does not indicate a desire to contest the seizure he is not sent a notice of the libel. Notice is by advertisement. The uncontested proceeding before the judge becomes a mere formality. Frequently neither the judge nor the United States Attorney has seen the condemned material. Once the libel is completed the material is either destroyed or sent to the Library of Congress, as a repository for world publications. If relevant to scholarly fields it is kept and at times catalogued.

In the case of suspect first class mail, which cannot be opened without permission from the addressee, forfeiture proceedings are begun only when permission to open the mail has been granted and customs officials believe after examination that their suspicion was correct. A notice of the forfeiture and a request for the addressee's assent are sent out. Where assent is denied a libel action is instituted. Where not even permission to open the suspected mail has been obtained, the mail may still be returned to the sender. Cf. Note 4 supra on the Post Office.

In United States v. 18 Packages of Magazines, 238 F. Supp. 846 (N.D. Calif. 1964), the district court declared the customs procedure unconstitutional on the basis of A Quantity of Copies of Books v. Kansas, 378 U.S. 205, supra. The decision, which ordered the customs officials to "return and deliver" the material in question subject to compliance with ordinary customs obligations, was accompanied by an opinion which read in part as follows:

"The Government attempts to avoid [the A Quantity of Books] case by arguing that the First Amendment has no inhibitory effect on Congress's 'complete' control of foreign commerce. This novel theory is not buttressed by citation to a single court opinion which has ever intimated such a possibility. The only rationale offered in support of the theory is to the effect that unless it be accepted, there will be practical limitations on the ability of Congress to restrict the importation of 'obscene' books or other material. This may well be. However, Constitutional guarantees may not be subverted to expediency. The Constitution, as it is written and construed by the United States Supreme Court, must be strictly respected.

"The Government goes on to argue that even if the First Amendment does apply to Congressional powers over foreign commerce, it would not prohibit a law authorizing summary seizure of foreign magazines. It is 'manifest' 'without argument,' the Government contends, that the language of the First Amendment could not refer to the 'foreign press.' Even if it be conceded, arguendo, that the 'foreign press' is not a direct beneficiary of the Amendment, the concession gains nought for the Government in this case. The First

Amendment does protect the public of this country. As Mr. Justice Brennan pointed out in A Quantity of Copies of Books v. State of Kansas, supra, there is a *'right of the public* in a free society to unobstructed circulation of non-obscene books' (emphasis added). The First Amendment surely was designed to protect the rights of readers and distributors of publications no less than those of writers or printers. Indeed, the essence of the First Amendment right to freedom of the press is not so much the right to print as it is the right to read. The rights of readers are not to be curtailed because of the geographical origin of printed materials." 238 F. Supp. at 847-848.

But see United States v. One Carton Positive Motion Picture Film Entitled "491," 248 F. Supp. 373, 247 F. Supp. 450 (S.D. N.Y. 1965) (distinguishing 18 Packages as decided prior to Supreme Court's indication in Freedman, supra, that some time may elapse prior to judicial determination).

REFERENCES

See Paul and Schwartz, Federal Censorship: Obscenity in the Mail 88-91, 117-130, 169-172, 270-279, 282-283 (1961). This reference includes descriptions of rulings on the "classics" and "scientific merits" exceptions. See also Sigler, Customs Censorship, 15 Clev.-Mar. L. Rev. 58 (1966). Cf. United States v. 31 Photographs, 156 F. Supp. 350 (S.D. N.Y 1957), and see Mounce v. United States, 247 F.2d 148 (9th Cir. 1957), vacated on the basis of the Roth case, 355 U.S. 180 (1957) (dealing with imported nudist magazines). See also United States Bureau of Customs, Customs Regulations of the United States; Cairns, Freedom of Expression in Literature, 200 Annals of the Am. Acad. of Pol. and Soc. Sci. 76 (1938) (views held by special Under Secretary of the Treasury in charge of allegedly obscene material); Chafee, Government and Mass Communications 242-275 (1947).

C. EXTRA-LEGAL CONTROLS

1. Self-Regulation

THE MOTION PICTURE PRODUCTION CODE
Motion Picture Association of America, 1956

GENERAL PRINCIPLES

1. No picture shall be produced which will lower the moral standards of those who see it. Hence the sympathy of the audience shall never be thrown to the side of crime, wrong-doing, evil or sin.

2. Correct standards of life, subject only to the requirements of drama and entertainment, shall be presented.

3. Law — divine, natural or human — shall not be ridiculed, nor shall sympathy be created for its violation.

Particular Applications

I. Crime: 1. Crime shall never be presented in such a way as to throw sympathy with the crime as against law and justice, or to inspire others with a desire for imitation.

2. Methods of crime shall not be explicitly presented or detailed in a manner calculated to glamorize crime or inspire imitation.

3. Action showing the taking of human life is to be held to the minimum. Its frequent presentation tends to lessen regard for the sacredness of life.

4. Suicide, as a solution of problems occurring in the development of screen drama, is to be discouraged unless absolutely necessary for the development of the plot, and shall never be justified, or glorified, or used specifically to defeat the ends of justice.

5. Excessive flaunting of weapons by criminals shall not be permitted.

6. There shall be no scenes of law-enforcing officers dying at the hands of criminals, unless such scenes are absolutely necessary to the plot.

7. Pictures dealing with criminal activities in which minors participate, or to which minors are related, shall not be approved if they tend to incite demoralizing imitation on the part of youth.

8. Murder:

(a) The technique of murder must not be presented in a way that will inspire imitation.

(b) Brutal killings are not to be presented in detail.

(c) Revenge in modern times shall not be justified.

(d) Mercy killing shall never be made to seem right or permissible.

9. Drug addiction or the illicit traffic in addiction-producing drugs shall not be shown if the portrayal:

(a) Tends in any manner to encourage, stimulate or justify the use of such drugs; or

(b) Stresses, visually or by dialogue, their temporarily attractive effects; or

(c) Suggests that the drug habit may be quickly or easily broken; or

(d) Shows details of drug procurement or of the taking of drugs in any manner; or

(e) Emphasizes the profits of the drug traffic; or

(f) Involves children who are shown knowingly to use or traffic in drugs.

10. Stories on the kidnapping or illegal abduction of children are acceptable under the Code only (1) when the subject is handled with restraint and discretion and avoids details, gruesomeness and undue horror, and (2) the child is returned unharmed.

II. Brutality: Excessive and inhumane acts of cruelty and brutality shall not be presented. This includes all detailed and protracted presentation of physical violence, torture and abuse.

III. Sex: The sanctity of the institution of marriage and the home shall be upheld. No film shall infer that casual or promiscuous sex relationships are the accepted or common thing.

1. Adultery and illicit sex, sometimes necessary plot material, shall not be explicitly treated, nor shall they be justified or made to seem right and permissible.

2. Scenes of passion:

(a) These should not be introduced except where they are definitely essential to the plot.

(b) Lustful and open-mouth kissing, lustful embraces, suggestive posture and gestures are not to be shown.

(c) In general, passion should be treated in such manner as not to stimulate the baser emotions.

3. Seduction or rape:

(a) These should never be more than suggested, and then only when essential to the plot. They should never be shown explicitly.

(b) They are never acceptable subject matter for comedy.

(c) They should never be made to seem right and permissible.

4. The subject of abortion shall be discouraged, shall never be more than suggested, and when referred to shall be condemned. It must never be treated lightly or made the subject of comedy. Abortion shall never be shown explicitly or by inference, and a story must not indicate that an abortion has been performed. The word "abortion" shall not be used.

5. The methods and techniques of prostitution and white slavery shall never be presented in detail, nor shall the subjects be presented unless shown in contrast to right standards of behavior. Brothels in any clear identification as such may not be shown.

6. Sex perversion or any inference of it is forbidden.[1]

7. Sex hygiene and venereal diseases are not acceptable subject matter for theatrical motion pictures.

8. Children's sex organs are never to be exposed. This provision shall not apply to infants.

IV. Vulgarity: Vulgar expressions and double meanings having the same effect are forbidden. This shall include but not be limited to such words and expressions as chippie, fairy, goose, nuts, pansy, S.O.B., son-of-a. The treatment of low, disgusting, unpleasant, though not necessarily evil, subjects should be guided always by the dictates of good taste and a proper regard for the sensibilities of the audience.

V. Obscenity: 1. Dances suggesting or representing sexual actions or emphasizing indecent movements are to be regarded as obscene.

---

[1] Changed in 1961 to permit treatment of "sex aberration" when done with "care, discretion and restraint." — ED.

2. Obscenity in words, gesture, reference, song, joke or by suggestion, even when likely to be understood by only part of the audience, is forbidden.

VI. Blasphemy and Profanity: 1. Blasphemy is forbidden. Reference to the Deity, God, Lord, Jesus, Christ, shall not be irreverent.

2. Profanity is forbidden. The words "hell" and "damn," while sometimes dramatically valid will if used without moderation be considered offensive by many members of the audience. Their use shall be governed by the discretion and prudent advice of the Code Administration.

VII. Costumes: 1. Complete nudity, in fact or in silhouette, is never permitted, nor shall there be any licentious notice by characters in the film of suggested nudity.

2. Indecent or undue exposure is forbidden.

(a) The foregoing shall not be interpreted to exclude actual scenes photographed in a foreign land of the natives of that land, showing native life, provided:

(1) Such scenes are included in a documentary film or travelogue depicting exclusively such land, its customs and civilization; and

(2) Such scenes are not in themselves intrinsically objectionable.

VIII. Religion: 1. No film or episode shall throw ridicule on any religious faith.

2. Ministers of religion, or persons posing as such, shall not be portrayed as comic characters or as villains so as to cast disrespect on religion.

3. Ceremonies of any definite religion shall be carefully and respectfully handled.

IX. Special Subjects: The following subjects must be treated with discretion and restraint and within the careful limits of good taste:

1. Bedroom scenes.

2. Hangings and electrocutions.

3. Liquor and drinking.

4. Surgical operations and childbirth.

5. Third degree methods.

X. National Feelings: 1. The use of the flag shall be consistently respectful.

2. The history, institutions, prominent people and citizenry of all nations shall be represented fairly.

3. No picture shall be produced that tends to incite bigotry or hatred among people of differing races, religions or national origins. The use of such offensive words as Chink, Dago, Frog, Greaser, Hunkie, Kike, Nigger, Spig, Wop, Yid, should be avoided.

XI. Titles: The following titles shall not be used:

1. Titles which are salacious, indecent, obscene, profane or vulgar.

2. Titles which violate any other clause of this Code.

XII. Cruelty to Animals: In the production of motion pictures involving animals the producer shall consult with the authorized representative of the

American Humane Association, and invite him to be present during the staging of such animal action. There shall be no use of any contrivance or apparatus for tripping or otherwise treating animals in any unacceptably harsh manner.

NOTES

1. This 1956 version of the Motion Picture Code is more liberal in some respects than earlier codes, especially with regard to the depiction of drug addiction, kidnapping of children, childbirth, and miscegenation. While blasphemy is still prohibited, the words "hell" and "damn" may sometimes be used. See, e.g., the Code reprinted in the first edition of this book 715-718 (1952). For discussion of these changes see N.Y. Times, Dec. 16, 1956, §II, June 14, 1957, and Sept. 18, 1957; America, Jan. 5, 1957, p. 384, Dec. 29, 1956, p. 367; Driver, The New Movie Code, Christian Century, Jan. 2, 1957, p. 6.

2. The actual administration of the Code does not consist of merely passing on the final film. Producers are advised on the properties they buy for adaptation, on the script in various stages of preparation, on casting, and on specific sequences as they are being filmed. An unfavorable ruling by the Hollywood Censor may be appealed to a board consisting of the heads of the major movie distributing companies, four independent producers, and six persons representing theater owners. Between 1954 and 1964 there were only six appeals. On appeal the board views the film and listens to arguments by the appellant. It reads the ruling of the Hollywood Censor. For discussion see Schumach, The Face on the Cutting Room Floor 36 et seq. (1964); Vizzard, The Production Code of the Motion Picture Association, in Lectures on Communications Media, Legal and Policy Problems 127 (Summer Institute on International and Comparative Law, Mich. L. School 1954); Shurlock, The Motion Picture Production Code, 254 Annals of the Am. Acad. of Pol. and Soc. Sci. 140 (1947); Inglis, Freedom of the Movies 152 et seq. (1947); Moley, The Hays Office (1945).

3. Recent troubles with the motion picture "The Pawnbroker" may have provided the incentive to make a fundamental revision of the Code for the first time in thirty-five years. The film was originally denied a Seal of Approval because it showed a woman's breasts, but it won a reversal from the industry's appeals board. It was thought that the shots were necessary to show concentration camp horror. Cf. the introduction of a diamond-studded navel in "Cleopatra" to avoid the prohibition against showing a navel. Schumach, The Face on the Cutting Room Floor 168 (1964). Though nothing specific is known about the proposed Code revision, it is thought that the following prohibitions will be eliminated or at least revised: (a) the humorous treatment of "impure love," (b) the use of the word "abortion" and the identification of a brothel, (c) the nudity prohibition, (d) the "lustful embraces" or "suggestive posture" prohibition, and (e) the ban on the use of words like "chippie," "pansy," or "S.O.B." N.Y. Times, April 7, 1965. A later announcement indicates that the new Code will eliminate specific prohibitions and substitute a statement of general principles. Films with obvious adult themes will be cleared if labeled "for mature audiences" in advertising and promotion. N.Y. Times, Sept. 14, 1966. (The N.Y. Times story also indicates that "Who's Afraid of

Virginia Woolf" and "Alfie" were approved only after receiving individual exemptions by the Code Review Board.)

Amendment of the Code is accomplished by a difficult procedure. Arguments must be presented to a special subcommittee which may then recommend changes to the full Code committee, which is headed by the president of the Association. Other members are the heads of the Paramount, Universal, and Columbia studios. Final approval may only be obtained from the full board of governors, which consists of representatives of the eight major movie companies now in the Association. See Schumach, id. at 40.

4. For the view that self-censorship frequently extends beyond the Code because producers are not aware of the extent of liberality in the Code, see id. at 33 et seq., which also describes the use of censorship consultants.

5. A television Code, similar to the Motion Picture Production Code, was adopted in 1952. The National Association of Broadcasters Code Authority on the whole has only advisory power, though it may expel stations from the Code. This power to expel was exercised once against 30 stations advertising remedies for hemorrhoids. The stations were reinstated when they promised not to broadcast such ads in the future. Approximately one third of the stations are not signatories to the Code.

The Code contains many general admonitions, such as the emphasis on the audience as a "home audience" and the underscoring of the relationship of the medium to the viewers as one "between a guest and host." Respect for the "special need of children, for community responsibility, for the advancement of education and culture . . . and for propriety in advertising" are also stressed. Restrictive provisions are largely contained in a section on "General Program Standards" prohibiting profanity, obscenity, and vulgarity, and words that deride any race, color, religion, or nationality unless they are used in the context of combating prejudice. Religion may not be attacked at all, marriage must be respected, and physical deformities must not be used to get a laugh. Cruelty, greed, and selfishness cannot be depicted as worthy motivations and the exploitation of others may not be praised. In addition the Code opposes lewd presentations and takes the expected stand on such subjects as the treatment of policemen, crime, revenge as a motive for murder, suicide, sex crimes, illicit sex, drunkenness, and narcotic addiction. Programs should not incite gambling, present horror for its own sake, or encourage belief in fortune telling and similar arts. Costumes must not expose or emphasize "anatomical detail" in such a way as to "embarrass or offend home viewers." News must be "adequate and well balanced" and must not arouse "panic and unnecessary alarm." Pictures must not distort the story, and commentary or analysis must be labeled as such. There should be no "morbid, sensational or alarming details not essential to the factual report, especially in connection with stories of crime or sex." The Code urges stations to seek out programs that present controversial issues. In their presentations the programs must be identified as programs presenting controversy and the persons involved must be knowledgeable and have a sense of responsibility. The Code also contains twenty-five paragraphs against advertising abuse. Advertising should, as far as the station knows, be truthful. It should be presented courteously and with "good taste," and offensive description of distress and morbid situations should be avoided.

Administration of the Code does not involve the right of prior restraint. But synopses of scripts are sent to the Authority usually more than two weeks before shooting and informal consultations may result in script changes. The broadcasters are not pledged to stop a show that does not get approval. Code personnel also monitor programs, and a program's violation of the Code has to be explained, which presumably tends to discourage repetition of the violation. See National Association of Broadcasters, The Television Code (7th ed. 1962), described in Schumach, The Face on the Cutting Room Floor 227-233 (1964). See also National Association of Broadcasters, Code of Conduct For Broadcasting Public Proceedings — Meetings, Hearings, Trials (n.d.).

6. For self-regulation in the magazine and comic book industries see Note, 71 Harv. L. Rev. 326, 358 et seq. (1957); Code of the Comics Magazine Association of America, reprinted in 1 Catholic Law. 60 (1955); Fact Kit issued by the Association; Report of Comics Code Administrator, printed in Report of N.Y. State Joint Legislative Committee, Legis. Doc. No. 32, Studying Publication of and Dissemination of Offensive and Obscene Materials, App. VI (1956). See also N.Y. Times, May 10, 1961, describing decline of the industry after seven years of self-regulation.

2. Pressure Groups

SLOUGH and McANANY, OBSCENITY AND CONSTITUTIONAL FREEDOM
8 St. Louis U.L.J. 449, 485-496 (1964)

The effect of concerted private action and private group pressures upon the reading and viewing habits of Americans cannot be underestimated, much less overlooked. We can recall that Anthony Comstock's New York Society for the Suppression of Vice, which grew out of a Y.M.C.A. committee in 1873, became a potent force that would endure for two generations.[405] Its Bostonian counterpart, The New England Watch and Ward Society, launched in 1876, successfully inhibited a daring performance by Mary Garden in Salome and raised a substantial hue and cry over the distribution of Elinor Glyn's controversial Three Weeks.[406] As late as 1926, the Reverend J.

---

[405] See text accompanying notes 32-35 *supra.* An annual society report released in 1881 indicated that during the society's first eight years, Comstock had confiscated 203,238 obscene pictures and photographs, destroyed 27,584 pounds of books, and seized 1,376,939 circulars, catalogues, songs, poems, and the like.

[406] The controversy over Three Weeks resulted in prosecution. Commonwealth v. Buckley, 200 Mass. 346, 86 N.E. 910 (1909). Anthony Comstock is supposed to have delivered a speech on "impure literature" at Boston's Park Street Church and doubtless his guiding influence had much to do with the initial success of the New England Society. Doctor Frederick Baylies Allen, a leading Boston Episcopalian and father of social historian Frederick Lewis Allen, is credited with having founded the society. Contrary to popular belief that the charter members of the society were simply a group of repressed "smut sniffers," an early society roster reveals that its officers and directors were people bent upon solid reform. Allen, Frederick Baylies Allen (1929); Boyer, Boston Book Censorship in the Twenties, 15 American Quarterly 3 (Spring 1963).

Frank Chase, who was the moving spirit of Watch and Ward, would draw the fire of H. L. Mencken who sued Chase and the Society because of their vigorous attempts to ban an issue of the American Mercury.[407]

Thirty years later, Editor John Fischer of Harper's would level almost identical charges against Monsignor Thomas Fitzgerald and the National Office for Decent Literature.[408] Organized in 1938 by the Catholic Bishops of America, NODL, as it is popularly known, has become a national successor of the earlier New York and New England Societies.[409] Originally established

---

[407] In September 1925, the American Mercury had published an article entitled "Keeping the Puritans Pure" which hit hard at Watch and Ward and its secretary Reverend Chase. Six months later, Boston newsdealers were warned by the society not to sell the April 1926 issue of the American Mercury and a Cambridge dealer was actually prosecuted and fined for disregarding the injunction. At that juncture, editor Mencken appeared in Boston and personally sold a copy of the banned issue to Reverend Chase before a large assembly in front of the Park Street Church. Mencken was arrested on Chase's complaint, but acquitted in Municipal Court. Following acquittal Mencken sued, charging illegal restraint of trade, and ultimately secured an injunction prohibiting further molestation.

[408] Fischer, The Harm Good People Do, Harpers, Oct. 1956, p. 14. Fischer, with no lack of vehemence, charged that a little band of Catholics was conducting a shocking attack on the rights of their fellow citizens and drew alarming comparisons between their tactics and those employed by the Communists. He accused the NODL of putting pressure on news dealers, drug stores and booksellers, to force them to remove from their stocks every item blacklisted by the organization. Blacklisted, he claimed, were reprint editions of books by Ernest Hemingway, William Faulkner, John Dos Passos, George Orwell, John O'Hara, Émile Zola, Arthur Koestler and other great literary figures. Condemning boycott techniques, he took issue with the NODL for its tactics compelling readers of all faiths to bow to its dislikes by denying them a free choice in what they buy. Reverend John Courtney Murray, S.J. by way of reply took issue with the Fischer tactic of slapping the label "Communist" on his adversary's position and referred to such as the tactic of unreason. He found fault with Fischer's failure to distinguish between the "idea" of the NODL, which is the substantive issue, and the applications of the idea which raise issues of procedure. In good "liberal" fashion, therefore, Fischer had assigned the primacy to the procedural over the substantive. Although Father Murray did hold that private agencies such as the NODL could perform an indispensable public function, he did observe that irresponsible procedures effected by local zealots could likewise effect considerable harm. Murray, the Bad Arguments Intelligent Men Make, America, Nov. 3, 1956, p. 120. See also, Bourke, Moral Problems Related to Censoring the Media of Mass Communications, 40 Marq. L. Rev. 57 (1956); Murray, Literature and Censorship, 14 Books on Trial 393 (1956).

[409] The National Organization for Decent Literature was formed in 1938 by an Episcopal Committee of the Catholic heirarchy "to devise a plan for organizing a systematic campaign in all dioceses of the United States against the publication and sale of lewd magazines and brochure literature." Drive for Decency in Print, Report of the Bishops' Committee Sponsoring the National Organization for Decent Literature 5 (1939); Noll, Manual of the N.O.D.L. 17 (n.d.). A national office was acquired in Fort Wayne, Indiana, but in April 1955 NODL moved to 33 E. Congress Parkway, Chicago 5, Illinois. Apparently in an effort to disassociate itself from the activities and procedures of local extremists, NODL has changed its name from the "National *Organization* for Decent-Literature" to the "National *Office* for Decent Literature." Fitzgerald, NODL States Its Case, America, June 1, 1957, pp. 280-81. Monsignor Fitzgerald emphatically denied that NODL had entered the field of adult reading, and observed that Catholics already have the law of the Church, clear and binding in conscience, which forbids the reading of *ex professo* obscene publications. NODL's appeal to adults outside the Church, he comments, is to their sense of decency and their individual responsibility to the common

to review magazines, the NODL has been active since 1947 in reviewing comic books and paperback editions. Recognizing that its sole purpose is one of discouraging dissemination of objectionable literature harmful to young people, the NODL hits hardest at publications and other media which: (1) glorify crime or the criminal, (2) describe in detail ways to commit criminal acts, (3) hold lawful authority in disrespect, (4) exploit horror, cruelty, or violence, (5) portray sex facts offensively, (6) feature indecent, lewd, or suggestive photographs or illustrations, (7) carry advertising which is offensive in content or advertise products which may lead to physical or moral harm, (8) use blasphemous, profane, or obscene speech indiscriminately and repeatedly, or (9) hold up to ridicule any national, religious, or racial group.

Initial determination of what material shall be placed on current NODL lists is made by a corps of voluntary readers who work regularly for the organization. Reviewers must have a college education and many members of Protestant and Jewish persuasion serve on the reviewing board. Methods of review are thorough rather than haphazard, and neither magazines nor paperbacks can be placed on the objectionable list until six persons have agreed that they violate the NODL Code. For organizations that do not find it convenient to prepare their own lists, NODL provides a monthly list of current books and magazines and acceptable comic books that have been evaluated according to the Code. The NODL indicates, however, that lists as such are merely an expression of a publication's disconformity with the Code, and states categorically that lists are not to be used for purposes of legal action, boycott, or coercion.[410]

---

good. He did not deny that the NODL list carried many mature literary works, a few of which were award winners, but cautioned that these had been evaluated by NODL reviewers as too advanced for the youthful mind. Thus, ideally and practically, NODL considers that these books should be made available for adults but kept out of the hands of youth through a program of self-regulation on the part of the publishing and distributing industries.

[410] Criticism of the NODL by anti-censorship forces has been steady and vocal since the moment of it inception, but it is unlikely that any single voice of disapproval has received more publicity than that accorded a statement issued by the American Civil Liberties Union in May 1957. The statement, signed by some 168 persons prominent in literature and the arts, deplored any form of boycott, general or secondary, and charged that NODL activities were especially contrary to the spirit of the Constitution in the field of communication. American Civil Liberties Union Statement on Censorship Activity by Private Organizations and the National Organization for Decent Literature (n.d.); ACLU, Civil Liberties, May 1957, p. 1. Shortly after the ACLU issued its appeal for authors, publishers, editors, and other influential people to sign their "statement of 1957," an editorial in the magazine America, among other points, raised the question whether the distinguished persons who stood behind the ACLU's charges had ever read the policy statements of the NODL. Did each signer know accurately just what the NODL was atempting to accomplish? America, May 18, 1957, p. 218. On August 14, 1957, Patrick Murphy Malin, executive director of the ACLU, replied by letter to America, in which he noted that the signers were well informed people. In an effort to control the activities of its local committees more effectively, NODL has recently reached an agreement with the ACLU and the American Book Publishers' Council. According to the terms of this agreement, in any instance where these organizations can present evidence that NODL listings are being misused, NODL has agreed to contact the offending party or group and state its position. America, March 18, 1961, p. 779.

The national office suggests that a parish committee visit those local outlets which attract youthful customers, check the publications displayed, and, using the list as a guide, request the store owner to remove objectionable material.[411] Teams or committees are instructed to visit retail stores at a slack time when the owner or manager is not too busy to talk to them. If objectionable titles are on display, one team member is to request in a courteous manner that they be removed from sale. If the dealer agrees, the team thanks him. In case of refusal, the team must leave quietly and report refusal to the local pastor who can determine future action.

As NODL policies and activities mellowed with age, a new type of organization, entitled Citizens for Decent Literature, was inaugurated in Cincinnati, Ohio, in 1957.[412] CDL is aggressive and admits as much, but it counsels against telling any bookseller or newsdealer what not to display or what not to sell. Chairman Charles H. Keating, Jr., a Cincinnati lawyer, believes in going to court. Relying less on the book list technique, the newer organization seeks to arouse public feelings and convictions with respect to the prevalence of obscene materials, and its asserted goal is one of encouraging if not assisting public officials in the prosecution of obscenity cases.[413]

The story of CDL's clean-up campaign in Cincinnati, known as Operation Newsstand, has been related by Kay Sullivan in Catholic Digest.[414] A small group of business and professional men, motivated by a mutual concern over the volume of pornographic objects offered for sale in local outlets, formed a speakers bureau and through this office spread the gospel of decency throughout the metropolitan area. Programs were presented before professional groups, service clubs, women's clubs, schools, and parent-teacher associations; immediate citizen response reflected the ardor and enthusiasm of the pilot group. Local police, once assured of substantial community support, descended upon newsstands trafficking in hard-core materials, and within a period of two years at least seven successful prosecutions resulted.[415]

---

[411] Although the NODL does operate out of a national office, it does not attempt to act on the basis of national uniformity. Its policy is to encourage the formation of autonomous local committees, nonsectarian in nature, which will represent not only Catholic interests but a number of social, fraternal, and religious groups also. A plan of organization suggests how such committees may be brought into being for effective action. Copies of sample local constitutions and bylaws are distributed from the NODL office at 33 East Congress Street Parkway, Chicago 5, Illinois. In some areas, Protestant groups may join in the implementation of the NODL list. See Lockhart & McClure, Literature, the Law of Obscenity, and the Constitution, 38 Minn. L. Rev. 295, 315 (1954).

[412] A national office is currently maintained by CDL at 3701 Carew Tower, Cincinnati, Ohio 45202.

[413] See, e.g., City of Cincinnati v. King, 168 N.E.2d 633 (Ohio 1960). Lockhart and McClure have noted correctly that prior to 1957, criminal prosecution of reputable news dealers were relatively rare and seldom successful. Lockhart & McClure, supra note 411, at 309.

[414] Sullivan, Cincinnati v. Pornography, Catholic Digest, June 1959, p. 12.

[415] In December 1958, a Cincinnati jury found Joseph L. Marshall, a major local distributor, guilty of selling an assortment of magazines, contents ranging from the sextease to the pornographic. Among these were Gent, Dude, Men, Real Men, and Man's

Success in Cincinnati soon prompted similar citizen response in other Ohio cities, and in 1958 a statewide organization was formed. By 1960, national organization had been accomplished. Community efforts in other cities have as a rule followed the original organizational blueprint adopted in Cincinnati. A core of ten or twelve individuals will volunteer as speakers before selected audiences, making certain that one of their number is prepared to offer professional advice on questions of law and legislation. Local units in major cities will generally publish a monthly newsletter which aims at supplying current news relative to judicial action and legislation, and supplementary information that will make for an informed citizenry.[416] Members are encouraged to write to their community newspapers, to the district attorney, the chief of police and to all responsible public representatives.[417] At once revered and respected by CDL is the oft-quoted admonition of Edmund Burke: "The only thing necessary for the triumph of evil is that good men do nothing."

A third organization active in the campaign for decent literature is the Churchmen's Commission for Decent Publications, formed in 1956 as the outgrowth of a meeting called in Washington, D.C., by O. K. Armstrong, a former member of Congress from Missouri. The Churchmen's Commission has outlined specific recommendations for local action, suggesting that local units carefully study published materials in light of obscenity laws, that they

---

Life. Subsequently, the distributor voluntarily discontinued circulation of Playboy, Nugget, Rogue, Stag and several other semi-prurient publications. Letter from Charles H. Keating, Jr. to Father Paul Bussard, Publisher of the Catholic Digest.

[416] The February 1962 edition of a monthly newsletter entitled Stamp Out Smut, published by the Citizens for Decent Literature of Greater Milwaukee, provides a fair sample. Under a banner headline "Drive For Decency Takes Hold" the newsletter informs the reader that hundreds of new members are active in reporting obscenity as they see it, that the District Attorney's office is getting letters every day demanding action. It advises of a state obscenity probe, the purpose of which is not to censor books but to find out why dirty books could exist in Wisconsin. Observing that members of the CDL Speakers Bureau are in constant demand, readers are invited to contact the Bureau for a speaker who will appear at any community forum. Two half-hour films in sound and color, Pages of Death and Perversion for Profit, are listed as being available for sale or rental from CDL. Positive reading guides are noted, selections ranging from CDL pamphlets to works by Sorokin and Wertham. One entire page of the letter is devoted to a book list containing the titles of some 200 publications of which typical titles are: Autosex, Impotent Male, Lesbos Is for Lonnie, Passionate Professor, Sin Swap, and Warped Desires. Lady Chatterley's Lover, Lolita, and the Tropics were likewise listed. The books were not banned as such, but readers were advised to examine those listed, and to report their findings to an area chief of police if they should find that the dominant theme of any book was obscene.

[417] Apparently most "write-in" efforts have been accomplished without undue agitation, however, the exertion of pressure upon members of the judiciary has not been effected without incident. In 1960, CDL in Indianapolis felt the scorn of Municipal Judge Joseph N. Meyers who voiced the opinion that write-in campaigns were outright attempts to coerce the court while suggesting that writers could be held in contempt. Indianapolis Star, January 5, 1960. Cincinnati Judge Frank M. Gusweiler had earlier criticized pressure groups for attempting to influence the courts. Cincinnati Enquirer, Nov. 4, 1958. See text accompanying notes 459-462 infra.

grant retail dealers every opportunity to rid their shelves of objectionable books and magazines, and that matters be presented to law-enforcement authorities only when gentler methods fail.[418]

Americans for Moral Decency, popularly recognized as AFMD, operates primarily on the thesis that good reading habits constitute a ready antidote for the threat posed by wanton circulation of indecent literature.[419] Parents, in particular, are urged to encourage their children to take advantage of the wealth of instructive reading materials available at nominal cost, while community groups are invited to sponsor book reviews, book fairs, and similar programs designed to promote an appreciation for better literature. Nevertheless, AFMD does assert the right of every citizen to protest the dissemination of objectionable publications, and in the interest of protecting this right, suggests that the citizen may make a courteous request of any dealer to remove indecent materials from his shelves.

In May 1959, the Board for Christian Social Action of the American Lutheran Church issued a statement in which it decried the flood of sex-centered or violence-saturated products appearing on the magazine racks, bookshelves, and motion picture screens. The Lutheran program called for systematic individual action in avoiding purchase of objectionable material and in seeking to influence public opinion against obscenity. Although recourse to the courts was not foreclosed in its estimation, greater stress was placed upon efforts aimed at obtaining voluntary support from the newsdealers and booksellers themselves. The Board suggested that lists of cooperating dealers pledged to standards of review, distribution, and sale be published, and approved the practice of supplying dealers with emblems of participation which they might display. While recognizing that parents and schools must share a responsibility for seeing that young people receive a sound, sensible perspective of sex, the role of the church in warning of the evils inherent in obscenity was realized without question.[420]

With the advent of the '60's, interfaith movements directed at expressing community standards have become increasingly significant. Typical of such is New York City's "Operation Yorkville" which was organized as an interfaith campaign to protect the parental-civil right to keep obscene literature out of the hands of children. Founders included Reverend Robert E. Wiltenberg, Pastor of the Immanuel Lutheran Church, Reverend William T. Wood, S.J., Rector of the Church of St. Ignatius Loyola, and Doctor Julius G. Neumann, Rabbi of the Congregation Zichron Moshe. Each month Operation Yorkville selects a prime target, and targets will as a rule include the local newspapers, the local dealer, or the area distributor. A man or woman who has made a signal contribution to the campaign against indecent litera-

---

[418] A newsletter is published by a research committee headed by Reverend Ralph A. Cannon, 113 Franklin Village, Spartanburg, South Carolina.

[419] Headquarters for AFMD are located at Room 1105, 173 West Madison Street, Chicago, Illinois.

[420] Kilpatrick, The Smut Peddlers 250 (1960).

ture is afforded the honor of being named man or lady of the month. In December 1963, man of the month was Judge Benjamin Gassman, a New York jurist.[421] Mrs. Yetta Panken, reputable bookdealer, was chosen lady of the month for January 1964.[422] Man of the month for February 1964 was Thomas H. Esch, driver for the city's sanitation department.[423] The organization has enlisted the support of Mayor Robert F. Wagner, District Attorney Frank S. Hogan, and other New York officials in its effort to stamp out obscenity in metropolitan New York.[424]

Authors, publishers, distributors, and booksellers are just beginning to feel

[421] In a ruling handed down by three criminal court judges, one of whom was Judge Gassman, on November 14, 1963, Irwin Weisfeld, operator of Bookcase, Inc. in New York City, and clerk John Downs were found guilty of violating Section 484(h) of the New York State Penal Code (Supp. 1963). Section 484(h) prohibits lending, giving away, selling or showing to persons under 18 any book, pocketbook, pamphlet or magazine that exploits or is devoted to, or is principally made up of descriptions of illicit sex or sexual immorality. Weisfeld was sentenced to 30 days in jail; Downs to 10 days; and the corporate owner was fined $500. A hardbound copy of John Cleland's Fanny Hill had been sold at the Bookcase to a minor, and on the advice of Operation Yorkville, the mother in the case promptly filed a complaint against the offending seller. Bookdealer Weisfeld had actually displayed a "pile of books" in his window and had drawn attention to same by placing a sign in the window which announced Fanny Hill in bold letters, alluding to the fact that "the barriers are now down, and it is happening in our time."

[422] Mrs. Yetta Panken and her husband operate a bookstore on Lexington Avenue and have attested to the fact that they have never once sold a piece of filth. Reporting that her husband goes through all of the material which comes in and returns it if it is undesirable, Mrs. Panken says that this does involve work but notes that it's just part of a day's business. States Operation Yorkville: "They will not even touch the much touted bunny-rag, the house organ of the 'bunny club' addicts.' Operation Yorkville Newsletter, Jan. 1964, p. 3.

[423] As a driver for the Sanitation Department, Mr. Esch has become acutely aware of the tons of filth the Department shovels in off the streets of New York each day. Well aware of the scope of Section 484(h), he lately gave his 16 year old daughter the price of a hard bound copy of Fanny Hill and instructed her to see if she could buy it. Buy it she did at the Fordham Bookcase in the Bronx. As a result of this purchase, one Mr. Ed Gross, Bronx bookseller, was found guilty on January 6, 1964 of violating Section 484(h).

[424] Operation Yorkville Newsletter, Dec. 1963, p. 4. It is taken for granted that public officials in metropolitan America will experience pressures from an aroused and indignant citizenry, yet this arousal is not confined to big city groups. The urge to stamp out smut prevails as well in the small city and the rural community as a partial list of citizens' organizations will reveal. The following organizations typify an expanding movement: Newport (R.I.) Citizens' Committee on Literature, Inc.; Citizens' Committee for Decent Literature, Joliet, Illinois; Decent Literature Council, Coral Gables, Florida; Committee for Decent Literature, Exchange Club, Orlando, Florida; City of Poughkeepsie's Committee on Questionable Literature, Poughkeepsie, N.Y.; Committee for Decent Literature, Carlstadt and East Rutherford, N.J.; Advisory Committee on Literature for Youth, Westfield, New York; Parent Teachers' Association Committee, Kalamazoo, Michigan; Wyandotte Civic Organization for Decent Literature, Wyandotte, Michigan; Committee on Decent Literature, Stevens Point, Wisconsin; Organization for Clean Publications, Williamsport, Pennsylvania; Clean Comics Committee of the Lancaster County Community Council, Lancaster, Pennsylvania; Literature Review Committee of Chatham County, Georgia; Springfield Church Group for Promotion of Decent Literature, Springfield, Vermont; Committee for Clean Literature, Corpus Christi, Texas; Women's Civic League, Hills, Minnesota.

the sting of the private group pressure that the motion picture producer has known and lived with for forty-five years. Following World War I, picture producers became quite venturesome with their offerings of risqué titles and daring photographic realism.[425] For example, Barrie's story The Admirable Crichton was released as Male and Female, and a film based on the play Du Barry was given the florid title Passion. Even Cecil B. DeMille was known to rock the complacency of the early twentieth century conscience with titles such as Don't Change Your Husband and Forbidden Fruit.[426]

In those times, lust was to become equated with glamor; sex was something colossal that spelled big money; and the trials and tragedies of Fatty Arbuckle would scarcely palliate the indignation of a public skeptical of the wiles and ways of this new Babylon by the Mojave.[427]

By the early thirties, the motion picture industry had just about hit rock bottom in terms of measuring the moral qualities of its productions. The National Board of Review,[428] the Hays Office,[429] and the industry Production Code[430] had been designed to upgrade values and restore public faith, but

[425] From 1918 to 1920, several critical surveys of motion picture content were conducted by voluntary organizations across the country. A study by the Chicago Political Equality League for the General Federation of Women's Clubs examined 1,765 films and declared that 20 per cent were "good," 21 per cent "bad" and 59 per cent "not worth while." Young, Motion Pictures: A Study in Social Legislation 22 (1922). The International Reform Federation and the Lord's Day Alliance actively promoted restrictive legislation while the 1920 convention of the Central Conference of America Rabbis protested the demoralization of drama and the motion picture. Other resolutions demanding industry reform were passed by Baptists, Episcopal, Methodist, and Presbyterian groups. Inglis, Freedom of the Movies 62 (1947).

[426] In an obvious attempt to achieve the air of sophistication then apparent in the contemporary novel and play, producers in their own unsubtle imitative fashion made a clean break with long held canons of decency and morality. Whatever made good box office made good sense, social taboos to the contrary.

[427] Roscoe "Fatty" Arbuckle became front page news in the summer of 1921 after he gave a party at the St. Francis Hotel in San Francisco at which one of his female guests died. Although acquitted of a charge of manslaughter, he was forced to abandon his film career as a result of copious and absurd publicity. The mysterious slaying of English director William Desmond Taylor likewise insured circulation for tabloids ever conscious of Hollywood's foibles and sins.

[428] The National Board of Review was established in 1909 as the result of the showing of sensational motion pictures in New York City, notably The Great Thaw Trial. Originally formed as the National Board of Censorship, the Board in 1916 adopted a more decorous title while sponsoring a slogan: "Selection Not Censorship." Failing to satisfy various pressure groups working for legal censorship, it soon became apparent that producers could not depend upon the Board's seal of approval, and its influence as a reviewing body gradually diminished.

[429] Legally, the Hays Office was incorporated as the Motion Picture Producers and Distributors of America (M.P.P.D.A.) and such was its official name until Eric Johnson shortened it to Motion Picture Association of America (M.P.A.A.) in 1945. Will H. Hays, Postmaster-General in the Harding administration, assumed active direction of the agency in March 1922. For a more detailed account of the activities of the MPAA, see Inglis, Freedom of the Movies 83-151 (1947).

[430] In 1930 a detailed code was drafted for the MPAA by Daniel A. Lord, S.J. and Martin Quigley, a Catholic editor. This code flatly prohibited certain themes and scenes, yet despite its clarity, no apparent decrease in the output of sensational films was evident by the time the Legion of Decency was launched in 1934.

efforts at self-regulation had failed to achieve what could approximate a satisfactory solution. In October 1933, at a Catholic Charities convention in New York City, Archbishop Cicognani, the newly appointed apostolic delegate to the United States, issued a call to action for purification of the screen. A month later, the Catholic bishops of America at their annual meeting formulated plans to organize the National Legion of Decency* and appointed an Episcopal Committee on Motion Pictures to insure realization of its objectives. From the moment of its inception, the Legion disassociated itself from all forces of political censorship and eschewed any attempt to employ the power of government to strengthen its arm.[431] The work of the Legion, to this day, is confined exclusively to the evaluation of the moral aspects of motion picture production; therefore, it does not judge the artistic qualities of films, nor the social and political content unless a political issue in fact presents a moral problem of its very nature.

In December 1957, the Legion adopted five principal classifications for motion pictures.[432] Class "A-1" films, which are deemed morally unobjectionable for general patronage, typically comprise in excess of forty percent of the domestically produced films. Class "A-2" films, morally unobjectionable for adults and adolescents, include mature movie subjects which bear witness to the fact that certain motion pictures can and do contribute to the intellectual and emotional maturation of the adolescent. The "A-3" classification, morally unobjectionable for adults, represents an attempt to provide for truly adult subject matter, provided that the themes in question and their treatment be consonant with the moral law and with traditionally accepted moral standards. Class "B" films, which are morally objectionable in part for all, are so judged because they contain material which, in itself or in its offensive treatment, is contrary to traditional morality, thereby constituting a threat to personal spiritual life as well as to the wider pattern of public morality. Class "C" pictures, which are condemned, are considered to constitute a definite moral danger to the "average" or "normal" Catholic; yet as a group, they rarely comprise more than one percent of domestic productions.[433]

* Now known as the National Catholic Office for Motion Pictures, N.Y. Times, Dec. 8, 1956. — Ed.

[431] The Legion takes no affirmative action to enforce recognition of the list, nor does it have any official liaison with the Production Code Administration or local law enforcement units. Its force is principally felt through its moral influence on the more than 40,000,000 Catholics in the United States. Note, 71 Harv. L. Rev. 326 (1957).

[432] Prior to this date, the Legion had provided for only four classifications: A-1; A-2; B; and C. The list was expanded to aid the adolescent in his search for more mature movie subjects and to afford reasonable moral controls upon the adolescent choice. Gardiner, Catholic Viewpoint on Censorship 98 (1961). In 1963, a sixth classification, "A-4," was added to include films morally unobjectionable for adults, with reservations. Listed here are films which are not morally objectionable in themselves, yet the Legion advises that analysis and explanation are in order to insulate the uninformed against wrong interpretations and false conclusions. The new classification incorporates such typically adult productions as Advise and Consent, La Dolce Vita, Lolita, and Divorce Italian Style.

[433] In addition to the Legion effort, two other organizations of national scope pre-

While it may be conceded that interest in censorship by private groups exists as a natural concomitant of the right to preserve a well ordered society, it must be recognized that private group activity all too frequently and unnecessarily unleashes disruptive forces which only aggravate pre-existing social conflicts. No one can deny the right of the private citizen to make judgments with respect to what is decent and proper, nor can one question his right to implement that judgment or belief, because the concept of freedom of expression is basic in a society governed by constitutional principles.[434] On the other hand, the history of censorship has forever been a history of excess, and private action in this regard has provided many examples of history repeating itself.

The interest of a group in expressing its will freely and openly must be balanced against an individual's interest in remaining free from unfair economic pressure and the public's interest in securing access to material it desires to read and to see. National organizations such as the NODL and CDL do present principled objectives, and they do fill a need which formal governmental action cannot supply.[435] Yet regardless of the wisdom and sanity reflected by a national goal, there will inevitably remain the case of the local zealot who "has the zeal of God indeed, but not according to understanding." [436] Certainly each organization should exert unstinting efforts to control the activities of its local representatives in the interest of preserving an image that will enhance rather than denigrate the aims and intentions of private action.[437]

Just how far private action may be carried, or in which direction it may proceed, one cannot say with confidence. The law is virtually unformulated

---

pare lists evaluating the content of motion pictures. The "green sheet," formally known as the Joint Estimates of Current Entertainment Films, is compiled through the cooperation of twelve national organizations which include the General Federation of Women's Clubs, The National Congress of Parents and Teachers, the Daughters of the American Revolution, and the Protestant Motion Picture Council. The National Board of Review, discussed supra note 428, publishes a monthly magazine, Films in Review, which reviews and rates motion pictures according to their educational, ethical, and artistic values.

[434] The American Civil Liberties Union has supported the right to judge and to act non-governmentally in this respect. ACLU Policy Statement on Censorship, 1962.

[435] "It is for this reason that we need private agencies to evaluate communications on the basis of moral standards higher than those practicable for civil law, and then to publicize these evaluations and to seek by legal means the cooperation of like-minded persons in the vindication of their rights as parents and citizens." Hayes, A Position on the Control of Obscenity, 51 Ky. L.J. 641, 650 (1963).

[436] Romans 10:2.

[437] That real and grave dangers do derive from the excesses of private groups cannot be denied. Organized reform so often degenerates to organized intolerance, and particularly so, when emotional, irrational private pressure is commingled with the overanxious drives of ambitious public officials. The amateurish sleuthing procedures, alluded to supra at note 423, symbolize a type of private crusade that constitutes an unwarranted interference with established legal process. For a clear description and denunciation of excesses to be avoided, see Bantam Books v. Melko, 25 N.J. Super. 292, 96 A.2d 47 (1953).

due to the apparent fact that few conflicts of this order have reached the arena of judicial decision. It could, for example, be argued that there is a distinction between picketing a theatre during the showing of an objectionable motion picture, and calling for a boycott of the theatre after the film has completed its run. Picketing in the first instance is designed primarily to warn others of an apprehended evil and is, therefore, justified by a privilege so to act.[438] Conduct in the latter instance could possibly be actionable in tort,[439] depending upon the measure of good-faith responsibility evidenced by the actor for the welfare of third persons in the community. Certainly the purpose of the actor would constitute a signal factor in assessing the legality of the boycott in question, because the prima facie tort of intentional interference with reasonable business expectations may be justified by a lawful purpose where no other unlawful means are used.[440]

NOTE

See also Emerson and Haber, Political and Civil Rights in the United States 959-964 (2d ed. 1958); Mark, Censorship, Fanatics and Fallacies, The Nation, July 5, 1965, p. 5; Amen, The Church vs. Obscene Literature, 24 The Jurist 261 (1964), 11 Cath. Law. 21 (1965); Church Legislation on Obscenity, 10 Cath. Law. 109 (1964). See further N.Y. Times, Oct. 29, 1963 (New York City drive against obscenity started by priest's fast); N.Y. Times, Aug. 7, 1964 (Cardinal Spellman calls for protest against Supreme Court decision and boycott of doctors who "traffic in pornography").

[438] Restatement, Torts §§766, 767 (1938).

[439] Cf. Morasse v. Brochu, 151 Mass. 567, 25 N.E. 74 (1890). If it could be demonstrated that the motivation for boycott, even after the objectionable picture has been exhibited, is still remedial in that the boycotting group hopes to dissuade the theatre owner from booking objectionable films in the future, good faith would likely be established.

[440] In Watch Tower Bible & Tract Soc'y v. Dougherty, 337 Pa. 286, 11 A.2d 147 (1940), a secondary boycott was held not to be tortious. Catholic Bishops had induced their congregation to refrain from patronizing a store which owned and operated a radio station which carried a Watch Tower Society program highly critical of Catholic beliefs. As a result of this action by the Bishops, the Society's broadcasting contract was not renewed. Similarly in Kuryer Publishing Co. v. Messler, 162 Wis. 565, 156 N.W. 948 (1916), Catholic Bishops had ordered their congregations not to purchase or read a secular newspaper, and this action was held not to be tortious. Action by laymen was held privileged in Rosman v. United Strictly Kosher Butchers, 164 Misc. 378, 298 N.Y. Supp. 343 (1937). See Coons, Non-Commercial Purpose as a Sherman Act Defense, 56 Nw. U.L. Rev. 705 (1962).

CDL has lately been sued in the United States District Court of Northern Illinois by the Universal Publishing and Distributing Corporation of New York. American Book Publishers Council [ABPC], Freedom-To-Read Bull., (Fall 1963). A particular target of CDL has been Universal's line of Beacon-Signal books. Universal charged that retailers have been threatened with boycott by individuals and by the CDL, as a group, and where dealers did not comply, they have been boycotted. Boycott has extended to all items carried by the retailer.

LEGAL RESPONSIBILITY FOR EXTRA-LEGAL
CENSURE
62 Colum. L. Rev. 475, 476-493 (1962)

II REMEDIES AGAINST CENSURE BY PRIVATE INDIVIDUALS

A. *Liability in Tort*

There appear to be at least four different causes of action sounding in tort that may be available to one injured by extra-legal censure: defamation, interference with contractual relations or prospective advantage, trade libel, and prima facie tort. While this Note will touch only briefly on the first, the other three will be considered in greater detail. Because of the relative paucity of reported cases involving extra-legal censure, the discussion will comprehend other decisions that are thought to illuminate principles that would probably be applicable to censure cases.

1. *Defamation.* In the course of a campaign of extra-legal censure, statements tending to reflect unfavorably on the plaintiff's person or business standing will frequently be made. When the statements are defamatory,[2] one available remedy may be a suit for libel or slander, which will enable the plaintiff to recover some or all of the damages suffered consequent to the censuring activities.[3]

All the principles generally governing actions for defamation are applicable in cases in which the actionable statement is an incident of attempted censure. However, the defense of truth and that of privileged comment on matters of public concern are of particular interest, since they are addressed to the problem, predominant throughout the area of relief from censure, of balancing

---

[2] Certain statements of a kind that might arise with relative frequency in censure cases are clearly thought to be defamatory. For example, liability can be imposed for publishing falsely and without privilege that a person is an anarchist, Cerveny v. Chicago Daily News Co., 139 Ill. 345, 28 N.E. 692 (1891), pro-nazi, Derounian v. Stokes, 168 F.2d 305 (10th Cir. 1948), a communist or communist sympathizer, e.g., Utah State Farm Bureau Fed'n v. National Farmers Union Serv. Corp., 198 F.2d 20 (10th Cir. 1952); Grant v. Reader's Digest Ass'n, 151 F.2d 733 (2d Cir. 1945), cert denied, 326 U.S. 797 (1946); Foltz v. News Syndicate Co., 114 F. Supp. 559 (S.D.N.Y. 1953); Mencher v. Chesley, 297 N.Y. 94, 75 N.E.2d 257 (1947). See also Natchez Times Publishing Co. v. Dunigan, 221 Miss. 320, 72 So. 2d 681 (1954) (insinuation that white person is colored); Collins v. Oklahoma State Hosp., 76 Okla. 229, 184 Pac. 946 (1916) (same).

[3] In some situations, proof of special damages is a necessary element of the cause of action. See Prosser, Torts 584-96 (2d ed. 1955). When the defamatory publication is actionable per se, or once the requisite pecuniary loss has been proven, the damages recoverable are those thought to be the proximate result of the defamatory publication. See Williams v. Riddle, 145 Ky. 459, 140 S.W. 661 (1911); Field v. Colson, 93 Ky. 347, 20 S.W. 264 (1892); Clark v. Morrison, 80 Ore. 240, 156 Pac. 429 (1916).

protection from injury against the desirability of untrammeled communication of knowledge, ideas, and opinions.

As a general rule, a defendant who can establish the truth of an allegedly defamatory publication[4] will escape liability although no justification for his conduct can be advanced — that is, even though he believed the published matter to be false[5] or was prompted to make the harmful statement solely by ill-will.[6] A few states, however, have enacted legislation abrogating the availability of truth as an absolute defense by requiring that publication of the defamatory mater must have been for good motives or justifiable ends.[7] Despite the creation of a requirement of justification, the defense of truth will usually be adequate in censure situations, since publication for "public information" has been recognized as sufficient justification for the defendant's conduct.[8]

The process of weighing opposing interests is also implicit in the recognized defense of fair comment on matters of public interest. Expressions of opinion[9] that are made in good faith, are based on true facts that are stated,

[4] The burden of establishing the truth of his defamatory statements may as a practical matter pose serious problems for the defendant. Thus, for example, in Utah State Farm Bureau Fed'n v. National Farmers Union Serv. Corp., 198 F.2d 20 (10th Cir. 1952), the defendant had published that the plaintiff union was "communist dominated." The defense of truth was held not established, although evidence was received of speeches by the union's president assailing the profit system and calling for cooperative farming and militant organization of tenant farmers, and of a pamphlet circulated by the union recommending books by communist authors, denouncing current un-American investigations, criticizing foreign aid plans, and advocating "closer ties with Russia." Id. at 24.

[5] See Foss v. Hildreth, 92 Mass. (10 Allen) 76 (1865); Restatement, Torts §582, comment g (1938).

[6] See, e.g., McCuddin v. Dickinson, 230 Iowa 1141, 300 N.W. 308 (1941); Herald Publishing Co. v. Feltner, 158 Ky. 35, 164 S.W. 670 (1914); Restatement, Torts §582, comment a (1938).

[7] E.g., Florida Const., Declaration of Rights §13; Ill. Const. art. II, §4; Maine Rev. Stat. ch. 113, §47 (1954); Neb. Const. art. I, §5; Neb. Rev. Stat. §25-840 (1943). One state reached a similar result without legislation. Hutchins v. Page, 75 N.H. 215, 72 Atl. 689 (1909).

This tendency to protect one defamed even when the statements are true perhaps parallels the enlarging scope of the action for invasion of privacy, which is based on a recognition that there are certain indignities to which people should not be subjected even though the information published is correct. See generally 1 Harper & James, Torts 677-81 (1956).

[8] See e.g., Del. Code Ann. tit. 10, §3920 (1953); Pa Stat. Ann. tit. 12, §1582 (1953); Star Publishing Co. v. Donahoe, 58 Atl. 513 (Del. Sup. Ct. 1904).

[9] Although a few states apparently recognize a privilege protecting good faith misrepresentations of fact about candidates for public office, see Salinger v. Cowles, 195 Iowa 873, 191 N.W. 167 (1922); Mulderig v. Wilkes-Barre Times, 215 Pa. 470, 64 Atl. 636 (1906); cf. Harris v. Curtis Publishing Co., 49 Cal. App. 2d 340, 121 P.2d 761 (4th Dist. Ct. App.), this privilege is not properly a part of the defense of fair comment, which, it is generally agreed, is limited to expressions of opinion and is not available to protect misstatements of fact. See, e.g., Foltz v. News Syndicate Co., 114 F. Supp. 599 (S.D.N.Y. 1953); Mencher v. Chesley, 297 N.Y. 94, 75 N.E.2d 257 (1947); 1 Harper & James, Torts 458 (1956); Prosser, Torts 621-22 (2d ed. 1955). The case of Julian v. American Business Consultants, Inc., 2 N.Y.2d 1, 137 N.E.2d 1, 155 N.Y.S.2d 1 (1956), illustrates how the characterization of an alleged defamatory statement as fact or opinion can affect the outcome of a case. The court there charac-

generally known, or readily accessible, and are such as a reasonable man might entertain on the basis of the facts will be protected although they prove injurious to the plaintiff.[10] The existence of the defense of fair comment, originally directed at those who put themselves or their achievements in the public eye, would clearly have a more adverse effect on the claims of plaintiffs who are in some way public figures than on the prospects for recovery of private individuals injured by censure.[11] However, by virtue of the public interest element usually present in the subject matter of censure cases, the defense will probably have a restrictive effect on use of the defamation remedy in many of these situations.

An action for defamation is of limited utility to individuals injured by extra-legal censure, not only because the defenses of truth and fair comment drastically reduce the chances of success, but also because the means employed by censuring groups frequently do not include publication of statements governed by the laws of defamation. While a defamation action may provide an adequate remedy when the censuring group calls on the populace not to patronize plaintiff because he is a communist, it clearly will be of little avail if the reason urged is that plaintiff sells books written by communists. Relief must then be sought under some other theory.

---

terized as a privileged assertion of opinion the inference that plaintiff, because of his association with communist organizations knowingly or otherwise, was thereby unfit for employment in the entertainment industry. The dissent maintained that to say "plaintiff advanced the Communist cause, whether knowingly or not" is a statement of fact that should be actionable as an imputation disparaging plaintiff in his business capacity. Id. at 29, 137 N.E.2d at 19, 155 N.Y.S.2d at 27. See also Utah State Farm Bureau Fed'n v. National Farmers Union Serv. Corp., 198 F.2d 20 (10th Cir. 1952) (calling union "communist dominated" is "statement of a bald and unambiguous fact"); Potts v. Dies, 132 F.2d 734 (D.C. Cir. 1942), cert. denied, 319 U.S. 762 (1943) (calling excerpt from plaintiff's newspaper an example of "the Nazi Trojan Horse" held a privileged expression of opinion).

[10] See 1 Harper & James, Torts 456-63 (1956); Prosser, Torts 623 (2d ed. 1955).

[11] Thus, while the defense of fair comment will clearly serve to protect much criticism of the behavior or character of public officials and candidates for public office and of the quality of artistic works or production of various sorts, the cases reflect a concern with restricting the fair comment privilege to the public aspects of such persons' lives or to the artistic works themselves. Comment will not be permitted on the private or personal affairs of those whose activities or works are dedicated to the public. See 1 Harper & James, Torts 460-62 (1956).

Consequently, the range of permissible comment on the activities of private individuals should, in principle, be fairly limited. If a private person makes a public speech, however, comment thereon is permissible. Kellems v. California CIO Council, 68 F. Supp. 277 (N.D. Cal. 1946). And when the comment is on a matter deemed to be of considerable public concern, wide latitude appears to be allowed. In Julian v. American Business Consultants, Inc., 2 N.Y.2d 1, 137 N.E.2d 1, 155 N.Y.S.2d 1 (1956), defendants, in order to show the extent to which communists had infiltrated the entertainment industry, published a list of actors and artists who, knowingly or otherwise, had been associated with communist organizations on some occasions. In answer to the assertion that although the publication did not say plaintiff was a communist, inclusion of his name in this list was defamatory, the court held that the defamatory inference that plaintiff was unfit for employment in the industry was legitimate comment on a matter of public interest.

2. *Interference with contractual relations or prospective advantage.* The area of tort law designed to safeguard the security of economic relations is of particular relevance in cases of extra-legal censure. Existing contractual agreements[12] and reasonable expectancy of future gain, such as the possibility of obtaining potential customers,[13] employees,[14] or employment,[15] are to some extent protected from intentional invasion in all jurisdictions by actions for causing breach of contract and for interference with prospective economic advantage.

To state a cause of action for interference with economic relations, the plaintiff must first establish intent on the part of defendant, a requirement usually presenting no great difficulty in cases of extra-legal censure. The term "malice" is often used to describe the requisite intent, and at one time the defendant's motive had to be the desire to do harm for harm's sake.[16] It is now generally agreed, however, that the "malice" required to impose liability for injury to economic relations exists when there is intent to interfere in plaintiff's affairs without justification.[17] In addition, actual damage to the plaintiff, caused or threatened by defendant's conduct, is a prerequisite to relief.[18]

When the requisite intent and damage to the plaintiff have been established, a prima facie case has been made out and liability will then turn on the issue of justification for the alleged tortious conduct. To be exonerated from liability, the defendant must show that the interest he sought to further,

[12] See, e.g., Blum v. William Goldman Theatres, Inc., 69 F. Supp. 468 (E.D. Pa. 1946); Campbell v. Gates, 236 N.Y. 457, 141 N.E. 914 (1923); Lumley v. Gye, 2 El. & Bl. 216, 118 Eng. Rep. 749 (Q.B. 1853). See generally 1 Harper & James, Torts 489-510 (1956); Restatement, Torts §§766-74 (1938).

Interference with contractual agreements presupposes knowledge of the contract or of facts reasonably indicating its existence. See Twitchell v. Glenwood-Inglewood Co., 131 Minn. 375, 155 N.W. 621 (1915); S. C. Posner Co. v. Jackson, 223 N.Y. 325, 119 N.E. 573 (1918). Liability will not be imposed if the contract interfered with is illegal or contrary to public policy. See Gunnels v. Atlanta Bar Ass'n, 191 Ga. 366, 12 S.E.2d 609 (1940) (usurious contracts); Seitz v. Michel, 148 Minn. 474, 181 N.W. 106 (1921) (contract contravening public policy).

[13] See, e.g., Boggs v. Duncan-Schell Furniture Co., 163 Iowa 106, 143 N.W. 482 (1913); Graham v. Saint Charles St. R.R., 47 La. Ann. 214, 16 So. 806 (1895).

[14] See, e.g., Vegelahn v. Guntner, 167 Mass. 92, 44 N.E. 1077 (1896); Jersey City Printing Co. v. Cassidy, 63 N.J. Eq. 759, 53 Atl. 230 (Ch. 1902).

[15] See, e.g., Kamara v. Livanos & Co., 97 F. Supp. 435 (S.D.N.Y. 1951); Carnes v. Saint Paul Union Stockyards Co., 164 Minn. 457, 205 N.W. 630 (1925); Huskie v. Griffin, 75 N.H. 345, 74 Atl. 595 (1909).

[16] See Lumley v. Gye, 2 El. & Bl. 216, 118 Eng. Rep. 749 (Q.B. 1853); Gregory v. Duke of Brunswick, 6 Man. & G. 205, 134 Eng. Rep. 866 (C.P. 1843) (defendant liable for having actor hissed off stage).

[17] See Meyer v. Washington Times Co., 76 F.2d 988 (D.C. Cir. 1935); Campbell v. Gates, 236 N.Y. 457, 141 N.E. 914 (1923); 1 Harper & James, Torts 492, 511 (1956); Prosser, Torts 720-22 (2d ed. 1955). Intentional interference with economic relations has been analogized to interference with the person, which is wrongful unless justification for the invasion exists. See 1 Harper & James, Torts 493 (1956).

[18] Max Ams Mach. Co. v. International Ass'n of Machinists, 92 Conn. 297, 102 Atl. 706 (1917). In cases of interference with contracts, an available cause of action against the person breaching the contract is no defense to an action for inducing the breach. Hornstein v. Podwitz, 254 N.Y. 443, 173 N.E. 674 (1930).

in view of the means used to achieve his purpose, would produce a result desirable enough to merit the sacrifice of conflicting interests of the plaintiff. Although justified conduct thus depends on the balancing of relative values in each case, some general limits can be ascertained.

When defendant's dominant motive was solely to do harm, liability will ensue regardless of the means employed.[19] Liability may also result from the means utilized by the defendant to interfere in the plaintiff's affairs. It is the general rule that modes of action tortious in themselves, such as violence, threats of harm, or use of false, misleading, or defamatory statements, are unjustified regardless of the motive prompting such conduct.[20] Thus, in an action by a publishing company against the New England Watch and Ward Society for preventing the sale of plaintiff's magazine by threatening distributors with prosecution for handling obscene literature, temporary injunctive relief was granted, the court noting that in spite of defendants' sincere desire to benefit the public interest, they could not enforce their views about the desirability of plaintiff's publication by "organized threats and intimidation." [21]

When defendant's conduct is not tainted by actual malice or unlawful means, the balancing of conflicting interests is more difficult. Conduct has more readily been found privileged when the defendant acted to further his own economic interests. Thus, the common law has long recognized a right to use reasonable means to protect an existing economic advantage or curtail the prospective gain of a business competitor.[22] Similarly, the competing interests of labor and management may justify considerable interference with economic operations by labor organizations seeking improved terms and conditions of employment.[23]

[19] See Boggs v. Duncan-Schell Furniture Co., 163 Iowa 106, 143 N.W. 482 (1913); Graham v. Saint Charles St. R.R., 47 La. Ann. 214, 16 So. 806 (1895). But see Guethler v. Altman, 26 Ind. App. 587, 60 N.E. 355 (1901).

[20] See, e.g., Maytag v. Meadows Mfg. Co., 35 F.2d 403 (7th Cir. 1929), cert. denied, 283 U.S. 843 (1931) (false statements); Gomez v. United Office & Professional Workers, 73 F. Supp. 79 (D.D.C. 1947) (method "involving fraud"); Standard Oil Co. v. Doyle, 118 Ky. 662, 82 S.W. 271 (1904) (threats and false statements); Godin v. Niebuhr, 236 Mass. 350, 128 N.E. 406 (1920) (libelous statements); Vegelahn v. Guntner, 167 Mass. 92, 44 N.E. 1077 (1896) (intimidation).

[21] American Mercury, Inc. v. Chase, 13 F.2d 224 (D. Mass. 1926); accord, Green v. Samuelson, 168 Md. 421, 178 Atl. 109 (1935) (intimidation and possible violence permit enjoining picketing against discriminatory hiring practices); A. S. Beck Shoe Corp. v. Johnson, 153 Misc. 363, 274 N.Y. Supp. 946 (Sup. Ct. 1934) (same).

[22] See, e.g., Katz v. Kapper, 7 Cal. App. 2d 1, 44 P.2d 1060 (2d Dist. Ct. App. 1935); Hansberry v. Holloway, 332 Ill. 334, 163 N.E. 662 (1928); Restatement, Torts §768 (1938). Interference with contracts requires greater justification than interference with prospective advantage. See Friedberg, Inc. v. McClary, 173 Ky. 579, 191 S.W. 300 (1917).

[23] See, e.g., Pierce v. Stablemen's Union, 156 Cal. 70, 103 Pac. 324 (1909); Kirmse v. Adler, 311 Pa. 78, 166 Atl. 566 (1933); Restatement, Torts §§775, 784-96 (1938). Labor union activity, although for the most part economically motivated, involves frequent use of censure techniques. These practices are now closely regulated by state and federal legislation and a discussion of them is beyond the scope of this Note.

Justification sufficient to bar the plaintiff's claim is not restricted to areas of economic conflict. A privilege will frequently arise when the defendant is forwarding the interests of some group to which he bears a relation of responsibility. For example, when the officers of a private college passed a rule that students could use only the college eating facilities, consequently injuring plaintiff's college-patronized restaurant business, the court denied plaintiff all relief, relying not on defendants' possible economic motives but mainly on their privilege to make rules for the well-being of the students.[24] So, too, on an allegation that students had been prevented by threat of expulsion from patronizing plaintiff's store, the court again found justification in the right to make regulations for the management of the school.[25] To the same effect is dictum of a Tennessee court that justification will be found if defendant's act tends to promote some legitimate and reasonable advantage, although the court held that the privilege to interfere was lost when purely malicious motives underlay the action of a school in forbidding its students and faculty to live at plaintiff's boarding house.[26]

The protection of one's religious group has also generally been held to be sufficient justification. In an action against bishops of the Roman Catholic Church who had circulated a pastoral letter forbidding parishioners to read plaintiff's newspaper, the claim for relief was denied, although it was noted that the result might have been otherwise had the bishops "attempted to forbid social or business intercourse with the plaintiff . . . [that] could not affect the faith of the members." [27] Interference by a religious group was also held privileged in an action against officers of a church who had threatened boycott of a department store, thereby inducing a radio station controlled by the store to refuse renewal of plaintiff's contract for religious broadcasts.[28] The court declared that the defendants, who claimed the broadcasts fomented bigotry, could not be mulcted in damages for protecting themselves against a believed attack on their church.

Except for cases involving threats of violence, see UAW v. Wisconsin Employment Relations Bd., 351 U.S. 266 (1956), it is only when injurious labor activity is not "arguably within" the scope of §§7 or 8 of the National Labor Relations Act that a state or federal court has jurisdiction to entertain common law actions for damages or injunctive relief by the injured individual. See San Diego Bldg. Trades Council v. Garmon, 359 U.S. 236 (1959).

[24] Gott v. Berea College, 156 Ky. 376, 161 S.W. 204 (1913); accord, Jones v. Cody, 132 Mich. 13, 92 N.W. 495 (1902).

[25] Guethler v. Altman, 26 Ind. App. 587, 60 N.E. 355 (1901). Defendant's conduct was held justified although actual malice was alleged and there was no showing that the regulation in question bore any relation to the welfare of the school or its students.

[26] Hutton v. Watters, 132 Tenn. 527, 179 S.W. 134 (1915). To the same effect, requiring some showing of benefit to defendant or those for whom he is responsible, see Graham v. Saint Charles St. R.R., 47 La. Ann. 214, 16 So. 806 (1895); International & G.N. Ry. v. Greenwood, 2 Tex. Civ. App. 76, 21 S.W. 559 (Civ. App. 1893).

[27] Kuryer Publishing Co. v. Messmer, 162 Wis. 565, 568, 156 N.W. 948, 949 (1916).

[28] Watch Tower Bible & Tract Soc'y v. Dougherty, 337 Pa. 286, 288, 11 A.2d 147, 148 (1940).

Advancement of a limited or general public interest is another source of justification for injury to plaintiff's economic affairs.[29] Consequently, relief against interference with trade was held not available to a butcher seeking to restrain pickets from truthfully stating that his advertising the sale of kosher poultry did not mean the meat sold was kosher[30] or to a bakery picketed by a neighborhood organization protesting the high price of bread.[31]

The foregoing discussion indicates that censure or other forms of interference in economic affairs may usually be justified if it can be shown that the action taken was related to the protection or information of the public or any significant, socially acceptable segment thereof. Although the defendant's motive is thus of great importance, his interference with another's business will not be justified by good motives if the ends sought or achieved by his actions, even if not clearly legal, in any way contravene judicially declared public policy.[32] Thus, an injunction was granted to store owners against pickets protesting racially discriminatory hiring practices when the defendants' object was to achieve an employment quota of Negroes proportionate to their patronage, which would violate the state's policy against hiring on a racial rather than merit basis.[33]

[29] See, e.g., Anora Amusement Corp. v. Doe, 171 Misc. 279, 12 N.Y.S.2d 400 (Sup. Ct. 1939) (relief denied theatre owner against negro association picketing to promote employment for its members); 1621, Inc. v. Wilson, 402 Pa. 94, 166 A.2d 271 (1961) (denial of relief against picketing of bar to force its relocation, the court having found the bar detrimental to neighborhood interests); cf. People ex rel. Burnham v. Flynn, 189 N.Y. 180, 82 N.E. 169 (1907) (exclusion of drama critic by association of theatre owners because he ridiculed their religion not punishable under statute forbidding conspiracy to prevent exercise of lawful trade).

[30] Rosman v. United Strictly Kosher Butchers, 164 Misc. 378, 298 N.Y. Supp. 343 (Sup. Ct. 1937).

[31] Julie Baking Co. v. Graymond, 152 Misc. 846, 274 N.Y. Supp. 250 (Sup. Ct. 1934).

[32] See cases cited note 33 infra.

[33] Hughes v. Superior Court, 32 Cal. 2d 850, 198 P.2d 835 (1948), aff'd, 339 U.S. 460 (1950). Justices Carter and Traynor, dissenting separately, suggested that the real object of the boycott was nondiscrimination. Id. at 866, 868, 198 P.2d at 893, 895. See Green v. Samuelson, 168 Md. 421, 178 Atl. 109 (1935) (boycott to force store owner in negro neighborhood to employ only colored help).

Compare a recent New York case, Levine v. Dempsey, 45 N.Y.L.J. 14 (Sup. Ct. Jan. 11, 1961), in which the supreme court, on motion for injunction pendente lite, restrained the Economic Action Committee, a Harlem group, from picketing plaintiff's liquor store in an attempt to force the owner to deal only with a "preferred" list of salesmen, largely Negro. The court found the defendants were "seeking to enforce discriminatory racial practices" and circumvent an injunction obtained earlier by the Liquor Salesmen's Union, Brandenburg v. Metropolitan Package Store Ass'n, 143 N.Y.L.J. 13 (Sup. Ct. Mar. 30, 1960), prohibiting any acts which would induce or coerce any liquor store proprietor to refrain from purchasing from any of the plaintiffs because of race or color. See N.Y. Times, Mar. 31, 1960, p. 27, col. 7; id., Jan. 12, 1961, p. 22, col. 2.

Although no employer-employee relationship is involved in these cases, a court may hold that the boycott is a "labor dispute" and thus subject to a no-injunction statute. See New Negro Alliance v. Sanitary Grocery Co., 303 U.S. 552 (1938) (Norris-La Guardia Act §13); Lifshitz v. Straughn, 261 App. Div. 757, 27 N.Y.S.2d 193 (2d Dep't 1941) (N.Y.C.P.A. §876(a)). But see, rejecting the labor dispute rationale, Green v.

3. *Trade libel.* Closely related to the torts of defamation and interference with contractual agreements or prospective economic advantage is a distinct but not always distinguishable cause of action for trade libel. Also known as disparagement, this tort is defined as the publication to third persons of direct or indirect [34] aspersions on the quality of plaintiff's goods or on the character or conduct of his business.[35] Disparagements may take the form either of statements of fact [36] or expressions of unfavorable opinion.[37] To recover on this theory, the plaintiff must establish that the disparaging statements were untrue,[38] and that the disparagement played a substantial part in causing him the required special damage — present or prospective pecuniary loss.[39]

In an action for trade libel, a defense of privilege, similar to that of justification recognized in the other economic torts,[40] is available to defeat the plaintiff's claim, even though it is proved that the defamatory statement was in fact false. In addition to certain privileges permitted to economic

---

Samuelson, supra; A. S. Beck Shoe Corp. v. Johnson, 153 Misc. 363, 274 N.Y. Supp. 946 (Sup. Ct. 1934).

[34] See Dale System, Inc. v. Time, Inc., 116 F. Supp. 527 (D. Conn. 1953) (statement that certain business is unique held to be defamatory of plaintiff's identical business; cf. Pendleton v. Time, Inc., 339 Ill. App. 188, 89 N.E.2d 435 (1949); Advance Music Corp. v. American Tobacco Co., 296 N.Y. 79, 70 N.E.2d 401 (1946).

[35] Trade libel is sometimes difficult to distinguish from defamation of the plaintiff himself in his business capacity. Generally, if the statements charge personal misconduct on the part of the plaintiff, such as dishonesty or the knowing perpetration of a fraud on the public, they may be actionable as libel or slander affecting plaintiff in his business. *Compare* Rosenberg v. J.C. Penney Co., 30 Cal. App. 2d 609, 86 P.2d 696 (3d Dist. Ct. App. 1939) (selling shoddy garments; personal), *and* Craig v. Pueblo Press Publishing Co., 5 Colo. App. 208, 37 Pac. 945 (1894) (selling bad food; personal), *with* Nonpareil Cork Mfg. Co. v. Keasbey & Mattison Co., 108 Fed. 721 (E.D. Pa. 1899) (article made by plaintiff is a "fraud"; trade libel), *and* Bosi v. New York Herald Co., 33 Misc. 622, 68 N.Y. Supp. 898 (Sup. Ct.), aff'd mem., 58 App. Div. 619, 68 N.Y. Supp. 1134 (1st Dep't 1901) (plaintiff's boarding house is "resort for anarchists"; trade libel).

This distinction can be of considerable importance, for in trade libel cases, unlike actions for personal defamation, the plaintiff has the burden of proving the falsity of the defamatory statement. Restatement, Torts §651(c) (1938). Also, in trade libel, the plaintiff must prove special damages, see notes 48-49 infra and accompanying text, whereas statements defamatory of the plaintiff personally and injuring him in his business capacity are actionable per se, see 1 Harper & James, Torts 381-82 (1956).

Slander of title, a parallel cause of action not generally relevant to cases of extralegal censure, exists to impose liability for statements impugning plaintiff's title to land or goods. See generally 1 id. at 474-86.

[36] See Kennedy v. Press Publishing Co., 41 Hun 422 (N.Y. Sup. Ct. 1886); Restatement, Torts §627 (1938).

[37] See Dooling v. Budget Publishing Co., 144 Mass. 258, 10 N.E. 809 (1887); Restatement, Torts §627 (1938).

[38] 1 Harper & James, Torts 481 (1956); Restatement, Torts §651(c) (1938). Truth is an absolute defense. See id. §634.

[39] See Dudley v. Briggs, 141 Mass. 582, 6 N.E. 717 (1886); Houston Chronicle Publishing Co. v. Martin, 5 S.W.2d 170 (Tex. Civ. App. 1928); cf. Fleming v. McDonald, 230 Pa. 75, 79 Atl. 226 (1911).

[40] See notes 22-23 supra and accompanying text.

competitors,[41] the law recognizes a qualified privilege for comment designed to advance some interest of a group or of the general public.[42] Thus, in the absence of otherwise illegal conduct by a picketing NAACP group, a complaint charging conspiracy to malign plaintiff's production of Uncle Tom's Cabin as "an instrument of race ridicule" was held insufficient.[43] Similarly, in the absence of intended malicious injury to plaintiffs or their business, no injunction would issue against publication of a book containing allegedly false statements disparaging the quality of plaintiff's cancer drug, the public interest in discussion of cancer being deemed paramount.[44]

However, qualified privilege, like justification, can be defeated if it is shown that the defendant was motivated by actual malice.[45] Thus, repeated false editorials were enjoined when intended only to injure the business of a bank by persuading depositors to discontinue their patronage,[46] and an allegedly false and malicious statement by a priest to his congregation that plaintiff's business establishment was a "bad place of resort" and should be avoided was held, inter alia, to give rise to a cause of action for loss of parishioners' business.[47]

The decided cases do not clearly illuminate the scope of the privilege to disparage in good faith, and it is uncertain whether participants in a program of censure would be entitled to invoke this privilege. Undoubtedly those, such as religious leaders or school administrators, whose occupations make them responsible to a segment of society, would be permitted to invoke the privilege when acting in furtherance of their obligations. But the availability of the privilege to individuals who claim to be acting in the public interest or in the interest of a particular group to which they owe no special obligation is less certain. That the privilege has been extended to protect injurious comment about cancer medication does not mean that it will be extended to those who seek to foster their own conception of public morality.

In addition to the possible availability of the defense of privilege, a plaintiff who has been injured by a trade libel made in the course of a campaign of

[41] See generally 1 Harper & James, Torts 483-85 (1956); Restatement, Torts §649 (1938).

[42] See, e.g., Browning v. Van Rensselaer, 97 Fed. 531 (E.D. Pa. 1899); Fahey v. Shafer, 98 Wash. 517, 167 Pac. 1118 (1917); cf. Purofied Down Prod. Corp. v. National Ass'n of Bedding Mfrs., 97 N.Y.S.2d 683 (Sup. Ct. 1950). This justification may be analogized to the defense of fair comment in personal defamation.

[43] Lawton v. Murray, 61 N.Y.S.2d 721 (Sup. Ct. 1946); cf. People v. Johnson, 117 Misc. 133, 191 N.Y. Supp. 750 (Sup. Ct. 1921) (reversal of conviction for distributing "do not patronize" circulars to protest showing of film that defendant said exalted activities of the Ku Klux Klan).

[44] Krebiozen Research Foundation v. Beacon Press, Inc., 334 Mass. 86, 134 N.E.2d 1, cert. denied, 352 U.S. 848 (1956).

[45] See, e.g., A. B. Farquhar Co. v. National Harrow Co., 102 Fed. 714 (3d Cir. 1900); cases cited notes 46-47 infra.

[46] Lawrence Trust Co. v. Sun-American Publishing Co., 245 Mass. 262, 139 N.E. 655 (1923).

[47] Fitzgerald v. Robinson, 112 Mass. 371 (1873).

censure must cope with other limitations on the cause of action. Unlike personal defamation maligning plaintiff in his business capacity, trade libel is not actionable per se, and special damages must be proved with considerable particularity; many courts declare a mere showing of decline in business to be insufficient and require proof of loss of specific sales or customers to establish the requisite injury.[48] Such proof may be virtually impossible in many cases, but only occasionally have courts excused a plaintiff from these exactitudes.[49] Although the gist of trade libel is protection from unjust interference with economic relations, many courts raise a further difficulty by analogizing trade libel to personal defamation and therefore denying injunctive relief, frequently the most effective weapon against extra-legal censure.[50]

4. *Prima facie tort.* The doctrine of prima facie tort originated from dictum in the English case of Mogul S.S. Co. v. McGregor, Gow & Co. to the effect that "intentionally to do that which is calculated in the ordinary course of events to damage, and which does, in fact, damage another . . . is actionable if done without just cause or excuse."[51] Prima facie tort has been accorded increasing recognition by American courts, especially to redress injury to economic relations. To recover, it is not necessary to show malicious intent, but

[48] See, e.g., Shaw Cleaners & Dyers v. Des Moines Dress Club, 215 Iowa 1130, 245 N.W. 231 (1932); Le Massena v. Storm, 62 App. Div. 150, 70 N.Y. Supp. 882 (1st Dep't 1901).

[49] See Dale System, Inc. v. Time, Inc., 116 F. Supp. 527 (D. Conn. 1953); Houston Chronicle Publishing Co. v. Martin, 5 S.W.2d 170 (Tex. Civ. App. 1928); Erick Bowman Remedy Co. v. Jensen Salsbery Labs., Inc., 17 F. 2d 255, 261 (8th Cir. 1926) (dictum).

[50] In both defamation and trade libel actions, courts are frequently reluctant to grant injunctive relief, the use of injunctions being associated with an unlawful prior restraint on freedom of expression. See, e.g., Citizens' Light, Heat & Power Co. v. Montgomery Light & Water Power Co., 171 Fed. 553, 556 (C.C.M.D. Ala. 1909) (trade libel; "after he has spoken or written falsely, the criminal law can punish him, and the civil courts amerce him in damages. . . . but the remedies named are all that the Constitution permits any court to employ"); Willis v. O'Connell, 231 Fed. 1004 (S.D. Ala. 1916)) (trade libel); Kwass v. Kersey, 139 W. Va. 497, 81 S.E.2d 237 (1954) (personal defamation). However, since statements found defamatory are beyond the scope of constitutional protection, see note 99 infra and accompanying text, it seems that the first and fourteenth amendments should not be considered to prohibit injunctions against publication of defamatory matter. A few courts of equity, apparently proceeding on this assumption, have granted injunctive relief in trade libel cases, relying on equity's inherent jurisdiction to prevent irreparable injury to property, or professedly restraining the libelous utterances as mere verbal conduct incident to some other enjoinable tort. See, e.g., Maytag Co. v. Meadows Mfg. Co., 35 F.2d 403 (7th Cir. 1929), cert. denied, 283 U.S. 843 (1931); Dehydro, Inc. v. Treolite Co., 53 F.2d 273 (N.D. Okla. 1931); Menard v. Houle, 298 Mass. 546, 11 N.E.2d 436 (1937); Lawrence Trust Co. v. Sun-American Publishing Co., 245 Mass. 262, 139 N.E. 655 (1923); Saxon Motor Sales, Inc. v. Torino, 166 Misc. 863, 2 N.Y.S.2d 885 (Sup. Ct. 1938). At least one federal court has explicitly recognized the right to enjoin publication of a trade libel as such. Black & Yates, Inc. v. Mahogany Ass'n, 129 F.2d 227, 231 (3d Cir. 1941), cert. denied, 317 U.S. 672 (1942). But such relief might nevertheless be denied when the subject matter of the defamatory publication is one of vital public concern. See Krebiozen Research Foundation v. Beacon Press, Inc., 334 Mass. 86, 134 N.E.2d 1, cert. denied, 352 U.S. 848 (1956).

[51] 23 Q.B.D. 598, 613 (1889), aff'd, [1892] A.C. 25 (1891).

merely that defendant acted deliberately and with the knowledge or reasonable expectancy that damage to the plaintiff would result from his acts.[52] The elements of intent, damage, and justification are governed by substantially the same rules as in the torts of interference with contract or prospective advantage, and some courts use the prima facie tort rationale as an alternative to these more traditional causes of action.[53]

Prima facie tort is similarly useful as a substitute for[54] or supplement to the cause of action for trade libel and may permit recovery when a false statement falls short of actual disparagement of the quality of plaintiff's goods or services, yet interferes with the success of his economic operations by affecting the conduct of third persons.[55] Thus, a statement by a Catholic priest that he would attend no one employing the plaintiff doctor, with the implication that plaintiff was unfit to be employed because his marriage violated church regulations, was sufficient to permit recovery for the doctor's resulting loss of parishioner-patients.[56] The prima facie tort doctrine may also serve to relax the strict trade libel requirement of proof of special damages.[57]

The possible usefulness of prima facie tort as an additional theory of recovery for extra-legal censure should not be overlooked. Although few censure cases proceeding under this theory have been found, the prima facie tort rationale has been the basis for recovery in unusual situations of interference with trade expectancy and injury to professional reputation.[58] However, the element of justification, with its underlying consideration of balancing the desirability of free action and expression against resultant harm to the public generally and to the plaintiff will, as in the case of other economic torts, be the primary factor in determining the success of the plaintiff's claim.

5. *Adequacy of the tort remedies in censure cases.* Although extra-legal censure is probably as ancient a phenomenon as competitive economic struggle, recognition of the need for relief from injurious censure practices seems

---

[52] See, e.g., Gale v. Ryan, 263 App. Div. 76, 31 N.Y.S.2d 732 (1st Dep't 1941); Schauder v. Weiss, 88 N.Y.S.2d 317 (Sup. Ct. 1949), aff'd, 276 App. Div. 967, 94 N.Y.S.2d 748 (2d Dep't 1950).

[53] See, e.g., Original Ballet Russe, Ltd. v. Ballet Theatre, Inc., 133 F.2d 187 (2d Cir. 1943); Owen v. Williams, 322 Mass. 356, 77 N.E.2d 318 (1948); Opera on Tour, Inc. v. Weber, 285 N.Y. 348, 34 N.E.2d 349, cert. denied, 314 U.S. 615 (1941); Barile v. Fisher, 197 Misc. 493, 94 N.Y.S.2d 346 (Sup. Ct 1949).

[54] See Purofied Down Prods. Corp. v. National Ass'n of Bedding Mfrs., 97 N.Y.S.2d 683 (Sup. Ct. 1950).

[55] See, e.g., Pendleton v. Time, Inc., 339 Ill. App. 188, 89 N.E.2d 435 (1949); Davis v. New England Ry. Publishing Co., 203 Mass. 470, 89 N.E. 565 (1909). In contrast, there have been statements of a nondefamatory type that were treated as trade libel rather than prima facie tort. See, e.g., Dale System, Inc. v. Time, Inc., 116 F. Supp. 527 (D. Conn. 1953); Dudley v. Briggs, 141 Mass. 582, 6 N.E. 717 (1886) (no cause of action in trade libel).

[56] Morasse v. Brochu, 151 Mass. 567, 25 N.E. 74 (1890).

[57] See Pendleton v. Time, Inc., 339 Ill. App. 188, 89 N.E.2d 435 (1949); Rochester Brewing Co. v. Certo Bottling Works, Inc., 192 Misc. 629, 80 N.Y.S.2d 925 (Sup. Ct. 1948). Compare trade libel cases cited notes 48-49 supra.

[58] See generally Note, 52 Colum. L. Rev. 503 (1952) and cases cited therein.

to have lagged behind the development of adequate remedies for abusive competitive practices. With the exception of defamation, the tort remedies discussed above developed largely in the context of preventing persons from gaining unjust advantage over competitors or affording relief from economic injury caused by purely spiteful conduct, and it might well be wondered whether the principles governing these causes of action are adequate to cope with the many subtleties of contemporary censure activities.

The treatment of the concept of justification is the focal point in an analysis of judicial disposition of censure cases. From the previous discussion of justification it appears that the courts are most interested in the object sought by the censurers and their standing to pursue such a goal. The religious leader may use nearly any means short of defamatory speech or threatened or actual violence to prevent exposure of his communicants to objectionable books and movies,[59] and the housewife may similarly protest the high price of food and other household commodities.[60] All that is generally necessary is that the matter be one of legitimate concern to the censurers.

It is submitted that the courts have, in many cases, been unnecessarily generous in finding that the activities of defendants who inflict economic harm by censure practices are legally justified. Admittedly, the considerations that usually govern their decisions are relevant and important ones. And great wariness should certainly attend a determination to curtail the means of voicing disapproval.[61] But censure cases rarely involve individual action or mere expression of disapprobation. Rather, there is concerted action bringing economic as well as moral pressure to bear on those who dissent from the censurer's views.[62] A greater effort to separate the legitimate expression of

[59] In Watch Tower Bible & Tract Soc'y v. Dougherty, 337 Pa. 286, 11 A.2d 147 (1940), once the court determined that the defendant priest had a legitimate interest in endeavoring to curtail what he considered an attack on his church by the plaintiff, it expressed no concern with the means employed to effectuate that purpose, which included a threatened secondary boycott of a department store by church members in order to force the store-owned radio station to refuse renewal of the plaintiff's broadcasting contract. Cf. Guethler v. Altman, 26 Ind. App. 587, 60 N.E. 355 (1901), which upheld the right of a school officer to forbid students from patronizing plaintiff's store on the theory that the officer had a responsibility to make regulations for the conduct of the school. Apparently the court accorded no weight to the fact that actual malice allegedly motivated regulation which was not shown to have any bearing on the welfare of the students.

[60] See Julie Baking Co. v. Graymond, 152 Misc. 846, 274 N.Y. Supp. 250 (Sup. Ct. 1934). The brevity of the opinion in this case indicates that the court apparently thought it unnecessary, in reaching its result, to go beyond a finding that defendants, as members of the public, were entitled to advance the public interest in obtaining a lower price for bread. It failed to mention other factors that seem relevant in determining justification, such as whether the picketed bakery was the only one selling bread at an objectionable price, or whether, if the high price was prevalent throughout the local area, the plaintiff was the only bakery singled out as a target for economic pressure.

[61] The extent to which constitutional principles limit judicial proscription of censuring activities is considered at notes 98-108 infra and accompanying text.

[62] In cases of censure activity carried on by a number of individuals acting in concert, the impetus to comply with the censurers' demands comes largely from threats

disapproval directed against the objectionable commodity or practice from the exertion of economic pressure in a manner threatening or causing unnecessarily or improperly broad injury may be desirable.

While it may frequently be difficult to ascertain which element predominates in a given fact situation or to reconcile the conflicting interests when both are present to a substantial degree, certain standards for evaluating the means employed by censurers may be suggested. The most significant factor is probably the degree of correlation between the subject of the censure and subject of the boycott. The greater the degree of correlation, the more likely it is that the censuring activity has been kept within proper bounds. Thus, for example, a boycott of buses because of racially discriminatory seating would not give rise to liability, whereas a boycott of an entire shopping center because one of numerous, independently operated stores practices racial discrimination would be impermissible. Similarly, a religious leader might be acting properly in urging his communicants to refrain from attending a movie that he honestly considers will endanger their faith or morals, but improperly in threatening the exhibitor with a six-month boycott as punishment for showing the film and as a deterrent to future refusal to comply with recommendations not to show a film.[63]

Naturally, cases will arise in which this standard will be more difficult to apply. An example might be the recent nationwide picketing of the Woolworth chain in protest against its segregated lunch-counter policy in southern stores. Stores at which no discrimination was practiced were picketed in order to bring national pressure to bear on the company. If the quarrel were viewed as one with the company, this practice may be justifiable despite the extended scope of the boycott, but it might well be argued that the scope of the boycott was improperly wide.[64]

In deciding borderline cases, there are at least two factors, apart from the scope of the economic pressure exerted, that would appear relevant. One is the presence of injury to innocent third parties. For instance, in the Woolworth situation, if the sales or local management personnel, who have no voice in national company policy, were paid in whole or in part on a commis-

---

of economic injury rather than moral pressure. A threatened boycott by a large group of persons may often be as effective in compelling compliance as threats of violence or physical harm and, if carried into effect, the results of such economic coercion may often be just as destructive.

[63] See Gellhorn, American Rights 183-186 (1961), for a discussion of the measures taken by leaders of the Catholic Church to prevent exhibition of the movie Baby Doll. The measures covered a substantial portion of the spectrum of possible censure activities.

[64] The argument finding that the scope of this boycott was [im]permissible would probably emphasize that no interference with the business of Woolworth stores in the North could be justified, because these branches of the company were already acting in compliance with the censurers' views. It might even be argued that since the objection of the censures was directed solely at discriminatory seating at the lunch counters, the picketing of the southern stores should be limited to exhortations not to patronize the lunch counter rather than appeals to boycott the entire store.

sion basis, this factor would tend to render the boycott illegal, especially in a suit brought by them.

A second element of considerable significance is that of the public interest. The effects of extra-legal censure are not always limited to economic injury to the boycotted party. A successful campaign against a book, magazine, or movie may result in its complete suppression in the community, thus depriving those who seek it of their liberty to obtain something the law does not prohibit them from having. This feature is not present in all censure cases,[65] but when it is, the injury to the public would tend to offset the justification of furthering a similar but diametrically opposed private interest.

B. *Possible Relief Under the Sherman Act*

For the most part, individuals injured by extra-legal censure must seek relief under state tort law, utilizing one or more of the judicially evolved causes of action described in the preceding section. In certain cases, however, there appears to be a substantial possibility that relief may be obtained by suit for violation of the Sherman Act's prohibition of restraints of trade.[66] Although little thought was apparently given, prior to recent years, to application of Section 1 of the Sherman Act to activities outside the realm of competitive economic conflict, the language of the statute itself seems sufficiently broad to encompass situations in which interference with normal trade relations by use of economic devices is prompted by noneconomic motives.

Of the devices employed by censure groups, the group boycott appears to be the one most susceptible to attack through antitrust legislation. Two examples of censure activities falling within the concept of group boycott may be noted: agreement by members of an industry to pursue a given course of action with respect to individuals or groups with whom they have dealings (blacklisting); agreement by private individuals to pool their economic power to bring about or prevent specified conduct by others (frequently used to further efforts to suppress the distribution or exhibition of books, magazines, or movies).

The Supreme Court has exhibited continuing hostility toward group boycotts, regularly striking them down as unlawful restraints of trade in viola-

---

[65] There are few cases apart from those involving suppression of films or publications in which there is likely to be a substantial public interest affecting the decision. In such situations as the Woolworth boycott there is not likely to be a resulting suppression of commodities, and hence the public will not be deprived or injured. Even in cases of this sort, however, a public interest may become relevant in the event the boycotted party closes his business, thus impairing competition in the local market or removing an important source of goods and services not otherwise readily available.

[66] "Every contract, combination . . . or conspiracy, in restraint of trade or commerce among the several States, or with foreign nations, is hereby declared to be illegal . . . ." 26 Stat. 209 (1890), as amended, 15 U.S.C. §1 (1958). Private actions for treble damages and injunctive relief are available to persons injured by any violation of the antitrust provisions. 38 Stat. 731 (1914), 15 U.S.C. §15 (1958); 38 Stat. 737 (1914), 15 U.S.C. §26 (1958).

tion of the Sherman Act.[67] In Fashion Originators' Guild of America, Inc. v. FTC,[68] the Court held unlawful a boycott by a combination of dress designers controlling a substantial portion of the relevant market against retailers of competing dresses whose styles had been copied, or "pirated," from dresses designed by members of the Guild. Mr. Justice Black wrote for a unanimous Court that "even if copying were an acknowledged tort under the law of every state, that situation would not justify petitioners in combining together to regulate and restrain interstate commerce in violation of federal law." [69] In its most recent decision on the subject, Klor's, Inc. v. Broadway-Hale Stores, Inc.,[70] the Court rejected the defense that the challenged boycott had no significant impact on market conditions, asserting that Congress had "determined its own criteria of public harm and it was not for the courts to decide whether in an individual case injury [to the market] had actually occurred." [71] The Supreme Court has thus apparently laid down a rule of per se illegality of group boycotts, seemingly applicable regardless of the purpose of the boycott, but it is by no means clear that this position will be adhered to when economic profit is not the underlying motive of the boycott, or even, perhaps, that this approach will be followed when the case is less appealing than Klor's, which involved an attempt to cut off all sources of supply available to the plaintiff, a small businessman who was competing with one of the defendants.[72]

There are at least two instances in which the federal courts have found conduct motivated chiefly by ideological rather than economic considerations to be violative of federal antitrust legislation. In one case, an injunction was issued against a boycott of all Hearst publications by a substantial number of newsdealers and local "defense councils" [73] in the state of New Mexico, even

---

[67] E.g., Northern Pac. Ry. v. United States, 356 U.S. 1 (1958); Kiefer-Stewart Co. v. Joseph E. Seagram & Sons, 340 U.S. 211 (1951); Binderup v. Pathe Exchange, Inc., 263 U.S. 291 (1923); Eastern States Retail Lumber Dealers' Ass'n v. United States, 234 U.S. 600 (1914).

[68] 312 U.S. 457 (1941).

[69] Id. at 468.

[70] 359 U.S. 207 (1959).

[71] Id. at 211.

[72] It has been urged that the rule of per se illegality of group boycotts is now absolute. Handler, Recent Developments in Antitrust Law: 1958-1959, 59 Colum. L. Rev. 843, 862-66 (1959). However, it might be noted that in Fashion Originators' Guild, the defendants controlled from 38% to 60% of the relevant markets. On the other hand, in Klor's, in which no appreciable effect on the market did in fact result from the boycott, the defendants' motive was reprehensible. Thus, the decided cases do not entirely foreclose the possibility of a permissible group boycott in an instance in which there are both justifiable motive and negligible effect on the market.

[73] The state and county "councils of defense" were organizations created by legislative authorization to deal with matters of public defense during World War I. In furtherance of this purpose, the state council circulated a newspaper known as the "New Mexico War News," in which it allegedly published an "honor roll" of newsdealers throughout the state who had complied with the councils' request to suppress all Hearst publications for the duration of the war.

though the reason for the boycott was objection to the political views of the majority stockholder of the publishing company rather than any possible or supposed economic benefit.[74] In the second instance, a strike by members of a movie projectionists' union who refused to project a film because of ideological objection to its content was held to violate the Sherman Act.[75] However, the precedential value of these cases in combatting contemporary instances of censure is questionable. Both were decided by district courts and were not appealed, and neither has been invoked as authority in subsequent Sherman Act litigation, although the latter phenomenon may be explained by the paucity of litigation raising similar issues.

It can not be denied that the authority supporting application of the Sherman Act to ideologically motivated censure activity conducted with economic weapons is far from overwhelming. On the other hand, proponents of a more restrictive application of that legislation will have some difficulty marshalling superior judicial precedent in support of their contentions. There are, however, two recent decisions that do indicate some restriction on the sweep of the act.

In Molinas v. National Basketball Ass'n,[76] a player who had been blacklisted for betting on his own team brought an antitrust action against the Association. The district judge dismissed the complaint, holding that the plaintiff had "patently failed to establish an unreasonable restraint of trade within the meaning of the anti-trust laws. A rule . . . providing for the suspension of those who place wagers on games in which they are participating seems not only reasonable, but necessary for the survival of the league." [77] There was no mention of, or attempt to distinguish, the line of cases indicating that group boycotts are illegal per se under the act.

In Eastern R.R. Presidents Conference v. Noerr Motor Freight, Inc.,[78] decided early in 1961, the Supreme Court was confronted with the question whether the Sherman Act should be extended to control concerted activities designed to obtain competitive benefits through political rather than economic pressures. The techniques employed were not those of group boycott, but of lobbying and other overt and covert activities calculated to elicit favorable legislative action. A unanimous Court held that the Sherman Act does not reach this type of concerted activity, notwithstanding the finding of the district court [79] that the activities of the railroads were aimed primarily at inflicting injury on their major competitor, the trucking industry, and that the means employed were not only of dubious propriety but also had consequences extending beyond influence of legislative action. The Court observed

[74] Council of Defense v. International Magazine Co., 267 Fed. 390 (8th Cir. 1920).
[75] IPC Distribs., Inc. v. Chicago Moving Picture Mach. Operators Union, 132 F. Supp. 294 (N.D. Ill. 1955).
[76] 190 F. Supp. 241 (S.D.N.Y. (1961).
[77] Id. at 243
[78] 365 U.S. 127 (1961).
[79] 155 F. Supp. 768 (E.D. Pa. 1957).

that a contrary decision could have raised important constitutional questions by creating a possible conflict with the first amendment's protection of the right of petition. The opinion also stated, in passing, that "the proscriptions of the Act, tailored as they are for the business world, are not at all appropriate for application in the political arena." [80]

The fate of censure cases brought under the Sherman Act is, as appears from the above discussion, largely a matter of conjecture. Both Klor's and Fashion Originators' Guild express considerable concern with the relation of the boycott to the acquisition of monopoly power.[81] It is unlikely that the Supreme Court, in deciding these cases and others reaching similar conclusions, had in mind the types of situations likely to arise in the censure context. Moreover, the Molinas case reached a result seemingly inconsistent with the principle of per se illegality, yet there can be little disagreement with the fairness of the decision.

On the other hand, even if group boycotts are not always illegal under the Sherman Act, an important distinction may be drawn between Molinas and other instances of blacklisting, such as the refusal of the movie industry to employ actors and screenwriters who were or are suspected communists or who have refused to testify before congressional investigating committees, a boycott that is presently the subject of an antitrust suit brought by blacklisted artists.[82] Molinas' gambling activities clearly impaired his usefulness to any basketball team and his exclusion served to protect the integrity of the sport. The justification proffered by the Basketball Association was, consequently, considerably stronger than it would have been had a player been boycotted because of the commission of some other wrong unrelated to his professional activities. In the case of the actors and screenwriters, there may very well not be the necessary relation between the supposed wrong for which they have been blacklisted and the talents that they have thereby been prevented from putting to gainful use.

The scope of the Noerr decision is unclear, and it would certainly seem possible to argue that the limitation there imposed on the sweep of the Sher-

---

[80] 365 U.S. at 141.

[81] In Klor's, the Court observed that defendants' practice "clearly has, by its 'nature' and 'character,' a 'monopolistic tendency.' As such it is not to be tolerated merely because the victim is just one merchant whose business is so small that his destruction makes little difference to the economy." 359 U.S. at 213. But this consideration seems to have been relied on as additional support rather than as an essential ingredient of the decision.

[82] See N.Y. Times, Dec. 30, 1960, p. 1, col. 8. Prior to the institution of this action for Sherman Act violation, several blacklisted writers had attempted unsuccessfully to establish the illegality, on the basis of their unemployment contracts, of their discharge or of their employers' refusal to give them screen credit. 20th Century-Fox Film Corp. v. Lardner, 216 F.2d 844 (9th Cir. 1954), cert. denied, 348 U.S. 944 (1955); Loew's Inc. v. Cole, 185 F.2d 641 (9th Cir. 1950), cert. denied, 340 U.S. 954 (1951); RKO Radio Pictures, Inc. v. Jarrico, 128 Cal. App. 2d 172, 274 P.2d 928 (2d Dist. Ct. App. 1954), cert. denied, 349 U.S. 928 (1955). See also Screen Writers' Guild v. Motion Picture Ass'n of America, 8 F.R.D. 487 (S.D.N.Y. 1948) (complaint under Sherman Act dismissed).

man Act should not be extended to conduct not so clearly political and so arguably protected by a specific constitutional provision. The situation presented in Noerr, the use of political influence to achieve an economic objective, is, in a sense, the converse of that likely to arise in censure cases, and a similar result in the latter type of case, though possible, is by no means compelled.

The development of this yet ill-defined area of antitrust law is likely to be slow and winding, unless, as is possible, it is strangled at the outset by a firm extension of the principle enunciated in Noerr. The variety of configurations in which these problems might present themselves to the courts is substantial, as is the number of distinctions that the courts may draw among them. Consideration of these questions must, however, await resolution of the threshold question whether antitrust legislation is applicable at all to ideologically motivated activities. Opponents of its application to censuring practices would probably suggest that the sole legitimate concern of the antitrust laws is the preservation of competition in the marketplace and that they should apply only to combinations of entities engaged in business or mercantile activity seeking to protect or obtain a competitive advantage. The history of their application has, by and large, exhibited little deviation from this economic context. Proponents of broader application would probably argue, however, that the primary purpose of the law is to control abusive use of economic power regardless of the motivation underlying the abuse. It is probable that the drafters of the Sherman Act were concerned with the large social implications of the economic power wielded by the giant trusts that had emerged during the last quarter of the nineteenth century.[83] The trusts, in addition to wielding enormous economic power, had substantial social and political influence. If it is true that the sponsors of the Sherman Act sought to curb the power of the trusts in all fields, it is arguable that this broad underlying purpose should be accorded vitality in dealing with modern situations. The answer to the problems here posed may well depend on which of the two divergent views of the primary purpose of antitrust legislation ultimately prevails.[84]

[83] See Samuelson, Economics 493 (4th ed. 1958).

[84] Apart from the basic question of the applicability of the Sherman Act to censure cases generally, the attempt to bring censuring activity within the scope of §1 may present additional problems. First, the activity affected by the challenged restrictive practice must be "trade or commerce." This language has been held to include the sale or exchange of goods or the furnishing of services in many economic operations that are likely to be adversely affected by attempted censure. See, e.g., United States v. Shubert, 348 U.S. 222 (1955) (production and booking of legitimate stage attractions); United States v. Paramount Pictures, 334 U.S. 131 (1948) (production, distribution, and exhibition of motion pictures); Associated Press v. United States, 326 U.S. 1 (1945) (gathering and distribution of news); Council of Defense v. International Magazine Co., 267 Fed. 390 (8th Cir. 1920) (sale of publications); Evening News Publishing Co. v. Allied Newspaper Carriers, 160 F. Supp. 568 (D.N.J. 1958), aff'd, 263 F.2d 715 (3d Cir. 1959) (sale of newspapers); H. B. Marienelli, Ltd. v. United Booking Offices of America, 227 Fed. 165 (S.D.N.Y. 1914) (vaudeville booking). Several professional

REFERENCES

See Note, Extralegal Censorship of Literature, 33 N.Y.U.L. Rev. 989 (1958); Note, Use of Economic Sanctions by Private Groups: Illegality Under the Sherman Act, 30 U. Chi. L. Rev. 171 (1962).

---

sports are also within the ambit of trade or commerce. See Radovitch v. National Football League, 352 U.S. 445 (1957); United States v. International Boxing Club, 348 U.S. 236 (1955). But see Federal Baseball Club v. National League, 259 U.S. 200 (1922).

The jurisdictional requirement that the trade or commerce restrained by the challenged practices be "interstate" may also raise interesting questions in censure cases. Because much censuring activity is quite local in scope, it will often be necessary to ascertain when, in the process of distribution, goods shipped in interstate commerce lose their interstate character. For example, publications shipped interstate will clearly be protected by the Sherman Act against intrastate censuring activity that prevents or inhibits their introduction into the state. See Council of Defense v. International Magazine Co., supra; cf. IPC Distribs., Inc. v. Chicago Moving Picture Mach. Operators Union, 132 F. Supp. 294 (N.D. Ill. 1955) (preventing local showing of film). If, on the other hand, interference occurs at a more remote stage of distribution, such as after the publications are in the hands of an intrastate distributor or retailer, it may be found that the effect of the interference on interstate commerce is too slight to subject it to Sherman Act regulation. Cf. C. S. Smith Metropolitan Mkt. Co. v. Food & Grocery Bureau, 33 F. Supp. 539 (S.D. Calif. 1939) (holding insufficient complaint alleging interference with intrastate retail sale of national brand foods shipped in interstate commerce).

It appears, however, that the courts will go far in finding the requisite interstate element when local restraints have a considerable effect on the market in which such restraints are operative. See Evening News Publishing Co. v. Allied Newspaper Carriers, supra (gathering of news and some printing of newspaper done out of state; newspaper publisher permitted to invoke Sherman Act against practices restricting the sale of that portion of his paper destined solely for local distribution); 1955 Att'y Gen. Nat'l Comm. Antitrust Rep. 64.

In the event relief is unavailable under federal antitrust legislation because the particular activity is not considered to have the requisite effect on interstate commerce, there remains a possibility that the party injured by censure activities will have a remedy under state antitrust laws. No cases of this sort have been found, but this is not surprising in light of the similar paucity of federal litigation proceeding under the same theory. Local antitrust legislation varies considerably from state to state, and a study of potential relief under these statutes is beyond the scope of this Note. See generally Note, 61 Colum. L. Rev. 1469 (1961).

PART TWO

Freedom of Religion
and Other Individual Rights

CHAPTER VIII

Freedom of Religion

A. HERITAGE — AND NOW

EVERSON v. BOARD OF EDUCATION
330 U.S. 1, 33-43, 67 S. Ct. 504, 520-524, 91 L. Ed. 711
732-737 (1947)

MR. JUSTICE RUTLEDGE, dissenting.

No provision of the Constitution is more closely tied to or given content by its generating history than the religious clause of the First Amendment. It is at once the refined product and the terse summation of that history. The history includes not only Madison's authorship and the proceedings before the First Congress, but also the long and intensive struggle for religious freedom in America, more especially in Virginia,[11] of which the Amendment was

[11] Conflicts in other states, and earlier in the colonies, contributed much to generation of the Amendment, but none so directly as that in Virginia or with such formative influence on the Amendment's content and wording. See Cobb, Rise of Religious Liberty in America (1902); Sweet, The Story of Religion in America (1939). The Charter of Rhode Island of 1663, II Poore, Constitutions (1878) 1595, was the first colonial charter to provide for religious freedom.

The climactic period of the Virginia struggle covers the decade 1776-1786, from adoption of the Declaration of Rights to enactment of the Statute for Religious Freedom. For short accounts see Padover, Jefferson (1942) c. V; Brant, James Madison, The Virginia Revolutionist (1941) cc. XII, XV; James, The Struggle for Religious Liberty in Virginia (1900) cc. X, XI; Eckenrode, Separation of Church and State in Virginia (1910). These works and Randall [The Life of Thomas Jefferson (1858)] will be cited in this opinion by the names of their authors. Citations to "Jefferson" refer to The Works of Thomas Jefferson (ed. by Ford, 1904-1905); to "Madison," to The Writings of James Madison (ed. by Hunt, 1901-1910).

the direct culmination.[12] In the documents of the times, particularly of Madison, who was leader in the Virginia struggle before he became the Amendment's sponsor, but also in the writings of Jefferson and others and in the issues which engendered them is to be found irrefutable confirmation of the Amendment's sweeping content.

For Madison, as also for Jefferson, religious freedom was the crux of the struggle for freedom in general. Remonstrance, Par. 15, Appendix hereto. Madison was coauthor with George Mason of the religious clause in Virginia's great Declaration of Rights of 1776. He is credited with changing it from a mere statement of the principle of tolerance to the first official legislative pronouncement that freedom of conscience and religion are inherent rights of the individual.[13] He sought also to have the Declaration expressly condemn the existing Virginia establishment.[14] But the forces supporting it were then too strong.

Accordingly Madison yielded on this phase but not for long. At once he resumed the fight, continuing it before succeeding legislative sessions. As a member of the General Assembly in 1779 he threw his full weight behind Jefferson's historic Bill for Establishing Religious Freedom. That bill was a prime phase of Jefferson's broad program of democratic reform undertaken on his return from the Continental Congress in 1776 and submitted for the General Assembly's consideration in 1779 as his proposed revised Virginia code.[15] With Jefferson's departure for Europe in 1784, Madison became the Bill's prime sponsor.[16] Enactment failed in successive legislatures from its introduction in June, 1779, until its adoption in January, 1786. But during all this time the fight for religious freedom moved forward in Virginia on various fronts with growing intensity. Madison led throughout, against Patrick

[12] Brant, cc. XII, XV; James, cc. X, XI; Eckenrode.

[13] See Brant, c. XII, particularly at 243. Cf. Madison's Remonstrance, Appendix to this opinion. Jefferson of course held the same view. See note 15. . . .

[14] See Brant, 245-246. Madison quoted liberally from the Declaration in his Remonstrance and the use made of the quotations indicates that he considered the Declaration to have outlawed the prevailing establishment in principle, if not technically.

[15] Jefferson was chairman of the revising committee and chief draftsman. Corevisers were Wythe, Pendleton, Mason and Lee. The first enacted portion of the revision, which became known as Jefferson's Code, was the statute barring entailments. Primogeniture soon followed. Much longer the author was to wait for enactment of the Bill for Religious Freedom; and not until after his death was the corollary bill to be accepted in principle which he considered most important of all, namely, to provide for common education at public expense. See V Jefferson, 153. However, he linked this with disestablishment as corollary prime parts in a system of basic freedoms. I Jefferson, 78.

Jefferson, and Madison by his sponsorship, sought to give the Bill for Establishing Religious Freedom as nearly constitutional status as they could at the time. Acknowledging that one legislature could not "restrain the acts of succeeding Assemblies . . . and that therefore to declare this act irrevocable would be of no effect in law," the Bill's concluding provision as enacted nevertheless asserted: "Yet we are free to declare, and do declare, that the rights hereby asserted are of the natural rights of mankind, and that if any act shall be hereafter passed to repeal the present or to narrow its operation, such act will be an infringement of natural right." 1 Randall, 220.

[16] See I Jefferson, 70-71; XII Jefferson, 447; Padover, 80.

Henry's powerful opposing leadership until Henry was elected governor in November, 1784.

The climax came in the legislative struggle of 1784-1785 over the Assessment Bill. . . . This was nothing more nor less than a taxing measure for the support of religion, designed to revive the payment of tithes suspended since 1777. So long as it singled out a particular sect for preference it incurred the active and general hostility of dissentient groups. It was broadened to include them, with the result that some subsided temporarily in their opposition.[17] As altered, the bill gave to each taxpayer the privilege of designating which church should receive his share of the tax. In default of designation the legislature applied it to pious uses.[18] But what is of the utmost significance here, "in its final form the bill left the taxpayer the option of giving his tax to education." [19]

Madison was unyielding at all times, opposing with all his vigor the general and nondiscriminatory as he had the earlier particular and discriminatory assessments proposed. The modified Assessment Bill passed second reading in December, 1784, and was all but enacted. Madison and his followers, however, maneuvered deferment of final consideration until November, 1785. And before the Assembly reconvened in the fall he issued his historic Memorial and Remonstrance.[20]

This is Madison's complete, though not his only, interpretation of religious liberty.[21] It is a broadside attack upon all forms of "establishment" of religion, both general and particular, nondiscriminatory or selective. Reflecting not only the many legislative conflicts over the Assessment Bill and the Bill for Establishing Religious Freedom but also, for example, the struggles for religious incorporations and the continued maintenance of the glebes, the Remonstrance is at once the most concise and the most accurate statement of the views of the First Amendment's author concerning what is "an establishment of religion." . . .

The Remonstrance, stirring up a storm of popular protest, killed the Assessment Bill.[22] It collapsed in committee shortly before Christmas, 1785. With

[17] Madison regarded this action as desertion. See his letter to Monroe of April 12, 1785; II Madison, 129, 131-132; James, cc. X, XI. But see Eckenrode, 91, suggesting it was surrender to the inevitable. . . .

[18] Eckenrode, 99, 100.

[19] Id., 100; II Madison, 113. . . .

[20] See generally Eckenrode, c. V; Brant, James, and other authorities cited in note 11 above.

[21] II Madison, 183; and the Appendix to this opinion. Eckenrode, 100 ff. See also Fleet, Madison's "Detached Memoranda" (1946) III William & Mary Q. (3d Series) 534, 554-562.

[22] The major causes assigned for its defeat include the elevation of Patrick Henry to the governorship in November of 1784; the blunder of the proponents in allowing the Bill for Incorporations to come to the floor and incur defeat before the Assessment Bill was acted on; Madison's astute leadership, taking advantage of every "break" to convert his initial minority into a majority, including the deferment of action on the third reading to the fall; the Remonstrance, bringing a flood of protesting petitions; and the general poverty of the time. See Eckenrode, c. V, for an excellent short, detailed account.

this, the way was cleared at last for enactment of Jefferson's Bill for Establishing Religious Freedom. Madison promptly drove it through in January of 1786, seven years from the time it was first introduced. This dual victory substantially ended the fight over establishments, settling the issue against them. See note 33.

The next year Madison became a member of the Constitutional Convention. Its work done, he fought valiantly to secure the ratification of its great product in Virginia as elsewhere, and nowhere else more effectively.[23] Madison was certain in his own mind that under the Constitution "there is not a shadow of right in the general government to intermeddle with religion"[24] and that "this subject is, for the honor of America, perfectly free and unshackled. The government has no jurisdiction over it . . . ."[25] Nevertheless he pledged that he would work for a Bill of Rights, including a specific guaranty of religious freedom, and Virginia, with other states, ratified the Constitution on this assurance.[26]

Ratification thus accomplished, Madison was sent to the first Congress. There he went at once about performing his pledge to establish freedom for the nation as he had done in Virginia. Within a little more than three years from his legislative victory at home he had proposed and secured the submission and ratification of the First Amendment as the first article of our Bill of Rights.[27]

All the great instruments of the Virginia struggle for religious liberty thus became warp and woof of our constitutional tradition, not simply by the course of history, but by the common unifying force of Madison's life, thought and sponsorship. He epitomized the whole of that tradition in the Amendment's compact, but nonetheless comprehensive, phrasing.

As the Remonstrance discloses throughout, Madison opposed every form and degree of official relation between religion and civil authority. For him religion was a wholly private matter beyond the scope of civil power either to restrain or to support.[28] Denial or abridgment of religious freedom was a

---

[23] See James, Brant, op. cit. supra note 11.

[24] V Madison, 176. Cf. notes 33, 37.

[25] V Madison, 132.

[26] Brant, 250. . . .

[27] The amendment with respect to religious liberties read, as Madison introduced it: "The civil rights of none shall be abridged on account of religious belief or worship, nor shall any national religion be established, nor shall the full and equal rights of conscience be in any manner, or on any pretext, infringed." 1 Annals of Congress 434. In the process of debate this was modified to its present form. See especially 1 Annals of Congress 729-731, 765; also note 34.

[28] See text of the Remonstrance, Appendix; also notes 13, 15, 24, 25 supra and text. Madison's one exception concerning restraint was for "preserving public order." Thus he declared in a private letter, IX Madison, 484, 487, written after the First Amendment was adopted: "The tendency to a usurpation on one side or the other, or to a corrupting coalition or alliance between them, will be best guarded agst. by an entire abstinance of the Govt. from interference in any way whatever, beyond the necessity of preserving public order, & protecting each sect agst. trespasses on its legal rights by others." . . .

violation of rights both of conscience and of natural equality. State aid was no less obnoxious or destructive to freedom and to religion itself than other forms of state interference. "Establishment" and "free exercise" were correlative and coextensive ideas, representing only different facets of the single great and fundamental freedom. The Remonstrance, following the Virginia statute's example, referred to the history of religious conflicts and the effects of all sorts of establishments, current and historical, to suppress religion's free exercise. With Jefferson, Madison believed that to tolerate any fragment of establishment would be by so much to perpetuate restraint upon that freedom. Hence he sought to tear out the institution not partially but root and branch, and to bar its return forever.

In no phase was he more unrelentingly absolute than in opposing state support or aid by taxation. Not even "three pence" contribution was thus to be exacted from any citizen for such a purpose. Remonstrance, Par. 3.[29] Tithes had been the lifeblood of establishment before and after other compulsions disappeared. Madison and his coworkers made no exceptions or abridgments to the complete separation they created. Their objection was not to small tithes. It was to any tithes whatsoever. "If it were lawful to impose a small tax for religion, the admission would pave the way for oppressive levies." [30] Not the amount but "the principle of assessment was wrong." And the principle was as much to prevent "the interference of law in religion" as to restrain religious intervention in political matters.[31] In this field the authors of our freedom would not tolerate "the first experiment on our liberties" or "wait till usurped power had strengthened itself by exercise, and entangled the question in precedents." Remonstrance, Par. 3. Nor should we.

In view of this history no further proof is needed that the Amendment forbids any appropriation, large or small, from public funds to aid or support any and all religious exercises. But if more were called for, the debates in the First Congress and this Court's consistent expressions, whenever it has touched on the matter directly, supply it.

By contrast with the Virginia history, the congressional debates on consideration of the Amendment reveal only sparse discussion, reflecting the fact

[29] The third ground of remonstrance . . . bears repetition for emphasis here: "Because, it is proper to take alarm at the first experiment on our liberties . . . The freemen of America did not wait till usurped power had strengthened itself by exercise, and entangled the question in precedents. They saw all the consequences in the principle, and they avoided the consequences by denying the principle. We revere this lesson too much, soon to forget it. Who does not see that . . . the same authority which can force a citizen to *contribute three pence* only of his property for the support of any one establishment, may force him to conform to any other establishment in all cases whatsoever?" (Emphasis added.) II Madison 183, 185-186.

[30] Eckenrode, 105, in summary of the Remonstrance.

[31] "Because the bill implies either that the Civil Magistrate is a competent Judge of Religious truth; or that he may employ Religion as an engine of Civil policy. The first is an arrogant pretention falsified by the contradictory opinions of Rulers in all ages, and throughout the world: The second an unhallowed perversion of the means of salvation." Remonstrance, Appendix, Par. 5; II Madison 183, 187.

that the essential issues had been settled.[33] Indeed the matter had become so well understood as to have been taken for granted in all but formal phrasing. Hence, the only enlightening reference shows concern, not to preserve any power to use public funds in aid of religion, but to prevent the Amendment from outlawing private gifts inadvertently by virtue of the breadth of its wording.[34] . . .

REFERENCES

1. For another discussion throwing a different light on the views of Jefferson and Madison see the dissenting opinion of Mr. Justice Reed in the McCollum case, printed infra.

2. On the movement toward separation and religious freedom in Virginia and other colonies see discussions and materials in 1 Stokes, Church and State in the United States (1950); Howe, Cases on Church and State in the United States, ch. 1 (1952); Littell,

[33] See text supra at notes 24, 25. Madison, of course, was but one of many holding such views, but nevertheless agreeing to the common understanding for adoption of a Bill of Rights in order to remove all doubt engendered by the absence of explicit guaranties in the original Constitution.

By 1791 the great fight over establishments had ended, although some vestiges remained then and later, even in Virginia. The glebes, for example, were not sold there until 1802. Cf. Eckenrode, 147. Fixing an exact date for "disestablishment" is almost impossible, since the process was piecemeal. Although Madison failed in having the Virginia Bill of Rights declare explicitly against establishment in 1776, cf. note 14 and text supra, in 1777 the levy for support of the Anglican clergy was suspended. It was never resumed. Eckenrode states: "This act, in effect, destroyed the establishment. Many dates have been given for its end, but it really came on January 1, 1777, when the act suspending the payment of tithes became effective. This was not seen at the time. . . . But in freeing almost half of the taxpayers from the burden of the state religion, the state religion was at an end. Nobody could be forced to support it, and an attempt to levy tithes upon Anglicans alone would be to recruit the ranks of dissent." P. 53. See also pp. 61, 64. The question of assessment however was revived "with far more strength than ever, in the summer of 1784." Id., 64. It would seem more factual therefore to fix the time of disestablishment as of December, 1785-January, 1786, when the issue in large was finally settled.

[34] At one point the wording was proposed: "No religion shall be established by law, nor shall the equal rights of conscience be infringed." 1 Annals of Congress 729. Cf. note 27. Representative Huntington of Connecticut feared this might be construed to prevent judicial enforcement of private pledges. He stated "that he feared . . . that the words might be taken in such latitude as to be extremely hurtful to the cause of religion. He understood the amendment to mean what had been expressed by the gentleman from Virginia; but others might find it convenient to put another construction upon it. The ministers of their congregations to the Eastward were maintained by the contributions of those who belonged to their society; the expense of building meeting-houses was contributed in the same manner. These things were regulated by by-laws. If an action was brought before a Federal Court on any of these cases, the person who had neglected to perform his engagements could not be compelled to do it; for a support of ministers or building of places of worship might be construed into a religious establishment." 1 Annals of Congress 730.

To avoid any such possibility, Madison suggested inserting the word "national" before "religion," thereby not only again disclaiming intent to bring about the result Huntington feared but also showing unmistakably that "establishment" meant public "support" of religion in the financial sense. 1 Annals of Congress 731. See also IX Madison, 484-487.

From State Church to Pluralism: A Protestant Interpretation of Religion in American History (1962); Thorning, Religious Liberty in Transition (1931); Blau, Cornerstones of Religious Freedom in America (1949); Greene, Religion and the State, The Making and Testing of an American Tradition (1941); Konvitz, Separation of Church and State: The First Freedom, 14 Law & Contemp. Prob. 44 (1949). See also Eliot, in Pioneers of Religious Liberty in America (1903); Meyer, The Blaine Amendment and the Bill of Rights, 64 Harv. L. Rev. 939 (1951); Ernst, The Political Thought of Roger Williams (1929) and Roger Williams, New England Firebrand (1932); Greene, The Development of Religious Liberty in Connecticut (1905); Purcell, Connecticut in Transition 1775-1818 (1918); Meyer, Church and State in Massachusetts from 1740 to 1833 (1930); Sweet, The Story of Religion in America (1950), Religion in Colonial America (1942), and The American Churches, An Interpretation (1947 and 1948); Weigle, American Idealism, chs. IV, V, and VI (1928) (title pages, documents, pictures, contemporary with the establishment of religious freedom in the United States); Cobb, The Rise of Religious Liberty in America (1902); Bryce, The American Commonwealth, chs. III and IV (1888); Campbell, The Puritan in Holland, England and America (1893); Eaton, Freedom of Thought in the Old South (1940) (decline of liberalism in the Old South); Altfeld, The Jew's Struggle for Religious and Civil Liberty in Maryland (1924); Nevins, The American States During and After the Revolution, ch. X (1927) (South Carolina).

For history of the struggle for religious liberty throughout the ages, see Bainton, The Struggle for Religious Liberty (1941); Bury, A History of Freedom of Thought, chs. V and VIII (1913); Geffcken, Church and State, Their Relations Historically Developed (1877); Garrison, Intolerance (1934); Jordan, The Development of Religious Toleration in England (1940); Lecky, Democracy and Liberty, chs. VI and VII (1899); Ruffini, Religious Liberty (1912); Hearnshaw (ed.), The Social and Political Ideas of Some Great Thinkers of the Renaissance and Reformation (1939).

3. For the Catholic point of view, see Abbott (ed.), The Documents of Vatican II 675-696 (religious freedom), 637-651 (Christian education) (1966). See also Casad, The Establishment Clause and the Ecumenical Movement, 62 Mich. L. Rev. 419 (1964); Giacchi, Freedom of Religion and the State, 11 Catholic Law. 271 (1965); O'Gorman, Church, State and Rome (1963); Rubinstein, Church and State: the Jewish Posture, in Giannella (ed.), 1963 Religion and the Public Order (1964); Murray, The Problem of Pluralism in America, 1 Catholic Law. 223 (1955); Murray, Law or Prepossessions? 14 Law & Contemp. Prob. 23 (1949) (partially reprinted in the second edition of this book, 1120-1123); Maritain, Education at the Crossroads (1943); Maritain, Man and the State (1951) (partially reprinted in the second edition of this book, 1123-1124); O'Brien, Justice Reed and the First Amendment: The Religion Clauses (1958). For medieval points of view see Hearnshaw (ed.), The Social and Political Ideas of Some Great Medieval Thinkers (1950); Dunning, A History of Political Theories Ancient and Medieval (1923). For later development see Taylor, Thought and Expression in the Sixteenth Century (2d ed. 1930); Waring, The Political Theories of Martin Luther (1916).

4. For secular discussion of the relation of religious education to democratic theory, see Kallen, The Education of Free Men 224-229 (1949); Mannheim, Freedom, Power, and Democratic Planning 286-289 (1950). Cf. T. S. Eliot, The Idea of a Christian Society (1939), and Notes Toward the Definition of Culture (1948).

5. On definitions of religion see Note, Defining Religion: Of God, the Constitution and the D.A.R., 32 U. Chi. L. Rev. 533, 550-551 (1965):

"An individual or group belief is religious if it occupies the same place in the lives of its adherents that orthodox beliefs occupy in the lives of their adherents. Four characteristics should be present: (1) a belief regarding the meaning of life; (2) a psychological commitment by the individual adherent (or if a group, by the members generally) to this belief; (3) a system of moral practice resulting from adherence to this belief; and,

(4) an acknowledgement by its adherents that the belief (or belief system) is their exclusive or supreme system of ultimate beliefs."

Cf. Kolbeck v. Kramer, 84 N.J. Super. 569, 574, 202 A.2d 889, 892, (1964) to the effect that it is invalid for "a state . . . to determine that a cause is not a religious one." See also Stahmer, Defining Religion: Federal Aid and Academic Freedom, in Giannella (ed.), 1963 Religion and the Public Order (1964); Weiss, Privilege, Posture and Protection: "Religion" in the Law, 73 Yale L.J. 593 (1964) (taking a position similar to Kolbeck, supra, that any definition would restrict freedom of religion); Robinson, Honest to God (1963); Edwards (ed.), The Honest to God Debate (1963).

6. For treatment of rationalism as a type of American religious thought, see Koch, Republican Religion: The American Revolution and the Cult of Reason (1933). See also Morais, Deism in Eighteenth Century America (1934). Compare also Cox, The Secular City: Secularization and Urbanization in Theological Perspective (1965); Altizer and Hamilton, Radical Theology and the Death of God (1966).

7. The following are standard reference works on the subjects of this chapter: Stokes, Church and State in the United States (1950); Pfeffer, Church, State and Freedom (1953); Stokes and Pfeffer, Church and State in the United States (rev. ed. 1964); Fellman, Religion in American Public Law (1965); Johnson and Yost, Separation of Church and State in the United States (1948); Torpey, Judicial Doctrines of Religious Rights in America (1948). See also Religious Liberty Association, American State Papers on Freedom in Religion (1943); Greene, Religion and the State: The Making and Testing of an American Tradition (1941); Brady, Confusion Twice Confounded (1955); Zabel, God and Caesar in Nebraska (1955). For further discussions, both legal and nonlegal, see Howe, The Garden and the Wilderness (1965); Moore, The Supreme Court and the Relationship Between the "Establishment" and "Free Exercise" Clauses, 42 Texas L. Rev. 142 (1963); Drinan, Religion, the Courts, and Public Policy (1963); Kurland, Religion and the Law of Church and State and the Supreme Court (1962); Corwin, A Constitution of Powers in a Secular State (1951); Kauper, Religion and the Constitution (1964); Kauper, Church and State: Cooperative Separatism, 60 Mich. L. Rev. 7 (1961); Griswold, Absolute is in the Dark — A Discussion of the Approach of the Supreme Court to Constitutional Questions, 8 Utah L. Rev. 167 (1963); Katz, Religion and American Constitutions (1964); Howe, The Constitutional Question, in Religion and the Free Society 49 (Fund for the Republic 1958); Pfeffer, Religion-Blind Government, 15 Stan. L. Rev. 389 (1963); Center for the Study of Democratic Institutions, The Churches and the Public (1960); Special Committee on Church and State, Report of the Special Committee on Relations between Church and State in the U.S.A., 7 The United Presbyterian Church in the United States of America, General Assembly, Journal 1963, 180 (published also separately); Commission on Church and State Relations in a Pluralistic Society, Board of Social Ministry, Lutheran Church in America, Church and State: A Lutheran Perspective (1963); Marvell, The First Amendment: The History of Religious Freedom in America (1964); Antieau, Downey, and Roberts, Freedom from Federal Establishment (1964); Van Alstyne, Constitutional Separation of Church and State: The Quest for a Coherent Position, 57 Am. Pol. Sci. Rev. 865 (1963); Villanova University, Institute of Church and State, Proceedings: vol. 3. Secularism and Religious Freedom, vol. 4. Law and Religious Pluralism (1963); Giannella (ed.), Religion and the Public Order 1963, 1964, and 1965; Note, The Free Exercise and Establishment Clauses: Conflict or Coordination? 48 Minn. L. Rev. 929 (1964); Note, Church-State — Religious Institutions and Values: A Legal Survey — 1963-1964, 39 Notre Dame Law. 427 (1964) (appears periodically); Oaks (ed.), The Wall Between Church and State (1963); Harper, Justice Rutledge and the Bright Constellation (1965); Dunsford, The Establishment Syndrome and Religious Liberty, 2 Duquesne L. Rev. 139 (1964); Odegard, Religion and Politics (1960) (collection of materials); Cahn, The "Establishment of Religion" Puzzle, 36 N.Y.U.L. Rev. 1274 (1961); Konvitz, Fundamental Liberties of a Free People, Pt. I

(1957); Chafee, The Blessings of Liberty, ch. IX (1956); Beth, Toward a Modern American Theory of Church-State Relationships, 70 Pol. Sci. Q. 573 (1955); Steinhardt, Christian Science: Religious Freedom and State Control, 7 Miami L.Q. 358 (1953); Sutherland, Due Process and Disestablishment, 62 Harv. L. Rev. 1306 (1949); Van Dusen, Church and State in the Modern World (1937).

8. For discussion of religions in America see Cogley (ed.), Religion in America (1958); Ellis, American Catholicism (1956); Organized Religions in the United States, 256 Annals Am. Acad. Pol. & Soc. Sci. (1948); May, Protestant Churches and Industrial America (1949); Maynard, The Story of American Catholicism (1941); Finkelstein, Ross and Brown, The Religions of Democracy: Judaism, Catholicism, Protestantism in Creed and Life (1946); Smith and Jamison (eds.), 4 vols., Religion in American Life (Princeton 1961); Lambert (ed.), Religion in American Society, 332 Annals Am. Acad. Pol. & Soc. Sci. (1960); Mays and Nicholson, Negro's Church (1933); Clark, The Small Sects in America (1949); Stroup, The Jehovah's Witnesses (1945). See also Greene (ed.), Roger Williams and the Massachusetts Magistrates (1964).

9. For critical evaluation of the connection of religious thought and institutions with the development of political and economic theory in America see Bates, American Faith: Its Religious, Political and Economic Foundations (1940); Gabriel, The Course of American Democratic Thought (1943); Curti, Growth of American Thought (1951); Dorfman, The Economic Mind in American Civilization, 1606-1918 (1946-1949); Schneider, History of American Philosophy (1946); Perry, Puritanism and Democracy (1944); Blanshard, American Freedom and Catholic Power (1958); Blanshard, God and Man in Washington (1960).

10. For a brief scholarly discussion of the history, development and teachings of the various major religions of the world see Bouquet, Comparative Religion (1941). See also Jurji (ed.), The Great Religions of the Modern World (1946). For a sociological study of religion, including the nature of religious experience and its expression, the impact of religion on society, the nature of religious groups and of religious authority, and the relation of religion to the state throughout the world and throughout history, see Wach, Sociology of Religion (1944). The study contains extensive bibliographical references. For critical philosophical treatments of religion see Hume, Dialogues Concerning Natural Religion (1779); Feuerbach, Das Wesen der Religion (1849); Santayana, Reason in Religion (1905); Russell, Religion and Science (1935); Koehler, The Place of Value in a World of Facts (1938). For an extensive bibliography of philosophical treatments of religion see Brightman, A Philosophy of Religion 490-522 (1940). See also Kaufman, Critique of Religion and Philosophy (1958); Muller, Religion and Freedom in the Modern World (1963); Hocking, Living Religions and a World Faith (1940); Mumford, The Conduct of Life (1951); Whyte, The Next Development in Man (1948); Burtt, Types of Religious Philosophy (1939); Collingwood, Religion and Philosophy (1916); D'Arcy, The Mind and Heart of Love, Lion and Unicorn: A Study in Eros and Agape (1947) (theology and psychoanalysis); Dewey, A Common Faith (1934); Freud, The Future of an Illusion (1928); Fromm, Psychoanalysis and Religion (1950); Jung, Psychology and Religion (1938); Macmurray, The Structure of Religious Experience (1836).

B. Organized Religion and Education

1. History of Secular and Religious Education in the United States

ILLINOIS ex rel. McCOLLUM v. BOARD OF EDUCATION
333 U.S. 203, 213-225, 68 S. Ct. 461, 466-472,
92 L. Ed. 649, 660-665 (1948)

Mr. Justice Frankfurter concurring.

. . . Traditionally, organized education in the Western world was Church education. It could hardly be otherwise when the education of children was primarily study of the Word and the ways of God. Even in the Protestant countries, where there was a less close identification of Church and State, the basis of education was largely the Bible, and its chief purpose inculcation of piety. To the extent that the State intervened, it used its authority to further aims of the Church.

The emigrants who came to these shores brought this view of education with them. Colonial schools certainly started with a religious orientation. When the common problems of the early settlers of the Massachusetts Bay Colony revealed the need for common schools, the object was the defeat of "one chief project of that old deluder, Satan, to keep men from the knowledge of the Scriptures." The Laws and Liberties of Massachusetts, 1648 edition (Cambridge 1929) 47.[1]

The evolution of colonial education, largely in the service of religion, into the public school system of today is the story of changing conceptions regarding the American democratic society, of the functions of State-maintained education in such a society, and of the role therein of the free exercise of religion by the people. The modern public school derived from a philosophy of freedom reflected in the First Amendment. It is appropriate to recall that the Remonstrance of James Madison, an event basic in the history of religious liberty, was called forth by a proposal which involved support to religious education. . . . As the momentum for popular education increased and in turn evoked strong claims for State support of religious education, contests not unlike that which in Virginia had produced Madison's Remonstrance appeared in various forms in other States. New York and Massachusetts provide famous chapters in the history that established dissociation of religious teaching from State-maintained schools. In New York, the rise of the com-

[1] For an exposition of the religious origins of American education, see S. W. Brown, The Secularization of American Education (1912) cc. I, II; Knight, Education in the United States (2d rev. ed. 1941) cc. III, V; Cubberley, Public Education in the United States (1934) cc. II, III.

mon schools led, despite fierce sectarian opposition, to the barring of tax
funds to church schools, and later to any school in which sectarian doctrine
was taught.[2] In Massachusetts, largely through the efforts of Horace Mann,
all sectarian teachings were barred from the common school to save it from
being rent by denominational conflict.[3] The upshot of these controversies,
often long and fierce, is fairly summarized by saying that long before the
Fourteenth Amendment subjected the States to new limitations, the prohibition of furtherance by the State of religious instruction became the guiding
principle, in law and feeling, of the American people. In sustaining Stephen
Girard's will, this Court referred to the inevitable conflicts engendered by
matters "connected with religious polity" and particularly "in a country composed of such a variety of religious sects as our country." Vidal v. Girard's
Executors, 2 How. 127, 198. That was more than one hundred years ago.

Separation in the field of education, then, was not imposed upon unwilling
States by force of superior law. In this respect the Fourteenth Amendment
merely reflected a principle then dominant in our national life. To the extent
that the Constitution thus made it binding upon the States, the basis of the
restriction is the whole experience of our people. Zealous watchfulness
against fusion of secular and religious activities by Government itself,
through any of its instruments but especially through its educational agencies, was the democratic response of the American community to the particular needs of a young and growing nation, unique in the composition of its
people.[4] . . . The secular public school did not imply indifference to the
basic role of religion in the life of the people, nor rejection of religious education as a means of fostering it. The claims of religion were not minimized by
refusing to make the public schools agencies for their assertion. The non-
sectarian or secular public school was the means of reconciling freedom in
general with religious freedom. The sharp confinement of the public schools
to secular education was a recognition of the need of a democratic society to
educate its children, insofar as the State undertook to do so, in an atmosphere
free from pressures in a realm in which pressures are most resisted and where
conflicts are most easily and most bitterly engendered. . . .

This development of the public school as a symbol of our secular unity was

---

[2] See Boese, Public Education in the City of New York (1869) c. XIV; Hall, Reli-
gious Education in the Public Schools of the State and City of New York (1914) cc.
VI, VII; Palmer, The New York Public School (1905) cc. VI, VII, X, XII. And see
New York Laws 1842, c. 150, §14, amended, New York Laws 1844, c. 320, §12.

[3] S. M. Smith, The Relation of the State to Religious Education in Massachusetts
(1926) c. VII; Culver, Horace Mann and Religion in the Massachusetts Public Schools
(1929).

[4] It has been suggested that secular education in this country is the inevitable
"product of the utter impossibility of harmonizing multiform creeds." T. W. M.
Marshall, Secular Education in England and the United States, 1 American Catholic
Quarterly Review 278, 308. It is precisely because of this "utter impossibility" that
the fathers put into the Constitution the principle of complete "hands-off," for a people
as religiously heterogeneous as ours.

not a sudden achievement nor attained without violent conflict.[5] While in small communities of comparatively homogeneous religious beliefs, the need for absolute separation presented no urgencies, elsewhere the growth of the secular school encountered the resistance of feeling strongly engaged against it. . . .

[By] 1875 the separation of public education from Church entanglements, of the State from the teaching of religion, was firmly established in the consciousness of the nation. In that year President Grant made his famous remarks to the Convention of the Army of the Tennessee:

"Encourage free schools, and resolve that not one dollar appropriated for their support shall be appropriated to the support of any sectarian schools. Resolve that neither the State nor nation, nor both combined, shall support institutions of learning other than those sufficient to afford every child growing up in the land the opportunity of a good common-school education, unmixed with sectarian, pagan, or atheistical dogmas. Leave the matter of religion to the family altar, the church, and the private school, supported entirely by private contributions. Keep the church and the state forever separate." "The President's Speech at Des Moines," 22 Catholic World 433, 434-35 (1876).

So strong was this conviction, that rather than rest on the comprehensive prohibitions of the First and Fourteenth Amendments, President Grant urged that there be written into the United States Constitution particular elaborations, including a specific prohibition against the use of public funds for sectarian education,[6] such as had been written into many State constitu-

---

[5] See Cubberley, Public Education in the United States (1934) pp. 230 et seq.; Zollmann, The Relation of Church and State, in Lotz and Crawford, Studies in Religious Education (1931) 403, 418 et seq.; Payson Smith, The Public Schools and Religious Education, in Religion and Education (Sperry, Editor, 1945) pp. 32 et seq.; also Mahoney, The Relation of the State to Religious Education in Early New York 1633-1825 (1941) c. VI; McLaughlin, A History of State Legislation Affecting Private Elementary and Secondary Schools in the United States, 1870-1945 (1946) c. I; and see note 10, infra.

[6] President Grant's Annual Message to Congress, December 7, 1875, 4 Cong. Rec. 175 et seq.; Ames, The Proposed Amendments to the Constitution of the United States During the First Century of its History, H.R. Doc. No. 353, Pt. 2, 54th Cong., 2d Sess., pp. 277-78. In addition to the first proposal, "The Blaine Amendment," five others to similar effect are cited by Ames. The reason for the failure of these attempts seems to have been in part that the "provisions of the State constitutions are in almost all instances adequate on this subject, and no amendment is likely to be secured." Id.

In the form in which it passed the House of Representatives, the Blaine Amendment read as follows: "No State shall make any law respecting an establishment of religion, or prohibiting the free exercise thereof; and no religious test shall ever be required as a qualification to any office or public trust under any State. No public property, and no public revenue of, nor any loan of credit by or under the authority of, the United States, or any State, Territory, District, or municipal corporation, shall be appropriated to, or made or used for, the support of any school, educational or other institution, under the control of any religious or anti-religious sect, organization, or denomination, or wherein the particular creed or tenets of any religious or anti-religious sect, organization, or denomination shall be taught. And no such particular creed or tenets shall be read or taught in any school or institution supported in whole or in part by such revenue or loan of credit; and no such appropriation or loan of credit shall be made

tions.[7] By 1894, in urging the adoption of such a provision in the New York Constitution, Elihu Root was able to summarize a century of the nation's history: "It is not a question of religion, or of creed, or of party; it is a question of declaring and maintaining the great American principle of eternal separation between Church and State." Root, Addresses on Government and Citizenship, 137, 140. The extent to which this principle was deemed a presupposition of our Constitutional system is strikingly illustrated by the fact that every State admitted into the Union since 1876 was compelled by Congress to write into its constitution a requirement that it maintain a school system "free from sectarian control."

Prohibition of the commingling of sectarian and secular instruction in the public school is of course only half the story. A religious people was naturally concerned about the part of the child's education entrusted "to the family altar, the church, and the private school." The promotion of religious education took many forms. Laboring under financial difficulties and exercising only persuasive authority, various denominations felt handicapped in their task of religious education. Abortive attempts were therefore frequently made to obtain public funds for religious schools.[10] But the major efforts of religious inculcation were a recognition of the principle of Separation by the establishment of church schools privately supported. Parochial schools were maintained by various denominations. These, however, were often beset by serious handicaps, financial and otherwise, so that the religious aims which they represented found other directions. There were experiments with vacation schools, with Saturday as well as Sunday schools.[11] They all fell short of their

---

to any religious or anti-religious sect, organization, or denomination, or to promote its interests or tenets. This article shall not be construed to prohibit the reading of the Bible in any school or institution; and it shall not have the effect to impair rights of property already vested. . . ." H. Res. 1, 44th Cong., 1st Sess. (1876).

[7] See Constitutions of the States and United States, III Report of the New York State Constitutional Convention Committee (1938) Index, pp. 1766-67.

[10] See, e.g., the New York experience, including, inter alia, the famous Hughes controversy of 1840-42, the conflict culminating in the Constitutional Convention of 1894, and the attempts to restore aid to parochial schools by revision of the New York City Charter, in 1901, and at the State Constitutional Convention of 1938. See McLaughlin, A History of State Legislation Affecting Private Elementary and Secondary Schools in the United States, 1870-1945 (1946) pp. 119-25; Mahoney, The Relation of the State to Religious Education in Early New York 1633-1825 (1941) c. VI; Hall, Religious Education in the Public Schools of the State and the City of New York (1914) pp. 46-47; Boese, Public Education in the City of New York (1869) c. XIV; compare New York Laws 1901, vol. 3 §1152, p. 492, with amendment, id., p. 668; see Nicholas Murray Butler, Religion and Education (Editorial) in 22 Educational Review 101, June, 1901; New York Times, April 8, 1901, p. 1, col. 1; April 9, 1901, p. 2 col. 5; April 19, 1901, p. 2, col. 2; April 21, 1901, p. 1, col. 3; Editorial, April 22, 1901, p. 6, col. 1.

Compare S. 2499, 79th Cong., 2d Sess., providing for Federal aid to education, and the controversy engendered over the inclusion in the aid program of sectarian schools, fully discussed in, e.g., "The Nation's Schools," January through June, 1947.

[11] For surveys of the development of private religious education, see e.g., A. A. Brown, A History of Religious Education in Recent Times (1923); Athearn, Religious Education and American Democracy (1917); Burns and Kohlbrenner, A History of

purpose. It was urged that by appearing to make religion a one-day-a-week matter, the Sunday school, which acquired national acceptance, tended to relegate the child's religious education, and thereby his religion, to a minor role not unlike the enforced piano lesson.

Out of these inadequate efforts evolved the week-day church school, held on one or more afternoons a week after the close of the public school. But children continued to be children; they wanted to play when school was out, particularly when other children were free to do so. Church leaders decided that if the week-day church school was to succeed, a way had to be found to give the child his religious education during what the child conceived to be his "business hours."

The initiation of the movement[12] may fairly be attributed to Dr. George U. Wenner. The underlying assumption of his proposal, made at the Interfaith Conference on Federation held in New York City in 1905, was that the public school unduly monopolized the child's time and that the churches were entitled to their share of it.[13] This, the schools should "release." Accordingly, the Federation, citing the example of the Third Republic of France,[14] urged that

---

Catholic Education in the United States (1937); Lotz and Crawford, Studies in Religious Education (1931) Parts I and IV.

[12] Reference should be made to Jacob Gould Schurman, who in 1903 proposed a plan bearing close resemblance to that of Champaign. See Symposium, 75 The Outlook 635, 636, November 14, 1903; Crooker, Religious Freedom in American Education (1903) pp. 39 et seq.

[13] For the text of the resolution, a brief in its support, as well as an exposition of some of the opposition it inspired, see Wenner's book, Religious Education and the Public School (rev. ed. 1913).

[14] The French example is cited not only by Wenner but also by Nicholas Murray Butler, who thought released time was "restoring the American system in the state of New York." The Place of Religious Instruction in Our Educational System, 7 Vital Speeches 167, 168 (Nov. 28, 1940); see also Report of the President of Columbia University, 1934, pp. 22-24. It is important to note, however, that the French practice must be viewed as the result of the struggle to emancipate the French schools from control by the Church. The leaders of this revolution, men like Paul Bert, Ferdinand Buisson, and Jules Ferry, agreed to this measure as one part of a great step towards, rather than a retreat from, the principle of Separation. The history of these events is described in Muzzey, State, Church, and School in France, The School Review, March through June, 1911.

In effect, moreover, the French practice differs in crucial respects from both the Wenner proposal and the Champaign system. The law of 1882 provided that "Public elementary schools will be closed one day a week in addition to Sunday in order to permit parents, if they so desire, to have their children given religious instruction outside of school buildings." Law No. 11,696, March 28, 1882, Bulletin des Lois, No. 690. This then approximates that aspect of released time generally known as "dismissed time." No children went to school on that day, and the public school was therefore not an alternative used to impel the children towards the religious school. The religious education was given "outside of school buildings."

The Vichy Government attempted to introduce a program of religious instruction within the public school system remarkably similar to that in effect in Champaign. The proposal was defeated by intense opposition which included the protest of the French clergy, who apparently feared State control of the Church. See Schwartz, Religious Instruction under Petain, 58 Christian Century 1170 (Sept. 24, 1941).

upon the request of their parents children be excused from public school on Wednesday afternoon, so that the churches could provide "Sunday school on Wednesday." This was to be carried out on church premises under church authority. Those not desiring to attend church school would continue their normal classes. Lest these public school classes unfairly compete with the church education, it was requested that the school authorities refrain from scheduling courses or activities of compelling interest or importance.

The proposal aroused considerable opposition and it took another decade for a "released time" scheme to become part of a public school system. Gary, Indiana, inaugurated the movement. At a time when industrial expansion strained the communal facilities of the city, Superintendent of Schools Wirt suggested a fuller use of the school buildings. Building on theories which had become more or less current, he also urged that education was more than instruction in a classroom. The school was only one of several educational agencies. The library, the playground, the home, the church, all have their function in the child's proper unfolding. Accordingly, Wirt's plan sought to rotate the schedules of the children during the school-day so that some were in class, others were in the library, still others in the playground. And some, he suggested to the leading ministers of the City, might be released to attend religious classes if the churches of the City cooperated and provided them. They did, in 1914, and thus was "released time" begun. The religious teaching was held on church premises and the public schools had no hand in the conduct of these church schools. They did not supervise the choice of instructors or the subject matter taught. Nor did they assume responsibility for the attendance, conduct or achievement of the child in a church school; and he received no credit for it. The period of attendance in the religious schools would otherwise have been a play period for the child, with the result that the arrangement did not cut into public school instruction or truly affect the activities or feelings of the children who did not attend the church schools.[15]

From such a beginning "released time" has attained substantial proportions. In 1914-15, under the Gary program, 619 pupils left the public schools for the church schools during one period a week. According to responsible figures almost 2,000,000 in some 2,200 communities participated in "released time" programs during 1947.[16]

REFERENCES

1. See Butts, The American Tradition in Religion and Education (1950); Moehlman, School and Church: The American Way (1944); Sweets, Church and Education (1939); Punke, Religious Issues in American Public Education, 20 Law & Contemp. Prob. 138

[15] Of the many expositions of the Gary plan, see, e.g., A. A. Brown, The Week-Day Church Schools of Gary, Indiana, 11 Religious Education 5 (1916); Wirt, The Gary Public Schools and the Churches, id. at 221 (1916).

[16] See the 1947 Yearbook, International Council of Religious Education, p. 76; also New York Times, September 21, 1947, p. 22, col. 1.

(1955); Rodes, Religious Education and the Historical Method of Constitutional Interpretation, 9 Rutgers L. Rev. 682 (1955); Kruse, The Historical Meaning and Judicial Construction of the Establishment of Religion Clause of the First Amendment, 2 Washburn L.J. 65 (1962); Pfeffer, Religion, Education and the Constitution, 8 Law. Guild Rev. 387 (1948); Stewart, A History of Religious Education in Connecticut to the Middle of the Nineteenth Century (1924); Healey, Jefferson on Religion in Public Education (1962).

2. On religion and education in general see: Boles, The Bible, Religion, and the Public Schools (3d ed. 1965); McLean and Kimber, The Teaching of Religion in State Universities: Description of Programs in Twenty-five Institutions (1960); Dierenfield, The Extent of Religious Influence in American Public Schools, 56 Religious Education 173 (1961), and Religion in American Public Schools (1962) (containing statistical survey based on sample of 4000 communities); National Education Association, The Status of Religious Education in the Public Schools (1949) (contains extensive bibliography); American Council on Education, The Relation of Religion to Public Education (1947); Chave, A Functional Approach to Religious Education (1947); Mattox, The Teaching of Religion in the Public Schools (1948); Moehlman, The Church As Educator (1947); Lotz (ed.), Orientation in Religious Education (1950); Williams, The New Education and Religion, A Challenge to Secularism in Education (1945); Kilpatrick, Religion in Education: The Issues, Prog. Ed. 98 (1949); Thayer, Religion in Public Education (1947); Weary, Democracy's Case Against Religious Education on School Time (1947); Synagogue Council of America, Conference on Religious Education and the Public Schools (1941); Brubacher (ed.), The Public Schools and Spiritual Values (1944); Meiklejohn, Educational Cooperation Between Church and State, 14 Law & Contemp. Prob. 61 (1949); American Jewish Committee, Church, State and Education (1951); Cushman, Public Support of Religious Education in American Constitutional Law, 45 Ill. L. Rev. 333 (1950); Cosway and Toepfer, Religion and the Schools, 17 U. Cinc. L. Rev. 117 (1948); Burke, Busses, Released Time and the Political Process, 32 Marq. L. Rev. 311 (1948); Note, Catholic Schools and Public Money, 50 Yale L.J. 917 (1941).

2. Aid to Education

EVERSON v. BOARD OF EDUCATION
330 U.S. 1, 67 S. Ct. 504, 91 L. Ed. 711 (1947)

Mr. Justice Black delivered the opinion of the Court.

A New Jersey statute authorizes its local school districts to make rules and contracts for the transportation of children to and from schools.[1] The appellee, a township board of education, acting pursuant to this statute, authorized reimbursement to parents of money expended by them for the bus transporta-

---

[1] "Whenever in any district there are children living remote from any schoolhouse, the board of education of the district may make rules and contracts for the transportation of such children to and from school, including the transportation of school children to and from school other than a public school, except such school as is operated for profit in whole or in part.

"When any school district provides any transportation for public school children to and from school, transportation from any point in such established school route to any other point in such established school route shall be supplied to school children residing in such school district in going to and from school other than a public school, except such school as is operated for profit in whole or in part." New Jersey Laws, 1941, c. 191, p. 581; N.J.R.S. Cum. Supp., tit. 18, c. 14, §8.

tion of their children on regular busses operated by the public transportation system. Part of this money was for the payment of transportation of some children in the community to Catholic parochial schools. These church schools give their students, in addition to secular education, regular religious instruction conforming to the religious tenets and modes of worship of the Catholic Faith. The superintendent of these schools is a Catholic priest.

The appellant, in his capacity as a district taxpayer, filed suit in a state court challenging the right of the Board to reimburse parents of parochial school students. He contended that the statute and the resolution passed pursuant to it violated both the State and the Federal Constitutions. That court held that the legislature was without power to authorize such payment under the state constitution. 132 N.J.L. 98, 39 A.2d 75. The New Jersey Court of Errors and Appeals reversed, holding that neither the statute nor the resolution passed pursuant to it was in conflict with the State constitution or the provisions of the Federal Constitution in issue. 133 N.J.L. 350, 44 A.2d 333. The case is here on appeal under 28 U.S.C. §344(a).

Since there has been no attack on the statute on the ground that a part of its language excludes children attending private schools operated for profit from enjoying State payment for their transportation, we need not consider this exclusionary language; it has no relevancy to any constitutional question here presented.[2] Furthermore, if the exclusion clause had been properly challenged, we do not know whether New Jersey's highest court would construe its statutes as precluding payment of the school transportation of any group of pupils, even those of a private school run for profit. Consequently, we put to one side the question as to the validity of the statute against the claim that it does not authorize payment for the transportation generally of school children in New Jersey.

The only contention here is that the state statute and the resolution, insofar as they authorized reimbursement to parents of children attending parochial schools, violate the Federal Constitution in these two respects, which to some extent overlap. *First*. They authorize the State to take by taxation the private property of some and bestow it upon others, to be used for their own private

[2] Appellant does not challenge the New Jersey statute or the resolution on the ground that either violates the equal protection clause of the Fourteenth Amendment by excluding payment for the transportation of any pupil who attends a "private school run for profit." Although the township resolution authorized reimbursement only for parents of public and Catholic school pupils, appellant does not allege, nor is there anything in the record which would offer the slightest support to an allegation, that there were any children in the township who attended or would have attended, but for want of transportation, any but public and Catholic schools. It will be appropriate to consider the exclusion of students of private schools operated for profit when and if it is proved to have occurred, is made the basis of a suit by one in a position to challenge it, and New Jersey's highest court has ruled adversely to the challenger. Striking down a state law is not a matter of such light moment that it should be done by a federal court ex mero motu on a postulate neither charged nor proved, but which rests on nothing but a possibility. Cf. Liverpool, N.Y. & P.S.S. Co. v. Comm'rs of Emigration, 113 U.S. 33, 39.

purposes. This, it is alleged, violates the due process clause of the Fourteenth Amendment. *Second.* The statute and the resolution forced inhabitants to pay taxes to help support and maintain schools which are dedicated to, and which regularly teach, the Catholic Faith. This is alleged to be a use of state power to support church schools contrary to the prohibition of the First Amendment which the Fourteenth Amendment made applicable to the states.

First. The due process argument that the state law taxes some people to help others carry out their private purposes is framed in two phases. The first phase is that a state cannot tax A to reimburse B for the cost of transporting his children to church schools. This is said to violate the due process clause because the children are sent to these church schools to satisfy the personal desires of the parents, rather than the public's interest in the general education of all children. This argument, if valid, would apply equally to prohibit state payment for the transportation of children to any non-public school, whether operated by a church or any other non-government individual or group. But, the New Jersey legislature has decided that a public purpose will be served by using tax-raised funds to pay the bus fares of all school children, including those who attend parochial schools. The New Jersey Court of Errors and Appeals has reached the same conclusion. The fact that a state law, passed to satisfy a public need, coincides with the personal desires of the individuals most directly affected is certainly an inadequate reason for us to say that a legislature has erroneously appraised the public need. . . .

It is much too late to argue that legislation intended to facilitate the opportunity of children to get a secular education serves no public purpose. Cochran v. Louisiana State Board of Education, 281 U.S. 370; Holmes, J., in Interstate Ry. v. Massachusetts, 207 U.S. 79, 87. See opinion of Cooley, J., in Stuart v. School District No. 1 of Kalamazoo, 30 Mich. 69 (1874). The same thing is no less true of legislation to reimburse needy parents, or all parents, for payment of the fares of their children so that they can ride in public busses to and from schools rather than run the risk of traffic and other hazards incident to walking or "hitchhiking." See Barbier v. Connolly [113 U.S. 27, 31]. See also cases collected 63 A.L.R. 413; 118 A.L.R. 806. Nor does it follow that a law has a private rather than a public purpose because it provides that tax-raised funds will be paid to reimburse individuals on account of money spent by them in a way which furthers a public program. See Carmichael v. Southern Coal & Coke Co., 301 U.S. 495, 518. Subsidies and loans to individuals such as farmers and homeowners, and to privately owned transportation systems, as well as many other kinds of businesses, have been commonplace practice in our state and national history. . . .

Second. The New Jersey statute is challenged as a "law respecting an establishment of religion." The First Amendment, as made applicable to the states by the Fourteenth, Murdock v. Pennsylvania, 319 U.S. 105, commands that a state "shall make no law respecting an establishment of religion, or prohibiting the free exercise thereof. . . ." These words of the First Amendment reflected in the minds of early Americans a vivid mental picture of conditions and practices which they fervently wished to stamp out in order to preserve liberty for themselves and for their posterity. Doubtless their goal has not been entirely reached; but so far has the Nation moved toward it that the expression "law respecting an establishment of religion," probably does not so vividly remind present-day Americans of the evils, fears, and political problems that caused that expression to be written into our Bill of Rights. Whether this New Jersey law is one respecting an "establishment of religion" requires an understanding of the meaning of that language, particularly with respect to the imposition of taxes. Once again, therefore, it is not inappropriate briefly to review the background and environment of the period in which that constitutional language was fashioned and adopted. . . .

[The opinion here reviews the history of the First Amendment.]

The meaning and scope of the First Amendment, preventing establishment of religion or prohibiting the free exercise thereof, in the light of its history and the evils it was designed forever to suppress, have been several times elaborated by the decisions of this Court prior to the application of the First Amendment to the states by the Fourteenth.[21] The broad meaning given the Amendment by these earlier cases has been accepted by this Court in its decisions concerning an individual's religious freedom rendered since the Fourteenth Amendment was interpreted to make the prohibitions of the First applicable to state action abridging religious freedom. There is every reason to give the same application and broad interpretation to the "establishment of religion" clause. The interrelation of these complementary clauses was well summarized in a statement of the Court of Appeals of South Carolina,[23] quoted with approval by this Court in Watson v. Jones, 13 Wall. 679, 730: "The structure of our government has, for the preservation of civil liberty, rescued the temporal institutions from religious interference. On the other hand, it has secured religious liberty from the invasion of the civil authority."

The "establishment of religion" clause of the First Amendment means at least this: Neither a state nor the Federal Government can set up a church. Neither can pass laws which aid one religion, aid all religions, or prefer one religion over another. Neither can force nor influence a person to go to or to remain away from church against his will or force him to profess a belief or disbelief in any religion. No person can be punished for entertaining or professing religious beliefs or disbeliefs, for church attendance or non-attendance. No tax in any amount, large or small, can be levied to support any religious activities or institutions, whatever they may be called, or whatever form they

---

[21] Terrett v. Taylor, 9 Cranch 43; Watson v. Jones, 13 Wall. 679; Davis v. Beason, 133 U.S. 333; Cf. Reynolds v. United States [98 U.S. 145, 162]; Reuben Quick Bear v. Leupp, 210 U.S. 50.

[23] Harmon v. Dreher, Speer's Equity Reports (S.C., 1843), 87, 120.

may adopt to teach or practice religion. Neither a state nor the Federal Government can, openly or secretly, participate in the affairs of any religious organizations or groups and vice versa. In the words of Jefferson, the clause against establishment of religion by law was intended to erect "a wall of separation between church and State." Reynolds v. United States, supra at 164.

We must consider the New Jersey statute in accordance with the foregoing limitations imposed by the First Amendment. But we must not strike that state statute down if it is within the State's constitutional power even though it approaches the verge of that power. See Interstate Ry. v. Massachusetts, Holmes, J., supra at 85, 88. New Jersey cannot consistently with the "establishment of religion" clause of the First Amendment contribute tax-raised funds to the support of an institution which teaches the tenets and faith of any church. On the other hand, other language of the amendment commands that New Jersey cannot hamper its citizens in the free exercise of their own religion. Consequently, it cannot exclude individual Catholics, Lutherans, Mohammedans, Baptists, Jews, Methodists, Non-believers, Presbyterians, or the members of any other faith, *because of their faith, or lack of it,* from receiving the benefits of public welfare legislation. While we do not mean to intimate that a state could not provide transportation only to children attending public schools, we must be careful, in protecting the citizens of New Jersey against state-established churches, to be sure that we do not inadvertently prohibit New Jersey from extending its general state law benefits to all its citizens without regard to their religious belief.

Measured by these standards, we cannot say that the First Amendment prohibits New Jersey from spending tax-raised funds to pay the bus fares of parochial school pupils as a part of a general program under which it pays the fares of pupils attending public and other schools. It is undoubtedly true that children are helped to get to church schools. There is even a possibility that some of the children might not be sent to the church schools if the parents were compelled to pay their children's bus fares out of their own pockets when transportation to a public school would have been paid for by the State. The same possibility exists where the state requires a local transit company to provide reduced fares to school children including those attending parochial schools, or where a municipally owned transportation system undertakes to carry all school children free of charge. Moreover, state-paid policemen, detailed to protect children going to and from church schools from the very real hazards of traffic, would serve much the same purpose and accomplish much the same result as state provisions intended to guarantee free transportation of a kind which the state deems to be best for the school children's welfare. And parents might refuse to risk their children to the serious danger of traffic accidents going to and from parochial schools, the approaches to which were not protected by policemen. Similarly, parents might be reluctant to permit their children to attend schools which the state had cut off from such general government services as ordinary police and fire protection, connections for sewage disposals, public highways and sidewalks. Of course, cutting off church schools from these services, so separate and so indisputably marked off from the religious function, would make it far more difficult for the schools to operate. But such is obviously not the purpose of the First Amendment. That Amendment requires the state to be a neutral in its relations with groups of religious believers and non-believers; it does not require the state to be their adversary. State power is no more to be used so as to handicap religions than it is to favor them.

This Court has said that parents may, in the discharge of their duty under state compulsory education laws, send their children to a religious rather than a public school if the school meets the secular educational requirements which the state has power to impose. See Pierce v. Society of Sisters, 268 U.S. 510. It appears that these parochial schools meet New Jersey's requirements. The State contributes no money to the schools. It does not support them. Its legislation, as applied, does no more than provide a general program to help parents get their children, regardless of their religion, safely and expeditiously to and from accredited schools.

The First Amendment has erected a wall between church and state. That wall must be kept high and impregnable. We could not approve the slightest breach. New Jersey has not breached it here.

Affirmed.

Mr. Justice Jackson, dissenting. . . .

Whether the taxpayer constitutionally can be made to contribute aid to parents of students because of their attendance at parochial schools depends upon the nature of those schools and their relation to the Church. The Constitution says nothing of education. It lays no obligation on the states to provide schools and does not undertake to regulate state systems of education if they see fit to maintain them. But they cannot, through school policy any more than through other means, invade rights secured to citizens by the Constitution of the United States. West Virginia State Board of Education v. Barnette, 319 U.S. 624. One of our basic rights is to be free of taxation to support a transgression of the constitutional command that the authorities "shall make no law respecting an establishment of religion, or prohibiting the free exercise thereof. . . ." U.S. Const., Amend. I; Cantwell v. Connecticut, 310 U.S. 296.

The function of the Church school is a subject on which this record is meager. It shows only that the schools are under superintendence of a priest and that "religion is taught as part of the curriculum." But we know that such schools are parochial only in name — they, in fact, represent a world-wide and age-old policy of the Roman Catholic Church. Under the rubric "Catholic Schools," the Canon Law of the Church, by which all Catholics are bound, provides:

"1215. Catholic children are to be educated in schools where not only nothing contrary to Catholic faith and morals is taught, but rather in schools where religious and moral training occupy the first place. . . . (Canon 1372.)"

"1216. In every elementary school the children must, according to their age, be instructed in Christian doctrine.

"The young people who attend the higher schools are to receive a deeper religious knowledge, and the bishops shall appoint priests qualified for such work by their learning and piety. (Canon 1373.)"

"1217. Catholic children shall not attend non-Catholic, indifferent, schools that are mixed, that is to say, schools open to Catholics and non-Catholics alike. The bishop of the diocese only has the right, in harmony with the instructions of the Holy See, to decide under what circumstances, and with what safeguards to prevent loss of faith, it may be tolerated that Catholic children go to such schools. (Canon 1374.)"

"1224. The religious teaching of youth in any schools is subject to the authority and inspection of the Church.

"The local Ordinaries have the right and duty to watch that nothing is taught contrary to faith or good morals, in any of the schools of their territory.

"They, moreover, have the right to approve the books of Christian doctrine and the teachers of religion, and to demand, for the sake of safeguarding religion and morals, the removal of teachers and books. (Canon 1381.)" (Woywod, Rev. Stanislaus, The New Canon Law, under imprimatur of Most Rev. Francis J. Spellman, Archbishop of New York and others, 1940.)

It is no exaggeration to say that the whole historic conflict in temporal policy between the Catholic Church and non-Catholics comes to a focus in their respective school policies. The Roman Catholic Church, counseled by experience in many ages and many lands and with all sorts and conditions of men, takes what, from the viewpoint of its own progress and the success of its mission, is a wise estimate of the importance of education to religion. It does not leave the individual to pick up religion by chance. It relies on early and indelible indoctrination in the faith and order of the Church by the word and example of persons consecrated to the task.

Our public school, if not a product of Protestantism, at least is more consistent with it than with the Catholic culture and scheme of values. It is a relatively recent development dating from about 1840.[1] It is organized on the premise that secular education can be isolated from all religious teaching so that the school can inculcate all needed temporal knowledge and also maintain a strict and lofty neutrality as to religion. The assumption is that after the individual has been instructed in worldly wisdom he will be better fitted to choose his religion. Whether such a disjunction is possible, and if possible whether it is wise, are questions I need not try to answer.

[1] See Cubberley, Public Education in the United States (1934) ch. VI; Knight, Education in the United States (1941) ch. VIII.

I should be surprised if any Catholic would deny that the parochial school is a vital, if not the most vital, part of the Roman Catholic Church. If put to the choice, that venerable institution, I should expect, would forego its whole service for mature persons before it would give up education of the young, and it would be a wise choice. Its growth and cohesion, discipline and loyalty, spring from its schools. Catholic education is the rock on which the whole structure rests, and to render tax aid to its Church school is indistinguishable to me from rendering the same aid to the Church itself. . . .

It is of no importance in this situation whether the beneficiary of this expenditure of tax-raised funds is primarily the parochial school and incidentally the pupil, or whether the aid is directly bestowed on the pupil with indirect benefits to the school. The state cannot maintain a Church and it can no more tax its citizens to furnish free carriage to those who attend a Church. The prohibition against establishment of religion cannot be circumvented by a subsidy, bonus or reimbursement of expense to individuals for receiving religious instruction and indoctrination.

The Court, however, compares this to other subsidies and loans to individuals and says, "Nor does it follow that a law has a private rather than a public purpose because it provides that tax-raised funds will be paid to reimburse individuals on account of money spent by them in a way which furthers a public program. See Carmichael v. Southern Coal & Coke Co., 301 U.S. 495, 518." Of course, the state may pay out tax-raised funds to relieve pauperism, but it may not under our Constitution do so to induce or reward piety. It may spend funds to secure old age against want, but it may not spend funds to secure religion against skepticism. It may compensate individuals for loss of employment, but it cannot compensate them for adherence to a creed.

It seems to me that the basic fallacy in the Court's reasoning, which accounts for its failure to apply the principles it avows, is in ignoring the essentially religious test by which beneficiaries of this expenditure are selected. A policeman protects a Catholic of course — but not because he is a Catholic; it is because he is a man and a member of our society. The fireman protects the Church school — but not because it is a Church school; it is because it is property, part of the assets of our society. Neither the fireman nor the policeman has to ask before he renders aid "Is this man or building identified with the Catholic Church —" But before these school authorities draw a check to reimburse for a student's fare they must ask just that question, and if the school is a Catholic one they may render aid because it is such, while if it is of any other faith or is run for profit, the help must be withheld. To consider the converse of the Court's reasoning will best disclose its fallacy. That there is no parallel between police and fire protection and this plan of reimbursement is apparent from the incongruity of the limitation of this Act if applied to police and fire service. Could we sustain an Act that said the police shall protect pupils on the way to or from public schools and Catholic schools but not while going to and coming from other schools, and firemen shall extinguish a blaze in public or Catholic school buildings but shall not put out a blaze in Protestant Church schools or private schools operated for profit? That is the true analogy to the case we have before us and I should think it pretty plain that such a scheme would not be valid. . . .

Mr. Justice Frankfurter joins in this opinion.

MR. JUSTICE RUTLEDGE, with whom Mr. Justice Frankfurter, Mr. Justice Jackson, and Mr. Justice Burton agree dissenting. . . .

[The first part of Mr. Justice Rutledge's opinion has been printed supra.]

It is not because religious teaching does not promote the public or the individual's welfare, but because neither is furthered when the state promotes religious education, that the Constitution forbids it to do so. Both legislatures and courts are bound by that distinction. In failure to observe it lies the fallacy of the "public function" — "social legislation" argument, a fallacy facilitated by easy transference of the argument's basing from due process unrelated to any religious aspect to the First Amendment.

By no declaration that a gift of public money to religious uses will promote the general or individual welfare, or the cause of education generally, can legislative bodies overcome the Amendment's bar. Nor may the courts sustain their attempts to do so by finding such consequences for appropriations which in fact give aid to or promote religious uses. Cf. Norris v. Alabama, 294 U.S. 587, 590; Hooven & Allison Co. v. Evatt, 324 U.S. 652, 659; Akins v. Texas, 325 U.S. 398, 402. Legislatures are free to make, and courts to sustain, appropriations only when it can be found that in fact they do not aid, promote, encourage or sustain religious teaching or observances, be the amount large or small. No such finding has been or could be made in this case. The Amendment has removed this form of promoting the public welfare from legislative and judicial competence to make a public function. It is exclusively a private affair.

The reasons underlying the Amendment's policy have not vanished with time or diminished in force. Now as when it was adopted the price of religious freedom is double. It is that the church and religion shall live both within and upon that freedom. There cannot be freedom of religion, safeguarded by the state, and intervention by the church or its agencies in the state's domain or dependency on its largesse. Madison's Remonstrance, Par. 6, 8.[44] The great condition of religious liberty is that it be maintained free from sustenance, as also from other interferences, by the state. For when it comes to rest upon that secular foundation it vanishes with the resting. Id., Par. 7,

[44] "Because the establishment proposed by the Bill is not requisite for the support of the Christian Religion. To say that it is, is a contradiction to the Christian Religion itself; for every page of it disavows a dependence on the powers of this world. . . . Because the establishment in question is not necessary for the support of Civil Government. . . . What influence in fact have ecclesiastical establishments had on Civil Society? . . . in no instance have they been seen the guardians of the liberties of the people." II Madison 183, 187, 188.

8.[45] Public money devoted to payment of religious costs, educational or other, brings the quest for more. It brings too the struggle of sect against sect for the larger share or for any. Here one by numbers alone will benefit most, there another. That is precisely the history of societies which have had an established religion and dissident groups. Id., Par. 8, 11. It is the very thing Jefferson and Madison experienced and sought to guard against, whether in its blunt or in its more screened forms. Ibid. The end of such strife cannot be other than to destroy the cherished liberty. The dominating group will achieve the dominant benefit; or all will embroil the state in their dissensions. Id., Par. 11.[46]

Exactly such conflicts have centered of late around providing transportation to religious schools from public funds.[47] The issue and the dissension work typically, in Madison's phrase, to "destroy that moderation and harmony which the forbearance of our laws to intermeddle with Religion, has produced amongst its several sects." Id., Par. 11. This occurs, as he well knew, over measures at the very threshold of departure from the principle. Id., Par. 3, 9, 11.

In these conflicts wherever success has been obtained it has been upon the contention that by providing the transportation the general cause of education, the general welfare, and the welfare of the individual will be forwarded; hence that the matter lies within the realm of public function, for legislative determination. State courts have divided upon the issue, some taking the view that only the individual, others that the institution receives the benefit. A few have recognized that this dichotomy is false, that both in fact are aided.

The majority here does not accept in terms any of those views. But neither does it deny that the individual or the school or indeed both, are benefited directly and substantially. . . .

Notwithstanding the recognition that this two-way aid is given and the absence of any denial that religious teaching is thus furthered, the Court concludes that the aid so given is not "support" of religion. . . .

---

[45] "Because experience witnesseth that ecclesiastical establishments, instead of maintaining the purity and efficacy of Religion, have had a contrary operation." II Madison 183, 187.

[46] "At least let warning be taken at the first fruits of the threatened innovation. The very appearance of the Bill has transformed that 'Christian forbearance, love and charity,' which of late mutually prevailed, into animosities and jealousies, which may not soon be appeased." II Madison 183, 189.

[47] In this case briefs amici curiae have been filed on behalf of various organizations representing three religious sects, one labor union, the American Civil Liberties Union, and the states of Illinois, Indiana, Louisiana, Massachusetts, Michigan and New York. All these states have laws similar to New Jersey's and all of them, with one religious sect, support the constitutionality of New Jersey's action. The others oppose it. Maryland and Mississippi have sustained similar legislation. . . . No state without legislation of this sort has filed an opposing brief. But at least six states have held such action invalid, namely, Delaware, Oklahoma, New York, South Dakota, Washington and Wisconsin. . . . The New York ruling was overturned by amendment to the state constitution in 1938. Constitution of New York, Art. XI, 4. . . .

[This] approach, if valid, supplies a ready method for nullifying the Amendment's guaranty, not only for this case and others involving small grants in aid for religious education, but equally for larger ones. The only thing needed will be for the Court again to transplant the "public welfare — public function" view from its proper nonreligious due process bearing to First Amendment application, holding that religious education is not "supported" though it may be aided by the appropriation, and that the cause of education generally is furthered by helping the pupil to secure that type of training. . . .

[Mr. Justice Rutledge goes on to say that no discrimination against those attending religious schools is involved, for they can always choose to attend public schools. The hardship entailed by those attending religious schools is a necessary consequence of the principle of separation. He states further that even if it were shown that all religions received aid under the statute, it could not stand.]

For then the adherent of one creed still would pay for the support of another, the childless taxpayer with others more fortunate. Then too there would seem to be no bar to making appropriations for transportation and other expenses of children attending public or other secular schools, after hours in separate places and classes for their exclusively religious instruction. The person who embraces no creed also would be forced to pay for teaching what he does not believe. Again, it was the furnishing of "contributions of money for the propagation of opinions which he disbelieves" that the fathers outlawed. That consequence and effect are not removed by mutliplying to all-inclusiveness the sects for which support is exacted. The Constitution requires, not comprehensive identification of state with religion, but complete separation. . . .

I have chosen to place my dissent upon the broad ground I think decisive, though strictly speaking the case might be decided on narrower issues. The New Jersey statute might be held invalid on its face for the exclusion of children who attend private, profit-making schools.[58] I cannot assume, as does the majority, that the New Jersey courts would write off this explicit limitation from the statute. Moreover, the resolution by which the statute was applied expressly limits its benefits to students of public and Catholic schools.[59] There is no showing that there are no other private or religious schools in this

---

[58] It would seem at least a doubtfully sufficient basis for reasonable classification that some children should be excluded simply because the only school feasible for them to attend, in view of geographic or other situation, might be one conducted in whole *or in part* for profit. . . .

[59] . . . The resolution was as follows, according to the school board's minutes read in proof: "The transportation committee recommended the transportation of pupils of Ewing to the Trenton and Pennington High Schools *and Catholic Schools* by way of public carrier as in recent years. On Motion of Mr. Ralph Ryan and Mr. M. French the same was adopted." (Emphasis added.) The New Jersey court's holding that the resolution was within the authority conferred by the state statute is binding on us. Reinman v. Little Rock, 237 U.S. 171, 176; Hadacheck v. Sebastian, 239 U.S. 394, 414.

populous district.[60] I do not think it can be assumed there were none. But in the view I have taken, it is unnecessary to limit grounding to these matters. . . .

NOTES

1. Several jurisdictions have held that the furnishing of free transportation to pupils of non-public schools is prohibited. For cases since the Everson case, see: McVey v. Hawkins, 364 Mo. 44, 258 S.W.2d 927 (1953), noted in 3 St. Louis U.L.J. 273 (1955); Visser v. Nooksack Valley School Dist., 33 Wash. 2d 699, 207 P.2d 198 (1949); School Dist. of Robinson Township v. Houghton (Ct. Com. Pl., Allegheny County, Pa., May 29, 1956); Board of Education v. Antone, 384 P.2d 911 (Okla. 1963); State ex rel. Reynolds v. Nusbaum, 17 Wis. 2d 148, 115 N.W.2d 761 (1962) (holding unconstitutional a law for transporting private school children to the public school they were permitted to attend and contemplating their fending for themselves thereafter; only ten private schools in the state were not operated by religious groups; see Setzler and Linford, A Constitutional Analysis of the Wisconsin School Bus Law, 1962 Wis. L. Rev. 500); Matthews v. Quinton, 362 P.2d 932 (Alaska 1961), app. dis., 368 U.S. 517 (1962) (act of territorial legislature violates Organic Act of Alaska, 37 Stat. 512 §9, at 515 (1912), in providing free transportation to non-public schools despite statement that purpose of statute is "to protect the health and safety of all school children in Alaska, and to achieve the objectives of the compulsory education laws of Alaska").

Prior to the Everson case some of the cases are: Gurney v. Ferguson, 190 Okla. 254, 122 P.2d 1002 (1941); Mitchell v. Consolidated School Dist., 17 Wash. 2d 61, 135 P.2d 79 (1943); Sherrard v. Jefferson County Bd. of Education, 294 Ky. 469, 171 S.W.2d 963 (1942) (not for a "public purpose," but a similar expenditure under a modified enabling law was later upheld as a proper police measure, Nichols v. Henry, 301 Ky. 434, 191 S.W.2d 930 (1945), but cf. Rawlings v. Butler, 290 S.W.2d 801 (Ct. of App. Ky., 1956)); State ex rel. Van Straten v. Milquet, 180 Wis. 109, 192 N.W. 392 (1928); State ex rel. Traub v. Brown, 36 Del. 181, 172 Atl. 835 (1934), writ of error dismissed, 39 Del. 187, 197 Atl. 478 (1938); Judd v. Board of Education, 278 N.Y. 200, 15 N.E.2d 576 (1938), but see N.Y. Const. Art. XI, Sec. 4 (amending State Constitution by explicitly authorizing free transportation to parochial school students).

To the same effect as the Everson case, see Quinn v. School Committee of Plymouth, 332 Mass. 410, 125 N.E.2d 410 (1955) (granting mandamus to force committee to provide transportation for parochial school students); Bowker v. Baker, 73 Cal. App. 653, 167 P.2d 256 (1946); Adams v. St. Mary's County, 180 Md. 550, 26 A.2d 377 (1942); Zellers v. Huff, 55 N.M. 501, 236 P.2d 949 (1951); Snyder v. Town of Newtown, 147 Conn. 374, 161 A.2d 770 (1960), app. dis., 365 U.S. 299 (1961); see Powell, The School Bus Law (1960); Connecticut Civil Liberties Union, The Connecticut School Bus Law: A Controversial Problem in Church and State Relations (1958) (distinguishing Everson reimbursement from

---

[60] The population of Ewing Township, located near the City of Trenton, was 10,146 according to the census of 1940. Sixteenth Census of the United States, Population, Vol. 1, 674.

direct provision for free transportation); Squires v. Inhabitants of the City of Augusta, 155 Me. 151, 153 A.2d 80 (1959) (neither federal nor state constitution forbids free transportation but city could not transport without proper state enabling act).

See Tockman, The Constitutionality of Furnishing Publicly Financed Transportation to Private and Parochial School Students in Missouri, 1963 Wash. U.L.Q. 455; Note, The School Bus Law: Transportation of Parochial and Private School Pupils in Pennsylvania, 27 U. Pitt. L. Rev. 71 (1965). For a review of pending litigation in 1966 in Michigan (Alexander v. Bartlett), Minnesota (Cornwall v. Common School Dist. No. 2065, Schulz v. Common School Dist. No. 2065), Ohio (Honohan v. Holt), and Pennsylvania (Worrell v. Matters, Bowerman v. O'Connor), see American Jewish Congress, Commission on Law and Social Action, Litigation Docket of Pending Cases Affecting Freedom of Religion and Separation of Church and State (Jan. 17, 1966; issued periodically), hereinafter referred to as A.J.C. Litigation Docket.

2. The Everson case is discussed in Blum, Religious Liberty and Bus Transportation, 30 Notre Dame Law. 384 (1955); Boyer, Public Transportation of Parochial School Pupils, 1952 Wis. L. Rev. 64; Cosgrove and Flattery, Transportation of Parochial School Pupils, 22 Notre Dame Law. 192 (1947); Cahill, Constitutionality of Indirect State Aid to Sectarian Schools, 3 Intramural L. Rev. 147 (1948); Hopkins, State Transportation of Students to Parochial Schools, 36 Ky. L.J. 328 (1948).

TOTAL AND PARTIAL INTEGRATION OF RELIGIOUS AND PUBLIC SCHOOL SYSTEMS

In Zellers v. Huff, 55 N.M. 501, 236 P.2d 949 (1951), the Supreme Court of New Mexico enjoined the State Board of Education from continuing its support of parochial schools and schools substantially managed by the Roman Catholic Church. The schools were part of the public school system, the state had to maintain two sets of textbooks, and in some communities they were the only schools even for non-Catholics. Religious instruction and religious exercises were part of the program and religious comic books, prayer books and other equipment were used. The court held that the following violated the religious provisions of federal and state constitutions: (1) the wearing of religious garbs by teachers in public schools; (2) the teaching of sectarian religion and the dissemination of religious literature; (3) the supervision of school teachers and public school system by a church. The court authorized, in accordance with provisions of a state statute, the discharge of teachers who knowingly taught sectarian doctrine. But it held that the payment by teachers of their salaries to religious orders did not render state payment of those salaries state aid to religion. Cf. Miller v. Cooper, 56 N.M. 355, 244 P.2d 520 (1952) (baccalaureate services and commencement exercises may be held in churches where these are the only buildings which can accommodate the number of people invited).

For an account of the background of this case, see 2 Stokes, Church and

State in the United States, pp. 662-671 (1950). To the same effect as the Zellers case see also Berghorn v. Reorganized School District, 364 Mo. 121, 260 S.W.2d 573 (1953); Outcalt v. Hoefler (Dist. Ct. Colo., Logan County Aug. 1952); Knowlton v. Baumhover, 182 Iowa 691, 166 N.W. 202 (1918) (appropriating rent for schoolroom with relics and teaching by sister with garb, as alternative to requiring public school room, held invalid); State ex rel. Public School District v. Taylor, 122 Neb. 454, 240 N.W. 573 (1932); Harfst v. Hoegen, 349 Mo. 808, 163 S.W.2d 609 (1942) (Roman Catholic school made part of public school system — state textbooks and course of instruction adopted, name of building, graven images, holy water fonts, garbed teachers and religious instruction persisted — held invalid); Wright v. School District, 151 Kan. 485, 99 P.2d 737 (1940); Williams v. Stanton School Dist., 173 Ky. 708, 191 S.W. 507 (1917); Richter v. Cordes, 100 Mich. 278, 58 N.W. 1110 (1894); Moore v. Board of Education of Southwest Local School District, 4 Ohio Misc. 257, 330 O.2d 406, 212 N.E.2d 833 (C. P. Mercer Co. 1965) (court found improper use of public funds for providing sectarian instruction and for making public school sectarian schools; contentions about clerical garb and the segregation of Catholic children into three of the four public schools operated by the District, rejected). See A.J.C. Litigation Docket, supra, p. 8.

For cases upholding the use and renting of religious property for public schools and the right of garbed nuns to teach in such schools, see Rawlings v. Butler, 290 S.W. 801 (Ct. App. Ky. 1956); cf. Wooley v. Superintendent of Schools, 293 S.W.2d 563 (Ct. App. Ky. 1956) (holding that a school board may not discriminatorily close a high school in what seemed to be a predominantly Protestant area, thus forcing students into the schools where garbed nuns were teaching); Hysong v. School Dist., 164 Pa. 629, 30 Atl. 482 (1894), changed by statute, Penn. Stat. Ann. tit. 24, §11-1112 (1950), constitutionality upheld in Commonwealth v. Herr, 229 Pa. 132, 78 Atl. 68 (1910); Millard v. Board of Education, 121 Ill. 297, 10 N.E. 669 (1887) (emergency measure — there were religious exercises but no compulsion against wishes of parents); Scripture v. Burns, 59 Iowa 70, 12 N.W. 760 (1882) (public funds available only for a six-month school; justification was that by using sectarian school building and contributions by the church, school could be taught for ten months); New Haven v. Torrington, 132 Conn. 194, 43 A.2d 455 (1945) (Board of Education ran school in Catholic orphanage taught in part by garbed nuns who conducted religious exercises but not immediately prior to classes; the school was open to all children in the neighborhood but attended only by Catholics; held that a city whose residents were taught in it must reimburse the city which ran the school; the school met the two prerequisites of (1) exclusive control by Board of Education and (2) no sectarian instruction); State ex rel. Johnson v. Boyd, 217 Ind. 348, 28 N.E.2d 256 (1940); Crain v. Walker, 222 Ky. 828, 2 S.W.2d 654 (1928); Matter of Roche, 26 N.Y. St. Dept. Rep. 217 (1921). See discussions, Blum, Religious Liberty and the Religious Garb, 22 U. Chi. L. Rev. 875 (1955); Notes, 22 U. Chi. L. Rev. 888 (1955); 3 Wayne L. Rev. 57 (1956). See also Craig v. Mercy Hospital — Street Memorial, 209 Miss. 427, 47 So. 2d 867 (1950) (program of nursing education in sectarian hospital to be conducted in return for grant in aid held merely incidental to rendering of general hospital services and therefore not barred by constitutional provisions against appropriations for sectarian schools); to the same effect see Opinion of Justices, 99 N.H. 519, 113 A.2d 114 (1955); Quick Bear v. Leupp, 210 U.S. 50, 28 S. Ct. 690, 52 L. Ed. 954 (1908) (payment of Indian claims by Federal Government intended to be used in support of Catholic parochial system, did not constitute violation of separation of church and state).

OTHER AIDS TO RELIGIOUS SCHOOLS

Tuition. Some of the cases which hold use of state funds to pay parochial school tuition invalid are: Swart v. South Burlington Town School Dist., 122 Vt. 177, 167 A.2d 514 (1961), cert. den., 366 U.S. 925 (1961), noted 29 Fordham L. Rev. 578 (1961); Almond v. Day, 197 Va. 419, 89 S.E.2d 851 (1955), noted in 42 Va. L. Rev. 437 (1956) (appropriation for tuition for orphans of members of the armed forces to be expended at any educational institution approved by Superintendent of Public Instruction invalid in so far as tuition may be paid to sectarian schools); Otken v. Lamkin, 56 Miss. 758 (1879) (holding unconstitutional a statute permitting child attending private school to receive from the school fund share he would have been entitled to were he attending public school); Synod of Dakota v. State, 2 S.D. 366, 50 N.W. 632 (1891) (tuition of students being trained as public school teachers in sectarian college could not be paid out of state funds); Williams v. Stanton School Dist., 173 Ky. 708, 191 S.W. 507 (1917) (payment of tuition fees of public school students taught in rooms, and in part by teachers, of a sectarian college unlawful). See Note, 81 A.L.R.2d 1309 (1962).

Free textbooks to parochial school students. In addition to the Cochran case mentioned in the Everson case (upholding loans of books to nonpublic school students on "public purpose" grounds, apparently without deciding disestablishment issue), see Dickman v. School Dist. No. 62C, 232 Ore. 238, 366 P.2d 533 (1961), cert. den., 371 U.S. 823 (1962) (invalid); Bordon v. Louisiana State Board of Educ., 168 La. 1005, 123 So. 655 (1929) (valid); Haas v. Independent School Dist., 69 S.D. 303, 9 N.W.2d 707 (1943) (invalid); see also Bowerman v. O'Connor (Sup. Ct. Rhode Island, pending), A.J.C. Litigation Docket, supra, p. 5; Chance v. Mississippi State Textbook Rating and Purchasing Board, 190 Miss. 453, 200 So. 706 (1941) (valid); Smith v. Donahue, 202 App. Div. 656, 195 N.Y. Supp. 715 (1922) (invalid); Donahoe v. Richards, 38 Me. 376 (1854) (invalid); Board of Education of East Greenbush v. Allen, — Misc. 2d —, — N.Y.S.2d — (Sup. Ct., Albany Co.

1966) (declaring invalid New York law requiring free loan of textbooks to certain parochial school students). See Notes, 93 A.L.R.2d 986 (1964); 67 A.L.R. 1196 (1930); 17 A.L.R. 299 (1922).

Use of school property. Primarily in connection with the Sunday School movement a number of cases have dealt with the question of the use of public school property for religious purposes. Cases authorizing use are: Southsides Estates Baptist Church v. Board of Trustees, 115 So. 2d 697 (Fla. 1959); Nichols v. School Directors, 93 Ill. 61 (1879) (statute explicitly authorizing use of public school building for religious meetings, and Sunday School sessions not interfering with regular school work, held not to violate constitutional provision that no person should be required to support a place of worship against his consent, nor any preference given to any denomination; the "incidental benefit" received by the religious organizations did not constitute state aid to religion); to the same effect see, State ex rel. Gilbert v. Dilley, 95 Neb. 527, 145 N.W. 999 (1914) (the occasional use of school for Sunday Schools did not convert it into a place of worship — mandamus not available to taxpayer who cannot show extent of his contribution to cost of Sunday meetings); Davis v. Boget, 50 Iowa 11 (1878) (relies on earlier case, Townsend v. Hagen, 35 Iowa 194 (1872), for holding that statute broadly authorizing disposition by electors of school building for religious purposes is constitutional). See also Bull v. Stichman, 298 N.Y. 516, 80 N.E.2d 661 (1948) (appropriation by Emergency Joint Housing Board to remodel building of a Jesuit college; held taxpayer and citizen without any special or personal interest has no standing to sue). Cases prohibiting use are: Spencer v. School District, 15 Kan. 259 (1875) (religious and other private uses violate prohibition of expending funds for "private purpose"); Hysong v. Gallitzin School Dist., 164 Pa. 629, 30 Atl. 482 (1894) (violates financial aid to religion provisions); Bender v. Streabich, 17 Pa. County Ct. 609 (1896) (violates financial aid to religion provisions). See also Scofield v. Eighth School District, 27 Conn. 499 (1858); George v. Second School District, 6 Met. (Mass.) 497 (1843); cf. Lawrence v. Buchmueller, 40 Misc. 2d 300, 243 N.Y.S.2d 87 (Sup. Ct. 1963) (taxpayers' erection of Nativity scene upon school grounds during holidays when school not in session without school personnel participation or public expense does not violate establishment clause); Lowe v. City of Eugene (Cir. Ct. Lune County, Oregon, pending) A.J.C. Litigation Docket, supra, p. 11 (suit against citizens erecting cross in public park and officials granting building permit); Horace Mann League v. Board of Public Works, — Md. —, 220 A.2d 51 (1966) (allocation of construction funds to religiously connected colleges invalid).

Tax exemption. For a decision since the Everson case, see: Lundberg v. County of Alameda, 46 Cal. 2d 644, 298 P.2d 1 (1956), app. dis., 352 U.S. 921 (1956) (upholding exemption in favor of a non-profit school operated by religious organizations on the following grounds: (1) benefit to religious denominations is merely incidental; the paramount purpose is to exempt all educational institutions to promote the general welfare; (2) even if a substantial benefit to religious groups exists, tax exemption is the type of benefit that has been permitted by longstanding practice and by all cases where the issue was raised). See also the cases on tax exemption of church property cited below. Exemption of parochial school childrens' parents from paying state taxes has been held invalid. Underwood v. Wood, 93 Ky. 177, 19 S.W. 405 (1892).

Other aids to education are treated in connection with Federal Aid to Education, infra.

FEDERAL AID TO EDUCATION

A most important controversy over aid to religion has been over federal aid to education. The first large-scale comprehensive bill dealing with elementary and secondary school education, Elementary and Secondary Education Act of 1965, Pub. L. 89-10, 79 Stat. 27 (1965), codified in 20 U.S.C. §§821-885 et al., avoids direct grants or loans to parochial schools or parochial school students and specifically provides: "Nothing contained in this Act shall be construed to authorize the making of any payment under this Act . . . for religious worship or instruction." 20 U.S.C. §885. However, several provisions of the Act do provide certain types of aid to private, including parochial, schools or their students:

Title I, Section 205(a)(2), 20 U.S.C. §241e(2), makes money available for special educational services and arrangements for the benefit of "educationally deprived children . . . who are enrolled in private elementary and secondary schools." These include "dual enrollment" (also called "shared time") programs, permitting private school students to take certain courses in public schools, "educational radio and television, and mobile educational services and equipment." Under this section, according to Senate Report No. 146 (89th Cong., 1st Sess. 1965), U.S. Code, Cong. & Ad. News, 89th Cong., 1st Sess. 1457, "public school teachers will be made available to other than public school facilities only to provide specialized services which contribute particularly to meeting the special educational needs of educationally deprived children (such as therapeutic, remedial or welfare services)." [1]

[1] For statements that the sending of teachers to parochial schools is to be limited to those remedial programs which "would not be part of the regular instructional program of the nonpublic schools," and could be authorized only when the local agency deems it advisable, see the remarks of Congressman Perkins, manager of the bill, Congressman Thompson, and others, 111 Cong. Rec. 5743-5748, 6096-6097, 6099-6100 (1965). See also H.R. Rep. No. 1814, 89th Cong., 2d Sess. 4 (1966) ("normally" programs should be on "public property," except "remedial, health and therapeutic services" which "consistent with local and state law" might "by necessity" be provided on nonpublic school premises). But cf. id., pt. 2 at 3 (a supplemental report emphasizing that a real effort should be made to help nonpublic school students wherever they are found). For indications that one of the purposes of the program is the commingling of public and nonpublic school children, see statements by Congressmen Perkins, Carey, and Scheuer, 111 Cong. Rec. 6114-6115 (1965). See also H.R. Rep. No. 1814, supra, at pp. 2-3. For implementa-

Title II, Section 203(a)(2), 20 U.S.C. §823(a)(2), makes available grants for the acquisition of "library resources (. . . books, periodicals, documents, audio-visual materials, and other related library materials), textbooks, and other printed and published instructional materials for the use of children and teachers in public elementary and secondary schools." Commenting on this and related sections the Senate Report states: "The committee has taken care to assure that funds provided under this title will not inure to the enrichment or benefit of any private institution by providing that —

"(1) Library resources, textbooks . . . [etc.] . . . are to be made available to children and teachers and not to institutions;

"(2) Such materials are made available on a loan basis only;

. . .

"(4) Such material must be that approved for use by public school authority in the State; and

"(5) Books and materials must not supplant . . . but must supplement library resources . . . [etc.] . . . to assure that the legislation will furnish increased opportunities for learning. . . . [Nor must they] be used to supplant or duplicate, inappropriately, functions of the public library system of the State." The law provides that these sections must be administered in conformity with state law. The Committee report suggests as one possible means of administering this aid program a central public depository "from which all elementary and secondary schoolchildren and teachers could 'check out' library resources, textbooks . . . [etc.]." U.S. Code, Cong. & Ad. News, 89th Cong., 1st Sess. 1468.

Title III of the Act, 20 U.S.C. §842 et seq., authorizes grants to "local educational . . . agencies," 20 U.S.C. §844(a), for supplemental educational centers and services to provide guidance, counseling, remedial instruction, school health, and psychological and social work services. Also included might be educational programs operated when schools are not regularly in session. According to the Committee report, various programs, including equipment and personnel for teaching art and music, might be made "available . . . on a temporary basis to public and other nonprofit schools, organizations, and institutions." U.S. Code, Cong. & Ad. News 1472. In general, however, there is no authorization "for the payment of private school teachers . . . [nor] . . . the financing of instruction for nonpublic schools. Facilities are not to be constructed nor equipment procured which will be to the pecuniary advantage of any nonpublic institution. Rather it is intended that the local public educational agency, through its preserved autonomy over local school matters, will have wide latitude in fashioning programs of direct benefit and

tion in New York City, providing for remedial reading, remedial arithmetic, speech therapy and guidance services in nonpublic schools, see Board of Education of the City of New York, Statement on Title I Proposals (mimeo, Aug. 31, 1966). For a pending case on a state program see Special District for the Education and Training of Handicapped Children of St. Louis County, Mo. v. Wheeler, A.J.C. Litigation Docket, supra, pp. 7-8.

advantage to elementary and secondary school pupils regardless of whether they are enrolled in public schools." Id. at 1473. The "local public educational agencies" to which the grants are to be made "must involve persons broadly representative of the cultural and educational resources of the area. . . . Such resources include . . . nonprofit private schools. . . ." Id. at 1470.[2]

In 1965 Congress also passed the Higher Education Act of 1965, granting broad aid to public and private institutions of higher learning and their students. Pub. L. 89-329, 79 Stat. 1219, codified in 20 U.S.C. §§1001-1144 et al. Some of the limitations in the Act do address themselves to the church-state issues but are perhaps not broad enough to foreclose all constitutional questions. For example, the provisions for college library assistance and library training and research in Title II, Section 207, 20 U.S.C. §1027, provide that no grants be used for materials for sectarian instruction or religious worship or in connection with any part of a program in a school or department of divinity. Similar restrictions obtain as to grants for strengthening developing institutions. §302(h), 20 U.S.C. §1052(h). Provisions for scholarship assistance do not limit the schools a student may attend nor the type of instruction or activities for which the funds obtained by the student through his scholarship may be used.

NOTES

1. Programs of federal aid to religious institutions prior to 1965 included aid to private denominational hospitals under the Hospital Survey and Construction Act, 60 Stat. 1041 (1946) as amended, 42 U.S.C. §291; see Drinan, Religion, the Courts, and Public Policy 37 (1963); lunches to parochial school childern under the National School Lunch Act, 60 Stat. 233 (1946) as amended, 42 U.S.C. §1759; payment for the education of Supreme Court pages in private schools, 60 Stat. 839 (1946), 2 U.S.C. §88a; grants and loans for tuition and educational materials to private schools, regardless of their religious character, provided for Korean War Veterans, 72 Stat. 1177 (1958), 38 U.S.C. §1620, and in connection with the National Defense Education program, 72 Stat. 1590 (1958), as amended, 20 U.S.C. §445; and loans and grants for construction by private colleges and universities, 64 Stat. 78 (1950), as amended, 12 U.S.C. §1749a; 77 Stat. 366 (1963), 20 U.S.C. §714. For a more comprehensive list of federal projects which in part bestow financial aid on religious institutions, see Hearings before the Subcommittee of the Senate Committee on Labor and Public Welfare, on S. 370, 89th Cong., 1st Sess. 146-157 (1965); see also id. at 2642-2646 for aid granted to church-related projects by the Office of Economic Opportunity under the anti-poverty program. And see letter by T. I. Emerson, N.Y. Times, June 27, 1964, concerning elimination of provision in original anti-poverty bill that "elementary or secondary school education programs . . . shall be administered by the public educational agency . . . principally responsible."

[2] For a detailed analysis of the statute and the Federal Regulations, 30 Fed. Reg. 11810-11822, 13138-13142, and guidelines, see American Jewish Congress, Commission on Law and Social Action, Federal Aid to Religiously Affiliated Schools (1966).

For discussion of the legal issues, see United States Department of Health, Education, and Welfare, Memorandum on the Impact of the First Amendment to the Constitution upon Federal Aid to Education, 50 Geo. L.J. 349 (1961); Legal Department, National Catholic Welfare Conference, The Constitutionality of the Inclusion of Church-Related Schools in Federal Aid to Education, 50 Geo. L.J. 397; Subcommittee on Education of the Senate Committee on Labor and Public Welfare, Constitutionality of Federal Aid to Education in its Various Aspects, Sen. Doc. No. 29, 87th Cong., 1st Sess. (1961); Hayes, The Constitutional Permissibility of the Participation of Church-Related Schools in the Administration's Proposed Program of Massive Federal Aid to Education, 11 De Paul L. Rev. 161 (1962); Hearings before the Subcommittee on Education of the Senate Committee on Labor and Public Welfare on S. 600, 89th Cong., 1st Sess. (1965) (Higher Education); Hearings before the Special Subcommittee on Education of the House Committee on Education and Labor on H.R. 3220, 89th Cong., 1st Sess. (1965) (Higher Education); Hearings before the Subcommittee on Education of the Senate Committee on Labor and Public Welfare on S. 370, 89th Cong., 1st Sess. (1965) (Elementary and Secondary Education); LaNoue, Public Funds for Parochial Schools? (1963); The Arthur Garfield Hays Civil Liberties Conference: Public Aid to Parochial Schools and Standing to Bring Suit, 12 Buffalo L. Rev. 35 (1962); North, An Exposition and Analysis of Policy Arguments Against Federal Aid to Parochial Schools, 9 Catholic Law. 43 (1963); Drinan, Should the State Aid Private Schools? 37 Conn. B.J. 361 (1963); Drinan, State and Federal Aid to Parochial Schools, 7 J. Ch. and State 67 (1965); Callahan (ed.), Federal Aid and Catholic Schools (1964); Pfeffer, Federal Funds for Parochial Schools? No, 37 Notre Dame Law. 309 (1962); Butler, The Effect of State Aid to Church Schools on Public Education, 6 J. Church and State 74 (1964). See also Symposium, Shared Time: A Proposal for the Education of Children (critiques by religious and educational leaders), 57 Religious Education 5 (1962); Wakin and Powell, The "Shared Time" Experiment, Saturday Review, Feb. 15, 1964, p. 68.

For a decision indicating that shared time may not violate prohibitions against aid to non-public schools, see Commonwealth ex rel. Wehrle v. Plummer, 21 Pa. Dist. R. 182, 184 (1911), aff'd on narrower grounds, 241 Pa. 224, 88 Atl. 481 (1913). See also Morton v. Board of Education of Chicago, A.J.C. Litigation Docket, supra, p. 7.

On the question whether government aid to denominational schools or other institutions might become so extensive as to subject them to non-discrimination requirements of the Fifth and Fourteenth Amendments even with respect to religious requirements, see Note, Public Control of Private Sectarian Institutions Receiving Public Funds, 63 Mich. L. Rev. 142 (1964); cf. Simkins v. Moses H. Cone Memorial Hospital, 323 F.2d 959 (4th Cir. 1963), cert. den., 376 U.S. 938 (1964) (Negro physicians and patients entitled to declaratory and injunctive relief from discrimination by hospitals using funds distributed under the Hospital Survey and Construction Act). Cf. Abernathy v. City of Irvine, 355 S.W.2d 159 (Ky. 1962), cert. den., 371 U.S. 831 (1962) (upholding "dollar a year" lease of public hospital to a religious group, the lease providing that admission not be denied for race, creed or color, but failing to deal with other religious issues). See Black, Religion, "Standing," and the Supreme Court's Role, 13 J. Pub. L. 459, 471 (1964).

2. While aid in connection with education has been the major subject of current

litigation, other government aids to religion have also been challenged on constitutional grounds:

(a) *Tax exemption relating to churches:* Religious organizations are generally exempt from federal income taxation except for so-called "unrelated business income." Churches as such are exempt from taxes even on such income. See Scripture Press Foundation v. United States, 285 F.2d 800 (Ct. Cl. 1961); Note, Preventing the Operation of Untaxed Businesses by Tax Exempt Organizations, 32 U. Chi. L. Rev. 581 (1965). For a challenge to this exemption, see Seversmith v. Machiz, A.J.C. Litigation Docket, supra, p. 9. Contributions to them are deductible. Gifts and bequests to religious organizations are also deductible for purposes of federal gift and estate tax.

States grant tax exemptions to religious organizations either under state statutes or under constitutional provisions. For state cases upholding the exemptions see Lundberg v. County of Alameda, 46 Cal. 2d 644, 298 P.2d 1 (1956), app. dis. sub nom. Heisey v. County of Alameda, 352 U.S. 921 (1956); General Finance Corp. v. Archetto, 93 R.I. 392, 176 A.2d 73 (1961), app. dis., 369 U.S. 423 (1962); Murray v. Comptroller of the Treasury, 241 Md. 383, 216 A.2d 897 (1966), petition for certiorari filed in Supreme Court sub nom. Murray v. Goldstein, May 13, 1966; Garrett Biblical Inst. v. Elmhurst State Bank, 331 Ill. 308, 163 N.E.1 (1928); Trustees of Griswold College v. Iowa, 46 Iowa 275 (1877). For cases upholding exemption on the ground that it is not the inculcation of dogma that is supported but rather the public welfare in inculcation of morality and respect for the law, see Fellowship of Humanity v. County of Alameda, 153 Cal. App. 2d 673, 696-697, 315 P.2d 394, 408-409 (1957); Trustees of the First Methodist Episcopal Church v. City of Atlanta, 76 Ga. 181, 191-194 (1886) (also arguing that such exemption aids free exercise of religion, id. at 195-196); cf. State ex rel. Anshe Chesed Congregation v. Bruggemeier, 97 Ohio App. 67, 75-76, 115 N.E.2d 65, 69 (1953). See also First Unitarian Church v. County of Los Angeles, 357 U.S. 545, 78 S. Ct. 1350, 2 L. Ed. 2d 1484 (1958); Speiser v. Randall, 357 U.S. 513, 78 S. Ct. 1332, 2 L. Ed. 2d 1460 (1958); Braunfeld v. Brown, 366 U.S. 599, 81 S. Ct. 1144, 6 L. Ed. 2d 563 (1961), all implicitly approving aid by way of tax exemption.

The exemption for "religious purposes" has been extended to so-called nontheistic sects on grounds that the courts are constitutionally prohibited from determining theological truth or error. See Fellowship of Humanity v. County of Alemeda, supra; Saint Germain Foundation v. County of Siskiyou, 212 Cal. App. 2d 911, 28 Cal. Rptr. 393 (1963). See also A. A. Allen Revivals, Inc., 22 CCH Tax Ct. Mem. 1435 (1963); Washington Ethical Society v. District of Columbia, 249 F.2d 127 (D.C. Cir. 1957); cf. Rider v. Commissioner, 244 F.2d 220 (9th Cir. 1957), cert. den., 355 U.S. 839 (1957) (restaurant operated for profit does not become church by calling itself "Christ's Church of the Golden Rule"); Golden Rule Church Assn, 41 T.C. 719 (1964).

The statutes limit tax exemptions either in terms of the area of church holdings or in terms of their total value, or in terms of their use. Use exemptions give birth to a great deal of litigation. For a collection of cases see Fellman, Religion in American Public Law, 44 B.U.L. Rev. 287, 329-337 (1964); Torpey, Judicial Doctrines of Religious Rights in America 171-197 (1948).

For a general discussion see Pfeffer, Church, State, and Freedom 183-190

(1953). For discussion of the constitutional question see Kauper, The Constitutionality of Tax Exemptions for Religious Activities, in Oaks (ed.), The Wall Between Church and State (1963); Van Alstyne, Tax Exemption of Church Property, 20 Ohio St. L.J. 461 (1959); Symposium, Law and Philanthropy, 46 Va. L. Rev. 391 (1960); Note, Constitutionality of Tax Exemptions Accorded American Church Property, 30 Albany L. Rev. 58 (1966); Paulsen, Preferment of Religious Institutions in Tax and Labor Legislation, 14 Law & Contemp. Prob. 144 (1949). See also Note, 58 Colum. L. Rev. 417 (1958); testimony of Paul Blanshard in Hearings before Subcommittee of House Committee on Ways and Means, Technical Amendments to Internal Revenue Code, 84th Cong., 2d Sess. 46-57 (1956).

(b) *Appropriations for institutions other than schools:* Cases holding these invalid under specific constitutional prohibitions are: State ex rel. Neveda Orphan Asylum v. Hallock, 16 Nev. 373 (1882) (sectarian asylum); Cook County v. Chicago Industrial School for Girls, 125 Ill. 540, 18 N.E. 183 (1888) (tuition, board, clothing, and medical care furnished delinquent girls committed to Catholic institutions); Bennett v. City of La Grange, 153 Ga. 428, 112 S.E. 482 (1922) (Salvation Army aided by contract with city whereby the former assumed care of the poor of the city at actual cost). Direct financial aid to sectarian institutions is sometimes permitted because they are explicitly exempt from the state constitutional prohibition, or because they allegedly service the general community: Sargent v. Board of Education, 177 N.Y. 317, 69 N.E. 722 (1904) (explicit exemption); cf. People ex rel. Orphan Asylum v. Board of Education, 13 Barb. 400 (N.Y. Sup. Ct. 1851); Craig v. Mercy Hospital–Street Memorial, 209 Miss. 427, 47 So. 2d 867 (1950); Kentucky Building Commission v. Effron, 310 Ky. 355, 220 S.W.2d 836 (1949) (state funds allocated for hospitals which serviced patients regardless of creed and conducted no religious ceremonies). To the same effect see Opinion of the Justices, 99 N.H. 519, 113 A.2d 114 (1955). See also Bradfield v. Roberts, 175 U.S. 291, 20 S. Ct. 121, 44 L. Ed. 168 (1899) (appropriation for building in connection with congressionally chartered hospital run by a monastic order upheld as long as hospital carried out purposes of charter). Payments to sectarian institutions for support and maintenance of neglected or dependent children under jurisdiction of a juvenile court have also been upheld. Shade v. Allegheny County, 386 Pa. 507, 126 A.2d 911 (1956) (relying in part on the Everson case for disposing of objections based on the United States Constitution). See Johnson and Yost, Separation of Church and State in the United States 100-114 (1948); Stokes, Church and State in the United States (1950).

3. Released Time

ILLINOIS ex rel. McCOLLUM v. BOARD OF EDUCATION
333 U.S. 203, 68 S. Ct. 461, 92 L. Ed. 649 (1948)

Mr. Justice Black delivered the opinion of the Court.

This case relates to the power of a state to utilize its tax-supported public school system in aid of religious instruction insofar as that power may be restricted by the First and Fourteenth Amendments to the Federal Constitution.

The appellant, Vashti McCollum, began this action for mandamus against the Champaign Board of Education in the Circuit Court of Champaign County, Illinois. Her asserted interest was that of a resident and taxpayer of Champaign and of a parent whose child was then enrolled in the Champaign public schools. Illinois has a compulsory education law which, with exceptions, requires parents to send their children, aged seven to sixteen, to its tax-supported public schools where the children are to remain in attendance during the hours when the schools are regularly in session. Parents who violate this law commit a misdemeanor punishable by fine unless the children attend private or parochial schools which meet educational standards fixed by the State. District boards of education are given general supervisory powers over the use of the public school buildings within the school districts. Ill. Rev. Stat. ch. 122, §§123, 301 (1943).

Appellant's petition for mandamus alleged that religious teachers, employed by private religious groups, were permitted to come weekly into the school buildings during the regular hours set apart for secular teaching, and then and there for a period of thirty minutes substitute their religious teaching for the secular education provided under the compulsory education law. The petitioner charged that this joint public-school religious-group program violated the First and Fourteenth Amendments to the United States Constitution. The prayer of her petition was that the Board of Education be ordered to "adopt and enforce rules and regulations prohibiting all instruction in and teaching of religious education in all public schools in Champaign School District Number 71, . . . and in all public school houses and buildings in said district when occupied by public schools." . . .

[The Court holds that the appellant has standing to maintain the action.]

Although there are disputes between the parties as to various inferences that may or may not properly be drawn from the evidence concerning the religious program, the following facts are shown by the record without dispute.[1] In 1940 interested members of the Jewish, Roman Catholic, and a few of the Protestant faiths formed a voluntary association called the Champaign Council on Religious Education. They obtained permission from the Board of Education to offer classes in religious instruction to public school pupils in grades four to nine inclusive. Classes were made up of pupils whose parents

---

[1] Appellant, taking issue with the facts found by the Illinois courts, argues that the religious education program in question is invalid under the Federal Constitution for any one of the following reasons: (1) In actual practice certain Protestant groups have obtained an overshadowing advantage in the propagation of their faiths over other Protestant sects; (2) the religious education program was voluntary in name only because in fact subtle pressures were brought to bear on the students to force them to participate in it; and (3) the power given the school superintendent to reject teachers selected by religious groups and the power given the local Council on Religious Education to determine which religious faiths should participate in the program was a prior censorship of religion.

In view of our decision we find it unnecessary to consider these arguments or the disputed facts upon which they depend.

signed printed cards requesting that their children be permitted to attend;[2] they were held weekly, thirty minutes for the lower grades, forty-five minutes for the higher. The council employed the religious teachers at no expense to the school authorities, but the instructors were subject to the approval and supervision of the superintendent of schools.[3] The classes were taught in three separate religious groups by Protestant teachers,[4] Catholic priests, and a Jewish rabbi, although for the past several years there have apparently been no classes instructed in the Jewish religion. Classes were conducted in the regular classrooms of the school building. Students who did not choose to take the religious instruction were not released from public school duties; they were required to leave their classrooms and go to some other place in the school building for pursuit of their secular studies. On the other hand, students who were released from secular study for the religious instructions were required to be present at the religious classes. Reports of their presence or absence were to be made to their secular teachers.[5]

[2] The Supreme Court described the request card system as follows: ". . . Admission to the classes was to be allowed only upon the express written request of parents, and then only to classes designated by the parents. . . . Cards were distributed to the parents of elementary students by the public-school teachers requesting them to indicate whether they desired their children to receive religious education. After being filled out, the cards were returned to the teachers of religious education classes either by the public-school teachers or the children. . . ." On this subject the trial court found that ". . . those students who have obtained the written consent of their parents therefor are released by the school authorities from their secular work, and in the grade schools for a period of thirty minutes' instruction in each week during said school hours, and forty-five minutes during each week in the junior high school, receive training in religious education. . . . Certain cards are used for obtaining permission of parents for their children to take said religious instruction courses, and they are made available through the offices of the superintendent of schools and through the hands of principals and teachers to the pupils of the school district. Said cards are prepared at the cost of the council of religious education. The handling and distribution of said cards does not interfere with the duties or suspend the regular secular work of the employees of the defendant. . . ."

[3] The State Supreme Court said: "The record further discloses that the teachers conducting the religious classes were not teachers in the public schools but were subject to the approval and supervision of the superintendent. . . ." The trial court found: "Before any faith or other group may obtain permission from the defendant for the similar, free and equal use of rooms in the public school buildings said faith or group must make application to the superintendent of schools of said School District Number 71, who in turn will determine whether or not it is practical for said group to teach in said school system." The president of the local school board testified: ". . . The Protestants would have one group and the Catholics, and would be given a room where they would have the class and we would go along with the plan of the religious people. They were all to be treated alike, with the understanding that the teachers they would bring into the school were approved by the superintendent. . . . The superintendent was the last word so far as the individual was concerned. . . ."

[4] There were two teachers of the Protestant faith. One was a Presbyterian and had been a foreign missionary for that church. The second testified as follows: "I am affiliated with the Christian church. I also work in the Methodist Church and I taught at the Presbyterian. I am married to a Lutheran."

[5] The director of the Champaign Council on Religious Education testified: ". . . If any pupil is absent we turn in a slip just like any teacher would to the superintendent's office. The slip is a piece of paper with a number of hours in the school day and a

The foregoing facts, without reference to others that appear in the record, show the use of tax-supported property for religious instruction and the close cooperation between the school authorities and the religious council in promoting religious education. The operation of the State's compulsory education system thus assists and is integrated with the program of religious instruction carried on by separate religious sects. Pupils compelled by law to go to school for secular education are released in part from their legal duty upon the condition that they attend the religious classes. This is beyond all question a utilization of the tax-established and tax-supported public school system to aid religious groups to spread their faith. And it falls squarely under the ban of the First Amendment (made applicable to the States by the Fourteenth Amendment) as we interpreted it in Everson v. Board of Education, 330 U.S. 1. . . . The majority in the Everson case, and the minority . . . , agreed that the First Amendment's language, properly interpreted, had erected a wall of separation between Church and State. They disagreed as to the facts shown by the record and as to the proper application of the First Amendment's language to those facts.

Recognizing that the Illinois program is barred by the First and Fourteenth Amendments if we adhere to the views expressed both by the majority and the minority in the Everson case, counsel for the respondents challenge those views as dicta and urge that we reconsider and repudiate them. They argue that historically the First Amendment was intended to forbid only government preference of one religion over another, not an impartial governmental assistance of all religions. In addition they ask that we distinguish or overrule our holding in the Everson case that the Fourteenth Amendment made the "establishment of religion" clause of the First Amendment applicable as a prohibition against the States. After giving full consideration to the arguments presented we are unable to accept either of these contentions.

To hold that a state cannot consistently with the First and Fourteenth Amendments utilize its public school system to aid any or all religious faiths or sects in the dissemination of their doctrines and ideals does not, as counsel urge, manifest a governmental hostility to religion or religious teachings. A manifestation of such hostility would be at war with our national tradition as embodied in the First Amendment's guaranty of the free exercise of religion. For the First Amendment rests upon the premise that both religion and government can best work to achieve their lofty aims if each is left free from the other within its respective sphere. Or, as we said in the Everson case, the First Amendment has erected a wall between Church and State which must be kept high and impregnable.

Here not only are the State's tax-supported public school buildings used for

_____

square, and the teacher of the particular room for the particular hour records the absentees. It has their names and the grade and the section to which they belong. It is the same sheet that the geography and history teachers and all the other teachers use, and is furnished by the school. . . ."

the dissemination of religious doctrines. The State also affords sectarian groups an invaluable aid in that it helps to provide pupils for their religious classes through use of the State's compulsory public school machinery. This is not separation of Church and State.

The cause is reversed and remanded to the State Supreme Court for proceedings not inconsistent with this opinion.

Reversed and remanded.

[Mr. Justice Frankfurter delivered a concurring opinion in which Justices Jackson, Rutledge, and Burton joined. Part of this opinion has been reprinted supra. The remainder of the opinion makes the following points: The Champaign plan works "an obvious pressure upon children to attend" and "sharpens the consciousness of religious differences at least among some of the children." These "are precisely the consequences against which the Constitution was directed." The problem is not simply one of the short period of time allocated to religious education. "If that were all, Champaign might have drawn upon the French system, known in its American manifestation as 'dismissed time,' whereby one school day is shortened to allow all children to go where they please, leaving those who so desire to go to a religious school. The momentum of the whole school atmosphere and school planning is presumably put behind religious instruction, as given in Champaign, precisely in order to secure for the religious instruction such momentum and planning." "Separation means separation, not something less." "The public school is at once the symbol of our democracy and the most pervasive means for promoting our common destiny."

Mr. Justice Jackson's concurring opinion in part warns that the Court went too far in granting without qualification Mrs. McCollum's sweeping request that it not only end released time but "ban every form of teaching which suggests or recognizes that there is a God. . . . The fact is that, for good or ill, nearly everything in our culture worth transmitting, everything which gives meaning to life, is saturated with religious influences, derived from paganism, Judaism, Christianity — both Catholic and Protestant — and other faiths accepted by a large part of the world's peoples. One can hardly respect a system of education that would leave the student wholly ignorant of the currents of religious thought that move the world society for a part in which he is being prepared." Mr. Justice Jackson adds: "The opinions in this case show that public educational authorities have evolved a considerable variety of practices in dealing with the religious problem. . . . [It] must be expected that, no matter what practice prevails, there will be many discontented and possibly belligerent minorities. We must leave some flexibility to meet local conditions, some chance to progress by trial and error. . . . To lay down a sweeping constitutional doctrine as demanded by complainant . . . is to decree a uniform, rigid and . . . unchanging standard for countless school boards. . . . It seems to me that to do so is to allow zeal for our own ideas of what is good in public instruction to induce us to accept the role of a super board of education for every school district in the nation." Neither the Constitution nor any other "legal source" is a guide to where the "secular ends and the sectarian begins."]

MR. JUSTICE REED, dissenting. . . .

The phrase "an establishment of religion" may have been intended by Congress to be aimed only at a state church. When the First Amendment was pending in Congress in substantially its present form, "Mr. Madison said, he apprehended the meaning of the words to be, that Congress should not establish a religion, and enforce the legal observation of it by law, nor compel men to worship God in any manner contrary to their conscience." [7] Passing years, however, have brought about acceptance of a broader meaning, although never until today, I believe, has this Court widened its interpretation to any such degree as holding that recognition of the interest of our nation in religion, through the granting, to qualified representatives of the principal faiths, of opportunity to present religion as an optional, extracurricular subject during released school time in public school buildings, was equivalent to an establishment of religion. A reading of the general statements of eminent statesmen of former days, referred to in the opinions in this case and in Everson v. Board of Education, supra, will show that circumstances such as those in this case were far from the minds of the authors. The words and spirit of those statements may be wholeheartedly accepted without in the least impugning of the judgment of the State of Illinois.[8]

Mr. Jefferson, as one of the founders of the University of Virginia, a school which from its establishment in 1819 has been wholly governed, managed and controlled by the State of Virginia, was faced with the same problem that is before this Court today: the question of the constitutional limitation upon religious education in public schools. In his annual report as Rector, to the President and Directors of the Literary Fund, dated October 7, 1822, approved by the Visitors of the University of whom Mr. Madison was one,[10] Mr. Jefferson set forth his views at some length.[11] These suggestions of Mr. Jeffer-

---

[7] 1 Annals of Congress 730.

[8] For example, Mr. Jefferson's striking phrase as to the "wall of separation between church and State" appears in a letter acknowledging "The affectionate sentiments of esteem and approbation" included in a testimonial to himself. In its context it reads as follows:

"Believing with you that religion is a matter which lies solely between man and his God, that he owes account to none other for his faith or his worship, that the legislative powers of Government reach actions only, and not opinions, I contemplate with sovereign reverence that act of the whole American people which declared that their legislature should 'make no law respecting an establishment of religion, or prohibiting the free exercise thereof,' thus building a wall of separation between church and State." 8 The Writings of Thomas Jefferson (Washington ed., 1861) 113.

[10] 19 The Writings of Thomas Jefferson (Memorial edition, 1904) 408, 409.

[11] Id., pp. 414-17:

"It was not, however, to be understood that instruction in religious opinion and

son were adopted [12] and ch. II, §1, of the Regulations of the University of October 4, 1824, provided that:

"Should the religious sects of this State, or any of them, according to the invitation held out to them, establish within, or adjacent to, the precincts of the University, schools for instruction in the religion of their sect, the students of the University will be free, and expected to attend religious worship at the establishment of their respective sects, in the morning, and in time to meet their school in the University at its stated hour." [13]

Thus, the "wall of separation between church and State" that Mr. Jefferson built at the University which he founded did not exclude religious education from that school. The difference between the generality of his statements on the separation of church and state and the specificity of his conclusions on education are considerable. A rule of law should not be drawn from a figure of speech.

Mr. Madison's Memorial and Remonstrance against Religious Assessments,[14] relied upon by the dissenting Justices in Everson, is not applicable

---

duties was meant to be precluded by the public authorities, as indifferent to the interests of society. On the contrary, the relations which exist between man and his Maker, and the duties resulting from those relations, are the most interesting and important to every human being, and the most incumbent on his study and investigation. The want of instruction in the various creeds of religious faith existing among our citizens presents, therefore, a chasm in a general institution of the useful sciences. . . . A remedy, however, has been suggested of promising aspect, which, while it excludes the public authorities from the domain of religious freedom, will give to the sectarian schools of divinity the full benefit the public provisions made for instruction in the other branches of science. . . . It has, therefore, been in contemplation, and suggested by some pious individuals, who perceive the advantages of associating other studies with those of religion, to establish their religious schools on the confines of the University, so as to give to their students ready and convenient access and attendance on the scientific lectures of the University; and to maintain, by that means, those destined for the religious professions on as high a standing of science, and of personal weight and respectability, as may be obtained by others from the benefits of the University. Such establishments would offer the further and greater advantage of enabling the students of the University to attend religious exercises with the professor of their particular sect, either in the rooms of the building still to be erected, and destined to that purpose under impartial regulations, as proposed in the same report of the commissioners, or in the lecturing room of such professor. . . . Such an arrangement would complete the circle of the useful sciences embraced by this institution, and would fill the chasm now existing, on principles which would leave inviolate the constitutional freedom of religion, the most inalienable and sacred of all human rights, over which the people and authorities of this state, individually and publicly, have ever manifested the most watchful jealousy; and could this jealousy be now alarmed, in the opinion of the legislature, by what is here suggested, the idea will be relinquished on any surmise of disapprobation which they might think proper to express."

Mr. Jefferson commented upon the report on November 2, 1822, in a letter to Dr. Thomas Cooper, as follows: "And by bringing the sects together, and mixing them with the mass of other students, we shall soften their asperities, liberalize and neutralize their prejudices, and make the general religion a religion of peace, reason, and morality." 12 Ford, The Works of Thomas Jefferson (Fed. ed., 1905) 272.

[12] 3 Randall, Life of Thomas Jefferson (1858) 471.

[13] 19 The Writings of Thomas Jefferson (Memorial edition, 1904) 449.

[14] The texts of the Memorial and Remonstrance and the bill against which it was

here. Mr. Madison was one of the principal opponents in the Virginia General Assembly of A Bill Establishing a Provision for Teachers of the Christian Religion. The monies raised by the taxing section of that bill were to be appropriated "by the Vestries, Elders, or Directors of each religious society, . . . to a provision for a Minister or Teacher of the Gospel of their denomination, or the providing places of divine worship, and to none other use whatsoever . . ." The conclusive legislative struggle over this act took place in the fall of 1785, before the adoption of the Bill of Rights. The Remonstrance had been issued before the General Assembly convened and was instrumental in the final defeat of the act, which died in committee. Throughout the Remonstrance, Mr. Madison speaks of the "establishment" sought to be effected by the act. It is clear from its historical setting and its language that the Remonstrance was a protest against an effort by Virginia to support Christian sects by taxation. Issues similar to those raised by the instant case were not discussed. Thus, Mr. Madison's approval of Mr. Jefferson's report as Rector gives, in my opinion, a clearer indication of his views on the constitutionality of religious education in public schools than his general statements on a different subject.

This Court summarized the amendment's accepted reach into the religious field, as I understand its scope, in Everson v. Board of Education, supra. The Court's opinion quotes the gist of the Court's reasoning in Everson. I agree, as there stated, that none of our governmental entities can "set up a church." I agree that they cannot "aid" all or any religions or prefer one "over another." But "aid" must be understood as a purposeful assistance directly to the church itself or to some religious group or organization doing religious work of such a character that it may fairly be said to be performing ecclesiastical functions. "Prefer" must give an advantage to one "over another." I agree that pupils cannot "be released in part from their legal duty" of school attendance upon condition that they attend religious classes. But as Illinois has held that it is within the discretion of the School Board to permit absence from school for religious instruction no legal duty of school attendance is violated. 396 Ill. 14, 71 N.E.2d 161. If the sentence in the Court's opinion, concerning the pupils' release from legal duty, is intended to mean that the Constitution forbids a school to excuse a pupil from secular control during school hours to attend voluntarily a class in religious education, whether in or out of school buildings, I disagree. Of course, no tax can be levied to support organizations intended "to teach or practice religion." I agree too that the state cannot influence one toward religion against his will or punish him for his beliefs. Champaign's religious education course does none of these things. . . .

---

aimed, to wit, A Bill Establishing a Provision for Teachers of the Christian **Religion** are set forth in Everson v. Board of Education, 330 U.S. 1, 28, 63-74.

NOTES

1. In Zorach v. Clauson, 343 U.S. 306, 72 S. Ct. 679, 96 L. Ed. 954 (1952), the Supreme Court upheld the New York City released time system. The New York system provides for the release of the students on written request of parents, for purposes of attending religious instruction and devotional exercises in religious centers outside of school. Students not released under the system stay in classrooms. The churches send weekly reports to the schools on attendance of the released pupils. Mr. Justice Douglas, writing for the Court, distinguished the McCollum case as follows:

"In the McCollum case the classrooms were used for religious instruction and the force of the public school was used to promote that instruction. Here, as we have said, the public schools do no more than accommodate their schedules to a program of outside religious instruction. We follow the McCollum case. But we cannot expand it to cover the present released time program unless separation of Church and State means that public institutions can make no adjustments of their schedules to accommodate the religious needs of the people. We cannot read into the Bill of Rights such a philosophy of hostility to religion."

Concerning the principle of separation the Court said:

"The First Amendment within the scope of its coverage permits no exception; the prohibition is absolute. The First Amendment, however, does not say that in every and all respects there shall be a separation of Church and State. Rather, it studiously defines the manner, the specific ways, in which there shall be no concert or union or dependency one on the other. That is the common sense of the matter. Otherwise the state and religion would be aliens to each other — hostile, suspicious, and even unfriendly. Churches could not be required to pay even property taxes. Municipalities would not be permitted to render police or fire protection to religious groups. Policemen who helped parishioners into their places of worship would violate the Constitution. Prayers in our legislative halls; the appeals to the Almighty in the messages of the Chief Executive; the proclamations making Thanksgiving Day a holiday; 'so help me God' in our courtroom oaths — these and all other references to the Almighty that run through our laws, our public rituals, our ceremonies would be flouting the First Amendment. A fastidious atheist or agnostic could even object to the supplication with which the Court opens each session: 'God save the United United States and this Honorable Court.'"

Mr. Justice Douglas added:

"Government may not finance religious groups nor undertake religious instruction nor blend secular and sectarian education nor use secular institutions to force one or some religion on any person. But we find no constitutional requirement which makes it necessary for government to be hostile to religion and to throw its weight against efforts to widen the effective scope of religious influence. The government must be neutral when it comes to competition between sects. It may not thrust any sect on any person. It may not make a religious observance compulsory. It may not coerce anyone to attend church, to observe a religious holiday, or to take religious instruction. But it can close its doors or suspend its operations as to those who want to repair to their religious sanctuary for worship or instruction. No more than that is undertaken here."

Justices Black, Frankfurter, and Jackson dissented. They felt that the state was involved in the administration of the system and both explicitly and implicitly used its coercive power to implement the program.

2. In the courts below the plaintiffs had sought to introduce evidence that the system on the administrative level actually worked coercively. See paragraph 3 of this Note, infra. This evidence was not admitted. One of Mr. Justice Douglas' grounds for upholding the system was that the record showed no actual coercion. Mr. Justice Frankfurter's dissent levels special criticism at this aspect of the opinion.

For an earlier New York case upholding the New York released time system see Lewis v. Spaulding, 193 Misc. 66, 85 N.Y.S.2d 682 (1948).

3. The following extract from Note, Released Time Reconsidered: The New York Plan Is Tested, 61 Yale L.J. 405, 411-415 (1952), describes released time systems in operation, based primarily upon the New York experience. The Note was written prior to the Supreme Court's opinion in the Zorach case:

"Continuance of released time would sanction infringement of the 'separation doctrine' by state aid existing in three aspects of the program's operation. One element of aid is the New York Education Law. It requires through its truancy provisions that those students who are released actually attend their religious classes. A released child who fails to attend religious classes has no excused absence from public school and is thus a truant. In enforcing the truancy law upon released time truants some school districts interview the child to find out why he did not attend the religious instruction. Other districts, if the child is frequently truant, refuse him permission to be released for religious instruction. Still others use these techniques jointly. In addition to the actual enforcement sanctions, the very existence of the law may influence the released child to attend his religious classes. Use of the compulsory education law in a released time program was expressly condemned in the McCollum decision.

"The machinery of the public school also makes a substantial contribution to the operation and success of released time. Time and labor of teachers and school officials is required to administer the program. They must obtain and file cards of excused children; prepare, distribute, and keep current lists for classroom teachers of released time students; supervise an additional classroom dismissal; and secure and check absence reports of religious centers. Some teachers, despite the Board of Education's prohibition of comment on the attendance or non-attendance of pupils at religious classes, encourage children to attend religious classes or actually recruit them for such instruction.[37] The persistence of this practice over the years, despite its prohibition, suggests that this is an abuse inherent in the program.[39] The

[37] Examples of this type of coercion are: "Miss Jeffries (a teacher) distributed blank consent cards to the children in her class and asked the children publicly for a show of hands of those who were going to participate in the released time program . . . Miss Jeffries scolded those students who had participated in the released time program the term before but who did not raise their hands to show that they were continuing." Affidavit of Wendy Gluck, Affidavits, Kings County Clerk's Number 10327/1948 Supreme Court of the State of New York, County of Kings. "A student in her class became ill and vomited in the classroom. Miss Jeffries said to the sick student that she did not object at looking at the vomit as much as she objected to looking at the student's face because he did not participate in the released time program." Affidavit of Esta Gluck, ibid. See also affidavit of Anne Stewart. . . .

[39] It is important to study the actual practice since there are indications that the rules are not always literally followed. Rule 4 of the New York City Board of Education's Regulations before September 24, 1941 read, "Pupils of any grade will be dis-

teacher exerts considerable influence on the children,[40] and her contribution to the religious education program can be important.[41] Moreover, high schools aid the released time program by allowing scholastic credit for religious instruction.[42]

"Further state aid for religion exists in the substantial contribution made by the school milieu to the recruitment of children for religious classes. The public school environment is a significant factor in motivating behavior,[43] and it must be considered in evaluating the total contribution of the school, as an institution, to religious education. Holding religious classes during school hours aids religious instruction since it can more easily compete with classroom time than with recreational time. Such encouragement may be lessened in some schools because the released time period activities may be enjoyable, or may include important school work which the children may not want to miss. In addition, group interactions are an effective assistance to recruitment of children for religious classes and this has been regarded as 'state action' in aid of religion. Children belong to social groups not ordinarily based on religion or released time attendance.[51] Studies have shown that

---

missed from school for the last hour of each week, except that in classes on a departmental schedule release will be limited to the last period of the program." Mr. William Hendrie, who was then a principal in a school employing the departmental schedule, released his children at 2:30 as instructed by the regulation. Mr. Jansen, then Associate Superintendent of Schools and now Superintendent of Schools called and told Mr. Hendrie not to interpret the rules literally and to dismiss the students in the departmentally scheduled classes promptly at 2:00 p.m. Affidavit of Mr. William Hendrie, Kings County Clerk's Number 10327/1948, Supreme Court of the State of New York, County of Kings.

[40] See National Education Association, Department of School Principals, Personality Adjustment of the Elementary School Child 385 (1936); Carrington, Teacher Personality as a Factor in Child Adjustment, National Education Association of the United States, Department of Elementary School Principals 15th Yearbook 586-594 (1936).

[41] Another, though more infrequent, practice used by teachers to induce attendance at the released time program is the giving of onerous work to the children who remain in the public school. A student reports, "My sixth grade teacher, Miss Croft, urged the children in the class to participate in the released time program and she stated that those students who did not participate would be required to do long division arithmetic problems during every released time hour, whereas those children who did participate were to be excused from this exercise. While I was in Miss Croft's class, the students who remained in the public school after 2 o'clock on Thursdays were given long division arithmetic problems beyond the level of the normal expectation of sixth grade." Affidavit of Anne Stewart, Affidavits, King County Clerk's Number 10327/1948, Supreme Court of the State of New York, County of Kings. Also Affidavit of Mrs. Gussie Finer, ibid. . . .

[42] . . . A study of released time programs in high school indicates that one of the principal motivations for students to take released time courses in high school was to obtain credit toward graduation. McClure, Weekday Religious Education at the High School Level, 46 Religious Education 345, 352 (1951).

[43] For a description of the school environment and its impact on the individual see: Bossard, The Sociology of Child Development 459-92 (1948); Lee & Lee, The Child and His Curriculum 74, 95-103 (2d ed. 1950); Waller, The Sociology of Teaching c. 2 (1932).

[51] Group unity forms among children in the early primary school. Hurlock, Child Development 236 (1942); Thorpe, Child Psychology and Development 558 (1946). The primary bases for friendship formation of primary school children are: propinquity of the children, same mental and physical age. Hurlock, op. cit. supra at 247; Murphy, Murphy, & Newcomb, Experimental Social Psychology 513 (1931); Thorpe, op. cit. supra at 595.

a group influences children so strongly that they frequently accept its judgment even when they know that judgment is wrong,[52] and in matters of opinion, children follow their friends almost completely.[53] Thus, when a child in the public school sees his friends leave to attend religious classes, the social interactions of the school, as an institution, impel him toward religious instruction. When parents refuse to allow children to attend religious classes with their friends, the children may become emotionally disturbed.[54] This reaction indicates the coercion on the children to attend religious classes. Such coercion, even though not completely successful in forcing conformity in all situations, was regarded in the McCollum case as one of the abridgments of the separation doctrine."

4. See also on the New York released time system, Public Education Association, Released Time For Religious Education in New York City Schools (1949). For a full discussion of the variety of released time systems in the United States and an extensive bibliography see Mr. Justice Frankfurter's opinion in the McCollum case, 333 U.S. at 222-231.

5. For discussion of the legal issues see Reed, Church-State and the Zorach Case, 27 Notre Dame Law. 529 (1952); Kauper, Church, State and Freedom: A Review, 52 Mich. L. Rev. 829 (1954); Pfeffer, Released Time and Religious Liberty: A Reply, 53 Mich. L. Rev. 91 (1954); Kauper, Released Time and Religious Liberty: A Further Reply, 53 Mich. L. Rev. 233 (1954); Notes, 1 J. Pub. L. 212 (1952), 52 Colum. L. Rev. 1033 (1952); Lassiter, The McCollum Decision and the Public School, 37 Ky. L.J. 402 (1949); Manion, The Church, The State and Mrs. McCollum, 23 Notre Dame Law. 456 (1948); Owen, The McCollum Case, 22 Temple L.Q. 159 (1948); Michenfelder, The McCollum Decision: A

[52] . . . Berenda, Influence of the Group on the Judgment of Children 14-32 (1950). On the strong control of the peer group see, Brown, Sociology of Childhood 164, 169-70 (1939); Bossard, op. cit. supra note 43, at 504, 507; Hurlock, op. cit. supra note 51 at 218, 233, 236-7; Lee & Lee, op. cit. supra note 43, at 74.

[53] In a test of food preferences there was virtually complete identification of choices between close friends. Duncker, Experimental Modification of Children's Food Preference Through Social Suggestion, 33 Jour. of Abnormal and Social Psychology 489 (1938). Cf. Riesman, The Lonely Crowd (1950).

[54] A former non-released student describes her experiences as follows: "When the released time children departed at 2:00 p.m. on Wednesdays, I felt left behind. The released children made remarks about my being Jewish and I was made very much aware of the fact that I did not participate with them in the released time program. I endured a great deal of anguish as a result of this and decided that I would like to go along with the other children to the church center rather than continue to expose myself to such embarrassment. I asked my mother for permission to participate in the released time program to accompany my Catholic classmates to their religious center, but she forbade it. The divisiveness created by the released time program among the public school children became a part of our after school play. Following the introduction of released time at P.S. 163, Brooklyn, I began to notice I was ostracized by other children in after school activities. I was not permitted to share in their play, and they made unflattering remarks about my not going to the church center because I was Jewish. As a result of arguments about my nonparticipation in released time, my classmates called me such names as 'Christ killer' and 'dirty Jew.' I still live in the same neighborhood and to this day I do not talk to many of the girls with whom I went to school because of the arguments and fights which developed among us as a result of our differences which developed from the released time program." Statement of Leah Cunn, Affidavits, Kings County Clerk's Number 10327/1948, New York Supreme Court, County of Kings. See also affidavits by Gussie Finer and Charles Stewart, ibid.

Criticism, 1 Intramural L. Rev. 26 (St. Louis Univ. 1949); Notes, 49 Colum. L. Rev. 836 (1949); 61 Harv. L. Rev. 1248 (1948). See also McCollum, One Woman's Fight (1951).

6. Compare the "shared time" provisions in the federal aid to education legislation, supra, and the material on "shared time" cited at the end of the previous section.

4. Bible Reading and Prayers

ENGEL v. VITALE
370 U.S. 421, 82 S. Ct. 1261, 8 L. Ed. 2d 601 (1962)

MR. JUSTICE BLACK delivered the opinion of the Court.

The respondent Board of Education of Union Free School District No. 9, New Hyde Park, New York, acting in its official capacity under state law, directed the School District's principal to cause the following prayer to be said aloud by each class in the presence of a teacher at the beginning of each school day:

"Almighty God, we acknowledge our dependence upon Thee, and we beg Thy blessings upon us, our parents, our teachers and our Country."

This daily procedure was adopted on the recommendation of the State Board of Regents, a governmental agency created by the State Constitution to which the New York Legislature has granted broad supervisory, executive, and legislative powers over the State's public school system.[1] These state officials composed the prayer which they recommended and published as a part of their "statement on Moral and Spiritual Training in the Schools," saying: "We believe that this Statement will be subscribed to by all men and women of good will, and we call upon all of them to aid in giving life to our program."

Shortly after the practice of reciting the Regents' prayer was adopted by the School District, the parents of ten pupils brought this action in a New York State Court insisting that use of this official prayer in the public schools was contrary to the beliefs, religions, or religious practices of both themselves and their children. Among other things, these parents challenged the constitutionality of both the state law authorizing the School District to direct the use of prayer in public schools and the School District's regulation ordering the recitation of this particular prayer on the ground that these actions of official governmental agencies violate that part of the First Amendment of the Federal Constitution which commands that "Congress shall make no law respecting an establishment of religion" — a command which was "made applicable to the State of New York by the Fourteenth Amendment of the said Constitution." The New York Court of Appeals, over the dissents of Judges

---

[1] See New York Constitution, Art. V, §4; New York Education Law, §§101, 120 et seq., 202, 214-219, 224, 245 et seq., 704, and 801 et seq.

Dye and Fuld, sustained an order of the lower state courts which had upheld the power of New York to use the Regents' prayer as a part of the daily procedures of its public schools so long as the schools did not compel any pupil to join in the prayer over his or his parents' objection.[2] We granted certiorari to review this important decision involving rights protected by the First and Fourteenth Amendments.

We think that by using its public school system to encourage recitation of the Regents' prayer, the State of New York has adopted a practice wholly inconsistent with the Estabishment Clause. There can, of course, be no doubt that New York's program of daily classroom invocation of God's blessings as prescribed in the Regents' prayer is a religious activity. It is a solemn avowal of divine faith and supplication for the blessings of the Almighty. The nature of such a prayer has always been religious, none of the respondents has denied this and the trial court expressly so found. . . .

The petitioners contend among other things that the state laws requiring or permitting use of the Regents' prayer must be struck down as a violation of the Establishment Clause because that prayer was composed by governmental officials as a part of a governmental program to further religious beliefs. For this reason, petitioners argue, the State's use of the Regents' prayer in its public school system breaches the constitutional wall of separation between Church and State. We agree with that contention since we think that the constitutional prohibition against laws respecting an establishment of religion must at least mean that in this country it is no part of the business of government to compose official prayers for any group of the American people to recite as a part of a religious program carried on by government.

It is a matter of history that this very practice of establishing governmentally composed prayers for religious services was one of the reasons which

---

[2] 10 N.Y.2d 174, 176 N.E.2d 579. The trial court's opinion, which is reported at 18 Misc. 2d 659, 191 N.Y.S.2d 453, had made it clear that the Board of Education must set up some sort of procedures to protect those who objected to reciting the prayer: "This is not to say that the rights accorded petitioners and their children under the 'free exercise' clause do not mandate safeguards against such embarrassments and pressures. It is enough on this score, however, that regulations, such as were adopted by New York City's Board of Education in connection with its released time program, be adopted, making clear that neither teachers nor any other school authority may comment on participation or nonparticipation in the exercise nor suggest or require that any posture or language be used or dress be worn or be not used or not worn. Nonparticipation may take the form either of remaining silent during the exercise, or if the parent or child so desires, of being excused entirely from the exercise. Such regulations must also make provision for those nonparticipants who are to be excused from the prayer exercise. The exact provision to be made is a matter for decision by the board, rather than the court, within the framework of constitutional requirements. Within that framework would fall a provision that prayer participants proceed to a common assembly while nonparticipants attend other rooms, or that nonparticipants be permitted to arrive at school a few minutes late or to attend separate opening exercises, or any other method which treats with equality both participants and nonparticipants." 18 Misc. 2d, at 696, 191 N.Y.S.2d, at 492-493. See also the opinion of the Appellate Division affirming that of the trial court, reported at 11 App. Div. 2d 340, 206 N.Y.S.2d 183.

caused many of our early colonists to leave England and seek religious freedom in America. The Book of Common Prayer, which was created under governmental direction and which was approved by Acts of Parliament in 1548 and 1549,[5] set out in minute detail the accepted form and content of prayer and other religious ceremonies to be used in the established, tax-supported Church of England.[6] The controversies over the Book and what should be its content repeatedly threatened to disrupt the peace of that country as the accepted forms of prayer in the established church changed with the views of the particular ruler that happened to be in control at the time.[7] Powerful groups representing some of the varying religious views of the people struggled among themselves to impress their particular views upon the Government and obtain amendments of the Book more suitable to their respective notions of how religious services should be conducted in order that the official religious establishment would advance their particular religious beliefs.[8] Other groups, lacking the necessary political power to influence the Government on the matter, decided to leave England and its established

---

[5] 2 & 3 Edward VI, c. 1, entitled "An Act for Uniformity of Service and Administration of the Sacraments throughout the Realm"; 3 & 4 Edward VI, c. 10, entitled "An Act for the abolishing and putting away of divers Books and Images."

[6] The provisions of the various versions of the Book of Common Prayer are set out in broad outline in the Encyclopaedia Britannica, Vol. 18 (1957 ed.), pp. 420-423. For a more complete description, see Pullan, The History of the Book of Common Prayer (1900).

[7] The first major revision of the Book of Common Prayer was made in 1552 during the reign of Edward VI. 5 & 6 Edward VI, c. 1. In 1553, Edward VI died and was succeeded by Mary who abolished the Book of Common Prayer entirely. 1 Mary, c. 2. But upon the accession of Elizabeth in 1558, the Book was restored with important alterations from the form it had been given by Edward VI. 1 Elizabeth, c. 2. The resentment to this amended form of the Book was kept firmly under control during the reign of Elizabeth but, upon her death in 1603, a petition signed by more than 1,000 Puritan ministers was presented to King James I asking for further alterations in the Book. Some alterations were made and the Book retained substantially this form until it was completely suppressed again in 1645 as a result of the successful Puritan Revolution. Shortly after the restoration in 1660 of Charles II, the Book was again reintroduced, 13 & 14 Charles II, c. 4, and again with alterations. Rather than accept this form of the Book some 2,000 Puritan ministers vacated their benefices. See generally Pullan, The History of the Book of Common Prayer (1900), pp. vii-xvi; Encyclopaedia Britannica (1957 ed.), Vol. 18, pp. 421-422.

[8] For example, the Puritans twice attempted to modify the Book of Common Prayer and once attempted to destroy it. The story of their struggle to modify the Book in the reign of Charles I is vividly summarized in Pullan, History of the Book of Common Prayer, at p. xiii: "The King actively supported those members of the Church of England who were anxious to vindicate its Catholic character and maintain the ceremonial which Elizabeth had approved. Laud, Archbishop of Canterbury, was the leader of this school. Equally resolute in his opposition to the distinctive tenets of Rome and of Geneva, he enjoyed the hatred of both Jesuit and Calvinist. He helped the Scottish bishops, who had made large concessions to the uncouth habits of Presbyterian worship, to draw up a Book of Common Prayer for Scotland. It contained a Communion Office resembling that of the book of 1549. It came into use in 1637, and met with a bitter and barbarous opposition. The vigour of the Scottish Protestants strengthened the hands of their English sympathisers. Laud and Charles were executed, Episcopacy was abolished, the use of the Book of Common Prayer was prohibited."

church and seek freedom in America from England's governmentally ordained and supported religion.

It is an unfortunate fact of history that when some of the very groups which had most strenuously opposed the established Church of England found themselves sufficiently in control of colonial governments in this country to write their own prayers into law, they passed laws making their own religion the official religion of their respective colonies.[9] Indeed, as late as the time of the Revolutionary War, there were established churches in at least eight of the thirteen former colonies and established religions in at least four of the other five.[10] But the successful Revolution against English political domination was shortly followed by intense opposition to the practice of establishing religion by law. This opposition crystallized rapidly into an effective political force in Virginia where the minority religious groups such as Presbyterians, Lutherans, Quakers and Baptists had gained such strength that the adherents to the established Episcopal Church were actually a minority themselves. In 1785-1786, those opposed to the established Church, led by James Madison and Thomas Jefferson, who, though themselves not members of any of these dissenting religious groups, opposed all religious establishments by law on grounds of principle, obtained the enactment of the famous "Virginia Bill for Religious Liberty" by which all religious groups were placed on an equal footing so far as the State was concerned.[11] Similar though less far-reaching legislation was being considered and passed in other States.[12]

By the time of the adoption of the Constitution, our history shows that there was a widespread awareness among many Americans of the dangers of a union of Church and State. These people knew, some of them from bitter

[9] For a description of some of the laws enacted by early theocratic governments in New England, see Parrington, Main Currents in American Thought (1930), Vol. 1, pp. 5-50; Whipple, Our Ancient Liberties (1927), pp. 63-78; Wertenbaker, The Puritan Oligarchy (1947).

[10] The Church of England was the established church of at least five colonies: Maryland, Virginia, North Carolina, South Carolina and Georgia. There seems to be some controversy as to whether that church was officially established in New York and New Jersey but there is no doubt that it received substantial support from those States. See Cobb, The Rise of Religious Liberty in America (1902), pp. 338, 408. In Massachusetts, New Hampshire and Connecticut, the Congregationalist Church was officially established. In Pennsylvania and Delaware, all Christian sects were treated equally in most situations but Catholics were discriminated against in some respects. See generally Cobb, The Rise of Religious Liberty in America (1902). In Rhode Island all Protestants enjoyed equal privileges but it is not clear whether Catholics were allowed to vote. Compare Fiske, The Critical Period in American History (1899), p. 76 with Cobb, The Rise of Religious Liberty in America (1902), pp. 437-438.

[11] 12 Hening, Statutes of Virginia (1823), 84, entitled "An act for establishing religious freedom." The story of the events surrounding the enactment of this law was reviewed in Everson v. Board of Education, 330 U.S. 1, both by the Court, at pp. 11-13, and in the dissenting opinion of Mr. Justice Rutledge, at pp. 33-42. See also Fiske, The Critical Period in American History (1899), pp. 78-82; James, The Struggle for Religious Liberty in Virginia (1900); Thom, The Struggle for Religious Freedom in Virginia: The Baptists (1900); Cobb, The Rise of Religious Liberty in America (1902), pp. 74-115, 482-499.

[12] See Cobb, The Rise of Religious Liberty in America (1902), pp. 482-509.

personal experience, that one of the greatest dangers to the freedom of the individual to worship in his own way lay in the Government's placing its official stamp of approval upon one particular kind of prayer or one particular form of religious services. They knew the anguish, hardship and bitter strife that could come when zealous religious groups struggled with one another to obtain the Government's stamp of approval from each King, Queen, or Protector that came to temporary power. The Constitution was intended to avert a part of this danger by leaving the government of this country in the hands of the people rather than in the hands of any monarch. But this safeguard was not enough. Our Founders were no more willing to let the content of their prayers and their privilege of praying whenever they pleased be influenced by the ballot box than they were to let these vital matters of personal conscience depend upon the succession of monarchs. The First Amendment was added to the Constitution to stand as a guarantee that neither the power nor the prestige of the Federal Government would be used to control, support or influence the kinds of prayer the American people can say — that the people's religions must not be subjected to the pressures of government for change each time a new political administration is elected to office. Under that Amendment's prohibition against governmental establishment of religion, as reinforced by the provisions of the Fourteenth Amendment, government in this country, be it state or federal, is without power to prescribe by law any particular form of prayer which is to be used as an official prayer in carrying on any program of governmentally sponsored religious activity.

There can be no doubt that New York's state prayer program officially establishes the religious beliefs embodied in the Regents' prayer. The respondents' argument to the contrary, which is largely based upon the contention that the Regents' prayer is "non-denominational" and the fact that the program, as modified and approved by state courts, does not require all pupils to recite the prayer but permits those who wish to do so to remain silent or be excused from the room, ignores the essential nature of the program's constitutional defects. Neither the fact that the prayer may be denominationally neutral nor the fact that its observance on the part of the students is voluntary can serve to free it from the limitations of the Establishment Clause, as it might from the Free Exercise Clause, of the First Amendment, both of which are operative against the States by virtue of the Fourteenth Amendment. Although these two clauses may in certain instances overlap, they forbid two quite different kinds of governmental encroachment upon religious freedom. The Establishment Clause, unlike the Free Exercise Clause, does not depend upon any showing of direct governmental compulsion and is violated by the enactment of laws which establish an official religion whether those laws operate directly to coerce nonobserving individuals or not. This is not to say, of course, that laws officially prescribing a particular form of religious worship do not involve coercion of such individuals. When the power, prestige and financial support of government is placed behind a particular religious belief, the indirect coercive pressure upon religious minorities to conform to the prevailing officially approved religion is plain. But the purposes underlying the Establishment Clause go much further than that. Its first and most immediate purpose rested on the belief that a union of government and religion tends to destroy government and to degrade religion. The history of governmentally established religion, both in England and in this country, showed that whenever government had allied itself with one particular form of religion, the inevitable result had been that it had incurred the hatred, disrespect and even contempt of those who held contrary beliefs.[13] That same history showed that many people had lost their respect for any religion that had relied upon the support of government to spread its faith.[14] The Establishment Clause thus stands as an expression of principle on the part of the Founders of our Constitution that religion is too personal, too sacred, too holy, to permit its "unhallowed perversion" by a civil magistrate.[15] Another purpose of the Establishment Clause rested upon an awareness of the historical fact that governmentally established religions and religious persecutions go hand in hand.[16] The Founders knew that only a few years after the Book of Common Prayer became the only accepted form of religious services in the established Church of England, an Act of Uniformity was passed to compel all Englishmen to attend those services and to make it a

[13] "[A]ttempts to enforce by legal sanctions, acts obnoxious to so great a proportion of Citizens, tend to enervate the laws in general, and to slacken the bands of Society. If it be difficult to execute any law which is not generally deemed necessary or salutary, what must be the case where it is deemed invalid and dangerous? and what may be the effect of so striking an example of impotency in the Government, on its general authority." Memorial and Remonstrance against Religious Assessments, II Writings of Madison 183, 190.

[14] "It is moreover to weaken in those who profess this Religion a pious confidence in its innate excellence, and the patronage of its Author; and to foster in those who still reject it, a suspicion that its friends are too conscious of its fallacies, to trust it to its own merits. . . . [E]xperience witnesseth that ecclesiastical establishments, instead of maintaining the purity and efficacy of Religion, have had a contrary operation. During almost fifteen centuries, has the legal establishment of Christianity been on trial. What have been its fruits? More or less in all places, pride and indolence in the Clergy; ignorance and servility in the laity; in both, superstition, bigotry and persecution. Enquire of the Teachers of Christianity for the ages in which it appeared in its greatest lustre; those of every sect, point to the ages prior to its incorporation with Civil policy." Id., at 187.

[15] Memorial and Remonstrance against Religious Assessments, II Writings of Madison, at 187.

[16] "[T]he proposed establishment is a departure from that generous policy, which, offering an asylum to the persecuted and oppressed of every Nation and Religion, promised a lustre to our country, and an accession to the number of its citizens. What a melancholy mark is the Bill of sudden degeneracy? Instead of holding forth an asylum to the persecuted, it is itself a signal of persecution. . . . Distant as it may be, in its present form, from the Inquisition it differs from it only in degree. The one is the first step, the other the last in the career of intolerance. The magnanimous sufferer under this cruel scourge in foreign Regions, must view the Bill as a Beacon on our Coast, warning him to seek some other haven, where liberty and philanthropy in their due extent may offer a more certain repose from his troubles." Id., at 188.

criminal offense to conduct or attend religious gatherings of any other kind [17] —a law which was consistently flouted by dissenting religious groups in England and which contributed to widespread persecutions of people like John Bunyan who persisted in holding "unlawful [religious] meetings . . . to the great disturbance and distraction of the good subjects of this kingdom. . . ." [18] And they knew that similar persecutions had received the sanction of law in several of the colonies in this country soon after the establishment of official religions in those colonies.[19] It was in large part to get completely away from this sort of systematic religious persecution that the Founders brought into being our Nation, our Constitution, and our Bill of Rights with its prohibition against any governmental establishment of religion. The New York laws officially prescribing the Regents' prayer are inconsistent both with the purposes of the Establishment Clause and with the Establishment Clause itself.

It has been argued that to apply the Constitution in such a way as to prohibit state laws respecting an establishment of religious services in public schools is to indicate a hostility toward religion or toward prayer. Nothing, of course, could be more wrong. The history of man is inseparable from the history of religion. And perhaps it is not too much to say that since the beginning of that history many people have devoutly believed that "More things are wrought by prayer than this world dreams of." It was doubtless largely due to men who believed this that there grew up a sentiment that caused men to leave the cross-currents of officially established state religions and religious persecution in Europe and come to this country filled with the hope that they could find a place in which they could pray when they pleased to the God of their faith in the language they chose.[20] And there were men of

[17] 5 & 6 Edward VI, c. 1, entitled "An Act for the Uniformity of Service and Administration of Sacraments throughout the Realm." This Act was repealed during the reign of Mary but revived upon the accession of Elizabeth. See note 7, supra. The reasons which led to the enactment of this statute were set out in its preamble: "Where there hath been a very godly Order set forth by the Authority of Parliament, for Common Prayer and Administration of the Sacraments to be used in the Mother Tongue within the Church of *England*, agreeable to the Word of God and the Primitive Church, very comfortable to all good People desiring to live in Christian Conversation, and most profitable to the Estate of this Realm, upon which the Mercy, Favour and Blessing of Almighty God is in no wise so readily and plenteously poured as by Common Prayers, due using of the Sacraments, and often preaching of the Gospel, with the Devotion of the Hearers: (1) And yet this notwithstanding, a great Number of People in divers Parts of this Realm, following their own Sensuality, and living either without Knowledge or due Fear of God, do wilfully and damnably before Almighty God abstain and refuse to come to their Parish Churches and other Places where Common Prayer, Administration of the Sacraments, and Preaching of the Word of God, is used upon *Sundays* and other Days ordained to be Holydays."

[18] Bunyan's own account of his trial is set forth in A Relation of the Imprisonment of Mr. John Bunyan, reprinted in Grace Abounding and The Pilgrim's Progress (Brown ed. 1907), at 103-132.

[19] For a vivid account of some of these persecutions, see Wertenbaker, The Puritan Oligarchy (1947).

[20] Perhaps the best example of the sort of men who came to this country for precisely that reason is Roger Williams, the founder of Rhode Island, who has been de-

this same faith in the power of prayer who led the fight for adoption of our Constitution and also for our Bill of Rights with the very guarantees of religious freedom that forbid the sort of governmental activity which New York has attempted here. These men knew that the First Amendment, which tried to put an end to governmental control of religion and of prayer, was not written to destroy either. They knew rather that it was written to quiet well-justified fears which nearly all of them felt arising out of an awareness that governments of the past had shackled men's tongues to make them speak only the religious thoughts that government wanted them to speak and to pray only to the God that government wanted them to pray to. It is neither sacrilegious nor antireligious to say that each separate government in this country should stay out of the business of writing or sanctioning official prayers and leave that purely religious function to the people themselves and to those the people choose to look to for religious guidance.[21]

NOTES

1. Neither Mr. Justice Frankfurter nor Mr. Justice White participated. Mr. Justice Douglas concurred, stressing that it is the financing of religious exercises by the government which constitutes the violation of the establishment clause not

---

scribed as "the truest Christian amongst many who sincerely desired to be Christian." Parrington, Main Currents in American Thought (1930), Vol. 1, at p. 74. Williams, who was one of the earliest exponents of the doctrine of separation of church and state, believed that separation was necessary in order to protect the church from the danger of destruction which he thought inevitably flowed from control by even the best-intentioned civil authorities: "The unknowing zeale of *Constantine* and other Emperours, did more hurt to *Christ Jesus* his Crowne and Kingdome, then the raging fury of the most bloody *Neroes*. In the *persecutions* of the later, *Christians* were sweet and fragrant, like spice pounded and beaten in morters: But those *good* Emperours, persecuting some erroneous persons, *Arrius, &c.* and advancing the professours of some Truths of Christ (for there was no small number of *Truths* lost in those times) and maintaining their *Religion* by the materiall Sword, I say by this meanes *Christianity* was *ecclipsed,* and the Professors of it fell asleep . . . ." Williams, The Bloudy Tenent, of Persecution, for cause of Conscience, discussed in A Conference betweene Truth and Peace (London, 1644), reprinted in Narragansett Club Publications, Vol. III, p. 184. To Williams, it was no part of the business or competence of a civil magistrate to interfere in religious matters: "[W]hat imprudence and *indiscretion* is it in the most common affaires of Life, to conceive that *Emperours, Kings* and *Rulers* of the earth must not only be qualified with *politicall* and *state abilities* to *make* and *execute* such *Civill Lawes* which may concerne the common *rights, peace* and *safety* (which is worke and businesse, load and burthen enough for the ablest shoulders in the Commonweal) but also furnished with such *Spirituall* and heavenly *abilities* to governe the *Spirituall* and *Christian Commonweale* . . . ." Id., at 366. See also id., at 136-137.

[21] There is of course nothing in the decision reached here that is inconsistent with the fact that school children and others are officially encouraged to express love for our country by reciting historical documents such as the Declaration of Independence which contain references to the Deity or by singing officially espoused anthems which include the composer's professions of faith in a Supreme Being, or with the fact that there are many manifestations in our public life of belief in God. Such patriotic or ceremonial occasions bear no true resemblance to the unquestioned religious exercise that the State of New York has sponsored in this instance.

only in schools but also as it takes place in the Supreme Court, Congress, and elsewhere. In this connection he also stated his belief that Everson "seems in retrospect to be out of line with the First Amendment. Its result is appealing, as it allows aid to be given to needy children. Yet by the same token, public funds could be used to satisfy other needs of children in parochial schools — lunches, books, and tuition being obvious examples." 370 U.S. at 443.

Mr. Justice Stewart dissented, also stressing the religious ceremonies in the Court and Congress and other official references to God, but concluding: "I do not believe that this Court, or the Congress, or the President has by the actions and practices I have mentioned established an 'official religion' in violation of the Constitution. And I do not believe that the State of New York has done so in this case. What each has done has been to recognize and to follow the deeply entrenched and highly cherished spiritual traditions of our Nation — traditions which come down to us from those who almost two hundred years ago avowed their 'firm Reliance on the Protection of divine Providence' when they proclaimed the freedom and independence of this brave new world." [Footnote reference to Declaration of Independence omitted.] 370 U.S. at 450.

2. See also Chamberlin v. Dade County Bd. of Public Instruction, 143 So. 2d 21 (Fla. 1962), vacated and remanded for further consideration, 374 U.S. 487 (1963), aff'd, 160 So. 2d 97 (Fla. 1964), rev'd per curiam, 377 U.S. 402 (1964). In Stein v. Oshinsky, 348 F.2d 999 (2d Cir. 1965), cert. den., 382 U.S. 957 (1965), children in kindergarten before they ate their cookies and milk in the morning session recited: "God is Great, God is Good and We Thank Him for our Food, Amen!." Kindergarten classes in the afternoon session recited: "Thank You for the World so Sweet, Thank You for the Food We Eat, Thank You for the Birds that Sing — Thank You, God, for Everything." 348 F.2d at 1000. An injunction to stop the school principal from interfering with this "student initiated" prayer was denied, the court saying that no constitutional provision requires a "state to permit persons to engage in public prayer in state-owned facilities wherever and whenever they desire. . . . We are not here required to consider such cases as that of a Moslem, obliged to prostrate himself five times daily in the direction of Mecca, or of a child whose beliefs forbade his partaking of milk and cookies without saying the blessings of his faith. . . . So far as appears, the school authorities might well permit students to withdraw momentarily for such necessary observances — or to forego the milk and cookies, just as they excuse children on holidays important to their religions." 348 F.2d at 1001-1002. Compare Reed v. van Hoven, 237 F. Supp. 48 (W.D. Mich. 1965), denying injunction against school authorities to prohibit their permitting the saying of prayers and reading of scriptures by children who wish to do so before school day begins or after school day ends, this to be done in a room other than the home room and in silence if during lunch hour, and no bell must announce a prayer period.

SCHOOL DISTRICT OF ABINGTON TOWNSHIP v. SCHEMPP
374 U.S. 203, 83 S. Ct. 1560, 10 L. Ed. 2d 844 (1963)

Mr. Justice Clark delivered the opinion of the Court.

Once again we are called upon to consider the scope of the provision of the

First Amendment to the United States Constitution which declares that "Congress shall make no law respecting an establishment of religion, or prohibiting the free exercise thereof . . . ." These companion cases present the issues in the context of state action requiring that schools begin each day with readings from the Bible. While raising the basic questions under slightly different factual situations, the cases permit of joint treatment. In light of the history of the First Amendment and of our cases interpreting and applying its requirements, we hold that the practices at issue and the laws requiring them are unconstitutional under the Establishment Clause, as applied to the States through the Fourteenth Amendment.

I

The Facts in Each Case: No. 142. The Commonwealth of Pennsylvania by law, 24 Pa. Stat. §15-1516, as amended, Pub. Law 1928 (Supp. 1960) Dec. 17, 1959, requires that "At least ten verses from the Holy Bible shall be read, without comment, at the opening of each public school on each school day. Any child shall be excused from such Bible reading, or attending such Bible reading, upon the written request of his parent or guardian." The Schempp family, husband and wife and two of their three children, brought suit to enjoin enforcement of the statute, contending that their rights under the Fourteenth Amendment to the Constitution of the United States are, have been, and will continue to be violated unless this statute be declared unconstitutional as violative of these provisions of the First Amendment. They sought to enjoin the appellant school district, wherein the Schempp children attend school, and its officers and the Superintendent of Public Instruction of the Commonwealth from continuing to conduct such readings and recitation of the Lord's Prayer in the public schools of the district pursuant to the statute. A three-judge statutory District Court for the Eastern District of Pennsylvania held that the statute is violative of the Establishment Clause of the First Amendment as applied to the States by the Due Process Clause of the Fourteenth Amendment and directed that appropriate injunctive relief issue. 201 F. Supp. 815. On appeal by the District, its officials and the Superintendent, under 28 U.S.C. §1253, we noted probable jurisdiction. 371 N.S. 807.

The appellees Edward Lewis Schempp, his wife Sidney, and their children, Roger and Donna, are of the Unitarian faith and are members of the Unitarian Church in Germantown, Philadelphia, Pennsylvania, where they, as well as another son, Ellory, regularly attend religious services. The latter was originally a party but having graduated from the school system pendente lite was voluntarily dismissed from the action. The other children attend the Abington Senior High School, which is a public school operated by appellant district.

On each school day at the Abington Senior High School between 8:15 and 8:30 A.M., while the pupils are attending their home rooms or advisory sections, opening exercises are conducted pursuant to the statute. The exercises are broadcast into each room in the school building through an intercommunications system and are conducted under the supervision of a teacher by students attending the school's radio and television workshop. Selected students from this course gather each morning in the school's workshop studio for the exercises, which include readings by one of the students of 10 verses of the Holy Bible, broadcast to each room in the building. This is followed by the recitation of the Lord's Prayer, likewise over the intercommunications system, but also by the students in the various classrooms, who are asked to stand and join in repeating the prayer in unison. The exercises are closed with the flag salute and such pertinent announcements as are of interest to the students. Participation in the opening exercises, as directed by the statute, is voluntary. The student reading the verses from the Bible may select the passages and read from any version he chooses, although the only copies furnished by the school are the King James version, copies of which were circulated to each teacher by the school district. During the period in which the exercises have been conducted the King James, the Douay and the Revised Standard versions of the Bible have been used, as well as the Jewish Holy Scriptures. There are no prefatory statements, no questions asked or solicited, no comments or explanations made and no interpretations given at or during the exercises. The students and parents are advised that the student may absent himself from the classroom or, should he elect to remain, not participate in the exercises.

It appears from the record that in schools not having an intercommunications system the Bible reading and the recitation of the Lord's Prayer were conducted by the home-room teacher,[2] who chose the text of the verses and read them herself or had students read them in rotation or by volunteers. This was followed by a standing recitation of the Lord's Prayer, together with the Pledge of Allegiance to the Flag by the class in unison and a closing announcement of routine school items of interest.

At the first trial Edward Schempp and the children testified as to specific religious doctrines purveyed by a literal reading of the Bible "which were contrary to the religious beliefs which they held and to their familial teaching." 177 F. Supp. 398, 400. The children testified that all of the doctrines to which they referred were read to them at various times as part of the exercises. Edward Schempp testified at the second trial that he had considered having Roger and Donna excused from attendance at the exercises but decided against it for several reasons, including his belief that the children's relationships with their teachers and classmates would be adversely affected.[3]

---

[2] The statute as amended imposes no penalty upon a teacher refusing to obey its mandate. However, it remains to be seen whether one refusing could have his contract of employment terminated for "wilful violation of the school laws." 24 Pa. Stat. (Supp. 1960) §11-1122.

[3] The trial court summarized his testimony as follows:

"Edward Schempp, the children's father, testified that after careful consideration he

Expert testimony was introduced by both appellants and appellees at the first trial, which testimony was summarized by the trial court as follows: "Dr. Solomon Grayzel testified that there were marked differences between the Jewish Holy Scriptures and the Christian Holy Bible, the most obvious of which was the absence of the New Testament in the Jewish Holy Scriptures. Dr. Grayzel testified that portions of the New Testament were offensive to Jewish tradition and that, from the standpoint of Jewish faith, the concept of Jesus Christ as the Son of God was 'practically blasphemous.' He cited instances in the New Testament which, assertedly, were not only sectarian in nature but tended to bring the Jews into ridicule or scorn. Dr. Grayzel gave as his expert opinion that such material from the New Testament could be explained to Jewish children in such a way as to do no harm to them. But if portions of the New Testament were read without explanation, they could be, and in his specific experience with children Dr. Grayzel observed, had been, psychologically harmful to the child and had caused a divisive force within the social media of the school.

"Dr. Grayzel also testified that there was significant difference in attitude with regard to the respective Books of the Jewish and Christian Religions in that Judaism attaches no special significance to the reading of the Bible per se and that the Jewish Holy Scriptures are source materials to be studied. But Dr. Grayzel did state that many portions of the New, as well as of the Old, Testament contained passages of great literary and moral value.

"Dr. Luther A. Weigle, an expert witness for the defense, testified in some detail as to the reasons for and the methods employed in developing the King James and the Revised Standard Versions of the Bible. On direct examination, Dr. Weigle stated that the Bible was non-sectarian. He later stated that the phrase 'non-sectarian' meant to him non-sectarian within the Christian faiths. Dr. Weigle stated that his definition of the Holy Bible would include the Jewish Holy Scriptures, but also stated that the 'Holy Bible' would not be complete without the New Testament. He stated that the New Testament 'conveyed the message of Christians.' In his opinion, reading of the Holy Scriptures to the exclusion of the New Testament would be a sectarian practice. Dr. Weigle stated that the Bible was of great moral, historical and liter-

---

had decided that he should not have Roger or Donna excused from attendance at these morning ceremonies. Among his reasons were the following. He said that he thought his children would be 'labeled as "odd balls"' before their teachers and classmates every school day; that children, like Roger's and Donna's classmates, were liable 'to lump all particular religious difference[s] or religious objections [together] as "atheism"' and that today the word 'atheism' is often connected with 'atheistic communism,' and has 'very bad' connotations, such as 'un-American' or 'anti-Red,' with overtones of possible immorality. Mr. Schempp pointed out that due to the events of the morning exercises following in rapid succession, the Bible reading, the Lord's Prayer, the Flag Salute, and the announcements, excusing his children from the Bible reading would mean that probably they would miss hearing the announcements so important to children. He testified also that if Roger and Donna were excused from Bible reading they would have to stand in the hall outside their 'homeroom' and that this carried with it the imputation of punishment for bad conduct." 201 F. Supp., at 818.

ary value. This is conceded by all the parties and is also the view of the court." 177 F. Supp. 398, 401-402.

The trial court, in striking down the practices and the statute requiring them, made specific findings of fact that the children's attendance at Abington Senior High School is compulsory and that the practice of reading 10 verses from the Bible is also compelled by law. It also found that:

"The reading of the verses, even without comment, possesses a devotional and religious character and constitutes in effect a religious observance. The devotional and religious nature of the morning exercises is made all the more apparent by the fact that the Bible reading is followed immediately by a recital in unison by the pupils of the Lord's Prayer. The fact that some pupils, or theoretically all pupils, might be excused from attendance at the exercises does not mitigate the obligatory nature of the ceremony for . . . Section 1516 . . . unequivocally requires the exercises to be held every school day in every school in the Commonwealth. The exercises are held in the school buildings and perforce are conducted by and under the authority of the local school authorities and during school sessions. Since the statute requires the reading of the 'Holy Bible,' a Christian document, the practice . . . prefers the Christian religion. The record demonstrates that it was the intention of . . . the Commonwealth . . . to introduce a religious ceremony into the public schools of the Commonwealth." 201 F. Supp., at 819.

No. 119. In 1905 the Board of School Commissioners of Baltimore City adopted a rule pursuant to Art. 77, §202 of the Annotated Code of Maryland. The rule provided for the holding of opening exercises in the schools of the city, consisting primarily of the "reading, without comment, of a chapter in the Holy Bible and/or the use of the Lord's Prayer." The petitioners, Mrs. Madalyn Murray and her son, William J. Murray III, are both professed atheists. Following unsuccessful attempts to have the respondent school board rescind the rule, this suit was filed for mandamus to compel its rescission and cancellation. It was alleged that William was a student in a public school of the city and Mrs. Murray, his mother, was a taxpayer therein; that it was the practice under the rule to have a reading on each school morning from the King James version of the Bible; that at petitioners' insistence the rule was amended [4] to permit children to be excused from the exercise on request of the parent and that William had been excused pursuant thereto; that nevertheless the rule as amended was in violation of the petitioners' rights "to freedom of religion under the First and Fourteenth Amendments"

---

[4] The rule as amended provides as follows:

"Opening Exercises. Each school, either collectively or in classes, shall be opened by the reading, without comment, of a chapter in the Holy Bible and/or the use of the Lord's Prayer. The Douay version may be used by those pupils who prefer it. Appropriate patriotic exercises should be held as a part of the general opening exercise of the school or class. Any child shall be excused from participating in the opening exercises or from attending the opening exercises upon the written request of his parent or guardian."

and in violation of "the principle of separation between church and state, contained therein. . . ." The petition particularized the petitioners' atheistic beliefs and stated that the rule, as practiced, violated their rights "in that it threatens their religious liberty by placing a premium on belief as against non-belief and subjects their freedom of conscience to the rule of the majority; it pronounces belief in God as the source of all moral and spiritual values, equating these values with religious values, and thereby renders sinister, alien and suspect the beliefs and ideals of your Petitioners, promoting doubt and question of their morality, good citizenship and good faith."

The respondents demurred and the trial court, recognizing that the demurrer admitted all facts well pleaded, sustained it without leave to amend. The Maryland Court of Appeals affirmed, the majority of four justices holding the exercise not in violation of the First and Fourteenth Amendments, with three justices dissenting. 228 Md. 239, 179 A.2d 698. We granted certiorari. 371 U.S. 809.

I I

It is true that religion has been closely identified with our history and government.

[Here the opinion after quoting from Engel and Zorach mentions among other things the Mayflower Compact, the reference to the Supreme Being in the Constitution and oaths of office, the opening prayers in Congress, the Court's opening ceremony, and the provision for religious services in the armed forces.]

This is not to say, however, that religion has been so identified with our history and government that religious freedom is not likewise as strongly imbedded in our public and private life. . . .

III

Almost a hundred years ago in Minor v. Board of Education of Cincinnati, Judge Alphonso Taft, father of the revered Chief Justice, in an unpublished opinion stated the ideal of our people as to religious freedom as one of "absolute equality before the law, of all religious opinions and sects. . . .

. . .

"The government is neutral, and, while protecting all, it prefers none, and it *disparages* none."

Before examining this "neutral" position in which the Establishment and Free Exercise Clauses of the First Amendment place our Government it is well that we discuss the reach of the Amendment under the cases of this Court.

First, this Court has decisively settled that the First Amendment's mandate that "Congress shall make no law respecting an establishment of religion, or prohibiting the free exercise thereof" has been made wholly applicable to the States by the Fourteenth Amendment. . . .

Second, this Court has rejected unequivocally the contention that the Establishment Clause forbids only governmental preference of one religion over another. . . .

While none of the parties to either of these cases has questioned these basic conclusions of the Court, both of which have been long established, recognized and consistently reaffirmed, others continue to question their history, logic and efficacy. Such contentions, in the light of the consistent interpretation in cases of this Court, seem entirely untenable and of value only as academic exercises.

IV

The interrelationship of the Establishment and the Free Exercise Clauses was first touched upon by Mr. Justice Roberts for the Court in Cantwell v. Connecticut . . .

[Here the opinion reviews the position of the Court and occasional dissenting justices in Everson, McCollum, Zorach, and Engel, as well as McGowan and Torcaso, infra.]

V

The wholesome "neutrality" of which this Court's cases speak thus stems from a recognition of the teachings of history that powerful sects or groups might bring about a fusion of governmental and religious functions or a concert or dependency of one upon the other to the end that official support of the State or Federal Government would be placed behind the tenets of one or of all orthodoxies. This the Establishment Clause prohibits. And a further reason for neutrality is found in the Free Exercise Clause, which recognizes the value of religious training, teaching and observance and, more particularly, the right of every person to freely choose his own course with reference thereto, free of any compulsion from the state. This the Free Exercise Clause guarantees. Thus, as we have seen, the two clauses may overlap. As we have indicated, the Establishment Clause has been directly considered by this Court eight times in the past score of years and, with only one Justice dissenting on the point, it has consistently held that the clause withdrew all legislative power respecting religious belief or the expression thereof. The test may be stated as follows: what are the purpose and the primary effect of the enactment? If either is the advancement or inhibition of religion then the enactment exceeds the scope of legislative power as circumscribed by the Constitution. That is to say that to withstand the strictures of the Establishment Clause there must be a secular legislative purpose and a primary effect that neither advances nor inhibits religion. Everson v. Board of Education, supra; McGowan v. Maryland, [366 U.S.] at 442. The Free Exercise Clause, likewise considered many times here, withdraws from legislative power, state and federal, the exertion of any restraint on the free exercise of religion. Its purpose is to secure religious liberty in the individual by prohibiting any invasions thereof by civil authority. Hence it is necessary in a free exercise case for one to show the coercive effect of the enactment as it operates against him in the practice of his religion. The distinction between the two clauses is apparent — a violation of the Free Exercise Clause is predicated on coercion while the Establishment Clause violation need not be so attended.

Applying the Establishment Clause principles to the cases at bar we find that the States are requiring the selection and reading at the opening of the school day of verses from the Holy Bible and the recitation of the Lord's Prayer by the students in unison. These exercises are prescribed as part of the curricular activities of students who are required by law to attend school. They are held in the school buildings under the supervision and with the participation of teachers employed in those schools. None of these factors, other than compulsory school attendance, was present in the program upheld in Zorach v. Clauson. The trial court in No. 142 has found that such an opening exercise is a religious ceremony and was intended by the State to be so. We agree with the trial court's finding as to the religious character of the exercises. Given that finding, the exercises and the law requiring them are in violation of the Establishment Clause.

There is no such specific finding as to the religious character of the exercises in No. 119, and the State contends (as does the State in No. 142) that the program is an effort to extend its benefits to all public school children without regard to their religious belief. Included within its secular purposes, it says, are the promotion of moral values, the contradiction to the materialistic trends of our times, the perpetuation of our institutions and the teaching of literature. The case came up on demurrer, of course, to a petition which alleged that the uniform practice under the rule had been to read from the King James version of the Bible and that the exercise was sectarian. The short answer, therefore, is that the religious character of the exercise was admitted by the State. But even if its purpose is not strictly religious, it is sought to be accomplished through readings, without comment, from the Bible. Surely the place of the Bible as an instrument of religion cannot be gainsaid, and the State's recognition of the pervading religious character of the ceremony is evident from the rule's specific permission of the alternative use of the Catholic Douay version as well as the recent amendment permitting nonattendance at the exercises. None of these factors is consistent with the contention that the Bible is here used either as an instrument for nonreligious moral inspiration or as a reference for the teaching of secular subjects.

The conclusion follows that in both cases the laws require religious exercises and such exercises are being conducted in direct violation of the rights of the appellees and petitioners.[9] Nor are these required exercises mitigated by the fact that individual students may absent themselves upon parental request, for that fact furnishes no defense to a claim of unconstitutionality under the Establishment Clause. See Engel v. Vitale, supra, at 430. Further, it is no defense to urge that the religious practices here may be relatively minor encroachments on the First Amendment. The breach of neutrality that is today a trickling stream may all too soon become a raging torrent and, in the words of Madison, "it is proper to take alarm at the first experiment on our liberties." Memorial and Remonstrance Against Religious Assessments, quoted in Everson, supra, at 65.

It is insisted that unless these religious exercises are permitted a "religion of secularism" is established in the schools. We agree of course that the State may not establish a "religion of secularism" in the sense of affirmatively opposing or showing hostility to religion, thus "preferring those who believe in no religion over those who do believe." Zorach v. Clauson, supra, at 314. We do not agree, however, that this decision in any sense has that effect. In addition, it might well be said that one's education is not complete without a study of comparative religion or the history of religion and its relationship to the advancement of civilization. It certainly may be said that the Bible is worthy of study for its literary and historic qualities. Nothing we have said here indicates that such study of the Bible or of religion, when presented objectively as part of a secular program of education, may not be effected consistently with the First Amendment. But the exercises here do not fall into those categories. They are religious exercises, required by the States in violation of the command of the First Amendment that the Government maintain strict neutrality, neither aiding nor opposing religion.

Finally, we cannot accept that the concept of neutrality, which does not permit a State to require a religious exercise even with the consent of the majority of those affected, collides with the majority's right to free exercise of religion.[10] While the Free Exercise Clause clearly prohibits the use of state

[9] It goes without saying that the laws and practices involved here can be challenged only by persons having standing to complain. But the requirements for standing to challenge state action under the Establishment Clause, unlike those relating to the Free Exercise Clause, do not include proof that particular religious freedoms are infringed. McGowan v. Maryland, supra, at 429-430. The parties here are school children and their parents, who are directly affected by the laws and practices against which their complaints are directed. These interests surely suffice to give the parties standing to complain. See Engel v. Vitale, supra. Cf. McCollum v. Board of Education, supra; Everson v. Board of Education, supra. Compare Doremus v. Board of Education, 342 U.S. 429 (1952), which involved the same substantive issues presented here. The appeal was there dismissed upon the graduation of the school child involved and because of the appellants' failure to establish standing as taxpayers.

[10] We are not of course presented with and therefore do not pass upon a situation such as military service, where the Government regulates the temporal and geographic environment of individuals to a point that, unless it permits voluntary religious services to be conducted with the use of government facilities, military personnel would be unable to engage in the practice of their faiths.

action to deny the rights of free exercise to *anyone,* it has never meant that a majority could use the machinery of the State to practice its beliefs. Such a contention was effectively answered by Mr. Justice Jackson for the Court in West Virginia Board of Education v. Barnette, 319 U.S. 624, 638 (1943):

"The very purpose of a Bill of Rights was to withdraw certain subjects from the vicissitudes of political controversy, to place them beyond the reach of majorities and officials and to establish them as legal principles to be applied by the courts. One's right to . . . freedom of worship . . . and other fundamental rights may not be submitted to vote; they depend on the outcome of no elections." . . .

[On the basis of this principle the Court affirmed the judgment in No. 192 and in No. 119 remanded to the Maryland Court of Appeals for further proceedings consistent with the opinion.]

Mr. Justice Douglas' concurrence stressed in addition to the states' conducting of religious exercises the states' employment of its "facilities or funds in a way that gives any church, or all churches, greater strength in our society than it would have by relying on its members alone." He added: "Financing a church either in its strictly religious activities or in its other activities is equally unconstitutional . . . [T]he institution is an inseparable whole . . . which is strengthened in proselytizing when it is strengthened in any department by contributions from other than its own members." 374 U.S. at 229.

Mr. Justice Brennan's extensive concurring opinion addressed itself to various questions raised over the years with respect to the establishment and free exercise clauses. Some of these are:

(1) Would Jefferson and Madison have proscribed devotional exercises in public educational institutions? "A too literal quest for the advice of the founding fathers upon the issues of these cases seems to me futile and misdirected." The historical evidence is ambiguous. The question should rather be whether given present day America "the practices here challenged threaten those consequences which the Framers deeply feared; whether, in short, they tend to promote that type of interdependence between religion and state which the First Amendment was designed to prevent." Since the adoption of the First Amendment public education has become much more widespread and the diversity of religion has increased. As a consequence it has become "implicit in the history and the character of American public education that the public schools serve a uniquely *public* function: the training of American citizens in an atmosphere free of parochial, divisive, or separatist influences of any sort — an atmosphere in which children may assimilate a heritage common to all American groups and religions." Moreover, "[a]ttendance at the public schools has never been compulsory; parents remain morally and constitutionally free to choose the academic environment in which they wish

their children to be educated. The relationship of the Establishment Clause of the First Amendment to the public school system is preeminently that of reserving such a choice to the individual parent, rather than vesting it in the majority of voters of each State or school district. The choice which is thus preserved is between a public secular education with its uniquely democratic values, and some form of private or sectarian education, which offers values of its own. In my judgment the First Amendment forbids the State to inhibit that freedom of choice by diminishing the attractiveness of either alternative — either by restricting the liberty of the private schools to inculcate whatever values they wish, or by jeopardizing the freedom of the public schools from private or sectarian pressures. The choice between these very different forms of education is one — very much like the choice of whether or not to worship — which our Constitution leaves to the individual parent. It is no proper function of the state or local government to influence or restrict that election. The lesson of history — drawn more from the experiences of other countries than from our own — is that a system of free public education forfeits its unique contribution to the growth of democratic citizenship when that choice ceases to be freely available to each parent." 374 U.S. at 234-242.

(2) May the religious attributes of Bible reading be overlooked on the grounds that it serves the secular purposes of establishing discipline and inculcating general spiritual and moral values? To the extent that these secular purposes depend "upon an immediately religious experience shared by the participating children," "the purpose as well as the means is so plainly religious that the exercise is necessarily forbidden by the Establishment Clause. The fact that purely secular benefits may eventually result does not seem to me to justify the exercises." To the extent that the religious exercises may have a direct secular effect of "fostering harmony and tolerance among the pupils, enhancing the authority of the teacher, and inspiring better discipline," "it would seem that less sensitive materials might equally well serve the same purpose." "[This] principle is readily applied to these cases. It has not been shown that readings from the speeches and messages of great Americans, for example, or from the documents of our heritage of liberty, daily recitation of the Pledge of Allegiance, or even the observance of a moment of reverent silence at the opening of class, may not adequately serve the solely secular purposes of the devotional activities without jeopardizing either the religious liberties of any members of the community or the proper degree of separation between the spheres of religion and government. Such substitutes would, I think, be unsatisfactory or inadequate only to the extent that the present activities do in fact serve religious goals. While I do not question the judgment of experienced educators that the challenged practices may well achieve valuable secular ends, it seems to me that the State acts unconstitutionally if it either sets about to attain even indirectly religious ends by religious means, or if it uses religious means to serve secular ends where secular means would suffice." 374 U.S. at 278-281.

(3) Are the practices in these cases unobjectionable "because they prefer no particular sect or sects at the expense of others"? Any "version of the Bible is inherently sectarian" and even to "vary the version as the Abington and Baltimore schools have done" still results in a preference for the majority sects. The "basic flaw" in the contention is that there "are persons in every community — often deeply devout — to whom any version of the Judaeo-Christian Bible is offensive," and there "are others whose reverence for the Holy Scriptures demands private study or reflection and to whom public reading or recitation is sacrilegious." 374 U.S. at 281-283.

(4) Does the excuse or exemption of those who do not wish to participate absolve those practices from the Constitutional ban? The "availability of excusal or exemption simply has no relevance to the establishment question, if it is once found that these practices are essentially religious exercises designed at least in part to achieve religious aims through the use of public school facilities during the school day." The "more difficult question" arises with respect to the free exercise clause:

"While it is enough to decide these cases to dispose of the establishment questions, questions of free exercise are so inextricably interwoven into the history and present status of these practices as to jusify disposition of this second aspect of the excusal issue. The answer is that the excusal procedure itself necessarily operates in such a way as to infringe the rights of free exercise of those children who wish to be excused. We have held in Barnette and Torcaso, respectively, that a State may require neither public school students nor candidates for an office of public trust to profess beliefs offensive to religious principles. By the same token the State could not constitutionally require a student to profess publicly his disbelief as the prerequisite to the exercise of his constitutional right of abstention. And apart from Torcaso and Barnette, I think Speiser v. Randall, 357 U.S. 513, suggests a further answer. We held there that a State may not condition the grant of a tax exemption upon the willingness of those entitled to the exemption to affirm their loyalty to the Government, even though the exemption was itself a matter of grace rather than of constitutional right. We concluded that to impose upon the eligible taxpayers the affirmative burden of proving their loyalty impermissibly jeopardized the freedom to engage in constitutionally protected activities close to the area to which the loyalty oath related. Speiser v. Randall seems to me to dispose of two aspects of the excusal or exemption procedure now before us. First, by requiring what is tantamount in the eyes of teachers and schoolmates to a profession of disbelief, or at least of nonconformity, the procedure may well deter those children who do not wish to participate for any reason based upon the dictates of conscience from exercising an indisputably constitutional right to be excused.[68] Thus the excusal provision in its

---

[68] See the testimony of Edward L. Schempp, the father of the children in the Abington schools and plaintiff-appellee in No. 142, concerning his reasons for not asking that his children be excused from the morning exercises after excusal was made available

operation subjects them to a cruel dilemma. In consequence, even devout children may well avoid claiming their right and simply continue to participate in exercises distasteful to them because of an understandable reluctance to be stigmatized as atheists or nonconformists simply on the basis of their request.

"Such reluctance to seek exemption seems all the more likely in view of the fact that children are disinclined at this age to step out of line or to flout 'peer-group norms.' Such is the widely held view of experts who have studied the behaviors and attitudes of children.[69]. . .

"Speiser v. Randall also suggests the answer to a further argument based on

---

through amendment of the statute [quoted in the majority opinion]. . . . A recent opinion of the Attorney General of California gave as one reason for finding devotional exercises unconstitutional the likelihood that "[c]hildren forced by conscience to leave the room during such exercises would be placed in a position inferior to that of students adhering to the State-endorsed religion." 25 Cal. Op. Atty. Gen. 316, 319 (1955). Other views on this question, and possible effects of the excusal procedure, are summarized in Rosenfield, Separation of Church and State in the Public Schools, 22 U. of Pitt. L. Rev. 561, 581-585 (1961); Note, Separation of Church and State: Religious Exercises in the Schools, 31 U. of Cinc. L. Rev. 408, 416 (1962); Note, 62 W. Va. L. Rev. 353, 358 (1960).

[69] Extensive testimony by behavioral scientists concerning the effect of similar practices upon children's attitudes and behaviors is discussed in Tudor v. Board of Education, 14 N.J. 31, 50-52, 100 A.2d 857, 867-868. See also Choper, Religion in the Public Schools: A Proposed Constitutional Standard, 47 Minn. L. Rev. 329, 344 (1963). There appear to be no reported experiments which bear directly upon the question under consideration. There have, however, been numerous experiments which indicate the susceptibility of school children to peer-group pressures, especially where important group norms and values are involved. See, e.g., Berenda, The Influence of the Group on the Judgments of Children (1950), 26-33; Argyle, Social Pressure in Public and Private Situations, 54 J. Abnormal & Social Psych. 172 (1957); cf. Rhine, The Effect of Peer Group Influence Upon Concept-Attitude Development and Change, 51 J. Social Psych. 173 (1960); French, Morrison and Levinger, Coercive Power and Forces Affecting Conformity, 61 J. Abnormal and Social Psych. 93 (1960). For a recent and important experimental study of the susceptibility of students to various factors in the school environment, see Zander, Curtis and Rosenfeld, The Influence of Teachers and Peers on Aspirations of Youth (U.S. Office of Education Cooperative Research Project No. 451, 1961), 24-25, 78-79. It is also apparent that the susceptibility of school children to prestige suggestion and social influence within the school environment varies inversely with the age, grade level, and consequent degree of sophistication of the child, see Patel and Gordon, Some Personal and Situational Determinants of Yielding to Influence, 61 J. Abnormal and Social Psych. 411, 417 (1960).

Experimental findings also shed some light upon the probable effectiveness of a provision for excusal when, as is usually the case, the percentage of the class wishing not to participate in the exercises is very small. It has been demonstrated, for example, that the inclination even of adults to depart or dissent overtly from strong group norms varies proportionately with the size of the dissenting group — that is, inversely with the apparent or perceived strength of the norm itself — and is markedly slighter in the case of the sole or isolated dissenter. See, e.g., Asch, Studies of Independence and Conformity: I. A Minority of One Against a Unanimous Majority (Psych. Monographs No. 416, 1956), 69-70; Asch, Effects of Group Pressure upon the Modification and Distortion of Judgments, in Cartwright and Zander, Group Dynamics (2d ed. 1960), 189-199; Luchins and Luchins, On Conformity With True and False Communications, 42 J. Social Psych. 283 (1955). Recent important findings on these questions are summarized in Hare, Handbook of Small Group Research (1962), c. II.

the excusal procedure. It has been suggested by the School Board, in Schempp, that we ought not pass upon the appellees' constitutional challenge at least until the children have availed themselves of the excusal procedure and found it inadequate to redress their grievances. Were the right to be excused not itself of constitutional stature, I might have some doubt about this issue. But we held in Speiser that the constitutional vice of the loyalty oath procedure discharged any obligation to seek the exemption before challenging the constitutionality of the conditions upon which it might have been denied. 357 U.S., at 529. Similarly, we have held that one need not apply for a permit to distribute constitutionally protected literature, Lovell v. Griffin, 303 U.S. 444, or to deliver a speech, Thomas v. Collins, 323 U.S. 516, before he may attack the constitutionality of a licensing system of which the defect is patent. Insofar as these cases implicate only questions of establishment, it seems to me that the availability of an excuse is constitutionally irrelevant. Moreover, the excusal procedure seems to me to operate in such a way as to discourage the free exercise of religion on the part of those who might wish to utilize it, thereby rendering it unconstitutional in an additional and quite distinct respect." 374 U.S. at 287-293.

(5) Does the invalidation of Bible reading in public schools imply the unconstitutionality of "every vestige, however slight, of cooperation or accommodation between religion and government"? "I cannot accept that contention." What is forbidden are "those involvements of religions with secular institutions which (a) serve the essentially religious activities of religious institutions; (b) employ the organs of government for essentially religious purposes; or (c) use essentially religious means to serve governmental ends, where secular means would suffice." On the other hand "nothing in the Establishment Clause forbids the application of legislation having purely secular ends in such a way as to alleviate burdens upon the free exercise of an individual's religious beliefs." Thus provisions for churches and chaplains in the military services and penal institutions as well as draft exemptions for ministers or conscientious objectors, though not required, are permissible. Similarly excusing children from school on their religious holidays, or allowing churches to use public buildings where church buildings are unavailable because of disaster or emergency, does not violate the establishment clause:

"Such activities and practices seem distinguishable from the sponsorship of daily Bible reading and prayer recital. For one thing, there is no element of coercion present in the appointment of military or prison chaplains; the soldier or convict who declines the opportunities for worship would not ordinarily subject himself to the suspicion or obloquy of his peers. Of special significance to this distinction is the fact that we are here usually dealing with adults, not with impressionable children as in the public schools. Moreover, the school exercises are not designed to provide the pupils with general opportunities for worship denied them by the legal obligation to attend school. The student's compelled presence in school for five days a week in no way renders the regular religious facilities of the community less accessible to him than they are to others. The situation of the school child is therefore plainly unlike that of the isolated soldier or the prisoner.

"The State must be steadfastly neutral in all matters of faith, and neither favor nor inhibit religion. In my view, government cannot sponsor religious exercises in the public schools without jeopardizing that neutrality. On the other hand, hostility, not neutrality, would characterize the refusal to provide chaplains and places of worship for prisoners and soldiers cut off by the State from all civilian opportunities for public communion, the withholding of draft exemptions for ministers and conscientious objectors, or the denial of the temporary use of an empty public building to a congregation whose place of worship has been destroyed by fire or flood. I do not say that government *must* provide chaplains or draft exemptions, or that the courts should intercede if it fails to do so."

The fact that adults are involved who might readily excuse themselves also suggests that legislative and other invocational exercises may not violate the establishment clause. Other problems here are the "political question" issue and the question of who would have standing to challenge the practice.

Of course, teaching about religion and about the differences between religious sects in classes in literature or history is not foreclosed. "If it should sometime hereafter be shown that in fact religion can play no part in the teaching of a given subject without resurrecting the ghost of the practices we strike down today, it will then be time enough to consider questions we must now defer."

As for tax exemptions and deductions which "incidentally benefit churches and religious institutions, along with many secular charities and non-profit organizations," if "religious institutions benefit, it is in spite of rather than because of their religious character. . . . There is no indication that taxing authorities have used such benefits in any way to subsidize the worship or foster belief in God. And as among religious beneficiaries, the tax exemption or deduction can be truly non-discriminatory, available on equal terms . . . to those . . . which reject as well as those which accept a belief in God."

Finally, there are public displays and activities which though religious in origin have ceased to have religious meaning. Included are the motto "In God We Trust" on currency and public buildings, and "various patriotic exercises and activities used in the public schools and elsewhere." "The reference to divinity in the revised pledge of allegiance . . . may merely recognize the historical fact that our Nation was believed to have been founded 'under God.'" 374 U.S. at 294-304.

Mr. Justice Goldberg's concurrence, in which Mr. Justice Harlan joined, read the Court's opinion as not foreclosing the government's "cognizance of the existence of religion." Under "certain circumstances the First Amendment may require that it do so." The opinion continues:

"The practices here involved do not fall within any sensible or acceptable concept of compelled or permitted accommodation and involve the state so significantly and directly in the realm of the sectarian as to give rise to those very divisive influences and inhibitions of freedom which both religion clauses of the First Amendment preclude. The state has ordained and has utilized its facilities to engage in unmistakably religious exercises — the devotional reading and recitation of the Holy Bible — in a manner having substantial and significant import and impact. That it has selected, rather than written, a particular devotional liturgy seems to me without constitutional import. The pervasive religiosity and direct governmental involvement inhering in the prescription of prayer and Bible reading in the public schools, during and as part of the curricular day, involving young impressionable children whose school attendance is statutorily compelled, and utilizing the prestige, power, and influence of school administration, staff, and authority, cannot realistically be termed simply accommodation, and must fall within the interdiction of the First Amendment. I find nothing in the opinion of the Court which says more than this. And, of course, today's decision does not mean that all incidents of government which import of the religious are therefore and without more banned by the strictures of the Establishment Clause. . . . The First Amendment does not prohibit practices which by any realistic measure create none of the dangers which it is designed to prevent and which do not so directly or substantially involve the state in religious exercises or in the favoring of religion as to have meaningful and practical impact. It is of course true that great consequences can grow from small beginnings, but the measure of constitutional adjudication is the ability and willingness to distinguish between real threat and mere shadow." 374 U.S. at 306-308.

Mr. Justice Stewart's dissent read in part as follows:

"It has become accepted that the decision in Pierce v. Society of Sisters, 268 U.S. 510, upholding the right of parents to send their children to nonpublic schools, was ultimately based upon the recognition of the validity of the free exercise claim involved in that situation. It might be argued here that parents who wanted their children to be exposed to religious influences in school could, under Pierce, send their children to private or parochial schools. But the consideration which renders this contention too facile to be determinative has already been recognized by the Court: 'Freedom of speech, freedom of the press, freedom of religion are available to all, not merely to those who can pay their own way.' Murdock v. Pennsylvania, 319 U.S. 105, 111.

"It might also be argued that parents who want their children exposed to religious influences can adequately fulfill that wish off school property and outside school time. With all its surface persuasiveness, however, this argument seriously misconceives the basic constitutional justification for permitting the exercises at issue in these cases. For a compulsory state educational system so structures a child's life that if religious exercises are held to be an impermissible activity in schools, religion is placed at an artificial and state-created disadvantage. Viewed in this light, permission of such exercises for those who want them is necessary if the schools are truly to be neutral in the matter of religion. And a refusal to permit religious exercises thus is seen, not as the realization of state neutrality, but rather as the establishment of a religion of secularism, or at the least, as government support of the beliefs of those who think that religious exercises should be conducted only in private.

"What seems to me to be of paramount importance, then, is recognition of the fact that the claim advanced here in favor of Bible reading is sufficiently substantial to make simple reference to the constitutional phrase 'establishment of religion' as inadequate an analysis of the cases before us as the ritualistic invocation of the nonconstitutional phrase 'separation of church and state.' What these cases compel, rather, is an analysis of just what the 'neutrality' is which is required by the interplay of the Establishment and Free Exercise Clauses of the First Amendment, as imbedded in the Fourteenth. . . .

"The dangers both to government and to religion inherent in official support of instruction in the tenets of various religious sects are absent in the present cases, which involve only a reading from the Bible unaccompanied by comments which might otherwise constitute instruction. Indeed, since, from all that appears in either record, any teacher who does not wish to do so is free not to participate,[5] it cannot even be contended that some infinitesimal part of the salaries paid by the State are made contingent upon the performance of a religious function.

"In the absence of evidence that the legislature or school board intended to prohibit local schools from substituting a different set of readings where parents requested such a change, we should not assume that the provisions before us — as actually administered — may not be construed simply as authorizing religious exercises, nor that the designations may not be treated simply as indications of the promulgating body's view as to the community's preference.

". . . I shall for the balance of this dissenting opinion treat the provisions before us as making the variety and content of the exercises, as well as a choice as to their implementation, matters which ultimately reflect the consensus of each local school community. In the absence of coercion upon those who do not wish to participate — because they hold less strong beliefs, other beliefs, or no beliefs at all — such provisions cannot, in my view, be held to represent the type of support of religion barred by the Establishment Clause. For the only support which such rules provide for religion is the withholding of state hostility — a simple acknowledgment on the part of secular authori-

---

[5] The Pennsylvania statute was specifically amended to remove the compulsion upon teachers. Act of December 17, 1959, P.L. 1928, 24 Purdon's Pa. Stat. Ann. §15-1516. Since the Maryland case is here on a demurrer, the issue of whether or not a teacher could be dismissed for refusal to participate seems, among many others, never to have been raised.

ties that the Constitution does not require extirpation of all expression of religious belief. . . .

"The governmental neutrality which the First and Fourteenth Amendments require in the cases before us, in other words, is the extension of even-handed treatment to all who believe, doubt, or disbelieve — a refusal on the part of the State to weight the scales of private choice. In these cases, therefore, what is involved is not state action based on impermissible categories, but rather an attempt by the State to accommodate those differences which the existence in our society of a variety of religious beliefs makes inevitable. The Constitution requires that such efforts be struck down only if they are proven to entail the use of the secular authority of government to coerce a preference among such beliefs.

"It may well be, as has been argued to us, that even the supposed benefits to be derived from noncoercive religious exercises in public schools are incommensurate with the administrative problems which they would create. The choice involved, however, is one for each local community and its school board, and not for this Court. For, as I have said, religious exercises are not constitutionally invalid if they simply reflect differences which exist in the society from which the school draws its pupils. They become constitutionally invalid only if their administration places the sanction of secular authority behind one or more particular religious or irreligious beliefs.

"To be specific, it seems to me clear that certain types of exercises would present situations in which no possibility of coercion on the part of secular officials could be claimed to exist. Thus, if such exercises were held either before or after the official school day, or if the school schedule were such that participation were merely one among a number of desirable alternatives,[6] it could hardly be contended that the exercises did anything more than to provide an opportunity for the voluntary expression of religious belief. On the other hand, a law which provided for religious exercises during the school day and which contained no excusal provision would obviously be unconstitutionally coercive upon those who did not wish to participate. And even under a law containing an excusal provision, if the exercises were held during the school day, and no equally desirable alternative were provided by the school authorities, the likelihood that children might be under at least some psychological compulsion to participate would be great. In a case such as the latter, however, I think we would err if we assumed such coercion in the absence of any evidence.

"Viewed in this light, it seems to me clear that the records in both of the cases before us are wholly inadequate to support an informed or responsible decision. Both cases involve provisions which explicitly permit any student who wishes, to be excused from participation in the exercises. There is no

---

[6] See, e.g., the description of a plan permitting religious instruction off school property contained in McCollum v. Board of Education, 333 U.S. 203, 224 (separate opinion of Mr. Justice Frankfurter).

evidence in either case as to whether there would exist any coercion of any kind upon a student who did not want to participate. No evidence at all was adduced in the Murray case, because it was decided upon a demurrer. All that we have in that case, therefore, is the conclusory language of a pleading. While such conclusory allegations are acceptable for procedural purposes, I think that the nature of the constitutional problem involved here clearly demands that no decision be made except upon evidence. In the Schempp case the record shows no more than a subjective prophecy by a parent of what he thought would happen if a request were made to be excused from participation in the exercises under the amended statute. No such request was ever made, and there is no evidence whatever as to what might or would actually happen, nor of what administrative arrangements the school actually might or could make to free from pressure of any kind those who do not want to participate in the exercises. There were no District Court findings on this issue, since the case under the amended statute was decided exclusively on Establishment Clause grounds. 201 F. Supp. 815." 374 U.S. at 312-319.

NOTES

1. See also Johns v. Allen, 231 F. Supp. 852 (D. Del. 1964).

2. Amendments to the Constitution have been proposed to alter the effect of the school prayer decisions. The most prominent is one offered by Congressman Becker, which reads in part:

"Section 1. Nothing in this Constitution shall be deemed to prohibit the offering, reading from, or listening to prayers or biblical scriptures, if participation therein is on a voluntary basis, in any governmental or public school, institution, or place.

"Sec. 2. Nothing in this Constitution shall be deemed to prohibit making reference to belief in, reliance upon, or invoking the aid of God or a Supreme Being in any governmental or public document, proceeding, activity, ceremony, school, institution, or place, or upon any coinage, currency, or obligation of the United States.

"Sec. 3. Nothing in this Article shall constitute an establishment of religion." H.J. Res. No. 693, 88th Cong., 1st Sess. (1963).

For a proposed amendment offered by Senator Dirksen authorizing the "providing for or permitting" of "voluntary participation" in prayer but prohibiting school authorities from prescribing the "form or content" of the prayer, see S.J. Res. 148, 89th Cong., 2d Sess. (1966).

See Hearings before the House Committee on the Judiciary, School Prayers, 88th Cong., 2d Sess. (1964). See also, Hearings before the Senate Committee on the Judiciary, Prayers in Public Schools and Other Matters, 87th Cong., 2d Sess. (1962). For a general discussion of the political aftermath of the school prayer decisions including incidents illustrating degrees of compliance, see Beaney and Beiser, Prayer and Politics: The Impact of Engel and Schempp on the Political Process, 13 J. Pub. L. 475 (1964). See also Note, School Prayer and the Becker Amendment, 53 Geo. L.J. 192 (1964); Miller, No Constitutional Amendment to

Allow Prayer in Public Schools (American Civil Liberties Union 1965). See generally, O'Brien, The States and "No Establishment": Proposed Amendments to the Constitution Since 1798, 4 Washburn L. Rev. 183 (1965).

3. In Tudor v. Board of Education, 14 N.J. 31, 100 A.2d 857 (1953), cert. den., 348 U.S. 816 (1954), the issue was whether the board had the power to authorize the free distribution in the schools of the Gideon Bible to children whose parents were willing to sign a request slip. The New Jersey court held that the King James Bible is sectarian and that authorization for its distribution coupled with the administration of request slips would violate at least that phase of the First Amendment which prohibits preference for one religion over another. See also Miller v. Cooper, 56 N.M. 355, 244 P.2d 520 (1952) (dissemination of religious literature by teacher by putting it on a table in his classroom, enjoined) and Wooley v. Spalding, 293 S.W.2d 563 (Ct. App. Ky. 1956) (enjoining school authorities from buying sectarian literature for school libraries). In Evans v. Selma Union High School Dist., 193 Cal. 54, 222 Pac. 801, 31 A.L.R. 1121 (1924), objections were raised to a purchase for the High School's library of Bibles in the King James version. The statute provided that "No publication of a sectarian, partisan, or denominational character must be used or distributed in any school or be made part of any school library; nor must any sectarian or denominational doctrine be taught therein." The court, holding that the King James version of the Bible is not a sectarian book, said that neither the authorship of a book, nor its predominant use by particular sects, nor the fact that it states the doctrine of a particular sect necessarily makes it sectarian.

4. Religion also appears in the public schools in the form of Christmas and Easter parties and other celebrations of religious holidays. For a brief outline of the extent and variety of practices and some suggestions as to community attitudes and effects see Synagogue Council of America and National Community Relations Advisory Council, Joint Conference on Religious Holiday Observances in the Public Schools, Fact Sheet (1949); American Jewish Congress, Public School Sectarianism and the Jewish Child — A Report of Experiences (1957). See also Decision by N.Y. State Commissioner of Education, to the effect that Handel's Messiah may be presented in connection with Christmas celebrations in the public schools: "Many of the greatest works in music, as in other arts, have some religious implications. Nevertheless, in my view to prevent the mention or teaching of these works in the public schools would be obviously failing to provide adequately for the educational background of our children. . . . During a holiday such as Christmas, which is universally celebrated whether as a religious holiday or simply as the occasion for the visits of Santa Claus, it would be a strange situation if the public schools were prevented from taking any notice of the holiday." In the Matter of Appeal of Arthur G. Cromwell, 72 N.Y. State Dept. Reps. 116 (1951). For an approach to the problem in terms of joint celebrations of the holidays of various groups, see Edman and Collins, Promising Practices in Intergroup Education (1947).

5. Compare with the prohibition of religious devotional exercises, prayer and devotional reading of the Bible, celebration of religious holidays, religious pageants, and baccalaureate church services, the almost universally stated goal that the public schools should teach "moral and spiritual" values. See, e.g., Educational Policies Commission, N.E.A., Moral and Spiritual Values in the Public Schools

(1951). Even moral values alone, though based on systems of belief such as secular humanism, might still be regarded as religious today. See United States v. Seeger, 380 U.S. 163, 85 S. Ct. 850, 13 L. Ed. 2d 733 (1965), infra. See Hunt, Policy Problems Arising from Current Trends and Recent Court Decisions, in 59 Religious Education 313, 316-317 (1964); Ladd, Public Education and Religion, 13 J. Pub. L. 310, 326-328 (1964); Ramsey, Teaching "Virtue" in the Public Schools, in Giannella (ed.), 1963 Religion and the Public Order 336 (1964).

On the general issue of teaching religion or about religion in the public schools, principally public universities, see in addition to Ladd, supra, Note, The Supreme Court, The First Amendment, and Religion in the Public Schools, 63 Colum. L. Rev. 73 (1963); Michaelsen, The Supreme Court and Religion in Public Higher Education, 13 J. Pub. L. 343 (1964); Louisell and Jackson, Religion, Theology and Public Higher Education, 50 Calif. L. Rev. 751 (1962); Casad, On Teaching Religion at the State University, 12 Kan. L. Rev. 405 (1964); McLean and Kimber, The Teaching of Religion in State Universities, Description of Programs in Twenty-five Institutions (1960); Note, Church and State — The Place of Religion in the Schools of the State of Iowa, 49 Iowa L. Rev. 771 (1964); Society for Religion in Higher Education, A Report on an Invitational Conference on the Study of Religion in the State University (1964); Stahmer, Religion and Moral Values in the Public Schools, 61 Religious Education 20 (1966). See also materials on the meaning of "religion" cited in Section A.

6. On the question of chaplains in the armed services and in legislatures see Figinski, Military Chaplains — A Constitutionally Permissible Accommodation Between Church and State, 24 Md. L. Rev. 377 (1964). An early case refused to decide the question because of lack of standing. Elliott v. White, 23 F.2d 997 (D.C. Cir. 1928). See generally President's Committee on Religion and Welfare in the Armed Forces, The Military Chaplaincy (1950); David Moulton and Mordecai Myers: Report of the Select Committee of the New York State Assembly on the Several Memorials Against Appointing Chaplains to the Legislature (1832), in Blau (ed.), Cornerstones of Religious Freedom in America 141 (1949). See also Barish (ed.), Rabbis in Uniform (1962).

7. In Doremus v. Board of Education, 342 U.S. 429, 72 S. Ct. 394, 96 L. Ed. 475 (1952), the plaintiffs sought a declaratory judgment to declare unconstitutional as in violation of the First Amendment a state statute which provided for reading without comment five verses of the Old Testament at the opening of each public-school day. No issue was raised under the state Constitution. The Supreme Court held that it lacked jurisdiction because of the plaintiff's lack of standing and was not bound by the state court's willingness to consider the case on the merits. One plaintiff was the father of a child in school, but the child had graduated before the appeal reached the Supreme Court. Mr. Justice Jackson gave as further reasons for lack of standing: "There is no assertion that she was injured or even offended . . . or that she was compelled to accept, approve or confess agreement with any dogma or creed or even to listen when the Scriptures were read. . . . [There] was a . . . stipulation that any student, at his own or his parents' request, could be excused. . . . [No] such excuse was asked." As to the plaintiffs' standing as taxpayers he stated in part: "There is no allegation that this activity is supported by any separate tax or paid for from any particular appropriation or that it adds any sum whatever to the cost of conducting the school. No information is given as to

what kind of taxes are paid by appellants and there is no averment that the Bible reading increases any tax they do pay or that as taxpayers they are, will, or possibly can be out of pocket because of it." The Court, relying on Massachusetts v. Mellon, 262 U.S. 447, 43 S. Ct. 597, 67 L. Ed. 1078 (1923), held that there is no "case or controversy" where the taxpayer cannot show any immediate special pecuniary injury. The Everson case was distinguished on the ground that "Everson showed a measurable appropriation or disbursement of school-district funds occasioned solely by the activities complained of." Justices Douglas, Reed and Burton dissented. They contended that Massachusetts v. Mellon does not limit the jurisdiction of the Court in cases involving state statutes where the state was willing to take the case on the merits.

See also State ex rel. Sholes v. University of Minnesota, 236 Minn. 452, 54 N.W.2d 122 (1952) (mandamus to compel Board of Regents to adopt rules prohibiting use of University property for religious teaching denied on ground that before seeking mandamus against a "body corporate" demand must first be made of the defendant to grant the relief requested).

For the view that the Court's decisions in the school prayer and Bible reading cases do not imply an expansion of the concept of "standing" so as to permit any member of the public to ask for judicial enforcement of the establishment clause, see Black, Religion, "Standing," and the Supreme Court's Role, 13 J. Pub. L. 459 (1964). See also Dorsen, The Arthur Garfield Hays Civil Liberties Conference: Public Aid to Parochial Schools and Standing to Bring Suit, 12 Buffalo L. Rev. 35 (1962); Davis, Standing to Sue in Religion Cases, 110 Cong. Rec. 3258-3262 (1964); Sutherland, Due Process and Disestablishment, 62 Harv. L. Rev. 1306 (1949). On standing generally see, Jaffe, Judicial Control of Administrative Action, chs. 12 and 13 (1965).

REFERENCES

On the subject of Bible reading and school prayers generally, see Freund and Ulich, Religion and the Public Schools: The Legal Issue, The Educational Issue (1965); Blanshard, Religion and the Schools: The Great Controversy (1963); Rodes, The Passing of Non-Sectarianism: Some Reflections on the School Prayer Case, 38 Notre Dame Law. 115 (1963); Pollak, Public Prayers in Public Schools, 77 Harv. L. Rev. 62 (1963); Kauper, Schempp and Sherbert: Studies in Neutrality and Accommodation, in Gianella (ed.), 1963 Religion and the Public Order 3 (1964); Brown, Quis Custodiet Ipsos Custodes? — The School Prayer Cases, 1963 Supreme Court Rev. 1; Sutherland, Establishment According to Engel, 76 Harv. L. Rev. 25 (1962); Kurland, The Regents' Prayer Case: "Full of Sound and Fury Signifying . . . ," 1962 Supreme Court Rev. 1; Cahn, On Government and Prayer, 37 N.Y.U.L. Rev. 981 (1962); Hanft, The Prayer Decisions, 42 N.C.L. Rev. 567 (1964); Rice, The Supreme Court and Public Prayer: The Need for Restraint (1964); Religion and the Constitution — A Symposium on the Supreme Court Decisions on Prayer and Bible Reading in the Public Schools, 13 J. Pub. L. 247 (1964); Boles, The Bible, Religion, and the Public Schools (rev. ed. 1963); Choper, Religion in the Public Schools: A Proposed Constitutional Standard, 47 Minn. L. Rev. 329 (1963); Kauper, Law and Public Opinion, in Walter (ed.), Religion and the State University 69 (1958); Weclew, The Establishment Clause and "Coercion," 47 Marq. L. Rev. 359 (1963-1964); Note, School Prayer and the Becker Amendment, 53 Geo. L.J. 192 (1964) (Appendix at 224 collects state rulings on religious observances in public schools); Harrison, The Bible, the Constitution and Public Education, 29 Tenn. L. Rev. 363 (1962) (case study of practices in Knox County, Tennessee).

On Mr. Justice Douglas' position see Louisell, The Man and the Mountain: Douglas on Religious Freedom, 73 Yale L.J. 975 (1964); Manning, The Douglas Concept of God in Government, 39 Wash. L. Rev. 47 (1964).

5. *Flag Salute and Other Compulsory Practices Offensive to Certain Religions*

In Minersville School District v. Gobitis, 310 U.S. 586, 60 S. Ct. 1010, 84 L. Ed. 1375 (1940), the Supreme Court upheld the expulsion of Jehovah's Witnesses' children for refusing to salute the flag, as they were required to do by state law, on the ground that the salute was contrary to their religious belief. The opinion, written by Mr. Justice Frankfurter, and a dissent written by Mr. Justice Stone were the subject of a great deal of public debate. In West Virginia State Board of Education v. Barnette, 319 U.S. 624, 63 S. Ct. 1178, 87 L. Ed. 1628 (1943), the issue came up a second time. Mr. Justice Jackson's opinion, overruling the Court's Gobitis decision, formulated the principal issue as whether the state has power to compel affirmance of a belief and reasoned that the clear and present danger test is just as applicable where the government compels affirmance of a belief as where it seeks to suppress one. The opinion rejected the view of the Gobitis case that the matter was one within the special province of local school boards and legislatures and one in which the Court had little competence, and asserted that in matters of fundamental constitutional rights the Court acted by virtue of its commission and not its competence. Mr. Justice Jackson concluded:

"Lastly, and this is the very heart of the Gobitis opinion, it reasons that 'National unity is the basis of national security', that the authorities have 'the right to select appropriate means for its attainment', and hence reaches the conclusion that such compulsory measures toward 'national unity' are constitutional. Id. at 595. Upon the verity of this assumption depends our answer in this case.

"National unity as an end which officials may foster by persuasion and example is not in question. The problem is whether under our Constitution compulsion as here employed is a permissible means for its achievement.

"Struggles to coerce uniformity of sentiment in support of some end thought essential to their time and country have been waged by many good as well as by evil men. Nationalism is a relatively recent phenomenon but at other times and places the ends have been racial or territorial security, support of a dynasty or regime, and particular plans for saving souls. As first and moderate methods to attain unity have failed, those bent on its accomplishment must resort to an ever-increasing severity. As governmental pressure toward unity becomes greater, so strife becomes more bitter as to whose unity it shall be. Probably no deeper division of our people could proceed from any provocation than from finding it necessary to choose what doctrine and whose program public educational officials shall compel youth to unite in embracing. Ultimate futility of such attempts to compel coherence is the lesson of every such effort from the Roman drive to stamp out Christianity as a disturber of its pagan unity, the Inquisition, as a means to religious and dynastic unity, the Siberian exiles as a means to Russian unity, down to the fast failing efforts of our present totalitarian enemies. Those who begin coercive elimination of dissent soon find themselves exterminating dissenters. Compulsory unification of opinion achieves only the unanimity of the graveyard.

"It seems trite but necessary to say that the First Amendment to our Constitution was designed to avoid these ends by avoiding these beginnings. There is no mysticism in the American concept of the State or of the nature or origin of its authority. We set up government by the consent of the governed, and the Bill of Rights denies those in power any legal opportunity to coerce that consent. Authority here is to be controlled by public opinion, not public opinion by authority.

"The case is made difficult not because the principles of its decision are obscure but because the flag involved is our own. Nevertheless, we apply the limitations of the Constitution with no fear that freedom to be intellectually and spiritually diverse or even contrary will disintegrate the social organization. To believe that patriotism will not flourish if patriotic ceremonies are voluntary and spontaneous instead of a compulsory routine is to make an unflattering estimate of the appeal of our institutions to free minds. We can have intellectual individualism and the rich cultural diversities that we owe to exceptional minds only at the price of occasional eccentricity and abnormal attitudes. When they are so harmless to others or to the State as those we deal with here, the price is not too great. But freedom to differ is not limited to things that do not matter much. That would be a mere shadow of freedom. The test of its substance is the right to differ as to things that touch the heart of the existing order.

"If there is any fixed star in our constitutional constellation, it is that no official, high or petty, can prescribe what shall be orthodox in politics, nationalism, religion, or other matters of opinion or force citizens to confess by word or act their faith therein. If there are any circumstances which permit an exception, they do not now occur to us.[19]

"We think the action of the local authorities in compelling the flag salute and pledge transcends constitutional limitations on their power and invades the sphere of intellect and spirit which it is the purpose of the First Amendment to our Constitution to reserve from all official control." 319 U.S. at 640-642.

Mr. Justice Frankfurter, dissenting, said in part:

---

[19] The Nation may raise armies and compel citizens to give military service. Selective Draft Law Cases, 245 U.S. 366. It follows, of course, that those subject to military discipline are under many duties and may not claim many freedoms that we hold inviolable as to those in civilian life.

"We are told that a flag salute is a doubtful substitute for adequate understanding of our institutions. The states that require such a school exercise do not have to justify it as the only means for promoting good citizenship in children, but merely as one of diverse means for accomplishing a worthy end. We may deem it a foolish measure, but the point is that this Court is not the organ of government to resolve doubts as to whether it will fulfill its purpose. Only if there be no doubt that any reasonable mind could entertain can we deny to the states the right to resolve doubts their way and not ours.

"That which to the majority may seem essential for the welfare of the state may offend the consciences of a minority. But, so long as no inroads are made upon the actual exercise of religion by the minority, to deny the political power of the majority to enact laws concerned with civil matters, simply because they may offend the consciences of a minority, really means that the consciences of a minority are more sacred and more enshrined in the Constitution than the consciences of a majority.

"We are told that symbolism is a dramatic but primitive way of communicating ideas. Symbolism is inescapable. Even the most sophisticated live by symbols. But it is not for this Court to make psychological judgments as to the effectiveness of a particular symbol in inculcating concededly indispensable feelings, particularly if the state happens to see fit to utilize the symbol that represents our heritage and our hopes. And surely only flippancy could be responsible for the suggestion that constitutional validity of a requirement to salute our flag implies equal validity of a requirement to salute a dictator. The significance of a symbol lies in what it represents. To reject the swastika does not imply rejection of the Cross. And so it bears repetition to say that it mocks reason and denies our whole history to find in the allowance of a requirement to salute our flag on fitting occasions the seeds of sanction for obeisance to a leader. To deny the power to employ educational symbols is to say that the state's educational system may not stimulate the imagination because this may lead to unwise stimulation. . . .

"To talk about 'clear and present danger' as the touchstone of allowable educational policy by the states whenever school curricula may impinge upon the boundaries of individual conscience, is to take a felicitous phrase out of the context of the particular situation where it arose and for which it was adapted. Mr. Justice Holmes used the phrase 'clear and present danger' in a case involving mere speech as a means by which alone to accomplish sedition in time of war. By that phrase he meant merely to indicate that, in view of the protection given to utterance by the First Amendment, in order that mere utterance may not be proscribed, 'the words used are used in such circumstances and are of such a nature as to create a clear and present danger that they will bring about the substantive evils that Congress has a right to prevent.' Schenck v. United States, 249 U.S. 47, 52. The 'substantive evils' about which he was speaking were inducement of insubordination in the military and naval forces of the United States and obstruction of enlistment while the country was at war. He was not enunciating a formal rule that there can be no restriction upon speech and, still less, no compulsion where conscience balks, unless imminent danger would thereby be wrought 'to our institutions or our government.'

"The flag salute exercise has no kinship whatever to the oath tests so odious in history. For the oath test was one of the instruments for suppressing heretical beliefs. Saluting the flag suppresses no belief nor curbs it. Children and their parents may believe what they please, avow their belief and practice it. It is not even remotely suggested that the requirement for saluting the flag involves the slightest restriction against the fullest opportunity on the part both of the children and of their parents to disavow as publicly as they choose to do so the meaning that others attach to the gesture of salute. All channels of affirmative free expression are open to both children and parents. Had we before us any act of the state putting the slightest curbs upon such free expression, I should not lag behind any member of this Court in striking down such an invasion of the right to freedom of thought and freedom of speech protected by the Constitution." 319 U.S. at 661-664.

NOTES

1. See Manwaring, Render unto Caesar: The Flag-Salute Controversy, (1962), reviewed by Roche, 30 U. Chi. L. Rev. 406 (1963). See also Matter of Lewis v. Allen, 5 Misc. 2d 68, 159 N.Y.S.2d 807 (1957), aff'd, 11 A.D.2d 447, 207 N.Y.S.2d 862 (3d Dept. 1960), aff'd, 14 N.Y.2d 867, 252 N.Y.S.2d 80 (1964), cert. den., 379 U.S. 923 (1964), in which the petitioners sought to compel the Commissioner of Education to revoke a regulation recommending the use of the pledge of allegiance including the words "under God." The petition was denied on the ground that a voluntary pledge does not violate Constitutional prohibitions. The words "under God" were added to the pledge of allegiance to the flag by Act of Congress June 14, 1954, 68 Stat. 249, 36 U.S.C. §172. See further Sheldon v. Fannin, 221 F. Supp. 766 (D. Ariz. 1963) (forcing students to stand during singing of National Anthem where this violates their religious beliefs held unconstitutional interference with "free exercise," citing Barnette).

2. Instances other than those involving compulsory flag salute where children have objected to public school requirements on religious grounds are: (1) Absence from school on religious holiday: Commonwealth v. Bey, 166 Pa. Super. 136, 70 A.2d 693 (1950), noted in 98 U. Pa. L. Rev. 923 (1950) (Moslem students absent on Friday; held prosecution under compulsory education law constitutional). See also Wooley v. Spalding, 293 S.W.2d 563 (Ct. App. Ky. 1956) (enjoining the school board from stopping the operation of school buses on non-legal religious holidays). (2) Compulsory dancing lessons: Hardwick v. Board of School Trustees, 54 Cal. App. 696, 205 Pac. 49 (1921) (held unreasonable). (3) Compulsory military training: Hamilton v. Regents of the Univ. of Calif., 293 U.S. 245, 55 S. Ct. 197, 79 L. Ed. 343 (1934); Hanauer v. Elkins, 217 Md. 213, 141 A.2d 903 (1958), app. dis., 358 U.S. 643 (1959) (students voluntarily attending state-maintained university cannot refuse to accept military training which

offended their religious beliefs). (4) Course requirements: See, N.Y. Educ. Laws §3204(5) (exempting certain pupils from attending hygiene courses); Starr, Religion, Science and the Curriculum, in Ladd and Sayres (eds.), Social Aspects of Education: A Casebook 330 (1962); Willgoose, Health, Welfare, and Religious Freedom, 73 School and Society 198 (March 31, 1951). See also Univ. of Md. v. Coale, 165 Md. 224, 167 Atl. 54 (1933). In Miami Military Institute v. Leff, 129 Misc. 481, 220 N.Y. Supp. 799 (1926), it was held that a private school may not compel Jewish students to attend Christian churches.

C. Police Regulation

1. General

UNITED STATES v. BALLARD
322 U.S. 78, 64 S. Ct. 882, 88 L. Ed. 1148 (1944)

[Guy, Edna, and Donald Ballard were indicted for conspiracy and mail fraud in connection with organizing a religious sect known as the I Am movement. The indictment charged that the defendants falsely represented with the intent to defraud certain religious doctrines and beliefs, well knowing the falsity thereof, in order to convert money and valuable property obtained from their followers for their own benefit. Some of the beliefs were as follows: (1) That Guy Ballard, alias Saint Germain, and the other Ballards, had been selected as divine messengers to transmit the words of the alleged divine entity Saint Germain to mankind under teachings commonly known as the I Am movement; (2) that by reason of their supernatural attainments they could cure persons of diseases either curable or incurable and had in fact cured hundreds of persons. With the acquiescence of both sides the charge to the jury eliminated the question of truth and falsity of the religious belief. The District Court presented the issue as follows: "Did these defendants honestly and in good faith believe these things? If they did they should be acquitted." Defendants were convicted. The Court of Appeals reversed on the ground that the allegations in the indictment required a finding by the jury that at least some of the representations were false. Defendants attacked the constitutionality of the indictment as violative of the guarantees of free exercise of religion extended by the First and Fourteenth Amendments. They also attacked the charge to the jury as error on the theory that it amounted to an amendment of the indictment.]

Mr. Justice Douglas delivered the opinion of the Court. . . .

[We] do not agree that the truth or verity of respondents' religious doctrines or beliefs should have been submitted to the jury. Whatever this particular indictment might require, the First Amendment precludes such a course, as the United States seems to concede. "The law knows no heresy, and is committed to the support of no dogma, the establishment of no sect." Watson v. Jones, 13 Wall. 679, 728. The First Amendment has a dual aspect. It not only "forestalls compulsion by law of the acceptance of any creed or the practice of any form of worship" but also "safeguards the free exercise of the chosen form of religion." Cantwell v. Connecticut, 310 U.S. 296, 303. "Thus the Amendment embraces two concepts, — freedom to believe and freedom to act. The first is absolute but, in the nature of things, the second cannot be." Id., pp. 303-304. Freedom of thought, which includes freedom of religious belief, is basic in a society of free men. Board of Education v. Barnette, 319 U.S. 624. It embraces the right to maintain theories of life and of death and of the hereafter which are rank heresy to followers of the orthodox faiths. Heresy trials are foreign to our Constitution. Men may believe what they cannot prove. They may not be put to the proof of their religious doctrines or beliefs. Religious experiences which are as real as life to some may be incomprehensible to others. Yet the fact that they may be beyond the ken of mortals does not mean that they can be made suspect before the law. Many take their gospel from the New Testament. But it would hardly be supposed that they could be tried before a jury charged with the duty of determining whether those teachings contained false representations. The miracles of the New Testament, the Divinity of Christ, life after death, the power of prayer are deep in the religious convictions of many. If one could be sent to jail because a jury in a hostile environment found those teachings false, little indeed would be left of religious freedom. The Fathers of the Constitution were not unaware of the varied and extreme views of religious sects, of the violence of disagreement among them, and of the lack of any one religious creed on which all men would agree. They fashioned a charter of government which envisaged the widest possible toleration of conflicting views. Man's relation to his God was made no concern of the state. He was granted the right to worship as he pleased and to answer to no man for the verity of his religious views. The religious views espoused by respondents might seem incredible, if not preposterous, to most people. But if those doctrines are subject to trial before a jury charged with finding their truth or falsity, then the same can be done with the religious beliefs of any sect. When the triers of fact undertake that task, they enter a forbidden domain. The First Amendment does not select any one group or any one type of religion for preferred treatment. It puts them all in that position. Murdock v. Pennsylvania, 319 U.S. 105. As stated in Davis v. Beason, 133 U.S. 333, 342, "With man's relations to his Maker and the obligations he may think they impose, and the manner in which an expression shall be made by him of his belief on those subjects, no interference can be permitted, provided always the laws of society, designed to secure its peace and prosperity, and the morals of its people, are not interfered with." See Prince v. Massachusetts, 321 U.S. 158. So we conclude that the District Court ruled properly when it withheld from the jury all questions concerning the truth or falsity of the religious beliefs or doctrines of respondents. . . .

[The case was reversed and remanded to the Court of Appeals to consider other grounds urged by the defendants which that court had not reached.]

MR. CHIEF JUSTICE STONE, dissenting:

I am not prepared to say that the constitutional guaranty of freedom of religion affords immunity from criminal prosecution for the fraudulent procurement of money by false statements as to one's religious experiences, more than it renders polygamy or libel immune from criminal prosecution. Davis v. Beason, 133 U.S. 333; see Chaplinsky v. New Hampshire, 315 U.S. 568, 572; cf. Patterson v. Colorado, 205 U.S. 454, 462; Near v. Minnesota, 283 U.S. 697, 715. I cannot say that freedom of thought and worship includes freedom to procure money by making knowingly false statements about one's religious experiences. To go no further, if it were shown that a defendant in this case had asserted as a part of the alleged fraudulent scheme, that he had physically shaken hands with St. Germain in San Francisco on a day named, or that, as the indictment here alleges, by the exertion of his spiritual power he "had in fact cured . . . hundreds of persons afflicted with diseases and ailments," I should not doubt that it would be open to the Government to submit to the jury proof that he had never been in San Francisco and that no such cures had ever been effected. In any event I see no occasion for making any pronouncement on this subject in the present case. . . .

With the assent of the prosecution and the defense the trial judge withdrew from the consideration of the jury the question whether the alleged religious experiences had in fact occurred, but submitted to the jury the single issue whether petitioners honestly believed that they had occurred, with the instruction that if the jury did not so find, then it should return a verdict of guilty. . . . The state of one's mind is a fact as capable of fraudulent misrepresentation as is one's physical condition or the state of his bodily health. See Seven Cases v. United States, 239 U.S. 510, 517; cf. Durland v. United States, 161 U.S. 306, 313. . . . Since the indictment and the evidence support the conviction, it is irrelevant whether the religious experiences alleged did or did not in fact occur or whether that issue could or could not, for constitutional reasons, have been rightly submitted to the jury. Certainly none of respondents' constitutional rights are violated if they are prosecuted for the fraudulent procurement of money by false representations as to their beliefs, religious or otherwise. . . .

[Justices Roberts and Frankfurter joined in the Stone opinion. Mr. Justice Jackson dissented in a separate opinion.]

NOTES

1. When the case reached the Supreme Court for a second time, the indictment was ordered dismissed on the ground that women were intentionally and systematically excluded from the federal grand jury panel. The Court again refused to

pass on the central issue of whether the mail may be used to obtain money by fraud when the fraud is a false claim of belief concerning religion. Ballard v. United States, 329 U.S. 187, 67 S. Ct. 261, 91 L. Ed. 181 (1946).

2. Compare Brown v. Father Divine, 163 Misc. 796, 298 N.Y. Supp. 642 (1937), in which a follower of Father Divine sought appointment of a receiver for the rents and profits of the property of the Peace Mission on the ground that the money contributed had not been deposited in the Heavenly Treasure. The plaintiff was successful.

3. Employees will not be excused from joining a union in compliance with a union shop contract because of religious scruples. See Wicks v. Southern Pac. Co., 231 F.2d 130 (9th Cir. 1956), cert. den., 351 U.S. 946 (1956); Note, 3 St. Louis U.L.J. 293 (1955); Otten v. Baltimore and O.R. Co., 205 F.2d 58 (2d Cir. 1953), where Judge Learned Hand had the following to say: "The First Amendment protects one against action by the government . . . but it gives no one the right to insist that in the pursuit of their own interests others must conform their conduct to his own religious necessities. . . . We must accommodate our idiosyncrasies, religious as well as secular, to the compromises necessary in communal life; and we can hope for no reward for the sacrifices this may require beyond our satisfaction from within, or our expectations of a better world." 205 F.2d at 61.

It has also been held that a corporation doing religious work is not exempt from complying with the Fair Labor Standards Act. Mitchell v. Pilgrim Holiness Church Corp., 210 F.2d 879 (7th Cir. 1954), cert. den., 347 U.S. 1013 (1954); Note, 3 St. Louis U.L.J. 282 (1955).

4. In Cabinet v. Shapiro, 17 N.J. Super. 540, 86 A.2d 314 (1952), defendants, a rabbi and a corporation formed to enforce Hebrew Kosher Law, distributed circulars stating that the plaintiff's chickens were non-Kosher. The charge was based on the fact that plaintiff did not kill poultry under supervision of defendant rabbi as required by an ordinance of the Jewish community. Defendants sought to dismiss plaintiff's libel suit on the ground that the court lacked power to interfere in matters of a purely ecclesiastical nature. The court in deciding that it validly could take jurisdiction stated: "We feel that the principles involved . . . are not of a purely ecclesiastical nature. The civil and property rights of the plaintiffs are involved. The *issur* on which the defendants rely as a defense for their proclamation applies only to animals slaughtered within the City of Atlantic City. There is no allegation that the poultry . . . did not [otherwise] meet all kosher requirements . . . This court does not claim, nor does it have the right, authority or jurisdiction, to declare or to find what is kosher and what is non-kosher . . . We do have the right and the jurisdiction to determine a matter in violation of civil and property rights of a citizen even though such rights involve the fundamental concepts and dogma of the Hebrew religion and law." 17 N.J. Super. at 546-7. See also Cohen v. Eisenberg, 173 Misc. 1089, 19 N.Y.S.2d 678 (Sup. Ct. 1940), aff'd, 260 App. Div. 1014, 24 N.Y.S.2d 1004 (1940); cf. S S & B Live Poultry Corp. v. Kashruth Assoc., 158 Misc. 358, 285 N.Y. Supp. 879 (Sup. Ct., 1936).

5. In Pencovic v. Pencovic, 45 Cal. 2d 97, 287 P.2d 501 (1955), the court held that the head and founder of a religious communal society must pay an increased child-support award, though the communal society would not increase its "gifts" to him to meet the child's increased needs. The court stated: "Although freedom of conscience and the freedom to believe are absolute, the freedom to act is not

. . . Certainly there are few interests of greater importance to the state than the proper discharge by parents of their duties to their children, and the Constitution does not compel the subordination of the statutory duty of a parent . . . to a rule of religious conduct prohibiting gainful employment." 45 Cal. 2d at 103.

6. Among state police regulations that have been challenged on religious grounds are:

(1) *Statutes forbidding fortune-telling and spiritualism or vagrancy laws construed to cover these practices.* State v. De Laney, 122 Atl. 890 (N.J. 1923) (charter of church permitted teaching of spiritualism; freedom of religion defense upheld); People v. Miller, 46 N.Y.S.2d 206 (1943) (statute specifically exempted spiritualists acting in good faith and without personal fee; client made contribution; defense upheld); for an earlier case prior to the statute in which a spiritualist was convicted, see People v. Ashley, 184 App. Div. 520, 172 N.Y. Supp. 282 (1918). To the same effect see People v. Neitzel, 69 Wash. 567, 125 Pac. 939 (1912); City of St. Louis v. Hellscher, 295 Mo. 293, 242 S.W. 652 (1922); McMasters v. State, 21 Okla. Crim. 318, 207 Pac. 566 (1922). For full description and historical background see Rubenstein, A Treatise on Contemporary Religious Jurisprudence (1948).

(2) *Liquor prohibition.* The granting of an exemption for sacramental wine has been upheld against challenges that it is discriminatory or an aid to religion. See People v. Marquis, 291 Ill. 121, 125 N.E. 757 (1919); cf. State v. Kramer, 49 S.D. 56, 206 N.W. 468 (1925) (refusal by a state to exempt an unlimited quantity for sacramental purposes has been held not to violate freedom of religion).

(3) *Building and zoning laws.* Spieth v. City of Pomona (Sup. Ct. Cal., Los Angeles, Jan. 15, 1953) (City Planning Commission and City Council may not discriminatorily deny building permit to Jehovah's Witnesses because of disagreement with the sect's tenets); Columbus Park Congregation of Jehovah's Witnesses, Inc. v. Board of Appeals of Chicago, 25 Ill. 2d 65, 182 N.E.2d 722 (1962) ("The right of freedom of religion, and other first amendment freedoms, rise above mere property rights. They rise 'far above mere public inconvenience, annoyance, or unrest.'" Board's denial of special use permit to plaintiffs was "arbitrary and capricious and . . . denied their constitutional rights."). See also Congregation Temple Israel v. City of Creve Coeur, 320 S.W.2d 451 (Mo. 1959) (free exercise argument); North Shore Unitarian Soc. v. Village of Plandome, 200 Misc. 524, 109 N.Y.S.2d 803 (Sup. Ct. Nassau Co. 1951) (discrimination argument); State ex rel. Synod of Ohio of Lutheran Church v. Joseph, 139 Ohio St. 229, 22 Ohio Op. 241, 39 N.E.2d 515, 138 A.L.R. 1274 (1942) (no substantial relation to public health, safety, morals or general welfare).

It has been held, however, that churches may be excluded from certain residential zones. See Latter-Day Saints v. City of Porterville, 90 Cal. App. 2d 656, 203 P.2d 823 (1949), app. dis., 338 U.S. 805 (1949). But see North Shore Unitarian Society v. Village of Plandome, 200 Misc. 524, 109 N.Y.S.2d 803 (Sup. Ct. 1951); Bishop of Reno v. Hill, 59 Nev. 231, 90 P.2d 217 (1939); State ex rel. Synod of Ohio v. Joseph, 139 Ohio St. 229, 39 N.E.2d 515 (1942). For a tendency to set a standard which requires that the "benefit to the public health, morals, general welfare and safety outweighs the restriction which such regulation places upon the right of freedom of worship and assembly," see Board of Zoning Appeals v. Decatur Ind. Co. of Jehovah's Witnesses, 233 Ind. 83, 91, 117 N.E.2d 115, 119 (1954) (setback regulation valid but off-street parking requirement held contrary to First and Fourteenth Amendments). See also State ex rel. Tampa, Fla. v. City of Tampa, 48 So. 2d 78 (Sup. Ct. Fla. 1950). In general, see Note, Zoning Laws and the Church, 27 St. John's L. Rev. 93 (1952); Brindel, Zoning Out Religious Institutions, 32 Notre Dame Law. 627 (1957); Note, Churches and Zoning, 70 Harv. L. Rev. 1428 (1957); Curry, Public Regulation of the Religious Use of Land: A Detailed and Critical Analysis of a Hundred Court Cases (1964); Religious Institutions and Values: A Legal Survey (1955-1957), 33 Notre Dame Law. 416, Zoning, 418-420 (1958); [same title] (1958-1959), 35 Notre Dame Law. 405, 406-412 (1960); [same title] (1960-1962), 37 Notre Dame Law. 649, 656-660 (1962); [same title] (1963-1964), 39 Notre Dame Law. 427, 435-439 (1964). Cf. Note, Zoning, Aesthetics, and the First Amendment, 64 Colum. L. Rev. 81 (1964).

For a case holding valid a restrictive covenant excluding churches, despite previous waiver of restriction for Catholic church, see Willis v. New Orleans East Unit of Jehovah Witnesses, Inc., 156 So. 2d 310 (La. App. 4th Cir. 1963), rev. den., 245 La. 88, 157 So. 2d 232 (1963). On parochial school exclusion see Trinity Evangelical Lutheran Church v. Board of Adjustment of Borough of Morris Plains, 72 N.J. Super. 425, 179 A.2d 45 (1962) (under statute proscribing zoning discrimination between public and private day schools, private school cannot reasonably be excluded from district where public school could be located). Cf. St. Cassian's Catholic Church v. Allen, 40 N.J. 46, 190 A.2d 667 (1963); St. John's Roman Catholic Church Corp. v. Town of Darien, 149 Conn. 712, 184 A.2d 42 (1962) (where zoning affecting private schools is functional equivalent of other regulations which affect only public schools, applying zoning laws to private schools only is not discriminatory).

7. Many health regulations have also been challenged on constitutional grounds. The following are examples:

(1) *Prohibition of spiritual healing.* For an account of the controversy subsequent to the founding of the Christian Science movement and the eventual recognition of Christian Science healing in most states, see 2 Stokes, Church and State in the United States, 322-325 (1950). For report on present legal and professional status of Christian Science healing, see N.Y. Times, June 3, 1952. See generally, Cawley, Criminal Liability in Faith Healing, 39 Minn. L. Rev. 48 (1954). The religious right to heal by prayer does not extend so far as to compel a state to permit the practice of medicine for a fee to an unqualified and unlicensed physician. People v. Handzik, 410 Ill. 295, 102 N.E.2d 340 (1951); cert. den., 343 U.S. 927 (1952); People v. Estep, 346 Ill. App. 132, 104 N.E.2d 562, writ of error dis., 413 Ill. 437, 109 N.E.2d 762 (1952), cert. den., 345 U.S. 970 (1953); Fealy v. City of Birmingham, 15 Ala. App. 367, 73 So. 296 (1916); Smith v. People, 51 Colo. 270, 117 Pac. 612 (1911); State v. Verbon, 167 Wash. 140, 8 P.2d 1083 (1932); State v. Miller, 59 N.D. 286, 229 N.W. 569 (1930); People v. Vogelgesang, 221 N.Y. 290, 116 N.E. 977 (1917); State v. Buswell, 40 Neb. 158, 58 N.W. 728 (1894); People v. Cole, 219 N.Y. 98, 113 N.E. 790 (1916); State v. Marble, 72 Ohio St. 21, 73 N.E. 1063 (1905). The problem also arises in prosecution of parents for breach of duty imposed by statute to furnish recognized medical care to a child. The defense that medical care contradicts the defendant's religious beliefs, such as Divine Healing through prayer, is not accepted on ground that the law is directed at acts which the state could regulate under the police power, not beliefs. People v. Pierson, 176

N.Y. 201, 68 N.E. 243 (1903); State v. Chenoweth, 163 Ind. 94, 71 N.E. 197 (1904); Owens v. State, 6 Okla. Crim. 110, 116 Pac. 345, 36 L.R.A.N.S. 633 (1911); Beck v. State, 29 Okla. Crim. 240, 233 Pac. 495 (1925); see also Mitchell v. Davis, 205 S.W.2d 812 (Tex. Civ. App. 1947) (mother loses custody of dying child); Note, 12 A.L.R.2d 1042. For other custody cases involving the elements of religious upbringing and health and well-being of child, see supra.

(2) *Vaccination and physical examination.* The well-established power of a state to require vaccination, Jacobson v. Massachusetts, 197 U.S. 11, 25 S. Ct. 358, 49 L. Ed. 643 (1905); Zucht v. King, 260 U.S. 174, 43 S. Ct. 24, 67 L. Ed. 194 (1922), has been challenged specifically on the ground that it interferes with religious freedom. The cases on the whole involve prosecution of parents under the compulsory education laws, for failing to vaccinate children as a condition for admission to the public school: Seubold v. Fort Smith Special School District, 218 Ark. 560, 237 S.W.2d 884 (1951); Anderson v. State, 84 Ga. App. 259, 65 S.E.2d 848 (1951); Vonnegut v. Baun, 206 Ind. 172, 188 N.E. 677 (1934); Mosier v. Barren County Board of Health, 308 Ky. 829, 215 S.W.2d 967 (1948); Commonwealth v. Green, 268 Mass. 585, 168 N.E. 101 (1929); State v. Drew, 89 N.H. 54, 192 Atl. 629 (1937); Sadlock v. Board of Education, 137 N.J. 85, 58 A.2d 218 (1948); In re Whitmore, 47 N.Y.S.2d 143 (1944); Viemeister v. White, 179 N.Y. 235, 72 N.E. 97 (1904); City of New Braunfels v. Waldschmidt, 109 Tex. 302, 207 S.W. 303 (1918); see also, Walker v. Dallas Independant School District, 75 F. Supp. 552 (N.D. Tex., 1948). Cf. Kolbeck v. Kramer, 84 N.J. Super. 569, 202 A.2d 889 (1964), noted supra, (state university which exempted Christian Scientists from vaccination requirements could not require membership in organized religious group as a condition for religious exemption from vaccination), jud. modified and preserved for declaratory value to plaintiff, 46 N.J. 46, 214 A.2d 408 (1965) (evidence sustained finding that plaintiff had objected to vaccination on religious grounds). For a case in which the court upheld a requirement of physical examination and report by a physician as prerequisite of admission to public school against religious freedom objections, see Streich v. Board of Education, 34 S.D. 169, 147 N.W. 779 (1914). In Peterson v. Widule, 157 Wis. 641, 147 N.W. 966 (1914), the court held that it was not a violation of freedom of religion for a state to require examination for venereal disease prior to obtaining a marriage license.

(3) *Blood transfusions.* For cases granting application for permission to administer blood transfusions though patient and close relatives object on religious grounds, see Application of President and Directors of Georgetown College, Inc., 331 F.2d 1000, rehearing en banc denied 331 F.2d 1010 (D.C. Cir. 1964), cert. den. (sub nom. Jones v. President, etc.), 377 U.S. 978 (1964); Raleigh Fitkin–Paul Morgan Memorial Hospital v. Anderson, 42 N.J. 421, 201 A.2d 537 (1964), cert. den., 377 U.S. 985 (1964); Note, Transfusions Ordered for Dying Woman Over Religious Objections, 113 U. Pa. L. Rev. 290 (1964). But cf. In re Estate of Brooks, 32 Ill. 2d 361, 205 N.E.2d 435 (1965) (distinguishing Georgetown College and Anderson cases). For discussion, see Note, The Refused Blood Transfusion: An Ultimate Challenge for Law and Morals, 10 Natural L. For. 202 (1965). See also State v. Perricone, 37 N.J. 463, 181 A.2d 751 (1962), cert. den., 371 U.S. 890 (1962) (Jehovah's Witness parents held guilty of child neglect for refusing consent to transfusion despite statute guaranteeing right to have ill child treated "in

accordance with the religious tenets of any church," N.J. Stat. Ann. 9:6-1.1); In the Matter of Santos v. Goldstein, 16 App. Div. 2d 755, 227 N.Y.S.2d 450 (1st Dept. 1962), motion for leave to appeal dismissed for lack of jurisdiction, 12 N.Y.2d 672, 233 N.Y.S.2d 465 (1962) (parents' refusal of consent to blood transfusion warrants finding child "neglected" within meaning of Family Court Act §312, Dom. Rel. Ct. Act §2 subd. 17 (g)).

(4) *Snake handling.* Some religious sects make snake handling part of their religious ritual. Statutes outlawing these practices have been upheld. Hill v. State, 38 Ala. App. 404, 88 So. 2d 880 (1956), cert. den., 264 Ala. 697, 88 So. 2d 887 (1956); Harden v. State, 188 Tenn. 17, 216 S.W.2d 708 (1948), noted in 2 Vand. L. Rev. 694 (1949); State v. Massey, 229 N.C. 734, 51 S.E.2d 179 (1949), app. dis. sub nom. Bunn v. N.C., 336 U.S. 942 (1949); Lawson v. Commonwealth, 291 Ky. 437, 164 S.W.2d 972 (1942); cf. Kirk v. Commonwealth, 186 Va. 839, 44 S.E.2d 409 (1947) (defense of religious belief not available in prosecution for death due to snake handling).

(5) *Drugs.* In People v. Woody, 61 Cal. 2d 716, 40 Cal. Rptr. 69, 394 P.2d 813, (1964), the conviction of Navajo Indians for using peyote in religious ceremonies of the Native American Church of the State of California was reversed.

(6) *Fluoridation.* The use of fluoridation has been upheld against objection from members of sects opposed to medication that such a program violates their religious liberty. Baer v. City of Bend, 206 Ore. 221, 292 P.2d 134 (1956); Kraus v. City of Cleveland, 121 N.E.2d 311 (Ohio Ct. App., 1954), aff'd, 163 Ohio St. 559, 127 N.E.2d 609 (1955), app. dis., 351 U.S. 935 (1956), noted in 3 St. Louis U.L.J. 284 (1955).

2. *Sunday Laws*

McGOWAN v. MARYLAND
366 U.S. 420, 81 S. Ct. 1101, 6 L. Ed. 2d 393 (1961)

MR. CHIEF JUSTICE WARREN delivered the opinion of the Court.

The issues in this case concern the constitutional validity of Maryland criminal statutes, commonly known as Sunday Closing Laws or Sunday Blue Laws. These statutes, with exceptions to be noted hereafter, generally proscribe all labor, business and other commercial activities on Sunday. The questions presented are whether the classifications within the statutes bring about a denial of equal protection of the law, whether the laws are so vague as to fail to give reasonable notice of the forbidden conduct and therefore violate due process, and whether the statutes are laws respecting an establishment of religion or prohibiting the free exercise thereof.

Appellants are seven employees of a large discount department store located on a highway in Anne Arundel County, Maryland. They were indicted for the Sunday sale of a three-ring loose-leaf binder, a can of floor wax, a stapler and staples, and a toy submarine in violation of Md. Ann. Code, Art. 27, §521. Generally, this section prohibited, throughout the State, the Sunday sale of all merchandise except the retail sale of tobacco products, confectioneries, milk, bread, fruits, gasoline, oils, greases, drugs and medicines, and newspapers and periodicals. Recently amended, this section also now excepts from the general prohibition the retail sale in Anne Arundel County of all foodstuffs, automobile and boating accessories, flowers, toilet goods, hospital supplies and souvenirs. It now further provides that any retail establishment in Anne Arundel County which does not employ more than one person other than the owner may operate on Sunday.

Although appellants were indicted only under §521, in order properly to consider several of the broad constitutional contentions, we must examine the whole body of Maryland Sunday laws. Several sections of the Maryland statutes are particularly relevant to evaluation of the issues presented. Section 492 of Md. Ann. Code, Art. 27, forbids all persons from doing any work or bodily labor on Sunday and forbids permitting children or servants to work on that day or to engage in fishing, hunting and unlawful pastimes or recreations. The section excepts all works of necessity and charity. Section 522 of Md. Ann. Code, Art. 27, disallows the opening or use of any dancing saloon, opera house, bowling alley or barber shop on Sunday. However, in addition to the exceptions noted above, Md. Ann. Code, Art. 27, §509, exempts, for Anne Arundel County, the Sunday operation of any bathing beach, bathhouse, dancing saloon and amusement park, and activities incident thereto and retail sales of merchandise customarily sold at, or incidental to, the operation of the aforesaid occupations and businesses. Section 90 of Md. Ann. Code, Art. 2B, makes generally unlawful the sale of alcoholic beverages on Sunday. However, this section, and immediately succeeding ones, provide various immunities for the Sunday sale of different kinds of alcoholic beverages, at different hours during the day, by vendors holding different types of licenses, in different political divisions of the State — particularly in Anne Arundel County. See Md. Ann. Code, Art. 2B, §28(a).

The remaining statutory sections concern a myriad of exceptions for various counties, districts of counties, cities and towns throughout the State. Among the activities allowed in certain areas on Sunday are such sports as football, baseball, golf, tennis, bowling, croquet, basketball, lacrosse, soccer, hockey, swimming, softball, boating, fishing, skating, horseback riding, stock car racing and pool or billiards. Other immunized activities permitted in some regions of the State include group singing or playing of musical instruments; the exhibition of motion pictures; dancing; the operation of recreation centers, picnic grounds, swimming pools, skating rinks and miniature golf courses. The taking of oysters and the hunting or killing of game is generally forbidden, but shooting conducted by organized rod and gun clubs is permitted in one county. In some of the subdivisions within the State, the exempted Sunday activities are sanctioned throughout the day; in others, they may not commence until early afternoon or evening; in many, the activities may only be conducted during the afternoon and late in the evening. Certain localities do not permit the allowed Sunday activity to be carried on within one hundred yards of any church where religious services are being held. Local ordinances and regulations concerning certain limited activities supplement the State's statutory scheme. In Anne Arundel County, for example, slot machines, pin-ball machines and bingo may be played on Sunday. . . .

I

Appellants argue that the Maryland statutes violate the "Equal Protection" Clause of the Fourteenth Amendment on several counts. First, they contend that the classifications contained in the statutes concerning which commodities may or may not be sold on Sunday are without rational and substantial relation to the object of the legislation.[2] Specifically, appellants allege that the statutory exemptions for the Sunday sale of the merchandise mentioned above render arbitrary the statute under which they were convicted. Appellants further allege that §521 is capricious because of the exemptions for the operation of the various amusements that have been listed and because slot machines, pin-ball machines, and bingo are legalized and are freely played on Sunday.

The standards under which this proposition is to be evaluated have been set forth many times by this Court. Although no precise formula has been developed, the Court has held that the Fourteenth Amendment permits the States a wide scope of discretion in enacting laws which affect some groups of citizens differently than others. The constitutional safeguard is offended only if the classification rests on grounds wholly irrelevant to the achievement of the State's objective. State legislatures are presumed to have acted within their constitutional power despite the fact that, in practice, their laws result in some inequality. A statutory discrimination will not be set aside if any state of facts reasonably may be conceived to justify it. See Kotch v. Board of River Port Pilot Comm'rs, 330 U.S. 552; Metropolitan Casualty Ins. Co. v. Brownell, 294 U.S. 580; Lindsley v. Natural Carbonic Gas Co., 220 U.S. 61; Atchison, T. & S. F. R. Co. v. Matthews, 174 U.S. 96.[3]

It would seem that a legislature could reasonably find that the Sunday sale

[2] Companion arguments made by appellants are that the exceptions to the Sunday sale's prohibition so undermine the alleged purpose of Sunday as a day of rest as to bear no rational relationship to it and thereby render the statutes violative of due process; that the distinctions drawn by the statutes are so unreasonable as to violate due process.

[3] More recently we declared: "The problem of legislative classification is a perennial one, admitting of no doctrinaire definition. Evils in the same field may be of different dimensions and proportions, requiring different remedies. Or so the legislature may think. Tigner v. Texas, 310 U.S. 141. Or the reform may take one step at a time, addressing itself to the phase of the problem which seems most acute to the legislative mind. Semler v. Dental Examiners, 294 U.S. 608. The legislature may select one phase of one field and apply a remedy there, neglecting the others. A. F. of L. v. American Sash Co., 335 U.S. 538. The prohibition of the Equal Protection Clause goes no further than the *invidious discrimination*." Williamson v. Lee Optical, 348 U.S. 483, 489. (Emphasis added.)

of the exempted commodities was necessary either for the health of the populace or for the enhancement of the recreational atmosphere of the day — that a family which takes a Sunday ride into the country will need gasoline for the automobile and may find pleasant a soft drink or fresh fruit; that those who go to the beach may wish ice cream or some other item normally sold there; that some people will prefer alcoholic beverages or games of chance to add to their relaxation; that newspapers and drug products should always be available to the public.

The record is barren of any indication that this apparently reasonable basis does not exist, that the statutory distinctions are invidious, that local tradition and custom might not rationally call for this legislative treatment. . . .

Secondly, appellants contend that the statutory arrangement which permits only certain Anne Arundel County retailers to sell merchandise essential to, or customarily sold at, or incidental to, the operation of bathing beaches, amusement parks et cetera is contrary to the "Equal Protection" Clause because it discriminates unreasonably against retailers in other Maryland counties. But we have held that the Equal Protection Clause relates to equality between persons as such, rather than between areas and that territorial uniformity is not a constitutional prerequisite. With particular reference to the State of Maryland, we have noted that the prescription of different substantive offenses in different counties is generally a matter for legislative discretion. We find no invidious discrimination here. See Salsburg v. Maryland, [346 U.S. 545].

Thirdly, appellants contend that this same statutory provision, Art. 27, §509, violates the "Equal Protection" Clause because it permits only certain merchants within Anne Arundel County (operators of bathing beaches and amusement parks et cetera) to sell merchandise customarily sold at these places while forbidding its sale by other vendors of this merchandise, such as appellants' employer. Here again, it would seem that a legislature could reasonably find that these commodities, necessary for the health and recreation of its citizens, should only be sold on Sunday by those vendors at the locations where the commodities are most likely to be immediately put to use. . . .

II

Another question presented by appellants is whether Art. 27, §509, which exempts the Sunday retail sale of "merchandise essential to, or customarily sold at, or incidental to, the operation of" bathing beaches, amusement parks et cetera in Anne Arundel County, is unconstitutionally vague. We believe that business people of ordinary intelligence in the position of appellants' employer would be able to know what exceptions are encompassed by the statute either as a matter of ordinary commercial knowledge or by simply making a reasonable investigation at a nearby bathing beach or amusement park within the county. . . .

III

The final questions for decision are whether the Maryland Sunday Closing Laws conflict with the Federal Constitution's provisions for religious liberty. First, appellants contend here that the statutes applicable to Anne Arundel County violate the constitutional guarantee of freedom of religion in that the statutes' effect is to prohibit the free exercise of religion in contravention of the First Amendment, made applicable to the States by the Fourteenth Amendment. But appellants allege only economic injury to themselves; they do not allege any infringement of their own religious freedoms due to Sunday closing. . . . Since the general rule is that "a litigant may only assert his own constitutional rights or immunities," United States v. Raines, 362 U.S. 17, 22, we hold that appellants have no standing to raise this contention. Tileston v. Ullman, 318 U.S. 44, 46. Furthermore, since appellants do not specifically allege that the statutes infringe upon the religious beliefs of the department store's present or prospective patrons, we have no occasion here to consider the standing question of Pierce v. Society of Sisters, 268 U.S. 510, 535-536. Those persons whose religious rights are allegedly impaired by the statutes are not without effective ways to assert these rights. Cf. N.A.A.C.P. v. Alabama, 357 U.S. 449, 459-460; Barrows v. Jackson, 346 U.S. 249, 257. Appellants present no weighty countervailing policies here to cause an exception to our general principles. See United States v. Raines, supra.

Secondly, appellants contend that the statutes violate the guarantee of separation of church and state in that the statutes are laws respecting an esablishment of religion contrary to the First Amendment, made applicable to the States by the Fourteenth Amendment. If the purpose of the "establishment" clause was only to insure protection for the "free exercise" of religion, then what we have said above concerning appellants' standing to raise the "free exercise" contention would appear to be true here. However, the writings of Madison, who was the First Amendment's architect, demonstrate that the establishment of a religion was equally feared because of its tendencies to political tyranny and subversion of civil authority. . . . Appellants here concededly have suffered direct economic injury, allegedly due to the imposition on them of the tenets of the Christian religion. We find that, in these circumstances, these appellants have standing to complain that the statutes are laws respecting an establishment of religion.

The essence of appellants' "establishment" argument is that Sunday is the Sabbath day of the predominant Christian sects; that the purpose of the enforced stoppage of labor on that day is to facilitate and encourage church attendance; that the purpose of setting Sunday as a day of universal rest is to induce people with no religion or people with marginal religious beliefs to join the predominant Christian sects; that the purpose of the atmosphere of tranquility created by Sunday closing is to aid the conduct of church services and religious observance of the sacred day. In substantiating their "establishment" argument, appellants rely on the wording of the present Maryland statutes, on earlier versions of the current Sunday laws and on prior judicial characterizations of these laws by the Maryland Court of Appeals. Although only the constitutionality of §521, the section under which appellants have been convicted, is immediately before us in this litigation, inquiry into the history of Sunday Closing Laws in our country, in addition to an examination of the Maryland Sunday closing statutes in their entirety and of their history, is relevant to the decision of whether the Maryland Sunday law in question is one respecting an establishment of religion. There is no dispute that the original laws which dealt with Sunday labor were motivated by religious forces. But what we must decide is whether present Sunday legislation, having undergone extensive changes from the earliest forms, still retains its religious character.

Sunday Closing Laws go far back into American history, having been brought to the colonies with a background of English legislation dating to the thirteenth century. . . . Observation of [the language of such legislation] reveals clearly that the English Sunday legislation was in aid of the established church.

The American colonial Sunday restrictions arose soon after settlement. Starting in 1650, the Plymouth Colony proscribed servile work, unnecessary travelling, sports, and the sale of alcoholic beverages on the Lord's day and enacted laws concerning church attendance. The Massachusetts Bay Colony and the Connecticut and New Haven Colonies enacted similar prohibitions, some even earlier in the seventeenth century. The religious orientation of the colonial statutes was equally apparent. . . .

But, despite the strongly religious origin of these laws, beginning before the eighteenth century, nonreligious arguments for Sunday closing began to be heard more distinctly and the statutes began to lose some of their totally religious flavor. In the middle 1700's Blackstone wrote, "[T]he keeping one day in the seven holy, as a time of relaxation and refreshment as well as for public worship, is of admirable service to a state considered merely as a civil institution. It humanizes, by the help of conversation and society, the manners of the lower classes; which would otherwise degenerate into a sordid ferocity and savage selfishness of spirit; it enables the industrious workman to pursue his occupation in the ensuing week with health and cheerfulness." 4 Bl. Comm. 63. . . .

More recently, further secular justifications have been advanced for making Sunday a day of rest, a day when people may recover from the labors of the week just passed and may physically and mentally prepare for the week's work to come. . . .

The proponents of Sunday closing legisation are no longer exclusively representatives of religious interests. . . .

Throughout the years, state legislatures have modified, deleted from and added to their Sunday statutes. . . . Almost every State in our country presently has some type of Sunday regulation and over forty possess a relatively comprehensive system. Note, 73 Harv. L. Rev. 732-733; Note, 12 Rutgers L. Rev. 506. Some of our States now enforce their Sunday legislation through Departments of Labor, e.g., 6 S.C. Code Ann. (1952), §64-5. Thus have Sunday laws evolved from the wholly religious sanctions that originally were enacted.

Moreover, litigation over Sunday closing laws is not novel. Scores of cases may be found in the state appellate courts relating to sundry phases of Sunday enactments.[12] Religious objections have been raised there on numerous occasions but sustained only once, in Ex parte Newman, 9 Cal. 502 (1858); and that decision was overruled three years later, in Ex parte Andrews, 18 Cal. 678. . . .

Before turning to the Maryland legislation now here under attack, an investigation of what historical position Sunday Closing Laws have occupied with reference to the First Amendment should be undertaken, Everson v. Board of Education, [330 U.S. 1, 14].

This Court has considered the happenings surrounding the Virginia General Assembly's enactment of "An act for establishing religious freedom," 12 Hening's Statutes of Virginia 84, written by Thomas Jefferson and sponsored by James Madison, as best reflecting the long and intensive struggle for religious freedom in America, as particularly relevant in the search for the First Amendment's meaning. See the opinions in Everson v. Board of Education, supra. . . . In 1799, Virginia pronounced "An act for establishing religious freedom" as "a true exposition of the principles of the bill of rights and constitution," and repealed all subsequently enacted legislation deemed inconsistent with it. 2 Shepherd, Statutes at Large of Virginia, 149. Virginia's statute banning Sunday labor stood. . . .

But in order to dispose of the case before us, we must consider the standards by which the Maryland statutes are to be measured. Here, a brief review of the First Amendment's background proves helpful.

. . . [T]he First Amendment in its final form, did not simply bar a congressional enactment *establishing a church;* it forbade all laws *respecting an establishment of religion.* Thus, this Court has given the Amendment a "broad interpretation . . ." It has found that the First and Fourteenth Amendments afford protection against religious establishment far more extensive than merely to forbid a national or state church. . . .

However, it is equally true that the "Establishment" Clause does not ban federal or state regulation of conduct whose reason or effect merely happens to coincide or harmonize with the tenets of some or all religions. In many instances, the Congress or state legislatures conclude that the general welfare of society, wholly apart from any religious considerations, demands such

---

[12] See cases collected at 50 Am. Jur. 802 et seq.; 24 A.L.R.2d 813 et seq.; 57 A.L.R.2d 975 et seq.

regulation. Thus, for temporal purposes, murder is illegal. And the fact that this agrees with the dictates of the Judaeo-Christian religions while it may disagree with others does not invalidate the regulation. So too with the questions of adultery and polygamy. Davis v. Beason, 133 U.S. 333; Reynolds v. United States, [98 U.S. 145]. The same could be said of theft, fraud, etc., because those offenses were also proscribed in the Decalogue. . . .

In light of the evolution of our Sunday Closing Laws through the centuries, and of their more or less recent emphasis upon secular considerations, it is not difficult to discern that as presently written and administered, most of them, at least, are of a secular rather than of a religious character, and that presently they bear no relationship to establishment of religion as those words are used in the Constitution of the United States.

Throughout this century and longer, both the federal and state governments have oriented their activities very largely toward improvement of the health, safety, recreation and general well-being of our citizens. Numerous laws affecting public health, safety factors in industry, laws affecting hours and conditions of labor of women and children, week-end diversion at parks and beaches, and cultural activities of various kinds, now point the way toward the good life for all. Sunday Closing Laws, like those before us, have become part and parcel of this great governmental concern wholly apart from their original purposes or connotations. The present purpose and effect of most of them is to provide a uniform day of rest for all citizens; the fact that this day is Sunday, a day of particular significance for the dominant Christian sects, does not bar the State from achieving its secular goals. To say that the States cannot prescribe Sunday as a day of rest for these purposes solely because centuries ago such laws had their genesis in religion would give a constitutional interpretation of hostility to the public welfare rather than one of mere separation of church and State.

We now reach the Maryland statutes under review. The title of the major series of sections of the Maryland Code dealing with Sunday closing — Art. 27, §§492-534C — is "Sabbath Breaking"; §492 proscribes work or bodily labor on the "Lord's day," and forbids persons to "profane the Lord's day" by gaming, fishing et cetera; §522 refers to Sunday as the "Sabbath day." As has been mentioned above, many of the exempted Sunday activities in the various localities of the State may only be conducted during the afternoon and late evening; most Christian church services, of course, are held on Sunday morning and early Sunday evening. Finally, as previously noted, certain localities do not permit the allowed Sunday activities to be carried on within one hundred yards of any church where religious services are being held. This is the totality of the evidence of religious purpose which may be gleaned from the face of the present statute and from its operative effect.

The predecessors of the existing Maryland Sunday laws are undeniably religious in origin. . . .

Considering the language and operative effect of the current statutes, we no longer find the blanket prohibition against Sunday work or bodily labor. To the contrary, we find that §521 of Art. 27, the section which appellants violated, permits the Sunday sale of tobaccos and sweets and a long list of sundry articles which we have enumerated above; we find that §509 of Art. 27 permits the Sunday operation of bathing beaches, amusement parks and similar facilities; we find that Art. 2B, §28, permits the Sunday sale of alcoholic beverages, products strictly forbidden by predecessor statutes; we are told that Anne Arundel County allows Sunday bingo and the Sunday playing of pinball machines and slot machines, activities generally condemned by prior Maryland Sunday legislation. Certainly, these are not works of charity or necessity. Section 521's current stipulation that shops with only one employee may remain open on Sunday does not coincide with a religious purpose. These provisions, along with those which permit various sports and entertainments on Sunday, seem clearly to be fashioned for the purpose of providing a Sunday atmosphere of recreation, cheerfulness, repose and enjoyment. Coupled with the general proscription against other types of work, we believe that the air of the day is one of relaxation rather than one of religion.

The existing Maryland Sunday laws are not simply verbatim re-enactments of their religiously oriented antecedents. Only §492 retains the appellation of "Lord's day" and even that section no longer makes recitation of religious purpose. It does talk in terms of "profan[ing] the Lord's day," but other sections permit the activities previously thought to be profane. Prior denunciation of Sunday drunkenness is now gone. Contemporary concern with these statutes is evidenced by the dozen changes made in 1959 and by the recent enactment of a majority of the exceptions.

Finally, the relevant pronouncements of the Maryland Court of Appeals dispel any argument that the statutes' announced purpose is religious. . . . After engaging in the close scrutiny demanded of us when First Amendment liberties are at issue, we accept the State Supreme Court's determination that the statutes' present purpose and effect is not to aid religion but to set aside a day of rest and recreation.

But this does not answer all of appellants' contentions. We are told that the State has other means at its disposal to accomplish its secular purpose, other courses that would not even remotely or incidentally give state aid to religion. On this basis, we are asked to hold these statutes invalid on the ground that the State's power to regulate conduct in the public interest may only be executed in a way that does not unduly or unnecessarily infringe upon the religious provisions of the First Amendment. See Cantwell v. Connecticut, [310 U.S. 296, 304-305]. However relevant this argument may be, we believe that the factual basis on which it rests is not supportable. It is true that if the State's interest were simply to provide for its citizens a periodic respite from work, a regulation demanding that everyone rest one day in seven, leaving the choice of the day to the individual, would suffice.

However, the State's purpose is not merely to provide a one-day-in-seven work stoppage. In addition to this, the State seeks to set one day apart from all others as a day of rest, repose, recreation and tranquility — a day which all members of the family and community have the opportunity to spend and enjoy together, a day on which there exists relative quiet and disassociation from the everyday intensity of commercial activities, a day on which people may visit friends and relatives who are not available during working days.

Obviously, a State is empowered to determine that a rest-one-day-in-seven statute would not accomplish this purpose; that it would not provide for a general cessation of activity, a special atmosphere of tranquility, a day which all members of the family or friends and relatives might spend together. Furthermore, it seems plain that the problems involved in enforcing such a provision would be exceedingly more difficult than those in enforcing a common-day-of-rest provision.

Moreover, it is common knowledge that the first day of the week has come to have special significance as a rest day in this country. People of all religions and people with no religion regard Sunday as a time for family activity, for visiting friends and relatives, for late sleeping, for passive and active entertainments, for dining out, and the like. . . . Sunday is a day apart from all others.[22] The cause is irrelevant; the fact exists. It would seem unrealistic for enforcement purposes and perhaps detrimental to the general welfare to require a State to choose a common day of rest other than that which most persons would select of their own accord. For these reasons, we hold that the Maryland statutes are not laws respecting an establishment of religion.

The distinctions between the statutes in the case before us and the state action in McCollum v. Board of Education, [333 U.S. 203], the only case in this Court finding a violation of the "Establishment" Clause, lend further substantiation to our conclusion. In McCollum . . . [t]he Court found that [the practices] had the effect of coercing the children to attend religious classes; no such coercion to attend church services is present in the situation at bar. In McCollum, the only alternative available to the nonattending students was to remain in their classrooms; the alternatives open to nonlaboring persons in the instant case are far more diverse. In McCollum, there was direct cooperation between state officials and religious ministers; no such direct participation exists under the Maryland laws. In McCollum, tax-supported buildings were used to aid religion; in the instant case, no tax monies are being used in aid of religion.

Finally, we should make clear that this case deals only with the constitutionality of §521 of the Maryland statute before us. We do not hold that Sunday legislation may not be a violation of the "Establishment" Clause if it can be demonstrated that its purpose — evidenced either on the face of the legislation, in conjunction with its legislative history, or in its operative effect — is to use the State's coercive power to aid religion.

---

[22] The Constitution itself provides for a Sunday exception in the calculation of the ten days for presidential veto. U.S. Const., Art. I, §7.

Accordingly, the decision is
Affirmed.

Mr. Justice Frankfurter, whom Mr. Justice Harlan joined, in a concurring opinion took the following position on the applicability of the establishment clause to the McGowan type of case: "Neither the National Government nor, under the Due Process Clause of the Fourteenth Amendment, a State, may, by any device, support belief or the expression of belief for its own sake, whether from conviction of the truth of that belief, or from conviction that by the propagation of that belief the civil welfare of the State is served, or because a majority of its citizens, holding that belief, are offended when all do not hold it. With regulations which have other objectives the Establishment Clause, and the fundamental separationist concept which it expresses, are not concerned. Those regulations may fall afoul of the constitutional guarantee against infringement of the free exercise or observance of religion. Where they do, they must be set aside at the instance of those whose faith they prejudice. But once it is determined that a challenged statute is supportable as implementing other substantial interests than the promotion of belief, the guarantee prohibiting religious 'establishment' is satisfied. . . . If the primary end achieved by a form of regulation is the affirmation or promotion of religious doctrine — primary, in the sense that all secular ends which it purportedly serves are derivative from, not wholly independent of, the advancement of religion — the regulation is beyond the power of the state. This was the case in McCollum. Or if a statute furthers both secular and religious ends by means unnecessary to the effectuation of the secular ends alone — where the same secular ends could equally be attained by means which do not have the consequences for promotion of religion — the statute cannot stand." 366 U.S. at 466-467. Applying these standards Mr. Justice Frankfurter concluded that Sunday had become in part at least a secular institution and that Sunday restrictions can "reasonably be said" to serve a "substantial non-ecclesiastical purpose relevant to a well-ordered social life." 366 U.S. at 504-505. As to the possibility that other means for securing a day of rest could have been used by the legislature Mr. Justice Frankfurter stated: "in all fairness, certainly, it would be impossible to call unreasonable a legislative finding that these suggested alternatives were unsatisfactory." 366 U.S. at 506. Mr. Justice Frankfurter's opinion also included a lengthy concurrence in Braunfeld v. Brown, infra, and an appendix summarizing the provisions of the various Sunday closing laws.

Mr. Justice Douglas, dissenting, stated in part: "The Court picks and chooses language from various decisions to bolster its conclusion that these Sunday laws in modern setting are 'civil regulations.' No matter how much is written, no matter what is said, the parentage of those laws is the Fourth Commandment. . . . Cases are put where acts that are immoral by our standards but not by the standards of other religious groups are made criminal. That category of cases, until today, has been a very restricted one confined to polygamy . . . and other extreme situations. The latest example is Prince v. Massachusetts, 321 U.S. 158, which upheld a statute making it criminal for a child under twelve to sell papers, periodicals, or merchandise on a street or in any public place. It was sustained in spite of the finding that the child thought it was her religious duty to perform the act. But that was a narrow holding which turned on the effect which street solicitation might have on the child-solicitor . . . None of the acts involved here implicates minors. None of the actions made constitutionally criminal today involves the doing of any act that any society has deemed to be immoral. . . . The Court balances the need of the people for rest, recreation, late-sleeping, family visiting and the like against the command of the First Amendment that no one need bow to the religious beliefs of another. There is in this realm no room for balancing. . . . The State can, of course, require one day of rest a week: one day when every shop or factory is closed. . . . Then the 'day of rest' becomes purely and simply a health measure. But the Sunday laws operate differently. They force minorities to obey the majority's religious feelings of what is due and proper for a Christian community. . . . There is an 'establishment' of religion in the constitutional sense if any practice of any religious group has the sanction of law behind it." 366 U.S. at 572-576.

In Braunfeld v. Brown, 366 U.S. 599, 81 S. Ct. 1144, 6 L. Ed. 2d 563 (1961), an injunction against enforcing the Pennsylvania Sunday closing law, 18 Purdon's Pa. Stat. Ann. (1960 Cum. Supp.) §4699.10, was sought by orthodox Jewish clothing merchants who raised the issue among others that the law interfered with the free exercise of their religion and discriminated against their religion. Their religion, they claimed, forced them to close on Saturday. By being forced to close on Sunday as well they claimed to be faced with the alternative of either giving up their Sabbath adherence or of being put to a serious economic disadvantage. They claimed further that the law thus discouraged the winning of new followers to their faith.

The Chief Justice's opinion after referring to Reynolds v. United States, 98 U.S. 145 (1878) (the polygamy case), and Prince v. Massachusetts, 321 U.S. 158 (1944) (the child labor case), stated:

"It is to be noted that, in the two cases just mentioned, the religious practices themselves conflicted with the public interest. In such cases, to make accommodation between the religious action and an exercise of state authority is a particularly delicate task, id., at 165, because resolution in favor of the State results in the choice to the individual of either abandoning his religious principle or facing criminal prosecution.

"But, again, this is not the case before us because the statute at bar does not make unlawful any religious practices of appellants; the Sunday law simply regulates a secular activity and, as applied to appellants, operates so as to make the practice of their religious beliefs more expensive. Furthermore, the law's effect does not inconvenience all members of the Orthodox Jewish faith but only those who believe it necessary to work on Sunday. And even these are not faced with as serious a choice as forsaking their religious practices or subjecting themselves to criminal prosecution. Fully recognizing that the alternatives open to appellants and others similarly situated — retaining their present occupations and incurring economic disadvantage or engaging in some other commercial activity which does not call for either Saturday or Sunday labor — may well result in some financial sacrifice in order to observe their religious beliefs, still the option is wholly different than when the legislation attempts to make a religious practice itself unlawful.

"To strike down, without the most critical scrutiny, legislation which imposes only an indirect burden on the exercise of religion, i.e., legislation which does not make unlawful the religious practice itself, would radically restrict the operating latitude of the legislature. Statutes which tax income and limit the amount which may be deducted for religious contributions impose an indirect economic burden on the observance of the religion of the citizen whose religion requires him to donate a greater amount to his church; statutes which require the courts to be closed on Saturday and Sunday impose a similar indirect burden on the observance of the religion of the trial lawyer whose religion requires him to rest on a weekday. The list of legislation of this nature is nearly limitless. . . .

"Of course, to hold unassailable all legislation regulating conduct which imposes solely an indirect burden on the observance of religion would be a gross oversimplification. If the purpose or effect of a law is to impede the observance of one or all religions or is to discriminate invidiously between religions, that law is constitutionally invalid even though the burden may be characterized as being only indirect. But if the State regulates conduct by enacting a general law within its power, the purpose and effect of which is to advance the State's secular goals, the statute is valid despite its indirect burden on religious observance unless the State may accomplish its purpose by means which do not impose such a burden. See Cantwell v. Connecticut, [310 U.S. 296, 304-305].[4] . . .

"[In] McGowan, we examined several suggested alternative means by which it was argued that the State might accomplish its secular goals without even remotely or incidentally affecting religious freedom. Ante, at pp. 450-452. We found there that a State might well find that those alter-

[4] Thus in cases like Murdock v. Pennsylvania, 319 U.S. 105, and Follett v. McCormick, 321 U.S. 573, this Court struck down municipal ordinances which, in application, required religious colporteurs to pay a license tax as a condition to the pursuit of their activities because the State's interest, the obtaining of revenue, could be easily satisfied by imposing this tax on nonreligious sources.

natives would not accomplish bringing about a general day of rest. We need not examine them again here.

"However, appellants advance yet another means at the State's disposal which they would find unobjectionable. They contend that the State should cut an exception from the Sunday labor proscription for those people who, because of religious conviction, observe a day of rest other than Sunday. By such regulation, appellants contend, the economic disadvantages imposed by the present system would be removed and the State's interest in having all people rest one day would be satisfied.

"A number of States provide such an exemption, and this may well be the wiser solution to the problem. But our concern is not with the wisdom of legislation but with its constitutional limitation. Thus, reason and experience teach that to permit the exemption might well undermine the State's goal of providing a day that, as best possible, eliminates the atmosphere of commercial noise and activity. Although not dispositive of the issue, enforcement problems would be more difficult since there would be two or more days to police rather than one and it would be more difficult to observe whether violations were occurring.

"Additional problems might also be presented by a regulation of this sort. To allow only people who rest on a day other than Sunday to keep their businesses open on that day might well provide these people with an economic advantage over their competitors who must remain closed on that day;[6] this might cause the Sunday-observers to complain that their religions are being discriminated against. With this competitive advantage existing, there could well be the temptation for some, in order to keep their businesses open on Sunday, to assert that they have religious convictions which compel them to close their businesses on what had formerly been their least profitable day. This might make necessary a state-conducted inquiry into the sincerity of the individual's religious beliefs,[7] a practice which a State might believe would itself run afoul of the spirit of constitutionally protected religious guarantees. Finally, in order to keep the disruption of the day at a minimum, exempted employers would probably have to hire employees who themselves qualified for the exemption because of their own religious beliefs, a practice which a State might feel to be opposed to its general policy prohibiting religious discrimination in

[6] "If he [the Orthodox Jewish storekeeper] opens on Saturday, he is subjected to very fierce competition indeed from Christian shopkeepers, whereas on Sunday, supposing he closes on Saturday, he has an absolutely free run and no competition from Christian shopkeepers at all." 311 Parliamentary Debates, Commons, 492.

"It is true that the orthodox Jew will only be allowed to trade until two o'clock on Sunday, but during that time he will have a monopoly. That is a tremendous advantage. In many districts he will be the only trader with a shop open in that district." 101 Parliamentary Debates, Lords, 430.

[7] Connecticut, which has such an exemption statute, requires that Sabbatarians, in order to qualify, file a written notice of religious belief with the prosecuting attorney. Conn. Gen. Stat. Rev. §53-303.

hiring. For all of these reasons, we cannot say that the Pennsylvania statute before us is invalid, either on its face or as applied." 366 U.S. at 605-609.

Mr. Justice Brennan's dissent first challenged the Court's standard of judicial review in these cases: "The Court in such cases is not confined to the narrow inquiry whether the challenged law is rationally related to some legitimate legislative end. Nor is the case decided by a finding that the State's interest is substantial and important, as well as rationally justifiable." 366 U.S. at 611. Quoting from Mr. Justice Jackson's opinion in the Barnette case, supra, Mr. Justice Brennan accepted "grave and immediate danger to interests the State may lawfully protect" as the only ground for infringing the free exercise of religion. Mr. Justice Brennan then observed that, while the Pennsylvania law did not compel belief in a particular religion nor "prohibit outright" anyone's religious practices, it nevertheless constituted a "clog upon the exercise of religion." It "has exactly the same economic effect as a tax levied upon the sale of religious literature." The only state interest involved "is the mere convenience of having everyone rest on the same day. It is to defend this interest that the Court holds that a State need not follow the alternative route of granting an exemption for those who in good faith observe a day of rest other than Sunday." Mr. Justice Brennan continues:

"It is true, I suppose, that the granting of such an exemption would make Sundays a little noisier, and the task of police and prosecutor a little more difficult. It is also true that a majority — 21 — of the 34 States which have general Sunday regulations have exemptions of this kind.[1] We are not told that those States are significantly noisier, or that their police are significantly more burdened, than Pennsylvania's. Even England, not under the compulsion of a written constitution, but simply influenced by considerations of fairness, has such an exemption for some activities.[2] The Court conjures up several difficulties with such a system which seem to me more fanciful than real. Non-Sunday observers might get an unfair advantage, it is said. A similar contention against the draft exemption for conscientious objectors (another example of the exemption technique) was rejected with the observation that 'its unsoundness is too apparent to require' discussion. Selective Draft Law Cases, 245 U.S. 366, 390 (1918).

---

[1] Conn. Gen. Stat., 1958 rev., §53-303; Fla. Laws 1959, c. 59-1650, §2; Ill. Rev. Stat., 1959, c. 38, §549; Burns' Ind. Ann. Stat., 1956 repl., §10-4301; Kan. Gen. Stat. Ann., 1949, §21-953; Ky. Rev. Stat., 1959, §436.160(2); Me. Rev. Stat., 1954, c. 134, §44; Mass. Gen. Laws Ann., 1958, c. 136, §6; Mich. Stat. Ann., 1957 rev., §§18.855, 18.122, 9.2702; Mo. Rev. Stat., 1959, §563.700; Neb. Rev. Stat., 1943, §28-940; N.J. Stat. Ann., 1953, §2A:171-4; McKinney's N.Y. Laws, Penal Law §2144; N.D. Rev. Code, 1943, §12-2117; Page's Ohio Rev. Code Ann., 1954, §3773.24; Okla. Stat. Ann., 1958, Tit. 21, §909; R.I. Gen. Laws, 1956, §11-40-4; S.D. Code, 1939, §13.1710; Tex. Pen. Code Art. 284; Va. Code, 1950, §18.1-359; Wash. Rev. Code, 1951, §9.76.020; W. Va. Code Ann., 1955, c. 61, Art. 8, §6073. Cf. Wis. Stat. Ann., 1958, §301.33.
[2] E.g., Shops Act, 1950, 14 Geo. VI, c. 28, §53.

However widespread the complaint, it is legally baseless, and the State's reliance upon it cannot withstand a First Amendment claim. We are told that an official inquiry into the good faith with which religious beliefs are held might be itself unconstitutional. But this Court indicated otherwise in United States v. Ballard, 322 U.S. 78 (1944). Such an inquiry is no more an infringement of religious freedom than the requirement imposed by the Court itself in McGowan v. Maryland, ante, p. 420, decided this day, that a plaintiff show that his good-faith religious beliefs are hampered before he acquires standing to attack a statute under the Free-Exercise Clause of the First Amendment. Finally, I find the Court's mention of a problem under state antidiscrimination statutes almost chimerical. Most such statutes provide that hiring may be made on a religious basis if religion is a bona fide occupational qualification.[3] It happens, moreover, that Pennsylvania's statute has such a provision.[4] " 366 U.S. at 611-615.

NOTES

Other cases decided by the Court in 1961 which involve in part application of the principles of the McGowan and Braunfeld cases, are Two Guys from Harrison-Allenstown, Inc. v. McGinley, 366 U.S. 582, 81 S. Ct. 1135, 6 L. Ed. 2d 551 (1961), and Gallagher v. Crown Kosher Market, 366 U.S. 617, 81 S. Ct. 1122, 6 L. Ed. 2d 536 (1961). In the Gallagher case the plaintiffs included customers who claimed that the statutes "deprive them, from Friday afternoon until Monday of each week, of the opportunity to purchase the kosher food sanctioned by their faith." In denying this claim the Chief Justice's opinion stated that the question of standing need not be decided, since the issue was decided on the merits in the Braunfeld case. 366 U.S. at 630-631.

In the Two Guys from Harrison case, an injunction proceeding, the opinion upheld the statute involved in the Braunfeld case against equal protection and disestablishment challenges. In that case there was also challenged another Pennsylvania statute, 18 Purdon's Pa. Stat. Ann. §4699.4, which with some exceptions generally forbids all worldly employment, business, and sports on Sunday. The Supreme Court upheld the lower court's ruling that it need not decide the constitutionality of this statute in the injunction proceedings because there was no serious threat of prosecution. Another contention, that the statute was being discriminatorily enforced was also put aside because the previous District Attorney was no longer in office and the defense of discriminatory enforcement would be available in a criminal prosecution.

See also Cardinal Sporting Goods Company v. Eagleton, 213 F. Supp. 207 (E.D. Mo. 1963) (upholding Missouri Sunday Selling Law), dis. as moot, 374 U.S. 496 (1963); Moss v. Hornig, 314 F.2d 89 (2d Cir. 1963) (denying injunction against alleged discriminatory enforcement of Connecticut Sunday Closing Law).

---

[3] E.g., Mass. Gen. Laws Ann., 1958, c. 151B, §4, par. 1.
[4] 43 Purdon's Pa. Stat. Ann. (1960 Cum. Supp.) §955.

REFERENCES

For discussion of the Sunday laws, see Note, Sunday, the Sabbath, and Blue Laws, 30 Tenn. L. Rev. 249 (1963); Note, Sunday Laws, 43 N.C.L. Rev. 123 (1964); Hopp, Sunday Laws — The McGowan Decision, 13 Baylor L. Rev. 225 (1961); Note, A Braunfeld v. Brown Test For Indirect Burdens on the Free Exercise of Religion, 48 Minn. L. Rev. 1165 (1964) (application to license tax, compulsory military training in universities, and qualification for unemployment compensation cases); Mann and Garfinkel, The Sunday Closing Laws Decisions — A Critique, 37 Notre Dame Law. 323 (1962); Dyson, General Laws and Blue Laws: A Criticism of the Sunday Closing Case, 13 Kan. L. Rev. 103 (1964). See also Barron, Sunday in North America, 79 Harv. L. Rev. 42 (1965) (comparing Canadian law).

3. Denial of Privileges

In Sherbert v. Verner, 374 U.S. 398, 83 S. Ct. 1790, 10 L. Ed. 2d 965 (1963), the issue was whether a Seventh Day Adventist could be denied unemployment benefits after she was discharged by her employer for refusing to work on Saturday contrary to her religious belief. Benefits were denied because she "failed, without good cause . . . to accept available suitable work when offered . . . by the employment office or the employer." The Court declared that the state may not "constitutionally apply the eligibility provisions so as to constrain a worker to abandon his religious convictions respecting the day of rest." 374 U.S. at 410. Mr. Justice Brennan, writing for the Court, noted first that unlike the child labor or polygamy cases "appellant's conscientious objection to Saturday work constitutes no conduct prompted by religious principles of a kind within the reach of state legislation." He went on to say that therefore, if the state court's decision is to withstand constitutional challenge, "it must be either because her disqualification as a beneficiary represents no infringement by the State of her constitutional rights of free exercise, or because any incidental burden on the free exercise of appellant's religion may be justified by a 'compelling state interest in the regulation of a subject within the State's constitutional power to regulate . . . .' NAACP v. Button, 371 U.S. 415, 438." 374 U.S. at 403.

Stating that withholding of unemployment benefits interferes with "free exercise" to the same extent as a fine imposed for Saturday worship, Mr. Justice Brennan emphasized that the mere fact that such benefits are not a "right" but a mere "privilege" makes no difference. The opinion discusses a number of cases, such as Flemming v. Nestor, 363 U.S. 603 (Social Security benefits); Speiser v. Randall, 357 U.S. 513 (tax exemption), holding that the denial of privilege can violate due process and First Amendment rights.

As to the second ground, Mr. Justice Brennan concluded that no "compelling state interest . . . justifies the substantial infringement of appellant's First Amendment right." He disposed of the contention that "the filing of fraudulent claims by unscrupulous claimants feigning religious objections to

Saturday work might not only dilute the unemployment compensation fund but also hinder the scheduling by employers of necessary Saturday work." The opinion noted that this contention was not made below and was at any rate not supported by the record. Even were this not so, "it would plainly be incumbent upon the appellees to demonstrate that no alternative forms of regulation would combat such abuses without infringing First Amendment rights.[7] " Mr. Justice Brennan went on to distinguish Braunfeld v. Brown, supra, asserting that there the statute "was . . . saved by a countervailing factor which finds no equivalent in the instant case — a strong state interest in providing one uniform day of rest for all workers. That secular objective could be achieved, the Court found, only by declaring Sunday to be that day of rest. Requiring exemptions for Sabbatarians, while theoretically possible, appeared to present an administrative problem of such magnitude, or to afford the exempted class so great a competitive advantage, that such a requirement would have rendered the entire statutory scheme unworkable. In the present case no such justifications underlie the determination of the state court that appellant's religion makes her ineligible to receive benefits.[9] " 374 U.S. at 406-409.

[7] We note that before the instant decision, state supreme courts had, without exception, granted benefits to persons who were physically available for work but unable to find suitable employment solely because of a religious prohibition against Saturday work. E.g., In re Miller, 243 N.C. 509, 91 S.E.2d 241; Swenson v. Michigan Employment Security Comm'n, 340 Mich. 430, 65 N.W.2d 709; Tary v. Board of Review, 161 Ohio St. 251, 119 N.E.2d 56. Cf. Kut v. Albers Super Markets, Inc., 146 Ohio St. 522, 66 N.E.2d 643, appeal dismissed sub nom. Kut v. Bureau of Unemployment Compensation, 329 U.S. 669. One author has observed, "the law was settled that conscientious objections to work on the Sabbath made such work unsuitable and that such objectors were nevertheless available for work. . . . A contrary opinion would make the unemployment compensation law unconstitutional, as a violation of freedom of religion. Religious convictions, strongly held, are so impelling as to constitute good cause for refusal. Since availability refers to suitable work, religious observers were not unavailable because they excluded Sabbath work." Altman, Availability for Work: A Study in Unemployment Compensation (1950), 187. See also Sanders, Disqualification for Unemployment Insurance, 8 Vand. L. Rev. 307, 327-328 (1955); 34 N.C.L. Rev. 591 (1956); cf. Freeman, Able To Work and Available for Work, 55 Yale L.J. 123, 131 (1945). Of the 47 States which have eligibility provisions similar to those of the South Carolina statute, only 28 appear to have given administrative rulings concerning the eligibility of persons whose religious convictions prevented them from accepting available work. Twenty-two of those States have held such persons entitled to benefits, although apparently only one such decision rests exclusively upon the federal constitutional ground which constitutes the basis of our decision. See 111 U. of Pa. L. Rev. 253, and n.3 (1962); 34 N.C.L. Rev. 591, 602, n.60 (1956).

[9] These considerations also distinguish the quite different case of Flemming v. Nestor, supra, upon which appellees rely. In that case the Court found that the compelling federal interests which underlay the decision of Congress to impose such a disqualification justified whatever effect the denial of social security benefits may have had upon the disqualified class. See 363 U.S., at 612. And compare Torcaso v. Watkins, [367 U.S. 488], in which an undoubted state interest in ensuring the veracity and trustworthiness of Notaries Public was held insufficient to justify the substantial infringement upon the religious freedom of applicants for that position which resulted from a required oath of belief in God. See 74 Harv. L. Rev. 611, 612-613 (1961); 109 U. of Pa. L. Rev. 611, 614-616 (1961).

Mr. Justice Brennan's opinion then disposed of several other contentions: "In holding as we do, plainly we are not fostering the 'establishment' of the Seventh-day Adventist religion in South Carolina, for the extension of unemployment benefits to Sabbatarians in common with Sunday worshippers reflects nothing more than the governmental obligation of neutrality in the face of religious differences, and does not represent that involvement of religious with secular institutions which it is the object of the Establishment Clause to forestall. See School District of Abington Township v. Schempp, [374 U.S. 203]. Nor does the recognition of the appellant's right to unemployment benefits under the state statute serve to abridge any other person's religious liberties. Nor do we, by our decision today, declare the existence of a constitutional right to unemployment benefits on the part of all persons whose religious convictions are the cause of their unemployment. This is not a case in which an employee's religious convictions serve to make him a nonproductive member of society. . . . Finally, nothing we say today constrains the States to adopt any particular form or scheme of unemployment compensation." 374 U.S. at 409-410.

Mr. Justice Douglas and Mr. Justice Stewart both wrote separate concurring opinions based on their disagreement with Braunfeld v. Brown, and Mr. Justice Stewart added his disagreement with the Court's "mechanistic concept of the Establishment Clause" as a further ground for his concurrence. Mr. Justice Harlan's dissent, in which Mr. Justice White joined, asserted that the decision violated both Braunfeld v. Brown and the disestablishment precedents.

In Torcaso v. Watkins. 367 U.S. 488, 81 S. Ct. 1680, 6 L. Ed. 982 (1961), a newly appointed notary public was denied his commission because he failed to declare his belief in God as required by the Maryland Constitution. In upholding Torcaso's right to obtain the Commission Mr. Justice Black declared in part: "The fact . . . that a person is not compelled to hold public office cannot possibly be an excuse for barring him from office by state-imposed criteria forbidden by the Constitution . . . This Maryland religious test for public office unconstitutionally invades the appellant's freedom of belief and religion and therefore cannot be enforced against him." 367 U.S. at 495-496.

See also In re Jenison, 265 Minn. 96, 120 N.W.2d 515 (1963), vacated and remanded in the light of Sherbert v. Verner, 375 U.S. 14 (1963); on remand, 267 Minn. 136, 125 N.W.2d 588 (1963) (contempt conviction of a juror refusing to serve because judging others violated religious principles, reversed). To the same effect see United States v. Hillyard, 52 F. Supp. 612 (E.D. Wash. 1943). Cf. Schowgurow v. State, 240 Md. 121, 213 A.2d 475 (1965) (reversing murder conviction of Buddhist whose religion does not teach belief in the existence of a Supreme Being; jurors were required to affirm a belief in the existence of God as a condition of jury service). See also State v. Madison, 240 Md. 265, 213 A.2d 880 (1965) (defendant, who was member of Apostolic

faith, which believes in the existence of a Supreme Being, and who was therefore not in the class excluded from jury service, may nevertheless challenge
jury selection).

NOTE

Recently a growing number of cases have dealt with attempts by members of the
Nation of Islam (called Black Muslims) to practice their religion in prison:

In Sewell v. Pegelow, 291 F.2d 196 (4th Cir. 1961), the court held that prisoners' allegations that they were isolated and treated discriminatorily solely because of their religious beliefs stated enough to require a hearing on suit for
injunction under the Civil Rights Act of 1871, 42 U.S.C. §1983. In a later development the appeal was dismissed without prejudice to the plaintiffs on the basis of a
letter from counsel outlining reforms to be put into effect in the District of Columbia reformatory at Lorton, Virginia. 304 F.2d 670 (1962). The proposed reforms included the following: (1) Inmates who become Muslims in prison will be
recognized as such. (2) Copies of the Koran and Islam prayer books will be permitted and furnished on the same basis as copies of the Bible are made available to
inmates of the Catholic and Protestant faiths. (3) Muslim inmates will be permitted to correspond with Muslim ministers in conformity with normal prison
procedures (including the usual censorship), to meet at reasonable times and
places for prayer and study, to carry religious medals to the same extent as Christian and other medals are permitted, and to discuss their religion with other inmates to the same extent as Christians and others are permitted to do so.
(4) Upon request the superintendent will extend to the local Muslim minister the
same privilege of conducting religious meetings at the reformatory as he extends
to ministers of other religions. (5) Complaints by inmates of discriminatory treatment will be forwarded without alteration or delay to the Secretary of the Board of
Commissioners of the District of Columbia. (6) "For the present, inmates are not
to be permitted to subscribe to the Los Angeles Herald Dispatch [subject to later
re-evaluation]." 304 F.2d at 671. See also Sewell v. Kennedy, 222 F. Supp. 15
(E.D. Va. 1963) (rejecting contention that plaintiff did not authorize his court-
appointed counsel to consent to dismissal of his appeal in 304 F.2d 670); Roberts v.
Pegelow, 313 F.2d 548 (4th Cir. 1963) (complaint alleging interference with
rights to practice religion and to complain to District of Columbia Board of
Commissioners properly dismissed as moot in view of adoption of new policies
regarding treatment of Muslim inmates incorporated in assurances addressed to
court in Sewell v. Pegelow, supra).

In litigation alleging religious persecution of Muslims in New York state
prisons, including solitary confinement and deprivation of "good time" for leaders
of the "Muslim Brotherhood," the Court of Appeals for the Second Circuit held
that the District Courts must entertain such claims under the Federal Civil Rights
Act. Pierce v. LaVallee, 293 F.2d 233 (1961). Subsequently the District Court
dismissed the complaint. 212 F. Supp. 865 (N.D. N.Y. 1962). The Court of Appeals affirmed, on the ground that the District Court's finding that plaintiffs had
failed to establish that their punishment resulted from their religious beliefs "was
not clearly erroneous." 319 F.2d 844 (2d Cir. 1963), cert. den. sub nom. Sostre v.

Wilkins, 374 U.S. 850 (1963). Prison officials had claimed that the Brotherhood had "overtones of secrecy and intrigue," although its avowed objective was the study and furtherance of Islam, and that the leaders were disciplined for "agitating." In a further action for relief against interference with practice of the Muslim religion, a complaint was dismissed by the Federal District Court for the Western District of New York pending state action. The Court of Appeals agreed that the state authorities should be given an opportunity to propose workable rules and regulations which would permit Muslim inmates to practice their religion so far as possible within the prison discipline but directed the District Court to retain jurisdiction so it could act if the state delayed unreasonably. Sostre v. McGinnis, 334 F.2d 906 (2d Cir. 1964), cert. den., 379 U.S. 892 (1964).

In Cooper v. Pate, 378 U.S. 546, 84 S. Ct. 1733, 12 L. Ed. 2d 1030 (1964), the Supreme Court cited the Pierce and Sewell cases in a per curiam decision upholding the right of an inmate at the Illinois State Penitentiary to bring an action under the Civil Rights Act, 42 U.S.C. §§1983, 1979, alleging that "solely because of his religious beliefs he was denied permission to purchase certain religious publications and denied other privileges enjoyed by other prisoners." The prisoner's principal complaint had been "that he was placed in solitary confinement because he insisted upon obtaining a Muslim bible, termed by him 'Quran' and language books 'Arabic' and 'Swahli.' " 324 F.2d 165, 166 (7th Cir. 1963).

See also Williford v. People of California, 352 F.2d 474 (9th Cir. 1965), reversing 217 F. Supp. 245 (N.D. Cal. 1963); Banks v. Havener, 234 F. Supp. 27 (E.D. Va. 1964); Matter of Shaw v. McGinnis, 14 N.Y.2d 864, 251 N.Y.S.2d 972, 200 N.E.2d 636 (1964); Matter of Brown v. McGinnis, 10 N.Y.2d 531, 225 N.Y.S.2d 497, 180 N.E.2d 791 (1962); Fulwood v. Clemmor, 295 F.2d 171 (D.C. Cir. 1961), 206 F. Supp. 370 (D. D.C. 1962). Cf. Childs v. Pegelow, 321 F.2d 487 (4th Cir. 1963), cert. den., 376 U.S. 932 (1964); Cooke v. Tramberg, 43 N.J. 514, 205 A.2d 889 (1964); In re Ferguson, 55 Cal. 2d 663, 12 Cal. Rptr. 753, 361 P.2d 417 (1961), cert. den., 368 U.S. 864, 879 (1961). For discussion see Frankino, The Manacles and the Messenger: A Short Study in Religious Freedom in the Prison Community, 14 Catholic U.L. Rev. 30 (1965). For a police officer's view of the Muslim movement reviewing some of the literature and concluding that it "does not pose a threat to the police," and that former criminals who become Muslims "become law-abiding citizens and very few, if any, ever return to a life of crime," see Brown, Black Muslims and the Police, 56 J. Crim. L., C. & P.S. 119 (1965). And see The Autobiography of Malcolm X, chs. 10-15 (with Haley, 1965).

4. Conscientious Objection

UNITED STATES v. SEEGER
380 U.S. 163, 85 S. Ct. 850, 13 L. Ed. 2d 733 (1965)

MR. JUSTICE CLARK delivered the opinion of the Court.

These cases involve claims of conscientious objectors under §6(j) of the Universal Military Training and Service Act, 50 U.S.C. App. §456(j) (1958 ed.), which exempts from combatant training and service in the armed forces of the United States those persons who by reason of their religious training and belief are conscientiously opposed to participation in war in any form. The cases were consolidated for argument and we consider them together although each involves different facts and circumstances. The parties raise the basic question of the constitutionality of the section which defines the term "religious training and belief," as used in the Act, as "an individual's belief in a relation to a Supreme Being involving duties superior to those arising from any human relation, but [not including] essentially political, sociological, or philosophical views or a merely personal moral code." The constitutional attack is launched under the First Amendment's Establishment and Free Exercise Clauses and is twofold: (1) The section does not exempt nonreligious conscientious objectors; and (2) it discriminates between different forms of religious expression in violation of the Due Process Clause of the Fifth Amendment. Jakobson (No. 51) and Peter (No. 29) also claim that their beliefs come within the meaning of the section. Jakobson claims that he meets the standards of §6(j) because his opposition to war is based on belief in a Supreme Reality and is therefore an obligation superior to one resulting from man's relationship to his fellow man. Peter contends that his opposition to war derives from his acceptance of the existence of a universal power beyond that of man and that this acceptance in fact constitutes belief in a Supreme Being, qualifying him for exemption. We granted certiorari in each of the cases because of their importance in the administration of the Act. 377 U.S. 922.

We have concluded that Congress, in using the expression "Supreme Being" rather than the designation "God," was merely clarifying the meaning of religious training and belief so as to embrace all religions and to exclude essentially political, sociological, or philosophical views. We believe that under his construction, the test of belief "in a relation to a Supreme Being" is whether a given belief that is sincere and meaningful occupies a place in the life of its possessor parallel to that filled by the orthodox belief in God of one who clearly qualifies for the exemption. Where such beliefs have parallel positions in the lives of their respective holders we cannot say that one is "in a relation to a Supreme Being" and the other is not. We have concluded that the beliefs of the objectors in these cases meet these criteria, and, accordingly, we affirm the judgments in Nos. 50 and 51 and reverse the judgment in No. 29.

The Facts in the Cases

No. 50: Seeger was convicted in the District Court for the Southern District of New York of having refused to submit to induction in the armed forces. He was originally classified 1-A in 1953 by his local board, but this classification was changed in 1955 to 2-S (student) and he remained in this status until 1958 when he was reclassified 1-A. He first claimed exemption as a conscientious objector in 1957 after successive annual renewals of his student classification. Although he did not adopt verbatim the printed Selective Service System form, he declared that he was conscientiously opposed to participation in war in any form by reason of his "religious" belief; that he preferred to leave the question as to his belief in a Supreme Being open, "rather than answer 'yes' or 'no' "; that his "skepticism or disbelief in the existence of God" did "not necessarily mean lack of faith in anything whatsoever"; that his was a "belief in and devotion to goodness and virtue for their own sakes, and a religious faith in a purely ethical creed." R. 69-70, 73. He cited such personages as Plato, Aristotle and Spinoza for support of his ethical belief in intellectual and moral integrity "without belief in God, except in the remotest sense." R. 73. His belief was found to be sincere, honest, and made in good faith; and his conscientious objection to be based upon individual training and belief, both of which included research in religious and cultural fields. Seeger's claim, however, was denied solely because it was not based upon a "belief in a relation to a Supreme Being" as required by §6(j) of the Act. At trial Seeger's counsel admitted that Seeger's belief was not in relation to a Supreme Being as commonly understood, but contended that he was entitled to the exemption because "under the present law Mr. Seeger's position would also include definitions of religion which have been stated more recently," R. 49, and could be "accommodated" under the definition of religious training and belief in the Act, R. 53. He was convicted and the Court of Appeals reversed, holding that the Supreme Being requirement of the section distinguished "between internally derived and externally compelled beliefs" and was, therefore, an "impermissible classification" under the Due Process Clause of the Fifth Amendment. 326 F.2d 846.

No. 51: Jakobson was also convicted in the Southern District of New York on a charge of refusing to submit to induction. On his appeal the Court of Appeals reversed on the ground that rejection of his claim may have rested on the factual finding, erroneously made, that he did not believe in a Supreme Being as required by §6(j). 325 F.2d 409.

Jakobson was originally classified 1-A in September 1953 and enjoyed a student classification until June 1956. It was not until April 1958 that he made claim to non-combatant classification (1-A-O) as a conscientious objector. He stated on the Selective Service System form that he believed in a "Supreme Being" who was "Creator of Man" in the sense of being "ultimately responsible for the existence of" man and who was "the Supreme Reality" of which "the existence of man is the *result.*" R. 44. (Emphasis in the original.) He explained that his religious and social thinking had developed after much meditation and thought. He had concluded that man must be "partly spiritual" and, therefore, "partly akin to the Supreme Reality"; and that his "most important religious law" was that "no man ought ever to wilfully sacrifice another man's life as a means to any other end . . . ." R. 45-46. In December 1958 he requested a 1-O classification since he felt that participation in any form of military service would involve him in "too many situations and relationships that would be a strain on [his] conscience that [he felt he] must avoid." R. 70. He submitted a long memorandum of "notes on religion" in which he defined religion as the *"sum and essence of one's basic attitudes to the fundamental problems of human existence,"* R. 72 (emphasis in the original); he said that he believed in "Godness" which was "the Ultimate Cause for the fact of the Being of the Universe"; that to deny its existence would but deny the existence of the universe because "anything that Is, has an Ultimate Cause for its Being." R. 73. There was a relationship to Godness, he stated, in two directions, i.e., "vertically, towards Godness directly," and "horizontally, towards Godness through Mankind and the World." R. 74. He accepted the latter one. The Board classified him 1-A-O and Jakobson appealed. The hearing officer found that the claim was based upon a personal moral code and that he was not sincere in his claim. The Appeal Board classified him 1-A. It did not indicate upon what ground it based its decision, i.e., insincerity or a conclusion that his belief was only a personal moral code. The Court of Appeals reversed, finding that his claim came within the requirements of §6(j). Because it could not determine whether the Appeal Board had found that Jakobson's beliefs failed to come within the statutory definition, or whether it had concluded that he lacked sincerity, it directed dismissal of the indictment.

No. 29: Forest Britt Peter was convicted in the Northern District of California on a charge of refusing to submit to induction. In his Selective Service System form he stated that he was not a member of a religious sect or organization; he failed to execute section VII of the questionnaire but attached to it a quotation expressing opposition to war, in which he stated that he concurred. In a later form he hedged the question as to his belief in a Supreme Being by saying that it depended on the definition and he appended a statement that he felt it a violation of his moral code to take human life and that he considered this belief superior to his obligation to the state. As to whether his conviction was religious, he quoted with approval Reverend John Haynes Holmes' definition of religion as "the consciousness of some power manifest in nature which helps man in the ordering of his life in harmony with its demands . . . [; it] is the supreme expression of human nature; it is man thinking his highest, feeling his deepest, and living his best." R. 27. The source of his conviction he attributed to reading and meditation "in our democratic American culture, with its values derived from the western religious and philosophical tradition." Ibid. As to his belief in a Supreme Being, Peter stated that he supposed "you could call that a belief in the Supreme Being or God. These just do not happen to be the words I use." R. 11. In 1959 he was classified 1-A, although there was no evidence in the record that he was not sincere in his beliefs. After his conviction for failure to report for induction the Court of Appeals, assuming arguendo that he was sincere, affirmed, 324 F.2d 173.

INTERPRETATION OF §6(J)

[Here the Court discusses at length the history of draft exemption and the legislative history of Section 6(j). The Court notes that between 1940 and 1948 two cases, United States v. Kauten, 133 F.2d 703 (2d Cir. 1943), and Berman v. United States, 156 F.2d 377 (9th Cir. 1946), held that the phrase "religious training and belief" found in the 1940 statute did not include philosophical, social or political policy. The Berman case, which was cited in the Senate report, also made the point that religious belief is belief in a relation to God, and it was argued by the Government that the words "Supreme Being" as used in the 1948 statute were an attempt to make clear that belief in God as mentioned in Berman was essential for qualification as a conscientious objector. The Court rejected this contention stating that only the exclusion of philosophical, moral, and social policy mentioned in the 1948 statute was adopted from Berman. The deliberate use of "Supreme Being" rather than God indicated that Congress in clarifying the 1940 statute meant to exempt a broader category of "religious belief." This broader category is in accord with the "understanding of the modern religious community" as evidenced by statements of Paul Tillich and David Muzzey as well as excerpts from a draft Schema of the Ecumenical Council which the opinion quotes.]

We recognize the difficulties that have always faced the trier of fact in these cases. We hope that the test that we lay down proves less onerous. The examiner is furnished a standard that permits consideration of criteria with which he has had considerable experience. While the applicant's words may differ, the test is simple of application. It is essentially an objective one, namely, does the claimed belief occupy the same place in the life of the objector as an orthodox belief in God holds in the life of one clearly qualified for exemption?

Moreover, it must be remembered that in resolving these exemption problems one deals with the beliefs of different individuals who will articulate them in a multitude of ways. In such an intensely personal area, of course, the claim of the registrant that his belief is an essential part of a religious faith must be given great weight. . . . The validity of what he believes cannot be questioned. Some theologians, and indeed some examiners, might be tempted to question the existence of the registrant's "Supreme Being" or the truth of his concepts. But these are inquiries foreclosed to Government. . . . Local boards and courts in this sense are not free to reject beliefs because they consider them "incomprehensible." Their task is to decide whether the beliefs professed by a registrant are sincerely held and whether they are, in his own scheme of things, religious.

But we hasten to emphasize that while the "truth" of a belief is not open to question, there remains the significant question whether it is "truly held." This is the threshold question of sincerity which must be resolved in every case. It is, of course, a question of fact — a prime consideration to the validity of every claim for exemption as a conscientious objector. The Act provides a comprehensive scheme for assisting the Appeal Boards in making this determination, placing at their service the facilities of the Department of Justice, including the Federal Bureau of Investigation and hearing officers. Finally, we would point out that in Estep v. United States, 327 U.S. 114 (1946), this Court held that:

"The provision making the decisions of the local boards 'final' means to us that Congress chose not to give administrative action under this Act the customary scope of judicial review which obtains under other statutes. It means that the courts are not to weigh the evidence to determine whether the classification made by the local boards was justified. The decisions of the local boards made in conformity with the regulations are final even though they may be erroneous. The question of jurisdiction of the local board is reached only if there is no basis in fact for the classification which it gave the registrant." At 122-123.

APPLICATION OF §6(J) TO THE INSTANT CASES

As we noted earlier, the statutory definition excepts those registrants whose beliefs are based on a "merely personal moral code." The records in these cases, however, show that at no time did any one of the applicants suggest that his objection was based on a "merely personal moral code." Indeed at the outset each of them claimed in his application that his objection was based on a religious belief. We have construed the statutory definition broadly and it follows that any exception to it must be interpreted narrowly. The use by Congress of the words "merely personal" seems to us to restrict the exception to a moral code which is not only personal but which is the sole basis for the registrant's belief and is in no way related to a Supreme Being. It follows, therefore, that if the claimed religious beliefs of the respective registrants in these cases meet the test that we lay down then their objections cannot be based on a "merely personal" moral code.

In Seeger, No. 50, the Court of Appeals failed to find sufficient "externally compelled beliefs." However, it did find that "it would seem impossible to say with assurance that [Seeger] is not bowing to 'external commands' in virtually the same sense as is the objector who defers to the will of a supernatural power." 326 F.2d, at 853. It found little distinction between Jakobson's devotion to a mystical force of "Godness" and Seeger's compulsion to "goodness." Of course, as we have said, the statute does not distinguish between externally and internally derived beliefs. Such a determination would, as the Court of Appeals observed, prove impossible as a practical matter, and we have found that Congress intended no such distinction.

The Court of Appeals also found that there was no question of the applicant's sincerity. He was a product of a devout Roman Catholic home; he was a close student of Quaker beliefs from which he said "much of [his] thought is derived"; he approved of their opposition to war in any form; he devoted his spare hours to the American Friends Service Committee and was assigned to hospital duty.

In summary, Seeger professed "religious belief" and "religious faith." He did not disavow any belief "in a relation to a Supreme Being"; indeed he stated that "the cosmic order does, perhaps, suggest a creative intelligence." He decried the tremendous "spiritual" price man must pay for his willingness to destroy human life. In light of his beliefs and the unquestioned sincerity with which he held them, we think the Board, had it applied the test we propose today, would have granted him the exemption. We think it clear that the beliefs which prompted his objection occupy the same place in his life as the belief in a traditional diety holds in the lives of his friends, the Quakers. We are reminded once more of Dr. Tillich's thoughts:

"And if that word [God] has not much meaning for you, translate it, and speak of the depths of your life, of the source of your being, of your ultimate concern, *of what you take seriously without any reservation*. Perhaps, in order to do so, you must forget everything traditional that you have learned about God . . . ." Tillich, The Shaking of the Foundations 57 (1948). (Emphasis supplied.)

It may be that Seeger did not clearly demonstrate what his beliefs were with regard to the usual understanding of the term "Supreme Being." But as we have said Congress did not intend that to be the test. We therefore affirm the judgment in No. 50.

In Jakobson, No. 51, the Court of Appeals found that the registrant demonstrated that his belief as to opposition to war was related to a Supreme Being. We agree and affirm that judgment.

We reach a like conclusion in No. 29. It will be remembered that Peter acknowledged "some power manifest in nature . . . the supreme expresssion" that helps man in ordering his life. As to whether he would call that belief in a Supreme Being, he replied, "you could call that a belief in the Supreme Being or God. These just do not happen to be the words I use." We think that under the test we establish here the Board would grant the exemption to Peter and we therefore reverse the judgment in No. 29.

It is so ordered.

[Mr. Justice Douglas' concurring opinion emphasized that the attitude of Buddhism, Taoism, and Confucianism to God requires the broader view of Supreme Being adopted by the Court. With so much of our country including possessions and the State of Hawaii now populated by adherents of these religions, Congress must have had the broad view in mind when it used the phrase "Supreme Being" in the 1948 statute. Any other view of the statute would have rendered it unconstitutional.]

NOTES

1. See Note, Conscientious Objectors — The New "Parallel Belief" Test — United States v. Seeger, 14 Catholic U.L. Rev. 238 (1965); Conklin, Conscientious Objector Provisions: A View in the Light of Torcaso v. Watkins, 51 Geo. L.J. 252 (1963); Clancy and Weiss, The Conscientious Objector Exemption: Problems in Conceptual Clarity and Constitutional Consideration, 17 Me. L. Rev. 143 (1965); Note, The Three Eras of the Conscientious Objector, 34 U. Cinc. L. Rev. 487 (1965).

2. In 1966 the American Civil Liberties Union adopted a statement on conscientious objection which read in part as follows:

"Government under law means that the conduct of those who disagree will yield to the command of government when democratic processes have resolved the subject of debate. The individuals who should qualify as conscientious objectors to a particular war are rather those who find such participation in such a war to be so great a wrong that even government's command will not relieve them of responsibility for committing that wrong. For civil libertarians conscience so central to a man's belief becomes an aspect of religious liberty protected by the First Amendment — whether or not the objector calls his conscience 'religious.'" American Civil Liberties Union Bull., March 14, 1966.

3. For the treatment of Jehovah's Witnesses who claim exemption as "ministers" for many active members of their sect, see cases cited in second edition of this book, 1193-1194. See also United States v. Stewart, 213 F. Supp. 497 (D. Md. 1963); United States v. Willard, 211 F. Supp. 643 (N.D. Ohio 1962); United States v. Zasadni, 206 F. Supp. 318 (W.D. Pa. 1962). For case upholding denial of admission to bar for refusing to take oath which includes willingness to serve in state militia see In re Summers, 325 U.S. 561, 65 S. Ct. 1307, 89 L. Ed. 1795 (1945). Knowingly counseling to fail and refuse to register has not been excused on the ground of religious belief. Warren v. United States, 177 F.2d 596 (10th Cir. 1949), cert. den., 338 U.S. 947 (1950); Gara v. United States, 178 F.2d 38 (6th Cir. 1949), aff'd by equally divided Court, 340 U.S. 857, 71 S. Ct. 87, 95 L. Ed. 628 (1950).

4. The Supreme Court had held prior to 1946 that an alien who refuses to bear arms will not be admitted to citizenship. United States v. Schwimmer, 279 U.S. 644, 49 S. Ct. 448, 73 L. Ed. 889 (1929); United States v. MacIntosh, 283 U.S. 605, 51 S. Ct. 570, 75 L. Ed. 1302 (1931); United States v. Bland, 282 U.S. 636, 51 S. Ct. 569, 75 L. Ed. 1319 (1931). In Girouard v. United States, 328 U.S. 61, 66 S. Ct. 826, 90 L. Ed. 1084 (1946), the Court held that an alien who is willing to serve as a non-combatant and take the oath of allegiance but does not want to bear arms because of his religious beliefs can become a citizen under the provisions of the Nationality Act. The earlier cases were overruled. See also Cohnstaedt v. Immigration and Naturalization Service, 339 U.S. 901, 70 S. Ct. 516, 94 L. Ed. 1331 (1950) (refusal to manufacture munitions or deliver them to combat troops on religious grounds is no bar); cf. In re Clarke, 301 Pa. 321, 152 A.92 (1930) (citizenship refused where petitioner wanted to add to customary oath: "So far as they are in accord with the moral law of the United States"). The statutory oath has been

changed to permit those who refuse to bear arms on religious grounds to become citizens. See 66 Stat. 258 (1952), 8 U.S.C.A. §1448. Cf. Petition of Plywacki, 107 F. Supp. 593 (D. Haw. 1952) (naturalization denied where petitioner sought to substitute "I hereby declare . . . in honor and sincerity" for "I hereby declare on oath" and wanted to omit the closing phrase "so help me God"), reversed upon confession of error by the United States, 205 F.2d 423 (9th Cir. 1953). For discussion of the lower court opinion see Note, 1 Kan. L. Rev. 343 (1953).

D. OTHER ASPECTS OF FREEDOM OF RELIGION

Laws prohibiting polygamy and bigamy have been upheld against the objection that they interfered with religious beliefs of members of the Mormon Church that permitted and required these practices. See Reynolds v. United States, 98 U.S. 145, 25 L. Ed. 244 (1878); Davis v. Beason, 133 U.S. 333, 10 S. Ct. 299, 33 L. Ed. 637 (1890) (upholding Utah territorial law requiring that every voter swear that he does not practice and advocate polygamy privately or publicly). See also Church of Latter-Day Saints v. United States, 136 U.S. 1, 10 S. Ct. 792, 34 L. Ed. 478 (1890), where the Court said: ". . . the Thugs of India imagined that their belief in the right of assassination was a religious belief; but their thinking so did not make it so . . . The offering of human sacrifices by our own ancestors in Britain was no doubt sanctioned by an equally conscientious impulse. But no one, on that account, would hesitate to brand these practices, now, as crimes against society, and obnoxious to condemnation and punishment by the civil authority." 136 U.S. at 49-50. See further State v. Barlow, 107 Utah 292, 153 P.2d 647 (1944), app. dis., 324 U.S. 829 (1945) (state bigamy law); Cleveland v. United States, 329 U.S. 14, 67 S. Ct. 13, 91 L. Ed. 12 (1946) (federal anti-white slave law); In re State in interest of Black, 3 Utah 2d 315, 283 P.2d 887 (1955), app. dis., 350 U.S. 923 (1955) (parents who insist on teaching their children that polygamy is proper may be deprived of custody). See Linford, The Mormons and the Law: The Polygamy Cases, Part II, Civil Disabilities, 9 Utah L. Rev. 543 (1965). For a discussion of British cases see Bartholomew, Polygamous Marriages, 15 Mod. L. Rev. 35 (1952).

In People ex rel. Bernat v. Bicek, 405 Ill. 510, 91 N.E.2d 588 (1950), the Illinois Domestic Relations Act of 1949 authorized divorce courts to seek the assistance of representatives of religious denominations to which the parties belonged for purposes of effecting a reconciliation. The Court in holding the Act invalid gave as one of its reasons that it violated the principle of separation of Church and State. It relied principally on the McCollum case, printed in Section B.

It is generally held that only the state may dissolve marriages and religious divorces are not recognized. Certain grounds for seeking a divorce also touch on the issue of separation of Church and State and religious freedom. These include religious oppression and refusal to cohabit on religious grounds. See

Frantzen v. Frantzen, 349 S.W.2d 765 (Tex. Civ. App. 1961) (husband's concern about wife's being a Jehovah's Witness whose faith might affect family relationship because of that faith's objection to saluting the flag, serving in the armed forces, and permitting blood transfusions, held insufficient ground for divorce or child custody); Hughes v. Holman, 110 Ore. 415, 223 Pac. 730 (1924) (alienation of affection of wife by church; held that proof of intent and causal connection insufficient). Cf. Wood v. Wood, 227 Md. 211, 176 A.2d 229 (1961) (too much church-going by wife and her ultimately leaving the house to do work of the Lord held to constitute desertion). For a collection of cases see Torpey, Judicial Doctrines of Religious Rights in America, 207 et seq. (1948).

Some other Church-State problems not covered in this chapter are: (1) disputes between factions within religious organizations; (2) incorporation of church property; (3) enforceability of testamentary provisions restricting religious faith or marriage; (4) appointment of ambassador to Vatican; (5) adoption of religious mottos or principles by government, except to the extent discussed in the context of the Supreme Court opinions, supra. See the second edition of this book 1195-1196.

CHAPTER IX

Individual Rights Within
Private Associations

As has frequently been pointed out, Americans have always formed and joined associations created for a great variety of purposes. In modern times these private, or non-governmental, associations have assumed increasing importance in the national life of the country and in the individual life of its citizens. Organizations have grown in size, power, influence, and techniques of operation. Some have taken on quasi-public powers or functions, exert pressures which seriously affect the lives of non-belongers, or indeed make participation in the association compulsory. In other chapters we have dealt with the power of government to control the activities of private associations and their members. This chapter considers the rights of individual members, or persons seeking to become members, vis-à-vis the association itself or its officialdom.

The matters with which we are particularly concerned here relate to the power of private associations to exclude persons from membership, to expel or otherwise discipline members, and to control the funds contributed by members. Problems involving discriminatory action because of race, religion, nationality, or similar factors are taken up in other chapters.

The issues have been framed in various forms. One concerns the power of the courts to afford relief to an individual complaining against the action of the association. If the courts assume jurisdiction, questions arise as to the basis for judicial action, whether constitutional, statutory, or some form of relief founded on contract, tort, property right, fiduciary relation, or other similar principle. The problems include not only the substantive standards to which the association must conform but the extent to which the courts will require the association to afford procedural safeguards. In some instances, particularly in the labor field, statutory controls have been enacted, administered by executive agencies as well as the judiciary. The materials below present some samples of these issues as they have arisen in recent years.

REFERENCES

The seminal article on the subject is Chafee, The Internal Affairs of Associations Not for Profit, 43 Harv. L. Rev. 993 (1930). A recent extensive treatment of most aspects of the problem is Note, Judicial Control of Actions of Private Associations, 76 Harv. L.

Rev. 983 (1963). Much of the material cited in Chapter V, Section A, on the "right of association" is concerned with these issues. From a broader point of view, see Wyzanski, The Open Window and the Open Door, 35 Calif. L. Rev. 336 (1947); Hale, Freedom Through Law: Public Control of Private Governing Power (1952); Wirtz, Government by Private Groups, 13 La. L. Rev. 440 (1953); A Symposium on Group Interests and the Law, 13 Rutgers L. Rev. 429 (1959); Symposium, Freedom in the Modern American Economy, 55 Nw. U.L. Rev. 1 (1960); Hanslowe, Regulation By Visible Public and Invisible Private Government, 40 Texas L. Rev. 88 (1961).

For the proposition that certain constitutional protections under the Bill of Rights should be made available to members of certain private associations, see Miller, The Constitutional Law of the "Security State," 10 Stan. L. Rev. 620 (1958); Malick, Toward a New Constitutional Status for Labor Unions: A Proposal, 21 Rocky Mt. L. Rev. 260 (1949); Read, Minority Rights and the Union Shop: A Basis For Constitutional Attack, 49 Minn. L. Rev. 227 (1964); but cf. Wellington, The Constitution, the Labor Union, and "Governmental Action," 70 Yale L.J. 345 (1961). Along the same lines see Berle, Constitutional Limitations on Corporate Activity — Protection of Personal Rights from Invasion Through Economic Power, 100 U. Pa. L. Rev. 933 (1952); Friedman, Corporate Power, Government by Private Groups, and the Law, 57 Colum. L. Rev. 155 (1957); Latham, The Commonwealth of the Corporation, 55 Nw. U.L. Rev. 25 (1960).

For a detailed account of the operations of one of the best known private associations, see The American Medical Association: Power, Purpose, and Politics in Organized Medicine, 63 Yale L.J. 937 (1954).

NOTE, EXCLUSION FROM PRIVATE ASSOCIATIONS
74 Yale L.J. 1313 (1965)

Students of politics and law have long recognized the public influence of private associations as well as their immense power over members of the associations.[1] However, there is considerable disagreement among commentators about what role, if any, courts ought to play in regulating the exercise of either the influence or the power.[2] Generally, judicial action concerning private associations has been limited to reviewing the society's duties towards its members.[3] In suits involving non-members seeking admission, only a few

---

[1] One of the earliest comments on the importance of private associations was II De Tocqueville, Democracy in America (chap. V) (1862). For examples of other works by political scientists see, Mills, White Collar (1951); Truman, The Governmental Process (1955). In the legal field the classic discussion is Chafee, The Internal Affairs of Associations Not for Profit, 43 Harv. L. Rev. 993 (1930). For a complete survey of the "law of private associations" see Developments in the Law — Judicial Control of Actions of Private Associations, 76 Harv. L. Rev. 983 (1963). Most other studies have concentrated on particular associations. See, e.g., Note, The American Medical Association: Power, Purposes, and Politics in Organized Medicine, 63 Yale L.J. 938 (1954).

[2] Some commentators would have courts review the actions of every association strong enough to affect a large number of people. See, e.g., Miller, Private Governments and the Constitution 12-14 (1959); Berle, Constitutional Limitations on Corporate Activity — Protection of Personal Rights from Invasion Through Economic Power, 100 U. Pa. L. Rev. 933 (1952). Others emphasize the importance of group autonomy and advocate judicial intervention only under special circumstances which pose a particular threat to democratic government. See, e.g., Summers, Democracy in Private Groups and Democracy in Government at 5 (1960) (unpublished speech); Chafee, supra note 1.

[3] See Developments in the Law, supra note 1, at 1006-37.

courts have ordered a private association to admit an excluded applicant.[4] Review of the internal actions of private associations raises many problems, for the interests of an excluded applicant must be balanced against the values of free association, group autonomy and private ordering of society. In each case a court must determine whether the particular association is a proper subject of judicial review; whether the harm to the excluded applicant justifies intervention; and whether there are suitable standards to test the validity of the group's action. This Note will examine one type of private organization — the professional association[5] — in an attempt to isolate some of the factors which might justify intervening in exclusion disputes. Also the Note will suggest a workable standard for the courts to apply.

Historically, courts have treated professional associations as private, voluntary groups, and have been reluctant to intervene in their affairs.[6] This policy of non-interference has been more pronounced in cases involving exclusion from membership rather than expulsion from an association. In expulsion cases, courts have justified intervention on the grounds that the expelled member has been deprived of "property rights" or that the association's actions were in breach of a contractual agreement between the member and the society.[7] However, an individual cannot have a property right in an organization of which he is not a member.[8] Nor can he establish the existence of a contractual relationship which will protect him. Generally there has been no legal remedy available to the practitioner denied admission to a professional society. Such associations have been free to refuse admission on any grounds. They are treated by the courts no differently from country clubs, college fra-

---

[4] See Falcone v. County Medical Soc'y, 34 N.J. 582, 170 A.2d 791 (1961), affirming 62 N.J. Super. 184, 162 A.2d 324 (1960). Blende v. County Medical Soc'y, 96 Ariz. 240, 393 P.2d 926 (1964). For critical comment see, Note, Judicially Compelled Admission to Medical Societies: The Falcone Case, 75 Harv. L. Rev. 1186 (1962); Note, 15 Rutgers L. Rev. 327 (1961).

[5] Several characteristics of professional associations make them of particular concern to our government and legal system. Professional service is extremely important to society, yet the general public has little means of judging the competence of this service. Thus, professional associations, by promoting higher standards of competence and ethics, are performing an important public service. This frequently results in the delegation of public powers to these associations. See, infra notes 37-40 and accompanying text. . . .

[6] For a full discussion of the reasons for this policy see Chafee, supra note 1, at 1021-23.

[7] As examples of the "property" theory see State ex rel. Waring v. Medical Soc'y, 38 Ga. 608 (1869); Dawkins v. Antrobus, 17 Ch. D. 615 (1881). As examples of the "contract" theory see Smith v. County Medical Ass'n, 19 Cal. 2d 263, 120 P.2d 874 (1942); Polin v. Kaplan, 257 N.Y. 277, 177 N.E. 833 (1931). Both of these theories have been extensively criticized, and the absence of a "contractual" or "property" right does not appear to be a valid reason for non-intervention in exclusion disputes. See Note, 15 Rutgers L. Rev. 327, 330-32 (1961); Chafee, supra note 1, at 1001-07; Developments in the Law, supra note 1, at 999, 1002.

[8] Courts have usually used the term "property interest" in connection with a right to use the association's physical property or to share in the society's assets in the event of dissolution. See, e.g., Davis v. Scher, 356 Mich. 291, 97 N.W.2d 137 (1959); Stein v. Marks, 44 Misc. 140, 89 N.Y. Supp. 921 (Sup. Ct. 1904).

ternities or the Masons. The typical judicial attitude is expressed in Harris v. Thomas[9] which involved the exclusion of an osteopath from a local medical society in Texas. The court stated that:

"A voluntary association has the power to enact laws governing the admission of members. . . . Membership therein is a privilege which the society may accord or withhold at its pleasure, with which a court of equity will not interfere, even though the arbitrary rejection of the candidate may prejudice his material interests.[10] "

Only in certain special circumstances have the courts made exceptions to this general policy. Where the state requires membership in a professional society as a prerequisite to practice, some courts have compelled the admission of duly licensed members of the profession.[11] Furthermore, a few state courts have intervened when there was a showing that the association's actions were designed solely to eliminate competition in violation of state antitrust law.[12] However, state antitrust laws afford relief only in limited circumstances, and at best provide an infrequent basis for intervention in exclusion cases.[13]

The New Jersey Supreme Court, in the case of Falcone v. Medical Soc'y,[14] was the first court to break completely from the traditional judicial approach toward professional societies. Dr. Falcone, a graduate of the Philadelphia College of Osteopathy, passed the New Jersey State Medical Examination, and was licensed to "practice Medicine and Surgery in the State of New Jersey." [15] The Philadelphia College of Osteopathy offered a complete medical

---

[9] 217 S.W. 1068 (Tex. Civ. App. 1920); accord, Medical Soc'y v. Walker, 245 Ala. 135, 16 So. 2d 321 (1944).

[10] 217 S.W. at 1076-77.

[11] See People ex rel. Bartlett v. Medical Soc'y, 32 N.Y. 187 (1865).

[12] See, e.g., Group Health Co-op v. County Medical Soc'y, 39 Wash. 2d 586, 237 P.2d 737 (1951); Tatkin v. Superior Court, 160 Cal. App. 2d 745, 326 P.2d 201 (Dist. Ct. App. 1958). See, contra, Levin v. Sinai Hosp., 186 Md. 174, 46 A.2d 298 (Ct. App. 1946).

[13] Generally, courts have limited application of anti-trust laws to cases where the AMA was trying to destroy a group-health plan. See, e.g., Group Health Co-op v. County Medical Soc'y, supra note 12. Most anti-trust actions have been brought under state anti-trust laws because of the difficulty of proving a violation of the Sherman Act. In American Medical Ass'n v. United States, 317 U.S. 519 (1943), an action brought under §3 of the Sherman Act, the Court enjoined the association's activity, but avoided ruling on whether the Sherman Act would apply to professions outside of the District of Columbia. However, in United States v. State Medical Soc'y, 343 U.S. 326 (1952), the Court held that the practice of medicine could not be covered by the Sherman Act since it did not involve interstate commerce. (This would seem to apply to other professions as well.) Consequently, the Court refused to compel admission into the society. Another obstacle to use of the Sherman Act is the difficulty of proving a conspiracy or injury to the public. See, e.g., Riggall v. County Medical Soc'y, 249 F.2d 266 (8th Cir. 1957), cert. denied, 355 U.S. 954 (1958). For a general discussion of the application of anti-trust laws to medical associations see Comment, 22 U. Chi. L. Rev. 694 (1955).

[14] 34 N.J. 582, 170 A.2d 791 (1961), affirming 62 N.J. Super. 184, 162 A.2d 324 (1960).

[15] 34 N.J. 582, 584, 170 A.2d 791, 793. The facts of this case are set forth at 34 N.J. at 584-87, 170 A.2d at 793-96.

course and was accredited by the New Jersey State Board of Medical Examiners, but not by the American Medical Association (AMA). Dr. Falcone later acquired a full medical degree, based partially on his previous education, from the AMA-accredited University of Milan in Italy. After starting practice in New Jersey, and becoming a staff member of several hospitals there,[16] Dr. Falcone applied for admission to the Middlesex County Medical Society. He was denied membership because he was a Doctor of Osteopathy, not of Medicine. The Society considered his degree from Milan unsatisfactory since that institution had given credit for his prior study. He was unable to continue serving on the hospitals' staffs because the AMA, by threatening to withdraw accreditation, forced the hospitals to hire only members of local medical societies. Since Dr. Falcone required hospital facilities in order to maintain his practice, he alleged that his rejection from the Society severely limited his professional practice, and that consequently he would suffer serious economic hardship.

The Superior Court of Middlesex County ordered Dr. Falcone admitted into the society.[17] In affirming this decision, the New Jersey Supreme Court recognized the traditional reluctance of courts to interfere in the affairs of private associations, but found that the economic hardship caused by the society's action justified the lower court's decision.[18] The Supreme Court agreed that the AMA's stranglehold over accredited hospitals gave the Middlesex society a monopoly over hospital staffing. Consequently, the Court considered it unreasonable to accept the traditional categorization of the medical society as a voluntary association, since membership in it was an economic necessity.[19] After a further finding that Dr. Falcone's exclusion bore "no relation to the advancement of medical science or the elevation of public standards," [20] the Court held that the society's action "[ran] counter to the public policy of our State" [21] by reducing the value of Dr. Falcone's license.[22]

Most commentators criticized the Falcone decision,[23] although they conceded that plaintiff's substantial economic injury provided some justification for the court's intervention.[24] It is submitted, however, that not only was Falcone decided correctly, but that its impact should not be limited to the situation in which an individual suffers economic harm as a result of the monop-

[16] Dr. Falcone had been accepted to these hospital staffs while a provisional member of the Middlesex Society. 34 N.J. at 586, 170 A.2d at 793.

[17] 62 N.J. Super. 184, 162 A.2d 324 (1960).

[18] 34 N.J. at 592, 170 A.2d at 796-97.

[19] 34 N.J. at 596, 170 A.2d at 799.

[20] 34 N.J. at 598, 170 A.2d at 800.

[21] Ibid.

[22] 34 N.J. at 597, 598, 170 A.2d at 799, 800.

[23] See, e.g., Note, 75 Harv. L. Rev. 1186, 1193 (1961); Note, 15 Rutgers L. Rev. 327, 356 (1961). The notewriters argued that if an association is compelled to admit all practitioners this would result in lower standards for the profession in general, and would damage the reputation of the society.

[24] Note, 75 Harv. L. Rev. 1186, 1198 (1961); Note, 15 Rutgers L. Rev. 327, 354 (1961).

oly power exercised by the excluding association.[25] Exclusion from a professional association may result in harm which is not measurable in economic terms. An association's monopoly power in regulating and supervising professional practice[26] deprives the excluded practitioner of the important right to participate in decision-making concerning regulation of his occupation.[27] Because this regulation may have a substantial effect on the individual's practice, his exclusion appreciably diminishes the value of his license.[28] The practitioner can be compared to a person denied admission to a union which has a closed shop arrangement with an employer. Usually courts will order that the union either admit a qualified applicant or that the closed shop arrangement be disregarded.[29] However, under the latter alternative the worker earns a livelihood, but is deprived of the right to participate in union policy making which might materially affect the conditions of his employment. Thus, a sounder approach in both the union and professional context is to compel admission into the excluding organization.[30]

This argument was advanced by the plaintiff in a recent exclusion case, *Salter v. Psychological Ass'n.*[31] Salter, a psychologist certified by New York, claimed that the court should compel his admission because "the Association was an arm of the state" or at the very least, exercised monopoly power over his profession, and that the association's action harmed him substantially.[32] Salter emphasized the non-economic interests that were jeopardized by exclusion,[33] chiefly his inability to be heard in the forum most concerned with the

---

[25] While economic injury does provide a valid basis for intervention, there are several problems in applying an economic test. It is not clear what degree of economic harm is necessary to justify intervention. There are economic injuries, less serious than total loss of ability to practice, which might deprive an excluded applicant of the ability to practice successfully. Membership in the association may be necessary to obtain social and professional contracts necessary for referral business and professional advancement; access to publications, libraries, and meetings which help the professional keep abreast of developments in his profession; or malpractice insurance necessary for practice. Moreover, there may be instances where substantial economic injury is alleged but a court would not be justified in intervening. Exclusion from a local Elks or country club may result in substantial economic injury. (This might occur when most of a town's business leaders belong to the club and make it a practice to deal only with other members.) Yet, if a court were to intervene when an individual was excluded from such a club, all the values of private association and group autonomy would be endangered.

[26] For a description of these powers see text accompanying notes 37-39 infra.

[27] See note 43 infra and accompanying text.

[28] See discussion in note 41 infra and accompanying text.

[29] See James v. Marinship Corp., 25 Cal. 2d 721, 155 P.2d 329 (1944).

[30] Although only one court has adopted this approach in the area of union activity, Thorman v. International Alliance of Theatrical, Stage Employees, 49 Cal. 2d 629, 320 P.2d 494 (1958), it has been advocated by many commentators. See, e.g., Summers, The Right to Join a Union, 47 Colum. L. Rev. 33, 73 (1947).

[31] 14 N.Y.2d 100, 198 N.E.2d 250, 248 N.Y.S.2d 867 (1964).

[32] Brief for Appellant, pp. 10, 17, Salter v. Psychological Ass'n, supra note 31.

[33] He also alleged that he would suffer economic harm resulting from injury to reputation and loss of prestige due to his exclusion from the psychological association. Id. at 19, 27.

regulation and development of the practice of psychology in New York.[34] The court rejected Salter's petition on the grounds that he failed to prove either that the association's actions were state action, or that the association exerted monopolistic control over the profession.[35] However, the court did leave open the possibility that Salter's non-economic arguments might justify judicial intervention if state action were established.[36]

Actually, with regard to many professional associations, there exists sufficient formal nexus between the state and the association to support a finding of state action. If, then, the exclusion is unreasonable, the association's action would violate the equal protection clause of the fourteenth amendment. For example, unlike the situation in the Salter case, extensive power over the regulation of most professions has been given to licensing boards, which are in turn formally controlled by a professional association.[37] Furthermore, in

[34] Id. at 15. Salter alleged that
"[b]ecause of its size, power and position, the Association obtained the legislation governing petitioner's profession and means of livelihood. It is performing the duties of the statutory State Advisory Council by undertaking to construe and implement that legislation . . . all of this having a direct impact on petitioner's professional existence. And yet, as one certified under this legislation and governed by it, petitioner is denied the right to have a voice . . . in the implementation and interpretation of the law and in any proposals for new legislation." Ibid.

[35] 14 N.Y.2d at 105, 248 N.Y.S.2d at 870.

[36] 14 N.Y.2d at 104, 248 N.Y.S.2d at 869, 870. Due to the peculiar fact situation presented in this case the court was probably justified in reaching its decision. Not only did Salter fail to satisfy the educational requirements for membership in the association, but also these requirements were lower than those of the state certification standard. Salter had received his certification through a "grandfather" clause in the certification statute, which provided that individuals practicing in New York for twelve years prior to the passage of the certification law need not meet the educational requirements. 14 N.Y.2d at 103, 248 N.Y.S.2d at 869. Furthermore, Salter was a successful practitioner and could not show economic harm. Finally, as noted above, Salter failed to prove ties between the association and the government sufficient to constitute state action. 14 N.Y.2d at 105-06, 248 N.Y.S.2d at 870-71.
Salter's claims, however, were not entirely without merit. There was ample evidence that he was a very competent psychologist. Brief for Appellant, at 3. He was at least considered competent enough to merit state licensure, since the state statute required that individuals without the requisite educational background prove their competency to a state board of examiners. N.Y. Education Law §7601 (1956). Moreover, there were significant ties, albeit informal ones, between the association and the state. It was primarily through the efforts of the association that the state certification law had been passed, and the legislature had worked closely with the association in drafting the statute. Brief for Appellant, at 10. Eight of the seventeen members of the State Advisory Board were also directors of the association. Id. at 11. The association itself recognized these connections with the state by proclaiming itself the voice of all New York State psychologists and claiming to be the organ through which the psychologist could have a voice in regulation of the profession. Id. at 11, 12. Finally, the association had frequently made exceptions to its general qualifications and admitted those with qualifications similar to Salter's, id. at 14, indicating that its standards were not absolute. Yet, in this instance, it refused to give Salter a hearing. Ibid. These facts might justify a finding that the association's actions were state action and that the society acted arbitrarily in excluding Salter.

[37] In most states the licensing boards are either chosen directly by the professional association or from a list of nominees submitted by the association. For a detailed breakdown of the methods by which these boards are chosen see Council of State

many states, professional groups have been delegated the authority to accredit professional schools.[38] This power is particularly important in states where licensure is restricted to graduates of accredited institutions.[39] Finally, a number of states authorize professional societies to make up and grade the licensing examination.[40] In all of these instances, the association exercises a significant degree of control over the individual practitioner and his manner of practice.[41]

Delegations of this nature have been defended on the grounds that:

"They guarantee expert understanding of the problems faced by practitioners in the occupation. Above all, they give the practitioners being regulated a sense of participation in selecting their regulators and thus ensure their close cooperation in maintaining high standards of practice.[42]"

It should be apparent then, that the most persuasive reason for reposing state regulatory authority in a professional society — its responsiveness to the members of the profession — is also the most persuasive argument for enforcing the claim of duly licensed practitioners to admission to the association. The democratic process is best satisfied when those persons most directly affected by the licensing and regulation of professions are accorded the fullest right to participate in the decision-making process.[43] Since the state delegates regulatory power to a specific organization, any practitioner outside the organization is silenced. Moreover, the public benefits when all viewpoints within a particular profession are heard before an association exercising public powers. Dissenting opinion should not be stifled by denial of admission to applicants with unpopular views. In Falcone, for example, it would seem that a major reason why the AMA denied Dr. Falcone admission was that he had

---

Governments, Occupational Licensing Legislation in the States at 88-90 (1952). For a typical statute see N.C. Gen. Stat. §90-93 (1958).

[38] E.g., W. Va. Code Ann. §2869(b) (1961); Mont. Rev. Codes §66-1003(a) (1947).

[39] Ibid.

[40] The American Institute of Certified Public Accountants makes up and grades the licensing exam in every state. (It has instituted a uniform test.) See, Penny, The American Institute of CPAs — Past and Future, Journal of Accountancy at 33 (Jan. 1962). Similar powers have been granted other professional associations. Council of State Governments, op. cit. supra note 37, at 51.

[41] These boards issue, suspend, and revoke licenses (and often establish the grounds for these actions), enforce the licensing statute — even to the extent of evaluating the work of licensees, establish license fees, and examine applicants for admission to the profession. They frequently determine ethical standards which may regulate how a professional may obtain clients or what fees he may charge. Council of State Governments, op. cit. supra note 37, at 40-47.

[42] Council of State Governments, op. cit. supra note 37, at 38.

[43] See Summers, supra note 2, at 12, 13. In fact, our entire system of government is based on the right of participation in governmental decision — either directly or through elected representatives. It is not a long jump from this premise to the conclusion that there should be a right to participate in decisions of private groups, when, in effect, these groups have authority to make decisions as a result of a delegation of governmental power.

studied osteopathy, a science abhorred by the Association.[44] Thus, while securing the rights of qualified practitioners seeking admission to professional associations, the court protects also the broader public interest in having a fully representative professional forum.

Judicial intervention, then, seems justified in exclusion cases involving associations to which the state has formally delegated regulatory authority. (The majority of professional organizations probably fall within this class.)[45] The argument for intervention, of course, may seem weaker when no formal delegation of authority exists. But, informal ties between the association and the state may be just as significant as those established by legislative enactment. Even in the absence of formal delegation, a strong society may exercise effective regulatory power over a profession. A state legislature, faced with the need to enact legislation in a short period, cannot consider extensively varying professional viewpoints concerning regulation of the profession. Instead, the legislature relies heavily upon the associations, under the assumption that internal differences among members of the profession have been resolved within the association itself. Therefore, an association may have been primarily responsible for drafting and amending the state's licensing statute;[46] or, as a matter of practice, the state licensing board may be composed of the association's officers.[47] In such a situation the harm to the professional resulting from exclusion by the association is just as substantial as the harm caused by exclusion from an association formally performing state functions. The type of economic injury considered in Falcone may readily result from exclusion by either type of association. Also, access to effective decisional arenas may be just as completely blocked in either situation.

For these reasons the courts should intervene in exclusion disputes when the association has established substantial informal ties with the state, although there has been no formal delegation.[48] In analogous areas the courts

---

[44] There is at present a trend toward absorption of osteopaths into the AMA. Note, The American Medical Association, supra note 1, at 966-67. Thus the cleavage between osteopaths and the AMA may be disappearing. However, in local societies the breach may still be significant. Ideology also seemed to be the major reason Salter was excluded. According to several members of the profession, Salter espoused an approach to psychology repugnant to the majority of the Psychological Association.

[45] Council of State Governments, op. cit. supra note 37, at 88-90.

[46] See discussion supra note 36. Council of State Governments, op. cit. supra note 37, at 57.

[47] See discussion supra note 36. Power in professional associations tends to be centered in relatively few hands, and this may be reflected in the composition of licensing boards. For a general discussion of the tendency towards oligarchies see Note, The American Medical Association, supra note 1; Kahn-Freund, Trade Union Democracy and the Law, 22 Ohio St. L.J. 4 (1961).

[48] Courts would have to proceed on a case by case basis in determining whether an association was de facto a quasi-public body. The plaintiff would have the burden of proving that the association was performing functions supposedly performed by the state. See supra notes 46, 47 for two factors a court should consider. See also Lewis, The Meaning of State Action, 60 Colum. L. Rev. 1083 (1960).

have recognized that private associations may exercise public power and thus should be prohibited from taking arbitrary or unconstitutional action. For example, in the case of Terry v. Adams,[49] the Supreme Court compelled admission of Negroes into a private association which in reality controlled a state's electoral process. And in Marsh v. Alabama[50] the Court held that a company town, though a private body, had assumed public characteristics and should be held to the same constitutional standards as government itself.[51] Similarly, in the area of professional regulation, a clear de facto exercise of regulatory power by the association should justify its being treated in the same manner as an association formally performing governmental functions. Alternatively, the economic monopoly position of the association might justify a state court's intervention.

Once a decision has been made to intervene in an exclusion dispute, a court must determine what standards it should apply in testing the validity of the association's action. This problem is seen by many commentators as the most serious obstacle to judicial intervention in exclusion disputes. They argue that a court, lacking expertise, cannot, and therefore should not, substitute its judgment for that of the association.[52]

It is submitted, however, that certification or licensure by the state provides a workable standard of review. When an applicant has been certified or licensed by the state there should be a presumption that the applicant is qualified for admission to the professional association. This rule follows the logical implications of the Falcone decision. Although the Falcone court claimed it was not evaluating standards, it did exactly that in saying that the society's rules had "no relation to the advancement of medical science or the evaluation of professional standards." [53] In effect, the court said that the state of New Jersey found Dr. Falcone qualified, and therefore any contrary finding by the medical society was unacceptable. Making state licensure prima facie evidence of qualification for membership in a professional association places upon the association the burden of proving that a particular applicant should be excluded. The society would have to demonstrate that although the applicant had a license his admission was not in the public interest.[54] Absent a clear

---

[49] 345 U.S. 461 (1953).

[50] 326 U.S. 501 (1946).

[51] Id. at 506-07.

[52] See note 23 supra.

[53] 34 N.J. at 598, 170 A.2d at 800. This was the standard suggested by the lower court. 62 N.J. Super. at 202, 162 A.2d at 333.

[54] The association would have to show that, although the applicant was licensed, he had violated ethical standards applicable to a member of the entire profession, or had practiced in a manner sufficient to warrant delicensure. Thus if the applicant lost a malpractice suit, advertised in a manner contrary to professional standards, or was guilty of other professional misconduct, the association might justifiably exclude him. Basically, this eliminates qualifications based on arbitrary factors such as race or political ideology, and qualifications based on educational background — since the state educational standard is determinative. However, it is possible that in rare cases an association will be able to show that the state's educational requirements are so low that the asso-

and convincing showing, a court should accept the fact of licensure as suffi-cient evidence of qualification and order the applicant admitted to the associ-ation.

The standard based on state licensure is clear-cut, objective and readily applicable in most cases. It minimizes the need for courts to make technical or policy determinations concerning professional qualifications. Also, it pro-tects the right of the individual practitioner without sacrificing high stand-ards of professional practice, since every applicant will have been judged qualified by a state board of examiners.[55] Moreover, the important role of professional associations in raising the ethical (as opposed to educational) standards of the profession will not be affected by applying this standard. And when an association believes that the state educational or competence qualifications are too low, it can lobby to get them raised. In the past the associations have had great success in convincing the states to impose stricter licensing laws.[56] Finally, adoption of the standard proposed in this Note will prevent the professional association from using its power of exclusion to form an economic cartel. Frenquently, associations have adopted restrictive qualifi-cations only to further their economic interests.[57]

---

ciation had to have higher standards in order to insure the public of competent pro-fessional service.

[55] Generally, professional associations accept state licensure as sufficient evidence of qualification. Occasionally, different classes of membership will be created, based on the number of years of practical experience, but the rights of all members will not vary significantly. See, By-Laws, American Pharmaceutical Association, Art. II §1; By-Laws, American Institute of Certified Public Accountants, Art. II §2; By-Laws, American Dental Association, Chap. I §20. Very few associations have higher educational require-ments.

[56] The fact that the impetus for licensing legislation generally comes from occupa-tional associations themselves, and the success of these associations in prompting the pas-sage of this type of legislation has been noted by many commentators. See, e.g., Jaffe, Law Making by Private Groups, 51 Harv. L. Rev. 201, 229-30 (1937); Council of State Governments, op. cit. supra note 37, at 57; Grant, The Gild Returns to America I, 4 J. of Politics 303, 316-17 (1942).

[57] Numerous commentators have noted the cartelizing efforts of these associations. See, e.g., Grant, supra note 56, at 316-17; Gilb, Self-Regulating Professions and the Public Welfare — A Case Study of the California Bar (unpublished thesis, Radcliffe, 1956); Note, The American Medical Association, Power, Purpose, and Politics in Organized Medicine, 63 Yale L.J. 938, 947 (1954). Often this is accomplished by en-couraging the passage of licensing legislation. See, Council of State Governments, op. cit. supra note 37, at 57. Sometimes the methods are less subtle. The attempts of the AMA to destroy group health plans and to regulate fees are two examples. See Group Health Co-op v. County Medical Soc'y, 39 Wash. 2d 586, 237 P.2d 737 (1951); Tatkin v. Superior Court, 160 Cal. App. 2d 745, 326 P.2d 201 (Dist. Ct. App. 1958). In a related context see Brazier, The Ohio Architects' Guild, Cases in State and Local Government at 41 (Frost ed. 1961).

When a private association is in a position to function as a cartel, a court should be even more willing to see that it exercises its power consonant with public policy. Such an attitude was expressed by the Supreme Court in Silver v. Stock Exchange, 373 U.S. 341 (1963), in which the stock exchange was found to be subject to the Sherman Act. The Court stated:

"The exchanges are by their nature bodies with a limited number of members. . . .

Judicial intervention in exclusion cases might result in some disharmony within the affected association. Actually, there is no reason to expect that there will be very many cases in which the courts will be called upon to enforce admission, since most applicants do not have any particular difficulty in gaining entrance to professional associations. However, there will always be a few individuals excluded because of race, unpopular professional or political views, or because of other unreasonable restraints imposed by the association. In these situations, judicial intervention is justified. The resulting interference with private associations will be both insignificant and infrequent. For the most part private ordering will not be supplanted by judicial fiat, and the societies will be left a free hand in the management of their affairs.

REFERENCES

For additional discussion of the exclusion problem, see Note, Judicial Control of Actions of Private Association, 76 Harv. L. Rev. 983, 1037-1055 (1963); Pasley, Exclusion and Expulsion From Non-Profit Organizations — The Civil Rights Aspect, 14 Clev.-Mar. L. Rev. 203 (1965). Most of the earlier cases dealt with the problem of expulsion or discipline. See Chafee, The Internal Affairs of Associations Not for Profit, 43 Harv. L. Rev. 993 (1930); Note, Equitable Jurisdiction to Protect Membership in a Voluntary Association, 58 Yale L.J. 999 (1949); Fellman, The Constitutional Right of Association, ch. III (1963); Note, supra, 76 Harv. L. Rev. at 998-1020. See also Lloyd, The Disciplinary Powers of Professional Bodies, 13 Mod. L. Rev. 281 (1950), and Judicial Review of Expulsion by a Domestic Tribunal, 15 Mod. L. Rev. 413 (1952).

More specifically on procedural requirements, see Note, Exhaustion of Remedies in Private Voluntary Associations, 65 Yale L.J. 369 (1956); Note, supra, 76 Harv. L. Rev. at 1020-1037, 1069-1100.

On rights involved in cases of schism or factional disputes, see Note, Judicial Intervention in Disputes Over the Use of Church Property, 75 Harv. L. Rev. 1142 (1962). See also Note, The Power of Courts Over the Internal Affairs of Religious Groups, 43 Calif. L. Rev. 322 (1955); Note, Judicial Intervention in Disputes Within Independent Church Bodies, 54 Mich. L. Rev. 102 (1955).

All these problems are discussed in great detail in the materials dealing specifically with the internal affairs of labor organizations, collected in the references following the extracts from the Labor-Management Reporting and Disclosure Act of 1959.

This limited-entry feature of exchanges led historically to their being treated by courts as private clubs, . . . and to their being given great latitude in disciplining errant members. . . . As exchanges became a more and more important element in our Nation's economic . . . system, however, the private-club analogy became increasingly inapposite and the ungoverned self-regulation became more and more obviously inadequate. . . ." Id. at 350-51.

Because of this change in character, the Court held that the stock exchange was covered by the Sherman Act, and that it could not arbitrarily exclude an individual from use of its services. Since the Sherman Act is not applicable to professional associations, see supra note 13, a court must find other ways of checking the actions of these groups.

LABOR – MANAGEMENT REPORTING AND
DISCLOSURE ACT OF 1959, TITLE I, BILL OF RIGHTS
OF MEMBERS OF LABOR ORGANIZATIONS
73 Stat. 522-523 (1959), 29 U.S.C. §§411-413

§411. Bill of rights; constitution and bylaws of labor organizations.
(a)(1) Equal rights.

Every member of a labor organization shall have equal rights and privileges within such organization to nominate candidates, to vote in elections or referendums of the labor organizations, to attend membership meetings, and to participate in the deliberations and voting upon the business of such meetings, subject to reasonable rules and regulations in such organization's constitution and bylaws.

(2) Freedom of speech and assembly.

Every member of any labor organization shall have the right to meet and assemble freely with other members; and to express any views, arguments, or opinions; and to express at meetings of the labor organization his views, upon candidates in an election of the labor organization or upon any business properly before the meeting, subject to the organization's established and reasonable rules pertaining to the conduct of meetings: *Provided,* That nothing herein shall be construed to impair the right of a labor organization to adopt and enforce reasonable rules as to the responsibility of every member toward the organization as an institution and to his refraining from conduct that would interfere with its performance of its legal or contractual obligations.

(3) Dues, initiation fees, and assessments.

Except in the case of a federation of national or international labor organizations, the rates of dues and initiation fees payable by members of any labor organization in effect on September 14, 1959 shall not be increased, and no general or special assessment shall be levied upon such members, except—

(A) in the case of a local labor organization, (i) by majority vote by secret ballot of the members in good standing voting at a general or special membership meeting, after reasonable notice of the intention to vote upon such question, or (ii) by majority vote of the members in good standing voting in a membership referendum conducted by secret ballot; or

(B) in the case of a labor organization, other than a local labor organization or a federation of national or international labor organizations, (i) by majority vote of the delegates voting at a regular convention, or at a special convention of such labor organization held upon not less than thirty days' written notice to the principal office of each local or constituent labor organization entitled to such notice, or (ii) by majority vote of the members in good standing of such labor organization voting in a membership referendum conducted by secret ballot, or (iii) by majority vote of the members of the executive board or similar governing body of such labor organization, pursuant to express authority contained in the constitution and bylaws of such labor organization: *Provided,* That such action on the part of the executive board or similar governing body shall be effective only until the next regular convention of such labor organization.

(4) Protection of the right to sue.

No labor organization shall limit the right of any member thereof to institute an action in any court, or in a proceeding before any administrative agency, irrespective of whether or not the labor organization or its officers are named as defendants or respondents in such action or proceeding, or the right of any member of a labor organization to appear as a witness in any judicial, administrative, or legislative proceeding, or to petition any legislature or to communicate with any legislator: *Provided,* That any such member may be required to exhaust reasonable hearing procedures (but not to exceed a four-month lapse of time) within such organization, before instituting legal or administrative proceedings against such organizations or any officer thereof: *And provided further,* That no interested employer or employer association shall directly or indirectly finance, encourage, or participate in, except as a party, any such action, proceeding, appearance, or petition.

(5) Safeguards against improper disciplinary action.

No member of any labor organization may be fined, suspended, expelled, or otherwise disciplined except for nonpayment of dues by such organization or by any officer thereof unless such member has been (A) served with written specific charges; (B) given a reasonable time to prepare his defense; (C) afforded a full and fair hearing.

(b) Any provision of the constitution and bylaws of any labor organization which is inconsistent with the provisions of this section shall be of no force or effect.

§412. Civil action for infringement of rights; jurisdiction.

Any person whose rights secured by the provisions of this subchapter have been infringed by any violation of this subchapter may bring a civil action in a district court of the United States for such relief (including injunctions) as may be appropriate. Any such action against a labor organization shall be brought in the district court of the United States for the district where the alleged violation occurred, or where the principal office of such labor organization is located.

§413. Retention of existing rights of members.

Nothing contained in this subchapter shall limit the rights and remedies of any member of a labor organization under any State or Federal law or before any court or other tribunal, or under the constitution and bylaws of any labor organization.

REFERENCES

1. Sections 401 to 403 of the Labor-Management Reporting and Disclosure Act contain provisions designed to secure fair union elections. 73 Stat. 532-534 (1959), 29 U.S.C.

§§481-483. Other sections provide for reporting by unions and their officers and employees of various matters affecting the membership, including finances, 73 Stat. 524-530, 29 U.S.C. §§431-440, and contain provisions regulating union trusteeships, 73 Stat. 530-532, 29 U.S.C. §§461-466. For the legislative history of the Bill of Rights provisions, see 2 Legislative History of the Labor-Management Reporting and Disclosure Act of 1959, 1102-1119, 1220-1239 (1959); Rothman, Legislative History of the "Bill of Rights" for Union Members, 45 Minn. L. Rev. 199 (1960); Sherman, The Individual Member and the Union: The Bill of Rights Title in the Labor-Management Reporting and Disclosure Act of 1959, 54 Nw. U.L. Rev. 803 (1960).

2. The courts have tended to interpret the Bill of Rights provisions liberally. See Salzhandler v. Caputo, 316 F.2d 445 (2d Cir. 1963), cert. den., 375 U.S. 946 (1963); Farowitz v. Associated Musicians, 330 F.2d 999 (2d Cir. 1964); Nelson v. Johnson, 212 F. Supp. 233 (D. Minn. 1963), aff'd, 325 F.2d 646 (8th Cir. 1963); cf. Grand Lodge, International Association of Machinists v. King, 335 F.2d 340 (9th Cir. 1964), cert. den., 379 U.S. 920 (1964). Leading cases on the reaction of the courts to issues involving the rights of union members, decided apart from the Act, include Polin v. Kaplan, 257 N.Y. 277, 177 N.E. 833 (1931); and Mitchell v. International Association of Machinists, 196 Cal. App. 2d 796, 16 Calif. Rptr. 816 (Cal. Dist. Ct. App. 1961), pet. for hearing den., 196 Cal. App. 2d 808 (1961). For a collection of cases decided outside and under the Act, see Williams (ed.), Labor Relations and the Law, Pt. Five (3d ed. 1965).

3. More has been written concerning the rights of members of labor organizations than on any other aspect of this general field. Material prior to passage of the Labor-Management Reporting and Disclosure Act includes Summers, The Right to Join a Union, 47 Colum. L. Rev. 33 (1947); Kovner, The Legal Protection for Civil Liberties Within Unions, 1948 Wis. L. Rev. 18; Note, Procedural "Due Process" in Union Disciplinary Proceedings, 57 Yale L.J. .1302 (1948); Aaron and Komaroff, Statutory Regulation of Internal Affairs, 44 Ill. L. Rev. 425, 631 (1949); Forkosch, Internal Affairs of Unions: Government Control or Self Regulation? 18 U. Chi. L. Rev. 729 (1951); Hewitt, The Right to Membership in a Labor Union, 99 U. Pa. L. Rev. 919 (1951); Summers, Legal Limitations on Union Discipline, 64 Harv. L. Rev. 1049 (1951), and Judicial Settlement of Internal Union Disputes, 7 Buffalo L. Rev. 405 (1958); Cox, The Role of Law in Preserving Union Democracy, 72 Harv. L. Rev. 609 (1959).

4. Material published after passage of the Labor-Management Reporting and Disclosure Act includes Aaron, The Labor-Management Reporting and Disclosure Act of 1959, 73 Harv. L. Rev. 851 (1960); Affeldt, The Labor Bill of Rights — Its Impact Upon Personal Rights, 37 U. Det. L.J. 500 (1960); Cox, Internal Affairs of Labor Unions Under the Labor Reform Act of 1959, 58 Mich. L. Rev. 819 (1960); Smith, The Labor-Management Reporting and Disclosure Act of 1959, 46 Va. L. Rev. 195 (1960); Summers, The Law of Union Discipline: What the Courts Do In Fact, 70 Yale L.J. 175 (1960); Rothman, Judicial Interpretation of the "Bill of Rights" for Union Members, 45 Minn. L. Rev. 995 (1961); Summers, Judicial Regulation of Union Elections, 70 Yale L.J. Landrum-Griffin and the Trusteeship Imbroglio, 71 Yale L.J. 1460 (1962); Blumrosen, 1221 (1961); Symposium, Internal Union Affairs, 22 Ohio St. L.J. 1 (1961); Anderson, The Worker and Three Phases of Unionism: Administrative and Judicial Control of the Worker-Union Relationship, 61 Mich. L. Rev. 1435 (1963); Thatcher, Rights of Individual Union Members Under Title I and Section 610 of the Landrum-Griffin Act, 52 Geo. L.J. 339 (1964); Symposium, Comparative Labor Law and the Law of the Employment Relation, Part One, Internal Relations Between Unions and Their Members, 18 Rutgers L. Rev. 236 (1964); Note, Bill of Rights of Members of Labor Organizations, 1959-1964, 40 Notre Dame Law. 86 (1964); Note, Free Speech, Fair Trials and Factionalism in Union Discipline, 73 Yale L.J. 472 (1964); Note, Election Remedies Under the Labor-Management Reporting and Disclosure Act, 78 Harv. L. Rev. 1617 (1965).

5. With respect to the United Automobile Workers Public Review Board, a board of

outsiders created by the union to review disputes between the union and its members, see Stieber, Oberer, and Harrington, Democracy and Public Review, An Analysis of the UAW Public Review Board (Center for the Study of Democratic Institutions 1960); Brooks, Impartial Public Review of Internal Union Disputes: Experiment in Democratic Self-Discipline, 22 Ohio St. L.J. 64 (1961); and other materials collected in Williams (ed.), Labor Relations and the Law 1037-1048 (3d ed. 1965).

INTERNATIONAL ASSOCIATION OF MACHINISTS v. STREET
367 U.S. 740, 81 S. Ct. 1784, 6 L. Ed. 2d 1141 (1961)

Mr. Justice Brennan delivered the opinion of the Court.

A group of labor organizations, appellants here, and the carriers comprising the Southern Railway System, entered into a union-shop agreement pursuant to the authority of §2, Eleventh of the Railway Labor Act. The agreement requires each of the appellees, employees of the carriers, as a condition of continued employment, to pay the appellant union representing his particular class or craft the dues, initiation fees and assessments uniformly required as a condition of acquiring or retaining union membership. The appellees, in behalf of themselves and of employees similarly situated, brought this action in the Superior Court of Bibb County, Georgia, alleging that the money each was thus compelled to pay to hold his job was in substantial part used to finance the campaigns of candidates for federal and state offices whom he opposed, and to promote the propagation of political and economic doctrines, concepts and ideologies with which he disagreed. The Superior Court found that the allegations were fully proved and entered a judgment and decree enjoining the enforcement of the union-shop agreement on the ground that §2, Eleventh violates the Federal Constitution to the extent that it permits such use by the appellants of the funds exacted from employees. The Supreme Court of Georgia affirmed, 215 Ga. 27, 108 S.E.2d 796. . . .

I

The Hanson Decision

We held in Railway Employes' Dept. v. Hanson, 351 U.S. 225, that enactment of the provision of §2, Eleventh authorizing union-shop agreements between interstate railroads and unions of their employees was a valid exercise by Congress of its powers under the Commerce Clause and did not violate the First Amendment or the Due Process Clause of the Fifth Amendment. It is argued that our disposition of the First Amendment claims in Hanson disposes of appellees' constitutional claims in this case adversely to their contentions. We disagree. As appears from its history, that case decided only that §2, Eleventh, in authorizing collective agreements conditioning employees' continued employment on payment of union dues, initiation fees and assessments, did not on its face impinge upon protected rights of association. . . . We therefore reserved decision of the constitutional questions which the appellees present in this case. We said: "It is argued that compulsory membership will be used to impair freedom of expression. But that problem is not presented by this record. . . . if the exaction of dues, initiation fees, or assessments is used as a cover for forcing ideological conformity or other action in contravention of the First Amendment, this judgment will not prejudice the decision in that case. For we pass narrowly on §2, Eleventh of the Railway Labor Act. We only hold that the requirements for financial support of the collective-bargaining agency by all who receive the benefits of its work is within the power of Congress under the Commerce Clause and does not violate either the First or the Fifth Amendments." Id., p. 238. See also p. 242 (concurring opinion). Thus all that was held in Hanson was that §2, Eleventh was constitutional in its bare authorization of union-shop contracts requiring workers to give "financial support" to unions legally authorized to act as their collective bargaining agents. We sustained this requirement — and only this requirement — embodied in the statutory authorization of agreements under which "all employees shall become members of the labor organization representing their craft or class." Clearly we passed neither upon forced association in any other aspect nor upon the issue of the use of exacted money for political causes which were opposed by the employees.

The record in this case is adequate squarely to present the constitutional questions reserved in Hanson. These are questions of the utmost gravity. However, the restraints against unnecessary constitutional decisions counsel against their determination unless we must conclude that Congress, in authorizing a union shop under §2, Eleventh, also meant that the labor organization receiving an employee's money should be free, despite that employee's objection, to spend his money for political causes which he opposes. Federal statutes are to be so construed as to avoid serious doubt of their constitutionality. . . . Each named appellee in this action has made known to the union representing his craft or class his dissent from the use of his money for political causes which he opposes. We have therefore examined the legislative history of §2, Eleventh in the context of the development of unionism in the railroad industry under the regulatory scheme created by the Railway Labor Act to determine whether a construction is "fairly possible" which denies the authority to a union, over the employee's objection, to spend his money for political causes which he opposes. We conclude that such a construction is not only "fairly possible" but entirely reasonable, and we therefore find it unnecessary to decide the correctness of the constitutional determinations made by the Georgia courts.

II

The Rail Unions and Union Security

The history of union security in the railway industry is marked *first*, by a strong and long-standing tradition of voluntary unionism on the part of the standard rail unions; *second*, by the declaration in 1934 of a congressional policy of complete freedom of choice of employees to join or not to join a union; *third*, by the modification of the firm legislative policy against compulsion, but only as a specific response to the recognition of the expenses and burdens incurred by the unions in the administration of the complex scheme of the Railway Labor Act. . . .

[The Court then reviews the history of railroad labor legislation.]

In sum, in prescribing collective bargaining as the method of settling railway disputes, in conferring upon the unions the status of exclusive representatives in the negotiation and administration of collective agreements, and in giving them representation on the statutory board to adjudicate grievances, Congress has given the unions a clearly defined and delineated role to play in effectuating the basic congressional policy of stabilizing labor relations in the industry. "It is fair to say that every stage in the evolution of this railroad labor code was progressively infused with the purpose of securing self-adjustment between the effectively organized railroads and the equally effective railroad unions and, to that end, of establishing facilities for such self-adjustment by the railroad community of its own industrial controversies. . . . The assumption as well as the aim of that Act [of 1934] is a process of permanent conference and negotiation between the carriers on the one hand and the employees through their unions on the other." Elgin, J. & E. R. Co. v. Burley, 325 U.S. 711, 752-753 (dissenting opinion).

Performance of these functions entails the expenditure of considerable funds. Moreover, this Court has held that under the statutory scheme, a union's status as exclusive bargaining representative carries with it the duty fairly and equitably to represent all employees of the craft or class, union and nonunion. Steele v. Louisville & N. R. Co., 323 U.S. 192; Tunstall v. Brotherhood of Locomotive Firemen & Enginemen, 323 U.S. 210. The principal argument made by the unions in 1950 was based on their role in this regulatory framework. They maintained that because of the expense of performing their duties in the congressional scheme, fairness justified the spreading of the costs to all employees who benefited. They thus advanced as their purpose the elimination of the "free riders" — those employees who obtained the benefits of the unions' participation in the machinery of the Act without financially supporting the unions. . . .

This argument was decisive with Congress. . . . The conclusion to which this history clearly points is that §2, Eleventh contemplated compulsory unionism to force employees to share the costs of negotiating and administering collective agreements, and the costs of the adjustment and settlement of disputes. One looks in vain for any suggestion that Congress also meant in §2, Eleventh to provide the unions with a means for forcing employees, over their objection, to support political causes which they oppose.

III

THE SAFEGUARDING OF RIGHTS OF DISSENT

To the contrary, Congress incorporated safeguards in the statute to protect dissenters' interests. Congress became concerned during the hearings and debates that the union shop might be used to abridge freedom of speech and beliefs. The original proposal for authorization of the union shop was qualified in only one respect. It provided "That no such agreement shall require such condition of employment with respect to employees to whom membership is not available upon the same terms and conditions as are generally applicable to any other member . . . ." This was primarily designed to prevent discharge of employees for nonmembership where the union did not admit the employee to membership on racial grounds. See House Hearings, p. 68; Senate Hearings, pp. 22-25. But it was strenuously protested that the proposal provided no protection for an employee who disagreed with union policies or leadership. It was argued, for example, that "the right of free speech is at stake. . . . A man could feel that he was no longer able freely to express himself because he could be dismissed on account of criticism of the union . . . ." House Hearings, p. 115; see also Senate Hearings, pp. 167-169, 320. Objections of this kind led the rail unions to propose an addition to the proviso to §2, Eleventh to prevent loss of job for lack of union membership "with respect to employees to whom membership was denied or terminated for any reason other than the failure of the employee to tender the periodic dues, fees, and assessments uniformly required as a condition of acquiring or retaining membership." House Hearings, p. 247. Mr. Harrison presented this text and stated, "It is submitted that this bill with the amendment as suggested in this statement remedies the alleged abuses of compulsory union membership as claimed by the opposing witnesses, yet makes possible the elimination of the 'free rider' and the sharing of the burden of maintenance by all of the beneficiaries of union activity." House Hearings, p. 253. . . .

A congressional concern over possible impingements on the interests of individual dissenters from union policies is therefore discernible. It is true that opponents of the union shop urged that Congress should not allow it without explicitly regulating the amount of dues which might be exacted or prescribing the uses for which the dues might be expended. We may assume that Congress was also fully conversant with the long history of intensive involvement of the railroad unions in political activities. But it does not follow that §2, Eleventh places no restriction on the use of an employee's money, over his objection, to support political causes he opposes merely because Congress did not enact a comprehensive regulatory scheme governing expenditures. For it is abundantly clear that Congress did not completely abandon the policy of full freedom of choice embodied in the 1934 Act, but rather made inroads on it for the limited purpose of eliminating the problems created by the "free rider." That policy survives in §2, Eleventh in the safeguards intended to protect freedom of dissent. Congress was aware of the conflicting interests involved in the question of the union shop and sought to achieve their accommodation. . . . We respect this congressional purpose when we construe §2, Eleventh as not vesting the unions with unlimited power to spend exacted money. We are not called upon to delineate the precise limits of that power in this case. We have before us only the question whether the power is restricted to the extent of denying the unions the right, over the employee's objection, to use his money to support political causes which he opposes. Its use to support candidates for public office, and advance political programs, is not a use which helps defray the expenses of the negotiation or administration of collective agreements, or the expenses entailed in the adjustment of grievances and disputes. In other words, it is a use which falls clearly outside the reasons advanced by the unions and accepted by Congress why authority to make union-shop agreements was justified. On the other hand, it is equally clear that it is a use to support activities within the area of dissenters' interests which Congress enacted the proviso to protect. We give §2, Eleventh the construction which achieves both congressional purposes when we hold, as we do, that §2, Eleventh is to be construed to deny the unions, over an employee's objection, the power to use his exacted funds to support political causes which he opposes.

We express no view as to other union expenditures objected to by an employee and not made to meet the costs of negotiation and administration of collective agreements, or the adjustment and settlement of grievances and disputes. We do not understand, in view of the findings of the Georgia courts and the question decided by the Georgia Supreme Court, that there is before us the matter of expenditures for activities in the area between the costs which led directly to the complaint as to "free riders," and the expenditures to support union political activities. We are satisfied, however, that §2, Eleventh is to be interpreted to deny the unions the power claimed in this case. The appellant unions, in insisting that §2, Eleventh contemplates their use of exacted funds to support political causes objected to by the employee, would have us hold that Congress sanctioned an expansion of historical practices in the political area by the rail unions. This we decline to do. Both by tradition and, from 1934 to 1951, by force of law, the rail unions did not rely upon the compulsion of union security agreements to exact money to support the political activities in which they engage. Our construction therefore involves no curtailment of the traditional political activities of the railroad unions. It means only that those unions must not support those activities, against the expressed wishes of a dissenting employee, with his exacted money.

I V

THE APPROPRIATE REMEDY

Under our view of the statute, however, the decision of the court below was erroneous and cannot stand. The appellees who have participated in this action have in the course of it made known to their respective unions their objection to the use of their money for the support of political causes. In that circumstance, the respective unions were without power to use payments thereafter tendered by them for such political causes. However, the union-shop agreement itself is not unlawful. Railway Employes' Dept. v. Hanson, supra. The appellees therefore remain obliged, as a condition of continued employment, to make the payments to their respective unions called for by the agreement. Their right of action stems not from constitutional limitations on Congress' power to authorize the union shop, but from §2, Eleventh itself. In other words, appellees' grievance stems from the spending of their funds for purposes not authorized by the Act in the face of their objection, not from the enforcement of the union-shop agreement by the mere collection of funds. If their money were used for purposes contemplated by §2, Eleventh, the appellees would have no grievance at all. We think that an injunction restraining enforcement of the union-shop agreement is therefore plainly not a remedy appropriate to the violation of the Act's restriction on expenditures. Restraining the collection of all funds from the appellees sweeps too broadly, since their objection is only to the uses to which some of their money is put. Moreover, restraining collection of the funds as the Georgia courts have done might well interfere with the appellant unions' performance of those functions and duties which the Railway Labor Act places upon them to attain its goal of stability in the industry. . . .

Since the case must therefore be remanded to the court below for consideration of a proper remedy, we think that it is appropriate to suggest the limits within which remedial discretion may be exercised consistently with the Railway Labor Act and other relevant public policies. As indicated, an injunction against enforcement of the union shop itself through the collection of funds is unwarranted. We also think that a blanket injunction against all expenditures of funds for the disputed purposes, even one conditioned on cessation of improper expenditures, would not be a proper exercise of equitable discretion. Nor would it be proper to issue an interim or temporary blanket injunction of this character pending a final adjudication. . . . [T]he fact that these expenditures are made for political activities is an additional reason for reluctance to impose such an injunctive remedy. Whatever may be the powers of Congress or the States to forbid unions altogether to make various types of political expenditures, as to which we express no opinion here,[21] many of the

[21] No contention was made below or here that any of the expenditures involved

expenditures involved in the present case are made for the purpose of disseminating information as to candidates and programs and publicizing the positions of the unions on them. As to such expenditures an injunction would work a restraint on the expression of political ideas which might be offensive to the First Amendment. For the majority also has an interest in stating its views without being silenced by the dissenters. To attain the appropriate reconciliation between majority and dissenting interests in the area of political expression, we think the courts in adminstering the Act should select remedies which protect both interests to the maximum extent possible without undue impingement of one on the other.

Among possible remedies which would appear appropriate to the injury complained of, two may be enforced with a minimum of administrative difficulty and with little danger of encroachment on the legitimate activities or necessary functions of the unions. Any remedies, however, would properly be granted only to employees who have made known to the union officials that they do not desire their funds to be used for political causes to which they object. The safeguards of §2, Eleventh were added for the protection of dissenters' interest, but dissent is not to be presumed — it must affirmatively be made known to the union by the dissenting employee. The union receiving money exacted from an employee under a union-shop agreement should not in fairness be subjected to sanctions in favor of an employee who makes no complaint of the use of his money for such activities. From these considerations, it follows that the present action is not a true class action, for there is no attempt to prove the existence of a class of workers who had specifically objected to the exaction of dues for political purposes. See Hansberry v. Lee, 311 U.S. 32, 44. Thus we think that only those who have identified themselves as opposed to political uses of their funds are entitled to relief in this action.

One remedy would be an injunction against expenditure for political causes opposed by each complaining employee of a sum, from those moneys to be spent by the union for political purposes, which is so much of the moneys exacted from him as is the proportion of the union's total expenditures made for such political activities to the union's total budget. The union should not be in a position to make up such sum from money paid by a nondissenter, for this would shift a disproportionate share of the costs of collective bargaining to the dissenter and have the same effect of applying his money to support such political activities. A second remedy would be restitution to each individual employee of that portion of his money which the union expended, despite his notification, for the political causes to which he had advised the union he was opposed. There should be no necessity, however, for the employee to trace his money up to and including its expenditure; if the money goes into general funds and no separate account of receipts and expenditures of the funds of individual employees are maintained, the portion of his

---

in this case were made in violation of the Federal Corrupt Practices Act, 18 U.S.C. §610, or any state corrupt practices legislation.

money the employee would be entitled to recover would be in the same proportion that the expenditures for political purposes which he had advised the union he disapproved bore to the total union budget.

The judgment is reversed and the case is remanded to the court below for proceedings not inconsistent with this opinion.

Reversed and remanded.

Mr. Justice Douglas, concurring.

Some forced associations are inevitable in an industrial society. One who of necessity rides busses and street cars does not have the freedom that John Muir and Walt Whitman extolled. The very existence of a factory brings into being human colonies. Public housing in some areas may of necessity take the form of apartment buildings which to some may be as repulsive as ant hills. Yet people in teeming communities often have no other choice.

Legislatures have some leeway in dealing with the problems created by these modern phenomena.

Collective bargaining is a remedy for some of the problems created by modern factory conditions. The beneficiaries are all the members of the laboring force. We therefore concluded in Railway Employes' Dept. v. Hanson, 351 U.S. 225, that it was permissible for the legislature to require all who gain from collective bargaining to contribute to its cost. That is the narrow and precise holding of the Hanson case, as Mr. Justice Black shows.

Once an association with others is compelled by the facts of life, special safeguards are necessary lest the spirit of the First, Fourth, and Fifth Amendments be lost and we all succumb to regimentation. I expressed this concern in Public Utilities Comm'n v. Pollak, 343 U.S. 451, 467 (dissenting opinion), where a "captive audience" was forced to listen to special radio broadcasts. If an association is compelled, the individual should not be forced to surrender any matters of conscience, belief, or expression. He should be allowed to enter the group with his own flag flying, whether it be religious, political, or philosophical; nothing that the group does should deprive him of the privilege of preserving and expressing his agreement, disagreement, or dissent, whether it coincides with the view of the group, or conflicts with it in minor or major ways; and he should not be required to finance the promotion of causes with which he disagrees.

In a debate on the Universal Declaration of Human Rights, later adopted by the General Assembly of the United Nations on December 10, 1948, Mr. Malik of Lebanon stated what I think is the controlling principle in cases of the character now before us:

"The social group to which the individual belongs, may, like the human person himself, be wrong or right: the person alone is the judge." [2]

This means that membership in a group cannot be conditioned on the

[2] Commission on Human Rights, Summary Record of the Fourteenth Meeting, February 4, 1947, U.N. Doc. E/CN.4/SR.14, p. 4.

individual's acceptance of the group's philosophy. Otherwise, First Amendment rights are required to be exchanged for the group's attitude, philosophy, or politics. I do not see how that is permissible under the Constitution. Since neither Congress nor the state legislatures can abridge those rights, they cannot grant the power to private groups to abridge them. As I read the First Amendment, it forbids any abridgment by government whether directly or indirectly.

The collection of dues for paying the costs of collective bargaining of which each member is a beneficiary is one thing. If, however, dues are used, or assessments are made, to promote or oppose birth control, to repeal or increase the taxes on cosmetics, to promote or oppose the admission of Red China into the United Nations, and the like, then the group compels an individual to support with his money causes beyond what gave rise to the need for group action.

I think the same must be said when union dues or assessments are used to elect a Governor, a Congressman, a Senator, or a President. It may be said that the election of a Franklin D. Roosevelt rather than a Calvin Coolidge might be the best possible way to serve the cause of collective bargaining. But even such a selective use of union funds for political purposes subordinates the individual's First Amendment rights to the views of the majority. I do not see how that can be done, even though the objector retains his rights to campaign, to speak, to vote as he chooses. For when union funds are used for that purpose, the individual is required to finance political projects against which he may be in rebellion. The furtherance of the common cause leaves some leeway for the leadership of the group. As long as they act to promote the cause which justified bringing the group together, the individual cannot withdraw his financial support merely because he disagrees with the group's strategy. If that were allowed, we would be reversing the Hanson case, sub silentio. But since the funds here in issue are used for causes other than defraying the costs of collective bargaining, I would affirm the judgment below with modifications. Although I recognize the strength of the arguments advanced by my Brothers BLACK and WHITTAKER against giving a "proportional" relief to appellees in this case, there is the practical problem of mustering five Justices for a judgment in this case. Cf. Screws v. United States, 325 U.S. 91, 134. So I have concluded dubitante to agree to the one suggested by MR. JUSTICE BRENNAN, on the understanding that all relief granted will be confined to the six protesting employees. This suit, though called a "class" action, does not meet the requirements as the use or nonuse of any dues or assessments depends on the choice of each individual, not the group. See Hansberry v. Lee, 311 U.S. 32, 44.

[Mr. Justice Whittaker concurred in Parts I, II, and III of Mr. Justice Brennan's opinion, but dissented as to Part IV, believing the remedy formulated by the Georgia courts should be approved.]

Mr. Justice Black, dissenting. . . .

[N]o one has suggested that the Court's statutory construction of §2, Eleventh could possibly be supported without the crutch of its fear of unconstitutionality. This is why I think the Court's avoidance of the constitutional issue in both cases today is wholly unfair to the unions as well as to Congress. I must consider this case on the basis of my belief as to the constitutionality of §2, Eleventh, interpreted so as to authorize compulsion of workers to pay dues to a union for use in advocating causes and political candidates that the protesting workers are against. . . .

[T]he Hanson case held only that workers could be required to pay their part of the cost of actual bargaining carried on by a union selected as bargaining agent under authority of Congress, just as Congress doubtless could have required workers to pay the cost of such bargaining had it chosen to have the bargaining carried on by the Secretary of Labor or any other appropriately selected bargaining agent. The Hanson case did not hold that railroad workers could be compelled by law to forego their constitutionally protected freedom of association by participating as union "members" against their will. That case cannot, therefore, properly be read to rest on a principle which would permit government — in furtherance of some public interest, be that interest actual or imaginary — to compel membership in Rotary Clubs, fraternal organizations, religious groups, chambers of commerce, bar associations, labor unions, or any other private organizations Government may decide it wants to subsidize, support or control. In a word, the Hanson case did not hold that the existence of union-shop contracts could be used as an excuse to force workers to asosciate with people they do not want to associate with, or to pay their money to support causes they detest. . . .

Probably no one would suggest that Congress could, without violating this Amendment, pass a law taxing workers, or any persons for that matter (even lawyers), to create a fund to be used in helping certain political parties or groups favored by the Government to elect their candidates or promote their controversial causes. Compelling a man by law to pay his money to elect candidates or advocate laws or doctrines he is against differs only in degree, if at all, from compelling him by law to speak for a candidate, a party, or a cause he is against. The very reason for the First Amendment is to make the people of this country free to think, speak, write and worship as they wish, not as the Government commands.

There is, of course, no constitutional reason why a union or other private group may not spend its funds for political or ideological causes if its members voluntarily join it and can voluntarily get out of it. Labor unions made up of voluntary members free to get in or out of the unions when they please have played important and useful roles in politics and economic affairs. How to spend its money is a question for each voluntary group to decide for itself in the absence of some valid law forbidding activities for which the money is spent. But a different situation arises when a federal law steps in and author-izes such a group to carry on activities at the expense of persons who do not choose to be members of the group as well as those who do. Such a law, even though validly passed by Congress, cannot be used in a way that abridges the specifically defined freedoms of the First Amendment. And whether there is such abridgment depends not only on how the law is written but also on how it works.

There can be no doubt that the federally sanctioned union-shop contract here, as it actually works, takes a part of the earnings of some men and turns it over to others, who spend a substantial part of the funds so received in efforts to thwart the political, economic and ideological hopes of those whose money has been forced from them under authority of law. This injects fed-eral compulsion into the political and ideological processes, a result which I have supposed everyone would agree the First Amendment was particularly intended to prevent. . . .

In my view, §2, Eleventh can constitutionally authorize no more than to make a worker pay dues to a union for the sole purpose of defraying the cost of acting as his bargaining agent. Our Government has no more power to compel individuals to support union programs or union publications than it has to compel the support of political programs, employer programs or church programs. And the First Amendment, fairly construed, deprives the Government of all power to make any person pay out one single penny against his will to be used in any way to advocate doctrines or views he is against, whether economic, scientific, political, religious or any other.

I would therefore hold that §2, Eleventh of the Railway Labor Act, in authorizing application of the union-shop contract to the named protesting employees who are appellees here, violates the freedom of speech guarantee of the First Amendment.

[Mr. Justice Black also dissented from the remedy provided by the Court. In his view, "The three workers who paid under protest here were forced under authority of a federal statute to pay *all* current dues or lose their jobs. They should get back *all* they paid with interest."]

Mr. Justice Frankfurter, whom Mr. Justice Harlan joins, dissent-ing. . . .

[W]e unanimously held that the plaintiffs in Hanson had not been denied any right protected by the First Amendment. Despite our holding, the gist of the complaint here is that the expenditure of a portion of mandatory funds for political objectives denies free speech — the right to speak or to remain silent — to members who oppose, against the constituted authority of union desires, this use of their union dues. No one's desire or power to speak his mind is checked or curbed. The individual member may express his views in any public or private forum as freely as he could before the union collected his dues. Federal taxes also may diminish the vigor with which a citizen can give partisan support to a political belief, but as yet no one would place such an impediment to making one's views effective within the reach of constitutionally protected "free speech."

This is too fine-spun a claim for constitutional recognition. The framers of the Bill of Rights lived in an era when overhanging threats to conduct deemed "seditious" and lettres de cachet were current issues. Their concern was in protecting the right of the individual freely to express himself — especially his political beliefs — in a public forum, untrammeled by fear of punishment or of governmental censure.

But were we to assume, arguendo, that the plaintiffs have alleged a valid constitutional objection if Congress had specifically ordered the result, we must consider the difference between such compulsion and the absence of compulsion when Congress acts as platonically as it did, in a wholly non-coercive way. Congress has not commanded that the railroads shall employ only those workers who are members of authorized unions. Congress has only given leave to a bargaining representative, democratically elected by a majority of workers, to enter into a particular contractual provision arrived at under the give-and-take of duly safeguarded bargaining procedures. (The statute forbids distortion of these procedures as, for instance, through racial discrimination. Steele v. Louisville & Nashville R. Co., 323 U.S. 192.) Congress itself emphasized this vital distinction between authorization and compulsion. S. Rep. No. 2262, 81st Cong., 2d Sess. 2. And this Court in Hanson noted that "The union shop provision of the Railway Labor Act is only permissive. Congress has not . . . required carriers and employees to enter into union shop agreements." 351 U.S., at 231. When we speak of the Government "acting" in permitting the union shop, the scope and force of what Congress has done must be heeded. There is not a trace of compulsion involved — no exercise of restriction by Congress on the freedom of the carriers and the unions. On the contrary, Congress expanded their freedom of action. Congress lifted limitations upon free action by parties bargaining at arm's length.

The plaintiffs have not been deprived of the right to participate in determining union policies or to assert their respective weight in defining the purposes for which union dues may be expended. Responsive to the actualities of our industrial society, in which unions as such play the role that they do, the law regards a union as a self-contained, legal personality exercising rights and subject to responsibilities wholly distinct from its individual members. See United Mine Workers of America v. Coronado Coal Co., 259 U.S. 344. It is a commonplace of all organizations that a minority of a legally recognized group may at times see an organization's funds used for promotion of ideas opposed by the minority. The analogies are numerous. On the largest scale, the Federal Government expends revenue collected from individual taxpayers to propagandize ideas which many taxpayers oppose. Or, as this Court noted in Hanson, many state laws compel membership in the integrated bar as a prerequisite to practicing law, and the bar association uses its funds to urge

legislation of which individual members often disapprove. . . . Again, under
the Securities Exchange Act of 1934, Congress specifically authorized the formation of "national securities associations," membership in which is of practical necessity to many brokers and dealers. The Association has urged the
passage of several legislative reforms which one can confidently assume did
not represent the convictions of all members. To come closer to the heart of
the immediate matter, is the union's choice of when to picket or to go out on
strike unconstitutional? Picketing is still deemed also a form of speech, but
surely the union's decision to strike under its statutory aegis as a bargaining
unit is not an unconstitutional compulsion forced upon members who
strongly oppose a strike, as minorities not infrequently do. Indeed, legislative
reform intended to insure the fair representation of the minority workers in
internal union politics would be redundant if, despite all precautions, the
union were constitutionally forbidden because of minority opposition to
spend money in accordance with the majority's desires. . . .

For us to hold that these defendant unions may not expend their moneys
for political and legislative purposes would be completely to ignore the long
history of union conduct and its pervasive acceptance in our political life.
American labor's initial role in shaping legislation dates back 130 years. With
the coming of the AFL in 1886, labor on a national scale was committed not
to act as a class party but to maintain a program of political action in furtherance of its industrial standards. British trade unions were supporting members of the House of Commons as early as 1867. The Canadian Trades Congress in 1894 debated whether political action should be the main objective of
the labor force. And in a recent Australian case, the High Court upheld the
right of a union to expel a member who refused to pay a political levy. That
Britain, Canada and Australia have no explicit First Amendment is beside
the point. For one thing, the freedoms safeguarded in terms in the First
Amendment are deeply rooted and respected in the British tradition, and are
part of legal presuppositions in Canada and Australia. And in relation to
our immediate concern, the British Commonwealth experience establishes
the pertinence of political means for realizing basic trade-union interests.

The expenditures revealed by the AFL – CIO Executive Council Reports
emphasize that labor's participation in urging legislation and candidacies is a
major one. In the last three fiscal years, the Committee on Political Education
(COPE) expended a total of $1,681, 990.42; the AFL – CIO News cost $756,-
591.99; the Legislative Department reported total expenses of $741,918.24. . . .

When one runs down the detailed list of national and international problems on which the AFL – CIO speaks, it seems rather naive for a court to
conclude — as did the trial court — that the union expenditures were "not reasonably necessary to collective bargaining or to maintaining the existence and
position of said union defendants as effective bargaining agents." The notion
that economic and political concerns are separable is pre-Victorian. Presidents
of the United States and Committees of Congress invite views of labor on

matters not immediately concerned with wages, hours, and conditions of employment. And this Court accepts briefs as amici from the AFL – CIO on issues that cannot be called industrial, in any circumscribed sense. It is not true in life that political protection is irrelevant to, and insulated from, economic interests. . . .

In conclusion, then, we are asked by union members who oppose these expenditures to protect their right to free speech — although they are as free to speak as ever — against governmental action which has permitted a union elected by democratic process to bargain for a union shop and to expend the funds thereby collected for purposes which are controlled by internal union choice. To do so would be to mutilate a scheme designed by Congress for the purpose of equitably sharing the cost of securing the benefits of union exertions; it would greatly embarrass if not frustrate conventional labor activities which have become institutionalized through time. To do so is to give constitutional sanction to doctrinaire views and to grant a miniscule claim constitutional recognition. . . .

I would reverse and remand the case for dismissal in the Georgia courts.

NOTES

1. In a sequel to the Street case, the Court dealt in more detail with the problem of remedies. Brotherhood of Railway & Steamship Clerks v. Allen, 373 U.S. 113, 83 S. Ct. 1158, 10 L. Ed. 2d 235 (1963). The Court reiterated that (1) each employee seeking relief must affirmatively prove that he objects to the use of the funds for political purposes; no class action is permissible; (2) an injunction relieving employees of all payments, including interim relief of this nature, will not be approved. The Court then went on:

"On remand, in order to frame a decree embodying the suggested remedies, two determinations will have to be made: (1) what expenditures disclosed by the record are political; (2) what percentage of total union expenditures are political expenditures. As to (1) we presently intimate no view, . . . because here, as in Street, see 367 U.S., at 768-770, the courts below made no attempt to draw the boundary between political expenditures and those germane to collective bargaining, and it would be inappropriate for this Court to do so in the first instance and upon the present record. As to (2) the present record is insufficient to enable any calculation.

"Since the unions possess the facts and records from which the proportion of political to total union expenditures can reasonably be calculated, basic considerations of fairness compel that they, not the individual employees, bear the burden of proving such proportion. Absolute precision in the calculation of such proportion is not, of course, to be expected or required; we are mindful of the difficult accounting problems that may arise. And no decree would be proper which appeared likely to infringe the unions' right to expend uniform exactions under the union-shop agreement in support of activities germane to collective bargaining and, as well, to expend nondissenters' such exactions in support of political activities.

". . . While adhering to the principles governing remedy which we announced in Street, see 367 U.S., at 771-775, we think it appropriate to suggest, in addition, a practical decree to which each respondent proving his right to relief would be entitled. Such a decree would order (1) the refund to him of a portion of the exacted funds in the same proportion that union political expenditures bear to total union expenditures, and (2) a reduction of future such exactions from him by the same proportion. We recognize that practical difficulties may attend a decree reducing an employee's obligations under the union-shop agreement by a fixed proportion, since the proportion of the union budget devoted to political activities may not be constant. The difficulties in judicially administered relief, although not insurmountable (a decree once entered would of course be modifiable upon a showing of changed circumstances), should, we think, encourage petitioner unions to consider the adoption by their membership of some voluntary plan by which dissenters would be afforded an internal union remedy." 373 U.S. at 121-122.

2. In Lathrop v. Donohue, 367 U.S. 820, 81 S. Ct. 1826, 6 L. Ed. 2d 1191 (1961), decided the same day as the Street case, the Court considered similar issues as they arose in connection with the integrated bar of Wisconsin. Under this system all lawyers in the state were required to become members of an association called "The State Bar of Wisconsin." A Wisconsin lawyer brought an action to recover his dues, alleging that they were being used for political and propaganda activities of which he disapproved. Mr. Justice Brennan, in an opinion which Mr. Chief Justice Warren and Justices Clark and Stewart joined, held that, within the principle of the Hanson case, the state could legitimately require lawyers to pay dues to an association designed to improve the quality of legal services in Wisconsin, and that the First Amendment claim based on the use of dues for political purposes was not ripe for adjudication. Justices Frankfurter and Harlan, concurring, reached the First Amendment issues and found no infringement. Mr. Justice Whittaker also concurred. Justices Black and Douglas dissented on the ground that the use of compulsory dues for political purposes violated First Amendment rights.

3. Article 20 of the Universal Declaration of Human Rights, adopted by the General Assembly of the United Nations on December 10, 1948, provides:

"(1) Everyone has the right to freedom of peaceful assembly and association.

"(2) No one may be compelled to belong to an association."

REFERENCES

On the Street and Lathrop cases, see Wellington, The Constitution, the Labor Union and "Governmental Action," 70 Yale L.J. 345 (1961), and Machinists v. Street: Statutory Interpretation and the Avoidance of Constitutional Issues, 1961 Sup. Ct. Rev. 49; Blumrosen, Significant Supreme Court Decisions Affecting Labor Relations, 1960 Term; Herein of Political Use of Union Dues and of Hiring Halls, 16 Sw. L.J. 57 (1962); Note, Freedom From Political Association: The Street and Lathrop Decisions, 56 Nw. U.L. Rev. 777 (1962); Note, 1962 Wis. L. Rev. 138; Read, Minority Rights and the Union Shop: A Basis for Constitutional Attack, 49 Minn. L. Rev. 227 (1964).

CHAPTER X

Right of Privacy

GRISWOLD v. CONNECTICUT
381 U.S. 479, 85 S. Ct. 1678, 14 L. Ed. 2d 510 (1965)

Mr. Justice Douglas delivered the opinion of the Court.

Appellant Griswold is Executive Director of the Planned Parenthood League of Connecticut. Appellant Buxton is a licensed physician and a professor at the Yale Medical School who served as Medical Director for the League at its Center in New Haven — a center open and operating from November 1 to November 10, 1961, when appellants were arrested.

They gave information, instruction, and medical advice to *married persons* as to the means of preventing conception. They examined the wife and prescribed the best contraceptive device or material for her use. Fees were usually charged, although some couples were serviced free.

The statutes whose constitutionality is involved in this appeal are §§53-32 and 54-196 of the General Statutes of Connecticut (1958 rev.). The former provides:

"Any person who uses any drug, medicinal article or instrument for the purpose of preventing conception shall be fined not less than fifty dollars or imprisoned not less than sixty days nor more than one year or be both fined and imprisoned."

Section 54-196 provides:

"Any person who assists, abets, counsels, causes, hires or commands another to commit any offense may be prosecuted and punished as if he were the principal offender."

The appellants were found guilty as accessories and fined $100 each, against the claim that the accessory statute as so applied violated the Fourteenth Amendment. The Appellate Division of the Circuit Court affirmed. The Supreme Court of Errors affirmed that judgment. 151 Conn. 544, 200 A.2d 479. We noted probable jurisdiction. 379 U.S. 926.

We think that appellants have standing to raise the constitutional rights of the married people with whom they had a professional relationship. Tileston v. Ullman, 318 U.S. 44, is different, for there the plaintiff seeking to represent others asked for a declaratory judgment. In that situation we thought that the requirements of standing should be strict, lest the standards of "case or controversy" in Article III of the Constitution become blurred. Here those doubts are removed by reason of a criminal conviction for serving married couples in violation of an aiding-and-abetting statute. Certainly the accessory should have standing to assert that the offense which he is charged with assisting is not, or cannot constitutionally be, a crime.

This case is more akin to Truax v. Raich, 239 U.S. 33, where an employee was permitted to assert the rights of his employer; to Pierce v. Society of Sisters, 268 U.S. 510, where the owners of private schools were entitled to assert the rights of potential pupils and their parents; and to Barrows v. Jackson, 346 U.S. 249, where a white defendant, party to a racially restrictive covenant, who was being sued for damages by the covenantors because she had conveyed her property to Negroes, was allowed to raise the issue that enforcement of the covenant violated the rights of prospective Negro purchasers to equal protection, although no Negro was a party to the suit. And see Meyer v. Nebraska, 262 U.S. 390; Adler v. Board of Education, 342 U.S. 485; NAACP v. Alabama, 357 U.S. 449; NAACP v. Button, 371 U.S. 415. The rights of husband and wife, pressed here, are likely to be diluted or adversely affected unless those rights are considered in a suit involving those who have this kind of confidential relation to them.

Coming to the merits, we are met with a wide range of questions that implicate the Due Process Clause of the Fourteenth Amendment. Overtones of some arguments suggest that Lochner v. New York, 198 U.S. 45, should be our guide. But we decline that invitation as we did in West Coast Hotel Co. v. Parrish, 300 U.S. 379; Olsen v. Nebraska, 313 U.S. 236; Lincoln Union v. Northwestern Co., 335 U.S. 525; Williamson v. Lee Optical Co., 348 U.S. 483; Giboney v. Empire Storage Co., 336 U.S. 490. We do not sit as a superlegislature to determine the wisdom, need, and propriety of laws that touch economic problems, business affairs, or social conditions. This law, however, operates directly on an intimate relation of husband and wife and their physician's role in one aspect of that relation.

The association of people is not mentioned in the Constitution nor in the Bill of Rights. The right to educate a child in a school of the parents' choice — whether public or private or parochial — is also not mentioned. Nor is the right to study any particular subject or any foreign language. Yet the First Amendment has been construed to include certain of those rights.

By Pierce v. Society of Sisters, supra, the right to educate one's children as one chooses is made applicable to the States by the force of the First and Fourteenth Amendments. By Meyer v. Nebraska, supra, the same dignity is given the right to study the German language in a private school. In other words, the State may not, consistently with the spirit of the First Amendment, contract the spectrum of available knowledge. The right of freedom of speech and press includes not only the right to utter or to print, but the right to distribute, the right to receive, the right to read (Martin v. Struthers, 319 U.S. 141, 143) and freedom of inquiry, freedom of thought, and freedom to teach (see Wieman v. Updegraff, 344 U.S. 183, 195) — indeed the freedom of the entire university community. Sweezy v. New Hampshire, 354 U.S. 234, 249-250, 261-262; Barenblatt v. United States, 360 U.S. 109, 112; Baggett v. Bullitt, 377 U.S. 360, 369. Without those peripheral rights the specific rights would be less secure. And so we reaffirm the principle of the Pierce and the Meyer cases.

In NAACP v. Alabama, 357 U.S. 449, 462, we protected the "freedom to associate and privacy in one's associations," noting that freedom of association was a peripheral First Amendment right. Disclosure of membership lists of a constitutionally valid association, we held, was invalid "as entailing the likelihood of a substantial restraint upon the exercise by petitioner's members of their right to freedom of association." Ibid. In other words, the First Amendment has a penumbra where privacy is protected from governmental intrusion. In like context, we have protected forms of "association" that are not political in the customary sense but pertain to the social, legal, and economic benefit of the members. NAACP v. Button, 371 U.S. 415, 430-431. In Schware v. Board of Bar Examiners, 353 U.S. 232, we held it not permissible to bar a lawyer from practice, because he had once been a member of the Communist Party. The man's "association with that Party" was not shown to be "anything more than a political faith in a political party" (id., at 244) and was not action of a kind proving bad moral character. Id., at 245-246.

Those cases involved more than the "right of assembly" — a right that extends to all irrespective of their race or ideology. De Jonge v. Oregon, 299 U.S. 353. The right of "association," like the right of belief (Board of Education v. Barnette, 319 U.S. 624), is more than the right to attend a meeting; it includes the right to express one's attitudes or philosophies by membership in a group or by affiliation with it or by other lawful means. Association in that context is a form of expression of opinion; and while it is not expressly included in the First Amendment its existence is necessary in making the express guarantees fully meaningful.

The foregoing cases suggest that specific guarantees in the Bill of Rights have penumbras, formed by emanations from those guarantees that help give them life and substance. See Poe v. Ullman, 367 U.S. 497, 516-522 (dissenting opinion). Various guarantees create zones of privacy. The right of association contained in the penumbra of the First Amendment is one, as we have seen. The Third Amendment in its prohibition against the quartering of soldiers "in any house" in time of peace without the consent of the owner is another facet of that privacy. The Fourth Amendment explicitly affirms the "right of the people to be secure in their persons, houses, papers, and effects, against unreasonable searches and seizures." The Fifth Amendment in its Self-Incrimination Clause enables the citizen to create a zone of privacy which government may not force him to surrender to his detriment. The Ninth Amendment provides: "The enumeration in the Constitution, of certain rights, shall not be construed to deny or disparage others retained by the people."

The Fourth and Fifth Amendments were described in Boyd v. United States, 116 U.S. 616, 630, as protection against all governmental invasions "of the sanctity of a man's home and the privacies of life." * We recently referred in Mapp v. Ohio, 367 U.S. 643, 656, to the Fourth Amendment as creating a "right to privacy, no less important than any other right carefully and particularly reserved to the people." See Beaney, The Constitutional Right to Privacy, 1962 Sup. Ct. Rev. 212; Griswold, The Right to be Let Alone, 55 Nw. U.L. Rev. 216 (1960).

We have had many controversies over these penumbral rights of "privacy and repose." See, e.g., Breard v. Alexandria, 341 U.S. 622, 626, 644; Public Utilities Comm'n v. Pollak, 343 U.S. 451; Monroe v. Pape, 365 U.S. 167; Lanza v. New York, 370 U.S. 139; Frank v. Maryland, 359 U.S. 360; Skinner v. Oklahoma, 316 U.S. 535, 541. These cases bear witness that the right of privacy which presses for recognition here is a legitimate one.

The present case, then, concerns a relationship lying within the zone of privacy created by several fundamental constitutional guarantees. And it concerns a law which, in forbidding the *use* of contraceptives rather than regulating their manufacture or sale, seeks to achieve its goals by means having a maximum destructive impact upon that relationship. Such a law cannot stand in light of the familiar principle, so often applied by this Court, that a "governmental purpose to control or prevent activities constitutionally subject to state regulation may not be achieved by means which sweep unnecessarily broadly and thereby invade the area of protected freedoms." NAACP v. Alabama, 377 U.S. 288, 307. Would we allow the police to search the sacred precincts of marital bedrooms for telltale signs of the use of contraceptives? The very idea is repulsive to the notions of privacy surrounding the marriage relationship.

We deal with a right of privacy older than the Bill of Rights — older than our political parties, older than our school system. Marriage is a coming to-

---

* The Court said in full about this right of privacy:

"The principles laid down in this opinion [by Lord Camden in Entick v. Carrington, 19 How. St. Tr. 1029] affect the very essence of constitutional liberty and security. They reach farther than the concrete form of the case then before the court, with its adventitious circumstances; they apply to all invasions on the part of the government and its employees of the sanctity of a man's home and the privacies of life. It is not the breaking of his doors, and the rummaging of his drawers, that constitutes the essence of the offence; but it is the invasion of his indefeasible right of personal security, personal liberty and private property, where that right has never been forfeited by his conviction of some public offence, — it is the invasion of his sacred right which underlies and constitutes the essence of Lord Camden's judgment. Breaking into a house and opening boxes and drawers are circumstances of aggravation; but any forcible and compulsory extortion of a man's own testimony or of his private papers to be used as evidence to convict him of crime or to forfeit his goods, is within the condemnation of that judgment. In this regard the Fourth and Fifth Amendments run almost into each other." 116 U.S., at 630.

gether for better or for worse, hopefully enduring, and intimate to the degree of being sacred. It is an association that promotes a way of life, not causes; a harmony in living, not political faiths; a bilateral loyalty, not commercial or social projects. Yet it is an association for as noble a purpose as any involved in our prior decisions.

Reversed.

MR. JUSTICE GOLDBERG, whom The Chief Justice and Mr. Justice Brennan join, concurring.

I agree with the Court that Connecticut's birth-control law unconstitutionally intrudes upon the right of marital privacy, and I join in its opinion and judgment. Although I have not accepted the view that "due process" as used in the Fourteenth Amendment incorporates all of the first eight Amendments (see my concurring opinion in Pointer v. Texas, 380 U.S. 400, 410, and the dissenting opinion of MR. JUSTICE BRENNAN in Cohen v. Hurley, 366 U.S. 117, 154), I do agree that the concept of liberty protects those personal rights that are fundamental, and is not confined to the specific terms of the Bill of Rights. My conclusion that the concept of liberty is not so restricted and that it embraces the right of marital privacy though that right is not mentioned explicitly in the Constitution[1] is supported both by numerous decisions of this Court, referred to in the Court's opinion, and by the language and history of the Ninth Amendment. In reaching the conclusion that the right of marital privacy is protected, as being within the protected penumbra of specific guarantees of the Bill of Rights, the Court refers to the Ninth Amendment. . . . I add these words to emphasize the relevance of that Amendment to the Court's holding. . . .

This Court, in a series of decisions, has held that the Fourteenth Amendment absorbs and applies to the States those specifics of the first eight amendments which express fundamental personal rights. The language and history of the Ninth Amendment reveal that the Framers of the Constitution believed that there are additional fundamental rights, protected from govern-

---

[1] My Brother Stewart dissents on the ground that he "can find no . . . general right of privacy in the Bill of Rights, in any other part of the Constitution, or in any case ever before decided by this Court." Post, at 530. He would require a more explicit guarantee than the one which the Court derives from several constitutional amendments. This Court, however, has never held that the Bill of Rights or the Fourteenth Amendment protects only those rights that the Constitution specifically mentions by name. See, e.g., Bolling v. Sharpe, 347 U.S. 497; Aptheker v. Secretary of State, 378 U.S. 500; Kent v. Dulles, 357 U.S. 116; Carrington v. Rash, 380 U.S. 89, 96; Schware v. Board of Bar Examiners, 353 U.S. 232; NAACP v. Alabama, 360 U.S. 240; Pierce v. Society of Sisters, 268 U.S. 510; Meyer v. Nebraska, 262 U.S. 390. To the contrary, this Court, for example, in Bolling v. Sharpe, supra, while recognizing that the Fifth Amendment does not contain the "explicit safeguard" of an equal protection clause, id., at 499, nevertheless derived an equal protection principle from that Amendment's Due Process Clause. And in Schware v. Board of Bar Examiners, supra, the Court held that the Fourteenth Amendment protects from arbitrary state action the right to pursue an occupation, such as the practice of law.

mental infringement, which exist alongside those fundamental rights specifically mentioned in the first eight constitutional amendments.

The Ninth Amendment reads, "The enumeration in the Constitution, of certain rights, shall not be construed to deny or disparage others retained by the people." The Amendment is almost entirely the work of James Madison. It was introduced in Congress by him and passed the House and Senate with little or no debate and virtually no change in language. It was proffered to quiet expressed fears that a bill of specifically enumerated rights[3] could not be sufficiently broad to cover all essential rights and that the specific mention of certain rights would be interpreted as a denial that others were protected.[4]

In presenting the proposed Amendment, Madison said:

"It has been objected also against a bill of rights, that, by enumerating particular exceptions to the grant of power, it would disparage those rights which were not placed in that enumeration; and it might follow by implication, that those rights which were not singled out, were intended to be assigned into the hands of the General Government, and were consequently insecure. This is one of the most plausible arguments I have ever heard urged against the admission of a bill of rights into this system; but, I conceive, that it may be guarded against. I have attempted it, as gentlemen may see by turning to the last clause of the fourth resolution [the Ninth Amendment]." I Annals of Congress 439 (Gales and Seaton ed. 1834).

Mr. Justice Story wrote of this argument against a bill of rights and the meaning of the Ninth Amendment:

"In regard to . . . [a] suggestion, that the affirmance of certain rights might disparage others, or might lead to argumentative implications in favor of other powers, it might be sufficient to say that such a course of reasoning could never be sustained upon any solid basis. . . . But a conclusive answer is, that such an attempt may be interdicted (as it has been) by a positive

---

[3] Madison himself had previously pointed out the dangers of inaccuracy resulting from the fact that "no language is so copious as to supply words and phrases for every complex idea." The Federalist, No. 37 (Cooke ed. 1961), at 236.

[4] Alexander Hamilton was opposed to a bill of rights on the ground that it was unnecessary because the Federal Government was a government of delegated powers and it was not granted the power to intrude upon fundamental personal rights. The Federalist, No. 84 (Cooke ed. 1961), at 578-579. He also argued,

"I go further, and affirm that bills of rights, in the sense and in the extent in which they are contended for, are not only unnecessary in the proposed constitution, but would even be dangerous. They would contain various exceptions to powers which are not granted; and on this very account, would afford a colourable pretext to claim more than were granted. For why declare that things shall not be done which there is no power to do? Why for instance, should it be said, that the liberty of the press shall not be restrained, when no power is given by which restrictions may be imposed? I will not contend that such a provision would confer a regulating power; but it is evident that it would furnish, to men disposed to usurp, a plausible pretence for claiming that power." Id., at 579.

The Ninth Amendment and the Tenth Amendment, which provides, "The powers not delegated to the United States by the Constitution, nor prohibited by it to the States, are reserved to the States respectively, or to the people," were apparently also designed in part to meet the above-quoted argument of Hamilton.

declaration in such a bill of rights that the enumeration of certain rights shall not be construed to deny or disparage others retained by the people." II Story, Commentaries on the Constitution of the United States 626-627 (5th ed. 1891).

He further stated, referring to the Ninth Amendment:

"This clause was manifestly introduced to prevent any perverse or ingenious misapplication of the well-known maxim, that an affirmation in particular cases implies a negation in all others; and, e converso, that a negation in particular cases implies an affirmation in all others." Id., at 651.

These statements of Madison and Story make clear that the Framers did not intend that the first eight amendments be construed to exhaust the basic and fundamental rights which the Constitution guaranteed to the people.[5]

While this Court has had little occasion to interpret the Ninth Amendment,[6] "[i]t cannot be presumed that any clause in the constitution is intended to be without effect." Marbury v. Madison, 1 Cranch 137, 174. In interpreting the Constitution, "real effect should be given to all the words it uses." Myers v. United States, 272 U.S. 52, 151. The Ninth Amendment to the Constitution may be regarded by some as a recent discovery and may be forgotten by others, but since 1791 it has been a basic part of the Constitution which we are sworn to uphold. To hold that a right so basic and fundamental and so deep-rooted in our society as the right of privacy in marriage may be infringed because that right is not guaranteed in so many words by the first eight amendments to the Constitution is to ignore the Ninth Amendment and to give it no effect whatsoever. Moreover, a judicial construction that this fundamental right is not protected by the Constitution because it is not mentioned in explicit terms by one of the first eight amendments or elsewhere in the Constitution would violate the Ninth Amendment, which specifically states that "[t]he enumeration in the Constitution, of certain rights, shall not

[5] The Tenth Amendment similarly made clear that the States and the people retained all those powers not expressly delegated to the Federal Government.

[6] This Amendment has been referred to as "The Forgotten Ninth Amendment," in a book with that title by Bennett B. Patterson (1955). Other commentary on the Ninth Amendment includes Redlich, Are There "Certain Rights . . . Retained by the People"? 37 N.Y.U.L. Rev. 787 (1962), and Kelsey, The Ninth Amendment of the Federal Constitution, 11 Ind. L.J. 309 (1936). As far as I am aware, until today this Court has referred to the Ninth Amendment only in United Public Workers v. Mitchell, 330 U.S. 75, 94-95; Tennessee Electric Power Co. v. TVA, 306 U.S. 118, 143-144; and Ashwander v. TVA, 297 U.S. 288, 330-331. See also Calder v. Bull, 3 Dall. 386, 388; Loan Assn. v. Topeka, 20 Wall. 655, 662-663.

In United Public Workers v. Mitchell, supra, at 94-95, the Court stated: "We accept appellants' contention that the nature of political rights reserved to the people by the Ninth and Tenth Amendments [is] involved. The right claimed as inviolate may be stated as the right of a citizen to act as a party official or worker to further his own political views. Thus we have a measure of interference by the Hatch Act and the Rules with what otherwise would be the freedom of the civil servant under the First, Ninth and Tenth Amendments. And, if we look upon due process as a guarantee of freedom in those fields, there is a corresponding impairment of that right under the Fifth Amendment."

be *construed* to deny or disparage others retained by the people." (Emphasis added.)

A dissenting opinion suggests that my interpretation of the Ninth Amendment somehow "broaden[s] the powers of this Court." . . . With all due respect, I believe that it misses the import of what I am saying. I do not take the position of my Brother Black in his dissent in Adamson v. California, 332 U.S. 46, 68, that the entire Bill of Rights is incorporated in the Fourteenth Amendment, and I do not mean to imply that the Ninth Amendment is applied against the States by the Fourteenth. Nor do I mean to state that the Ninth Amendment constitutes an independent source of rights protected from infringement by either the States or the Federal Government. Rather, the Ninth Amendment shows a belief of the Constitution's authors that fundamental rights exist that are not expressly enumerated in the first eight amendments and an intent that the list of rights included there not be deemed exhaustive. As any student of this Court's opinions knows, this Court has held, often unanimously, that the Fifth and Fourteenth Amendments protect certain fundamental personal liberties from abridgment by the Federal Government or the States. See, e.g., Bolling v. Sharpe, 347 U.S. 497; Aptheker v. Secretary of State, 378 U.S. 500; Kent v. Dulles, 357 U.S. 116; Cantwell v. Connecticut, 310 U.S. 296; NAACP v. Alabama, 357 U.S. 449; Gideon v. Wainwright, 372 U.S. 335; New York Times Co. v. Sullivan, 376 U.S. 254. The Ninth Amendment simply shows the intent of the Constitution's authors that other fundamental personal rights should not be denied such protection or disparaged in any other way simply because they are not specifically listed in the first eight constitutional amendments. I do not see how this broadens the authority of the Court; rather it serves to support what this Court has been doing in protecting fundamental rights.

Nor am I turning somersaults with history in arguing that the Ninth Amendment is relevant in a case dealing with a *State's* infringement of a fundamental right. While the Ninth Amendment — and indeed the entire Bill of Rights — originally concerned restrictions upon *federal* power, the subsequently enacted Fourteenth Amendment prohibits the States as well from abridging fundamental personal liberties. And, the Ninth Amendment, in indicating that not all such liberties are specifically mentioned in the first eight amendments, is surely relevant in showing the existence of other fundamental personal rights, now protected from state, as well as federal, infringement. In sum, the Ninth Amendment simply lends strong support to the view that the "liberty" protected by the Fifth and Fourteenth Amendments from infringement by the Federal Government or the States is not restricted to rights specifically mentioned in the first eight amendments. Cf. United Public Workers v. Mitchell, 330 U.S. 75, 94-95.

In determining which rights are fundamental, judges are not left at large to decide cases in light of their personal and private notions. Rather, they must look to the "traditions and [collective] conscience of our people" to determine whether a principle is "so rooted [there] . . . as to be ranked as fundamental." Snyder v. Massachusetts, 291 U.S. 97, 105. The inquiry is whether a right involved "is of such a character that it cannot be denied without violating those 'fundamental principles of liberty and justice which lie at the base of all our civil and political institutions'. . . ." Powell v. Alabama, 287 U.S. 45, 67. "Liberty" also "gains content from the emanations of . . . specific [constitutional] guarantees" and "from experience with the requirements of a free society." Poe v. Ullman, 367 U.S. 497, 517 (dissenting opinion of Mr. Justice Douglas).

I agree fully with the Court that, applying these tests, the right of privacy is a fundamental personal right, emanating "from the totality of the constitutional scheme under which we live." Id., at 521. Mr. Justice Brandeis, dissenting in Olmstead v. United States, 277 U.S. 438, 478, comprehensively summarized the principles underlying the Constitution's guarantees of privacy:

"The protection guaranteed by the [Fourth and Fifth] Amendments is much broader in scope. The makers of our Constitution undertook to secure conditions favorable to the pursuit of happiness. They recognized the significance of man's spiritual nature, of his feelings and of his intellect. They knew that only a part of the pain, pleasure and satisfactions of life are to be found in material things. They sought to protect Americans in their beliefs, their thoughts, their emotions and their sensations. They conferred, as against the Government, the right to be let alone — the most comprehensive of rights and the right most valued by civilized men."

The Connecticut statutes here involved deal with a particularly important and sensitive area of privacy — that of the marital relation and the marital home. This Court recognized in Meyer v. Nebraska, supra, that the right "to marry, establish a home and bring up children" was an essential part of the liberty guaranteed by the Fourteenth Amendment. 262 U.S., at 399. In Pierce v. Society of Sisters, 268 U.S. 510, the Court held unconstitutional an Oregon Act which forbade parents from sending their children to private schools because such an act "unreasonably interferes with the liberty of parents and guardians to direct the upbringing and education of children under their control." 268 U.S., at 534-535. As this Court said in Prince v. Massachusetts, 321 U.S. 158, at 166, the Meyer and Pierce decisions "have respected the private realm of family life which the state cannot enter."

I agree with Mr. Justice Harlan's statement in his dissenting opinion in Poe v. Ullman, 367 U.S. 497, 551-552: "Certainly the safeguarding of the home does not follow merely from the sanctity of property rights. The home derives its pre-eminence as the seat of family life. And the integrity of that life is something so fundamental that it has been found to draw to its protection the principles of more than one explicitly granted Constitutional right. . . . Of this whole 'private realm of family life' it is difficult to imagine what is more private or more intimate than a husband and wife's marital relations."

The entire fabric of the Constitution and the purposes that clearly underlie its specific guarantees demonstrate that the rights to marital privacy and to marry and raise a family are of similar order and magnitude as the fundamental rights specifically protected.

Although the Constitution does not speak in so many words of the right of privacy in marriage, I cannot believe that it offers these fundamental rights no protection. The fact that no particular provision of the Constitution explicitly forbids the State from disrupting the traditional relation of the family — a relation as old and as fundamental as our entire civilization — surely does not show that the Government was meant to have the power to do so. Rather, as the Ninth Amendment expressly recognizes, there are fundamental personal rights such as this one, which are protected from abridgment by the Government though not specifically mentioned in the Constitution. . . .

The logic of the dissents would sanction federal or state legislation that seems to me even more plainly unconstitutional than the statute before us. Surely the Government, absent a showing of a compelling subordinating state interest, could not decree that all husbands and wives must be sterilized after two children have been born to them. Yet by their reasoning such an invasion of marital privacy would not be subject to constitutional challenge because, while it might be "silly," no provision of the Constitution specifically prevents the Government from curtailing the marital right to bear children and raise a family. While it may shock some of my Brethren that the Court today holds that the Constitution protects the right of marital privacy, in my view it is far more shocking to believe that the personal liberty guaranteed by the Constitution does not include protection against such totalitarian limitation of family size, which is at complete variance with our constitutional concepts. Yet, if upon a showing of a slender basis of rationality, a law outlawing voluntary birth control by married persons is valid, then, by the same reasoning, a law requiring compulsory birth control also would seem to be valid. In my view, however, both types of law would unjustifiably intrude upon rights of marital privacy which are constitutionally protected. . . .

Although the Connecticut birth-control law obviously encroaches upon a fundamental personal liberty, the State does not show that the law serves any "subordinating [state] interest which is compelling" or that it is "necessary . . . to the accomplishment of a permissible state policy." The State, at most, argues that there is some rational relation between this statute and what is admittedly a legitimate subject of state concern — the discouraging of extra-marital relations. It says that preventing the use of birth-control devices by married persons helps prevent the indulgence by some in such extra-marital relations. The rationality of this justification is dubious, particularly in light of the admitted widespread availability to all persons in the State of Connecticut, unmarried as well as married, of birth-control devices for the prevention of disease, as distinguished from the prevention of conception, see Tileston v. Ullman, 129 Conn. 84, 26 A.2d 582. But, in any event, it is clear that the state interest in safeguarding marital fidelity can be served by a more discriminately tailored statute, which does not, like the present one, sweep unnecessarily broadly, reaching far beyond the evil sought to be dealt with and intruding upon the privacy of all married couples. . . .

Finally, it should be said of the Court's holding today that it in no way interferes with a State's proper regulation of sexual promiscuity or misconduct. As my Brother Harlan so well stated in his dissenting opinion in Poe v. Ullman, supra, at 553.

"Adultery, homosexuality and the like are sexual intimacies which the State forbids . . . but the intimacy of husband and wife is necessarily an essential and accepted feature of the institution of marriage, an institution which the State not only must allow, but which always and in every age it has fostered and protected. It is one thing when the State exerts its power either to forbid extra-marital sexuality . . . or to say who may marry, but it is quite another when, having acknowledged a marriage and the intimacies inherent in it, it undertakes to regulate by means of the criminal law the details of that intimacy."

In sum, I believe that the right of privacy in the marital relation is fundamental and basic — a personal right "retained by the people" within the meaning of the Ninth Amendment. Connecticut cannot constitutionally abridge this fundamental right, which is protected by the Fourteenth Amendment from infringement by the States. I agree with the Court that petitioners' convictions must therefore be reversed.

Mr. Justice Harlan, concurring in the judgment.

I fully agree with the judgment of reversal, but find myself unable to join the Court's opinion. The reason is that it seems to me to evince an approach to this case very much like that taken by my Brothers Black and Stewart in dissent, namely: the Due Process Clause of the Fourteenth Amendment does not touch this Connecticut statute unless the enactment is found to violate some right assured by the letter or penumbra of the Bill of Rights.

In other words, what I find implicit in the Court's opinion is that the "incorporation" doctrine may be used to *restrict* the reach of Fourteenth Amendment Due Process. For me this is just as unacceptable constitutional doctrine as is the use of the "incorporation" approach to *impose* upon the States all the requirements of the Bill of Rights as found in the provisions of the first eight amendments and in the decisions of this Court interpreting them. See, e.g., my concurring opinions in Pointer v. Texas, 380 U.S. 400, 408, and Griffin v. California, 380 U.S. 609, 615, and my dissenting opinion in Poe v. Ullman, 367 U.S. 497, 522, at pp. 539-545.

In my view, the proper constitutional inquiry in this case is whether this Connecticut statute infringes the Due Process Clause of the Fourteenth Amendment because the enactment violates basic values "implicit in the concept of ordered liberty," Palko v. Connecticut, 302 U.S. 319, 325. For reasons stated at length in my dissenting opinion in Poe v. Ullman, supra, I believe that it does. While the relevant inquiry may be aided by resort to one or more of the provisions of the Bill of Rights, it is not dependent on them or any of their radiations. The Due Process Clause of the Fourteenth Amendment stands, in my opinion, on its own bottom. . . .

MR. JUSTICE WHITE, concurring in the judgment.

In my view this Connecticut law as applied to married couples deprives them of "liberty" without due process of law, as that concept is used in the Fourteenth Amendment. I therefore concur in the judgment of the Court reversing these convictions under Connecticut's aiding and abetting statute.

. . . Surely the right invoked in this case, to be free of regulation of the intimacies of the marriage relationship, "come[s] to this Court with a momentum for respect lacking when appeal is made to liberties which derive merely from shifting economic arrangements." Kovacs v. Cooper, 336 U.S. 77, 95 (opinion of Frankfurter, J.).

The Connecticut anti-contraceptive statute deals rather substantially with this relationship. For it forbids all married persons the right to use birth-control devices, regardless of whether their use is dictated by considerations of family planning, Trubek v. Ullman, 147 Conn. 633, 165 A.2d 158, health, or indeed even of life itself. Buxton v. Ullman, 147 Conn. 48, 156 A.2d 508. The anti-use statute, together with the general aiding and abetting statute, prohibits doctors from affording advice to married persons on proper and effective methods of birth control. Tileston v. Ullman, 129 Conn. 84, 26 A.2d 582. And the clear effect of these statutes, as enforced, is to deny disadvantaged citizens of Connecticut, those without either adequate knowledge or resources to obtain private counseling, access to medical assistance and up-to-date information in respect to proper methods of birth control. State v. Nelson, 126 Conn. 412, 11 A.2d 856; State v. Griswold, 151 Conn. 544, 200 A.2d 479. In my view, a statute with these effects bears a substantial burden of justification when attacked under the Fourteenth Amendment. Yick Wo v. Hopkins, 118 U.S. 356; Skinner v. Oklahoma, 316 U.S. 535; Schware v. Board of Bar Examiners, 353 U.S. 232; McLaughlin v. Florida, 379 U.S. 184, 192. . . .

In these circumstances one is rather hard pressed to explain how the ban on use by married persons in any way prevents use of such devices by persons engaging in illicit sexual relations and thereby contributes to the State's policy against such relationships. Neither the state courts nor the State before the bar of this Court has tendered such an explanation. It is purely fanciful to believe that the broad proscription on use facilitates discovery of use by persons engaging in a prohibited relationship or for some other reason makes such use more unlikely and thus can be supported by any sort of administrative consideration. . . . At most the broad ban is of marginal utility to the declared objective. A statute limiting its prohibition on use to persons engaging in the prohibited relationship would serve the end posited by Connecticut in the same way, and with the same effectiveness, or ineffectiveness, as the broad anti-use statute under attack in this case. I find nothing in this record justifying the sweeping scope of this statute, with its telling effect on the freedoms of married persons, and therefore conclude that it deprives such persons of liberty without due process of law.

Mr. Justice Black, with whom Mr. Justice Stewart joins, dissenting.

I agree with my Brother Stewart's dissenting opinion. And like him I do not to any extent whatever base my view that this Connecticut law is constitutional on a belief that the law is wise or that its policy is a good one. . . .

The Court talks about a constitutional "right of privacy" as though there is some constitutional provision or provisions forbidding any law ever to be passed which might abridge the "privacy" of individuals. But there is not. There are, of course, guarantees in certain specific constitutional provisions which are designed in part to protect privacy at certain times and places with respect to certain activities. Such, for example, is the Fourth Amendment's guarantee against "unreasonable searches and seizures." But I think it belittles that Amendment to talk about it as though it protects nothing but "privacy." To treat it that way is to give it a niggardly interpretation, not the kind of liberal reading I think any Bill of Rights provision should be given. The average man would very likely not have his feelings soothed any more by having his property seized openly than by having it seized privately and by stealth. He simply wants his property left alone. And a person can be just as much, if not more, irritated, annoyed and injured by an unceremonious public arrest by a policeman as he is by a seizure in the privacy of his office or home.

One of the most effective ways of diluting or expanding a constitutionally guaranteed right is to substitute for the crucial word or words of a constitutional guarantee another word or words, more or less flexible and more or less restricted in meaning. This fact is well illustrated by the use of the term "right of privacy" as a comprehensive substitute for the Fourth Amendment's guarantee against "unreasonable searches and seizures." "Privacy" is a broad, abstract and ambiguous concept which can easily be shrunken in meaning but which can also, on the other hand, easily be interpreted as a constitutional ban against many things other than searches and seizures. I have expressed the view many times that First Amendment freedoms, for example, have suffered from a failure of the courts to stick to the simple language of the First Amendment in construing it, instead of invoking multitudes of words substituted for those the Framers used. See, e.g., New York Times Co. v. Sullivan, 376 U.S. 254, 293 (concurring opinion); cases collected in City of El Paso v. Simmons, 379 U.S. 497, 517, n. 1 (dissenting opinion); Black, The Bill of Rights, 35 N.Y.U.L. Rev. 865. For these reasons I get nowhere in this case by talk about a constitutional "right of privacy" as an emanation from one or more constitutional provisions. I like my privacy as well as the next one, but I am nevertheless compelled to admit that government has a right to invade it unless prohibited by some specific constitutional provision. For these reasons I cannot agree with the Court's judgment and the reasons it gives for holding this Connecticut law unconstitutional. . . .

My Brother GOLDBERG has adopted the recent discovery that the Ninth Amendment as well as the Due Process Clause can be used by this Court as authority to strike down all state legislation which this Court thinks violates "fundamental principles of liberty and justice," or is contrary to the "traditions and [collective] conscience of our people." He also states, without proof satisfactory to me, that in making decisions on this basis judges will not consider "their personal and private notions." One may ask how they can avoid considering them. Our Court certainly has no machinery with which to take a Gallup Poll. And the scientific miracles of this age have not yet produced a gadget which the Court can use to determine what traditions are rooted in the "[collective] conscience of our people." Moreover, one would certainly have to look far beyond the language of the Ninth Amendment to find that the Framers vested in this Court any such awesome veto powers over lawmaking, either by the States or by the Congress. Nor does anything in the history of the Amendment offer any support for such a shocking doctrine. The whole history of the adoption of the Constitution and Bill of Rights points the other way, and the very material quoted by my Brother GOLDBERG shows that the Ninth Amendment was intended to protect against the idea that "by enumerating particular exceptions to the grant of power" to the Federal Government, "those rights which were not singled out, were intended to be assigned into the hands of the General Government [the United States], and were consequently insecure." [15] That Amendment was passed, not to broaden the powers of this Court or any other department of "the General Government," but, as every student of history knows, to assure the people that the Constitution in all its provisions was intended to limit the Federal Government to the powers granted expressly or by necessary implication. If any broad, unlimited power to hold laws unconstitutional because they offend what this Court conceives to be the "[collective] conscience of our people" is vested in this Court by the Ninth Amendment, the Fourteenth Amendment, or any other provision of the Constitution, it was not given by the Framers, but rather has been bestowed on the Court by the Court. This fact is perhaps responsible for the peculiar phenomenon that for a period of a century and a half no serious suggestion was ever made that the Ninth Amendment, enacted to protect state powers against federal invasion, could be used as a weapon of federal power to prevent state legislatures from pass-

[15] 1 Annals of Congress 439. See also II Story, Commentaries on the Constitution of the United States (5th ed. 1891): "This clause was manifestly introduced to prevent any perverse or ingenious misapplication of the well-known maxim, that an affirmation in particular cases implies a negation in all others; and, e converso, that a negation in particular cases implies an affirmation in all others. The maxim, rightly understood, is perfectly sound and safe; but it has often been strangely forced from its natural meaning into the support of the most dangerous political heresies." Id., at 651 (footnote omitted).

ing laws they consider appropriate to govern local affairs. Use of any such broad, unbounded judicial authority would make of this Court's members a day-to-day constitutional convention. . . .

I realize that many good and able men have eloquently spoken and written, sometimes in rhapsodical strains, about the duty of this Court to keep the Constitution in tune with the times. The idea is that the Constitution must be changed from time to time and that this Court is charged with a duty to make those changes. For myself, I must with all deference reject that philosophy. The Constitution makers knew the need for change and provided for it. Amendments suggested by the people's elected representatives can be submitted to the people or their selected agents for ratification. That method of change was good for our Fathers, and being somewhat old-fashioned I must add it is good enough for me. And so, I cannot rely on the Due Process Clause or the Ninth Amendment or any mysterious and uncertain natural law concept as a reason for striking down this state law. . . . The Due Process Clause with an "arbitrary and capricious" or "shocking to the conscience" formula was liberally used by this Court to strike down economic legislation in the early decades of this century, threatening, many people thought, the tranquility and stability of the Nation. See, e.g., Lochner v. New York, 198 U.S. 45. That formula, based on subjective considerations of "natural justice," is no less dangerous when used to enforce this Court's views about personal rights than those about economic rights. I had thought that we had laid that formula, as a means for striking down state legislation, to rest once and for all in cases like West Coast Hotel Co. v. Parrish, 300 U.S. 379; Olsen v. Nebraska ex rel. Western Reference & Bond Assn., 313 U.S. 236, and many other opinions. . . .

MR. JUSTICE STEWART, whom Mr. Justice Black joins, dissenting.

Since 1879 Connecticut has had on its books a law which forbids the use of contraceptives by anyone. I think this is an uncommonly silly law. As a practical matter, the law is obviously unenforceable, except in the oblique context of the present case. As a philosophical matter, I believe the use of contraceptives in the relationship of marriage should be left to personal and private choice, based upon each individual's moral, ethical, and religious beliefs. As a matter of social policy, I think professional counsel about methods of birth control should be available to all, so that each individual's choice can be meaningfully made. But we are not asked in this case to say whether we think this law is unwise, or even asinine. We are asked to hold that it violates the United States Constitution. And that I cannot do.

In the course of its opinion the Court refers to no less than six Amendments to the Constitution: the First, the Third, the Fourth, the Fifth, the Ninth, and the Fourteenth. But the Court does not say which of these Amendments, if any, it thinks is infringed by this Connecticut law.

We *are* told that the Due Process Clause of the Fourteenth Amendment is not, as such, the "guide" in this case. With that much I agree. There is no claim that this law, duly enacted by the Connecticut Legislature, is unconstitutionally vague. There is no claim that the appellants were denied any of the elements of procedural due process at their trial, so as to make their convictions constitutionally invalid. And, as the Court says, the day has long passed since the Due Process Clause was regarded as a proper instrument for determining "the wisdom, need, and propriety" of state laws. Compare Lochner v. New York, 198 U.S. 45, with Ferguson v. Skrupa, 372 U.S. 726. My Brothers HARLAN and WHITE to the contrary, "[w]e have returned to the original constitutional proposition that courts do not substitute their social and economic beliefs for the judgment of legislative bodies, who are elected to pass laws." Ferguson v. Skrupa, supra, at 730.

As to the First, Third, Fourth, and Fifth Amendments, I can find nothing in any of them to invalidate this Connecticut law, even assuming that all those Amendments are fully applicable against the States. It has not even been argued that this is a law "respecting an establishment of religion, or prohibiting the free exercise thereof." And surely, unless the solemn process of constitutional adjudication is to descend to the level of a play on words, there is not involved here any abridgment of "the freedom of speech, or of the press; or the right of the people peaceably to assemble, and to petition the Government for a redress of grievances." No soldier has been quartered in any house. There has been no search, and no seizure. Nobody has been compelled to be a witness against himself.

The Court also quotes the Ninth Amendment, and my Brother GOLDBERG's concurring opinion relies heavily upon it. But to say that the Ninth Amendment has anything to do with this case is to turn somersaults with history. The Ninth Amendment, like its companion the Tenth, which this Court held "states but a truism that all is retained which has not been surrendered," United States v. Darby, 312 U.S. 100, 124, was framed by James Madison and adopted by the States simply to make clear that the adoption of the Bill of Rights did not alter the plan that the *Federal* Government was to be a government of express and limited powers, and that all rights and powers not delegated to it were retained by the people and the individual States. Until today no member of this Court has ever suggested that the Ninth Amendment meant anything else, and the idea that a federal court could ever use the Ninth Amendment to annul a law passed by the elected representatives of the people of the State of Connecticut would have caused James Madison no little wonder.

What provision of the Constitution, then, does make this state law invalid? The Court says it is the right of privacy "created by several fundamental constitutional guarantees." With all deference, I can find no such general right of privacy in the Bill of Rights, in any other part of the Constitution, or in any case ever before decided by this Court.

. . . It is the essence of judicial duty to subordinate our own personal views, our own ideas of what legislation is wise and what is not. If, as I should surely hope, the law before us does not reflect the standards of the people of Connecticut, the people of Connecticut can freely exercise their true Ninth and Tenth Amendment rights to persuade their elected representatives to repeal it. That is the constitutional way to take this law off the books.

NOTES

1. For discussion of the Griswold case, see Symposium on the Griswold Case and the Right of Privacy, 64 Mich. L. Rev. 197 (1965); Notes, 15 Catholic U.L. Rev. 126 (1965); 69 Dick. L. Rev. 417 (1965).

2. While the Griswold case was the first to explicitly map out a broad constitutional right of privacy and thus indirectly suggested the problem of resolving a possible conflict between this right and constitutional guarantees of free speech, this issue already lurked behind the developing tort remedy for invasion of privacy and certain statutes that sought to protect similar interests. A classical article, Warren and Brandeis, The Right to Privacy, 4 Harv. L. Rev. 193 (1890), virtually shaped the law. Today the following classes of cases are said by some to be encompassed within this right: (1) intrusion upon the plaintiff's seclusion or solitude or into his private affairs; (2) public disclosure of embarassing facts about the plaintiff; (3) publicity which places the plaintiff in a false light in the public eye; (4) appropriation, for the defendant's advantage, of the plaintiff's name or likeness. Truth is no defense. See Prosser, Privacy, 48 Calif. L. Rev. 383 (1960). There has been a dispute as to whether a separate right of privacy existed, or whether several different rights protecting different interests were simply inadequately lumped under a single name. Cf. Prosser, supra, with Blousten, Privacy as an Aspect of Human Dignity: An Answer to Dean Prosser, 39 N.Y.U.L. Rev. 963 (1964). It would seem, in view of the Griswold opinion, that those who hold out for a separate right of privacy based on the need of protecting the dignity of the human personality are gaining judicial support.

The law today, without being too explicit, tends to reach results which are sensitive to the free speech issue while on the whole rejecting any express defense made on that ground. Thus, the cases treat liberally any coverage of activities of a notorious or important individual who is thought to have implicitly consented to publicity by becoming famous. Some limits may be put if the material goes beyond community standards of decency. Inaccurate and misleading versions as well as fictionalized accounts, whether for literary or advertising purposes, may not fare as well. But cf. Youssoupoff v. Columbia Broadcasting System, 6 Pike & Fischer Radio Reg. 2d 2036 (N.Y. Sup. Ct. 1965) (mere use of author's "original" dialogue not enough to sustain finding of fictionalization; broadcast in regular course of network business not enough to show statutory "commercial purpose"). The unimportant individual who through no fault of his own is caught in a web of publicity is at times given tort protection. The courts today, however, tend to permit coverage of anything that is considered news. While definitions of news differ, the general tendency is to treat as news any matter that is of interest to the general public rather than merely what ought to be of interest. Cf. Hubbard v. Journal Publishing Co., 69 N.M. 473, 368 P.2d 147 (1962) (publication of verbatim copy of official juvenile court records of sexual assault on minor female by her brother (identifying the female) not actionable because (1) privileged, as report of a judicial proceeding, even as to involuntary participant, and (2) newsworthy), with Barber v. Time, Inc., 348 Mo. 1199, 159 S.W.2d 291 (1942) (news account of private hospital diagnosis of voraciously hungry person who did not gain weight, naming name and publishing photograph obtained without consent, held actionable not simply because of the manner in which photograph was obtained but also because the identity of the person who suffered the ailment was not a matter of public interest). The Barber case rejected a constitutional free speech defense on the ground that a determination of "proper public interest" is for the court, and that such a rule only limits "abuse" and not "freedom" of the press. Cf. Sarat Lahiri v. Daily Mirror, 162 Misc. 776, 295 N.Y.S. 382 (1937) (if statutory right of privacy is to cover news items, as opposed to use of photo for advertising or in connection with fiction, "it should be the result of a clear expression of legislative policy").

Criminal statutes in the area prohibit the naming or identification of a female victim of a rape or similar criminal assault. Fla. Stat. Ann. §794.03; Geo. Code Ann. §§26-2105; Code of Laws of S.C. §16-81 (only naming prohibited; but see Nappier v. Jefferson Standard Life Ins. Co., 322 F.2d 502 (4th Cir. 1963), holding statutory word "name" to be read as equivalent of "identify"); Wis. Stat. Ann. §942.02 (predecessor statute Wis. Stat. Ann. §348.412 (1925) held unconstitutional by trial court but the Supreme Court sustained the statute's validity, State v. Evjue, 253 Wis. 146, 33 N.W.2d 305, 13 A.L.R.2d 1201 (1948), relying on Chaplinsky v. New Hampshire, 315 U.S. 568, 62 S. Ct. 766, 86 L. Ed. 1031 (1942)). Examples of similar statutes in other areas are Fla. Stat. §398.18(1) (narcotics addicts; records "open for public inspection only to person named . . . or his counsel or by narcotics officers"; publication implicitly prohibited, Patterson v. Tribune Co., 146 So. 2d 623 (2d D.C. App. Fla. 1962), cert. den., 153 So. 2d 306 (Fla. 1963)); Ga. Code Ann. §§24-2432, 24-9905 (juvenile first offenders).

It remains to be seen to what extent the constitutional right of privacy enunciated in the Griswold case will further retard any attempts to challenge the remaining common law or statutory protection of privacy interests on free speech or free press grounds. See Hill v. Hayes and Time Inc., 15 N.Y.2d 986, 260 N.Y.S.2d 7, 207 N.E.2d 604 (1965), prob. juris. noted sub nom. Time Inc. v. Hill, 382 U.S. 936 (1965), reargument ordered, 384 U.S. 995 (1966). The Hill case involved a suit by persons who were victims of a crime, on which a book of fiction, "The Desperate Hours," was based. A Life Magazine article reported that the episode would be made into a play. Members of the cast were transported to the plaintiff's former home — his home at the time of the crime. Photos taken there illustrated the story. The plaintiff claimed this caused renewed emotional upset to his family and that the account was "fictionalized." The Supreme Court probably will consider whether to reverse the damage award on First Amendment grounds. Cf. Youssoupoff v. Columbia Broadcasting System, supra (N.Y. Times v. Sullivan dealt with public officials; free speech does not permit invasion of privacy of public figure); Spahn v. Messner, 23 App. Div. 2d 216, 260 N.Y.S.2d 451 (1965); University of Notre Dame Du Lac v. 20th Century Fox, 22 App. Div. 2d 452, 256 N.Y.S.2d 301 (1st Dept. 1965), aff'd, 15 N.Y.2d 940, 259 N.Y.S.2d 832, 207 N.E.2d 508 (1965) (right of privacy case involving fictionalized story referring to University). See also N.Y. Times, Sunday, May 15, 1966, Sec. 4, reporting a Baltimore decision basing on Justice Douglas' reference to the status of privacy rights in Griswold, an injunction against picketing the home of a tavern owner by residents who objected to the tavern in their neighborhood. The article also discussed the growing number of right of privacy actions in the wake of Griswold.

For discussion of state cases in relation to Sullivan, see Silver, Privacy and the First Amendment, 36 Fordham L. Rev. 553 (1966). Further, on the relation of privacy rights to the First Amendment see Prosser, Privacy, 48 Calif. L. Rev. at 410-419; Wade, Defamation and the Right of Privacy, 15 Vand. L. Rev. 1093 (1962). For other discussion see, in addition to Blaustein, supra, Pound, The Fourteenth Amendment and the Right of Privacy, 13 W. Res. L. Rev. 34 (1961); Beaney, The Constitutional Right to Privacy in the Supreme Court, 1962 Sup. Ct. Rev. 212; Franklin, A Constitutional Problem in Privacy Protection: Legal Inhibitions on Reporting of Fact, 16 Stan. L. Rev. 107 (1963). See also Geis, Publicity and Juvenile Court Proceedings, 30 Rocky Mt. L. Rev. 101 (1958); Zelermyer, Invasion of Privacy (1959); Note, The Right of Privacy in News Photographs, 44 Va. L. Rev. 1303 (1958); Note, The Right of Privacy: Normative-Descriptive Confusion in the Defense of Newsworthiness, 30 U. Chi. L. Rev. 722 (1963); Hofstadter and Horowitz, The Right of Privacy (1964); McCarthy, Privacy: Burgeoning Rights and Remedies, 38 Conn. B.J. 555 (1964); Ezer, Intrusion on Solitude: Herein of Civil Rights and Civil Wrongs, 21 Law in Trans. 63 (1961).

3. More generally on the right of privacy, see Reynard, The Right of Privacy, in 6 Southern Methodist University Studies in Jurisprudence, Fundamental Law in Criminal Prosecutions 85 (Harding, ed., 1959); Hurst, Law and the Limits of Individuality, in Spiller (ed.), Social Control in a Free Society 97 (1960); Ernst and Schwartz, Privacy: The Right to be Let Alone (1962); Lamoreaux, The Right of Privacy: A Bibliography, 71 Years, 1890-1961 (Wash. State U., Dept. of Journalism, 1962); Note, Advertising and the Right of Privacy, 9 Vill. L. Rev. 274 (1964); Gordon, Invasion of Privacy: The Unsolicited Telephone Call, 2 Lex et Scientia 206 (1965); Note, The Right to Privacy in the Name, Reputation and Personality of a Deceased Relative, 40 Notre Dame Law. 324 (1965); Westin, Science, Privacy, and Freedom: Issues and Proposals for the 1970's, 66 Colum. L. Rev. 1003, — (1966).

4. On the use of psychological questionnaires and personality tests on federal employees and job applicants and census methods, particularly the 1964 Census of Agriculture with detailed questions about outside income, see Hearings before a Subcommittee of the House Committee on Government Operations, Special Inquiry on Invasion of Privacy, 89th Cong. 1st Sess. (1965); Hearings before Subcommittee on Constitutional Rights of the Senate Committee on the Judiciary, Psychological Tests and Constitutional Rights, 89th Cong., 1st Sess. (1965); Mirel, The Limits of Governmental Inquiry into the Private Lives of Government Employees, 46 B.U.L. Rev. 1 (1966). See further Gross, The Brain Watchers (1952); Brenton, The Privacy Invaders (1964); Packard, The Naked Society (1964); Michael, Speculation on the Relation of the Computer to Individual Freedom and Right to Privacy, 33 Geo. Wash. L. Rev. 270 (1964); Ridgeway, The Snoops, Private Lives and Public Service, The New Republic, Dec. 19, 1964, p. 13; Ruebhausen and Brim, Privacy and Behavioral Research. 65 Colum. L. Rev. 1184 (1965); Special Issue, Testing and Public Policy, 20 American Psychologist 857-

993, November 1965. See also Schubert, Constitutional Politics, ch. 12, The Implications of Ordered Liberty: Physiological and Psychological Privacy (1960); Whyte, The Organization Man (1956). For organized labor opposition to the use of lie detectors by public and private employers, see N.Y. Times, Feb. 26, 1965. See also Note, Lie Detectors in Private Employment: A Proposal for Balancing Interests, 33 Geo. Wash. L. Rev. 932 (1965). For a report that lie detector use by the C.I.A. "tended to weed out the active, all-American, conscientious and virile types most urgently needed as spies" and that "overreliance on the lie detector helps open the way for employment of homosexuals, laggards and trained Communist agents," see N.Y. Times, Nov. 24, 1964. Cf. Dew v. Halaby, 317 F.2d 582, 4 A.L.R. 3d 474 (D.C. Cir. 1963), cert. dis., 379 U.S. 951 (1964) (dismissal of government employee for pre-employment homosexual acts and smoking of marijuana). Lookouts from which postal inspectors can observe postal employees have been discontinued in post-office washrooms. N.Y. Times, Dec. 12, 1964. For a case denying relief from round-the-clock F.B.I. suveillance, see Giancana v. Hoover, 322 F.2d 789 (7th Cir. 1963). On mail covers see Chapter VII, Section B, subsection 2. In July, 1966, the Subcommittee of the House Committee on Government Operations, supra, held hearings on a proposal to establish a Federal Data Center which would collect and make available through computers all the data available in the different federal agencies on each individual.

5. Prior to Griswold the protection of privacy stemmed from the constitutional prohibition against unauthorized search and self-incrimination, not separately covered in this text. For general reference, see, e.g., Paulsen and Kadish, Criminal Law and Its Processes, chs. 10, 12 (1962). See also Note, Do We Have to Live with Eavesdropping: A Legislative Proposal, 38 So. Cal. L. Rev. 622 (1965); King, Electronic Surveillance and Constitutional Rights: Some Recent Developments and Observations, 33 Geo. Wash. L. Rev. 240 (1964). On midnight searches of homes of welfare recipients see Reich, Midnight Welfare Searches and the Social Security Act, 72 Yale L.J. 1347 (1963), and pending case, Benny Parrish v. Civil Service Commission of Alameda County, 1 Civ. No. 22, 556 (Cal. Dist. Ct. App., 1st Dist. 1965) (social worker discharged for refusal to participate in midnight raid on welfare recipient's home).

On the relation of patient-doctor privilege to the problem of privacy, see Goldstein and Katz, Psychiatrist-Patient Privilege: The GAP Proposal and the Connecticut Statute, 36 Conn. B.J. 175 (1962).

6. In Rochin v. California, 342 U.S. 165, 72 S. Ct. 205, 96 L. Ed. 183 (1952), the Court held it violated due process to obtain evidence by pumping the stomach of a narcotics seller who had swallowed morphine capsules to avoid having them seized by the police. But in Breithaupt v. Abram, 352 U.S. 432, 77 S. Ct. 408, 1 L. Ed. 2d 448 (1957), the Court held that it did not violate due process to take blood from an unconscious driver for use as evidence in a prosecution for drunken driving. In both cases Justices Black and Douglas dissented in part on the ground that the pumping and taking of blood samples involved compulsion to force an individual to give evidence against himself. See Note, Blood Tests and the Bill of Rights — Breithaupt Revisited, 17 Hastings L.J. 139 (1965); Note, Destruction of Evidence — A Rationale for Blood Tests Without an Arrest? 18 Stan. L. Rev. 243 (1965); Santos, Does Blood Test Violate the Right Against Self-Incrimination? 9 9 Far Eastern L. Rev. 357 (1962).

For statutes which provide for a so-called implied consent by motorists to have their blood and breath tested, see, e.g., Conn. Gen. Stat. §§14-227a, 14-227b; Idaho Code §§49-352 to 49-355; N.Y. Vehicle and Traffic Law §1192-1194. For discussion, see LaPlante, Alcohol Testing: Connecticut's Implied Consent Statute, 38 Conn. B.J. 16 (1964); LaPlante, Alcohol Testing: Some Recent Decisions Dealing with Implied Consent Statutes, 39 Conn. B.J. 72 (1965); Weinstein, Statute Compelling Submission to a Chemical Test for Intoxication, 45 J. Crim. L., C. & P.S. 551 (1955); Note, Virginia's Implied Consent Statute, 49 Va. L. Rev. 386 (1963); Goff, Constitutionality of Compulsory Chemical Tests to Determine Intoxication, 49 J. Crim. L., C. & P.S. 58 (1958); Slough and Wilson, Alcohol and the Motorist: Practical and Legal Problems of Chemical Testing, 44 Minn. L. Rev. 673 (1960); Cadd and Gibson, Legal Medical Aspects of Blood Tests to Determine Intoxication, 29 Va. L. Rev. 749 (1943); Note, Implied Consent to a Chemical Test for Intoxication: Doubts about Section 6-205 of the Uniform Vehicle Code, 31 U. Chi. L. Rev. 603 (1964); cf. also People v. Young, 42 Misc. 2d 540, 248 N.Y.S.2d 287 (Sup. Ct. Westchester Co. 1964); People v. Huber, 232 Adv. Cal. App. 84, 43 Cal. Rptr. 65 (Dist. Ct. App. 1965) (analysis of blood extracted without warrant from unconscious suspect admissible), noted in 79 Harv. L. Rev. 677 (1966).

Schmerber v. California, 384 U.S. 757, 86 St. Ct. 1826, 16 L. Ed. 2d 908 (1966), involved the legality of the use of blood samples, withdrawn over the defendant's objection, to effect a conviction for drunken driving. The Court held that such a withdrawal did not offend that "sense of justice" required by the due process clause, citing Breithaupt v. Abram, supra, where the withdrawal was made while the driver was unconscious. The Court also rejected arguments under the Fourth and Sixth Amendments and the self-incrimination clause of the Fifth Amendment which, the Court reiterated, became applicable to the states under recent Supreme Court decisions in Mapp. v. Ohio, 367 U.S. 643, 81 S. Ct. 1684, 6 L. Ed. 2d 1081 (1961); Malloy v. Hogan, 378 U.S. 1, 84 S. Ct. 1489, 12 L. Ed. 2d 653 (1964); and Escobedo v. Illinois, 378 U.S. 478, 84 S. Ct. 1774, 12 L. Ed. 2d 977 (1964). As to self-incrimination, the Court stated that the privilege applies only to compelled communications. While there are concededly borderline cases such as the use of lie detectors, here not "even a shadow of testimonial compulsion upon or enforced communication by the accused was involved either in the extraction or in the chemical analysis. Petitioner's testimonial capacities were in no way implicated; indeed, his participation, except as a donor, was irrelevant to the results of the test . . ." Nor was petitioner, according to the opinion, denied his Sixth Amendment right to counsel: "Since petitioner was not entitled to assert the [self-incrimination] privilege, he has no greater right because counsel erroneously advised him he could assert it." On search and seizure protections of the Fourth Amendment the Court's opinion first states that "[t]he overriding function of the Fourth Amendment is to protect personal privacy and dignity against unwarranted intrusion by the State," and reaffirms the application of the Federal exclusionary rule to the states. It then goes on to say, in part:

"Because we are dealing with intrusions into the human body rather than with state interferences with property relationships or private papers — 'houses, papers, and effects' — we write on a clean slate. Limitations on the kinds of property which may be seized under warrant, as distinct from the procedures for search and the permissible scope of search, are not instructive in this context. We begin with the assumption that once the privilege against self-incrimination has been found not to bar compelled intrusions into the body for blood to be analyzed for alcohol content, the Fourth Amendment's proper function is to constrain, not against all intrusions as such, but against intrusions which are not justified in the circumstances, or which are made in an improper manner. In other words, the questions we must decide in this case are whether the police were justified in requiring petitioner to submit to the blood test, and whether the means and procedures employed in taking his blood respected relevant Fourth Amendment standards of reasonableness.

"In this case, as will often be true when charges of driving under the influence of alcohol are pressed, these questions arise in the context of an arrest made by an officer without a warrant. . . .

"While early cases suggest that there is an unrestricted 'right on the part of the Government, always recognized under English and American law, to search the person of the accused when legally arrested to discover and seize the fruits or evidences of crime,' Weeks v. United States, 232 U.S. 383, 392; People v. Chiagles, 237 N.Y. 193, 142 N.E. 583 (1923) (Cardozo, J.), the mere fact of a lawful arrest does not end our inquiry. . . . The interests in human dignity and privacy which the Fourth Amendment protects forbid any such intrusions on the mere chance that desired evidence might be obtained. In the absence of a clear indication that in fact such evidence will be found, these fundamental human interests require law officers to suffer the risk that such evidence may disappear unless there is an immediate search.

"Although the facts which established probable cause to arrest in this case also suggested the required relevance and likely success of a test of petitioner's blood for alcohol, the question remains whether the arresting officer was permitted to draw these inferences himself, or was required instead to procure a warrant before proceeding with the test. . . .

"The officer in the present case, however, might reasonably have believed that he was confronted with an emergency, in which the delay necessary to obtain a warrant, under the circumstances, threatened 'the destruction of evidence,' Preston v. United States, 376 U.S. 364, 367. . . .

"Similarly, we are satisfied that the test chosen to measure petitioner's blood-alcohol level was a reasonable one. Extraction of blood samples for testing is a highly effective means of determining the degree to which a person is under the influence of alcohol. See Breithaupt v. Abram, 352 U.S., at 436, n.3. . . . Petitioner is not one of the few who on grounds of fear, concern for health, or religious scruple might prefer some other means of testing, such as the 'breathalyzer' test petitioner refused, see n. 9, supra. We need not decide whether such wishes would have to be respected.

"Finally, the record shows that the test was performed in a reasonable manner. Petitioner's blood was taken by a physician in a hospital environment according to accepted medical practices. . . ."

Among the dissenters, consisting of Mr. Chief Justice Warren and Justices Black, Douglas, and Fortas, only Mr. Justice Douglas put a degree of emphasis on the spirit of constitutional interpretation in the Griswold case.

See also Jacobson v. Massachusetts, 197 U.S. 11, 25 S. Ct. 358, 49 L. Ed. 643 (1905) (upholding the Massachusetts compulsory vaccination law); Buck v. Bell,

274 U.S. 200, 47 S. Ct. 584, 71 L. Ed. 1000 (1927) (upholding sterilization of inmate of mental institution); Skinner v. Oklahoma, 316 U.S. 535, 62 S. Ct. 1110, 86 L. Ed. 1655(1942) (invalidating the Oklahoma Habitual Criminal Sterilization Act on the ground that it embodied an arbitrary classification). See on the related subject of compulsory mental examinations, Note, Compulsory Mental Examinations and the Privilege Against Self-Incrimination, 1964 Wis. L. Rev. 67.

CHAPTER XI

The Right to Travel

A. Domestic

EDWARDS v. CALIFORNIA
314 U.S. 160, 62 S. Ct. 164, 86 L. Ed. 119 (1941)

MR. JUSTICE BYRNES delivered the opinion of the Court.

The facts of this case are simple and are not disputed. Appellant is a citizen of the United States and a resident of California. In December, 1939, he left his home in Marysville, California, for Spur, Texas, with the intention of bringing back to Marysville his wife's brother, Frank Duncan, a citizen of the United States and a resident of Texas. When he arrived in Texas, appellant learned that Duncan had last been employed by the Works Progress Administration. Appellant thus became aware of the fact that Duncan was an indigent person and he continued to be aware of it throughout the period involved in this case. The two men agreed that appellant should transport Duncan from Texas to Marysville in appellant's automobile. Accordingly, they left Spur on January 1, 1940, entered California by way of Arizona on January 3, and reached Marysville on January 5. When he left Texas, Duncan had about $20. It had all been spent by the time he reached Marysville. He lived with appellant for about ten days until he obtained financial assistance from the Farm Security Administration. During the ten day interval, he had no employment.

In Justice Court a complaint was filed against appellant under §2615 of the Welfare and Institutions Code of California, which provides: "Every person, firm or corporation or officer or agent thereof that brings or assists in bringing into the State any indigent person who is not a resident of the State, knowing him to be an indigent person, is guilty of a misdemeanor." On demurrer to the complaint, appellant urged that the Section violated several provisions of the Federal Constitution. The demurrer was overruled, the cause was tried, appellant was convicted and sentenced to six months imprisonment in the county jail, and sentence was suspended.

On appeal to the Superior Court of Yuba County, the facts as stated above were stipulated. The Superior Court, although regarding as "close" the question of the validity of the Section, felt "constrained to uphold the statute as a valid exercise of the police power of the State of California." Consequently, the conviction was affirmed. No appeal to a higher state court was open to appellant. We noted probable jurisdiction early last term, and later ordered reargument (313 U.S. 545) which has been held.

At the threshold of our inquiry a question arises with respect to the interpretation of §2615. On reargument, the Attorney General of California has submitted an exposition of the history of the Section, which reveals that statutes similar, though not identical, to it have been in effect in California since 1860. (See Cal. Stat. (1860) 213; Cal. Stat. (1901) 636; Cal. Stat. (1933) 2005). Neither under these forerunners nor under §2615 itself does the term "indigent person" seem to have been accorded an authoritative interpretation by the California courts. The appellee claims for the Section a very limited scope. It urges that the term "indigent person" must be taken to include only persons who are presently destitute of property and without resources to obtain the necessities of life, and who have no relatives or friends able and willing to support them. It is conceded, however, that the term is not confined to those who are physically or mentally incapacitated. While the generality of the language of the Section contains no hint of these limitations, we are content to assign to the term this narrow meaning.

Article I, §8 of the Constitution delegates to the Congress the authority to regulate interstate commerce. And it is settled beyond question that the transportation of persons is "commerce," within the meaning of that provision.[1] It is nevertheless true, that the States are not wholly precluded from exercising their police power in matters of local concern even though they may thereby affect interstate commerce. California v. Thompson, 313 U.S. 109, 113. The issue presented in this case, therefore, is whether the prohibition embodied in §2615 against the "bringing" or transportation of indigent persons into California is within the police power of that State. We think that it is not, and hold that it is an unconstitutional barrier to interstate commerce.

The grave and perplexing social and economic dislocation which this statute reflects is a matter of common knowledge and concern. We are not unmindful of it. We appreciate that the spectacle of large segments of our population constantly on the move has given rise to urgent demands upon the ingenuity of government. Both the brief of the Attorney General of California and that of the Chairman of the Select Committee of the House of Representatives of the United States, as amicus curiae, have sharpened this appreciation. The State asserts that the huge influx of migrants into California in recent years has resulted in problems of health, morals, and especially finance, the proportions of which are staggering. It is not for us to say that this is not true. We have repeatedly and recently affirmed, and we now reaffirm, that we

---

[1] Gloucester Ferry Co. v. Pennsylvania, 114 U.S. 196, 203; Leisy v. Hardin, 135 U.S. 100, 112; Covington Bridge Co. v. Kentucky, 154 U.S. 204, 218; Hoke v. United States, 227 U.S. 308, 320; Caminetti v. United States, 242 U.S. 470, 491; United States v. Hill, 248 U.S. 420, 423; Mitchell v. United States, 313 U.S. 80. Cf. The Federal Kidnaping Act of 1932, U.S.C., Title 18, §§408a-408c. It is immaterial whether or not the transportation is commercial in character. See Caminetti v. United States, supra.

do not conceive it our function to pass upon "the wisdom, need, or appropriateness" of the legislative efforts of the States to solve such difficulties. See Olsen v. Nebraska, 313 U.S. 236, 246.

But this does not mean that there are no boundaries to the permissible area of State legislative activity. There are. And none is more certain than the prohibition against attempts on the part of any single State to isolate itself from difficulties common to all of them by restraining the transportation of persons and property across its borders. It is frequently the case that a State might gain a momentary respite from the pressure of events by the simple expedient of shutting its gates to the outside world. But, in the words of Mr. Justice Cardozo: "The Constitution was framed under the dominion of a political philosophy less parochial in range. It was framed upon the theory that the peoples of the several States must sink or swim together, and that in the long run prosperity and salvation are in union and not division." Baldwin v. Seelig, 294 U.S. 511, 523.

It is difficult to conceive of a statute more squarely in conflict with this theory than the Section challenged here. Its express purpose and inevitable effect is to prohibit the transportation of indigent persons across the California border. The burden upon interstate commerce is intended and immediate; it is the plain and sole function of the statute. Moreover, the indigent non-residents who are the real victims of the statute are deprived of the opportunity to exert political pressure upon the California legislature in order to obtain a change in policy. South Carolina Highway Dept. v. Barnwell Bros., 303 U.S. 177, 185, n.2. We think this statute must fail under any known test of the validity of State interference with interstate commerce. . . .

There remains to be noticed only the contention that the limitation upon State power to interfere with the interstate transportation of persons is subject to an exception in the case of "paupers." It is true that support for this contention may be found in early decisions of this Court. In City of New York v. Miln, 11 Pet. 102, at 143, it was said that it is "as competent and as necessary for a State to provide precautionary measures against the moral pestilence of paupers, vagabonds, and possibly convicts, as it is to guard against the physical pestilence, which may arise from unsound and infectious articles imported, . . ." This language has been casually repeated in numerous later cases up to the turn of the century. See, e.g., Passenger Cases, 7 How. 283, 426 and 466-467; Railway Company v. Husen, 95 U.S. 465, 471; Plumley v. Massachusetts, 155 U.S. 461, 478; Missouri, K. & T. Ry. Co. v. Haber, 169 U.S. 613, 629. In none of these cases, however, was the power of a State to exclude "paupers" actually involved.

Whether an able-bodied but unemployed person like Duncan is a "pauper" within the historical meaning of the term is open to considerable doubt. See 53 Harvard L. Rev. 1031, 1032. But assuming that the term is applicable to him and to persons similarly situated, we do not consider ourselves bound by the language referred to. City of New York v. Miln was decided in 1837.

Whatever may have been the notion then prevailing, we do not think that it will now be seriously contended that because a person is without employment and without funds he constitutes a "moral pestilence." Poverty and immorality are not synonymous.

We are of the opinion that §2615 is not a valid exercise of the police power of California; that it imposes an unconstitutional burden upon interstate commerce, and that the conviction under it cannot be sustained. In the view we have taken it is unnecessary to decide whether the Section is repugnant to other provisions of the Constitution.

Reversed.

Mr. Justice Douglas, concurring:

I express no view on whether or not the statute here in question runs afoul of Art. I, §8 of the Constitution granting to Congress the power "to regulate Commerce with foreign Nations, and among the several States." But I am of the opinion that the right of persons to move freely from State to State occupies a more protected position in our constitutional system than does the movement of cattle, fruit, steel and coal across state lines. While the opinion of the Court expresses no view on that issue, the right involved is so fundamental that I deem it appropriate to indicate the reach of the constitutional question which is present.

The right to move freely from State to State is an incident of *national* citizenship protected by the privileges and immunities clause of the Fourteenth Amendment against state interference. Mr. Justice Moody in Twining v. New Jersey, 211 U.S. 78, 97, stated, "Privileges and immunities of citizens of the United States . . . are only such as arise out of the nature and essential character of the National Government, or are specifically granted or secured to all citizens or persons by the Constitution of the United States." And he went on to state that one of those rights of *national* citizenship was "the right to pass freely from State to State." Id., p. 97. Now it is apparent that this right is not specifically granted by the Constitution. Yet before the Fourteenth Amendment it was recognized as a right fundamental to the national character of our Federal government. It was so decided in 1867 by Crandall v. Nevada, 6 Wall. 35. In that case this Court struck down a Nevada tax "upon every person leaving the State" by common carrier. Mr. Justice Miller writing for the Court held that the right to move freely throughout the nation was a right of *national* citizenship. That the right was implied did not make it any the less "guaranteed" by the Constitution. Id., p. 47. To be sure, he emphasized that the Nevada statute would obstruct the right of a citizen to travel to the seat of his national government or its offices throughout the country. And see United States v. Wheeler, 254 U.S. 281, 299. But there is not a shred of evidence in the record of the Crandall case that the persons there involved were en route on any such mission any more than it appears in this case that Duncan entered California to interview some federal agency. The point which Mr. Justice Miller made was merely in illustration of the damage and havoc which would ensue if the States had the power to prevent the free movement of citizens from one State to another. This is emphasized by his quotation from Chief Justice Taney's dissenting opinion in the Passenger Case, 7 How. 283, 492: "We are all citizens of the United States; and as members of the same community, must have the right to pass and repass through every part of it without interruption, as freely as in our own States." Hence the dictum in United States v. Wheeler, supra, p. 299, which attempts to limit the Crandall case to a holding that the statute in question directly burdened "the performance by the United States of its governmental functions" and limited the "rights of the citizens growing out of such functions," does not bear analysis.

So, when the Fourteenth Amendment was adopted in 1868, it had been squarely and authoritatively settled that the right to move freely from State to State was a right of *national* citizenship. As such it was protected by the privileges and immunities clause of the Fourteenth Amendment against state interference. Slaughter House Cases, 16 Wall. 36, 74, 79. In the latter case Mr. Justice Miller recognized that it was so "protected by implied guarantees" of the Constitution. Id., p. 79. That was also acknowledged in Twining v. New Jersey, supra. And Chief Justice Fuller in Williams v. Fears, 179 U.S. 270, 274, stated: "Undoubtedly the right of locomotion, the right to remove from one place to another according to inclination, is an attribute of personal liberty, and the right, ordinarily, of free transit from or through the territory of any State is a right secured by the Fourteenth Amendment and by other provisions of the Constitution."

In the face of this history I cannot accede to the suggestion (Helson & Randolph v. Kentucky, 279 U.S. 245, 251; Colgate v. Harvey, 296 U.S. 404, 444) that the commerce clause is the appropriate explanation of Crandall v. Nevada, supra. . . .

To be sure, there are expressions in the cases that this right of free movement of persons is an incident of *state* citizenship protected against discriminatory state action by Art. IV, §2 of the Constitution. Corfield v. Coryell, 4 Wash. C.C. 371, 381; Paul v. Virginia, 8 Wall. 168, 180; Ward v. Maryland, 12 Wall. 418, 430; United States v. Wheeler, supra, pp. 298-299. Under the dicta of those cases the statute in the instant case would not survive, since California is curtailing only the free movement of indigents who are non-residents of that State. But the thrust of the Crandall case is deeper. Mr. Justice Miller adverted to Corfield v. Coryell, Paul v. Virginia, and Ward v. Maryland, when he stated in the Slaughter House Cases that the right protected by the Crandall case was a right of *national* citizenship arising from the "implied guarantees" of the Constitution. 16 Wall. at pp. 75-79. But his failure to classify that right as one of *state* citizenship protected solely by Art. IV, §2, underscores his view that the free movement of persons throughout this nation was a right of *national* citizenship. It likewise emphasizes that Art. IV,

§2, whatever its reach, is primarily concerned with the incidents of residence (the matter involved in United States v. Wheeler, supra) and the exercise of rights within a State, so that a citizen of one State is not in a "condition of alienage when he is within or when he removes to another State." Blake v. McClung, 172 U.S. 239, 256. Furthermore, Art. IV, §2, cannot explain the Crandall decision. The statute in that case applied to citizens of Nevada as well as to citizens of other States. That is to say, Nevada was not "discriminating against citizens of other States in favor of its own." Hague v. Committee for Industrial Organization, 307 U.S. 496, 511 and cases cited. Thus it is plain that the right of free ingress and egress rises to a higher constitutional dignity than that afforded by *state* citizenship.

The conclusion that the right of free movement is a right of *national* citizenship stands on firm historical ground. If a state tax on that movement, as in the Crandall case, is invalid, a fortiori a state statute which obstructs or in substance prevents that movement must fall. That result necessarily follows unless perchance a State can curtail the right of free movement of those who are poor or destitute. But to allow such an exception to be engrafted on the rights of *national* citizenship would be to contravene every conception of national unity. It would also introduce a caste system utterly incompatible with the spirit of our system of government. It would permit those who were stigmatized by a State as indigents, paupers, or vagabonds to be relegated to an inferior class of citizenship. It would prevent a citizen because he was poor from seeking new horizons in other States. It might thus withhold from large segments of our people that mobility which is basic to any guarantee of freedom of opportunity. The result would be a substantial dilution of the rights of *national* citizenship, a serious impairment of the principles of equality. Since the state statute here challenged involves such consequences, it runs afoul of the privileges and immunities clause of the Fourteenth Amendment.

Mr. Justice Black and Mr. Justice Murphy join in this opinion.

Mr. Justice Jackson, concurring:

I concur in the result reached by the Court, and I agree that the grounds of its decision are permissible ones under applicable authorities. But the migrations of a human being, of whom it is charged that he possesses nothing that can be sold and has no wherewithal to buy, do not fit easily into my notions as to what is commerce. To hold that the measure of his rights is the commerce clause is likely to result eventually either in distorting the commercial law or in denaturing human rights. I turn, therefore, away from principles by which commerce is regulated to that clause of the Constitution by virtue of which Duncan is a citizen of the United States and which forbids any State to abridge his privileges or immunities as such.

This clause was adopted to make United States citizenship the dominant and paramount allegiance among us. The return which the law had long associated with allegiance was protection. The power of citizenship as a shield against oppression was widely known from the example of Paul's Roman citizenship, which sent the centurion scurrying to his higher-ups with the message: "Take heed what thou doest: for this man is a Roman." I suppose none of us doubts that the hope of imparting to American citizenship some of this vitality was the purpose of declaring in the Fourteenth Amendment: "All persons born or naturalized in the United States, and subject to the jurisdiction thereof, are citizens of the United States and of the State wherein they reside. No State shall make or enforce any law which shall abridge the privileges or immunities of citizens of the United States . . ."

But the hope proclaimed in such generality soon shriveled in the process of judicial interpretation. For nearly three-quarters of a century this Court rejected every plea to the privileges and immunities clause. The judicial history of this clause and the very real difficulties in the way of its practical application to specific cases have been too well and recently reviewed to warrant repetition.[1]

While instances of valid "privileges or immunities" must be but few, I am convinced that this is one. I do not ignore or belittle the difficulties of what has been characterized by this Court as an "almost forgotten" clause. But the difficulty of the task does not excuse us from giving these general and abstract words whatever of specific content and concreteness they will bear as we mark out their application, case by case. That is the method of the common law, and it has been the method of this Court with other no less general statements in our fundamental law. This Court has not been timorous about giving concrete meaning to such obscure and vagrant phrases as "due process," "general welfare," "equal protection," or even "commerce among the several States." But it has always hesitated to give any real meaning to the privileges and immunities clause lest it improvidently give too much.

This Court should, however, hold squarely that it is a privilege of citizenship of the United States, protected from state abridgment, to enter any state of the Union, either for temporary sojourn or for the establishment of permanent residence therein and for gaining resultant citizenship thereof. If national citizenship means less than this, it means nothing. . . .

The right of the citizen to migrate from state to state which, I agree with Mr. Justice Douglas, is shown by our precedents to be one of national citizenship, is not, however, an unlimited one. In addition to being subject to all constitutional limitations imposed by the federal government, such citizen is subject to some control by state governments. He may not, if a fugitive from justice, claim freedom to migrate unmolested, nor may he endanger others by carrying contagion about. These causes, and perhaps others that do not occur to me now, warrant any public authority in stopping a man where it finds him and arresting his progress across a state line quite as much as from place to place within the state.

---

[1] See dissenting opinion of Mr. Justice Stone in Colgate v. Harvey, 296 U.S. 404, 436, et seq.

It is here that we meet the real crux of this case. Does "indigence" as defined by the application of the California statute constitute a basis for restricting the freedom of a citizen, as crime or contagion warrants its restriction? We should say now, and in no uncertain terms, that a man's mere property status, without more, cannot be used by a state to test, qualify, or limit his rights as a citizen of the United States. "Indigence" in itself is neither a source of rights nor a basis for denying them. The mere state of being without funds is a neutral fact — constitutionally an irrelevance, like race, creed, or color. I agree with what I understand to be the holding of the Court that cases which may indicate the contrary are overruled.

Any measure which would divide our citizenry on the basis of property into one class free to move from state to state and another class that is poverty-bound to the place where it has suffered misfortune is not only at war with the habit and custom by which our country has expanded, but is also a short-sighted blow at the security of property itself. Property can have no more dangerous, even if unwitting, enemy than one who would make its possession a pretext for unequal or exclusive civil rights. Where those rights are derived from national citizenship no state may impose such a test, and whether the Congress could do so we are not called upon to inquire.

I think California had no right to make the condition of Duncan's purse, with no evidence of violation by him of any law or social policy which caused it, the basis of excluding him or of punishing one who extended him aid. . . .

NOTES

1. Conn. Gen. Stat. §17-273a, provided for the removal of welfare applicants from the State to another to which they belong, after a finding by the Commissioner of Welfare and a court warrant ordering an officer to transport such person. This statute was before the Supreme Court of Connecticut in a declaratory judgment action brought by the Commissioner seeking a determination of its constitutionality. The court refused to rule on the constitutional issue. State v. Doe, 149 Conn. 216, 231, 178 A.2d 271, 278 (1962). Later the statute was repealed. 1963 Public Act 501, §4. See also Interstate Compact on Welfare Services, Conn. Gen. Stat. §17-21a; Me. Stat. Tit. 22, §§4101 et seq. Cf. Matter of Chirillo, 283 N.Y. 417, 28 N.E.2d 895 (1940). See Note, 37 Conn. Bar J. 504 (1963).

2. The Universal Declaration of Human Rights, adopted by the United Nations General Assembly on December 10, 1948, declares in Article 13:

"(1) Everyone has the right of freedom of movement and residence within the borders of each state.

"(2) Everyone has the right to leave any country, including his own, and return to his country."

REFERENCES

For discussion of the Edwards problem and freedom of movement generally, see Note, Interstate Migration and Personal Liberty, 40 Colum. L. Rev. 1032 (1940); Roback,

Legal Barriers to Interstate Migration, 28 Cornell L.Q. 286 (1943); Meyers, Federal Privileges and Immunities: Application to Ingress and Egress, 29 Cornell L.Q. 489 (1944); Rutledge, Regulation of the Movement of Workers: Freedom of Passage Within the United States, 1953 Wash. U.L.Q. 270; Vestal, Freedom of Movement, 41 Iowa L. Rev. 6 (1955); Chafee, Three Human Rights in the Constitution of 1787, ch. III (1956). See also Notes, 26 Calif. L. Rev. 603 (1938); 40 Mich. L. Rev. 711 (1942).

B. INTERNATIONAL

The chief restrictions imposed upon freedom of movement in recent times have been in connection with the denial of passports to citizens wishing to travel abroad and the denial of visas to persons desiring to visit the United States.

Shortly after the end of World War II a series of controversies arose over the policy of the State Department in denying passports to persons whose travel abroad, in the opinion of the Department, would not be in the "best interests of the United States." In May 1952 Secretary of State Acheson issued a formal statement of the Department's position:

"It was decided that, in view of the findings by the court [in the Dennis case] and the Congress [in the Internal Security Act of 1950], it would be inappropriate and inconsistent for the Department to issue a passport to a person if information in its files *gave reason to believe* that he is knowingly a member of a Communist organization or that his conduct abroad is likely to be contrary to the best interests of the United States. This policy has been followed since February 1951, and, in view of the national emergency proclaimed by President Truman and the conditions existing in various areas of the world, it is believed that it should be closely adhered to.

"A passport certifies to foreign governments not only the citizenship and identity of the bearer, but requests them to permit him safely and freely to pass and, in case of need, to give all lawful aid and protection. Possession of the passport indicates the right of the bearer to receive the protection and good offices of American diplomatic and consular officers abroad. The right to receive the protection of this Government is correlative with the obligation to give undivided allegiance to the United States. A person whose activities, either at home or abroad, promote the interests of a foreign country or a political faction therein to the detriment of the United States or of friendly foreign countries should not be the bearer of an American passport." [1]

On August 28, 1952, the State Department issued regulations embodying the above policy. 17 Fed. Reg. 8013, 22 C.F.R. §§51.135 to 51.143. These provided in part:

"51.135 *Limitations on issuance of passports to persons supporting Communist movement.* In order to promote the national interest by assuring that persons who support the world Communist movement of which the Com-

---

[1] Department of State Press Release, May 24, 1952, reprinted in The Department of State Bulletin, June 9, 1952, pp. 919-920.

munist Party is an integral unit may not, through use of United States passports, further the purposes of that movement, no passport, except one limited for direct and immediate return to the United States, shall be issued to:

"(a) Persons who are members of the Communist Party or who have recently terminated such membership under such circumstances as to warrant the conclusion — not otherwise rebutted by the evidence — that they continue to act in furtherance of the interests and under the discipline of the Communist Party;

"(b) Persons, regardless of the formal state of their affiliation with the Communist Party, who engage in activities which support the Communist movement under such circumstances as to warrant the conclusion — not otherwise rebutted by the evidence — that they have engaged in such activities as a result of direction, domination, or control exercised over them by the Communist movement;

"(c) Persons, regardless of the formal state of their affiliation with the Communist Party, as to whom there is reason to believe, on the balance of all the evidence, that they are going abroad to engage in activities which will advance the Communist movement for the purpose, knowingly and willfully of advancing that movement."

"51.142 *Oath or affirmation by applicant as to membership in Communist Party*. At any stage of the proceedings in the Passport Division or before the Board, if it is deemed necessary, the applicant may be required, as a part of his application, to subscribe, under oath or affirmation, to a statement with respect to present or past membership in the Communist Party. If applicant states that he is a Communist, refusal of a passport in his case will be without further proceedings."

Pursuant to this policy the Department of State prior to 1958 revoked or refused to issue passports in a number of cases. Some of the better known instances included the revocation of the passport of Paul Robeson (N.Y. Times, Aug. 4, 1950); the refusal to issue a passport to Corliss Lamont, lecturer at Columbia University (N.Y. Times, Oct. 15 and 16, 1951); the denial of a passport to Dr. Otto Nathan, executor under the will of Albert Einstein, until court proceedings were brought (see infra); the same with respect to the passport of former Judge William D. Clark (N.Y. Times, Dec. 29, 1953; July 24, 1955); the refusal of a passport to Arthur Miller, who had planned to go to Brussels for the opening of his play "The Crucible" (N.Y. Times, Mar. 31, 1954); the refusal for two years to renew the passport of Carl N. Foreman, screen writer who wrote the scripts for "High Noon" and "Home of the Brave" (N.Y. Times, Jan. 14, 1956); denial of a passport to Dr. W. E. B. Du Bois who wished to visit Ghana at the invitation of Premier Kwame Nkrumah (N.Y. Times, Mar. 5, 1957); and the refusal to issue passports to correspondents of the Communist newspaper, the Daily Worker (N.Y. Times, Nov. 11 and Dec. 12, 1957). Dr. Linus Pauling of the California Institute of Technology was refused a passport on three occasions in 1952, 1953 and 1954, was granted a limited passport in 1953 and, after receiving the Nobel Prize in 1954, was granted an unlimited passport. See Pauling, My Efforts to Obtain a Passport, Bull. of the Atomic Scientists, October 1952, p. 253; id., January 1956, p. 28.

In 1952 Paul Robeson was prevented by United States officials from entering Canada, although no passport is required to visit countries in the Western Hemisphere. N.Y. Times, Feb. 1, 1952. Later in 1952, the State Department announced that it had notified the Customs Bureau not to permit Owen Lattimore to leave the country, on the basis of an allegation that he planned to visit the Soviet Union; but the ban was revoked a few days later when the allegation proved unfounded. N.Y. Times, June 21, 22, 25, 26, 28 and 29, 1952. The prohibition against Robeson's traveling in the Western Hemisphere was lifted in August 1957. N.Y. Times, April 20, 1958.

The State Department also refused to issue passports for anyone to visit certain countries, and stamped all passports as invalid in those countries. The major controversy over this practice arose in connection with the refusal to issue passports to visit Communist China. See, e.g., N.Y. Times, June 26, 1957 (Mrs. Roosevelt refused passport to China); N.Y. Times, Sept. 19, 1957 (announcement of revocation of passports of 42 students who visited China); N.Y. Times, Sept. 26, 1957 (modification of order to withhold revocation where student could satisfy Department of no intention to commit a new violation); N.Y. Times, Aug. 23, 1957 (Secretary of State Dulles announced policy of permitting 24 named news agencies to send correspondents to China for a seven-month trial period).

The State Department's policy and practice with respect to granting visas to persons desiring to visit the United States temporarily was also the subject of controversy. Thus, in March 1950 the State Department denied entry to twelve members of the World Congress of Partisans of Peace, including Pablo Picasso, the French artist, and Rev. Hewlett Johnson, Dean of Canterbury, for the reason that they were "known Communists and fellow-travelers." N.Y. Times, March 4, 1950.

The Internal Security Act of 1950 (64 Stat. 987, 1006) and the Immigration and Nationality Act of 1952 (66 Stat. 163, 8 U.S.C. §1182(a)(28)) tightened the restrictions on foreign visitors. Under the latter statute aliens "who are members of . . . the Communist or any other totalitarian party" of any country, with the exception of those whose membership was involuntary, who were under 16, who joined to obtain food, or who have been actively opposed for five years, are denied visas; but the Attorney General has discretion to make exceptions on recommendation of the Secretary of State or a consular officer (8 U.S.C. §1182(d)(3)). Under these provisions a number of well known foreign visitors were barred from entry. Thus in September 1951 "a dozen of the world's leading chemists, some of them official delegates to the International Congress of Pure and Applied Chemistry," were denied visas. N.Y. Times, Sept. 7, 1951. And in December of that year the Depart-

ment refused to grant a visa to Dr. Ernest B. Chain, German-born English
subject and winner of the Nobel Prize in biochemistry. N.Y. Times, Dec. 16,
1951. The Federation of American Scientists, at its annual meeting in 1952,
reported that "United States visa restrictions had prevented or 'indefinitely
delayed' the visits of more than 200 foreign scientists in the last year and one-
half." N.Y. Times, April 30, 1952.

Numerous protests, from scientists and others, were made against this visa
policy. Typical was the statement of four members of the University of Chicago to Secretary of State Acheson: "It has become very difficult for a reputable university in the United States to invite foreign scholars to participate
even temporarily in the intellectual life of the institution and this at a time at
which a feeling of communion among the universities of the free world is
greatly to be desired." N.Y. Times, Jan. 31, 1952. And in December 1957,
Lloyd V. Berkner, a member of President Eisenhower's Scientific Advisory
Committee, stated that State Department rules forbidding scientists from
Communist China to come to the United States were preventing many scientific organizations from meeting in this country:

"Since no truly international organization can accept an invitation to meet
in any country that excludes some of its members, our ban on the entry of
Communist scientists into the U.S. prevents any meetings of such organizations from being held in this country.

"In the meantime, however, Moscow is inviting all scientific organizations
willing to come. Consequently, many important international scientific meetings . . . will be held in Moscow in 1958. The effect of our attitude is to
increase the importance of Moscow as a scientific capital and on occasion to
isolate American scientists unless they will travel to Moscow." Berkner, Earth
Satellites and Foreign Policy, Foreign Affairs, January 1958, p. 221, 229-230.

The State Department's passport policy was challenged in a number of
legal actions, all arising in the District of Columbia courts. In the spring of
1958 the Supreme Court considered the matter in the Kent, Briehl and Dayton cases.

KENT v. DULLES
357 U.S. 116, 78 S. Ct. 1113, 2 L. Ed. 2d 1204 (1958)

MR. JUSTICE DOUGLAS delivered the opinion of the Court.

This case concerns two applications for passports, denied by the Secretary
of State. One was by Rockwell Kent who desired to visit England and attend
a meeting of an organization known as the "World Council of Peace" in
Helsinki, Finland. The Director of the Passport Office informed Kent that
issuance of a passport was precluded by §51.135 of the Regulations promulgated by the Secretary of State on two grounds: (1) that he was a Communist and (2) that he had had "a consistent and prolonged adherence to the
Communist Party line." . . .

[In the case of Dr. Walter Briehl, a psychiatrist, the State Department also denied the passport on the same grounds as in the Kent case.]

A passport not only is of great value — indeed necessary — abroad; it is also an aid in establishing citizenship for purposes of re-entry into the United States. See Browder v. United States, 312 U.S. 335, 339; 3 Moore, International Law Digest (1906), §512. But throughout most of our history — until indeed quite recently — a passport, though a great convenience in foreign travel, was not a legal requirement for leaving or entering the United States. See Jaffe, The Right to Travel, 35 Foreign Affairs 17. Apart from minor exceptions to be noted, it was first made a requirement by §215 of the Act of June 27, 1952, 66 Stat. 190, 8 U.S.C. §1185, which states that, after a prescribed proclamation by the President, it is "unlawful for any citizen of the United States to depart from or enter, or attempt to depart from or enter, the United States unless he bears a valid passport." And the Proclamation necessary to make the restrictions of this Act applicable and in force has been made.[5]

[The Court then reviews the legislation and executive practices relating to the "minor exceptions."]

. . . By the Act of August 18, 1856, 11 Stat. 52, 60-61, 22 U.S.C. §211a, Congress put an end to those practices.[6] This provision, as codified by the Act of July 3, 1926, 44 Stat., Part 2, 887, reads,

"The Secretary of State may grant and issue passports . . . under such rules as the President shall designate and prescribe for and on behalf of the United States, and no other person shall grant, issue, or verify such passports." . . .

The right to travel is a part of the "liberty" of which the citizen cannot be deprived without due process of law under the Fifth Amendment. So much is conceded by the Solicitor General. In Anglo-Saxon law that right was emerging at least as early as the Magna Carta.[12] Chafee, Three Human Rights in the Constitution of 1787 (1956), 171-181, 187 et seq., shows how deeply engrained in our history this freedom of movement is. Freedom of movement across frontiers in either direction, and inside frontiers as well, was a part of our heritage. Travel abroad, like travel within the country, may be necessary for a livelihood. It may be as close to the heart of the individual as the choice of what he eats, or wears, or reads. Freedom of movement is basic in our scheme of values. See Crandall v. Nevada, 6 Wall. 35, 44; Williams v. Fears, 179 U.S. 270, 274; Edwards v. California, 314 U.S. 160. "Our nation," wrote

[5] Proc. No. 3004, 64 Stat. C31.
[6] See 9 Op. Atty. Gen. 350, 352.
[12] Article 42 reads as follows: "It shall be lawful to any person, for the future, to go out of our kingdom, and to return, safely and securely, by land or by water, saving his allegiance to us, unless it be in time of war, for some short space, for the common good of the kingdom: excepting prisoners and outlaws, according to the laws of the land, and of the people of the nation at war against us, and Merchants who shall be treated as it is said above." And see Jaffe, op. cit. supra, 19-20; Sibley, The Passport System, 7 J. Soc. Comp. Leg. (N.S.) 26, 32-33; 1 Blackstone Commentaries 134-135.

Chafee, "has thrived on the principle that, outside areas of plainly harmful conduct, every American is left to shape his own life as he thinks best, do what he pleases, go where he pleases." Id., at 197.

Freedom of movement also has large social values. As Chafee put it:

"Foreign correspondents and lecturers on public affairs need first-hand information. Scientists and scholars gain greatly from consultations with colleagues in other countries. Students equip themselves for more fruitful careers in the United States by instruction in foreign universities.[13] Then there are reasons close to the core of personal life — marriage, reuniting families, spending hours with old friends. Finally, travel abroad enables American citizens to understand that people like themselves live in Europe and helps them to be well-informed on public issues. An American who has crossed the ocean is not obliged to form his opinions about our foreign policy merely from what he is told by officials of our government or by a few correspondents of American newspapers. Moreover, his views on domestic questions are enriched by seeing how foreigners are trying to solve similar problems. In many different ways direct contact with other countries contributes to sounder decisions at home." Id., at 195-196. And see Vestal, Freedom of Movement, 41 Iowa L. Rev. 6, 13-14.

Freedom to travel is, indeed, an important aspect of the citizen's "liberty." We need not decide the extent to which it can be curtailed. We are first concerned with the extent, if any, to which Congress has authorized its curtailment.

The difficulty is that while the power of the Secretary of State over the issuance of passports is expressed in broad terms, it was apparently long exercised quite narrowly. So far as material here, the cases of refusal of passports generally fell into two categories. First, questions pertinent to the citizenship of the applicant and his allegiance to the United States had to be resolved by the Secretary, for the command of Congress was that "No passport shall be granted or issued to or verified for any other persons than those owing allegiance, whether citizens or not, to the United States." 32 Stat. 386, 22 U.S.C. §212. Second, was the question whether the applicant was participating in illegal conduct, trying to escape the toils of the law, promoting passport frauds, or otherwise engaging in conduct which would violate the laws of the United States. See 3 Moore, Digest of International Law (1906), §512; 3 Hackworth, Digest of International Law (1942), §268; 2 Hyde, International Law (2d rev. ed.), §401.

The grounds for refusal asserted here do not relate to citizenship or allegiance on the one hand or to criminal or unlawful conduct on the other. Yet, so far as relevant here, those two are the only ones which it could fairly be argued were adopted by Congress in light of prior administrative practice. One can find in the records of the State Department rulings of subordinates

---

[13] The use of foreign travel to promote educational interests is reviewed by Francis J. Colligan in 30 Dept. State Bull. 663.

covering a wider range of activities than the two indicated. But as respects Communists these are scattered rulings and not consistently of one pattern. We can say with assurance that whatever may have been the practice after 1926, at the time the Act of July 3, 1926, was adopted, the administrative practice, so far as relevant here, had jelled only around the two categories mentioned. We, therefore, hesitate to impute to Congress, when in 1952 it made a passport necessary for foreign travel and left its issuance to the discretion of the Secretary of State, a purpose to give him unbridled discretion to grant or withhold a passport from a citizen for any substantive reason he may choose.

More restrictive regulations were applied in 1918 and in 1941 as war measures. We are not compelled to equate this present problem of statutory construction with problems that may arise under the war power. Cf. Youngstown Sheet & Tube Co. v. Sawyer, 343 U.S. 579.

In a case of comparable magnitude, Korematsu v. United States, 323 U.S. 214, 218, we allowed the Government in time of war to exclude citizens from their homes and restrict their freedom of movement only on a showing of "the gravest imminent danger to the public safety." There the Congress and the Chief Executive moved in coordinated action; and, as we said, the Nation was then at war. No such condition presently exists. No such showing of extremity, no such showing of joint action by the Chief Executive and the Congress to curtail a constitutional right of the citizen has been made here.

Since we start with an exercise by an American citizen of an activity included in constitutional protection, we will not readily infer that Congress gave the Secretary of State unbridled discretion to grant or withhold it. If we were dealing with political questions entrusted to the Chief Executive by the Constitution we would have a different case. But there is more involved here. In part, of course, the issuance of the passport carries some implication of intention to extend the bearer diplomatic protection, though it does no more than "request all whom it may concern to permit safely and freely to pass, and in case of need to give all lawful aid and protection" to this citizen of the United States. But that function of the passport is subordinate. Its crucial function today is control over exit. And, as we have seen, the right of exit is a personal right included within the word "liberty" as used in the Fifth Amendment. If that "liberty" is to be regulated, it must be pursuant to the law-making functions of the Congress. Youngstown Sheet & Tube Co. v. Sawyer, supra. And if that power is delegated, the standards must be adequate to pass scrutiny by the accepted tests. See Panama Refining Co. v. Ryan, 293 U.S. 388, 420-430. Cf. Cantwell v. Connecticut, 310 U.S. 296, 307; Niemotko v. Maryland, 340 U.S. 268, 271. Where activities or enjoyment, natural and often necessary to the well-being of an American citizen, such as travel, are involved, we will construe narrowly all delegated powers that curtail or dilute them. See Ex parte Endo, 323 U.S. 283, 301-302. Cf. Hannegan v.

Esquire Inc., 327 U.S. 146, 156; United States v. Rumely, 345 U.S. 41, 46. We hesitate to find in this broad generalized power an authority to trench so heavily on the rights of the citizen.

Thus we do not reach the question of constitutionality. We only conclude that §1185 and §211a do not delegate to the Secretary the kind of authority exercised here. We deal with beliefs, with associations, with ideological matters. We must remember that we are dealing here with citizens who have neither been accused of crimes nor found guilty. They are being denied their freedom of movement solely because of their refusal to be subjected to inquiry into their beliefs and associations. They do not seek to escape the law nor to violate it. They may or may not be Communists. But assuming they are, the only law which Congress has passed expressly curtailing the movement of Communists across our borders has not yet become effective. It would therefore be strange to infer that pending the effectiveness of that law, the Secretary has been silently granted by Congress the larger, the more pervasive power to curtail in his discretion the free movement of citizens in order to satisfy himself about their beliefs or associations.

To repeat, we deal here with a constitutional right of the citizen, a right which we must assume Congress will be faithful to respect. We would be faced with important constitutional questions were we to hold that Congress by §1185 and §211a had given the Secretary authority to withhold passports to citizens because of their beliefs or associations. Congress has made no such provision in explicit terms; and absent one, the Secretary may not employ that standard to restrict the citizens' right of free movement.

Reversed.

[Mr. Justice Clark's dissent, in which Justices Burton, Harlan and Whittaker joined, is omitted.]

NOTES

1. In a third case, decided the same day on the same grounds, the Supreme Court held that the Secretary of State could not deny a passport to physicist Weldon B. Dayton, despite his findings that Dayton had Communist associations and there was "reason to believe . . . that the applicant is going abroad to engage in activities which will advance the Communist movement for the purpose, knowingly and wilfully of advancing that movement." Dayton v. Dulles, 357 U.S. 144, 78 S. Ct. 1127, 2 L. Ed 1221 (1958). In the courts below the Dayton case had turned primarily on the issue of whether the Department could refuse a passport on the basis of evidence not disclosed to the applicant, but the Supreme Court did not reach this issue.

2. Shortly after the above decisions the State Department announced that it had granted passports, not only to Kent, Briehl and Dayton, but to Robeson and Lamont as well. N.Y. Times, June 25 and 27, 1958. Legislation to revise the passport

laws was already pending in Congress at the time of the Kent decision. See e.g., H.R. 9937 (Rep. Walters), S. 2416 (Sen. Stennis and Cotton), and S. 2770 (Sen. Fulbright), all 85th Cong., 1st Session. The Stennis-Cotton bill embodied the recommendations made in the Report of the Commission on Government Security 475-495 (G.P.O. 1957). Following the Supreme Court decisions additional bills were introduced, but no new legislation was enacted.

3. After the Kent case the State Department abandoned its policy of refusing passports on grounds of Communist Party membership or the other grounds stated in Section 51.135 of its 1952 regulations. In June 1961, however, the Supreme Court upheld the order of the Subversive Activities Control Board requiring the Communist Party to register as a Communist-action organization under the Internal Security Act of 1950. Communist Party v. Subversive Activities Control Board, 367 U.S. 1, 81 S. Ct. 1357, 6 L. Ed. 2d 625 (1961). This brought into operation the provisions of Section 6 of the Subversive Activities Control Act (Title I of the Internal Security Act) which made it unlawful for a member of an organization ordered to register to obtain a passport. The State Department then reinstituted its ban against giving passports to members of the Communist Party. See 22 C.F.R. 51.135. The validity of Section 6 came before the Court in the Aptheker case, set forth below.

4. Lower federal court decisions prior to Kent, discussing the basic constitutional issues involved in the State Department's pre-Kent policy include, in addition to the Kent, Briehl and Dayton cases, Schactman v. Dulles, 225 F.2d 938 (D.C. Cir. 1955). See also Stewart v. Dulles, 248 F.2d 602 (D.C. Cir. 1957).

5. Much of the passport litigation prior to Kent centered around procedural issues. In the first passport case decided on the merits under the post-war policy, a three-judge court held that due process required that a hearing be held before the State Department could revoke or refuse to renew a passport. Bauer v. Acheson, 106 F. Supp. 445 (D.D.C. 1952). Thereafter the State Department issued the regulations of August 28, 1952, which contained provision for an appearance by the applicant before the Passport Division and an appeal to a Board of Passport Appeals. 22 C.F.R. §§51.137 to 51.141. In January 1954 the Secretary of State approved regulations providing for the procedure before the Board of Passport Appeals. 19 Fed. Reg. 161 (1954), 22 C.F.R. §§51.151 to 51.170.

In Dulles v. Nathan, 225 F.2d 29 (D.C. Cir. 1955), the Court of Appeals, reaffirming the Bauer case, in effect ordered the State Department to give Dr. Nathan "a quasi judicial hearing . . . with opportunity provided to the government and to the appellee to offer evidence." See also Clark v. Dulles, 129 F. Supp. 950 (D.D.C. 1955). In Boudin v. Dulles, 136 F. Supp. 218 (D.D.C. 1955), Judge Youngdahl ruled that "All evidence upon which the [Passport] Office may rely for its decision under Section 51.135 must appear on record so that the applicant may have the opportunity to meet it and the court to review it." 136 F. Supp. at 222. The Court of Appeals, sitting en banc, did not reach the question of secret evidence but ruled that the Secretary of State must, under his regulations, make specific findings indicating under which of the classifications of Section 51.135 the passport application is denied. 235 F.2d 532 (D.C. Cir. 1956). See also Dayton v. Dulles, 237 F.2d 43 (D.C. Cir. 1956).

In the Briehl case, however, the prevailing opinion in the Court of Appeals stated that "due process in passport proceedings does not prevent the use of confidential information when foreign affairs or the national security is involved." 248 F.2d at 575. And a majority sitting in the second stage of the Dayton case made the same holding. 254 F.2d at 74-77.

The doctrine of exhaustion of administrative hearings has been applied in the passport situation. Robeson v. Dulles, 235 F. 2d 810 (D.C. Cir. 1956), cert. den., 352 U.S. 895 (1956).

6. In addition to other limitations on the issuance of passports the State Department regulations provide:

"51.136. *Limitations on issuance of passports to certain other persons*. In order to promote and safeguard the interests of the United States, passport facilities, except for direct and immediate return to the United States, shall be refused to a person when it appears to the satisfaction of the Secretary of State that the person's activities abroad would: (a) Violate the laws of the United States; (b) be prejudicial to the orderly conduct of foreign relations; or (c) otherwise be prejudicial to the interests of the United States."

The limitations set forth in §§51.135 and 51.136 are not intended to be exclusive, and the Secretary of State refuses passports to individuals on other grounds, including persons who are mentally ill, persons likely to become public charges, habitual criminals, fugitives from justice, and persons under court restraining orders. See Hearings before Subcommittee on Constitutional Rights of the Senate Judiciary Committee, Security and Constitutional Rights, 84th Cong., 1st Sess. 163-164 (1955); Hearings before the Senate Committee on Foreign Relations, Department of State Passport Policies, 85th Cong. 1st Sess. 39 (1957). See also Kraus v. Dulles, 235 F.2d 840 (D.C. Cir. 1956), remanding for further proceedings a case involving denial of a passport unless the applicant could show he had or could obtain the necessary funds to travel abroad and return. With the exception of the Kraus case issues of denial of a passport on these grounds do not appear to have been litigated.

REFERENCES

1. For accounts of the State Department practice in refusing passports on political grounds, prior to the Kent decision, see Note, Passport Refusals for Political Reasons: Constitutional Issues and Judicial Review, 61 Yale L.J. 171, 174-178 (1952); Parker, The Right to Go Abroad: To Have and to Hold a Passport, 40 Va. L. Rev. 853, 857-861 (1954); Hearings before the Subcommittee on Constitutional Rights of the Senate Judiciary Committee, Security and Constitutional Rights, 84th Cong., 1st. Sess. 85-216 (1955); Report of the Commission on Government Security, 462-475 (1957). On the policy and practice with respect to visas see American Visa Policy and Foreign Scientists, October 1952 issue of the Bulletin of the Atomic Scientists; American Visa Policy: A Report, Bull. of the Atomic Scientists, December 1955, p. 367; Bruce, Consular Curtain, The Nation, Nov. 27, 1954, p. 462. With respect to the announcement of Attorney General McGranery that he had ordered an investigation to be made of the subversive tendencies of Charlie Chaplin when Chaplin returned from a trip abroad, as a result of which Chaplin decided to surrender his re-entry permit to the United States, see N.Y. Times, Sept. 20, 1952, Apr. 16 and 18, 1953.

2. For legal discussion of the various issues raised by the passport cases, published

prior to the Kent case, see Note, Passport Refusals for Political Reasons: Constitutional Issues and Judicial Review, 61 Yale L.J. 171 (1952); Note, Passports and Freedom of Travel: The Conflict of a Right and a Privilege, 41 Geo. L.J. 63 (1952); Barnett, Passport Administration and the Courts, 32 Ore. L. Rev. 193 (1953); Parker, The Right to Go Abroad: To Have and to Hold a Passport, 40 Va. L. Rev. 853 (1954); Boudin, The Constitutional Right to Travel, 56 Colum. L. Rev. 47 (1956); Note, The Passport Puzzle, 23 U. Chi. L. Rev. 260 (1956); Doman, A Comparative Analysis: Do Citizens Have the Right to Travel? 43 A.B.A.J. 307 (1957).

On the secret evidence issue see Note, supra, 23 U. Chi. L. Rev. 260, 282 et seq. (1956); Note, Denial of Passport Upon Undisclosed Information, 44 Calif. L. Rev. 579 (1956); Note, Appraisal, Confrontation and the Passport Applicant, 8 Stan. L. Rev. 673 (1956). See also the materials cited in reference to the loyalty programs, Chapter III, Section E.

3. For pre-Kent discussions of some of the non-legal aspects of the problem see Wyzanski, Freedom to Travel, Atlantic Monthly, October 1952, p. 66; Fanelli, Passport — Right or Privilege? 300 Annals of the Am. Acad. of Pol. and Soc. Sci. 36 (1955); Fosdick, The Passport — And the Right to Travel, N.Y. Times Magazine, July 17, 1955, p. 8; Jaffe, The Right to Travel: The Passport Problem, Foreign Affairs, October 1956, p. 17; Why U.S. Bans Travel to Communist China, U.S. News and World Report, Apr. 12, 1957 (statement by Deputy Under Secretary of State Robert D. Murphy before Senate Foreign Relations Committee); debate on passport policy between Roderic L. O'Connor, head of the State Department's Bureau of Security and Consular Affairs, and Joseph N. Welch, Saturday Review, Jan. 11, 1958, p. 10; Commager, A Nation of Travelers, id., p. 24.

See also Report by the American Civil Liberties Union on the Issuance of Passports (Feb. 18, 1952); Hearings before Subcommittee No. 1 of the House Judiciary Committee, U.S. Passports: Denial and Review, 84th Cong., 2d Sess. (1956); Hearings before the Subcommittee on Constitutional Rights of the Senate Judiciary Committee, The Right to Travel, 85th Cong., 1st Sess. (1957).

4. For discussion of the Kent case, see McNamara and Mitchell, Beliefs, Associations, and Passports: Recent Cases and Proposed Legislation, 27 Geo. Wash. L. Rev. 77 (1958); Note, Passport Denial as a Security Measure, 43 Minn. L. Rev. 126 (1958); Notes, 72 Harv. L. Rev. 77, 172-176 (1958); 8 DePaul L. Rev. 376 (1959); 37 N.C.L. Rev. 172 (1959). Other material following the Kent case can be found in Association of the Bar of the City of New York, Report of the Special Committee to Study Passport Procedure, Freedom To Travel (1958); Hearings before the Senate Committee on Foreign Relations, Passport Legislation, 85th Cong., 2d Sess. (1958).

APTHEKER v. SECRETARY OF STATE
378 U.S. 500, 84 S. Ct. 1659, 12 L. Ed. 2d 992 (1964)

Mr. Justice Goldberg delivered the opinion of the Court.

This appeal involves a single question: the constitutionality of §6 of the Subversive Activities Control Act of 1950, 64 Stat. 993, 50 U.S.C. §785. Section 6 provides in pertinent part that:

"(a) When a Communist organization . . . is registered, or there is in effect a final order of the Board requiring such organization to register, it shall be unlawful for any member of such organization, with knowledge or notice that such organization is so registered or that such order has become final —

"(1) to make application for a passport, or the renewal of a passport, to be issued or renewed by or under the authority of the United States; or

"(2) to use or attempt to use any such passport." [2] . . .

[After the decision in Communist Party v. Subversives Activities Control Board, 367 U.S. 1, upholding the order directing the Communist Party to register, the Department of State revoked the passports held by the appellants. Appellants brought suit to compel return. A three-judge Court granted the Secretary of State's motion for summary judgment. 219 F. Supp. 709.]

The substantiality of the restrictions cannot be doubted. The denial of a passport, given existing domestic and foreign laws, is a severe restriction upon, and in effect a prohibition against, world-wide foreign travel. Present laws and regulations make it a crime for a United States citizen to travel outside the Western Hemisphere or to Cuba without a passport. By its plain import §6 of the Control Act effectively prohibits travel anywhere in the world outside the Western Hemisphere by members of any "Communist organization" — including "Communist-action" and "Communist-front" organizations. The restrictive effect of the legislation cannot be gainsaid by emphasizing, as the Government seems to do, that a member of a registering organization could recapture his freedom to travel by simply in good faith abandoning his membership in the organization. Since freedom of association is itself guaranteed in the First Amendment, restrictions imposed upon the right to travel cannot be dismissed by asserting that the right to travel could be fully exercised if the individual would first yield up his membership in a given association.

Although previous cases have not involved the constitutionality of statutory restrictions upon the right to travel abroad, there are well-established principles by which to test whether the restrictions here imposed are consistent with the liberty guaranteed in the Fifth Amendment. It is a familiar and basic principle, recently reaffirmed in N.A.A.C.P. v. Alabama, 377 U.S. 288, 307, that "a governmental purpose to control or prevent activities constitutionally subject to state regulation may not be achieved by means which sweep unnecessarily broadly and thereby invade the area of protected freedoms." . . .

This principle requires that we consider the congressional purpose underlying §6 of the Control Act.[8] The Government emphasizes that the legislation

---

[2] Section 6(b) provides that: "When an organization is registered, or there is in effect a final order of the Board requiring an organization to register, as a Communist-action organization, it shall be unlawful for any officer or employee of the United States to issue a passport to, or renew the passport of, any individual knowing or having reason to believe that such individual is a member of such organization."

The criminal penalties for violations of §6 are specified in §15(c) of the Act which provides in pertinent part that: "Any individual who violates any provision of section 5, 6, or 10 of this title shall, upon conviction thereof, be punished for each such violation by a fine of not more than $10,000 or by imprisonment for not more than five years, or by both such fine and imprisonment." 64 Stat. 1003, 50 U.S.C. §794(c).

[8] The purpose of the Act is stated in §2. 64 Stat. 987, 50 U.S.C. §781. Congress found,

in question flows, as the statute itself declares, from the congressional desire to protect our national security. That Congress under the Constitution has power to safeguard our Nation's security is obvious and unarguable. . . .

Section 6 provides that any member of a Communist organization which has registered or has been ordered to register commits a crime if he attempts to use or obtain a United States passport. The section applies to members who act "with knowledge or notice" that the organization is under a final registration order. "Notice" is specifically defined in §13(k). That section provides that publication in the Federal Register of the fact of registration or of issuance of a final registration order "shall constitute notice to all members of such organization that such order has become final." Thus the terms of §6 apply whether or not the member actually knows or believes that he is associated with what is deemed to be a "Communist-action" or a "Communist-front" organization. The section also applies whether or not one knows or believes that he is associated with an organization operating to further aims of the world Communist movement and "to establish a Communist totalitarian dictatorship in the countries throughout the world. . . ." 64 Stat. 987, 50 U.S.C. §781(1). The provision therefore sweeps within its prohibition both knowing and unknowing members. In related contexts this Court has had occasion to consider the substantiality of the relationship between an individual and a group where, as here, the fact of membership in that group has been made the sole criterion for limiting the individual's freedom. In Wieman v. Updegraff, 344 U.S. 183, the Court held that the due process guarantee of the Constitution was violated when a State, in an attempt to bar disloyal individuals from its employ, excluded persons solely on the basis of organizational memberships without regard to their knowledge concerning the organizations to which they had belonged. The Court concluded that: "Indiscriminate classification of innocent with knowing activity must fall as an assertion of arbitrary power." Id., at 191.

Section 6 also renders irrelevant the member's degree of activity in the organization and his commitment to its purpose. These factors, like knowledge, would bear on the likelihood that travel by such a person would be attended by the type of activity which Congress sought to control. As the Court has

---

as is generally stated in §2(1), that there "exists a world Communist movement . . . whose purpose it is, by treachery, deceit, infiltration . . . , espionage, sabotage, terrorism, and any other means deemed necessary, to establish a Communist totalitarian dictatorship in the countries throughout the world through the medium of a worldwide Communist organization." Congress concluded, as stated in §2(15), that the "Communist organization in the United States" and the world Communist movement present a danger to the security of the United States, a danger requiring legislative action. The congressional purpose in adopting §6 is more specifically stated in §2(8):

"Due to the nature and scope of the world Communist movement, with the existence of affiliated constituent elements working toward common objects in various countries of the world, travel of Communist members, representatives, and agents from country to country facilitates communication and is a prerequisite for the carrying on of activities to further the purposes of the Communist movement."

elsewhere noted, "men in adhering to a political party or other organization notoriously do not subscribe unqualifiedly to all of its platforms or asserted principles." Cf. Schneiderman v. United States, 320 U.S. 118, 136. It was in this vein that the Court in Schware v. Board of Bar Examiners, 353 U.S., at 246, stated that even "[a]ssuming that some members of the Communist Party . . . had illegal aims and engaged in illegal activities, it cannot automatically be inferred that all members shared their evil purposes or participated in their illegal conduct." Section 6, however, establishes an irrebuttable presumption that individuals who are members of the specified organizations will, if given passports, engage in activities inimical to the security of the United States.[9]

In addition to the absence of criteria linking the bare fact of membership to the individual's knowledge, activity or commitment, §6 also excludes other considerations which might more closely relate the denial of passports to the stated purpose of the legislation. The prohibition of §6 applies regardless of the purposes for which an individual wishes to travel. Under the Statute it is a crime for a notified member of a registered organization to apply for a passport to travel abroad to visit a sick relative, to receive medical treatment, or for any other wholly innocent purpose.[10] In determining whether there has been an abridgment of the Fifth Amendment's guarantee of liberty, this Court must recognize the danger of punishing a member of a Communist organization "for his adherence to lawful and constitutionally protected purposes, because of other and unprotected purposes which he does not necessarily share." Noto v. United States, 367 U.S. 290, 299-300; Scales v. United States, 367 U.S. 203, 229-230. In addition it must be noted that §6 applies to a member regardless of the security-sensitivity of the areas in which he wishes to travel.

---

[9] The provision in question cannot, as the Government admits, be limited by adopting an interpretation analogous to this Court's interpretation of the so-called "membership clause" in the Smith Act. In Scales v. United States, 367 U.S. 203, the Smith Act, which imposes criminal penalties for membership, was interpreted to include only "'active' members having also a guilty knowledge and intent." Id., at 228. The membership clause in that case, however, explicitly required "that a defendant must have knowledge of the organization's illegal advocacy." Id., at 221. That requirement was intimately connected with the construction limiting membership to "active" members. With regard to the Control Act, however, as the Government concedes, "neither the words nor history of Section 6 suggests limiting its application to 'active' members."

[10] In denying appellants passports the Secretary of State made no finding as to their purposes in traveling abroad. The statute, as noted, supports the Secretary's implicit conclusion that such a finding was irrelevant. Appellants, however, in their respective complaints stated their purposes. Appellant Aptheker alleged that:

"He desires to travel to countries of Europe and elsewhere for study and recreation, to observe social, political and economic conditions abroad, and thereafter to write, publish, teach and lecture in this country about his observations. He also desires to travel abroad in order to attend meetings of learned societies and to fulfill invitations to lecture abroad."

Appellant Flynn alleged that:

"[She] desires to travel to countries of Europe and elsewhere for recreation and study, to observe social, political and economic conditions abroad, and thereafter to write, publish and lecture about her observations."

As a result, if a notified member of a registered organization were to apply for a passport to visit a relative in Ireland, or to read rare manuscripts in the Bodleian Library of Oxford University, the applicant would be guilty of a crime; whereas, if he were to travel to Canada or Latin America to carry on criminal activities directed against the United States, he could do so free from the prohibitive reach of §6.

In determining the constitutionality of §6, it is also important to consider that Congress has within its power "less drastic" [11] means of achieving the congressional objective of safeguarding our national security. Shelton v. Tucker, 364 U.S., at 488. The Federal Employee Loyalty Program, which was before this Court in Joint Anti-Fascist Refugee Comm. v. McGrath, 341 U.S. 123, provides an example. Under Executive Order No. 9835, membership in a Communist organization is not considered conclusive but only as one factor to be weighed in determining the loyalty of an applicant or employee. It is relevant to note that less than a month after the decision in Kent v. Dulles, supra, President Eisenhower sent a message to Congress stating that: "Any limitations on the right to travel can only be tolerated in terms of overriding requirements of our national security, and must be subject to substantive and procedural guaranties." Message from the President — Issuance of Passports, H. Doc. No. 417, 85th Cong., 2d Sess.; 104 Cong. Rec. 13046. The legislation which the President proposed did not make membership in a Communist organization, without more, a disqualification for obtaining a passport. S. 4110, H.R. 13318, 85th Cong., 2d Sess. Irrespective of views as to the validity of this or other such proposals, they demonstrate the conviction of the Executive Branch that our national security can be adequately protected by means which, when compared with §6, are more discriminately tailored to the constitutional liberties of individuals.

In our view the foregoing considerations compel the conclusion that §6 of the Control Act is unconstitutional on its face. The section, judged by its plain import and by the substantive evil which Congress sought to control, sweeps too widely and too indiscriminately across the liberty guaranteed in the Fifth Amendment. The prohibition against travel is supported only by a tenuous relationship between the bare fact of organizational membership and the activity Congress sought to proscribe. The broad and enveloping prohibition indiscriminately excludes plainly relevant considerations such as the individual's knowledge, activity, commitment, and purposes in and places for travel. The section therefore is patently not a regulation "narrowly drawn to

[11] The abridgment of liberty involved in this case is more "drastic" than, and distinguishable from, that involved in American Communications Assn. v. Douds, 339 U.S. 382. In Douds the Court upheld §9(h) of the National Labor Relations Act as amended by the Taft-Hartley Act, 61 Stat. 136, 146, 29 U.S.C. §159(h), which conditions trade-union access to the facilities of the National Labor Relations Board upon the submission of non-Communist affidavits by officers of the union. Although the requirement undoubtedly discouraged unions from choosing officers with Communist affiliations, it did not prohibit their election and did not affect basic individual rights to work and to union membership.

prevent the supposed evil," cf. Cantwell v. Connecticut, 310 U.S., at 307, yet here, as elsewhere, precision must be the touchstone of legislation so affecting basic freedoms, N.A.A.C.P. v. Button, 371 U.S., at 438.

The Government alternatively urges that, if §6 cannot be sustained on its face, the prohibition should nevertheless be held constitutional as applied to these particular appellants. The Government argues that "surely Section 6 was reasonable as applied to the top-ranking Party leaders involved here." [13] It is not disputed that appellants are top-ranking leaders: Appellant Aptheker is editor of Political Affairs, the "theoretical organ" of the Party in this country and appellant Flynn is chairman of the Party. . . .

The clarity and preciseness of the provision in question make it impossible to narrow its indiscriminately cast and overly broad scope without substantial rewriting. . . . [A]n attempt to "construe" the statute and to probe its recesses for some core of constitutionality would inject an element of vagueness into the statute's scope and application; the plain words would thus become uncertain in meaning only if courts proceeded on a case-by-case basis to separate out constitutional from unconstitutional areas of coverage. This course would not be proper, or desirable, in dealing with a section which so severely curtails personal liberty.

Since this case involves a personal liberty protected by the Bill of Rights, we believe that the proper approach to legislation curtailing that liberty must be that adopted by this Court in N.A.A.C.P. v. Button, 371 U.S. 415, and Thornhill v. Alabama, 310 U.S. 88. In N.A.A.C.P. v. Button the Court stated that:

"[I]n appraising a statute's inhibitory effect upon such rights, this Court has not hesitated to take into account possible applications of the statute in other factual contexts besides that at bar. . . . The objectionable quality of vagueness and overbreadth does not depend upon absence of fair notice to a criminally accused or upon unchanneled delegation of legislative powers, but upon the danger of tolerating, in the area of First Amendment freedoms, the existence of a penal statute susceptible of sweeping and improper application." [371 U.S. at 432-433].

For essentially the same reasons this Court had concluded that the constitutionality of the statute in Thornhill v. Alabama should be judged on its face:

"An accused, after arrest and conviction under such a statute [on its face unconstitutionally abridging freedom of speech], does not have to sustain the burden of demonstrating that the State could not constitutionally have written a different and specific statute covering his activities as disclosed by the charge and the evidence introduced against him." 310 U.S., at 98.

Similarly, since freedom of travel is a constitutional liberty closely related to rights of free speech and association, we believe that appellants in this case

---

[13] The Government recognizes, however, that: "Membership, or even leadership, in the Communist Party is not automatically a crime." Brief for Petitioner on Petition for a Writ of Certiorari, p. 11, United States v. Communist Party of the United States, No. 1027, O.T. 1963, cert. denied, 377 U.S. 968.

should not be required to assume the burden of demonstrating that Congress could not have written a statute constitutionally prohibiting their travel.[16]

Accordingly the judgment of the three-judge District Court is reversed and the cause remanded for proceedings in conformity with this opinion.

Reversed and remanded.

MR. JUSTICE BLACK, concurring.

. . . I concur in the Court's holding that this section of the Act is unconstitutional, but not on the ground that the Due Process Clause of the Fifth Amendment, standing alone, confers on all our people a constitutional liberty to travel abroad at will. Without reference to other constitutional provisions, Congress has, in my judgment, broad powers to regulate the issuance of passports under its specific power to regulate commerce with foreign nations. The Due Process Clauses of the Fifth and Fourteenth Amendments do mean to me, however, that neither the Secretary of State nor any other government agent can deny people in this country their liberty to travel or their liberty to do anything else except in accordance with the "law of the land" as declared by the Constitution or by valid laws made pursuant to it. For reasons stated in my dissenting opinion in Communist Party v. Subversive Activities Control Board, 367 U.S. 1, 137, I think the whole Act, including §6, is not a valid law . . .

MR. JUSTICE DOUGLAS, concurring.

While I join the opinion of the Court, I add only a few words to indicate what I think is the basic reach of the problem before us.

We noted in Kent v. Dulles, 357 U.S. 116, 126, that "freedom of movement," both internally and abroad, is "deeply engrained" in our history. I would not suppose that a Communist, any more than an indigent, could be barred from traveling interstate. I think that a Communist, the same as anyone else, has this right. Being a Communist certainly is not a crime; and while traveling may increase the likelihood of illegal events happening, so does being alive. If, as I think, the right to move freely from State to State is a privilege and immunity of national citizenship (see Edwards v. California, 314 U.S. 160, 178), none can be barred from exercising it, though anyone who uses it as an occasion to commit a crime can of course be punished. But the right remains sacrosanct, only illegal conduct being punishable.

Free movement by the citizen is of course as dangerous to a tyrant as free expression of ideas or the right of assembly and it is therefore controlled in most countries in the interests of security. That is why riding boxcars carries extreme penalties in Communist lands. That is why the ticketing of people

---

[16] Nor in our opinion should the Secretary of State or other government officers be exposed to the risk of criminal penalties for violating §6(b) by issuing a passport to a member of a registered Communist-action organization who is subsequently found by a court to be a person whose travel, contrary to the belief of the government officer, could constitutionally be prohibited.

and the use of identification papers are routine matters under totalitarian regimes, yet abhorrent in the United States.

Freedom of movement, at home and abroad, is important for job and business opportunities — for cultural, political, and social activities — for all the commingling which gregarious man enjoys. Those with the right of free movement use it at times for mischievous purposes. But that is true of many liberties we enjoy. We nevertheless place our faith in them, and against restraint, knowing that the risk of abusing liberty so as to give rise to punishable conduct is part of the price we pay for this free society.

Freedom of movement is kin to the right of assembly and to the right of association. These rights may not be abridged, De Jonge v. Oregon, 299 U.S. 353; N.A.A.C.P. v. Alabama, 357 U.S. 449, 460-462, only illegal conduct being within the purview of crime in the constitutional sense.

War may be the occasion for serious curtailment of liberty. Absent war, I see no way to keep a citizen from traveling within or without the country, unless there is power to detain him. Ex parte Endo, 323 U.S. 283. And no authority to detain exists except under extreme conditions, e.g., unless he has been convicted of a crime or unless there is probable cause for issuing a warrant of arrest by standards of the Fourth Amendment. This freedom of movement is the very essence of our free society, setting us apart. Like the right of assembly and the right of association, it often makes all other rights meaningful — knowing, studying, arguing, exploring, conversing, observing and even thinking. Once the right to travel is curtailed, all other rights suffer, just as when curfew or home detention is placed on a person.

America is of course sovereign; but her sovereignty is woven in an international web that makes her one of the family of nations. The ties with all the continents are close — commercially as well as culturally. Our concerns are planetary, beyond sunrises and sunsets. Citizenship implicates us in those problems and perplexities, as well as in domestic ones. We cannot exercise and enjoy citizenship in world perspective without the right to travel abroad; and I see no constitutional way to curb it unless, as I said, there is the power to detain.

Mr. Justice Clark, whom Mr. Justice Harlan joins and whom Mr. Justice White joins in part, dissenting.

I

The Court refuses to consider the constitutionality of §6 of the Subversive Activities Control Act as applied to the appellants in this case, Elizabeth Gurley Flynn, the Chairman of the Communist Party of the United States, and Herbert Aptheker, the editor of the Party's "theoretical organ," Political Affairs. Instead, the Court declares the section invalid on its face under the

Fifth Amendment. This is contrary to the long-prevailing practice of this Court. . . .

[The opinion quotes from United States v. Raines, 362 U.S. 17, 20-21, and distinguishes the Thornhill and Button cases on the ground that they were "First Amendment cases, while the holding of this case is based on the Fifth Amendment's guarantee of the right to travel abroad."]

As applied to the prosecution of the Communist Party's top dignitaries, the section is clearly constitutional. The only objections the Court finds to the language of Congress are that it makes the section applicable: (1) "whether or not the member [of the Party] actually knows or believes that he is associated with what is deemed to be a 'Communist-action' or a 'Communist-front' organization"; (2) "whether or not one knows or believes that he is associated with an organization operating to further aims of the world Communist movement and 'to establish a Communist totalitarian dictatorship in the countries throughout the world . . . .' " Let us discuss these objectives seriatim:

(1) There is a finding here — not under attack — that Mrs. Flynn "was an active, participating and continuous member of the Communist Party of the United States; was active in the Party's affairs and its organization; and indeed was and still is one of its principal officials." Likewise there is a finding — not under attack — as to Aptheker that he "[Aptheker] makes it quite clear in his own words that he has been a member of the Communist Party since 1939 and that he is very proud of this association and will do whatever he can to further the aims and goals of the Party." The record shows that both Flynn and Aptheker were witnesses in behalf of the Party in the registration proceeding which resulted in the Party's being ordered to register as a Communist-action organization. Communist Party v. Subversive Activities Control Board, 367 U.S. 1 (1961). In addition, Mrs. Flynn was convicted under the Smith Act. See United States v. Flynn, 216 F.2d 354 (1954). In view of these circumstances, no one could say with truth that the appellants did not know that they were associated with a Communist-action organization. In fact, neither appellant claims lack of notice or knowledge of the requirements of the section.

(2) As to knowledge that the Communist Party is involved in a world Communist movement aimed at establishing a totalitarian Communist dictatorship in countries throughout the world, Congress made specific findings in the Subversive Activities Control Act of 1950 (the very statute under which the hearing was held at which petitioners testified for the Party) and in the Communist Control Act of 1954 that: "the Communist Party of the United States . . . is in fact an instrumentality of a conspiracy to overthrow the Government of the United States" . . . It is, therefore, difficult for me to see how it can be said rationally that these appellants — top Party functionaries who testified on behalf of the Party in the registration proceeding involved in Communist Party v. Control Board, supra — did not know that they were

"associated with an organization operating to further aims of the world Communist movement and 'to establish a Communist totalitarian dictatorship in the countries throughout the world . . . .' "

How does the Court escape? It says that the section "sweeps within its prohibition both knowing and unknowing members." But we have no "unknowing members" before us. Neither appellant contests these findings. All we have are irrational imaginings: a member of the Party might wish "to visit a relative in Ireland, or to read rare manuscripts in the Bodleian Library of Oxford University . . . ." But no such party is here and no such claim is asserted. It will be soon enough to test this situation when it comes here.

II

Nor do I believe the section invalid "on its face." While the right to travel abroad is a part of the liberty protected by the Fifth Amendment, the Due Process Clause does not prohibit reasonable regulation of life, liberty or property. Here the restriction is reasonably related to the national security. . . . The right to travel is not absolute. Congress had ample evidence that use of passports by Americans belonging to the world Communist movement is a threat to our national security. Passports were denied to Communists from the time of the Soviet Revolution until the early 30's and then again later in the 40's. In 1950 Congress determined, in the Subversive Activities Control Act, that foreign travel "is a prerequisite for the carrying on of activities to further the purposes of the Communist movement." 64 Stat. 988. The Congress had before it evidence that such use of passports by Communist Party members: enabled the leaders of the world Communist movement in the Soviet Union to give orders to their comrades in the United States and to exchange vital secrets as well; facilitated the training of American Communist leaders by experts in sabotage and the like in Moscow; gave closer central control to the world Communist movement; and, of utmost importance, provided world Communist leaders with passports for Soviet secret agents to use in the United States for espionage purposes.* This evidence afforded the Congress a rational basis upon which to place the denial of passports to members of the Communist Party in the United States. The denial is reasonably related to the national security. The degree of restraint upon travel is outweighed by the dangers to our very existence.

The remedy adopted by the Congress is reasonably tailored to accomplish the purpose. It may be true that not every member of the Party would endan-

---

* In the proceeding which led to the order of the Subversive Activities Control Board directing the Communist Party to register, the Board heard evidence that the present leaders of the Communist Party in the United States have traveled to the Soviet Union on Party business, have been indoctrinated and trained in Communist strategy and policies and have acted as couriers between the Communist Parties of the two countries.

ger our national security by traveling abroad, but which Communist Party member is worthy of trust? Since the Party is a secret, conspiratorial organization subject to rigid discipline by Moscow, the Congress merely determined that it was not wise to take the risk which foreign travel by Communists entailed. The fact that all persons in a class may not engage in harmful conduct does not of itself make the classification invalid. . . .

Nor do I subscribe to the loose generalization that individual guilt may be conclusively presumed from membership in the Party. One cannot consider the matter in isolation but must relate it to the subject matter involved and the legislative findings upon which the action is based. It is true that in Scales v. United States, 367 U.S. 203 (1961), the Court found that the intention of the Congress in the Smith Act was "to reach only 'active' members having also a guilty knowledge and intent." At 228. But that was a criminal prosecution under the Smith Act which, of course, carried stricter standards. And, in addition, this requirement, as laid down in Scales, was not held to be a constitutional mandate. The Court was merely interpreting a criminal statute which directly prohibits membership in organizations that come within its terms. The Act here does not prohibit membership, but merely restricts members in a field in which the Congress has found danger to our security. Nor is Wieman v. Updegraff, 344 U.S. 183 (1952), cited by the majority, apposite here. That case dealt with an oath based on membership in organizations on the Attorney General's list of subversive groups. The Act condemned the employee who was a member of any listed organization regardless of whether he actually knew the organization was so listed; furthermore, the statute proscribed past membership in the listed organizations. Here proof of actual membership is necessary and notice of registration or entry of a final order directing registration under the Act is required. Finally, the member of the Party here can avoid the Act's sanctions by terminating his membership, which was not possible in Wieman. Appellants also depend on Adler v. Board of Education, 342 U.S. 485 (1952), which upheld a statute with a rebuttable presumption that members of the Party supported Communist objectives. The Court did not hold that the opportunity to rebut was constitutionally required in the circumstances of that case, but even if it had, Adler would not control here. The evidence before Congress as to the danger to national security was of such strength that it warranted the denial of passports, a much less onerous disability than loss of employment.

For these reasons, I would affirm.

[Mr. Justice White agreed with the first ground of Mr. Justice Clark's dissent.]

NOTES

1. For discussion of the Aptheker case, see Note, The Future of American Passports as Restrictions on Travel, 60 Nw. U.L. Rev. 511 (1965), which contains a

short summary of the development of State Department policy; Note, 78 Harv. L. Rev. 143, 195-199 (1965). Other materials are cited in the references following the Zemel case, infra.

2. As noted above, in addition to imposing restrictions upon individuals seeking passports, the State Department has also refused to grant passports for travel to particular countries. See Note, supra, 60 Nw. U.L. Rev. at 523-526. These area travel bans were upheld in the cases of Waldo Frank, a lecturer and newspaper man, who sought to travel to the University of Peking, Frank v. Herter, 269 F.2d 245 (D.C. Cir. 1959), cert. den., 361 U.S. 918 (1959); William Worthy, a newspaper reporter who was refused a passport valid for Communist China, Korea, Vietnam, and Hungary, after having previously violated restrictions by travelling to Communist China and Hungary, Worthy v. Herter, 270 F.2d 905 (D.C. Cir. 1959), cert. den., 361 U.S. 918 (1959); and Congressman Charles O. Porter, who was refused permission to go to Communist China, Porter v. Herter, 278 F.2d 280 (D.C. Cir. 1960), cert. den., 361 U.S. 918 (1959). The Supreme Court addressed itself to these issues in Zemel v. Rusk, set forth below.

ZEMEL v. RUSK
381 U.S. 1, 85 S. Ct. 1271, 14 L. Ed. 2d 179 (1965)

Mr. Chief Justice Warren delivered the opinion of the Court.

The questions for decision are whether the Secretary of State is statutorily authorized to refuse to validate the passports of United States citizens for travel to Cuba, and, if he is, whether the exercise of that authority is constitutionally permissible. We answer both questions in the affirmative.

Prior to 1961 no passport was required for travel anywhere in the Western Hemisphere. On January 3 of that year, the United States broke diplomatic and consular relations with Cuba. On January 16 the Department of State eliminated Cuba from the area for which passports were not required, and declared all outstanding United States passports (except those held by persons already in Cuba) to be invalid for travel to or in Cuba "unless specifically endorsed for such travel under the authority of the Secretary of State." A companion press release stated that the Department contemplated granting exceptions to "persons whose travel may be regarded as being in the best interests of the United States, such as newsmen or businessmen with previously established business interests."

Through an exchange of letters in early 1962, appellant, a citizen of the United States and holder of an otherwise valid passport, applied to the State Department to have his passport validated for travel to Cuba as a tourist. His request was denied. On October 30, 1962, he renewed the request, stating that the purpose of the proposed trip was "to satisfy my curiosity about the state of affairs in Cuba and to make me a better informed citizen." The request again was denied, on the ground that the purpose of the trip did not meet the previously prescribed standards for such travel.

On December 7, 1962, appellant instituted this suit against the Secretary of

State and the Attorney General in the United States District Court for the District of Connecticut . . .

[The first part of the opinion held that a three-judge court was properly convened and that the Supreme Court therefore had jurisdiction over the appeal.]

II

We think that the Passport Act of 1926, 44 Stat. 887, 22 U.S.C. §211a (1958 ed.), embodies a grant of authority to the Executive to refuse to validate the passports of United States citizens for travel to Cuba. That Act provides, in pertinent part:

"The Secretary of State may grant and issue passports . . . under such rules as the President shall designate and prescribe for and on behalf of the United States . . . ." [5]

This provision is derived from §23 of the Act of August 18, 1856, 11 Stat. 52, 60-61, which had, prior to 1926, been re-enacted several times without substantial change. The legislative history of the 1926 Act and its predecessors does not, it is true, affirmatively indicate an intention to authorize area restrictions. However, its language is surely broad enough to authorize area restrictions, and there is no legislative history indicating an intent to exclude such restrictions from the grant of authority; these factors take on added significance when viewed in light of the fact that during the decade preceding the passage of the Act, the Executive had imposed both peacetime and wartime area restrictions.

. . . The use in the 1926 Act of language broad enough to permit executive imposition of area restrictions, after the Executive had several times in the recent past openly asserted the power to impose such restrictions under predecessor statutes containing substantially the same language, supports the conclusion that Congress intended in 1926 to maintain in the Executive the authority to make such restrictions.

This construction of the Act is reinforced by the State Department's continued imposition of area restrictions during both times of war and periods of peace since 1926. . . .

On March 31, 1938, the President, purporting to act pursuant to the 1926 Act, specifically authorized the Secretary to impose area restrictions in the issuance of passports, Exec. Order No. 7856, 3 Fed. Reg. 681, 687:

---

[5] The Secretary of State, rather than the President, imposed the restriction on travel to Cuba. However, Congress has provided that "[t]he Secretary of State shall perform such duties as shall from time to time be enjoined on or intrusted to him by the President relative to . . . such . . . matters respecting foreign affairs as the President of the United States shall assign to the department . . . ." R.S. §202, 5 U.S.C. §156 (1958 ed.). The President, in turn, has authorized the Secretary in his discretion "to restrict a passport for use only in certain countries [or] to restrict it against use in certain countries . . . ." Exec. Order No. 7856, 3 Fed. Reg. 681, 687, 22 CFR §51.75.

"The Secretary of State is authorized in his discretion to refuse to issue a passport, to restrict a passport for use only in certain countries, to restrict it against use in certain countries, to withdraw or cancel a passport already issued, and to withdraw a passport for the purpose of restricting its validity or use in certain countries."

This Executive Order is still in force. 22 CFR §51.75. In September 1939, travel to Europe was prohibited except with a passport specially validated for such travel; passports were so validated only upon a showing of the "imperativeness" of the travel. Departmental Order No. 811, 4 Fed. Reg. 3892.

Area restrictions have also been imposed on numerous occasions since World War II. Travel to Yugoslavia was restricted in the late 1940's as a result of a series of incidents involving American citizens. Dept. State Press Conf., May 9, 1947. Travel to Hungary was restricted between December 1949 and May 1951, and after December 1951.[7] In June 1951, the State Department began to stamp passports "not valid for travel in Czechoslovakia," and declared that all passports outstanding at that time were not valid for such travel. 24 Dept. State Bull. 932. In May 1952, the Department issued a general order that all new passports would be stamped not valid for travel to Albania, Bulgaria, Communist China, Czechoslovakia, Hungary, Poland, Rumania and the Soviet Union. 26 id., at 736. In October 1955, the Secretary announced that passports would no longer require special validation for travel to Czechoslovakia, Hungary, Poland, Rumania and the Soviet Union, but would be stamped invalid for travel "to the following areas under control of authorities with which the United States does not have diplomatic relations: Albania, Bulgaria, and those portions of China, Korea and Viet-Nam under communist control." 33 id., at 777. In February 1956, the restriction on travel to Hungary was reimposed. 34 id., at 246-248. And in late 1956, passports were for a brief period stamped invalid for travel to or in Egypt, Israel, Jordan and Syria. 35 id., at 756.

Even if there had been no passport legislation enacted since the 1926 Act, the post-1926 history of executive imposition of area restrictions, as well as the pre-1926 history, would be of relevance to our construction of the Act. The interpretation expressly placed on a statute by those charged with its administration must be given weight by courts faced with the task of construing the statute. Udall v. Tallman, 380 U.S. 1, 16-18; Norwegian Nitrogen Co. v. United States, 288 U.S. 294, 315. Under some circumstances, Congress' failure to repeal or revise in the face of such administrative interpretation has been held to constitute persuasive evidence that that interpretation is the one intended by Congress.[8] In this case, however, the inference is supported by more than mere congressional inaction. For in 1952 Congress, substantially re-enacting laws which had been passed during the First and Second World

---

[7] 22 Dept. State Bull. 399; 26 id., at 7.

[8] Norwegian Nitrogen Co. v. United States, supra, at 313; Costanzo v. Tillinghast, 287 U.S. 341, 345; United States v. Midwest Oil Co., 236 U.S. 459, 472-473.

Wars,[9] provided that after the issuance of a presidential proclamation of war or national emergency, it would be unlawful to leave or enter the United States without a valid passport. Section 215 of the Immigration and Nationality Act of 1952, 66 Stat. 190, 8 U.S.C. §1185 (1958 ed.). The Solicitor General urges that in view of the issuance in 1953 of a presidential proclamation of national emergency which is still outstanding,[10] travel in violation of an area restriction imposed on an otherwise valid passport is unlawful under the 1952 Act. The correctness of this interpretation is a question we do not reach on this appeal . . . But whether or not the new legislation was intended to attach criminal penalties to the violation of area restrictions, it certainly was not meant to cut back upon the power to impose such restrictions. Despite 26 years of executive interpretation of the 1926 Act as authorizing the imposition of area restrictions, Congress in 1952, though it once again enacted legislation relating to passports, left completely untouched the broad rule-making authority granted in the earlier Act. Cf. Norwegian Nitrogen Co. v. United States, supra, at 313.[11]

This case is therefore not like Kent v. Dulles, [357 U.S. 116], where we were unable to find, with regard to the sort of passport refusal involved there, an administrative practice sufficiently substantial and consistent to warrant the conclusion that Congress had implicitly approved it. Appellant reminds us that in summarizing the Secretary's practice in Kent, we observed:

"So far as material here, the cases of refusal of passports generally fell into two categories. First, questions pertinent to the citizenship of the applicant and his allegiance to the United States had to be resolved by the Secretary . . . . Second, was the question whether the applicant was participating in illegal conduct, trying to escape the toils of the law, promoting passport frauds, or otherwise engaging in conduct which would violate the laws of the United States." 357 U.S., at 127.

It must be remembered, in reading this passage, that the issue involved in Kent was whether a citizen could be denied a passport because of his political beliefs or associations. In finding that history did not support the position of the Secretary in that case, we summarized that history "so far as material here" — that is, so far as material to passport refusals based on the character of the particular applicant. In this case, however, the Secretary has refused to validate appellant's passport not because of any characteristic peculiar to ap-

---

[9] Act of May 22, 1918, 40 Stat. 559; Act of June 21, 1941, 55 Stat. 252.

[10] Pres. Proc. No. 3004, 67 Stat. c31; cf. Exec. Order No. 11037, 3 CFR 621 (1959-1963 Comp.).

[11] Pres. Proc. No. 3004, 67 Stat. c31, which was issued in 1953 pursuant to §215, stated that the departure and entry of citizens would be governed by "sections 53.1 to 53.9, inclusive, of title 22 of the Code of Federal Regulations." 22 CFR §53.8 (1949 ed.) provided:

"Nothing in this part shall be construed to prevent the Secretary of State from exercising the discretion resting in him to refuse to issue a passport, to restrict its use to certain countries, to withdraw or cancel a passport already issued, or to withdraw a passport for the purpose of restricting its validity or use in certain countries."

pellant, but rather because of foreign policy considerations affecting all citizens.

III

Having concluded that the Secretary of State's refusal to validate appellant's passport for travel to Cuba is supported by the authority granted by Congress in the Passport Act of 1926, we must next consider whether that refusal abridges any constitutional right of appellant. Although we do not in this case reach the question of whether the 1952 Act should be read to attach criminal penalties to travel to an area for which one's passport is not validated, we must, if we are to approach the constitutional issues presented by this appeal candidly, proceed on the assumption that the Secretary's refusal to validate a passport for a given area acts as a deterrent to travel to that area. In Kent v. Dulles, supra, at 125, we held that "[t]he right to travel is a part of the 'liberty' of which the citizen cannot be deprived without due process of law under the Fifth Amendment." See also Aptheker v. Secretary of State, [378 U.S. 500], at 505-506. However, the fact that a liberty cannot be inhibited without due process of law does not mean that it can under no circumstances be inhibited.[12]

The requirements of due process are a function not only of the extent of the governmental restriction imposed,[13] but also of the extent of the necessity for the restriction. Cuba is the only area in the Western Hemisphere controlled by a Communist government. It is, moreover, the judgment of the State Department that a major goal of the Castro regime is to export its Communist revolution to the rest of Latin America.[14] The United States and other members of the Organization of American States have determined that travel between Cuba and the other countries of the Western Hemisphere is an important element in the spreading of subversion, and many have therefore undertaken measures to discourage such travel.[15] It also cannot be forgotten that in the early days of the Castro regime, United States citizens were arrested and imprisoned without charges. We think, particularly in view of

---

[12] Aptheker v. Secretary of State, supra, at 505-514; Shachtman v. Dulles, 96 U.S. App. D.C. 287, 290 (opinion of the court), 293 (Edgerton, J., concurring), 225 F.2d 938, 941, 944 (1955); cf. Bolling v. Sharpe, 347 U.S. 497, 499-500; Freedom to Travel (Report of Special Committee to Study Passport Procedures, Ass'n of the Bar of the City of New York), pp. 53, 55 (1958); Chafee, Three Human Rights in the Constitution of 1787, p. 192 (1956).

[13] Compare Kent v. Dulles, supra; Aptheker v. Secretary of State, supra; Universal Declaration of Human Rights, Art. 13 (quoted, S. Doc. No. 123, 81st Cong., 1st Sess., p. 1157); Korematsu v. United States, 323 U.S. 214, 218.

[14] Cuba, Dept. State Pub. No. 7171, pp. 25-36 (1961); see also Ball, U.S. Policy Toward Cuba, Dept. State Pub. No. 7690, p. 3 (1964); 47 Dept. State Bull. 598-600.

[15] See Report of the Special Committee to Study Resolutions II.1 and VIII of the Eighth Meeting of Consultation of Ministers of Foreign Affairs, OEA/Ser. G/IV, pp. 14-16 (1963); 48 Dept. State Bull. 517, 719; Resolution I, Final Act, Ninth Meeting of Consultation of Ministers of Foreign Affairs, OEA/Ser. F/II.9 (1964).

the President's statutory obligation to "use such means, not amounting to acts of war, as he may think necessary and proper" to secure the release of an American citizen unjustly deprived of his liberty by a foreign government,[16] that the Secretary has justifiably concluded that travel to Cuba by American citizens might involve the Nation in dangerous international incidents, and that the Constitution does not require him to validate passports for such travel.

The right to travel *within* the United States is of course also constitutionally protected, cf. Edwards v. California, 314 U.S. 160. But that freedom does not mean that areas ravaged by flood, fire or pestilence cannot be quarantined when it can be demonstrated that unlimited travel to the area would directly and materially interfere with the safety and welfare of the area or the Nation as a whole. So it is with international travel. That the restriction which is challenged in this case is supported by the weightiest considerations of national security is perhaps best pointed up by recalling that the Cuban missile crisis of October 1962 preceded the filing of appellant's complaint by less than two months.

Appellant also asserts that the Secretary's refusal to validate his passport for travel to Cuba denies him rights guaranteed by the First Amendment. His claim is different from that which was raised in Kent v. Dulles, supra, and Aptheker v. Secretary of State, supra, for the refusal to validate appellant's passport does not result from any expression or association on his part; appellant is not being forced to choose between membership in an organization and freedom to travel. Appellant's allegation is, rather, that the "travel ban is a direct interference with the First Amendment rights of citizens to travel abroad so that they might acquaint themselves at first hand with the effects abroad of our Government's policies, foreign and domestic, and with conditions abroad which might affect such policies." We must agree that the Secretary's refusal to validate passports for Cuba renders less than wholly free the flow of information concerning that country. While we further agree that this is a factor to be considered in determining whether appellant has been denied due process of law, we cannot accept the contention of appellant that it is a First Amendment right which is involved. For to the extent that the Secretary's refusal to validate passports for Cuba acts as an inhibition (and it would be unrealistic to assume that it does not), it is an inhibition of action.

---

[16] R.S. §2001, 22 U.S.C. §1732 (1958 ed.), provides:

"Whenever it is made known to the President that any citizen of the United States has been unjustly deprived of his liberty by or under the authority of any foreign government, it shall be the duty of the President forthwith to demand of that government the reasons of such imprisonment; and if it appears to be wrongful and in violation of the rights of American citizenship, the President shall forthwith demand the release of such citizen, and if the release so demanded is unreasonably delayed or refused, the President shall use such means, not amounting to acts of war, as he may think necessary and proper to obtain or effectuate the release; and all the facts and proceedings relative thereto shall as soon as practicable be communicated by the President to Congress."

There are few restrictions on action which could not be clothed by ingenious argument in the garb of decreased data flow. For example, the prohibition of unauthorized entry into the White House diminishes the citizen's opportunities to gather information he might find relevant to his opinion of the way the country is being run, but that does not make entry into the White House a First Amendment right. The right to speak and publish does not carry with it the unrestrained right to gather information.

Finally, appellant challenges the 1926 Act on the ground that it does not contain sufficiently definite standards for the formulation of travel controls by the Executive. It is important to bear in mind, in appraising this argument, that because of the changeable and explosive nature of contemporary international relations, and the fact that the Executive is immediately privy to information which cannot be swiftly presented to, evaluated by, and acted upon by the legislature, Congress — in giving the Executive authority over matters of foreign affairs — must of necessity paint with a brush broader than that it customarily wields in domestic areas. . . .

. . . This does not mean that simply because a statute deals with foreign relations, it can grant the Executive totally unrestricted freedom of choice. However, the 1926 Act contains no such grant. We have held, Kent v. Dulles, supra, and reaffirm today, that the 1926 Act must take its content from history: it authorizes only those passport refusals and restrictions "which it could fairly be argued were adopted by Congress in light of prior administrative practice." Kent v. Dulles, supra, at 128. So limited, the Act does not constitute an invalid delegation. . . .

Affirmed.

[Mr. Justice Black dissented on the ground that only Congress and not the President can make laws regarding the issuance of passports. To the extent that Congress in the 1926 Act attempted to delegate this power to the President and the Secretary of State such delegation was unconstitutional because it purports to confer a power "so broad . . . as to be marked by no bounds except an unlimited discretion."]

MR. JUSTICE DOUGLAS, with whom Mr. Justice Goldberg concurs, dissenting . . . .

I agree that there are areas to which Congress can restrict or ban travel. Pestilences may rage in a region making it necessary to protect not only the traveler but those he might infect on his return. A theatre of war may be too dangerous for travel. Other like situations can be put. But the only so-called danger present here is the Communist regime in Cuba. The world, however, is filled with Communist thought; and Communist regimes are on more than one continent. They are part of the world spectrum; and if we are to know them and understand them, we must mingle with them, as Pope John said. Keeping alive intellectual intercourse between opposing groups has always been important and perhaps was never more important than now.

The First Amendment presupposes a mature people, not afraid of ideas. The First Amendment leaves no room for the official, whether truculent or benign, to say nay or yea because the ideas offend or please him or because he believes some political objective is served by keeping the citizen at home or letting him go. Yet that is just what the Court's decision today allows to happen. We have here no congressional determination that Cuba is an area from which our national security demands that Americans be excluded. Nor do we have a congressional authorization of the Executive to make such a determination according to standards fixed by Congress. Rather we have only the claim that Congress has painted with such a "broad brush" that the State Department can ban travel to Cuba simply because it is pleased to do so. By permitting this, the Court ignores the "familiar and basic principle," Aptheker v. Secretary of State, supra, at 508, that "a governmental purpose to control or prevent activities constitutionally subject to state regulation may not be achieved by means which sweep unnecessarily broadly and thereby invade the area of protected freedoms." NAACP v. Alabama, 377 U.S. 288, 307.

As I have said, the right to travel is at the periphery of the First Amendment, rather than at its core, largely because travel is, of course, more than speech: it is speech brigaded with conduct. "Conduct remains subject to regulation for the protection of society. . . . [But i]n every case the power to regulate must be so exercised as not, in attaining a permissible end, unduly to infringe the protected freedom." Cantwell v. Connecticut, supra, at 304. Restrictions on the right to travel in times of peace should be so particularized that a First Amendment right is not precluded unless some clear countervailing national interest stands in the way of its assertion.

[Mr. Justice Goldberg wrote a separate dissenting opinion in which, after a review of the legislative history and administrative practice connected with the 1926 Act, and a review of the implications of the Kent and Aptheker decisions, he concluded that "it is clear Congress did not mean the 1926 Act to authorize the Executive to impose area restrictions in time of peace."]

NOTES

1. In MacEwan v. Rusk, 228 F. Supp. 306 (E.D. Pa. 1964), decided before Zemel, the District Court reached the same conclusion.

2. In December 1965, Professor Staughton Lynd, Herbert Aptheker, and Thomas Hayden made a trip to North Vietnam without passports valid for that country. On their return their passports were withdrawn by the State Department. Proceedings to regain the passports were instituted. N.Y. Times, Jan. 9 and 11, Feb. 3, 4, and 6, Mar. 16 and 25, 1966.

3. Beginning in December 1965 the State Department announced a series of exceptions to its area restriction policies. It ruled that journalists, public-health specialists, medical scientists, and graduate scholars would be given passports to Communist China, Albania, Cuba, North Korea, and North Vietnam, the coun-

tries then on the restricted list. In July 1966 it added athletes and businessmen to the excepted categories, N.Y. Times, July 12, 1966; and then "prominent American citizens" going as tourists, N.Y. Times, July 17, 1966. On October 19, 1966, the State Department issued revised regulations on passports, incorporating some of the foregoing exceptions. 31 Fed. Reg. 13450.

4. The decision in Zemel expressly left open the question whether a person travelling to a restricted area can be criminally prosecuted under Section 215(b) of the Immigration and Nationality Act of 1952, 8 U.S.C. §1185(b). That Section, violation of which is subject to a fine of not more than $5000, or imprisonment for not more than five years, or both, provides:

"After such proclamation as is provided for in subsection (a) has been made and published and while such proclamation is in force, it shall, except as otherwise provided by the President, and subject to such limitations and exceptions as the President may authorize and prescribe, be unlawful for any citizen of the United States to depart from or enter, or attempt to depart from or enter, the United States unless he bears a valid passport."

The issue, in one form, had previously arisen in Worthy v. United States, 328 F.2d 386 (5th Cir. 1964). Worthy, whose passport had been revoked (see Worthy v. Herter, noted above) had travelled to Cuba, then a restricted area under State Department regulations. Upon his return he was indicted under 8 U.S.C. §1185(b) for unlawfully entering the country without a valid passport. The Court of Appeals reversed his conviction, saying:

"The prohibitory provision of Section 1185(b) defines the offenses in the alternative, and makes it unlawful for a citizen 'to depart from or enter . . . the United States unless he bears a valid passport.' If the conviction of the appellant had been for a willful departure from the United States without a valid passport we would be confronted with a less difficult problem. A citizen, at an airport or pier, without a passport, can refrain from a violation of the statute by remaining in the country. So doing, the citizen can continue to exercise all of the rights and privileges of citizenship and enjoy the protection afforded to him by constitutions and laws incident to his citizenship. The situation of a citizen, outside the United States or at a port of entry, without a passport, is different. He can resume the enjoyment of a citizen's rights and privileges only by the commission of a criminal offense. The appellant had it within his power to avoid a violation of the prohibition against unlawful entry by refraining from an unlawful departure. But the penalty for an unlawful departure is a fine or imprisonment, or both; and the offense of unlawful departure does not include the offense of an unlawful entry. Neither does an unlawful entry include an unlawful departure although it may be improbable that an entry would be unlawful if the departure was lawful. The two offenses are separate. The appellant was not charged with an unlawful departure.

"In Browder v. United States, 312 U.S. 335, 61 S. Ct. 599, 85 L. Ed. 862, and Warzower v. United States, 312 U.S. 442, 61 S. Ct. 603, 85 L. Ed. 876, convictions were sustained for using passports secured by false statements where the passports were used for the purpose of establishing identity and citizenship and the consequent right of entry into the United States from abroad. The offense was the use of passports fraudulently secured, and not the act of entering the United States. If citizenship and identity had been established by other means than the passports no offense would have been committed, at least not the offense for which convictions were had. These decisions are not authority for sustaining the conviction of the appellant.

"The United States, by 18 U.S.C.A. §1407, has made it a criminal offense for narcotics addicts and violators to depart from or enter into the United States without registration at a point of entry or a border customs station. This provision has been sustained. Palma v. United States, 5th Cir. 1958, 261 F.2d 93; United States v. Juzwiak, 2nd Cir. 1958, 258 F.2d 844, cert. den., 359 U.S. 939, 79 S. Ct. 652, 3 L. Ed. 2d 639; Reyes v. United States, 9th Cir. 1958, 258 F.2d 774; United States v. Eramdjian, D.C. S.D. Cal. 1957, 155 F. Supp. 914. The offense proscribed by the narcotics act is the failure to register, not the entry as in the case before us. We get but little aid from these decisions in our search for a solution to the problem here posed.

"We think it is inherent in the concept of citizenship that the citizen, when absent from the country to which he owes allegiance, has a right to return, again to set foot on its soil. It is not to be wondered that the occasions for declaring this principle have been few. In United States v. Ju Toy, 198 U.S. 253, 25 S. Ct. 644, 49 L. Ed. 1040, it was assumed that to deny entrance of a citizen into the United States was a deprivation of a liberty secured by the Fifth Amendment. In the dissenting opinion in that case it was said that it is no crime for a citizen to come back to his native land. 198 U.S. 253, 269, 25 S. Ct. 644, 49 L. Ed. 1040. . . .

"We do not think that a citizen, absent from his country, can have his fundamental right to have free ingress thereto subject to a criminal penalty if he does not have a passport. The citizen, culpable though he may have been in leaving his country without a passport which he could not obtain, and subject, as he probably was, to a criminal penalty for departing without a passport, cannot, we think, be required to choose between banishment or expatriation on the one hand or crossing the border on the other hand, being faced with criminal punishment and the loss of some of the rights and privileges of citizenship as a felon. Citizenship, the Supreme Court has recently said, is a most precious right, expressly guaranteed by the Fourteenth Amendment to the Constitution. Kennedy v. Mendoza-Martinez, [372 U.S. 144]." 328 F.2d at 293-294.

The Government did not petition for certiorari.

In United States v. Laub, 253 F. Supp. 433 (E.D. N.Y. 1966), the District Court in an extensive opinion dismissed a prosecution for conspiring to arrange for a group of students to visit Cuba without passports valid for that country. A second indictment against some of the students who had travelled to Cuba was also dismissed. The contrary result was reached in Travis v. United States, 353 F.2d 506 (9th Cir. 1965), where the defendant travelled to Cuba via Mexico. The Supreme Court agreed to review both the Laub and the Travis cases. 384 U.S. 984, 903 (1966).

5. Bills have been introduced in Congress to strengthen the State Department's authority. Among them one, introduced by Senator Eastland, would authorize the Secretary of State upon Presidential approval to promulgate regulations "describing particular areas under foreign jurisdiction which may be entered or traveled within, by individuals who are nationals or residents of the United States or members of any reasonable designated class thereof, only after receiving, and in accordance with, written authorization therefor issued by the Secretary or his designee." The basis for the regulations is to be a finding that they are "necessary in the

national interest, for the protection of national security or the full, effective and successful conduct of the foreign affairs of the United States." S. 3243, 89th Cong., 2d Sess. (Apr. 19, 1966).

An Administration-supported bill would authorize the Secretary of State to "amend, limit, deny, or revoke passports," and would make it "unlawful for any national to travel abroad without a valid passport." Denial of passports is specifically authorized where "the Secretary determines that the applicant's activities abroad are causing or are likely to cause serious damage to the national security or the foreign policy of the United States." Another provision would authorize the Secretary, subject to the President's approval, to "restrict the travel of nationals and limit the validity of passports with respect to travel to the following places:

"(1) Countries with which the United States is at war;

"(2) Countries or areas where armed hostilities are in progress;

"(3) Countries or areas to which the Secretary determines that travel must be restricted in the national interest because such travel would seriously impair the conduct of United States foreign affairs." H.R. 14895, 89th Cong., 2d Sess. (introduced by Congressman Hays, May 5, 1966).

REFERENCES

On the area restriction problem, and the Zemel case, see Note, Passport Control in the National Interest and Freedom to Travel, 33 Temple L.Q. 332 (1960); Rauh and Pollitt, Restrictions on the Right to Travel, 13 W. Res. L. Rev. 128 (1961); Gould, The Right to Travel and National Security, 1961 Wash. U.L.Q. 334; Edelman, International Travel and Our Quarantine System, 37 Temple L.Q. 28 (1963); Note, Right to Travel versus Power to Conduct Foreign Affairs: Area Restrictions on Passports, 50 Cornell L.Q. 262 (1965); Note, The Future of American Passports as Restrictions on Travel, 60 Nw. U.L. Rev. 511 (1965); Notes, 1963 U. Ill. L.F. 709 (1963); 32 Brooklyn L. Rev. 181 (1965); 1966 Duke L.J. 244; 13 U.C.L.A.L. Rev. 470 (1966). See also United States Library of Congress, Legislative Reference Service, Passports and the Right to Travel: A Study of Administrative Control of the Citizen (1958). And see, generally, Commager, Passport Barrier: It Must Come Down, N.Y. Times, Oct. 20, 1963; Ingles, Study of Discrimination in Respect of the Right of Everyone to Leave Any Country, Including His Own, and to Return to His Country (United Nations 1963); Mayer, A Man With A Country, Harper's Magazine, March 1964, p. 88.

CHAPTER XII

The Right of Franchise

The right of franchise, basic as it is to the maintenance of all other rights of the individual in a democratic society, is considered at several places in this book. Chapter III deals with denial of the ballot to groups or candidates considered "subversive." Chapter V takes up corrupt practices legislation and similar restrictions upon the operation of the political process. And Chapter XIV treats at length the problems of discrimination in the right to vote by reason of race. This chapter considers certain other aspects of the right of franchise. The most significant issues, in constitutional terms, have been those arising in connection with reapportionment and with the rights of minority political parties.

A. Reapportionment

Problems in the reapportionment field fall into two categories. One concerns constitutional requirements as to whether voting districts must be of equal population. The second involves what is generally known as gerrymandering, that is, drawing district lines which contain equal numbers of voters, but which operate to the advantage or disadvantage of certain political, economic, social, racial, or similar groups.

1. Districts of Equal Population

In Colegrove v. Green, 328 U.S. 549, 66 S. Ct. 1198, 90 L. Ed. 1432 (1946), the Supreme Court refused to grant relief to three voters in Illinois who complained that the Congressional Districts in that state were seriously unequal in population and hence granted some citizens greater voting power than others in electing Representatives to Congress. As a result of Colegrove and a series of later cases it was taken as established that the federal courts would not "enter this political thicket" of taking jurisdiction over reapportionment issues. See the second edition of this book at 232-244. But 16 years later, in Baker v. Carr, 369 U.S. 186, 82 S. Ct. 691, 7 L. Ed. 2d 663 (1962), the Court ruled that these questions did present justiciable issues. Following Baker v. Carr suits were brought in three quarters of the states challenging the apportionment of Congressional and state legislative districts. A series of these cases soon reached the Supreme Court. In 1964 the Court ruled upon six cases which established the major guidelines in the field. The leading decision, Reynolds v. Sims, is set forth below. The opinion of the Court also summarizes the developments from Baker v. Carr up to that point.

REYNOLDS v. SIMS
377 U.S. 533, 84 S. Ct. 1362, 12 L. Ed. 2d 506 (1964)

MR. CHIEF JUSTICE WARREN delivered the opinion of the Court.

Involved in these cases are an appeal and two cross-appeals from a decision of the Federal District Court for the Middle District of Alabama holding invalid, under the Equal Protection Clause of the Federal Constitution, the existing and two legislatively proposed plans for the apportionment of seats in the two houses of the Alabama Legislature, and ordering into effect a temporary reapportionment plan comprised of parts of the proposed but judicially disapproved measures.

I

. . .

On July 12, 1962, an extraordinary session of the Alabama Legislature adopted two reapportionment plans to take effect for the 1966 elections. One was a proposed constitutional amendment, referred to as the "67-Senator Amendment." It provided for a House of Representatives consisting of 106 members, apportioned by giving one seat to each of Alabama's 67 counties and distributing the others according to population by the "equal proportions" method. Using this formula, the constitutional amendment specified the number of representatives allotted to each county until a new apportionment could be made on the basis of the 1970 census. The Senate was to be composed of 67 members, one from each county. The legislation provided that the proposed amendment should be submitted to the voters for ratification at the November 1962 general election.

The other reapportionment plan was embodied in a statutory measure adopted by the legislature and signed into law by the Alabama Governor, and was referred to as the "Crawford-Webb Act." It was enacted as standby legislation to take effect in 1966 if the proposed constitutional amendment should fail of passage by a majority of the State's voters, or should the federal courts refuse to accept the proposed amendment (though not rejected by the voters) as effective action in compliance with the requirements of the Fourteenth Amendment. The act provided for a Senate consisting of 35 members, representing 35 senatorial districts established along county lines, and altered only a few of the former districts. In apportioning the 106 seats in the Alabama House of Representatives, the statutory measure gave each county one seat, and apportioned the remaining 39 on a rough population basis, under a formula requiring increasingly more population for a county to be accorded additional seats. The Crawford-Webb Act also provided that it would be effective "until the legislature is reapportioned according to law," but provided no standards for such a reapportionment. Future apportionments would presumably be based on the existing provisions of the Alabama Constitution which the statute, unlike the proposed constitutional amendment, would not affect.

The evidence adduced at trial before the three-judge panel consisted primarily of figures showing the population of each Alabama county and senatorial district according to the 1960 census, and the number of representatives allocated to each county under each of the three plans at issue in the litigation — the existing apportionment (under the 1901 constitutional provisions and the current statutory measures substantially reenacting the same plan), the proposed 67-Senator constitutional amendment, and the Crawford-Webb Act. Under all three plans, each senatorial district would be represented by only one senator.

On July 21, 1962, the District Court held that the inequality of the existing representation in the Alabama Legislature violated the Equal Protection Clause of the Fourteenth Amendment, a finding which the Court noted had been "generally conceded" by the parties to the litigation, since population growth and shifts had converted the 1901 scheme, as perpetuated some 60 years later, into an invidiously discriminatory plan completely lacking in rationality. 208 F. Supp. 431. Under the existing provisions, applying 1960 census figures, only 25.1% of the State's total population resided in districts represented by a majority of the members of the Senate, and only 25.7% lived in counties which could elect a majority of the members of the House of Representatives. Population-variance ratios of up to about 41-to-1 existed in the Senate, and up to about 16-to-1 in the House. Bullock County, with a population of only 13,462, and Henry County, with a population of only 15,286, each were allocated two seats in the Alabama House, whereas Mobile County, with a population of 314,301, was given only three seats, and Jefferson County, with 634,864 people, had only seven representatives. With respect to senatorial apportionment, since the pertinent Alabama constitutional provisions had been consistently construed as prohibiting the giving of more than one Senate seat to any one county, Jefferson County, with over 600,000 people, was given only one senator, as was Lowndes County, with a 1960 population of only 15,417, and Wilcox County, with only 18,739 people.

The Court then considered both the proposed constitutional amendment and the Crawford-Webb Act to ascertain whether the legislature had taken effective action to remedy the unconstitutional aspects of the existing apportionment. In initially summarizing the result which it had reached, the Court stated:

"This Court has reached the conclusion that neither the '67-Senator Amendment,' nor the 'Crawford-Webb Act' meets the necessary constitutional requirements. We find that each of the legislative acts, when considered as a whole, is so obviously discriminatory, arbitrary and irrational that it becomes unnecessary to pursue a detailed development of each of the relevant factors of the [federal constitutional] test."

The Court stated that the apportionment of one senator to each county, under the proposed constitutional amendment, would "make the discrimination in the Senate even more invidious than at present." Under the 67-Senator Amendment, as pointed out by the court below, "[t]he present control of the Senate by members representing 25.1% of the people of Alabama would be reduced to control by members representing 19.4% of the people of the State," the 34 smallest counties, with a total population of less than that of Jefferson County, would have a majority of the senatorial seats, and senators elected by only about 14% of the State's population could prevent the submission to the electorate of any future proposals to amend the State Constitution (since a vote of two-fifths of the members of one house can defeat a proposal to amend the Alabama Constitution). . . . The Court concluded, however, that the apportionment of seats in the Alabama House, under the proposed constitutional amendment, was "based upon reason, with a rational regard for known and accepted standards of apportionment." Under the proposed apportionment of representatives, each of the 67 counties was given one seat and the remaining 39 were allocated on a population basis. About 43% of the State's total population would live in counties which could elect a majority in that body. And, under the provisions of the 67-Senator Amendment, while the maximum population-variance ratio was increased to about 59-to-1 in the Senate, it was significantly reduced to about 4.7-to-1 in the House of Representatives. Jefferson County was given 17 House seats, an addition of 10, and Mobile County was allotted eight, an increase of five. The increased representation of the urban counties was achieved primarily by limiting the State's 55 least populous counties to one House seat each, and the net effect was to take 19 seats away from rural counties and allocate them to the more populous counties. Even so, serious disparities from a population-based standard remained. Montgomery County, with 169,210 people, was given only four seats, while Coosa County, with a population of only 10,726, and Cleburne County, with only 10,911, were each allocated one representative.

Turning next to the provisions of the Crawford-Webb Act, the District Court found that its apportionment of the 106 seats in the Alabama House of Representatives, by allocating one seat to each county and distributing the remaining 39 to the more populous counties in diminishing ratio to their populations, was "totally unacceptable." Under this plan, about 37% of the State's total population would reside in counties electing a majority of the members of the Alabama House, with a maximum population-variance ratio of about 5-to-1. Each representative from Jefferson and Mobile Counties would represent over 52,000 persons while representatives from eight rural counties would each represent less than 20,000 people. The Court regarded the senatorial apportionment provided in the Crawford-Webb Act as "a step in the right direction, but an extremely short step," and but a "slight improvement over the present system of representation." The net effect of combining a few of the less populous counties into two-county districts and splitting up several of the larger districts into smaller ones would be merely to increase the minority which would be represented by a majority of the members of the Senate from 25.1% to only 27.6% of the State's population. The Court pointed out that, under the Crawford-Webb Act, the vote of a person in the senatorial district consisting of Bibb and Perry Counties would be worth 20 times that of a citizen in Jefferson County, and that the vote of a citizen in the six smallest districts would be worth 15 or more times that of a Jefferson County voter. The Court concluded that the Crawford-Webb Act was "totally unacceptable" as a "piece of permanent legislation" which, under the Alabama Constitution, would have remained in effect without alteration at least until after the next decennial census. . . .

The District Court then directed its concern to the providing of an effective remedy. It indicated that it was adopting and ordering into effect for the November 1962 election a provisional and temporary reapportionment plan composed of the provisions relating to the House of Representatives contained in the 67-Senator Amendment and the provisions of the Crawford-Webb Act relating to the Senate. The Court noted, however, that "[t]he proposed reapportionment of the Senate in the 'Crawford-Webb Act,' unacceptable as a piece of permanent legislation, may not even break the strangle hold." Stating that it was retaining jurisdiction and deferring any hearing on plaintiffs' motion for a permanent injunction "until the Legislature, as provisionally reapportioned . . . , has an opportunity to provide for a true reapportionment of both Houses of the Alabama Legislature," the Court emphasized that its "moderate" action was designed to break the strangle hold by the smaller counties on the Alabama Legislature and would not suffice as a permanent reapportionment. On July 25, 1962, the Court entered its decree in accordance with its previously stated determinations, concluding that "plaintiffs . . . are denied . . . equal protection . . . by virtue of the debasement of their votes since the Legislature of the State of Alabama has failed and continues to fail to reapportion itself as required by law." It enjoined the defendant state officials from holding any future elections under any of the apportionment plans that it had found invalid, and stated that the 1962 election of Alabama legislators could validly be conducted only under the apportionment scheme specified in the Court's order. . . .

No effective political remedy to obtain relief against the alleged malapportionment of the Alabama Legislature appears to have been available. No initiative procedure exists under Alabama law. Amendment of the State Constitution can be achieved only after a proposal is adopted by three-fifths of the members of both houses of the legislature and is approved by a majority of the people, or as a result of a constitutional convention convened after approval by the people of a convention call initiated by a majority of both houses of the Alabama Legislature. . . .

II

Undeniably the Constitution of the United States protects the right of all qualified citizens to vote, in state as well as in federal elections. A consistent line of decisions by this Court in cases involving attempts to deny or restrict the right of suffrage has made this indelibly clear. . . . The right to vote freely for the candidate of one's choice is of the essence of a democratic society, and any restrictions on that right strike at the heart of representative government. And the right of suffrage can be denied by a debasement or dilution of the weight of a citizen's vote just as effectively as by wholly prohibiting the free exercise of the franchise.

In Baker v. Carr, 369 U.S. 186, we held that a claim asserted under the Equal Protection Clause challenging the constitutionality of a State's apportionment of seats in its legislature, on the ground that the right to vote of certain citizens was effectively impaired since debased and diluted, in effect presented a justiciable controversy subject to adjudication by federal courts. The spate of similar cases filed and decided by lower courts since our decision in Baker amply shows that the problem of state legislative malapportionment is one that is perceived to exist in a large number of the States. In Baker, a suit involving an attack on the apportionment of seats in the Tennessee Legislature, we remanded to the District Court, which had dismissed the action, for consideration on the merits. We intimated no view as to the proper constitutional standards for evaluating the validity of a state legislative apportionment scheme. Nor did we give any consideration to the question of appropriate remedies. Rather, we simply stated:

"Beyond noting that we have no cause at this stage to doubt the District Court will be able to fashion relief if violations of constitutional rights are found, it is improper now to consider what remedy would be most appropriate if appellants prevail at the trial." [369 U.S. at 198].

We indicated in Baker, however, that the Equal Protection Clause provides discoverable and manageable standards for use by lower courts in determining the constitutionality of a state legislative apportionment scheme, and we stated:

"Nor need the appellants, in order to succeed in this action, ask the Court to enter upon policy determinations for which judicially manageable standards are lacking. Judicial standards under the Equal Protection Clause are well developed and familiar, and it has been open to courts since the enactment of the Fourteenth Amendment to determine, if on the particular facts they must, that a discrimination reflects *no* policy, but simply arbitrary and capricious action." [369 U.S. at 226].

Subsequent to Baker, we remanded several cases to the courts below for reconsideration in light of that decision.

In Gray v. Sanders, 372 U.S. 368, we held that the Georgia county unit system, applicable in statewide primary elections, was unconstitutional since it resulted in a dilution of the weight of the votes of certain Georgia voters merely because of where they resided. After indicating that the Fifteenth and Nineteenth Amendments prohibit a State from overweighting or diluting votes on the basis of race or sex, we stated:

"How then can one person be given twice or ten times the voting power of another person in a statewide election merely because he lives in a rural area or because he lives in the smallest rural county? Once the geographical unit for which a representative is to be chosen is designated, all who participate in the election are to have an equal vote — whatever their race, whatever their sex, whatever their occupation, whatever their income, and wherever their home may be in that geographical unit. This is required by the Equal Protection Clause of the Fourteenth Amendment. The concept of 'we the people' under the Constitution visualizes no preferred class of voters but equality among those who meet the basic qualifications. The idea that every voter is equal to every other voter in his State, when he casts his ballot in favor of one of several competing candidates, underlies many of our decisions." [372 U.S. at 379-380].

Continuing, we stated that "there is no indication in the Constitution that homesite or occupation affords a permissible basis for distinguishing between qualified voters within the State." And, finally, we concluded: "The conception of political equality from the Declaration of Independence, to Lincoln's Gettysburg Address, to the Fifteenth, Seventeenth, and Nineteenth Amendments can mean only one thing — one person, one vote." [372 U.S. at 381].

. . . Of course, in these cases we are faced with the problem not presented in Gray — that of determining the basic standards and stating the applicable guidelines for implementing our decision in Baker v. Carr.

In Wesberry v. Sanders, 376 U.S. 1, decided earlier this Term, we held that attacks on the constitutionality of congressional districting plans enacted by state legislatures do not present nonjusticiable questions and should not be dismissed generally for "want of equity." We determined that the constitutional test for the validity of congressional districting schemes was one of substantial equality of population among the various districts established by a state legislature for the election of members of the Federal House of Representatives.

In that case we decided that an apportionment of congressional seats which "contracts the value of some votes and expands that of others" is unconstitutional, since "the Federal Constitution intends that when qualified voters elect members of Congress each vote be given as much weight as any other vote . . . ." We concluded that the constitutional prescription for election of members of the House of Representatives "by the People," construed in its historical context, "means that as nearly as is practicable one man's vote in a congressional election is to be worth as much as another's." We further stated:

"It would defeat the principle solemnly embodied in the Great Compromise — equal representation in the House for equal numbers of people — for us to hold that, within the States, legislatures may draw the lines of congressional districts in such a way as to give some voters a greater voice in choosing a Congressman than others." [376 U.S. at 14].

We found further, in Wesberry, that "our Constitution's plain objective" was that "of making equal representation for equal numbers of people the fundamental goal . . . ." We concluded by stating:

"No right is more precious in a free country than that of having a voice in the election of those who make the laws under which, as good citizens, we must live. Other rights, even the most basic, are illusory if the right to vote is undermined. Our Constitution leaves no room for classification of people in a way that unnecessarily abridges this right." [376 U.S. at 17-18].

Gray and Wesberry are of course not dispositive of or directly controlling on our decision in these cases involving state legislative apportionment controversies. Admittedly, those decisions, in which we held that, in statewide and in congressional elections, one person's vote must be counted equally with those of all other voters in a State, were based on different constitutional considerations and were addressed to rather distinct problems. But neither are they wholly inapposite. Gray, though not determinative here since involving the weighting of votes in statewide elections, established the basic principle of equality among voters within a State, and held that voters cannot be classified, constitutionally, on the basis of where they live, at least with respect to voting in statewide elections. And our decision in Wesberry was of course grounded on that language of the Constitution which prescribes that members of the Federal House of Representatives are to be chosen "by the People," while attacks on state legislative apportionment schemes, such as that involved in the instant cases, are principally based on the Equal Protection Clause of the Fourteenth Amendment. Nevertheless, Wesberry clearly established that the fundamental principle of representative government in this country is one of equal representation for equal numbers of people, without regard to race, sex, economic status, or place of residence within a State. Our problem, then, is to ascertain, in the instant cases, whether there are any constitutionally cognizable principles which would justify departures from the basic standard of equality among voters in the apportionment of seats in state legislatures.

III

A predominant consideration in determining whether a State's legislative apportionment scheme constitutes an invidious discrimination violative of rights asserted under the Equal Protection Clause is that the rights allegedly impaired are individual and personal in nature. . . .

Legislators represent people, not trees or acres. Legislators are elected by voters, not farms or cities or economic interests. As long as ours is a representative form of government, and our legislatures are those instruments of government elected directly by and directly representative of the people, the right to elect legislators in a free and unimpaired fashion is a bedrock of our political system. It could hardly be gainsaid that a constitutional claim had been asserted by an allegation that certain otherwise qualified voters had been entirely prohibited from voting for members of their state legislature. And, if a State should provide that the votes of citizens in one part of the State should be given two times, or five times, or 10 times the weight of votes of citizens in another part of the State, it could hardly be contended that the right to vote of those residing in the disfavored areas had not been effectively diluted. It would appear extraordinary to suggest that a State could be constitutionally permitted to enact a law providing that certain of the State's voters could vote two, five, or 10 times for their legislative representatives, while voters living elsewhere could vote only once. And it is inconceivable that a state law to the effect that, in counting votes for legislators, the votes of citizens in one part of the State would be multiplied by two, five, or 10, while the votes of persons in another area would be counted only at face value, could be constitutionally sustainable. Of course, the effect of state legislative districting schemes which give the same number of representatives to unequal numbers of constituents is identical. Overweighting and overvaluation of the votes of those living here has the certain effect of dilution and undervaluation of the votes of those living there. The resulting discrimination against those individual voters living in disfavored areas is easily demonstrable mathematically. Their right to vote is simply not the same right to vote as that of those living in a favored part of the State. Two, five, or 10 of them must vote before the effect of their voting is equivalent to that of their favored neighbor. Weighting the votes of citizens differently, by any method or means, merely because of where they happen to reside, hardly seems justifiable. . . .

Logically, in a society ostensibly grounded on representative government, it would seem reasonable that a majority of the people of a State could elect a majority of that State's legislators. To conclude differently, and to sanction minority control of state legislative bodies, would appear to deny majority rights in a way that far surpasses any possible denial of minority rights that might otherwise be thought to result. Since legislatures are responsible for enacting laws by which all citizens are to be governed, they should be bodies which are collectively responsive to the popular will. And the concept of equal protection has been traditionally viewed as requiring the uniform treatment of persons standing in the same relation to the governmental action questioned or challenged. With respect to the allocation of legislative representation, all voters, as citizens of a State, stand in the same relation regardless of where they live. Any suggested criteria for the differentiation of citizens are insufficient to justify any discrimination, as to the weight of their votes, unless relevant to the permissible purposes of legislative apportionment. Since the achieving of fair and effective representation for all citizens is concededly the basic aim of legislative apportionment, we conclude that the Equal Protection Clause guarantees the opportunity for equal participation by all voters in the election of state legislators. Diluting the weight of votes because of place of residence impairs basic constitutional rights under the Fourteenth Amendment just as much as invidious discriminations based upon factors such as race, Brown v. Board of Education, 347 U.S. 483, or economic status, Griffin v. Illinois, 351 U.S. 12, Douglas v. California, 372 U.S. 353. Our constitutional system amply provides for the protection of minorities by means other than giving them majority control of state legislatures. And the democratic ideals of equality and majority rule, which have served this Nation so well in the past, are hardly of any less significance for the present and the future.

We are told that the matter of apportioning representation in a state legislature is a complex and many-faceted one. We are advised that States can rationally consider factors other than population in apportioning legislative representation. We are admonished not to restrict the power of the States to impose differing views as to political philosophy on their citizens. We are cautioned about the dangers of entering into political thickets and mathematical quagmires. Our answer is this: a denial of constitutionally protected rights demands judicial protection; our oath and our office require no less of us. . . . To the extent that a citizen's right to vote is debased, he is that much less a citizen. The fact that an individual lives here or there is not a legitimate reason for overweighting or diluting the efficacy of his vote. The complexions of societies and civilizations change, often with amazing rapidity. A nation once primarily rural in character becomes predominantly urban.[43] Representation schemes once fair and equitable become archaic and outdated. But the basic principle of representative government remains, and must remain, unchanged — the weight of a citizen's vote cannot be made to depend on where he lives. Population is, of necessity, the starting point for consideration and

---

[43] Although legislative apportionment controversies are generally viewed as involving urban-rural conflicts, much evidence indicates that presently it is the fast-growing suburban areas which are probably the most seriously underrepresented in many of our state legislatures. And, while currently the thrust of state legislative malapportionment results, in most States, in underrepresentation of urban and suburban areas, in earlier times cities were in fact overrepresented in a number of States. In the early 19th century, certain of the seaboard cities in some of the Eastern and Southern States possessed and struggled to retain legislative representation disproportionate to population, and bitterly opposed according additional representation to the growing inland areas. Conceivably, in some future time, urban areas might again be in a situation of attempting to acquire or retain legislative representation in excess of that to which, on a population basis, they are entitled. Malapportionment can, and has historically, run in various directions. However and whenever it does, it is constitutionally impermissible under the Equal Protection Clause.

the controlling criterion for judgment in legislative apportionment controversies. A citizen, a qualified voter, is no more nor no less so because he lives in the city or on the farm. This is the clear and strong command of our Constitution's Equal Protection Clause. This is an essential part of the concept of a government of laws and not men. This is at the heart of Lincoln's vision of "government of the people, by the people, [and] for the people." The Equal Protection Clause demands no less than substantially equal state legislative representation for all citizens, of all places as well as of all races.

IV

We hold that, as a basic constitutional standard, the Equal Protection Clause requires that the seats in both houses of a bicameral state legislature must be apportioned on a population basis. Simply stated, an individual's right to vote for state legislators is unconstitutionally impaired when its weight is in a substantial fashion diluted when compared with votes of citizens living in other parts of the State. Since, under neither the existing apportionment provisions nor either of the proposed plans was either of the houses of the Alabama Legislature apportioned on a population basis, the District Court correctly held that all three of these schemes were constitutionally invalid. Furthermore, the existing apportionment, and also to a lesser extent the apportionment under the Crawford-Webb Act, presented little more than crazy quilts, completely lacking in rationality, and could be found invalid on that basis alone. Although the District Court presumably found the apportionment of the Alabama House of Representatives under the 67-Senator Amendment to be acceptable, we conclude that the deviations from a strict population basis are too egregious to permit us to find that that body, under this proposed plan, was apportioned sufficiently on a population basis so as to permit the arrangement to be constitutionally sustained. Although about 43% of the State's total population would be required to comprise districts which could elect a majority in that body, only 39 of the 106 House seats were actually to be distributed on a population basis, as each of Alabama's 67 counties was given at least one representative, and population-variance ratios of close to 5-to-1 would have existed. While mathematical nicety is not a constitutional requisite, one could hardly conclude that the Alabama House, under the proposed constitutional amendment, had been apportioned sufficiently on a population basis to be sustainable under the requirements of the Equal Protection Clause. And none of the other apportionments of seats in either of the bodies of the Alabama Legislature, under the three plans considered by the District Court, came nearly as close to approaching the required constitutional standard as did that of the House of Representatives under the 67-Senator Amendment. . . .

V

. . .

We do not believe that the concept of bicameralism is rendered anachronistic and meaningless when the predominant basis of representation in the two state legislative bodies is required to be the same — population. A prime reason for bicameralism, modernly considered, is to insure mature and deliberate consideration of, and to prevent precipitate action on, proposed legislative measures. Simply because the controlling criterion for apportioning representation is required to be the same in both houses does not mean that there will be no differences in the composition and complexion of the two bodies. Different constituencies can be represented in the two houses. One body could be composed of single-member districts while the other could have at least some multimember districts. The length of terms of the legislators in the separate bodies could differ. The numerical size of the two bodies could be made to differ, even significantly, and the geographical size of districts from which legislators are elected could also be made to differ. And apportionment in one house could be arranged so as to balance off minor inequities in the representation of certain areas in the other house. In summary, these and other factors could be, and are presently in many States, utilized to engender differing complexions and collective attitudes in the two bodies of a state legislature, although both are apportioned substantially on a population basis.

V I

By holding that as a federal constitutional requisite both houses of a state legislature must be apportioned on a population basis, we mean that the Equal Protection Clause requires that a State make an honest and good faith effort to construct districts, in both houses of its legislature, as nearly of equal population as is practicable. We realize that it is a practical impossibility to arrange legislative districts so that each one has an identical number of residents, or citizens, or voters. Mathematical exactness or precision is hardly a workable constitutional requirement.

In Wesberry v. Sanders, supra, the Court stated that congressional representation must be based on population as nearly as is practicable. In implementing the basic constitutional principle of representative government as enunciated by the Court in Wesberry — equality of population among districts — some distinctions may well be made between congressional and state legislative representation. Since, almost invariably, there is a significantly larger number of seats in state legislative bodies to be distributed within a State than congressional seats, it may be feasible to use political subdivision lines to a greater extent in establishing state legislative districts than in congressional districting while still affording adequate representation to all parts of the State. To do so would be constitutionally valid, so long as the resulting apportionment was one based substantially on population and the equal-population principle was not diluted in any significant way. Somewhat more flexibility may therefore be constitutionally permissible with respect to state legislative apportionment than in congressional districting. Lower courts can and assuredly will work out more concrete and specific standards for evaluating state legislative apportionment schemes in the context of actual litigation. For the present, we deem it expedient not to attempt to spell out any precise constitutional tests. What is marginally permissible in one State may be unsatisfactory in another, depending on the particular circumstances of the case. Developing a body of doctrine on a case-by-case basis appears to us to provide the most satisfactory means of arriving at detailed constitutional requirements in the area of state legislative apportionment. Cf. Slaughter-House Cases, 16 Wall. 36, 78-79. Thus, we proceed to state here only a few rather general considerations which appear to us to be relevant.

A State may legitimately desire to maintain the integrity of various political subdivisions, insofar as possible, and provide for compact districts of contiguous territory in designing a legislative apportionment scheme. Valid considerations may underlie such aims. Indiscriminate districting, without any regard for political subdivision or natural or historical boundary lines, may be little more than an open invitation to partisan gerrymandering. Single-member districts may be the rule in one State, while another State might desire to achieve some flexibility by creating multimember or floterial districts. Whatever the means of accomplishment, the overriding objective must be substantial equality of population among the various districts, so that the vote of any citizen is approximately equal in weight to that of any other citizen in the State.

History indicates, however, that many States have deviated, to a greater or lesser degree, from the equal-population principle in the apportionment of seats in at least one house of their legislatures. So long as the divergences from a strict population standard are based on legitimate considerations incident to the effectuation of a rational state policy, some deviations from the equal-population principle are constitutionally permissible with respect to the apportionment of seats in either or both of the two houses of a bicameral state legislature. But neither history alone, nor economic or other sorts of group interests, are permissible factors in attempting to justify disparities from population-based representation. Citizens, not history or economic interests, cast votes. Considerations of area alone provide an insufficient justification for deviations from the equal-population principle. Again, people, not land or trees or pastures, vote. Modern developments and improvements in transportation and communications make rather hollow, in the mid 1960's, most claims that deviations from population-based representation can validly be based solely on geographical considerations. Arguments for allowing such deviations in order to insure effective representation for sparsely settled areas and to prevent legislative districts from becoming so large that the availability of access of citizens to their representatives is impaired are today, for the most part, unconvincing.

A consideration that appears to be of more substance in justifying some deviations from population-based representation in state legislatures is that of insuring some voice to political subdivisions, as political subdivisions. Several factors make more than insubstantial claims that a State can rationally consider according political subdivisions some independent representation in at least one body of the state legislature, as long as the basic standard of equality of population among districts is maintained. Local governmental entities are frequently charged with various responsibilities incident to the operation of state government. In many States much of the legislature's activity involves the enactment of so-called local legislation, directed only to the concerns of particular political subdivisions. And a State may legitimately desire to construct districts along political subdivision lines to deter the possibilities of gerrymandering. However, permitting deviations from population-based representation does not mean that each local governmental unit or political subdivision can be given separate representation, regardless of population. Carried too far, a scheme of giving at least one seat in one house to each political subdivision (for example, to each county) could easily result, in many States, in a total subversion of the equal-population principle in that legislative body. This would be especially true in a State where the number of counties is large and many of them are sparsely populated, and the number of seats in the legislative body being apportioned does not significantly exceed the number of counties. Such a result, we conclude, would be constitutionally impermissible. And careful judicial scrutiny must of course be given, in evaluating state apportionment schemes, to the character as well as the degree of deviations from a strict population basis. But if, even as a result of a clearly rational state policy of according some legislative representation to political subdivisions, population is submerged as the controlling consideration in the apportionment of seats in the particular legislative body, then the right of all of the State's citizens to cast an effective and adequately weighted vote would be unconstitutionally impaired. . . .

VIII

That the Equal Protection Clause requires that both houses of a state legislature be apportioned on a population basis does not mean that States cannot adopt some reasonable plan for periodic revision of their apportionment schemes. Decennial reapportionment appears to be a rational approach to readjustment of legislative representation in order to take into account population shifts and growth. Reallocation of legislative seats every 10 years coincides with the prescribed practice in 41 of the States, often honored more in the breach than the observance, however. Illustratively, the Alabama Constitution requires decennial reapportionment, yet the last reapportionment of the Alabama Legislature, when this suit was brought, was in 1901. Limitations on the frequency of reapportionment are justified by the need for stability and continuity in the organization of the legislative system, although undoubtedly reapportioning no more frequently than every 10 years leads to some imbalance in the population of districts toward the end of the decennial period and also to the development of resistance to change on the part of some incumbent legislators. In substance, we do not regard the Equal Protection Clause as requiring daily, monthly, annual or biennial reapportionment, so long as a State has a reasonably conceived plan for periodic readjustment of legislative representation. While we do not intend to indicate that decennial reapportionment is a constitutional requisite, compliance with such an approach would clearly meet the minimal requirements for maintaining a reasonably current scheme of legislative representation. And we do not mean to intimate that more frequent reapportionment would not be constitutionally permissible or practicably desirable. But if reapportionment were accomplished with less frequency, it would assuredly be constitutionally suspect. . . .

X

We do not consider here the difficult question of the proper remedial devices which federal courts should utilize in state legislative apportionment cases. Remedial techniques in this new and developing area of the law will probably often differ with the circumstances of the challenged apportionment and a variety of local conditions. It is enough to say now that, once a State's legislative apportionment scheme has been found to be unconstitutional, it would be the unusual case in which a court would be justified in not taking appropriate action to insure that no further elections are conducted under the invalid plan. However, under certain circumstances, such as where an impending election is imminent and a State's election machinery is already in progress, equitable considerations might justify a court in withholding the granting of immediately effective relief in a legislative apportionment case, even though the existing apportionment scheme was found invalid. In awarding or withholding immediate relief, a court is entitled to and should consider the proximity of a forthcoming election and the mechanics and complexities of state election laws, and should act and rely upon general equitable principles. With respect to the timing of relief, a court can reasonably endeavor to avoid a disruption of the election process which might result from requiring precipitate changes that could make unreasonable or embarrassing demands on a State in adjusting to the requirements of the court's decree. As stated by Mr. Justice Douglas, concurring in Baker v. Carr, "any relief accorded can be fashioned in the light of well-known principles of equity."

We feel that the District Court in this case acted in a most proper and commendable manner. It initially acted wisely in declining to stay the impending primary election in Alabama, and properly refrained from acting further until the Alabama Legislature had been given an opportunity to remedy the admitted discrepancies in the State's legislative apportionment scheme, while initially stating some of its views to provide guidelines for legislative action. And it correctly recognized that legislative reapportionment is primarily a matter for legislative consideration and determination, and that judicial relief becomes appropriate only when a legislature fails to reapportion according to federal constitutional requisites in a timely fashion after having had an adequate opportunity to do so. Additionally, the court below acted with proper judicial restraint, after the Alabama Legislature had failed to act effectively in remedying the constitutional deficiencies in the State's legislative apportionment scheme, in ordering its own temporary reapportionment plan into effect, at a time sufficiently early to permit the holding of elections pursuant to that plan without great difficulty, and in prescribing a plan admittedly provisional in purpose so as not to usurp the primary responsibility for reapportionment which rests with the legislature.

We find, therefore, that the action taken by the District Court in this case, in ordering into effect a reapportionment of both houses of the Alabama Legislature for purposes of the 1962 primary and general elections, by using the best parts of the two proposed plans which it had found, as a whole, to be invalid, was an appropriate and well-considered exercise of judicial power. Admittedly, the lower court's ordered plan was intended only as a temporary and provisional measure and the District Court correctly indicated that the plan was invalid as a permanent apportionment. In retaining jurisdiction while deferring a hearing on the issuance of a final injunction in order to give the provisionally reapportioned legislature an opportunity to act effectively, the court below proceeded in a proper fashion. Since the District Court evinced its realization that its ordered reapportionment could not be sustained as the basis for conducting the 1966 election of Alabama legislators, and avowedly intends to take some further action should the reapportioned Alabama Legislature fail to enact a constitutionally valid, permanent apportionment scheme in the interim, we affirm the judgment below and remand the cases for further proceedings consistent with the views stated in this opinion.

It is so ordered.

MR. JUSTICE CLARK, concurring in the affirmance.

The Court goes much beyond the necessities of this case in laying down a new "equal population" principle for state legislative apportionment. This principle seems to be an offshoot of Gray v. Sanders, 372 U.S. 368, 381 (1963), i.e., "one person, one vote," modified by the "nearly as is practicable" admonition of Wesberry v. Sanders, 376 U.S. 1, 8 (1964). Whether "nearly as is practicable" means "one person, one vote" qualified by "approximately equal" or "some deviations" or by the impossibility of "mathematical nicety" is not clear from the majority's use of these vague and meaningless phrases. But whatever the standard, the Court applies it to each house of the State Legislature.

It seems to me that all that the Court need say in this case is that each plan considered by the trial court is "a crazy quilt," clearly revealing invidious discrimination in each house of the Legislature and therefore violative of the Equal Protection Clause. See my concurring opinion in Baker v. Carr, 369 U.S. 186, 253-258 (1962).

I, therefore, do not reach the question of the so-called "federal analogy." But in my view, if one house of the State Legislature meets the population standard, representation in the other house might include some departure from it so as to take into account, on a rational basis, other factors in order to afford some representation to the various elements of the State. See my dissenting opinion in Lucas v. Forty-Fourth General Assembly of Colorado, . . . decided this date.

MR. JUSTICE STEWART.

All of the parties have agreed with the District Court's finding that legislative inaction for some 60 years in the face of growth and shifts in population has converted Alabama's legislative apportionment plan enacted in 1901 into one completely lacking in rationality. Accordingly, for the reasons stated in my dissenting opinion in Lucas v. Forty-Fourth General Assembly of Colorado, . . . I would affirm the judgment of the District Court holding that this apportionment violated the Equal Protection Clause. . . .

MR. JUSTICE HARLAN, dissenting.

In these cases the Court holds that seats in the legislatures of six States are apportioned in ways that violate the Federal Constitution. Under the Court's ruling it is bound to follow that the legislatures in all but a few of the other 44 States will meet the same fate. These decisions, with Wesberry v. Sanders, 376 U.S. 1, involving congressional districting by the States, and Gray v. Sanders, 372 U.S. 368, relating to elections for statewide office, have the effect of placing basic aspects of state political systems under the pervasive overlordship of the federal judiciary. Once again, I must register my protest. . . .

The Court's elaboration of its new "constitutional" doctrine indicates how far — and how unwisely — it has strayed from the appropriate bounds of its authority. The consequence of today's decision is that in all but the handful of States which may already satisfy the new requirements the local District Court or, it may be, the state courts, are given blanket authority and the constitutional duty to supervise apportionment of the State Legislatures. It is difficult to imagine a more intolerable and inappropriate interference by the judiciary with the independent legislatures of the States. . . .

With these cases the Court approaches the end of the third round set in motion by the complaint filed in Baker v. Carr. What is done today deepens my conviction that judicial entry into this realm is profoundly ill-advised and constitutionally impermissible. As I have said before, Wesberry v. Sanders, supra, at 48, I believe that the vitality of our political system, on which in the last analysis all else depends, is weakened by reliance on the judiciary for political reform; in time a complacent body politic may result.

These decisions also cut deeply into the fabric of our federalism. What must follow from them may eventually appear to be the product of state legislatures. Nevertheless, no thinking person can fail to recognize that the aftermath of these cases, however desirable it may be thought in itself, will have been achieved at the cost of a radical alteration in the relationship between the States and the Federal Government, more particularly the Federal Judiciary. Only one who has an overbearing impatience with the federal system and its political processes will believe that that cost was not too high or was inevitable.

Finally, these decisions give support to a current mistaken view of the Constitution and the constitutional function of this Court. This view, in a nutshell, is that every major social ill in this country can find its cure in some constitutional "principle," and that this Court should "take the lead" in promoting reform when other branches of government fail to act. The Constitution is not a panacea for every blot upon the public welfare, nor should this Court, ordained as a judicial body, be thought of as a general haven for reform movements. The Constitution is an instrument of government, fundamental to which is the premise that in a diffusion of governmental authority lies the greatest promise that this Nation will realize liberty for all its citizens. This Court, limited in function in accordance with that premise, does not serve its high purpose when it exceeds its authority, even to satisfy justified impatience with the slow workings of the political process. For when, in the name of constitutional interpretation, the Court *adds* something to the Constitution that was deliberately excluded from it, the Court in reality substitutes its view of what should be so for the amending process. . . .

NOTES

1. Another of the six cases decided the same day, Lucas v. Forty-Fourth General Assembly of Colorado, 377 U.S. 713, 84 S. Ct. 1472, 12 L. Ed. 2d 632 (1964), involved reapportionment in Colorado. At an election in November, 1962, Amendment No. 7 to the Colorado Constitution was adopted by a vote of 305,700 to 172,725. That Amendment provided for the apportionment of the House of Representatives of the state legislature on the basis of districts of equal population, but provided an apportionment for the Senate based upon a combination of population and other factors. At the same time the electorate defeated Amendment No. 8, by a vote of 311,749 to 149,822, that would have prescribed an apportionment plan under which seats in both houses would be apportioned on an equal population basis. Pursuant to Amendment No. 7 the Colorado legislature in 1963 enacted a statute establishing the House and Senate districts. Under the apportionment of

the House seats, districts in which about 45.1 per cent of the total population resided were represented by a majority of the members of the House. The maximum population-variance, between the most populous and the least populous district, was approximately 1.7 to 1. Under the Senate plan, counties containing 33.2 per cent of the total population elected a majority. And the maximum population-variance ratio between the largest and smallest district was 3.6 to 1. The Court held the apportionment invalid. It found it unnecessary to pass on the validity of the House apportionment, as it held that the Senate apportionment "clearly involves departures from population-based representation too extreme to be constitutionally permissible." With respect to the fact that the basic plan had been adopted by a majority of the Colorado electorate the Court said:

"As appellees have correctly pointed out, a majority of the voters in every county of the State voted in favor of the apportionment scheme embodied in Amendment No. 7's provisions, in preference to that contained in proposed Amendment No. 8, which, subject to minor deviations, would have based the apportionment of seats in both houses on a population basis. However, the choice presented to the Colorado electorate, in voting on these two proposed constitutional amendments, was hardly as clear-cut as the court below regarded it. One of the most undesirable features of the existing apportionment scheme was the requirement that, in counties given more than one seat in either or both of the houses of the General Assembly, all legislators must be elected at large from the county as a whole. Thus, under the existing plan, each Denver voter was required to vote for eight senators and 17 representatives. Ballots were long and cumbersome, and an intelligent choice among candidates for seats in the legislature was made quite difficult. No identifiable constituencies *within* the populous counties resulted, and the residents of those areas had no single member of the Senate or House elected specifically to represent them. Rather, each legislator elected from a multimember county represented the county as a whole. Amendment No. 8, as distinguished from Amendment No. 7, while purportedly basing the apportionment of seats in both houses on a population basis, would have perpetuated, for all practical purposes, this debatable feature of the existing scheme. Under Amendment No. 8, senators were to be elected at large in those counties given more than one Senate seat, and no provision was made for subdistricting within such counties for the purpose of electing senators. Representatives were also to be elected at large in multimember counties pursuant to the provisions of Amendment No. 8, at least initially, although subdistricting for the purpose of electing House members was permitted if the voters of a multimember county specifically approved a representative subdistricting plan for that county. Thus, neither of the proposed plans was, in all probability, wholly acceptable to the voters in the populous counties, and the assumption of the court below that the Colorado voters made a definitive choice between two contrasting alternatives and indicated that 'minority process in the Senate is what they want' does not appear to be factually justifiable. . . .

"Except as an interim remedial procedure justifying a court in staying its hand temporarily, we find no significance in the fact that a nonjudicial, political remedy may be available for the effectuation of asserted rights to equal representation in a state legislature. Courts sit to adjudicate controversies involving alleged denials of constitutional rights. While a court sitting as a court of equity might be justified in temporarily refraining from the issuance of injunctive relief in an apportionment case in order to allow for resort to an available political remedy, such as initiative and referendum, individual constitutional rights cannot be deprived, or denied judicial effectuation, because of the existence of a nonjudicial remedy through which relief against the alleged malapportionment, which the individual voters seek, might be achieved. An individual's constitutionally protected right to cast an equally weighted vote cannot be denied even by a vote of a majority of a State's electorate, if the apportionment scheme adopted by the voters fails to measure up to the requirements of the Equal Protection Clause. Manifestly, the fact that an apportionment plan is adopted in a popular referendum is insufficient to sustain its constitutionality or to induce a court of equity to refuse to act. As stated by this Court in West Virginia State Bd. of Educ. v. Barnette, 319 U.S. 624, 638, 'One's right to life, liberty, and property . . . and other fundamental rights may not be submitted to vote; they depend on the outcome of no elections.' A citizen's constitutional rights can hardly be infringed simply because a majority of the people choose that it be. We hold that the fact that a challenged legislative apportionment plan was approved by the electorate is without federal constitutional significance, if the scheme adopted fails to satisfy the basic requirements of the Equal Protection Clause, as delineated in our opinion in Reynolds v. Sims. And we conclude that the fact that a practicably available political remedy, such as initiative and referendum, exists under state law provides justification only for a court of equity to stay its hand temporarily while recourse to such a remedial device is attempted or while proposed initiated measures relating to legislative apportionment are pending and will be submitted to the State's voters at the next election." 377 U.S. at 731-732, 736-737.

Justices Harlan, Clark, and Stewart dissented.

2. In the other four cases the Court also held invalid the state legislative districting plans:

WMCA, Inc. v. Lomenzo, 377 U.S. 633, 84 S. Ct. 1418, 12 L. Ed. 2d 568 (1964): Under the New York apportionment plan, in the Assembly members representing 37.1 per cent of the State's citizens constituted a majority, and the population-variance ratio of largest to smallest was 11.9 to 1. In the Senate the figures were 40.9 per cent and 2.4 to 1.

Maryland Committee for Fair Representation v. Tawes, 377 U.S. 656, 84 S. Ct. 1442, 12 L. Ed. 2d 595 (1964): Only the apportionment plan of the Maryland Senate was under attack. The 15 least populous counties, with only 14.1 per cent of the population, could elect a majority in the Senate; the five most populous counties, with 75.3 per cent of the population, could elect only 10 out of 29 Senators; the maximum population-variance ratio was about 32 to 1.

David v. Mann, 377 U.S. 678, 84 S. Ct. 1453, 12 L. Ed. 2d 609 (1964): In the Virginia House, about 40.5 per cent of the population could elect a majority, and the maximum population-variance ratio was 4.36 to 1. In the Senate the figures were 44.1 per cent and 2.65 to 1.

Roman v. Sincock, 377 U.S. 695, 84 S. Ct. 1462, 12 L. Ed. 2d 620 (1964): In Delaware, 18.5 per cent of the population could elect a majority in the House, and the maximum population-variance was 35 to 1. In the Senate the figures were 22 per cent and 15 to 1.

Later, in a series of per curiam opinions the Court, citing Reynolds v. Sims, affirmed lower court decisions holding apportionment plans invalid in Iowa,

Washington, Connecticut, and Oklahoma; and reversed lower court rulings that had upheld plans in Illinois, Idaho, Michigan, Ohio, and Florida. Hill v. Davis, 378 U.S. 565, 84 S. Ct. 1918, 12 L. Ed. 2d 1037 (1964) (Iowa); Meyers v. Thigpen, 378 U.S. 554, 84 S. Ct. 1905, 12 L. Ed. 2d 1024 (1964) (Washington); Pinney v. Butterworth, 378 U.S. 564, 84 S. Ct. 1918, 12 L. Ed. 2d 1037 (1964) (Connecticut); Williams v. Moss, 378 U.S. 558, 84 S. Ct. 1907, 12 L. Ed. 2d 1026 (1964) (Oklahoma). It reversed the lower courts' actions that had upheld legislative apportionment in Germano v. Kerner, 378 U.S. 560, 84 S. Ct. 1908, 12 L. Ed. 2d 1034 (1964) (Illinois); Hearne v. Smylie, 378 U.S. 563, 84 S. Ct. 1917, 12 L. Ed. 2d 1036 (1964) (Idaho); Marshall v. Hare, 378 U.S. 561, 84 S. Ct. 1912, 12 L. Ed. 2d 1036 (1964) (Michigan); Nolan v. Rhodes, 378 U.S. 556, 84 S. Ct. 1906, 12 L. Ed. 2d 1034 (1964) (Ohio); Swann v. Adams, 378 U.S. 553, 84 S. Ct. 1904, 12 L. Ed. 2d 1033 (1964) (Florida).

3. Fortson v. Dorsey, 379 U.S. 433, 85 S. Ct. 498, 13 L. Ed. 2d 401 (1965), decided the following term, raised the question of multiple-member districts. Under the Georgia plan for districting of its Senate, the state was divided into districts of substantially equal population. Out of 54 seats, 33 members were elected from districts composed of one to eight counties. The other 21 districts were allocated to the seven most populous counties, each county having two to seven. But the voters in those counties, instead of electing on a district basis, elected all members at large. The Court upheld the apportionment, saying: "It is not accurate to treat a senator from a multi-district county as the representative of only that district within the county wherein he resides. The statute uses districts in multi-district counties merely as the basis of residence for candidates, not for voting or representation. Each district's senator must be a resident of that district, but since his tenure depends upon the county-wide electorate he must be vigilant to serve the interests of all the people in the county, and not merely those of people in his home district; thus in fact he is the county's and not merely the district's senator. If the weight of the vote of any voter in a Fulton County district, when he votes for seven senators to represent him in the Georgia Senate, is not the exact equivalent of that of a resident of a single-member constituency, we cannot say that his vote is not 'approximately equal in weight to that of any other citizen in the State.'" But the Court added: ". . . our opinion is not to be understood to say that in all instances or under all circumstances such a system as Georgia has will comport with the dictates of the Equal Protection Clause. It might well be that, designedly or otherwise, a multi-member constituency apportionment scheme, under the circumstances of a particular case, would operate to minimize or cancel out the voting strength of racial or political elements of the voting population. When this is demonstrated it will be time enough to consider whether the system still passes constitutional muster. This question, however, is not presented by the record before us." 379 U.S. at 438-439. Mr. Justice Harlan concurred.

Mr. Justice Douglas dissented, saying: "As appellees point out, even if a candidate for one of those districts obtained all of the votes in that district, he could still be defeated by the foreign vote, while he would of course be elected if he were running in a district in the first group. I have no idea how this weighted voting might produce prejudice race-wise, religion-wise, politics-wise. But to allow some candidates to be chosen by the electors in their districts and others to be defeated by the voters of foreign districts is in my view an 'invidious discrimination' — the test of unequal protection under the Fourteenth Amendment. Baker v. Carr, 369 U.S. 186, 244. I had assumed we had settled this question in Gray v. Sanders, 372 U.S. 368, 379, where we said: 'Once the geographical unit for which a representative is to be chosen is designated, all who participate in the election are to have an equal vote — whatever their race, whatever their sex, whatever their occupation, whatever their income, and wherever their home may be in that geographical unit. This is required by the Equal Protection Clause of the Fourteenth Amendment.' " 379 U.S. at 441-442.

Cf. Kruidenier v. McCulloch, 142 N.W.2d 355 (Iowa 1966), holding multi-member districts invalid.

4. In Burns v. Richardson, 384 U.S. 73, 86 S. Ct. 1286, 16 L. Ed. 2d 376 (1966), involving the Hawaiian legislature, the Court reiterated the holding of Fortson v. Dorsey that multiple-member districts were not invalid unless "invidious discrimination" was shown.

5. The Court has dealt with various problems of remedies and administration in Parsons v. Buckley, 379 U.S. 359, 85 S. Ct. 503, 13 L. Ed. 2d 352 (1965); Fortson v. Toombs, 379 U.S. 621, 85 S. Ct. 598, 13 L. Ed. 2d 527 (1965); Scott v. Germano, 381 U.S. 407, 85 S. Ct. 1525, 14 L. Ed. 2d 477 (1965); Travia v. Lomenzo, 381 U.S. 431, 85 S. Ct. 1582, 14 L. Ed. 2d 480 (1965).

6. The announcement of the "one-man, one-vote" standard in Reynolds v. Sims resulted in a serious effort to counter the Supreme Court decisions by legislative measures. On August 4, 1964, Senator Dirksen, Republican minority leader, introduced a bill, intended as a stop-gap measure until a constitutional amendment could be obtained, providing: "[In any federal court action] . . . in which there is placed in question the validity of the composition of either house of the legislature of . . . [a] State or the apportionment of the membership thereof, such action or proceding shall be stayed until the end of the second regular session of the legislature of that State which begins after the date of the enactment of this section." S. 3069, 88th Cong., 2d Sess. (1964). On August 19 the House passed a more drastic measure, the Tuck bill, which would deprive the lower federal courts of original jurisdiction and the Supreme Court of appellate jurisdiction over reapportionment cases. H.R. 11926, 88th Cong., 2d Sess. (1964); 110 Cong. Rec. 20300. Later the Senate passed a compromise bill declaring that the courts could "properly allow" state legislatures additional time for reapportionment, not to exceed six months, and "permit" the next election of members under the 1964 laws. 110 Cong. Rec. 22758. But the House did not accept the compromise, and no legislation resulted. For accounts of this legislative struggle and a discussion of the constitutional issues, see Dixon, Reapportionment in the Supreme Court and Congress: Constitutional Struggle for Fair Representation, 63 Mich. L. Rev. 290 (1964); McKay, Court, Congress, and Reapportionment, 63 Mich. L. Rev. 255 (1964), and Reapportionment: The Law and Politics of Equal Representation 203-208 (1965); Note, Reapportionment, 79 Harv. L. Rev. 1226, 1232-1235 (1966). On the question of limiting the federal courts' jurisdiction, see also Hart, The Power of Congress to Limit the Jurisdiction of Federal Courts: An Exercise in Dialectic, 66 Harv. L. Rev. 1362 (1953).

The following session of Congress Senator Dirksen introduced a constitutional amendment which provided: "The right and power to determine the composition of the legislature of a State and the apportionment of the membership thereof shall remain in the people of that State. Nothing in this Constitution shall prohibit the people from apportioning one house of a bicameral legislature upon the basis of factors other than population, or from giving reasonable weight to factors other than population in apportioning a unicameral legislature, if, in either case, such apportionment has been submitted to a vote of the people in accordance with law and with the provisions of this Constitution and has been approved by a majority of those voting on that issue." S.J. Res. 2, 89th Cong., 1st Sess. (1965). Later Senator Dirksen modified his proposal to substitute "population, geography, and political subdivisions" for the phrase "factors other than population"; and added a clause providing that an alternative plan based on equal population must be submitted to the voters along with any other plan. After long controversy the Dirksen plan came to a vote on August 4, 1965; it was approved 57 to 39, but fell seven voters short of the required two-thirds. 111 Cong. Rec. — N.Y. Times, Aug. 5, 1965. See McKay, supra, 211-213; Note, supra, 79 Harv. at 1235-1237. Senator Dirksen again modified his proposal and pressed it the following year. The measure reached a vote on April 20, 1966; it failed again by seven votes — 55 to 38 — to muster the two-thirds necessary. 112 Cong. Rec. —; N.Y. Times, Apr. 21, 1966.

Other opponents of the Supreme Court's reapportionment decisions, operating primarily through the states, instituted a program to obtain a constitutional amendment through the process of a constitutional convention called by Congress on the application of two-thirds of the states. The drive was officially sponsored by the Council of State Governments. A number of states, variously estimated from 20 to 25, petitioned Congress. By October 1965, however, 18 states — one more than the number necessary to prevent a petition by two-thirds — had rejected petition proposals. N.Y. Times, Oct. 26, 1965. See Note, supra, 79 Harv. L. Rev. at 1237-1238.

7. The Supreme Court's reapportionment decisions caused substantial changes in the apportionment plans of almost all the states. See, e.g., the survey of the 50 states made by the New York Times six months after the decision in Reynolds v. Sims. N.Y. Times, Dec. 28, 1964; U.S. News & World Report, Aug. 23, 1965, p. 42, and Feb. 14, 1966, p. 66. For a summary of the history of apportionment in each state, from its origin through October of 1965, see McKay, Reapportionment: The Law and Politics of Equal Representation, App. 271-475 (1965). Professor McKay summarizes his findings as follows: "It should be helpful to learn, for example, that a substantial majority of the apportionment formulas in the original constitutions of the 50 states were based primarily on population in both houses of the bicameral legislatures (as they nearly all were). It is now common knowledge that by 1962 nearly all the states had substantially abandoned the equal-population principle in one or both legislative houses, either by constitutional amendment or by legislative failure to satisfy state requirements for periodic reapportionment in accordance with population. Most revealing of all is the fact that by late 1965 the great majority of the states had returned to apportionment formulas in both houses based primarily on population; and in many cases, once the matter was settled, there appeared to be quiet relief and general satisfaction as with a job well done." Id. at viii.

8. A number of unresolved issues remain in the wake of the Supreme Court's "one-man, one-vote" decisions. Perhaps the most significant is the extent to which the principle applies beyond the area of Congressional Districts and state legisla-

tures. Questions have arisen, or can arise, as to county governments, city governments, special district governments, judicial bodies, appointive bodies, administrative agencies, party primaries, party conventions, constitutional conventions, and perhaps others. These issues have not yet reached the United States Supreme Court. The state and lower federal courts, however, have thus far almost uniformly indicated that the "one-man, one-vote" doctrine applies to county and city government. See Ellis v. Mayor and City Council of Baltimore, 234 F. Supp. 945 (D. Md. 1964), aff'd, 352 F.2d 123 (4th Cir. 1965); Bianchi v. Griffing, 238 F. Supp. 997 (E.D. N.Y. 1965), app. dis. for want of juris., 382 U.S. 15 (1965); Seaman v. Fedourich, 16 N.Y.2d 93, 262 N.Y.S.2d 444, 209 N.E.2d 778 (1965); State ex rel. Sonneborn v. Sylvester, 26 Wis. 2d 43, 132 N.W.2d 249 (1965). But cf. Johnson v. Genesee County, 232 F. Supp. 567 (E.D. Mich. 1964). In Delozier v. Tyrone Area School Board, 247 F. Supp. 30 (W.D. Pa. 1965), the court held that the Reynolds principle applied to a school board. But two courts have indicated the rule is otherwise as to the judiciary. Hamrick v. George, 378 P.2d 324 (Okla. 1963); Stokes v. Fortson, 234 F. Supp. 575 (N.D. Ga. 1964); cf. In re Court of Appeals, 372 Mich. 227, 125 N.W.2d 719 (1964). And another court has ruled that the principle does not extend to the election of party county chairmen, at least where party nominations of candidates are not directly involved. Lynch v. Torquato, 343 F.2d 370 (3d Cir. 1965). For discussion, see Weinstein, The Effect of the Federal Reapportionment Decisions on Counties and Other Forms of Municipal Government, 65 Colum. L. Rev. 21 (1965); King, The Reynolds Standard and Local Reapportionment, 15 Buffalo L. Rev. 120 (1965); Note, Reapportionment, 79 Harv. L. Rev. at 1269-1283 (1966).

REFERENCES

1. The two most comprehensive treatments of current reapportionment issues are, McKay, Reapportionment: The Law and Politics of Equal Representation (1965) (bibliography at 477-485), and Note, Reapportionment, 79 Harv. L. Rev. 1226 (1966). See also Dixon, Reapportionment Perspectives: What is Fair Representation? 51 A.B.A.J. 319 (1965).

2. For a survey of the legal situation prior to Baker v. Carr, see Lewis, Legislative Apportionment and the Federal Courts, 71 Harv. L. Rev. 1057 (1958). For discussion of the extent of malapportionment and its political implications, see Baker, State Constitutions: Reapportionment (1960), and Rural Versus Urban Political Power (1955). See also National Municipal League, Compendium on Legislative Apportionment (2d ed. 1962). Other materials, both legal and non-legal, on the pre-Baker situation are collected in the second edition of this book, 242-244.

3. The decision in Baker v. Carr was widely discussed. The material includes: The Problem of Malapportionment: A Symposium on Baker v. Carr, 72 Yale L.J. 7 (1962) (articles by Bickel, Black, Emerson, Goldberg, O'Brien, Pollak, Schattschneider, and Sindler); Dixon, Legislative Apportionment and the Federal Constitution, 27 Law & Contemp. Prob. 329 (1962); Israel, On Charting a Course Through the Mathematical Quagmire: The Future of Baker v. Carr, 61 Mich. L. Rev. 107 (1962); Katzenbach, Some Reflections on Baker v. Carr, 15 Vand. L. Rev. 829 (1962); McCloskey, The Reapportionment Case, 76 Harv. L. Rev. 54 (1962); Neal, Baker v. Carr: Politics in Search of Law, 1962 Sup. Ct. Rev. 252; Lucas, Legislative Apportionment and Representative Government: The Meaning of Baker v. Carr, 61 Mich. L. Rev. 711 (1963); McKay, Political Thickets and Crazy Quilts: Reapportionment and Equal Protection, 61

Mich. L. Rev. 645 (1963); Note, Challenges to Congressional Districting: After Baker v. Carr Does Colegrove v. Green Endure? 63 Colum. L. Rev. 98 (1963). See also Bonfield, Baker v. Carr: New Light on the Constitutional Guarantee of Republican Government, 50 Calif. L. Rev. 245 (1962).

4. For comment on Wesberry v. Sanders, see Carpenter, Wesberry v. Sanders: A Case of Oversimplification, 9 Vill. L. Rev. 415 (1964); Weiss, An Analysis of Wesberry v. Sanders, 38 So. Cal. L. Rev. 67 (1965). See also Note, 32 Geo. Wash. L. Rev. 1076 (1964).

5. On Reynolds v. Sims and accompanying cases, see Reapportionment Symposium, 63 Mich. L. Rev. 209 (1964) (articles by Dixon, Kauper, and McKay); Auerbach, The Reapportionment Cases: One Person, One Vote — One Vote, One Value, 1964 Sup. Ct. Rev. 1; Dix, The Apportionment Cases: An Expanded Concept of Equal Protection, 1965 Wis. L. Rev. 606; Notes, 33 U. Cinc. L. Rev. 483 (1964); 59 Nw. U.L. Rev. 500 (1964); 1965 Wis. L. Rev. 606.

6. For discussion of standards to be employed in determining whether an apportionment meets the requirements of the equal protection clause, see the following, all published before Reynolds v. Sims: Dixon, Apportionment Standards and Judicial Power, 38 Notre Dame Law. 367 (1963); Israel, Non-population Factors Relevant to an Acceptable Standard of Apportionment, 38 Notre Dame Law. 499 (1963); Krastin, The Implementation of Representative Government in a Democracy, 48 Iowa L. Rev. 549 (1963); Merrill, Blazes For a Trail Through the Thicket of Reapportionment, 16 Okla. L. Rev. 59 (1963); Note, Baker v. Carr and Legislative Apportionments: A Problem of Standards, 72 Yale L.J. 968 (1963). See also Perrin, In Defense of Country Votes, Yale Review, October 1962, p. 16. For a summary of the standards employed since Reynolds v. Sims, see Note, supra, 79 Harv. L. Rev. at 1248-1261. On the federal analogy, see McKay, The Federal Analogy and State Apportionment Standards, 38 Notre Dame Law. 487 (1963). See also, on the theory of representation, Dahl, A Preface to Democratic Theory 146-147 (1956); de Grazia, Apportionment and Representative Government (1963).

7. On the question of remedies and administration, see Lucas, Of Ducks and Drakes: Judicial Relief in Reapportionment Cases, 38 Notre Dame Law. 401 (1963); Sills and Handler, The Imbroglio of Constitutional Revision: Another By-Product of Reapportionment, 20 Rutgers L. Rev. 1 (1965); Note, Legislative Reapportionment: The Scope of Federal Judicial Relief, 1965 Duke L.J. 563; Note, The Case for District Court Management of the Reapportionment Process, 114 U. Pa. L. Rev. 504 (1966).

8. For a case holding that a conviction under a statute passed by a legislature which was elected under an unconstitutional apportionment plan is nevertheless valid, see United States ex rel. Watkins v. Pennsylvania, 214 F. Supp. 913 (W.D. Pa. 1963).

9. Other material on the reapportionment problem may be found in Boyd, Patterns of Apportionment (National Municipal League 1962); David and Eisenberg, Devaluation of the Urban and Suburban Vote (1961-1962), and State Legislative Redistricting (1962); Jewell, The Politics of Reapportionment (1962); United States Advisory Commission on Intergovernmental Relations, Apportionment of State Legislatures (G.P.O. 1962); Hacker, Congressional Districting: The Issue of Equal Representation (rev. ed. 1964); Schubert, Reapportionment (1965); Silva, Reapportionment and Redistricting, Scientific American, Nov. 1965, p. 20; Council of State Governments, Legislative Reapportionment in the States (1964 and 1965); United States Library of Congress, Legislative Reference Service, Apportionment of State Legislatures (G.P.O. 1965). For a detailed study of the problem in New York, see Silva, The Population Base for Apportionment of the New York Legislature, 32 Fordham L. Rev. 1 (1963). All the cases dealing with reapportionment are currently collected in National Municipal League, Court Decisions On Legislative Apportionment (1962 to date).

10. Bibliographies include Silva and Boyd, Selected Bibliography on Legislative Apportionment and Districting (National Municipal League 1963); United States Library

of Congress, Legislative Reference Service, Congressional Districting and Legislative Apportionment: Selected References (G.P.O. 1965).

2. *Gerrymandering*

GOMILLION v. LIGHTFOOT
364 U.S. 339, 81 S. Ct. 125, 5 L. Ed. 2d 110 (1960)

MR. JUSTICE FRANKFURTER delivered the opinion of the Court.

This litigation challenges the validity, under the United States Constitution, of Local Act No. 140, passed by the Legislature of Alabama in 1957, redefining the boundaries of the City of Tuskegee. Petitioners, Negro citizens of Alabama who were, at the time of this redistricting measure, residents of the City of Tuskegee, brought an action in the United States District Court for the Middle District of Alabama for a declaratory judgment that Act 140 is unconstitutional, and for an injunction to restrain the Mayor and officers of Tuskegee and the officials of Macon County, Alabama, from enforcing the Act against them and other Negroes similarly situated. Petitioners' claim is that enforcement of the statute, which alters the shape of Tuskegee from a square to an uncouth twenty-eight-sided figure, will constitute a discrimination against them in violation of the Due Process and Equal Protection Clauses of the Fourteenth Amendment to the Constitution and will deny them the right to vote in defiance of the Fifteenth Amendment.

The respondents moved for dismissal of the action for failure to state a claim upon which relief could be granted and for lack of jurisdiction of the District Court. The court granted the motion, stating, "This Court has no control over, no supervision over, and no power to change any boundaries of municipal corporations fixed by a duly convened and elected legislative body, acting for the people in the State of Alabama." 167 F. Supp. 405, 410. On appeal, the Court of Appeals for the Fifth Circuit, affirmed the judgment, one judge dissenting. 270 F.2d 594. We brought the case here since serious questions were raised concerning the power of a State over its municipalities in relation to the Fourteenth and Fifteenth Amendments. 362 U.S. 916.

At this stage of the litigation we are not concerned with the truth of the allegations, that is, the ability of petitioners to sustain their allegations by proof. The sole question is whether the allegations entitle them to make good on their claim that they are being denied rights under the United States Constitution. The complaint, charging that Act 140 is a device to disenfranchise Negro citizens, alleges the following facts: Prior to Act 140 the City of Tuskegee was square in shape; the Act transformed it into a strangely irregular twenty-eight-sided figure as indicated in the diagram appended to this opinion. The essential inevitable effect of this redefinition of Tuskegee's boundaries is to remove from the city all save only four or five of its 400 Negro voters while not removing a single white voter or resident. The result of the Act is to deprive the Negro petitioners discriminatorily of the benefits of residence in Tuskegee, including, inter alia, the right to vote in municipal elections.

These allegations, if proven, would abundantly establish that Act 140 was not an ordinary geographic redistricting measure even within familiar abuses of gerrymandering. If these allegations upon a trial remained uncontradicted or unqualified, the conclusion would be irresistible, tantamount for all practical purposes to a mathematical demonstration, that the legislation is solely concerned with segregating white and colored voters by fencing Negro citizens out of town so as to deprive them of their pre-existing municipal vote.

It is difficult to appreciate what stands in the way of adjudging a statute having this inevitable effect invalid in light of the principles by which this Court must judge, and uniformly has judged, statutes that, howsoever speciously defined, obviously discriminate against colored citizens. "The [Fifteenth] Amendment nullifies sophisticated as well as simple-minded modes of discrimination." Lane v. Wilson, 307 U.S. 268, 275.

The complaint amply alleges a claim of racial discrimination. Against this claim the respondents have never suggested, either in their brief or in oral argument, any countervailing municipal function which Act 140 is designed to serve. The respondents invoke generalities expressing the State's unrestricted power — unlimited, that is, by the United States Constitution — to establish, destroy, or reorganize by contraction or expansion its political subdivisions, to wit, cities, counties, and other local units. We freely recognize the breadth and importance of this aspect of the State's political power. To exalt this power into an absolute is to misconceive the reach and rule of this Court's decisions in the leading case of Hunter v. Pittsburgh, 207 U.S. 161, and related cases relied upon by respondents.

. . . [S]uch power, extensive though it is, is met and overcome by the Fifteenth Amendment to the Constitution of the United States, which forbids a State from passing any law which deprives a citizen of his vote because of his race. The opposite conclusion, urged upon us by respondents, would sanction the achievement by a State of any impairment of voting rights whatever so long as it was cloaked in the garb of the realignment of political subdivisions. "It is inconceivable that guaranties embedded in the Constitution of the United States may thus be manipulated out of existence." Frost & Frost Trucking Co. v. Railroad Commission of California, 271 U.S. 583, 594.

The respondents find another barrier to the trial of this case in Colegrove v. Green, 328 U.S. 549. In that case the Court passed on an Illinois law governing the arrangement of congressional districts within that State. The complaint rested upon the disparity of population between the different districts which rendered the effectiveness of each individual's vote in some districts far less than in others. This disparity came to pass solely through shifts in population between 1901, when Illinois organized its congressional districts, and 1946, when the complaint was lodged. During this entire period elections were held under the districting scheme devised in 1901. The Court affirmed

the dismissal of the complaint on the ground that it presented a subject not meet for adjudication. The decisive facts in this case, which at this stage must be taken as proved, are wholly different from the considerations found controlling in Colegrove.

That case involved a complaint of discriminatory apportionment of congressional districts. The appellants in Colegrove complained only of a dilution of the strength of their votes as a result of legislative inaction over a course of many years. The petitioners here complain that affirmative legislative action deprives them of their votes and the consequent advantages that the ballot affords. When a legislature thus singles out a readily isolated segment of a racial minority for special discriminatory treatment, it violates the Fifteenth Amendment. In no case involving unequal weight in voting distribution that has come before the Court did the decision sanction a differentiation on racial lines whereby approval was given to unequivocal withdrawal of the vote solely from colored citizens. Apart from all else, these considerations lift this controversy out of the so-called "political" arena and into the conventional sphere of constitutional litigation.

In sum, as Mr. Justice Holmes remarked, when dealing with a related situation, in Nixon v. Herndon, 273 U.S. 536, 540, "Of course the petition concerns political action," but "The objection that the subject matter of the suit is political is little more than a play upon words." A statute which is alleged to have worked unconstitutional deprivations of petitioners' rights is not immune to attack simply because the mechanism employed by the legislature is a redefinition of municipal boundaries. According to the allegations here made, the Alabama Legislature has not merely redrawn the Tuskegee city limits with incidental inconvenience to the petitioners; it is more accurate to say that it has deprived the petitioners of the municipal franchise and consequent rights and to that end it has incidentally changed the city's boundaries. While in form this is merely an act redefining metes and bounds, if the allegations are established, the inescapable human effect of this essay in geometry and geography is to despoil colored citizens, and only colored citizens, of their theretofore enjoyed voting rights. That was not Colegrove v. Green.

When a State exercises power wholly within the domain of state interest, it is insulated from federal judicial review. But such insulation is not carried over when state power is used as an instrument for circumventing a federally protected right. This principle has had many applications. It has long been recognized in cases which have prohibited a State from exploiting a power acknowledged to be absolute in an isolated context to justify the imposition of an "unconstitutional condition." What the Court has said in those cases is equally applicable here, viz., that "Acts generally lawful may become unlawful when done to accomplish an unlawful end, United States v. Reading Co., 226 U.S. 324, 357, and a constitutional power cannot be used by way of condition to attain an unconstitutional result." Western Union Telegraph Co. v.

Foster, 247 U.S. 105, 114. The petitioners are entitled to prove their allegations at trial.

For these reasons, the principal conclusions of the District Court and the Court of Appeals are clearly erroneous and the decision below must be
Reversed.

Mr. Justice Douglas, while joining the opinion of the Court, adheres to the dissents in Colegrove v. Green, 328 U.S. 549, and South v. Peters, 339 U.S. 276.

Mr. Justice Whittaker, concurring.

I concur in the Court's judgment, but not in the whole of its opinion. It seems to me that the decision should be rested not on the Fifteenth Amendment, but rather on the Equal Protection Clause of the Fourteenth Amendment to the Constitution. I am doubtful that the averments of the complaint, taken for present purposes to be true, show a purpose by Act No. 140 to abridge petitioners' "right . . . to vote," in the Fifteenth Amendment sense. It seems to me that the "right . . . to vote" that is guaranteed by the Fifteenth Amendment is but the same right to vote as is enjoyed by all others within the same election precinct, ward or other political division. And, inasmuch as no one has the right to vote in a political division, or in a local election concerning only an area in which he does not reside, it would seem to follow that one's right to vote in Division A is not abridged by a redistricting that places his residence in Division B *if* he there enjoys the same voting privileges as all others in that Division, even though the redistricting was done by the State for the purpose of placing a racial group of citizens in Division B rather than A.

But it does seem clear to me that accomplishment of a State's purpose — to use the Court's phrase — of "fencing Negro citizens out of" Division A and into Division B is an unlawful segregation of races of citizens, in violation of the Equal Protection Clause of the Fourteenth Amendment, Brown v. Board of Education, 347 U.S. 483; Cooper v. Aaron, 358 U.S. 1; and, as stated, I would think the decision should be rested on that ground — which, incidentally, clearly would not involve, just as the cited cases did not involve, the Colegrove problem.

WRIGHT v. ROCKEFELLER
376 U.S. 52, 84 S. Ct. 603, 11 L. Ed. 2d 512 (1964)

Mr. Justice Black delivered the opinion of the Court.

Appellants, citizens and registered voters of New York's Seventeenth, Eighteenth, Nineteenth, and Twentieth Congressional Districts, all in New York County (the Island of Manhattan), brought this action in the United States District Court for the Southern District of New York challenging the constitutionality of that part of Chapter 980 of New York's 1961 congressional apportionment statute which defined these four districts. The Governor and several other New York state officials were named as defendants. Congressman Adam Clayton Powell, who represents the Eighteenth Congressional District, and several other New York County political leaders were permitted to intervene as defendants supporting the constitutionality of the apportionment act. Appellants charged that the part of the New York Act in question deprived them of rights guaranteed by the Due Process and Equal Protection Clauses of the Fourteenth Amendment and by the Fifteenth Amendment, which provides that "The right of citizens of the United States to vote shall not be denied or abridged by the United States or by any State on account of race, color, or previous condition of servitude." Their complaint alleged that:

"Chapter 980 establishes irrational, discriminatory and unequal Congressional Districts in the County of New York and segregates eligible voters by race and place of origin. It is contrived to create one district, the 17th Congressional District, which excludes non-white citizens and citizens of Puerto Rican origin and which is over-represented in comparison to the other three districts in the County of New York. The 18th, 19th and 20th Congressional Districts have been drawn so as to include the overwhelming number of nonwhite citizens and citizens of Puerto Rican origin in the County of New York and to be under-represented in relation to the 17th Congressional District."

The case was heard by a District Court of three judges. During these hearings, counsel for appellants made it clear that their case did not depend on "under-representation because of the variation in the size of the Congressional districts"; it was rather, he said, "a case of ghettoizing the Island of Manhattan" so as "to create a white Congressional district and a non-white Congressional district." "I think," counsel said, "the only province of the Court in this area is to determine whether or not these districts have been created with racial considerations in mind, and, if they have, or if the results of this districting, the effect of the statute is to create racially segregated areas, we maintain that it violates the Fourteenth and Fifteenth Amendments." Appellants offered maps, statistics, and some oral evidence designed to prove their charge that it was impossible to have districts such as these were unless they "were drawn with regard to race." The statistics showed that the Eighteenth District contained 86.3% Negroes and Puerto Ricans; the Nineteenth, 28.5%; the Twentieth, 27.5%; and the Seventeenth, 5.1%. The evidence also showed irregularities in the boundaries of the districts and some variation in population among the four.[3] Appellees presented no oral testimony but did offer historical maps, a table from the Bureau of the Census, and a message from the President to the Congress on the subject of congressional apportionment.

A majority of the District Court found that appellants had not made out

---

[3] The population of the Seventeenth Congressional District was 382,320; the Eighteenth, 431, 330; the Nineteenth, 445,175; and the Twentieth, 439,456.

their case on the crucial factual issues.[4] Judge Moore broadly found that "[n]o proof was offered by any party that the specific boundaries created by Chapter 980 were drawn on racial lines or that the Legislature was motivated by considerations of race, creed or country of origin in creating the districts." He concluded, "Plaintiffs having failed upon the facts and the law to establish any violation of their constitutional rights as a result of the action of the New York Legislature in enacting Chapter 980 of the Laws of 1961, the complaint must be dismissed." Judge Feinberg concurred in Judge Moore's result because he, too, believed that appellants had

"not met their burden of proving that the boundaries of the new 17th, 18th, 19th, and 20th Congressional Districts were drawn along racial lines, as they allege. . . .

. . .

". . . Plaintiffs did introduce evidence which might justify an inference that racial considerations motivated the 1961 reapportionment of congressional districts in Manhattan. However, other inferences, as set forth below, are equally or more justifiable. Plaintiffs have a difficult burden to meet in attacking the constitutionality of this state statute. . . . Upon analysis, I do not think that burden has been met.

. . .

". . . In short, based upon the entire record, I do not feel that plaintiffs have proved their case."

Judge Murphy dissented. He viewed the evidence as "tantamount for all practical purposes, to a mathematical demonstration" that the legislation was "solely concerned with segregating" white voters from colored and Puerto Rican voters "by fencing colored and Puerto Rican citizens out of the 17th District and into a district of their own (the 18th)" and as establishing "per se a prima facie case of a legislative intent to draw congressional district lines in the 17th and 18th Districts on the basis of race and national origin."

While a number of other matters have been discussed, we find it necessary to decide only the first question presented in the jurisdictional statement, namely "[w]hether appellants sustained their burden of proving that the portion of Chapter 980 . . . which delineates the boundaries of the Congressional districts in Manhattan Island segregates eligible voters by race and place of origin in violation of the Equal Protection and Due Process Clauses of the Fourteenth Amendment and in violation of the Fifteenth Amendment." We accept the findings of the majority of the District Court that appellants failed to prove that the New York Legislature was either motivated by racial considerations or in fact drew the districts on racial lines. Compare Gomillion v. Lightfoot, 364 U.S. 339. It may be true, as Judge Feinberg thought, that there was evidence which could have supported inferences that racial considerations might have moved the state legislature, but, even if so, we agree that there also was evidence to support his finding that the

[4] 211 F. Supp. 460.

contrary inference was "equally, or more, persuasive." Where there are such conflicting inferences one group of them cannot, because labeled as "prima facie proof," be treated as conclusive on the fact finder so as to deprive him of his responsibility to choose among disputed inferences. And this is true whether the conflicting inferences are drawn from evidence offered by the plaintiff or by the defendant or by both. Hernandez v. Texas, 347 U.S. 475, does not support the dissenting view of Judge Murphy that appellants' evidence here established a prima facie case compelling the District Court, despite conflicting inferences which could be drawn from that evidence, to find that New York created these districts on the basis of race and place of origin. Hernandez followed the rule laid down in Norris v. Alabama, 294 U.S. 587, and other cases, that proof of a long-continued state practice of not calling Negroes as jurors made out a prima facie case sufficient to justify, but not necessarily to compel, a finding of discrimination on account of race. The conclusion of racial discrimination in those cases was reached only after an appraisal of this practice along with all the circumstances. It is plain to us that the District Court was not compelled to find that these districts were the product of a state contrivance to discriminate against colored or Puerto Rican voters. As the majority below pointed out, the concentration of colored and Puerto Rican voters in one area in the county made it difficult, even assuming it to be permissible, to fix districts so as to have anything like an equal division of these voters among the districts. Undoubtedly some of these voters, as shown by this lawsuit, would prefer a more even distribution of minority groups among the four congressional districts, but others, like the intervenors in this case, would argue strenuously that the kind of districts for which appellants contended would be undesirable and, because based on race or place of origin, would themselves be unconstitutional.

We accept the District Court's finding that appellants have not shown that the challenged part of the New York Act was the product of a state contrivance to segregate on the basis of race or place of origin. That finding was crucial to appellants' case as they presented it, and for that reason their challenge cannot be sustained. We do not pass on the question which appellants have not presented here, that is, whether the state apportionment is constitutionally invalid because it may fail in its objective to create districts based as nearly as practicable on equal population. See Wesberry v. Sanders, [376 U.S. 1]. Since no such challenge has been urged here, the issues have not been formulated to bring it into focus, and the evidence has not been offered or appraised to decide it, our holding has no bearing on that wholly separate question.

The judgment dismissing the complaint is
Affirmed.

Mr. Justice Harlan, concurring.
I join the opinion of the Court on the premise that the only issue in this

case involves alleged racially segregated districts. The case is thus, in my opinion, governed by entirely different constitutional considerations, see Gomillion v. Lightfoot, 364 U.S. 339, than those which I believe should govern in Wesberry v. Sanders, ante, p. 1, also decided today, in which I have filed a dissenting opinion, ante, p. 20.

Mr. Justice Douglas, with whom Mr. Justice Goldberg concurs, dissenting.

This case raises a question kin to that in Gomillion v. Lightfoot, 364 U.S. 339, where racial gerrymandering was used to deprive Negroes of the right to vote. Here no Negroes are deprived of the franchise. Rather, zigzag, tortuous lines are drawn to concentrate Negroes and Puerto Ricans in Manhattan's Eighteenth Congressional District and practically to exclude them from the Seventeenth Congressional District. Neighborhoods in our larger cities often contain members of only one race; and those who draw the lines of Congressional Districts cannot be expected to disregard neighborhoods in an effort to make each district a multiracial one. But where, as here, the line that is drawn can be explained only in racial terms, a different problem is presented.

I

Manhattan is divided into four districts and as a result of the serpentine path that the lines follow, those districts reflect substantial, though not complete, segregation by races:

District	White percent of district	Negro and Puerto Rican percent of district
17th	94.9	5.1
18th	13.7	86.3
19th	71.5	28.5
20th	72.5	27.5

In 1961 the legislature expanded the Seventeenth District by altering its boundaries in three respects: (1) it added an area on the upper East Side between 59th Street and 89th Street *of whose population Negroes and Puerto Ricans make up 2.7% of the total;* [2] (2) it added an area on the lower East Side called Stuyvesant Town *of whose population Negroes and Puerto Ri-*

---

[2] An area extending from 89th Street to 95th Street, between Third Avenue and the East River, was left in the Eighteenth District. This area of 10,507 persons is less than 5% Negro and Puerto Rican. There is, however, a new low-cost public housing project (of the type in which the average Negro-Puerto Rican occupancy in Manhattan will be about 75%) which has been scheduled for construction in that area. Because of that project and the general southward push of the Negro and Puerto Rican population, the area south of 95th Street appears to be but a temporary buffer zone.

cans make up 0.5% of the total; and (3) it dropped from the Seventeenth District and added to the Eighteenth District a two-block area from 98th Street to 100th Street between Fifth Avenue and Madison Avenue *of whose population Negroes and Puerto Ricans make up 44.5% of the total.*

To achieve this racial gerrymandering, careful manipulation of the boundaries of the Eighteenth District was necessary. The southeast corner is near the East River and from there it goes — west four blocks, north two blocks, west one block, north five blocks, west one block, north one block, west one block, north one block, west one block, north eleven blocks, west five blocks across the northern line of Central Park to Morningside, north along Morningside about twelve blocks, west one block, north along Amsterdam from 122d to 150th, east two blocks, north fifteen blocks to 165th, and east to East River.

The record strongly suggests that these twists and turns producing an 11-sided, step-shaped boundary between the Seventeenth and Eighteenth Districts were made to bring into the Eighteenth District and keep out of the Seventeenth as many Negroes and Puerto Ricans as possible. There is to be sure no finding to this effect by the three-judge District Court. One of the three judges thought, as I do, that the uncontradicted facts establish per se a prima facie case of a legislative purpose to design the Seventeenth and Eighteenth Districts on racial lines (211 F. Supp. 460, 472-473), saying that: "[In Gomillion] . . . it was a glaring exclusion of Negroes from a municipal district. Here it is a subtle exclusion from a 'silk stocking district' (as the 17th is so frequently referred to) and a jamming in of colored and Puerto Ricans into the 18th or the kind of segregation that appeals to the intervenors." Id., at 474-475.

A second judge concluded that petitioners "have not met their burden of proving" that the boundaries in question were "drawn along racial lines." Id., at 468. The third judge expressed no view on the precise issue.[3]

The evidence which I have summarized was not rebutted or challenged, the State introducing no evidence. We have not only inferences from conceded facts but also New York's frank concession that it is not possible to say "that race is irrelevant to districting."

Racial segregation that is state-sponsored should be nullified whatever may have been intended. In Johnson v. Virginia, 373 U.S. 61, we held segregation of a courtroom audience by race to be unconstitutional, without stopping to inquire what the motive may have been. A well-settled proposition applicable to many rights in the constitutional spectrum is that there may be an abridge-

---

[3] The closest intimation, though not on the precise issue, is contained in the following statement which he made in his opinion: "No proof was tendered that the Legislature in drawing the district lines in previous years was motivated or influenced by any considerations which have become unconstitutional during subsequent years. Plaintiffs wholly failed to support their allegation of 'repeated and energetic efforts' to seek legislative correction or that efforts were unavailing because of unconstitutional apportionment." 211 F. Supp., at 467

ment "even though unintended." See NAACP v. Alabama, 357 U.S. 449, 461, and cases cited. What the State has done is often conclusive irrespective of motive. Eubanks v. Louisiana, 356 U.S. 584, 587-588.

I had assumed that since Brown v. Board of Education, 347 U.S. 483, no State may segregate people by race *in the public areas.* The design of voting districts involves one important *public area* — as important as schools, parks, and courtrooms. We should uproot all vestiges of Plessy v. Ferguson, 163 U.S. 537, from *the public area.*

The intervenors are persons who apparently have a vested interest in control of the segregated Eighteenth District.[4] They and the State seem to support this segregation not on the "separate but equal" theory of Plessy v. Ferguson, supra, but on another theory. Their theory might be called the theory of "separate but better off" — a theory that has been used before. A like argument was made in Buchanan v. Warley, 245 U.S. 60, 81, in support of municipal segregation of residential areas; in District of Columbia v. Thompson, 346 U.S. 100, in support of segregation in restaurants; in Watson v. Memphis, 373 U.S. 526, in support of delayed integration of municipal parks. Indeed, the final argument of John W. Davis for South Carolina in Brown v. Board of Education, supra, ended with the words, "The good is sometimes better than the best."

The fact that Negro political leaders find advantage in this nearly solid Negro and Puerto Rican district is irrelevant to our problem. Rotten boroughs were long a curse of democratic processes. Racial boroughs are also at war with democratic standards.

II

What we have in the Seventeenth and Eighteenth Districts in Manhattan is comparable to the Electoral Register System which Britain introduced into India. That system gave a separate constituency to Sikhs, Muslims, Anglo-Indians, Europeans, and Indian Christians.[5] Religious minorities found comfort and safety in such an arrangement. A Muslim deputation made the following demand:[6]

"(1) That in the whole of India the Muslims number over 62 millions or between one-fifth and one-fourth of the total population;

"(2) that as their numbers exceed the entire population of any first-class

---

[4] Adam Clayton Powell has represented the Eighteenth District in Congress since 1945.

[5] Acharya, Indian Elections and Franchise (1937), p. 17:
"No one who is not a Sikh, a Muhammadan, Anglo Indian, European or an Indian Christian, is entitled to be included in a Sikh, Muhammadan, Anglo Indian, European or an Indian Christian constituency respectively. No person who is entitled to be included in a Sikh, Muhammadan, Anglo Indian, European or an Indian Christian constituency will be included in the electoral roll for a General Constituency in a province."

[6] Ahsan, Community Electorates in India (1934), pp. 6-7.

European Power, except Russia, Muslims might justly claim adequate recognition as an important factor in the State;

"(3) that the representation hitherto accorded to them, almost entirely by nomination, had been inadequate to their requirements and had not always carried with it the approval of those whom the nominees were selected to represent; and

"(4) that while Muslims are a distinct community with additional interests of their own, which are not shared by other communities, no Muslim would ever be returned by the existing electoral bodies, unless he worked in sympathy with the Hindu majority in all matters of importance."

Lord Morley made the following reply:[7]

"The Muslims demand three things. I had the pleasure of receiving a deputation from them and I know very well what is in their minds. They demand an election of their own representatives to these councils in all the stages just as in Cyprus, where, I think, Muslims vote by themselves; they have nine votes and the non-Muslims have three or the other way about; so in Bohemia where the Germans vote alone and have their own register; therefore we are not without a precedent and a parallel for the idea of a separate register. Secondly, they want a number of seats in excess of their numerical strength. These two demands we are quite ready and intend to meet in full."

Hindus responded favorably.[8] The Joint Report of 1918 stated:[9]

"Some persons hold that for a people, such as they deem those of India to be, so divided by race, religion and caste as to be unable to consider the interests of any but their own section, a system of communal electorates and class representation is not merely inevitable but is actually best. They maintain that it evokes and applies the principle of democracy over the widest range over which it is actually alive at all, by appealing to the instincts which are strongest; and that we must hope to develop the finer, which are also at present the weaker instincts by using the forces that really count. According to this theory communal representation is an inevitable and even a healthy stage in the development of a non-political people."

As already noted, the Electoral Register System was not peculiar to British India. Other nations used it. Lebanon today has a modified version: each of eight religious groups has electoral districts from which only a member of that faith can be chosen for the legislature.[11]

---

[7] Id., at 11.

[8] Id., at 12.

[9] Id., at 16.

[11] The 1927 Lebanese Constitution established a unicameral legislature. See II Patai, The Republic of Lebanon (1956), p. 533. The number of deputies now is 99. Statesman's Year-Book 1963-1964, p. 1222. Prior to that increase it had 66 members elected according to the following proportional division among religious groups: 20 Maronites; 26 Moslems, of whom 12 were Shi'ites; 7 Greek Orthodox; 4 Druses; 4 Greek Catholics; 3 Armenian Orthodox; 1 Armenian Catholic; 1 other religious minority. 17 Encyclopedia Americana (1963), p. 175. See I Khalil, The Arab States and the Arab League (1962), pp. 124, 133; Ziadeh, The Lebanese Elections, 14 Middle East J. 367 (1960).

Racial electoral registers, like religious ones, have no place in a society that honors the Lincoln tradition — "of the people, by the people, for the people." Here the individual is important, not his race, his creed, or his color. The principle of equality is at war with the notion that District A must be represented by a Negro, as it is with the notion that District B must be represented by a Caucasian, District C by a Jew, District D by a Catholic, and so on. Cf. Gray v. Sanders, 372 U.S. 368, 379. The racial electoral register system weights votes along one racial line more heavily than it does other votes. That system, by whatever name it is called, is a divisive force in a community, emphasizing differences between candidates and voters that are irrelevant in the constitutional sense. Of course race, like religion, plays an important role in the choices which individual voters make from among various candidates.[12] But government has no business designing electoral districts along racial or religious lines. We held in Akins v. Texas, 325 U.S. 398, 403, and in Brown v. Allen, 344 U.S. 443, 471, that courts in selecting juries need not — indeed should not — give each jury list the proportional racial complexion that the community has. If race is not a proper criterion for drawing a jury list, how can it be in designing an electoral district?

In Anderson v. Martin, 375 U.S. 399, we barred Louisiana from putting on a ballot opposite a Negro candidate's name the word, "Negro," as it was a device encouraging racial discrimination. When we said in that case that a State may not encourage its citizens "to vote for a candidate solely on account of race," id., at 404, I had assumed that we would hold a fortiori that no State could make an electoral district out of any racial bloc unless the electoral unit represented an actual neighborhood. Yet we violate that principle here.

When racial or religious lines are drawn by the State, the multiracial, multireligious communities that our Constitution seeks to weld together as one become separatist; antagonisms that relate to race or to religion rather than to political issues are generated; communities seek not the best representative but the best racial or religious partisan. Since that system is at war with the democratic ideal, it should find no footing here.

"Separate but equal" and "separate but better off" have no more place in voting districts than they have in schools, parks, railroad terminals, or any other facility serving the public.

Mr. Justice Goldberg, with whom Mr. Justice Douglas joins, dissenting.

I fully agree with and join what my Brother Douglas has written in dissent but wish to add these words by way of comment on the Court's opinion.

The question for decision in this case is whether appellants have sustained their burden of proving that the boundaries of the Seventeenth and Eighteenth Congressional Districts of New York were purposefully drawn on racial lines. The Court resolves this question against appellants by accepting "the District Court's finding that appellants have not shown that the chal-

[12] See Dawidowicz and Goldstein, Politics in a Pluralistic Democracy (1963).

lenged part of the New York Act was the product of a state contrivance to segregate on the basis of race or place of origin." Ante, at 58.

My difficulty with this conclusion is that the record does not support the Court's treatment of the District Court's finding. The District Court was a three-judge court and the three judges did not agree upon and, as a court, made no express findings of fact. Instead there were three separate and differing opinions. Judge Moore implied that racially segregated voting districts are constitutional absent a showing of serious under-representation or other specific harm to the individual complainants. 211 F. Supp. 460, 467-468. He also suggested that segregated voting districts could be constitutionally justified because they may enable persons of the same race or place of origin "to obtain representation in legislative bodies which otherwise would be denied to them." Id., at 467. Finally, Judge Moore intimated that factually segregated voting districts would be unconstitutional only where the legislature was "motivated or influenced" to create such districts. Ibid. To establish this motivation or influence complainants must introduce proof, and in this case no such proof was tendered by the appellants who, therefore, failed to make a case "upon the facts and the law." Id., at 468.

Judge Moore did not in my view apply the proper constitutional standard. The Constitution, I strongly believe, proscribes state-sanctioned racial segregation in legislative districting as well as in voting and in public schools and facilities. E.g., Brown v. Board of Education, 347 U.S. 483; Gomillion v. Lightfoot, 364 U.S. 339; Johnson v. Virginia, 373 U.S. 61; Watson v. City of Memphis, 373 U.S. 526; Goss v. Board of Education, 373 U.S. 683; Anderson v. Martin, 375 U.S. 399. Certainly in these areas the Fourteenth Amendment "nullifies sophisticated as well as simple-minded modes of discrimination." Cf. Lane v. Wilson, 307 U.S. 268, 275. This Court has declared state-sanctioned segregation invalid on the ground that, under the Constitution, distinctions by law between citizens because of their race, ancestry, color or religion "are by their very nature odious to a free people whose institutions are founded upon the doctrine of equality." Hirabayashi v. United States, 320 U.S. 81, 100. Given this settled principle that state-sanctioned racial segregation is unconstitutional per se, a showing of serious under-representation or other specific harm to individual complainants is irrelevant. I understand the Court's decisions since Brown v. Board of Education, supra, to hold that harm to the Nation as a whole and to whites and Negroes alike inheres in segregation. The Fourteenth Amendment commands equality, and racial segregation by law is inequality. Judge Moore, therefore, did not apply the proper constitutional standard.

Furthermore, as I shall point out, Judge Moore also erred in holding that in any event appellants' proof was insufficient to establish a prima facie case of unconstitutional racial districting.

Judge Feinberg disagreed both with Judge Moore's implication that segregated voting districts are constitutional absent serious under-representation and with the view that segregated districts could be constitutionally justified by alleged advantages to persons of a particular race or place of origin. Judge Feinberg stated that the "constitutional vice would be use by the legislature of an impermissible standard, and the harm to plaintiffs that need be shown is only that such a standard was used." 211 F. Supp., at 468. He then frankly acknowledged that:

"The case is a closer one for me than the opinion of Judge Moore would indicate it is for him. Plaintiffs did introduce evidence which might justify an inference that racial considerations motivated the 1961 reapportionment of congressional districts in Manhattan. However, other inferences . . . are equally or more justifiable. Plaintiffs have a difficult burden to meet in attacking the constitutionality of this state statute." Id., at 469.

Judge Feinberg, on this reasoning, cast his vote for Judge Moore's result on the ground that appellants failed to sustain the "difficult burden" of attacking the constitutionality of this statute: Even where such racially segregated districting results and complainants' evidence "might justify an inference that racial considerations motivated" the districting, still complainants fail to sustain their burden unless they also disprove every other permissible or reasonable purpose which the legislature might have had in mind.

Judge Murphy, in his dissent, agreed with Judge Feinberg as to the applicable constitutional standard. But, on Judge Murphy's view of the record, the appellants carried their burden of proving that "the legislation was solely concerned with segregating white, and colored and Puerto Rican voters by fencing colored and Puerto Rican citizens out of the 17th District and into a district of their own (the 18th)"; that the legislation had effected "obvious segregation"; and that the statute constituted a "subtle exclusion" of Negroes from the Seventeenth and a "jamming in of colored and Puerto Ricans into the 18th or the kind of segregation that appeals to the intervenors." Id., at 473-475. Accordingly, Judge Murphy thought appellants had met their burden of proving segregation and, in the absence of any proof by the State or by intervenors, were entitled to a judgment declaring the statute unconstitutional under the Equal Protection Clause of the Fourteenth Amendment.

In light of these conflicting opinions and analyses, this case cannot be fairly decided on the ground stated in the opinion of the Court, viz., that "[w]e accept the District Court's finding." . . . Which finding and under what constitutional standard — Judge Moore's, Judge Feinberg's or Judge Murphy's? Judges Moore and Feinberg, who comprised the majority below, differed both with regard to the constitutional standard and, as I read the opinions, with regard to the proof. It should not be forgotten that the conclusions of the District Court — both as to law and fact — have not been reviewed by an intermediate appellate tribunal. Instead the case has come directly to this Court from a three-judge District Court and presents a record containing variant and inconsistent legal and factual conclusions. Even where a three-judge District Court has made a unanimous finding of fact, this Court has given that finding less deference where, as here, it depends on evidence that is largely documentary and particularly where, as here, "the crucial issues involve mixed questions of law and fact." United States v. United States Gypsum Co., 333 U.S. 364, 396. In my view, we cannot, in light of the record in this case, rest our decision on the "finding" of the District Court without abdicating our responsibility for principled constitutional adjudication.

My Brother DOUGLAS in his dissent has set forth the virtually undisputed facts. I shall not repeat them here. He has also set forth the correct constitutional standard which I believe we should unhesitatingly reaffirm and apply. On the basis of the evidence,[1] I agree with Judge Murphy's conclusion "that the only available inference from the . . . uncontradicted figure picture establishes per se a prima facie case of a legislative intent to draw congressional

---

[1] Judge Murphy in his dissent stated:

"The uncontradicted proof submitted by plaintiffs, however, establishes a visual figure picture of the end results of the recent redistricting of Manhattan Isle (New York County) as follows:

"Manhattan has a population of 1,698,281 people and is entitled to four congressmen. The census figures of 1960 divided the ethnic groups into only two classes — white and non-white and Puerto Rican. These classes have been counted and according to the census 1,058,589 or 62.3% are white and 639,622 or 37.7% are non-white and Puerto Rican.

"The district lines as fixed by Chapter 980 created the four districts in question with the following make-up:

District	Total Population	White Population	% of District	Non-White and Puerto Rican Origin Population of District	
17th	382,320	362,668	94.9%	19,652	5.1%
18th	431,330	59,216	13.7%	372,114	86.3%
19th	445,175	318,223	71.5%	126,952	28.5%
20th	439,456	318,482	72.5%	120,974	27.5%
Total	1,698,281	1,058,589	62.3%	639,692	37.7%

"The following table shows the percent of non-white persons and persons of Puerto Rican origin in each congressional district in relation to the total number of such persons in the entire county:

District	% of Non-White and Puerto Rican of County
17th	3.1%
18th	58.2%
19th	19.8%
20th	18.9%
	100.0%

"The figure picture of the 17th District shows that the lines as drawn encompass a population 94.9% white and 5.1% non-white and Puerto Rican. It further shows it has a population of 382,320 people, or between 15.4% and 12% less than any of the adjoining districts. The 18th District encompasses a population that is 86.3% non-white and Puerto Rican and only 13.7% white. Its population of 431,330 people is 12% more than the 17th and 5% above the state average." 211 F. Supp. 460, 472.

district lines in the 17th and 18th Districts on the basis of race and national origin." Id., at 472-473. At least, however, appellants' proof made it appear probable that a racial criterion shaped the 1961 reapportionment and that an inference of reliance on such an impermissible criterion was more reasonable than an inference that other factors alone had been used. In my view, then, this justifiable inference was sufficient to raise a rebuttable presumption of unconstitutionality and, without shifting the ultimate burden of proof, to place on the State the burden of going forward and introducing rebuttal evidence. See Note, 72 Yale L.J. 1041, 1056-1061. It might be that the appellees and intervenors could have offered proof to counteract the inference of racial districting, but they chose not to do so. They might, for example, have attempted to prove that the lines were drawn in an attempt to equalize the population of districts or to follow neighborhood lines. The simple answer is that appellees made no attempt whatever to rebut the inference that race was a criterion in — or racial segregation a purpose of — the districting.[2]

The question therefore recurs: What more need appellants have proved? Judge Moore apparently would have required them to introduce proof that the legislature's actual motive was to create racially segregated voting districts. Appellants, however, by their evidence established a pattern of segregation not adequately explained on a geometric, geographic, equalization, party-compromise, neighborhood or other basis. To require a showing of racial motivation in the legislature would place an impossible burden on complainants. For example, in this case the redistricting bill was recommended and submitted to the legislature on November 9, 1961, passed on November 10, 1961, and signed by the Governor on that date. No public hearings were had on the bill and no statements by the bill's managers or published debates were available. Under these circumstances, appellants' evidence, showing the factual pattern of segregation outlined by Mr. Justice Douglas and by Judge Murphy, was sufficient to establish a prima facie case of unconstitutional racial districting. Once this had been done, appellees should have introduced evidence negating the inference that racial segregation was a purpose of the districting. In the absence of such proof by the State, I am compelled to conclude that racial segregation was a criterion in — or a purpose of — the districting of New York's Seventeenth and Eighteenth Congressional Districts. I, therefore, respectfully dissent.

NOTES

1. The Supreme Court has not directly addressed itself to the gerrymandering problem except in Gomillion and Wright v. Rockefeller. But in Fortson v. Dorsey, 379 U.S. 433, 85 S. Ct. 498, 13 L. Ed. 2d 401 (1965), noted above, it made clear that multi-member districts would be scrutinized to see whether, under the partic-

---

[2] In fact the State in its brief in this Court candidly asserts "that a Legislature may 'consider' race in drawing Congressional district lines and . . . that there is no per se prohibition against classifications by race."

ular circumstances, the districting "would operate to minimize or cancel out the voting strength of racial or political elements of the voting population." 379 U.S. at 439, 85 S. Ct. at 501, 13 L. Ed. 2d at 405.

2. The lower federal courts have dealt with claims of gerrymandering in several instances, but most frequently have rejected them. Thus in Mann v. Davis, 245 F. Supp. 241 (E.D. Va. 1965), aff'd sub nom. Burnette v. Davis, 382 U.S. 42 (1965), the Virginia apportionment plan grouped Henrico County (surrounding Richmond) and the City of Richmond in a single district, entitled to eight members in the House of Representatives. Voters in Henrico County contended that Henrico should be given a district of its own, entitled to three members. Voters in Richmond alleged that the fusion of Richmond and Henrico County "deprives Negro citizens of their chance to elect one of their race to the General Assembly," since it reduced the proportion of Negro voters from 42 per cent in the city to 29 per cent in the district as a whole, and did not subdivide the city into districts. Pointing out that neither Richmond nor any other city or county in Virginia "has in her history ever been sub-districted," a three-judge court found no "trespasses or fouls."

Other cases in which the courts have refused to grant relief include Honeywood v. Rockefeller, 214 F. Supp. 897 (E.D. N.Y. 1963), aff'd, 376 U.S. 222 (1964); Meeks v. Avery, 251 F. Supp. 245 (D. Kan. 1966).

But in Sims v. Baggett, 247 F. Supp. 96 (M.D. Ala. 1965), a three-judge court held invalid part of the Alabama reapportionment plan, adopted after Reynolds v. Sims: "The conclusion is inescapable that Elmore, Tallapoosa and Macon [counties] were combined needlessly into a single House district for the sole purpose of preventing the election of a Negro House member. In the Bullock-Pike-Coffee-Geneva House district to which the Legislature proposes to allot three members, the inference is also clear that there is no purpose other than racial considerations. The obvious effect of this grouping, from a racial standpoint, is to equalize the 71.9% of nonwhite citizens in Bullock County. . . . The court is permitted to find the intent of the Legislature from the consistency of inherent probabilities inferred from the record as a whole. We, therefore, hold that the Legislature intentionally aggregated predominantly Negro counties with predominantly white counties for the sole purpose of preventing the election of Negroes to House membership. The plan adopted by the Legislature can have no other effect." 247 F. Supp. at 109. Cf. Drew v. Scranton, 229 F. Supp. 310 (M.D. Pa. 1964), vac. and remanded, 379 U.S. 40 (1964).

State court decisions on gerrymandering, not infrequent even before Baker v. Carr and Reynolds v. Sims, are noted in Tabor, The Gerrymandering of State and Federal Legislative Districts, 16 Md. L. Rev. 277 (1956); Lewis, Legislative Apportionment and the Federal Courts, 71 Harv. L. Rev. 1057 (1958); McKay, Reapportionment: The Law and Politics of Equal Representation, App. (1965).

3. The most frequently used standard for controlling gerrymanders is that the districts must be "compact" and "contiguous." Such requirements were imposed by Congress for Congressional Districts, beginning as early as 1862, but were omitted from the 1929 legislation. Congressman Emanuel Celler, Chairman of the House Judiciary Committee, has long pressed for re-enactment of these standards. His bill passed the House in 1965, but the Senate has taken no action. 111 Cong. Rec. 5101; N.Y. Times, Mar. 17, 1965. For a history of the federal legislation, see Celler,

Congressional Apportionment — Past, Present, and Future, 17 Law & Contemp. Prob. 268 (1952).

4. Proposals have been made for the elimination of gerrymandering through the use of computers to form districts, or through mathematical tests for compactness and contiguity. See Reock, Measuring Compactness as a Requirement of Legislative Apportionment, 5 Midwest J. Pol. Sci. 70 (1961); Weaver and Hess, A Procedure for Nonpartisan Districting: Development of Computer Techniques, 73 Yale L.J. 288 (1963); Nagel, Simplified Bipartisan Computer Redistricting, 17 Stan. L. Rev. 863 (1965).

REFERENCES

Generally on the gerrymander, see Griffith, The Rise and Development of the Gerrymander (1907); Hacker, Congressional Districting 54-78 (rev. ed. 1964). With respect to the legal issues as they have been posed since the abandonment of Colegrove v. Green, see Lucas, Dragon in a Thicket: A Perusal of Gomillion v. Lightfoot, 1961 Sup. Ct. Rev. 194; Neal, Baker v. Carr: Politics in Search of Law, 1962 Sup. Ct. Rev. 252, 275-278; Note, Wright v. Rockefeller and Legislative Gerrymanders: The Desegregation Decisions Plus a Problem of Proof, 72 Yale L.J. 1041 (1963); Note, Apportionment and the Courts — A Synopsis and Prognosis: Herein of Gerrymanders and Other Dragons, 59 Nw. U.L. Rev. 500 (1964); Notes, 78 Harv. L. Rev. 143, 252-254 (1964); 39 N.Y.U.L. Rev. 264, 278-285 (1964); Note, Legislative Reapportionment: The Scope of Federal Judicial Relief, 1965 Duke L.J. 563, 590-595; McKay, Reapportionment: The Law and Politics of Equal Representation 255-258 (1965); Note, Reapportionment, 79 Harv. L. Rev. 1226, 1283-1287 (1966).

B. Minority Parties

MacDOUGALL v. GREEN
335 U.S. 281, 69 S. Ct. 1, 93 L. Ed. 3 (1948)

Per Curiam.

This action was brought before a three-judge court convened in the Northern District of Illinois under 28 U.S.C. §2281 and §2284. The object of the action is an injunction against the enforcement of a provision which, in 1935, was added to a statute of Illinois and which requires that a petition to form and to nominate candidates for a new political party be signed by at least 25,000 qualified voters, "Provided, that included in the aggregate total of twenty-five thousand (25,000) signatures are the signatures of two hundred (200) qualified voters from each of at least fifty (50) counties within the State." Ill. Rev. Stat. c. 46, §10-2 (1947). Appellants are the "Progressive Party," its nominees for United States Senator, Presidential Electors, and State offices, and several Illinois voters. Appellees are the Governor, the Auditor of Public Accounts, and the Secretary of State of Illinois, members of the Boards of Election Commissioners of various cities, and the County Clerks of various counties. The District Court found want of jurisdiction and denied the injunction. 80 F. Supp. 725. Appellants invoke the jurisdiction of this Court under 28 U.S.C. §1253.

The action arises from the finding of the State Officers Electoral Board that appellants had not obtained the requisite number of signatures from the requisite number of counties and its consequent ruling that their nominating petition was "not sufficient in law to entitle the said candidates' names to appear on the ballot." The appellants' claim to equitable relief against this ruling is based upon the peculiar distribution of population among Illinois' 102 counties. They allege that 52% of the State's registered voters are residents of Cook County alone, 87% are residents of the 49 most populous counties, and only 13% reside in the 53 least populous counties. Under these circumstances, they say, the Illinois statute is so discriminatory in its application as to amount to a denial of the due-process, equal-protection, and privileges-and-immunities clauses of the Fourteenth Amendment, as well as Article I, §§2 and 4, Article II, §1, and the Seventeenth Amendment of the Constitution of the United States.

It is clear that the requirement of 200 signatures from at least 50 counties gives to the voters of the less populous counties of Illinois the power completely to block the nomination of candidates whose support is confined to geographically limited areas. But the State is entitled to deem this power not disproportionate: of 25,000 signatures required, only 9,800, or 39%, need be distributed; the remaining 61% may be obtained from a single county. And Cook County, the largest, contains not more than 52% of the State's voters. It is allowable State policy to require that candidates for state-wide office should have support not limited to a concentrated locality. This is not a unique policy. See New York Laws 1896, c. 909, §57, now N.Y. Elec. Law §137(4); 113 Laws of Ohio 349, Gen. Code, §4785-91 (1929), now Ohio Code Ann. (Cum. Supp. 1947) §4785-91; Mass. Acts 1943, c. 334, §2, now Mass. Ann. Laws c. 53, §6 (1945). To assume that political power is a function exclusively of numbers is to disregard the practicalities of government. Thus, the Constitution protects the interests of the smaller against the greater by giving in the Senate entirely unequal representation to populations. It would be strange indeed, and doctrinaire, for this Court, applying such broad constitutional concepts as due process and equal protection of the laws, to deny a State the power to assure a proper diffusion of political initiative as between its thinly populated counties and those having concentrated masses, in view of the fact that the latter have practical opportunities for exerting their political weight at the polls not available to the former. The Constitution — a practical instrument of government — makes no such demands on the States. Colegrove v. Green, 328 U.S. 549, and Colegrove v. Barrett, 330 U.S. 804.

On the record before us, we need not pass upon purely local questions, also urged by appellants, having no federal constitutional aspect.

Judgment affirmed.

[Mr. Justice Rutledge concurred in the result on the ground that the Court should decline to exercise its equity jurisdiction for the reason that, with only 12 days remaining before the election, the ballots already printed and absentee ballots already distributed, judicial action might prove ineffective and disrupt the entire Illinois electoral process.]

Mr. Justice Douglas, with whom Mr. Justice Black and Mr. Justice Murphy concur, dissenting.

I think that the 1935 amendment of the Illinois Election Code, Ill. Rev. Stat. c. 46, §10-2 (1947), as construed and applied in this case, violates the Equal Protection Clause of the Fourteenth Amendment.

That statute requires the nominating petition of a new political party, which places candidates on the ballot for the general election, to contain 200 signatures from each of at least 50 of the 102 counties in the state. The statute does not attempt to make the required signatures proportionate to the population of each county. One effect of this requirement is that the electorate in 49 of the counties which contain 87% of the registered voters could not form a new political party and place its candidates on the ballot. Twenty-five thousand of the remaining 13% of registered voters, however, properly distributed among the 53 remaining counties could form a new party to elect candidates to office. That regulation thus discriminates against the residents of the populous counties of the state in favor of rural sections. It therefore lacks the equality to which the exercise of political rights is entitled under the Fourteenth Amendment. . . .

None would deny that a state law giving some citizens twice the vote of other citizens in either the primary or general election would lack that equality which the Fourteenth Amendment guarantees. See Nixon v. Herndon, 273 U.S. 536. The dilution of political rights may be as complete and effective if the same discrimination appears in the procedure prescribed for nominating petitions. See State v. Junkin, 85 Neb. 1, 122 N.W. 473. It would, of course, be palpably discriminatory in violation of the Equal Protection Clause if this law were aimed at the Progressive Party in the manner that the state law in Nixon v. Herndon, supra, was aimed at negroes. But the effect of a state law may bring it under the condemnation of the Equal Protection Clause however innocent its purpose. It is invalid if discrimination is apparent in its operation. The test is whether it has some foundation in experience, practicality, or necessity. See Skinner v. Oklahoma, 316 U.S. 535, 541-542.

It is not enough to say that this law can stand that test because it is designed to require statewide support for the launching of a new political party rather than support from a few localities. There is no attempt here, as I have said, to make the required signatures even approximately proportionate to the distribution of voters among the various counties of the state. No such proportionate allocation could of course be mathematically exact. Nor would it be required. But when, as here, the law applies a rigid, arbitrary formula to sparsely settled counties and populous counties alike, it offers no basis whatever to justify giving greater weight to the individual votes of one group of citizens than to those of another group. This legislation therefore has the same inherent infirmity as that which some of us saw in Colegrove v. Green, 328 U.S. 549, 569. The fact that the Constitution itself sanctions inequalities in some phases of our political system does not justify us in allowing a state to create additional ones. The theme of the Constitution is equality among citizens in the exercise of their political rights. The notion that one group can be granted greater voting strength than another is hostile to our standards for popular representative government.

Federal courts should be most hesitant to use the injunction in state elections. See Wilson v. North Carolina, 169 U.S. 586, 596. If federal courts undertook the role of superintendence, disruption of the whole electoral process might result, and the elective system that is vital to our government might be paralyzed. Cf. Johnson v. Stevenson, 170 F.2d 108. The equity court, moreover, must always be alert in the exercise of its discretion to make sure that its decree will not be a futile and ineffective thing. But the case, as made before us, does not indicate that either of those considerations should deter us in striking down this unconstitutional statute and in freeing the impending Illinois election of its impediments. The state officials who are responsible for the election and who at this bar confessed error in the decision of the District Court make no such intimation or suggestion. We are therefore not authorized to assume that our decree would interfere with the orderly process of the election.

REFERENCES

For discussion see Note, Legal Obstacles to Minority Party Success, 57 Yale L.J. 1276 (1948); Note, Denial of Equal Voting Facilities to Minor Parties, 50 Colum. L. Rev. 712 (1950); Note, The Right to Form a Political Party, 43 Ill. L. Rev. 832 (1949); Note, Legal Barriers Confronting Third Parties, 16 U. Chi. L. Rev. 499 (1949); Note, 34 Cornell L.Q. 620 (1949); Nader and Jacobs, Do Third Parties Have a Chance? Harv. Law Record, Oct. 9, 1958. See also American Civil Liberties Union, Minority Parties on the Ballot (rev. 1943); Smith, Voting and Election Laws (1960).

C. OTHER ASPECTS OF THE RIGHT OF FRANCHISE

Other problems involving the right of franchise include the following:

In Carrington v. Rash, 380 U.S. 89, 85 S. Ct. 775, 13 L. Ed. 2d 675 (1965), the Supreme Court held invalid, as a denial of equal protection, a provision of Texas Constitution which provided: "Any member of the Armed Forces of the United States or component branches thereof, or in the military service of the United States, may vote only in the county in which he or she resided at the time of entering such service so long as he or she is a member of the Armed Forces." The effect of the provision was that no serviceman, previously resident of another state, could acquire a voting residence in Texas so long as he remained in the service. The Court, while recognizing that "Texas has unquestioned power to impose reasonable residence restrictions on the availability of the ballot," declared that the right to vote "cannot constitutionally be obliterated because of a fear of the political views of a particular group of bona fide residents." 380 U.S. at 91, 94. Mr. Justice Harlan dissented.

In Ray v. Blair, 343 U.S. 214, 72 S. Ct. 654, 96 L. Ed. 894 (1952), the Court ruled that candidates for Presidential electors could be required by the Alabama State Democratic Committee, as a condition of running in the Democratic primary, to pledge that they would "aid and support the nominees of the National Convention of the Democratic Party for President and Vice President," even though such nominees had not yet been selected. Justices Jackson and Douglas dissented. Justices Black and Frankfurter did not participate. See Note, 4 Ala. L. Rev. 245 (1952). For other material on the efforts of state parties to avoid supporting the national candidate of the party, see Note, 34 Va. L. Rev. 619 (1948). See also Note, 34 Cornell L.Q. 430 (1949). Generally on the subject, see Mitau, Judicial Determination of Political Party Organizational Autonomy, 42 Minn. L. Rev. 245 (1957).

On the right of previously unaffiliated voters to enroll in a party and vote in a party primary, see Alexander v. Todman, 337 F.2d 962 (3d Cir. 1964), cert. den., 380 U.S. 915 (1965). With respect to changing party affiliation after voting in a primary, see Clark v. Meyland, 261 N.C. 140, 134 S.E.2d 168 (1964).

The Connecticut statute requiring that voting machines be equipped with a mandatory party lever was challenged in Voorhes v. Dempsey, 231 F. Supp. 975 (D. Conn. 1964), aff'd, 379 U.S. 648 (1965). In using voting machines so equipped the voter had first to pull one of the party levers, which turned down all the keys on the machine for candidates of that party, and then push up the particular key of any candidate he did not wish to vote for. A three-judge court said: "While the wisdom of mandatory party lever statute may be questionable, it can hardly be termed fundamentally unfair or unreasonably discriminatory in contravention of the Fourteenth Amendment." 231 F. Supp. at 977.

In Voltaggio v. Caputo, 210 F. Supp. 337 (D. N.J. 1962), a three-judge court upheld a New Jersey statute which gave first choice of position on the ballot to political parties, with those nominated as independent candidates listed thereafter; and prohibited independent candidates from using as a slogan on the ballot the name or designation of any party entitled to appear on the ballot.

The requirement of the New York Election Law that only persons who were registered to vote at the last preceding general election were qualified to sign nominating petitions for independent candidates was upheld in Davis v. Board of Elections of the City of New York, 5 N.Y.2d 66, 179 N.Y.S.2d 513, 153 N.E.2d 879 (1959).

With respect to the right to a secret ballot see Nutting, Freedom of Silence: Constitutional Protection Against Governmental Intrusions in Political Affairs, 47 Mich. L. Rev. 181, 181-200 (1948); Smith v. Blackwell, 115 F.2d 186 (4th Cir. 1940).

On the right of Indians to vote, see Harrison v. Laveen, 67 Ariz. 337, 196 P.2d 456 (1948); Allen v. Merrell, 6 Utah 2d 32, 305 P.2d 490 (1956), remanded as moot, 353 U.S. 932 (1957); Note, Denial of Voting Rights to Reservation Indians, 5 Utah L. Rev. 247 (1956).

REFERENCES

Generally, on voting behavior, see Burdick and Brodbeck, American Voting Behavior (1959); Campbell, Converse, Miller, and Stokes, The American Voter (1960); Lipset, Political Man (1960); Report of President's Commission on Registration and Voting Participation (1963); Key, The Responsible Electorate (1966). See also Berelson, Lazarsfeld, and McPhee, Voting: A Study of Opinion Formation in a Presidential Campaign (1955); Thomson and Shattuck, The 1956 Presidential Campaign (1960); David, Goldman, and Bain, The Politics of National Party Conventions (1960); Dawidowicz and Goldstein, Politics in a Pluralist Democracy: Studies of Voting in the 1960 Election (1963); Scammon, America at the Polls: A Handbook of American Presidential Election Statistics 1920-1964 (1965).

INDEX

995*a*